THE SCOUTING NOTEBOOK: 1998

Produced by STATS, Inc.
(Sports Team Analysis and Tracking Systems, Inc.)

John Dewan & Don Zminda, Editors
Jim Callis, Associate Editor

Statistics by STATS, Inc.

STATS
PUBLISHING

Most of the player photographs which appear in THE SCOUTING NOTEBOOK: 1998 were furnished individually by the 30 teams that comprise Major League Baseball. Their cooperation is gratefully acknowledged: Anaheim Angels, Baltimore Orioles, Boston Red Sox, Chicago White Sox, Cleveland Indians, Detroit Tigers, Kansas City Royals, Minnesota Twins, New York Yankees, Oakland Athletics, Seattle Mariners, Tampa Bay Devil Rays, Texas Rangers, Toronto Blue Jays, Arizona Diamondbacks, Atlanta Braves, Chicago Cubs, Cincinnati Reds, Colorado Rockies, Florida Marlins, Houston Astros, Los Angeles Dodgers, Milwaukee Brewers, Montreal Expos, New York Mets, Philadelphia Phillies, Pittsburgh Pirates, St. Louis Cardinals, San Diego Padres and San Francisco Giants. Thanks also to *Baseball America*, which filled our last few photo holes. Magglio Ordonez photo (page 107) by Rodger Wood.

Cover by Ron Freer

Cover photos by Tony Inzerillo, *The Sporting Views*, Bensenville, IL

STATS is a trademark of Sports Team Analysis and Tracking Systems, Inc.

First Edition: January, 1998

ISBN 1-884064-47-7

Acknowledgments

The Scouting Notebook is by far the biggest annual book we produce at STATS, Inc. This year's edition is 720 pages and required the efforts of seemingly as many people. Thanks for a job well done.

John Dewan, STATS President and CEO, continues to make us the No. 1 source for sports statistics. He's assisted by Heather Schwarze, who somehow manages to keep up with everything John has his hand in. The newest member of the STATS executive team is Chief Operating Officer Marty Gilbert, who came on board on the day this book went to press. Welcome to your first STATS publication, Marty!

This book is filled with statistics, rankings and other assorted numbers, all gathered by the Operations Department headed by Doug Abel. His staff consists of Jeff Chernow, Brian Cousins, Jason Kinsey, Jim Osborne, John Sasman, Matt Senter, Joe Weindel and Peter Woelflein, and they oversee a vast reporter network.

After the data is gathered, our Systems Departement works its magic. Sue Dewan, Mike Canter and Art Ashley run Systems, and Jeff Schinski, Allan Spear and David Pinto did the bulk of the programming for this book. The rest of Systems, which also includes Andrew Bernstein, Dave Carlson, Drew Faust, Kevin Goldstein, Mike Hammer, Stefan Kretschmann, Steve Moyer, Brent Osland, Dean Peterson, Pat Quinn and Kevin Thomas, also made valuable contributions.

Then it's up to the Publications Department, led by Don Zminda, to interpret all that data and present it to the reader. The Publications staff consists of Ethan Cooperson, Kevin Fullam, Jim Henzler, Chuck Miller, Tony Nistler, Mat Olkin and yours truly. As usual, the look of STATS books is the result of Chuck's hard work and countless hours. Special thanks also are in order for part-time Publications employees Thom Henninger and Chad Huebner, who did the bulk of the fact-checking for this book, and also to Sharon Zminda, who was a big help in cutting and pasting the photographs and diagrams. Don also oversees our Fantasy Department, which includes Dan Ford, Jim Musso, Oscar Palacios and Mike Wenz, and produces the best sports games on the market.

Steve Byrd's Marketing Department spreads the word about STATS to a worldwide client base. Marc Elman, Ron Freer, Corey Roberts, Lori Smith and Walter Lis assist Steve in his efforts. Jim Capuano's Sales Department pays most of our bills, and he's helped out by Kristen Beauregard and Leena Sheth.

Bob Meyerhoff's Finance and Administrative Departments ensure that everything runs smoothly at our Skokie, Ill., headquarters. Controller Steve Drago crunches the financial numbers, with the assistance of Angela Gabe, Mark Hong and Betty Moy. Susan Zamechek oversees the Administrative staff of Grant Blair, Ken Gilbert, Sherlinda Johnson, Antoinette Kelly, Kacey Schueler Poulos, Carol Savier and Taasha Schroeder. Stephanie Seburn handles the Human Resources Department's responsibilities with help from Tracy Lickton.

—Jim Callis

The Scouting Staff

The Scouting Notebook writing staff is a mix of beat writers and STATS reporters who cover major league games on a regular basis. They truly know their baseball, and STATS would like to thank them for their efforts.

The scouting reports were written by the following people, in conjunction with our editors:

Anaheim Angels	Phil Rogers *Chicago Tribune*
Baltimore Orioles	Mike Mittleman *STATS, Inc.*
Boston Red Sox	Peter Gammons *ESPN/Boston Globe/* *Baseball America*
Chicago White Sox	Phil Rogers *Chicago Tribune*
Cleveland Indians	Paul Hoynes *Cleveland Plain Dealer*
Detroit Tigers	Pat Caputo *Oakland (Mich.) Press/* *Baseball America*
Kansas City Royals	Marc Bowman *STATS, Inc.*
Minnesota Twins	John Sickels *STATS, Inc.*
New York Yankees	Peter Pascarelli *ESPN/Baseball Weekly*
Oakland Athletics	Lawr Michaels *CREATiVESPORTS*
Seattle Mariners	David Schoenfield *Starwave/ESPN SportsZone*
Tampa Bay Devil Rays	Mat Olkin/Jim Callis *STATS, Inc.*
Texas Rangers	Phil Rogers *Chicago Tribune*
Toronto Blue Jays	Mike Mittleman *STATS, Inc.*
Arizona Diamondbacks	Mat Olkin/Jim Callis *STATS, Inc.*
Atlanta Braves	Mat Olkin *STATS, Inc.*
Chicago Cubs	Mat Olkin *STATS, Inc.*
Cincinnati Reds	Peter Pascarelli *ESPN/Baseball Weekly*
Colorado Rockies	Alan Smithee
Florida Marlins	Alan Smithee
Houston Astros	Jim Molony *Baseball America*
Los Angeles Dodgers	Don Hartack *STATS, Inc.*
Milwaukee Brewers	Mat Olkin *STATS, Inc.*
Montreal Expos	Jeff Blair *The Globe & Mail (Toronto)/* *Baseball America*
New York Mets	Peter Pascarelli *ESPN/Baseball Weekly*
Philadelphia Phillies	Tony Blengino *Diamond Library*
Pittsburgh Pirates	John Perrotto *Beaver County (Pa.) Times/* *Baseball America*
St. Louis Cardinals	Mike Eisenbath *St. Louis Post-Dispatch/* *Baseball America*
San Diego Padres	Peter Pascarelli *ESPN/Baseball Weekly*
San Francisco Giants	Peter Pascarelli *ESPN/Baseball Weekly*

The minor league prospect reports were written by yours truly, and I'd like to thank the player-development personnel from 27 of the 30 major league teams who were willing to discuss their farm systems. The "Other Anaheim Angels," etc., for each team were written by Kevin Fullam, Tony Nistler, Mat Olkin, Don Zminda and yours truly.

This is STATS' fourth edition of *The Scouting Notebook*, and before that we produced the 1990-94 editions with a different publisher. Kudos to the three writers who have written for all nine editions STATS has worked on: Marc Bowman, Paul Hoynes and John Perrotto. Special thanks are also in order for Peter Gammons and Peter Pascarelli, two of the busiest and most knowledgable writers in baseball.

I'd also like to offer my personal thanks to *Baseball America* editor Allan Simpson, who gave me my first job. Allan also gave me an appreciation for evaluating players and helped me hone my skills at doing so.

—Jim Callis

Table of Contents

This book is dedicated to my mom and dad, the two special people who taught me all about the importance of kindness, courtesy, honesty and love. Priceless lessons that will last a lifetime.

—Your daughter,

Heather Schwarze

Foreword

by Paul Snyder
Director of Scouting and Player Development, Atlanta Braves

All baseball people know how important scouting is to a successful franchise.

To a large extent, general managers, directors of player development and scouting directors make their personnel decisions based on reports from their scouts. The men at the top might get their names in the news, but it's the guys who are in the field day in and day out, evaluating talent and grading players at all levels, who do the groundwork.

No team relies on the opinion of one man. That's where *The Scouting Notebook* comes in. We count on it to provide us with statistics, analysis, tendencies and performance ratings to supplement the reports from our scouts and crosscheckers.

In this business, it's almost impossible to have too much information if it's presented in a concise way. *The Scouting Notebook* does that. It's well organized and thorough, discussing every major leaguer from 1997 and every team's top prospects.

Not only is *The Scouting Notebook* a valuable tool for professional teams, but sportswriters and broadcasters also use it as a reliable source of information and background. Years ago, material such as this was available only to those in the baseball business. Now, thanks to *The Scouting Notebook*, fans can enjoy it as well.

Introduction

Welcome to the fourth edition of *The Scouting Notebook*. This is the ninth annual book of scouting reports that STATS, Inc., has created. We produced the annual *Scouting Report* from 1990-94. No matter the title or the publisher, the underlying philosophy of these books has remained the same: get several intelligent baseball analysts, people who collectively cover thousands of games every season, and have them give us detailed reports on every major league player who saw significant action last season. Our scouting staff includes some of the top baseball minds around, such as Peter Gammons, Peter Pascarelli, Paul Hoynes, John Perrotto and Phil Rogers.

The result is a veritable encyclopedia of contemporary major league baseball. Every year, we tell you about the strengths and weaknesses of hundreds of players. Our analysis extends beyond major league players, too, covering each club's top minor league prospects. We study the statistics, we talk to the scouts and we watch the games with a keen eye. We look for the true ability that may have been exaggerated or obscured by the hype.

The expansion teams began putting their rosters together right before we went to print. That didn't stop us from putting together scouting reports on the players likely to make the biggest impact on the Devil Rays and Diamondbacks in 1998. Those teams get the same treatment as the 28 established clubs.

Let's take a look at our lineup:

Major League Leaders

The chapter immediately following this introduction is a complete listing of Major League Leaders. The top three players in each category are shown for the American and National Leagues. You'll notice a STATS flavor to these leaders. Not only do we show the leaders for the common categories such as batting average, home runs and ERA, but you'll also find less traditional categories like steals of third and pitches thrown. Tony Gwynn led the majors in hitting last year, but did you know that Ron Coomer led the majors in hitting versus lefthanders? Or that Jamie Moyer had the best run support in baseball?

Stars, Bums and Sleepers

This section is useful to traditional fans and fantasy baseball players alike. We tell you what to expect from each player in 1998: whether they'll improve, decline, remain consistent or come out of nowhere to surprise. We like Tino Martinez, but don't count on 44 homers and 141 RBI from him again.

The Managers

On these pages, we analyze each manager's strengths and weaknesses, style and strategy, and outlook for 1998. We list his 1997 and career managerial record, and we also show how often he used starting pitchers on various days of rest. We compare his use and the performance of his starters to the league average.

We also provide statistical breakdowns detailing his handling of his pitching staff and his use of strategies like the sacrifice, the hit- and-run and defensive substitutions. To qualify for the rankings, a manager had to have his team for at least 100 games in 1997. Some of the terms listed in the statistics and rankings sections may be unfamiliar. They include:

Hit & Run Success %: The percentage of hit-and-runs resulting in baserunner advancement with no double play.

Platoon Pct.: Frequency that the manager gets his hitters the platoon advantage (lefty vs. righty and vice versa). Switch- hitters always have the advantage.

Defensive Subs: The number of straight defensive substitutions with the team leading by four runs or fewer.

High-Pitch Outings: The number of times a starting pitchers threw more than 120 pitches in a ballgame.

Quick/Slow Hooks: A Quick Hook occurs when a pitcher is removed after having pitched less than six innings and given up three runs or fewer. A Slow Hook occurs when a pitcher works more than nine innings, allows seven or more runs, or whose total innings and runs equal 13 or more.

First-Batter Platoon Percentage: The percentage of times the managers' relievers had a platoon advantage over the first hitter they faced (lefty vs. lefty, righty vs. righty).

Mid-Inning Changes: The number of times the manager changed pitchers in the middle of an inning.

Pitchouts with a Runner Moving: The number of times the opposition was running when the manager called a pitchout.

Sacrifice Bunt Percentage: The percentage of bunts resulting in sacrifices or hits with runners on.

Starting Lineups Used: Based on batting order, 1-8 for National Leaguers, 1-9 for American Leaguers.

2+ Pitching Changes in Low-Scoring Games: The number of times a manager used at least three pitchers in a game in which his team allowed two runs or fewer.

The Players

For each major league team, we give extensive reports on 21 or more players. Most of them get a full page of scouting information, while some receive half-page reports. Because we like to get this book into your hands as soon as possible, players are listed with their 1997 clubs—with the exception of the two expansion teams. We keep abreast of postseason transactions, and all player moves that took place through December 7, 1997, are noted and discussed. If you can't find a particular player, check the detailed index in the back.

Pages for primary players have two columns. The left column provides an in-depth report by an expert analyst. The right column contains statistical information. Starting at the top of the column, it lists:

Position: The first position shown is the player's most common position in 1997. Positions at which he played 10 or more games also are shown. For pitchers, SP stands for starting pitcher and RP for relief pitcher. A second pitching position is shown if a starter relieved at least four times or if a reliever started at least twice.

Bats and Throws: L stands for lefthanded, R stands for righthanded, and B stands for both (switch-hitter).

Ht: Height.

Wt: Weight.

Opening Day Age: This is the player's age on March 31, 1998, the Sunday night on which the season is expected to begin.

Born: Birthdate and birthplace.

ML Seasons: This number indicates the number of different major league seasons in which the player has appeared. For example, if a player was called up to play in September in each of the last three seasons, the number shown would be three (3). This is different from major league service, which counts the actual number of days a player appears on a big league roster and is used to determine arbitration and free-agency eligibility.

Overall Statistics: These are traditional major league statistics for the player's 1997 season and his career.

Where He Hits The Ball

The hitting diagrams are state-of-the-art. For every major league game in 1997, STATS-trained reporters entered into our computers every ball hit into play. They kept track of the type of batted balls—grounders, fly balls, pop-ups, line drives and bunts—as well as the distance each ball traveled. Direction was tracked by dividing the field into 26 "wedges" projecting out from home plate. Distance was measured in 10-foot increments outward from home plate.

Below are lefthanded-hitting Tony Gwynn's hitting diagrams. The chart on the left shows where Gwynn hit the ball against lefthanders, while the chart on the right shows what he did against righties.

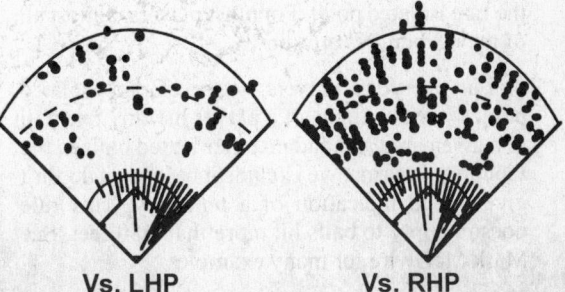

Vs. LHP   Vs. RHP

In the diagrams, ground balls and short line drives are shown by the lines of various lengths in the infield. The longer the line, the more ground balls and line drives were hit in that direction. As you can see from the charts above, Gwynn sprays grounders and liners all over the field against righthanders, but is more likely to pull them against lefties. With southpaws on the mound, shortstops and third baseman should cheat a few steps toward right field.

In the outfield, batted balls are shown by dots. The dotted line in the outfield is 300 feet away from home plate, a rough approximation of typical outfield defensive positions. Taking another look at Gwynn, he again sprays balls all over the outfield against righties, though he now is more apt to use the opposite field against lefties. Though an infield shift would make sense with southpaws on the mound, left fielders ought to play Gwynn straight-away.

A lot of experimentation went into producing the hitting diagrams. When we first started, we tried to show every single batted ball that was put into play by each player. We found that the charts became very cluttered for everyday players, so we began experimenting with trying to show only the most meaningful information. When all was said and done, here's what we ended up with:

a. Pop-ups and bunts are excluded. We excluded pop-ups because 95 percent of these are caught regardless of how fielders are positioned. We excluded bunts because defensing a bunt is an entirely different strategy primarily used against a select number of players or in specific situations.

b. Ground balls under 50 feet are excluded. These are mostly swinging bunts and are somewhat rare. We exclude them because they don't provide a true indication of the direction of a batted ball reaching an infielder or going through the infield.

c. For ground balls over 50 feet, we excluded only the rare isolated point. For most players, almost all of their grounders are shown.

d. For everyday players, we excluded isolated points in the outfield. If a player hit only one ball in a given area and had no other batted balls in the vicinity all season, we exclude it because it doesn't give a true indication of a tendency. This rule doesn't apply to balls hit more than 380 feet. See Mark McGwire for many examples.

e. For non-everyday players, we expanded the data sample to create a more complete pattern of outfield dots. Otherwise, it would present a misleading picture of these players' power.

Other notes of interest:

The field itself is drawn to precise scale, with the outfield fence reaching 400 feet in center and 330 feet down the lines. Ballparks are configured differently, so a dot inside of the fence might have been a home run. Similarly, a dot outside the fence might actually have been in play.

Line drives under 170 feet are part of the infield. We give responsibility for short liners to the infielders.

No distinction is made between hits and outs.

How Often He Throws Strikes

Our STATS reporters also tracked every pitch thrown in a major league game in 1997. The pitching graphs show how often the hurler throws strikes in different situations. Our data shows most pitchers will toss a strike between 40 and 80 percent of the time. Therefore we've constructed the chart to represent the 40-80 percent range.

The strike count includes swinging strikes, taken strikes, foul balls and balls put in play. Even though not all batted balls are strikes, our theory is that most are and the ones that aren't would be difficult to judge. Our charts reflect these assumptions.

The charts are broken into four categories. *All Pitches* is straightforward, as is *First Pitch*. We define *Ahead* as counts with more strikes than balls. *Behind* includes counts with more balls than strikes. The appropriate league average is shown in each chart. The Brewers are compared to the American League average, while pitchers on expansion teams are compared to the league in which they pitched last year.

Below are the 1997 league averages. The National League threw a slightly higher percentage of strikes than the American League, as it has in all nine years we have tracked this.

Strike Percentage by League — 1997		
	American	National
All Pitches	61.8%	62.1%
First Pitch	56.6%	57.4%
Ahead in the Count	59.4%	60.1%
Behind in the Count	67.0%	66.5%

1997 Situational Stats

There are eight situational breakdowns for every primary player. *Home* and *Road* show performance in his home ballpark and on the road. *First Half* and *Scnd Half* show performance before and after the 1997 All-Star break. For hitters, *LHP* and *RHP* show how the player hit against lefthanders and righthanders. For pitchers, *LHB* and *RHB* show how the opposition lefthanders and righthanders hit against the pitcher. *Sc Pos* shows batting or pitching performance with runners in scoring position. *Clutch* shows batting or pitching performance in clutch situations, defined as the seventh inning or later with the batting team ahead by one run, tied or with the tying run on base, at bat or on deck. Our definition is consistent with save situations.

1997 Rankings

This section shows how the player ranked against his league, other league players at his position and his teammates. Because of space considerations, we omitted some of the less interesting rankings when a player placed high in numerous categories.

As we do in the League Leaders section, we include many less traditional categories. The Definitions and Qualifications section below provides details for these statistics.

Definitions and Qualifications

The following are definitions and qualifications for the Major League Leaders and Rankings.

Definitions:

Times on Base — Hits plus walks plus hit-by-pitch.

Ground/Fly Ratio — Ground balls hit divided by the total of fly balls and pop-ups hit. Bunts and line drives are excluded.

Runs/Times on Base — Runs scored divided by times on base.

Clutch — A player's batting average in the late innings of close games, defined as the seventh inning or later with the batting team ahead by one run, tied or with the tying run on base, at bat or on deck.

Bases Loaded — A player's batting average in bases-loaded situations.

GDP per GDP situation — Ground-ball double plays divided by ground-ball double-play situations, defined as a man on first base with less than two out.

Percentage of Pitches Taken — The percentage of pitches a player lets go by without swinging.

Percentage Swings Put In Play — The percentage of swings resulting in a batted ball into fair territory or a foul-ball out.

Run Support per Nine Innings — The number of runs scored for a pitcher while he was pitching, scaled to a nine-inning figure.

Baserunners per Nine Innings — The total of hits, walks and hit batsmen allowed per nine innings.

Strikeout/Walk Ratio — Strikeouts divided by walks.

Stolen Base Percentage Allowed — Stolen bases divided by stolen-base attempts.

Save Percentage — Saves divided by save opportunities. Save opportunities include saves plus blown saves.

Blown Saves — A blown save is charged any time a pitcher enters a game in a save situation and loses the lead. A save situation is defined as any time a reliever enters the game with a lead, isn't the pitcher of record and either a) pitches at least one inning with a lead of no more than three runs; b) enters the game with the potential tying run on base, at bat or on deck; or c) pitches effectively for at least three innings.

Holds — A hold is given to a pitcher when he enters a game in a save situation and is removed before the end of the game while maintaining his team's lead. The pitcher must retire at least one batter to get a hold.

Percentage of Inherited Runners Scored — Percentage of runners already on base when a pitcher enters a game that he allows to score.

First Batter Efficiency — The batting average allowed by a reliever to the first batter he faces in a game.

Qualifications:

In order to be ranked, a player had to qualify with a minimum number of opportunities, as follows:

Batters

Batting average, slugging percentage, on-base percentage, home run frequency, ground/fly ratio, runs scored per time reached base and pitches seen per plate appearance — 3.1 plate appearances per team game

Percentage of pitches taken, lowest percentage of swings that missed and percentage of swings put into play — 9.26 pitches seen per team game

Percentage of extra bases taken as a runner — .09

opportunities to advance per team game

Stolen base percentage — .12 stolen-base attempts per team game

Runners in scoring position — .62 plate appearances with runners in scoring position per team game

Clutch — .31 plate appearances in the clutch per team game

Bases loaded — .06 plate appearances with the bases loaded per team game

GDP per GDP situation — .31 plate appearances in GDP situations per team game

Vs LHP — .77 plate appearances against lefthanders per team game

Vs RHP — 2.33 plate appearances against righthanders per team game

BA at home — 1.55 plate appearances at home per team game

BA on the road — 1.55 plate appearances on the road per team game

Leadoff on-base percentage — .93 plate appearances in the No. 1 lineup spot per team game

Cleanup slugging percentage — .93 plate appearances in the No. 4 lineup spot per team game

BA on 3-1 count — .06 plate appearances with a 3-1 count per team game

BA with 2 strikes — .62 plate appearances with two strikes per team game

BA on 0-2 count — .12 plate appearances with an 0-2 count per team game

BA on 3-2 count — .12 plate appearances with a 3-2 count per team game

Pitchers

Earned run average, run support per nine innings, baserunners per nine innings, batting average allowed, slugging percentage allowed, on-base percentage allowed, home runs per nine innings, strikeouts per nine innings, strikeout/walk ratio, stolen base percentage allowed, GDPs per nine innings, pitches thrown per batter and ground/fly ratio against — one inning per team game

Winning percentage — .09 decisions per team game

GDPs induced per GDP situation — .19 batters faced in GDP situations per team game

BA allowed, runners in scoring position — .93 batters faced with runners in scoring position per

team game

ERA at home — .5 innings at home per team game

ERA on the road — .5 innings on the road per team game

Vs LHB — .77 lefthanders faced per team game

Vs RHB — 2.33 righthanders faced per team game

Relievers

ERA, batting average allowed, baserunners per nine innings, strikeouts per nine innings — .33 relief innings per team game

Save percentage — .12 save opportunities per team game

Percentage of inherited runners scoring — .19 inherited runners per team game

First batter efficiency — .25 games in relief per team game

Fielders

Percentage caught stealing by catchers — .46 stolen-base attempts per team game

Fielding percentage — .62 games at a position per team game (.19 chances per team game for pitchers)

Other Players

Some players didn't play enough to merit a full- or half-page essay, and aren't young enough or good enough to deserve a prospect report. But they did play in the majors last year, so we give them a brief evaluation. Following the half-page reports for each team, you'll find a page devoted to these part-timers under the heading "Other Anaheim Angels," etc. Each player gets a short summary and his 1998 Outlook is graded as follows:

A — Should be an important contributor.
B — Should play at least part of the season in the majors and contribute.
C — Unlikely to play much time in the majors or contribute much if he does.
D — Unlikely to play in the majors.

Minor League Prospects

We present two pages of minor league prospects for each team, again including Arizona and Tampa Bay. Former *Baseball America* managing editor Jim Callis spoke directly to player-development personnel for most major league teams and also looked beyond athletic tools by analyzing statistics. Each club has eight featured prospects. We try to include most of the top phenoms, but our primary emphasis is on advanced players with the best chance of contributing in the majors in 1998.

For featured prospects who are hitters and played in Double-A or Triple-A in 1997, we include major league equivalencies. Developed by Bill James, The MLE translates minor league statistics into major league numbers. It does this by making a series of adjustments for a player's home ballpark, his league, his level of competition and his future major league home park. The MLE irons out many of the misleading illusions in minor league stats and indicates how the hitter would have done in 1997 at the major league level.

We also include an organization overview for each team. We tell you which clubs are the best and worst at developing talent, and we tell you why. In addition, we summarize another half-dozen or so notable prospects per team in a section called "Others to Watch." You can find them in the index, along with every other player in this book.

Where we mention that managers voted a player as the best in a specific category in his league, our source is *Baseball America*.

1997 American League Leaders

Batters

Batting Average
Frank Thomas	.347
Edgar Martinez	.330
David Justice	.329

Home Runs
Ken Griffey Jr	56
Tino Martinez	44
Juan Gonzalez	42

Runs Batted In
Ken Griffey Jr	147
Tino Martinez	141
Juan Gonzalez	131

Games Played
Cal Ripken	162
Brian L. Hunter	162
Albert Belle	161

At Bats
N. Garciaparra	684
Brian L. Hunter	658
Derek Jeter	654

Runs Scored
Ken Griffey Jr	125
Nomar Garciaparra	122
Chuck Knoblauch	117

Hits
N. Garciaparra	209
Rusty Greer	193
Derek Jeter	190

Singles
Garret Anderson	142
Derek Jeter	142
Brian L. Hunter	137

Doubles
John Valentin	47
Jeff Cirillo	46
Albert Belle	45

Triples
N. Garciaparra	11
Chuck Knoblauch	10
Johnny Damon	8
Jeromy Burnitz	8

Stolen Bases
Brian L. Hunter	74
Chuck Knoblauch	62
Tom Goodwin	50

Caught Stealing
Brian L. Hunter	18
Tom Goodwin	16
Ray Durham	16

Walks
Jim Thome	120
Edgar Martinez	119
Jay Buhner	119

Intentional Walks
Ken Griffey Jr	23
Mo Vaughn	17
Chili Davis	16

Hit by Pitch
Brady Anderson	19
Chuck Knoblauch	17
2 players tied with	16

Strikeouts
Jay Buhner	175
Melvin Nieves	157
Mo Vaughn	154

Ground into DP
Albert Belle	26
Mike Bordick	23
Jay Buhner	23

Sacrifice Bunts
Omar Vizquel	16
Deivi Cruz	14
Mike Bordick	12

Sacrifice Flies
Tino Martinez	13
3 players tied with	12

Plate Appearances
Derek Jeter	748
Brian L. Hunter	738
Nomar Garciaparra	734

Times on Base
Edgar Martinez	309
Frank Thomas	296
2 players tied with	279

Total Bases
Ken Griffey Jr	393
Nomar Garciaparra	365
Tino Martinez	343

Slugging Percentage
Ken Griffey Jr	.646
Frank Thomas	.611
David Justice	.596

Slugging off LHP
Dan Wilson	.651
Juan Gonzalez	.649
Matt Williams	.647

Slugging off RHP
Ken Griffey Jr	.699
Jim Thome	.638
Tino Martinez	.636

Cleanup Slugging
Mark McGwire	.603
Juan Gonzalez	.592
Jim Edmonds	.567

On-Base Average
Frank Thomas	.456
Edgar Martinez	.456
Jim Thome	.423

OBA off LHP
Ron Coomer	.459
Jay Buhner	.449
Geronimo Berroa	.444

OBA off RHP
Edgar Martinez	.469
Frank Thomas	.461
Jim Thome	.445

Leadoff OBA
Tim Raines	.417
Brady Anderson	.398
Derek Jeter	.394

AB/HR Frequency
Ken Griffey Jr	10.9
Jim Thome	12.4
Juan Gonzalez	12.7

Ground/Fly Ratio
Julio Franco	3.7
Derek Jeter	3.0
Reggie Jefferson	2.2

% Extra Bases Taken
Dave Hollins	73.2%
Dave Martinez	72.7
Damion Easley	71.2

Runs/Time On Base
N. Garciaparra	48.8%
Ken Griffey Jr	46.5
Tom Goodwin	45.9

SB Success %
Mike Cameron	92.0%
Chuck Knoblauch	86.1
Bip Roberts	85.7

Steals of third
Brian L. Hunter	14
Chuck Knoblauch	12
Alex Rodriguez	11

BA Scoring Position
Paul O'Neill	.428
Frank Thomas	.417
Ron Coomer	.370

BA Late & Close
Sandy Alomar Jr	.397
Omar Vizquel	.382
Darin Erstad	.381

BA Bases Loaded
Ken Griffey Jr	.857
Jeff Cirillo	.625
Joe Carter	.600

GDP/GDP Situation
Brady Anderson	0.9%
Johnny Damon	3.1
Dave Martinez	3.7

BA vs LH Pitchers
Ron Coomer	.415
Tony Fernandez	.407
Jose Offerman	.380

BA vs RH Pitchers
Reggie Jefferson	.352
Paul O'Neill	.346
Edgar Martinez	.345

BA at Home
Rusty Greer	.370
David Justice	.353
Ivan Rodriguez	.347

BA on the Road
Frank Thomas	.373
Bernie Williams	.353
Edgar Martinez	.339

BA on 3-1 Count
Alex Gonzalez	1.000
Benji Gil	.750
Russ Davis	.714

BA With 2 Strikes
Rusty Greer	.281
Mark Loretta	.277
Paul O'Neill	.273

BA on 0-2 Count
Will Clark	.391
Harold Baines	.348
Jim Thome	.316

BA on 3-2 Count
Paul Molitor	.481
Jorge Fabregas	.478
Mark Loretta	.421

Pitches Seen
Derek Jeter	2923
Chuck Knoblauch	2896
Brian L. Hunter	2820

Pitches Seen per PA
Jim Thome	4.46
Julio Franco	4.22
Jay Buhner	4.20

% Pitches Taken
Edgar Martinez	66.5%
Jim Thome	65.6
Wade Boggs	64.9

% of Missed Swings
Joey Cora	6.8%
Wade Boggs	7.4
Chuck Knoblauch	9.3

% Swings Put Into Play
Gary DiSarcina	60.5%
Wade Boggs	55.3
Joey Cora	54.2

Bunts in Play
Tom Goodwin	41
Otis Nixon	41
Omar Vizquel	29

Pitchers

Earned Run Average
Roger Clemens	2.05
Randy Johnson	2.28
David Cone	2.82

Wins
Roger Clemens	21
Brad Radke	20
Randy Johnson	20

Losses
Cal Eldred	15
James Baldwin	15
Tim Wakefield	15

Win-Loss Percentage
Randy Johnson	.833
Jamie Moyer	.773
Roger Clemens	.750

Games Pitched
Mike Myers	88
Buddy Groom	78
2 players tied with	77

Games Started
Andy Pettitte	35
Pat Hentgen	35
Brad Radke	35
Jeff Fassero	35

Complete Games
Pat Hentgen	9
Roger Clemens	9
3 players tied with	5

Shutouts
Pat Hentgen	3
Roger Clemens	3
6 players tied with	2

Games Finished
Doug Jones	73
Heathcliff Slocumb	61
John Wetteland	58

Innings Pitched
Roger Clemens	264.0
Pat Hentgen	264.0
Andy Pettitte	240.1

Hits Allowed
Jaime Navarro	267
Pat Hentgen	253
Charles Nagy	253

Batters Faced
Pat Hentgen	1085
Roger Clemens	1044
Jeff Fassero	1010

Runs Allowed
Jaime Navarro	155
Tim Belcher	128
James Baldwin	128

Earned Runs Allowed
Jaime Navarro	135
Tim Belcher	119
James Baldwin	117

Home Runs Allowed
Allen Watson	37
Bobby Witt	33
2 players tied with	32

Walks Allowed
Ken Hill	95
Cal Eldred	89
Tim Wakefield	87

Hit Batters
Tim Wakefield	16
Aaron Sele	15
Omar Olivares	13

Strikeouts
Roger Clemens	292
Randy Johnson	291
David Cone	222

Wild Pitches
James Baldwin	14
Kevin Appier	14
David Cone	14
Jaime Navarro	14

Balks
LaTroy Hawkins	3
Hideki Irabu	3
Paul Spoljaric	3
James Baldwin	3

Run Support per 9 IP
Jamie Moyer	7.7
Tim Belcher	6.5
Andy Pettitte	6.5

Baserunners per 9 IP
Roger Clemens	9.7
Randy Johnson	9.9
Mike Mussina	10.2

BA Allowed
Randy Johnson	.194
Roger Clemens	.213
David Cone	.218

BA Allowed Scor Pos
Randy Johnson	.154
Jimmy Key	.179
Roger Clemens	.180

Slugging Pct Allowed
Roger Clemens	.290
Randy Johnson	.318
Tom Gordon	.319

On-Base Pct Allowed
Roger Clemens	.273
Randy Johnson	.277
Mike Mussina	.282

Home Runs per 9 IP
Andy Pettitte	.262
Roger Clemens	.307
Tom Gordon	.493

Strikeouts per 9 IP
Randy Johnson	12.3
David Cone	10.2
Roger Clemens	10.0

Walks per 9 IP
John Burkett	1.4
Bob Tewksbury	1.7
Brad Radke	1.8

Strikeout/Walk Ratio
John Burkett	4.6
Roger Clemens	4.3
Mike Mussina	4.0

Stolen Bases Allowed
Jeff Suppan	25
Tim Wakefield	25
Scott Kamieniecki	25

Caught Stealing Off
Tim Wakefield	18
Randy Johnson	16
Pat Hentgen	15

SB% Allowed
Orel Hershiser	33.3%
Jason Dickson	41.7
Omar Olivares	42.9

GDPs induced
Andy Pettitte	36
Scott Erickson	33
Orel Hershiser	31

GDPs induced per 9 IP
Orel Hershiser	1.4
Andy Pettitte	1.3
Scott Erickson	1.3

GDPs/GDP Situation
Joe Hudson	22.2%
Rick Krivda	21.1
Scott Aldred	20.3

Grd/Fly Ratio Off
Scott Erickson	2.9
Charles Nagy	2.3
Orel Hershiser	2.2

Pitches Thrown
Roger Clemens	4106
Pat Hentgen	3914
Kevin Appier	3735

Pitches per Batter
Bob Tewksbury	3.43
Scott Erickson	3.46
David Wells	3.52

Pickoff Throws
Allen Watson	253
Jimmy Key	223
Scott Kamieniecki	215

ERA at Home
Roger Clemens	1.52
Randy Johnson	1.89
Andy Pettitte	2.65

ERA on the Road
David Cone	2.49
Roger Clemens	2.71
Randy Johnson	2.73

BA Off by LH Batters
Roger Clemens	.205
David Cone	.213
Mike Mussina	.221

BA Off by RH Batters
Randy Johnson	.186
Jose Mercedes	.215
Tom Gordon	.220

Relief ERA
Randy Myers	1.51
Mariano Rivera	1.88
John Wetteland	1.94

Relief Wins
Arthur Rhodes	10
Danny Patterson	10
Bobby Ayala	10

Relief Losses
H. Slocumb	9
Norm Charlton	8
Jeff Nelson	7
Paul Quantrill	7

Saves
Randy Myers	45
Mariano Rivera	43
Doug Jones	36

Blown Saves
Norm Charlton	11
Mariano Rivera	9
Mike Timlin	8

Save Opportunities
Mariano Rivera	52
Randy Myers	46
Doug Jones	38

Save Percentage			Relief Strikeouts/9 IP			Errors by Catcher			Errors by Left Field	
Randy Myers	97.8%		Armando Benitez	13.0		Sandy Alomar Jr	12		Rusty Greer	11
Doug Jones	94.7		Arthur Rhodes	9.6		Scott Hatteberg	11		Albert Belle	10
Troy Percival	87.1		Mike Stanton	9.4		Raul Casanova	9		Bob Higginson	6
R. Hernandez	87.1									

Holds / **% Inher Rnnrs Scored** / **Errors by First Base** / **Errors by Center Field**

Bob Wickman	28		Jeff Nelson	20.8%		Mo Vaughn	14		Ken Griffey Jr	6
Dan Plesac	27		Buddy Groom	20.8		Carlos Delgado	12		Rich Becker	5
Mike Stanton	26		Armando Benitez	21.1		Frank Thomas	11		Jim Edmonds	5
						Darin Erstad	11		Mike Cameron	5

Relief Innings / **First Batter Efficiency** / **Errors by Second Base** / **Errors by Right Field**

Greg Swindell	112.0		Jesse Orosco	.070		Ray Durham	18		Tim Salmon	11
Aaron Small	96.2		Troy Percival	.106		Joey Cora	17		Manny Ramirez	7
Bobby Ayala	96.2		John Wetteland	.107		Damion Easley	12		Jeromy Burnitz	7

Relief BA Allowed

Fielding

Errors by Third Base / **% CS off Catchers**

John Wetteland	.182		**Errors by Pitcher**			Dave Hollins	29		Ivan Rodriguez	56.0%
Armando Benitez	.191		Scott Erickson	6		Cal Ripken	22		Jim Leyritz	43.5
Jeff Nelson	.191		Bartolo Colon	5		Dean Palmer	19		Dan Wilson	43.1
			Chad Ogea	5						

Runners/9 IP - Relief

			Ariel Prieto	5		**Errors by Shortstop**				
Doug Jones	8.3					Alex Rodriguez	24			
John Wetteland	8.9					Nomar Garciaparra	21			
Greg Swindell	9.8					Pat Meares	20			
						Jose Valentin	20			

1997 National League Leaders

Batters

Batting Average

Tony Gwynn	.372
Larry Walker	.366
Mike Piazza	.362

Home Runs

Larry Walker	49
Jeff Bagwell	43
Andres Galarraga	41

Runs Batted In

Andres Galarraga	140
Jeff Bagwell	135
Larry Walker	130

Games Played

Jeff Bagwell	162
Craig Biggio	162
Sammy Sosa	162
Eric Karros	162

At Bats

M. Grudzielanek	649
Sammy Sosa	642
Tony Womack	641

Runs Scored

Craig Biggio	146
Larry Walker	143
Barry Bonds	123

Hits

Tony Gwynn	220
Larry Walker	208
Mike Piazza	201

Singles

Tony Gwynn	152
Edgar Renteria	143
Tony Womack	137

Doubles

M. Grudzielanek	54
Tony Gwynn	49
Larry Walker	46

Triples

Delino DeShields	14
Neifi Perez	10
3 players tied with	9

Stolen Bases

Tony Womack	60
Deion Sanders	56
Delino DeShields	55

Caught Stealing

Kenny Lofton	20
Edgar Renteria	15
Raul Mondesi	15

Walks

Barry Bonds	145
Jeff Bagwell	127
Gary Sheffield	121

Intentional Walks

Barry Bonds	34
Jeff Bagwell	27
Todd Hundley	16

Hit by Pitch

Craig Biggio	34
Jason Kendall	31
F.P. Santangelo	25

Strikeouts

Sammy Sosa	174
Ron Gant	162
Henry Rodriguez	149

Ground into DP

Fred McGriff	22
Butch Huskey	21
2 players tied with	20

Sacrifice Bunts

Edgar Renteria	19
Tom Glavine	17
Brett Butler	15

Sacrifice Flies

Tony Gwynn	12
Bernard Gilkey	12
2 players tied with	10

Plate Appearances

Craig Biggio	744
Eric Young	718
Jeff Bagwell	717

Times on Base

Craig Biggio	309
Barry Bonds	308
Jeff Bagwell	305

Total Bases

Larry Walker	409
Mike Piazza	355
Andres Galarraga	351

Slugging Percentage

Larry Walker	.720
Mike Piazza	.638
Jeff Bagwell	.592

Slugging off LHP

Vinny Castilla	.698
Ray Lankford	.662
Andres Galarraga	.643

Slugging off RHP

Larry Walker	.788
Mike Piazza	.644
Jeff Bagwell	.630

Cleanup Slugging

Barry Bonds	.579
Ray Lankford	.578
Todd Hundley	.578

On-Base Average

Larry Walker	.452
Barry Bonds	.446
Mike Piazza	.431

OBA off LHP

Mike Piazza	.450
Edgardo Alfonzo	.448
Craig Biggio	.444

OBA off RHP
Larry Walker	.470
Barry Bonds	.455
Ray Lankford	.426

Leadoff OBA
F.P. Santangelo	.427
Craig Biggio	.418
Rickey Henderson	.417

AB/HR Frequency
Larry Walker	11.6
Jeff Bagwell	13.2
Barry Bonds	13.3

Ground/Fly Ratio
Jose Vizcaino	2.3
Kenny Lofton	2.2
Quilvio Veras	2.1

% Extra Bases Taken
Larry Walker	70.7%
Craig Biggio	68.7
Steve Finley	67.7

Runs/Time On Base
Steve Finley	52.6%
Larry Walker	47.7
Doug Glanville	47.3

SB Success %
Tony Womack	89.6%
Stan Javier	89.3
Rickey Henderson	87.9

Steals of third
Deion Sanders	21
Tony Womack	16
Craig Biggio	14

BA Scoring Position
Tony Gwynn	.459
Edgardo Alfonzo	.417
John Olerud	.385

BA Late & Close
Tony Gwynn	.395
Jeff Blauser	.382
Jason Kendall	.373

BA Bases Loaded
Tony Young	.615
Edgardo Alfonzo	.600
J. Allensworth	.600

GDP/GDP Situation
Craig Biggio	0.0%
F.P. Santangelo	1.6
Pokey Reese	2.0

BA vs LH Pitchers
Vinny Castilla	.380
Edgardo Alfonzo	.378
Mike Piazza	.363

BA vs RH Pitchers
Larry Walker	.389
Tony Gwynn	.378
Mike Piazza	.361

BA at Home
Larry Walker	.384
Tony Gwynn	.378
Dante Bichette	.362

BA on the Road
Mike Piazza	.368
Tony Gwynn	.365
Larry Walker	.346

BA on 3-1 Count
Henry Rodriguez	1.000
Jon Nunnally	.800
Jim Eisenreich	.800

BA With 2 Strikes
Tony Gwynn	.358
Mike Piazza	.311
Bill Spiers	.310

BA on 0-2 Count
Tony Gwynn	.400
Doug Glanville	.359
Carlos Baerga	.341

BA on 3-2 Count
Bill Spiers	.485
Mark Lewis	.400
Mike Lieberthal	.385

Pitches Seen
Jeff Bagwell	2818
Todd Zeile	2757
Craig Biggio	2730

Pitches Seen per PA
Todd Hundley	4.30
Ray Lankford	4.25
Ron Gant	4.17

% Pitches Taken
R. Henderson	68.4%
Todd Zeile	65.7
Walt Weiss	64.7

% of Missed Swings
Tony Gwynn	8.0%
Gregg Jefferies	8.3
Lance Johnson	8.6

% Swings Put Into Play
Eric Young	60.3%
Lance Johnson	58.3
Tony Gwynn	58.0

Bunts in Play
Delino DeShields	40
Brett Butler	33
Edgar Renteria	32

Pitchers

Earned Run Average
Pedro Martinez	1.90
Greg Maddux	2.20
Darryl Kile	2.57

Wins
Denny Neagle	20
Darryl Kile	19
Shawn Estes	19
Greg Maddux	19

Losses
Mark Leiter	17
Steve Cooke	15
Jon Lieber	14

Win-Loss Percentage
Greg Maddux	.826
Denny Neagle	.800
Shawn Estes	.792

Games Pitched
Julian Tavarez	89
Stan Belinda	84
Jeff Shaw	78

Games Started
John Smoltz	35
Curt Schilling	35
4 players tied with	34

Complete Games
Pedro Martinez	13
Carlos Perez	8
3 players tied with	7

Shutouts
Carlos Perez	5
Denny Neagle	4
Darryl Kile	4
Pedro Martinez	4

Games Finished
Rod Beck	66
Robb Nen	65
Jeff Shaw	62

Innings Pitched
John Smoltz	256.0
Darryl Kile	255.2
Curt Schilling	254.1

Hits Allowed
John Smoltz	234
Steve Trachsel	225
Frank Castillo	220

Batters Faced
Darryl Kile	1056
John Smoltz	1043
Curt Schilling	1009

Runs Allowed
Mark Leiter	132
Frank Castillo	121
Jamey Wright	113

Earned Runs Allowed
Mark Leiter	115
Frank Castillo	111
Jamey Wright	104

Home Runs Allowed
Steve Trachsel	32
Mark Gardner	28
Kevin Foster	27
Roger Bailey	27

Walks Allowed
Shawn Estes	100
Darryl Kile	94
Hideo Nomo	92

Hit Batters
Kevin Brown	14
Roger Bailey	13
5 players tied with	12

Strikeouts
Curt Schilling	319
Pedro Martinez	305
John Smoltz	241

Wild Pitches
Mike Remlinger	12
Mark Leiter	11
3 players tied with	10

Balks
Hideo Nomo	4
6 players tied with	3

Run Support per 9 IP
Mike Hampton	6.2
Shawn Estes	6.0
Roger Bailey	5.9

Baserunners per 9 IP
Pedro Martinez	8.7
Greg Maddux	8.7
Curt Schilling	9.6

BA Allowed
Pedro Martinez	.184
Chan Ho Park	.213
Shawn Estes	.223

Slugging Pct Allowed
Pedro Martinez	.277
Greg Maddux	.311
Shawn Estes	.311

On-Base Pct Allowed
Pedro Martinez	.250
Greg Maddux	.256
Curt Schilling	.271

Home Runs per 9 IP
Greg Maddux	.348
Kevin Brown	.379
Andy Benes	.458

Strikeouts per 9 IP
Pedro Martinez	11.4
Curt Schilling	11.3
Hideo Nomo	10.1

Walks per 9 IP
Greg Maddux	0.8
Rick Reed	1.3
Denny Neagle	1.9

Strikeout/Walk Ratio
Greg Maddux	8.9
Curt Schilling	5.5
Pedro Martinez	4.6

Stolen Bases Allowed
Jeff Juden	41
Jim Bullinger	34
Andy Ashby	30

Caught Stealing Off
Al Leiter	16
Mark Gardner	16
Frank Castillo	15

SB% Allowed
Terry Mulholland	20.0%
Rick Reed	33.3
Mike Hampton	36.4

GDPs induced
Tom Glavine	33
Mike Hampton	27
Kevin Brown	26
Roger Bailey	26

GDPs induced per 9 IP
John Thomson	1.4
Tom Glavine	1.2
Roger Bailey	1.2

GDPs/GDP Situation
Mike Munoz	27.3%
Julian Tavarez	22.8
Marc Wilkins	21.1

Grd/Fly Ratio Off
Kevin Brown	3.6
Steve Cooke	2.9
Andy Ashby	2.4

BA Allowed Scor Pos
Darryl Kile	.171
Tom Glavine	.183
Ramon Martinez	.190

Pitches Thrown
Curt Schilling	4132
Darryl Kile	3826
John Smoltz	3698

Pitches per Batter
Greg Maddux	3.18
Carlos Perez	3.35
Roger Bailey	3.38

Pickoff Throws
Mark Gardner	220
Ismael Valdes	213
Kirk Rueter	210

ERA at Home
Pedro Martinez	1.99
Ismael Valdes	2.07
Tom Glavine	2.13

ERA on the Road
Pedro Martinez	1.78
Greg Maddux	2.24
Darryl Kile	2.55

BA Off by LH Batters
Pedro Martinez	.183
Brett Tomko	.190
Greg Maddux	.213

BA Off by RH Batters
Pedro Martinez	.184
Chan Ho Park	.187
Todd Stottlemyre	.189

Relief ERA
Tom Martin	2.09
Antonio Osuna	2.19
Darren Hall	2.30

Relief Wins
Marc Wilkins	9
Robb Nen	9
6 players tied with	7

Relief Losses
Greg McMichael	10
Terry Adams	9
4 players tied with	8

Saves
Jeff Shaw	42
Trevor Hoffman	37
Rod Beck	37

Blown Saves
Greg McMichael	11
Todd Worrell	9
Rod Beck	8

Save Opportunities
Jeff Shaw	49
Rod Beck	45
Todd Worrell	44
Trevor Hoffman	44

Save Percentage
Jeff Shaw	85.7%
John Franco	85.7
Rich Loiselle	85.3

Holds
Stan Belinda	28
Julian Tavarez	26
Scott Radinsky	26

Relief Innings
Stan Belinda	99.1
Scott Sullivan	97.1
Jerry Dipoto	95.2

Relief BA Allowed
Trevor Hoffman	.200
Darren Dreifort	.202
Billy Wagner	.204

Runners/9 IP - Relief
Bob Patterson	8.6
Jeff Shaw	8.7
Trevor Hoffman	9.2

Relief Strikeouts/9 IP
Billy Wagner	14.4
Trevor Hoffman	12.3
Russ Springer	12.0

% Inher Rnnrs Scored
Tony Fossas	10.0%
Alan Embree	14.0
Mike Remlinger	16.0

First Batter Efficiency
Doug Bochtler	.026
Darren Dreifort	.128
Trevor Hoffman	.147

Fielding

Errors by Pitcher
Matt Morris	5
4 players tied with	4

Errors by Catcher
Mike Piazza	16
Mike Lieberthal	12
3 players tied with	11

Errors by First Base
Andres Galarraga	15
Fred McGriff	13
Jeff Bagwell	11
Eric Karros	11

Errors by Second Base
Tony Womack	20
Delino DeShields	19
Craig Biggio	18
Eric Young	18

Errors by Third Base
Todd Zeile	26
Ken Caminiti	24
Scott Rolen	24

Errors by Shortstop
M. Grudzielanek	32
Royce Clayton	19
Edgar Renteria	17

Errors by Left Field
Ron Gant	6
Al Martin	6
Ryan Klesko	6

Errors by Center Field
Ray Lankford	9
Lance Johnson	7
Darryl Hamilton	5
Kenny Lofton	5

Errors by Right Field
Vladimir Guerrero	12
Glenallen Hill	9
Jose Guillen	9

% CS off Catchers
Brad Ausmus	49.5%
Charles Johnson	47.5
Jason Kendall	37.1

Stars, Bums and Sleepers — Who's Who in 1998

Who will be the next Nomar Garciaparra? No one has the answer, but everyone has an opinion. Here at STATS, we have our own ideas about 1998's surprise players. As we do every year, we present our choices and much more in this section.

Last year, we hit on several of our choices for sleepers: Garciaparra, Tony Clark, Damion Easley, Darin Erstad, Jeffrey Hammonds, Scott Rolen, Justin Thompson and Rondell White. Our success involved a lot more than luck. There were good reasons to expect those three players to perform beyond their established expectations. There are several similar players on the horizon for 1998, and we'll tip you off on all of them.

In addition to the always-in-demand sleeper picks, we also tell you which players are most likely to improve, decline, or remain consistent. We'll admit that certain players don't present much of a challenge. We're quite confident that Greg Maddux will remain one of baseball's best pitchers and that Tony Gwynn will contend for another batting title. But we don't just make the easy picks. We make all the picks.

How do we do it? Well, we don't want give away all our secrets, but we assure you that the office dartboard plays absolutely no part in the process. Those of you familiar with the work of Bill James, particularly *The Bill James Baseball Abstract*, may recall that he designed a system to predict a player's future performance. The heart of the system is the simple truth that a player's past history is the best indicator of his future production. Over the past few years, Bill and STATS President John Dewan have refined the system further. Its results, combined with the subjective advice of our scouts and staff experts, help us form the lists that follow.

The system is quite complex. If we apply it to a .300 hitter, it won't just tell us that the guy will hit .300 next year and leave it at that. The system also takes into account general truths about how a player's production changes over time. For example, younger players tend to get better, while older players tend to decline, with age 27 typically being the peak offensive season for a position player. Age 27 is also the most common year for a player to have a "career year," which we also take into account. It's likely that a player who has an unexpectedly good year will have trouble repeating it. A player who improves the previous season will tend to decline the next, and vice versa. We've developed several other reliable indicators as well.

How To Use This Section

Every position is broken into four groups: Expect A Better Year in '98, Look for Consistency, Production Will Drop and 1998 Sleepers. A player is put into one of the first three groups based on his 1997 performance only. For example, Sandy Alomar Jr. is listed under Production Will Drop. That means he shouldn't be expected him to hit .324 with a .545 slugging percentage again. That doesn't mean he's going to turn into Kirt Manwaring. It just indicates that Alomar's production will drop, not that it will disappear.

We do things a little differently with the 1998 Sleepers. Not every pick will turn out as well as Garciaparra, but many of this year's selections will wake up the baseball world. The statistics we show in this section are combined major and minor league totals, in order to show what the players are capable of doing. We factored projected playing time into the equation as this book went to press in late 1997.

How We Developed This Section

We broke down all the regular major league players from this book into their most common position played in 1997, and made a few adjustments if the player projected to start at a different spot in 1998. Cliff Floyd is one example. We then developed statistical analysis and subjective ratings for each player.

For our statistical model, we looked at historical

patterns of performance. Here are some of the factors that we plugged into our computers:

Career Trends — A player should not be judged simply on his most recent year of performance, though most fans and many experts tend to do just that. While it's possible that a player who had a good year in relation to the rest of his career suddenly has become a better ballplayer, it's much more likely that it was simply a good year. Larry Walker hit .295 with 38 homers per 150 games in his first two seasons in Colorado, then jumped to .366 with 49 longballs last year. He might contend for another National League Most Valuable Player Award in 1998, but his production likely will settle in between last year's and his previously established levels. In short, it's a lot easier to have a fluke year than a fluke career. The same is true about a player who suffered through an off year. If his slump doesn't result in a severe reduction in playing time, the player usually will rebound to some extent.

Player Age — Based on historical studies, the prime year for a hitter to have his best year is age 27. The rule of thumb is that if a batter is younger than 27, he can be expected to improve over his established level of play. If a batter is older than 27, he can be expect to decline. The age when a pitcher reaches his peak is more difficult to pin down. Instead of defining a specific peak age as we do for hitters, we identify other factors that

indicate whether a pitcher should improve or decline.

Minor League Performance — Bill James found that minor league performance, when properly adjusted, is just as reliable as major league performance for predicting how a player will do in the big leagues. Therefore, we've looked at minor league performance to help us project 1998, especially for the players we call "Sleepers."

We then add our own thoughts:

Playing Time — When considering how productive a player will be, we estimate how often he'll play by evaluating him compared to his teammates. As this book goes to press, Cliff Floyd hasn't been guaranteed an everday job by the Marlins. But they have an opening at first base and Floyd can hit, so we think he'll start there for Florida. Spring training will shed more light on playing time, but we don't have the luxury of waiting. We also take into account a player's injury history. We project that Cal Ripken will be in Baltimore's lineup every day, but we're not as confident about Eric Davis.

Pitchers' Inconsistency — For every five hitters who are reasonably consistent from year to year, there's probably one pitcher who's as reliable. Pitchers are full of surprises, so we use many subjective considerations when evaluating them.

Catcher

Expect A Better Year in '98

| | 1997 Statistics | | | |
	Avg.	HR	RBI	SB
Benito Santiago	.243	13	42	1
Joe Girardi	.264	1	50	2
Scott Servais	.260	6	45	0
Eddie Taubensee	.268	10	34	0
Mike Macfarlane	.237	8	35	0
Tony Eusebio	.274	1	18	0
Charlie O'Brien	.218	4	27	0

Look for Consistency

| | 1997 Statistics | | | |
	Avg.	HR	RBI	SB
Mike Piazza	.362	40	124	5
Ivan Rodriguez	.313	20	77	7
Jason Kendall	.294	8	49	18
Javy Lopez	.295	23	68	1
Dan Wilson	.270	15	74	7
Charles Johnson	.250	19	63	0
Darrin Fletcher	.277	17	55	1
Terry Steinbach	.248	12	54	6
Jorge Fabregas	.258	7	51	1
Joe Oliver	.258	14	43	1
Scott Hatteberg	.277	10	44	0
Brad Ausmus	.266	4	44	14
John Flaherty	.273	9	46	4
Brian Johnson	.261	13	45	1
Jesse Levis	.285	1	19	1
Gregg Zaun	.301	2	20	1
Jorge Posada	.250	6	25	1
Mike Matheny	.244	4	32	0
Chris Widger	.234	7	37	2

Look for Consistency (continued)

Kirt Manwaring	.226	1	27	1
Mike Difelice	.238	4	30	1
Rick Wilkins	.198	7	27	0

Production Will Drop

| | 1997 Statistics | | | |
	Avg.	HR	RBI	SB
Sandy Alomar Jr	.324	21	83	0
Mike Lieberthal	.246	20	77	3
Jim Leyritz	.277	11	64	2
Todd Hundley	.273	30	86	2
Jeff Reed	.297	17	47	2
Lenny Webster	.255	7	37	0
Brent Mayne	.289	6	22	1

1998 Sleepers

| | 1997 Statistics (includes minor leagues) | | | |
	Avg.	HR	RBI	SB
Todd Greene	.333	34	99	7
Chris Hoiles	.257	12	51	1
Mike Sweeney	.240	17	60	3
Eli Marrero	.270	22	75	8
Raul Casanova	.238	6	27	1
Todd Pratt	.295	11	53	1
George Williams	.286	4	28	0
Bill Haselman	.228	8	30	1
Bobby Estalella	.240	20	74	3

First Base

Expect A Better Year in '98

| | 1997 Statistics | | | |
	Avg.	HR	RBI	SB
John Jaha	.247	11	26	1
Jeff Conine	.242	17	61	2
Hal Morris	.276	1	33	3
Mike Blowers	.293	5	20	0
Scott Stahoviak	.229	10	33	5
Mark Johnson	.215	4	29	1

Look for Consistency

| | 1997 Statistics | | | |
	Avg.	HR	RBI	SB
Frank Thomas	.347	35	125	1
Jeff Bagwell	.286	43	135	31
Mark McGwire	.274	58	123	3
Mo Vaughn	.315	35	96	2
Jim Thome	.286	40	102	1
Rafael Palmeiro	.254	38	110	5
Mark Grace	.319	13	78	2
Will Clark	.326	12	51	0
John Olerud	.294	22	102	0
Eric Karros	.266	31	104	15
Carlos Delgado	.262	30	91	0
Eduardo Perez	.253	16	52	5
Dave Nilsson	.278	20	81	2
Darin Erstad	.299	16	77	23
Fred McGriff	.277	22	97	5
David Segui	.307	21	68	1
Dmitri Young	.258	5	34	6

Production Will Drop

| | 1997 Statistics | | | |
	Avg.	HR	RBI	SB
Tino Martinez	.296	44	141	3
Andres Galarraga	.318	41	140	15
Tony Clark	.276	32	117	1
J.T. Snow	.281	28	104	6
Jeff King	.238	28	112	16
Paul Sorrento	.269	31	80	0
Wally Joyner	.327	13	83	3
Lee Stevens	.300	21	74	1
Rico Brogna	.252	20	81	12
Kevin Young	.300	18	74	11

1998 Sleepers

| | 1997 Statistics (includes minor leagues) | | | |
	Avg.	HR	RBI	SB
Cliff Floyd	.299	15	52	13
Ryan McGuire	.277	6	32	6
Brad Fullmer	.307	25	87	7
Larry Sutton	.298	21	80	0
David Arias	.318	32	130	4

Second Base

Expect A Better Year in '98

	1997 Statistics			
	Avg.	HR	RBI	SB
Roberto Alomar	.333	14	60	9
Scott Spiezio	.243	14	65	9
Quilvio Veras	.265	3	45	33
Jose Offerman	.297	2	39	9
Mark Loretta	.287	5	47	5
Wilton Guerrero	.291	4	32	6
Mark Lemke	.245	2	26	2
Carlos Garcia	.220	3	23	11
Tony Graffanino	.258	8	20	6

Look for Consistency

	1997 Statistics			
	Avg.	HR	RBI	SB
Chuck Knoblauch	.291	9	58	62
John Valentin	.306	18	77	7
Ray Durham	.271	11	53	33
Tony Phillips	.275	8	57	13
Mike Lansing	.281	20	70	11
Carlos Baerga	.281	9	52	2
Kurt Abbott	.274	6	30	3
Keith Lockhart	.279	6	32	0
Mariano Duncan	.236	1	25	6

Production Will Drop

	1997 Statistics			
	Avg.	HR	RBI	SB
Craig Biggio	.309	22	81	47
Delino DeShields	.295	11	58	55
Eric Young	.280	8	61	45
Jeff Kent	.250	29	121	11
Damion Easley	.264	22	72	28
Mickey Morandini	.295	1	39	16
Joey Cora	.300	11	54	6
Tony Womack	.278	6	50	60
Luis Alicea	.253	5	37	22
Domingo Cedeno	.282	4	36	3
Jeff Frye	.312	3	51	19
Tony Fernandez	.286	11	44	6

1998 Sleepers

	1997 Statistics (includes minor leagues)			
	Avg.	HR	RBI	SB
Craig Counsell	.324	6	79	13
Fernando Vina	.290	5	36	8
Bret Boone	.224	7	47	6
Mark McLemore	.262	1	29	9
Ralph Milliard	.260	4	25	9
Luis Castillo	.277	0	13	24
Jed Hansen	.276	12	58	11
Miguel Cairo	.278	5	47	40
Jason Hardtke	.281	14	57	4
Tony Batista	.247	7	39	4

Third Base

Expect A Better Year in '98

	1997 Statistics			
	Avg.	HR	RBI	SB
Dean Palmer	.256	23	86	2
Wade Boggs	.292	4	28	0
Tim Naehring	.286	9	40	1
Ed Sprague	.228	14	48	0
Scott Brosius	.203	11	41	9
Jose Hernandez	.273	7	26	2

Look for Consistency

	1997 Statistics			
	Avg.	HR	RBI	SB
Chipper Jones	.295	21	111	20
Vinny Castilla	.304	40	113	2
Travis Fryman	.274	22	102	16
Matt Williams	.263	32	105	12
Scott Rolen	.283	21	92	16
Ken Caminiti	.290	26	90	11
Jeff Cirillo	.288	10	82	4
Bobby Bonilla	.297	17	96	6
Cal Ripken	.270	17	84	1
Willie Greene	.253	26	91	6
Ron Coomer	.298	13	85	4
Russ Davis	.271	20	63	6
Bill Mueller	.292	7	44	4
Brent Gates	.238	3	20	0
Mark Lewis	.267	10	42	3
Dave Magadan	.303	4	30	1

Production Will Drop

	1997 Statistics			
	Avg.	HR	RBI	SB
Todd Zeile	.268	31	90	8
Edgardo Alfonzo	.315	10	72	11
Dave Hollins	.288	16	85	16
Joe Randa	.302	7	60	4
Gary Gaetti	.251	17	69	7
Bill Spiers	.320	4	48	10
Charlie Hayes	.258	11	53	3
Dale Sveum	.261	12	47	0

1998 Sleepers

	1997 Statistics (includes minor leagues)			
	Avg.	HR	RBI	SB
Robin Ventura	.274	9	33	0
Todd Walker	.310	14	69	12
Fernando Tatis	.293	32	90	20
Paul Konerko	.320	37	127	2
Kevin Orie	.286	11	58	2
Mark Bellhorn	.280	17	65	13
Sean Berry	.258	8	43	1
Greg Norton	.275	26	77	3

Shortstop

Expect A Better Year in '98

| | 1997 Statistics | | | |
	Avg.	HR	RBI	SB
Alex Rodriguez	.300	23	84	29
Barry Larkin	.317	4	20	14
Jose Valentin	.253	17	58	19
Alex Gonzalez	.239	12	35	15
Kevin Elster	.225	7	25	0
Rey Ordonez	.216	1	33	11
Orlando Miller	.234	2	10	1

Look for Consistency

| | 1997 Statistics | | | |
	Avg.	HR	RBI	SB
Derek Jeter	.291	10	70	23
Edgar Renteria	.277	4	52	32
Mark Grudzielanek	.273	4	51	25
Jose Vizcaino	.266	5	50	8
Walt Weiss	.270	4	38	5
Pat Meares	.276	10	60	7
Pokey Reese	.219	4	26	25
Benji Gil	.224	5	31	1
Chris Gomez	.253	5	54	5
Kevin Stocker	.266	4	40	11
Gary DiSarcina	.246	4	47	7
Mike Bordick	.236	7	46	0
Deivi Cruz	.241	2	40	3
Ricky Gutierrez	.261	3	34	5
Denny Hocking	.257	2	25	3

Production Will Drop

| | 1997 Statistics | | | |
	Avg.	HR	RBI	SB
Nomar Garciaparra	.306	30	98	22
Jay Bell	.291	21	92	10
Omar Vizquel	.280	5	49	43
Royce Clayton	.266	9	61	30
Jeff Blauser	.308	17	70	5
Shawon Dunston	.300	14	57	32
Ozzie Guillen	.245	4	52	5
Greg Gagne	.251	9	57	2
Tim Bogar	.249	4	30	4

1998 Sleepers

| | 1997 Statistics (includes minor leagues) | | | |
	Avg.	HR	RBI	SB
Neifi Perez	.326	13	77	12
Enrique Wilson	.307	11	40	9
Miguel Tejada	.263	24	107	17
Manny Alexander	.266	3	22	13
Damian Jackson	.279	5	22	26
Desi Relaford	.261	9	59	32
Lou Collier	.313	1	51	13

Left Field

Expect A Better Year in '98

| | 1997 Statistics | | | |
	Avg.	HR	RBI	SB
Albert Belle	.274	30	116	4
Brian Giles	.268	17	61	13
Ryan Klesko	.261	24	84	4
Bernard Gilkey	.249	18	78	7
Ron Gant	.229	17	62	14
Gregg Jefferies	.256	11	48	12
Greg Vaughn	.216	18	57	7
Tim Raines	.321	4	38	8

Look for Consistency

| | 1997 Statistics | | | |
	Avg.	HR	RBI	SB
Barry Bonds	.291	40	101	37
Dante Bichette	.308	26	118	6
Al Martin	.291	13	59	23
Garret Anderson	.303	8	92	10
Jason Giambi	.293	20	81	0
Luis Gonzalez	.258	10	68	10
Henry Rodriguez	.244	26	83	3
Mark Smith	.285	9	35	3
Jim Eisenreich	.280	2	34	0
Phil Nevin	.235	9	35	0

Production Will Drop

| | 1997 Statistics | | | |
	Avg.	HR	RBI	SB
Rusty Greer	.321	26	87	9
David Justice	.329	33	101	3
Bob Higginson	.299	27	101	12
Moises Alou	.292	23	115	9
B.J. Surhoff	.284	18	88	1
Wil Cordero	.281	18	72	1
Rickey Henderson	.248	8	34	45
Chad Curtis	.284	15	55	12
Doug Glanville	.300	4	35	19
Bip Roberts	.302	4	44	18

1998 Sleepers

| | 1997 Statistics (includes minor leagues) | | | |
	Avg.	HR	RBI	SB
Todd Helton	.338	21	99	3
Jose Cruz Jr	.255	32	98	10
Marty Cordova	.254	16	55	6
Chris Stynes	.305	15	89	18
Marc Newfield	.245	2	21	0
Todd Dunn	.284	21	75	8
Yamil Benitez	.285	29	92	14
Billy McMillon	.277	14	61	12
Rod Myers	.259	4	22	10
Jeff Abbott	.322	12	65	12
Todd Hollandsworth	.275	5	47	7
Karim Garcia	.282	21	74	11
Patrick Lennon	.312	11	53	0
Brian Lesher	.300	25	94	18

Center Field

Expect A Better Year in '98

	1997 Statistics			
	Avg.	HR	RBI	SB
Kenny Lofton	.333	5	48	27
Brian McRae	.242	11	43	17
Marquis Grissom	.262	12	66	22
Johnny Damon	.275	8	48	16
Lance Johnson	.307	5	39	20
Rich Becker	.264	10	45	17
Devon White	.245	6	34	13
Midre Cummings	.264	4	31	2
Thomas Howard	.247	3	22	1
Curtis Goodwin	.253	1	12	22

Look for Consistency

	1997 Statistics			
	Avg.	HR	RBI	SB
Ken Griffey Jr	.304	56	147	15
Brady Anderson	.288	18	73	18
Jim Edmonds	.291	26	80	5
Steve Finley	.261	28	92	15
Ellis Burks	.290	32	82	7
Rondell White	.270	28	82	16
Darryl Hamilton	.270	5	43	15
Darren Bragg	.257	9	57	10
Quinton McCracken	.292	3	36	28
Shane Mack	.315	3	17	2
Tom Goodwin	.260	2	39	50
Damon Buford	.224	8	39	18
Damon Mashore	.247	3	18	5
Jason Mcdonald	.263	4	14	13

Production Will Drop

	1997 Statistics			
	Avg.	HR	RBI	SB
Bernie Williams	.328	21	100	15
Ray Lankford	.295	31	98	21
Brian L. Hunter	.269	4	45	74
Gerald Williams	.253	10	41	23
Otis Nixon	.266	2	44	59
Carl Everett	.248	14	57	17

1998 Sleepers

	1997 Statistics (includes minor leagues)			
	Avg.	HR	RBI	SB
Mike Cameron	.263	20	72	27
Jon Nunnally	.293	29	72	15
Shannon Stewart	.319	5	46	19
Mark Kotsay	.294	20	81	20
J. Allensworth	.262	3	44	15
Richard Hidalgo	.282	13	84	7
Ernie Young	.276	14	60	6
Roger Cedeno	.303	5	26	14
Todd Dunwoody	.262	25	69	27
Dante Powell	.246	12	45	35
Michael Coleman	.299	21	79	25
Ryan Christenson	.330	17	77	27

Right Field

Expect A Better Year in '98

	1997 Statistics			
	Avg.	HR	RBI	SB
Gary Sheffield	.250	21	71	11
Andruw Jones	.231	18	70	20
Derek Bell	.276	15	71	15
Matt Lawton	.248	14	60	7
Shawn Green	.287	16	53	14
Orlando Merced	.266	9	40	7
Melvin Nieves	.228	20	64	1
John Mabry	.284	5	36	0
Glenallen Hill	.261	11	64	7
Eric Davis	.304	8	25	6
Alex Ochoa	.244	3	22	3
Danny Tartabull	.000	0	0	0
Matt Mieske	.249	5	21	1

Look for Consistency

	1997 Statistics			
	Avg.	HR	RBI	SB
Tim Salmon	.296	33	129	9
Manny Ramirez	.328	26	88	2
Jay Buhner	.243	40	109	0
Raul Mondesi	.310	30	87	32
Sammy Sosa	.251	36	119	22
Matt Stairs	.298	27	73	3
Geronimo Berroa	.283	26	90	4
Jeromy Burnitz	.281	27	85	20
Troy O'Leary	.309	15	80	0
Michael Tucker	.283	14	56	12
Jeffrey Hammonds	.264	21	55	15
Mark Sweeney	.280	2	23	2
Butch Huskey	.287	24	81	8
Jose Guillen	.267	14	70	1

Look for Consistency (continued)

	Avg.	HR	RBI	SB
Roberto Kelly	.291	12	59	9
F.P. Santangelo	.249	5	31	8

Production Will Drop

	1997 Statistics			
	Avg.	HR	RBI	SB
Larry Walker	.366	49	130	33
Paul O'Neill	.324	21	117	10
Tony Gwynn	.372	17	119	12
Dave Martinez	.286	12	55	12
Darren Daulton	.263	14	63	6
Stan Javier	.286	8	50	25
Willie McGee	.300	3	38	8

1998 Sleepers

	1997 Statistics (includes minor leagues)			
	Avg.	HR	RBI	SB
Ben Grieve	.344	34	160	5
Vladimir Guerrero	.304	11	42	4
Bubba Trammell	.244	32	88	5
Reggie Sanders	.260	20	60	13
Brian Jordan	.224	0	12	6
Magglio Ordonez	.328	18	101	15
Jacob Cruz	.351	12	98	18
Jermaine Dye	.260	17	47	2
Juan Encarnacion	.316	27	95	20
Brent Brede	.324	12	97	11
Bob Abreu	.256	5	48	14
Raul Ibanez	.295	16	88	7
Phil Plantier	.293	11	40	2
Tony Tarasco	.204	9	32	2

Designated Hitter

Expect A Better Year in '98

| | 1997 Statistics | | | |
	Avg.	HR	RBI	SB
Cecil Fielder	.260	13	61	0
Jose Canseco	.235	23	74	8

Look for Consistency

| | 1997 Statistics | | | |
	Avg.	HR	RBI	SB
Juan Gonzalez	.296	42	131	0
Edgar Martinez	.330	28	108	2
Reggie Jefferson	.319	13	67	1
Harold Baines	.301	16	67	0
Mike Stanley	.297	16	65	0
Bob Hamelin	.270	18	52	2

Production Will Drop

| | 1997 Statistics | | | |
	Avg.	HR	RBI	SB
Chili Davis	.279	30	90	6
Paul Molitor	.305	10	89	11
Joe Carter	.234	21	102	8
Julio Franco	.270	7	44	15

1998 Sleepers

| | 1997 Statistics (includes minor leagues) | | | |
	Avg.	HR	RBI	SB
Bubba Trammell	.245	32	88	5
Brooks Kieschnick	.247	25	78	1

Starting Pitchers

Expect A Better Year in '98

| | 1997 Statistics | | | | |
	W	L	ERA	Sv	BR/IP
Bret Saberhagen	0	1	6.58	0	1.62
Kevin Appier	9	13	3.40	0	1.24
Andy Benes	10	7	3.10	0	1.21
Ismael Valdes	10	11	2.65	0	1.12
Hideo Nomo	14	12	4.25	0	1.42
Kenny Rogers	6	7	5.65	0	1.59
Andy Ashby	9	11	4.13	0	1.30
John Smiley	11	14	5.31	0	1.50
Jack McDowell	3	3	5.09	0	1.55
Ramon Martinez	10	5	3.64	0	1.47
James Baldwin	12	15	5.26	0	1.47
Jaime Navarro	9	14	5.79	0	1.64
Steve Karsay	3	12	5.77	0	1.67
Erik Hanson	0	0	7.80	0	1.40
Tom Gordon	6	10	3.74	11	1.29
Brian Anderson	4	2	4.69	0	1.38
Kevin Ritz	6	8	5.87	0	1.76
Steve Avery	6	7	6.42	0	1.84
Scott Aldred	2	10	7.68	0	1.72
Glendon Rusch	6	9	5.50	0	1.56
Tony Saunders	4	6	4.61	0	1.48
Amaury Telemaco	0	3	6.16	0	1.53
Pete Schourek	5	8	5.42	0	1.42
Juan Guzman	3	6	4.95	0	1.35
Jeff Suppan	7	3	5.69	0	1.60
Rheal Cormier	0	1	33.75	0	3.75
Pat Rapp	5	8	4.83	0	1.66
Shane Reynolds	9	10	4.23	0	1.32
Willie Adams	3	5	8.18	0	1.87
Jose Rosado	9	12	4.69	0	1.40
Jeff D'Amico	9	7	4.71	0	1.40
Jamey Wright	8	12	6.25	0	1.87
Mike Busby	0	2	8.79	0	1.95
W. VanLandingham	4	7	4.96	0	1.56
Mike Johnson	2	6	6.83	2	1.61
Mark Thompson	3	3	7.89	0	1.92
Felipe Lira	5	11	6.34	0	1.74
Glenn Dishman	1	2	5.28	0	1.38
Bryan Rekar	1	0	5.79	0	1.82
S. Wojciechowski	0	2	7.84	0	1.74
Terrell Wade	2	3	5.36	0	1.86
Osvaldo Fernandez	3	4	4.95	0	1.58
Esteban Yan	0	1	15.83	0	3.00
John Thomson	7	9	4.71	0	1.50
Matt Perisho	0	2	6.00	0	2.00
Chris Brock	0	0	5.58	0	1.73
Sean Lowe	0	2	9.35	0	2.19

Look for Consistency

| | 1997 Statistics | | | | |
	W	L	ERA	Sv	BR/IP
Brett Tomko	11	7	3.43	0	1.25
Danny Darwin	5	11	4.35	0	1.45
Mike Morgan	9	12	4.78	0	1.37
Orel Hershiser	14	6	4.47	0	1.43
Dwight Gooden	9	5	4.91	0	1.66
Mark Portugal	0	2	4.61	0	1.61
Bob Tewksbury	8	13	4.22	0	1.38
Bobby Witt	12	12	4.82	0	1.54
Doug Drabek	12	11	5.74	0	1.44
Chuck Finley	13	6	4.23	0	1.35
David Cone	12	6	2.82	0	1.26
Greg Maddux	19	4	2.20	0	0.97
Terry Mulholland	6	13	4.24	0	1.35
Kevin Brown	16	8	2.69	0	1.24
Cal Eldred	13	15	4.99	0	1.51
Tim Belcher	13	12	5.02	0	1.49
David Wells	16	10	4.21	0	1.33
John Burkett	9	12	4.56	0	1.45
Tom Glavine	14	7	2.96	0	1.17
Chan Ho Park	14	8	3.38	0	1.18
Al Leiter	11	9	4.34	0	1.56
Ken Hill	9	12	4.55	0	1.54
Todd Stottlemyre	12	9	3.88	0	1.28
Terry Clark	1	7	6.00	0	1.67
John Smoltz	15	12	3.02	0	1.16
Curt Schilling	17	11	2.97	0	1.07
Randy Johnson	20	4	2.28	0	1.10
Mark Gardner	12	9	4.29	0	1.36
Kevin Tapani	9	3	3.39	0	1.20
Wilson Alvarez	13	11	3.48	0	1.30
Steve Cooke	9	15	4.30	0	1.61
Woody Williams	9	14	4.35	0	1.40
Jason Bere	4	2	4.71	0	1.40
Bobby Munoz	1	5	8.91	0	1.92
Ben McDonald	8	7	4.06	0	1.21
Charles Nagy	15	11	4.28	0	1.48
Mark Leiter	10	17	5.67	0	1.58
Omar Olivares	6	10	4.97	0	1.61
LaTroy Hawkins	6	12	5.84	0	1.79
Dave Burba	11	10	4.72	0	1.49
Jeff Fassero	16	9	3.61	0	1.34
Frank Castillo	12	12	5.42	0	1.61
Mike Mussina	15	8	3.20	0	1.13
Armando Reynoso	6	3	4.53	0	1.42
Pat Hentgen	15	10	3.68	0	1.25
Mark Clark	14	8	3.82	0	1.35
Jeff Juden	11	6	4.46	0	1.48
Jim Bullinger	7	12	5.56	0	1.62

Look For Consistency (cont.)

	W	L	ERA	Sv	BR/IP
Pedro Astacio	12	10	4.14	0	1.33
Tim Wakefield	12	15	4.25	0	1.47
Roger Bailey	9	10	4.29	0	1.53
Esteban Loaiza	11	11	4.13	0	1.44
Sterling Hitchcock	10	11	5.20	0	1.43
Dave Mlicki	8	12	4.00	0	1.42
Tyler Green	4	4	4.93	0	1.54
Mike Hampton	15	10	3.83	0	1.33
Rich Robertson	8	12	5.69	0	1.67
Dave Telgheder	4	6	6.06	0	1.69
Kevin Foster	10	7	4.61	0	1.43
Aaron Sele	13	12	5.38	0	1.64
Allen Watson	12	12	4.93	0	1.51
Kirk Rueter	13	6	3.45	0	1.29
Bobby Jones	15	9	3.63	0	1.25
Darren Oliver	13	12	4.20	0	1.52
Mark Langston	2	4	5.85	0	1.51
Dennis Springer	9	9	5.18	0	1.45
Steve Trachsel	8	12	4.51	0	1.49
Chad Ogea	8	9	4.99	0	1.51
Jon Lieber	11	14	4.49	0	1.30
Joey Hamilton	12	7	4.25	0	1.45
Andrew Lorraine	3	1	6.37	0	2.06
Scott Karl	10	13	4.47	0	1.46
Andy Pettitte	18	7	2.88	0	1.25
Tanyon Sturtze	1	1	8.27	0	1.93
Carlos Perez	12	13	3.88	0	1.25
Ariel Prieto	6	8	5.04	0	1.84
Rick Krivda	4	2	6.30	0	1.70
Bob Wolcott	5	6	6.03	0	1.63
Mike Grace	3	2	3.46	0	1.10
Robert Person	5	10	5.61	0	1.48
Doug Creek	1	2	6.75	0	1.95
Francisco Cordova	11	8	3.63	0	1.30
Greg Keagle	3	5	6.55	0	1.79
Matt Beech	4	9	5.07	0	1.53
John Burke	2	5	6.56	0	1.95
Travis Miller	1	5	7.63	0	1.82
Calvin Maduro	3	7	7.23	0	1.79
Jeremi Gonzalez	11	9	4.25	0	1.37
Matt Morris	12	9	3.19	0	1.31

Production Will Drop

	1997 Statistics				
	W	L	ERA	Sv	BR/IP
Roger Clemens	21	7	2.05	0	1.08
Denny Neagle	20	5	2.97	0	1.11
Jimmy Key	16	10	3.43	0	1.40
Alex Fernandez	17	12	3.59	0	1.21
Rick Reed	13	9	2.89	0	1.07
Kent Mercker	8	11	3.92	0	1.38
Brian Bohanon	6	4	3.82	0	1.41

Production Will Drop (cont.)

	W	L	ERA	Sv	BR/IP
Willie Blair	16	8	4.17	0	1.34
Scott Erickson	16	7	3.69	0	1.28
Darryl Kile	19	7	2.57	0	1.22
Scott Kamieniecki	10	6	4.01	0	1.39
Pedro Martinez	17	8	1.90	0	0.97
Mike Oquist	4	6	5.02	0	1.49
Gabe White	2	2	4.39	1	1.17
Jose Mercedes	7	10	3.79	0	1.28
Paul Menhart	2	3	4.70	0	1.25
Brad Radke	20	10	3.87	0	1.21
Jason Schmidt	10	9	4.60	0	1.48
Dustin Hermanson	8	8	3.69	0	1.27
Jim Pittsley	5	8	5.46	0	1.61
Mike Sirotka	3	0	2.25	0	1.31
Jimmy Haynes	3	6	4.42	0	1.58
Shawn Estes	19	5	3.18	0	1.34
Alan Benes	9	9	2.89	0	1.24
Justin Thompson	15	11	3.02	0	1.15
Dan Serafini	2	1	3.42	0	1.44
Jamie Moyer	17	5	3.86	0	1.26
Garrett Stephenson	8	6	3.15	0	1.24
Jason Dickson	13	9	4.29	0	1.47
Chris Holt	8	12	3.52	0	1.34
Livan Hernandez	9	3	3.18	0	1.27
Brian Moehler	11	12	4.67	0	1.51

1998 Sleepers

	1997 Statistics (includes minor leagues)				
	W	L	ERA	Sv	BR/IP
Mark Gubicza	0	2	20.77	0	3.35
Pete Harnisch	3	3	6.18	0	1.60
Donovan Osborne	3	8	4.90	0	1.35
Roger Pavlik	3	5	3.69	0	1.40
Jason Isringhausen	4	4	4.75	0	1.64
Donne Wall	10	12	4.51	0	1.35
Rocky Coppinger	3	4	4.98	0	1.54
Brad Rigby	9	11	4.61	0	1.50
Bartolo Colon	11	8	4.36	0	1.48
Chris Carpenter	7	16	4.74	0	1.57
Bobby M. Jones	8	12	5.55	0	1.71
Jaret Wright	15	7	3.57	0	1.25
Hideki Irabu	9	5	4.71	0	1.32
Kevin Millwood	15	8	3.32	0	1.26
Brian Rose	17	5	3.16	0	1.28
Steve Woodard	18	6	3.45	0	1.19
Scott Eyre	17	9	4.23	0	1.41
Manny Aybar	7	12	3.73	0	1.36
Ken Cloude	15	9	4.21	0	1.42
Kirt Ojala	9	9	3.44	0	1.42
Jim Crowell	13	7	2.95	0	1.26

Relief Pitchers

Expect A Better Year in '98

	1997 Statistics				
	W	L	ERA	Sv	BR/IP
Dennis Eckersley	1	5	3.91	36	1.11
Darren Dreifort	5	2	2.86	4	1.27
Armando Benitez	4	5	2.45	9	1.27
Jay Powell	7	2	3.28	2	1.32
Dan Plesac	2	4	3.58	1	1.31
Eric Plunk	4	5	4.66	0	1.51
Ed Vosberg	2	3	4.42	1	1.60
Norm Charlton	3	8	7.27	14	2.02
Jose Mesa	4	4	2.40	16	1.38
Jose Bautista	2	2	6.66	0	1.65
Jeff Brantley	1	1	3.86	1	1.54
Troy Percival	5	5	3.46	27	1.27
Tony Castillo	4	4	4.91	1	1.57
Mark Guthrie	1	4	5.32	1	1.46
Jim Poole	3	1	7.11	0	2.07

Expect A Better Year in '98 (cont.)

	W	L	ERA	Sv	BR/IP
Chris Hammond	3	4	5.92	1	1.68
Mel Rojas	0	6	4.64	15	1.42
Darren Holmes	9	2	5.34	3	1.67
Heathcliff Slocumb	0	9	5.16	27	1.83
Ramon Garcia	9	8	3.69	1	1.36
Terry Mathews	4	4	4.41	1	1.56
Doug Henry	4	5	4.71	3	1.58
Ricky Bones	4	8	6.75	0	1.83
Barry Manuel	0	1	5.26	0	1.91
Yorkis Perez	0	1	8.31	0	2.19
Bill Risley	0	1	8.31	0	1.15
Richie Lewis	2	0	8.88	0	1.93
Blas Minor	1	0	4.50	1	1.58
Mike Trombley	2	3	4.37	1	1.34
Mike Mohler	1	10	5.13	1	1.74
John Cummings	2	0	5.47	0	1.86
Rene Arocha	0	0	11.32	0	2.23

Expect A Better Year in '98 (cont.)

Name	W	L	ERA	Sv	BR/IP
Lance Painter	1	1	4.76	0	1.24
Sean Bergman	2	4	6.09	0	1.69
Mark Hutton	3	2	4.48	0	1.72
Salomon Torres	0	0	9.82	0	1.95
Tim Crabtree	3	3	7.08	2	2.07
Omar Daal	2	3	7.06	1	1.83
Albie Lopez	3	7	6.93	0	1.89
Scott Sanders	6	14	5.86	2	1.56
Tim Worrell	4	8	5.16	3	1.63
Cory Bailey	0	1	8.38	0	1.97
Dan Miceli	3	2	5.01	3	1.40
Huck Flener	0	1	9.87	0	2.65
Terry Adams	2	9	4.62	18	1.78
Nate Minchey	0	0	13.50	0	3.00
Jeff Granger	0	0	18.00	0	3.60
Carlos Reyes	3	4	5.82	0	1.66
Jose Lima	1	6	5.28	2	1.33
Paul Shuey	4	2	6.20	2	1.80
John Hudek	1	3	5.98	4	1.82
T.J. Mathews	10	6	3.01	3	1.43
Bob Wells	2	0	5.75	2	1.62
Terry Burrows	0	2	10.45	0	2.03
Kurt Miller	0	1	9.82	0	2.73
Jeff Darwin	0	1	5.27	0	1.76
Joey Eischen	0	0	6.75	0	2.25
Ricky Bottalico	2	5	3.65	34	1.51
Vaughn Eshelman	3	3	6.33	0	1.80
Michael Mimbs	0	3	7.53	0	2.13
Eric Ludwick	1	5	8.51	0	2.18
Ricardo Jordan	1	2	5.33	0	1.78
Larry Thomas	0	0	8.10	0	1.50
Rodney Myers	0	0	6.00	0	2.22
Jose Paniagua	1	2	12.00	0	2.72
Ron Blazier	1	1	5.03	0	1.55
Dario Veras	2	1	5.11	0	1.70
Joey Long	0	0	8.18	0	2.36
Marc Kroon	0	1	7.15	0	1.76
Wayne Gomes	5	1	5.27	0	1.64
Roberto Duran	0	0	7.59	0	2.34
Gary Haught	0	0	7.15	0	1.76
Chris Clemons	0	2	8.53	0	2.45
Mike Misuraca	0	0	11.32	0	2.13
Jason Johnson	0	0	6.00	0	1.83
Oscar Henriquez	0	1	4.50	0	1.50

Look for Consistency

Name	1997 Statistics				
	W	L	ERA	Sv	BR/IP
John Wetteland	7	2	1.94	31	0.98
Billy Wagner	7	8	2.85	23	1.24
Tom Candiotti	10	7	3.60	0	1.33
John Franco	5	3	2.55	36	1.17
Ugueth Urbina	5	8	3.78	27	1.27
Rick Aguilera	5	4	3.82	26	1.30
Mike Jackson	2	5	3.24	15	1.23
Stan Belinda	1	5	3.71	1	1.27
Greg Cadaret	0	0	3.29	0	1.54
Tony Fossas	2	7	3.83	0	1.72
Jim Corsi	5	3	3.43	2	1.40
Dave Veres	2	3	3.48	1	1.56
Scott Service	0	3	6.45	0	1.52
Chuck McElroy	1	3	3.84	1	1.29
Xavier Hernandez	0	4	4.56	0	1.52
Alan Mills	2	3	4.89	0	1.94
Shawn Boskie	6	6	6.43	1	1.60
Anthony Telford	4	6	3.24	1	1.29
Danny Patterson	10	6	3.42	1	1.31
Arthur Rhodes	10	3	3.02	1	1.10
Larry Casian	0	3	5.70	0	1.57
Rich Garces	0	1	4.61	0	1.76
Roberto Hernandez	10	3	2.45	31	1.31
Mike Timlin	6	4	3.22	10	1.24
Frank Rodriguez	3	6	4.62	0	1.48
Brad Clontz	5	1	3.75	1	1.48
Dennis Cook	1	2	3.90	0	1.51
Mark Petkovsek	4	7	5.06	2	1.52
David Wainhouse	0	1	8.04	0	1.93
Mark Wohlers	5	7	3.50	33	1.37

Look For Consistency (cont.)

Name	W	L	ERA	Sv	BR/IP
Josias Manzanillo	0	1	5.40	0	1.96
Ricky Trlicek	3	4	5.57	0	1.86
Butch Henry	7	3	3.52	6	1.28
Jeff Nelson	3	7	2.86	2	1.19
Hipolito Pichardo	3	5	4.22	11	1.55
Buddy Groom	2	2	5.15	3	1.53
Mike Williams	0	2	6.43	1	2.07
Kent Bottenfield	2	3	3.86	2	1.42
Bob Patterson	1	6	3.34	0	0.96
Matt Whiteside	4	1	5.08	0	1.57
Steve Reed	4	6	4.04	6	1.30
Bobby Ayala	10	5	3.82	8	1.40
Robb Nen	9	3	3.89	35	1.51
Trevor Hoffman	6	4	2.66	37	1.02
Billy Brewer	1	2	4.13	0	1.33
Angel Miranda	0	0	3.86	0	2.07
Scott Ruffcorn	0	3	7.71	0	2.14
Pedro A. Martinez	1	1	9.45	0	2.40
Todd Jones	5	4	3.09	31	1.37
Cory Lidle	7	2	3.53	2	1.33
Julian Tavarez	6	4	3.87	0	1.46
Kelvim Escobar	3	2	2.90	14	1.52
Richard Batchelor	3	1	5.97	0	1.99
John Johnstone	0	0	3.24	0	1.60
Hector Carrasco	2	8	4.40	0	1.50
Kevin Jarvis	0	4	7.68	1	1.90
Eddie Guardado	0	4	3.91	1	1.39
Turk Wendell	3	5	4.36	5	1.61
Paul Spoljaric	0	3	3.69	3	1.42
Tim Davis	0	0	6.75	0	1.65
Billy Taylor	3	4	3.82	23	1.52
Graeme Lloyd	1	1	3.31	1	1.55
Jeff Tabaka	0	0	4.50	0	2.00
Mark Acre	2	0	5.74	0	1.85
Jason Jacome	2	0	5.84	0	1.60
Bryce Florie	4	4	4.32	0	1.59
Mike James	5	5	4.31	7	1.63
Antonio Osuna	3	4	2.19	0	1.07
Greg Hansell	0	0	9.64	0	1.50
Mike Myers	0	4	5.70	2	1.58
Al Reyes	1	2	5.46	1	1.48
Jose Alberro	0	3	7.94	0	1.94
Ron Villone	1	0	3.42	0	1.73
Juan Acevedo	3	1	3.59	0	1.64
Doug Bochtler	3	6	4.77	2	1.69
Felix Rodriguez	0	0	4.30	0	1.78
Ramon Morel	0	0	4.76	0	1.85
Joe Borowski	2	3	4.15	0	1.88
Mark Brandenburg	0	2	5.49	0	1.63
Mike Bertotti	0	0	7.36	0	3.00
Paul Byrd	4	4	5.26	0	1.49
Bill Simas	3	1	4.14	1	1.74
John Wasdin	4	6	4.40	0	1.30
Jim Mecir	0	4	5.88	0	1.43
Luis Andujar	0	6	6.48	0	1.94
Steve Montgomery	0	1	9.95	0	2.84
Alvin Morman	0	0	5.89	2	1.85
Matt Ruebel	3	2	6.32	0	1.74
Brian Bevil	1	2	6.61	1	1.59
Al Levine	2	2	6.91	0	1.94
Jay Witasick	0	0	5.73	0	1.82
Mike Holtz	3	4	3.32	2	1.27
Chris Peters	2	2	4.58	0	1.66
Mark Davis	0	0	5.51	0	1.65
Ken Grundt	0	0	9.00	0	1.67
Felix Heredia	5	3	4.29	0	1.55
Pep Harris	5	4	3.62	0	1.53
Kerry Lacy	1	1	6.11	3	1.80
Greg McCarthy	1	1	5.46	0	1.45
S. Hasegawa	3	7	3.93	0	1.43
Julio Santana	4	6	6.75	0	1.87
Ricardo Rincon	4	8	3.45	4	1.28
Will Cunnane	6	3	5.81	0	1.84
Tom Fordham	0	1	6.23	0	1.62
Todd Ritchie	2	3	4.58	0	1.57
Ramon Tatis	1	1	5.34	0	1.76
Jamie Walker	3	3	5.44	0	1.60
Takashi Kashiwada	3	1	4.31	0	1.79
Chad Fox	0	1	3.29	0	1.46

Look For Consistency (cont.)

	W	L	ERA	Sv	BR/IP
Rick DeHart	2	1	5.52	0	1.60
Curtis King	4	2	2.76	0	1.70
Tim Kubinski	0	0	5.68	0	1.50
Steve Falteisek	0	0	3.38	0	1.50
Nelson Cruz	0	2	6.49	0	1.44
Eric Moody	0	1	4.26	0	1.47
Mike Bovee	0	0	5.40	0	1.20

Production Will Drop

	1997 Statistics				
	W	L	ERA	Sv	BR/IP
Jesse Orosco	6	3	2.32	0	1.17
Tom Martin	5	3	2.09	2	1.36
Randy Myers	2	3	1.51	45	1.16
Greg Swindell	7	4	3.58	1	1.12
Paul Assenmacher	5	0	2.94	4	1.20
Doug Jones	6	6	2.02	36	0.92
Pete Smith	7	6	4.81	1	1.47
Randy Veres	4	0	3.31	1	1.30
Mike Stanton	6	1	2.57	3	1.30
Mike Munoz	3	3	4.53	2	1.42
Scott Radinsky	5	1	2.89	3	1.22
Reggie Harris	1	3	5.30	0	1.90
Eric Gunderson	2	1	3.26	1	1.25
Jeff Shaw	4	2	2.38	42	0.97
Rich Rodriguez	4	3	3.17	1	1.33
Rich DeLucia	6	4	3.89	3	1.43
Mike Perez	2	0	3.54	0	1.18
Mike Magnante	3	1	2.27	1	1.05
Rod Beck	7	4	3.47	37	1.10
Mike Remlinger	8	8	4.14	2	1.35
Willie Banks	3	0	1.93	0	1.14
Brian Williams	0	0	3.00	0	1.58
Russ Springer	3	3	4.23	3	1.43
Paul Quantrill	6	7	1.94	5	1.38
Bob Wickman	7	6	2.73	1	1.39
Doug Brocail	3	4	3.23	2	1.45
Alan Embree	3	1	2.54	0	1.26
Greg McMichael	7	10	2.98	7	1.16
Jerry DiPoto	5	3	4.70	16	1.52
Jim Converse	0	0	3.60	0	1.80
Jerry Spradlin	4	8	4.74	1	1.40
Erik Plantenberg	0	0	4.91	0	1.48
Mark Holzemer	0	0	6.00	1	1.89
A.J. Sager	3	4	4.18	3	1.26
Rick Helling	5	9	4.47	0	1.40
Darren Hall	3	2	2.30	2	1.54
Dane Johnson	4	1	4.53	2	1.80
Aaron Small	9	5	4.28	4	1.57
John Frascatore	5	2	2.47	1	1.41
Brian Boehringer	3	2	2.63	0	1.48
Wilson Heredia	1	0	3.20	0	1.53
Jason Christiansen	3	0	2.94	0	1.66
Don Wengert	5	11	6.04	2	1.69
Scott Sullivan	5	3	3.24	1	1.19
Jeff McCurry	1	4	4.43	0	1.55
Rafael Carmona	0	0	3.18	0	0.88
Mariano Rivera	6	4	1.88	43	1.19
Joe Hudson	3	1	3.53	0	1.60

Production Will Drop (continued)

	W	L	ERA	Sv	BR/IP
Ryan Karp	1	1	5.40	0	1.53
John Ericks	1	0	1.93	6	1.18
Matt Karchner	3	1	2.91	15	1.44
Ken Robinson	0	0	2.70	0	0.60
Jim Bruske	4	1	3.63	0	1.41
Marc Valdes	4	4	3.13	2	1.38
Darrell May	2	1	5.23	0	1.57
Clint Sodowsky	2	2	3.63	0	1.63
Joe Roa	2	5	5.21	0	1.64
Joel Adamson	5	3	3.54	0	1.34
Marty Janzen	2	1	3.60	0	1.44
Marc Wilkins	9	5	3.69	2	1.35
Ramiro Mendoza	8	6	4.24	2	1.42
Nerio Rodriguez	2	1	4.91	0	1.36
Robbie Beckett	0	0	5.40	0	1.20
Jose Silva	2	1	5.94	0	1.90
Donn Pall	0	0	3.86	0	1.71
Rich Loiselle	1	5	3.10	29	1.39
Jose Santiago	0	0	1.93	0	2.14
Anthony Chavez	0	0	0.93	0	1.24

1998 Sleepers

	1997 Statistics (includes minor leagues)				
	W	L	ERA	Sv	BR/IP
Bruce Ruffin	0	2	5.11	7	1.50
Jeff Montgomery	1	4	3.38	14	1.19
Gregg Olson	7	4	4.64	1	1.49
Mike Fetters	1	5	3.63	6	1.36
Oscar Henriquez	4	6	2.88	12	1.32
Chris Haney	2	3	3.93	0	1.29
Tim Scott	1	1	5.30	3	1.40
Ken Ryan	2	0	8.10	1	2.10
Curt Leskanic	4	0	5.08	4	1.48
Ron Mahay	7	3	2.69	5	1.09
Dan Naulty	1	2	6.37	1	1.39
Carlos Castillo	2	1	4.23	4	1.47
Steve Kline	7	5	5.02	1	1.61
Robinson Checo	7	7	4.15	0	1.22
Joe Crawford	12	5	3.45	0	1.30
Brady Raggio	9	13	4.68	0	1.44
Matt Whisenant	3	1	5.85	0	1.85
Derek Lowe	9	10	4.42	0	1.35
Mike DeJean	5	2	4.24	6	1.62
Keith Foulke	9	9	5.44	3	1.45
Rigo Beltran	6	4	2.90	1	1.21
Todd Erdos	3	4	3.72	27	1.24
Antonio Alfonseca	8	5	4.50	7	1.51
Marc Pisciotta	9	3	2.68	22	1.23
Dennis Reyes	16	7	4.05	0	1.53
Mike Cather	7	6	2.94	4	1.20
Eddie Gaillard	2	4	4.54	29	1.42
Kerry Ligtenberg	4	4	2.99	18	0.98
Mike Thurman	11	9	4.16	0	1.20
Manuel Barrios	4	8	3.57	0	1.33
Scott Winchester	4	2	2.05	33	1.09
Rick Gorecki	7	5	3.43	0	1.26

American League Players

Terry Collins

1997 Season

After three winning seasons with the Astros, Terry Collins succeeded in his first year working for Team Disney. The fiery Collins enjoyed his fourth consecutive winning season, but it wasn't easy. He found himself in the middle of the mess that followed Tony Phillips' August arrest for cocaine possession.

Offense

Collins is a big believer in putting runners in motion and making things happen. The Angels lacked a top basestealing threat but had six runners swipe at least 10 bases. He also used the hit-and-run more than any American League manager except for Buddy Bell. As a result of the aggressive approach, Anaheim ranked fifth in runs while having the AL's seventh-best batting average and eighth-most homers.

Pitching & Defense

Collins did a terrific job to solve the Angels' Rubik's Cube riddle last season, fitting four talented outfielders into the lineup by converting the willing and able Darin Erstad to first base. Collins isn't afraid to gamble with his rotation. He went to a four-man rotation in some stretches after injuries hit the staff and might be willing to give it a try again this year. He makes lots of pitching changes and does a good job of breaking in young pitchers.

1998 Outlook

Collins weathered a stormy season well, though he isn't guaranteed an easier time in 1998. The Angels raised expectations with their unexpected success in 1997, but haven't had back-to-back winning seasons in over 10 years. The health of key players such as center fielder Jim Edmonds, lefthander Chuck Finley and catcher Todd Greene is essential.

Born: 5/27/49 in Midland, MI

Playing Experience: No major league experience

Managerial Experience: 4 seasons

Manager Statistics

Year	Team, Lg	W	L	Pct	GB	Finish
1997	Anaheim, AL	84	78	.519	6.0	2nd West
4 Seasons		308	275	.528	—	—

1997 Starting Pitchers by Days Rest

	≤3	4	5	6+
Angels Starts	20	72	36	24
Angels ERA	3.92	5.57	3.91	5.88
AL Avg Starts	5	89	34	24
AL ERA	4.38	4.60	4.61	5.37

1997 Situational Stats

	Terry Collins	AL Average
Hit & Run Success %	32.1	36.5
Stolen Base Success %	63.6	67.3
Platoon Pct.	69.7	59.5
Defensive Subs	22	22
High-Pitch Outings	15	15
Quick/Slow Hooks	10/16	19/15
Sacrifice Attempts	55	53

1997 Rankings (American League)

⇒ 1st in starts on three days rest (20)
⇒ 2nd in steals of home plate (1), hit-and-run attempts (109), pitchouts (60), pitchouts with a runner moving (18) and starts with over 140 pitches (2)
⇒ 3rd in stolen base attempts (198), least caught steals of home plate (1), mid-inning pitching changes (207) and first batter platoon percentage (66.5%)

Garret Anderson

1997 Season

After signing a three-year contract in spring training, Garret Anderson responded by leading the Angels with 36 doubles and ranking second with 92 RBI. He batted .303, inching up his career average to .301, and was solid in left field, surprising those who viewed him as a defensive liability.

Hitting

Most lefthanded hitters love the ball at the knees, but Anderson is different. He does a good job hitting high pitches, even against lefties. Most of his value is contained in his batting average, as he has just 61 unintentional walks and 36 homers in 415 major league games, not the kind of numbers you want to see in a left fielder. Anderson keeps his average up against lefties by using the whole field, but they take away his modest power and he didn't homer off them in 1997. He's a tough hitter to put away, batting .249 with two-strike counts. Because he hits the ball hard, he is prone to hitting into double plays.

Baserunning & Defense

Anderson seemed likely to wind up at designated hitter after the Angels traded Chili Davis, but he played primarily in left field. He also filled in for center fielder Jim Edmonds, starting 27 games there. Teams challenged Anderson's arm all season, allowing him to collect 14 assists, which ranked third among AL outfielders. He does cover a lot of ground in the outfield. He has good speed but lacks the instincts to be a serious threat stealing bases, though he went 10-for-14 in 1997.

1998 Outlook

With the emergence of Darin Erstad, Anderson might have become expendable. The Angels decided to trade Davis instead, holding on to the runner-up for 1995 American League Rookie of the Year. Anderson is a fine hitter for average, but offers below-average production for a left fielder and probably deserves to be ranked as one of baseball's most overrated players. Anaheim has discussed trading him for a much-needed starting pitcher, but hasn't found any takers.

Position: LF/CF
Bats: L **Throws:** L
Ht: 6' 3" **Wt:** 190

Opening Day Age: 25
Born: 6/30/72 in Los Angeles, CA
ML Seasons: 4

Overall Statistics

	G	AB	R	H	D	T	HR	RBI	SB	BB	SO	Avg	OBP	Slg
1997	154	624	76	189	36	3	8	92	10	30	70	.303	.334	.409
Career	415	1618	205	487	88	6	36	234	23	76	221	.301	.331	.430

Where He Hits the Ball

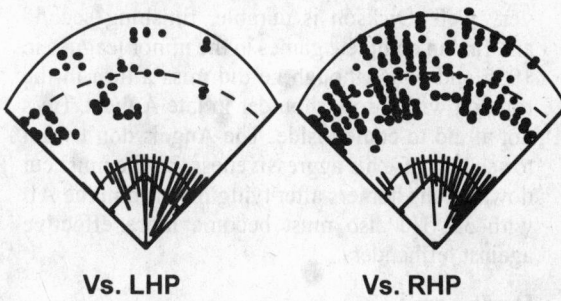

Vs. LHP   **Vs. RHP**

1997 Situational Stats

	AB	H	HR	RBI	Avg		AB	H	HR	RBI	Avg
Home	327	107	5	45	.327	LHP	184	54	0	29	.293
Road	297	82	3	47	.276	RHP	440	135	8	63	.307
First Half	327	102	2	47	.312	Sc Pos	185	56	3	80	.303
Scnd Half	297	87	6	45	.293	Clutch	111	37	3	23	.333

1997 Rankings (American League)

⇒ 1st in singles
⇒ 4th in hits and fielding percentage in left field (.989)
⇒ 5th in errors in left field (3)
⇒ 6th in at-bats, GDPs (20) and lowest HR frequency (78.0 ABs per HR)
⇒ 8th in least pitches seen per plate appearance (3.44) and batting average at home
⇒ 10th in lowest on-base percentage vs. lefthanded pitchers (.296)
⇒ Led the Angels in batting average, at-bats, hits, singles, doubles, intentional walks (6), GDPs (20), batting average with the bases loaded (.500), batting average vs. righthanded pitchers and batting average at home

Jason Dickson

1997 Season

Unassuming righthander Jason Dickson was an American League All-Star in his first full season by virtue of an 8-4 record at the break. He struggled afterward but was a savior for an Angel pitching staff that lost Chuck Finley, Mark Langston and Mark Gubicza to injury. Dickson was the only Anaheim pitcher with more than 200 innings, a very solid first full season in the majors.

Pitching

Dickson doesn't have an overpowering fastball but succeeds by having command of three pitches, including a changeup that was his best pitch in 1997. He changes speeds and locates his pitchers very well. Dickson is durable, finishing second and first in complete games in the minor leagues in 1995 and 1996, though he did miss a turn in the rotation with a sore shoulder in late August. He's not afraid to come inside. The Angels don't want to see him lose his aggressiveness, but he must cut down on his homers after tying for third in the AL with 32. He also must become more effective against lefthanders.

Defense

Dickson does an excellent job holding runners on base. He allowed only five stolen bases in 12 attempts in 1997, an amazing performance considering the mediocre cast of catchers he worked with. He fields his position well, but sometimes tries to force the action and makes hurried mistakes.

1998 Outlook

There was some concern that Dickson's subpar second half was caused by his rushing to get warmed up in the bullpen at the All-Star Game. The Angels hope he can maintain his effectiveness all year this time around. They'll be counting on the Canadian to be one of the leaders of their staff, and need him to eat a significant number of innings once again.

Position: SP
Bats: L **Throws:** R
Ht: 6' 0" **Wt:** 190

Opening Day Age: 25
Born: 3/30/73 in London, Canada
ML Seasons: 2

Overall Statistics

	W	L	Pct.	ERA	G	GS	Sv	IP	H	BB	SO	HR	Ratio
1997	13	9	.591	4.29	33	32	0	203.2	236	56	115	32	1.43
Career	14	13	.519	4.34	40	39	0	247.0	288	74	135	38	1.47

How Often He Throws Strikes

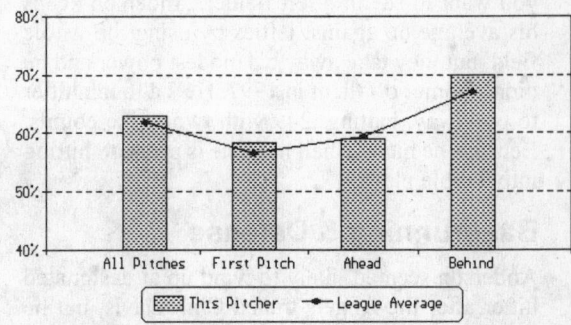

1997 Situational Stats

	W	L	ERA	Sv	IP		AB	H	HR	RBI	Avg
Home	7	5	4.67	0	113.2	LHB	438	135	21	59	.308
Road	6	4	3.80	0	90.0	RHB	378	101	11	42	.267
First Half	8	4	3.41	0	118.2	Sc Pos	188	44	3	61	.234
Scnd Half	5	5	5.51	0	85.0	Clutch	47	15	1	3	.319

1997 Rankings (American League)

⇒ 2nd in lowest stolen base percentage allowed (41.7%)

⇒ 3rd in home runs allowed

⇒ Led the Angels in wins, shutouts (1), innings pitched, hits allowed, batters faced (888), GDPs induced (20), lowest stolen base percentage allowed (41.7%), most GDPs induced per 9 innings (0.9), ERA on the road and lowest batting average allowed with runners in scoring position

Gary DiSarcina

1997 Season

Most teams would be happy with Gary DiSarcina's steady play at shortstop and quiet leadership. But he had improved so much as a hitter before tearing ligaments in his left thumb late in the 1995 season that the Angels have been disappointed by his play the last two years. He had a typical DiSarcina season last year, starting 150 games and ranking among the AL's most reliable fielders, but he was an almost automatic out at the plate.

Hitting

DiSarcina swings at so many borderline pitches that it's amazing when he draws a walk. He seldom takes a pitch and thus drew just 17 free passes in 1997. He's hard to strike out, but seldom hits the ball with authority. He does his best hitting when he can line a first-pitch fastball somewhere, though pitchers don't often throw him one because they know he'll offer at anything. He was especially anemic against lefthanders last season, which is strange for a righthanded hitter and hadn't been the case in the past.

Baserunning & Defense

DiSarcina appeared to regain his confidence after spending most of 1996 in a fielding slump. He combines good range with steady hands, and is quick on the double play. He's not as quick on the basepaths, showing average speed and stealing bases only when pitchers ignore him. He's usually caught more than he's successful.

1998 Outlook

After a move to the leadoff spot in 1995, DiSarcina has returned to the No. 9 hole, where he'll probably spend the rest of his career. He has two more guaranteed years and an option year left on a contract he signed in 1996. The Angels are happy with him for the moment, and have no middle-infield alternatives in their farm system. He's the kind of player who might be best appreciated by his own team after he's gone.

Position: SS
Bats: R **Throws:** R
Ht: 6' 2" **Wt:** 190

Opening Day Age: 30
Born: 11/19/67 in Malden, MA
ML Seasons: 9
Pronunciation: dee-sar-SEE-na

Overall Statistics

	G	AB	R	H	D	T	HR	RBI	SB	BB	SO	Avg	OBP	Slg
1997	154	549	52	135	28	2	4	47	7	17	29	.246	.271	.326
Career	836	2884	333	731	138	16	23	259	34	117	220	.253	.287	.336

Where He Hits the Ball

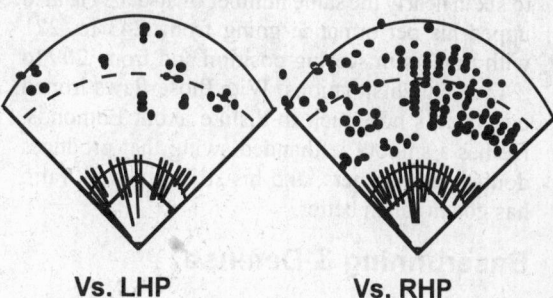

Vs. LHP   **Vs. RHP**

1997 Situational Stats

	AB	H	HR	RBI	Avg		AB	H	HR	RBI	Avg
Home	288	80	2	30	.278	LHP	158	33	1	9	.209
Road	261	55	2	17	.211	RHP	391	102	3	38	.261
First Half	290	74	3	33	.255	Sc Pos	143	34	1	43	.238
Scnd Half	259	61	1	14	.236	Clutch	90	22	2	8	.244

1997 Rankings (American League)

⇒ 1st in highest percentage of swings put into play (60.5%)
⇒ 2nd in lowest on-base percentage, least pitches seen per plate appearance (2.98) and lowest batting average on the road
⇒ 3rd in lowest slugging percentage and lowest HR frequency (137.3 ABs per HR)
⇒ Led the Angels in sacrifice bunts (8), highest groundball/flyball ratio (1.7), lowest percentage of swings that missed (10.4%) and highest percentage of swings put into play (60.5%)

Jim Edmonds

1997 Season

Jim Edmonds had another solid season. Playing through thumb, knee, wrist and back ailments, he topped 25 homers and a .500 or better slugging percentage for the third straight season. He batted mainly in the second through fifth slots in the order, and most frequently was used as the cleanup hitter. He became a staple on "SportsCenter," making one acrobatic catch after another in center field en route to his first Gold Glove.

Hitting

Edmonds reversed a couple of trends in 1997. He improved his batting average from .189 to .273 against lefthanders, tripling his homers from two to six in nearly the same number of at-bats. He also upped his performance going from .243 to .271 with runners in scoring position and from .209 to .242 in clutch situations. With those flaws ironed out, there's not much to dislike about Edmonds. He has a smooth lefthanded swing that produces doubles and homers, and his strikeout/walk ratio has gotten much better.

Baserunning & Defense

Edmonds is fearless in center field, sacrificing his body by diving or running into the wall in an attempt to catch anything he can reach. This takes a toll on him, but he knows no other way to play and still produces offensively. The only regular center fielder to reach more balls per nine innings in 1997 was White Sox rookie Mike Cameron. Edmonds' arm is fine, and only San Diego's Steve Finley could top his nine assists from center. Edmonds isn't as good a baserunner as he is a defender. He's 14-for-29 in his career as a basestealer and doesn't always get good jumps, making it difficult to take the extra base.

1998 Outlook

Edmonds will remain a key player for Anaheim. He'll continue to hit and produce runs unless he puts himself on the disabled list with his reckless defense. As one of the more valuable Angels, he has been rumored to be on the block for an established starting pitcher. If that trade happened, Darin Estad would move from first base to center.

Position: CF/1B
Bats: L **Throws:** L
Ht: 6' 1" **Wt:** 190

Opening Day Age: 27
Born: 6/27/70 in Fullerton, CA
ML Seasons: 5

Overall Statistics

	G	AB	R	H	D	T	HR	RBI	SB	BB	SO	Avg	OBP	Slg
1997	133	502	82	146	27	0	26	80	5	60	80	.291	.368	.500
Career	500	1841	315	533	102	9	91	294	14	189	399	.290	.358	.503

Where He Hits the Ball

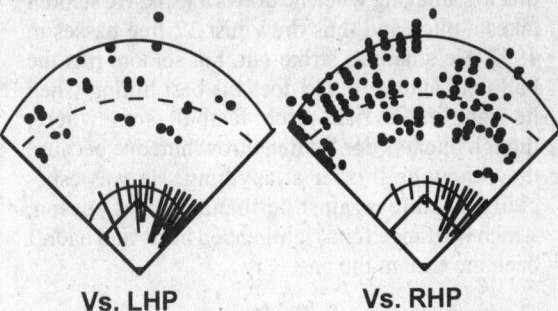

Vs. LHP   Vs. RHP

1997 Situational Stats

	AB	H	HR	RBI	Avg		AB	H	HR	RBI	Avg
Home	237	70	14	42	.295	LHP	143	39	6	24	.273
Road	265	76	12	38	.287	RHP	359	107	20	56	.298
First Half	297	90	14	49	.303	Sc Pos	129	35	2	48	.271
Scnd Half	205	56	12	31	.273	Clutch	91	22	4	12	.242

1997 Rankings (American League)

⇒ 2nd in errors in center field (5)
⇒ 3rd in cleanup slugging percentage (.567) and lowest fielding percentage in center field (.985)
⇒ 10th in batting average with two strikes (.252)
⇒ Led the Angels in cleanup slugging percentage (.567), slugging percentage vs. righthanded pitchers (.532) and batting average with two strikes (.252)

Darin Erstad

Position: 1B
Bats: L **Throws:** L
Ht: 6' 2" **Wt:** 210

Opening Day Age: 23
Born: 6/4/74 in Jamestown, North Dakota
ML Seasons: 2

Anaheim Angels

1997 Season

There's no doubt that Darin Erstad is a quick learner. The first overall pick in the 1995 draft, he got to Anaheim to stay after just 114 minor league games. He spent his first half-season with the Angels playing the outfield, his natural position, then made a smooth conversion to first base in 1997. Erstad led the Angels with 23 steals and placed second with 99 runs and 34 doubles, a very impressive first full season in the majors.

Hitting

Not many first basemen bat leadoff, but the Angels gave Erstad a long look there. He was willing to take pitches and work counts, but didn't get on base nearly as much leading off as when he hit second in the order. He has good power but doesn't rely on it. He's a pure hitter who drives the ball in the gaps. He almost never swings at the first pitch and is comfortable hitting with two-strike counts. Erstad hangs in well against lefthanders and hit five points higher off them than righties in 1997. He kills low fastballs.

Baserunning & Defense

Erstad is a fine athlete who punted and kicked long-range field goals on a national championship football team at the University of Nebraska. He has proven that he can steal a base, with a ceiling of perhaps 30 a season. There were times last year when he played first base well, but he was inconsistent. His .990 fielding percentage ranked third-worst among regular American League first basemen, but he should improve the longer he plays there. He's a versatile player whom manager Terry Collins will use in all three outfield spots. Erstad's best defensive position is left field. His arm is unimpressive.

1998 Outlook

What's not to like? On one of his off days last April, Erstad returned to his family home in Jamestown, N.D., to help his neighbors stack sand bags as they fought flooding. The Angels believe he'll develop into an All-Star first baseman, and he could make that jump this year. At worst, he seems a safe bet for gradual improvement.

Overall Statistics

	G	AB	R	H	D	T	HR	RBI	SB	BB	SO	Avg	OBP	Slg
1997	139	539	99	161	34	4	16	77	23	51	86	.299	.360	.466
Career	196	747	133	220	39	5	20	97	26	68	115	.295	.353	.440

Where He Hits the Ball

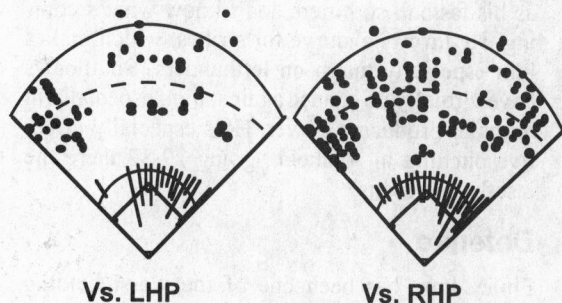

Vs. LHP   **Vs. RHP**

1997 Situational Stats

	AB	H	HR	RBI	Avg		AB	H	HR	RBI	Avg
Home	276	85	8	40	.308	LHP	159	48	8	31	.302
Road	263	76	8	37	.289	RHP	380	113	8	46	.297
First Half	299	91	10	43	.304	Sc Pos	124	41	5	59	.331
Scnd Half	240	70	6	34	.292	Clutch	84	32	2	14	.381

1997 Rankings (American League)

⇒ 2nd in lowest percentage of swings on the first pitch (12.3%)
⇒ 3rd in batting average in the clutch, errors at first base (11) and lowest fielding percentage at first base (.990)
⇒ 5th in lowest on-base percentage for a leadoff hitter (.318)
⇒ 8th in least GDPs per GDP situation (4.8%)
⇒ 9th in stolen bases
⇒ Led the Angels in stolen bases, least GDPs per GDP situation (4.8%), batting average in the clutch and lowest percentage of swings on the first pitch (12.3%)

Chuck Finley

1997 Season

The surprising Angels were giving Seattle a good race until Aug. 19, when Chuck Finley broke his left wrist backing up home plate. Finley had overcome a slow start to win 10 consecutive decisions, and the injury was a crippling blow for Anaheim's rotation. He remained the leader of the staff in his 10th year as a starter for the Angels, reaching double figures in victories for the eighth time in nine seasons.

Pitching

Finley combines a good fastball with a plus fork-ball. His forkball has good sink and produces grounders, and he throws it with the same motion as his fastball so hitters don't know what's coming. He throws a slurve for strikes, which makes him especially tough on lefthanders. Southpaws have virtually no chance against him, especially in terms of producing power. He's especially effective pitching in Anaheim, going 29-12 there the last three seasons.

Defense

Finley long has been one of the worst-fielding pitchers in the American League. He somehow managed to avoid making an error in 1997 after committing three or more in each of the five previous seasons. His height causes him trouble making plays on low comebackers, and he doesn't move especially well. Finley has always been one of the easiest lefties for basestealers to run against, though he was better last season.

1998 Outlook

Finley is expected to be ready to go when he reports to spring training. Few pitchers are as consistent as Finley, who has kept his ERA between 4.16 and 4.32 for each of the last four years, and he's arguably as good as any AL southpaw this side of Randy Johnson. The Angels are counting on him to continue to stabilize their rotation. Coming off his lightest workload in 10 years, he's expected to be as strong as ever.

Position: SP
Bats: L   **Throws:** L
Ht: 6' 6"   **Wt:** 214

Opening Day Age: 35
Born: 11/26/62 in Monroe, LA
ML Seasons: 12

Overall Statistics

	W	L	Pct.	ERA	G	GS	Sv	IP	H	BB	SO	HR	Ratio
1997	13	6	.684	4.23	25	25	0	164.0	152	65	155	20	1.32
Career	142	120	.542	3.69	369	312	0	2238.1	2137	915	1739	211	1.36

How Often He Throws Strikes

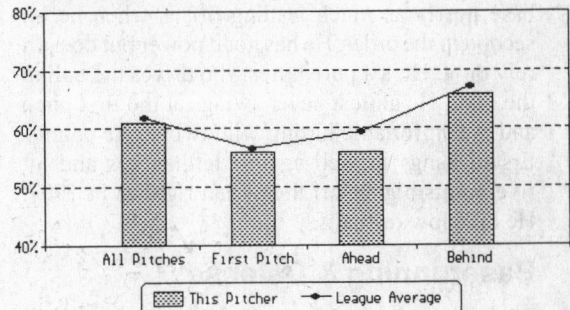

1997 Situational Stats

	W	L	ERA	Sv	IP		AB	H	HR	RBI	Avg
Home	8	1	3.36	0	83.0	LHB	62	10	0	3	.161
Road	5	5	5.11	0	81.0	RHB	551	142	20	64	.258
First Half	5	6	4.89	0	103.0	Sc Pos	132	36	3	45	.273
Scnd Half	8	0	3.10	0	61.0	Clutch	49	9	1	5	.184

1997 Rankings (American League)

⇒ 2nd in most pitches thrown per batter (4.00)
⇒ 5th in balks (2) and most strikeouts per 9 innings (8.5)
⇒ Led the Angels in ERA, wins, complete games (3), shutouts (1), strikeouts, wild pitches (10), balks (2), winning percentage, highest strikeout/walk ratio (2.4), lowest batting average allowed (.248), lowest slugging percentage allowed (.387), lowest on-base percentage allowed (.323), highest groundball/flyball ratio allowed (1.4), least baserunners allowed per 9 innings (12.2), most run support per 9 innings (6.3), least home runs allowed per 9 innings (1.10), most strikeouts per 9 innings (8.5), ERA at home and lowest batting average allowed vs. righthanded batters

Todd Greene (Top Prospect)

1997 Season

After a disappointing 1996 season, catcher Todd Greene made the Angels comfortable enough to trade both of their frontline catchers, Jorge Fabregas and Jim Leyritz, in 1997. The third-leading home-run hitter in NCAA history, Greene put up some eye-popping numbers between Triple-A and Anaheim. He smashed 34 longballs in 98 games before his season ended with a broken wrist in late August. The converted outfielder also was better than expected behind the plate.

Hitting

Greene began to shed his reputation as an all-or-nothing hitter, collecting enough singles to hit .354 at Triple-A and then challenging .300 in his 34-game stint with the Angels. But Mike Piazza-style power is his drawing card. He had a 40-home run season in the minor leagues in 1995 and could hit 30-plus in a full season in the majors. He still chases too many pitches, which results in a high strikeout total, but he should become more selective as he settles into the big leagues. He swings at the first pitch a lot and can put a charge into a first-pitch fastball.

Baserunning & Defense

Greene's movements behind the plate are a little slow, but he has improved dramatically since allowing 44 passed balls in the minors in 1994. His throwing has improved much more than his receiving, however. Opponents figured him for an easy target but he often surprised them with accurate throws. Greene is a good athlete who runs well for a catcher.

1998 Outlook

Greene appears to be in the big leagues to stay. If he's healthy, he's expected to be Anaheim's No. 1 catcher and occasional designated hitter. He could develop into an All-Star, but the Angels will be happy if he simply gives them the stability behind the plate they've lacked since Bob Boone moved on.

Position: C
Bats: R **Throws:** R
Ht: 5'10" **Wt:** 200

Opening Day Age: 26
Born: 5/8/71 in Augusta, GA
ML Seasons: 2

Overall Statistics

	G	AB	R	H	D	T	HR	RBI	SB	BB	SO	Avg	OBP	Slg
1997	34	124	24	36	6	0	9	24	2	7	25	.290	.328	.556
Career	63	203	33	51	7	0	11	33	4	11	36	.251	.293	.448

Where He Hits the Ball

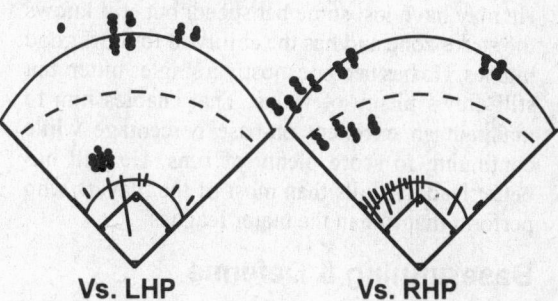

Vs. LHP   **Vs. RHP**

1997 Situational Stats

	AB	H	HR	RBI	Avg		AB	H	HR	RBI	Avg
Home	72	23	5	13	.319	LHP	44	14	3	8	.318
Road	52	13	4	11	.250	RHP	80	22	6	16	.275
First Half	21	4	0	1	.190	Sc Pos	42	11	2	16	.262
Scnd Half	103	32	9	23	.311	Clutch	13	3	0	1	.231

1997 Rankings (American League)

⇒ Did not rank near the top or bottom in any category

Rickey Henderson   (Hall of Famer)

1997 Season

People have been trying to write Rickey Henderson off for years. It appeared that his time finally might have come when he opened 1997 as the Padres' fourth outfielder. He was hitting only .164 at the end of May, then got hot at midseason and created trade interest. After Tony Phillips was arrested for cocaine possession, the Angels traded prospects George Arias and Ryan Hancock to San Diego to get Henderson. He failed to take advantage of his opportunity, hitting .183 in 32 games with Anaheim.

Hitting

Few hitters work a pitcher harder than Henderson. He may have lost some bat speed, but still knows the strike zone and has the ability to foul off good pitches. He has become mostly a singles hitter, but still draws plenty of walks. That enables him to maintain an excellent on-base percentage while continuing to score plenty of runs. He still has better leadoff skills than most of the players who perform that role in the major leagues.

Baserunning & Defense

Henderson doesn't have the speed that made him the most feared baserunner in the major leagues a decade ago. But he gets great jumps and can still steal a base even when the opposing team knows he's going to run. Henderson still covers a lot of ground in left field but his wet-noodle arm has become a liability. Teams run on him constantly.

1998 Outlook

The 39-year-old Henderson will finish his second decade in the majors this year, and seems in no hurry to retire. If he's willing to play for a reduced salary, he should have a job for the forseeable future. The Angels envision him as a DH and leadoff hitter, and may try to re-sign him as a free agent. He's headed to the Hall of Fame five years after he announces his retirement.

Position: LF/CF/DH
Bats: R   **Throws:** L
Ht: 5'10"   **Wt:** 190

Opening Day Age: 39
Born: 12/25/58 in Chicago, IL
ML Seasons: 19

Overall Statistics

	G	AB	R	H	D	T	HR	RBI	SB	BB	SO	Avg	OBP	Slg
1997	120	403	84	100	14	0	8	34	45	97	85	.248	.400	.342
Career	2460	8931	1913	2550	426	59	252	921	1231	1772	1276	.286	.406	.431

Where He Hits the Ball

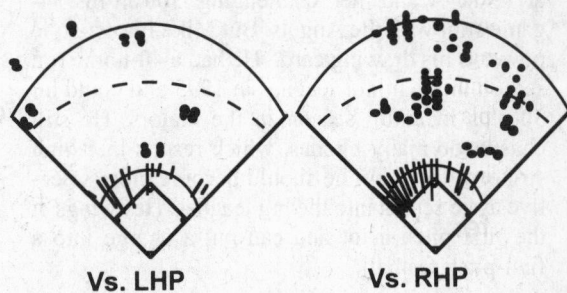

Vs. LHP   Vs. RHP

1997 Situational Stats

	AB	H	HR	RBI	Avg		AB	H	HR	RBI	Avg
Home	209	48	6	18	.230	LHP	77	21	4	9	.273
Road	194	52	2	16	.268	RHP	326	79	4	25	.242
First Half	180	52	5	20	.289	Sc Pos	61	17	1	26	.279
Scnd Half	223	48	3	14	.215	Clutch	59	15	1	3	.254

1997 Rankings (American League)

⇒ 7th in stolen base percentage (80.0%)
⇒ Led the Angels in stolen base percentage (80.0%)

Ken Hill

1997 Season

After a workhorse 1996 season that helped Texas win its first-ever division title, Ken Hill struggled through a difficult 1997. He never seemed quite right after straining his right shoulder on a cold April night at Comiskey Park. He was unusually inconsistent, and the Rangers dealt him to Anaheim for Jim Leyritz at the trading deadline. The Angels expected a lot from Hill, but he had problems with his mechanics and won only four of 12 starts with them.

Pitching

When he's on, Hill is a power pitcher who can get his fastball into the low-90s. He has a very good forkball, which enables him to combat lefthanders effectively, and can throw both his slider and changeup for strikes. He usually gets lots of ground balls and generates a good number of double plays. Hill struggled with his control in 1997, leading the American League with 95 walks and having the worst strikeout/walk ratio of his career.

Defense

Hill is a fairly easy target for basestealers. He's slow to home plate and has an ordinary pickoff move. Even though he spent two-thirds of the season throwing to Ivan Rodriguez, opponents were successful on 19 of 27 steal attempts with Hill on the mound. He does a great job fielding comebackers and keeps his head in the game. He didn't commit an error in 1997.

1998 Outlook

Anaheim re-signed Hill after he filed for free agency. He should be able to bounce back and become as effective as he has been in the past, but a declining strikeout/walk ratio usually is the first sign a pitcher is beginning to fade.

Position: SP
Bats: R **Throws:** R
Ht: 6' 2" **Wt:** 205

Opening Day Age: 32
Born: 12/14/65 in Lynn, MA
ML Seasons: 10

Overall Statistics

	W	L	Pct.	ERA	G	GS	Sv	IP	H	BB	SO	HR	Ratio
1997	9	12	.429	4.55	31	31	0	190.0	194	95	106	19	1.52
Career	99	83	.544	3.76	264	257	0	1652.2	1569	665	996	122	1.35

How Often He Throws Strikes

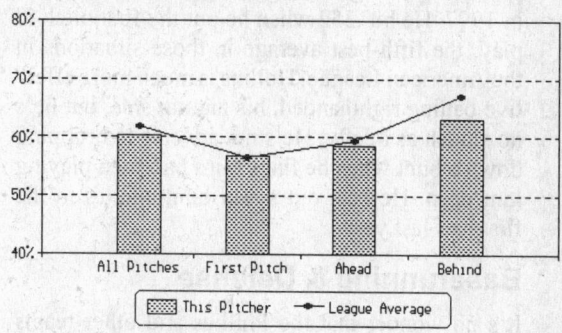

1997 Situational Stats

	W	L	ERA	Sv	IP		AB	H	HR	RBI	Avg
Home	2	6	5.11	0	86.1	LHB	387	102	12	43	.264
Road	7	6	4.08	0	103.2	RHB	338	92	7	48	.272
First Half	5	5	4.17	0	90.2	Sc Pos	189	52	4	73	.275
Scnd Half	4	7	4.89	0	99.1	Clutch	32	10	1	4	.313

1997 Rankings (American League)

⇒ 1st in walks allowed (95) and fielding percentage at pitcher (1.000)
⇒ 2nd in lowest strikeout/walk ratio (1.1)
⇒ 5th in highest on-base percentage allowed (.352) and most baserunners allowed per 9 innings (13.8)
⇒ 8th in highest ERA at home (5.11)
⇒ 9th in least strikeouts per 9 innings (5.0)
⇒ 10th in losses (12) and most GDPs induced per 9 innings (0.9)

Dave Hollins

1997 Season

Dave Hollins resurrected a sinking career with a very good season for the Angels, his fifth team in three years. The switch-hitting third baseman spent most of the season as the Angels' No. 3 hitter. He led the Angels with 101 runs and ranked third with 85 RBI. The ultimate compliment for Hollins came in August, when GM Bill Bavasi included third-base prospect George Arias in the Rickey Henderson trade with San Diego.

Hitting

Hollins always has been one of the most patient hitters in baseball, though he did surprise opposing pitchers by being more aggressive on the first pitch in 1997. He hit .352 when he put the first pitch in play, the fifth-best average in those situations in the American League. Hollins is much more effective batting righthanded, his natural side, but he's no slouch as a lefty. He's not adverse to dropping down a bunt when he finds third basemen playing him deep. He beat out seven bunt singles in the first half last year.

Baserunning & Defense

It's no wonder that the Phillies and other teams have tried Hollins at first base and in the outfield. He's a liability at third base, largely because he gets in some extended slumps throwing the ball. He doesn't just short-hop throws; he also sails them into the seats. He has limited range at third base as well. Hollins does a decent job at first base, where he played occasionally in 1997. He's surprisingly aggressive on the bases, setting a career high with 16 stolen bases last season and leading the American League with the highest percentage of extra bases taken (73.2).

1998 Outlook

Manager Terry Collins is counting on Hollins to produce another big season hitting in the middle of the order. Hollins did have surgery to clean out his right knee but is expected to be 100 percent for spring training. The Angels will work hard in the spring training to improve his fielding at third base, and may move him to first base if the roster allows.

Position: 3B/1B
Bats: B **Throws:** R
Ht: 6' 1" **Wt:** 210

Opening Day Age: 31
Born: 5/25/66 in Orchard Park, NY
ML Seasons: 8

Overall Statistics

	G	AB	R	H	D	T	HR	RBI	SB	BB	SO	Avg	OBP	Slg
1997	149	572	101	165	29	2	16	85	16	62	124	.288	.363	.430
Career	839	2862	505	757	145	15	99	437	36	414	591	.265	.366	.429

Where He Hits the Ball

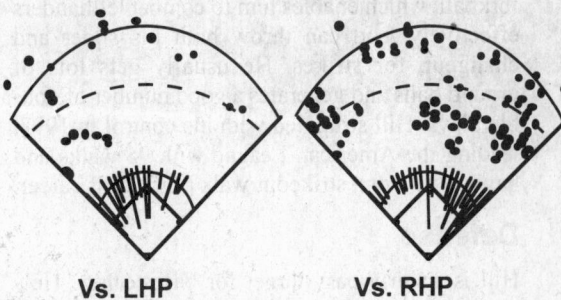

Vs. LHP   Vs. RHP

1997 Situational Stats

	AB	H	HR	RBI	Avg		AB	H	HR	RBI	Avg
Home	290	92	15	60	.317	LHP	175	57	8	29	.326
Road	282	73	1	25	.259	RHP	397	108	8	56	.272
First Half	301	88	11	48	.292	Sc Pos	161	41	5	70	.255
Scnd Half	271	77	5	37	.284	Clutch	99	29	2	15	.293

1997 Rankings (American League)

⇒ 1st in errors at third base (29), lowest fielding percentage at third base (.922) and highest percentage of extra bases taken as a runner (73.2%)
⇒ 6th in bunts in play (20)
⇒ 8th in highest percentage of swings on the first pitch (37.5%)
⇒ 10th in batting average on an 0-2 count (.279)
⇒ Led the Angels in runs scored, hit by pitch (8), batting average vs. lefthanded pitchers, slugging percentage vs. lefthanded pitchers (.526), bunts in play (20) and highest percentage of extra bases taken as a runner (73.2%)

Mark Langston

1997 Season

In three of the last four seasons, veteran southpaw Mark Langston has been seriously affected by arm injuries. He made only eight starts in 1997 before undergoing elbow surgery. He had a few setbacks in his rehabilitation before returning to the Angels on Aug. 20. He lasted only one inning and didn't pitch again. Anaheim missed him badly.

Pitching

Langston has entered the stage in his career where he's more often described as a crafty lefty than a fireballer. He has relied largely on his changeup since elbow surgery in 1994. His fastball seldom reaches the high 80s anymore. He throws a curveball and a slider, and both breaking pitches tend to look alike. Langston uses his fastball-changeup combination to neutralize lefthanders but lacks an out pitch against righties. Because he can't afford to fall behind in the count with his diminished stuff, he's fairly predictable and starts hitters with fastballs. He has become prone to homers now that he doesn't throw as hard. He dominated lefthanders in 1997, but righties had their way with him.

Defense

Seven Gold Gloves say a lot about Langston's knowledge of his position, but his reactions have slowed down. He's technically sound, especially holding runners on base. He gave up just one stolen base in 1997, and basestealers usually are caught more often than not against him.

1998 Outlook

Langston averaged 247 innings a year between 1986-93, and has paid the price since then. He may be at the end of the road. An offseason of rest might have healed his elbow, though expecting him to win more than 10 games may prove too optimistic. He's a free agent who should have a few job offers because the market is weak in pitchers.

Position: SP
Bats: R **Throws:** L
Ht: 6' 2" **Wt:** 184

Opening Day Age: 37
Born: 8/20/60 in San Diego, CA
ML Seasons: 14

Overall Statistics

	W	L	Pct.	ERA	G	GS	Sv	IP	H	BB	SO	HR	Ratio
1997	2	4	.333	5.85	9	9	0	47.2	61	29	30	8	1.89
Career	174	150	.537	3.88	410	407	0	2819.2	2547	1219	2365	291	1.34

How Often He Throws Strikes

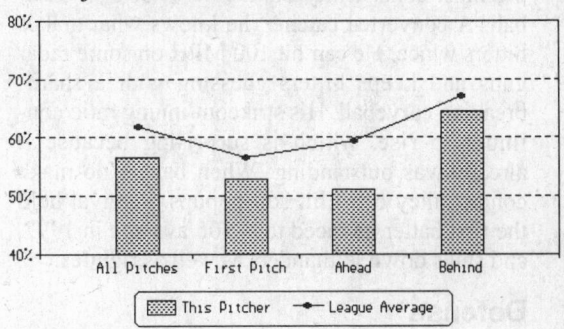

1997 Situational Stats

	W	L	ERA	Sv	IP		AB	H	HR	RBI	Avg
Home	1	3	5.97	0	31.2	LHB	27	5	1	1	.185
Road	1	1	5.63	0	16.0	RHB	166	56	7	31	.337
First Half	2	3	5.01	0	46.2	Sc Pos	54	16	3	24	.296
Scnd Half	0	1	45.00	0	1.0	Clutch	3	0	0	0	.000

1997 Rankings (American League)

⇒ Did not rank near the top or bottom in any category

Troy Percival

1997 Season

Scouts noticed in spring training that Troy Percival didn't have his usual velocity. They soon found out why, as he went on the disabled list with a sore shoulder from April 9 through May 17. He was his old self when he returned, piling up strikeouts while seldom failing in a save situation. Percival was once again the key for a bullpen built around unproven kids. He converted 27 of 31 save opportunities, making him 63 for 70 the last two years. He's money in the bank for manager Terry Collins.

Pitching

Over the last two years, Percival has been one of the most consistently unhittable closers in baseball. A converted catcher, he knows what makes hitters wince. He can hit 100 MPH on some radar guns and keeps hitters guessing with a sharp-breaking curveball. His strikeout/inning ratio continues to rise, which is surprising because it already was outstanding. When batters do make contact, they often hit soft popups. Percival held the first batter he faced to a .106 average in 1997, and shuts down lefthanders as well as righties.

Defense

Percival is no natural on the mound. He has trouble holding runners, who have gone 26-for-29 against him during his major league career, and had only four defensive chances in 52 innings. It's surprising that more teams don't bunt on him, as good things can happen for the opposition when he's in the middle of a play.

1998 Outlook

With a good spring training, Percival should get off to the type of start that will attract All-Star mention. He's a good bet for 40-plus saves, especially if the Angels surround him with a little more talent in the bullpen. They haven't had a dominant setup man since he was in that role in 1995.

Position: RP
Bats: R **Throws:** R
Ht: 6' 3" **Wt:** 200

Opening Day Age: 28
Born: 8/9/69 in Fontana, CA
ML Seasons: 3

Overall Statistics

	W	L	Pct.	ERA	G	GS	Sv	IP	H	BB	SO	HR	Ratio
1997	5	5	.500	3.46	55	0	27	52.0	40	22	72	6	1.19
Career	8	9	.471	2.48	179	0	66	200.0	115	79	266	20	0.97

How Often He Throws Strikes

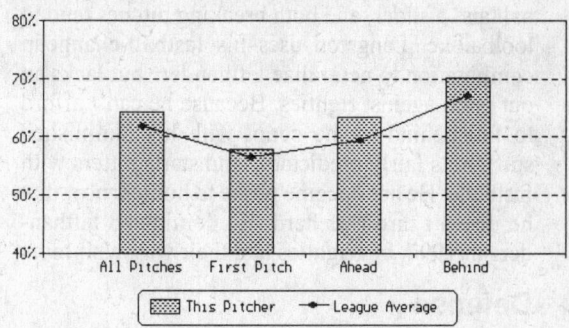

1997 Situational Stats

	W	L	ERA	Sv	IP		AB	H	HR	RBI	Avg
Home	4	3	3.03	14	29.2	LHB	102	24	2	10	.235
Road	1	2	4.03	13	22.1	RHB	93	16	4	11	.172
First Half	3	4	3.24	10	25.0	Sc Pos	67	12	1	15	.179
Scnd Half	2	1	3.67	17	27.0	Clutch	137	28	6	19	.204

1997 Rankings (American League)

⇒ 2nd in first batter efficiency (.106)
⇒ 3rd in save percentage (87.1%)
⇒ 6th in saves
⇒ 8th in games finished (46) and save opportunities (31)
⇒ 10th in lowest batting average allowed in relief with runners on base (.194)
⇒ Led the Angels in saves, games finished (46), save opportunities (31), save percentage (87.1%), first batter efficiency (.106) and lowest batting average allowed in relief with runners in scoring position (.179)

Tony Phillips

1997 Season

Over the last two seasons, Tony Phillips has been an outstanding leadoff hitter and an unquestioned lightning rod for controversy. In 1997, he prompted the White Sox to trade him by accusing AL president Gene Budig of being a racist after receiving a two-game suspension. He got off to a great start with Anaheim but was arrested in August on drug charges. When the Angels suspended him, the union got the suspension overturned. He retained the right to finish the season in uniform but virtually ensured that he wouldn't be back with the Disney Co.'s Angels in 1998.

Hitting

Phillips get on base as effectively as anyone in baseball. He works pitchers into deep counts almost every time up to the plate. The switch-hitting Phillips is equally tough from either side of the plate. He annoys pitchers with a deep crouch and a penchant for backing out of the box. His personal troubles seemed to drag him down in 1997, as his on-base percentage dropped 60 points after the All-Star break. His power is pretty much limited to doubles, but he can be very effective at the top of a lineup.

Baserunning & Defense

Versatility is Phillips' calling card. He was the White Sox' regular left fielder in 1996, then moved to right field after the addition of Albert Belle. He played second base, third base, left field and DH after he was traded to Anaheim. Phillips is a liability at third but remains a passable second baseman, with left field being his best position. He does cover lots of ground in the outfield but has a below-average arm. He has good speed but is no longer a serious basestealing threat. He had 13 swipes in 1997 but was caught 10 times.

1998 Outlook

Phillips entered the free-agent market in the off-season. Though he remains a good leadoff man, he'll have to walk a straight line to restore his reputation. He's also 38, another factor working against him. But it would be surprising if he couldn't find a job.

Position: 2B/LF/RF/DH
Bats: B **Throws:** R
Ht: 5'10" **Wt:** 175

Opening Day Age: 38
Born: 4/25/59 in Atlanta, GA
ML Seasons: 16

Overall Statistics

	G	AB	R	H	D	T	HR	RBI	SB	BB	SO	Avg	OBP	Slg
1997	141	534	96	147	34	2	8	57	13	102	118	.275	.392	.391
Career	1990	6975	1190	1865	320	46	141	749	165	1201	1355	.267	.375	.387

Where He Hits the Ball

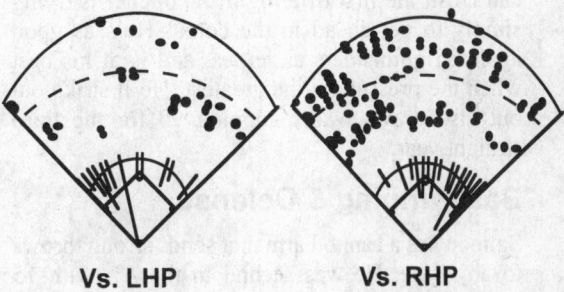

Vs. LHP   **Vs. RHP**

1997 Situational Stats

	AB	H	HR	RBI	Avg		AB	H	HR	RBI	Avg
Home	272	67	5	35	.246	LHP	139	34	1	12	.245
Road	262	80	3	22	.305	RHP	395	113	7	45	.286
First Half	307	89	4	25	.290	Sc Pos	117	38	2	49	.325
Scnd Half	227	58	4	32	.256	Clutch	74	17	0	6	.230

1997 Rankings (American League)

⇒ 2nd in lowest stolen base percentage (56.5%)
⇒ 4th in most pitches seen per plate appearance (4.15)
⇒ 5th in walks (102) and on-base percentage for a leadoff hitter (.389)
⇒ 9th in lowest HR frequency (66.8 ABs per HR) and highest percentage of pitches taken (61.5%)
⇒ 10th in lowest batting average at home (.246)
⇒ Led the Angels in on-base percentage for a leadoff hitter (.371) and highest percentage of pitches taken (61.1%)

Tim Salmon

1997 Season

Tim Salmon recovered from a slow start to enjoy another strong season. His .296 average and 33 homers were standard from him, and he drove in a career-high 129 runs. He also continued to play right field well, displaying one of the strongest throwing arms around. His presence in the lineup made it possible for the Angels to recover from a disappointing 1996.

Hitting

Salmon has a short, controlled swing and covers the entire plate. He has wrists like a lumberjack, allowing him to drive the ball to all fields. He's a patient hitter who prefers to get the ball down. He can crush the first offering if the pitcher is trying simply to get ahead in the count. He's as good against righthanders as lefties, and is at his best when the pressure is the greatest. He'll strike out but also draws walks, topping 90 for the third straight year.

Baserunning & Defense

Salmon has a cannon arm that sends strong throws to any base. He was second in the AL with 15 outfield assists. He has mastered the sliding catch, which allows him to play deep, but he sometimes has trouble going back to the warning track on balls. He has good range and is solid in the field despite leading American League right fielders with 11 errors in 1997. He's an average baserunner but will take an extra base when outfielders take him for granted. He was successful on just nine of 21 steal attempts and should stop running as much.

1998 Outlook

It's hard to believe that Salmon never has made an All-Star team. The Angels point to his chronic slow starts, and will try to address them this spring. There's talk that he'll play as many innings as he can in Arizona to see if he can find his midseason form in April. If he does, he just might put together the best season of his career.

Position: RF
Bats: R **Throws:** R
Ht: 6' 3" **Wt:** 220

Opening Day Age: 29
Born: 8/24/68 in Long Beach, CA
ML Seasons: 6
Pronunciation: SA-men

Overall Statistics

	G	AB	R	H	D	T	HR	RBI	SB	BB	SO	Avg	OBP	Slg
1997	157	582	95	172	28	1	33	129	9	95	142	.296	.394	.517
Career	721	2667	464	782	143	11	153	503	25	426	638	.293	.392	.527

Where He Hits the Ball

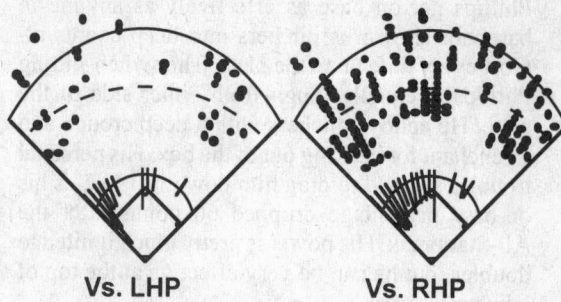

Vs. LHP   Vs. RHP

1997 Situational Stats

	AB	H	HR	RBI	Avg		AB	H	HR	RBI	Avg
Home	297	84	17	62	.283	LHP	139	40	9	25	.288
Road	285	88	16	67	.309	RHP	443	132	24	104	.298
First Half	305	86	15	60	.282	Sc Pos	178	62	10	99	.348
Scnd Half	277	86	18	69	.310	Clutch	102	25	4	26	.245

1997 Rankings (American League)

⇒ 1st in lowest stolen base percentage (42.9%) and errors in right field (11)
⇒ 2nd in lowest fielding percentage in right field (.971)
⇒ 3rd in lowest percentage of swings put into play (33.8%)
⇒ 4th in RBI
⇒ 5th in sacrifice flies (11) and times on base (274)
⇒ Led the Angels in home runs, total bases (301), RBI, sacrifice flies (11), caught stealing (12), walks, times on base (274), strikeouts, pitches seen (2,787), plate appearances (695), games played (157), slugging percentage, on-base percentage, HR frequency (17.6 ABs per HR), most pitches seen per plate appearance (4.01) and batting average with runners in scoring position

Luis Alicea

Position: 2B/3B
Bats: B **Throws:** R
Ht: 5' 9" **Wt:** 177

Opening Day Age: 32
Born: 7/29/65 in
Santurce, PR
ML Seasons: 8
Pronunciation:
ah-la-SAY-ya

Overall Statistics

	G	AB	R	H	D	T	HR	RBI	SB	BB	SO	Avg	OBP	Slg
1997	128	388	59	98	16	7	5	37	22	69	65	.253	.375	.369
Career	826	2384	310	608	115	36	27	254	64	321	387	.255	.347	.367

1997 Situational Stats

	AB	H	HR	RBI	Avg		AB	H	HR	RBI	Avg
Home	187	44	2	23	.235	LHP	110	27	0	9	.245
Road	201	54	3	14	.269	RHP	278	71	5	28	.255
First Half	240	69	4	25	.288	Sc Pos	82	25	2	32	.305
Scnd Half	148	29	1	12	.196	Clutch	71	19	1	5	.268

1997 Season

Luis Alicea signed a minor league contract last season with Anaheim, his third team in three years. It proved to be a good investment for the Angels, as he inherited the second-base job in Anaheim when Randy Velarde was injured. Alicea played well in the field while setting career highs in on-base percentage (.375) and stolen bases (22). He lost playing time late in the year when Tony Phillips became the regular second baseman after the acquisition of Rickey Henderson.

Hitting, Baserunning & Defense

A switch-hitter, Alicea generally hits for a better average righthanded. He seemed to benefit from hitting coach Rod Carew, showing more patience at the plate. Alicea had more walks than strikeouts and flashed occasional power. He has good speed but doesn't get many infield hits. He doesn't have quite the speed he had when he came up, but has become a skilled basestealer. He has good range at second base, making more than his share of spectacular plays. He cut down his error total last year.

1998 Outlook

A free agent, Alicea might have to move on to play regularly. Alicea could be a valuable utilityman for someone, but might have some time left as a No. 1 second baseman in the right situation.

Craig Grebeck

Position: 2B/3B/SS
Bats: R **Throws:** R
Ht: 5' 7" **Wt:** 150

Opening Day Age: 33
Born: 12/29/64 in
Johnstown, PA
ML Seasons: 8
Pronunciation:
GRAY-beck
Nickname: Little Hurt

Overall Statistics

	G	AB	R	H	D	T	HR	RBI	SB	BB	SO	Avg	OBP	Slg
1997	63	126	12	34	9	0	1	6	0	18	11	.270	.359	.365
Career	527	1292	149	327	72	6	14	125	2	157	177	.253	.337	.351

1997 Situational Stats

	AB	H	HR	RBI	Avg		AB	H	HR	RBI	Avg
Home	53	12	1	2	.226	LHP	75	22	0	3	.293
Road	73	22	0	4	.301	RHP	51	12	1	3	.235
First Half	92	28	1	6	.304	Sc Pos	24	8	0	3	.333
Scnd Half	34	6	0	0	.176	Clutch	21	6	0	1	.286

1997 Season

Craig Grebeck began 1997 as a valuable reserve, but his batting average and value decreased as the season progressed. He started the year by hitting well and earned himself some playing time, but he batted .176 in the second half and became a virtually forgotten man down the stretch.

Hitting, Baserunning & Defense

Grebeck always has been an outstanding fastball hitter and still can hold his own against all but the nastiest heat. He never has adjusted to good breaking pitches and copes by fouling lots of them off. He's a tough guy to strike out, but doesn't often drive the ball and hits too many fly balls considering his poor power. Grebeck lacks the speed to be a top-notch bench player; he has stolen just two bases in his major league career. He's versatile in the field, starting games at second base, shortstop, third base and left field in 1997. He seldom makes defensive mistakes.

1998 Outlook

Grebeck went into the offseason looking for work, and signed a minor league contract with the Blue Jays. It will take either a great spring or solid start in the minors to earn him another spot on a big league bench.

Shigetoshi Hasegawa

Position: RP/SP
Bats: R **Throws:** R
Ht: 5'11" **Wt:** 160

Opening Day Age: 29
Born: 8/1/68 in Kobe, Japan
ML Seasons: 1
Pronunciation: shig-eh-TOE-shee HOS-eh-gah-wah

Overall Statistics

	W	L	Pct.	ERA	G	GS	Sv	IP	H	BB	SO	HR	Ratio
1997	3	7	.300	3.93	50	7	0	116.2	118	46	83	14	1.41
Career	3	7	.300	3.93	50	7	0	116.2	118	46	83	14	1.41

1997 Situational Stats

	W	L	ERA	Sv	IP			AB	H	HR	RBI	Avg
Home	0	4	4.23	0	66.0	LHB		176	49	5	16	.278
Road	3	3	3.55	0	50.2	RHB		262	69	9	40	.263
First Half	1	4	4.21	0	66.1	Sc Pos		110	25	3	39	.227
Scnd Half	2	3	3.58	0	50.1	Clutch		69	20	2	9	.290

1997 Season

Compared to Hideki Irabu, Hideo Nomo and other Japanese imports, Shigetoshi Hasegawa has received minimal attention. He spent six years pitching in Japan before joining the Angels as a free agent. He spent all season with Anaheim, making seven awful starts but pitching fairly effectively out of the bullpen.

Pitching & Defense

Hasegawa is a control specialist who knows how to pitch. His fastball got better as the year went along, topping out at 90 MPH in the last two months. He hits his spots with it, seldom making mistakes out over the plate. He has an excellent changeup and a good curveball. He was equally effective against lefthanders and righthanders as a rookie. He's a skilled fielder who does a good job starting double plays. Basestealers found him hard to run on, going just 3-for-7.

1998 Outlook

Given the cultural adjustments he had to make, Hasegawa did a tremendous job in 1997. He could develop into a setup man for Troy Percival, but seems most valuable as a long reliever. It will be interesting to see if he can maintain the 90-MPH fastball he showed at the end of the season.

Jack Howell

Position: 3B/1B/DH
Bats: L **Throws:** R
Ht: 6' 0" **Wt:** 190

Opening Day Age: 36
Born: 8/18/61 in Tucson, AZ
ML Seasons: 9

Overall Statistics

	G	AB	R	H	D	T	HR	RBI	SB	BB	SO	Avg	OBP	Slg
1997	77	174	25	45	7	0	14	34	1	13	36	.259	.305	.540
Career	880	2568	339	614	122	16	106	329	14	288	605	.239	.317	.423

1997 Situational Stats

	AB	H	HR	RBI	Avg			AB	H	HR	RBI	Avg
Home	81	22	5	16	.272	LHP		23	6	0	4	.261
Road	93	23	9	18	.247	RHP		151	39	14	30	.258
First Half	72	20	3	9	.278	Sc Pos		58	12	3	19	.207
Scnd Half	102	25	11	25	.245	Clutch		27	8	2	6	.296

1997 Season

He'll never be confused with Mark McGwire, but retread Jack Howell put up some amazing power numbers for the second straight season after taking a four-year sabbatical in Japan. Batting almost exclusively against righthanders, Howell performed well in periodic starts at third base, first base and designated hitter. Though he was only 3-for-21 as a pinch hitter, the Angels were thrilled with the production he provided.

Hitting, Baserunning & Defense

Howell has a compact swing that lets him catch up to all but the very best fastballs. He can be fooled by pitchers who are willing to throw breaking balls on fastball counts. He always has struggled against southpaws and is now considered strictly a platoon player. Howell is a slow runner and is limited defensively both at first and third base. He makes most routine plays at the hot corner but has little range and a below-average arm.

1998 Outlook

Howell filed for free agency but is expected to return to the Angels. He provides some depth and versatility. His role isn't likely to expand, due to his defensive limitations and inability to hit lefties, but he's a valuable role player.

Mike James

Position: RP
Bats: R **Throws:** R
Ht: 6' 3" **Wt:** 185

Opening Day Age: 30
Born: 8/15/67 in Fort Walton, FL
ML Seasons: 3

Overall Statistics

	W	L	Pct.	ERA	G	GS	Sv	IP	H	BB	SO	HR	Ratio
1997	5	5	.500	4.31	58	0	7	62.2	69	28	57	3	1.55
Career	13	10	.565	3.52	173	0	9	199.1	180	96	158	16	1.38

1997 Situational Stats

	W	L	ERA	Sv	IP		AB	H	HR	RBI	Avg
Home	5	2	2.94	3	33.2	LHB	92	29	0	9	.315
Road	0	3	5.90	4	29.0	RHB	152	40	3	24	.263
First Half	4	2	4.85	6	39.0	Sc Pos	68	20	0	27	.294
Scnd Half	1	3	3.42	1	23.2	Clutch	170	47	2	22	.276

1997 Season

Despite a three-month slump and a brief stay on the disabled list with an inflamed elbow, reliever Mike James posted another fairly strong season. He filled in as the closer early in the year when Troy Percival was sidelined. After Percival returned and James' arm came around, the two of them teamed up to present major problems for opponents in the eighth and ninth innings.

Pitching & Defense

James comes right at hitters with a three-quarters motion that makes him especially tough on righthanders. His fastball rides in on righties' fists, jamming them or breaking their bats. He has a decent slider which he uses when his fastball isn't at his best, but it sometimes flattens out. He could use another pitch to keep lefthanders off balance. James is not afraid to pitch inside and gives up very few home runs. He's an average fielder. He can be slow going to the plate but is difficult for basestealers to time.

1998 Outlook

James should remain one of the Angels' primary setup men. He's an excellent bet to pitch often in the late innings. He could become a major force by improving his work against lefthanders.

Chad Kreuter

Position: C
Bats: B **Throws:** R
Ht: 6' 2" **Wt:** 200

Opening Day Age: 33
Born: 8/26/64 in Greenbrae, CA
ML Seasons: 10
Pronunciation: CREW-ter

Overall Statistics

	G	AB	R	H	D	T	HR	RBI	SB	BB	SO	Avg	OBP	Slg
1997	89	255	25	59	9	2	5	21	0	29	66	.231	.310	.341
Career	540	1413	170	333	68	6	33	149	2	186	346	.236	.325	.362

1997 Situational Stats

	AB	H	HR	RBI	Avg		AB	H	HR	RBI	Avg
Home	121	25	3	13	.207	LHP	77	19	3	10	.247
Road	134	34	2	8	.254	RHP	178	40	2	11	.225
First Half	122	28	2	10	.230	Sc Pos	64	11	0	12	.172
Scnd Half	133	31	3	11	.233	Clutch	38	6	0	2	.158

1997 Season

No one doubts Chad Kreuter's determination. Last spring he put himself through hell to recover from a career-threatening injury to his left shoulder, along with complications involving internal bleeding that actually became life-threatening, in time to win a job with the White Sox. His playing time increased with a trade to Anaheim, especially after Jim Leyritz went to Texas in a deal for Ken Hill. Kreuter was consistently mediocre, showing a good knowledge of the game without the tools to put that knowledge to use.

Hitting, Baserunning & Defense

Kreuter has hit for very little power since his 1993 season, when he hit 15 home runs. The switch-hitting Kreuter is better from the right side but gets most of his at-bats from the left. If pitchers get ahead in the count, he's almost an automatic out. His best offensive skill is drawing walks. Kreuter does a great job calling games and working with pitchers. He throws well and is willing to block the plate. He hasn't stolen a base since '93.

1998 Outlook

Kreuter probably won't return to the Angels, who acquired Matt Walbeck in the offseason. Kreuter's reputation as a team player should land him a job as a backup catcher somewhere.

Orlando Palmeiro

Position: CF
Bats: L **Throws:** R
Ht: 5'11" **Wt:** 160

Opening Day Age: 29
Born: 1/19/69 in Hoboken, NJ
ML Seasons: 3
Pronunciation: pall-MARE-oh

Overall Statistics

	G	AB	R	H	D	T	HR	RBI	SB	BB	SO	Avg	OBP	Slg
1997	74	134	19	29	2	2	0	8	2	17	11	.216	.307	.261
Career	139	241	28	61	8	3	0	15	2	26	25	.253	.332	.311

1997 Situational Stats

	AB	H	HR	RBI	Avg		AB	H	HR	RBI	Avg
Home	65	14	0	6	.215	LHP	37	13	0	2	.351
Road	69	15	0	2	.217	RHP	97	16	0	6	.165
First Half	72	18	0	5	.250	Sc Pos	30	5	0	8	.167
Scnd Half	62	11	0	3	.177	Clutch	29	11	0	2	.379

1997 Season

While scouts like Orlando Palmeiro's tools, he consistently disappoints his managers. He's quickly overexposed when entrusted with any responsibility. Palmeiro was sidelined with back spasms briefly in August, but otherwise spent a full season as the Angels' fourth outfielder. He did a good job defensively filling in when Jim Edmonds was injured, but otherwise struggled. He failed to hit a home run in 134 at-bats.

Hitting, Baserunning & Defense

Palmeiro is a lefthanded hitter who is a tough out against lefthanders. He has developed a mental block when hitting righties. He hit nearly 200 points higher against lefties than righties in 1997. He takes lefties to the opposite field but seems intent on pulling righties. He's a contact hitter who's able to get into deep counts without striking out too often. Palmeiro plays all three outfield positions. He does a good job running down fly balls but isn't an accurate thrower. He has good speed, though he hasn't developed into a basestealing threat.

1998 Outlook

Palmeiro's low salary is his major asset at this point. He's an inexpensive reserve who needs to hit better in order to prolong his big league career.

Allen Watson

Position: SP
Bats: L **Throws:** L
Ht: 6' 3" **Wt:** 195

Opening Day Age: 27
Born: 11/18/70 in Jamaica, NY
ML Seasons: 5

Overall Statistics

	W	L	Pct.	ERA	G	GS	Sv	IP	H	BB	SO	HR	Ratio
1997	12	12	.500	4.93	35	34	0	199.0	220	73	141	37	1.47
Career	39	45	.464	4.91	123	119	0	700.2	755	264	441	108	1.45

1997 Situational Stats

	W	L	ERA	Sv	IP		AB	H	HR	RBI	Avg
Home	5	7	5.85	0	104.2	LHB	142	36	4	19	.254
Road	7	5	3.91	0	94.1	RHB	646	184	33	96	.285
First Half	7	5	5.23	0	94.2	Sc Pos	170	50	7	73	.294
Scnd Half	5	7	4.66	0	104.1	Clutch	25	6	1	2	.240

1997 Season

Former Cardinals first-round pick Allen Watson pitched for his third team in three years after the Angels acquired him from the Giants for first baseman J.T. Snow. Watson continued to make slow progress, but did win a career-high 12 games. He held up well enough to pitch 199 innings, and four of his five starts on three days rest were quality outings.

Pitching & Defense

Watson is a traditional three-pitch lefty, with a slightly above-average fastball, a curveball and a change. He's an aggressive pitcher who challenges hitters. He works high in the strike zone and gives up a lot of fly balls. That hurt him at his new home park, and he led all American League pitchers with 37 homers allowed. His high leg kick makes him a fairly easy target for basestealers, but he used his pickoff move to great effect in 1997. A good athlete, he can field his position well—and swing a bat. He's a career .255 hitter who was used as a pinch hitter by the Giants.

1998 Outlook

Watson has good stuff for a lefthander, so he'll keep getting opportunities to pitch. The Angels see him as a No. 3 or 4 starter. To move beyond that level, he'll need to work on keeping the ball down.

Other Anaheim Angels

Greg Cadaret (Pos: LHP, Age: 36)

	W	L	Pct.	ERA	G	GS	Sv	IP	H	BB	SO	HR	Ratio
1997	0	0	-	3.29	15	0	0	13.2	11	8	11	1	1.39
Career	37	30	.552	3.97	401	35	13	679.2	667	385	497	51	1.55

Cadaret, who hadn't pitched in the majors in three years, resurfaced last summer in Anaheim. He pitched reasonably well and signed a minor league deal with the Angels after the season. 1998 Outlook: C

Rich DeLucia (Pos: RHP, Age: 33)

	W	L	Pct.	ERA	G	GS	Sv	IP	H	BB	SO	HR	Ratio
1997	6	4	.600	3.89	36	0	3	44.0	35	27	44	5	1.41
Career	36	44	.450	4.62	253	49	4	543.0	521	244	422	77	1.41

DeLucia came to the Angels in an early season deal with the Giants. He was pitching very well when he came down with a blood clot in his pitching shoulder. If healthy, he can be a useful pitcher. 1998 Outlook: B

Robert Eenhoorn (Pos: SS, Age: 25, Bats: R)

	G	AB	R	H	D	T	HR	RBI	SB	BB	SO	Avg	OBP	Slg
1997	11	20	2	7	1	0	1	6	0	0	2	.350	.333	.550
Career	37	67	7	16	3	0	1	10	0	3	10	.239	.260	.328

Still waiting for a real chance at a major league job, Eenhoorn spent most of 1997 at Triple-A Vancouver, where he batted .308. Expansion might enable him to get a shot at last. 1998 Outlook: B

Angelo Encarnacion (Pos: C, Age: 24, Bats: R)

	G	AB	R	H	D	T	HR	RBI	SB	BB	SO	Avg	OBP	Slg
1997	11	17	2	7	1	0	1	4	2	0	1	.412	.412	.647
Career	76	198	23	50	10	2	3	15	3	13	34	.253	.299	.369

Encarnacion began last year with the Pirates but was dealt to the Padres. After hitting .245 at Las Vegas, he was picked up by the Angels. Still only 24, he might get a chance this year. 1998 Outlook: C

Kevin Gross (Pos: RHP, Age: 36)

	W	L	Pct.	ERA	G	GS	Sv	IP	H	BB	SO	HR	Ratio
1997	2	1	.667	6.75	12	3	0	25.1	30	20	20	4	1.97
Career	142	158	.473	4.11	474	368	5	2487.2	2519	986	1727	230	1.41

Gross began last year with the Rangers, got released, then was picked up by the Angels. He got into 12 games with the Angels, showed little and then was dropped. His career is probably over. 1998 Outlook: D

Mark Gubicza (Pos: RHP, Age: 35)

	W	L	Pct.	ERA	G	GS	Sv	IP	H	BB	SO	HR	Ratio
1997	0	1	.000	25.07	2	2	0	4.2	13	3	5	2	3.43
Career	132	136	.493	3.96	384	329	2	2223.1	2239	786	1371	155	1.36

After coming to Anaheim in the Chili Davis deal, Gubicza came down with shoulder problems. He made only two harrowing starts before undergoing survery in June. His future is shaky. 1998 Outlook: C

Pep Harris (Pos: RHP, Age: 25)

	W	L	Pct.	ERA	G	GS	Sv	IP	H	BB	SO	HR	Ratio
1997	5	4	.556	3.62	61	0	0	79.2	82	38	56	7	1.51
Career	7	4	.636	3.70	72	3	0	112.0	113	55	76	11	1.50

After getting a taste of the big leagues in 1996, Harris arrived to stay in 1997. He throws a hard sinker that can reach the low 90s. 1998 Outlook: A

Mike Holtz (Pos: LHP, Age: 25)

	W	L	Pct.	ERA	G	GS	Sv	IP	H	BB	SO	HR	Ratio
1997	3	4	.429	3.32	66	0	2	43.1	38	15	40	7	1.22
Career	6	7	.462	2.97	96	0	2	72.2	59	34	71	8	1.28

Holtz has found a niche in Anaheim as a lefty specialist. He took a 1.63 ERA into September before running out of gas. 1998 Outlook: A

Darrell May (Pos: LHP, Age: 25)

	W	L	Pct.	ERA	G	GS	Sv	IP	H	BB	SO	HR	Ratio
1997	2	1	.667	5.23	29	2	0	51.2	56	25	42	6	1.57
Career	2	2	.500	6.31	41	4	0	67.0	84	31	49	12	1.72

May, who had previously pitched for the Braves and Pirates, got his first extended major league trial with the Angels last year. He didn't dazzle anyone, but he *is* lefthanded. 1998 Outlook: C

Chris Turner (Pos: C, Age: 29, Bats: R)

	G	AB	R	H	D	T	HR	RBI	SB	BB	SO	Avg	OBP	Slg
1997	13	23	4	6	1	1	1	2	0	5	8	.261	.393	.522
Career	105	260	37	65	13	2	3	29	4	25	56	.250	.316	.350

Turner missed considerable time with a wrist injury last year, but when he played he hit pretty well for the Angels. The Twins signed him to a minor league contract after the season. 1998 Outlook: C

Randy Velarde (Pos: C, Age: 35, Bats: R)

	G	AB	R	H	D	T	HR	RBI	SB	BB	SO	Avg	OBP	Slg
1997	1	0	0	0	0	0	0	0	0	0	0			
Career	795	2465	345	662	126	13	57	262	29	256	500	.269	.342	.400

After signing a free-agent contract with the Angels, Velarde hurt his elbow in spring training and got into only one game all year. If healthy, he could be Anaheim's second baseman this year. 1998 Outlook: B

Shad Williams (Pos: RHP, Age: 27)

	W	L	Pct.	ERA	G	GS	Sv	IP	H	BB	SO	HR	Ratio
1997	0	0	-	0.00	1	0	0	1.0	1	1	0	0	2.00
Career	0	2	.000	8.59	14	2	0	29.1	43	22	26	7	2.22

A long-time minor league veteran who's pitched at Triple-A Vancouver in each of the last four years, Williams got into only one game with the Angels last year. He's looking for a new employer. 1998 Outlook: C

Anaheim Angels Minor League Prospects

Organization Overview:

You have to give the Angels credit for developing their own major league talent. More than half of their regulars, two of their top three starting pitchers and their closer have come directly from the Anaheim system. You don't have to give the Angels credit for anything else. What they have in Anaheim is what they've got. Several of their most advanced pitching prospects struggled in 1997, and their most advanced position player might miss all of 1998. The lack of depth is the result of the Autrys cutting back on bonus money in the amateur draft before selling part of the team to the Disney Co. The Angels have gotten what they've paid for.

Mike Bovee

Position: P   **Opening Day Age:** 24
Bats: R **Throws:** R   **Born:** 8/21/73 in San
Ht: 5' 10" **Wt:** 200   Diego, CA

Recent Statistics

	W	L	ERA	G	GS	Sv	IP	H	R	BB	SO	HR
97 AA Midland	8	2	4.24	20	13	0	102.0	117	53	23	61	7
97 AAA Vancouver	4	3	3.44	12	12	0	89.0	92	38	25	71	7
97 AL Anaheim	0	0	5.40	3	0	0	3.1	3	2	1	5	1

A sixth-round draft pick in 1991, Bovee was a throw-in in the October 1996 trade that sent Chili Davis to the Royals for Mark Gubicza. He consistently has posted good strikeout-walk ratios, mainly a tribute to his ability to locate all four of his pitches. His curve is probably his best, and his fastball is slightly below average at 88 MPH. Despite his lack of overwhelming stuff, he succeeded in the hitter-friendly Pacific Coast League, albeit in the PCL's best pitchers' park. Whether he can make it as a No. 5 starter remains to be seen, but he can fall back on a middle-relief role.

Jamie Burke

Position: 3B   **Opening Day Age:** 26
Bats: R **Throws:** R   **Born:** 9/24/71 in
Ht: 6' 0" **Wt:** 195   Roseburg, OR

Recent Statistics

	G	AB	R	H	D	T	HR	RBI	SB	BB	SO	AVG
96 AA Midland	45	144	24	46	8	2	2	16	1	20	22	.319
96 AAA Vancouver	41	156	12	39	5	0	1	14	2	7	18	.250
97 AA Midland	116	428	77	141	44	3	6	72	2	40	46	.329
97 AAA Vancouver	8	27	4	8	1	0	0	3	0	3	2	.296
97 MLE	124	428	59	122	36	1	4	54	1	26	52	.285

Burke isn't going to be an all-star, but he could be a useful player. A 1993 ninth-round pick out of Oregon State, he's trying to enhance his chances by learning to catch. Normally a third baseman, he went behind the plate for 30 games in 1997 and further honed his catching skills in the Arizona Fall League. He's 26 and hasn't hit for the power the Angels expected, but he did bat .327 with 45 doubles and nearly as many walks as

strikeouts. If he can add versatility to his hitting ability, he just might get a chance.

Anthony Chavez

Position: P   **Opening Day Age:** 27
Bats: R **Throws:** R   **Born:** 10/22/70 in
Ht: 5' 11" **Wt:** 180   Turlock, CA

Recent Statistics

	W	L	ERA	G	GS	Sv	IP	H	R	BB	SO	HR
97 AA Midland	1	2	4.21	33	1	6	47.0	53	23	15	35	1
97 AAA Vancouver	4	1	2.54	28	0	15	28.1	21	8	6	22	2
97 AL Anaheim	0	0	0.93	7	0	0	9.2	7	1	5	10	1

That Chavez is included in this section is 1) a tribute to his perseverance and 2) a knock on the Angels system. He began his pro career in 1992 with two strikes against him: He was a 50th-round draft pick (out of San Jose State) and a 5-foot-10 righthander, two resume lines not often seen in the major leagues. Slowly but surely, he climbed the ladder with an average fastball and a good split-finger pitch, until he reached Anaheim at the end of 1997. He's not overpowering and he's not going to get any better at age 27, but he throws strikes and gets outs. Middle relievers have succeeded with less.

Troy Glaus

Position: 3B/SS   **Opening Day Age:** 21
Bats: R **Throws:** P   **Born:** 8/3/76 in
Ht: 6' 5" **Wt:** 215   Tarzana, CA

Recent Statistics

	G	AB	R	H	D	T	HR	RBI	SB	BB	SO	AVG
97				Did Not Play								

Glaus has yet to make his pro debut because he took all of last summer to negotiate a $2.25 million bonus as the No. 3 overall pick in the draft. The UCLA product was the third baseman on the 1996 U.S. Olympic team, but played shortstop last year for the Bruins. Though he's stiff at short, his contract mandates that he'll start his pro career there. He's got plenty of power and arm strength, and eliminate some holes in his swing as a UCLA junior, but he's not a junior. He'll be on the fast track and breathing down Dave Hollins' neck once he moves to third.

Bret Hemphill

Position: C   **Opening Day Age:** 26
Bats: B **Throws:** R   **Born:** 12/17/71 in Santa
Ht: 6' 3" **Wt:** 210   Clara, CA

Recent Statistics

	G	AB	R	H	D	T	HR	RBI	SB	BB	SO	AVG
96 A Lk Elsinore	108	399	64	105	21	3	17	64	4	52	93	.263
97 AA Midland	78	266	46	82	15	2	10	63	0	47	56	.308
97 MLE	78	252	33	68	11	1	8	45	0	28	61	.270

The good news is that Hemphill proved that his surge in the second half of 1996 wasn't a complete fluke. The bad news is that he injured his throwing shoulder in a collision and required reconstructive surgery, which could shelve him for all of 1998. A 14th-round pick in 1994 out of Cal State Fullerton, Hemphill was the Angels' most advanced position-player prospect. His arm has always been his best tool, which is more cause for concern. He has improved his plate discipline and developed some power in the last season and a half, but his age and his injury are working against him.

Ramon Ortiz

Position: P **Opening Day Age:** 21
Bats: R **Throws:** R **Born:** 5/23/76 in Las
Ht: 6' 0" **Wt:** 150 Matas Cotui, DR

Recent Statistics

	W	L	ERA	G	GS	Sv	IP	H	R	BB	SO	HR
96 R Angels	5	4	2.12	16	8	1	68.0	55	28	27	78	5
96 A Boise	1	1	3.66	3	3	0	19.2	21	10	6	18	3
97 A Cedar Rapds	11	10	3.58	27	27	0	181.0	156	78	53	225	22

The jewel of the system, Ortiz is a product of the Angels' now-defunct baseball academy in the Dominican Republic. Not only does he have a 95-MPH fastball and an 86-MPH slider, but he can maintain the velocity on both pitches for nine innings. He throws strikes and throws *good* strikes, keeping the ball down in the zone. He led the minors in strikeouts pitching in his first full pro season, and the only negative at this point would be the 181 innings he worked at age 21. His stuff and his small, wiry body have the Angels dreaming that he can become Pedro Martinez.

Scott Schoeneweis

Position: P **Opening Day Age:** 24
Bats: L **Throws:** L **Born:** 10/2/73 in Long
Ht: 6' 0" **Wt:** 180 Branch, NY

Recent Statistics

	W	L	ERA	G	GS	Sv	IP	H	R	BB	SO	HR
96 A Lk Elsinore	8	3	3.94	14	12	0	93.2	86	47	27	83	6
97 AA Midland	7	5	5.96	20	20	0	113.1	145	84	39	94	7

Schoeneweis has proven he can come back from adversity, which should serve him well after a rocky 1997. After winning Freshman All-America honors at Duke, he battled testicular cancer and arm problems, but rebounded to become a third-round pick in 1996. He had a strong pro debut that year, in high Class A ball to boot, showing an average fastball and above-average slider. He continued to throw strikes last year, but got pounded in Midland because he wouldn't throw his fastball inside and because his slider regressed. He also needs to throw his changeup more often and locate it better. If not, he's only fodder for the back end of a rotation.

Jarrod Washburn

Position: P **Opening Day Age:** 23
Bats: L **Throws:** L **Born:** 8/13/74 in La
Ht: 6' 1" **Wt:** 185 Crosse, WI

Recent Statistics

	W	L	ERA	G	GS	Sv	IP	H	R	BB	SO	HR
96 A Lk Elsinore	6	3	3.30	14	14	0	92.2	79	38	33	93	5
96 AAA Vancouver	0	2	10.80	2	2	0	8.1	12	16	12	5	1
96 AA Midland	5	6	4.40	13	13	0	88.0	77	44	25	58	11
97 AA Midland	15	12	4.80	29	29	0	189.1	211	115	65	146	23
97 AAA Vancouver	0	0	3.60	1	1	0	5.0	4	2	2	6	0

Few minor league lefthanders throw harder than Washburn, a 1995 second-round pick who pitched in relative obscurity at the University of Wisconsin-Oshkosh. Like Schoeneweis, he greatly disappointed the Angels after a banner 1996 season. If his fastball wasn't at its peak velocity of 93 MPH, he got rocked. He has a curveball, but it's very inconsistent, and he hasn't shown any aptitude for a changeup in three pro seasons. He has the best stuff in the upper levels of the Angels system, but may wind up in relief if he can't improve his offspeed stuff and command. As with Ortiz, he has been handed a surprisingly heavy workload, working 189 and 194 innings the last two years at ages 21 and 22.

Others to Watch

First baseman **Larry Barnes**, signed out of Fresno State as an undrafted free agent, continues to put up good raw numbers (.287-13-71 at Class A Lake Elsinore). But he was also a bit old for the California League at age 23, and his combined on-base and slugging percentage (.808) was just 8 percent above the league average. . . 23-year-old shortstop **Justin Baughman** has outstanding speed and stole 68 bases in the Cal League, but his bat is still a question mark. He also may face a move to second base. . . The best middle-infield prospect in the system is 21-year-old shortstop **Nelson Castro**, who has yet to reach full-season ball. His best tools are his speed and arm, and he also has some hitting ability. . . As they did with Devon White, the Angels signed **Norm Hutchins** out of an inner-city New York high school. Hutchins has similar athletic gifts, but has struggled to put his offensive game together. Now 22, he's a gifted center fielder with leadoff speed, but not the on-base ability. . . Outfielder **Marcus Knight**, 19, may be the best pure hitter in the system. His bat will have to carry him, because the rest of his tools are nothing special. . . Outfielder **Rich Stuart**, 21, had been the Angels' brightest young hitter until he was supplanted by Knight. That might not have happened had he not lost most of 1997 to elbow surgery. Stuart has more power than Knight, and a right-field arm.

Ray Miller

1997 Season

After serving as Baltimore's pitching coach from 1978-85 and the Pirates' pitching coach from 1986-96, Ray Miller served the Orioles in the same capacity in 1997. He was an immediate success, helping lower the pitching staff's ERA by more than a full run. After Baltimore lost to Cleveland in the ALCS, manager Davey Johnson resigned and Miller was appointed his successor. Though Miller has nearly 19 years of experience as a major league pitching coach, his only managerial stint came in 1985-86 with the Twins.

Offense

Miller has spent 16 of his 19 years coaching for either Earl Weaver or Jim Leyland, two managers who platoon extensively. In his short stint with the Twins, however, Miller used a set eight-man lineup and hardly platooned. He stuck with the lineup he inherited. Developing the bench wasn't a priority, and he didn't seem interested in the running game or using other one-run strategies.

Pitching & Defense

While Miller has been one of the most successful pitching coaches of the last 20 years, the Minnesota staff showed surprisingly little development under his reign as manager. The staff ERA went up after he arrived and declined again after he left, and the team's three young starters—Frank Viola, Mike Smithson and John Butcher—each regressed during his tenure. He was unable to sort out his bullpen and forced his starters to throw a lot of complete games as a result. The one significant lineup change he made was to replace a good-hitting, weak-fielding second baseman, Tim Teufel, with a non-hitting glove man, Steve Lombardozzi.

1998 Outlook

Unless Brady Anderson leaves via free agency, Miller won't face many tough lineup decisions. The pitching staff is strong, and even the possible departure of Randy Myers shouldn't create a problem as Armando Benitez seems ready to step in at closer. In Minnesota, Miller made few changes and the team stagnated. Ironically, that same approach may be exactly what Baltimore needs.

Born: 4/30/45 in Takoma Park, MD

Playing Experience: None

Managerial Experience: 2 seasons

Manager Statistics

Year	Team, Lg	W	L	Pct	GB	Finish
1997		—	—	—	—	—
2 Seasons		109	130	.456	—	—

1997 Starting Pitchers by Days Rest

	≤3	4	5	6+
Orioles Starts	—	—	—	—
Orioles ERA	—	—	—	—
AL Avg Starts	5	89	34	24
AL ERA	4.38	4.60	4.61	5.37

1997 Situational Stats

	Ray Miller	AL Average
Hit & Run Success %	—	36.5
Stolen Base Success %	—	67.3
Platoon Pct.	—	59.5
Defensive Subs	—	22
High-Pitch Outings	—	15
Quick/Slow Hooks	—	19/15
Sacrifice Attempts	—	53

1997 Rankings (American League)

⇒ Did not manage in the majors last year

Roberto Alomar

1997 Season

One of the best tests of a player's greatness is how well he handles adversity. In 1997, Roberto Alomar hit a career-high .333 while being booed relentlessly during virtually every road appearance because of his distasteful altercation with umpire John Hirschbeck in 1996. Alomar was limited to 112 games because of a five-game suspension and a myriad of injuries, including a sprained ankle, pulled groin, and finally a sore shoulder which forced him to bat exclusively lefthanded in the second half of the season.

Hitting

The tougher the situation, the better Alomar performs, which is why he's so devastating during high-pressure postseason series and pennant races. He batted .500 with a .532 on-base percentage, hitting exclusively lefthanded, during the tough month of September. Normally a switch-hitter, Alomar will make something happen with anything he can reach—inside or out—and is an incredible two-strike hitter. He has good power from the left side with pitches left out over the plate. Sharp sliders up and in will jam him, but he will rarely strike out.

Baserunning & Defense

Alomar is still capable of stealing 20 bases or more because of his excellent first-step quickness and good open speed, but his injuries in 1997 prevented any such thoughts. He has the best range of any second baseman in baseball, and often gets his glove on balls hit to the right side even when it appears he should have no chance. His double-play relays became somewhat erratic after his shoulder injury.

1998 Outlook

Alomar should stay away from playing Puerto Rican winter ball this year to nurse himself back to perfect health; whether he will remains an open question. Assuming he enters spring training healthy, Alomar will again be one of the most productive all-around players in the game and the Orioles' most important position player in their run for another division title.

Position: 2B
Bats: B **Throws:** R
Ht: 6' 0" **Wt:** 185

Opening Day Age: 30
Born: 2/5/68 in Ponce, PR
ML Seasons: 10
Pronunciation: AL-a-mar
Nickname: Robby

Overall Statistics

	G	AB	R	H	D	T	HR	RBI	SB	BB	SO	Avg	OBP	Slg
1997	112	412	64	137	23	2	14	60	9	40	43	.333	.390	.500
Career	1416	5460	893	1659	296	54	113	653	322	600	630	.304	.372	.440

Where He Hits the Ball

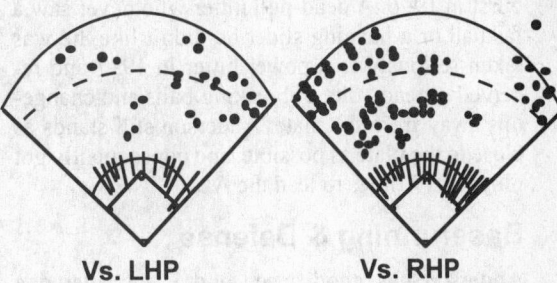

Vs. LHP   **Vs. RHP**

1997 Situational Stats

	AB	H	HR	RBI	Avg		AB	H	HR	RBI	Avg
Home	211	80	10	39	.379	LHP	113	28	0	8	.248
Road	201	57	4	21	.284	RHP	299	109	14	52	.365
First Half	274	84	8	36	.307	Sc Pos	91	26	2	39	.286
Scnd Half	138	53	6	24	.384	Clutch	56	15	1	4	.268

1997 Rankings (American League)

⇒ 2nd in fielding percentage at second base (.988)
⇒ 4th in batting average with two strikes (.269)
⇒ 6th in lowest slugging percentage vs. lefthanded pitchers (.292) and lowest percentage of swings that missed (10.2%)
⇒ 8th in batting average on a 3-2 count (.375)
⇒ Led the Orioles in batting average on a 3-2 count (.375), batting average with two strikes (.269) and lowest percentage of swings that missed (10.2%)

Brady Anderson

1997 Season

It would have been unrealistic for anyone to have expected Brady Anderson to repeat his 50-homer performance of 1996. A cracked rib suffered at the end of spring training ensured that he wouldn't. Anderson lost a significant amount of power, but became a more effective situational hitter, batting .296 with runners in scoring position, 89 points better than his 1996 mark. His .398 on-base percentage while hitting first was among the American League's best for leadoff hitters.

Hitting

Besides having to curtail his swing because of his rib injury, Anderson also had to deal with pitchers making adjustments on him after his power outburst in 1996. A dead-pull hitter who never saw a fastball or a hanging slider he didn't like, he was taken seriously as a power hitter in 1997 and received a steady diet of breaking balls and change-ups away from the plate. Anderson still stands as close to the plate as possible, and consequently got plunked 19 times to lead the AL.

Baserunning & Defense

Anderson has good speed and is considered a basestealing threat. His 1997 success rate of 60 percent was the worst of his career, possibly a result of the cracked rib or merely an indicator that he's slowing with age. Anderson is a very dependable center fielder with good range, but he was not able to throw as well as he did in previous years because of the injury.

1998 Outlook

Very few teams can start off every game with a hitter like Anderson. He has power, speed and an ability to hit for average and get on base, making him one of the best leadoff men in the game today. He was a free agent this winter, and re-signed with Baltimore for five years and $31 million. With his ribs finally healed, Anderson should be in store for a solid 1998 campaign.

Position: CF/DH
Bats: L **Throws:** L
Ht: 6' 1" **Wt:** 195

Opening Day Age: 34
Born: 1/18/64 in Silver Spring, MD
ML Seasons: 10

Overall Statistics

	G	AB	R	H	D	T	HR	RBI	SB	BB	SO	Avg	OBP	Slg
1997	151	590	97	170	39	7	18	73	18	84	105	.288	.393	.469
Career	1245	4440	726	1159	240	56	140	529	226	619	804	.261	.361	.435

Where He Hits the Ball

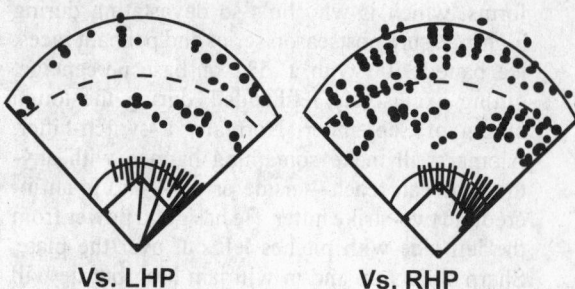

Vs. LHP   **Vs. RHP**

1997 Situational Stats

	AB	H	HR	RBI	Avg		AB	H	HR	RBI	Avg
Home	271	68	8	29	.251	LHP	192	54	5	23	.281
Road	319	102	10	44	.320	RHP	398	116	13	50	.291
First Half	313	94	7	41	.300	Sc Pos	115	34	2	53	.296
Scnd Half	277	76	11	32	.274	Clutch	75	26	2	17	.347

1997 Rankings (American League)

⇒ 1st in hit by pitch (19) and least GDPs per GDP situation (0.9%)

⇒ 2nd in on-base percentage for a leadoff hitter (.398)

⇒ 3rd in lowest stolen base percentage (60.0%)

⇒ 5th in triples and lowest fielding percentage in center field (.989)

⇒ Led the Orioles in batting average, runs scored, hits, doubles, triples, stolen bases, caught stealing (12), walks, hit by pitch (19), times on base (273), pitches seen (2,581), plate appearances (696), on-base percentage, stolen base percentage (60.0%), most pitches seen per plate appearance (3.71), least GDPs per GDP situation (0.9%), batting average in the clutch and batting average vs. righthanded pitchers

Harold Baines

1997 Season

After signing his second one-year contract in as many seasons with the White Sox, Harold Baines was traded back to his hometown Orioles as part of Chicago owner Jerry Reinsdorf's midseason purge. Baines carried on in typical fashion and finished another solid season at the plate, batting over .300 for the sixth time in his 18-year career. He had a solid postseason, batting a combined .364 and homering in both the division and championship series.

Hitting

Baines is a consummate hitter with keen strike-zone judgment and lots of power still left in his 39-year-old body. He remains successful by continually making adjustments. By turning his front foot inward and toward the catcher, Baines has kept his shoulder tucked in and hit to the opposite field more. He always has been an excellent low-and-inside fastball hitter, and hits lefthanders surprisingly well.

Baserunning & Defense

Baines hardly ever attempts to steal a base or play in the field, though he did manage to get two innings in right field in 1997. His long history of knee problems has relegated him to a DH role and limited him on the basepaths. Playing him in the field for an extended period of time or having him run wild on the basepaths would just be inviting injury.

1998 Outlook

Baines seems to be a perennial free agent because of his age, which makes teams reluctant to issue him a multi-year contract. The Orioles are likely to re-sign him because there aren't too many lefthanded bats as dangerous and as inexpensive as his. The White Sox had payroll problems that caused them to part with Baines, but the Orioles have more financial flexibility. He's also a quiet, classy presence in any clubhouse. He's still at least three seasons away, but he's sneaking up on 3,000 hits and 400 homers for his career.

Position: DH
Bats: L **Throws:** L
Ht: 6' 2" **Wt:** 195

Opening Day Age: 39
Born: 3/15/59 in St. Michaels, MD
ML Seasons: 18

Overall Statistics

	G	AB	R	H	D	T	HR	RBI	SB	BB	SO	Avg	OBP	Slg
1997	137	452	55	136	23	0	16	67	0	55	62	.301	.375	.458
Career	2463	8818	1168	2561	439	48	339	1423	33	932	1287	.290	.356	.466

Where He Hits the Ball

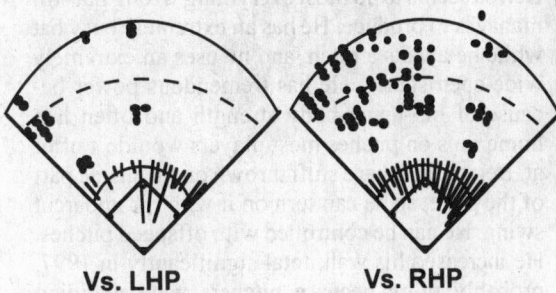

Vs. LHP   **Vs. RHP**

1997 Situational Stats

	AB	H	HR	RBI	Avg		AB	H	HR	RBI	Avg
Home	231	59	6	34	.255	LHP	92	25	3	19	.272
Road	221	77	10	33	.348	RHP	360	111	13	48	.308
First Half	252	74	9	42	.294	Sc Pos	129	38	4	54	.295
Scnd Half	200	62	7	25	.310	Clutch	66	21	2	15	.318

1997 Rankings (American League)

⇒ 2nd in batting average on an 0-2 count (.348)
⇒ 7th in intentional walks (11)
⇒ 8th in lowest batting average on a 3-1 count (.105)

Geronimo Berroa

1997 Season

Geronimo Berroa was 29 before he got a chance to play regularly in the majors, and has made the most of his opportunity. Traded from Oakland to Baltimore last June for minor league pitchers Jimmy Haynes and Mark Seaver, Berroa provided the righthanded bat the Orioles needed after Eric Davis went on the disabled list with colon cancer. Berroa's offensive output tailed off somewhat after his move into hitter-friendly Camden Yards, but he continued to terrorize lefthanded pitching, compiling a season-long .358 average against southpaws.

Hitting

Berroa seems to do most everything wrong but still manages to produce. He has an extremely busy bat while he awaits a pitch, and he uses an extremely wide-open stance. He has tremendous power because of his upper-body strength and often hits home runs on pitches most players wouldn't offer at. Berroa likes hard stuff thrown on the inside part of the plate, so he can turn on it with his uppercut swing. He can be controlled with offspeed pitches. He increased his walk total significantly in 1997, probably more becuase pitchers were avoiding him than a greater awareness of the strike zone.

Baserunning & Defense

Not blessed with much speed, Berroa rarely attempts to swipe a base. He motors around the diamond adequately on hits, but is by no means a heads-up baserunner. As a right fielder, Berroa is a liability because of his less-than-accurate arm, error-prone fly ball judgment and limited range. He played more in right field than he normally would have for the Orioles because Davis was sidelined.

1998 Outlook

Should Davis reclaim his position in right field, at-bats will be few and far between for Berroa. It's hard to see the Orioles using him as just a DH against lefthanders or as a fourth outfielder. His arbitration award will be significantly higher than the $3.3 million he earned in 1997, possibly forcing another trade.

Position: RF/DH
Bats: R **Throws:** R
Ht: 6' 0" **Wt:** 195

Opening Day Age: 33
Born: 3/18/65 in Santo Domingo, DR
ML Seasons: 8

Overall Statistics

	G	AB	R	H	D	T	HR	RBI	SB	BB	SO	Avg	OBP	Slg
1997	156	561	88	159	25	0	26	90	4	76	120	.283	.369	.467
Career	661	2222	343	629	103	6	99	358	18	239	443	.283	.352	.468

Where He Hits the Ball

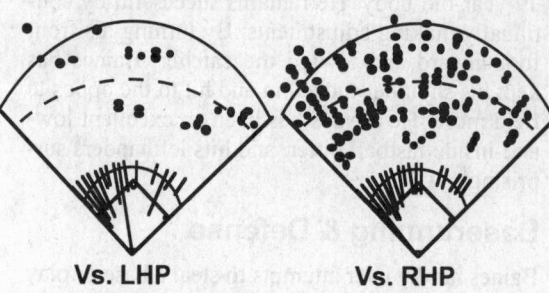

Vs. LHP   **Vs. RHP**

1997 Situational Stats

	AB	H	HR	RBI	Avg		AB	H	HR	RBI	Avg
Home	273	74	11	43	.271	LHP	148	53	7	29	.358
Road	288	85	15	47	.295	RHP	413	106	19	61	.257
First Half	298	87	17	46	.292	Sc Pos	151	40	4	66	.265
Scnd Half	263	72	9	44	.274	Clutch	81	21	4	12	.259

1997 Rankings (American League)

⇒ 3rd in on-base percentage vs. lefthanded pitchers (.444)
⇒ 4th in batting average vs. lefthanded pitchers (.358)
⇒ 6th in lowest cleanup slugging percentage (.431)
⇒ 7th in errors in right field (4)
⇒ 9th in GDPs (18) and batting average on an 0-2 count (.286)
⇒ Led the Orioles in cleanup slugging percentage (.431)

Mike Bordick

Position: SS
Bats: R **Throws:** R
Ht: 5'11" **Wt:** 175

Opening Day Age: 32
Born: 7/21/65 in Marquette, MI
ML Seasons: 8

Baltimore Orioles

1997 Season

At the conclusion of the 1996 season, the Orioles set out to find a shortstop good enough to move Cal Ripken to third base. Mike Bordick was signed as a free agent after spending seven years in Oakland, and his superior range helped to give Baltimore one of the best defensive infields in the league. However, Bordick's bat was disappointing as he hit .236, the lowest mark of his career.

Hitting

Bordick always has been a light-hitting shortstop who chops downward on the ball, generating a lot of grounders. He's better suited for artificial turf, and playing on the high grass at Camden Yards certainly hurt his average. He uses an open stance which makes him vulnerable to southpaws who throw changeups on the outside part of the plate. He closes his stance against righthanders and can even hit them straightaway with occasional power. Bordick should have been more patient at the plate, as he walked just 33 times in 1997.

Baserunning & Defense

Bordick is quick, but he doesn't have top-end speed and he is on base infrequently, making stolen bases rare. Hitting ninth in the order, usually ahead of Brady Anderson, Bordick stayed put when occupying first base. He has exceptional range as a shortstop, especially up the middle, and no one can get to his feet any quicker after diving for a ball. He has a powerful arm to go with his outstanding defensive package.

1998 Outlook

Bordick signed a three-year deal with the Orioles and will unquestionably be their shortstop through the 1999 season as Ripken's conversion to third base is complete. Despite a below-average year at the plate, Bordick figures to improve as he becomes more comfortable in his new surroundings—as he did during the latter part of the year. He was sought primarily for his glove and lived up to every expectation defensively.

Overall Statistics

	G	AB	R	H	D	T	HR	RBI	SB	BB	SO	Avg	OBP	Slg
1997	153	509	55	120	19	1	7	46	0	33	66	.236	.283	.318
Career	976	3152	328	802	113	16	28	298	48	273	375	.254	.318	.327

Where He Hits the Ball

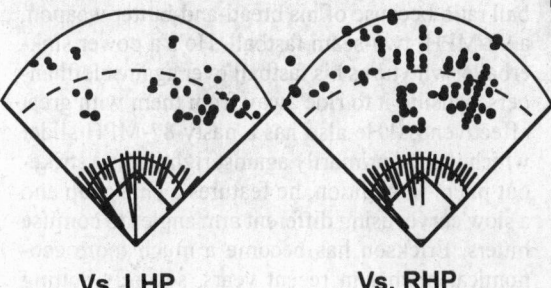

Vs. LHP   **Vs. RHP**

1997 Situational Stats

	AB	H	HR	RBI	Avg		AB	H	HR	RBI	Avg
Home	231	53	5	24	.229	LHP	154	30	1	9	.195
Road	278	67	2	22	.241	RHP	355	90	6	37	.254
First Half	287	63	3	25	.220	Sc Pos	110	27	0	34	.245
Scnd Half	222	57	4	21	.257	Clutch	70	16	0	2	.229

1997 Rankings (American League)

⇒ 2nd in GDPs (23), lowest slugging percentage and lowest on-base percentage vs. lefthanded pitchers (.233)

⇒ 3rd in sacrifice bunts (12), lowest batting average vs. lefthanded pitchers and lowest slugging percentage vs. lefthanded pitchers (.234)

⇒ 4th in lowest batting average, lowest batting average at home and highest fielding percentage at shortstop (.980)

⇒ 5th in lowest on-base percentage, most GDPs per GDP situation (20.9%) and highest percentage of swings put into play (53.0%)

⇒ Led the Orioles in sacrifice bunts (12), GDPs (23), bunts in play (16) and highest percentage of swings put into play (53.0%)

Scott Erickson

1997 Season

Scott Erickson enjoyed his best season in the majors since winning 20 games for Minnesota in 1991. Normally a slow starter who finishes strongly, he came out of the gate quicker than ever, thanks to a new offseason workout regimen devised by new pitching coach Ray Miller. Less weightlifting and more of an emphasis on throwing led to an 11-4 first half and a career-best strikeout-to-walk ratio. He sputtered somewhat in September, and missed a chance to record his 100th career win.

Pitching

Erickson again led the league in groundball/flyball ratio because of his bread-and-butter weapon, a 94-MPH, two-seam fastball. He's a power sinkerballer who turns his fastball over against lefthanders, causing it to ride away from them with great effectiveness. He also has a nasty 87-MPH slider which is used primarily against righties as a strikeout pitch. In addition, he features a changeup and a slow curve, using different arm angles to confuse hitters. Erickson has become a much more economical pitcher in recent years, severely cutting down on his walks.

Defense

Erickson remains one of the weaker pitchers in the American League at holding runners. He gave up 21 steals because he keeps his focus on the hitter and doesn't allow himself to be distracted by the runner at first, something which used to affect him severely. He comes off the mound ready for defense, but is prone to panicking and made six errors in 1997.

1998 Outlook

Erickson is enjoying the prime of his career right now. He teams with Mike Mussina to give the Orioles one of the best one-two punches in the game. His sinker is tailor-made for Camden Yards, and if he keeps improving his command, he could have an even better year in 1998.

Position: SP
Bats: R **Throws:** R
Ht: 6' 4" **Wt:** 230

Opening Day Age: 30
Born: 2/2/68 in Long Beach, CA
ML Seasons: 8

Overall Statistics

	W	L	Pct.	ERA	G	GS	Sv	IP	H	BB	SO	HR	Ratio
1997	16	7	.696	3.69	34	33	0	221.2	218	61	131	16	1.26
Career	99	83	.544	4.24	240	236	0	1532.0	1626	529	819	127	1.41

How Often He Throws Strikes

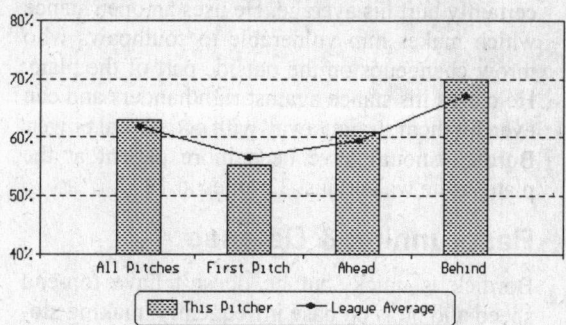

1997 Situational Stats

	W	L	ERA	Sv	IP		AB	H	HR	RBI	Avg
Home	8	4	3.29	0	109.1	LHB	452	112	10	47	.248
Road	8	3	4.09	0	112.1	RHB	397	106	6	37	.267
First Half	11	4	3.81	0	115.2	Sc Pos	174	49	7	73	.282
Scnd Half	5	3	3.57	0	106.0	Clutch	82	24	2	7	.293

1997 Rankings (American League)

⇒ 1st in highest groundball/flyball ratio allowed (2.9) and errors at pitcher (6)
⇒ 2nd in GDPs induced (33) and least pitches thrown per batter (3.46)
⇒ 3rd in shutouts (2) and most GDPs induced per 9 innings (1.3)
⇒ 5th in least home runs allowed per 9 innings (.65)
⇒ Led the Orioles in wins, shutouts (2), hits allowed, batters faced (922), hit batsmen (5), wild pitches (11), GDPs induced (33), winning percentage, lowest slugging percentage allowed (.362), highest groundball/flyball ratio allowed (2.9), least pitches thrown per batter (3.46), least home runs allowed per 9 innings (.65) and most GDPs induced per 9 innings (1.3)

Jeffrey Hammonds

1997 Season

After several years of unfulfilled promise, in part because of bothersome injuries, Jeffrey Hammonds made a semi-breakthrough. He hit 21 home runs in just 118 games, and was one of Baltimore's primary catalysts during June and July. He made the most of a starting role which he inherited early on, manning center field after Brady Anderson was limited to DH duties and then sliding over to right after Eric Davis went on the disabled list.

Hitting

Hammonds is a straight fastball hitter who likes his pitches on the inner half of the plate, where he can pull the ball with his great bat speed. He's particularly effective against lefthanders who fail to pitch him outside. He has learned to be a little more selective than he was in previous seasons, but he still has difficulty both with offspeed pitches and when behind in the count. He's unusually strong for a player his size, and has surprising power. He smacked an Eric Plunk fastball 460 feet in 1997, the second-longest home run ever hit at Camden Yards.

Baserunning & Defense

Hammonds is extremely fast and will attempt to steal when he's sure he has an advantage. He was caught stealing just once in 16 attempts for a 94-percent success rate. Any hesitation or miscue by an outfielder will result in an extra base for Hammonds. His great speed helps him cover a lot of ground in the outfield, but he often gets a late start on the ball. His arm isn't very strong, making him better suited for left field rather than center or right.

1998 Outlook

Hammonds has proven himself to be a valuable commodity in Baltimore as a fourth outfielder, ready to step into a starting role whenever one of the regulars goes down. Should Davis fail to return from cancer, Hammonds likely will be his successor. He's still a year away from free agency and has shown what he can do when healthy.

Position: RF/LF/CF
Bats: R **Throws:** R
Ht: 6' 0" **Wt:** 195

Opening Day Age: 27
Born: 3/5/71 in Plainfield, NJ
ML Seasons: 5

Overall Statistics

	G	AB	R	H	D	T	HR	RBI	SB	BB	SO	Avg	OBP	Slg
1997	118	397	71	105	19	3	21	55	15	32	73	.264	.323	.486
Career	347	1178	182	310	64	7	45	155	31	83	211	.263	.314	.444

Where He Hits the Ball

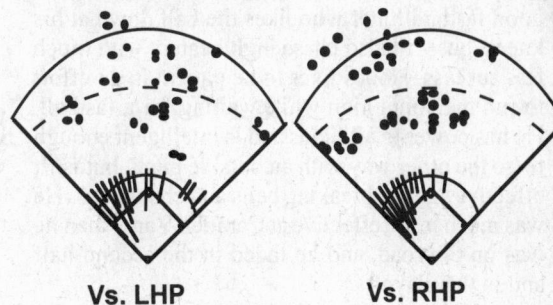

Vs. LHP   **Vs. RHP**

1997 Situational Stats

	AB	H	HR	RBI	Avg		AB	H	HR	RBI	Avg
Home	194	50	9	21	.258	LHP	148	41	8	18	.277
Road	203	55	12	34	.271	RHP	249	64	13	37	.257
First Half	230	66	14	37	.287	Sc Pos	91	19	1	24	.209
Scnd Half	167	39	7	18	.234	Clutch	64	15	4	14	.234

1997 Rankings (American League)

⇒ Led the Orioles in slugging percentage vs. lefthanded pitchers (.514)

Chris Hoiles

1997 Season

Chris Hoiles is the Orioles' version of a Timex watch: He takes a licking and just keeps on ticking. A sprain of the medial-collateral ligament in his right knee landed him on the disabled list from mid-June to mid-July, and he caught just 87 games, the fewest since Hoiles became a regular in 1991. He maintained his mediocre career average while his strikeout/at-bat ratio grew disturbingly higher.

Hitting

Hoiles has a compact uppercut stroke. He has a very high flyball/groundball ratio, lofting the majority of balls he puts in play into the air. He's a good fastball hitter who likes the ball down at his knees, but will also chase high heaters with much less success. Hoiles likes to be patient in an effort to run the count high while waiting for a fastball. He has power to all fields and is intelligent enough to go the other way with an outside pitch, but isn't effective against breaking balls and changeups. He was much more effective at Camden Yards than he was on the road, and he faded in the second half and in the playoffs.

Baserunning & Defense

Any catcher with knee problems won't scare too many opposing teams when he's on the basepaths, and Hoiles is no exception. His arm often has been criticized during the last few years. Last year he threw out just 15 percent of runners attempting to steal, the worst percentage in the American League. His knees also limit his mobility behind the plate, but he earns respect for his handling of pitchers.

1998 Outlook

Hoiles long has been the subject of trade rumors in Baltimore, but unless the Orioles sign a free-agent catcher, he's likely to return. The organization has no depth behind the plate, and because Hoiles was signed to a lucrative long-term contract extending through 1999, he will be extremely difficult to trade. He's probably past his prime, but the Orioles don't have any other options at this point.

Position: C
Bats: R **Throws:** R
Ht: 6' 0" **Wt:** 215

Opening Day Age: 33
Born: 3/20/65 in Bowling Green, OH
ML Seasons: 9

Overall Statistics

	G	AB	R	H	D	T	HR	RBI	SB	BB	SO	Avg	OBP	Slg
1997	99	320	45	83	15	0	12	49	1	51	86	.259	.375	.419
Career	797	2553	379	669	110	2	136	393	5	397	566	.262	.367	.467

Where He Hits the Ball

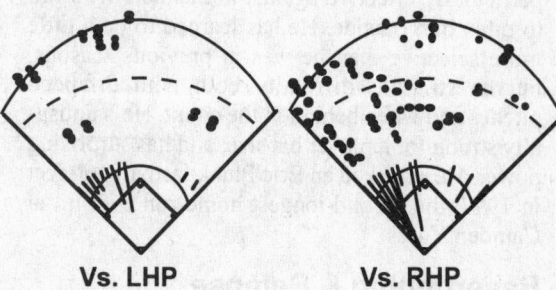

Vs. LHP   **Vs. RHP**

1997 Situational Stats

	AB	H	HR	RBI	Avg		AB	H	HR	RBI	Avg
Home	145	50	9	22	.345	LHP	94	23	5	18	.245
Road	175	33	3	27	.189	RHP	226	60	7	31	.265
First Half	176	50	8	30	.284	Sc Pos	75	25	2	37	.333
Scnd Half	144	33	4	19	.229	Clutch	55	14	1	8	.255

1997 Rankings (American League)

⇒ 1st in lowest percentage of runners caught stealing as a catcher (14.9%)
⇒ 9th in hit by pitch (10)
⇒ 10th in highest percentage of swings that missed (27.4%)
⇒ Led the Orioles in batting average with runners in scoring position and highest percentage of pitches taken (58.7%)

Jimmy Key

1997 Season

Signed by the Orioles as a free agent during the offseason, Jimmy Key was a huge factor early in the year as Baltimore built a solid lead in the American League East. His 2.55 ERA at the All-Star break was the best in the rotation and he was unquestionably the Orioles' best road starter throughout the entire year. Though he stayed healthy, Key tired in the second half, causing his location to wander and his walk totals to increase.

Pitching

Key is often referred to as an AL version of Tom Glavine. Like the Atlanta southpaw, he relies on changing speeds and working the corners. He'll tempt righthanded hitters with changeups and backdoor curveballs aimed at the outside corner. Because he tries to keep these hitters honest with the occasional inside fastball which tops out at only 89 MPH, he can be vulnerable. Key's slider is his best weapon against lefthanders, but he prefers throwing the backdoor curve to them. He has one of the most graceful windups and deliveries in the game and is a methodical worker.

Defense

Key has a deceptive move to first base, which was good enough for six pickoffs in 1997. More runners were caught stealing than were successful against him, which is remarkable considering he's somewhat of a soft thrower. Key is mobile off the mound and always makes intelligent decisions with bunts and slow rollers.

1998 Outlook

The Orioles signed Key as a free-agent replacement for David Wells, who took Key's place with the Yankees. Key answered the questions as to how far he has come after rotator-cuff surgery in 1995. He was able to throw over 200 innings for the first time since 1993 and was effective for most of them. Baltimore is counting on him to pitch in the front end of the rotation again.

Position: SP
Bats: R **Throws:** L
Ht: 6' 1" **Wt:** 185

Opening Day Age: 36
Born: 4/22/61 in Huntsville, AL
ML Seasons: 14

Overall Statistics

	W	L	Pct.	ERA	G	GS	Sv	IP	H	BB	SO	HR	Ratio
1997	16	10	.615	3.43	34	34	0	212.1	210	82	141	24	1.38
Career	180	114	.612	3.49	445	378	10	2512.1	2441	645	1485	249	1.23

How Often He Throws Strikes

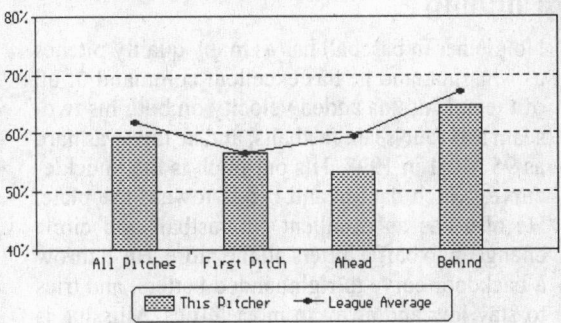

1997 Situational Stats

	W	L	ERA	Sv	IP		AB	H	HR	RBI	Avg
Home	6	8	3.93	0	100.2	LHB	140	38	5	17	.271
Road	10	2	2.98	0	111.2	RHB	664	172	19	60	.259
First Half	12	4	2.55	0	116.1	Sc Pos	156	28	7	54	.179
Scnd Half	4	6	4.50	0	96.0	Clutch	23	7	0	0	.304

1997 Rankings (American League)

⇒ 2nd in pickoff throws (223) and lowest batting average allowed with runners in scoring position
⇒ 3rd in most pitches thrown per batter (3.97)
⇒ 4th in runners caught stealing (13) and ERA on the road
⇒ 5th in games started
⇒ Led the Orioles in wins, losses, games started, walks allowed, hit batsmen (5), pitches thrown (3,585), pickoff throws (223), runners caught stealing (13), lowest stolen base percentage allowed (45.8%), ERA on the road and lowest batting average allowed with runners in scoring position

Mike Mussina

1997 Season

Though his 15 wins were his fewest since 1993, Mike Mussina pitched brilliantly. In 1997, his best exploits were reserved for the postseason, where he set an American League Championship Series record with 15 strikeouts in a single game. During the regular season, he logged the AL's sixth-best ERA (3.20) and third-best strikeout/walk ratio (4.04). Mussina's 218 strikeouts established a new career high as he remained the ace of the Baltimore staff. His career .682 winning percentage is the sixth-best in baseball history, and easily the top active mark among pitchers with 100 or more wins.

Pitching

No pitcher in baseball has as many quality pitches as Mussina, and he has excellent command of all of them. Mussina added velocity on both his two-seam and four-seam fastballs, and he threw as hard as 95 MPH in 1997. His out pitch is the knuckle-curve, which dances and bends toward the plate. He also has an excellent cut fastball and circle changeup to baffle hitters all the more. He'll throw a backdoor curve to righthanded batters, and tries to stay low and away to most lefties. Mussina is liable to throw anything on any count and isn't afraid to come inside. His one weakness is allowing home runs. He has yielded a total of 58 homers in the last two seasons, usually when he gets the ball up.

Defense

Mussina is famous for his deep-bend set position when holding runners on. He has a quick spin move to first base and is tough to steal against. He's also an excellent fielding pitcher, showing good mobility in getting to first base or coming in to field bunts. He won his second Gold Glove in 1997.

1998 Outlook

Mussina is a perennial Cy Young Award contender. The Orioles rewarded him last year with a three-year, $21 million contract extension, locking him up through 2000. He'll be gunning for the 20-win season which has eluded him thus far in his career.

Position: SP
Bats: L **Throws:** R
Ht: 6' 1" **Wt:** 180

Opening Day Age: 29
Born: 12/8/68 in Williamsport, PA
ML Seasons: 7
Pronunciation: myoo-SEE-nuh
Nickname: Moose

Overall Statistics

	W	L	Pct.	ERA	G	GS	Sv	IP	H	BB	SO	HR	Ratio
1997	15	8	.652	3.20	33	33	0	224.2	197	54	218	27	1.12
Career	105	49	.682	3.50	194	194	0	1362.1	1263	328	978	144	1.17

How Often He Throws Strikes

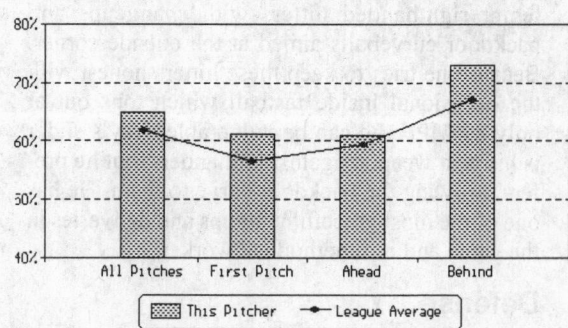

1997 Situational Stats

	W	L	ERA	Sv	IP		AB	H	HR	RBI	Avg
Home	8	4	2.68	0	117.2	LHB	423	94	14	41	.222
Road	7	4	3.79	0	107.0	RHB	420	103	13	37	.245
First Half	10	2	3.26	0	124.1	Sc Pos	161	31	4	41	.193
Scnd Half	5	6	3.14	0	100.1	Clutch	46	11	2	3	.239

1997 Rankings (American League)

⇒ 3rd in highest strikeout/walk ratio (4.0), lowest on-base percentage allowed (.282), least baserunners allowed per 9 innings (10.2) and lowest batting average allowed vs. lefthanded batters

⇒ 4th in strikeouts, most strikeouts per 9 innings (8.7), ERA at home and lowest batting average allowed with runners in scoring position

⇒ Led the Orioles in ERA, complete games (4), innings pitched, home runs allowed, strikeouts, highest strikeout/walk ratio (4.0), lowest batting average allowed (.234), lowest on-base percentage allowed (.282), least baserunners allowed per 9 innings (10.2), most run support per 9 innings (5.5), most strikeouts per 9 innings (8.7) and ERA at home

Randy Myers

Position: RP
Bats: L **Throws:** L
Ht: 6' 1" **Wt:** 225

Opening Day Age: 35
Born: 9/19/62 in
Vancouver, WA
ML Seasons: 13

1997 Season

Randy Myers deserves serious consideration as team MVP during the Orioles' best season since 1983. Myers slammed the door 45 out of 46 times to lead the majors in both saves and save percentage. He was a model of consistency throughout the year and was the primary reason why the Orioles were 87-1 in games they were leading after the eighth inning. Myers' save total was the second-highest of his career and his 1.51 ERA was his best ever. It was a much different story from 1996, when his ERA was more than two runs higher and he blew seven saves. He regained his status as an elite closer, as well as manager Davey Johnson's confidence, in '97.

Pitching

Myers' success was due in part to his ability to handle righthanded hitters with his 92-MPH, two-seam fastball. Righties pounded him in '96, and Johnson started using Armando Benitez against them in crucial situations. Myers rebounded last season when he began challenging righties again. He's at his best when he trusts his stuff and doesn't nibble. He has mastered the art of keeping the ball down and away from righthanders and getting called strikes. He'll also use the backdoor slider and has added a changeup as well. Myers' improvement was a direct result of getting ahead of hitters early.

Defense

As a lefthanded closer, Myers doesn't have to deal with a lot of stolen-base threats. Only one runner made an attempt and he was thwarted, though his pickoff move isn't particularly effective. As a fielder, Myers isn't particularly adept, though he made no errors in 1997.

1998 Outlook

The question becomes whether Myers, now 35, can continue to be as effective as he was in 1997. The Orioles wanted to re-sign him, but he went with division rival Toronto instead. His arm is sound and his pitching strategies are successful, boding well for his future.

Overall Statistics

	W	L	Pct.	ERA	G	GS	Sv	IP	H	BB	SO	HR	Ratio
1997	2	3	.400	1.51	61	0	45	59.2	47	22	56	2	1.16
Career	40	56	.417	3.08	666	12	319	828.0	699	370	843	63	1.29

How Often He Throws Strikes

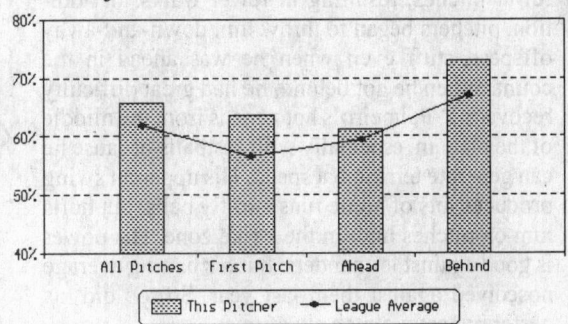

1997 Situational Stats

	W	L	ERA	Sv	IP		AB	H	HR	RBI	Avg
Home	1	2	2.40	22	30.0	LHB	48	9	1	5	.188
Road	1	1	0.61	23	29.2	RHB	169	38	1	13	.225
First Half	1	3	1.35	27	33.1	Sc Pos	59	13	2	17	.220
Scnd Half	1	0	1.71	18	26.1	Clutch	179	37	2	12	.207

1997 Rankings (American League)

⇒ 1st in saves, save percentage (97.8%) and relief ERA (1.51)
⇒ 2nd in save opportunities (46)
⇒ 4th in games finished (57)
⇒ 5th in least baserunners allowed per 9 innings in relief (10.4)
⇒ 6th in first batter efficiency (.154)
⇒ 7th in lowest batting average allowed in relief (.217)
⇒ Led the Orioles in saves, games finished (57), save opportunities (46), save percentage (97.8%) and relief ERA (1.51)

Baltimore Orioles

1997 Season

Rafael Palmeiro has been as dependable as any power hitter in the majors. He has driven in more than 100 runs every year he has been in Baltimore, with the exception of the strike-shortened 1994 campaign, and 1997 was no exception. Palmeiro slugged 38 home runs, but his .254 batting average was his lowest since he began playing regularly in 1987. He also struck out more than 100 times for the first time in his career.

Hitting

Palmeiro's batting average declined significantly for two reasons. He was less selective and took fewer pitches, resulting in fewer walks. In addition, pitchers began to throw him down-and-away offspeed stuff even when he was ahead in the count. When he got behind, he had great difficulty recovering. Palmeiro's hot zone is from the middle of the plate in, especially with fastballs because he can generate terrific bat speed. His uppercut swing produces lots of home runs and fly balls, but hurts him on pitches high in the strike zone. His power is good against lefthanders, but his batting average nosedived against them last year. So too did his performance in clutch situations.

Baserunning & Defense

Palmeiro is a slow runner and attempts very few steals. He sometimes appears to lack intensity on the basepaths and last season hit his fewest doubles since 1989. Defensively, he's a top-notch first baseman, even though he doesn't have a lot of range and has a slow first step on hard-hit balls down the line. He's an intelligent fielder who makes very few mental mistakes, and he won his first Gold Glove in 1997.

1998 Outlook

Palmeiro is likely to come back in 1998 because he realizes he gave away too many at-bats by not being patient enough at the plate. He has enormous physical talent and will make the necessary adjustments to offset what pitchers did to him last season. Palmeiro's durability speaks for itself, as he's rarely out of the lineup. He'll be counted on once again to be the Orioles' top run producer.

Position: 1B
Bats: L **Throws:** L
Ht: 6' 0" **Wt:** 190

Opening Day Age: 33
Born: 9/24/64 in Havana, Cuba
ML Seasons: 12
Pronunciation: pall-MARE-oh

Overall Statistics

	G	AB	R	H	D	T	HR	RBI	SB	BB	SO	Avg	OBP	Slg
1997	158	614	95	156	24	2	38	110	5	67	109	.254	.329	.485
Career	1620	6097	963	1792	360	31	271	958	73	656	746	.294	.364	.496

Where He Hits the Ball

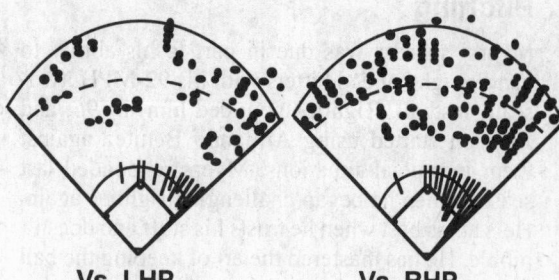

Vs. LHP　　　　**Vs. RHP**

1997 Situational Stats

	AB	H	HR	RBI	Avg		AB	H	HR	RBI	Avg
Home	299	74	20	50	.247	LHP	225	48	15	39	.213
Road	315	82	18	60	.260	RHP	389	108	23	71	.278
First Half	342	89	16	55	.260	Sc Pos	156	37	10	69	.237
Scnd Half	272	67	22	55	.246	Clutch	94	22	8	18	.234

1997 Rankings (American League)

⇒ 4th in lowest groundball/flyball ratio (0.7) and lowest cleanup slugging percentage (.426)
⇒ 5th in lowest batting average vs. lefthanded pitchers, lowest on-base percentage vs. lefthanded pitchers (.275), errors at first base (10) and lowest fielding percentage at first base (.993)
⇒ 6th in home runs and games played (158)
⇒ 8th in at-bats and lowest batting average on an 0-2 count (.053)
⇒ 10th in RBI, plate appearances (692) and highest percentage of swings on the first pitch (36.8%)
⇒ Led the Orioles in home runs, total bases (298), RBI, strikeouts, slugging percentage, HR frequency (16.2 ABs per HR) and slugging percentage vs. righthanded pitchers (.512)

Cal Ripken

1997 Season

Another season and The Streak just keeps on going for Cal Ripken, who now has played in 2,478 consecutive games. One thing did change, as he moved from shortstop to third base. Though his 22 errors were the second highest among American League third basemen, most of his miscues occurred during the first half of the season. At the plate, Ripken stayed close to his career averages in most categories despite a dreadful September, when lower-back pain took a toll on his swing.

Hitting

Ripken is known for continually changing his batting stance while trying to find new ways to adjust his timing. His bat speed isn't quite what it was in years past, but he still makes contact more often than not and remains a tough strikeout. He loves to extend his arms and can hit for good power on pitches from the middle to the inside part of the plate, especially the low ones. After experiencing late-season back problems, Ripken adjusted by punching balls to the opposite field, enabling him to contribute more in postseason play.

Baserunning & Defense

Ripken's move to third base wasn't as smooth as expected. He eventually got used to being closer to home plate, but it took half the season. His tall, lanky frame helped him plug holes to his left, but going to his right on balls hit down the line was a different story. Ripken has limited speed and isn't a stolen-base threat, but is an intelligent baserunner.

1998 Outlook

Some critics believe both Orioles management and Ripken are placing the importance of The Streak above the best interests of the team. The thinking is that occasional rest could refuel his energy and make him more productive. However, Ripken's competitive nature and the lack of a suitable backup will keep him in the lineup every day. Obviously, he knows how to condition himself and should be able to match his 1997 numbers.

Position: 3B
Bats: R **Throws:** R
Ht: 6' 4" **Wt:** 220

Opening Day Age: 37
Born: 8/24/60 in Havre de Grace, MD
ML Seasons: 17
Nickname: Junior

Baltimore Orioles

Overall Statistics

	G	AB	R	H	D	T	HR	RBI	SB	BB	SO	Avg	OBP	Slg
1997	162	615	79	166	30	0	17	84	1	56	73	.270	.331	.402
Career	2543	9832	1445	2715	517	43	370	1453	36	1016	1106	.276	.344	.450

Where He Hits the Ball

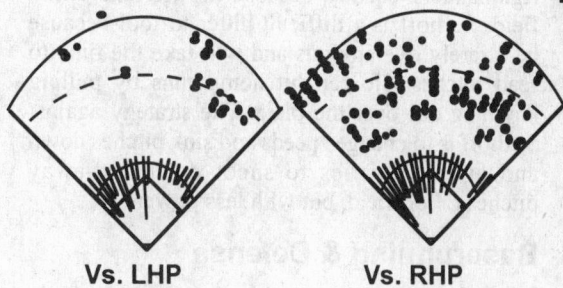

Vs. LHP	Vs. RHP

1997 Situational Stats

	AB	H	HR	RBI	Avg		AB	H	HR	RBI	Avg
Home	290	79	10	44	.272	LHP	181	47	5	22	.260
Road	325	87	7	40	.268	RHP	434	119	12	62	.274
First Half	341	101	11	57	.296	Sc Pos	153	42	5	68	.275
Scnd Half	274	65	6	27	.237	Clutch	104	31	5	13	.298

1997 Rankings (American League)

⇒ 1st in games played (162)
⇒ 2nd in errors at third base (22)
⇒ 5th in lowest fielding percentage at third base (.949)
⇒ 7th in at-bats, sacrifice flies (10) and GDPs (19)
⇒ 8th in highest groundball/flyball ratio (1.8)
⇒ 10th in singles
⇒ Led the Orioles in at-bats, singles, sacrifice flies (10), games played (162), highest groundball/flyball ratio (1.8) and batting average at home

B.J. Surhoff

1997 Season

B.J. Surhoff has been a model of consistency ever since he arrived in Baltimore two seasons ago. He evolved from a catcher to a third baseman in Milwaukee. Now an everyday left fielder, Surhoff exemplifies the depth and flexibilty the Orioles have in their lineup. He continues to be one of the team's most dependable hitters in key situations, batting .302 with runners on base and .588 with the bases loaded.

Hitting

Like most of the Orioles, Surhoff is a dangerous fastball hitter. He prefers his heat belt-high, occasionally a bit higher. He hits both lefthanders and righthanders equally because he uses the entire field. Surhoff is a difficult hitter to fool because he's rarely overanxious and will take the time to read pitches. He can hit home runs by pulling anything out over the plate. The strategy against Surhoff is to change speeds and sink pitches down and away. He tries to shoot down-and-away pitches to left field, but with less power.

Baserunning & Defense

Surhoff's days as a modest basestealing threat were left behind him in Milwaukee, as he rarely attempts to run any longer. He has average speed, but plays hard and is fearless when it comes to initiating contact on the basepaths. Surhoff's biggest improvement last season was in his defensive game, as he committed only two errors in left field. He has a strong, accurate throwing arm and was among the American League leaders in outfield assists with 11.

1998 Outlook

Surhoff has found a home in left field at Camden Yards and has become a cornerstone player in the Orioles' lineup. Since recovering from abdominal surgery that caused him to miss most of the 1994 season and hang up his catcher's gear, he has been relatively injury-free. He's under contract for 1998 and should continue to be productive.

Position: LF
Bats: L **Throws:** R
Ht: 6' 1" **Wt:** 200

Opening Day Age: 33
Born: 8/4/64 in Bronx, NY
ML Seasons: 11

Overall Statistics

	G	AB	R	H	D	T	HR	RBI	SB	BB	SO	Avg	OBP	Slg
1997	147	528	80	150	30	4	18	88	1	49	60	.284	.345	.458
Career	1392	4949	626	1371	251	34	96	694	103	390	462	.277	.328	.400

Where He Hits the Ball

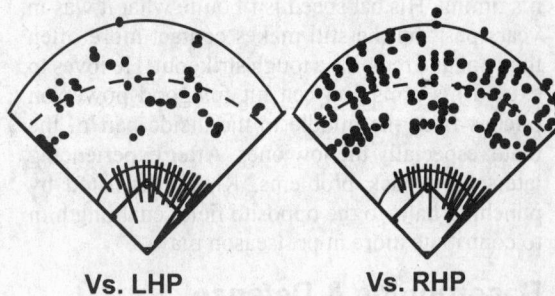

Vs. LHP   **Vs. RHP**

1997 Situational Stats

	AB	H	HR	RBI	Avg		AB	H	HR	RBI	Avg
Home	238	64	10	34	.269	LHP	160	46	3	28	.288
Road	290	86	8	54	.297	RHP	368	104	15	60	.283
First Half	272	81	11	54	.298	Sc Pos	130	39	4	66	.300
Scnd Half	256	69	7	34	.270	Clutch	83	22	0	11	.265

1997 Rankings (American League)

⇒ 2nd in fielding percentage in left field (.992)
⇒ 4th in intentional walks (14) and batting average with the bases loaded (.588)
⇒ 7th in sacrifice flies (10) and lowest batting average on a 3-2 count (.087)
⇒ 8th in highest percentage of extra bases taken as a runner (62.2%)
⇒ Led the Orioles in sacrifice flies (10), intentional walks (14), batting average with the bases loaded (.588), batting average vs. lefthanded pitchers, batting average on an 0-2 count (.222), highest percentage of extra bases taken as a runner (62.2%) and lowest percentage of swings on the first pitch (21.1%)

Armando Benitez (Unhittable)

Position: RP
Bats: R **Throws:** R
Ht: 6' 4" **Wt:** 220

Opening Day Age: 25
Born: 11/3/72 in Ramon Santana, DR
ML Seasons: 4
Pronunciation: buh-NEE-tezz

Overall Statistics

	W	L	Pct.	ERA	G	GS	Sv	IP	H	BB	SO	HR	Ratio
1997	4	5	.444	2.45	71	0	9	73.1	49	43	106	7	1.25
Career	6	10	.375	3.53	136	0	15	145.1	101	90	196	17	1.31

1997 Situational Stats

	W	L	ERA	Sv	IP		AB	H	HR	RBI	Avg
Home	2	4	3.89	3	34.2	LHB	102	20	3	12	.196
Road	2	1	1.16	6	38.2	RHB	155	29	4	16	.187
First Half	0	3	3.25	6	36.0	Sc Pos	89	13	1	21	.146
Scnd Half	4	2	1.69	3	37.1	Clutch	161	27	2	17	.168

1997 Season

Benitez enjoyed a superb regular season, only to face difficulties once again in the playoffs. The big righthander struck out 13 batters for every nine innings pitched and led all AL pitchers by holding opponents to a .125 average with runners on base. But he also surrendered the homer to Tony Fernandez that won Cleveland the AL pennant.

Pitching & Defense

Benitez used to be a one-dimensional pitcher who would depend on a devastating 99-MPH fastball and rarely use his slider. After working with pitching coach Ray Miller during the offseason, Benitez gained more confidence in the slider and also learned to throw a split-fingered fastball and a changeup. The slider will hang occasionally, as it did once too often in the playoffs. His control is getting better, but still needs improvement. Benitez is easy pickings for basestealers, but he's a decent fielder.

1998 Outlook

Benitez has shown that despite his awesome tools and explosive fastball, he's still not ready to step into the closer role, as he gets burned at the most inopportune times. But with Randy Myers defecting to Toronto, the Orioles may need Benitez to finish games.

Eric Davis

Position: RF/DH
Bats: R **Throws:** R
Ht: 6' 3" **Wt:** 190

Opening Day Age: 35
Born: 5/29/62 in Los Angeles, CA
ML Seasons: 13

Overall Statistics

	G	AB	R	H	D	T	HR	RBI	SB	BB	SO	Avg	OBP	Slg
1997	42	158	29	48	11	0	8	25	6	14	47	.304	.358	.525
Career	1271	4268	775	1124	180	20	239	753	335	617	1143	.263	.357	.483

1997 Situational Stats

	AB	H	HR	RBI	Avg		AB	H	HR	RBI	Avg
Home	88	33	7	22	.375	LHP	55	21	3	7	.382
Road	70	15	1	3	.214	RHP	103	27	5	18	.262
First Half	129	39	7	21	.302	Sc Pos	47	14	1	17	.298
Scnd Half	29	9	1	4	.310	Clutch	26	10	1	5	.385

1997 Season

After signing as a free agent with the Orioles, Eric Davis became a compelling study in courage as he waged a battle with colon cancer. Davis started his tenure in Baltimore with a hot bat, hitting .377 with five homers in April, but left the team in May after his cancer was diagnosed. He returned to the lineup in September and played in the postseason, serving as an inspiration to his teammates.

Hitting, Baserunning & Defense

Davis is an exceptionally good fastball hitter who uses his well-developed wrists to generate excellent bat speed. He stands wide open with his bat held low and in front of him. He does this to keep his shoulder locked as he steps into the ball. Pitchers throw him a lot of breaking stuff, trying to get his shoulder to fly open early. Davis is an exceptional defensive player with a very accurate arm and three Gold Gloves to his credit. Because of various leg injuries, he no longer steals bases as he once did, but he rarely is caught when he does go.

1998 Outlook

Davis is receiving chemotherapy treatments as he continues his recovery from cancer. The Orioles showed plenty of class by picking up his option for 1998.

Scott Kamieniecki

Position: SP
Bats: R **Throws:** R
Ht: 6' 0" **Wt:** 195

Opening Day Age: 33
Born: 4/19/64 in Mt.
Clemens, MI
ML Seasons: 7
Pronunciation:
kam-uh-NICK-ee

Overall Statistics

	W	L	Pct.	ERA	G	GS	Sv	IP	H	BB	SO	HR	Ratio
1997	10	6	.625	4.01	30	30	0	179.1	179	67	109	20	1.37
Career	46	45	.505	4.26	143	124	1	806.2	823	349	432	85	1.45

1997 Situational Stats

	W	L	ERA	Sv	IP		AB	H	HR	RBI	Avg
Home	6	3	3.41	0	105.2	LHB	344	90	8	34	.262
Road	4	3	4.89	0	73.2	RHB	342	89	12	47	.260
First Half	6	4	3.92	0	96.1	Sc Pos	182	47	5	60	.258
Scnd Half	4	2	4.12	0	83.0	Clutch	19	3	1	2	.158

1997 Season

Scott Kamieniecki was one of the better comeback stories of 1997. After elbow surgery ruined his 1996 season with the Yankees, he signed a minor league contract with the Orioles and fought his way into the rotation. He became the No. 4 starter after Rocky Coppinger went on the DL in May.

Pitching & Defense

Kamieniecki mixes three basic pitches in a simple repertoire. He throws a 91-MPH, four-seam fastball that usually rides high in the strike zone. Kamieniecki will change speeds with his curveball and mix in his changeup as well. He's successful at keeping his offspeed pitches low, inducing ground balls and getting batters to chase his fastball for strikeouts. He's one of the slowest workers in the AL and makes countless pickoff throws, though runners steal on him at will because of his deliberate motion. He's an average fielder.

1998 Outlook

Kamieniecki has proven to be a useful asset at the end of the rotation. He became a free agent and got a two-year, $6.2 million contract from the Orioles after getting his career on track. He'll be two years removed from his 1996 surgery, and should be able to average more innings per start.

Terry Mathews

Position: RP
Bats: L **Throws:** R
Ht: 6' 2" **Wt:** 225

Opening Day Age: 33
Born: 10/5/64 in
Alexandria, LA
ML Seasons: 6

Overall Statistics

	W	L	Pct.	ERA	G	GS	Sv	IP	H	BB	SO	HR	Ratio
1997	4	4	.500	4.41	57	0	1	63.1	63	36	39	8	1.56
Career	20	19	.513	4.12	283	4	9	362.1	359	155	271	40	1.42

1997 Situational Stats

	W	L	ERA	Sv	IP		AB	H	HR	RBI	Avg
Home	1	2	6.41	0	26.2	LHB	83	22	3	14	.265
Road	3	2	2.95	1	36.2	RHB	153	41	5	18	.268
First Half	1	1	3.34	0	32.1	Sc Pos	63	12	3	23	.190
Scnd Half	3	3	5.52	1	31.0	Clutch	89	23	4	12	.258

1997 Season

Veteran reliever Terry Mathews thought he had found a home in Baltimore after signing a new two-year deal before the start of the season. He started out strongly, but his ability to get men out seriously eroded by August, and manager Davey Johnson stopped using him in critical situations.

Pitching & Defense

Mathews uses two basic pitches, the fastball and the slider, and tries to vary speeds enough with both offerings to enhance his limited arsenal. On a good day he might hit 90 MPH with his hardest pitch, but in general he has below-average velocity. Because neither pitch has outstanding movement, he tries to pitch around the zone rather than challenge within, consequently issuing too many walks. His slow delivery makes him vulnerable to the steal, and he doesn't move well coming off the mound.

1998 Outlook

The Orioles have various options in their bullpen, making Mathews expendable as a result of his disappointing 1997 performance. He does not represent a big investment for Baltimore, and the fact that he comes cheap could work in his favor. But he must improve his control if he expects to stick around.

Alan Mills

Position: RP
Bats: B **Throws:** R
Ht: 6' 1" **Wt:** 195

Opening Day Age: 31
Born: 10/18/66 in Lakeland, FL
ML Seasons: 8

Overall Statistics

	W	L	Pct.	ERA	G	GS	Sv	IP	H	BB	SO	HR	Ratio
1997	2	3	.400	4.89	39	0	0	38.2	41	33	32	5	1.91
Career	28	22	.560	3.93	278	5	11	423.1	376	256	305	50	1.49

1997 Situational Stats

	W	L	ERA	Sv	IP		AB	H	HR	RBI	Avg
Home	1	1	5.29	0	17.0	LHB	48	16	2	10	.333
Road	1	2	4.57	0	21.2	RHB	104	25	3	13	.240
First Half	1	1	4.85	0	13.0	Sc Pos	46	9	2	17	.196
Scnd Half	1	2	4.91	0	25.2	Clutch	63	17	1	8	.270

1997 Season

Alan Mills got off to a rocky start as a result of a pregame collision in mid-April with catcher Lenny Webster, which put him on the DL for two months with a damaged nerve in his non-throwing shoulder. He compiled a streak of 14 straight scoreless appearances after the All-Star break through mid-August.

Pitching & Defense

Mills is your basic late-inning, two-pitch flamethrower. He mixes a 94-MPH fastball with an 87-MPH slider, and uses a deceptively slow delivery similar to that of Yankees closer Mariano Rivera. He doesn't appear to be putting forth much effort, but generates severe heat nonetheless. His biggest problem is control. He throws too many pitches, allowing hitters to time him more easily. He's susceptible to stolen bases because of his deliberate delivery and lack of concentration. He's an average fielder.

1998 Outlook

Mills has had serious injury problems and has missed considerable time in each of the last two years. He's an inexpensive reliever to maintain, and since Baltimore values its bullpen depth, it will keep him around as one of three righthanded middle-relief options.

Jesse Orosco

Position: RP
Bats: R **Throws:** L
Ht: 6' 2" **Wt:** 205

Opening Day Age: 40
Born: 4/21/57 in Santa Barbara, CA
ML Seasons: 18
Pronunciation: oh-ROSS-koh

Overall Statistics

	W	L	Pct.	ERA	G	GS	Sv	IP	H	BB	SO	HR	Ratio
1997	6	3	.667	2.32	71	0	0	50.1	29	30	46	6	1.17
Career	80	72	.526	2.95	956	4	133	1127.1	896	490	1018	90	1.23

1997 Situational Stats

	W	L	ERA	Sv	IP		AB	H	HR	RBI	Avg
Home	2	1	2.66	0	23.2	LHB	79	8	1	7	.101
Road	4	2	2.03	0	26.2	RHB	93	21	5	19	.226
First Half	2	1	2.13	0	25.1	Sc Pos	58	9	4	22	.155
Scnd Half	4	2	2.52	0	25.0	Clutch	100	19	4	15	.190

1997 Season

Jesse Orosco seems to keep getting better with age. The 40-year-old lefthander enjoyed a career-high 71 appearances and posted his lowest ERA in eight years, proving to be a vital component of the best bullpen in baseball last season.

Pitching & Defense

Orosco isn't just another southpaw specialist. In fact, he faced more righthanded than lefthanded batters last year. He likes to run his 91-MPH fastball in on righthanders, and mix it up with a back-door curve. To lefties, he'll throw more sliders low and away. He walks a lot of batters, but works out of jams because he excels with runners on base.

1998 Outlook

Jesse Orosco had vested options placed in his 1997 contract and easily reached those goals, meaning he's poised to return for another year with the Orioles. The team should be glad to have him, as he offers his services at bargain-basement prices.

Jeff Reboulet

Position: 2B/3B/SS
Bats: R **Throws:** R
Ht: 6' 0" **Wt:** 171

Opening Day Age: 33
Born: 4/30/64 in
Dayton, OH
ML Seasons: 6
Pronunciation:
REB-uh-lay

Overall Statistics

	G	AB	R	H	D	T	HR	RBI	SB	BB	SO	Avg	OBP	Slg
1997	99	228	26	54	9	0	4	27	3	23	44	.237	.307	.329
Career	549	1244	161	306	55	2	13	127	16	151	198	.246	.330	.325

1997 Situational Stats

	AB	H	HR	RBI	Avg		AB	H	HR	RBI	Avg
Home	104	23	2	11	.221	LHP	101	20	3	10	.198
Road	124	31	2	16	.250	RHP	127	34	1	17	.268
First Half	90	18	2	16	.200	Sc Pos	58	13	0	21	.224
Scnd Half	138	36	2	11	.261	Clutch	37	9	1	8	.243

1997 Season

Signed to a minor league contract after departing from Minnesota, Jeff Reboulet proved valuable to the Orioles in a utility role, especially as a fill-in for an injured Roberto Alomar at second base. His season highlight was hitting two homers off the Mariners' Randy Johnson, including one during the American League Division Series.

Hitting, Baserunning & Defense

Reboulet always has been a lightweight hitter. He's a good bunter, but has very little pop in his bat. He's often used as a pinch runner, and though he doesn't steal often, Reboulet has good awareness on the basepaths and makes few mistakes. He is more used to playing third base or shortstop than second base, but has a dependable glove and turns double plays easily.

1998 Outlook

Reboulet has been on the fringe over the last few years and is seen strictly as a utility player and defensive replacement. Baltimore's infield is rock solid and had it not been for Alomar's injury, Reboulet likely would have seen little playing time. The Orioles re-signed him as insurance.

Arthur Rhodes

Position: RP
Bats: L **Throws:** L
Ht: 6' 2" **Wt:** 205

Opening Day Age: 28
Born: 10/24/69 in
Waco, TX
ML Seasons: 7

Overall Statistics

	W	L	Pct.	ERA	G	GS	Sv	IP	H	BB	SO	HR	Ratio
1997	10	3	.769	3.02	53	0	1	95.1	75	26	102	9	1.06
Career	36	28	.563	5.01	150	61	2	492.1	467	237	437	62	1.43

1997 Situational Stats

	W	L	ERA	Sv	IP		AB	H	HR	RBI	Avg
Home	6	1	3.81	0	49.2	LHB	119	26	3	13	.218
Road	4	2	2.17	1	45.2	RHB	225	49	6	20	.218
First Half	6	2	2.45	1	51.1	Sc Pos	79	16	1	23	.203
Scnd Half	4	1	3.68	0	44.0	Clutch	118	26	0	6	.220

1997 Season

Arthur Rhodes continued to do what he does best, which is win games in relief. Over the last two years, Rhodes has compiled a 19-4 record. In 1997 he posted a career-best 3.02 ERA while surpassing the century mark in strikeouts for the first time.

Pitching & Defense

Rhodes is a high-fastball pitcher who uses a 95-MPH four-seamer as his main weapon. He likes to work from the belt upward and loves to jam both lefty and righty hitters inside. He makes the four-seamer appear even faster by mixing it up with a decent curveball and a changeup. Rhodes also throws a slider to lefthanded batters. He has good control, and posted his best strikeout/walk ratio ever in 1997. He's poor at holding runners, but isn't a bad fielder.

1998 Outlook

Rhodes is the Orioles' primary middle reliever and no one in the majors has been better at winning games in that role. He's under contract for another season, and his improved control has him poised for another good year in 1998.

Tony Tarasco

Position: RF
Bats: L **Throws:** R
Ht: 6' 1" **Wt:** 205

Opening Day Age: 27
Born: 12/9/70 in New York, NY
ML Seasons: 5
Pronunciation: tuh-RASS-koh

Overall Statistics

	G	AB	R	H	D	T	HR	RBI	SB	BB	SO	Avg	OBP	Slg
1997	100	166	26	34	8	1	7	26	2	25	33	.205	.313	.392
Career	368	855	126	207	37	5	27	96	36	92	148	.242	.317	.392

1997 Situational Stats

	AB	H	HR	RBI	Avg		AB	H	HR	RBI	Avg
Home	74	16	4	15	.216	LHP	25	4	1	1	.160
Road	92	18	3	11	.196	RHP	141	30	6	25	.213
First Half	118	27	6	19	.229	Sc Pos	43	12	1	16	.279
Scnd Half	48	7	1	7	.146	Clutch	29	5	1	6	.172

1997 Season

Tony Tarasco began the year at Triple-A Rochester, but quickly found himself back with the big club after Jerome Walton went on the disabled list. Tarasco was simply caught in a squeeze after the Orioles signed both Walton and Eric Davis.

Hitting, Baserunning & Defense

Tarasco's main problem in holding onto a full-time job in the majors is his ineptitude against southpaws. He also has difficulty playing a supporting role, which affects his capability against righthanders and has kept him from breaking through when he's gotten his chances. He does have occasional power, but it's usually all or nothing. Tarasco is fleet afoot, but is on base so seldom that he rarely gets any steals. He covers a lot of ground in right field, and has a terrific arm.

1998 Outlook

Tarasco's future with the Orioles is in jeopardy because of the club's outfield depth. The less Tarasco plays, the more his skills will erode. He hasn't realized the promise he exhibited while with the Braves in 1994. He is 27, and time is starting to work against him.

Lenny Webster

Position: C
Bats: R **Throws:** R
Ht: 5' 9" **Wt:** 195

Opening Day Age: 33
Born: 2/10/65 in New Orleans, LA
ML Seasons: 9

Overall Statistics

	G	AB	R	H	D	T	HR	RBI	SB	BB	SO	Avg	OBP	Slg
1997	98	259	29	66	8	1	7	37	0	22	46	.255	.317	.375
Career	418	1010	113	257	53	2	23	121	1	109	150	.254	.332	.379

1997 Situational Stats

	AB	H	HR	RBI	Avg		AB	H	HR	RBI	Avg
Home	134	29	3	16	.216	LHP	81	21	3	12	.259
Road	125	37	4	21	.296	RHP	178	45	4	25	.253
First Half	125	32	3	18	.256	Sc Pos	68	18	2	28	.265
Scnd Half	134	34	4	19	.254	Clutch	40	9	1	5	.225

1997 Season

After beginning the year as the Orioles' No. 2 catcher, Lenny Webster was thrust into the starting role at midseason when Chris Hoiles was sidelined with a knee sprain. Webster hit .316 during Hoiles' absence and subsequently received more playing time even after Hoiles returned from the DL.

Hitting, Baserunning & Defense

Webster's numbers don't appear to make him much of a threat, but he can drive fastballs with good power if pitchers aren't careful. He has limited plate coverage which hurts him substantially when he's either behind in the count or facing junk pitchers. Webster has no speed to speak of and won't steal. He's an adequate receiver, nothing special with his glove or at blocking the plate. Webster does have a decent arm, throwing out 25 percent of enemy basestealers.

1998 Outlook

Webster would be a good No. 2 catcher with any franchise, but in Baltimore his role is increased because Hoiles' injury problems have sapped his durability. If they need to replace Hoiles on a full-time basis, the Orioles are more likely to go outside the organization than to promote Webster.

Other Baltimore Orioles

Shawn Boskie (**Pos**: RHP, **Age**: 31)

	W	L	Pct.	ERA	G	GS	Sv	IP	H	BB	SO	HR	Ratio
1997	6	6	.500	6.43	28	9	1	77.0	95	26	50	14	1.57
Career	48	60	.444	5.06	212	127	1	852.2	948	288	484	128	1.45

Boskie was used as a swingman by the Orioles before he was bothered by elbow problems. He eventually went on the disabled list with tendinitis, and wasn't offered a new contract. 1998 Outlook: C

Rocky Coppinger (**Pos**: RHP, **Age**: 24)

	W	L	Pct.	ERA	G	GS	Sv	IP	H	BB	SO	HR	Ratio
1997	1	1	.500	6.30	5	4	0	20.0	21	16	22	2	1.85
Career	11	7	.611	5.34	28	26	0	145.0	147	76	126	27	1.54

Coppinger won 10 games as a rookie in 1996, but 1997 was a nightmare. He made only five appearances because of elbow problems which needed surgery. If he's healthy, he'll get the ball. 1998 Outlook: B

Charlie Greene (**Pos**: C, **Age**: 27, **Bats**: R)

	G	AB	R	H	D	T	HR	RBI	SB	BB	SO	Avg	OBP	Slg
1997	5	2	0	0	0	0	0	1	0	0	1	.000	.000	.000
Career	7	3	0	0	0	0	0	1	0	0	1	.000	.000	.000

A defensive specialist acquired on waivers from the Mets, Greene never has produced with the bat. If he has a major league future, it's probably as a coach. 1998 Outlook: D

Rick Krivda (**Pos**: LHP, **Age**: 28)

	W	L	Pct.	ERA	G	GS	Sv	IP	H	BB	SO	HR	Ratio
1997	4	2	.667	6.30	10	10	0	50.0	67	18	29	7	1.70
Career	9	14	.391	5.13	45	34	0	207.0	232	82	136	30	1.52

Krivda has gone 66-30 in the minors, but just 9-14 for Baltimore. He was the fifth starter down the stretch, but may be squeezed out of the rotation if Rocky Coppinger is healthy. 1998 Outlook: B

Tim Laker (**Pos**: C, **Age**: 28, **Bats**: R)

	G	AB	R	H	D	T	HR	RBI	SB	BB	SO	Avg	OBP	Slg
1997	7	14	0	0	0	0	0	1	0	2	9	.000	.118	.000
Career	142	287	28	60	13	2	3	32	3	20	77	.209	.263	.300

Laker showed some power at Triple-A Rochester, and his arm strength has always been considered his strong suit. He might have a shot as a backup. 1998 Outlook: B

Aaron Ledesma (**Pos**: 2B/3B, **Age**: 26, **Bats**: R)

	G	AB	R	H	D	T	HR	RBI	SB	BB	SO	Avg	OBP	Slg
1997	43	88	24	31	5	1	2	11	1	13	9	.352	.437	.500
Career	64	121	28	39	5	1	2	14	1	19	16	.322	.415	.430

Ledesma scored plenty of points with his performance in 1997. That .352 average is really pushing it, but the Devil Rays took him in the third round of the expansion draft. 1998 Outlook: B

Mel Rosario (**Pos**: C, **Age**: 24, **Bats**: B)

	G	AB	R	H	D	T	HR	RBI	SB	BB	SO	Avg	OBP	Slg
1997	4	3	0	0	0	0	0	0	0	0	1	.000	.000	.000
Career	4	3	0	0	0	0	0	0	0	0	1	.000	.000	.000

Rosario provides a little bit of power and a little bit of throwing, but probably not enough to be an everyday big leaguer. He may need another year in the minors before he's ready to be a backup. 1998 Outlook: C

Bill Swift (**Pos**: RHP, **Age**: 36)

	W	L	Pct.	ERA	G	GS	Sv	IP	H	BB	SO	HR	Ratio
1997	4	6	.400	6.34	14	13	0	65.1	85	26	29	11	1.70
Career	83	69	.546	3.76	374	194	27	1455.0	1505	456	690	95	1.35

Swift was signed after asking for his release from the Rockies, for whom he was an oft-injured free-agent bust. His return to health is a major question. 1998 Outlook: C

Jerome Walton (**Pos**: RF, **Age**: 32, **Bats**: R)

	G	AB	R	H	D	T	HR	RBI	SB	BB	SO	Avg	OBP	Slg
1997	26	68	8	20	1	0	3	9	0	4	10	.294	.333	.441
Career	586	1539	237	412	74	8	25	129	58	136	274	.268	.332	.375

The 1989 National League Rookie of the Year has found his niche coming off the bench. Repeated groin and hamstring problems have hampered his effectiveness, however. Now a free agent. 1998 Outlook: B

Brian Williams (**Pos**: RHP, **Age**: 29)

	W	L	Pct.	ERA	G	GS	Sv	IP	H	BB	SO	HR	Ratio
1997	0	0	-	3.00	13	0	0	24.0	20	18	14	0	1.58
Career	23	36	.390	5.34	177	59	5	485.2	535	266	324	52	1.65

Remember when Williams was going to be Detroit's closer? Now he'd be happy to have a guaranteed big league job. Add him to the list of failed first-round draft picks. 1998 Outlook: C

Baltimore Orioles Minor League Prospects

Organization Overview:

Baseball America ranked the Orioles' minor league talent as the worst in baseball at the outset of the 1997 season. Since Peter Angelos bought the franchise, the emphasis has been on winning at the major league level at all costs, be it trading prospects for pennant-drive acquisitions or forfeiting draft picks to sign free agents. As a result, the Baltimore system has produced little talent in recent years. Only two key members of the club with the best record in the American League were developed by the Orioles: third baseman Cal Ripken, who was signed almost 20 years ago, and Mike Mussina, a 1991 first-round pick. Where Baltimore has excelled recently is finding foreign talent, especially in cornering the market in Aruba, and gambling on athletes who were stars in other sports. Former Big Eight Conference Basketball Player of the Year Ryan Minor has the best upside of any Orioles minor leaguer, and Baltimore signed supposedly unsignable University of Texas running-back recruit Darnell McDonald as a 1997 first-round pick.

Danny Clyburn

Position: OF
Bats: R **Throws:** R
Ht: 6' 3" **Wt:** 217

Opening Day Age: 23
Born: 4/6/74 in Lancaster, SC

Recent Statistics

	G	AB	R	H	D	T	HR	RBI	SB	BB	SO	AVG
97 AAA Rochester	137	520	91	156	33	5	20	76	14	53	107	.300
97 AL Baltimore	2	3	0	0	0	0	0	0	0	0	2	.000
97 MLE	137	505	79	141	29	3	18	66	10	46	113	.279

A second-round pick of the Pirates in 1992, Clyburn since has been sent to the Reds (for Jacob Brumfield) and Orioles (for Brad Pennington). He has made plenty of progress in his two full seasons in the Baltimore system, leading the Eastern League in homers before straining a hamstring in 1996, and learning how to do more than just swing for the fences last year. His strikeout and walk rates were the best of his career, and he also added his share of doubles to the mix. He has decent speed but few instincts, relegating him to left field. If he can continue to improve, he could have a future.

Chris Fussell

Position: P
Bats: R **Throws:** R
Ht: 6' 2" **Wt:** 185

Opening Day Age: 21
Born: 5/19/76 in Oregon, OH

Recent Statistics

	W	L	ERA	G	GS	Sv	IP	H	R	BB	SO	HR
96 A Frederick	5	2	2.81	15	14	0	86.1	71	36	44	94	8
97 AA Bowie	1	8	7.11	19	18	0	82.1	102	71	58	71	12
97 A Frederick	3	3	3.96	9	9	0	50.0	42	23	31	54	5

Professional baseball was good for Fussell, a ninth-round pick in 1994, until mid-1996. He had a 16-6

career record and was overmatching the high Class A Carolina League when shoulder soreness abruptly ended his year. He didn't need surgery and returned in 1997, but struggled to make the adjustment to Double-A. His stuff was as good as ever, as he showed a 92-93 MPH fastball, a good curve and a developing change. The problem was command, which went from spotty to dreadful. He'll open this season at age 21, so there's plenty of time for him to regain his previous form.

Eugene Kingsale

Position: OF
Bats: B **Throws:** R
Ht: 6' 3" **Wt:** 170

Opening Day Age: 21
Born: 8/20/76 in Aruba, Aruba

Recent Statistics

	G	AB	R	H	D	T	HR	RBI	SB	BB	SO	AVG
96 A Frederick	49	166	26	45	6	4	0	9	23	19	32	.271
97 R Orioles	6	17	2	5	0	0	0	0	1	2	2	.294
97 AA Bowie	13	46	8	19	6	0	0	4	5	5	4	.413

The first Aruban to play in the major leagues, Kingsale has blazing speed but has been unable to showcase it because of injuries. He dislocated his left shoulder sliding headfirst in 1996, costing him the last three months, and appeared in just 19 games last year because of hand injuries. Kingsale's wheels give him good center-field range, and he also uses them to his advantage on offense. He draws walks and is working on his bunting, knowing he'll have to use his speed because he has little power. Kingsale could be Baltimore's leadoff man of the future.

Ryan Minor

Position: 3B
Bats: R **Throws:** R
Ht: 6' 7" **Wt:** 225

Opening Day Age: 24
Born: 1/5/74 in Canton, OH

Recent Statistics

	G	AB	R	H	D	T	HR	RBI	SB	BB	SO	AVG
96 R Bluefield	25	87	14	22	6	0	4	9	1	7	32	.253
97 A Delmarva	134	488	83	150	42	1	24	97	7	51	102	.307

The Orioles successfully gambled a 33rd-round pick in 1996 on Minor, whom most teams figured would play in the NBA after a stellar basketball career at the University of Oklahoma. But Minor was cut by the Philadelphia 76ers, who drafted him in the second round, and Baltimore is reaping the dividends. Minor, who also pitched on the Sooners' 1994 College World Series championship team, has big-time power and is an agile third baseman despite his size. At 23 he was a bit old for the Class-A South Atlantic League, and he may need to shorten his stroke against better competition. His contract allows him to explore the possibility of playing basketball after the 1998 season, but if he has another big year, the Orioles are hoping he won't want to.

Julio Moreno

Position: P

Bats: R **Throws:** R

Ht: 6' 1" **Wt:** 145

Opening Day Age: 22

Born: 10/23/75 in San Pedro De Macoris, DR

Recent Statistics

	W	L	ERA	G	GS	Sv	IP	H	R	BB	SO	HR
96 A Frederick	9	10	3.50	28	26	0	162.0	167	80	38	147	14
97 AA Bowie	9	6	3.83	27	25	0	138.2	141	76	64	106	20

Moreno easily had the best year of any of the prospects in the Double-A Bowie rotation. His stuff is fairly average, but he knows how to mix his fastball, slider and changeup to keep batters off balance. He also pitches on the corners of the plate, which makes him difficult to hit but leads to a few too many walks. His command had been very good in past years, so it's probably just a case of a little too much nibbling. Signed out of the Dominican Republic, Moreno was promoted to Triple-A for the International League playoffs and won the championship-clinching game. He'll probably spend most of 1998 in the minors unless a rash of injuries strikes Baltimore's rotation.

Sidney Ponson

Position: P

Bats: R **Throws:** R

Ht: 6' 1" **Wt:** 200

Opening Day Age: 21

Born: 11/2/76 in Aruba, Aruba

Recent Statistics

	W	L	ERA	G	GS	Sv	IP	H	R	BB	SO	HR
96 A Frederick	7	6	3.45	18	16	0	107.0	98	56	28	110	6
97 AA Bowie	2	7	5.42	13	13	0	74.2	77	51	32	56	11
97 R Orioles	1	0	0.00	1	0	0	2.0	0	0	0	1	0

Like his fellow Aruban Kingsale, Ponson also lost most of 1997 to injury. He strained a forearm muscle in June, with the good news being that he required only rest and not surgery. His best pitch is a fastball that has hit 95 MPH, and he complements it with an above-average changeup and a curveball. His command has been spectacular in the past, but just so-so in Double-A, where he was hit much harder than he was accustomed. He's six months younger than Fussell, so Ponson also has plenty of time to make the necessary adjustments. Considered Baltimore's best prospect entering last season, he's still on the fast track despite his subpar year.

Nerio Rodriguez

Position: P

Bats: R **Throws:** R

Ht: 6' 1" **Wt:** 195

Opening Day Age: 25

Born: 3/22/73 in Bani, DR

Recent Statistics

	W	L	ERA	G	GS	Sv	IP	H	R	BB	SO	HR
97 AAA Rochester	11	10	3.90	27	27	0	168.1	124	82	62	160	23
97 AL Baltimore	2	1	4.91	6	2	0	22.0	21	15	8	11	2

Rodriguez was a light-hitting minor league catcher for the White Sox when the Orioles took him in the Triple-A Rule 5 draft in December 1994. Baltimore liked his arm strength, and after he continued to struggle with the bat, moved him to the mound in the middle of 1995.

Little more than a year later, he made his major league debut. Rodriguez throws a hard, sinking fastball that's devastating as it bores in on righthanded hitters, and also has a big league changeup. Only his slider is in need of much refinement. Jumping from Class-A to Triple-A last year, he continued to throw strikes and showed that his 1996 success was no fluke. It would be no surprise if he made the Orioles' rotation out of spring training.

Everett Stull

Position: P

Bats: R **Throws:** R

Ht: 6' 3" **Wt:** 195

Opening Day Age: 26

Born: 8/24/71 in Fort Riley, GA

Recent Statistics

	W	L	ERA	G	GS	Sv	IP	H	R	BB	SO	HR
97 AAA Ottawa	8	10	5.82	27	27	0	159.1	166	110	86	130	25
97 NL Montreal	0	1	16.20	3	0	0	3.1	7	7	4	2	1

Stull was the player to be named in the trade that sent Mike Johnson to Montreal. A 1992 third-round pick out of Tennessee State, Stull has frustrated the Expos with his inability to adjust to Triple-A, where he has gone 10-16, 5.97 in the last two seasons. He throws a mid-90s fastball, an above-average curveball and a decent change, so he has the stuff to be a big winner. His biggest drawback is his extremely shaky command, and after six pro seasons it's becoming increasingly unlikely he'll ever throw enough strikes to be successful.

Others to Watch

Baltimore's top 1996 draft pick (second round), righthander **Brian Falkenborg**, was poised enough to get a brief taste of Double-A as a teenager. He has good life on his fastball. . . Don't get too excited about **Jim Foster's** .317-23-110 season. He's 26, nothing special as a catcher and spent half the year in the Carolina League, where he played the two previous seasons. . . Outfielder **Darnell McDonald** seemed headed to the University of Texas to play tailback, but Baltimore drafted him in the first round and signed him for $1.9 million. He's 19, has five-tool talent and probably could make it as a pitcher with a 95-MPH fastball. . . There aren't many prospects who are bigger or can hit the ball farther than 6-foot-5, 283-pound first baseman **Calvin Pickering**. He's not much defensively, but he's fairly athletic and isn't afraid to take the occasional walk. If he stays in shape, the 21 year old could be special. . . Few players throw harder than 23-year-old righthander **Alvie Shepherd**, a 1995 first-rounder, but he has shown little more than a plus fastball. Envisioned as a closer, he has poor command and hasn't dominated hitters while being used as a starter. . . Australian bonus baby **John Stephens** couldn't have had a more impressive debut. A three-pitch pitcher with an improving fastball, he went 7-0, 1.67 while striking out 77 and walking 14 in 57 innings between the Rookie-level Gulf Coast and Appalachian leagues. That's a strikeout-walk ratio of greater than 5-1, and he was only 17.

Jimy Williams

1997 Season

After waiting seven years for his second managerial assignment, Jimy Williams inherited a difficult situation with the 1997 Red Sox. First, he had to deal with a clubhouse that seemed to be on the verge of a mutiny after the acrimonious departures of Roger Clemens and Mike Greenwell. In the spring, he had to defuse a potentially explosive situation stemming from the competition between rookie Nomar Garciaparra and veteran John Valentin. In June, Wil Cordero was charged with spousal abuse, and the story was a major distraction for the rest of the season. Throughout, Williams did his best to maintain an even keel.

Offense

Williams shows little interest in bunting or the running game, and prefers to let his bats do the work. He's aggressive with the running game early in the inning, but hates to see an inning end with a runner caught stealing. He likes to platoon, but is willing to give a platoon player the chance to play full-time. By season's end, four players who'd begun the year as platoon players had earned significant playing time against all types of pitching.

Pitching & Defense

The two biggest moves Williams made in '97 involved moving players to less demanding positions. Cordero, a defensively-challenged infielder, was moved to left field, and shortstop John Valentin was moved to second base, all to accommodate Garciaparra. The changes worked, as Garciaparra became Rookie of the Year, Valentin and Cordero accepted their new positions, and the Red Sox turned 27 more double plays than they had in 1996. Williams was similarly courageous in handling the pitchers, shifting Tom Gordon from starter to closer.

1998 Outlook

No one in Boston would dare to admit it, but 1997 was basically a rebuilding year. The Red Sox' seven-game decline pales in comparison to what was accomplished for the future. With ace Pedro Martinez in tow and several more hot youngsters on the way, the club seems to be looking up.

Born: 10/04/43 in Santa Maria, CA

Playing Experience: 1966-1967, StL

Managerial Experience: 4 seasons

Manager Statistics

Year	Team, Lg	W	L	Pct	GB	Finish
1997	Boston, AL	78	84	.481	20.0	4th East
4 Seasons		359	325	.524	—	—

1997 Starting Pitchers by Days Rest

	≤3	4	5	6+
Red Sox Starts	4	85	40	21
Red Sox ERA	4.74	5.06	5.19	4.54
AL Avg Starts	5	89	34	24
AL ERA	4.38	4.60	4.61	5.37

1997 Situational Stats

	Jimy Williams	AL Average
Hit & Run Success %	44.7	36.5
Stolen Base Success %	58.6	67.3
Platoon Pct.	56.3	59.5
Defensive Subs	16	22
High-Pitch Outings	13	15
Quick/Slow Hooks	17/13	19/15
Sacrifice Attempts	30	53

1997 Rankings (American League)

⇒ 1st in pitchouts (108), pitchouts with a runner moving (29) and intentional walks (40)

⇒ 2nd in hit-and-run percentage (44.7%)

⇒ 3rd in starts with over 140 pitches (1), relief appearances (417) and saves with over 1 inning pitched (11)

Steve Avery

1997 Season

Steve Avery was signed to replace Roger Clemens, when the Red Sox figured out—too late—that Clemens wouldn't be back. Avery was the only big-name pitcher left on the market, so the Sox went for him. Things worked out so badly that the club yanked him from the rotation one start before his $3.9 million option for 1998 was to kick in. Manager Jimy Williams later opted to give him another start, but the decision had little to do with Avery's pitching.

Pitching

What happened? Avery is only 27, but in his last three seasons he's 20-30. He used to hit the low 90s on the gun, but for much of last season his fastball only reached the mid-80s. The .320 batting average against him speaks volumes. So does the .400 average by lefties, an indication that he has never come close to throwing the sharp curveball that he had early in his career. Some believe he hurt his arm three years ago and never recovered. Others think it's a combination of his arm and mechanics that were messed up when he had a rib problem in 1996. A mechanical adjustment in September helped push his velocity back up to 89 MPH, an indication that he may be able to come back.

Defense

Avery's natural athleticism carries over to his fielding. There's some thought that he could play the outfield if asked. His pickoff move is above-average, which helps because his delivery to the plate is slow.

1998 Outlook

The Red Sox may not want Avery back, both for his pitching and for the lingering ill feelings over the contract option. But to move him, Boston would have to eat a good chunk of his contract. Pitching coach Joe Kerrigan has turned around less talented pitchers, so a rebound is always a possibility.

Position: SP
Bats: L **Throws:** L
Ht: 6' 4" **Wt:** 205

Opening Day Age: 27
Born: 4/14/70 in Trenton, MI
ML Seasons: 8

Overall Statistics

	W	L	Pct.	ERA	G	GS	Sv	IP	H	BB	SO	HR	Ratio
1997	6	7	.462	6.42	22	18	0	96.2	127	49	51	15	1.82
Career	78	69	.531	4.02	225	219	0	1319.0	1307	420	866	118	1.31

How Often He Throws Strikes

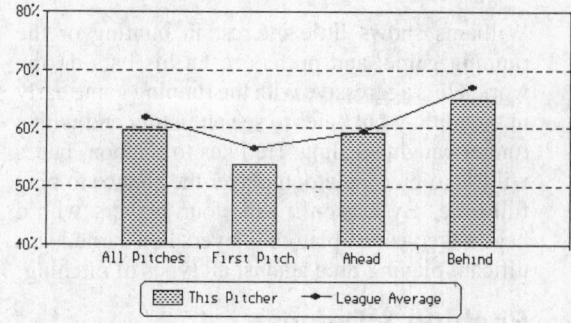

1997 Situational Stats

	W	L	ERA	Sv	IP		AB	H	HR	RBI	Avg
Home	2	4	8.59	0	36.2	LHB	65	26	2	9	.400
Road	4	3	5.10	0	60.0	RHB	332	101	13	60	.304
First Half	2	2	5.55	0	35.2	Sc Pos	103	38	4	55	.369
Scnd Half	4	5	6.93	0	61.0	Clutch	15	5	0	3	.333

1997 Rankings (American League)

⇒ 3rd in highest batting average allowed vs. righthanded batters

Darren Bragg

1997 Season

The New England prep school football legend is that when Darren Bragg was playing safety for Taft High School in Connecticut, he hit an opposing fullback named Maurice Vaughn so hard that he knocked him out cold. That makeup is what Bragg brings to the park every day. He runs into walls, dives headlong into fences, gets turf burns and breaks up double plays. When he doesn't play so much that he wears down, he hits. He began 1997 as the platoon center fielder. He started out hot, shedding his platoon role, but cooled after the first couple of months.

Hitting

Bragg is an aggressive fastball hitter, but he also has patience and will run out some tough battles with opposing pitchers. When fresh, the former Georgia Tech teammate of Nomar Garciaparra and Jason Varitek is a dead-fastball hitter who will stay back enough to get the breaking ball into the air. He hits a good number of doubles as well as some home runs, but he strikes out quite a bit because he swings so hard. Teams try to get him out by throwing a lot of offspeed stuff up and away and down and in, making him lose the feel of the strike zone.

Baserunning & Defense

Bragg is also very aggressive on the bases. He is very tough, and that hardened, heavy-metal makeup makes it easy for him to play in Boston. He's a good baserunner, albeit an average basestealer. He's considered lacking as a center fielder, but he tries to make up for his unremarkable range with his hustle and fearlessness. He has worked hard to improve his arm and has become an adequate thrower with above-average accuracy.

1998 Outlook

Bragg's numbers don't jump out at you, but his intangibles make him a better player than his statistics would indicate. The Red Sox may look elsewhere for a center fielder and picked up Damon Buford in the Jim Leyritz trade. Bragg is sure to see plenty of playing time, perhaps as a fourth outfielder or a platoon right fielder.

Position: CF/RF
Bats: L   **Throws:** R
Ht: 5' 9"   **Wt:** 180

Opening Day Age: 28
Born: 9/7/69 in Waterbury, CT
ML Seasons: 4

Overall Statistics

	G	AB	R	H	D	T	HR	RBI	SB	BB	SO	Avg	OBP	Slg
1997	153	513	65	132	35	2	9	57	10	61	102	.257	.337	.386
Career	340	1094	163	278	67	5	22	118	33	150	218	.254	.346	.385

Where He Hits the Ball

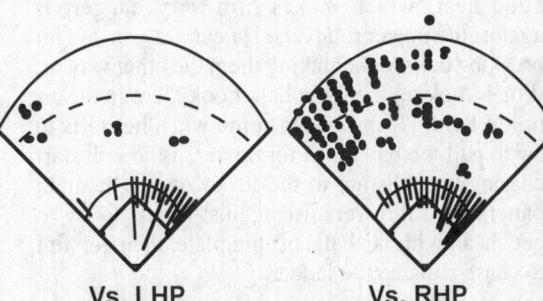

Vs. LHP   **Vs. RHP**

1997 Situational Stats

	AB	H	HR	RBI	Avg		AB	H	HR	RBI	Avg
Home	260	72	3	28	.277	LHP	120	29	1	10	.242
Road	253	60	6	29	.237	RHP	393	103	8	47	.262
First Half	296	79	8	37	.267	Sc Pos	133	33	5	48	.248
Scnd Half	217	53	1	20	.244	Clutch	94	28	2	21	.298

1997 Rankings (American League)

⇒ 2nd in fielding percentage in center field (.993)
⇒ 5th in lowest batting average on the road
⇒ 9th in highest groundball/flyball ratio (1.8) and lowest batting average on an 0-2 count (.056)
⇒ Led the Red Sox in sacrifice bunts (5), games played (153), most pitches seen per plate appearance (3.99), bunts in play (8) and highest percentage of extra bases taken as a runner (60.5%)

Wil Cordero

1997 Season

Wilfredo Cordero's Boston career came to an inglorious end amid clamor over spousal-abuse charges. He was on the brink of being one of the prime middle-order righthanded bats in the game. When he was gone from the team, the lineup wasn't the same. He played in 76 games the second half of the season, but his mindset was to swing at the first decent pitch and get away from the booing.

Hitting

Cordero is a classic hitter and can drive the ball hard to all fields. It sometimes looks as if he takes fastballs right out of the catcher's mitt. He can hit good heat, which makes him very dangerous against the power relievers. He can stay on and hit breaking balls, either taking them the other way or, if he is looking breaking ball, hook them in the air to left field. His problems come when he starts to try to pull the ball or hit for power, as he will start chasing fastballs out of the strike zone. The main pattern hard throwers use against him is to try to get ahead with fastballs off the plate, then get him to chase balls up the ladder.

Baserunning & Defense

After moving around the infield, Cordero last season appeared to be developing into a decent left fielder. Wilfredo may have had problems with range and throwing at shortstop, but in left field he utilitizes his very good hands and quick infielder's release. He has the ability to charge balls and also to go back on balls, which enables him to play shallow. Cordero's speed is average at best and he is not an aggressive baserunner.

1998 Outlook

In spite of his defensive and personal problems, Cordero can really hit. If he's able to put his problems behind him and get another opportunity, he can spend the next five years as a 100-RBI producer.

Position: LF
Bats: R **Throws:** R
Ht: 6' 2" **Wt:** 195

Opening Day Age: 26
Born: 10/3/71 in Mayaguez, PR
ML Seasons: 6
Pronunciation: cor-DAIR-oh

Overall Statistics

	G	AB	R	H	D	T	HR	RBI	SB	BB	SO	Avg	OBP	Slg
1997	140	570	82	160	26	3	18	72	1	31	122	.281	.320	.432
Career	623	2298	313	642	141	11	58	287	40	162	394	.279	.333	.426

Where He Hits the Ball

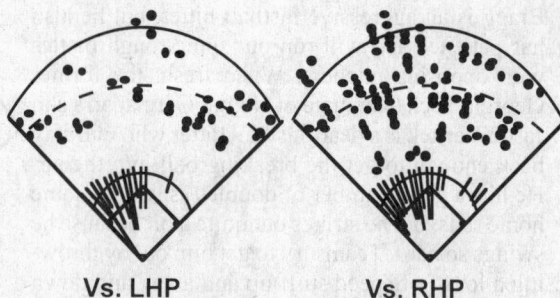

Vs. LHP   Vs. RHP

1997 Situational Stats

	AB	H	HR	RBI	Avg		AB	H	HR	RBI	Avg
Home	273	73	11	35	.267	LHP	174	50	4	19	.287
Road	297	87	7	37	.293	RHP	396	110	14	53	.278
First Half	280	84	11	41	.300	Sc Pos	144	38	7	56	.264
Scnd Half	290	76	7	31	.262	Clutch	96	29	3	10	.302

1997 Rankings (American League)
⇒ 1st in fielding percentage in left field (.992)

Nomar Garciaparra

Position: SS
Bats: R **Throws:** R
Ht: 6' 0" **Wt:** 167

Opening Day Age: 24
Born: 7/23/73 in Whittier, CA
ML Seasons: 2
Pronunciation:
NO-mar
gar-see-uh-PARR-uh

1997 Season

Everyone in the Red Sox organization knew Nomar Garciaparra was going to be a franchise defensive shortstop. What they never anticipated was that he could produce like *this*. As a leadoff man and potential Gold Glove winner, Garciaparra hit 30 homers, had 44 doubles and 11 triples, knocked in 98 runs, had 209 hits, scored 122 runs, stole 22 bases and slugged .534.

Hitting

Garciaparra may look skinny, but offseason weight training has left him with surprising strength. With his strong, wiry wrists, he has the rare ability to maintain bat control with two strikes without sacrificing power. At first, he seemed to be vulnerable to the fastball up and out of the strike zone and breaking balls down and away, but one of his greatest tools is his ability to adjust. He jumps on first-pitch fastballs, and he'll likely get more breaking balls early in his second season, but his teamates believe he will adjust.

Baserunning & Defense

Nomar quickly was dubbed "Spiderman" by Mo Vaughn for his acrobatic fielding. He is unusual in the way he fields balls one-handed, but he has such body control that he makes it look easy. Omar Vizquel is the only shortstop in the game who might be better. He developed his footwork and body control playing soccer as a kid. He has tremendous range into the hole, has a strong arm and sometimes exhibits instincts that make even veteran baseball men scratch their heads. Ted Simmons, for instance, believes Garciaparra has the finest instincts of any infielder in the last 20 years.

1998 Outlook

Near the end of the season, National League President Leonard Coleman asked Ted Williams who he thought were the best players in the American League. "Griffey's the best," replied Williams, "but I'm not sure the shortstop in Boston isn't the next best." He can bunt, he can run, and the one question some had—staying healthy—was not a problem his rookie season. At the moment, his future seems limitless.

Overall Statistics

	G	AB	R	H	D	T	HR	RBI	SB	BB	SO	Avg	OBP	Slg
1997	153	684	122	209	44	11	30	98	22	35	92	.306	.342	.534
Career	177	771	133	230	46	14	34	114	27	39	106	.298	.334	.527

Where He Hits the Ball

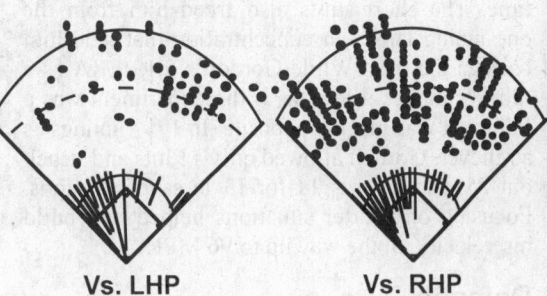

Vs. LHP **Vs. RHP**

1997 Situational Stats

	AB	H	HR	RBI	Avg		AB	H	HR	RBI	Avg
Home	356	106	11	49	.298	LHP	184	49	9	30	.266
Road	328	103	19	49	.314	RHP	500	160	21	68	.320
First Half	357	104	13	44	.291	Sc Pos	154	49	5	64	.318
Scnd Half	327	105	17	54	.321	Clutch	106	34	3	15	.321

1997 Rankings (American League)

⇒ 1st in at-bats, hits and triples
⇒ 2nd in runs scored, total bases (365), errors at shortstop (21) and highest percentage of swings on the first pitch (44.9%)
⇒ 3rd in plate appearances (734) and least pitches seen per plate appearance (3.23)
⇒ Led the Red Sox in at-bats, runs scored, hits, singles, triples, total bases (365), RBI, sacrifice flies (7), stolen bases, caught stealing (9), plate appearances (734), games played (153), stolen base percentage (71.0%), batting average with the bases loaded (.583), on-base percentage for a leadoff hitter (.342), slugging percentage vs. righthanded pitchers (.542) and batting average on the road

Boston Red Sox

Tom Gordon

1997 Season

Tom Gordon began the season as Boston's best starter and ended it as its best closer. His 5-9 record over the first four months of the season wasn't impressive, but he got minimal run support and he had one of those seasons where very little went right. When Heathcliff Slocumb was sent packing at the trading deadline, manager Jimy Williams decided to try Gordon as his closer. The move brought out the best in the fiery Gordon, and his future appears to lie in the bullpen.

Pitching

Relieving enabled Gordon to concentrate on throwing his best two pitches, his curveball and fastball, as he prefers to throw them—hard, all the time. The short stints also freed him from the one-inning lapses in concentration that held him back in the past. While Gordon's 5.19 ERA as a reliever makes it look as if the experiment was a failure, it was just the opposite. In 17⅓ innings as a reliever, Gordon allowed only 11 hits and struck out 25, and he was 11-for-13 in save situations. Focusing on shorter situations helped him build his velocity all the way up to 96 MPH.

Defense

Gordon always has been a decent fielder because he is an agile athlete. He is not proficient at holding runners because of his leg kick, but that flaw is less important now that he's a closer rather than a starter.

1998 Outlook

The Red Sox think the move to the bullpen will give Gordon a second career. He has what it takes to close out a lot of wins. The Red Sox have gone through several closers in recent seasons, and they'd like nothing more than for Gordon to be a stabilizing force in that role.

Position: SP/RP
Bats: R **Throws:** R
Ht: 5' 9" **Wt:** 180

Opening Day Age: 30
Born: 11/18/67 in Sebring, FL
ML Seasons: 10
Nickname: Flash

Overall Statistics

	W	L	Pct.	ERA	G	GS	Sv	IP	H	BB	SO	HR	Ratio
1997	6	10	.375	3.74	42	25	11	182.2	155	78	159	10	1.28
Career	97	90	.519	4.21	350	203	14	1548.0	1444	770	1329	129	1.43

How Often He Throws Strikes

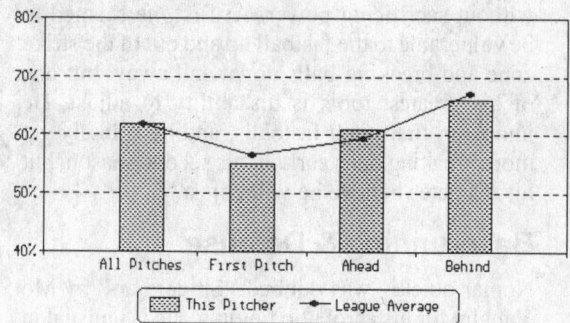

1997 Situational Stats

	W	L	ERA	Sv	IP		AB	H	HR	RBI	Avg
Home	2	6	4.34	3	112.0	LHB	363	84	3	37	.231
Road	4	4	2.80	8	70.2	RHB	323	71	7	40	.220
First Half	5	7	3.22	0	114.2	Sc Pos	164	42	2	66	.256
Scnd Half	1	3	4.63	11	68.0	Clutch	90	18	2	11	.200

1997 Rankings (American League)

⇒ 3rd in lowest slugging percentage allowed (.319), least home runs allowed per 9 innings (.49) and lowest batting average allowed vs. righthanded batters

⇒ 4th in lowest batting average allowed (.226) and lowest batting average allowed vs. lefthanded batters

⇒ 5th in highest groundball/flyball ratio allowed (2.0)

⇒ Led the Red Sox in ERA, strikeouts, highest strikeout/walk ratio (2.0), lowest batting average allowed (.226), lowest slugging percentage allowed (.319), lowest on-base percentage allowed (.306), highest groundball/flyball ratio allowed (2.0) and least baserunners allowed per 9 innings (11.6)

Scott Hatteberg

1997 Season

There wasn't a lot that went well for the Red Sox in 1997, but Scott Hatteberg was one of their more pleasant surprises. The lefthanded-hitting back-stop hit for both average and power in a platoon role and was one of baseball's lesser-known rookies to have a breakthrough season.

Hitting

Hatteberg worked very hard to build up his strength throughout his six-year climb through the minors, and he showed good production potential last year. He came up as a dead-fastball, low-ball hitter, and showed the intelligence to make adjustments, becoming more adept at laying back on breaking balls as the season wore on. By season's end, he had 34 extra-base hits in 350 at-bats. While he chased a lot of pitches up and out of the strike zone and finished with 70 strikeouts, he also showed a good eye, drawing 40 walks. He hasn't faced many lefthanders over the last three years and has yet to prove that he can handle them.

Baserunning & Defense

Hatteberg does not have a strong defensive reputation, but he has passable hands, understands the game and has a personality pitchers like. He threw out only 23 percent of opposing basestealers, but throwing is not one of his tools. The Sox believe that in time he will develop into an adept handler of pitchers, especially when he becomes more relaxed and comfortable at the major league level. He runs poorly and conservatively, even for a catcher.

1998 Outlook

Even with Jim Leyritz on board, Hatteberg figures to hold onto a good share of the playing time behind the dish this year. His production from the left side of the plate is useful, and he may have a future as a Darrin Fletcher-type player.

Position: C
Bats: L **Throws:** R
Ht: 6' 1" **Wt:** 195

Opening Day Age: 28
Born: 12/14/69 in Salem, OR
ML Seasons: 3

Overall Statistics

	G	AB	R	H	D	T	HR	RBI	SB	BB	SO	Avg	OBP	Slg
1997	114	350	46	97	23	1	10	44	0	40	70	.277	.354	.434
Career	126	363	50	100	24	1	10	44	0	43	72	.275	.355	.430

Where He Hits the Ball

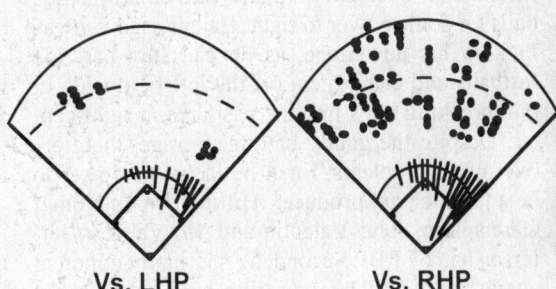

Vs. LHP   **Vs. RHP**

1997 Situational Stats

	AB	H	HR	RBI	Avg		AB	H	HR	RBI	Avg
Home	179	50	5	24	.279	LHP	80	18	0	12	.225
Road	171	47	5	20	.275	RHP	270	79	10	32	.293
First Half	161	46	5	19	.286	Sc Pos	90	21	2	32	.233
Scnd Half	189	51	5	25	.270	Clutch	58	12	1	6	.207

1997 Rankings (American League)

⇒ 1st in lowest fielding percentage at catcher (.983)
⇒ 2nd in errors at catcher (11)
⇒ 4th in highest percentage of pitches taken (63.1%)
⇒ Led the Red Sox in highest percentage of pitches taken (63.1%)

Reggie Jefferson

1997 Season

With the trade of Jose Canseco, Reggie Jefferson took over the bulk of the Red Sox' DH chores last year. Playing primarily against righthanders, he remained among the American League batting leaders for most of the year. In August, he successfully petitioned manager Jimy Williams for full-time play in order to gain enough plate appearances to qualify for the batting crown. Jefferson finally got to face lefties, but they continued to befuddle him as they always have and he dropped out of the race.

Hitting

Jefferson can hit. He's a low-ball hitter who lines fastballs all over the field and can yank breaking balls for some power to right. He has used Fenway Park to his advantage, as he can stay back on fastballs and clank them off the left-field wall, or pull breaking balls into the vast area in right-center. Despite the gaudy batting average, there are two major problems. First, he lacks the power to be a premier run producer. Hitting behind Nomar Garciaparra, John Valentin and Mo Vaughn, Jefferson had 67 RBI. Second, he's virtually impotent against lefties. The one-time switch-hitter has given up trying to bat righthanded, but it hasn't done any good. Over the last three years, he has hit .239 with one home run in 163 at-bats against southpaws.

Baserunning & Defense

The rest of Jefferson's game is also a problem. He can't run, so when he gets a single he clogs the bases. He also has no position. The Red Sox have tried him in left field and first base with no success, as he can't run or throw enough to play left, and his hands and throwing keep him off first.

1998 Outlook

Reggie Jefferson is a lifetime .302 hitter who has batted .347 and .319 the last two seasons. But when 1997 was over, it was clear the Red Sox were trying to find someone to take him off their hands. While he has a magic swing, Jefferson now needs to find the right team and situation to keep his career going.

Position: DH/1B
Bats: L **Throws:** L
Ht: 6' 4" **Wt:** 215

Opening Day Age: 29
Born: 9/25/68 in Tallahassee, FL
ML Seasons: 7

Overall Statistics

	G	AB	R	H	D	T	HR	RBI	SB	BB	SO	Avg	OBP	Slg
1997	136	489	74	156	33	1	13	67	1	24	93	.319	.358	.470
Career	535	1721	240	520	102	9	59	252	2	108	357	.302	.347	.475

Where He Hits the Ball

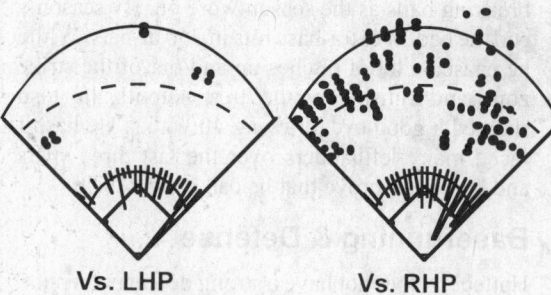

Vs. LHP   **Vs. RHP**

1997 Situational Stats

	AB	H	HR	RBI	Avg		AB	H	HR	RBI	Avg
Home	246	83	6	34	.337	LHP	106	21	0	6	.198
Road	243	73	7	33	.300	RHP	383	135	13	61	.352
First Half	229	78	8	36	.341	Sc Pos	128	37	3	50	.289
Scnd Half	260	78	5	31	.300	Clutch	72	15	2	8	.208

1997 Rankings (American League)

⇒ 1st in batting average vs. righthanded pitchers
⇒ 3rd in highest groundball/flyball ratio (2.2)
⇒ 5th in batting average at home and highest percentage of swings on the first pitch (39.4%)
⇒ 6th in batting average on an 0-2 count (.289)
⇒ 8th in batting average
⇒ 10th in least pitches seen per plate appearance (3.49) and cleanup slugging percentage (.509)
⇒ Led the Red Sox in batting average, highest groundball/flyball ratio (2.2), batting average vs. righthanded pitchers, batting average on an 0-2 count (.289), cleanup slugging percentage (.509) and batting average with two strikes (.251)

Tim Naehring

1997 Season

When one talks of players with soul, one has to mention Tim Naehring. He is always dirty and always plays hard. He's willing to stand up in the middle of the clubhouse and say what needs to be said, and because of the respect he carries he gets every teammate's ear. But there is one major problem: durability. In 1997, Naehring was on his way to one of his best years when he went down for the season in June and underwent reconstructive surgery on his elbow.

Hitting

A healthy Naehring is a solid hitter. He was on his way to a 20-homer, 80-RBI season last year when he went down. He is a very competitive hitter who is strong enough to take the fastball on his hands and fist it into right-center. When he guesses correctly, he can pull for better-than-average power. He's a savvy hitter who gets his share of walks and rarely strikes out. His health is always a concern, as he tends to wear down over the course of a season, even when he's able to stay in the lineup.

Baserunning & Defense

Naehring was far from quick when he came up as a shortstop in 1990, and after major back surgery in 1991, other injuries and intense weight-training, his speed is now well below average. His headiness and aggressiveness make up for some of that lack of blazing ability. Defensively, he is one of the league's premier third basemen. He has great hands, a quick release and strong arm. He charges balls well and has two strengths vital to third base: a fearlessness on hard-hit balls and the capacity to give the second baseman the ball where he needs it on the 5-4-3 double play.

1998 Outlook

Naehring plays and works so hard that his career has been ravaged by injuries. He has hit more than 10 homers once, had as many as 60 RBI once and once again faces a major comeback. He has come back from serious injuries before, and he ought to be able to overcome this one, too.

Position: 3B
Bats: R **Throws:** R
Ht: 6' 2" **Wt:** 203

Opening Day Age: 31
Born: 2/1/67 in Cincinnati, OH
ML Seasons: 8
Pronunciation: NAIR-ring

Overall Statistics

	G	AB	R	H	D	T	HR	RBI	SB	BB	SO	Avg	OBP	Slg
1997	70	259	38	74	18	1	9	40	1	38	40	.286	.375	.467
Career	547	1872	254	527	104	4	49	250	5	236	312	.282	.365	.420

Where He Hits the Ball

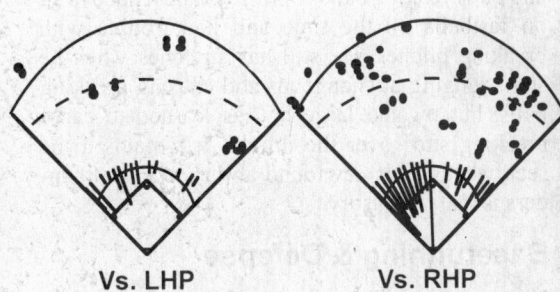

Vs. LHP   Vs. RHP

1997 Situational Stats

	AB	H	HR	RBI	Avg		AB	H	HR	RBI	Avg
Home	117	33	4	23	.282	LHP	72	21	2	5	.292
Road	142	41	5	17	.289	RHP	187	53	7	35	.283
First Half	259	74	9	40	.286	Sc Pos	66	17	3	34	.258
Scnd Half	0	0	0	0	-	Clutch	42	7	0	5	.167

1997 Rankings (American League)

⇒ Did not rank near the top or bottom in any category

Troy O'Leary

1997 Season

Troy O'Leary can hit, and last season he came close to shedding his label as a mere platoon player. In the past, O'Leary has been cast in tweener roles, partially because he was never a big RBI producer and mainly because managers doubted he could hit lefties or play the outfield with any degree of reliability. In 1997 he showed new toughness against southpaws and put himself in line to solidify his status as a full-timer.

Hitting

O'Leary has a sweet, laid-back swing. He can stay behind balls and use the left-field wall, drive fastballs hard from the left-field corner to right-center, and pull breaking balls. Until 1997, he tended to sit on fastballs all the time and had trouble with breaking pitches. He still has stretches when he starts lunging at changeups and chasing breaking balls, but by and large he has learned to carve breaking stuff over the infield. It remains to be seen whether his newfound ability to hit lefthanders is real or illusory.

Baserunning & Defense

No one ever will gush over O'Leary's baseball instincts. If the Red Sox follow through on their plan to move him to left field, he will be more comfortable there than he was in Fenway's spacious right field, where he was lost. He can run balls down, but has rocky hands and a below-average arm and he takes poor angles to balls. He is not a prime baserunner, as his 0-for-5 basestealing log indicates. But O'Leary is in there to hit, and he always has done that.

1998 Outlook

In 1998, O'Leary likely will get a chance to prove he can play every day—even against lefthanders—for the first time in his career. The move to left should help, and the Red Sox believe that he is on the road to becoming a valuable run producer.

Position: RF/LF
Bats: L **Throws:** L
Ht: 6' 0" **Wt:** 198

Opening Day Age: 28
Born: 8/4/69 in Compton, CA
ML Seasons: 5

Overall Statistics

	G	AB	R	H	D	T	HR	RBI	SB	BB	SO	Avg	OBP	Slg
1997	146	499	65	154	32	4	15	80	0	39	70	.309	.358	.479
Career	453	1502	205	436	95	16	42	220	9	125	235	.290	.346	.459

Where He Hits the Ball

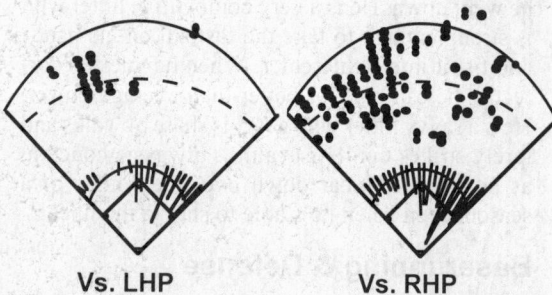

Vs. LHP   Vs. RHP

1997 Situational Stats

	AB	H	HR	RBI	Avg		AB	H	HR	RBI	Avg
Home	246	78	5	40	.317	LHP	101	28	2	18	.277
Road	253	76	10	40	.300	RHP	398	126	13	62	.317
First Half	248	74	8	38	.298	Sc Pos	132	45	3	62	.341
Scnd Half	251	80	7	42	.319	Clutch	84	26	0	15	.310

1997 Rankings (American League)

⇒ 3rd in fielding percentage in right field (.983)
⇒ 7th in errors in right field (4)
⇒ 9th in batting average with runners in scoring position
⇒ Led the Red Sox in batting average with runners in scoring position, batting average on a 3-2 count (.359) and lowest percentage of swings on the first pitch (24.5%)

Aaron Sele

Position: SP
Bats: R **Throws:** R
Ht: 6' 5" **Wt:** 215

Opening Day Age: 27
Born: 6/25/70 in Golden Valley, MN
ML Seasons: 5
Pronunciation: SEE-lee

1997 Season

After such a promising beginning, Aaron Sele's career in Boston finally came to an end following the 1997 season when he was traded to the Rangers in a deal for Jim Leyritz. Sele managed to stay healthy enough to make 33 starts last year, but still wasn't the pitcher he was before suffering shoulder problems in 1995. He was rarely effective for more than a few starts at a time, and he worked past the seventh inning only once all year.

Pitching

With an 86-88 MPH fastball, Sele is not overpowering, but his fastball has enough sink to get him a decent number of grounders. At times last season, he demonstrated an ability to work both sides of the plate and to come inside on lefthanders. However, he was inconsistent in that commitment, and the hard, over-the-top power curveball that was the hallmark of his early career hasn't been as prevalent since he hurt his shoulder. His softer curve hasn't fooled lefties, which is becoming a major problem. He has gained confidence in a cutter which keeps righthanders in check.

Defense

Sele is neither quick nor agile afield, though he has worked hard to improve himself. His move to first is ordinary, and because of his lengthened delivery and the big curveball, holding runners has become a concern.

1998 Outlook

The best thing for Sele will be to get out of Boston and start over again. The knock on Sele with the Red Sox was that he wasn't tough enough, and he probably wasn't going to be able to shake that perception. He just needs to go to Texas, regain his confidence and focus on his ability. As long as he has his curveball, he's a major league starter.

Overall Statistics

	W	L	Pct.	ERA	G	GS	Sv	IP	H	BB	SO	HR	Ratio
1997	13	12	.520	5.38	33	33	0	177.1	196	80	122	25	1.56
Career	38	33	.535	4.41	108	108	0	622.0	660	269	478	60	1.49

How Often He Throws Strikes

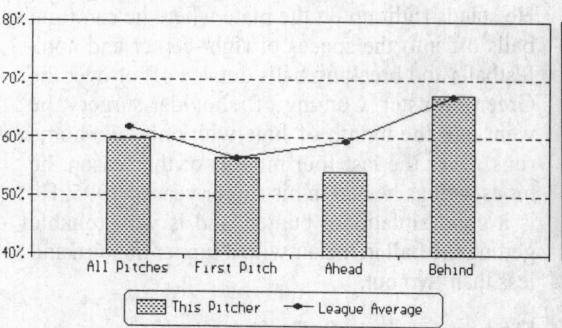

1997 Situational Stats

	W	L	ERA	Sv	IP		AB	H	HR	RBI	Avg
Home	8	6	4.49	0	102.1	LHB	377	123	15	48	.326
Road	5	6	6.60	0	75.0	RHB	326	73	10	50	.224
First Half	10	6	5.13	0	100.0	Sc Pos	187	44	3	66	.235
Scnd Half	3	6	5.70	0	77.1	Clutch	25	9	3	4	.360

1997 Rankings (American League)

⇒ 1st in highest on-base percentage allowed (.361) and most baserunners allowed per 9 innings (14.8)
⇒ 2nd in hit batsmen (15)
⇒ 4th in highest ERA
⇒ 5th in pickoff throws (196), most run support per 9 innings (6.4) and least GDPs induced per 9 innings (0.5)
⇒ Led the Red Sox in wins, games started, hits allowed, home runs allowed, wild pitches (7), pickoff throws (196), winning percentage, least pitches thrown per batter (3.75), most run support per 9 innings (6.4) and lowest batting average allowed with runners in scoring position

John Valentin

1997 Season

The 1997 season was often confusing for John Valentin. He had finished the 1996 season at third base because of the arrival of Nomar Garciaparra, but when Tim Naehring was re-signed, Valentin went into spring training as a shortstop. Halfway through, he moved to second base. When Naehring went down in July, Valentin went to third, where he finished the season strong, hitting .328 with 12 homers after the All-Star break.

Hitting

Valentin has made himself into a very good offensive player, particularly in Fenway Park, where he has hit .319 and slugged .525 the last five seasons. He stands right up on the plate where he can fight balls off into the spaces of right-center and hook fastballs and breaking balls outside off or over the Green Monster. Coming off shoulder surgery, he went into the month of June with only two home runs. Over the last four months of the season, he hit as well as he had in his career year of 1995. He is a good situational bunter, and is very reliable getting the ball in the air with a runner on third and less than two out.

Baserunning & Defense

Because Valentin came up as a shortstop, he still believes he can and should play there, despite having made a decision six years ago to bulk up and trade range for power. Some believe that his range at short is now below-average and that he doesn't anticipate well. When he went to second, not only did he work hard with Garciaparra, he did an adequate job on the pivot without ever being comfortable with his back to the runner. Third is clearly his best position, best suited for his hands, his arm and concentration. Valentin isn't a basestealer, but he sees the field well as a runner and has good first-to-home speed.

1998 Outlook

Trade rumors have followed Valentin ever since he agreed to move off short. Unless he's dealt, he'll go into 1998 as the Red Sox' starting second baseman. Starting the season at full strength without the distraction of playing a new position, he may be in line for one of his best years yet.

Position: 2B/3B
Bats: R **Throws:** R
Ht: 6' 0" **Wt:** 180

Opening Day Age: 31
Born: 2/18/67 in Mineola, NY
ML Seasons: 6
Nickname: Val

Overall Statistics

	G	AB	R	H	D	T	HR	RBI	SB	BB	SO	Avg	OBP	Slg
1997	143	575	95	176	47	5	18	77	7	58	66	.306	.372	.499
Career	695	2576	411	763	192	15	83	378	43	313	324	.296	.375	.479

Where He Hits the Ball

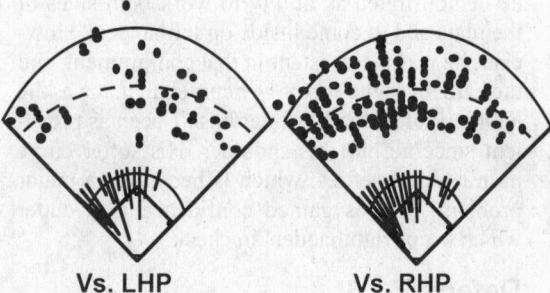

Vs. LHP   Vs. RHP

1997 Situational Stats

	AB	H	HR	RBI	Avg		AB	H	HR	RBI	Avg
Home	287	94	11	47	.328	LHP	154	34	5	12	.221
Road	288	82	7	30	.285	RHP	421	142	13	65	.337
First Half	304	87	6	39	.286	Sc Pos	141	44	3	55	.312
Scnd Half	271	89	12	38	.328	Clutch	99	37	0	12	.374

1997 Rankings (American League)

⇒ 1st in doubles
⇒ 4th in GDPs (21) and errors at second base (11)
⇒ 5th in batting average in the clutch and batting average vs. righthanded pitchers
⇒ 6th in lowest batting average vs. lefthanded pitchers
⇒ 7th in batting average at home
⇒ 9th in most GDPs per GDP situation (17.6%)
⇒ 10th in highest percentage of swings put into play (51.4%)
⇒ Led the Red Sox in doubles, GDPs (21) and batting average in the clutch

Mo Vaughn

1997 Season

Last season was one of constant turmoil and struggle for Mo Vaughn. He was distressed about the direction of Boston management, said so and became embroiled in a brouhaha that lasted well into the season. He hurt his knee, requiring arthroscopic surgery in June that sidelined him close to a month. When he came back more quickly than the doctors had predicted, he wasn't the same for the rest of the season and couldn't work hard enough to fight off weight gains. A lot of people would love to have 35 homers and 96 RBI called an off year, but while he still managed to bat .315 he considered it one of his poorer seasons.

Hitting

Vaughn's knee problems affected him at the plate, where he needs flexibility to uncoil his vicious uppercut swing. He's sometimes vulnerable to the fastball up and out of the strike zone, but when he's zoned in, he can lay off that pitch and catch up to almost any fastball from the knees to the letters. His approach is tailored for Fenway Park, where he can stay back, drive fastballs against or over the Green Monster, and pull offspeed pitches for power. Early in his career, Vaughn was vulnerable against lefties, but he has learned to hang in against southpaws.

Baserunning & Defense

Vaughn's problems on defense last year were much worsened by his knee problems. When healthy and in top shape, he has quick feet. Still, his hands aren't extraordinary, he sometimes loses sight of throws, and like most righthanded first basemen he has trouble throwing through runners on the 3-6-3 double play. Despite his lack of speed, he's actually a good baserunner who runs aggressively and will steal a base when ignored.

1998 Outlook

In many ways, both the Red Sox' and Vaughn's performance this year will depend on the resolution of his contract situation. Not only is he the central offensive player on the team, but he's also a key presence in the clubhouse and in the community.

Position: 1B
Bats: L **Throws:** R
Ht: 6' 1" **Wt:** 240

Opening Day Age: 30
Born: 12/15/67 in Norwalk, CT
ML Seasons: 7
Nickname: The Hit Dog

Overall Statistics

	G	AB	R	H	D	T	HR	RBI	SB	BB	SO	Avg	OBP	Slg
1997	141	527	91	166	24	0	35	96	2	86	154	.315	.420	.560
Career	892	3219	521	960	168	8	190	637	28	458	810	.298	.393	.532

Where He Hits the Ball

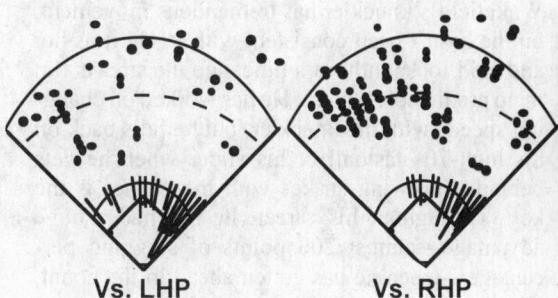

Vs. LHP   Vs. RHP

1997 Situational Stats

	AB	H	HR	RBI	Avg		AB	H	HR	RBI	Avg
Home	260	88	20	55	.338	LHP	196	66	15	33	.337
Road	267	78	15	41	.292	RHP	331	100	20	63	.302
First Half	239	80	20	45	.335	Sc Pos	146	44	10	62	.301
Scnd Half	288	86	15	51	.299	Clutch	76	21	6	17	.276

1997 Rankings (American League)

⇒ 1st in errors at first base (14) and lowest fielding percentage at first base (.988)
⇒ 2nd in intentional walks (17) and lowest percentage of extra bases taken as a runner (27.5%)
⇒ 3rd in strikeouts and highest percentage of swings that missed (31.3%)
⇒ Led the Red Sox in home runs, walks, intentional walks (17), hit by pitch (12), times on base (264), strikeouts, pitches seen (2,466), slugging percentage, on-base percentage, HR frequency (15.1 ABs per HR), least GDPs per GDP situation (7.9%), batting average vs. lefthanded pitchers, slugging percentage vs. lefthanded pitchers (.607), on-base percentage vs. lefthanded pitchers (.440) and on-base percentage vs. righthanded pitchers (.409)

Tim Wakefield

1997 Season

As usual, knuckleballer Tim Wakefield had an up-and-down year. A strained elbow put him out of action for a few weeks early on, and in his sixth game after his return, manager Jimy Williams had him throw 168 pitches in a June game in Milwaukee. After that, he fell into a monthlong slump so severe that he was banished to the bullpen. After returning to the rotation, he went 9-6, 3.71 for the balance of the schedule. Although he led the American League in losses, he saved Boston's beleaguered staff by working on short rest six times, winning four of the six games.

Pitching

Wakefield's knuckler has tremendous movement, but he hasn't been consistent with it. He runs hot and cold for months at a time, and the streaks run in no predictable pattern. He has worked on changing speeds with the knuckler, but he falls back on his high-70s fastball or his slider when he gets behind. Throwing strikes with the floater is the key. Throughout his career, he has had a huge advantage—almost 200 points of slugging percentage—when he has gotten ahead in the count. His slump in late 1995 has caused some to question his mental toughness, but he pitched well in the 1992 stretch run and postseason.

Defense

Wakefield, who is both a good athlete and a former first baseman, is a sound fielder. He has quick feet and therefore has a dangerous pickoff move, and he gets rid of the ball to the plate so quickly that he is far more difficult to run on than most knuckleballers. Eighteen runners were caught stealing against him last year, the highest figure in the majors.

1998 Outlook

Wakefield has led the AL in losses the last two years, but he throws lots of innings. At 31, he is at the age where knuckleballers Hoyt Wilhelm, Wilbur Wood and Charlie Hough put it all together. Boston GM Dan Duquette believes Wakefield is on the verge of becoming an 18-win, 250-inning pitcher, which is why he got offered a three-year, $12 million contract. He quickly signed.

Position: SP/RP
Bats: R **Throws:** R
Ht: 6' 2" **Wt:** 206

Opening Day Age: 31
Born: 8/2/66 in Melbourne, FL
ML Seasons: 5

Overall Statistics

	W	L	Pct.	ERA	G	GS	Sv	IP	H	BB	SO	HR	Ratio
1997	12	15	.444	4.25	35	29	0	201.1	193	87	151	24	1.39
Career	56	48	.538	4.15	131	121	0	828.2	815	355	520	101	1.41

How Often He Throws Strikes

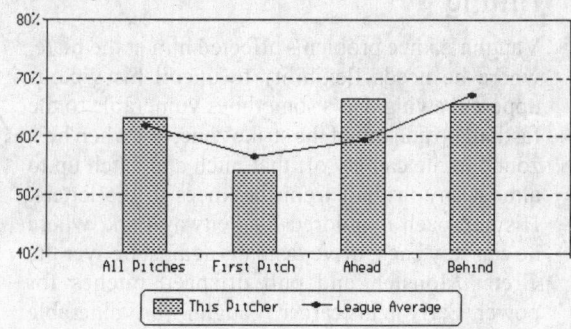

This Pitcher ▨   League Average ◆

1997 Situational Stats

	W	L	ERA	Sv	IP			AB	H	HR	RBI	Avg
Home	4	8	4.18	0	97.0	LHB		346	96	8	36	.277
Road	8	7	4.31	0	104.1	RHB		407	97	16	52	.238
First Half	3	9	4.95	0	87.1	Sc Pos		182	44	5	62	.242
Scnd Half	9	6	3.71	0	114.0	Clutch		73	17	4	10	.233

1997 Rankings (American League)

⇒ 1st in losses, hit batsmen (16), stolen bases allowed (25) and runners caught stealing (18)

⇒ 3rd in shutouts (2) and walks allowed

⇒ 4th in lowest groundball/flyball ratio allowed (0.8)

⇒ Led the Red Sox in losses, complete games (4), shutouts (2), innings pitched, batters faced (866), walks allowed, hit batsmen (16), pitches thrown (3,256), stolen bases allowed (25), runners caught stealing (18), GDPs induced (15), lowest stolen base percentage allowed (58.1%), ERA at home and ERA on the road

Jim Corsi

Position: RP
Bats: R **Throws:** R
Ht: 6' 1" **Wt:** 220

Opening Day Age: 36
Born: 9/9/61 in
Newton, MA
ML Seasons: 8

Overall Statistics

	W	L	Pct.	ERA	G	GS	Sv	IP	H	BB	SO	HR	Ratio
1997	5	3	.625	3.43	52	0	2	57.2	56	21	40	1	1.34
Career	18	19	.486	3.26	273	1	7	378.0	352	148	219	21	1.32

1997 Situational Stats

	W	L	ERA	Sv	IP		AB	H	HR	RBI	Avg
Home	5	1	2.78	1	35.2	LHB	85	19	0	15	.224
Road	0	2	4.50	1	22.0	RHB	135	37	1	16	.274
First Half	1	1	4.67	1	27.0	Sc Pos	79	20	0	28	.253
Scnd Half	4	2	2.35	1	30.2	Clutch	131	35	1	24	.267

1997 Season

It was a long, hard road for Jim Corsi to finally get to Fenway Park in a Red Sox uniform. At 36, the career workhorse who grew up eight miles from Fenway finally got his chance. When he did and stayed healthy, he was a solid workman who threw sinkers and gave up one home run in 52 appearances. He went 5-3, saved two games and ended up as one of Boston's most reliable relievers.

Pitching & Defense

Corsi is your basic sinker-slider reliever. His ball sinks and runs, it's hard to get into the air, and he throws strikes and works quickly. His fastball bores in on lefthanders, allowing him to get them out consistently, and his slider is effective against righthanders. As a groundball pitcher, he's ideally suited for Fenway, where he hasn't allowed a homer in 38 career appearances. With his quick delivery to the plate, Corsi always has been tough to run on. He has allowed five steals and had four runners caught in the last five seasons. To state that he's a below-average fielder is being kind.

1998 Outlook

Corsi became a free agent at season's end, then re-signed with the Red Sox. He'd be most valuable as a middle reliever in a home-run park with a grass surface.

Jeff Frye

Position: 2B/3B/DH
Bats: R **Throws:** R
Ht: 5' 9" **Wt:** 165

Opening Day Age: 31
Born: 8/31/66 in
Oakland, CA
ML Seasons: 5

Overall Statistics

	G	AB	R	H	D	T	HR	RBI	SB	BB	SO	Avg	OBP	Slg
1997	127	404	56	126	36	2	3	51	19	27	44	.312	.352	.433
Career	446	1540	229	451	107	10	12	151	47	150	196	.293	.358	.399

1997 Situational Stats

	AB	H	HR	RBI	Avg		AB	H	HR	RBI	Avg
Home	181	59	2	21	.326	LHP	115	37	1	17	.322
Road	223	67	1	30	.300	RHP	289	89	2	34	.308
First Half	135	36	1	17	.267	Sc Pos	105	33	0	43	.314
Scnd Half	269	90	2	34	.335	Clutch	70	18	0	9	.257

1997 Season

Just about everyone was surprised at how good an everyday player Jeff Frye was in 1997. He opened last season as a utilityman, but when Tim Naehring blew out his elbow, Frye regained his everyday job at second base, batted .335 over the second half and re-established himself as a regular.

Hitting, Baserunning & Defense

Frye is a pesky line-drive hitter who can bunt and play hit-and-run. He seldom swings at the first pitch and consistently forces pitchers to throw four pitches per at-bat. The Red Sox believe he's such an intelligent, studious player that he hits good pitchers' best pitches as well as anyone on the ballclub. He has above-average speed and is an intelligent baserunner who is very aggressive taking the extra base. Defensively, his hands are solid, he has better-than-average range, he turns the double play well and his alertness adds to any club. Last year, he saw some action at every position on the infield as well as all three outfield spots.

1998 Outlook

Frye is the classic example of the down-and-dirty type of player that managers love. If Naehring comes back healthy and John Valentin is still around, Frye will be left without a starting spot, but he'll be there to plug a hole when one opens.

Boston
Red Sox

Chris Hammond

Position: RP/SP
Bats: L **Throws:** L
Ht: 6' 1" **Wt:** 195

Opening Day Age: 32
Born: 1/21/66 in
Atlanta, GA
ML Seasons: 8

Overall Statistics

	W	L	Pct.	ERA	G	GS	Sv	IP	H	BB	SO	HR	Ratio
1997	3	4	.429	5.92	29	8	1	65.1	81	27	48	5	1.65
Career	46	53	.465	4.51	188	133	1	830.0	882	305	505	78	1.43

1997 Situational Stats

	W	L	ERA	Sv	IP		AB	H	HR	RBI	Avg
Home	3	2	3.57	1	40.1	LHB	75	22	1	17	.293
Road	0	2	9.72	0	25.0	RHB	186	59	4	23	.317
First Half	3	4	5.92	1	65.1	Sc Pos	72	28	2	34	.389
Scnd Half	0	0	-	0	0.0	Clutch	37	12	2	8	.324

1997 Season

Chris Hammond was signed by the Red Sox as a free agent in December 1996. He pitched middle relief early on before moving into the starting rotation in late April. His first three starts were solid, but after that he slumped and dropped out of the rotation. In June, he went down for the season with bone spurs in his elbow, and after the season ended he was released.

Pitching & Defense

Hammonds' mid-80s fastball is hittable, but he must be aggressive with it in order to set up his best pitch, his changeup. He also has a good slider and was learning to mix his pitches well before all his physical ailments cropped up. He has one of the best pickoff moves around and virtually neutralizes the running game. Though he's just a fair fielder, he'll help himself with the bat if he lands back in the National League.

1998 Outlook

In mid-July of 1995, Hammond owned a 6-2, 2.28 record. Since then, his career has unraveled. It remains to be seen whether he can recapture the form he showed a couple of years ago, when he seemed so close to establishing himself as a fine pitcher. As a lefty, he's probably got several more chances coming.

Bill Haselman

' Traded To —
RANGERS

Position: C
Bats: R **Throws:** R
Ht: 6' 3" **Wt:** 223

Opening Day Age: 31
Born: 5/25/66 in Long Branch, NJ
ML Seasons: 7
Pronunciation: HASS-ul-mun

Overall Statistics

	G	AB	R	H	D	T	HR	RBI	SB	BB	SO	Avg	OBP	Slg
1997	67	212	22	50	15	0	6	26	0	15	44	.236	.290	.392
Career	319	853	110	210	49	3	25	110	7	67	168	.246	.304	.399

1997 Situational Stats

	AB	H	HR	RBI	Avg		AB	H	HR	RBI	Avg
Home	96	24	3	13	.250	LHP	102	27	4	10	.265
Road	116	26	3	13	.224	RHP	110	23	2	16	.209
First Half	149	36	3	18	.242	Sc Pos	53	14	1	17	.264
Scnd Half	63	14	3	8	.222	Clutch	35	6	0	2	.171

1997 Season

The long, hard road traveled by Bill Haselman got him a starting job in Boston. The former Rangers first-round pick, whose Texas career was ruined by shoulder problems, got hurt again. He had slight shoulder and back problems, and was run over by the Mets' Carl Everett and suffered a severe neck injury. He also broke a thumb in June. By season's end, he was sent back to Texas in a deal for Jim Leyritz.

Hitting, Baserunning & Defense

It has appeared that Haselman could hit if given the opportunity. He is big and strong, and if he is sitting on fastballs he can pull them or react and get breaking balls in the air with power. When he's hitting well, he'll take both outside fastballs and inside pitches to the opposite field with power. Haselman is very athletic, but he has some problems receiving and his hands are merely adequate. His throwing is below average. Basestealing is not part of his game.

1998 Outlook

Moving in behind Pudge Rodriguez, it may be that Haselman's window of opportunity passed. Still, he's very intelligent. Even if he never gets another chance to play every day, he can carve out a decent long-term career as a backup.

Butch Henry

Position: RP/SP
Bats: L **Throws:** L
Ht: 6' 1" **Wt:** 205

Opening Day Age: 29
Born: 10/7/68 in El Paso, TX
ML Seasons: 5

Overall Statistics

	W	L	Pct.	ERA	G	GS	Sv	IP	H	BB	SO	HR	Ratio
1997	7	3	.700	3.52	36	5	6	84.1	89	19	51	6	1.28
Career	31	33	.484	3.77	139	85	7	587.0	639	136	324	58	1.32

1997 Situational Stats

	W	L	ERA	Sv	IP		AB	H	HR	RBI	Avg
Home	3	1	2.37	0	38.0	LHB	65	20	1	5	.308
Road	4	2	4.47	6	46.1	RHB	256	69	5	28	.270
First Half	2	2	2.96	4	27.1	Sc Pos	82	19	3	28	.232
Scnd Half	5	1	3.79	2	57.0	Clutch	106	30	3	11	.283

1997 Season

Last September, nearly two full years after breaking down and undergoing Tommy John surgery, Butch Henry was back in a major league rotation. Henry actually was throwing 2-3 MPH harder than he had at his peak in 1995. Manager Jimy Williams brought Henry along slowly. He began the season in the extended-spring program in Florida and worked out of the Red Sox bullpen through August. In five starts down the stretch, Henry was 2-1, 1.48.

Pitching & Defense

Henry's sinker runs away from righthanders, and by the end of the season was up to 88 MPH. Because he didn't get as many ground balls in 1997 as he had in the past, there's every reason to believe his sinker will have more consistent bite this season. His best pitch is his changeup, which he will throw at any time. His breaking ball is fair. With his compact delivery, basestealers haven't been a problem. His fielding is acceptable.

1998 Outlook

If Henry holds up, the Red Sox believe they have a quality lefthanded starter, as evidenced by their decision to protect him in the expansion draft over Jeff Suppan. But Henry hasn't pitched as many as 127 innings in a year since 1992.

Shane Mack

Position: CF
Bats: R **Throws:** R
Ht: 6' 0" **Wt:** 190

Opening Day Age: 34
Born: 12/7/63 in Los Angeles, CA
ML Seasons: 8

Overall Statistics

	G	AB	R	H	D	T	HR	RBI	SB	BB	SO	Avg	OBP	Slg
1997	60	130	13	41	7	0	3	17	2	9	24	.315	.368	.438
Career	854	2648	405	795	140	27	74	369	82	241	473	.300	.366	.457

1997 Situational Stats

	AB	H	HR	RBI	Avg		AB	H	HR	RBI	Avg
Home	69	19	2	8	.275	LHP	59	18	1	5	.305
Road	61	22	1	9	.361	RHP	71	23	2	12	.324
First Half	95	30	3	12	.316	Sc Pos	41	10	0	13	.244
Scnd Half	35	11	0	5	.314	Clutch	23	6	0	3	.261

1997 Season

It was a bitter homecoming for Shane Mack. After spending two years in Japan, he signed with the Red Sox and was expected to help them in center field. But he hurt his hand in the spring, and the Sox found out that chronic shoulder problems had rendered his throwing arm virtually useless. Although he hit like the Mack of old when given the chance, he spent most of the season on the bench.

Hitting, Baserunning & Defense

At the plate, Mack still makes his living by ripping into the first good pitch he sees. He hits hard liners to all fields and has the speed to turn them into doubles and triples when they split the gaps. He still excels against lefthanders. He still has the mobility to cover center field, but his arm is such a liability that even left field would be a challenge. He used to steal a base from time to time, but hasn't run much since he left for Japan.

1998 Outlook

Mack became a free agent after the season, and unless he's able to convince people that he still can play the field, his options may be severely limited. Although he's still a good pure hitter, he lacks the power to make it as a DH. He'd make a good fourth outfielder if he can prove that he can get by defensively.

Bret Saberhagen

Position: SP
Bats: R **Throws:** R
Ht: 6' 1" **Wt:** 200

Opening Day Age: 33
Born: 4/11/64 in
Chicago Heights, IL
ML Seasons: 13

Overall Statistics

	W	L	Pct.	ERA	G	GS	Sv	IP	H	BB	SO	HR	Ratio
1997	0	1	.000	6.58	6	6	0	26.0	30	10	14	5	1.54
Career	141	101	.583	3.30	343	315	1	2253.2	2130	431	1524	182	1.14

1997 Situational Stats

	W	L	ERA	Sv	IP		AB	H	HR	RBI	Avg
Home	0	0	2.70	0	10.0	LHB	61	20	4	16	.328
Road	0	1	9.00	0	16.0	RHB	43	10	1	3	.233
First Half	0	0	-	0	0.0	Sc Pos	31	9	2	14	.290
Scnd Half	0	1	6.58	0	26.0	Clutch	0	0	0	0	-

1997 Season

In spring training it was a test for Bret Saberhagen to throw a baseball just 60 feet, but he built up his arm as the season went along. He went through three farm teams and finally made it to a major league mound for the first time in two years in the last week of August. He threw well at times, reaching the mid-90s on the radar gun, but the rust showed in his six starts.

Pitching & Defense

As he rehabbed last summer, it took Saberhagen only a few starts to rediscover the command of the fastball that made him so good. When he had his best seasons, he had command and full use of his curveball, which was not back in 1997 but may yet return. Saberhagen is a very agile fielder. He is so self-confident on the mound that he seldom makes bad decisions, and his delivery is so compact that basestealers never have been a problem.

1998 Outlook

Saberhagen goes to spring training at a crossroads. His physical well-being always will be a concern. It has been nine years since he last won as many as 15 games or threw 200 innings. The most likely scenario is that he'll pitch well when healthy, whenever that may be.

John Wasdin

Position: RP/SP
Bats: R **Throws:** R
Ht: 6' 2" **Wt:** 190

Opening Day Age: 25
Born: 8/5/72 in Fort
Belvoir, VA
ML Seasons: 3

Overall Statistics

	W	L	Pct.	ERA	G	GS	Sv	IP	H	BB	SO	HR	Ratio
1997	4	6	.400	4.40	53	7	0	124.2	121	38	84	18	1.28
Career	13	14	.481	5.17	83	30	0	273.1	280	91	165	46	1.36

1997 Situational Stats

	W	L	ERA	Sv	IP		AB	H	HR	RBI	Avg
Home	2	4	5.04	0	60.2	LHB	235	64	10	43	.272
Road	2	2	3.80	0	64.0	RHB	247	57	8	28	.231
First Half	3	3	4.93	0	76.2	Sc Pos	124	34	6	55	.274
Scnd Half	1	3	3.56	0	48.0	Clutch	89	26	4	15	.292

1997 Season

John Wasdin was the player the Red Sox got from Oakland for Jose Canseco. While there were flashes of promise, the former first-round pick's guiding word is still "potential." He dropped out of the starting rotation by the middle of May. By September, he was hitting 94 MPH on the radar gun and pitching effectively, giving a glimmer of what the Athletics saw when they took him in the first round of the 1993 draft.

Pitching & Defense

The problem throughout Wasdin's brief major league career has been that he leaves his fastball up in the strike zone, where it flattens out and gets crushed. He has an erratic release point on his breaking ball, and he rushes his delivery. In stretches where he overcame his bad habits, he was very tough with his fastball, a hard slider and changeup. Wasdin is an average fielder, although he is quick on his feet. He's relatively easy to run on.

1998 Outlook

Wasdin is only 25 and he has made 30 big league starts. It took Curt Schilling two years of relief work to put it together. Wasdin doesn't have quite the same stuff, but he eventually may develop into a useful starter.

Mike Benjamin (**Pos**: 3B/SS, **Age**: 32, **Bats**: R)

	G	AB	R	H	D	T	HR	RBI	SB	BB	SO	Avg	OBP	Slg
1997	49	116	12	27	9	1	0	7	2	4	27	.233	.262	.328
Career	383	856	104	175	40	5	17	71	26	52	190	.204	.260	.322

Utilityman Benjamin played four positions and even pitched an inning for the Red Sox last year. He re-upped with Boston as a free agent. 1998 Outlook: B

Toby Borland (**Pos**: RHP, **Age**: 28)

	W	L	Pct.	ERA	G	GS	Sv	IP	H	BB	SO	HR	Ratio
1997	0	1	.000	7.56	16	0	1	16.2	17	21	8	2	2.28
Career	9	7	.563	3.96	159	0	8	215.2	212	115	169	15	1.52

Borland walked seven batters in 3⅓ innings after coming over from the Mets in a minor trade. Confidence may be a problem. He signed a minor league deal with the Reds in the offseason. 1998 Outlook: C

Mark Brandenburg (**Pos**: RHP, **Age**: 27)

	W	L	Pct.	ERA	G	GS	Sv	IP	H	BB	SO	HR	Ratio
1997	0	2	.000	5.49	31	0	0	41.0	49	16	34	3	1.59
Career	5	8	.385	4.49	97	0	0	144.1	161	56	121	16	1.50

The sidearmer missed most of the first half with shoulder problems and got bombed when he returned. He pitched well in the second half, then went to the Rangers in the Aaron Sele deal. 1998 Outlook: B

Rich Garces (**Pos**: RHP, **Age**: 26)

	W	L	Pct.	ERA	G	GS	Sv	IP	H	BB	SO	HR	Ratio
1997	0	1	1.000	4.61	12	0	0	13.2	14	9	12	2	1.68
Career	3	5	.375	4.32	75	0	2	91.2	89	59	93	8	1.61

Garces got demoted in June but pitched well enough in the minors in the second half to get another chance. 1998 Outlook: C

Ken Grundt (**Pos**: LHP, **Age**: 28)

	W	L	Pct.	ERA	G	GS	Sv	IP	H	BB	SO	HR	Ratio
1997	0	0	-	9.00	2	0	0	3.0	5	0	0	0	1.67
Career	0	0	-	10.80	3	0	0	3.1	6	0	0	0	1.80

Grundt is a lefty, and his virtues end there. He's 28 and did nothing in Triple-A last year that would suggest that he could help a major league team. 1998 Outlook: D

Joe Hudson (**Pos**: RHP, **Age**: 27)

	W	L	Pct.	ERA	G	GS	Sv	IP	H	BB	SO	HR	Ratio
1997	3	1	.750	3.53	26	0	0	35.2	39	14	14	1	1.49
Career	6	7	.462	4.41	101	0	2	126.2	149	69	62	7	1.72

The groundballer spent two stints with the Red Sox last year, posting unremarkable numbers in middle relief. He has little value. 1998 Outlook: C

Kerry Lacy (**Pos**: RHP, **Age**: 25)

	W	L	Pct.	ERA	G	GS	Sv	IP	H	BB	SO	HR	Ratio
1997	1	1	.500	6.11	33	0	3	45.2	60	11	21	7	1.55
Career	3	1	.750	5.59	44	0	3	56.1	75	30	27	9	1.86

Lacy posted a 2.30 ERA in May, but that mark soared to 8.10 in the following months. There was some thought he was Boston's closer of the future, but that's a reach. 1998 Outlook: B

Derek Lowe (**Pos**: RHP, **Age**: 24)

	W	L	Pct.	ERA	G	GS	Sv	IP	H	BB	SO	HR	Ratio
1997	2	6	.250	6.13	20	9	0	69.0	74	23	52	11	1.41
Career	2	6	.250	6.13	20	9	0	69.0	74	23	52	11	1.41

Lowe emerged as a prospect in the Mariners chain last year and was dealt to Boston in the Heathcliff Slocumb deal. After the deal, he pitched well in Triple-A and with Boston. A decent sleeper pick. 1998 Outlook: B

Ron Mahay (**Pos**: LHP, **Age**: 26)

	W	L	Pct.	ERA	G	GS	Sv	IP	H	BB	SO	HR	Ratio
1997	3	0	1.000	2.52	28	0	0	25.0	19	11	22	3	1.20
Career	3	0	1.000	2.52	28	0	0	25.0	19	11	22	3	1.20

The converted outfielder proved to a valuable lefthanded reliever in the second half, when he limited opponents to a .204 batting average. He can pitch. 1998 Outlook: B

Pat Mahomes (**Pos**: RHP, **Age**: 27)

	W	L	Pct.	ERA	G	GS	Sv	IP	H	BB	SO	HR	Ratio
1997	1	0	1.000	8.10	10	0	0	10.0	15	10	5	2	2.50
Career	21	28	.429	5.88	135	51	5	389.0	428	205	228	72	1.63

The Red Sox converted Mahomes to a closer at Triple-A, but appeared unwilling to give him an extended trial in the majors. He signed to play in Japan in late June, and didn't encounter much success there. 1998 Outlook: D

Jose Malave (**Pos**: LF, **Age**: 26, **Bats**: R)

	G	AB	R	H	D	T	HR	RBI	SB	BB	SO	Avg	OBP	Slg
1997	4	4	0	0	0	0	0	0	0	0	2	.000	.000	.000
Career	45	106	12	24	3	0	4	17	0	2	27	.226	.248	.368

All Malave has is power, and he hasn't come close to duplicating his remarkable 1994 season. He's 26 and righthanded, and his chance seems to have passed him by. 1998 Outlook: C

Walt McKeel (**Pos**: C, **Age**: 26, **Bats**: R)

	G	AB	R	H	D	T	HR	RBI	SB	BB	SO	Avg	OBP	Slg
1997	5	3	0	0	0	0	0	0	0	0	1	.000	.000	.000
Career	6	3	0	0	0	0	0	0	0	0	1	.000	.000	.000

After enjoying a breakout year with the bat in '96, McKeel receded in '97. He's a decent catcher with a strong arm, but he's 26 and probably too similar to Jim Leyritz for his own good. 1998 Outlook: C

Rudy Pemberton (**Pos**: RF, **Age**: 28, **Bats**: R)

	G	AB	R	H	D	T	HR	RBI	SB	BB	SO	Avg	OBP	Slg
1997	27	63	8	15	2	0	2	10	0	4	13	.238	.314	.365
Career	52	134	22	45	13	1	3	23	3	7	22	.336	.395	.515

Pemberton seemed to have won a spot as Boston's platoon right fielder in the spring, but the Red Sox gave up on him after nine weeks for reasons that are still unclear. He ended up in Japan, but can hit anywhere. 1998 Outlook: D

Boston Red Sox

Arquimedez Pozo (**Pos**: 3B, **Age**: 24, **Bats**: R)

	G	AB	R	H	D	T	HR	RBI	SB	BB	SO	Avg	OBP	Slg
1997	4	15	0	4	1	0	0	3	0	0	5	.267	.250	.333
Career	26	74	4	14	4	1	1	14	1	2	15	.189	.215	.311

Pozo continues to hit well for age while receiving absolutely zero respect. If he's really as young as he says he is, he could hit enough in the majors to help as a second or third baseman. 1998 Outlook: C

Curtis Pride (**Pos**: LF/DH, **Age**: 29, **Bats**: L)

	G	AB	R	H	D	T	HR	RBI	SB	BB	SO	Avg	OBP	Slg
1997	81	164	22	35	4	4	3	20	6	24	46	.213	.316	.341
Career	234	503	87	130	23	10	14	58	21	60	128	.258	.338	.427

The Red Sox claimed Pride off the Detroit roster late in the year. He may factor into their outfield mix next year but won't be anything more than a backup. 1998 Outlook: C

Jesus Tavarez (**Pos**: CF, **Age**: 27, **Bats**: B)

	G	AB	R	H	D	T	HR	RBI	SB	BB	SO	Avg	OBP	Slg
1997	42	69	12	12	3	1	0	9	0	4	9	.174	.216	.246
Career	220	412	61	99	12	3	2	32	13	28	59	.240	.289	.299

Tavarez spent half the year in Boston as a backup center fielder. He's fast and he switch-hits, but he hasn't shown he can do anything else of interest. He became a free agent over the winter. 1998 Outlook: C

Boston Red Sox Minor League Prospects

Organization Overview:

After years of producing nothing but one-dimensional hitters, the Red Sox now have one of the deepest systems in the game. When Wayne Britton was promoted to scouting director after the 1992 season, Boston started drafting multi-talented athletes and power pitchers, and paying what it took to sign them. The Red Sox' instructional efforts used to be widely ridiculed, but have improved greatly under director of player development Bob Schaefer. Boston even has made inroads on signing international talent, an area it once ignored. Shortstop Nomar Garciaparra is just the first of a wave of talented young players who will arrive in Fenway Park in the next few years.

Robinson Checo

Position: P   **Opening Day Age:** 26
Bats: R **Throws:** R   **Born:** 9/9/71 in
Ht: 6' 1" **Wt:** 165   Santiago, DR

Recent Statistics

	W	L	ERA	G	GS	Sv	IP	H	R	BB	SO	HR
97 A Sarasota	1	4	5.30	11	11	0	56.0	54	37	27	63	9
97 AA Trenton	1	0	2.35	1	1	0	7.2	6	3	1	9	0
97 AAA Pawtucket	4	2	3.42	9	9	0	55.1	41	22	16	56	8
97 AL Boston	1	1	3.38	5	2	0	13.1	12	5	3	14	0

Originally signed by the Angels in 1989 and released a year later, Checo pitched for five seasons in Japan and Korea before the Red Sox purchased him from the Hiroshima Toyo Carp in December 1996. They envisioned him immediately becoming a Mariano Riveraesque setup man, but elbow tendinitis meant Checo started the year in extended spring training. He has the stuff to succeed either as a starter or reliever, throwing a 93-94 MPH fastball and a tough slider. He's also developing a two-seam fastball that sinks, as well as a changeup. He also throws strikes with that impressive arsenal, and looked very good in a September cameo in Boston. He should have a prominent role on the Red Sox staff in 1998, whether it be in the rotation or the bullpen.

Michael Coleman

Position: OF   **Opening Day Age:** 22
Bats: R **Throws:** R   **Born:** 8/16/75 in
Ht: 5' 11" **Wt:** 180   Nashville, TN

Recent Statistics

	G	AB	R	H	D	T	HR	RBI	SB	BB	SO	AVG
97 AA Trenton	102	385	56	116	17	8	14	58	20	41	89	.301
97 AAA Pawtucket	28	113	27	36	9	2	7	19	4	12	27	.319
97 AL Boston	8	24	2	4	1	0	0	2	1	0	11	.167
97 MLE	130	488	71	142	26	7	17	65	15	40	123	.291

Coleman is typical of Boston's new approach to scouting. Headed to the University of Alabama as a blue-chip running back recruit, Coleman instead signed with the Red Sox after they astutely spent an 18th-round pick on

him in 1994. He struggled playing in the spacious ballparks of the high Class A Florida State League in 1996, but rebounded at Double-A Trenton last year and will compete for Boston's center-field job in 1998. His speed makes him a threat on the basepaths and an excellent defensive player, and he has all five tools. He has a quick bat with power and has improved his approach at the plate, though he still strikes out a lot. His arm, which is average, is his worst tool.

Jimmy Hurst

Position: OF   **Opening Day Age:** 26
Bats: R **Throws:** R   **Born:** 3/1/72 in
Ht: 6' 6" **Wt:** 225   Tuscaloosa, AL

Recent Statistics

	G	AB	R	H	D	T	HR	RBI	SB	BB	SO	AVG
97 AA Jacksnville	5	17	5	8	2	0	2	6	0	3	6	.471
97 AAA Toledo	110	377	51	102	11	3	18	58	14	47	115	.271
97 AL Detroit	13	17	1	3	1	0	1	1	0	2	6	.176
97 MLE	115	385	49	101	11	2	18	57	10	44	126	.262

Hurst hit a total of 45 homers in the White Sox system in 1993-94, but tailed off and joined the Tigers on waivers last spring. A member of a national championship basketball team at Three Rivers (Mo.) Junior College that also included the NBA's Latrell Sprewell, Hurst was a 12th-round draft-and-follow in 1990. His age is working against him, but he's a multitool player who can hit for power and run. Managers voted his outfield arm the best in the Triple-A International League. He probably could hit 20-plus homers in the majors, albeit with a lot of strikeouts, and his chances would be enhanced if he'd shorten his swing. Boston picked him up when Detroit designated him for assignment.

Cole Liniak

Position: 3B   **Opening Day Age:** 21
Bats: R **Throws:** R   **Born:** 8/23/76 in
Ht: 6' 1" **Wt:** 181   Encinitas, CA

Recent Statistics

	G	AB	R	H	D	T	HR	RBI	SB	BB	SO	AVG
96 A Michigan	121	437	65	115	26	2	3	46	7	59	59	.263
97 A Sarasota	64	217	32	73	16	0	6	42	1	22	31	.336
97 AA Trenton	53	200	20	56	11	0	2	18	0	17	29	.280

A seventh-round pick out of high school in 1995, Liniak is probably the best pure hitter in the Boston system. He uses the whole field and makes hard contact. How good a player he becomes will depend on how much stronger he gets after hitting just eight homers last year, though to be fair he reached Double-A at 20 and still is developing. Though he doesn't strike out much, he doesn't walk much either. Liniak doesn't run particularly well, but he's no slouch defensively, showing a good first step and an accurate arm. He's between one and two years away from being ready for Boston.

Peter Munro

Position: P

Bats: R **Throws:** R

Ht: 6' 2" **Wt:** 185

Opening Day Age: 22

Born: 6/14/75 in Flushing, NY

Recent Statistics

	W	L	ERA	G	GS	Sv	IP	H	R	BB	SO	HR
96 A Sarasota	11	6	3.60	27	25	1	155.0	153	76	62	115	4
97 AA Trenton	7	10	4.95	22	22	0	116.1	113	76	47	109	12

It was considered a coup when the Red Sox signed Munro for $300,000 in 1994, as a draft-and-follow out of Okaloosa-Walton (Fla.) Community College after spending a sixth-round pick on him a year earlier. He hasn't received the fanfare of a Carl Pavano or Brian Rose, but is a solid prospect in his own right. His 1997 numbers weren't especially pretty, but Boston officials were pleased with his development. He began to locate his 92-93 MPH fastball better, and started to throw his hard curveball and his changeup more often. The Red Sox also like his aggressive approach and could see him in their rotation within a year to a year and a half.

Trot Nixon

Position: OF

Bats: L **Throws:** L

Ht: 6' 1" **Wt:** 195

Opening Day Age: 23

Born: 4/11/74 in Durham, NC

Recent Statistics

	G	AB	R	H	D	T	HR	RBI	SB	BB	SO	AVG
96 AA Trenton	123	438	55	110	11	4	11	63	-7	50	65	.251
97 AAA Pawtucket	130	475	80	116	18	3	20	61	11	63	86	.244
97 MLE	130	469	70	110	18	2	17	54	7	55	90	.235

Nixon was Boston's first draft pick and cost $890,000 to buy away from North Carolina State football in 1993. He was immediately compared to Carl Yastrzemski and to Lenny Dykstra (with more power), but first back problems and now his intensity have curtailed him. Because of his desire to succeed and to make up for lost time, he puts too much pressure on himself. He still has the swing that got him drafted seventh overall, and he has become a solid right fielder. Interestingly, his .244 average in 1997 isn't as bad as it looks (he improved it steadily throughout the year) and his 20 homers aren't as good as they look (Triple-A Pawtucket is a launching pad, and 20 homers there are the equivalent of 13 elsewhere in the International League).

Brian Rose

Position: P

Bats: R **Throws:** R

Ht: 6' 3" **Wt:** 215

Opening Day Age: 22

Born: 2/13/76 in New Bedford, MA

Recent Statistics

	W	L	ERA	G	GS	Sv	IP	H	R	BB	SO	HR
97 AAA Pawtucket	17	5	3.02	27	26	0	190.2	188	74	46	116	21
97 AL Boston	0	0	12.00	1	1	0	3.0	5	4	2	3	0

Rose tied for the minor league lead with 17 wins and was named International League pitcher of the year in 1997. A 1994 third-round pick, he throws a 90-92 MPH fastball with nice movement. He has a good changeup

and throws both a curveball and slider. As good as Rose's stuff is, his strikeouts/innings and hits/innings ratios were rather ordinary last year. He could be in Boston's rotation at the start of 1998.

Donnie Sadler

Position: 2B-SS

Bats: R **Throws:** R

Ht: 5' 6" **Wt:** 165

Opening Day Age: 22

Born: 6/17/75 in Clifton, TX

Recent Statistics

	G	AB	R	H	D	T	HR	RBI	SB	BB	SO	AVG
96 AA Trenton	115	454	68	121	20	8	6	46	34	38	75	.267
97 AAA Pawtucket	125	481	74	102	18	2	11	36	20	57	121	.212
97 MLE	125	476	65	97	18	1	9	31	14	50	127	.204

The Red Sox have touted Sadler as perhaps the fastest player in organization history since signing him as an 11th-rounder in 1994. He signed as a shortstop, had two productive seasons, then took a step back in 1996 when Boston tried to turn him into a center fielder. When that didn't take, he shifted to second because of the presence of Nomar Garciaparra in the system, and took another step back in 1997 at Triple-A Pawtucket. He tried to hit homers, and the result was that he struck out too much and didn't get on base enough to take advantage of his speed. Sadler played a lot of shortstop in the latter months and was adequate, but he's a better defender at second base because his range is better than average. He's not going to displace Garciaparra, and he needs another year in Triple-A to straighten himself out.

Others to Watch

Righthander **Tony Armas Jr.** was supposed to be untouchable in the Yankees system, but George Steinbrenner just had to have Mike Stanley. Boston gladly snapped up the son of the former Red Sox slugger. Tony Jr., 19, has a good curveball and a very projectable fastball. . . The Red Sox think **Matt Kinney**, 21, could be as good as any righthander they have in their system. His fastball and curve are both above-average pitches, with innings and command his primary needs. . . Righthander **Juan Pena** struggled a little bit in Double-A, but he was only 20. His best pitches are his curveball and a changeup, and he's able to locate those and his fastball extremely well. . . Righthander **Chris Reitsma**, 20, was considered one of the steals of the 1996 draft, which is saying something considering that he was a supplemental first-round pick (34th overall). He broke his elbow throwing a pitch, though the Red Sox say that sounds more serious than it was. . . Another player whose 1997 season was ruined by injury was 21-year-old catcher **Damian Sapp**, who didn't make it into a game and required back surgery. Before that, he showed a strong arm and 20-homer potential. . . The Boston catching prospect closest to the majors is **Jason Varitek**, acquired in the Heathcliff Slocumb trade with the Mariners. After an All-America career at Georgia Tech, the 25-year-old Varitek hasn't hit as well as expected. His stroke may be a bit long.

Jerry Manuel

1997 Season

Jerry Manuel served as bench coach for the World Series champion Marlins, and in December he landed his first major league managerial position, taking the reins of the Chicago White Sox. Before coaching under Jim Leyland, he served as Felipe Alou's third-base coach for five years in Montreal. Manuel's low-key approach may be well suited for a clubhouse loaded with strong personalities.

Offense

In Montreal and Florida, Manuel worked with teams that incorporated young players into the lineup. Chicago's lineup figures to include several youngsters this year, and his experience may serve him well. Manuel's biggest challenges will be to plug the White Sox' holes at catcher and shortstop. Neither Alou nor Leyland has been a devotee of the sacrifice bunt or the running game. Manuel says he wants his team to be aggressive, so he may try to steal more often than his former bosses.

Pitching & Defense

During Manuel's brief minor league managerial career, his most obvious strength was his ability to make good use of his bullpen. This is another area in which the White Sox need his expertise, with the status of incumbent closer Matt Karchner uncertain after offseason elbow surgery. Chicago ended 1997 with a bullpen of unproven youngsters, so Manuel will have to choose the best arms and assign them the right roles. He'll also need to ease a couple of youngsters into the starting rotation. His decisions on the catcher and shortstop position may reveal a lot about his belief in the relative important of offense versus defense.

1998 Outlook

Manuel takes over an underachieving team with considerable offensive talent, and the White Sox figure to improve just by playing up to their ability. If Manuel can be at all civil, he'll be a stark contrast to his predecessor, Terry Bevington, who alienated his players, the fans and the media. Manuel has spent his big league coaching career with clubs that built successfully from within. The White Sox hope he can do the same for them.

Born: 12/23/53 in Hahira, GA

Playing Experience: 1975-1982, Det, Mon, SD

Managerial Experience: 0 seasons
Pronunciation: MAN-you-ell

Manager Statistics

Year	Team, Lg	W	L	Pct	GB	Finish
—	—	—	—	—	—	—
—	—	—	—	—	—	—

1997 Starting Pitchers by Days Rest

	≤3	4	5	6+
White Sox Starts	—	—	—	—
White Sox ERA	—	—	—	—
AL Avg Starts	5	89	34	24
AL ERA	4.38	4.60	4.61	5.37

1997 Situational Stats

	Jerry Manuel	AL Average
Hit & Run Success %	—	36.5
Stolen Base Success %	—	67.3
Platoon Pct.	—	59.5
Defensive Subs	—	22
High-Pitch Outings	—	15
Quick/Slow Hooks	—	19/15
Sacrifice Attempts	—	53

1997 Rankings (American League)

⇒ Did not manage in the majors last year

James Baldwin

1997 Season

After an impressive spring training, James Baldwin never got on a roll. He was tough to hit at times but couldn't keep anything going. He tied Doug Drabek for the most victories on the staff, but watched his ERA climb throughout the disappointing season. He had trouble with his control, finishing the season sixth in the American League in walks. Take away a strong run that Baldwin had working with former Sox catcher Chad Kreuter in the first half of 1996, and he's got a career record of 16-21. He was expected to be much better when he was coming up through the system.

Pitching

Baldwin was two different pitchers last year, a good one when he got the leadoff hitter out and a very bad one when teams put runners on base against him. He allowed a .285 batting average with runners in scoring position, and at times appeared to psyche himself out worrying that runners on second base were stealing signs. As a result, Baldwin gave up lots of big innings. He has good velocity on his fastball, but the key is whether he throws his curveball for strikes. He appears to lack the ability to dig deep and get himself out of trouble. As a result, he has only one complete game in 64 career starts.

Defense

Baldwin is a terrific athlete who works hard to keep himself in shape. He does a good job on comebackers and is generally fundamentally sound. He's decent at combatting basestealers, who went 11-for-18 against him in 1997.

1998 Outlook

This is a big season for Baldwin, who should be eligible for arbitration for the first time next winter. He gained lots of experience by hanging around veterans like Doug Drabek and Danny Darwin last year, and should be ready to put those lessons to use. He's no longer the kid of the staff, which means he'll be expected to deliver 15-18 victories. It could be that he's the victim of exaggerated expectations, however.

Position: SP
Bats: R **Throws:** R
Ht: 6' 3" **Wt:** 210

Opening Day Age: 26
Born: 7/15/71 in Southern Pines, NC
ML Seasons: 3

Overall Statistics

	W	L	Pct.	ERA	G	GS	Sv	IP	H	BB	SO	HR	Ratio
1997	12	15	.444	5.27	32	32	0	200.0	205	83	140	19	1.44
Career	23	22	.511	5.18	66	64	0	383.2	405	149	277	49	1.44

How Often He Throws Strikes

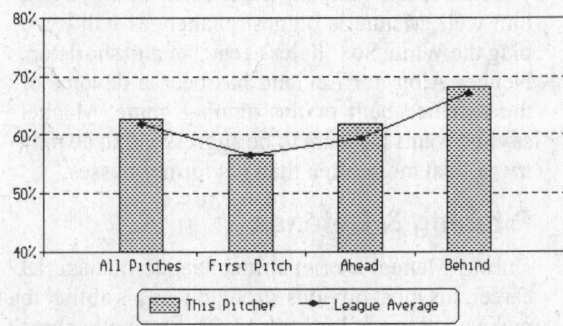

1997 Situational Stats

	W	L	ERA	Sv	IP		AB	H	HR	RBI	Avg
Home	5	7	5.17	0	94.0	LHB	386	107	8	55	.277
Road	7	8	5.35	0	106.0	RHB	396	98	11	55	.247
First Half	6	9	4.70	0	115.0	Sc Pos	207	59	5	87	.285
Scnd Half	6	6	6.04	0	85.0	Clutch	46	23	4	13	.500

1997 Rankings (American League)

⇒ 1st in losses, wild pitches (14) and balks (3)
⇒ 4th in least GDPs induced per 9 innings (0.4) and highest ERA on the road
⇒ 5th in highest ERA and lowest groundball/fly-ball ratio allowed (0.9)
⇒ 6th in walks allowed
⇒ 7th in highest ERA at home
⇒ 10th in least home runs allowed per 9 innings (.86)
⇒ Led the White Sox in ERA, wins, losses, walks allowed, hit batsmen (5), wild pitches (14), balks (3), runners caught stealing (7), lowest slugging percentage allowed (.421), lowest stolen base percentage allowed (61.1%), least home runs allowed per 9 innings (.86), most strikeouts per 9 innings (6.3) and ERA on the road

Albert Belle

Position: LF
Bats: R **Throws:** R
Ht: 6' 2" **Wt:** 210

Opening Day Age: 31
Born: 8/25/66 in Shreveport, LA
ML Seasons: 9

1997 Season

Albert Belle finally met expectations he couldn't fill. He struggled throughout the first year of the five-year, $55-million contract he signed. He didn't make good on his promises for a new start off the field and with the media, sitting out the White Sox' first scheduled autograph session and making himself available only occasionally for interviews. That would have been no big deal if he had led the American League in RBIs for a third consecutive season, but he slipped to eighth. Uncharacteristic slumps in April and July doomed Belle to a subpar season by his standards. He did grind it out, however, playing in all 161 games.

Hitting

Belle missed Jacobs Field badly. Two years after hitting 50 home runs, he didn't get his 30th until the final game of the season. He said he suspected it was more than 400 feet to center field at Comiskey Park, where many of his drives went to die. But his problem wasn't just his new home field. He managed only 16 homers and 55 RBIs on the road, compared to 26 and 79 in 1996. Belle struggled with his mechanics at the plate for much of the season, pulling off the ball. He was often unable to get to pitches on the outside part of the plate, which he normally drives to right field. He often lacked the discipline to take walks, striking out more times than in any season since 1992.

Baserunning & Defense

Belle has worked hard to improve his outfield play. He made several good catches against the fence at Comiskey Park, but he's average at best. He still makes too many errors, and teams run on him. Belle is a clever baserunner who could steal 20 bases a year if his manager let him run. But he's not getting $11 million a year to be Lou Brock.

1998 Outlook

Belle got himself into this mess. His career performance says he'll get himself out of it. After one year with the White Sox, he should be ready for a rebound. Belle could benefit by having Robin Ventura hitting behind him for a full year. Ventura was on the DL when Belle hit .206 in April, setting the tone for an underwhelming season.

Overall Statistics

	G	AB	R	H	D	T	HR	RBI	SB	BB	SO	Avg	OBP	Slg
1997	161	634	90	174	45	1	30	116	4	53	105	.274	.332	.491
Career	1074	4075	682	1188	268	17	272	867	65	449	727	.292	.364	.566

Where He Hits the Ball

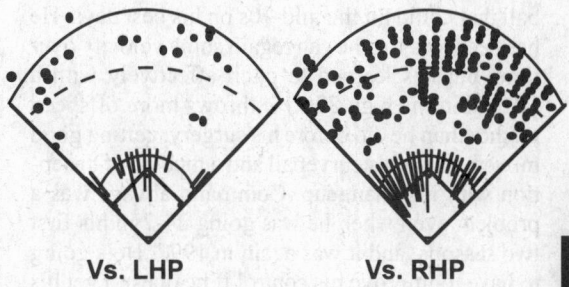

Vs. LHP   **Vs. RHP**

1997 Situational Stats

	AB	H	HR	RBI	Avg		AB	H	HR	RBI	Avg
Home	313	92	14	61	.294	LHP	122	36	7	21	.295
Road	321	82	16	55	.255	RHP	512	138	23	95	.270
First Half	339	101	18	70	.298	Sc Pos	198	50	9	86	.253
Scnd Half	295	73	12	46	.247	Clutch	86	25	4	16	.291

1997 Rankings (American League)

⇒ 1st in GDPs (26)
⇒ 2nd in errors in left field (10) and lowest fielding percentage in left field (.972)
⇒ 3rd in doubles and games played (161)
⇒ 4th in at-bats
⇒ Led the White Sox in at-bats, doubles, sacrifice flies (8), hit by pitch (6), strikeouts, GDPs (26), games played (161), batting average vs. lefthanded pitchers, cleanup slugging percentage (.491), slugging percentage vs. lefthanded pitchers (.525) and on-base percentage vs. lefthanded pitchers (.399)

1997 Season

There were times when the wunderkind of the White Sox' ultra-solid 1993 rotation wondered if he would ever make it back to Comiskey Park. Two years of elbow problems led to reconstructive surgery in September 1996, and the recovery was a torturous process for Jason Bere. He spent most of the season either rehabilitating in Sarasota, Florida, or wandering the minor leagues on rehab assignments. But he ended the season extremely encouraged, the result of four wins in six starts down the stretch. The best news was that he appeared to be healthy again.

Pitching

Bere came to the major leagues at 22 with a fastball that could hit the mid-90s on his best days. He has been told that he can regain some velocity over time, but has learned to pitch effectively with a fastball in the high 80s. He throws more offspeed pitches than he did before his surgery, getting good movement on his curveball and a nice bit of deception with his changeup. Command always was a problem even when he was going 24-7 in his first two seasons, and it was again in 1997. He's going to have to improve his control if he doesn't get his fastball back, or else he could fall victim to a lot of big innings.

Defense

Bere comes off the mound somewhat awkwardly but is an average fielder. He does a so-so job keeping runners close, though basestealers went 3-for-3 during his limited 1997 stint.

1998 Outlook

Until Bere holds together for 30 starts and 200 innings, he's going to be a question mark. He hasn't pitched more than 140 innings since 1994, when he led the American League in winning percentage and was an All-Star. But his late-season stint with the Sox last year suggested that he could become a frontline starter once again. He has gone through a lot at a young age, which could prove invaluable over the next decade if his elbow is able to take the wear and tear of pitching.

Position: SP
Bats: R **Throws:** R
Ht: 6' 3" **Wt:** 215

Opening Day Age: 26
Born: 5/26/71 in Cambridge, MA
ML Seasons: 5
Pronunciation: BURR-ay

Overall Statistics

	W	L	Pct	ERA	G	GS	Sv	IP	H	BB	SO	HR	Ratio
1997	4	2	.667	4.71	6	6	0	28.2	20	17	21	4	1.29
Career	36	25	.590	4.99	86	86	0	467.1	425	302	406	57	1.56

How Often He Throws Strikes

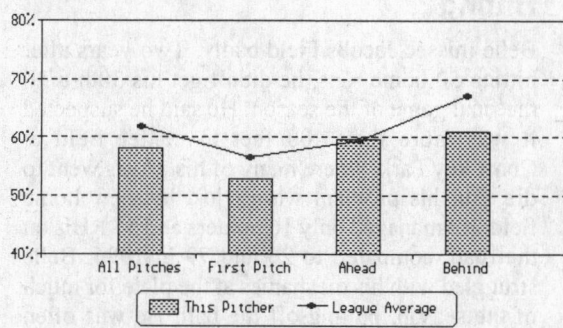

1997 Situational Stats

	W	L	ERA	Sv	IP		AB	H	HR	RBI	Avg
Home	3	1	4.15	0	21.2	LHB	50	14	2	8	.280
Road	1	1	6.43	0	7.0	RHB	51	6	2	6	.118
First Half	0	0	-	0	0.0	Sc Pos	23	8	0	9	.348
Scnd Half	4	2	4.71	0	28.2	Clutch	3	1	0	0	.333

1997 Rankings (American League)

⇒ Did not rank near the top or bottom in any category

Mike Cameron

Future All-Star

1997 Season

A slow start in spring training caused Mike Cameron to begin the year at Triple-A Nashville, but he quickly showed that his 1996 breakthrough season at Double-A Brimingham was no fluke. He joined the White Sox in early May and quickly established that he wasn't going back to the minor leagues. He gave the slow-footed Sox some needed speed on the bases and athleticism in the field. He established himself as a dangerous hitter despite some large holes in his swing. He played both center and right field, making the team's defensive play of the year by leaping above the Metrodome wall to make a running catch, robbing Roberto Kelly of a home run.

Hitting

Cameron has struck out at least 100 times for five consecutive seasons, but works his share of walks. He gave away some at-bats by chasing sliders before hitting instructor Ron Jackson worked with him to lay off them. He has good power to the gaps and can crush mistakes. He should hit 20-25 homers if he plays every day. There's no good reason to sit him down, as he hit better against righthanders than lefties in 1997.

Baserunning & Defense

Cameron should develop into a terrific center fielder but is going through some growing pains as he learns his way around the American League. He has the speed to cover lots of ground in the gaps, but often has to use that speed to make up for late breaks. He can leap against the wall to make catches, but misses catchable balls over his head. He has a strong arm, but wasn't an accurate thrower in 1997. He has great instincts on the bases and is a good basestealer who avoids getting picked off.

1998 Outlook

Barring injury, Cameron should start 130-150 games in center field. The defection of free agent Dave Martinez clears the way for Cameron. He has All-Star potential, but probably needs one or two more years to get to that level.

Position: CF/RF
Bats: R **Throws:** R
Ht: 6' 2" **Wt:** 190

Opening Day Age: 25
Born: 1/8/73 in La Grange, GA
ML Seasons: 3

Overall Statistics

	G	AB	R	H	D	T	HR	RBI	SB	BB	SO	Avg	OBP	Slg
1997	116	379	63	98	18	3	14	55	23	55	105	.259	.356	.433
Career	155	428	68	106	20	3	15	57	23	59	123	.248	.342	.414

Where He Hits the Ball

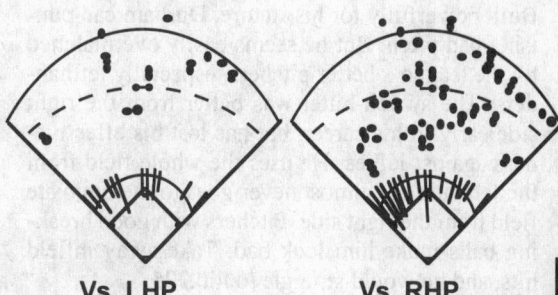

Vs. LHP   **Vs. RHP**

1997 Situational Stats

	AB	H	HR	RBI	Avg		AB	H	HR	RBI	Avg
Home	176	48	10	31	.273	LHP	114	26	4	15	.228
Road	203	50	4	24	.246	RHP	265	72	10	40	.272
First Half	137	34	6	16	.248	Sc Pos	93	29	2	41	.312
Scnd Half	242	64	8	39	.264	Clutch	43	11	0	8	.256

1997 Rankings (American League)

⇒ 1st in stolen base percentage (92.0%)
⇒ 2nd in errors in center field (5) and lowest fielding percentage in center field (.984)
⇒ 8th in lowest batting average vs. lefthanded pitchers
⇒ 9th in stolen bases
⇒ Led the White Sox in strikeouts and stolen base percentage (92.0%)

Chicago White Sox

Ray Durham

1997 Season

Suspicions about Tony Phillips' drug use probably had more to do with their decision to trade Phillips, but the White Sox believed Ray Durham was ready to be their leadoff hitter. Afterward, they wondered how they could have been so wrong watching the third-year second baseman get himself out repeatedly on pitches out of the strike zone. He vowed to use the same approach batting leadoff as he had when he was hitting elsewhere in the order. The result was 96 strikeouts and a .337 on-base average, poor figures for a top-of-the-order hitter.

Hitting

Built powerfully for his stature, Durham can punish a bad pitch. But he seems easily overmatched by the league's better pitchers, especially lefthanders. The switch-hitter was better from the right side early in his career, but has lost his effectiveness against lefties. He uses the whole field from the left side but almost never goes to the opposite field from the right side. Pitchers with good breaking balls make him look bad. Take away infield hits, and he would struggle to hit .225.

Baserunning & Defense

Durham looks like he should be a solid second baseman but remains subpar. He reacts to balls slowly off the bat, keeping him from covering much ground, and has only an average arm. He and Ozzie Guillen were among the worst double-play combinations in the major leagues last year. He hasn't learned how to fully exploit his speed on the bases. He was tied for second in the AL in caught stealings last year, making former manager Terry Bevington hesitant to give him the steal sign. He did better when running on his own.

1998 Outlook

With the White Sox having to replace Guillen, they're willing to give Durham another chance as the top second baseman. But he needs a good year in the leadoff spot to hold his position for the future. Some scouts believe Durham would make a very good left fielder, but the Sox aren't in the market for one.

Position: 2B
Bats: B **Throws:** R
Ht: 5' 8" **Wt:** 170

Opening Day Age: 26
Born: 11/30/71 in Charlotte, NC
ML Seasons: 3

Overall Statistics

	G	AB	R	H	D	T	HR	RBI	SB	BB	SO	Avg	OBP	Slg
1997	155	634	106	172	27	5	11	53	33	61	96	.271	.337	.382
Career	436	1662	253	446	87	16	28	169	81	150	274	.268	.334	.390

Where He Hits the Ball

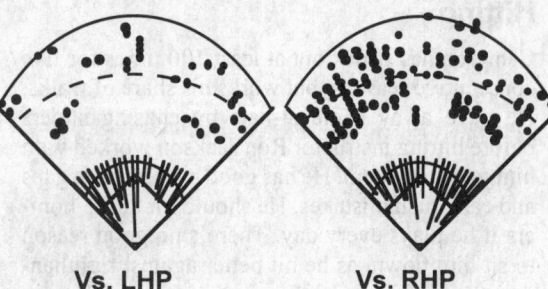

Vs. LHP   **Vs. RHP**

1997 Situational Stats

	AB	H	HR	RBI	Avg		AB	H	HR	RBI	Avg
Home	295	76	3	29	.258	LHP	177	42	3	10	.237
Road	339	96	8	24	.283	RHP	457	130	8	43	.284
First Half	344	87	5	29	.253	Sc Pos	130	31	1	43	.238
Scnd Half	290	85	6	24	.293	Clutch	91	23	0	5	.253

1997 Rankings (American League)

⇒ 1st in errors at second base (18)
⇒ 2nd in caught stealing (16) and lowest fielding percentage at second base (.974)
⇒ 4th in at-bats and pitches seen (2,807)
⇒ 5th in singles, plate appearances (711) and bunts in play (22)
⇒ Led the White Sox in at-bats, singles, sacrifice flies (8), stolen bases, caught stealing (16), hit by pitch (6), pitches seen (2,807), plate appearances (711), highest groundball/flyball ratio (1.6), bunts in play (22) and steals of third (5)

Ozzie Guillen

1997 Season

Ozzie Guillen's experience told him not to join in the spring-training optimism about the addition of Albert Belle meaning a 100-win season for the White Sox. "It will either be a great season", Guillen said, "or a miserable (bleeping) season." Bingo. No Sox player went through more angst than Guillen, who couldn't convince management to hold onto him for a 14th season in Chicago. He smashed a clubhouse television in one display of emotion and was uncharacteristically ejected from two games. He received five standing ovations from the Comiskey Park crowd in the season's final game, but it wasn't the farewell of his dreams.

Hitting

In the 6,451st and final plate appearance of his Sox career, the slap-hitting Guillen set up a big inning by working Kansas City's Scott Service for a walk. "I should take that approach and use it the rest of my career," he said afterward. Guillen considered 1997 a successful season because he had both 50 runs and 50 RBI for the first time since 1990, but his free-swinging nature left him as one of the easiest outs in the American League. He did hit lefthanders better than in previous years. He's a good contact hitter who can put fastballs and breaking pitches in play.

Baserunning & Defense

Guillen is still a reliable shortstop but is now limited both by his lack of range and arm strength. He seems a step slow going to his left, allowing too many balls to go up the middle. He is bettter going to his right but can't get many outs throwing across his body. He and Ray Durham were among the AL's worst double-play combinations. Guillen rarely tries to steal bases and is notorious for missing signs, probably because he carries on a running dialogue with umpires and opposing players.

1998 Outlook

Guillen believes he should be a regular for a few more years, but he could be headed for an end-of-the-career run as a backup middle infielder. That assumes he'll play for a fraction of the $4.5 million salary he had last year.

Position: SS
Bats: L **Throws:** R
Ht: 5'11" **Wt:** 164

Opening Day Age: 34
Born: 1/20/64 in Ocumare del Tuy, VZ
ML Seasons: 13
Pronunciation: GHEY-un

Overall Statistics

	G	AB	R	H	D	T	HR	RBI	SB	BB	SO	Avg	OBP	Slg
1997	142	490	59	120	21	6	4	52	5	22	24	.245	.275	.337
Career	1743	6067	693	1608	240	68	24	565	163	193	460	.265	.286	.339

Where He Hits the Ball

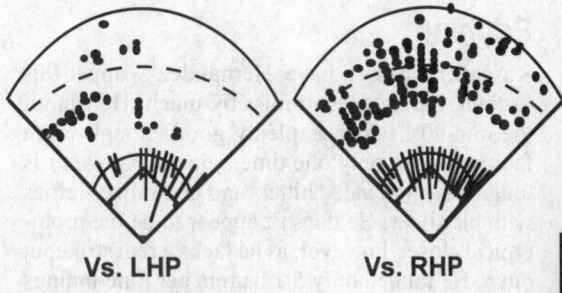

Vs. LHP   **Vs. RHP**

1997 Situational Stats

	AB	H	HR	RBI	Avg		AB	H	HR	RBI	Avg
Home	236	62	1	24	.263	LHP	108	30	1	9	.278
Road	254	58	3	28	.228	RHP	382	90	3	43	.236
First Half	271	74	1	18	.273	Sc Pos	102	29	2	45	.284
Scnd Half	219	46	3	34	.210	Clutch	86	22	1	11	.256

1997 Rankings (American League)

⇒ 1st in least pitches seen per plate appearance (2.78), lowest slugging percentage vs. righthanded pitchers (.325), lowest on-base percentage vs. righthanded pitchers (.262) and highest percentage of swings on the first pitch (45.2%)
⇒ 3rd in lowest on-base percentage
⇒ 4th in sacrifice bunts (11), lowest HR frequency (122.5 ABs per HR) and lowest batting average on the road
⇒ 5th in lowest slugging percentage
⇒ Led the White Sox in triples and sacrifice bunts (11)

Matt Karchner

1997 Season

Matt Karchner received a wakeup call in spring training, failing to break camp with a team most had penciled him on. He responded with the best season of his nine-year professional career. He pitched well in April at Triple-A Nashville, earning a return to the White Sox in mid-May. He worked his way up the pitching staff, going from long man to set-up man and—after Roberto Hernandez was traded to San Francisco—finally to closer. He set a career high with 52 appearances and opened eyes around the major leagues by converting 15 straight save opportunities from July 31-September 13. His season ended prematurely, as a sore elbow caused him to be shut down for the last two weeks.

Pitching

Karchner doesn't have Hernandez's upper-90s fastball, but he doesn't miss by much. He can hit the mid-90s, which is plenty good enough when facing a hitter only one time a game. Karchner is tough on righthanded hitters and neutralizes lefties with his slider. He doesn't appear to be the prototypical closer, however, as he lacks a real strikeout pitch. He fanned only 5.1 batters per nine innings with the Sox in 1997.

Fielding

The 6-foot-4 Karchner could be described as lumbering. He seldom seems to get to comebackers. He has an ordinary pickoff move but can be tough to run on because of his willingness to rely on his fastball.

1998 Outlook

Despite his sensational performance as Hernandez' replacement, the White Sox weren't expected to put Karchner on their 15-man protected list for the expansion draft. They believe they'll have to look elsewhere for the long-term answer in late relief, though Karchner could emerge as a key man in a bullpen-by-committee arrangement if he remains with the Sox. There's much concern about his durability. He has been on the disabled list in five different seasons and can't be counted on to be available every day.

Position: RP
Bats: R **Throws:** R
Ht: 6' 4" **Wt:** 210

Opening Day Age: 30
Born: 6/28/67 in Berwick, PA
ML Seasons: 3

Overall Statistics

	W	L	Pct.	ERA	G	GS	Sv	IP	H	BB	SO	HR	Ratio
1997	3	1	.750	2.91	52	0	15	52.2	50	26	30	4	1.44
Career	14	7	.667	3.81	133	0	16	144.0	144	79	100	16	1.55

How Often He Throws Strikes

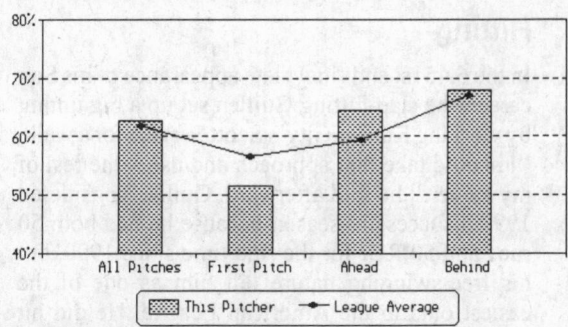

1997 Situational Stats

	W	L	ERA	Sv	IP		AB	H	HR	RBI	Avg
Home	3	1	3.38	8	26.2	LHB	71	18	1	8	.254
Road	0	0	2.42	7	26.0	RHB	123	32	3	14	.260
First Half	2	0	2.16	0	25.0	Sc Pos	65	15	0	17	.231
Scnd Half	1	1	3.58	15	27.2	Clutch	114	24	3	11	.211

1997 Rankings (American League)

⇒ Led the White Sox in most GDPs induced per GDP situation (17.0%)

Dave Martinez

1997 Season

Some guys get better with age. That continues to be the case with Dave Martinez, who opened the season as the White Sox' starting center fielder and split time between center, right field and first base after the emergence of rookie Mike Cameron. He was as reliable as anyone in the lineup except Frank Thomas, avoiding long slumps while setting career highs in at-bats and home runs. He was a valuable contributor off the bench when he wasn't in the lineup. Martinez is an upbeat presence in an often dreary clubhouse.

Hitting

The lefthanded-hitting Martinez once was looked at strictly as a platoon hitter. But he batted .259 against lefties in 1997, earning the opportunity to stay in the lineup against all but the toughest southpaws. He's got a quick, short stroke that allows him to hold his own against power pitchers. He pulled the ball well at times last season, which allowed him to hit for more power. Former Sox hitting coach Bill Buckner believes Martinez has the potential to hit 20-25 homers if he turns on the ball more, but he's valuable as a contact hitter with gap power. He's a good situational hitter and an excellent bunter, a trait devalued by the American League game.

Baserunning & Defense

There's nothing flashy about Martinez, but he's solid at all three outfield positions and at first base. His range at first base is above average. He seldom seems to make mistakes in the field, and he has a strong and accurate arm. He's an alert and aggressive baserunner.

1998 Outlook

Martinez signed with Tampa Bay as a free agent. He's a candidate to start on an outfield corner. If he's not an everyday player, he would be one of the American League's best fourth outfielders.

Position: RF/1B/CF
Bats: L **Throws:** L
Ht: 5'10" **Wt:** 175

Opening Day Age: 33
Born: 9/26/64 in Brooklyn, NY
ML Seasons: 12

Overall Statistics

	G	AB	R	H	D	T	HR	RBI	SB	BB	SO	Avg	OBP	Slg
1997	145	504	78	144	16	6	12	55	12	55	69	.286	.356	.413
Career	1433	4278	592	1181	172	59	75	427	151	401	648	.276	.339	.396

Where He Hits the Ball

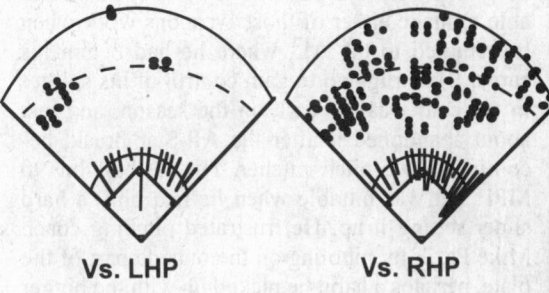

Vs. LHP   **Vs. RHP**

1997 Situational Stats

	AB	H	HR	RBI	Avg		AB	H	HR	RBI	Avg
Home	241	74	5	28	.307	LHP	85	22	3	8	.259
Road	263	70	7	27	.266	RHP	419	122	9	47	.291
First Half	256	72	10	38	.281	Sc Pos	117	31	4	40	.265
Scnd Half	248	72	2	17	.290	Clutch	77	26	1	11	.338

1997 Rankings (American League)

⇒ 2nd in highest percentage of extra bases taken as a runner (72.7%)
⇒ 3rd in least GDPs per GDP situation (3.7%)
⇒ 4th in lowest percentage of swings that missed (9.6%)
⇒ 5th in lowest percentage of swings on the first pitch (14.3%)
⇒ Led the White Sox in triples, most pitches seen per plate appearance (4.00), least GDPs per GDP situation (3.7%), batting average in the clutch, batting average with the bases loaded (.583), lowest percentage of swings that missed (9.6%), highest percentage of swings put into play (49.9%), highest percentage of extra bases taken as a runner (72.7%) and lowest percentage of swings on the first pitch (14.3%)

Chicago White Sox

99

Jaime Navarro

1997 Season

After being signed to a $20 million contract, Jaime Navarro gave the White Sox a performance that wasn't worth 20 cents on the dollar. The Sox handed him the mantle of staff ace upon the departure of Alex Fernandez, and he responded with the worst ERA in the American League. He was penciled in for 225-250 innings, and to ensure he got them former manager Terry Bevington left him in to allow nine-plus runs six times, including a career-worst 11 runs in two different starts.

Pitching

A good split-finger pitch and an ability to work on the outside corner of the plate helped Navarro win 15 games with the Cubs in 1996. But he wasn't able to make either of those weapons work when he returned to the AL, where he had begun his career. He struggled to gain control of his splitter in the cold weather early in the season, and just about abandoned it after the All-Star break, becoming a two-pitch pitcher. His fastball hit 90 MPH but was hittable when he had only a hard slider setting it up. He frustrated pitching coach Mike Pazik by nibbling on the outside part of the plate, perhaps a habit he picked up with the bigger strike zones of National League umpires. Navarro allowed hitters to become comfortable, almost never knocking them off the inside part of the plate.

Defense

Navarro appeared to gain weight throughout the season, costing him agility on the mound. His move to first is slow, making him a good target for opposing basestealers.

1998 Outlook

Because they still owe him $15 million, the White Sox have no choice but to try to get Navarro back on track. They hope that they can get him comfortable with one delivery in spring training after he experimented with several in 1997. Navarro has been durable, so count him for another 30 starts and 200-plus innings. He needs a fast start to regain the confidence he has lost.

Position: SP
Bats: R **Throws:** R
Ht: 6' 4" **Wt:** 230

Opening Day Age: 30
Born: 3/27/68 in Bayamon, PR
ML Seasons: 9
Pronunciation: JAY-mee nuh-VARR-oh

Overall Statistics

	W	L	Pct.	ERA	G	GS	Sv	IP	H	BB	SO	HR	Ratio
1997	9	14	.391	5.79	33	33	0	209.2	267	73	142	22	1.62
Career	100	91	.524	4.31	280	248	1	1689.2	1830	519	952	146	1.39

How Often He Throws Strikes

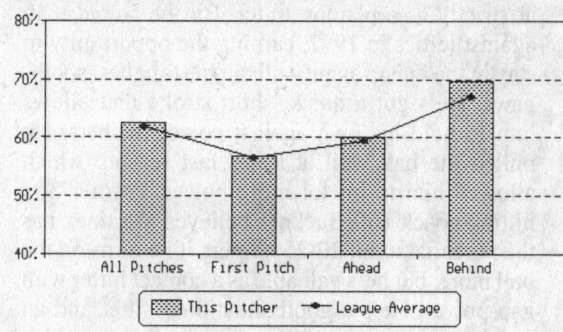

1997 Situational Stats

	W	L	ERA	Sv	IP		AB	H	HR	RBI	Avg
Home	6	6	4.57	0	102.1	LHB	396	127	9	61	.321
Road	3	8	6.96	0	107.1	RHB	469	140	13	79	.299
First Half	6	7	4.77	0	120.2	Sc Pos	248	81	8	117	.327
Scnd Half	3	7	7.18	0	89.0	Clutch	73	27	1	13	.370

1997 Rankings (American League)

⇒ 1st in highest ERA, hits allowed, wild pitches (14), highest batting average allowed (.309) and highest ERA on the road
⇒ 2nd in most baserunners allowed per 9 innings (14.7)
⇒ 3rd in highest on-base percentage allowed (.359)
⇒ Led the White Sox in games started, complete games (2), innings pitched, hits allowed, batters faced (957), strikeouts, wild pitches (14), pitches thrown (3,525), stolen bases allowed (23), runners caught stealing (7), highest strikeout/walk ratio (1.9), highest groundball/flyball ratio allowed (1.5), least pitches thrown per batter (3.68) and ERA at home

Chris Snopek

Position: 3B
Bats: R **Throws:** R
Ht: 6' 1" **Wt:** 185

Opening Day Age: 27
Born: 9/20/70 in Cynthiana, KY
ML Seasons: 3

1997 Season

Robin Ventura's broken leg provided an opportunity for Chris Snopek to play regularly, but the season turned into as much of a nightmare for the University of Mississippi product as for Ventura. Snopek's quick bat caught the eyes of scouts from other organizations in spring training, but he failed badly as a replacement for Ventura. A run of early errors hurt Snopek's confidence in the field. He got off to a decent start at the plate but lost playing time in late April when former manager Terry Bevington moved Tony Phillips from right field to third base to get Lyle Mouton's bat into the lineup. Snopek began a steady descent that ended with him being sent to Triple-A Nashville in August and not returning in September.

Hitting

Snopek is a scout's delight. He generates terrific bat speed from a fundamentally sound swing, covering both sides of the plate. He doesn't have great home-run power, but drives the ball in the gaps. He hurts himself by chasing too many bad pitches and does a poor job of working counts in his favor. Pitchers get him out with breaking balls away. As a part-time player in 1995, he crushed lefthanders while struggling against righties. He had trouble with pitchers of all kinds in 1997.

Baserunning & Defense

Snopek is a good athlete who has Ventura-like range at third base. He's hard on himself when he makes errors, seemingly developing mental blocks. He grew tentative in the field in 1997, often double-pumping on throws. He has good speed, especially for a third baseman, but couldn't get on base to use it.

1998 Outlook

While the White Sox seem to have lost interest in Snopek, it's easy to see him getting another chance. Ventura enters the final season of his contract and is likely to be traded if he can't be signed to an extension. Snopek could be a pleasant surprise, but needs to get mentally tougher because time is about to run out.

Overall Statistics

	G	AB	R	H	D	T	HR	RBI	SB	BB	SO	Avg	OBP	Slg
1997	86	298	27	65	15	0	5	35	3	18	51	.218	.263	.319
Career	154	470	57	114	25	1	12	60	4	33	79	.243	.293	.377

Where He Hits the Ball

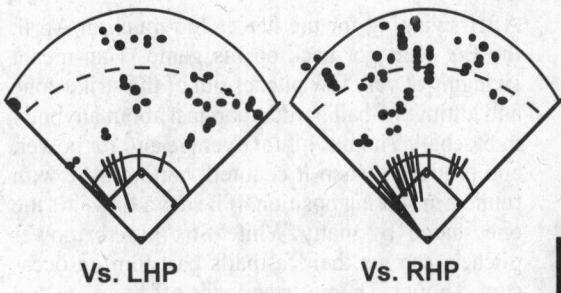

Vs. LHP   **Vs. RHP**

1997 Situational Stats

	AB	H	HR	RBI	Avg		AB	H	HR	RBI	Avg
Home	127	28	3	18	.220	LHP	115	25	2	11	.217
Road	171	37	2	17	.216	RHP	183	40	3	24	.219
First Half	236	53	5	33	.225	Sc Pos	84	20	0	28	.238
Scnd Half	62	12	0	2	.194	Clutch	46	8	0	4	.174

1997 Rankings (American League)

⇒ 3rd in lowest batting average in the clutch
⇒ 7th in errors at third base (16)

Frank Thomas

1997 Season

Gentlemen, start your superlatives. There haven't been many hitters better than Frank Thomas, who put together a vintage performance to overshadow White Sox newcomer Albert Belle. The arrival of Belle was supposed to force pitchers to challenge Thomas more often, but that seldom happened. Thomas got off to a slow start himself, but earned American League Player-of-the-Month honors by hitting .430 with 29 RBIs in May. He spent time on the disabled list with a strained oblique muscle but still wound up winning his first American League batting title. It would have been a dreary season for the Sox without Thomas.

Hitting

After swinging for the fences too much in April, the Big Hurt got back on his game. That meant swinging at very few pitches out of the strike zone and hitting the ball harder than just about anybody in baseball. Thomas hit for average and for power, and produced when it counted, batting .417 with runners in scoring position. If he has a flaw, it's the one shared by many White Sox hitters: power pitchers can get their fastballs past him on occasion. Though Thomas stands far off the plate and dives into pitches, not many pitchers go inside on him. As a result, he gets lots of hits to right field.

Baserunning & Defense

An admittedly challenged first baseman, Thomas accepted a midseason move to designated hitter with dignity. He does a decent job fielding ground balls at first, but lacks range as well as the instinct to react to fast-developing plays. Once he even allowed Detroit catcher Matt Walbeck to steal home on a double steal. He's a plodder on the bases who seems to protect himself from injury.

1998 Outlook

Thomas might not repeat as batting champion, but should have another ultra-productive year. He figures to be a full-time DH, playing first base only in National League parks. He scored 110 runs last year with Belle having a subpar year and No. 5 hitter Robin Ventura out two-thirds of the season with injury.

Position: 1B/DH
Bats: R **Throws:** R
Ht: 6' 5" **Wt:** 257

Opening Day Age: 29
Born: 5/27/68 in Columbus, GA
ML Seasons: 8
Nickname: Big Hurt

Overall Statistics

	G	AB	R	H	D	T	HR	RBI	SB	BB	SO	Avg	OBP	Slg
1997	146	530	110	184	35	0	35	125	1	109	69	.347	.456	.611
Career	1076	3821	785	1261	246	8	257	854	18	879	582	.330	.452	.600

Where He Hits the Ball

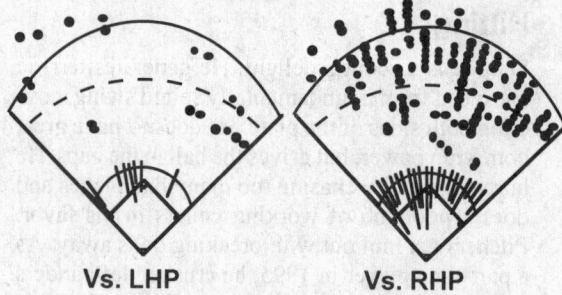

Vs. LHP   **Vs. RHP**

1997 Situational Stats

	AB	H	HR	RBI	Avg		AB	H	HR	RBI	Avg
Home	251	80	16	53	.319	LHP	106	38	12	31	.358
Road	279	104	19	72	.373	RHP	424	146	23	94	.344
First Half	261	96	17	63	.368	Sc Pos	139	58	10	87	.417
Scnd Half	269	88	18	62	.327	Clutch	78	26	4	20	.333

1997 Rankings (American League)

⇒ 1st in batting average, on-base percentage and batting average on the road
⇒ 2nd in times on base (296), slugging percentage, batting average with runners in scoring position and on-base percentage vs. righthanded pitchers (.461)
⇒ 3rd in errors at first base (11)
⇒ Led the White Sox in batting average, home runs, runs scored, hits, total bases (324), RBI, walks, times on base (296), slugging percentage, on-base percentage, HR frequency (15.1 ABs per HR), batting average with runners in scoring position, batting average vs. righthanded pitchers, batting average on an 0-2 count (.296) and batting average at home

Robin Ventura

1997 Season

Robin Ventura won't remember the 1997 season fondly. It began with him breaking his right leg and tearing ligaments in his right ankle with a slide into home plate in spring training, and ended with him saying farewell to longtime teammates Harold Baines, Ozzie Guillen and Roberto Hernandez. Ventura pushed himself hard in rehabilitating his ankle and beat even the most optimistic projections by returning to the lineup in late July. He handled a full workload at third base, convincing Chicago to exercise a $6 million option on his contract. Management rewarded him for his leadership as much as for his play.

Hitting

Ventura returned with a vengeance after coming off the disabled list, but he slowed down and never really regained his rhythm at the plate. He showed home-run power but didn't drive the ball as well as he had in 1996, when he hit 34 homers and drove in 105 runs. Some scouts question whether Ventura has lost a little bat speed, and he swung through a lot of fastballs. But make a mistake, and Ventura will make you pay.

Basrunning & Defense

Ventura has won four Gold Gloves with his quick reactions and constant alertness. There's no reason he shouldn't return to his previous form, but he raised some eyebrows by commiting seven errors. He didn't gobble up as many ground balls as usual, perhaps because he was bothered by his ankle. He lost half a step in range to his left and allowed a surprising number of balls to go down the line. Speed never has been an asset for Ventura, but he continued to run the bases aggressively.

1998 Outlook

With a year left on his contract, Ventura is at a crossroads. The Sox tried to sign him to an extension in the offseason, but negotiations were complicated by his feeling that management betrayed him by trading away several high-priced veterans. He'll be trade bait if he opens the year in Chicago.

Position: 3B
Bats: L **Throws:** R
Ht: 6' 1" **Wt:** 198

Opening Day Age: 30
Born: 7/14/67 in Santa Maria, CA
ML Seasons: 9

Overall Statistics

	G	AB	R	H	D	T	HR	RBI	SB	BB	SO	Avg	OBP	Slg
1997	54	183	27	48	10	1	6	26	0	34	21	.262	.373	.426
Career	1093	3952	574	1089	188	8	150	650	14	589	548	.276	.367	.441

Where He Hits the Ball

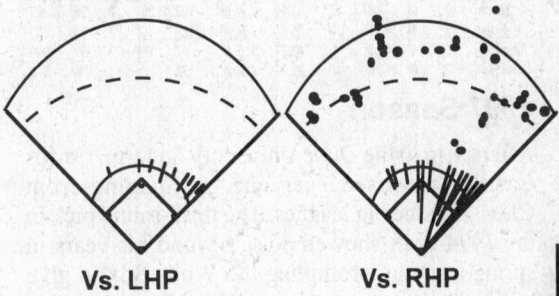

Vs. LHP   **Vs. RHP**

1997 Situational Stats

	AB	H	HR	RBI	Avg		AB	H	HR	RBI	Avg
Home	93	27	2	14	.290	LHP	39	10	0	7	.256
Road	90	21	4	12	.233	RHP	144	38	6	19	.264
First Half	0	0	0	0	-	Sc Pos	44	13	0	18	.295
Scnd Half	183	48	6	26	.262	Clutch	25	8	1	8	.320

1997 Rankings (American League)

⇒ Did not rank near the top or bottom in any category

Carlos Castillo

Position: RP
Bats: R **Throws:** R
Ht: 6' 2" **Wt:** 240

Opening Day Age: 22
Born: 4/21/75 in
Boston, MA
ML Seasons: 1
Pronunciation:
cas-TEE-oh

Overall Statistics

	W	L	Pct.	ERA	G	GS	Sv	IP	H	BB	SO	HR	Ratio
1997	2	1	.667	4.48	37	2	1	66.1	68	33	43	9	1.52
Career	2	1	.667	4.48	37	2	1	66.1	68	33	43	9	1.52

1997 Situational Stats

	W	L	ERA	Sv	IP		AB	H	HR	RBI	Avg
Home	0	0	4.88	0	31.1	LHB	128	38	8	26	.297
Road	2	1	4.11	1	35.0	RHB	129	30	1	14	.233
First Half	0	1	4.33	1	43.2	Sc Pos	67	18	4	32	.269
Scnd Half	2	0	4.76	0	22.2	Clutch	23	8	1	4	.348

1997 Season

After a trip to the Duke University fat farm, Carlos Castillo surprised everyone by jumping from Class-A to the big leagues. The third-round pick in the 1994 draft showed poise beyond his years in spring training, prompting the White Sox to give him a shot as a long reliever. He did an admirable job in a difficult role the first half of the season, then got a look both as a setup man and a starter in the second half. He was sent to Triple-A in late-August and never returned.

Pitching & Defense

Castillo can throw strikes both with a fastball that hits the low 90s and a hard slider. His changeup was inconsistent last year but has promise. He always has been a control pitcher and showed amazing command for a 22 year old who had never pitched in Double-A, challenging some of the best hitters in the game. He's not afraid to pitch inside. Castillo isn't a good fielder and can be very slow to home plate, allowing teams to run on him.

1998 Outlook

Barring a return of his weight problems, there's an excellent chance Castillo will earn a spot in the rotation. He's a good bet to win 12 games as the third or fourth starter, and probably will expect even more from himself.

Doug Drabek

Position: SP
Bats: R **Throws:** R
Ht: 6' 1" **Wt:** 185

Opening Day Age: 35
Born: 7/25/62 in
Victoria, TX
ML Seasons: 12
Pronunciation:
DRAY-bek

Overall Statistics

	W	L	Pct.	ERA	G	GS	Sv	IP	H	BB	SO	HR	Ratio
1997	12	11	.522	5.74	31	31	0	169.1	170	69	85	30	1.41
Career	149	123	.548	3.58	375	366	0	2426.1	2310	675	1539	226	1.23

1997 Situational Stats

	W	L	ERA	Sv	IP		AB	H	HR	RBI	Avg
Home	9	4	5.66	0	95.1	LHB	308	80	12	40	.260
Road	3	7	5.84	0	74.0	RHB	344	90	18	63	.262
First Half	6	6	6.80	0	87.1	Sc Pos	141	44	10	68	.312
Scnd Half	6	5	4.61	0	82.0	Clutch	23	6	2	4	.261

1997 Season

Not many teams would have let the graying Doug Drabek make 31 starts last year. He took an ERA of 6.80 into the All-Star break, which easily could have earned him his release. Drabek pitched better in the second half of the season but still finished with the highest ERA of his 12-year career. You have to give Drabek lots of credit for being a tough guy, though. He took his lumps and kept working to get better.

Pitching & Defense

Even when he won the NL Cy Young Award in 1990, Drabek could not throw his fastball past hitters. But that fastball has dropped from the high-80s to the low- to mid-80s, forcing him to hit his spots. His second-half improvement came largely because he shelved his slider in favor of a curve-ball. Drabek was once one of the best fielding pitchers around, but his reactions have slowed. Basestealers can take advantage of him.

1998 Outlook

Drabek's second-half performance encouraged him to continue a career that appeared near its end. He could be a good fit with an expansion team or a contender looking to fill a hole at the back of the rotation. What he lacks in stuff on the mound, he makes up for with character in the clubhouse.

Scott Eyre

Position: SP
Bats: L **Throws:** L
Ht: 6' 1" **Wt:** 190

Opening Day Age: 25
Born: 5/30/72 in
Inglewood, California
ML Seasons: 1
Pronunciation: IRE

Overall Statistics

	W	L	Pct.	ERA	G	GS	Sv	IP	H	BB	SO	HR	Ratio
1997	4	4	.500	5.04	11	11	0	60.2	62	31	36	11	1.53
Career	4	4	.500	5.04	11	11	0	60.2	62	31	36	11	1.53

1997 Situational Stats

	W	L	ERA	Sv	IP		AB	H	HR	RBI	Avg
Home	4	0	2.48	0	29.0	LHB	42	12	4	12	.286
Road	0	4	7.39	0	31.2	RHB	190	50	7	20	.263
First Half	0	0	-	0	0.0	Sc Pos	47	13	3	20	.277
Scnd Half	4	4	5.04	0	60.2	Clutch	5	1	0	0	.200

1997 Season

Three years after having Tommy John surgery, Scott Eyre led the White Sox organization with 17 victories. Four of those came after he was promoted from Double-A to replace the departed Wilson Alvarez in the starting rotation. The Rangers might spend the next decade explaining how they could have traded Eyre for backup infielder Esteban Beltre before the 1994 season.

Pitching & Defense

Eyre has an average major league fastball, which he uses to set up an excellent changeup. The changeup allows him to be successful against righthanders. He seems to know how to pitch, using both sides of the plate and moving hitters back. He can be wild at times, but is tough when he throws strikes. He's a good athlete who moves well on the mound. He has a good pickoff move and is tough to run on.

1998 Outlook

Eyre established himself as a strong favorite to fill one of the vacancies created by the trades of Wilson Alvarez and Danny Darwin. He'll be tested his second time around the American League as hitters learn more about him, but appears to have the stuff to survive for 30 starts and 180-plus innings.

Keith Foulke

Position: RP/SP
Bats: R **Throws:** R
Ht: 6' 0" **Wt:** 195

Opening Day Age: 25
Born: 10/19/72 in
Ellsworth AFB, SD
ML Seasons: 1
Pronunciation: FOLK

Overall Statistics

	W	L	Pct.	ERA	G	GS	Sv	IP	H	BB	SO	HR	Ratio
1997	4	5	.444	6.38	27	8	3	73.1	88	23	54	13	1.51
Career	4	5	.444	6.38	27	8	3	73.1	88	23	54	13	1.51

1997 Situational Stats

	W	L	ERA	Sv	IP		AB	H	HR	RBI	Avg
Home	3	0	3.67	2	41.2	LHB	132	45	5	15	.341
Road	1	5	9.95	1	31.2	RHB	163	43	8	25	.264
First Half	1	2	6.37	0	35.1	Sc Pos	66	21	3	26	.318
Scnd Half	3	3	6.39	3	38.0	Clutch	55	16	1	4	.291

1997 Season

After failing to take advantage of limited opportunities with San Francisco, Keith Foulke was included in the July 31 trade that sent Wilson Alvarez, Danny Darwin and Roberto Hernandez to the Giants. Foulke did better than the White Sox had expected in a late-season audition, perhaps because he was used as a middle reliever, not a starter. The Sox placed him on their 15-man protected list for the expansion draft, which wouldn't have happened in San Francisco.

Pitching & Defense

Foulke is a sinker-slider pitcher who isn't afraid to throw strikes. He walked fewer than two batters per nine innings with the White Sox. He has an average major league fastball that's effective because he locates it well. Foulke is an alert fielder who doesn't hurt himself. He is slow to the plate and runners can take advantage of him.

1998 Outlook

Foulke and the other minor leaguers acquired from San Francisco will get every opportunity to bloom with the Sox as owner Jerry Reinsdorf tries to justify pulling the plug when his team was only 3½ games behind Cleveland. Foulke figures to win a job next spring, most likely in the bullpen.

Ron Karkovice

Position: C
Bats: R **Throws:** R
Ht: 6' 1" **Wt:** 219

Opening Day Age: 34
Born: 8/8/63 in Union, NJ
ML Seasons: 12
Nickname: Officer Karkovice

Overall Statistics

	G	AB	R	H	D	T	HR	RBI	SB	BB	SO	Avg	OBP	Slg
1997	51	138	10	25	3	0	6	18	0	11	32	.181	.248	.333
Career	939	2597	336	574	120	6	96	335	24	233	749	.221	.289	.383

1997 Situational Stats

	AB	H	HR	RBI	Avg		AB	H	HR	RBI	Avg
Home	68	13	4	11	.191	LHP	56	12	2	4	.214
Road	70	12	2	7	.171	RHP	82	13	4	14	.159
First Half	98	17	3	12	.173	Sc Pos	35	4	1	11	.114
Scnd Half	40	8	3	6	.200	Clutch	13	4	1	2	.308

1997 Season

Despite his own protestations at the time, Ron Karkovice wasn't ready on Opening Day. His movement still was affected by knee surgery he underwent after the 1996 season. He nevertheless was the White Sox' regular catcher until Jorge Fabregas was acquired in mid-May. Karkovice, never a good hitter, was exposed as a defensive liability, throwing out only one of the first 20 runners attempting to steal against him. He improved behind the plate as the season went on, but received very limited playing time.

Hitting, Baserunning & Defense

Karkovice still has some pop in his bat, especially when he sits on fastballs. Watching Karkovice run can be a painful experience. The wear and tear of catching has left him with bone rubbing against bone in his knees. He calls a good game and his throwing improved after the horrible start last year.

1998 Outlook

Retirement can't be far away, but Karkovice wants to milk one or two more seasons out of his career. He showed an ability in the second half of the season to contribute after long stretches on the bench, which might make him a candidate to back up someone like Ivan Rodriguez.

Norberto Martin

Position: SS/3B
Bats: R **Throws:** R
Ht: 5'10" **Wt:** 164

Opening Day Age: 31
Born: 12/10/66 in Santo Domingo, DR
ML Seasons: 5
Pronunciation: mar-TEEN
Nickname: Paco

Overall Statistics

	G	AB	R	H	D	T	HR	RBI	SB	BB	SO	Avg	OBP	Slg
1997	71	213	24	64	7	1	2	27	1	6	31	.300	.320	.371
Career	266	658	93	197	28	6	6	76	20	25	90	.299	.323	.388

1997 Situational Stats

	AB	H	HR	RBI	Avg		AB	H	HR	RBI	Avg
Home	105	31	1	11	.295	LHP	81	28	1	13	.346
Road	108	33	1	16	.306	RHP	132	36	1	14	.273
First Half	114	32	2	15	.281	Sc Pos	57	22	1	26	.386
Scnd Half	99	32	0	12	.323	Clutch	42	15	1	5	.357

1997 Season

You can't start with a bigger bang than Norberto Martin did, hitting a pinch-hit homer on Opening Day to tie a game the White Sox would win in 10 innings. He was unable to build from his fast start. Often the Sox' only backup infielder, he failed to make a signficant contribution. He was bothered by a series of leg injuries and when healthy couldn't provide the defensive help up the middle that the Sox badly needed.

Hitting, Baserunning & Defense

Martin is a dangerous hitter with good bat speed. He often was used as a pinch hitter against righthanded closers. Only 10 of his 64 hits went for extra bases, a damning percentage for a free swinger who's reluctant to take a walk. Martin ran well in the minor leagues but now protects himself from injury on the bases. He can play second base, shortstop and third base decently, but he's not going to make anyone's team based on his glove.

1998 Outlook

The 31-year-old Martin wasn't seriously considered as a replacement for shortstop Ozzie Guillen, sending a message that his wave may have crested. He's a good enough hitter to get a look from someone else if the Sox cut him loose.

Chuck McElroy

Traded To ROCKIES

Position: RP
Bats: L **Throws:** L
Ht: 6' 0" **Wt:** 195

Opening Day Age: 30
Born: 10/1/67 in Port Arthur, TX
ML Seasons: 9
Pronunciation: MACK-ill-roy

Overall Statistics

	W	L	Pct.	ERA	G	GS	Sv	IP	H	BB	SO	HR	Ratio
1997	1	3	.250	3.84	61	0	1	75.0	73	22	62	5	1.27
Career	24	22	.522	3.53	428	0	15	478.2	449	222	402	34	1.40

1997 Situational Stats

	W	L	ERA	Sv	IP		AB	H	HR	RBI	Avg
Home	0	1	2.18	1	41.1	LHB	105	24	2	14	.229
Road	1	2	5.88	0	33.2	RHB	185	49	3	19	.265
First Half	0	1	4.35	0	39.1	Sc Pos	76	22	0	26	.289
Scnd Half	1	2	3.28	1	35.2	Clutch	91	26	3	14	.286

1997 Season

Chuck McElroy was deemed expendable by the Angels, but his reliable work out of the bullpen was missed after he was traded to the White Sox in mid-May. He greatly strengthened the Sox bullpen by giving former manager Terry Bevington another lefty to use when Tony Castillo was struggling. McElroy pitched in a variety of roles and proved to be very useful.

Pitching & Defense

McElroy's bread-and-butter pitch is a split-fingered fastball, and he can get outs with his other pitches as well. He also has a good fastball and a curveball he sometimes throws when he's behind in the count. The three pitches allow him to be effective against many righthanded hitters. As a good athlete should, he fields his position well. His pickoff move is outstanding.

1998 Outlook

McElroy was taken in the third round of the expansion draft by the Diamondbacks, who then traded him to Colorado for outfielder Harvey Pulliam. There's no reason why McElroy shouldn't continue to be effective in middle and long relief.

Magglio Ordonez

Position: RF
Bats: R **Throws:** R
Ht: 5'11" **Wt:** 170

Opening Day Age: 24
Born: 1/28/74 in Caracas, VZ
ML Seasons: 1
Pronunciation: or-DOAN-yez

Overall Statistics

	G	AB	R	H	D	T	HR	RBI	SB	BB	SO	Avg	OBP	Slg
1997	21	69	12	22	6	0	4	11	1	2	8	.319	.338	.580
Career	21	69	12	22	6	0	4	11	1	2	8	.319	.338	.580

1997 Situational Stats

	AB	H	HR	RBI	Avg		AB	H	HR	RBI	Avg
Home	46	15	2	9	.326	LHP	17	5	1	1	.294
Road	23	7	2	2	.304	RHP	52	17	3	10	.327
First Half	0	0	0	0	-	Sc Pos	15	4	1	6	.267
Scnd Half	69	22	4	11	.319	Clutch	11	4	1	1	.364

1997 Season

For a guy who didn't receive even a nonroster invitation to spring training, Magglio Ordonez turned in an outstanding season. The line drive-hitting right fielder was named Most Valuable Player of the American Association after winning a batting title with Triple-A Nashville. He was promoted ahead of Sounds teammate Jeff Abbott after Darren Lewis was traded in late August and made a favorable impression by hitting .319 in 21 games with the White Sox.

Hitting, Baserunning & Defense

Ordonez, a native of Venezuela, has an unusual stance at the plate, crouching with all his weight on his back foot, but is able to generate good bat speed. He's a smart hitter who sprays the ball to all fields. Ordonez runs well but isn't considered a basestealing threat. He has a strong arm and good range in right field.

1998 Outlook

Barring a bad spring, Ordonez will leave his first big league camp as a regular in right field. Unless last season was a mirage, he's worthy of Rookie-of-the-Year hype.

Bill Simas

Position: RP
Bats: R **Throws:** R
Ht: 6' 3" **Wt:** 220

Opening Day Age: 26
Born: 11/28/71 in Hanford, CA
ML Seasons: 3
Pronunciation: SEE-muss

Overall Statistics

	W	L	Pct.	ERA	G	GS	Sv	IP	H	BB	SO	HR	Ratio
1997	3	1	.750	4.14	40	0	1	41.1	46	24	38	6	1.69
Career	6	10	.375	4.22	118	0	3	128.0	136	73	119	12	1.63

1997 Situational Stats

	W	L	ERA	Sv	IP		AB	H	HR	RBI	Avg
Home	1	0	4.64	0	21.1	LHB	54	16	3	12	.296
Road	2	1	3.60	0	20.0	RHB	111	30	3	15	.270
First Half	3	0	4.54	0	33.2	Sc Pos	57	13	0	18	.228
Scnd Half	0	1	2.35	0	7.2	Clutch	45	10	1	5	.222

1997 Season

The White Sox had high expectations for Bill Simas. While he progressed from his erratic rookie season in 1996, he didn't display the kind of consistency needed from a setup man. He pitched really well in April and May, but seemed filled with self-doubt after the All-Star break. His season ended early with shoulder surgery that many members of the Sox' staff felt was unnecessary.

Pitching & Defense

Simas can be especially tough on righthanded hitters with his combination of a 92-MPH fastball and a hard slider. He is still searching for a quality offspeed pitch to make him more effective against lefties. He has a tendency to give up home runs. Simas is a big guy who moves slowly on the mound. He doesn't field his position well.

1998 Outlook

It's fortunate for Simas that he will get a fresh start with a new manager. While the White Sox organization values his potential, his unwillingness to pitch through pain dropped his stock with former manager Terry Bevington. This could be a make-or-break season for Simas.

Mario Valdez

Position: 1B
Bats: L **Throws:** L
Ht: 6' 2" **Wt:** 190

Opening Day Age: 23
Born: 11/19/74 in Obregon, Mexico
ML Seasons: 1

Overall Statistics

	G	AB	R	H	D	T	HR	RBI	SB	BB	SO	Avg	OBP	Slg
1997	54	115	11	28	7	0	1	13	1	17	39	.243	.350	.330
Career	54	115	11	28	7	0	1	13	1	17	39	.243	.350	.330

1997 Situational Stats

	AB	H	HR	RBI	Avg		AB	H	HR	RBI	Avg
Home	56	15	0	7	.268	LHP	16	3	0	0	.188
Road	59	13	1	6	.220	RHP	99	25	1	13	.253
First Half	16	5	0	3	.313	Sc Pos	35	7	0	12	.200
Scnd Half	99	23	1	10	.232	Clutch	15	3	0	1	.200

1997 Season

With no backup first basemen on the 40-man roster, the White Sox brought Mario Valdez to spring training to serve as a caddie for Frank Thomas. For someone who started 1996 in the Midwest League, Valdez was incredibly poised. He had good at-bats all spring against big league pitchers, earning a promotion to Triple-A. He played well enough there to get the call when Thomas went on the disabled list in June. Valdez returned to the White Sox after Harold Baines was traded July 29 and finished the season in the big leagues.

Hitting, Baserunning & Defense

Valdez is a big man with a short stroke. He always looks comfortable at the plate, but was unable to catch up to big league fastballs. Throw him a slider at the knees, however, and watch out. He's a gap hitter who should develop more power as he gets older. There's nothing wrong with his fielding. He has soft hands which should save teammates lots of errors. He's not much of a runner.

1998 Outlook

While it was the presence of Valdez that convinced Thomas to accept a switch to designated hitter, Valdez isn't a lock to open the season with the White Sox. Many in the organization think he needs at least another half-season at Triple-A.

Other Chicago White Sox

Mike Bertotti (**Pos**: LHP, **Age**: 28)

	W	L	Pct.	ERA	G	GS	Sv	IP	H	BB	SO	HR	Ratio
1997	0	0	-	7.36	9	0	0	3.2	9	2	4	0	3.00
Career	3	1	.750	7.63	28	6	0	46.0	60	33	38	11	2.02

Bertotti opened the year as a member of the Sox bullpen, but pitched poorly in nine appearances. Sent to Triple-A Nashville, he struggled with his control. The Sox are losing patience. 1998 Outlook: C

Tony Castillo (**Pos**: LHP, **Age**: 35)

	W	L	Pct.	ERA	G	GS	Sv	IP	H	BB	SO	HR	Ratio
1997	4	4	.500	4.91	64	0	4	62.1	74	23	42	6	1.56
Career	27	21	.563	3.71	378	6	22	499.2	517	168	319	45	1.37

One of those journeyman lefthanders who never seem to have trouble finding work, Castillo had a so-so year as a setup man in 1997. He figures to handle the same kind of role in '98. 1998 Outlook: A

Nelson Cruz (**Pos**: RHP, **Age**: 25)

	W	L	Pct.	ERA	G	GS	Sv	IP	H	BB	SO	HR	Ratio
1997	0	2	.000	6.49	19	0	0	26.1	29	9	23	6	1.44
Career	0	2	.000	6.49	19	0	0	26.1	29	9	23	6	1.44

A righthander who got a late-season shot with the Sox, Cruz showed good command of the strike zone but was plagued by the gopher ball. He'll get a long look this spring. 1998 Outlook: B

Jeff Darwin (**Pos**: RHP, **Age**: 28)

	W	L	Pct.	ERA	G	GS	Sv	IP	H	BB	SO	HR	Ratio
1997	0	1	.000	5.27	14	0	0	13.2	17	7	9	1	1.76
Career	0	2	.000	4.47	38	0	0	48.1	50	19	25	7	1.43

Danny Darwin's younger brother didn't pitch very well after being recalled from Triple-A Nashville in August. Chicago released him in the offseason. 1998 Outlook: C

Chad Fonville (**Pos**: 2B, **Age**: 27, **Bats**: B)

	G	AB	R	H	D	T	HR	RBI	SB	BB	SO	Avg	OBP	Slg
1997	18	23	2	3	0	0	0	2	2	3	4	.130	.231	.130
Career	223	544	79	133	10	2	0	31	29	43	77	.244	.301	.270

Former Expo and Dodger infielder Fonville came to the Sox in a late-season deal for Darren Lewis. He went to Cleveland on waivers in the offseason. 1998 Outlook: B

Al Levine (**Pos**: RHP, **Age**: 29)

	W	L	Pct.	ERA	G	GS	Sv	IP	H	BB	SO	HR	Ratio
1997	2	2	.500	6.91	25	0	0	27.1	35	16	22	4	1.87
Career	2	3	.400	6.31	41	0	0	45.2	57	23	34	5	1.75

After breaking in with the Sox in 1996, Levine spent the '97 season shuttling between Chicago and Triple-A Nashville. Wherever he went, the hitters were glad to see him. 1998 Outlook: C.

Robert Machado (**Pos**: C, **Age**: 24, **Bats**: R)

	G	AB	R	H	D	T	HR	RBI	SB	BB	SO	Avg	OBP	Slg
1997	10	15	1	3	0	1	0	2	0	1	6	.200	.250	.333
Career	14	21	2	7	1	1	0	4	0	1	6	.333	.364	.476

A catcher with solid defensive skills and a little bit of power, Machado got a brief shot with the White Sox late last year. If he hits this spring, he could stick as a reserve. 1998 Outlook: C

Lyle Mouton (**Pos**: RF/LF, **Age**: 28, **Bats**: R)

	G	AB	R	H	D	T	HR	RBI	SB	BB	SO	Avg	OBP	Slg
1997	88	242	26	65	9	0	5	23	4	14	66	.269	.308	.368
Career	233	635	74	182	33	1	17	89	8	55	162	.287	.345	.422

Mouton got off to a fast start, forcing his way into the lineup in April, but was sidelined after suffering a broken bone below his right eye in a collision with Dave Martinez. He signed a contract to play in Japan this year. 1998 Outlook: D

Mike Sirotka (**Pos**: LHP, **Age**: 26)

	W	L	Pct.	ERA	G	GS	Sv	IP	H	BB	SO	HR	Ratio
1997	3	0	1.000	2.25	7	4	0	32.0	36	5	24	4	1.28
Career	5	4	.556	4.37	28	14	0	92.2	109	34	54	9	1.54

After brief trials with the Sox in 1995 and '96, Sirotka got another chance late in 1997 and looked very impresive. He figures to be part of the club's rotation this year. 1998 Outlook: A

Larry Thomas (**Pos**: LHP, **Age**: 28)

	W	L	Pct.	ERA	G	GS	Sv	IP	H	BB	SO	HR	Ratio
1997	0	0	-	8.10	5	0	0	3.1	3	2	0	1	1.50
Career	2	3	.400	3.02	79	0	0	47.2	43	22	32	3	1.36

An effective setup man for the Sox in 1995 and '96, Thomas came down with elbow problems and spent most of last year at Triple-A Nashville. He pitched decently and could return in '98. 1998 Outlook: B

Chicago White Sox Minor League Prospects

Organization Overview:

The White Sox got a lot of acclaim, and deservedly so, when they spent their 1987-90 first-round picks on Jack McDowell, Robin Ventura, Frank Thomas and Alex Fernandez. They appeared to have a lot of talent coming up through the system, but it didn't quite work out that way. Jason Bere had some success before falling apart and then succumbing to injury. Chicago had high hopes for players such as James Baldwin, Jimmy Hurst, Scott Ruffcorn and Chris Snopek, all of whom have been disappointing thus far. As a result, the White Sox have had to go out and buy players, with the exceptions of second baseman Ray Durham and center fielder Mike Cameron. The strength of the system is hitters, especially at third base and the outfield. Bagging the 1997 season by trading Wilson Alvarez, Danny Darwin and Roberto Hernandez to San Francisco didn't endear the White Sox to their fans, but did land them some quality prospects in shortstop Mike Caruso and pitchers Lorenzo Barcelo and Ken Vining.

Jeff Abbott

Position: OF   **Opening Day Age:** 25
Bats: R **Throws:** L   **Born:** 8/17/72 in
Ht: 6' 2" **Wt:** 190   Decatur, GA

Recent Statistics

	G	AB	R	H	D	T	HR	RBI	SB	BB	SO	AVG
97 AAA Nashville	118	465	88	152	35	3	11	63	12	41	52	.327
97 AL Chicago	19	38	8	10	1	0	1	2	0	0	6	.263
97 MLE	118	454	80	141	32	2	9	57	9	37	54	.311

What does this guy have to do to get more respect? He has hit .325 and .327 in Triple-A the last two years, losing the 1997 American Association batting title to Nashville teammate Magglio Ordonez by .002. After a hot September, Ordonez is a favorite to start for Chicago next year while Abbott seemingly is without a job. Ordonez is considered more of a power hitter, but Abbott's slugging percentages have been higher. A fourth-round pick in 1994 out of the University of Kentucky, he's a career .340 hitter who draws more walks than Ordonez as well. The White Sox believe that Abbott is such a gifted hitter that he'll start turning doubles into homers once he turns on balls. He has decent speed, but is relegated to left field because he has had problems with a loose throwing shoulder. Abbott probably could have hit in the majors in 1997, and years of his career are going to waste.

Lorenzo Barcelo

Position: P   **Opening Day Age:** 20
Bats: R **Throws:** R   **Born:** 9/10/77 in San
Ht: 6' 4" **Wt:** 205   Pedro De Macoris, DR

Recent Statistics

	W	L	ERA	G	GS	Sv	IP	H	R	BB	SO	HR
96 A Burlington	12	10	3.54	26	26	0	152.2	138	70	46	139	19
97 A San Jose	5	4	3.94	16	16	0	89.0	91	45	30	89	13
97 AA Shreveport	2	0	4.02	5	5	0	31.1	30	19	8	20	4
97 AA Birmingham	2	1	4.86	6	6	0	33.1	36	20	9	29	2

Barcelo is the best player acquired in the nine-player deal with San Francisco that took Chicago out of contention. Signed out of the Dominican Republic, he was throwing 97 MPH in 1997—at age 19. His curveball has a chance to be an above-average pitch, and he'll need to develop a changeup to remain a starter. If he can't master the change, his fastball and curve are enough for him to become a closer. He was hit in Double-A, primarily because he only had 1½ effective pitches. Give him another season and a half, and he could be ready for Chicago before he turns 22.

Tom Fordham

Position: P   **Opening Day Age:** 24
Bats: L **Throws:** L   **Born:** 2/20/74 in San
Ht: 6' 2" **Wt:** 210   Diego, CA

Recent Statistics

	W	L	ERA	G	GS	Sv	IP	H	R	BB	SO	HR
97 AAA Nashville	6	7	4.74	21	20	0	114.0	113	64	53	90	14
97 AL Chicago	0	1	6.23	7	1	0	17.1	17	13	10	10	2

Fordham was only an 11th-round pick in 1993 out of Grossmont (Calif.) Junior College, but he had been a consistent winner in the minors until 1997. His best pitch is a changeup, and he also throws an 89-92 MPH fastball and an inconsistent curve. His curve is an above-average pitch at times, but the White Sox would settle for an average breaking ball with better command. He still walks a few too many hitters, and his control deserted him in his first taste of the big leagues. He's a candidate to fill any rotation spot that might open in Chicago in 1998.

Carlos Lee

Position: 3B   **Opening Day Age:** 21
Bats: R **Throws:** R   **Born:** 6/20/76 in
Ht: 6' 2" **Wt:** 202   Aguadulce, Panama

Recent Statistics

	G	AB	R	H	D	T	HR	RBI	SB	BB	SO	AVG
96 A Hickory	119	480	65	150	23	6	8	70	18	23	50	.313
97 A Winston-Sal	139	546	81	173	50	4	17	82	11	36	65	.317

Lee finally showed the power the White Sox knew he had. He tied for the minor league lead with 50 doubles in 1997, and his 17 homers nearly matched the total from his first 2½ pro seasons. Signed out of Panama, he should develop more power as he progresses and never has hit less than .302 in a full season. He has a very good arm and average hands at third base, but needs to improve his footwork to avoid making errors. Chicago is loaded at third base with Ventura, Snopek and Greg Norton, but will make room for Lee when he's ready.

Jeff Liefer

Position: OF   **Opening Day Age:** 23
Bats: L **Throws:** R   **Born:** 8/17/74 in
Ht: 6' 3" **Wt:** 195   Fontana, CA

Recent Statistics

	G	AB	R	H	D	T	HR	RBI	SB	BB	SO	AVG
96 A South Bend	74	277	60	90	14	0	15	58	6	30	62	.325
96 A Pr William	37	147	17	33	6	0	1	13	0	11	27	.224
97 AA Birmingham	119	474	67	113	24	9	15	71	2	38	115	.238
97 MLE	119	458	54	97	20	7	10	57	1	26	123	.212

Liefer was a third baseman when the White Sox made him a first-round pick out of Long Beach State in 1995, but didn't take to the position as a pro and required shoulder surgery in 1996. He was drafted for his bat, so he was moved to left field in 1997 and may get a look at first base in the future. Chicago is excited by his power potential and hitting ability, but both were hindered in Double-A as he recovered from the surgery. He doesn't do much besides hit, so he'll have to prove that 1997 was an aberration.

Greg Norton

Position: 3B   **Opening Day Age:** 25
Bats: B **Throws:** R   **Born:** 7/6/72 in San
Ht: 6' 1" **Wt:** 182   Leandro, CA

Recent Statistics

	G	AB	R	H	D	T	HR	RBI	SB	BB	SO	AVG
97 AAA Nashville	114	414	82	114	27	1	26	76	3	57	101	.275
97 AL Chicago	18	34	5	9	2	2	0	1	0	2	8	.265
97 MLE	114	404	74	104	24	0	21	69	2	51	106	.257

With Ventura carrying a $6 million price tag and Snopek having yet to establish himself with the White Sox, Norton could be Chicago's third baseman in 1998. A second-round pick in 1993 out of the University of Oklahoma, he exploded as a power hitter in 1997. His 26 homers were just six fewer than he had hit in 3½ pro seasons. The White Sox had projected him as a .300 hitter with 12-15 longballs per year. He has a quick first step and a strong arm at third base, and could play shortstop in a pinch.

Jim Parque

Position: P   **Opening Day Age:** 22
Bats: L **Throws:** L   **Born:** 2/8/76 in
Ht: 5' 10" **Wt:** 166   Norwalk, CA

Recent Statistics

	W	L	ERA	G	GS	Sv	IP	H	R	BB	SO	HR
97 A Winston-Sal	7	2	2.77	11	11	0	61.2	29	19	23	76	3
97 AAA Nashville	1	0	4.22	2	2	0	10.2	9	5	9	5	0

Parque always will have his share of doubters becuase he's 5-foot-10 and 166 pounds, but his size hasn't

stopped him. He was one of the most successful pitchers in UCLA history and made the 1996 U.S. Olympic team as a longshot. The only reason he lasted until the 46th pick of the 1997 draft was his size, and he uses such snubs as motivation. Indeed, he reached Triple-A in his first pro summer. His exceptional command and tough makeup make his good stuff even better. He throws an 88-92 MPH fastball, a good curveball and a changeup. He could join Chicago's depleted rotation at some point in 1998.

Brian Simmons

Position: OF   **Opening Day Age:** 24
Bats: B **Throws:** R   **Born:** 9/4/73 in
Ht: 6' 2" **Wt:** 191   Mcmurray, PA

Recent Statistics

	G	AB	R	H	D	T	HR	RBI	SB	BB	SO	AVG
96 A South Bend	92	356	73	106	29	6	17	58	14	48	69	.298
96 A Pr William	33	131	17	26	4	3	4	14	2	9	39	.198
97 AA Birmingham	138	546	108	143	28	12	15	72	15	88	124	.262
97 MLE	138	528	87	125	24	9	10	58	10	59	132	.237

As good as Mike Cameron was in center field for the White Sox, Simmons could push him in the near future. A 1995 second-round pick out of the University of Michigan, he has exceptional outfield instincts. He really struggled in high Class-A ball in 1996, but had no problem hitting in Double-A in a pitchers' park. He can produce for average and power, and has nice acceleration on the basepaths. Chicago has two outfield positions locked up with Albert Belle and Cameron, and it will be interesting to watch Simmons battle Abbott and Ordonez for the third in the next couple of years.

Others to Watch

Shortstop **Mike Caruso** was another part of the Giants trade. He's a 20-year-old line-drive hitter with some pop and good speed, and he has an aggessive makeup... Yet another part of the San Francisco trade, righthander **Bobby Howry** converted to relieving in 1997 and saved 24 games in Double-A at age 24. He's a three-pitch pitcher with an average fastball. . . Catcher **Mark Johnson**, 22, had been more of a defensive specialist, but really blossomed with the bat in 1997. He led the minors with 106 walks, making his .253 average at high Class-A Prince William more palatable, and continued to shine behind the plate. . . The White Sox aren't sure if **Josh Paul**, 22, will be a catcher or an outfielder. They're sure he'll hit with gap power and above-average speed. A broken hamate bone in his left hand cost him most of 1997. . . First baseman **Eddie Pearson** was supposed to develop into a big-time hitter when he was taken in the first round of the 1992 draft, but that hasn't happened. The 24 year old makes contact and hits doubles, but doesn't hit enough homers for his position. . . Lefthander **Ken Vining** was another valuable piece of the San Francisco trade. The 23 year old excels at locating his pitches, a good curveball and changeup, and an average fastball with nice movement.

Mike Hargrove

1997 Season

Mike Hargrove was embattled for much of 1997, but nearly finished the season with a World Series championship. His job was in danger after a 4-10 homestand in July, and the Indians were considered a disappointment because they won only 86 games during the regular season. When all was said and done, Cleveland came within two outs of winning its first World Series since 1948.

Offense

Hargrove had to manipulate his offense in 1997. The set linueps of the previous two years were gone. So, too, were Albert Belle and Kenny Lofton. Matt Williams couldn't handle the cleanup spot, and Marquis Grissom had to be taken out of the leadoff position. Every day seemed to bring a new lineup question. Hargrove did a fine job of finding the right answers. He even used the squeeze play to generate some offense. He used the sacrifice bunt often but only in traditional situations, and rarely called for the double steal because of the Tribe's poor baserunning.

Pitching & Defense

Hargrove did a masterful job with the pitching staff, keeping the rotation together despite losing Jack McDowell and John Smiley to injuries, and picking just the right time to reinsert Jose Mesa as closer after Mike Jackson ran out of steam in August. He worked rookie Jaret Wright and Bartolo Colon in as starters, and constantly juggled the bullpen roles because of the struggles of Mesa and Eric Plunk. Hargrove has a good feel for calling pitchouts. He religiously uses the intentional walk to avoid a dangerous hitter or to set up a double-play opportunity late in the game.

1998 Outlook

The Indians gave Hargrove a two-year extension with a club option for 2000. But his job has been in jeopardy at various times over the last two seasons, and probably will be again should the Indians hit hard times this year. Hargrove's teams have won 285 regular-season games, three division titles and two pennants in the last three years. He may be unappreciated, but he gets results.

Born: 10/26/49 in Perryton, TX

Playing Experience: 1974-1985, Tex, Cle, SD

Managerial Experience: 7 seasons
Nickname: Grover

Manager Statistics

Year	Team, Lg	W	L	Pct	GB	Finish
1997	Cleveland, AL	86	75	.534	—	1st Central
7 Seasons		535	453	.541	—	—

1997 Starting Pitchers by Days Rest

	≤3	4	5	6+
Indians Starts	3	85	32	29
Indians ERA	5.63	4.59	5.36	4.45
AL Avg Starts	5	89	34	24
AL ERA	4.38	4.60	4.61	5.37

1997 Situational Stats

	Mike Hargrove	AL Average
Hit & Run Success %	36.5	36.5
Stolen Base Success %	66.7	67.3
Platoon Pct.	58.3	59.5
Defensive Subs	14	22
High-Pitch Outings	14	15
Quick/Slow Hooks	21/13	19/15
Sacrifice Attempts	60	53

1997 Rankings (American League)

⇒ 1st in steals of home plate (2) and one-batter pitcher appearances (58)
⇒ 2nd in sacrifice bunt percentage (88.3%), squeeze plays (3) and relief appearances (429)
⇒ 3rd in steals of third base (17) and double steals (5)

Sandy Alomar Jr.

1997 Season

Sandy Alomar Jr. had the season of his dreams in 1997. Not only did he stay off the disabled list for the second straight year, the longest healthy stint of his career, but he also set career highs in batting average, doubles, homers and RBI. He had a 30-game hitting streak, was named MVP of the All-Star Game in Jacobs Field, hit homers in five straight games and set a postseason record by driving in 19 runs. After years of frustration, everything came together at once for Alomar.

Hitting

Alomar is a contact hitter with power potential that he's finally beginning to realize at the major league level. In the past, he always had been an aggressive first-pitch hitter who would choke up and try to go the other way if he worked deep into the count. In 1997, he tried to drive the ball regardless of the count. He's a low-ball hitter with power from left to center field. He rarely walks and will get himself out on first-pitch fastballs on the inner half of the plate.

Baserunning & Defense

Alomar worked hard behind the plate in 1997 as the Indians used several young pitchers because of injuries. His game-calling skills are finally becoming a strength. He's excellent at blocking balls in the dirt, but struggles throwing out basestealers despite a strong arm, because of bad knees and a team philosophy that makes pitchers concentrate on the batter instead of the runner. Alomar will occasionally beat out an infield hit, but don't ask him to steal a base as his knees make him an easy target.

1998 Outlook

Alomar signed a two-year deal last spring after the Indians gave him the opportunity to become a free agent by not picking up his 1997 option. He had the chance to be one the most sought-after free agents in baseball, but he always has preferred security. His career has been revived by his vigorous offseason training program, coupled with the realization that he shouldn't catch more than 120-130 games a year.

Position: C
Bats: R **Throws:** R
Ht: 6' 5" **Wt:** 215

Opening Day Age: 31
Born: 6/18/66 in Salinas, PR
ML Seasons: 10
Pronunciation: AL-a-mar

Overall Statistics

	G	AB	R	H	D	T	HR	RBI	SB	BB	SO	Avg	OBP	Slg
1997	125	451	63	146	37	0	21	83	0	19	48	.324	.354	.545
Career	742	2527	309	707	140	4	74	348	22	130	281	.280	.320	.426

Where He Hits the Ball

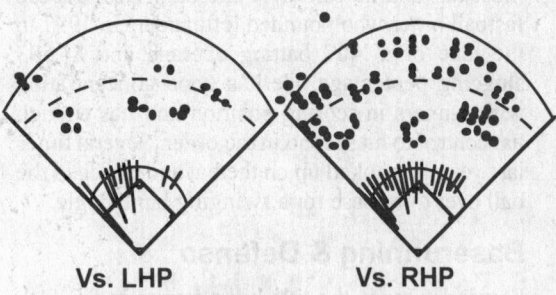

Vs. LHP   Vs. RHP

1997 Situational Stats

	AB	H	HR	RBI	Avg		AB	H	HR	RBI	Avg
Home	221	65	9	44	.294	LHP	119	40	5	23	.336
Road	230	81	12	39	.352	RHP	332	106	16	60	.319
First Half	240	90	11	44	.375	Sc Pos	137	44	6	61	.321
Scnd Half	211	56	10	39	.265	Clutch	63	25	2	10	.397

1997 Rankings (American League)

⇒ 1st in batting average in the clutch and errors at catcher (12)
⇒ 3rd in lowest fielding percentage at catcher (.985)
⇒ 6th in batting average with the bases loaded (.583)
⇒ 8th in lowest percentage of pitches taken (45.6%)
⇒ Led the Indians in batting average in the clutch and batting average with the bases loaded (.583)

Tony Fernandez

1997 Season

After missing all of the 1996 season with a broken right elbow, Tony Fernandez came back strong. He platooned at second base, facing mostly lefthanders, and in the second half was the Indians' best second baseman. After hitting .167 in June, he rallied to hit .375 in July. He also tied a career high with 11 homers and put the Indians in the World Series with his two-out blast off Baltimore's Armando Benitez in the 11th inning in Game 6 of the American League Championship Series.

Hitting

Fernandez is a line-drive hitter with deceiving power. He's tall and skinny, but his shoulders are muscular and he can drive the ball. He's a good fastball hitter who pounded lefthanders in 1997 to the tune of a .407 batting average and a .593 slugging percentage. He has good concentration with runners in scoring position and has enough bat control to hit second in the order. Several times last year, he choked up on the bat and punched the ball over third base for a swinging bunt single.

Baserunning & Defense

Fernandez made the title-killing error in the 11th inning of the seventh game of the World Series, but that didn't reflect his overall play. He showed great range going to his left but often wouldn't play far enough off the bag at second, a holdover from his days as a Gold Glove shortstop. His pivot on the double play improved, but it's still suspect because of his slow, submarine style of throwing. Fernandez still runs well at 35, but his days of 20-plus steals are long gone and he's prone to rookie mistakes on the bases.

1998 Outlook

Fernandez filed for free agency after the 1997 season. If he re-signs with the Indians, it would be as a utility infielder because prospect Enrique Wilson is expected to win the second-base job. Fernandez' return didn't seem likely, however. He said he wasn't respected by the Indians because they played Julio Franco and Bip Roberts in front of him. Fernandez, however, proved he still could be a valuable member of a contending team.

Position: 2B
Bats: B **Throws:** R
Ht: 6' 2" **Wt:** 175

Opening Day Age: 35
Born: 6/30/62 in San Pedro de Macoris, DR
ML Seasons: 14

Overall Statistics

	G	AB	R	H	D	T	HR	RBI	SB	BB	SO	Avg	OBP	Slg
1997	120	409	55	117	21	1	11	44	6	22	47	.286	.323	.423
Career	1802	6817	902	1925	333	90	77	682	226	560	652	.282	.338	.392

Where He Hits the Ball

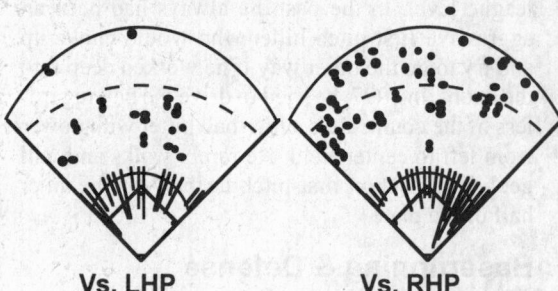

Vs. LHP   Vs. RHP

1997 Situational Stats

	AB	H	HR	RBI	Avg		AB	H	HR	RBI	Avg
Home	192	57	7	24	.297	LHP	123	50	5	18	.407
Road	217	60	4	20	.276	RHP	286	67	6	26	.234
First Half	201	55	3	19	.274	Sc Pos	91	28	0	31	.308
Scnd Half	208	62	8	25	.298	Clutch	65	23	2	12	.354

1997 Rankings (American League)

⇒ 2nd in batting average vs. lefthanded pitchers
⇒ 4th in lowest fielding percentage at second base (.981)
⇒ 6th in on-base percentage vs. lefthanded pitchers (.435)
⇒ 8th in slugging percentage vs. lefthanded pitchers (.594), errors at second base (10) and bunts in play (19)
⇒ 9th in batting average in the clutch and lowest batting average with two strikes (.133)
⇒ Led the Indians in batting average vs. lefthanded pitchers and on-base percentage vs. lefthanded pitchers (.435)

Brian Giles

1997 Season

Brian Giles made his first full season in the big leagues a memorable one, taking over the starting assignment in left field for the Indians when knee and elbow problems sidelined David Justice. Giles ended up playing all three outfield positions and batted in several different spots, but the shuffling didn't seem to hurt his production. He spent most of his time in the bottom third of the order, but hit .271 in the leadoff spot and .294 in the second slot. Bip Roberts' arrival on August 31 cost Giles time in left field, but he still managed to hit 17 homers and drive in 61 runs.

Hitting

Giles is built solid and low to the ground, and has good power against righthanders. He's disciplined at the plate and can drive low fastballs out of the park. He didn't face as many lefties as righties in 1997, but has no problem hitting southpaws for a decent average. He hit only one homer against lefties, however, and they can jam him. Despite walking more times than he struck out, Giles isn't hesitant about swinging at the first pitch. He hit .384 when he did so last season.

Baserunning & Defense

Giles played running back in high school. He runs with deceptive quickness, and stole 13 bases in 16 attempts. He probably could have swiped more if he'd gotten the green light more often. Giles comes in and goes back well on fly balls in the outfield. He played mostly right field in the minors, but made the move to left with no problem. He has the speed to cover the alleys in center and has a good, accurate arm.

1998 Outlook

Giles should be a solid fourth outfielder for the Indians this season if Justice is able to play the field. If not, Giles has shown he can play every day. With more playing time, he could be a 20-20 player who also hits for average.

Position: LF/CF/RF
Bats: L **Throws:** L
Ht: 5'11" **Wt:** 195

Opening Day Age: 27
Born: 1/21/71 in El Cajon, CA
ML Seasons: 3
Pronunciation: JYLES

Overall Statistics

	G	AB	R	H	D	T	HR	RBI	SB	BB	SO	Avg	OBP	Slg
1997	130	377	62	101	15	3	17	61	13	63	50	.268	.368	.459
Career	187	507	94	149	29	4	23	91	16	82	64	.294	.387	.503

Where He Hits the Ball

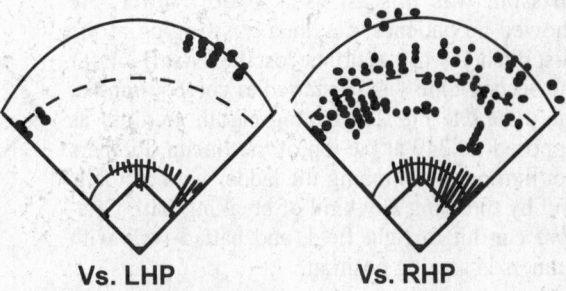

Vs. LHP　　　　**Vs. RHP**

1997 Situational Stats

	AB	H	HR	RBI	Avg		AB	H	HR	RBI	Avg
Home	197	47	7	28	.239	LHP	61	18	1	6	.295
Road	180	54	10	33	.300	RHP	316	83	16	55	.263
First Half	149	38	9	24	.255	Sc Pos	97	29	1	39	.299
Scnd Half	228	63	8	37	.276	Clutch	58	16	4	11	.276

1997 Rankings (American League)

⇒ 5th in errors in left field (3)
⇒ 8th in lowest percentage of swings that missed (10.7%)
⇒ Led the Indians in highest percentage of swings put into play (50.2%)

Marquis Grissom

1997 Season

When the Indians obtained Marquis Grissom from Atlanta last spring for Kenny Lofton, they expected a Gold Glove center fielder, a proven leadoff hitter and a basestealer. What they got was a hard-nosed player who didn't do anything exceptionally well. Maybe he had trouble adjusting to American League pitching, or maybe it was just a bad year. Grissom pulled his right hamstring in his first exhibition game with the Tribe, and the injury put him on the disabled list in late April. By the end of the year, his batting average had fallen 46 points from 1996.

Hitting

Grissom was miscast as a leadoff hitter. He showed no patience, continually swinging at the first pitch. It wasn't until he lost the leadoff job for the second time that he started to come around at the plate. He hit .289 batting eighth or ninth as opposed to .249 at the top of the lineup. Pitchers got him out by climbing the ladder with fastballs and by throwing any kind of breaking ball. Grissom can hit to right field, and batted well with runners in scoring position.

Baserunning & Defense

Maybe he didn't know the AL or maybe his hamstring never healed, but Grissom seemed slower than advertised. He stole 22 bases but was caught 13 times. He went from first to third well, and always went into second base hard to break up the double play. Grissom couldn't play as shallow as he normally did in center field because of the hamstring injury. Still, he went back on balls very well. His arm appeared average at best.

1998 Outlook.

Despite the poor season, the Indians extended Grissom's contract through 2002 with a club option for 2003. He might get another chance at leading off this year, and should be the Tribe's center fielder for many seasons to come. Cleveland expects Grissom to hit for more power now that he knows the league.

Position: CF
Bats: R **Throws:** R
Ht: 5'11" **Wt:** 190

Opening Day Age: 30
Born: 4/17/67 in Atlanta, GA
ML Seasons: 9
Pronunciation: mar-KEESE

Overall Statistics

	G	AB	R	H	D	T	HR	RBI	SB	BB	SO	Avg	OBP	Slg
1997	144	558	74	146	27	6	12	66	22	43	89	.262	.317	.396
Career	1139	4458	690	1242	212	42	101	458	345	339	596	.279	.330	.413

Where He Hits the Ball

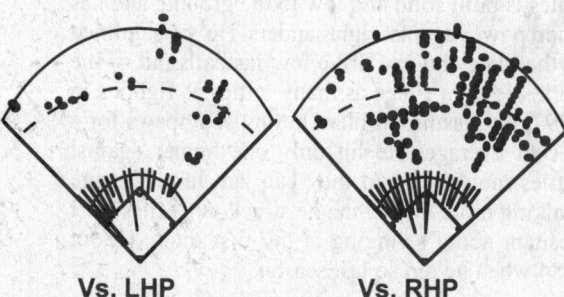

Vs. LHP   **Vs. RHP**

1997 Situational Stats

	AB	H	HR	RBI	Avg		AB	H	HR	RBI	Avg
Home	255	65	5	31	.255	LHP	138	36	5	18	.261
Road	303	81	7	35	.267	RHP	420	110	7	48	.262
First Half	273	71	2	32	.260	Sc Pos	132	40	4	56	.303
Scnd Half	285	75	10	34	.263	Clutch	70	19	3	12	.271

1997 Rankings (American League)

⇒ 4th in caught stealing (13) and lowest on-base percentage for a leadoff hitter (.312)
⇒ 5th in lowest batting average on a 3-2 count (.073) and fielding percentage in center field (.992)
⇒ 7th in errors in center field (3)
⇒ 8th in lowest stolen base percentage (62.9%)
⇒ 10th in triples
⇒ Led the Indians in triples, sacrifice flies (9) and caught stealing (13)

Orel Hershiser

1997 Season

Orel Hershiser was his consistent self in 1997. His 14 wins gave him a 45-21 record in three seasons with the Indians. He pitched better in the second half, despite going on the disabled list with back, groin and hip flexor soreness on August 4. He went 7-1 in 13 starts after the All-Star break, including a 3-0 record in August and a 5-1, 3.19 mark in his final nine starts after coming off the DL. After serving up 18 homers in the first half, Hershiser gave up just eight longballs after the break.

Pitching

At 39, Hershiser has become a five-inning pitcher. He's smart and crafty, but after five frames he's a danger to himself and his team. His best pitches are a sinking fastball and slider. He also has a splitter, curve and change. He throws between 87-90 MPH, but lost confidence in his sinker in 1997, especially in the postseason, and turned into a nibbler. He walked 69 batters, his highest single-season total since joining the Indians. Perhaps Hershiser should go on the disabled list at least once a year, whether he needs to or not. Following trips to the DL in 1995 and last season, he's a combined 16-4.

Defense

Hershiser knows how to stop basestealers. Eight of the 12 runners who attempted to steal on him in 1997 were thrown out. He fields his position well, but too often tries to turn low-percentage plays into outs. He made four errors.

1998 Outlook

Hershiser filed for free agency after a second straight postseason in which he failed to win a game. The Indians hoped to sign a No. 1 starter, which would make Hershiser expendable. He's still fiercely competitive, often yelling at hitters from the mound, and can get up for specific games. He wants to keep pitching, but there may not be a place for him in Cleveland.

Position: SP
Bats: R **Throws:** R
Ht: 6' 3" **Wt:** 195

Opening Day Age: 39
Born: 9/16/58 in Buffalo, NY
ML Seasons: 15
Nickname: Bulldog
Pronunciation: HER-shy-zer

Overall Statistics

	W	L	Pct.	ERA	G	GS	Sv	IP	H	BB	SO	HR	Ratio
1997	14	6	.700	4.47	32	32	0	195.1	199	69	107	26	1.37
Career	179	123	.593	3.25	434	394	5	2724.2	2522	831	1786	194	1.23

How Often He Throws Strikes

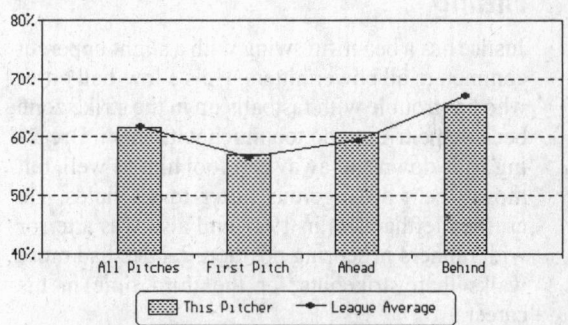

1997 Situational Stats

	W	L	ERA	Sv	IP		AB	H	HR	RBI	Avg
Home	6	1	3.87	0	100.0	LHB	340	96	12	49	.282
Road	8	5	5.10	0	95.1	RHB	392	103	14	48	.263
First Half	7	5	4.95	0	120.0	Sc Pos	164	48	7	69	.293
Scnd Half	7	1	3.70	0	75.1	Clutch	35	15	2	5	.429

1997 Rankings (American League)

⇒ 1st in lowest stolen base percentage allowed (33.3%) and most GDPs induced per 9 innings (1.4)
⇒ 3rd in GDPs induced (31) and highest ground-ball/flyball ratio allowed (2.2)
⇒ Led the Indians in complete games (1), hit batsmen (11), wild pitches (11), pickoff throws (90), GDPs induced (31), winning percentage, lowest batting average allowed (.272), lowest on-base percentage allowed (.340), lowest stolen base percentage allowed (33.3%), least pitches thrown per batter (3.53), least baserunners allowed per 9 innings (12.9), most run support per 9 innings (6.0), most GDPs induced per 9 innings (1.4), most GDPs induced per GDP situation (19.6%) and ERA at home

David Justice

1997 Season

David Justice made an easy transition to the American League in 1997, coming to Cleveland with Marquis Grissom in the blockbuster Kenny Lofton trade. Justice came back with a vengeance from the serious shoulder injury he suffered while taking a swing in 1996. He upped his games played from 40 to 139 and made the AL All-Star team. He was among the league batting leaders from start to finish, and topped the 30-homer and 100-RBI marks for the second time in his nine-year career. If it wasn't for a hyperextended left elbow and a torn patella tendon in his left knee, his offensive production would have been even better.

Hitting

Justice has a beautiful swing with a slight uppercut common to all power hitters. He's a low-ball hitter who has trouble with fastballs up in the strike zone because he tries to do too much with them. Breaking balls down and away can fool him as well, but mostly he's a dangerous hitter to all fields. He crushed lefthanders in 1997 and also was a terror with runners in scoring position. Justice had more walks than strikeouts for the third time in his career.

Baserunning & Defense

After the trade, Justice moved from right to left field. He felt awkward, but played well until injuries hit. He handled left field in the World Series with no problems, but looked most at ease during his three starts in right field during the regular season, displaying a strong arm. Justice runs the bases hard and well, but his knee injury stole any spring he had in his step.

1998 Outlook

Justice, who was scheduled to undergo knee surgery over the winter, should be in the Opening Day outfield this season. He signed a four-year contract extension last season with a club option for 2003. He was supposed to be a secondary player in the Kenny Lofton trade, but turned out to be the most valuable player in the deal.

Position: LF/DH
Bats: L **Throws:** L
Ht: 6' 3" **Wt:** 200

Opening Day Age: 31
Born: 4/14/66 in Cincinnati, OH
ML Seasons: 9

Overall Statistics

	G	AB	R	H	D	T	HR	RBI	SB	BB	SO	Avg	OBP	Slg
1997	139	495	84	163	31	1	33	101	3	80	79	.329	.418	.596
Career	956	3353	559	949	158	17	193	623	36	532	571	.283	.380	.513

Where He Hits the Ball

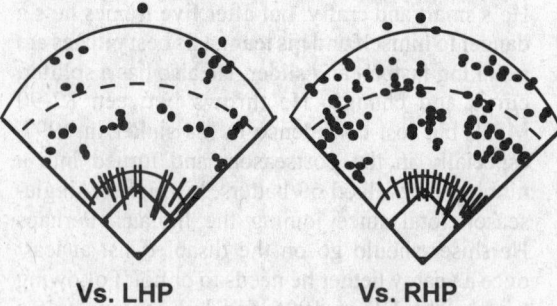

Vs. LHP   **Vs. RHP**

1997 Situational Stats

	AB	H	HR	RBI	Avg		AB	H	HR	RBI	Avg
Home	238	84	17	55	.353	LHP	146	47	11	32	.322
Road	257	79	16	46	.307	RHP	349	116	22	69	.332
First Half	218	73	17	47	.335	Sc Pos	127	45	11	74	.354
Scnd Half	277	90	16	54	.325	Clutch	65	22	5	18	.338

1997 Rankings (American League)

⇒ 2nd in batting average at home
⇒ 3rd in batting average and slugging percentage
⇒ 4th in on-base percentage vs. righthanded pitchers (.432)
⇒ 5th in on-base percentage, batting average with runners in scoring position, slugging percentage vs. lefthanded pitchers (.616) and lowest percentage of extra bases taken as a runner (28.8%)
⇒ Led the Indians in batting average, intentional walks (11), slugging percentage, batting average with runners in scoring position, batting average vs. righthanded pitchers and batting average at home

Jose Mesa

1997 Season

After memorable campaigns in 1995 and 1996, Jose Mesa had a season to forget in 1997. He started the year in court, where he was acquitted of sex and weapons charges. He ended it by blowing a 2-1 lead in the ninth inning of the seventh game of the World Series. In between, Mesa lost the closer's job at the end of April, and reclaimed it in August after he regained his confidence while working in long and middle relief. He showed flashes of his old dominance, going 4-1, 0.86 in his last 47 appearances of the regular season. From August 5 to September 8, he didn't allow an earned run in 17 straight appearances.

Pitching

Mesa is a power pitcher who can throw consistently between 96-98 MPH. He has a four-seam fastball that rises and two-seamer that sinks. He's strong and durable, and can easily pitch three or four days in a row. Mesa gets into problems when he stops throwing gas and goes to sliders and slow curves. That's what he did in Game 7 against the Marlins, and the Indians are still upset about it. He owned righthanders in 1997, but lefties hit .309 against him.

Defense

Mesa never has been a great fielder, but he does an adequate job covering his ground. He gets off the mound quickly and always hustles over to first base. He paid more attention to runners in long and middle relief, with three of five basestealers thrown out on his watch. His quick delivery is always appreciated by his batterymate.

1998 Outlook

Mesa earned saves to clinch the first two rounds of the playoffs, but his failure to finish off the World Series may cost him the closer's job. He was 4-for-7 in converting saves with one-run leads in 1997, and the Indians didn't protect him in the expansion draft. He still could be a valuable part of the bullpen as a setup man and middle reliever.

Position: RP
Bats: R **Throws:** R
Ht: 6' 3" **Wt:** 225

Opening Day Age: 31
Born: 5/22/66 in Azua, DR
ML Seasons: 9
Pronunciation: MAY-sa

Overall Statistics

	W	L	Pct.	ERA	G	GS	Sv	IP	H	BB	SO	HR	Ratio
1997	4	4	.500	2.40	66	0	16	82.1	83	28	69	7	1.35
Career	43	56	.434	4.28	346	95	103	862.2	899	335	539	74	1.43

How Often He Throws Strikes

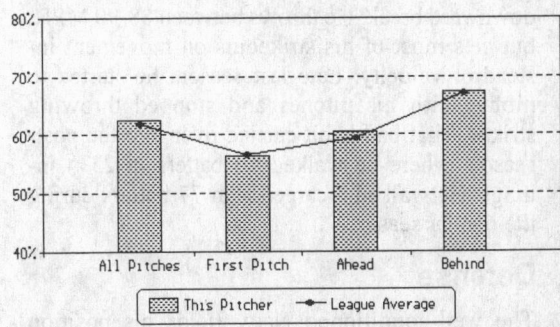

1997 Situational Stats

	W	L	ERA	Sv	IP		AB	H	HR	RBI	Avg
Home	2	1	2.09	7	47.1	LHB	149	46	1	13	.309
Road	2	3	2.83	9	35.0	RHB	172	37	6	17	.215
First Half	1	4	4.25	3	36.0	Sc Pos	88	17	0	22	.193
Scnd Half	3	0	0.97	13	46.1	Clutch	138	33	4	14	.239

1997 Rankings (American League)

⇒ 2nd in lowest save percentage (76.2%)
⇒ 6th in lowest percentage of inherited runners scored (22.2%)
⇒ 7th in relief ERA (2.40)
⇒ 10th in relief innings (82.1)
⇒ Led the Indians in saves, games finished (38), save opportunities (21), save percentage (76.2%), blown saves (5), lowest percentage of inherited runners scored (22.2%), relief ERA (2.40) and relief innings (82.1)

Charles Nagy

Position: SP
Bats: L **Throws:** R
Ht: 6' 3" **Wt:** 200

Opening Day Age: 30
Born: 5/5/67 in Fairfield, CT
ML Seasons: 8
Pronunciation: NAG-ee

1997 Season

Charles Nagy continued to be the quiet leader of the Cleveland pitching staff. He led the Indians in victories, innings and strikeouts for the third straight year. He pitched into the seventh inning in 28 of his 34 starts, but the workload may have caught up to him in the postseason. His ERA for September was 5.18. He then went 0-2, 4.94 in the playoffs and was passed over to start the seventh game of the World Series in favor of rookie Jaret Wright.

Pitching

Nagy throws a sinker, fastball, splitter and slurve. The slurve is Nagy's out pitch because of its sharp downward break. He throws between 88-90 MPH, but gets most of his strikeouts on movement instead of velocity. Late last season, he started to nibble with his pitches and stopped throwing strikes. That bad habit carried over into the postseason, where he walked 16 batters in 23⅔ innings. He walked a career-high 77 batters during the regular season.

Defense

The well-conditioned Nagy fields his position well, but does a poor job of holding runners. He improved somewhat in 1997, with 10 of 34 runners getting thrown out while attempting to steal with him on the mound. Defensively, he handles shots up the middle well, sometimes knocking them down with his feet. Nagy has played error-free baseball during the last two seasons.

1998 Outlook

The Indians exercised Nagy's option for 1998, but they have some major repair work to do. How do you bring the ace of the staff back after saying he's not good enough to start the seventh game of the World Series? Nagy may have been bothered by a breakdown in negotiations when the Indians tried to extend his contract but were put off when his agents asked for $7 million a year. He went through a similar slump in 1996 when negotiations went poorly.

Overall Statistics

	W	L	Pct.	ERA	G	GS	Sv	IP	H	BB	SO	HR	Ratio
1997	15	11	.577	4.28	34	34	0	227.0	253	77	149	27	1.45
Career	89	65	.578	3.93	202	201	0	1354.0	1436	404	897	122	1.36

How Often He Throws Strikes

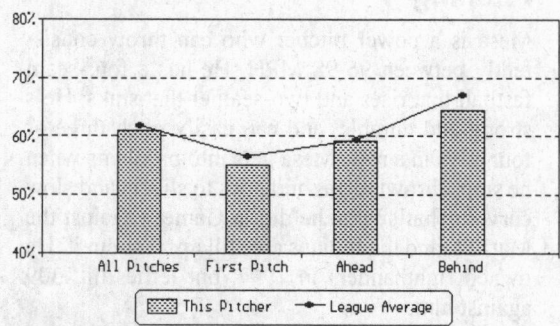

1997 Situational Stats

	W	L	ERA	Sv	IP		AB	H	HR	RBI	Avg
Home	9	6	4.37	0	129.2	LHB	419	117	13	49	.279
Road	6	5	4.16	0	97.1	RHB	476	136	14	59	.286
First Half	9	4	3.92	0	121.2	Sc Pos	223	59	5	80	.265
Scnd Half	6	7	4.70	0	105.1	Clutch	57	18	4	8	.316

1997 Rankings (American League)

⇒ 1st in fielding percentage at pitcher (1.000)
⇒ 2nd in hits allowed and highest groundball/flyball ratio allowed (2.3)
⇒ 4th in batters faced (991) and stolen bases allowed (24)
⇒ 5th in games started
⇒ Led the Indians in ERA, wins, losses, games started, complete games (1), shutouts (1), innings pitched, hits allowed, batters faced (991), home runs allowed, walks allowed, strikeouts, pitches thrown (3,606), stolen bases allowed (24), runners caught stealing (10), highest strikeout/walk ratio (1.9), lowest slugging percentage allowed (.434), highest groundball/flyball ratio allowed (2.3) and least home runs allowed per 9 innings (1.07)

Manny Ramirez

1997 Season

For the first time in five seasons in the big leagues, Manny Ramirez's power numbers didn't increase from the previous year. Ramirez ended 1997 with 26 homers and 88 RBI after hitting 33 homers and driving in 112 runs the year before. He did set new career highs, however, by hitting .328 and scoring 99 runs. Ramirez was bothered by hamstring problems early in the season. Some observers believe he began adopting Julio Franco's line-drive, opposite-field approach to hitting, which cost Ramirez power and RBI.

Hitting

Ramirez moved into the middle of the order full time in 1997, as the Indians looked to him to be one of the bats to replace the production of Albert Belle. Ramirez never looked comfortable, hitting .237 with runners in scoring position and grounding into a team-high 19 double plays. He always has been a patient hitter, but set a career high with 115 strikeouts last year. High fastballs and breaking balls away give him trouble. He has excellent power to all fields, especially to right. Ramirez, a .347 lifetime hitter against lefties, continued to pound them in 1997.

Baserunning & Defense

If Ramirez isn't the worst baserunner in the big leagues, he's the most confused. In a game against Detroit last year, he went to second on defensive indifference. But he thought the pitch had been fouled off and was tagged out walking back to first. As good as his instincts are at the plate, they're that bad on the bases. In right field, Ramirez continued to make strides even though he made seven errors. He usually hits the cutoff man, but some of his throws home lacked juice. He never appears to be running hard, but usually gets to the ball just in time.

1998 Outlook

There were rumors after the World Series that the Indians might trade Ramirez, but the team denied them. Ramirez should continue to improve offensively and defensively. As for running the bases, any chance for improvement seems slim. It's tough to teach speed and instincts.

Position: RF
Bats: R **Throws:** R
Ht: 6' 0" **Wt:** 190

Opening Day Age: 25
Born: 5/30/72 in Santo Domingo, DR
ML Seasons: 5

Overall Statistics

	G	AB	R	H	D	T	HR	RBI	SB	BB	SO	Avg	OBP	Slg
1997	150	561	99	184	40	0	26	88	2	79	115	.328	.415	.538
Career	552	1938	334	590	134	4	109	372	20	283	411	.304	.393	.546

Where He Hits the Ball

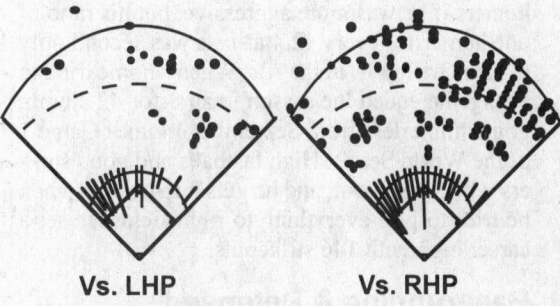

Vs. LHP   **Vs. RHP**

1997 Situational Stats

	AB	H	HR	RBI	Avg		AB	H	HR	RBI	Avg
Home	279	93	14	47	.333	LHP	137	48	6	26	.350
Road	282	91	12	41	.323	RHP	424	136	20	62	.321
First Half	263	90	13	49	.342	Sc Pos	152	36	5	62	.237
Scnd Half	298	94	13	39	.315	Clutch	62	22	4	8	.355

1997 Rankings (American League)

⇒ 2nd in errors in right field (7)
⇒ 3rd in lowest fielding percentage in right field (.975)
⇒ 4th in batting average on a 3-1 count (.667) and cleanup slugging percentage (.566)
⇒ 5th in batting average and batting average on the road
⇒ Led the Indians in hits, doubles, total bases (302), hit by pitch (7), times on base (270), GDPs (19), plate appearances (651), batting average on a 3-1 count (.667), cleanup slugging percentage (.566), batting average on the road and batting average with two strikes (.247)

Jim Thome

1997 Season

Jim Thome moved from third to first base in 1997, making way for Matt Williams at the hot corner. He continued to compile big offensive numbers with his second straight season of 100-plus runs, RBI and walks. He also chipped in with a career-high 40 homers, becoming the first Indian to hit 40 home runs and draw 100 walks in the same season. Thome, who led the American League with 120 walks, hit third and fourth in the lineup, and was equally effective in either spot.

Hitting

Critics say Thome takes too many good pitches in search of perfection. They say he'd hit even more homers if he was more aggressive, but his ratio of one homer for every 12.4 at-bats was second only to Ken Griffey Jr. in the AL. When Thome tried to change he ended the season in an 8-for-42 slump, going homerless from September 14 until Game 1 of the World Series. High fastballs and good sinkers will get him out, and he gets into trouble when he tries to pull everything to right field. He set a career high with 146 strikeouts.

Baserunning & Defense

Thome doesn't run badly for a big man, but he's no threat to beat out an infield single or steal a base. He goes from first to third well, will break up a double play at second and has a variety of nifty slides for close plays at the plate. Thome's play at first base needs work, but he scoops low throws well. He has limited range going to the line and still gets caught trying for grounders that belong to the second baseman. He's still adjusting to the position and should improve as he becomes more comfortable at first.

1998 Outlook

Thome's combination of power, walks and average is simply dynamite. If he ever hits for power against lefties, he'll be a strong candidate for an MVP season. He has signed a contract extension through 2001 and may one day pass Albert Belle as the Indians' all-time home-run leader.

Position: 1B
Bats: L **Throws:** R
Ht: 6' 4" **Wt:** 220

Opening Day Age: 27
Born: 8/27/70 in Peoria, IL
ML Seasons: 7
Pronunciation: TOE-mee

Overall Statistics

	G	AB	R	H	D	T	HR	RBI	SB	BB	SO	Avg	OBP	Slg
1997	147	496	104	142	25	0	40	102	1	120	146	.286	.423	.579
Career	647	2143	419	617	120	12	133	386	15	430	570	.288	.408	.541

Where He Hits the Ball

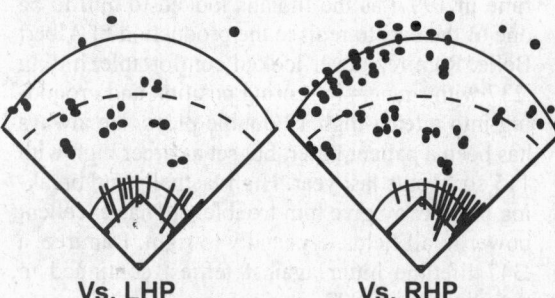

Vs. LHP   Vs. RHP

1997 Situational Stats

	AB	H	HR	RBI	Avg		AB	H	HR	RBI	Avg
Home	238	68	17	50	.286	LHP	131	36	4	22	.275
Road	258	74	23	52	.287	RHP	365	106	36	80	.290
First Half	258	77	24	62	.298	Sc Pos	132	38	7	63	.288
Scnd Half	238	65	16	40	.273	Clutch	54	14	4	13	.259

1997 Rankings (American League)

⇒ 1st in walks and most pitches seen per plate appearance (4.46)

⇒ 2nd in HR frequency (12.4 ABs per HR), slugging percentage vs. righthanded pitchers (.638) and highest percentage of pitches taken (65.6%)

⇒ 3rd in on-base percentage, batting average on an 0-2 count (.316), on-base percentage vs. righthanded pitchers (.445) and lowest percentage of swings on the first pitch (14.2%)

⇒ Led the Indians in home runs, runs scored, walks, strikeouts, pitches seen (2,799), on-base percentage, HR frequency (12.4 ABs per HR), most pitches seen per plate appearance (4.46), least GDPs per GDP situation (8.0%), batting average on an 0-2 count (.316) and slugging percentage vs. righthanded pitchers (.638)

Omar Vizquel

1997 Season

Omar Vizquel came back from surgery on his right shoulder after the 1996 season to win his fifth straight Gold Glove in 1997. He also provided some offense, hitting first, second, eighth and ninth in the lineup, and showing fine extra-base power for a shortstop. Vizquel continued to bloom as a baserunner with a career-high 43 steals. Only his .214 batting average in May kept him from hitting .300 for the year.

Hitting

There were times during his career in Seattle when Vizquel was called "Omar The Outmaker." That nickname has become a thing of the past as he has gotten stronger, more patient and more accustomed to switch-hitting. He's an excellent bunter, leading the American League with 16 sacrifice bunts in 1997, and is hard to strike out. High fastballs and inside breaking balls bother him, and he struggled with runners in scoring position. He's a better lefthanded hitter because he can pull the ball as well as slap breaking balls and sliders into left field.

Baserunning & Defense

Without Kenny Lofton, Vizquel was the Indians' running game In 1997. In four years with the Tribe, his steals have increased from 13 to 43. He relies on reading pitchers more than speed. Defensively, Vizquel may have the surest hands in the game. He often fields bouncers barehanded, has great range going to the hole and is acrobatic turning the double play. He has an average arm, but makes up for it with a quick release.

1998 Outlook

Vizquel has had a profound effect on the Indians' defense since he arrived in 1994. They have become a solid defensive team despite the revolving cast of characters on the rest of the infield. Vizquel batted .287 as a leadoff hitter in 1997, but felt uncomfortable in that role. The Indians went into the offseason trying to find a leadoff hitter to allow him to hit lower in the order.

Position: SS
Bats: B **Throws:** R
Ht: 5' 9" **Wt:** 165

Opening Day Age: 30
Born: 4/24/67 in Caracas, VZ
ML Seasons: 9
Pronunciation: viz-KELL

Overall Statistics

	G	AB	R	H	D	T	HR	RBI	SB	BB	SO	Avg	OBP	Slg
1997	153	565	89	158	23	6	5	49	43	57	58	.280	.347	.368
Career	1169	4046	536	1072	157	23	27	333	159	368	390	.265	.326	.335

Where He Hits the Ball

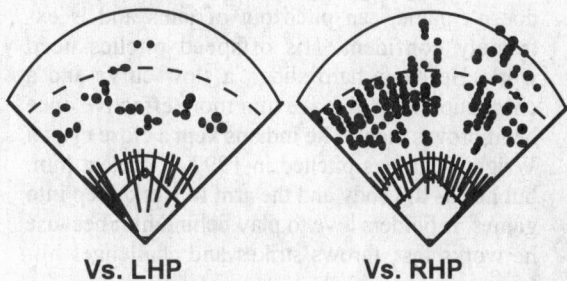

Vs. LHP   **Vs. RHP**

1997 Situational Stats

	AB	H	HR	RBI	Avg		AB	H	HR	RBI	Avg
Home	290	87	3	26	.300	LHP	151	40	2	14	.265
Road	275	71	2	23	.258	RHP	414	118	3	35	.285
First Half	290	81	2	27	.279	Sc Pos	143	32	1	42	.224
Scnd Half	275	77	3	22	.280	Clutch	68	26	0	10	.382

1997 Rankings (American League)

⇒ 1st in sacrifice bunts (16)
⇒ 2nd in batting average in the clutch and fielding percentage at shortstop (.985)
⇒ 3rd in bunts in play (29)
⇒ 4th in steals of third (10)
⇒ 5th in stolen bases, lowest HR frequency (113.0 ABs per HR) and lowest percentage of swings that missed (10.0%)
⇒ Led the Indians in singles, triples, sacrifice bunts (16), stolen bases, games played (153), highest groundball/flyball ratio (1.4), stolen base percentage (78.2%), on-base percentage for a leadoff hitter (.369), bunts in play (29), lowest percentage of swings that missed (10.0%), steals of third (10) and highest percentage of extra bases taken as a runner (43.9%)

Cleveland Indians

Jaret Wright

1997 Season

Jaret Wright had the kind of rookie season that even Hollywood would buy the rights to. He started the year in Double-A Akron and ended up being just the eighth rookie ever to start the deciding game in the Fall Classic. He was promoted to the big leagues on June 24 and won his major league debut the very same day. He went 5-1 in his last seven starts of the season and 3-0 in five starts in the postseason. All this came at the tender age of 21.

Pitching

Wright lives and dies with a 95-97 MPH fastball, but he's not just a thrower. Schooled by his father, former big league pitcher Clyde Wright, he doesn't panic, can pitch out of jams and is extremely confident. His offspeed pitches need work. He has a hard slider, a slow curve and a changeup that will make him more effective once he improves them. The Indians kept a close eye on Wright's innings pitched in 1997 to protect him, but he has the body and the arm to work deep into games. Infielders love to play behind him because he works fast, throws strikes and challenges hitters.

Defense

Like most young pitchers, Wright wasn't overly concerned about the running game. Only one of the 16 runners who attempted to steal a base with him on the mound was thrown out. Wright didn't make an error in 16 starts. He gets off the mound quickly and covers first base when he should. His big frame doesn't hamper him.

1998 Outlook

The Indians didn't figure Wright would pitch as well as he did. The next step in his maturation process will come when he assumes the role of No. 1 starter. It might not be this season, but the Indians think that day is quickly approaching. Cleveland may finally have found the lead-dog starter they've yearned for.

Position: SP
Bats: R **Throws:** R
Ht: 6' 2" **Wt:** 230

Opening Day Age: 22
Born: 12/29/75 in Anaheim, CA
ML Seasons: 1

Overall Statistics

	W	L	Pct.	ERA	G	GS	Sv	IP	H	BB	SO	HR	Ratio
1997	8	3	.727	4.38	16	16	0	90.1	81	35	63	9	1.28
Career	8	3	.727	4.38	16	16	0	90.1	81	35	63	9	1.28

How Often He Throws Strikes

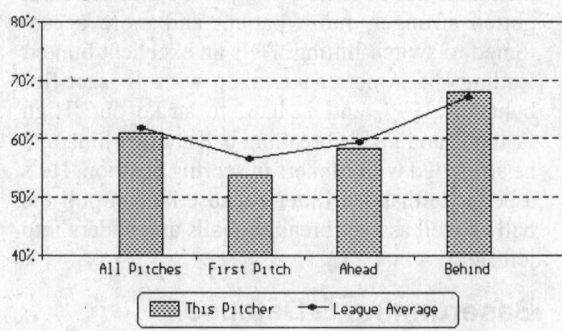

1997 Situational Stats

	W	L	ERA	Sv	IP		AB	H	HR	RBI	Avg
Home	3	2	5.20	0	36.1	LHB	175	49	4	22	.280
Road	5	1	3.83	0	54.0	RHB	166	32	5	16	.193
First Half	1	0	5.59	0	9.2	Sc Pos	88	24	3	32	.273
Scnd Half	7	3	4.24	0	80.2	Clutch	2	1	0	0	.500

1997 Rankings (American League)

⇒ Did not rank near the top or bottom in any category

Paul Assenmacher

Position: RP
Bats: L **Throws:** L
Ht: 6' 3" **Wt:** 210

Opening Day Age: 37
Born: 12/10/60 in Allen Park, MI
ML Seasons: 12
Pronunciation: AH-sen-mock-er

Overall Statistics

	W	L	Pct.	ERA	G	GS	Sv	IP	H	BB	SO	HR	Ratio
1997	5	0	1.000	2.94	75	0	4	49.0	43	15	53	5	1.18
Career	57	38	.600	3.35	760	1	53	775.2	713	279	735	62	1.28

1997 Situational Stats

	W	L	ERA	Sv	IP		AB	H	HR	RBI	Avg
Home	4	0	4.15	2	26.0	LHB	89	20	3	13	.225
Road	1	0	1.57	2	23.0	RHB	97	23	2	9	.237
First Half	2	0	5.66	0	20.2	Sc Pos	59	10	0	15	.169
Scnd Half	3	0	0.95	4	28.1	Clutch	82	14	0	7	.171

1997 Season

After a slow start because of family problems, Paul Assenmacher proved to be almost unhittable as a lefthanded setup man. His 75 appearances were the most in seven years for the 12-year vet and tied a career high. It was really a tale of two seasons. Assenmacher had a 7.63 ERA in his first 31 appearances and a 0.80 ERA in his last 44. In 30 appearances from June 18-August 26, he did not allow an earned run.

Pitching & Defense

Assenmacher's best pitch is a sharp-breaking curve that buckles lefties' knees. His fastball averages 88 MPH and can touch 90. He has made 520 appearances in the 1990s, the most in the big leagues. He's pressure-tested, allowing just 17 of 74 inherited runners to score last year. He hasn't committed an error since 1993. His slow delivery does little to shut down opposing running games.

1998 Outlook

The Indians almost gambled by not picking up Assenmacher's 1998 option. They made him a free agent so they could protect another player in November's expansion draft, then signed him anyway. If he had signed with another club, Cleveland's bullpen would have suffered a serious loss.

Jeff Branson

Position: 2B/3B/SS
Bats: L **Throws:** R
Ht: 6' 0" **Wt:** 180

Opening Day Age: 31
Born: 1/26/67 in Waynesboro, MS
ML Seasons: 6

Overall Statistics

	G	AB	R	H	D	T	HR	RBI	SB	BB	SO	Avg	OBP	Slg
1997	94	170	14	34	7	1	3	12	1	14	40	.200	.262	.306
Career	600	1417	161	353	67	10	33	147	9	118	281	.249	.305	.380

1997 Situational Stats

	AB	H	HR	RBI	Avg		AB	H	HR	RBI	Avg
Home	83	19	3	9	.229	LHP	18	7	0	0	.389
Road	87	15	0	3	.172	RHP	152	27	3	12	.178
First Half	91	13	1	5	.143	Sc Pos	31	3	1	9	.097
Scnd Half	79	21	2	7	.266	Clutch	45	6	1	3	.133

1997 Season

Jeff Branson went from almost being released by Cincinnati to the World Series with Cleveland. After he was outrighted off the 40-man roster by the Reds, Branson was part of the July 31 trade that brought John Smiley to the Indians. He started the season with Cincinnati in a 4-for-44 slump. In Cleveland, he platooned at second base with Tony Fernandez until the acquisition of Bip Roberts on August 31.

Hitting, Baserunning & Defense

Branson is a fastball hitter with a touch of power. He historically struggles against lefties, though he went 7-for-18 (.389) versus southpaws in 1997. He logged time in the field at second, third and short, with his best efforts coming at the hot corner. He doesn't run very well.

1998 Outlook

Branson didn't get much of a chance to show his skills with the Reds or the Indians. Eligible for arbitration, he wasn't expected to return to Cleveland. He's a decent utilityman who still has a few years left.

Bartolo Colon (Top Prospect)

Position: SP
Bats: R **Throws:** R
Ht: 6' 0" **Wt:** 185

Opening Day Age: 22
Born: 5/24/75 in Altamira, DR
ML Seasons: 1
Pronunciation: BAR-toe-loh ko-LONE

Overall Statistics

	W	L	Pct.	ERA	G	GS	Sv	IP	H	BB	SO	HR	Ratio
1997	4	7	.364	5.65	19	17	0	94.0	107	45	66	12	1.62
Career	4	7	.364	5.65	19	17	0	94.0	107	45	66	12	1.62

1997 Situational Stats

	W	L	ERA	Sv	IP		AB	H	HR	RBI	Avg
Home	2	3	4.53	0	43.2	LHB	200	56	5	26	.280
Road	2	4	6.62	0	50.1	RHB	174	51	7	29	.293
First Half	1	2	6.75	0	26.2	Sc Pos	107	29	2	41	.271
Scnd Half	3	5	5.21	0	67.1	Clutch	15	6	1	2	.400

1997 Season

Excuse Bartolo Colon if he didn't know where he was for most of his rookie season. He bounced between Cleveland and Triple-A Buffalo seven times. The Indians wanted to give Colon a full year at Buffalo, but injuries wouldn't allow them to do so. Colon's best month came in September, when he went 2-1 in five appearances.

Pitching & Defense

Colon's fastball has been timed anywhere from 95-99 MPH. Control of that fastball was a problem in 1997, as was his inability to throw his curve and changeup for strikes. In his second start of the season, Colon threw 61 pitches against Seattle—in the first inning. He committed five errors and certainly needs more seasoning when it comes to holding big league runners. Ten of 12 basestealers were successful against him.

1998 Outlook

The Indians would like to build their rotation around Colon and Jaret Wright, two young, hard-throwing righthanders. But they went into the off-season contemplating trading Colon to get an established No. 1 starter. He does come with a history of elbow problems, but he's also one of baseball's most coveted pitching prospects.

Mike Jackson

Position: RP
Bats: R **Throws:** R
Ht: 6' 2" **Wt:** 225

Opening Day Age: 33
Born: 12/22/64 in Houston, TX
ML Seasons: 12

Overall Statistics

	W	L	Pct.	ERA	G	GS	Sv	IP	H	BB	SO	HR	Ratio
1997	2	5	.286	3.24	71	0	15	75.0	59	29	74	3	1.17
Career	49	56	.467	3.33	694	7	59	885.0	698	375	795	86	1.21

1997 Situational Stats

	W	L	ERA	Sv	IP		AB	H	HR	RBI	Avg
Home	1	3	4.33	8	35.1	LHB	117	35	0	18	.299
Road	1	2	2.27	7	39.2	RHB	157	24	3	6	.153
First Half	1	1	2.27	11	43.2	Sc Pos	62	16	0	20	.258
Scnd Half	1	4	4.60	4	31.1	Clutch	151	29	1	11	.192

1997 Season

A case can be made for Mike Jackson being the Indians' MVP in 1997. With closer Jose Mesa hounded by legal problems at the start of the year, Jackson converted 14 of 16 save opportunities before returning to his setup role in August. He then turned in a splendid postseason, allowing one earned run with 16 strikeouts in 13 appearances covering 13⅓ innings.

Pitching & Defense

His hat pulled down to eye level, Jackson is intimidating on the mound. His slider and fastball are even more fearsome. He throws between 90-95 MPH, but the slider is his best pitch. He dominated righthanders in 1997, but lefties hurt him. Two runners attempted to steal against him and both were successful. He doesn't get many opportunities to flash the leather, but he has made only one error in the last four years.

1998 Outlook

Some Tribe scouts think Jackson has better stuff than Mesa and should be the closer. Jackson, however, isn't wild about finishing games. He's signed through 1998.

Jeff Juden

Position: SP
Bats: B **Throws:** R
Ht: 6' 8" **Wt:** 265

Opening Day Age: 27
Born: 1/19/71 in Salem, MA
ML Seasons: 6
Pronunciation: JOO-den

Overall Statistics

	W	L	Pct.	ERA	G	GS	Sv	IP	H	BB	SO	HR	Ratio
1997	11	6	.647	4.46	30	27	0	161.1	157	72	136	23	1.42
Career	19	17	.528	4.36	113	45	0	349.0	323	160	284	45	1.38

1997 Situational Stats

	W	L	ERA	Sv	IP		AB	H	HR	RBI	Avg
Home	7	3	4.17	0	90.2	LHB	281	84	10	35	.299
Road	4	3	4.84	0	70.2	RHB	330	73	13	44	.221
First Half	11	2	3.70	0	109.1	Sc Pos	157	32	4	51	.204
Scnd Half	0	4	6.06	0	52.0	Clutch	36	9	4	5	.250

1997 Season

Jeff Juden had the best first half of his career in 1997 with Montreal. He won his first five decisions and was 11-2 on July 6. Juden's season took a sharp downturn after the Indians acquired him on July 31. He was given three starts to win a job in the rotation, but went 0-1, 6.14 before being banished to the bullpen. He made an emergency start for injured John Smiley on September 20 and used it as a springboard to make the postseason roster.

Pitching & Defense

Juden is strictly a power pitcher. He's 6-foot-8 and isn't afraid to move hitters off the plate. He throws a 90-93 MPH fastball, cut fastball and slider. He was tough on righthanders in 1997. He couldn't hold a runner to save his life. He allowed 50 steals in 56 attempts last season, and no other major league pitcher permitted more than 34 swipes. His motion doesn't leave him in good fielding position, and he committed three errors in 1997.

1998 Outlook

There's a strong suspicion that Juden made the postseason roster only to salvage an otherwise disastrous trade. He has a bad reputation and didn't get along well with his Montreal teammates. He was eligible for arbitration over the winter, but the Indians planned on re-signing him as a swingman.

Chad Ogea

Position: SP
Bats: R **Throws:** R
Ht: 6' 2" **Wt:** 200

Opening Day Age: 27
Born: 11/9/70 in Lake Charles, LA
ML Seasons: 4
Pronunciation: OH-jay

Overall Statistics

	W	L	Pct.	ERA	G	GS	Sv	IP	H	BB	SO	HR	Ratio
1997	8	9	.471	4.99	21	21	0	126.1	139	47	80	13	1.47
Career	26	19	.578	4.44	74	57	0	395.2	406	128	249	48	1.35

1997 Situational Stats

	W	L	ERA	Sv	IP		AB	H	HR	RBI	Avg
Home	3	6	5.20	0	62.1	LHB	243	74	8	39	.305
Road	5	3	4.78	0	64.0	RHB	249	65	5	28	.261
First Half	5	8	5.49	0	98.1	Sc Pos	127	34	3	54	.268
Scnd Half	3	1	3.21	0	28.0	Clutch	15	5	0	3	.333

1997 Season

What appeared to be a lost season for Chad Ogea turned into a huge success. Ogea had lost five straight starts when he was placed on the disabled list with a sore right elbow and tender left knee on June 24. After more than two months on the DL, he was activated on September 1 and went 3-1 in his last five starts. Then he put together a strong postseason run, including two victories over Marlins ace Kevin Brown in the World Series.

Pitching & Defense

Ogea throws a changeup, curveball and fastball. His change is his best pitch, but he has to keep it down in the strike zone in order to be effective. He short-arms the ball but is deceptively fast, throwing between 87-91 MPH. He wears a brace on his left knee and isn't mobile on the mound, but he turned in another solid effort against basestealers.

1998 Outlook

Ogea's performance in the postseason all but guaranteed that he would be protected in the expansion draft and given a spot in the 1998 rotation. He rededicated himself to his physical conditioning during his stay on the disabled list, and that should help him.

Eric Plunk

Position: RP
Bats: R **Throws:** R
Ht: 6' 6" **Wt:** 220

Opening Day Age: 34
Born: 9/3/63 in Wilmington, CA
ML Seasons: 12

Overall Statistics

	W	L	Pct.	ERA	G	GS	Sv	IP	H	BB	SO	HR	Ratio
1997	4	5	.444	4.66	55	0	0	65.2	62	36	66	12	1.49
Career	64	51	.557	3.69	583	41	34	1003.0	861	574	944	98	1.43

1997 Situational Stats

	W	L	ERA	Sv	IP		AB	H	HR	RBI	Avg
Home	2	0	4.08	0	28.2	LHB	94	26	5	12	.277
Road	2	5	5.11	0	37.0	RHB	159	36	7	28	.226
First Half	3	2	5.54	0	37.1	Sc Pos	92	17	2	28	.185
Scnd Half	1	3	3.49	0	28.1	Clutch	61	16	4	9	.262

1997 Season

After five seasons of being one of the best setup men in baseball, Eric Plunk couldn't overcome a bone spur in his left heel in 1997. It cost him his job as Cleveland's go-to guy in close games. He allowed 12 homers in 65⅔ innings after allowing 14 in 212⅔ from 1994-96. He then capped his disappointing campaign with a miserable showing in the playoffs, posting a 12.60 ERA in five games.

Pitching & Defense

Plunk is a power pitcher with a fastball that travels between 92-95 MPH. He throws both a hard and a slow curve, as well as a slider. By the end of 1997, he was throwing a lot of slow curves because his fastball was getting hit so hard. Plunk seldom pays attention to baserunners, who went 8-for-10 stealing bases against him last season. Thanks to his limited innings he doesn't get many chances in the field, though he committed two errors in eight opportunities in '97.

1998 Outlook

Indians signed Plunk to a three-year deal with a club option before the 1997 season based on his track record. They could regret that contract unless he overcomes his heel problem, regains his confidence and becomes a viable part of the bullpen again.

Bip Roberts

Position: LF/2B
Bats: B **Throws:** R
Ht: 5' 7" **Wt:** 165

Opening Day Age: 34
Born: 10/27/63 in Berkeley, CA
ML Seasons: 11

Overall Statistics

	G	AB	R	H	D	T	HR	RBI	SB	BB	SO	Avg	OBP	Slg
1997	120	431	63	130	20	2	4	44	18	28	67	.302	.345	.385
Career	1107	3852	618	1141	186	31	29	328	248	365	510	.296	.359	.383

1997 Situational Stats

	AB	H	HR	RBI	Avg		AB	H	HR	RBI	Avg
Home	188	58	1	16	.309	LHP	145	47	2	15	.324
Road	243	72	3	28	.296	RHP	286	83	2	29	.290
First Half	196	63	1	23	.321	Sc Pos	100	29	0	34	.290
Scnd Half	235	67	3	21	.285	Clutch	69	23	0	4	.333

1997 Season

Bip Roberts got his first taste of the postseason after the Indians acquired him from Kansas City on August 31. He gave the Tribe a legitimate leadoff hitter for the first time since Cleveland traded Kenny Lofton to the Braves. Roberts, who hit .271 and scored 19 runs in 23 games after the trade, played second base against righthanders and left field against southpaws.

Hitting, Baserunning & Defense

Roberts is a contact hitter who likes the first pitch. He has almost no home-run power, but he turns high fastballs into doubles. He still can run and steal a base, and posted an outstanding stolen-base percentage of .857 (18 of 21) in 1997. Slightly built, Roberts isn't durable. He sat out the seventh game of the World Series with the flu. After the trade, he struggled defensively at second and left field. He turns a quick pivot, but his arm is below average, especially from the outfield.

1998 Outlook

If the Indians acquire a regular second baseman during the winter, the only way Roberts would return would be as a utility player. He could help the Tribe as a designated hitter out of the leadoff spot, but his inability to play when needed is a detriment.

Paul Shuey

Position: RP
Bats: R **Throws:** R
Ht: 6' 3" **Wt:** 215

Opening Day Age: 27
Born: 9/16/70 in Lima, OH
ML Seasons: 4
Pronunciation: SHOO-ee

Overall Statistics

	W	L	Pct.	ERA	G	GS	Sv	IP	H	BB	SO	HR	Ratio
1997	4	2	.667	6.20	40	0	2	45.0	52	28	46	5	1.78
Career	9	7	.563	4.78	103	0	11	116.2	116	71	111	12	1.60

1997 Situational Stats

	W	L	ERA	Sv	IP		AB	H	HR	RBI	Avg
Home	3	1	6.18	0	27.2	LHB	68	16	1	7	.235
Road	1	1	6.23	2	17.1	RHB	109	36	4	21	.330
First Half	2	1	5.16	2	22.2	Sc Pos	42	14	1	21	.333
Scnd Half	2	1	7.25	0	22.1	Clutch	34	9	1	6	.265

1997 Season

Just when Paul Shuey seemed to have established himself as a late-inning reliever, he slipped. He opened 1997 as Cleveland's closer because of Jose Mesa's legal problems, but he didn't last long in that role after posting a 9.31 ERA in nine April appearances. Shuey went on the disabled list three times, first with a strained right knee and twice with a pulled right hamstring. When he came off the DL the third time, he pitched so poorly that he didn't make the postseason roster.

Pitching & Defense

Shuey has a great arm and four quality pitches. He throws a fastball, changeup, splitter and curve. Wildness and injuries have hurt him, and he's been somewhat of a disappointment since being taken with the second overall pick in the 1992 draft. Shuey never has made an error in parts of four big league seasons, but he struggles to control the running game.

1998 Outlook

The Indians signed Shuey to a three-year deal last April, but ran the risk of losing him in the expansion draft because they couldn't afford to protect him based on his performance. He should continue as a middle reliever this year if his health allows.

John Smiley

Position: SP
Bats: L **Throws:** L
Ht: 6' 4" **Wt:** 210

Opening Day Age: 33
Born: 3/17/65 in Phoenixville, PA
ML Seasons: 12

Overall Statistics

	W	L	Pct.	ERA	G	GS	Sv	IP	H	BB	SO	HR	Ratio
1997	11	14	.440	5.31	26	26	0	154.1	184	41	120	26	1.46
Career	126	103	.550	3.80	361	280	4	1907.2	1842	496	1284	185	1.23

1997 Situational Stats

	W	L	ERA	Sv	IP		AB	H	HR	RBI	Avg
Home	4	6	7.57	0	54.2	LHB	107	41	5	12	.383
Road	7	8	4.06	0	99.2	RHB	511	143	21	77	.280
First Half	6	10	5.97	0	89.0	Sc Pos	144	44	5	57	.306
Scnd Half	5	4	4.41	0	65.1	Clutch	23	3	1	3	.130

1997 Season

The Indians acquired John Smiley from Cincinnati on July 31. He made six starts with the Tribe before breaking the humerus bone in his left arm while warming up for a start against Kansas City on September 20. He was throwing a curveball when he suffered a spiral fracture of the bone above his left elbow, a career-threatening injury.

Pitching & Defense

The Indians say Smiley wasn't damaged goods when they made the trade. But the fact is that when he broke his arm, he hadn't pitched in three weeks because of pain in his left elbow and shoulder. After the trade, he threw more changeups, sliders and curves than he had been throwing with the Reds. That combination may have put extra strain on his arm. Smiley's fastball is in the 90 MPH range and he has great control. Because Smiley doesn't have a smooth delivery or follow-through, he's a defensive liability. Basestealers get a good jump against him.

1998 Outlook

Smiley's arm was placed in a cast for six weeks, and he hoped to start throwing sometime in late March. Even the most optimistic projections don't have him pitching in game situations until late July or August—if at all in 1998.

Other Cleveland Indians

Pat Borders (Pos: C, Age: 34, Bats: R)

	G	AB	R	H	D	T	HR	RBI	SB	BB	SO	Avg	OBP	Slg
1997	55	159	17	47	7	1	4	15	0	9	27	.296	.341	.428
Career	935	2852	251	732	149	11	66	315	6	138	461	.257	.291	.386

The former World Series MVP made the Tribe as a non-roster player and served as a backup to Sandy Alomar Jr. When the year ended, Borders became a free agent. 1998 Outlook: B

Casey Candaele (Pos: 2B, Age: 37, Bats: B)

	G	AB	R	H	D	T	HR	RBI	SB	BB	SO	Avg	OBP	Slg
1997	14	26	5	8	1	0	0	4	1	1	1	.308	.333	.346
Career	754	1934	206	483	86	20	11	139	37	161	211	.250	.308	.332

Extending a career that just won't die, Candaele surfaced in Cleveland for the second straight year despite a .228 batting average in Triple-A. He has a winning personality, but he can't play any longer. 1998 Outlook: D

Trent Hubbard (Pos: LF, Age: 31, Bats: R)

	G	AB	R	H	D	T	HR	RBI	SB	BB	SO	Avg	OBP	Slg
1997	7	12	3	3	1	0	0	0	2	1	3	.250	.308	.333
Career	104	184	34	47	11	3	6	26	6	23	40	.255	.341	.446

Hubbard made three trips from Triple-A Buffalo to Cleveland, garnering a grand total of 12 at-bats. The Tribe has better outfield prospects on the way, which is why he signed with the Dodgers as a free agent. 1998 Outlook: C

Jason Jacome (Pos: LHP, Age: 27)

	W	L	Pct.	ERA	G	GS	Sv	IP	H	BB	SO	HR	Ratio
1997	2	0	1.000	5.84	28	4	0	49.1	58	20	27	10	1.58
Career	10	17	.370	5.17	105	33	1	256.0	313	95	139	36	1.59

Claimed off waivers from the Royals, Jacome made four starts when Orel Hershiser went on the disabled list. He's a lefthander who tries to beat hitters with guile but doesn't often succeed. 1998 Outlook: C

Jeff Manto (Pos: 3B, Age: 33, Bats: R)

	G	AB	R	H	D	T	HR	RBI	SB	BB	SO	Avg	OBP	Slg
1997	16	30	3	8	3	0	2	7	0	1	10	.267	.290	.567
Career	233	608	76	138	30	2	26	82	2	77	146	.227	.321	.411

Acquired from Toronto for Ryan Thompson, Manto briefly provided some power off the bench. In six years in the majors, he has played the equivalent of a full season and batted .227-26-82. 1998 Outlook: C

Jack McDowell (Pos: RHP, Age: 32)

	W	L	Pct.	ERA	G	GS	Sv	IP	H	BB	SO	HR	Ratio
1997	3	3	.500	5.09	8	6	0	40.2	44	18	38	6	1.52
Career	122	80	.604	3.76	259	257	0	1794.0	1727	582	1254	158	1.29

Black Jack grumbled when he was demoted to middle relief, but he was ineffective as a starter. He appeared only eight times before needing elbow surgery, and wasn't tendered a contract after the season. 1998 Outlook: C

Kevin Mitchell (Pos: DH, Age: 36, Bats: R)

	G	AB	R	H	D	T	HR	RBI	SB	BB	SO	Avg	OBP	Slg
1997	20	59	7	9	1	0	4	11	1	9	11	.153	.275	.373
Career	1172	4007	616	1144	217	24	232	739	30	482	693	.286	.363	.525

Brought in to provide power, Mitchell instead became a source of ridicule because of his poor physical condition. He was released in late May, shortly after fighting with teammate Chad Curtis. 1998 Outlook: C

Alvin Morman (Pos: LHP, Age: 29)

	W	L	Pct.	ERA	G	GS	Sv	IP	H	BB	SO	HR	Ratio
1997	0	0	-	5.89	34	0	2	18.1	19	14	13	2	1.80
Career	4	1	.800	5.22	87	0	2	60.1	62	38	44	10	1.66

Cleveland got Morman in a trade with the Astros, who got the better end of the deal. A lefthanded specialist, Morman had elbow problems but returned for the postseason. 1998 Outlook: B

Kevin Seitzer (Pos: DH/1B/3B, Age: 36, Bats: R)

	G	AB	R	H	D	T	HR	RBI	SB	BB	SO	Avg	OBP	Slg
1997	64	198	27	53	14	0	2	24	0	18	25	.268	.326	.369
Career	1439	5278	739	1557	285	35	74	613	80	669	617	.295	.375	.404

Ten years from now Seitzer still will be able to line a single to right field. But tired of playing on badly scarred knees, he retired after the World Series. 1998 Outlook: D.

Dave Weathers (Pos: RHP, Age: 28)

	W	L	Pct.	ERA	G	GS	Sv	IP	H	BB	SO	HR	Ratio
1997	1	3	.250	8.42	19	1	0	25.2	38	15	18	3	2.06
Career	18	27	.400	5.67	144	58	0	403.1	493	200	253	37	1.72

Weathers was acquired from the Yankees for Chad Curtis in what essentially was a salary dump. Despite a career 5.67 ERA, Weathers keeps getting chances to pitch. 1998 Outlook: C

Cleveland Indians Minor League Prospects

Organization Overview:

The Indians are in as good a position as any team in the game. Not only did they come within two outs of winning the World Series, but they have most of their players locked up with long-term contracts, compete in baseball's weakest division—and have one of the deepest farm systems in the game. That combination should ensure that they'll contend for the next few years. They've produced sluggers such as Manny Ramirez and Jim Thome, and pitchers such as Bartolo Colon, Charles Nagy and Jaret Wright. The upper levels of Cleveland's system have plenty of talent, which not only provides reinforcements but also trade bait. No team can match the Tribe's wherewithal to deal for established stars, because they can afford both to surrender prospects and pick up salary.

Bruce Aven

Position: OF
Bats: R **Throws:** R
Ht: 5' 9" **Wt:** 180
Opening Day Age: 26
Born: 3/4/72 in Orange, TX

Recent Statistics

	G	AB	R	H	D	T	HR	RBI	SB	BB	SO	AVG
97 AAA Buffalo	121	432	69	124	27	3	17	77	10	50	99	.287
97 AL Cleveland	13	19	4	4	1	0	0	2	0	1	5	.211
97 MLE	121	425	64	117	26	2	15	72	8	46	103	.275

Aven essentially is a righthanded version of Indians outfielder Brian Giles. A 30th-round draft pick out of Lamar in 1994, he would produce maybe a bit more power and a bit less average than Giles. Aven has hit 64 homers in the last three seasons while climbing from Class-A to Triple-A. He's an average runner, and his only mediocre tool is his arm. He has played all three outfield positions, though he's best suited for left field. At 26 he doesn't have much more to prove in the minors. He probably fits in Cleveland as a fourth outfielder or platoon player, but could start for other teams.

Russ Branyan

Position: 3B
Bats: L **Throws:** R
Ht: 6' 3" **Wt:** 195
Opening Day Age: 22
Born: 12/19/75 in Warner Robins, GA

Recent Statistics

	G	AB	R	H	D	T	HR	RBI	SB	BB	SO	AVG
96 A Columbus	130	482	102	129	20	4	40	106	7	62	166	.268
97 A Kinston	83	297	59	86	26	2	27	75	3	52	94	.290
97 AA Akron	41	137	26	32	4	0	12	30	0	28	56	.234

Branyan set a South Atlantic League record with 40 homers in 1996, then encored by leading the minors with 39 in 1997. A 1994 seventh-round pick, he has improved as a hitter each year, raising his batting aver-

age and walks annually. He has a little Ken Griffey Jr. in his stance, and teams covet his type of lefthanded power to all fields. He has an above-average arm, though he's not much of a third baseman, and average speed. His struggles in Double-A last season will earn him a return trip to Akron, but his timetable could be accelerated after the trade of Matt Williams.

Sean Casey

Position: 1B
Bats: L **Throws:** R
Ht: 6' 4" **Wt:** 215
Opening Day Age: 23
Born: 7/2/74 in Willingboro, NJ

Recent Statistics

	G	AB	R	H	D	T	HR	RBI	SB	BB	SO	AVG
97 AA Akron	62	241	38	93	19	1	10	66	0	23	34	.386
97 AAA Buffalo	20	72	12	26	7	0	5	18	0	9	11	.361
97 AL Cleveland	6	10	1	2	0	0	0	1	0	1	2	.200
97 MLE	82	297	39	103	22	0	11	65	0	22	47	.347

Casey is one of the best pure hitters in the minors, though acclaim has escaped him thus far. He won the 1995 NCAA Division I batting title for Richmond, then signed as a second-round pick and has hit .348 as a pro. He tore cartilage in his right wrist on a checked swing in 1997, costing him the first six weeks of the year, but returned to hit .380. He has good raw power, and the Indians believe he could hit 40 doubles and 20 homers per year. He's just adequate defensively, but Cleveland raves about his makeup and leadership skills. He's less than a year away from being ready for the big leagues, and probably will push Jim Thome to third base or designated hitter when he arrives.

Einar Diaz

Position: C
Bats: R **Throws:** R
Ht: 5' 10" **Wt:** 165
Opening Day Age: 25
Born: 12/28/72 in Chiriqui Rep., Panama

Recent Statistics

	G	AB	R	H	D	T	HR	RBI	SB	BB	SO	AVG
97 AAA Buffalo	109	336	40	86	18	2	3	31	2	18	34	.256
97 AL Cleveland	5	7	1	1	1	0	0	1	0	0	2	.143
97 MLE	109	331	37	81	17	1	2	29	1	16	35	.245

With backup catcher Pat Borders a free agent and not likely to return, Diaz is in line for the job as Sandy Alomar Jr.'s caddy. Signed out of Panama, Diaz has good defensive tools. He has an above-average arm, plus quick feet and hands, allowing him to combat basestealers and block pitches. He's still improving at calling games, and he offers no offense. That's no power, no speed, no walks and a mediocre batting average. If he were pressed into full-time duty at the major league level, Cleveland might be in trouble.

Willie Martinez

Position: P
Opening Day Age: 20
Bats: R **Throws:** R
Born: 1/4/78 in
Ht: 6' 2" **Wt:** 165
Barquisimeto, Ven

Recent Statistics

	W	L	ERA	G	GS	Sv	IP	H	R	BB	SO	HR
96 A Watertown	6	5	2.40	14	14	0	90.0	79	25	21	92	5
97 A Kinston	8	2	3.09	23	23	0	137.0	125	61	42	120	13

Jaret Wright took baseball by storm in 1997, and Bartolo Colon may do the same in 1998 if he's completely healthy. The next stud pitching prospect in the system is Martinez, who was signed out of Venezuela and went 0-7, 9.45 in his pro debut at Rookie-level Burlington in 1995. He has excelled since, pitching very well in high Class-A ball at age 19. He had minor surgery in January 1997 to remove a bone spur from his elbow, but that didn't affect his 94-MPH fastball. He has a sound delivery, shows a good feel for a curveball and is developing a changeup. He needs another two years in the minors, but the Indians weren't afraid to rush Wright when they needed him.

Alex Ramirez

Position: OF
Opening Day Age: 23
Bats: R **Throws:** R
Born: 10/3/74 in
Ht: 5' 11" **Wt:** 176
Caracas, Venez

Recent Statistics

	G	AB	R	H	D	T	HR	RBI	SB	BB	SO	AVG
96 AA Canton-Akrn	131	513	79	169	28	12	14	85	18	16	74	.329
97 AAA Buffalo	119	416	59	119	19	8	11	44	10	24	95	.286
97 MLE	119	409	55	112	18	6	10	41	8	22	99	.274

Ramirez signed out of Venezuela in 1991, the same year the Indians made Manny Ramirez (no relation) a first-round pick. Alex has very good bat speed and the Indians like his power potential, even if it really hasn't surfaced. He doesn't draw walks or steal bases, but he can play all three outfield positions. He faces the same dilemma as many Triple-A outfielders. He doesn't have the power to play on the corner in the majors, and he's not a true center fielder. He'll get another full season in Triple-A, and may have a difficult time making the Cleveland roster.

Richie Sexson

Position: 1B
Opening Day Age: 23
Bats: R **Throws:** R
Born: 12/29/74 in
Ht: 6' 6" **Wt:** 206
Portland, OR

Recent Statistics

	G	AB	R	H	D	T	HR	RBI	SB	BB	SO	AVG
97 AAA Buffalo	115	434	57	113	20	2	31	88	5	27	87	.260
97 AL Cleveland	5	11	3	3	0	0	0	0	0	0	2	.273
97 MLE	115	427	53	106	19	1	28	82	4	25	91	.248

How many first basemen could hit 31 homers in Triple-A yet be squeezed on both sides? Sexson, for one. He has the slugging Thome ahead of him and the sweet-swinging Casey coming up behind him. A 24th-round

pick in 1993, Sexson can hit for power and average, though his hitting has declined as pitchers have learned to exploit his inability to take a walk. He doesn't run much, but has worked very hard to make himself into an average first basemen. In most organizations, Sexson would be a premier prospect. The Indians like him, but he's third on the depth chart and may wind up as trade fodder.

Enrique Wilson

Position: SS-2B
Opening Day Age: 22
Bats: B **Throws:** R
Born: 7/27/75 in Santo
Ht: 5' 11" **Wt:** 160
Domingo, DR

Recent Statistics

	G	AB	R	H	D	T	HR	RBI	SB	BB	SO	AVG
97 AAA Buffalo	118	451	78	138	20	3	11	39	9	42	41	.306
97 AL Cleveland	5	15	2	5	0	0	1	0	0	0	2	.333
97 MLE	118	443	73	130	19	2	9	36	7	39	43	.293

Signed out of the Dominican Republic, Wilson was stolen in a 1994 spring-training trade with the Twins for lefthander Shawn Bryant, who was out of baseball a year later. Wilson has come up through the minors as a shortstop, but is expected to be Cleveland's second baseman in 1998. He's a legitimate shortstop, but the Tribe is set with Omar Vizquel. Wilson's range, arm and hands are all well above average, and he's expected to make the position change smoothly. He's a switch-hitter who hits for average and can steal an occasional base, but he has modest power and needs to draw more walks.

Others to Watch

Lefthander **Mike Matthews** has overcome major shoulder and elbow surgery. He still has a chance at 24, throwing an 88-90 MPH fastball with movement, though his slider isn't what it used to be. . . Outfielder **David Miller**, 24, was drafted in the first round ahead of Casey in 1995, but hasn't made the same progress. He hits for average and can run a little, but hasn't been able to translate his batting-practice power into game production. . . A former Gonzaga basketball player, 24-year-old outfielder **Scott Morgan** hit 25 homers last year, mostly in high Class-A, despite missing the final month with a bulging disc. He runs well and his arm is his only below-average tool. . . Outfielder **Danny Peoples** went in the first round of the 1996 draft only because he agreed to take less than market value, then hurt his shoulder and played like a bust that summer. He rebounded in 1997, smashing 34 homers at high Class-A Kinston at age 22. . . Outfielder **Chan Perry** isn't as athletic or as fast as his older brother Herb, a Devil Rays infielder, but he can hit. He's old at 25, but did hit .315 with 20 homers at Double-A Akron. . . Righthander **Jason Rakers** escapes notice because he's 25, but he has a 90-93 MPH fastball and a nice slider. He struck out 139 in 150⅔ innings in 1997 while going from Class-A to Triple-A.

Buddy Bell

1997 Season

Buddy Bell took a club that had hit rock bottom and brought it to respectability faster than had been expected. The Tigers' improvement from 1996 to 1997 was stunning. They went from worst to first in the American League in fielding percentage, cut 1.82 off their team ERA and led the AL in stolen bases. In his first year, Bell wasn't good at running a game and seemed a step behind his counterparts. That changed in 1997.

Offense

Under Bell, the Tigers no longer live and die with the three-run homer. Speester Brian Hunter and defensive whiz Deivi Cruz have been added. Bell isn't overly aggressive when it comes to bunting, but he did call for more hit-and-runs than any other AL manager and he expects his players to try to take the extra base. Detroit was shut out more than any other team in the majors in 1997, and its inability to adjust to top-flight pitching frustrates Bell. He preaches going to the plate with a plan and not throwing away at-bats. That message has gotten through to Tony Clark and Higginson, but it hasn't to many others.

Pitching & Defense

Bell, who played 18 years in the majors as a third baseman, will be the first to admit he's no expert on pitching. Yet he does a good job of relying on what pitching coach Rick Adair tells him and makes sound judgments. Bell balances things pretty well. He doesn't have a quick hook unless oft-injured ace Justin Thompson exceeds his pitch limit. That said, Bell seldom lets a spent pitcher linger too long. It took a while, but last season he placed all his pitchers in defined roles. Pitching actually has become Detroit's strength, along with defense. The Tigers are fundamentally sound with the glove and rarely throw to the wrong base.

1998 Outlook

Bell's players not only like him, but they also respect him. The fact that he was a very good player has helped him, as has his down-to-earth demeanor. He'll continue to put the pieces of a future contender in place.

Born: 8/27/51 in Pittsburgh, PA

Playing Experience: 1972-1989, Cle, Tex, Cin, Hou

Managerial Experience: 2 seasons

Manager Statistics

Year	Team, Lg	W	L	Pct	GB	Finish
1997	Detroit, AL	79	83	.488	19.0	3rd East
2 Seasons		132	192	.407	—	—

1997 Starting Pitchers by Days Rest

	≤3	4	5	6+
Tigers Starts	0	87	40	25
Tigers ERA	0.00	4.40	4.00	4.99
AL Avg Starts	5	89	34	24
AL ERA	4.38	4.60	4.61	5.37

1997 Situational Stats

	Buddy Bell	AL Average
Hit & Run Success %	33.0	36.5
Stolen Base Success %	69.1	67.3
Platoon Pct.	60.5	59.5
Defensive Subs	22	22
High-Pitch Outings	12	15
Quick/Slow Hooks	24/7	19/15
Sacrifice Attempts	44	53

1997 Rankings (American League)

⇒ 1st in stolen base attempts (233), steals of second base (135), steals of third base (25) and hit-and-run attempts (115)

⇒ 2nd in steals of home plate (1), double steals (7), squeeze plays (3) and mid-inning pitching changes (218)

⇒ 3rd in pinch hitters used (163), quick hooks (24), relief appearances (417), saves with over 1 inning pitched (11) and one-batter pitcher appearances (48)

Detroit Tigers

Willie Blair

1997 Season

Just 9-20 as a part-time starter over the previous five seasons, Willie Blair produced stunning results in his first full-time duty in a rotation. He won 16 games, 14 as a starter, despite missing a month with a fractured jaw courtesy of a Julio Franco line drive. Blair's sixth team proved to be a charm, as he had gone 25-41 in seven big league seasons with five clubs.

Pitching

Blair doesn't do anything fancy. He has neither a trick pitch nor anything that would be considered overpowering, His fastball consistently reached 90 MPH in 1997, and it's his main pitch along with his slider. He also shows hitters his curveball and changeup. What separated the Willie Blair of 1997 from the one in the past was his command. He got ahead in the count for the most part and it allowed him to work away from the middle of the plate toward the outside corner, where his slider is particularly effective against righthanders. When Blair's pitches drift toward the middle of the plate, he doesn't have enough to get them by batters and he gets punished. Blair really slows down his pace with runners on base.

Defense

Not a particularly good athlete, Blair is a below-average fielder. He has limited quickness off the mound and sometimes struggles with the routine play. Blair doesn't have a good pickoff move and can be stolen upon. One plus is that he doesn't have a high leg kick and is relatively quick to the plate.

1998 Outlook

Blair couldn't have picked a better year to have a breakout season, as he became eligible for free agency for the first time. The expansion Diamondbacks signed him to a three-year deal worth $11.5 million. The big question surrounding him is whether 1997 was just a fluke year. Will he go back to being a journeyman or has he turned a corner? Either way, he has value because he more than makes up for whatever he's lacking in raw talent with mental toughness.

Position: SP
Bats: R **Throws:** R
Ht: 6' 1" **Wt:** 185

Opening Day Age: 32
Born: 12/18/65 in Paintsville, KY
ML Seasons: 8

Overall Statistics

	W	L	Pct.	ERA	G	GS	Sv	IP	H	BB	SO	HR	Ratio
1997	16	8	.667	4.17	29	27	0	175.0	186	46	90	18	1.33
Career	41	49	.456	4.60	289	77	4	784.0	858	264	496	87	1.43

How Often He Throws Strikes

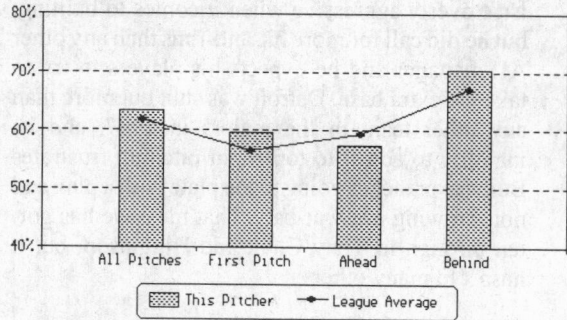

This Pitcher   —League Average

1997 Situational Stats

	W	L	ERA	Sv	IP		AB	H	HR	RBI	Avg
Home	8	4	4.65	0	69.2	LHB	347	95	8	40	.274
Road	8	4	3.84	0	105.1	RHB	334	91	10	35	.272
First Half	6	4	4.66	0	67.2	Sc Pos	155	39	5	55	.252
Scnd Half	10	4	3.86	0	107.1	Clutch	47	14	2	5	.298

1997 Rankings (American League)

⇒ 3rd in least strikeouts per 9 innings (4.6)
⇒ 6th in wins
⇒ 7th in most run support per 9 innings (6.3)
⇒ 9th in winning percentage
⇒ Led the Tigers in wins, balks (1), winning percentage, least pitches thrown per batter (3.68), most run support per 9 innings (6.3), lowest batting average allowed vs. lef thanded batters and lowest batting average allowed with runners in scoring position

Doug Brocail

1997 Season

Despite an 11-22 record in his first five major league seasons with San Diego and Houston, Doug Brocail was Detroit's Opening Day starter. When Todd Jones faltered early in the season, Brocail briefly became Detroit's closer. It wasn't until Jones rebounded that Brocail settled into the role of setup man. He has gone on the disabled list with elbow problems three times during his career, and missed two months in 1996 with a frayed biceps tendon. Healthy in 1997, he put up his best numbers and played an important role in Detroit's improvement.

Pitching

Brocail got stronger as 1997 went on. He began throwing in the 89-90 MPH range and struggling to find his breaking ball. By late August, he was touching 95 MPH. He scrapped his slider in favor of a knuckle-curve which he was able to throw for strikes. A tough competitor who isn't afraid to throw inside, he wears his emotions on his sleeve when he takes the mound. In the past that worked against him, but last season he used it to his advantage. When he was charged up, he hit his spots with crisp pitches instead of experiencing control problems or trying to blow fastballs down the middle like he used to.

Defense

Brocail holds runners well and is an above-average fielder. He'll make the right play at the right time. He's a solid athlete who has good hands and quickness, and he varies his moves to first and deliveries to the plate in order to keep runners honest.

1998 Outlook

As it did for Brian Hunter and Jones, the Detroit-Houston megatrade after the 1996 did wonders for Brocail. He walked into a clubhouse where he was expected to be a leader based on his experience. It was a role Brocail handled well, and in the process he learned to use his emotions to his advantage on the mound. His value comes not only in his performance, but also in his willingness to do whatever is asked of him. However, there will always be concerns about his health.

Position: RP/SP
Bats: L **Throws:** R
Ht: 6' 5" **Wt:** 235

Opening Day Age: 30
Born: 5/16/67 in Clearfield, PA
ML Seasons: 6
Pronunciation: broh-KALE

Overall Statistics

	W	L	Pct.	ERA	G	GS	Sv	IP	H	BB	SO	HR	Ratio
1997	3	4	.429	3.23	61	4	2	78.0	74	36	60	10	1.41
Career	14	26	.350	4.33	159	42	3	367.2	400	133	229	46	1.45

How Often He Throws Strikes

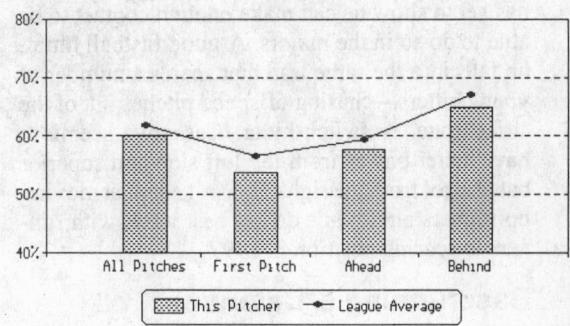

1997 Situational Stats

	W	L	ERA	Sv	IP		AB	H	HR	RBI	Avg
Home	2	0	2.45	0	40.1	LHB	131	36	3	15	.275
Road	1	4	4.06	2	37.2	RHB	158	38	7	26	.241
First Half	1	4	5.27	2	41.0	Sc Pos	71	22	1	28	.310
Scnd Half	2	0	0.97	0	37.0	Clutch	126	33	6	19	.262

1997 Rankings (American League)

⇒ 4th in blown saves (7) and highest percentage of inherited runners scored (43.3%)
⇒ 6th in relief ERA (2.38)
⇒ 9th in holds (16) and highest batting average allowed in relief with runners on base (.325)
⇒ 10th in lowest batting average allowed in relief (.233)
⇒ Led the Tigers in blown saves (7), first batter efficiency (.222) and relief ERA (2.38)

Detroit Tigers

Raul Casanova

1997 Season

Raul Casanova began 1997 at Triple-A Toledo and was expected to spend the entire season there. But a mid-April injury to Matt Walbeck brought Casanova to the majors, where he had an up-and-down season. He played well early, surprising Detroit's decision-makers and earning a starting job. That prompted Brian Johnson's demotion to the minor leagues and subsequent trade to San Francisco. Casanova tapered off after that, at times playing like a bona fide major league regular while at other times looking like he still belonged in Triple-A.

Hitting

Casanova hit for a high average in the minors, but has yet to show he can make enough contact to be able to do so in the majors. A good fastball hitter, he falls into the same trap that snares a number of young hitters—chasing offspeed pitches out of the strike zone. A switch-hitter, Casanova seems to have better power from the left side and superior bat control from the right. He isn't adept at moving up runners and didn't do his best work with runners in scoring position in 1997.

Baserunning & Defense

Casanova has a strong arm, but his throwing mechanics lack continuity. He gets in grooves where he throws accurately, and also has stretches where he's all over the place. Behind the plate, he seems to struggle when he's slumping with the bat. At times he displays soft hands, but he's also prone to untimely passed balls. The Tigers would like him to pay more attention to his conditioning program because he tends to put on weight. He's a below-average runner.

1998 Outlook

Casanova will enter 1998 as Detroit's regular catcher. The Tigers hope he learned a lot from his first extensive experience as a major league regular. He seemed to wear down as 1997 progressed, as his performance took a step back in the second half. GM Randy Smith had Casanova in San Diego and traded for him when he arrived in Detroit. One more point in Casanova's favor is the lack of catching depth in the organization.

Position: C
Bats: B **Throws:** R
Ht: 5'11" **Wt:** 200

Opening Day Age: 25
Born: 8/23/72 in Humacao, Puerto Rico
ML Seasons: 2

Overall Statistics

	G	AB	R	H	D	T	HR	RBI	SB	BB	SO	Avg	OBP	Slg
1997	101	304	27	74	10	1	5	24	1	26	48	.243	.308	.332
Career	126	389	33	90	11	1	9	33	1	32	66	.231	.294	.334

Where He Hits the Ball

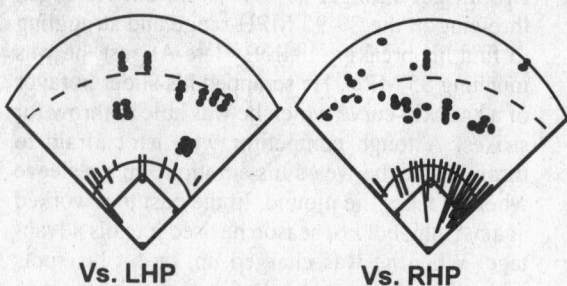

Vs. LHP   Vs. RHP

1997 Situational Stats

	AB	H	HR	RBI	Avg		AB	H	HR	RBI	Avg
Home	150	35	5	16	.233	LHP	59	14	1	5	.237
Road	154	39	0	8	.253	RHP	245	60	4	19	.245
First Half	146	38	4	11	.260	Sc Pos	78	15	2	20	.192
Scnd Half	158	36	1	13	.228	Clutch	47	10	0	0	.213

1997 Rankings (American League)

⇒ 2nd in lowest fielding percentage at catcher (.985)

⇒ 3rd in errors at catcher (9)

Tony Clark

Position: 1B
Bats: B **Throws:** R
Ht: 6' 7" **Wt:** 245

Opening Day Age: 25
Born: 6/15/72 in El Cajon, CA
ML Seasons: 3

1997 Season

Tony Clark closed the 1996 season with a flurry and it carried over to 1997. He was among the American League leaders in virtually every offensive department early in the season before his production declined during the second half. There were two main reasons for the dropoff. The first is that pitchers started to become careful about what they fed Clark. Second, he had a painful inflammation in his heel and seemed to wear down a bit from the grind of his first full season in the majors.

Hitting

Clark has as much raw power as any hitter in baseball not named Mark McGwire. A natural righthanded hitter, he started switch-hitting in high school. Easily jammed because of his long arms, Clark has compensated by taking inside pitches the other way with an inside-out swing. Though awkward, he still has enough strength to hit balls out of the park in this manner. He's good at fighting off tough pitches in clutch situations despite his high strikeout rate.

Baserunning & Defense

When Clark arrived in the majors in 1995, he had trouble handling even routine throws from his infielders. Thus the fact he's become at least an average fielder is impressive. He has excellent hands and is a former outfielder who has very good range on pop flies. He has below-average speed, a deficiency accentuated by his heel problems. He plays it safe on the bases.

1998 Outlook

The Tigers view Clark as a cornerstone of their rebuilding project, and the reasons go beyond his obvious tools. Despite his youth and inexperience, he already has become a clubhouse leader. He has a calm demeanor, an exceptional work ethic and is bright enough to know what to say and when. When Clark speaks, people listen. He's on the verge of becoming one of baseball's great sluggers, and Detroit signed him to a four-year deal in the offseason.

Overall Statistics

	G	AB	R	H	D	T	HR	RBI	SB	BB	SO	Avg	OBP	Slg
1997	159	580	105	160	28	3	32	117	1	93	144	.276	.376	.500
Career	286	1057	171	278	47	4	62	200	1	130	301	.263	.342	.491

Where He Hits the Ball

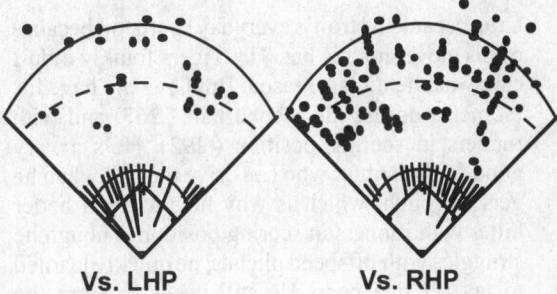

Vs. LHP   **Vs. RHP**

1997 Situational Stats

	AB	H	HR	RBI	Avg		AB	H	HR	RBI	Avg
Home	281	75	18	57	.267	LHP	181	48	10	35	.265
Road	299	85	14	60	.284	RHP	399	112	22	82	.281
First Half	299	87	22	73	.291	Sc Pos	149	47	11	86	.315
Scnd Half	281	73	10	44	.260	Clutch	86	23	4	17	.267

1997 Rankings (American League)

⇒ 4th in games played (159)
⇒ 5th in strikeouts, errors at first base (10), highest percentage of swings that missed (30.0%) and lowest percentage of extra bases taken as a runner (28.8%)
⇒ 6th in RBI, intentional walks (13) and fielding percentage at first base (.993)
⇒ 7th in walks
⇒ 10th in runs scored
⇒ Led the Tigers in home runs, total bases (290), RBI, walks, intentional walks (13), times on base (256), HR frequency (18.1 ABs per HR), cleanup slugging percentage (.499), on-base percentage vs. righthanded pitchers (.387) and batting average on the road

Detroit Tigers

137

Deivi Cruz

1997 Season

Teammates and club officials alike view Deivi Cruz as the biggest single factor in Detroit's resurgence. The Tigers went from last to first in fielding percentage in the American League, and Cruz was the major reason why. He played Class A ball in San Francisco's system until being acquired in a Rule 5 draft-day trade by Detroit at the 1996 Winter Meetings. GM Randy Smith expected Cruz to be capable enough in the field to serve as a backup while the team kept him on the roster throughout the entire season (or risk losing him, according to the Rule 5 guidelines). Cruz turned out to be so much more.

Hitting

Cruz became Detroit's everyday shortstop because of his glove, not his bat. The Tigers frankly didn't care what he hit last season. But Cruz did have his moments during the second half (.267) and with runners in scoring position (.292). He's a very good fastball hitter who can drive the ball when he gets his pitch, which is why he's a much better hitter with runners in scoring position. Though he struggles with offspeed pitches, he quickly learned to lay off bad ones. He still needs to learn the concept of drawing a walk. One added bonus has been that Cruz is an excellent bunter.

Baserunning & Defense

Cruz' hands are so good that he makes bad-hop groundballs appear routine. He also throws extremely well, particularly on relays from the outfield. Surgery to repair ligament damage on his right knee in 1994 has robbed Cruz of his speed. He's a below-average runner, especially for a shortstop, though he has decent range because of his superior instincts in the field. He turns the double play well.

1998 Outlook

The Tigers' concern over a lack of middle-infield prospects in their system led to their acquisition of Cruz as their shortstop of the future. It turned out that the future is now. Cruz will be Detroit's regular shortstop in 1998 and probably for years to come. It won't matter much what he hits.

Position: SS
Bats: R **Throws:** R
Ht: 5'11" **Wt:** 160

Opening Day Age: 22
Born: 6/11/75 in Nizao de Bani, DR
ML Seasons: 1
Pronunciation: DAY-vee CRUISE

Overall Statistics

	G	AB	R	H	D	T	HR	RBI	SB	BB	SO	Avg	OBP	Slg
1997	147	436	35	105	26	0	2	40	3	14	55	.241	.263	.314
Career	147	436	35	105	26	0	2	40	3	14	55	.241	.263	.314

Where He Hits the Ball

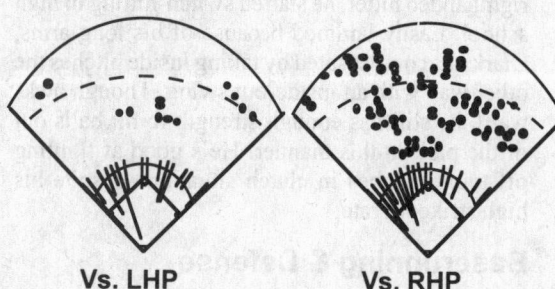

Vs. LHP   **Vs. RHP**

1997 Situational Stats

	AB	H	HR	RBI	Avg		AB	H	HR	RBI	Avg
Home	207	47	0	17	.227	LHP	112	24	0	8	.214
Road	229	58	2	23	.253	RHP	324	81	2	32	.250
First Half	219	47	1	21	.215	Sc Pos	96	28	0	33	.292
Scnd Half	217	58	1	19	.267	Clutch	56	12	0	6	.214

1997 Rankings (American League)

⇒ 2nd in sacrifice bunts (14)
⇒ 5th in batting average on a 3-2 count (.389) and fielding percentage at shortstop (.979)
⇒ 6th in bunts in play (20)
⇒ 7th in highest percentage of swings put into play (52.2%)
⇒ 9th in errors at shortstop (13)
⇒ Led the Tigers in sacrifice bunts (14), batting average on an 0-2 count (.239), batting average on a 3-2 count (.389), bunts in play (20) and highest percentage of swings put into play (52.2%)

Damion Easley

1997 Season

GM Randy Smith has made several good moves since taking over the Tigers, with his best thus far the trade that sent righthander Greg Gohr to the Angels for Damion Easley. Often injured in the past, Easley remained healthy for the entire season and exceeded any reasonable expectations by becoming a 20-20 man while Gohr dropped out of baseball. After a rigorous offseason conditioning program with teammate Tony Clark, Easley won the second-base job on the first day of spring training and just kept on hitting. He hit more homers and stole more bases than he did in his previous five years in the major leagues.

Hitting

Easley is very strong for a middle infielder and was able to translate that into power in 1997. Some of his homers were tape-measure shots. He has good balance in his stance, which adds to his pop. The weightlifting sessions with Clark helped. Easley still struggles with good breaking-ball pitchers, but did a much better job of not chasing offspeed stuff out of the strike zone. There are still times when he falls back into that bad habit.

Baserunning & Defense

Easley benefited greatly from Detroit's new aggressive approach on the bases. Because he has above-average speed, he was always on the move. One problem he does have is an all-or-nothing approach to stealing. He sometimes leaves before the pitcher delivers to the plate, and is susceptible to pickoffs. He has made significant progress defensively and has a strong arm for a second baseman. He's not the most fluid fielder, but makes the routine play consistently.

1998 Outlook

Now Easley has to do it again, not only in terms of productivity but in terms of remaining healthy. His 1997 performance made him part of Detroit's long-range future and won him a lucrative three-year contract, with which comes a certain amount of pressure. He would benefit again from hitting second in the order, where he saw a steady diet of fastballs with speedy Brian Hunter on base.

Position: 2B/SS
Bats: R **Throws:** R
Ht: 5'11" **Wt:** 185

Opening Day Age: 28
Born: 11/11/69 in New York, NY
ML Seasons: 6

Overall Statistics

	G	AB	R	H	D	T	HR	RBI	SB	BB	SO	Avg	OBP	Slg
1997	151	527	97	139	37	3	22	72	28	68	102	.264	.362	.471
Career	522	1693	234	425	87	8	39	188	55	175	283	.251	.330	.381

Where He Hits the Ball

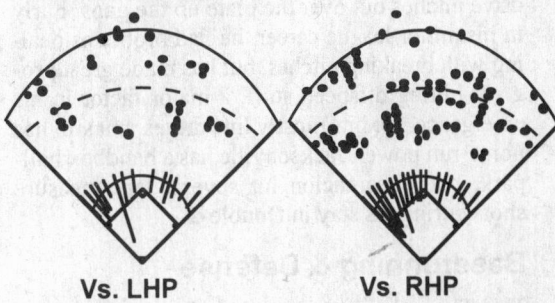

Vs. LHP   Vs. RHP

1997 Situational Stats

	AB	H	HR	RBI	Avg		AB	H	HR	RBI	Avg
Home	256	64	12	31	.250	LHP	143	33	7	20	.231
Road	271	75	10	41	.277	RHP	384	106	15	52	.276
First Half	265	72	13	34	.272	Sc Pos	126	29	6	49	.230
Scnd Half	262	67	9	38	.256	Clutch	72	25	2	11	.347

1997 Rankings (American League)

⇒ 3rd in hit by pitch (16), errors at second base (12) and highest percentage of extra bases taken as a runner (71.2%)

⇒ 4th in caught stealing (13) and fielding percentage at second base (.981)

⇒ 5th in steals of third (6)

⇒ 8th in stolen bases

⇒ 9th in GDPs (18) and lowest batting average vs. lefthanded pitchers

⇒ Led the Tigers in doubles, hit by pitch (16), GDPs (18), batting average in the clutch and highest percentage of extra bases taken as a runner (71.2%)

Juan Encarnacion

1997 Season

Juan Encarnacion had a breakout season at Double-A Jacksonville, applying his five-tool skills to the fullest for the first time. He never had hit more than 16 home runs in a season before, but he hit 26. He never had more than 72 RBI, but he had 90, and he hit above .300 for the first time. In the Southern League All-Star Game, he hit three home runs against the Seattle Mariners. He dazzled manager Buddy Bell with his exceptional skills in September before breaking his left hand.

Hitting

Encarnacion has an upright stance and a compact swing. He turns well on inside pitches and can drive pitches out over the plate up the gaps. Early in his minor league career, he had problems dealing with breaking pitches, but has made great progress hitting offspeed stuff, a major factor in his emergence. He hits mostly line drives, but still has home-run power. Jacksonville has a bandbox ballpark, but Encarnacion hit several tape-measure shots during his stay in Double-A.

Baserunning & Defense

The Tigers held a 60-yard dash competition in minor league camp during last spring training, and Encarnacion reached the finals with a 6.4-second time. A long strider, he goes from first to third and second to home very well. He's primarily a right fielder, but is capable of playing center. He has the best outfield arm in the organization, gets a good jump on the ball and has outstanding range.

1998 Outlook

The Tigers would like to have Encarnacion begin at Triple-A Toledo, perform well, and join them in June or July. Yet he's so impressive that it may be difficult not to take him north after spring training. In terms of tools, he's the best prospect Detroit has had since Howard Johnson arrived during the early 1980s. Encarnacion also has a solid work ethic and carries himself with a quiet confidence. If he makes the team out of spring training, he'll be a definite Rookie-of-the-Year candidate.

Position: RF
Bats: R **Throws:** R
Ht: 6' 2" **Wt:** 160

Opening Day Age: 22
Born: 3/8/76 in Las Matas de Faran, DR
ML Seasons: 1
Pronunciation: en-CAR-na-she-own

Overall Statistics

	G	AB	R	H	D	T	HR	RBI	SB	BB	SO	Avg	OBP	Slg
1997	11	33	3	7	1	1	1	5	3	3	12	.212	.316	.394
Career	11	33	3	7	1	1	1	5	3	3	12	.212	.316	.394

Where He Hits the Ball

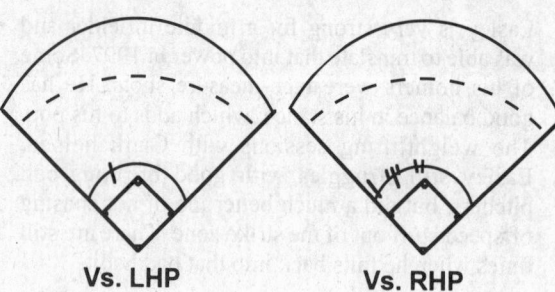

Vs. LHP   **Vs. RHP**

1997 Situational Stats

	AB	H	HR	RBI	Avg		AB	H	HR	RBI	Avg
Home	9	3	1	4	.333	LHP	12	2	1	2	.167
Road	24	4	0	1	.167	RHP	21	5	0	3	.238
First Half	0	0	0	0	-	Sc Pos	10	2	0	3	.200
Scnd Half	33	7	1	5	.212	Clutch	2	1	0	0	.500

1997 Rankings (American League)

⇒ Did not rank near the top or bottom in any category

Travis Fryman

Position: 3B
Bats: R **Throws:** R
Ht: 6' 1" **Wt:** 195

Opening Day Age: 29
Born: 3/25/69 in
Lexington, KY
ML Seasons: 8

1997 Season

Travis Fryman is very consistent. He usually hits about .275 with 20 home runs and 90 RBI. He established a career high in RBI in 1997, and did the same in stolen bases. He didn't make the American League All-Star team, something he has done four times in his career, but his statistics were comparable statistics to some of the participants.

Hitting

Fryman lives on the inside part of the plate and sits on fastballs. If he knows a fastball is coming, he'll connect no matter how hard it's thrown. He has hit more home runs (four) off Seattle's Randy Johnson than any other active hitter, though Johnson has wised up and now uses his slider more against Fryman. As consistent as he is, Fryman has several hot streaks and slumps each season. While he has improved his ability to hit breaking balls, he still strikes out frequently.

Baserunning & Defense

Fryman was drafted as a 6-foot-1, 170-pound shortstop who was taken as a supplemental first-round pick in 1987 primarily because of his hands and arm strength. He still has those tools, but outgrew shortstop and doesn't have particularly good range for a third baseman. He rarely makes throwing errors. His arm is not only strong, but it's on target. Like many of the Tigers, he was much more aggressive on the basepaths in 1997. Before then, he wasn't much of a basestealer.

1998 Outlook

Fryman is a $6.5 million-per-year player without the numbers to back up his salary. Thus it was no surprise when Detroit traded him to Arizona for three players on the night of the expansion draft. Two weeks later, he headed to Cleveland in a trade for Matt Williams. Joe Randa will take Fryman's place with the Tigers. Fryman may not be able to match Williams' home-run total, but he should measure up well against Williams in all the other areas.

Overall Statistics

	G	AB	R	H	D	T	HR	RBI	SB	BB	SO	Avg	OBP	Slg
1997	154	595	90	163	27	3	22	102	16	46	113	.274	.326	.440
Career	1096	4297	607	1176	229	29	149	679	58	390	931	.274	.334	.444

Where He Hits the Ball

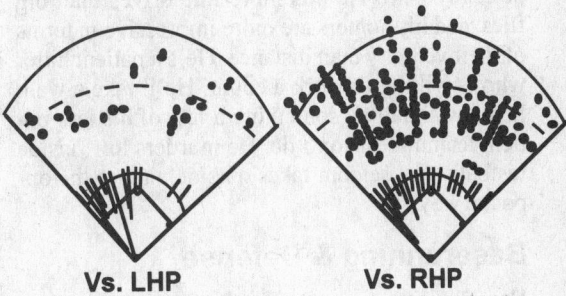

Vs. LHP   **Vs. RHP**

1997 Situational Stats

	AB	H	HR	RBI	Avg		AB	H	HR	RBI	Avg
Home	282	78	13	58	.277	LHP	151	45	5	21	.298
Road	313	85	9	44	.272	RHP	444	118	17	81	.266
First Half	301	91	12	54	.302	Sc Pos	167	46	4	79	.275
Scnd Half	294	72	10	48	.245	Clutch	88	23	4	14	.261

1997 Rankings (American League)

⇒ 1st in fielding percentage at third base (.978)
⇒ 5th in sacrifice flies (11)
⇒ 9th in highest percentage of extra bases taken as a runner (62.0%)
⇒ Led the Tigers in sacrifice flies (11)

Detroit Tigers

Bob Hamelin

1997 Season

Bob Hamelin's career appeared to be on the ropes. He was released by Kansas City during spring training and didn't receive a major league offer. He signed a Triple-A contract with Detroit because he knew Toledo manager Glenn Ezell, a former Royals coach. The Tigers called up Hamelin in May when they began to struggle offensively. He provided an immediate lift, becoming the club's everyday designated hitter versus righthanders.

Hitting

Hamelin has a short, compact stroke which generates plenty of power. Because of his size, there's a perception that he's a classic home-run hitter, but he really isn't. He hits more line drives than big flies, and his homers are more impressive in terms of their velocity than distance. He's a patient hitter who is willing to work a count. He'll take a walk in a key situation, something a few of his less-patient teammates won't do. He murders low, inside fastballs, but seldom takes outside pitches the opposite way.

Baserunning & Defense

Hamelin is by no means fast, but he is an excellent baserunner given his lack of speed. He displays solid judgment about when to go and when to stay, and he runs everything out to the fullest. He's not the base-clogger he would appear to be. Detroit used Hamelin strictly as a DH. He has OK hands as a first baseman, but his range is limited.

1998 Outlook

Hamelin is appreciated in Detroit. His ability as a hitter and his makeup have impressed manager Buddy Bell and GM Randy Smith. Hamelin provided good protection behind Tony Clark in the batting order and got results when others weren't producing. Don't expect Hamelin to see much time at first base, however, because Clark is the better fielder. His back has given him problems in the past, but as long as he's healthy he figures to remain productive.

Position: DH
Bats: L **Throws:** L
Ht: 6' 0" **Wt:** 235

Opening Day Age: 30
Born: 11/29/67 in Elizabeth, NJ
ML Seasons: 5
Pronunciation: HAM-lynn

Overall Statistics

	G	AB	R	H	D	T	HR	RBI	SB	BB	SO	Avg	OBP	Slg
1997	110	318	47	86	15	0	18	52	2	48	72	.270	.366	.487
Career	388	1126	164	281	64	3	60	187	11	190	263	.250	.359	.472

Where He Hits the Ball

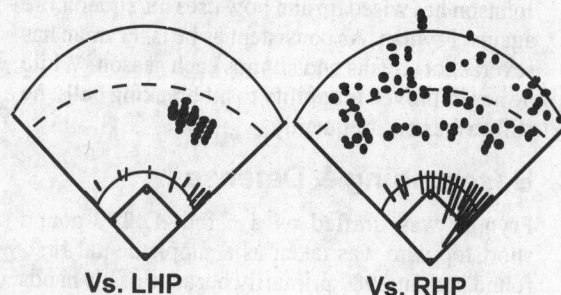

Vs. LHP   Vs. RHP

1997 Situational Stats

	AB	H	HR	RBI	Avg		AB	H	HR	RBI	Avg
Home	167	42	10	26	.251	LHP	43	9	2	4	.209
Road	151	44	8	26	.291	RHP	275	77	16	48	.280
First Half	132	40	9	25	.303	Sc Pos	84	23	4	32	.274
Scnd Half	186	46	9	27	.247	Clutch	37	11	2	6	.297

1997 Rankings (American League)

⇒ 1st in lowest batting average with the bases loaded (.000)

Bobby Higginson

1997 Season

If there were any doubts about Bobby Higginson's big year in 1996 being a fluke, they were erased last season. His RBI production rose by 20 and he kept his batting average around the .300 mark. He set a career high in home runs, including four in four straight at-bats to tie a major league record. Defensively, he moved back and forth between left and right field, leading the majors in outfield assists with 20.

Hitting

In his rookie season in 1995, Higginson kept trying to pull outside pitches and couldn't hit a fastball thrown above his waist. He corrected that deficiency and has become a very good all-around hitter. Though he still gets pull-happy at times, he has learned that he does his best hitting when he takes outside pitches to the opposite field. His main power zone remains low and inside, but it's no longer the only area from which he can drive a ball out of the park.

Baserunning & Defense

A below-average runner, Higginson disappointed club officials by being slower in 1997 than he was the year before, though he did appear to get quicker as the season went on. He doesn't cover a lot of ground in the outfield, but is sure-handed. His arm isn't overpowering, but is very accurate. His throws are almost always right on the bag, which is why he has led the American League in outfield assists two of his three big league seasons.

1998 Outlook

Higginson is a rarity, a homegrown product who predates GM Randy Smith's regime and is making it big. He's not the most physically gifted player around, but few are more productive. Manager Buddy Bell loves Higginson and will play him every day. Higginson does sit against tough southpaws, much to his dismay, but his increasing proficiency against them may put an end to that. He'll likely see more time in right field until top prospect Juan Encarnacion is called up to Detroit for good.

Position: LF/RF
Bats: L **Throws:** R
Ht: 5'11" **Wt:** 195

Opening Day Age: 27
Born: 8/18/70 in Philadelphia, PA
ML Seasons: 3

Overall Statistics

	G	AB	R	H	D	T	HR	RBI	SB	BB	SO	Avg	OBP	Slg
1997	146	546	94	163	30	5	27	101	12	70	85	.299	.379	.520
Career	407	1396	230	396	82	10	67	225	24	197	258	.284	.372	.501

Where He Hits the Ball

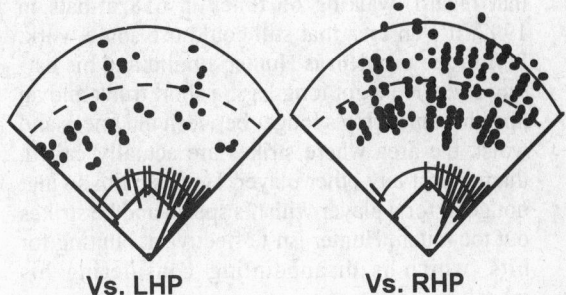

Vs. LHP   **Vs. RHP**

1997 Situational Stats

	AB	H	HR	RBI	Avg		AB	H	HR	RBI	Avg
Home	236	76	16	56	.322	LHP	156	47	7	35	.301
Road	310	87	11	45	.281	RHP	390	116	20	66	.297
First Half	258	69	14	49	.267	Sc Pos	151	51	10	79	.338
Scnd Half	288	94	13	52	.326	Clutch	76	20	1	6	.263

1997 Rankings (American League)

⇒ 3rd in errors in left field (6) and lowest fielding percentage in left field (.972)
⇒ Led the Tigers in batting average, slugging percentage, on-base percentage, most pitches seen per plate appearance (4.00), batting average with runners in scoring position, batting average with the bases loaded (.375), batting average vs. righthanded pitchers, batting average on a 3-1 count (.478), slugging percentage vs. righthanded pitchers (.518), on-base percentage vs. lefthanded pitchers (.375), batting average at home, highest percentage of pitches taken (61.0%), lowest percentage of swings that missed (15.5%) and lowest percentage of swings on the first pitch (17.3%)

Brian Hunter

1997 Season

Acquired from Houston in a nine-player trade prior to the 1997 season, Brian Hunter was put in center field on an everyday basis and turned loose on the bases. He had the type of season that was projected for him when he was a top prospect for the Astros. He led the majors in steals, the first Detroit player to do so since Ty Cobb in 1917, and topped the 400 mark in putouts while starting all 162 games in center field.

Hitting

The big knock on Hunter, especially after he walked just 17 times in 526 at-bats in 1996, was his lack of patience at the plate. He improved in that regard, walking 66 times in 658 at-bats in 1997. It's an area that still could use some work. Part of the problem is Hunter's build and his batting style. He's got long legs, a short trunk and an upright stance. He's longer between the knees and waist, the area where strikes are actually called, than almost any other player. He has a big swing, not good for a player with his speed, and he strikes out too much. Hunter isn't effective at bunting for hits, which is disappointing considering his wheels.

Baserunning & Defense

Few players can match Hunter's speed. He has long strides, but gets out of the batter's box quickly and off the mark well while stealing, possessing a good eye for pitchers' moves. In the field, he has been criticized for taking bad angles in pursuing line drives into the gaps, but there weren't many high flies that he wasn't able to outrun in Tiger Stadium's spacious center field. He has average arm strength, but he tends to press and overthrow in critical situations.

1998 Outlook

Acquiring Hunter was the biggest reason the Tigers made their nine-player deal with Houston. It looks like he'll be Detroit's leadoff man and center fielder for years to come. His speed alone gave Detroit a more balanced lineup after years of fielding a plodding, power-dependent club.

Position: CF
Bats: R **Throws:** R
Ht: 6' 4" **Wt:** 180

Opening Day Age: 27
Born: 3/5/71 in Portland, OR
ML Seasons: 4

Overall Statistics

	G	AB	R	H	D	T	HR	RBI	SB	BB	SO	Avg	OBP	Slg
1997	162	658	112	177	29	7	4	45	74	66	121	.269	.334	.353
Career	378	1529	240	425	71	14	11	108	135	105	271	.278	.323	.364

Where He Hits the Ball

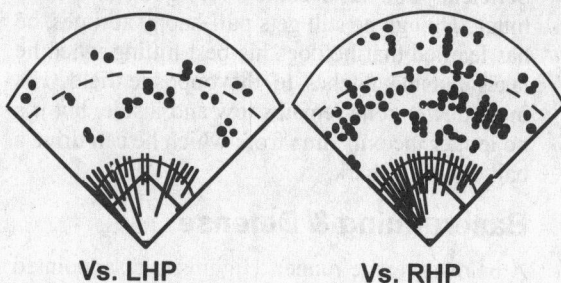

Vs. LHP   Vs. RHP

1997 Situational Stats

	AB	H	HR	RBI	Avg		AB	H	HR	RBI	Avg
Home	313	85	2	24	.272	LHP	159	42	1	9	.264
Road	345	92	2	21	.267	RHP	499	135	3	36	.271
First Half	347	89	4	32	.256	Sc Pos	130	39	1	41	.300
Scnd Half	311	88	0	13	.283	Clutch	100	22	0	7	.220

1997 Rankings (American League)

⇒ 1st in stolen bases, caught stealing (18), games played (162) and steals of third (14)
⇒ 2nd in at-bats, plate appearances (738) and lowest HR frequency (164.5 ABs per HR)
⇒ 3rd in singles and pitches seen (2,820)
⇒ 5th in runs scored, triples, highest groundball/flyball ratio (2.0) and errors in center field (4)
⇒ Led the Tigers in at-bats, runs scored, hits, singles, triples, stolen bases, caught stealing (18), pitches seen (2,820), plate appearances (738), games played (162), highest groundball/flyball ratio (2.0), stolen base percentage (80.4%), on-base percentage for a leadoff hitter (.332), batting average with two strikes (.227) and steals of third (14)

Todd Jones

1997 Season

A year that began with disappointment ended in joy for Todd Jones. Handled the closer's role out of spring training, he was so awful during the first couple of weeks of the season that he lost the job and was relegated to long relief. After tinkering with his motion and battling confidence problems, he decided to scrap his modifications and just get back to the basics. The results? A career high in saves and a new two-year, $5.7 million contract.

Pitching

Jones' bread-and-butter pitch is his fastball. He throws hard, consistently reaching the low 90s and topping out at 95 MPH. His fastball has a nasty running action that bores in on lefthanders and away from righties. Jones doesn't have a good breaking ball, but it doesn't matter. Hitters have to focus so much on his fastball that his curve is effective if he throws it for strikes. He also has a changeup, but seldom throws it. Jones has an odd motion. Instead of bringing his front leg straight up and down towards the plate, he brings his front foot back behind him, which results in a violent delivery, a balance problem and a tendency to throw across his body. But he has enough arm speed to compensate for the mechanical flaws.

Defense

Jones has a typical closer's mentality about baserunners, in that he doesn't worry too much about them, viewing the hitters as the only task at hand. Because of this, he can be run upon. As a fielder, he's average at best. He's not very athletic, but has good baseball sense and generally makes the routine play.

1998 Outlook

Jones, acquired in the nine-player deal with Houston last offseason, is very open about how unhappy he was with the Astros and how happy he is with the Tigers. GM Randy Smith chose to sign Jones to a multiyear contract because Smith believes Jones matured as a closer and he's still relatively young. Detroit's closer of the future, Francisco Cordero, also is still a couple of years away from the majors.

Position: RP
Bats: L **Throws:** R
Ht: 6' 3" **Wt:** 200

Opening Day Age: 29
Born: 4/24/68 in Marietta, GA
ML Seasons: 5

Overall Statistics

	W	L	Pct.	ERA	G	GS	Sv	IP	H	BB	SO	HR	Ratio
1997	5	4	.556	3.09	68	0	31	70.0	60	35	70	3	1.36
Career	23	16	.590	3.23	262	0	70	337.0	290	160	298	23	1.34

How Often He Throws Strikes

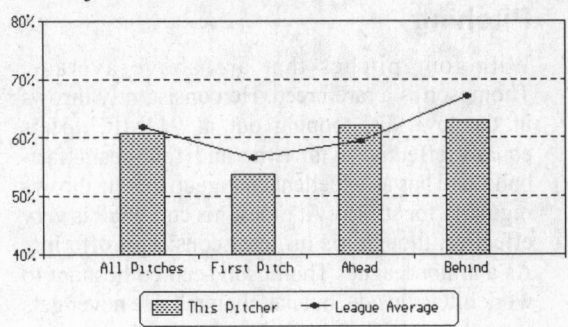

1997 Situational Stats

	W	L	ERA	Sv	IP		AB	H	HR	RBI	Avg
Home	1	2	3.66	16	32.0	LHB	134	33	3	15	.246
Road	4	2	2.61	15	38.0	RHB	126	27	0	11	.214
First Half	1	3	3.50	13	36.0	Sc Pos	74	11	1	22	.149
Scnd Half	4	1	2.65	18	34.0	Clutch	181	38	2	19	.210

1997 Rankings (American League)

⇒ 4th in saves and lowest batting average allowed in relief with runners on base (.175)
⇒ 5th in save opportunities (36), save percentage (86.1%) and lowest batting average allowed in relief with runners in scoring position (.149)
⇒ Led the Tigers in saves, games finished (51), wild pitches (7), save opportunities (36), save percentage (86.1%), lowest batting average allowed in relief with runners on base (.175), lowest batting average allowed in relief with runners in scoring position (.149), lowest percentage of inherited runners scored (28.6%), lowest batting average allowed in relief (.231) and most strikeouts per 9 innings in relief (9.0)

Detroit Tigers

145

Justin Thompson

1997 Season

The most-asked question about Justin Thompson in the past was: How well would he do if he could stay healthy for an entire year? After never throwing more than 147 innings in any professional season, Thompson worked 223 innings in 1997 and ranked among the best lefthanders in baseball. He pitched a scoreless inning in the All-Star Game and struck out Ken Griffey Jr. the first six times he faced him. Thompson did have one brief stint on the disabled list with an elbow ailment. But for someone who has suffered through numerous elbow and shoulder ailments and missed the entire 1994 season because of an elbow injury, it was a minor setback.

Pitching

With four pitches that are above average, Thompson is a rare breed. He consistently throws in the low 90s, topping out at 94 MPH. He's equally effective with two- and four-seam fastballs, and has an excellent changeup that he throws regularly for strikes. At times, his curveball is very effective, though it's his least consistent offering. As a minor leaguer Thompson seemed hesitant to work hitters inside, but has changed. He never gets flustered on the mound, but there are questions about his durability due to his injury-plagued past.

Defense

Thompson is a catcher's nightmare in that he's very poor at holding runners. Even though he's lefthanded, his move to first base is below average, and he has a high leg kick and a slow delivery toward the plate. He's a good fielder who hasn't made an error in 57 big league chances.

1998 Outlook

GM Randy Smith and manager Buddy Bell view Thompson as the anchor of their staff, and he relishes the responsibility. He averaged seven innings per start last season despite being on a 110-pitch limit each outing. With just a little better run support, Thompson might have won 20 games. He had a small bone spur shaved off and some loose bodies removed from his left elbow during arthroscopic surgery following the season, but should be 100 percent for spring training.

Position: SP
Bats: L **Throws:** L
Ht: 6' 4" **Wt:** 215

Opening Day Age: 25
Born: 3/8/73 in San Antonio, TX
ML Seasons: 2

Overall Statistics

	W	L	Pct.	ERA	G	GS	Sv	IP	H	BB	SO	HR	Ratio
1997	15	11	.577	3.02	32	32	0	223.1	188	66	151	20	1.14
Career	16	17	.485	3.35	43	43	0	282.1	250	97	195	27	1.23

How Often He Throws Strikes

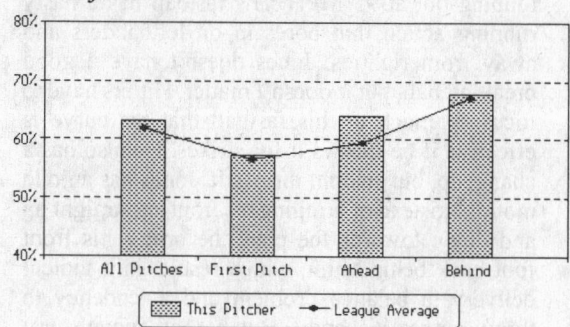

1997 Situational Stats

	W	L	ERA	Sv	IP			AB	H	HR	RBI	Avg
Home	11	5	2.88	0	131.1	LHB		127	24	4	11	.189
Road	4	6	3.23	0	92.0	RHB		680	164	16	65	.241
First Half	8	6	2.95	0	128.1	Sc Pos		148	39	1	50	.264
Scnd Half	7	5	3.13	0	95.0	Clutch		84	19	5	12	.226

1997 Rankings (American League)

⇒ 1st in fielding percentage at pitcher (1.000)
⇒ 4th in lowest on-base percentage allowed (.289) and least baserunners allowed per 9 innings (10.3)
⇒ 5th in ERA, runners caught stealing (11), GDPs induced (24), lowest batting average allowed (.233) and ERA at home
⇒ Led the Tigers in ERA, games started, complete games (4), innings pitched, batters faced (891), walks allowed, strikeouts, pitches thrown (3,330), pickoff throws (166), runners caught stealing (11), GDPs induced (24), highest strikeout/walk ratio (2.3), lowest batting average allowed (.233), lowest slugging percentage allowed (.354) and lowest on-base percentage allowed (.289)

Marcus Jensen

Position: C
Bats: B **Throws:** R
Ht: 6' 4" **Wt:** 195

Opening Day Age: 25
Born: 12/14/72 in
Oakland, CA
ML Seasons: 2

Overall Statistics

	G	AB	R	H	D	T	HR	RBI	SB	BB	SO	Avg	OBP	Slg
1997	38	85	6	13	2	0	1	4	0	8	28	.153	.226	.212
Career	47	104	10	17	3	0	1	8	0	16	35	.163	.275	.221

1997 Situational Stats

	AB	H	HR	RBI	Avg		AB	H	HR	RBI	Avg
Home	50	8	1	3	.160	LHP	31	4	0	1	.129
Road	35	5	0	1	.143	RHP	54	9	1	3	.167
First Half	73	11	1	3	.151	Sc Pos	19	4	1	4	.211
Scnd Half	12	2	0	1	.167	Clutch	16	1	0	0	.063

1997 Season

When it became evident the Tigers were going with Raul Casanova as their regular catcher, they dealt veteran Brian Johnson to San Francisco for Marcus Jensen. Detroit wanted a younger catcher to develop for the future, even if it's as a backup for Casanova. Jensen went to Triple-A Toledo before being promoted to Detroit in September.

Hitting, Baserunning & Defense

Jensen's strength lies with what he does behind the plate. He's an excellent receiver and pitchers love throwing to him. Despite being tall, he gets into a low stance and presents an excellent target, and is also very good at framing pitches. With above-average arm strength and a quick release, Jensen is a threat to basestealers. Offensively, he struggles. He has some bat speed, but it never has translated into the 15-plus homers a year the Giants expected. He also strikes out too much and has trouble with breaking pitches.

1998 Outlook

Jensen has some good tools defensively and should have a long major league career ahead of him. Unless he improves offensively, it's going to be mostly as a backup. That's what the Tigers envision him as.

Greg Keagle

Position: SP
Bats: R **Throws:** R
Ht: 6' 2" **Wt:** 195

Opening Day Age: 26
Born: 6/28/71 in
Corning, NY
ML Seasons: 2
Pronunciation:
KAY-gull

Overall Statistics

	W	L	Pct.	ERA	G	GS	Sv	IP	H	BB	SO	HR	Ratio
1997	3	5	.375	6.55	11	10	0	45.1	58	18	33	9	1.68
Career	6	11	.353	7.11	37	16	0	133.0	162	86	103	22	1.86

1997 Situational Stats

	W	L	ERA	Sv	IP		AB	H	HR	RBI	Avg
Home	2	2	5.63	0	24.0	LHB	109	35	8	20	.321
Road	1	3	7.59	0	21.1	RHB	79	23	1	9	.291
First Half	0	1	7.71	0	4.2	Sc Pos	55	11	0	15	.200
Scnd Half	3	4	6.42	0	40.2	Clutch	0	0	0	0	

1997 Season

After spending all of 1996 with Detroit as a major league Rule 5 draftee and struggling mightily, Greg Keagle spent most of 1997 season at Triple-A Toledo. He had a good season there, which served as a confidence booster. In the major leagues, however, he again didn't have success.

Pitching & Defense

Keagle usually tops 90 MPH with his fastball and his changeup can be a dazzling pitch when he's sharp. The problem is that he isn't sharp consistently enough. The flashes have been there on a couple of occasions, but Keagle has had trouble maintaining any level of consistency in the majors. When he gets into trouble, it's invariably because he falls behind in the count or walks hitters. He's a prime example of the importance of the baseball adage, trust your stuff. He needs to stop nibbling because his pitches aren't bad. Keagle is an average fielder and does an adequate job of holding runners.

1998 Outlook

Detroit GM Randy Smith is intrigued by Keagle and will give him another big league opportunity in 1998. But Keagle is approaching the age where he needs to start getting it done sooner. . . or there may not be a later.

Detroit Tigers

Dan Miceli

Traded To PADRES

Position: RP
Bats: R **Throws:** R
Ht: 6' 0" **Wt:** 216

Opening Day Age: 27
Born: 9/9/70 in Newark, NJ
ML Seasons: 5
Pronunciation: mah-SELL-ee

Overall Statistics

	W	L	Pct.	ERA	G	GS	Sv	IP	H	BB	SO	HR	Ratio
1997	3	2	.600	5.01	71	0	3	82.2	77	38	79	13	1.39
Career	11	17	.393	5.28	210	9	27	259.0	271	125	232	40	1.53

1997 Situational Stats

	W	L	ERA	Sv	IP		AB	H	HR	RBI	Avg
Home	1	1	2.70	0	40.0	LHB	127	33	5	26	.260
Road	2	1	7.17	3	42.2	RHB	183	44	8	33	.240
First Half	2	1	5.53	1	42.1	Sc Pos	86	29	2	43	.337
Scnd Half	1	1	4.46	2	40.1	Clutch	94	32	3	25	.340

1997 Season

The season started poorly for Dan Miceli when he was hit hard in his first three appearances. He was counted on to be Detroit's setup man, but never was able to regain that role. Miceli did recover to turn in some decent outings, but never was consistent.

Pitching & Defense

Miceli throws hard, sitting on 94-95 MPH on most nights. His fastball, however, lacks any type of tricky movement. If he doesn't spot his fastball well or falls behind in the count, he's in trouble. Miceli's breaking ball and changeup are below average, but he still can be effective when he's locating his fastball well and getting ahead in the count. He pitched well at home last season (2.70 ERA) but very poorly on the road (7.71 ERA). He's so intense that his teammates call him "Rambo," and he concentrates on hitters to the point that he forgets about runners. He's a below-average fielder.

1998 Outlook

Miceli is trying to recapture the magic of 1995, when he had 21 saves for Pittsburgh. In order to do that, he'll have to command his fastball better. He's now with San Diego after being part of a trade for Tim Worrell.

Orlando Miller

Claimed By ROYALS

Position: SS
Bats: R **Throws:** R
Ht: 6' 1" **Wt:** 180

Opening Day Age: 29
Born: 1/13/69 in Changuinola, Panama
ML Seasons: 4
Nickname: El Diablo

Overall Statistics

	G	AB	R	H	D	T	HR	RBI	SB	BB	SO	Avg	OBP	Slg
1997	50	111	13	26	7	1	2	10	1	5	24	.234	.289	.369
Career	297	943	95	244	53	5	24	113	8	43	223	.259	.305	.402

1997 Situational Stats

	AB	H	HR	RBI	Avg		AB	H	HR	RBI	Avg
Home	66	13	2	7	.197	LHP	32	8	1	4	.250
Road	45	13	0	3	.289	RHP	79	18	1	6	.228
First Half	49	11	2	6	.224	Sc Pos	25	4	0	7	.160
Scnd Half	62	15	0	4	.242	Clutch	20	2	0	2	.100

1997 Season

Orlando Miller knows how Wally Pipp felt. Acquired from Houston in a nine-player trade to be Detroit's regular shortstop, he had two bulging discs in his back and missed most of spring training and the first two months of the season. By the time he returned, the shortstop job belonged to rookie Deivi Cruz.

Hitting, Baserunning & Defense

Miller has good tools. Though he's not a good basestealer, he has decent speed and average range at shortstop. He also played reasonably well when put at third base in 1997. He has good power for a middle infielder and is capable of topping the 20-homer mark if he's playing regularly. His power and arm strength are his best tools, given his position. Miller's great weakness, however, is selectivity at the plate. He's impatient and doesn't take many pitches.

1998 Outlook

Miller's days of playing regularly in Detroit ended with the development of Cruz. He still has enough tools to be a regular in the major leagues. It remains to be seen how much his 1997 sabbatical will affect him. Waived in the offseason, he was claimed by the Royals.

Brian Moehler

Position: SP
Bats: R **Throws:** R
Ht: 6' 3" **Wt:** 220

Opening Day Age: 26
Born: 12/31/71 in
Rockingham, NC
ML Seasons: 2
Pronunciation:
MOE-ler

Overall Statistics

	W	L	Pct.	ERA	G	GS	Sv	IP	H	BB	SO	HR	Ratio
1997	11	12	.478	4.67	31	31	0	175.1	198	61	97	22	1.48
Career	11	13	.458	4.65	33	33	0	185.2	209	69	99	23	1.50

1997 Situational Stats

	W	L	ERA	Sv	IP		AB	H	HR	RBI	Avg
Home	5	6	4.90	0	82.2	LHB	374	120	12	48	.321
Road	6	6	4.47	0	92.2	RHB	321	78	10	32	.243
First Half	6	6	4.22	0	98.0	Sc Pos	145	45	1	54	.310
Scnd Half	5	6	5.24	0	77.1	Clutch	32	6	0	0	.188

1997 Season

Brian Moehler arrived at spring training with no Triple-A experience. He was a longshot to make the parent club, but earned a spot in the season-opening rotation. Moehler pitched well early in the season, but struggled after the All-Star break and was on the verge of being pulled from the rotation when he was disabled by a groin injury. The rest helped his arm strength, enabling Moehler to finish the season on an upbeat note.

Pitching & Defense

Moehler's career turned around at Jacksonville, where pitching coach Jeff Jones taught him a cut fastball. He doesn't have a trick pitch, generally going right after hitters with his fastball and slider. Moehler hit 95 MPH early in his minor league career and began to overthrow as a result. He stopped doing that in 1996 and now is generally in the 89-90 MPH range. He struggles against lefthanders and will give up more than his share of home runs when his cutter misses over the middle of the plate. Moehler moves well for his size and does a decent job holding runners.

1998 Outlook

Moehler is a tough, hard-nosed competitor who appears to be the ideal No. 3 or No. 4 starter for a contending team.

Phil Nevin

Traded To ANGELS

Position: LF/3B/DH
Bats: R **Throws:** R
Ht: 6' 2" **Wt:** 210

Opening Day Age: 27
Born: 1/19/71 in
Fullerton, California
ML Seasons: 3

Overall Statistics

	G	AB	R	H	D	T	HR	RBI	SB	BB	SO	Avg	OBP	Slg
1997	93	251	32	59	16	1	9	35	0	25	68	.235	.306	.414
Career	178	527	60	122	25	2	19	67	2	51	147	.231	.305	.395

1997 Situational Stats

	AB	H	HR	RBI	Avg		AB	H	HR	RBI	Avg
Home	112	24	4	15	.214	LHP	114	35	6	21	.307
Road	139	35	5	20	.252	RHP	137	24	3	14	.175
First Half	101	28	4	20	.277	Sc Pos	66	18	1	21	.273
Scnd Half	150	31	5	15	.207	Clutch	42	13	3	8	.310

1997 Season

Phil Nevin entered spring training primed to make a run for a regular position, either at designated hitter or in left field. Then he suffered a dislocated tendon in his left wrist and was out for all of the spring and the beginning of the season. As a result, the No. 1 overall pick in the 1992 draft never got untracked.

Hitting, Baserunning & Defense

Nevin has power, especially to the gap in right-center. He's much more effective against lefthanders than against righties. His best position is third base, where he's average in terms of his hands, range and arm strength. He's capable of getting by in left field in a pinch and spent the first half of the 1996 season learning to catch at Double-A Jacksonville, adding to his versatility. He's a below-average runner.

1998 Outlook

Nevin has some pop at the plate, can play the corner infield and outfield positions, and is an emergency catcher. He hasn't responded well the few times he's been given the opportunity to play regularly. He was traded to Anaheim in the offseason.

Detroit Tigers

Melvin Nieves

Traded To REDS

Position: RF/DH
Bats: B **Throws:** R
Ht: 6' 2" **Wt:** 210

Opening Day Age: 26
Born: 12/28/71 in San Juan, PR
ML Seasons: 6
Pronunciation: nee-AY-vuss

Overall Statistics

	G	AB	R	H	D	T	HR	RBI	SB	BB	SO	Avg	OBP	Slg
1997	116	359	46	82	18	1	20	64	1	39	157	.228	.311	.451
Career	375	1109	155	254	49	6	61	170	4	110	441	.229	.306	.449

1997 Situational Stats

	AB	H	HR	RBI	Avg		AB	H	HR	RBI	Avg
Home	162	38	7	23	.235	LHP	112	27	4	25	.241
Road	197	44	13	41	.223	RHP	247	55	16	39	.223
First Half	237	62	11	43	.262	Sc Pos	89	24	8	46	.270
Scnd Half	122	20	9	21	.164	Clutch	65	16	3	13	.246

1997 Season

After watching Melvin Nieves continually make the same mistakes for two straight years, manager Buddy Bell lost his patience and put him on the bench. Nieves struck out 157 times in only 359 at-bats and walked just 39 times.

Hitting, Baserunning & Defense

Few players can match Nieves drive for drive in batting practice, but his homers in game situations are few and far between. He does his best hitting when he relaxes at the plate and lets his natural ability take over. He doesn't handle failure well, and he's the one player the coaching staff wishes would spend less time watching videotape of his at-bats. Defensively, he's good at tracking fly balls and his arm is average. He has had problems picking up the ball off the ground, letting runners take extra bases. He has below-average speed.

1998 Outlook

Eligible for arbitration and no longer viewed as a prospect, Nieves is at a crossroads. He's no better a player than he was when the Tigers acquired him during spring training in 1996, and that's a shame considering his upside potential. Detroit tired of him and dealt him to Cincinnati for two fringe players.

A.J. Sager

Position: RP
Bats: R **Throws:** R
Ht: 6' 4" **Wt:** 220

Opening Day Age: 33
Born: 3/3/65 in Columbus, OH
ML Seasons: 4

Overall Statistics

	W	L	Pct.	ERA	G	GS	Sv	IP	H	BB	SO	HR	Ratio
1997	3	4	.429	4.18	38	1	3	84.0	81	24	53	10	1.25
Career	8	13	.381	5.05	92	13	3	224.1	253	76	141	25	1.47

1997 Situational Stats

	W	L	ERA	Sv	IP		AB	H	HR	RBI	Avg
Home	1	2	2.54	2	49.2	LHB	150	39	5	18	.260
Road	2	2	6.55	1	34.1	RHB	164	42	5	29	.256
First Half	2	2	3.02	3	44.2	Sc Pos	75	18	2	34	.240
Scnd Half	1	2	5.49	0	39.1	Clutch	94	17	2	13	.181

1997 Season

A.J. Sager was at his best both early in the season when the Tigers really needed him, and also in September when they made a run at .500. That has been his history with Detroit. Underrated and underappreciated, but surprisingly effective.

Pitching & Defense

Sager carries the reputation of a sinker-slider pitcher who's a little short with his fastball, but his stuff is better than generally believed. The key is how much time he has between appearances. He's always willing to take the ball, but he doesn't bounce back well on back-to-back days or even on two days rest. When he has three or more days rest between appearances, he consistently tops 90 MPH and has good sinking movement on his fastball. When he isn't rested, Sager doesn't touch 90 MPH and generally takes a beating. A former starting quarterback at the University of Toledo, Sager is a good athlete and a good fielder. He uses a slide-step delivery and holds runners well.

1998 Outlook

Because of the way his arm reacts, Sager is suited best for long relief. He's the ideal guy for quality innings early in a game when the starter has been knocked out or as a spot starter.

Scott Sanders

Position: RP/SP
Bats: R **Throws:** R
Ht: 6' 4" **Wt:** 220

Opening Day Age: 29
Born: 3/25/69 in
Hannibal, MO
ML Seasons: 5

Overall Statistics

	W	L	Pct.	ERA	G	GS	Sv	IP	H	BB	SO	HR	Ratio
1997	6	14	.300	5.86	47	20	2	139.2	152	62	120	30	1.53
Career	27	35	.435	4.54	142	80	3	537.0	505	212	511	68	1.34

1997 Situational Stats

	W	L	ERA	Sv	IP		AB	H	HR	RBI	Avg
Home	3	9	5.65	1	79.2	LHB	266	76	15	44	.286
Road	3	5	6.15	1	60.0	RHB	281	76	15	56	.270
First Half	2	6	6.68	2	62.0	Sc Pos	142	39	7	69	.275
Scnd Half	4	8	5.21	0	77.2	Clutch	39	16	3	11	.410

1997 Season

Scott Sanders had difficulty changing leagues and roles after being dealt to Seattle from San Diego last offseason for Sterling Hitchcock. He didn't perform well either as a starter or reliever for the Mariners, and was traded to Detroit with righthander Dean Crow in July for pitchers Omar Olivares and Felipe Lira. Sanders' struggles continued with the Tigers.

Pitching & Defense

Sanders brings plenty with him to the mound. He consistently tops 90 MPH and his slider is one of the best in baseball. The same can't be said for his command. He falls behind in the count frequently because he tends to rely on his slider too much, and tries to compensate with fastballs over the heart of the plate. As a result, he allowed 30 home runs in just 139 innings in 1997. Sanders moves well for a big man, has good hands and coordination, and holds runners well.

1998 Outlook

Sanders was one of the best pitchers in the National League during the second half of 1996 and one of the worst in the American League during the first half of 1997. How good is he? The answer probably lies somewhere in between.

Matt Walbeck

Position: C
Bats: B **Throws:** R
Ht: 5'11" **Wt:** 188

Opening Day Age: 28
Born: 10/2/69 in
Sacramento, CA
ML Seasons: 5

Overall Statistics

	G	AB	R	H	D	T	HR	RBI	SB	BB	SO	Avg	OBP	Slg
1997	47	137	18	38	3	0	3	10	3	12	19	.277	.331	.365
Career	333	1113	116	262	45	1	12	119	10	64	167	.235	.277	.310

1997 Situational Stats

	AB	H	HR	RBI	Avg		AB	H	HR	RBI	Avg
Home	61	17	1	6	.279	LHP	48	11	0	1	.229
Road	76	21	2	4	.276	RHP	89	27	3	9	.303
First Half	29	8	1	5	.276	Sc Pos	23	6	1	8	.261
Scnd Half	108	30	2	5	.278	Clutch	26	6	1	1	.231

1997 Season

Less than three weeks into the season, Matt Walbeck broke the hamate bone in his left hand while diving for a pop fly. When he returned to action, the Tigers chose to keep him over Brian Johnson to back up rookie Raul Casanova behind the plate. Walbeck hit a career-best .277 and was solid defensively.

Hitting, Baserunning & Defense

Walbeck is a switch-hitter and the big knock on him was that he couldn't hit lefthanded. In 1997, he batted .303 from the left side of the plate. In truth, he's not much of a threat from either side. However, he didn't reach the major leagues because of his bat. A good receiver with an accurate arm, Walbeck handles a pitching staff well and calls a good game. He's not much of a runner.

1998 Outlook

Walbeck is a solid defensive catcher, so he won't have trouble getting work. His bat keeps him from being an everyday player. Anaheim traded for him and will use him as a backup to Todd Greene.

Detroit Tigers

Kimera Bartee (**Pos**: LF, **Age**: 25, **Bats**: B)

	G	AB	R	H	D	T	HR	RBI	SB	BB	SO	Avg	OBP	Slg
1997	12	5	4	1	0	0	0	3	2	2	2	.200	.500	.200
Career	122	222	36	56	6	1	1	14	23	19	79	.252	.314	.302

Bartee was Detroit's primary center fielder in the second half of 1996, but watched Brian Hunter play every game there in 1997. His tools are similar to Hunter's, just not as good. 1998 Outlook: C

Vince Coleman (**Pos**: LF, **Age**: 36, **Bats**: B)

	G	AB	R	H	D	T	HR	RBI	SB	BB	SO	Avg	OBP	Slg
1997	6	14	0	1	0	0	0	0	1	3	.071	.133	.071
Career	1371	5406	849	1425	176	89	28	346	752	477	960	.264	.324	.345

It only took the Tigers the first two weeks of the season to realize that Coleman can run, but he can't play. He likely has finished his career with 752 stolen bases, sixth-best in big league history. 1998 Outlook: D

John Cummings (**Pos**: LHP, **Age**: 28)

	W	L	Pct.	ERA	G	GS	Sv	IP	H	BB	SO	HR	Ratio
1997	2	0	1.000	5.47	19	0	0	24.2	32	14	8	3	1.86
Career	10	15	.400	5.33	110	16	0	216.1	251	106	114	23	1.65

For the fifth straight season, Cummings split time between the majors and minors. His lack of control didn't endear him to the Tigers during his big league stint. 1998 Outlook: C

Glenn Dishman (**Pos**: LHP, **Age**: 27)

	W	L	Pct.	ERA	G	GS	Sv	IP	H	BB	SO	HR	Ratio
1997	1	2	.333	5.28	7	4	0	29.0	30	8	20	4	1.31
Career	5	10	.333	5.25	33	21	0	135.1	146	45	66	17	1.41

One of several former Padres who have joined the Tigers since GM Randy Smith went from San Diego to Detroit, Dishman pitched fairly well before having shoulder problems at the end of the season. 1998 Outlook: B

Roberto Duran (**Pos**: LHP, **Age**: 25)

	W	L	Pct.	ERA	G	GS	Sv	IP	H	BB	SO	HR	Ratio
1997	0	0	-	7.59	13	0	0	10.2	7	15	11	0	2.06
Career	0	0	-	7.59	13	0	0	10.2	7	15	11	0	2.06

In 1997, Duran led the Southern League in strikeouts per nine innings and ranked third in hits per nine innings. He has better stuff than Eddie Gaillard, the closer ahead of him in Triple-A. 1998 Outlook: C

Eddie Gaillard (**Pos**: RHP, **Age**: 27)

	W	L	Pct.	ERA	G	GS	Sv	IP	H	BB	SO	HR	Ratio
1997	1	0	1.000	5.31	16	0	1	20.1	16	10	12	2	1.28
Career	1	0	1.000	5.31	16	0	1	20.1	16	10	12	2	1.28

Gaillard was used as a minor league closer in 1995 and 1997, and responded with 25 and 28 saves, respectively. He won't get the same shot in Detroit, where Todd Jones is firmly established. 1998 Outlook: C

Joe Hall (**Pos**: RF, **Age**: 32, **Bats**: R)

	G	AB	R	H	D	T	HR	RBI	SB	BB	SO	Avg	OBP	Slg
1997	2	4	1	2	1	0	0	3	0	0	0	.500	.500	.750
Career	26	47	9	15	4	0	1	8	0	4	7	.319	.385	.468

Hall walks and hits doubles, but big league clubs don't covet 32-year-old corner outfielders with little home run power. 1997 was his second stint with the Tigers, and he probably won't return. 1998 Outlook: D

Fernando Hernandez (**Pos**: RHP, **Age**: 26)

	W	L	Pct.	ERA	G	GS	Sv	IP	H	BB	SO	HR	Ratio
1997	0	0	-	40.50	2	0	0	1.1	5	3	2	0	6.00
Career	0	0	-	40.50	2	0	0	1.1	5	3	2	0	6.00

Hernandez made the Opening Day roster, got bombed in two appearances and never returned. He averaged more than a strikeout per inning in Triple-A, as he has done throughout his minor league career. 1998 Outlook: C

Kevin Jarvis (**Pos**: RHP, **Age**: 28)

	W	L	Pct.	ERA	G	GS	Sv	IP	H	BB	SO	HR	Ratio
1997	0	4	.000	7.68	32	5	1	68.0	99	29	48	17	1.88
Career	12	18	.400	6.38	81	39	1	285.0	364	109	154	51	1.66

Jarvis pitched for the Reds and Twins before joining the Tigers off of waivers. He was much more effective in Detroit before he went on the disabled list with a back injury. 1998 Outlook: C

Mike Myers (**Pos**: LHP, **Age**: 28)

	W	L	Pct.	ERA	G	GS	Sv	IP	H	BB	SO	HR	Ratio
1997	0	4	.000	5.70	88	0	2	53.2	58	25	50	12	1.55
Career	2	9	.182	5.47	184	0	8	126.2	139	66	123	19	1.62

Myers has set club records for appearances in each of the last two seasons, but righthanders murder him and lefties hit him pretty well in 1997. He was traded to Milwaukee in a deal for Bryce Florie. 1998 Outlook: B

Tim Pugh (**Pos**: RHP, **Age**: 31)

	W	L	Pct.	ERA	G	GS	Sv	IP	H	BB	SO	HR	Ratio
1997	1	1	.500	5.00	2	2	0	9.0	6	5	4	0	1.22
Career	25	28	.472	4.97	107	58	0	416.2	479	158	214	51	1.53

Signed to a minor league contract after the 1996 season, Pugh made two starts for Detroit after Willie Blair took a liner off his forehead. Never matched the promise he showed in September 1992. 1998 Outlook: C

Jody Reed (**Pos**: 2B, **Age**: 35, **Bats**: R)

	G	AB	R	H	D	T	HR	RBI	SB	BB	SO	Avg	OBP	Slg
1997	52	112	6	22	2	0	0	8	3	10	15	.196	.278	.214
Career	1284	4554	566	1231	263	10	27	392	40	542	407	.270	.349	.350

Padres players raised a ruckus when Quilvio Veras beat him out for San Diego's second-base job, but Reed showed little in Detroit. Minor leaguer Frank Catalanotto can at least match Reed's performance. 1998 Outlook: C

Detroit Tigers Minor League Prospects

Organization Overview:

Baseball America selected the Tigers as the 1997 Organization of the Year, and while the award may have been a bit premature there's no question that Detroit has been much better off under GM Randy Smith. For years the Tigers were a joke when it came to player development. They lived off strong drafts in the late 1970s, then collapsed when those players aged. Outfielder Juan Encarnacion is the organization's most exciting prospect since Kirk Gibson. There are several quality arms at the upper levels, though many had off years in 1997, and Class-A West Michigan was as strong as any minor league club. Smith's plan has been for the Tigers to contend when they open a new ballpark in 1999, and they're on target.

Gabe Alvarez

Position: 3B   **Opening Day Age:** 24
Bats: R **Throws:** R   **Born:** 3/6/74 in
Ht: 6' 1" **Wt:** 185   Novojoa, Sonora, Mexico

Recent Statistics

	G	AB	R	H	D	T	HR	RBI	SB	BB	SO	AVG
96 AA Memphis	104	368	58	91	23	1	8	40	2	64	87	.247
97 AA Mobile	114	427	71	128	28	2	14	78	1	51	64	.300
97 MLE	114	407	52	108	22	1	11	57	0	31	67	.265

Alvarez was taken in the first round of the expansion draft by Arizona, then sent to Detroit in a trade for Travis Fryman. A 1995 second-round pick by the Padres out of the University of Southern California, Alvarez tore up the high Class-A California League in his pro debut but needed two seasons to master Double-A. He's capable of 20 or more homers per year, though he has yet to approach that total in the minors. He's a good hitter who'll draw a walk, but he has below-average speed and has struggled defensively. A converted shortstop, he has poor footwork at third and makes too many throwing errors. After a year in Triple-A, he'll press Joe Randa for the starting job in Detroit.

Frank Catalanotto

Position: 2B   **Opening Day Age:** 23
Bats: L **Throws:** R   **Born:** 4/27/74 in
Ht: 6' 0" **Wt:** 170   Smithtown, NY

Recent Statistics

	G	AB	R	H	D	T	HR	RBI	SB	BB	SO	AVG
97 AAA Toledo	134	500	75	150	32	3	16	68	12	47	80	.300
97 AL Detroit	13	26	2	8	2	0	0	3	0	3	7	.308
97 MLE	134	487	67	137	29	2	16	61	9	42	84	.281

Detroit briefly lost Catalanotto to Oakland in the major league Rule 5 draft, and gladly took him back when he couldn't stick with the Athletics. A 10th-round pick in 1992, he has very good pop for a middle infielder, hitting 33 homers in Double-A and Triple-A the last two seasons. He hits for average, though his walks dwindled in 1997, and can steal the occasional base. He has limited range at second base, and played some third in the Arizona Fall League to increase his options. The Tigers are satisfied with Damion Easley at second base, but Catalanotto possibly could emerge at the hot corner if Joe Randa disappoints.

Francisco Cordero

Position: P   **Opening Day Age:** 20
Bats: R **Throws:** R   **Born:** 8/11/77 in Santo
Ht: 6' 2" **Wt:** 170   Domingo, DR

Recent Statistics

	W	L	ERA	G	GS	Sv	IP	H	R	BB	SO	HR
96 A Fayetteville	0	0	2.57	2	1	0	7.0	2	2	6	7	0
96 A Jamestown	0	0	0.82	2	2	0	11.0	5	1	2	10	0
97 A W Michigan	6	1	0.99	50	0	35	54.1	36	13	15	67	2

Signed out of the Dominican Republic, Cordero had middling success as a starter in his first three pro seasons. Moved to the bullpen in 1997, he exploded onto the prospect scene. He finished second in the minors with 35 saves and was named the top prospect in the Class-A Midwest League, showing a 96-98 MPH fastball with good location. He also has a hard slider, and rarely throws his changeup because he has no reason to give hitters a break. The Tigers will jump him to Double-A at age 20 in 1998, and he could be their closer before he reaches the legal drinking age.

Dean Crow

Position: P   **Opening Day Age:** 25
Bats: R **Throws:** R   **Born:** 8/21/72 in
Ht: 6' 5" **Wt:** 212   Garland, TX

Recent Statistics

	W	L	ERA	G	GS	Sv	IP	H	R	BB	SO	HR
96 AA Port City	2	3	3.04	60	0	26	68.0	64	35	20	43	4
97 AAA Tacoma	4	2	4.78	33	0	7	43.1	56	25	19	36	3
97 AAA Toledo	3	0	7.85	18	0	2	18.1	26	16	10	10	1

Crow gives Detroit another potential closer, though you couldn't tell that by his 1997 performance. Seattle's 10th-round pick in 1993 out of Baylor, he went to the Tigers last year in a trade that sent Felipe Lira and Omar Olivares to the Mariners. Crow has a legitimate power arm, throwing in the mid-90s and getting grounders with good sinking action. Neither his splitter or slider is as reliable, and Triple-A hitters teed off on him by sitting on his fastball. With Todd Jones established in Detroit and Cordero closing fast, Crow is more likely to be used as a setup man by the Tigers.

Matt Drews

Position: P **Opening Day Age:** 23
Bats: R **Throws:** R **Born:** 8/29/74 in
Ht: 6' 8" **Wt:** 205 Sarasota, FL

Recent Statistics

	W	L	ERA	G	GS	Sv	IP	H	R	BB	SO	HR
96 AAA Columbus	0	4	8.41	7	7	0	20.1	18	27	27	7	4
96 A Tampa	0	3	7.13	4	4	0	17.2	26	20	12	12	0
96 AA Norwich	1	3	4.50	9	9	0	46.0	40	26	33	37	4
96 AA Jacksnville	0	4	4.35	6	6	0	31.0	26	18	19	40	3
97 AA Jacksnville	8	11	5.49	24	24	0	144.1	160	109	50	85	23
97 AAA Toledo	0	2	6.60	3	3	0	15.0	14	11	14	7	2

A first-round pick of the Yankees in 1993, Drews was rushed to Triple-A in his third pro season. He tried to overthrow, messed up his delivery and fell out of favor, so Detroit was able to grab him in the Cecil Fielder trade. His mechanics still are inconsistent and sometimes cost him velocity, but when he's on he can throw 93-94 MPH. He wasn't on often enough in 1997, and his statistics don't do justice to his fastball. He also has a good changeup and decent curveball, and began toying with a slider in the Arizona Fall League. He was taken in the second round of the expansion draft by Arizona, then returned to Detroit in a pre-arranged trade.

Mike Drumright

Position: P **Opening Day Age:** 23
Bats: L **Throws:** R **Born:** 4/19/74 in Salina,
Ht: 6' 4" **Wt:** 210 KS

Recent Statistics

	W	L	ERA	G	GS	Sv	IP	H	R	BB	SO	HR
96 AA Jacksnville	6	4	3.97	18	18	0	99.2	80	51	48	109	11
97 AA Jacksnville	1	1	1.57	5	5	0	28.2	16	7	13	24	0
97 AAA Toledo	5	10	5.06	23	23	0	133.1	134	78	91	115	22

A 1995 first-round pick out of Wichita State, Drumright had the best season and has the best upside of all the pitching prospects in the top half of the system. He returned at full strength after a weak shoulder bothered him the year before. He throws in the low to mid-90s and has a hard curveball, and can overpower hitters when he has command of both pitches. His control is still inconsistent, as is the changeup he needs as an offspeed pitch. It wouldn't be surprising to see him in Detroit's rotation at some point in 1998.

Seth Greisinger

Position: P **Opening Day Age:** 22
Bats: R **Throws:** R **Born:** 7/29/75 in
Ht: 6' 4" **Wt:** 190 Kansas City, KS

Recent Statistics

	W	L	ERA	G	GS	Sv	IP	H	R	BB	SO	HR
97 AA Jacksnville	10	6	5.20	28	28	0	159.1	194	103	53	105	29

Gresinger went 9-12 in his first two years at the University of Virginia before catching fire in 1996. He led NCAA Division I with a 1.76 ERA, made the U.S. Olympic team and became the first Team USA pitcher to win nine games in one summer. Detroit drafted him in the first round and sent him straight to Double-A to make his pro debut in 1997. He was the organization's best pitcher at any level in spring training, but scuffled while pitching in a Jacksonville ballpark conducive to home runs. His best pitch is a changeup, but he's not afraid to work inside with an average fastball. He may have thrown too many strikes, as he kept his walks down but was extremely hittable. Detroit views his debut as an aberration and just thinks he needs to trust his stuff a little more.

Willis Roberts

Position: P **Opening Day Age:** 22
Bats: R **Throws:** R **Born:** 6/19/75 in San
Ht: 6' 3" **Wt:** 175 Cristobal, DR

Recent Statistics

	W	L	ERA	G	GS	Sv	IP	H	R	BB	SO	HR
96 A Lakeland	9	7	2.89	23	22	0	149.1	133	60	69	105	5
97 AA Jacksnville	6	15	6.28	26	26	0	149.0	181	120	64	86	18

Roberts is proof that a pitcher can't survive on a fastball alone. He throws 93-95 MPH, but leaves his heat up in the zone and it gets hammered. His curveball is hard and so is his changeup, so hitters don't have to worry about him changing speeds. Signed out of the Dominican Republic, he has a deceptive motion. But his command is inconsistent, and if he can't develop a change he probably will be ticketed for relief. He was right with Drews, Drumright and Greisinger when 1997 opened, but took a huge step backward.

Others to Watch

Righthander **Matt Anderson** was the No. 1 overall draft pick, but remained unsigned in mid-November. If the Tigers sign him, they'll get a closer prospect with a high-90s fastball and a knuckle-curve. . . Outfielder **Trey Beamon**, 24, joined the Tigers in an offseason trade with San Diego. He hits for average, draws a few walks and steals a few bases, but lacks the power to play on the corners. . . Righthander **Dave Borkowski** went 15-3 at West Michigan at age 20 and is the best of the pitchers at the lower levels of the system. He has a hard 91-93 MPH sinker. . . Righthander **Clayton Bruner** matched Borkowski's age and record at West Michigan and had a better ERA, 2.38 to 3.46. Bruner's fastball is below average, but his breaking ball and changeup are quality pitches. . . First baseman **Robert Fick** was another West Michigan star, winning the Midwest League batting title (.341) and MVP honors at age 23. He won't move Tony Clark off first base, so he may try third base or catcher. He was an All-American at the latter position at Cal State Northridge. . . Right fielder **Gabe Kapler** has a bodybuilding physique and has been a model on the cover of fitness magazines. His stock has soared since he was drafted in the 57th round out of Moorpark (Calif.) Junior College in 1995. He batted .295-19-87 at Class-A Lakeland at age 22, and is a solid defender with average speed.

Tony Muser

1997 Season

Tony Muser spent the first half of 1997 as the Cubs' hitting coach, then took over the Royals' managerial reigns at the All-Star break. He arrived with a reputation for developing young position players. His first moves with Kansas City included inserting catching prospect Mike Sweeney into the regular lineup and moving Johnny Damon to center field. He also showed his commitment to youth by briefly recalling several of the Royals' prospects simply to get better acquainted with them.

Offense

The Royals' overall offensive approach changed little under Muser, and the club still ran the bases aggressively. But the platoon-laden lineups of former manager Bob Boone disappeared in favor of lineups designed to display talents of selected youngsters. Yamil Benitez, Jed Hansen and Rod Myers began playing regularly in August and September. In comparison to Boone, Muser used more conservative offensive strategies and played things mainly by the book.

Pitching & Defense

One of Muser's first big chores with the Royals was to rescue their tattered bullpen. He immediately reappointed Jeff Montgomery as the closer and began using other relievers where their specific skills were best suited. This was in contrast to Boone, who made frequent switches primarily to obtain platoon advantages. The new approach quickly paid dividends as Kansas City's bullpen immediately improved. Muser also demonstrated a quick hook and a commitment to good infield defense.

1998 Outlook

Muser knows his future is tied to the development of young talent, and his approach is very much in tune with the Royals' goal to build from the farm system. This may mean a quick turnover of veteran personnel, a sharp reversal from 1997. Keeping an even keel in the clubhouse during Kansas City's inevitable 1998 slumps will be a challenge for Muser.

Born: 8/1/47 in Los Angeles, CA

Playing Experience: 1969-1978, Bos, ChA, Bal, Mil

Managerial Experience: 1 season

Manager Statistics

Year	Team, Lg	W	L	Pct	GB	Finish
1997	Kansas City, AL	31	48	.392	19.0	5th Central
1 Season		31	48	.392	—	

1997 Starting Pitchers by Days Rest

	≤3	4	5	6+
Royals Starts	0	49	17	13
Royals ERA	—	5.97	4.80	6.35
AL Avg Starts	5	89	34	24
AL ERA	4.38	4.60	4.61	5.37

1997 Situational Stats

	Tony Muser*	AL Average
Hit & Run Success %	30.4	36.5
Stolen Base Success %	68.6	67.3
Platoon Pct.	60.3	59.5
Defensive Subs	14	22
High-Pitch Outings	4	15
Quick/Slow Hooks	9/11	19/15
Sacrifice Attempts	30	53

* Muser managed the Royals for 80 games

1997 Rankings (American League)

⇒ Did not rank near the top in any category

Kevin Appier

1997 Season

In his most frustrating major league season, Kevin Appier again placed among the American League leaders in ERA, innings and strikeouts, yet posted the first losing record of his career. He avoided his usual midseason shoulder troubles while still receiving his usual subpar run support. His insistence upon trying to strike out every hitter led to many long counts and triggered several rallies.

Pitching

Appier throws everything hard but has unusually good control. His straight, low-90s fastball and plus slider can be overpowering, but he lives and dies with his split-fingered fastball. Delivered at 90 MPH, it breaks late and drifts away from righthanders. When thrown near the strike zone, it's unhittable. However, he overthrows the splitter and buries it in the dirt too often. Learning to rely more on his other pitches might enable him to lower his pitch counts and go deeper into games.

Defense

Appier's glovework always has been below average. He falls off the mound toward the first-base line, leaving him off balance and out of position to field grounders through the box or bunts along the third-base line. His throws to the bases are unpredictable, though he has had reasonable success against the running game because he throws everything so hard. Most runners don't chance trying to steal a base because Appier's unruly splitter often results in wild pitches, allowing them to advance without risk.

1998 Outlook

Appier is an intense competitor, but his intensity can hinder his ability to win. He always takes the mound seemingly trying to pitch a perfect game. In the late innings of a close contest, he reaches back for a little extra and often grooves a fastball or bounces a splitter in the dirt. Yet he's still one of the best pitchers in the AL and might win a Cy Young Award one year if he ever received any run support. He separated his collarbone in an offseason fall at his home and had surgery, but was expected to be ready for spring training.

Position: SP
Bats: R **Throws:** R
Ht: 6' 2" **Wt:** 195

Opening Day Age: 30
Born: 12/6/67 in Lancaster, CA
ML Seasons: 9
Pronunciation: APE-ee-er

Overall Statistics

	W	L	Pct.	ERA	G	GS	Sv	IP	H	BB	SO	HR	Ratio
1997	9	13	.409	3.40	34	34	0	235.2	215	74	196	24	1.23
Career	104	78	.571	3.30	256	244	0	1665.1	1475	568	1364	113	1.23

How Often He Throws Strikes

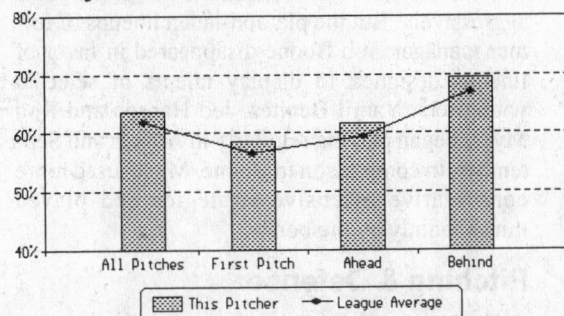

| | This Pitcher | League Average |

1997 Situational Stats

	W	L	ERA	Sv	IP		AB	H	HR	RBI	Avg
Home	3	7	3.50	0	121.0	LHB	467	120	14	48	.257
Road	6	6	3.30	0	114.2	RHB	419	95	10	39	.227
First Half	6	6	2.68	0	131.0	Sc Pos	192	46	4	63	.240
Scnd Half	3	7	4.30	0	104.2	Clutch	112	25	3	8	.223

1997 Rankings (American League)

⇒ 1st in wild pitches (14)
⇒ 2nd in least run support per 9 innings (4.0)
⇒ 3rd in pitches thrown (3,735)
⇒ 5th in games started, innings pitched and strikeouts
⇒ Led the Royals in ERA, losses, games started, complete games (4), shutouts (1), innings pitched, batters faced (972), walks allowed, strikeouts, wild pitches (14), pitches thrown (3,735), stolen bases allowed (14), runners caught stealing (9), highest strikeout/walk ratio (2.6), lowest batting average allowed (.243), lowest slugging percentage allowed (.378), lowest on-base percentage allowed (.303), least baserunners allowed per 9 innings (11.2) and least home runs allowed per 9 innings (.92)

Tim Belcher

Position: SP
Bats: R **Throws:** R
Ht: 6' 3" **Wt:** 220

Opening Day Age: 36
Born: 10/19/61 in Sparta, OH
ML Seasons: 11

1997 Season

Tim Belcher cruised into June among the American League leaders in several pitching categories, but the second half of the year proved more difficult for him. Frequent home runs contributed to a rising ERA, yet Belcher continued to win and led the staff in victories for the second straight season. He posted the only winning record among Kansas City starters, though he was helped considerably by the second-best run support in the AL (6.50).

Pitching

Working off an upper-80s four-seam fastball, Belcher also throws a sinking two-seamer, a cut fastball, a splitter and a curveball. His out pitch on any particular day depends upon what's working. He has the ability to quickly adjust to using his most effective pitch. His offspeed stuff often induces grounders, but he's extremely hittable. Opponents have batted over .280 against him each of the last four years. Belcher is most effective when he doesn't try to overpower opponents, and sticks to working both sides of the plate and changing speeds.

Defense

Belcher is a good fielder who rarely hurts himself with the glove. He works hard to field bunts and throws well to all bases. His pickoff move is above average. He possesses two different moves to first, using a softer move to lull unsuspecting runners to sleep, then throwing harder later in the sequence to pick them off.

1998 Outlook

Signed for an additional year, Belcher will return to the rotation as the No. 2 starter. Despite his age, he still has the competitive fire to succeed. A workhorse who always keeps his team in the game, he can win even when he doesn't have his best stuff. It's a valuable trait that Royals brass wish could be taught to younger members of their staff. Last year, his numbers were indirectly damaged by the Royals' weak bullpen. Belcher was left in the game to absorb seven or more runs on six separate occasions, significantly inflating his ERA.

Overall Statistics

	W	L	Pct.	ERA	G	GS	Sv	IP	H	BB	SO	HR	Ratio
1997	13	12	.520	5.02	32	32	0	213.1	242	70	113	31	1.46
Career	122	113	.519	3.93	327	306	5	2035.2	1963	719	1315	192	1.32

How Often He Throws Strikes

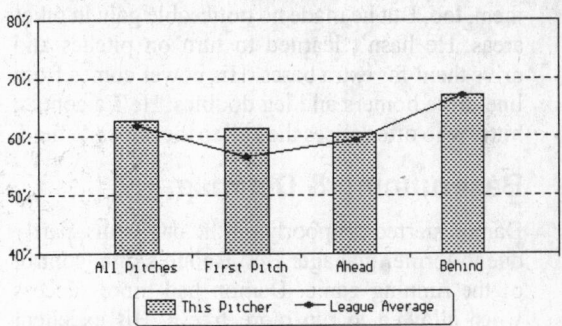

1997 Situational Stats

	W	L	ERA	Sv	IP		AB	H	HR	RBI	Avg
Home	7	8	5.87	0	112.0	LHB	407	113	17	50	.278
Road	6	4	4.09	0	101.1	RHB	434	129	14	65	.297
First Half	8	7	3.92	0	131.0	Sc Pos	196	58	9	84	.296
Scnd Half	5	5	6.78	0	82.1	Clutch	52	16	3	8	.308

1997 Rankings (American League)

⇒ 1st in fielding percentage at pitcher (1.000)
⇒ 2nd in most run support per 9 innings (6.5) and highest ERA at home
⇒ 5th in hits allowed, home runs allowed, least strikeouts per 9 innings (4.8) and highest batting average allowed vs. righthanded batters
⇒ Led the Royals in wins, shutouts (1), hits allowed, home runs allowed, GDPs induced (19), winning percentage, highest groundball/flyball ratio allowed (1.3), lowest stolen base percentage allowed (45.5%), least pitches thrown per batter (3.62) and most run support per 9 innings (6.5)

Johnny Damon

1997 Season

Johnny Damon had a slightly better year than in 1996, but didn't show the development expected from a young star. He only made marginal improvements and still has some glaring weaknesses. The questions that surrounded him before the 1997 season mostly remain unanswered. He played right field for most of the year, and shifted back to his natural position, center field, after Tom Goodwin was traded.

Hitting

Damon did improve upon his biggest weakness, hitting lefthanders. He looked far less tentative against most lefties and was more selective against them, too. But he made no noticeable gain in other areas. He hasn't learned to turn on pitches and drive them for extra bases. His power comes from line-drive homers and leg doubles. He's a contact hitter who often slices the ball to the opposite field.

Baserunning & Defense

Damon started off poorly on the basepaths, partly due to former manager Bob Boone's tight control of the running game. Damon had more success when allowed to run more freely. His excellent speed shows on balls hit to the spacious gaps at Kauffman Stadium, where he legged out six of his eight triples. His speed helps in the outfield, too, and he needs it because he still doesn't get a good jump on the ball. He has one of the major leagues' weakest outfield arms.

1998 Outlook

The center-field job belongs to Damon. With the distraction of shifting among outfield spots a thing of the past, he can focus on using his enormous talent to become the kind of player around which a team can be built. It's a huge responsibility, but the Royals clearly are casting him as a franchise player. He's only 24 and still can take a big stride forward, and 1998 could be the year that Damon makes his mark.

Position: CF/LF/RF
Bats: L **Throws:** L
Ht: 6' 2" **Wt:** 190

Opening Day Age: 24
Born: 11/5/73 in Fort Riley, KS
ML Seasons: 3
Pronunciation: DAY-mun

Overall Statistics

	G	AB	R	H	D	T	HR	RBI	SB	BB	SO	Avg	OBP	Slg
1997	146	472	70	130	12	8	8	48	16	42	70	.275	.338	.386
Career	338	1177	163	323	45	18	17	121	48	85	156	.274	.325	.387

Where He Hits the Ball

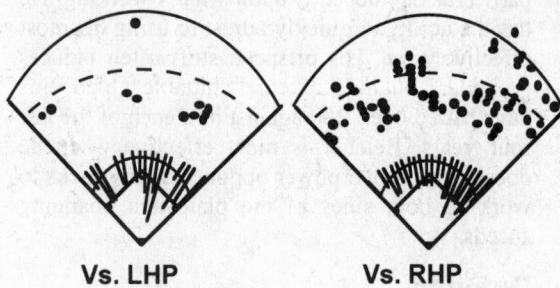

Vs. LHP   **Vs. RHP**

1997 Situational Stats

	AB	H	HR	RBI	Avg		AB	H	HR	RBI	Avg
Home	231	67	3	28	.290	LHP	117	29	2	9	.248
Road	241	63	5	20	.261	RHP	355	101	6	39	.285
First Half	215	68	4	26	.316	Sc Pos	114	36	1	36	.316
Scnd Half	257	62	4	22	.241	Clutch	95	22	1	9	.232

1997 Rankings (American League)

⇒ 2nd in least GDPs per GDP situation (3.1%)
⇒ 3rd in triples
⇒ 6th in lowest stolen base percentage (61.5%)
⇒ 7th in highest groundball/flyball ratio (1.9)
⇒ 8th in lowest slugging percentage vs. lefthanded pitchers (.316)
⇒ Led the Royals in triples, caught stealing (10), highest groundball/flyball ratio (1.9), least GDPs per GDP situation (3.1%), batting average with runners in scoring position, batting average with the bases loaded (.500), batting average at home and highest percentage of swings put into play (46.9%)

Chili Davis

1997 Season

As the Royals' first true designated hitter in several years, Chili Davis turned in one of his very best seasons at the age of 37. His occasional hot streaks included bursts of much-needed power and gave the team a credible RBI threat in the middle of the order. Even when he wasn't swinging a hot bat, his experience showed as he worked the count and frequently advanced runners by hitting behind them.

Hitting

As one of the all-time best switch-hitting power threats, Davis tries to pick on one pitch to drive for extra bases in each at-bat. Later in the same at-bat he'll try to just make contact. Davis has enough power to drive the ball to the opposite field but is more likely to pull pitches or hit them up the middle. He has been able to avoid grounding into double plays by getting some loft on most of his hits.

Baserunning & Defense

It's hard to imagine that Davis played center field and stole 24 bases as a rookie in 1982. Davis is a slow, station-to-station baserunner who is unlikely to take chances on the bases. Having appeared in just four games in the field over the last five years, he would be a serious liability with the glove at any position.

1998 Outlook

Free agent Davis wants to play for a winner in 1998. Whether he returns to the Royals or moves on to another club largely depends upon Kansas City's willingness to spend the necessary money to compete. If this condition isn't met, he may seek employment elsewhere. Despite his age, Davis can be expected to produce runs in an RBI position in the batting order. He still carries a potent bat.

Position: DH
Bats: B **Throws:** R
Ht: 6' 3" **Wt:** 217

Opening Day Age: 38
Born: 1/17/60 in Kingston, Jamaica
ML Seasons: 17

Overall Statistics

	G	AB	R	H	D	T	HR	RBI	SB	BB	SO	Avg	OBP	Slg
1997	140	477	71	133	20	0	30	90	6	85	96	.279	.386	.509
Career	2255	8094	1170	2222	392	29	328	1285	138	1107	1580	.275	.359	.452

Where He Hits the Ball

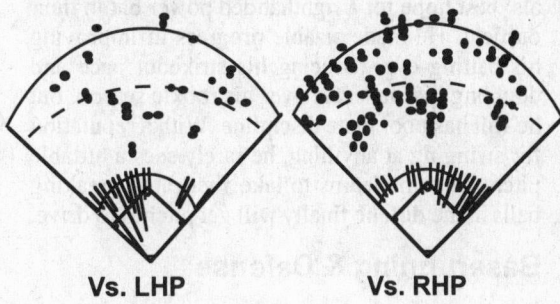

Vs. LHP   **Vs. RHP**

1997 Situational Stats

	AB	H	HR	RBI	Avg		AB	H	HR	RBI	Avg
Home	264	70	21	53	.265	LHP	147	48	9	32	.327
Road	213	63	9	37	.296	RHP	330	85	21	58	.258
First Half	228	68	13	48	.298	Sc Pos	118	37	7	60	.314
Scnd Half	249	65	17	42	.261	Clutch	83	25	5	16	.301

1997 Rankings (American League)

⇒ 3rd in intentional walks (16)
⇒ 9th in batting average vs. lefthanded pitchers
⇒ 10th in walks, HR frequency (15.9 ABs per HR) and slugging percentage vs. lefthanded pitchers (.585)
⇒ Led the Royals in home runs, intentional walks (16), GDPs (15), slugging percentage, on-base percentage, HR frequency (15.9 ABs per HR), batting average on a 3-1 count (.500), cleanup slugging percentage (.484), slugging percentage vs. lefthanded pitchers (.585) and batting average on the road

Jermaine Dye

1997 Season

When Jermaine Dye was acquired from Atlanta at the end of spring training for the popular Michael Tucker, expectations were high in Kansas City. The trade quickly looked lopsided when Tucker started the season on fire and Dye struggled and made two trips to the disabled list with a stress fracture in his left foot. Dye hit sporadically for most of the year and needed a late sprint to reach his meager final totals.

Hitting

Dye has a very quick batting stroke which lets him hit any fastballs and adjust to breaking pitches. His swing has natural power potential. He's the Royals' best hope for a righthanded power bat in their outfield. He made sizable progress in improving his batting eye, reducing his strikeout pace and doubling his walk rate over his rookie season, but he still has poor plate discipline. With a reputation for swinging at anything, he rarely sees a hittable pitch. Once he learns to take first-pitch breaking balls in the dirt, he finally will get pitches to drive.

Baserunning & Defense

Dye has by far the best outfield arm in the organization, showing both strength and accuracy. However, he occasionally played timidly in right field. He has decent speed, but isn't a burner in the field or on the bases. He ran the bases tentatively in 1997, but it's not fair to evaluate his major league basestealing ability because he spent the whole season favoring a fractured foot.

1998 Outlook

In 1998, Dye hopes to start his American League career afresh. He's determined to win the right-field job, then work his way into an RBI spot in the lineup. He's young, talented and focused, so there's no reason why he shouldn't have a fine season.

Position: RF
Bats: R **Throws:** R
Ht: 6' 4" **Wt:** 210

Opening Day Age: 24
Born: 1/28/74 in Oakland, CA
ML Seasons: 2

Overall Statistics

	G	AB	R	H	D	T	HR	RBI	SB	BB	SO	Avg	OBP	Slg
1997	75	263	26	62	14	0	7	22	2	17	51	.236	.284	.369
Career	173	555	58	144	30	0	19	59	3	25	118	.259	.294	.416

Where He Hits the Ball

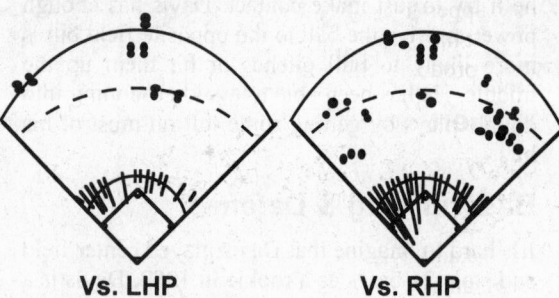

Vs. LHP   **Vs. RHP**

1997 Situational Stats

	AB	H	HR	RBI	Avg		AB	H	HR	RBI	Avg
Home	127	29	3	11	.228	LHP	84	24	4	8	.286
Road	136	33	4	11	.243	RHP	179	38	3	14	.212
First Half	117	25	2	9	.214	Sc Pos	56	10	1	14	.179
Scnd Half	146	37	5	13	.253	Clutch	49	9	1	1	.184

1997 Rankings (American League)

⇒ 1st in lowest batting average on an 0-2 count (.000)
⇒ 4th in errors in right field (6)
⇒ 5th in lowest batting average in the clutch

Jed Hansen

1997 Season

Jed Hansen's brief callup was designed to introduce him to new manager Tony Muser, but turned into a month-long stint as the Royals' regular second baseman when Jose Offerman went on the disabled list in mid-August. Hansen met every expectation by hitting very well while playing solid defense. His advancement in the organization has been steady.

Hitting

Hansen is a good all-around hitter. He sprays line drives to all fields and can turn on a pitch to drive it for extra bases. He has potential for double-digit homer totals. He has shown less plate discipline at the upper levels of the organization, however. He won't hit for a high average in the majors, but will be a productive hitter nonetheless.

Baserunning & Defense

Early scouting reports on Hansen's defense weren't encouraging, but he has made excellent progress and arrived in Kansas City with a fine glove and good range. He must keep his head in the game better as a baserunner. He was a victim of the hidden-ball trick in the Royals' final home series of the year.

1998 Outlook

Hansen's .309 average with the Royals marked the first time he'd batted .300 as a professional, and he's unlikely to remain at that level. However, his solid major league debut gives him a chance to challenge for a full-time job in 1998. He may not win the job outright, but he's sure to challenge for a big league role. Because the club wants him to play regularly, he'll go back to Triple-A if he doesn't win the starting job in spring training. When he returns to the majors, he'll provide all-around solid offense and surehanded defense.

Position: 2B
Bats: R **Throws:** R
Ht: 6' 1" **Wt:** 195

Opening Day Age: 25
Born: 8/19/72 in Tacoma, WA
ML Seasons: 1

Overall Statistics

	G	AB	R	H	D	T	HR	RBI	SB	BB	SO	Avg	OBP	Slg
1997	34	94	11	29	6	1	1	14	3	13	29	.309	.394	.426
Career	34	94	11	29	6	1	1	14	3	13	29	.309	.394	.426

Where He Hits the Ball

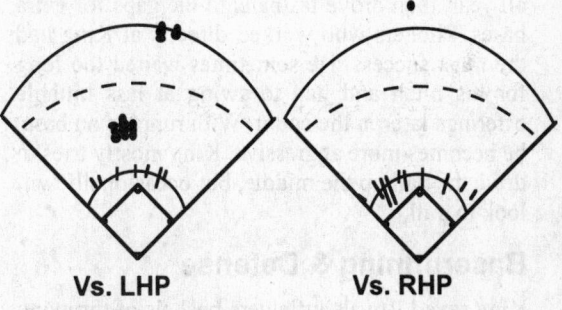

Vs. LHP   **Vs. RHP**

1997 Situational Stats

	AB	H	HR	RBI	Avg		AB	H	HR	RBI	Avg
Home	44	15	1	11	.341	LHP	42	15	0	3	.357
Road	50	14	0	3	.280	RHP	52	14	1	11	.269
First Half	0	0	0	0	-	Sc Pos	17	6	0	11	.353
Scnd Half	94	29	1	14	.309	Clutch	22	5	0	3	.227

1997 Rankings (American League)

⇒ Did not rank near the top or bottom in any category

Jeff King

1997 Season

A season filled with lengthy streaks and slumps from Jeff King resulted in an overall productive year. During his hot streaks, he drove in runs in bunches. His batting average was one of his poorest in years, but he finished high on the all-time Royal charts in RBI and walks. Because it was King's RBI production that Kansas City had coveted when it acquired him from Pittsburgh, the team was very happy with his performance. He also played outstanding defense at first base.

Hitting

An extremely patient hitter, King won't chase a bad pitch. He let pitchers fall behind in the count all year, then drove fastballs to the gaps for extra bases. Pitchers who worked directly at King had the most success. He sometimes waited too long for his pitch and had to swing at less hittable offerings later in the count. With runners on base, he becomes more aggressive. King mostly tries to drive the ball up the middle, but occasionally will look to pull.

Baserunning & Defense

King saved Royals infielders bushels of throwing errors, and his superior range and glove at first base are indicative of the years he spent as a top-notch third baseman with Pittsburgh. He's versatile in the field, capable of playing all the infield positions except shortstop. He played only at first base in 1997 to minimize the strain on his bad back. He's an astute baserunner who won't steal much, saving his attempts for the most crucial situations and usually having success.

1998 Outlook

The Royals moved quickly to re-sign King for 1998. His RBI ability and moderate salary expectations made for a good fit. Kansas City would be happy to see King repeat his 1997 numbers, and he is capable of doing that, at the very least. After the Royals traded for Jeff Conine, King could move to third base.

Position: 1B
Bats: R **Throws:** R
Ht: 6' 1" **Wt:** 184

Opening Day Age: 33
Born: 12/26/64 in Marion, IN
ML Seasons: 9

Overall Statistics

	G	AB	R	H	D	T	HR	RBI	SB	BB	SO	Avg	OBP	Slg
1997	155	543	84	129	30	1	28	112	16	89	96	.238	.341	.451
Career	1049	3704	503	946	203	17	127	605	63	385	501	.255	.323	.422

Where He Hits the Ball

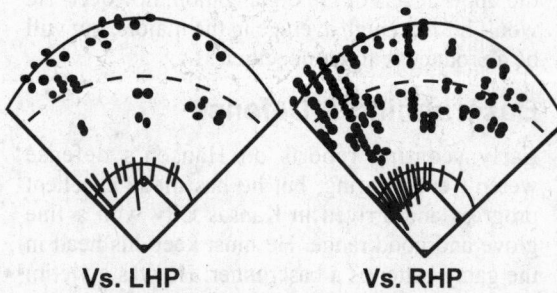

Vs. LHP   **Vs. RHP**

1997 Situational Stats

	AB	H	HR	RBI	Avg		AB	H	HR	RBI	Avg
Home	272	68	11	52	.250	LHP	149	40	9	28	.268
Road	271	61	17	60	.225	RHP	394	89	19	84	.226
First Half	279	72	15	57	.258	Sc Pos	148	41	7	76	.277
Scnd Half	264	57	13	55	.216	Clutch	95	19	5	23	.200

1997 Rankings (American League)

⇒ 1st in fielding percentage at first base (.996)
⇒ 2nd in sacrifice flies (12) and lowest ground-ball/flyball ratio (0.6)
⇒ 3rd in lowest batting average on the road
⇒ 5th in lowest batting average and lowest batting average vs. righthanded pitchers
⇒ 8th in walks and lowest cleanup slugging percentage (.467)
⇒ 9th in RBI
⇒ 10th in stolen base percentage (76.2%)
⇒ Led the Royals in doubles, RBI, sacrifice flies (12), walks, games played (155), highest percentage of pitches taken (60.2%) and highest percentage of extra bases taken as a runner (60.0%)

Jeff Montgomery

1997 Season

Offseason shoulder surgery left Jeff Montgomery unprepared to begin the 1997 season. After an extremely poor start, he went to Triple-A for a rehabilitation assignment and discovered a small flaw in his delivery. He returned to Kansas City, made adjustments and was once again a highly effective closer during the last part of the year. He posted a sparkling 0.80 ERA after the All-Star break.

Pitching

Montgomery no longer can bring his heater in the low 90s, but it's still an effective pitch when mixed with his slider, curveball and changeup. He tries to jump ahead of hitters with the fastball, then uses the slider to make them beat the ball into the ground. Keeping his pitches down in the strike zone is the key to his success. He no longer has the steam to blow his fastball past major league hitters. Montgomery has very good control but has had a problem with throwing pitches that are too hittable, which result in numerous homers (nine in only 59⅓ innings).

Defense

Montgomery has a decent pickoff move and has had success controlling the running game. He's quick to field his position and has the composure to make an accurate throw on bunts. For years, he has tried a desperate behind-the-back swipe at balls hit hard through the box to his right. It finally paid off in 1997 when he snared a hot grounder to save a run and escape the inning.

1998 Outlook

Montgomery's year-long battle to overcome tissue damage in his pitching shoulder is over and he has returned to his accustomed spot as an ace closer. He's Kansas City's all-time saves leader and the Royals are expected to exercise the option on his contract, giving him another year in his familiar role. Fully healthy again, he's among the more reliable closers in the American League.

Position: RP
Bats: R **Throws:** R
Ht: 5'11" **Wt:** 180

Opening Day Age: 36
Born: 1/7/62 in Wellston, OH
ML Seasons: 11

Overall Statistics

	W	L	Pct.	ERA	G	GS	Sv	IP	H	BB	SO	HR	Ratio
1997	1	4	.200	3.49	55	0	14	59.1	53	18	48	9	1.20
Career	43	43	.500	2.91	595	1	256	761.1	655	253	652	66	1.19

How Often He Throws Strikes

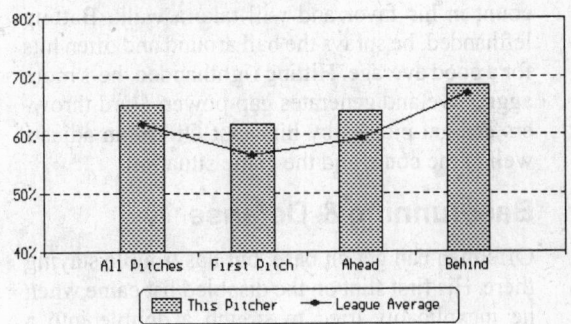

1997 Situational Stats

	W	L	ERA	Sv	IP		AB	H	HR	RBI	Avg
Home	0	1	4.13	5	32.2	LHB	101	27	6	16	.267
Road	1	3	2.70	9	26.2	RHB	120	26	3	16	.217
First Half	0	3	7.01	3	25.2	Sc Pos	56	15	0	21	.268
Scnd Half	1	1	0.80	11	33.2	Clutch	121	29	4	16	.240

1997 Rankings (American League)

⇒ 8th in least baserunners allowed per 9 innings in relief (10.8)

⇒ Led the Royals in games pitched, saves, games finished (37), save opportunities (17), relief ERA (3.49), relief innings (59.1), lowest batting average allowed in relief (.240), least baserunners allowed per 9 innings in relief (10.8) and most strikeouts per 9 innings in relief (7.3)

Jose Offerman

1997 Season

In between three separate trips to the disabled list, Jose Offerman gave the Royals an offensive sparkplug at the top of the batting order and steady defense at second base. He missed about two months, forcing Kansas City to look at other infield options, most notably rookie Jed Hansen. Offerman had a productive season when he was available.

Hitting

Offerman is a streaky hitter, but an accomplished switch-hitter who combines consistent contact with above-average plate discipline to produce fine on-base ability. He knows how to work the count in his favor and will take a walk. Batting lefthanded, he sprays the ball around and often hits for a good average. Hitting righthanded, he's more aggressive and generates gap power. Hard throwers can get pitches by him, but Offerman adjusts well to the count and the game situation.

Baserunning & Defense

Offerman can get on base, but has trouble staying there. His first stint on the disabled list came when he inexplicably tried to stretch a double into a triple while the Royals trailed by two runs in the ninth inning. That was indicative of the kind of poor decisions he frequently makes on the basepaths. Since shifting away from shortstop in 1996, Offerman has been a surehanded second baseman with decent range, though he's weaker going to his left than to his right. His throwing problems have disappeared since his shift to second base.

1998 Outlook

Offerman is in for a battle to retain his second-base job in Kansas City. Hansen impressed the Royals in his two-month major league trial and is clearly an organizational favorite for the long term. Another position or another team might be in Offerman's immediate future. Wherever he plays, he'll hit for a good average and get on base regularly. He'll also play acceptable defense—as long as he doesn't play shortstop.

Position: 2B
Bats: B **Throws:** R
Ht: 6' 0" **Wt:** 190

Opening Day Age: 29
Born: 11/8/68 in San Pedro de Macoris, DR
ML Seasons: 8

Overall Statistics

	G	AB	R	H	D	T	HR	RBI	SB	BB	SO	Avg	OBP	Slg
1997	106	424	59	126	23	6	2	39	9	41	64	.297	.359	.394
Career	836	2952	401	799	121	38	15	246	94	379	486	.271	.354	.353

Where He Hits the Ball

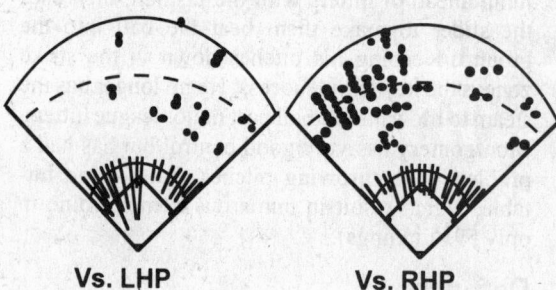

Vs. LHP   **Vs. RHP**

1997 Situational Stats

	AB	H	HR	RBI	Avg		AB	H	HR	RBI	Avg
Home	206	62	2	22	.301	LHP	129	49	0	11	.380
Road	218	64	0	17	.294	RHP	295	77	2	28	.261
First Half	260	81	2	28	.312	Sc Pos	98	26	1	38	.265
Scnd Half	164	45	0	11	.274	Clutch	76	19	0	3	.250

1997 Rankings (American League)

⇒ 3rd in batting average vs. lefthanded pitchers
⇒ 5th in fielding percentage at second base (.981)
⇒ 8th in on-base percentage vs. lefthanded pitchers (.433)
⇒ 9th in on-base percentage for a leadoff hitter (.366) and errors at second base (9)
⇒ 10th in triples
⇒ Led the Royals in caught stealing (10), batting average vs. lefthanded pitchers, on-base percentage for a leadoff hitter (.366), on-base percentage vs. lefthanded pitchers (.433) and lowest percentage of swings that missed (11.7%)

Dean Palmer

1997 Season

The midseason acquisition of Dean Palmer from the Rangers was an odd move by the Royals. Usually teams out of the pennant chase trade away high priced free-agents-to-be instead of acquiring them. Kansas City wanted to fill the gaping hole at third base and in the lineup. For two months he gave them that new look despite nagging injuries that diminished his play.

Hitting

Palmer is a free-swinging pull hitter with power. Pitchers can beat him by working the corners and getting him to chase pitches out of the strike zone, mostly on breaking balls away. But if a pitcher gets the ball in his wheelhouse, he'll hit it a mile. Because he lacks selectivity at the plate, he often hits behind in the count. Sinker-slider pitchers can get him to pound the ball into the turf for easy groundouts and double plays. American League pitchers are on to him and rarely throw him a first-pitch fastball for a strike.

Baserunning & Defense

Palmer is and always has been a below-average third baseman. His range is relatively poor and his reflexes at third base are merely average. He has trouble on balls hit directly at him. Palmer isn't a good baserunner. He lacks both agility and foot speed, and has been prone to making mental mistakes on the bases.

1998 Outlook

Palmer's two-month test-drive is over. His status as a respectable power threat will allow him to command a great deal of money as a free agent. The Royals liked what they saw and want to bring him back. The only question is whether they can afford him. Wherever Palmer plays in 1998, he'll hit for good power with a lot of strikeouts and subpar defense.

Position: 3B
Bats: R **Throws:** R
Ht: 6' 1" **Wt:** 210

Opening Day Age: 29
Born: 12/27/68 in Tallahassee, FL
ML Seasons: 8

Overall Statistics

	G	AB	R	H	D	T	HR	RBI	SB	BB	SO	Avg	OBP	Slg
1997	143	542	70	139	31	1	23	86	2	41	134	.256	.310	.445
Career	823	2932	448	729	144	9	163	482	29	294	807	.249	.321	.471

Where He Hits the Ball

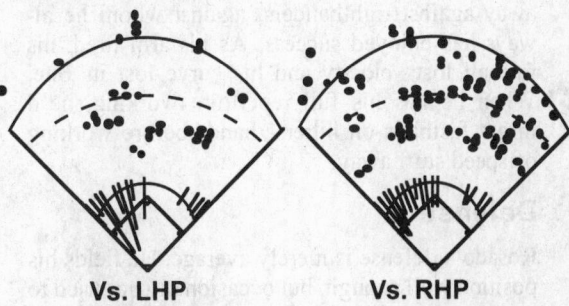

Vs. LHP   **Vs. RHP**

1997 Situational Stats

	AB	H	HR	RBI	Avg		AB	H	HR	RBI	Avg
Home	272	65	10	40	.239	LHP	146	35	8	17	.240
Road	270	74	13	46	.274	RHP	396	104	15	69	.263
First Half	297	71	8	42	.239	Sc Pos	145	37	5	63	.255
Scnd Half	245	68	15	44	.278	Clutch	83	24	5	16	.289

1997 Rankings (American League)

⇒ 3rd in errors at third base (19)
⇒ 4th in lowest fielding percentage at third base (.948)
⇒ 7th in strikeouts (134), lowest on-base percentage vs. lefthanded pitchers (.285) and lowest batting average at home (.239)
⇒ 10th in lowest on-base percentage (.310) and lowest percentage of swings put into play (35.8%)

Jose Rosado

1997 Season

Jose Rosado began 1997 the way he ended 1996, by enjoying unexpected success. He went 7-4 in the first half, and not only did he make the All-Star Game but he also won it. He seldom won afterward, displaying an increasingly tired arm down the stretch. Declining velocity and lack of sharpness made him an easy mark, and he rarely reached the sixth inning in the last two months. He had minor knee surgery after the season.

Pitching

Working off of a 90-MPH fastball, Rosado also throws a cut fastball, curveball and changeup. His changeup is very effective as it dips down and away against righthanders, against whom he always has enjoyed success. As his arm tired, his fastball lost velocity and his curve lost its bite. When he has his full repertoire working, he'll throw fastballs on hitters' hands before working offspeed stuff away.

Defense

Rosado's defense is merely average. He fields his position well enough, but occasionally has tried to make an overly difficult throw to retire lead runners instead of taking a sure out at first base. He lacks an impressive move to first, but counters basestealers by staying ahead in the count.

1998 Outlook

The Royals asked Rosado to avoid winter ball during the offseason. Hopefully, his poor second half was only the result of a tired arm and a troublesome knee. He should regain arm strength and once again have command of all his pitches. He enters 1998 as Kansas City's No. 3 starter and top lefthander. He already has the mound presence of an experienced veteran, and can develop into one of the American League's better southpaws.

Position: SP
Bats: L **Throws:** L
Ht: 6' 0" **Wt:** 175

Opening Day Age: 23
Born: 11/9/74 in Jersey City, NJ
ML Seasons: 2
Pronunciation: ro-SAH-doh

Overall Statistics

	W	L	Pct.	ERA	G	GS	Sv	IP	H	BB	SO	HR	Ratio
1997	9	12	.429	4.69	33	33	0	203.1	208	73	129	26	1.38
Career	17	18	.486	4.18	49	49	0	310.0	309	99	193	33	1.32

How Often He Throws Strikes

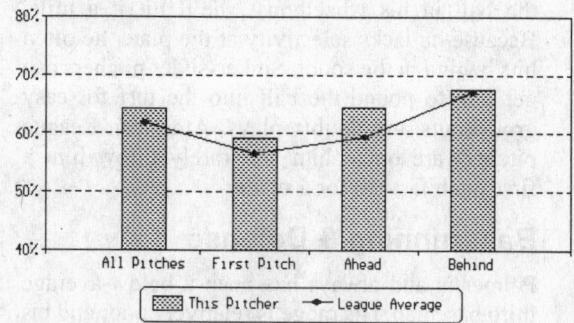

1997 Situational Stats

	W	L	ERA	Sv	IP		AB	H	HR	RBI	Avg
Home	5	6	4.33	0	95.2	LHB	145	36	7	17	.248
Road	4	6	5.02	0	107.2	RHB	642	172	19	75	.268
First Half	7	4	3.39	0	124.1	Sc Pos	162	39	0	60	.241
Scnd Half	2	8	6.75	0	78.2	Clutch	59	13	2	6	.220

1997 Rankings (American League)

⇒ 4th in highest stolen base percentage allowed (76.9%)
⇒ 5th in balks (2)
⇒ 6th in lowest groundball/flyball ratio allowed (1.0)
⇒ 8th in highest ERA on the road
⇒ 9th in least run support per 9 innings (4.6)
⇒ 10th in losses
⇒ Led the Royals in balks (2) and pickoff throws (143)

Glendon Rusch

Position: SP
Bats: L **Throws:** L
Ht: 6' 1" **Wt:** 195

Opening Day Age: 23
Born: 11/7/74 in Seattle, WA
ML Seasons: 1
Pronunciation: RUSH

1997 Season

As the Royals' top lefty pitching prospect, Glendon Rusch was thrust into a starting role last season. He struggled early in the year, and a swollen lymph node limited his mobility and required a short stay on the disabled list. He pitched much better after his return, gradually gaining confidence in his stuff. He pitched better in the second half than his 5.07 ERA would indicate.

Pitching

Rusch throws an above-average curveball and a fine cut fastball. His fastball only reaches the upper 80s, but he doesn't need a lot of steam to succeed. He's at his best when making batters put the ball in play. His repertoire is quite similar to teammate Jose Rosado's, and Rusch's outstanding changeup similarly moves down and away from righthanders. Rusch is hittable and gave up a lot of homers early in 1997. When he regained his usually sharp command later in the year the longballs became flyouts instead. He tended to make the wrong pitch at the wrong time and was prone to big innings. Lefties hammered him for a .354 average, but he fared better when he pitched inside.

Defense

Rusch's early-season tentativeness carried over to his fielding. He was timid when fielding bunts or covering first base, and he rarely dared to throw to first to keep runners honest. As he gained confidence, he became more aggressive in the field. He has an average pickoff move at best, and basestealers went 6-for-6 against him.

1998 Outlook

Rusch will be Kansas City's No. 4 or 5 starter, and should improve in his sophomore season. While he took his lumps last year, he was one of the youngest pitchers in the league, and should improve with experience. He learned to pitch over the last part of 1997 and is ready to take another step forward.

Overall Statistics

	W	L	Pct.	ERA	G	GS	Sv	IP	H	BB	SO	HR	Ratio
1997	6	9	.400	5.50	30	27	0	170.1	206	52	116	28	1.51
Career	6	9	.400	5.50	30	27	0	170.1	206	52	116	28	1.51

How Often He Throws Strikes

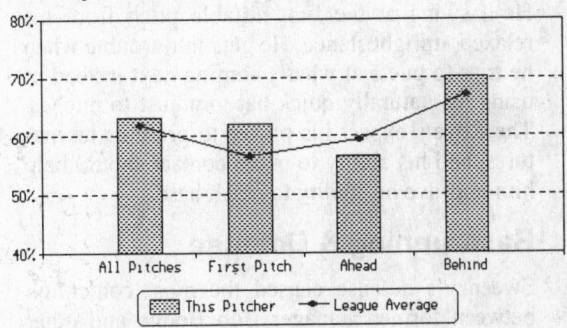

1997 Situational Stats

	W	L	ERA	Sv	IP		AB	H	HR	RBI	Avg
Home	0	6	6.10	0	76.2	LHB	164	58	9	25	.354
Road	6	3	5.00	0	93.2	RHB	520	148	19	73	.285
First Half	3	5	5.94	0	83.1	Sc Pos	143	49	4	66	.343
Scnd Half	3	4	5.07	0	87.0	Clutch	38	12	2	4	.316

1997 Rankings (American League)

⇒ 1st in highest slugging percentage allowed (.490) and highest stolen base percentage allowed (100.0%)
⇒ 2nd in highest batting average allowed with runners in scoring position
⇒ 3rd in highest ERA and highest batting average allowed (.301)
⇒ 4th in highest on-base percentage allowed (.353), most baserunners allowed per 9 innings (14.0) and most home runs allowed per 9 innings (1.48)
⇒ 5th in least run support per 9 innings (4.3)
⇒ 9th in highest ERA on the road
⇒ Led the Royals in hit batsmen (7) and most GDPs induced per 9 innings (0.9)

Mike Sweeney

1997 Season

Mike Sweeney endured a lot of turmoil to emerge as one of the Royals' better young position players. Twice demoted to Triple-A, he eventually was given the regular catching job in Kansas City with the arrival of new manager Tony Muser. He had bursts of excellent hitting surrounded by droughts in which he looked bad at the plate. It was another season of on-the-job training, and he mostly came through with flying colors.

Hitting

Sweeney has a good-looking swing from which he generates a little power, but he's mostly a line-drive hitter who hits the ball where it's pitched. He'll swing at the first hittable pitch from his relaxed, upright stance. He gets into trouble when he tries to guess at what's coming next instead of using his naturally quick bat to adjust to pitches. The Royals expect his power to grow as he matures, and his ability to make contact should help him improve his ability to reach base.

Baserunning & Defense

Sweeney's defense caused the most contention between former manager Bob Boone and other Royals staff members. Boone believed Sweeney needed to improve his game-calling skills at Triple-A, while others wanted him playing regularly at the major league level. Sweeney had success throwing out basestealers, nailing 20 of 52 (38.5 percent) in 1997. He has a good arm, but needs to work on blocking pitches in the dirt. He's not a good baserunner and occasionally runs into outs.

1998 Outlook

The stage is set for Sweeney to inherit the full-time catching chores. The organization obviously believes in him. He'll have the job to himself, and a solid first full major league season is expected. As a hitter, he should put up numbers roughly comparable to those of the man he'll be replacing, Mike Macfarlane.

Position: C
Bats: R **Throws:** R
Ht: 6' 1" **Wt:** 195

Opening Day Age: 24
Born: 7/22/73 in Orange, CA
ML Seasons: 3

Overall Statistics

	G	AB	R	H	D	T	HR	RBI	SB	BB	SO	Avg	OBP	Slg
1997	84	240	30	58	8	0	7	31	3	17	33	.242	.306	.363
Career	138	409	54	105	18	0	11	55	4	35	54	.257	.327	.381

Where He Hits the Ball

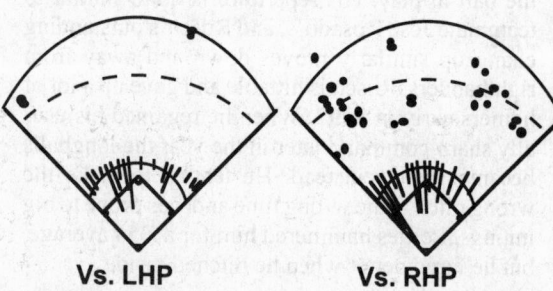

Vs. LHP   **Vs. RHP**

1997 Situational Stats

	AB	H	HR	RBI	Avg		AB	H	HR	RBI	Avg
Home	116	28	5	17	.241	LHP	74	14	1	8	.189
Road	124	30	2	14	.242	RHP	166	44	6	23	.265
First Half	70	17	4	12	.243	Sc Pos	58	13	3	25	.224
Scnd Half	170	41	3	19	.241	Clutch	46	11	3	8	.239

1997 Rankings (American League)
⇒ Led the Royals in hit by pitch (6)

David Howard

Position: 2B/RF
Bats: B **Throws:** R
Ht: 6' 0" **Wt:** 175

Opening Day Age: 31
Born: 2/26/67 in Sarasota, FL
ML Seasons: 7

Overall Statistics

	G	AB	R	H	D	T	HR	RBI	SB	BB	SO	Avg	OBP	Slg
1997	80	162	24	39	8	1	1	13	2	10	31	.241	.287	.321
Career	547	1399	151	320	52	13	8	130	23	118	262	.229	.289	.302

1997 Situational Stats

	AB	H	HR	RBI	Avg		AB	H	HR	RBI	Avg
Home	92	18	0	6	.196	LHP	51	12	0	3	.235
Road	70	21	1	7	.300	RHP	111	27	1	10	.243
First Half	104	29	1	12	.279	Sc Pos	38	9	1	13	.237
Scnd Half	58	10	0	1	.172	Clutch	33	9	0	1	.273

1997 Season

Solid infield play by new Royals imports returned David Howard to his accustomed utility role. As always, he played outstanding defense and provided very limited offense. A favorite of former manager Bob Boone, Howard lost second-half time to a shoulder strain and played sparingly under new manager Tony Muser. Shane Halter assumed Howard's super-sub role.

Hitting, Baserunning & Defense

Howard is a slap hitter who can be overmatched even by average pitching. He has no power and has trouble making contact. He possesses some speed but never has used it well on the bases, stealing few bases and occasionally running into outs. Defense is where Howard shines. He has outstanding reflexes, excellent range and a very good arm. He's a superior player at all infield positions and has learned to play the outfield well, too.

1998 Outlook

Howard signed a two-year, $1.8 million free-agent deal with St. Louis after the season. He's best used in small doses, primarily as a defensive replacement. He simply can't produce enough with the bat to play regularly. He serves a major league bench role very well, but won't succeed if pressed into more regular service.

Mike Macfarlane

Position: C
Bats: R **Throws:** R
Ht: 6' 1" **Wt:** 210

Opening Day Age: 33
Born: 4/12/64 in Stockton, CA
ML Seasons: 11

Overall Statistics

	G	AB	R	H	D	T	HR	RBI	SB	BB	SO	Avg	OBP	Slg
1997	82	257	34	61	14	2	8	35	0	24	47	.237	.316	.401
Career	1002	3158	405	798	192	17	118	449	11	270	612	.253	.327	.436

1997 Situational Stats

	AB	H	HR	RBI	Avg		AB	H	HR	RBI	Avg
Home	134	38	5	21	.284	LHP	80	16	2	12	.200
Road	123	23	3	14	.187	RHP	177	45	6	23	.254
First Half	148	27	3	17	.182	Sc Pos	63	18	2	26	.286
Scnd Half	109	34	5	18	.312	Clutch	44	12	1	5	.273

1997 Season

Two separate stints on the disabled list, first with an abdominal strain and then with a strained right shoulder, helped Mike Macfarlane get off to a horrible start. He was hitting below .200 in August before rebounding with a very strong finish.

Hitting, Baserunning & Defense

Macfarlane remains an extreme pull hitter. He crowds the plate and tries to drive everything deep to left. He's slowly learning to adjust and protect the plate with two strikes. His power stroke was severely limited by the shoulder injury. A return to health and better plate discipline helped fuel his late-season surge. Macfarlane is among the slowest baserunners in the majors. He's a hard-nosed catcher who blocks the plate and handles pitches in the dirt equally well. He has a reputation as a superb handler of pitchers and controls the running game well despite a merely average arm.

1998 Outlook

The Royals appear committed to expanding young Mike Sweeney's catching role. Macfarlane, who re-signed as a free agent, may see his playing time shrink. He can succeed as a reserve because he's a true professional and a well-respected clubhouse leader.

Rod Myers

Position: LF
Bats: L **Throws:** L
Ht: 6' 0" **Wt:** 190

Opening Day Age: 25
Born: 1/14/73 in
Conroe, TX
ML Seasons: 2

Overall Statistics

	G	AB	R	H	D	T	HR	RBI	SB	BB	SO	Avg	OBP	Slg
1997	31	101	14	26	7	0	2	9	4	17	22	.257	.370	.386
Career	53	164	23	44	14	0	3	20	7	24	38	.268	.365	.409

1997 Situational Stats

	AB	H	HR	RBI	Avg		AB	H	HR	RBI	Avg
Home	53	17	1	7	.321	LHP	19	4	0	3	.211
Road	48	9	1	2	.188	RHP	82	22	2	6	.268
First Half	0	0	0	0	-	Sc Pos	25	4	0	5	.160
Scnd Half	101	26	2	9	.257	Clutch	26	9	0	3	.346

1997 Season

Rod Myers was set to open the season in the Royals' starting lineup, but broke his wrist playing winter ball. He spent half the year on the disabled list, then made a triumphant return to Kansas City, hitting for average and power while playing sparkling outfield defense.

Hitting, Baserunning & Defense

Myers has decent tools. He's a line-drive hitter with a quick bat and surprising power. He has excellent speed and uses it well in the outfield and on the bases. He'll be a basestealing threat very soon. His arm and outfield range are both above average. Myers' difficulty hitting lefthanders and his occasional inability to make contact may be solved with more experience.

1998 Outlook

Having spent much of his career in Johnny Damon's shadow, Myers is a good prospect in his own right. He has the Royals anticipating a solid season as he opens the year playing regularly in left or center field. He has improved each step of the way and could take his biggest leap forward in 1998.

Gregg Olson

Position: RP
Bats: R **Throws:** R
Ht: 6' 4" **Wt:** 212

Opening Day Age: 31
Born: 10/11/66 in
Scribner, NE
ML Seasons: 10

Overall Statistics

	W	L	Pct.	ERA	G	GS	Sv	IP	H	BB	SO	HR	Ratio
1997	4	3	.571	5.58	45	0	1	50.0	58	28	34	3	1.72
Career	28	29	.491	3.20	456	0	173	500.1	441	253	449	25	1.39

1997 Situational Stats

	W	L	ERA	Sv	IP		AB	H	HR	RBI	Avg
Home	2	1	6.08	0	23.2	LHB	75	19	2	19	.253
Road	2	2	5.13	1	26.1	RHB	119	39	1	17	.328
First Half	0	0	16.20	0	10.0	Sc Pos	60	21	0	31	.350
Scnd Half	4	3	2.93	1	40.0	Clutch	64	22	2	15	.344

1997 Season

Gregg Olson earned his release from the Twins with 11 terrible outings, then was given a second chance in the Royals' decimated bullpen. He was suddenly marvelous, becoming their most consistent setup man at midseason and tied for the club lead in relief wins with Randy Veres. He ended the year in a slump, but must have been pleased with one of his best seasons in recent memory.

Pitching & Defense

Olson throws an upper-80s fastball and is working to add a changeup, but his out pitch is still the curveball. It's not the devastating knee-buckler that he used as a top closer for Baltimore some years ago, because arm problems have significantly diminished its sharpness. But it's still an effective pitch that works well against both lefthanders and righthanders. He's an above-average fielder with a decent pickoff move.

1998 Outlook

Olson has proven that he still can retire major league hitters, but must show he can be effective over the long haul. Opportunity is knocking in the Kansas City bullpen. He has an inside track to win an important role, though he'll probably never be a closer again.

Craig Paquette

Position: 3B
Bats: R **Throws:** R
Ht: 6' 0" **Wt:** 190

Opening Day Age: 29
Born: 3/28/69 in Long Beach, CA
ML Seasons: 5
Pronunciation: pah-KET

Overall Statistics

	G	AB	R	H	D	T	HR	RBI	SB	BB	SO	Avg	OBP	Slg
1997	77	252	26	58	15	1	8	33	2	10	57	.230	.263	.393
Career	419	1406	164	326	65	7	55	195	17	59	368	.232	.263	.405

1997 Situational Stats

	AB	H	HR	RBI	Avg		AB	H	HR	RBI	Avg
Home	124	33	7	18	.266	LHP	101	23	5	21	.228
Road	128	25	1	15	.195	RHP	151	35	3	12	.232
First Half	231	51	8	28	.221	Sc Pos	68	13	3	25	.191
Scnd Half	21	7	0	5	.333	Clutch	38	11	1	7	.289

1997 Season

The clock struck midnight for Craig Paquette when manager Bob Boone was fired at the All-Star break. Among new manager Tony Muser's first moves was a benching of Paquette, who was designated for assignment two weeks later. His occasional power paled beside his serious defensive deficiencies and unproductive hitting.

Hitting, Baserunning & Defense

Paquette tries to pull every pitch he sees. His uppercut and poor plate discipline make him easy pickings for most major league pitchers, though he can hit mistakes a long way. He can steal an occasional base but is otherwise a below-average baserunner. There have been few worse fielders at third base than Paquette in recent years. He has a strong arm but makes erratic throws, is error prone and has poor range.

1998 Outlook

Boone claimed Paquette would have a job as long as he ran the Royals, and he was right. Paquette works hard, but his skills don't warrant much consideration for another starting opportunity. He certainly could contend for a bench job, particularly if Boone hooks on as a manager somewhere.

Hipolito Pichardo

Position: RP
Bats: R **Throws:** R
Ht: 6' 1" **Wt:** 185

Opening Day Age: 28
Born: 8/22/69 in Esperanza, DR
ML Seasons: 6
Pronunciation: e-POL-ee-toe puh-CHAR-dough

Overall Statistics

	W	L	Pct.	ERA	G	GS	Sv	IP	H	BB	SO	HR	Ratio
1997	3	5	.375	4.22	47	0	11	49.0	51	24	34	7	1.53
Career	35	31	.530	4.34	254	49	18	557.1	604	206	285	39	1.45

1997 Situational Stats

	W	L	ERA	Sv	IP		AB	H	HR	RBI	Avg
Home	1	3	5.06	2	21.1	LHB	83	25	5	10	.301
Road	2	2	3.58	9	27.2	RHB	104	26	2	9	.250
First Half	2	4	5.61	9	33.2	Sc Pos	48	7	1	11	.146
Scnd Half	1	1	1.17	2	15.1	Clutch	120	35	5	14	.292

1997 Season

When all other Royals relievers were ineffective or injured in April, Hipolito Pichardo was the bullpen's only reliable righthander. He worked his way into the closer's role until Jeff Montgomery's effectiveness returned, and posted a 1.17 ERA after the All-Star break as a setup man. Overall it was a good year, as he showed he could handle an important bullpen role.

Pitching & Defense

Pichardo throws his fastball at 92 MPH. Control of his hard slider is his key to success against righthanders, but he lacks good command of his splitter. He sometimes overthrows his hard stuff, flattening the pitches out and making them very hittable. He's quick but not very smooth with the glove, and his slow delivery permits baserunners a good jump off first base.

1998 Outlook

Despite his half-season of success as closer, it's unlikely Pichardo will get extensive time in that role. Instead, he'll be counted on as a bridge from the starters to the relief ace.

Jim Pittsley

Position: SP
Bats: R **Throws:** R
Ht: 6' 7" **Wt:** 215

Opening Day Age: 23
Born: 4/3/74 in DuBois, PA
ML Seasons: 2

Overall Statistics

	W	L	Pct.	ERA	G	GS	Sv	IP	H	BB	SO	HR	Ratio
1997	5	8	.385	5.46	21	21	0	112.0	120	54	52	15	1.55
Career	5	8	.385	5.70	22	22	0	115.1	127	55	52	18	1.58

1997 Situational Stats

	W	L	ERA	Sv	IP		AB	H	HR	RBI	Avg
Home	4	5	4.82	0	74.2	LHB	205	61	8	30	.298
Road	1	3	6.75	0	37.1	RHB	228	59	7	36	.259
First Half	2	6	5.58	0	69.1	Sc Pos	116	31	3	47	.267
Scnd Half	3	2	5.27	0	42.2	Clutch	9	1	1	2	.111

1997 Season

Jim Pittsley's first major league season was a disappointment. He hasn't been the same pitcher since undergoing elbow surgery in 1995. He made very few starts in 1997 that could be classified as major league caliber and was easily the least effective Royals starter.

Pitching & Defense

Since elbow surgery Pittsley has lost about five MPH off his fastball. It now comes in very straight at 87 MPH, and his curve isn't as sharp as it once was. He throws a changeup and is adding a cut fastball, but they're less effective because his fastball is no longer overpowering. He must regain velocity to succeed against big league hitters. His size works against him when fielding the ball, as he's gangly and uncoordinated. His pickoff move is mediocre.

1998 Outlook

Formerly a top prospect, Pittsley is now a big question mark. If he can regain a little more pop on his heater he can take a big step forward, but that might not be possible. The Royals are committed to giving him every opportunity, so his struggles in a major league rotation are likely to continue.

Joe Vitiello

Position: RF/LF/DH
Bats: R **Throws:** R
Ht: 6' 3" **Wt:** 230

Opening Day Age: 27
Born: 4/11/70 in Cambridge, MA
ML Seasons: 3
Pronunciation: vit-ee-ELL-o

Overall Statistics

	G	AB	R	H	D	T	HR	RBI	SB	BB	SO	Avg	OBP	Slg
1997	51	130	11	31	6	0	5	18	0	14	37	.238	.322	.400
Career	189	517	53	126	25	1	20	79	2	60	131	.244	.331	.412

1997 Situational Stats

	AB	H	HR	RBI	Avg		AB	H	HR	RBI	Avg
Home	77	18	4	8	.234	LHP	72	17	3	11	.236
Road	53	13	1	10	.245	RHP	58	14	2	7	.241
First Half	102	23	2	14	.225	Sc Pos	40	10	1	13	.250
Scnd Half	28	8	3	4	.286	Clutch	14	3	0	1	.214

1997 Season

The 1997 season was a complete washout for Joe Vitiello. His first-base job was given to newcomer Jeff King, and Vitiello struggled at the plate and in occasional outfield roles. Eventually he succumbed to ongoing knee problems and was a nonfactor after undergoing arthroscopic knee surgery in June.

Hitting, Baserunning & Defense

Vitiello's hitting approach belies his size. With a controlled, level swing, he hits balls where they're pitched and only occasionally tries to pull the ball. He has shown sporadic bursts of power, but not enough to earn more than a bench job in the majors. He was slow before extensive knee operations, and now he's positively glacial. Former manager Bob Boone's attempt to play him in right field was an absolute disaster. Vitiello is a first baseman only, and not a good one.

1998 Outlook

Vitiello has little chance of winning a regular major league job in the near future. Returning from severe knee problems will be difficult. A more reasonable goal for 1998 will be to win a reserve job and remain healthy.

Other Kansas City Royals

Ricky Bones (**Pos**: RHP, **Age**: 28)

	W	L	Pct.	ERA	G	GS	Sv	IP	H	BB	SO	HR	Ratio
1997	4	8	.333	6.75	30	13	0	96.0	133	36	44	12	1.76
Career	55	70	.440	4.91	196	162	0	1040.0	1149	361	400	143	1.45

Bones began last year with the Reds, spent some time in the Brewers' farm system, then resurfaced with the Royals. ERAs last four years: 3.43, 4.63, 6.22, 6.75. But a lot of teams need pitching. 1998 Outlook: C

Larry Casian (**Pos**: LHP, **Age**: 32)

	W	L	Pct.	ERA	G	GS	Sv	IP	H	BB	SO	HR	Ratio
1997	0	3	.000	5.70	44	0	0	36.1	48	8	23	8	1.54
Career	11	13	.458	4.45	241	3	2	236.2	278	76	119	30	1.50

After getting off to a rocky start with the Cubs last year, Casian was sold to the Royals in a waiver deal. He continued to struggle and drew his release in August. Ah, but he's a lefty. . . 1998 Outlook: C

Jim Converse (**Pos**: RHP, **Age**: 26)

	W	L	Pct.	ERA	G	GS	Sv	IP	H	BB	SO	HR	Ratio
1997	0	0	-	3.60	3	0	0	5.0	4	5	3	2	1.80
Career	2	11	.154	7.21	35	13	1	97.1	128	75	66	9	2.09

Converse pitched briefly for the Royals last year but spent most of the year in the minors. He wound up pitching for the Yankees' Columbus farm team and might have earned himself another MLB chance. 1998 Outlook: C

Scott Cooper (**Pos**: 3B, **Age**: 30, **Bats**: L)

	G	AB	R	H	D	T	HR	RBI	SB	BB	SO	Avg	OBP	Slg
1997	75	159	12	32	6	1	3	15	1	17	32	.201	.283	.308
Career	592	1801	197	478	94	12	33	211	7	193	299	.265	.337	.386

After spending the 1996 season in Japan, Cooper returned to the majors last year as a reserve infielder/pinch hitter. He was basically awful, but expansion might help get him another chance. 1998 Outlook: C

Sal Fasano (**Pos**: C, **Age**: 26, **Bats**: R)

	G	AB	R	H	D	T	HR	RBI	SB	BB	SO	Avg	OBP	Slg
1997	13	38	4	8	2	0	1	1	0	1	12	.211	.231	.342
Career	64	181	24	37	4	0	7	20	1	15	37	.204	.273	.343

Fasano got into only 13 games with the Royals last year, spending most of the season in Double- and Triple-A. He hit for a low average in all three spots, but continued to show flashes of power. 1998 Outlook: B

Shane Halter (**Pos**: 2B/3B/RF, **Age**: 28, **Bats**: R)

	G	AB	R	H	D	T	HR	RBI	SB	BB	SO	Avg	OBP	Slg
1997	74	123	16	34	5	1	2	10	4	10	28	.276	.341	.382
Career	74	123	16	34	5	1	2	10	4	10	28	.276	.341	.382

The versatile Halter got his first major league chance last year and played six different positions while hitting for a respectable average. He figures to play the same role again this year. 1998 Outlook: A

Chris Haney (**Pos**: LHP, **Age**: 29)

	W	L	Pct.	ERA	G	GS	Sv	IP	H	BB	SO	HR	Ratio
1997	1	2	.333	4.38	8	3	0	24.2	29	5	16	1	1.38
Career	32	44	.421	4.82	120	109	0	651.0	720	222	350	69	1.45

After winning 10 games for the Royals in '96, Haney broke his ankle last April, then came down with arm trouble after he returned. If healthy, he can be a useful pitcher, but he'll have to prove it first. 1998 Outlook: C

Ryan Long (**Pos**: RF, **Age**: 25, **Bats**: R)

	G	AB	R	H	D	T	HR	RBI	SB	BB	SO	Avg	OBP	Slg
1997	6	9	2	2	0	0	0	2	0	0	3	.222	.300	.222
Career	6	9	2	2	0	0	0	2	0	0	3	.222	.300	.222

One of the Royals' better power prospects, Long saw brief action in Kansas City last year but spent most of the year at Triple-A Omaha, where he hit 19 homers. Lack of discipline is his biggest problem. 1998 Outlook: B

Allen McDill (**Pos**: LHP, **Age**: 26)

	W	L	Pct.	ERA	G	GS	Sv	IP	H	BB	SO	HR	Ratio
1997	0	0	-	13.50	3	0	0	4.0	3	8	2	1	2.75
Career	0	0	-	13.50	3	0	0	4.0	3	8	2	1	2.75

McDill got a brief chance with the Royals last May but couldn't get the ball over the plate, earning him a quick return trip to the minors. If he improves his control, he could be a useful reliever. 1998 Outlook: C

Mike Perez (**Pos**: RHP, **Age**: 33)

	W	L	Pct.	ERA	G	GS	Sv	IP	H	BB	SO	HR	Ratio
1997	2	0	1.000	3.54	16	0	0	20.1	15	8	17	2	1.13
Career	24	16	.600	3.56	313	0	22	346.0	334	120	224	26	1.31

Perez began last year at Triple-A Omaha, earned a midseason recall to the Royals, and then was released despite the fact that he pitched fairly well. Some team will probably give him another shot. 1998 Outlook: B

Jose Santiago (**Pos**: RHP, **Age**: 23)

	W	L	Pct.	ERA	G	GS	Sv	IP	H	BB	SO	HR	Ratio
1997	0	0	-	1.93	4	0	0	4.2	7	2	1	0	1.93
Career	0	0	-	1.93	4	0	0	4.2	7	2	1	0	1.93

A 70th-round draft pick in 1994, Santiago began last year in Class-A but made it all the way to Kansas City last summer. He was banned from the Carolina League after hitting a fan with a thrown ball. 1998 Outlook: C

Scott Service (**Pos**: RHP, **Age**: 31)

	W	L	Pct.	ERA	G	GS	Sv	IP	H	BB	SO	HR	Ratio
1997	0	3	.000	6.45	16	0	0	22.1	28	6	22	2	1.52
Career	7	8	.467	4.74	123	1	2	167.0	171	69	163	22	1.44

Service was traded to the Royals last July, spent some time in the minors, and then joined the big club for the final month. His overall numbers weren't great, but his K/BB ratio was excellent. 1998 Outlook: B

Andy Stewart (Pos: C, Age: 27, Bats: R)

	G	AB	R	H	D	T	HR	RBI	SB	BB	SO	Avg	OBP	Slg
1997	5	8	1	2	1	0	0	0	0	0	0	.250	.250	.375
Career	5	8	1	2	1	0	0	0	0	0	0	.250	.250	.375

A long-time member of the Royals' farm system, Stewart spent most of the year at Triple-A Omaha, where he batted .274. A catcher with a good arm, he could stick as a reserve receiver this year. 1998 Outlook: C

Randy Veres (Pos: RHP, Age: 32)

	W	L	Pct.	ERA	G	GS	Sv	IP	H	BB	SO	HR	Ratio
1997	4	0	1.000	3.31	24	0	1	35.1	36	7	28	4	1.22
Career	9	13	.409	4.60	135	1	3	174.0	179	74	116	24	1.45

Pitching for his fourth major league club in four years, Veres got off to a good start last year, then came down with shoulder problems. If healthy, he could be in someone's bullpen this year. 1998 Outlook: B

Jamie Walker (Pos: LHP, Age: 26)

	W	L	Pct.	ERA	G	GS	Sv	IP	H	BB	SO	HR	Ratio
1997	3	3	.500	5.44	50	0	0	43.0	46	20	24	6	1.53
Career	3	3	.500	5.44	50	0	0	43.0	46	20	24	6	1.53

An ex-Astro farmhand, Walker came to the Royals last year and spent most of the season as a lefthanded bullpen specialist. His pitching was so-so, but everyone needs lefties in their bullpen. 1998 Outlook: B

Matt Whisenant (Pos: LHP, Age: 26)

	W	L	Pct.	ERA	G	GS	Sv	IP	H	BB	SO	HR	Ratio
1997	1	0	1.000	4.57	28	0	0	21.2	19	18	20	0	1.71
Career	1	0	1.000	4.57	28	0	0	21.2	19	18	20	0	1.71

Whisenant began 1997 in the Marlins' system, then came to the Royals in a midseason deal. He struggled with his control at times but was tough to hit and kept the ball on the ground. 1998 Outlook: A

Mike Williams (Pos: RHP, Age: 29)

	W	L	Pct.	ERA	G	GS	Sv	IP	H	BB	SO	HR	Ratio
1997	0	2	.000	6.43	10	0	1	14.0	20	8	10	1	2.00
Career	13	27	.325	4.92	109	54	1	398.2	426	153	237	51	1.45

The ex-Phillie righthander was with the Red Sox last spring, got released and then hooked up with the Royals. He was unimpressive in 10 games and wound up back in the minors. 1998 Outlook: C

Mitch Williams (Pos: LHP, Age: 33)

	W	L	Pct.	ERA	G	GS	Sv	IP	H	BB	SO	HR	Ratio
1997	0	1	.000	10.80	7	0	0	6.2	11	7	10	2	2.70
Career	45	58	.437	3.63	619	3	192	691.1	537	544	660	49	1.56

Still trying to recover from that Joe Carter home run, Williams made another comeback attempt last year—this time with the Royals. He still hasn't recovered from that Joe Carter home run. 1998 Outlook: D

Organization Overview:

Over the last four years, the Kansas City Royals' farm system has become one of the most well-respected in the game. The system produced another good rookie crop last year, as home-grown youngsters Johnny Damon, Michael Tucker, Mike Sweeney and Jose Rosado all played prominent roles on the major league club. The strength of the system is an abundance of pitching, catching and infield prospects at the higher levels, a wave of talent that is expected to make an impact over the next couple of years. The entire organization has become one of the most development-oriented in baseball, and the youngsters will be given every opportunity to advance to the majors when their time comes.

Brian Bevil

Position: P **Opening Day Age:** 26
Bats: R **Throws:** R **Born:** 9/5/71 in
Ht: 6' 3" **Wt:** 190 Houston, TX

Recent Statistics

	W	L	ERA	G	GS	Sv	IP	H	R	BB	SO	HR
97 AA Wichita	0	0	5.63	4	2	0	8.0	11	8	4	10	0
97 AAA Omaha	2	1	4.38	26	3	1	39.0	34	22	22	47	8
97 AL Kansas City	1	2	6.61	18	0	1	16.1	16	13	9	13	1

Bevil had toiled in the minors for six seasons after signing as a 30th-round draft-and-follow out of Angelina (Texas) Community College, before a stellar 1997 spring-training performance established him as Kansas City's closer of the future. He showed a 91-94 MPH fastball and hard slider, more than enough ammunition to finish games. Then he came down with a tender elbow. He was hit somewhat hard in Triple-A and a lot in the majors. Now 26, he should serve as a setup man to Jeff Montgomery until the veteran falters.

Jaime Bluma

Position: P **Opening Day Age:** 25
Bats: R **Throws:** R **Born:** 5/18/72 in
Ht: 5' 11" **Wt:** 195 Beaufort, SC

Recent Statistics

	W	L	ERA	G	GS	Sv	IP	H	R	BB	SO	HR
96 AAA Omaha	1	2	3.12	52	0	25	57.2	57	22	20	40	7

Bluma's story is similar to Bevil's, only worse. A 1994 third-round pick out of Wichita State, where he earned more saves than teammate Darren Dreifort, Bluma shot through the minors. He earned five saves in as many tries during a September 1996 call-up, and appeared ready to open 1997 as Kansas City's closer while Montgomery made his way back from shoulder surgery. Instead Bluma went on the disabled list after needing shoulder surgery himself. When healthy, he mixes sinking fastballs with hard sliders and throws strikes. The Royals think he'll be ready for spring training, but his future and role are somewhat in doubt.

Dermal Brown

Position: OF **Opening Day Age:** 20
Bats: L **Throws:** R **Born:** 3/27/78 in Bronx,
Ht: 6' 1" **Wt:** 210 NY

Recent Statistics

	G	AB	R	H	D	T	HR	RBI	SB	BB	SO	AVG
96 R Royals	7	20	1	1	1	0	0	1	0	0	6	.050
97 A Spokane	73	298	67	97	20	6	13	73	17	38	65	.326

The Royals couldn't be more excited about the progress shown by Brown, a 1996 first-round pick who had the option of playing tailback at the University of Maryland. He was considered a raw athlete who would need time and patience, but put that idea to rest in 1997. He was named the top prospect in the low Class-A Northwest League, where he hit .326-13-73 with 17 steals in 73 games. Though he struck out a lot, he also proved willing to draw a walk. He's the organizations best power hitter since Bo Jackson, with his only drawbacks being a mediocre arm and instincts that limit him to left field. Brown has accelerated his timetable, though exactly by how much remains to be seen.

Enrique Calero

Position: P **Opening Day Age:** 23
Bats: R **Throws:** R **Born:** 1/9/75 in
Ht: 6' 2" **Wt:** 175 Santurce, Puerto Rico

Recent Statistics

	W	L	ERA	G	GS	Sv	IP	H	R	BB	SO	HR
96 A Spokane	4	2	2.52	17	11	1	75.0	77	34	18	61	5
97 AA Wichita	11	9	4.44	23	22	0	127.2	120	78	44	100	15

His strong winter in the Puerto Rican League convinced the Royals to let Calero begin 1997, his first full pro season, in Double-A. Though he was just a 27th-round pick in 1996 from little-known St. Thomas (Fla.) University, he held his own. He threw 90-94 MPH with good location, mixed in a slurve and used a forkball as a changeup. The only negative was shoulder discomfort that led to a one-month layoff at midseason. His repertoire might not quite be enough to start in the major leagues, but don't rule him out.

Jeremy Giambi

Position: OF

Bats: L **Throws:** L

Ht: 6' 0" **Wt:** 185

Opening Day Age: 23

Born: 9/30/74 in San Jose, CA

Recent Statistics

	G	AB	R	H	D	T	HR	RBI	SB	BB	SO	AVG
96 A Spokane	67	231	58	63	17	0	6	39	22	61	32	.273
97 A Lansing	31	116	33	39	11	1	5	21	5	23	16	.336
97 AA Wichita	74	268	50	86	15	1	11	52	4	44	47	.321
97 MLE	74	254	36	72	12	0	7	38	2	27	47	.283

Hitting must run in the Giambi family. Older brother Jason is a key part of Oakland's lineup, and Jeremy is heading toward Kansas City. A 1996 sixth-round pick out of Cal State Fullerton, he batted .326 with 16 homers in his first full season, spending the second half in Double-A. Like Jason, he can draw a walk, but Jeremy doesn't have his brother's 20-homer power. Neither brother is an outstanding defender, and though Jeremy saw some time in center field he's more at home in left. The Royals have plenty of youngsters in their outfield mix, and Giambi probably will add his name in 1999.

Mendy Lopez

Position: SS

Bats: R **Throws:** R

Ht: 6' 2" **Wt:** 165

Opening Day Age: 23

Born: 10/15/74 in Pimentel Provincia, DR

Recent Statistics

	G	AB	R	H	D	T	HR	RBI	SB	BB	SO	AVG
96 AA Wichita	93	327	47	92	20	5	6	32	14	26	67	.281
97 AAA Omaha	17	52	6	12	2	0	1	6	0	8	21	.231
97 AA Wichita	101	357	56	83	16	3	5	42	7	36	70	.232
97 MLE	118	394	45	80	14	2	3	35	4	28	91	.203

After spending most of 1996 at third base, Lopez returned to his original position of shortstop last season. Signed out of the Dominican Republic, he's the system's best defensive player at either spot and has an exceptional arm. The Royals also believe he'll hit for power as he fills out his 6'2" frame and learns to turn on pitches. He has just 20 homers in six pro seasons, but has the potential to hit that many in a single year. He still needs time to develop, but could be pushing for big league playing time by the end of 1999.

Felix Martinez

Position: SS

Bats: B **Throws:** R

Ht: 6' 0" **Wt:** 168

Opening Day Age: 23

Born: 5/18/74 in Nagua, DR

Recent Statistics

	G	AB	R	H	D	T	HR	RBI	SB	BB	SO	AVG
97 AAA Omaha	112	410	55	104	19	4	2	36	21	29	86	.254
97 AL Kansas City	16	31	3	7	1	0	3	0	6	8	.226
97 MLE	112	397	43	91	16	4	1	28	14	22	82	.229

A pure shortstop voted the best defensive player at that position in the American Association, Martinez is more spectacular but less consistent than Lopez. Martinez originally signed out of the Dominican Republic with Japan's Hiroshima Toyo Carp before the Royals purchased him in 1993. Kansas City views him as Omar Vizquel with a stronger arm, but he still has a long way to go to reach that level. Martinez commits too many careless errors, strikes out too much and doesn't draw enough walks to take advantage of his speed. He needs another full season in Triple-A to mature.

Larry Sutton

Position: 1B

Bats: L **Throws:** L

Ht: 5' 11" **Wt:** 175

Opening Day Age: 27

Born: 5/14/70 in W. Covina, CA

Recent Statistics

	G	AB	R	H	D	T	HR	RBI	SB	BB	SO	AVG
97 AAA Omaha	106	380	61	114	27	1	19	72	0	61	57	.300
97 AL Kansas City	27	69	9	20	2	0	2	8	0	5	12	.290
97 MLE	106	365	48	99	24	0	14	57	0	48	56	.271

Because he doesn't have light-tower power as a first baseman, Sutton generally is underappreciated. A 1992 21st-round pick out of the University of Illinois, he proved he could play by winning two league MVP awards in his first three seasons. A broken elbow slowed him down in 1995, but he has rebounded with two fine years since. He may not have 30-homer potential, but he has a solid hitting approach and has walked more than he has struck out in the minors. Though he has limited range, he's smooth around the bag and was named the American Association's best defensive first baseman. He should stick with the Royals in 1998 as at least a reserve.

Others to Watch

Carlos Beltran is a five-tool center fielder with above-average speed and a plus arm. But he hit just .229 in his first exposure to full-season ball at age 20 and looks like he'll need some time. . . Righthander **Roland de la Maza**, 26, joined the Royals in the Bip Roberts trade. He's not overpowering, just effective, and projects as a strike-throwing setup man. . . When he was drafted in the first round in 1995, outfielder **Juan LeBron** was compared to fellow Puerto Rican Juan Gonzalez as a power hitter. LeBron, 20, has been slow to develop because of a long swing, but the Royals remain high on him. . . Third baseman **Kit Pellow** hit 21 homers and reached Double-A in 1997, his first full pro season. The Royals tried the 24 year old at catcher in instructional league because of his arm strength, and were pleased with the results. . . Outfielder **Mark Quinn**, 23, has an odd stance where he steps in the bucket, but still can drive the ball to the opposite field. He has hit for power and average in his three years in the system. . . **Ken Ray's** stuff is as good as any pitcher's in the system, but he remains an enigma. Despite a 93-MPH fastball and an above-average curveball, the 23 year old hasn't been able to win above Class-A.

Tom Kelly

1997 Season

The Twins were expected to contend for a wild-card spot, but had one of the worst finishes in their history. Amid the carnage, Tom Kelly and his coaches came under fire, particularly for their handling of young players. Kelly remains a highly respected baseball man and one of the finest in-game managers around.

Offense

Kelly admits that Minnesota lacks the firepower of the elite-hitting teams in the AL. His team compensates with assertive, intelligent baserunning. Twins runners move up aggressively on fly balls and are the best-coached group in the league. Even the slow guys know what they are doing on the bases and everyone hustles. Kelly likes the hit-and-run and will give the steal sign, but eschews the bunt. He'll also platoon, especially with young players. He's not afraid to use all the men on his roster, and generally keeps his reserves sharp.

Pitching & Defense

For years, fans have been calling for the head of pitching coach Dick Such, but Kelly remains loyal to him. Such works well with veterans. But while the farm system has produced several promising mound prospects in recent years, only Brad Radke has lived up to his potential. Kelly prefers pitchers with good control and will seldom let a tired man stay on the mound. The Twins are traditionally excellent with the glove, and will sometimes keep a weak bat in the lineup if Kelly feels it gives him a defensive edge. He isn't an advocate of the intentional walk and is conservative with pitchouts.

1998 Outlook

Late last season, rumors surfaced that Kelly might take a another job, but the Minnesota native intends to stay with the organization. If the team moves to Charlotte, however, Kelly's situation may change. Kelly is a fine manager in many ways. His teams demonstrate extraordinary hustle. Veterans love playing for him, and he has made Minnesota attractive to free agents. Youngsters are the key for the future and Kelly's relationship with some of them is an open question at this point.

Born: 8/15/50 in Graceville, MN

Playing Experience: 1975, Min

Managerial Experience: 12 seasons

Minnesota Twins

Manager Statistics

Year	Team, Lg	W	L	Pct	GB	Finish
1997	Minnesota, AL	68	94	.420	18.5	4th Central
12 Seasons		853	885	.491	—	—

1997 Starting Pitchers by Days Rest

	≤3	4	5	6+
Twins Starts	5	96	27	22
Twins ERA	3.77	5.23	5.66	6.26
AL Avg Starts	5	89	34	24
AL ERA	4.38	4.60	4.61	5.37

1997 Situational Stats

	Tom Kelly	AL Average
Hit & Run Success %	34.0	36.5
Stolen Base Success %	74.4	67.3
Platoon Pct.	52.1	59.5
Defensive Subs	10	22
High-Pitch Outings	8	15
Quick/Slow Hooks	19/11	19/15
Sacrifice Attempts	26	53

1997 Rankings (American League)

⇒ 1st in stolen base percentage (74.4%), steals of second base (135) and starting lineups used (139)

⇒ 2nd in stolen base attempts (203), steals of home plate (1) and least caught steals of third base (3)

⇒ 3rd in pinch hitters used (163) and starts on three days rest (5)

Rick Aguilera

1997 Season

After a season as a starter in 1996, Rick Aguilera returned to his familiar bullpen habitat in 1997. The move was originally a temporary measure to spare Aguilera's sore knees, but a couple of weeks into the season the Twins made the move permanent. While Aguilera is no longer a premier closer, he's still consistent. After a slow start in April, he pitched very well.

Pitching

As a starter Aguilera used a four-pitch arsenal, but as a closer he relies primarily on his fastball and split-fingered pitch. His fastball is no longer overpowering, but the pitch still moves well and he can locate it with precision. The splitter remains excellent, and when he keeps his offerings down he's one of the best closers around. When his pitches are up, however, he can get hit hard. Aguilera will use his curveball and slider occasionally, but the fastball/splitter combination is usually enough. His strikeout rate remains excellent, and he was quite effective against lefthanded hitters last year.

Defense

Aguilera is a splendid athlete, handles his position with veteran aplomb and is alert and active on the field. His motion to the plate isn't quick, however, and his move to first isn't very effective, so he's vulnerable to the stolen base. Still, nearly as many basestealers were caught (four) as were successful (five) on his watch in 1997.

1998 Outlook

There are rumors that the Twins may trade Aguilera to a contender once again, but it's equally probable that they will keep him around, especially if they decide not to move to Charlotte. Aguilera enjoys playing for manager Tom Kelly and has made his home in Minnesota. The Twins like not having to worry about who will close games. If Aguilera stays, that shouldn't be a concern for two or three more years.

Position: RP
Bats: R **Throws:** R
Ht: 6' 5" **Wt:** 203

Opening Day Age: 36
Born: 12/31/61 in San Gabriel, CA
ML Seasons: 13
Pronunciation: ag-yuh-LAIR-uh

Overall Statistics

	W	L	Pct.	ERA	G	GS	Sv	IP	H	BB	SO	HR	Ratio
1997	5	4	.556	3.82	61	0	26	68.1	65	22	68	9	1.27
Career	72	66	.522	3.50	549	89	237	1101.2	1057	306	890	111	1.24

How Often He Throws Strikes

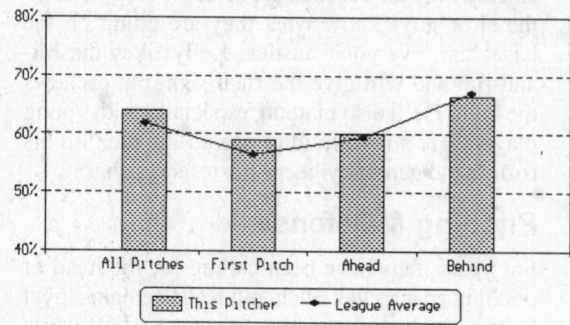

1997 Situational Stats

	W	L	ERA	Sv	IP		AB	H	HR	RBI	Avg
Home	3	2	2.75	12	36.0	LHB	115	27	5	17	.235
Road	2	2	5.01	14	32.1	RHB	138	38	4	20	.275
First Half	3	1	3.86	16	37.1	Sc Pos	61	14	4	29	.230
Scnd Half	2	3	3.77	10	31.0	Clutch	156	42	6	24	.269

1997 Rankings (American League)

⇒ 4th in games finished (57), lowest save percentage (78.8%) and blown saves (7)
⇒ 6th in save opportunities (33)
⇒ 8th in most strikeouts per 9 innings in relief (9.0)
⇒ 9th in saves
⇒ Led the Twins in saves, games finished (57), save opportunities (33), save percentage (78.8%), blown saves (7) and most strikeouts per 9 innings in relief (9.0)

Rich Becker

1997 Season

The Twins hoped that 1997 would be the year Rich Becker made the transition from a decent young player to a budding star. It didn't happen. While Becker overcame his usual slow start to post respectable numbers, he made no real progress in developing his skills. Becker lost playing time at various points in the season to veterans such as Darrin Jackson and Roberto Kelly, and ended the campaign without much of a flourish.

Hitting

Becker has good pop for a small guy and can be very patient. He strikes out a lot, however, and isn't a great contact hitter. Despite his good on-base percentage, he isn't the right match for the second spot in the order behind Chuck Knoblauch. Indeed, Becker does better lower in the order, hitting .331 in the eighth spot. Becker is susceptible to fastballs up and in, but usually does fairly well against breaking stuff. At this point, he's probably best cast as a platoon player. He continues to struggle against lefthanded pitching, and the Twins are increasingly reluctant to let him face southpaws.

Baserunning & Defense

Becker is a fine baserunner. He has above-average speed, is smart and aggressive, and steals bases at a good percentage. Defensively, he was excellent in 1996 but regressed in 1997. He had trouble tracking fly balls and made too many mental mistakes, as his five errors in center field would attest. Also, his assist total fell from a league-leading 19 in 1996 to just five in 1997. The decline can be blamed partly on an increased reluctance to challenge Becker's arm, but at times his throws were inaccurate.

1998 Outlook

Becker is at a crossroads. If he stays at his current level of performance, he's a useful, productive platoon outfielder. But the Twins are hoping for more. At times, he plays as if he has star ability, teasing the Minnesota brass with Lenny Dykstra-type production. He's young enough to break out and do that consistently, but it has yet to happen.

Position: CF/RF
Bats: L **Throws:** L
Ht: 5'10" **Wt:** 199

Opening Day Age: 26
Born: 2/1/72 in Aurora, IL
ML Seasons: 5

Overall Statistics

	G	AB	R	H	D	T	HR	RBI	SB	BB	SO	Avg	OBP	Slg
1997	132	443	61	117	22	3	10	45	17	62	130	.264	.354	.395
Career	417	1465	213	391	73	8	25	157	51	182	372	.267	.349	.379

Where He Hits the Ball

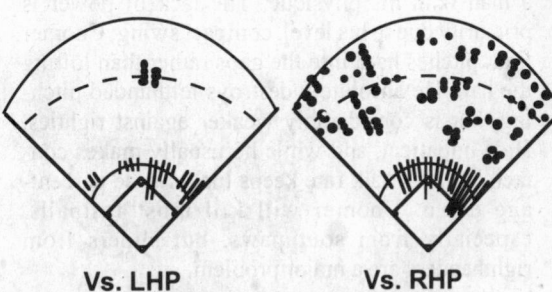

Vs. LHP   **Vs. RHP**

1997 Situational Stats

	AB	H	HR	RBI	Avg		AB	H	HR	RBI	Avg
Home	223	62	4	27	.278	LHP	64	10	0	3	.156
Road	220	55	6	18	.250	RHP	379	107	10	42	.282
First Half	250	64	6	22	.256	Sc Pos	103	25	5	36	.243
Scnd Half	193	53	4	23	.275	Clutch	70	17	1	4	.243

1997 Rankings (American League)

⇒ 1st in lowest fielding percentage in center field (.983)
⇒ 2nd in errors in center field (5)
⇒ 7th in least GDPs per GDP situation (4.6%)
⇒ 9th in strikeouts and stolen base percentage (77.3%)
⇒ Led the Twins in strikeouts and least GDPs per GDP situation (4.6%)

Ron Coomer

1997 Season

Ron Coomer opened the season platooning with Rookie-of-the-Year candidate Todd Walker. When Walker got off to a slow start, Coomer won the job full-time. In the process, he become one of manager Tom Kelly's favorite players. Coomer played very well throughout the first half, and hit better than .300 for much of the season. A late dry spell dropped him below that level, but it was still a good campaign from a player regarded as a career minor leaguer just three years ago.

Hitting

Coomer is very strong, but doesn't generate as much home-run power as one would expect from a man with his physique. The lack of power is primarily due to his level, compact swing; Coomer lines pitches hard into the gaps rather than lofting the ball. He absolutely destroys lefthanded pitching, but is considerably weaker against righties. He's impatient, and while he usually makes contact, his low walk rate keeps his on-base percentage down. Coomer will kill most fastballs, especially from southpaws, but sliders from righthanders are a major problem.

Baserunning & Defense

Coomer played mostly first base in 1996, but moved to third, his Triple-A position, last season. He's nothing more than a decent defensive player with average range and an average arm, but he doesn't make too many errors and is fundamentally sound. His glove at first is pretty steady, too, but he's much weaker as an outfielder. On the basepaths, he's slow and cautious, but seldom runs himself into outs.

1998 Outlook

Although Coomer saw action nearly every day in 1997, his future role remains as a platoon player. He devastates lefthanders, and his ability to play first or third base is an asset. The Twins also like his work ethic. How much playing time he receives in 1998 depends on what happens to the players around him, especially Walker and Scott Stahoviak.

Position: 3B
Bats: R **Throws:** R
Ht: 5'11" **Wt:** 195

Opening Day Age: 31
Born: 11/18/66 in Crest Hill, IL
ML Seasons: 3

Overall Statistics

	G	AB	R	H	D	T	HR	RBI	SB	BB	SO	Avg	OBP	Slg
1997	140	523	63	156	30	2	13	85	4	22	91	.298	.324	.438
Career	272	857	112	251	45	4	30	145	7	48	126	.293	.328	.460

Where He Hits the Ball

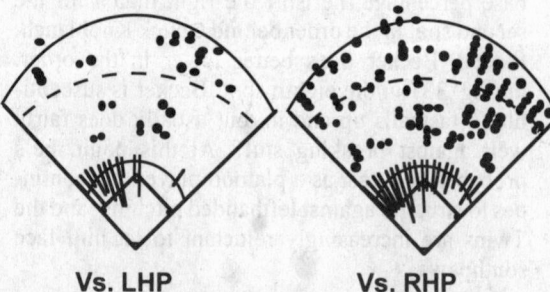

Vs. LHP   **Vs. RHP**

1997 Situational Stats

	AB	H	HR	RBI	Avg		AB	H	HR	RBI	Avg
Home	258	80	4	40	.310	LHP	123	51	3	24	.415
Road	265	76	9	45	.287	RHP	400	105	10	61	.263
First Half	233	71	8	41	.305	Sc Pos	135	50	4	73	.370
Scnd Half	290	85	5	44	.293	Clutch	69	18	1	5	.261

1997 Rankings (American League)

⇒ 1st in batting average vs. lefthanded pitchers and on-base percentage vs. lefthanded pitchers (.459)

⇒ 3rd in batting average with runners in scoring position

⇒ 4th in least pitches seen per plate appearance (3.37) and fielding percentage at third base (.966)

⇒ 5th in lowest on-base percentage vs. righthanded pitchers (.281)

⇒ Led the Twins in slugging percentage, batting average with runners in scoring position, batting average vs. lefthanded pitchers, slugging percentage vs. lefthanded pitchers (.594) and on-base percentage vs. lefthanded pitchers (.459)

Marty Cordova

1997 Season

Marty Cordova entered the season looking to so-lidify his reputation as one of the better players in the American League. It all came crashing down when he hurt his heel in spring training. The injury was diagnosed as plantar fasciitis, the same ailment that has plagued Mark McGwire. Though Cordova avoided surgery, he spent much of April and May on the disabled list. When he came back, he didn't look like the same player.

Hitting

When healthy, Cordova has a short, quick swing capable of producing high batting averages and power. When he came off the disabled list, how-ever, he looked like a player in pain. Struggling to adjust, he messed up his swing. The injury ap-peared to affect Cordova's ability to shift his weight properly at the plate. Trying to compensate, he became very impatient, and made the problem worse. Cordova struggled with men in scoring position, against lefties, and even in the hitter-friendly Metrodome. He did hit four home runs in September, and showed signs at the end of the season of regaining his healthy swing.

Baserunning & Defense

The heel injury certainly hurt Cordova's running ability. He stole only five bases after swiping a total of 31 the previous two seasons. His speed dropped from above-average to average, and he was more tentative on the basepaths than in the past. Defensively, Cordova still showed good range in left field and managed 12 assists despite average arm strength. He made only two errors, but mental mistakes and misplays in several games drew manager Tom Kelly's ire.

1998 Outlook

Cordova's work ethic remains excellent, and per-haps his intensity was part of his problem last year. He certainly looked like a player trying too hard to make up for lost time. Given that he returns healthy, there's no reason to believe he won't rebound.

Position: LF
Bats: R **Throws:** R
Ht: 6' 0" **Wt:** 193

Opening Day Age: 28
Born: 7/10/69 in Las Vegas, NV
ML Seasons: 3
Pronunciation: core-DOE-vuh

Overall Statistics

	G	AB	R	H	D	T	HR	RBI	SB	BB	SO	Avg	OBP	Slg
1997	103	378	44	93	18	4	15	51	5	30	92	.246	.305	.434
Career	385	1459	222	411	91	9	55	246	36	135	299	.282	.348	.469

Where He Hits the Ball

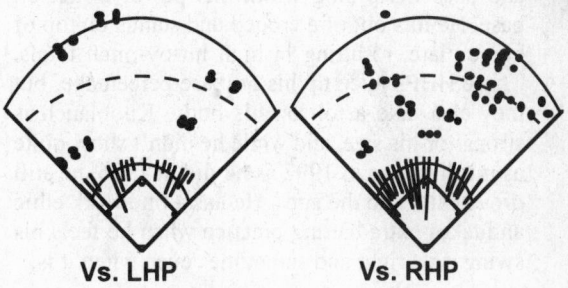

Vs. LHP   **Vs. RHP**

1997 Situational Stats

	AB	H	HR	RBI	Avg		AB	H	HR	RBI	Avg
Home	183	40	4	23	.219	LHP	99	21	7	20	.212
Road	195	53	11	28	.272	RHP	279	72	8	31	.258
First Half	145	39	5	19	.269	Sc Pos	98	21	3	30	.214
Scnd Half	233	54	10	32	.232	Clutch	52	19	4	11	.365

1997 Rankings (American League)

⇒ 2nd in lowest percentage of swings put into play (33.6%)
⇒ 3rd in fielding percentage in left field (.991)
⇒ 5th in lowest batting average with the bases loaded (.067)
⇒ 6th in batting average in the clutch
⇒ 9th in lowest percentage of pitches taken (46.2%)
⇒ Led the Twins in home runs and batting average in the clutch

Chuck Knoblauch

1997 Season

When Chuck Knoblauch signed a long-term contract after his incredible 1996 season, he became the frachise's most cherished asset. Knoblauch didn't perform quite as well in 1997, but he was still outstanding, leading the team in runs and setting a club record for stolen bases. He was henpecked by injuries to his ankles, elbows and forearms, mainly as a result of getting hit by pitches, but never stayed out of the lineup for more than a day at a time.

Hitting

Knoblauch is one of the best leadoff hitters in the American League. He's very patient at the plate and does everything within his power to get on base. He hits out of a crouch and stands on top of home plate, resulting in high hit-by-pitch totals. Those HBPs juice up his on-base percentage, but they also take a toll on his body. Knoblauch is strong for his size, and while he didn't show quite as much power in 1997 as he did in 1996, he still drove balls into the gaps. He has a fine work ethic and takes extra batting practice when he feels his swing isn't right and sometimes even when it is.

Baserunning & Defense

Knoblauch has above-average running speed and he's extraordinarily quick. He reads pitchers' minds like a psychic and doesn't just steal lots of bases, but steals them at a great percentage. His stolen-base success rate of 86.1 percent (62 of 72) was best in the AL among players with at least 30 attempts last year. Defensively, he's in the elite class, with a low error rate, great hands, well above-average range and a knack for decoying baserunners. He was awarded his first Gold Glove after the season.

1998 Outlook

The struggles of the 1997 Twins weighed heavily on Knoblauch and he has requested a trade to a contender. The Twins may oblige, but if they can prove to him that they are intent on improving the club immediately, he could be swayed to stay. If they do trade him, the prospects obtained in return would have to be outstanding, as the Twins would be giving up one of the best players in the league.

Position: 2B
Bats: R **Throws:** R
Ht: 5' 9" **Wt:** 181

Opening Day Age: 29
Born: 7/7/68 in Houston, TX
ML Seasons: 7
Pronunciation: NOB-lock

Overall Statistics

	G	AB	R	H	D	T	HR	RBI	SB	BB	SO	Avg	OBP	Slg
1997	156	611	117	178	26	10	9	58	62	84	84	.291	.390	.411
Career	1013	3939	713	1197	210	51	43	391	276	513	453	.304	.391	.416

Where He Hits the Ball

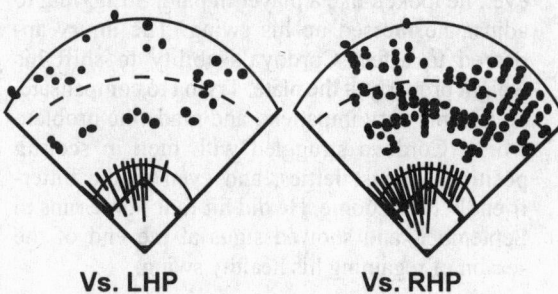

Vs. LHP   Vs. RHP

1997 Situational Stats

	AB	H	HR	RBI	Avg		AB	H	HR	RBI	Avg
Home	305	88	2	23	.289	LHP	132	39	3	17	.295
Road	306	90	7	35	.294	RHP	479	139	6	41	.290
First Half	325	94	5	36	.289	Sc Pos	131	41	0	45	.313
Scnd Half	286	84	4	22	.294	Clutch	73	13	1	7	.178

1997 Rankings (American League)

⇒ 2nd in triples, stolen bases, hit by pitch (17), pitches seen (2,896), stolen base percentage (86.1%) and steals of third (12)

⇒ 3rd in runs scored, times on base (279), fielding percentage at second base (.985) and lowest percentage of swings that missed (9.3%)

⇒ 4th in singles, plate appearances (716), lowest batting average in the clutch, on-base percentage for a leadoff hitter (.390), errors at second base (11) and lowest percentage of swings on the first pitch (14.3%)

⇒ Led the Twins in at-bats, runs scored, hits, singles, triples, total bases (251), stolen bases, caught stealing (10), walks, hit by pitch (17), times on base (279), pitches seen (2,896), plate appearances (716) and games played (156)

Matt Lawton

1997 Season

Matt Lawton opened the season as Minnesota's right fielder. He got off to a hot start, but a bout with unexplained dizziness in May cost him a few games and tossed him into a slump. His batting average hovered around .250 for the rest of the year, but he showed surprising pop in his bat for a small guy and hit better towards the end of the season, slugging .556 in September.

Hitting

Hitting out of an ardent crouch, Lawton is reminiscent of Tony Phillips. Though he hasn't developed Phillips' patience at the plate, Lawton does take more pitches than most Minnesota hitters, looking for balls to drive. He's extremely muscular and pitchers have learned not to give him a fastball anywhere on the inner half of the plate. He struggles against breaking stuff, though he has the hitting instincts to adjust. Lawton has done very well in limited exposure to lefties and isn't strictly a platoon player. Given further experience, it's conceivable that he could produce a few 20-homer seasons in the near future.

Baserunning & Defense

Lawton has above-average speed but isn't a skilled basestealer and isn't particularly assertive on the basepaths. Defensively, he's talented but erratic. He played all three outfield positions in 1997. While his range is pretty good, he has occasional problems tracking fly balls, especially in center field, and his arm isn't very strong. He'll make the spectacular play, but will muff the easy one.

1998 Outlook

Like teammate Rich Becker, Matt Lawton is a solid player who helps his team but isn't a dominant talent. If Lawton continues to develop his offensive skills, particularly his patience and power, the situation may change. He should start for the Twins in 1998, probably in right field.

Position: RF/LF/CF
Bats: L **Throws:** R
Ht: 5'10" **Wt:** 196

Opening Day Age: 26
Born: 11/3/71 in Gulfport, MS
ML Seasons: 3

Overall Statistics

	G	AB	R	H	D	T	HR	RBI	SB	BB	SO	Avg	OBP	Slg
1997	142	460	74	114	29	3	14	60	7	76	81	.248	.366	.415
Career	242	772	119	198	40	5	21	114	12	111	120	.256	.361	.403

Where He Hits the Ball

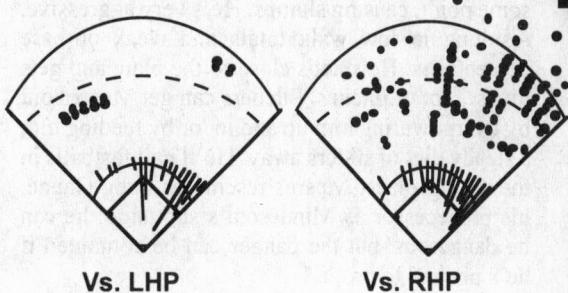

Vs. LHP   **Vs. RHP**

1997 Situational Stats

	AB	H	HR	RBI	Avg		AB	H	HR	RBI	Avg
Home	218	54	8	26	.248	LHP	84	23	1	12	.274
Road	242	60	6	34	.248	RHP	376	91	13	48	.242
First Half	261	67	6	29	.257	Sc Pos	104	29	4	42	.279
Scnd Half	199	47	8	31	.236	Clutch	65	20	2	10	.308

1997 Rankings (American League)

⇒ 7th in errors in center field (3)
⇒ 8th in lowest batting average vs. righthanded pitchers and highest percentage of pitches taken (61.5%)
⇒ 9th in hit by pitch (10)
⇒ 10th in lowest batting average
⇒ Led the Twins in HR frequency (32.9 ABs per HR) and highest percentage of pitches taken (61.5%)

Pat Meares

1997 Season

Pat Meares' 1997 season was similar to his previous seasons: a hot start followed by a midseason slump, then a strong finish to end with respectable numbers. Meares was bothered throughout the season by sore calves, a tender elbow and a bout with the flu, but he continued to impress observers with his hustle and intelligent play. At season's end, he was named *USA Today's* Mr. Average, as his stats approximated major league medians.

Hitting

When everything is right with Meares, he can drive pitches to all fields from a closed stance. But each year he becomes overly pull-conscious at some point, causing slumps. He's very aggressive, resulting in low walk totals and weak on-base percentages. He stands close to the plate and gets hit by a lot of pitches. Pitchers can get Meares out by overpowering him up and in, or by feeding him a steady diet of sliders away. He'll nail fastballs in the wrong place. Meares resembles Greg Gagne, his predecessor as Minnesota's shortstop: he can be dangerous, but the danger can be contained if he's pitched to properly.

Baserunning & Defense

Meares has good footspeed, but has never developed into a basestealing threat. He'll challenge outfielders on fly balls and is a determined, astute baserunner. Defensively, Meares does what he can with average ability. He has a strong arm, though sometimes his throws get away from him. His range is mediocre, and he doesn't possess the quickness of the ideal artificial turf shortstop. He does have good hands, isn't particularly error-prone and has developed a solid relationship with double-play partner Chuck Knoblauch.

1998 Outlook

Although being Mr. Average isn't highly coveted, in Meares' case it's very apt. Offensively and defensively, he's neither great nor ghastly. One thing that's not average about him is his work ethic. For that reason he's a favorite of coaches and teammates alike. He'll play shortstop for the Twins until a player with better skills arrives.

Position: SS
Bats: R **Throws:** R
Ht: 6' 0" **Wt:** 188

Opening Day Age: 29
Born: 9/6/68 in Salina, KS
ML Seasons: 5
Pronunciation: MEERS

Overall Statistics

	G	AB	R	H	D	T	HR	RBI	SB	BB	SO	Avg	OBP	Slg
1997	134	439	63	121	23	3	10	60	7	18	86	.276	.323	.410
Career	593	1921	248	512	94	18	32	233	35	71	346	.267	.303	.384

Where He Hits the Ball

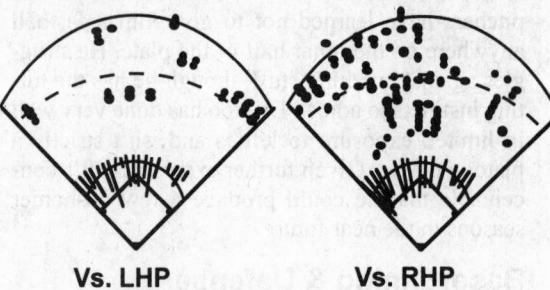

Vs. LHP   **Vs. RHP**

1997 Situational Stats

	AB	H	HR	RBI	Avg		AB	H	HR	RBI	Avg
Home	246	60	5	33	.244	LHP	99	18	1	12	.182
Road	193	61	5	27	.316	RHP	340	103	9	48	.303
First Half	261	72	8	38	.276	Sc Pos	114	35	4	51	.307
Scnd Half	178	49	2	22	.275	Clutch	58	19	2	9	.328

1997 Rankings (American League)

⇒ 3rd in hit by pitch (16) and errors at shortstop (20)
⇒ 4th in lowest fielding percentage at shortstop (.969)
⇒ 9th in lowest batting average at home
⇒ Led the Twins in bunts in play (8)

Paul Molitor

1997 Season

It's hard to believe Paul Molitor is 41. While he wasn't as consistently effective in 1997 as he was in 1996, Molitor still had a solid campaign, especially considering his age and the fact that he was bothered by nagging injuries, including an abdominal strain that landed him on the disabled list in April. The injury seemed to affect his hitting, but he finished on an up note, hitting .337 in September.

Hitting

Molitor is the prototype line-drive hitter. He will whack hard shots to all fields with his level swing, will nail breaking stuff and mediocre fastballs, and remains an exceptional contact hitter. His bat speed looked down at times in 1997, principally when he wasn't healthy, but he remains a threat whom few pitchers relish facing with men on base. He's especially effective in the Metrodome and against lefthanded pitchers.

Baserunning & Defense

Molitor still runs well, swiping 11 bases in 15 attempts in 1997, though he did look a bit slower than he did in 1996. He remains a shrewd baserunner who pressures the defense and can steal a critical base; he seldom blunders into an out. The Twins keep him at designated hitter most of the time to spare his body, though he did get some time at first base during interleague play and didn't embarrass himself.

1998 Outlook

Molitor wasn't happy about the Twins' possible move to North Carolina, but he re-signed for a year anyway. He already has expressed interest in becoming a field manager or front-office operative, and the Blue Jays considered hiring him as a player-manager before going with Tim Johnson. He'll continue to grace baseball with his class for years to come.

Position: DH/1B
Bats: R **Throws:** R
Ht: 6' 0" **Wt:** 190

Opening Day Age: 41
Born: 8/22/56 in St. Paul, MN
ML Seasons: 20
Pronunciation: MOLL-uh-ter
Nickname: The Igniter

Minnesota Twins

Overall Statistics

	G	AB	R	H	D	T	HR	RBI	SB	BB	SO	Avg	OBP	Slg
1997	135	538	63	164	32	4	10	89	11	45	73	.305	.351	.435
Career	2557	10333	1707	3178	576	109	230	1238	495	1049	1203	.308	.371	.451

Where He Hits the Ball

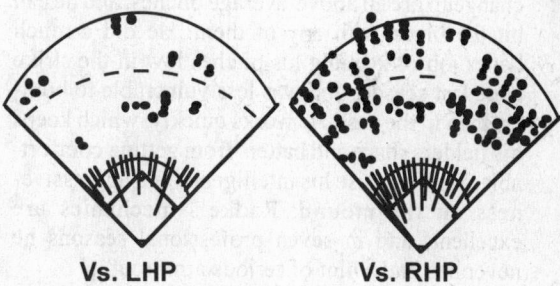

Vs. LHP   **Vs. RHP**

1997 Situational Stats

	AB	H	HR	RBI	Avg		AB	H	HR	RBI	Avg
Home	289	93	5	51	.322	LHP	113	38	0	16	.336
Road	249	71	5	38	.285	RHP	425	126	10	73	.296
First Half	264	84	4	47	.318	Sc Pos	169	55	3	75	.325
Scnd Half	274	80	6	42	.292	Clutch	63	19	2	14	.302

1997 Rankings (American League)

⇒ 1st in batting average on a 3-2 count (.481)
⇒ 2nd in sacrifice flies (12)
⇒ Led the Twins in batting average, doubles, RBI, sacrifice flies (12), intentional walks (8), highest groundball/flyball ratio (1.4), batting average vs. righthanded pitchers, batting average on a 3-1 count (.619), slugging percentage vs. righthanded pitchers (.442), batting average on a 3-2 count (.481), batting average at home, highest percentage of swings put into play (47.7%) and highest percentage of extra bases taken as a runner (55.0%)

Brad Radke

1997 Season

Brad Radke entered the 1997 season as a respected young pitcher who had yet to tap his ability completely. He exited the campaign as one of the aces of the American League. After a slow start, Radke got hot in midseason, posting a 12-game winning streak. He tired a bit in September, but still won 20 games, a tremendous achievement on a team as weak as the 1997 Twins.

Pitching

In his first two seasons, Radke's fastball seldom exceeded 87 MPH, but last year he regularly hit the low 90s, a result of physical maturity and small mechanical adjustments. His curveball, slider and changeup are all above-average pitches, and he can hit the black with any of them. He did a much better job of keeping his pitches low in the strike zone last season, and was less vulnerable to homers than in the past. He works quickly, which keeps his fielders sharp and batters from getting comfortable. Scouts praise his intelligence and aggressiveness on the mound. Radke's mechanics are excellent, and in seven professional seasons he never has had a hint of serious arm trouble.

Defense

Radke is a fine defensive player. He moves well around the infield, grasps all the fundamentals and demonstrates good situational judgement. His move to first is good for a righthander, and he's not particularly vulnerable to the stolen base. Seven of 17 would-be basestealers were gunned down on his watch.

1998 Outlook

The sky's the limit for Radke. Quiet in the clubhouse, he lets his pitching do the talking. For three months last year, he was nearly unbeatable. Assuming Radke remains in good health—given his mechanics and Tom Kelly's caution with pitching arms, there's no reason to anticipate he won't—he should continue to improve. He has established himself as an outstanding pitcher.

Position: SP
Bats: R **Throws:** R
Ht: 6' 2" **Wt:** 186

Opening Day Age: 25
Born: 10/27/72 in Eau Claire, WI
ML Seasons: 3

Overall Statistics

	W	L	Pct.	ERA	G	GS	Sv	IP	H	BB	SO	HR	Ratio
1997	20	10	.667	3.87	35	35	0	239.2	238	48	174	28	1.19
Career	42	40	.512	4.48	99	98	0	652.2	664	152	397	100	1.25

How Often He Throws Strikes

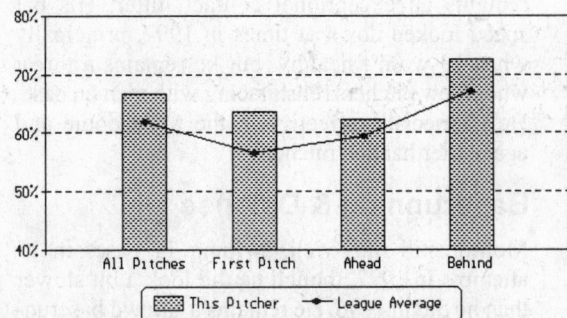

1997 Situational Stats

	W	L	ERA	Sv	IP		AB	H	HR	RBI	Avg
Home	11	5	4.00	0	135.0	LHB	471	137	15	52	.291
Road	9	5	3.70	0	104.2	RHB	456	101	13	52	.221
First Half	10	5	4.13	0	126.1	Sc Pos	169	53	5	72	.314
Scnd Half	10	5	3.57	0	113.1	Clutch	61	11	0	5	.180

1997 Rankings (American League)

⇒ 1st in games started and in fielding percentage at pitcher (1.000)
⇒ 2nd in wins
⇒ 4th in innings pitched and lowest batting average allowed vs. righthanded batters
⇒ 5th in batters faced (989), highest strikeout/walk ratio (3.6), lowest on-base percentage allowed (.293) and least baserunners allowed per 9 innings (10.9)
⇒ Led the Twins in ERA, wins, games started, innings pitched, hits allowed, batters faced (989), home runs allowed, strikeouts, pitches thrown (3,539), runners caught stealing (7), winning percentage, highest strikeout/walk ratio (3.6), lowest batting average allowed (.257) and lowest slugging percentage allowed (.412)

Frank Rodriguez

1997 Season

The Twins expected Frank Rodriguez and Brad Radke to form a productive one-two punch in the rotation in 1997. While Radke lived up to his end of the bargain, Rodriguez struggled early and was banished to the bullpen in May. His velocity was down from 1996 and his command wasn't good enough to compensate. Rodriguez adapted well to bullpen work and slowly regained the team's confidence. He rejoined the rotation late in the season and performed adequately. Though Rodriguez' final ERA wasn't terrible by current standards, he still had a disappointing season.

Pitching

Early in the year, Rodriguez' fastball was clocked only in the upper 80s, but by midseason it was back up to 93 MPH. His slider and curveball have excellent movement and his changeup is OK, but he still has problems throwing strikes. Rodriguez can look unbeatable in one outing, then get crushed in the first inning in his next start. Scouts say he must be more consistent and mature in order to get the most out of his arm. Rodriguez may be miscast as a starter, as he posted an excellent 2.88 ERA in relief. He's equally effective against lefties and righties, pitches well in the Metrodome and could have a future as a closer if he fails as a starter.

Defense

A shortstop in high school, Rodriguez is the best athlete on the team. He has extremely quick reactions and could win a Gold Glove as a pitcher if he cuts down on his errors. He holds runners well for a righthander.

1998 Outlook

At this stage, Rodriguez is penciled into the rotation again. Given his erratic history, it's hard to project what he may do or where he might end up. He has the arm of an All-Star, but needs better control and a more mature attitude. Given his solid bullpen performance last year, relieving may be his destiny.

Position: RP/SP
Bats: R **Throws:** R
Ht: 6' 0" **Wt:** 195

Opening Day Age: 25
Born: 12/11/72 in Brooklyn, NY
ML Seasons: 3

Overall Statistics

	W	L	Pct.	ERA	G	GS	Sv	IP	H	BB	SO	HR	Ratio
1997	3	6	.333	4.62	43	15	0	142.1	147	60	65	12	1.45
Career	21	28	.429	5.17	106	66	2	454.2	479	195	234	50	1.48

How Often He Throws Strikes

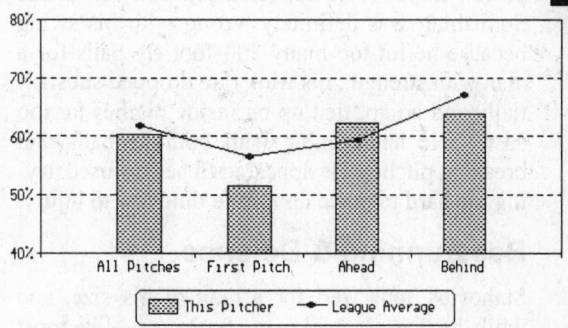

1997 Situational Stats

	W	L	ERA	Sv	IP		AB	•	H	HR	RBI	Avg
Home	1	2	2.97	0	69.2	LHB	233		66	7	29	.283
Road	2	4	6.19	0	72.2	RHB	310		81	5	45	.261
First Half	1	3	4.56	0	75.0	Sc Pos	137		45	3	62	.328
Scnd Half	2	3	4.68	0	67.1	Clutch	55		17	1	8	.309

1997 Rankings (American League)

⇒ 1st in least strikeouts per 9 innings in relief (4.0)
⇒ 3rd in highest batting average allowed with runners in scoring position
⇒ 10th in least baserunners allowed per 9 innings in relief (11.1)
⇒ Led the Twins in lowest batting average allowed vs. lefthanded batters and relief ERA (2.88)

Scott Stahoviak

1997 Season

Scott Stahoviak's 1997 campaign got off to a in-auspicious start when he broke his left pinky in early April. He did well when he came off the disabled list on May 16, hitting .339 in June, but in July his bat fell into a deep slumber and never woke up. He was woefully ineffective in the second half, hitting just .154 in 65 August at-bats. His poor performance was a major reason for the Twins' disappointing year.

Hitting

In 1996, Stahoviak was content to go with the pitch, and proved capable of driving the ball to the opposite field or occasionally pulling the ball for power. In 1997, he appeared too pull-conscious. Something was definitely wrong with his swing because he hit too many 300-foot fly balls for a man with strength, his walk rate dropped substantially and he got tied up on inside pitches far too easily. He had trouble with both fastballs and breaking pitches. He appeared to be confused, trying too hard to make up for the time lost to injury.

Baserunning & Defense

Stahoviak runs well for a man of his size, and while he doesn't steal many bases, he—like most Twins—is a smart baserunner who will take the extra base. He's a fine defensive first baseman, though he made more errors (seven) than usual last year. He continues to demonstrate very good range around the bag and makes the occasional spectacular stop on balls hit down the line.

1998 Outlook

With the emergence of prospect David Ortiz, Stahoviak's days in Minnesota are probably numbered. He works hard and hustles, and if he can get his swing and plate discipline back, there should be a place for him somewhere. Unless he shows more consistent power, his chance for a starting job is gone.

Position: 1B
Bats: L **Throws:** R
Ht: 6' 5" **Wt:** 222

Opening Day Age: 28
Born: 3/6/70 in Waukegan, IL
ML Seasons: 4
Pronunciation: sta-HO-vee-ak

Overall Statistics

	G	AB	R	H	D	T	HR	RBI	SB	BB	SO	Avg	OBP	Slg
1997	91	275	33	63	17	0	10	33	5	24	73	.229	.301	.400
Career	335	1000	134	259	70	3	26	118	13	116	270	.259	.339	.413

Where He Hits the Ball

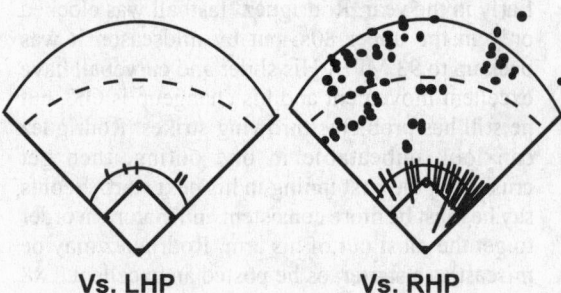

Vs. LHP   Vs. RHP

1997 Situational Stats

	AB	H	HR	RBI	Avg		AB	H	HR	RBI	Avg
Home	141	34	4	18	.241	LHP	14	4	0	2	.286
Road	134	29	6	15	.216	RHP	261	59	10	31	.226
First Half	106	29	6	17	.274	Sc Pos	59	13	2	22	.220
Scnd Half	169	34	4	16	.201	Clutch	37	6	0	1	.162

1997 Rankings (American League)

⇒ 9th in errors at first base (7)

Terry Steinbach

1997 Season

The Twins have made a habit of luring veteran players from Minnesota back to their home state, and Terry Steinbach was the 1997 catch. The club hoped he would provide some juice to a power-starved offense and a steadying presence behind home plate, but overall his season was a disappointment. While Steinbach played well defensively, he was unable to repeat his 1996 accomplishments at the plate.

Hitting

Steinbach may well have had his career year in 1996. While the Twins didn't realistically expect him to hit 35 home runs again, they had to be disappointed with his final total of 12. Steinbach's swing was confused at times. He suddenly had trouble catching up with the fastballs that he hammered the year before, and he struggled in the clutch. Historically good with men on base, he fared poorly with runners in scoring position and had trouble lifting the ball for power. He did do well against lefthanders and, despite his problems, he was certainly better than his predecessors behind the plate, Matt Walbeck and Greg Myers.

Baserunning & Defense

Steinbach is very slow, as one would expect with a catcher, but he isn't a terrible baserunner. He managed to steal six bases and was only caught once. With the glove, he was all the Twins had hoped for. Steinbach captains the infield like the veteran he is, moves well behind the plate, frames pitches nicely and has a strong, if occasionally inaccurate, arm. He worked extremely well with some of the Twins' young pitchers, especially Brad Radke.

1998 Outlook

While 1997 was not one of Steinbach's best seasons, he remains quite valuable as a durable catcher who combines solid defense with occasional power. It's quite possible that with a year in a Twins uniform under his belt, he could regain his power stroke. It's also possible that his best seasons are behind him. Still, the Twins don't regret signing him, and he figures to be in the lineup nearly every day.

Position: C
Bats: R **Throws:** R
Ht: 6' 1" **Wt:** 195

Opening Day Age: 36
Born: 3/2/62 in New Ulm, MN
ML Seasons: 12

Overall Statistics

	G	AB	R	H	D	T	HR	RBI	SB	BB	SO	Avg	OBP	Slg
1997	122	447	60	111	27	1	12	54	6	35	106	.248	.302	.394
Career	1321	4609	558	1255	232	15	144	649	21	342	795	.272	.325	.423

Where He Hits the Ball

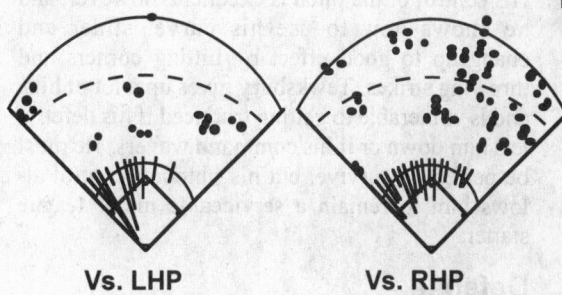

Vs. LHP   Vs. RHP

1997 Situational Stats

	AB	H	HR	RBI	Avg		AB	H	HR	RBI	Avg
Home	224	63	6	32	.281	LHP	117	36	4	18	.308
Road	223	48	6	22	.215	RHP	330	75	8	36	.227
First Half	242	66	8	38	.273	Sc Pos	127	26	2	40	.205
Scnd Half	205	45	4	16	.220	Clutch	61	12	1	6	.197

1997 Rankings (American League)

⇒ 3rd in lowest cleanup slugging percentage (.416)
⇒ 6th in lowest batting average with the bases loaded (.091) and highest fielding percentage at catcher (.993)
⇒ 7th in highest percentage of swings that missed (28.5%)
⇒ 8th in lowest batting average with runners in scoring position
⇒ 9th in errors at catcher (5)
⇒ 10th in lowest percentage of pitches taken (46.4%) and lowest percentage of extra bases taken as a runner (31.7%)
⇒ Led the Twins in GDPs (14) and cleanup slugging percentage (.416)

Bob Tewksbury

1997 Season

The Twins signed Bob Tewksbury as a free agent to bolster the staff for a wild-card run in 1997. The crafty veteran was extremely effective early in the season, but in mid-May he broke a pinky in the door of the team bus and landed on the disabled list. He returned before Memorial Day, but was bothered the rest of the way by a tender shoulder and by soreness in his back. He didn't pitch well in the second half, possibly as a result of the shoulder trouble, going just 4-6, 5.54 after the break.

Pitching

Tewksbury's fastball hits 87 MPH on a very good day. Most of the time he clocks in around 84 MPH. His control of the pitch is excellent, however, and he knows how to use his curve, slider and changeup to good effect by hitting corners and throwing strikes. Tewksbury gives up a lot of hits, and is vulnerable to getting trounced if his defense lets him down or if his command wavers. He must be perfect to survive, but his pinpoint control allows him to remain a serviceable major league starter.

Defense

Tewksbury isn't the best athlete around, and it shows when he fields bunts. His move to first is only average for a righthander. His delivery, while mechanically sound, is slow, leaving him susceptible to aggressive runners.

1998 Outlook

Despite his poor performance in the second half, the Twins like what Tewksbury did for them in 1997 and his overall ERA wasn't bad by current standards. He'll remain with the Twins after re-signing in early October, and the club will be more than pleased if he can make 25-30 starts in 1998. Manager Tom Kelly hopes that some of Tewksbury's guile will rub off on the team's younger pitchers.

Position: SP
Bats: R **Throws:** R
Ht: 6' 4" **Wt:** 205

Opening Day Age: 37
Born: 11/30/60 in Concord, NH
ML Seasons: 12
Pronunciation: TUKES-bury

Overall Statistics

	W	L	Pct.	ERA	G	GS	Sv	IP	H	BB	SO	HR	Ratio
1997	8	13	.381	4.22	26	26	0	168.2	200	31	92	12	1.37
Career	103	89	.536	3.84	276	252	1	1658.2	1869	272	752	123	1.29

How Often He Throws Strikes

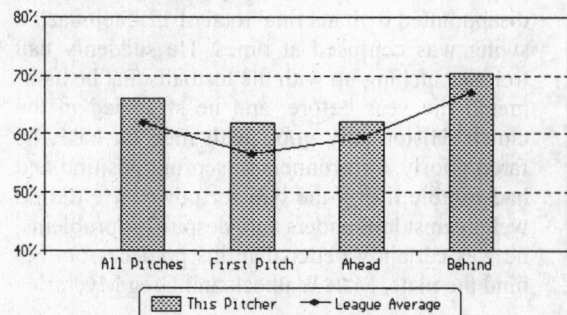

1997 Situational Stats

	W	L	ERA	Sv	IP		AB	H	HR	RBI	Avg
Home	3	7	4.44	0	77.0	LHB	351	108	6	41	.308
Road	5	6	4.03	0	91.2	RHB	323	92	6	34	.285
First Half	4	7	3.35	0	102.0	Sc Pos	171	55	4	64	.322
Scnd Half	4	6	5.54	0	66.2	Clutch	49	16	0	4	.327

1997 Rankings (American League)

⇒ 1st in least pitches thrown per batter (3.43) and in fielding percentage at pitcher (1.000)
⇒ 3rd in complete games (5), shutouts (2) and least run support per 9 innings (4.2)
⇒ 4th in highest batting average allowed (.297) and least home runs allowed per 9 innings (.64)
⇒ 5th in most GDPs induced per 9 innings (1.1) and highest batting average allowed with runners in scoring position
⇒ Led the Twins in losses, complete games (5), shutouts (2), GDPs induced (20), highest groundball/flyball ratio allowed (1.5), least pitches thrown per batter (3.43), least home runs allowed per 9 innings (.64) and most GDPs induced per 9 innings (1.1)

Todd Walker

1997 Season

Todd Walker was the preseason favorite for AL Rookie of the Year. Instead, he became Rookie Flop of the Year. He got off to a slow start, as is his norm, and began to press. Walker had difficulty sleeping, his swing deteriorated, and he ended up back in Triple-A Salt Lake. He played well in the minors, and when recalled in September he hit more like he was supposed to, with a .364 batting average and .591 slugging percentage.

Hitting

When Walker struggled in April and May, his timing looked off. He grounded out a lot, particularly with men on base, and had trouble with both breaking stuff and fastballs. Upon his return in September, his old stroke was back: short, sharp and sweet. Walker is hard to overpower and is seldom fooled by breaking stuff or changeups. He has excellent bat speed, and doesn't have the looping swing that did in former Twins phenom David McCarty. Despite his troubles last spring, Walker still projects as a successful major league hitter.

Baserunning & Defense

Walker isn't lightning fast, but he has refined his stealing technique: he stole seven bases in the majors without being caught. He's aggressive, has sound instincts and like most Twins will take the extra base from the defense. Manager Tom Kelly was critical of Walker's defense at third base, but his numbers there weren't bad. He doesn't have a strong arm, but his range factors and fielding percentage were above major league average. He was a second baseman in college and would move there should the Twins trade Chuck Knoblauch.

1998 Outlook

Walker has nothing left to prove in Triple-A and will be playing regularly in the Minnesota infield in 1998. Walker criticized the way he was handled by Kelly, who, in Walker's opinion, gave up on him too quickly. His frustration was understandable, but it probably wasn't wise to express it openly. Whatever the problems between Walker and Kelly, the front office still sees the youngster as a star in the making.

Position: 3B
Bats: L **Throws:** R
Ht: 6' 0" **Wt:** 170

Opening Day Age: 24
Born: 5/25/73 in Bakersfield, CA
ML Seasons: 2

Minnesota Twins

Overall Statistics

	G	AB	R	H	D	T	HR	RBI	SB	BB	SO	Avg	OBP	Slg
1997	52	156	15	37	7	1	3	16	7	11	30	.237	.288	.353
Career	77	238	23	58	13	1	3	22	9	15	43	.244	.286	.345

Where He Hits the Ball

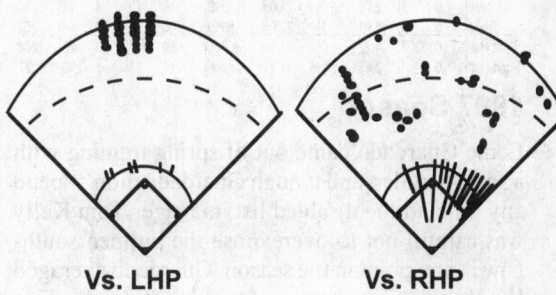

Vs. LHP   **Vs. RHP**

1997 Situational Stats

	AB	H	HR	RBI	Avg		AB	H	HR	RBI	Avg
Home	67	14	1	6	.209	LHP	14	5	0	3	.357
Road	89	23	2	10	.258	RHP	142	32	3	13	.225
First Half	108	21	1	6	.194	Sc Pos	47	10	1	13	.213
Scnd Half	48	16	2	10	.333	Clutch	23	8	0	2	.348

1997 Rankings (American League)

⇒ Did not rank near the top or bottom in any category

Eddie Guardado

Position: RP
Bats: R **Throws:** L
Ht: 6' 0" **Wt:** 193

Opening Day Age: 27
Born: 10/2/70 in
Stockton, CA
ML Seasons: 5
Pronunciation:
gwar-DAH-doe

Overall Statistics

	W	L	Pct.	ERA	G	GS	Sv	IP	H	BB	SO	HR	Ratio
1997	0	4	.000	3.91	69	0	1	46.0	45	17	54	7	1.35
Career	13	28	.317	5.47	226	25	7	322.2	354	135	253	48	1.52

1997 Situational Stats

	W	L	ERA	Sv	IP		AB	H	HR	RBI	Avg
Home	0	1	3.00	0	24.0	LHB	76	19	4	16	.250
Road	0	3	4.91	1	22.0	RHB	103	26	3	14	.252
First Half	0	3	4.22	0	21.1	Sc Pos	59	17	2	25	.288
Scnd Half	0	1	3.65	1	24.2	Clutch	47	13	2	9	.277

1997 Season

Eddie Guardado came out of spring training with a sore shoulder, and though Guardado didn't spend any time on the disabled list, manager Tom Kelly was careful not to overexpose the bullpen southpaw at any point in the season. Guardado averaged less than one inning per appearance, but was effective most of the time and finished the season healthy.

Pitching & Defense

Guardado has two good pitches, a 92-MPH fastball and a hard curve. The fastball has zip and he isn't afraid to throw it inside. The curve is a strikeout pitch but can be erratic. When he gives up home runs, it's usually because he hung a pitch. Guardado is generally effective against both lefties and righties, and his control is good. His mechanics are smooth and compact, and he can be difficult to steal against.

1998 Outlook

The last two seasons have established Guardado as a key member of the Minnesota bullpen. He continues to improve his consistency and control, and there's no reason to think he won't continue to be an effective pitcher as long as he remains healthy.

LaTroy Hawkins

Position: SP
Bats: R **Throws:** R
Ht: 6' 5" **Wt:** 193

Opening Day Age: 25
Born: 12/21/72 in
Gary, IN
ML Seasons: 3

Overall Statistics

	W	L	Pct.	ERA	G	GS	Sv	IP	H	BB	SO	HR	Ratio
1997	6	12	.333	5.84	20	20	0	103.1	134	47	58	19	1.75
Career	9	16	.360	6.72	33	32	0	156.2	215	68	91	30	1.81

1997 Situational Stats

	W	L	ERA	Sv	IP		AB	H	HR	RBI	Avg
Home	4	5	4.62	0	48.2	LHB	209	77	12	39	.368
Road	2	7	6.91	0	54.2	RHB	214	57	7	28	.266
First Half	1	4	4.78	0	26.1	Sc Pos	131	34	5	44	.260
Scnd Half	5	8	6.19	0	77.0	Clutch	8	1	0	0	.125

1997 Season

LaTroy Hawkins posted a 5.49 ERA in spring training, and found himself back at Triple-A Salt Lake to start the season. Hawkins criticized manager Tom Kelly and pitching coach Dick Such, leading to speculation that he might never pitch in Minneapolis again. He was recalled in June and spent the rest of the year in the rotation. Hawkins was occasionally impressive, but didn't do much to inspire the confidence of the coaching staff.

Pitching & Defense

Hawkins has the physical equipment to be a fine pitcher. His fastball, curve, slider and changeup are all major league quality. When he's sharp, Hawkins can hit spots with any of his pitches and make even the best hitters look foolish. When he isn't sharp, his fastball stays high in the zone, his breaking pitches hang and he gets knocked out quickly. Hawkins is a solid athlete and should develop into a fine defensive player with more experience. His move to first is average.

1998 Outlook

Hawkins enters 1998 the same way he entered 1997—as a big question mark. Will he gain some consistency and live up to the potential he showed in the minor leagues? After 32 major league starts, his career record stands at 9-16, 6.72.

Denny Hocking

Position: SS/2B/3B/RF
Bats: B **Throws:** R
Ht: 5'10" **Wt:** 174

Opening Day Age: 27
Born: 4/2/70 in Torrance, CA
ML Seasons: 5

Overall Statistics

	G	AB	R	H	D	T	HR	RBI	SB	BB	SO	Avg	OBP	Slg
1997	115	253	28	65	12	4	2	25	3	18	51	.257	.308	.360
Career	199	472	58	110	22	6	3	40	10	34	89	.233	.285	.324

1997 Situational Stats

	AB	H	HR	RBI	Avg		AB	H	HR	RBI	Avg
Home	95	27	0	9	.284	LHP	84	26	1	9	.310
Road	158	38	2	16	.241	RHP	169	39	1	16	.231
First Half	112	31	1	13	.277	Sc Pos	72	23	1	23	.319
Scnd Half	141	34	1	12	.241	Clutch	45	11	0	2	.244

1997 Season

Denny Hocking was Minnesota's jack-of-all-trades in 1997. He proved a worthy successor to Al Newman and Jeff Reboulet in the role, showing excellent defensive versatility, hustle and occasional sparks of offense.

Hitting, Baserunning & Defense

Hocking is a switch-hitter who's more effective from the right side. His impatience limits his on-base percentage, but he has some punch into the gaps and is capable of intermittent hot streaks. Though he's not much of a basestealer, he runs well and served as the Twins' primary pinch runner. Hocking's strongest attribute is his multipurpose glove. He can play all the infield positions very well and can handle the outfield without hurting the team. He also can catch in an emergency.

1998 Outlook

Manager Tom Kelly loves to have a guy like Hocking around. Newman and Reboulet lasted for years in Minnesota in similar roles. Hocking would have more value if he demonstrated more patience at the plate, but his defensive skills and hustle should keep him around for at least another season.

Dan Naulty

Position: RP
Bats: R **Throws:** R
Ht: 6'6" **Wt:** 211

Opening Day Age: 28
Born: 1/6/70 in Los Angeles, CA
ML Seasons: 2
Pronunciation: NAWL-tee

Overall Statistics

	W	L	Pct.	ERA	G	GS	Sv	IP	H	BB	SO	HR	Ratio
1997	1	1	.500	5.87	29	0	1	30.2	29	10	23	8	1.27
Career	4	3	.571	4.52	78	0	5	87.2	72	45	79	13	1.33

1997 Situational Stats

	W	L	ERA	Sv	IP		AB	H	HR	RBI	Avg
Home	1	1	5.25	1	12.0	LHB	41	11	4	10	.268
Road	0	0	6.27	0	18.2	RHB	73	18	4	13	.247
First Half	1	1	4.87	1	20.1	Sc Pos	43	7	2	15	.163
Scnd Half	0	0	7.84	0	10.1	Clutch	29	7	2	9	.241

1997 Season

Dan Naulty's 1996 rookie season was cut short by surgery to repair a problem with the blood flow to the muscles in his arm when he pitched. He recovered quickly and opened 1997 with the major league team, but went on the disabled list in May with a strained muscle on his right side. He didn't return until late in the season.

Pitching & Defense

When healthy, Naulty can dominate hitters with a 92-MPH fastball that bores in on righthanders, a hard slider, and a nasty forkball. Although his pitches had natural sink in 1996, he threw high in the zone in 1997 and was touched for eight homers. His control showed improvement, however. Naulty is mobile for a big guy, but his delivery is awkward and leaves him susceptible to the stolen base. He can field his position adequately.

1998 Outlook

When Naulty is healthy, he has the stuff and demeanor of a major league closer, though he needs to improve his command and keep his pitches low. To do that, he needs innings and experience. His future depends largely on the health of his arm.

Todd Ritchie

Position: RP
Bats: R **Throws:** R
Ht: 6' 3" **Wt:** 205

Opening Day Age: 26
Born: 11/7/71 in Portsmouth, VA
ML Seasons: 1

Overall Statistics

	W	L	Pct.	ERA	G	GS	Sv	IP	H	BB	SO	HR	Ratio
1997	2	3	.400	4.58	42	0	0	74.2	87	28	44	11	1.54
Career	2	3	.400	4.58	42	0	0	74.2	87	28	44	11	1.54

1997 Situational Stats

	W	L	ERA	Sv	IP		AB	H	HR	RBI	Avg
Home	1	0	3.91	0	46.0	LHB	110	24	8	18	.218
Road	1	3	5.65	0	28.2	RHB	190	63	3	23	.332
First Half	2	3	5.08	0	33.2	Sc Pos	88	21	2	29	.239
Scnd Half	0	0	4.17	0	41.0	Clutch	12	4	0	1	.333

1997 Season

A first-round pick in 1990, Todd Ritchie made the Twins in '97 because he was out of options and the team didn't want to lose him on waivers. After a minor league career plagued with injuries and inconsistency, Ritchie wasn't outstanding in his first major league season, but he wasn't terrible either. Manager Tom Kelly used Ritchie in long and middle relief, and he showed enough to give hope that he may eventually move beyond those roles.

Pitching & Defense

Ritchie has a fastball clocked around 93 MPH. He also has a sharp breaking pitch with nice movement, though he doesn't always have command of it. His changeup is mediocre at best, and he doesn't vary speeds consistently, leaving him best suited for bullpen work. He's also vulnerable to the gopher ball. His control was better than expected, but he grooves pitches when behind in the count and gives up hits. Ritchie is a fine athlete and a solid fielder.

1998 Outlook

Ritchie has the arm to move beyond the obscurity of the bullpen, though whether he has the command is another question. He'll probably make the staff again in 1998, and with improvement could move into a more critical role.

Rich Robertson

Position: SP/RP
Bats: L **Throws:** L
Ht: 6' 4" **Wt:** 175

Opening Day Age: 29
Born: 9/15/68 in Nacogdoches, TX
ML Seasons: 5

Overall Statistics

	W	L	Pct.	ERA	G	GS	Sv	IP	H	BB	SO	HR	Ratio
1997	8	12	.400	5.69	31	26	0	147.0	169	70	69	19	1.63
Career	17	30	.362	5.25	109	61	0	409.2	449	231	234	47	1.66

1997 Situational Stats

	W	L	ERA	Sv	IP		AB	H	HR	RBI	Avg
Home	5	7	6.42	0	82.2	LHB	116	39	2	20	.336
Road	3	5	4.76	0	64.1	RHB	463	130	17	65	.281
First Half	7	6	5.36	0	90.2	Sc Pos	143	44	6	66	.308
Scnd Half	1	6	6.23	0	56.1	Clutch	18	6	0	3	.333

1997 Season

Rich Robertson was either very good or very bad in 1996, but in 1997 he was mostly just bad. He stayed in the rotation for most of the season, but that was mainly because manager Tom Kelly and pitching coach Dick Such lacked confidence in farm products such as Dan Serafini and Travis Miller. Robertson was never effective for any length of time and ended the season in the bullpen.

Pitching & Defense

Robertson doesn't have great stuff, nor does he possess great command. That's a bad combination. He works with a fastball, slider, curve and change, but none of these pitches is outstanding. When he throws strikes he can get people out, but the trouble is he has finished with more walks than strikeouts for two consecutive years. No pitcher can survive such a poor ratio, especially not a finesse guy. Robertson is athletic but makes more fielding mistakes than he should. His move to first is average.

1998 Outlook

Robertson's major league career is on the line. The Twins have been patient with him, but haven't been rewarded. Miller and Serafini are nearly ready, so Robertson's days are numbered unless he shows sudden and dramatic improvement.

Greg Swindell

Position: RP
Bats: R **Throws:** L
Ht: 6' 3" **Wt:** 225

Opening Day Age: 33
Born: 1/2/65 in Fort Worth, TX
ML Seasons: 12
Pronunciation: swin-DELL

Overall Statistics

	W	L	Pct.	ERA	G	GS	Sv	IP	H	BB	SO	HR	Ratio
1997	7	4	.636	3.58	65	1	1	115.2	102	25	75	12	1.10
Career	110	102	.519	3.88	358	269	1	1915.2	2007	416	1299	213	1.26

1997 Situational Stats

	W	L	ERA	Sv	IP		AB	H	HR	RBI	Avg
Home	3	2	3.79	1	57.0	LHB	152	31	1	17	.204
Road	4	2	3.38	0	58.2	RHB	276	71	11	39	.257
First Half	4	2	3.97	0	59.0	Sc Pos	106	31	2	42	.292
Scnd Half	3	2	3.18	1	56.2	Clutch	138	31	4	18	.225

1997 Season

The Twins picked up free agent Greg Swindell before spring training, hoping that they could breathe some life into his moribund career. Swindell made the club, then exceeded everyone's expectations with a fine season out of the pen, establishing himself as a viable lefthanded option. He was consistent, durable and quite effective.

Pitching & Defense

Swindell was in his best physical shape in years in 1997, and the result was better stuff. His fastball had more life than it had shown in recent years, and his slider was much sharper. He adapted well to the bullpen role, showed a surprisingly resilient arm and was deadly against lefthanded hitters. Although Swindell did make one start, manager Tom Kelly resisted the temptation to put him in the rotation, and Swindell said he enjoyed the relief role. His defense is only adequate, though his pick-off move shuts down the running game.

1998 Outlook

Swindell isn't the first pitcher that Kelly and pitching coach Dick Such have picked off the reject pile and revived. Swindell will return to Minnesota, but there's no guarantee of a repeat performance. Relief pitchers who throw more than 100 innings in relief one season tend to struggle the next.

Mike Trombley

Position: RP
Bats: R **Throws:** R
Ht: 6' 2" **Wt:** 206

Opening Day Age: 30
Born: 4/14/67 in Springfield, MA
ML Seasons: 6
Pronunciation: TROM-blee

Overall Statistics

	W	L	Pct.	ERA	G	GS	Sv	IP	H	BB	SO	HR	Ratio
1997	2	3	.400	4.37	67	0	1	82.1	77	31	74	7	1.31
Career	22	20	.524	4.66	208	35	9	457.2	475	174	354	57	1.42

1997 Situational Stats

	W	L	ERA	Sv	IP		AB	H	HR	RBI	Avg
Home	0	1	4.78	1	43.1	LHB	109	23	2	13	.211
Road	2	2	3.92	0	39.0	RHB	202	54	5	26	.267
First Half	1	1	4.14	0	50.0	Sc Pos	91	26	2	31	.286
Scnd Half	1	2	4.73	1	32.1	Clutch	84	14	0	7	.167

1997 Season

The big question for Mike Trombley entering 1997 was whether he could repeat his solid 1996 performance and hold on to a spot on the staff. Though he wasn't quite as effective as he was the previous season, Trombley did throw well enough to not only hold his job, but also to remain the Twins' primary righthanded option in middle relief.

Pitching & Defense

Trombley has a slightly above-average fastball, but his two key pitches are a wicked curveball and a good split-fingered offering. The curve is useful against righthanders, while the splitter makes him effective against lefties. He keeps his stuff down, gets ground balls and isn't susceptible to the home run. Trombley stays healthy and can pitch on consecutive days without losing velocity or command. He's not especially good at holding basestealers, as they've gone 21 of 25 against him the past three seasons, but he fields his position adequately.

1998 Outlook

Trombley has proven his worth in the bullpen, and barring injury or trade, that's where he'll be in 1998. He doesn't dominate, but he's generally steady, consistent and dependable.

Other Minnesota Twins

Scott Aldred (**Pos**: LHP, **Age**: 29)

	W	L	Pct.	ERA	G	GS	Sv	IP	H	BB	SO	HR	Ratio
1997	2	10	.167	7.68	17	15	0	77.1	102	28	33	20	1.68
Career	15	33	.313	6.44	92	67	0	391.1	466	179	229	72	1.65

Aldred began the year in the Twins' rotation, pitched horribly, and was sent to Triple-A Salt Lake City in June. He continued to struggle and probably pitched his way out of the Twins' plans. 1998 Outlook: C

Shane Bowers (**Pos**: RHP, **Age**: 26)

	W	L	Pct.	ERA	G	GS	Sv	IP	H	BB	SO	HR	Ratio
1997	0	3	.000	8.05	5	5	0	19.0	27	8	7	2	1.84
Career	0	3	.000	8.05	5	5	0	19.0	27	8	7	2	1.84

Bowers doesn't throw hard, but he has a 40-21 career record in the minors. Given five starts by the Twins last year, he got lit up, but will probably get another chance. 1998 Outlook: C

Chris Latham (**Pos**: CF, **Age**: 24, **Bats**: B)

	G	AB	R	H	D	T	HR	RBI	SB	BB	SO	Avg	OBP	Slg
1997	15	22	4	4	1	0	0	1	0	0	8	.182	.182	.227
Career	15	22	4	4	1	0	0	1	0	0	8	.182	.182	.227

An ex-Dodger farmhand, Latham played pretty well at Triple-A Salt Lake City. He didn't show much in two brief stints with the Twins, but he has excellent speed and can get on base. 1998 Outlook: B

Minnesota Twins Minor League Prospects

Organization Overview:

As a small-revenue franchise, the Twins can't afford to go out and buy players. They didn't when they were winning World Series in 1987 and 1991, and they haven't since. Instead, Minnesota quietly has produced a number of major leaguers. Six of the nine regulars in its lineup and three of the its top five starters in 1997 were homegrown products. The Twins' development success tends to get overlooked because its top prospects tend to fail miserably. Remember Pat Mahomes and David McCarty? More recently, LaTroy Hawkins and Todd Walker have had little success, though Walker still looks like a keeper. The system would be even better had Minnesota been able to sign several premium draft picks who got away. Most notable among that group is first baseman Travis Lee, a 1996 first-round draft pick who became a free agent after a contract snafu and signed with the Arizona Diamondbacks for $10 million.

Jason Bell

Position: P   **Opening Day Age:** 23
Bats: R **Throws:** R   **Born:** 9/30/74 in Ocala,
Ht: 6' 3" **Wt:** 208   FL

Recent Statistics

	W	L	ERA	G	GS	Sv	IP	H	R	BB	SO	HR
96 A Ft. Myers	6	3	1.69	13	13	0	90.1	61	20	22	83	1
96 AA New Britain	2	6	4.40	16	16	0	94.0	93	54	38	94	13
97 AA New Britain	11	9	3.39	28	28	0	164.2	163	71	64	142	19

Bell was drafted in the second round in 1995 out of Oklahoma State not so much for his stuff as for his polish. His fastball averages 88 MPH, below the major league standard, but he mixes it well with a curveball and changeup and throws all three pitches for strikes. He keeps the ball down in the strike zone, getting a lot of ground balls. As a pro, he never has allowed more than a hit per inning and always has maintained a strikeout/walk ratio of greater than 2/1. His stuff isn't as good as some of the other pitching prospects in the system, but those guys can't match Bell's track record.

Torii Hunter

Position: OF   **Opening Day Age:** 22
Bats: R **Throws:** R   **Born:** 7/18/75 in Pine
Ht: 6' 2" **Wt:** 205   Bluff, AR

Recent Statistics

	G	AB	R	H	D	T	HR	RBI	SB	BB	SO	AVG
97 AA New Britain	127	471	57	109	22	2	8	56	8	47	94	.231
97 AL Minnesota	1	0	0	0	0	0	0	0	0	0	0	-
97 MLE	127	464	51	102	21	1	7	50	6	36	103	.220

A first-round pick in 1993, Hunter has yet to catch up to his potential. He has five-tool talent, yet never has hit better than .293 or totaled more than 10 homers or eight steals in a single season. He still struggles with offspeed pitches. To be fair, it must be noted that he has spent the last two years in one of the best pitchers' parks in the minors and is still just 22. He's much more accomplished defensively, showing center-field range and a right-field arm. The Twins are willing to be patient, which is what Hunter needs.

Jacque Jones

Position: OF   **Opening Day Age:** 22
Bats: L **Throws:** L   **Born:** 4/25/75 in San
Ht: 5' 10" **Wt:** 175   Diego, CA

Recent Statistics

	G	AB	R	H	D	T	HR	RBI	SB	BB	SO	AVG
96 A Ft. Myers	1	3	0	2	1	0	0	1	0	0	0	.667
97 A Ft. Myers	131	539	84	160	33	6	15	82	24	33	110	.297

If Hunter doesn't get going, Jones could pass him quickly as Minnesota's center fielder of the future. A second-round pick in 1996 out of the University of Southern California, his pro debut was delayed first by the Olympics and then by a strained knee ligament. His only exceptional tool is a quick bat, and he could become quite a hitter if he learns to draw a walk. His power is more to the gaps rather than over the fence, and he runs well but isn't a blazer. He can go get balls in center, and his arm is fine.

Travis Miller

Position: P   **Opening Day Age:** 25
Bats: R **Throws:** L   **Born:** 11/2/72 in
Ht: 6' 3" **Wt:** 205   Dayton, OH

Recent Statistics

	W	L	ERA	G	GS	Sv	IP	H	R	BB	SO	HR
97 AAA Salt Lake	10	6	4.73	21	21	0	125.2	140	73	57	86	11
97 AL Minnesota	1	5	7.63	13	7	0	48.1	64	49	23	26	8

Miller is one of several Twins pitching prospects who have struggled to make the jump from pitcher-friendly New Britain in Double-A to hitter-friendly Salt Lake in Triple-A. He has been bombed in Minnesota as well, going 2-7 the past two seasons. A supplemental first-round pick in 1994 out of Kent University, he uses a slider as his out pitch and has an average fastball. He needs to get ahead of hitters and stop leaving his fastball up in the strike zone. The upcoming season is an important one for Miller, who has failed his first two opportunities to show he can start in the major leagues.

David Ortiz

Position: 1B   **Opening Day Age:** 22
Bats: L **Throws:** L   **Born:** 11/18/75 in Santo
Ht: 6' 4" **Wt:** 230   Domingo, DR

Recent Statistics

	G	AB	R	H	D	T	HR	RBI	SB	BB	SO	AVG
97 A Ft. Myers	61	239	45	79	15	0	13	58	2	22	53	.331
97 AA New Britain	69	258	40	83	22	2	14	56	2	21	78	.322
97 AAA Salt Lake	10	42	5	9	1	0	4	10	0	2	11	.214
97 AL Minnesota	15	49	10	16	3	0	1	6	0	2	19	.327
97 MLE	79	293	39	85	21	1	16	57	1	17	97	.290

The Twins traded Dave Hollins to the Mariners in 1996, primarily to clear the way for Todd Walker at third base. As a bonus they got first baseman David Arias, who was signed out of the Dominican Republic and had begun to emerge as a power hitter with 18 homers in Class-A. Arias changed his surname to Ortiz in 1997 and developed even more power, hitting a total of 32 homers as he went from high Class-A Fort Myers to Minnesota. He's not much of a first baseman or a runner, but he doesn't need to be. His aggressive power is just what the Twins need, and he conceivably could start for them at some point in 1998.

Mark Redman

Position: P   **Opening Day Age:** 24
Bats: L **Throws:** L   **Born:** 1/5/74 in San
Ht: 6' 5" **Wt:** 220   Diego, CA

Recent Statistics

	W	L	ERA	G	GS	Sv	IP	H	R	BB	SO	HR
96 A Ft. Myers	3	4	1.85	13	13	0	82.2	63	24	34	75	1
96 AA New Britain	7	7	3.81	16	16	0	106.1	101	51	50	96	5
96 AAA Salt Lake	0	0	9.00	1	1	0	4.0	7	4	2	4	1
97 AAA Salt Lake	8	15	6.31	29	28	1	158.1	204	123	80	125	19

Redman is another Twins pitcher who hasn't been able to repeat his Double-A success in Triple-A. His ERA at Salt Lake was more than double what he had posted since being a first-round pick in 1995 out of the University of Oklahoma, where he pitched the Sooners to the 1994 College World Series championship. His top pitch is an outstanding changeup. His fastball has below-average velocity, but in the past he could locate it well enough to make it effective. His command slipped in 1997, which hurt him, as did a lackluster curveball that he doesn't have much confidence in. He needs a full year in Triple-A to re-establish himself.

Dan Serafini

Position: P   **Opening Day Age:** 24
Bats: B **Throws:** L   **Born:** 1/25/74 in San
Ht: 6' 1" **Wt:** 185   Francisco, CA

Recent Statistics

	W	L	ERA	G	GS	Sv	IP	H	R	BB	SO	HR
97 AAA Salt Lake	9	7	4.97	28	24	0	152.0	166	87	55	118	18
97 AL Minnesota	2	1	3.42	6	4	0	26.1	27	11	11	15	1

Add Serafini to the list of Twins lefthanders who have had difficulty making the climb to Triple-A. Unlike the others, however, he has maintained a good strike-out/walk ratio, which means he could be the best of the group. A first-round pick in 1992, he mixes three effective pitches. He has an average fastball, a curveball with good bite and a very good changeup. He has better stuff than Miller and Redman, and he was effective during a September call-up. He also has an excellent pickoff move that shuts down the running game. If the Twins have a rotation opening for a youngster in 1998, Serafini would be the logical choice.

Javier Valentin

Position: C   **Opening Day Age:** 22
Bats: B **Throws:** R   **Born:** 9/19/75 in
Ht: 5' 10" **Wt:** 191   Manati, PR

Recent Statistics

	G	AB	R	H	D	T	HR	RBI	SB	BB	SO	AVG
97 AA New Britain	102	370	41	90	17	0	8	50	2	30	61	.243
97 AL Minnesota	4	7	1	2	0	0	0	0	0	0	3	.286
97 MLE	102	364	37	84	16	0	7	45	1	23	68	.231

A third-round pick in 1993, Valentin originally went by Jose, which caused confusion because his brother Jose plays shortstop for the Brewers. He emerged as a prospect in 1995, when he hit .324 with 19 homers at Class-A Fort Wayne, but hasn't hit nearly as well since. Part of the problem is the park in New Britain, but he also isn't selective enough at the plate. His best asset is being a switch-hitter with power, but he also has a good arm. He could become a solid defensive player if he improves his blocking, calling and receiving. He has advanced quickly for a 22 year old, and probably is two years away from full-time duty in Minnesota.

Others to Watch

Hard-nosed left fielder **Chad Allen**, 23, played with Jones on the 1996 U.S. Olympic team. He sprays line drives to all fields and is a decent athlete. . . The Twins picked up outfielder **Marc Lewis**, 22, from Atlanta as the player to be named in the Greg Colbrunn trade. He has solid offensive tools, but he rarely draws a walk. . . Righthander **Dan Perkins**, 23, is a three-pitch pitcher with an average fastball and good command. He was hampered in 1997 by shoulder stiffness. . . **A.J. Pierzynski**, 21, has a good bat and decent power for a catcher. His arm is average, and he is still learning behind the plate. . . Outfielder **Ryan Radmanovich** (28 homers) and first baseman **Chad Rupp** (32 homers) battered Triple-A pitching, but get little mention as prospects because they're 26. Radmanovich has the better future, because he's lefthanded, has a quicker bat and is versatile enough to also play first and third. . . **Luis Rivas** didn't turn 18 until late August, but he was named the best defensive shortstop and infield arm in the Class-A Midwest League. He was overmatched at the plate, but he has outstanding speed and bears watching.

Joe Torre

1997 Season

In many ways, Joe Torre did a better job in 1997 than he had the year before, when he guided the Yankees to a World Series title. Despite constant on- and off-field distractions and several injuries, the 1997 Yankees won more games than they had in their championship year. Torre displayed the steady calm needed to manage in the Bronx and didn't back down from doing what he felt was best for the club. He was willing to bench a veteran like Wade Boggs or ride the hot hand of a reserve like Chad Curtis.

Offense

Torre prefers to grind things out one run at a time with bunts and hit-and-runs. He also recognizes that the Yankees don't have a lot of speed and thus he more often relied on the big-bang components of his lineup. He'll usually play a slugger over a glove man in his lineups. He also looked for ways to accomodate both Tim Raines and Derek Jeter in the same lineup, keeping Raines in his traditional leadoff role and looking for a spot for Jeter. The shuffling didn't work out for Jeter.

Pitching & Defense

Patience was needed early when closer Mariano Rivera and the whole bullpen got off to a brutal start. Torre's patience was rewarded when the relief corps turned into a strength. When he has the available flexibility, Torre will try to take advantage of platoon matchups with his relievers. He also tried to be careful with Rivera, monitoring his use so as not to overwork the young closer.

1998 Outlook

No manager has handled working for the impetuous George Steinbrenner better than Torre. In 1997 he felt the owner's wrath for the first time, and Torre's ability to maintain a steady hand will likely be tested even more this year. He remains a perfect man for the toughest job in baseball.

Born: 7/18/40 in Brooklyn, NY

Playing Experience: 1960-1977, Atl, StL, NYN

Managerial Experience: 16 seasons

Pronunciation: TORE-ee

Manager Statistics

Year	Team, Lg	W	L	Pct	GB	Finish
1997	New York, AL	96	66	.593	2.0	2nd East
16 Seasons		1082	1139	.486	—	—

1997 Starting Pitchers by Days Rest

	≤3	4	5	6+
Yankees Starts	5	90	35	24
Yankees ERA	5.34	3.68	4.65	4.43
AL Avg Starts	5	89	34	24
AL ERA	4.38	4.60	4.61	5.37

1997 Situational Stats

	Joe Torre	AL Average
Hit & Run Success %	46.4	36.5
Stolen Base Success %	63.1	67.3
Platoon Pct.	60.8	59.5
Defensive Subs	23	22
High-Pitch Outings	19	15
Quick/Slow Hooks	18/12	19/15
Sacrifice Attempts	54	53

1997 Rankings (American League)

⇒ 1st in least caught steals of home plate (0), hit-and-run percentage (46.4%) and saves with over 1 inning pitched (14)

⇒ 2nd in squeeze plays (3) and 2+ pitching changes in low scoring games (32)

⇒ 3rd in starts with over 120 pitches (19) and starts on three days rest (5)

Wade Boggs

1997 Season

For only the second time in 16 years, Wade Boggs failed to bat .300. He was benched on a number of occasions, becoming a part-time player for the first time since his rookie season. He did have a solid finish, batting .362 after the All-Star break and .417 in September.

Hitting

Boggs still shows flashes of his uncanny ability to serve singles into left field as if on automatic pilot. But for the first time in his career, he had extended stretches in which he was pulling off pitches and making weak contact. He was so helpless at certain times that there were concerns that he was suffering from vision problems. He also had fastballs thrown by him more often than at any time in memory. He still was his old self in terms of plate discipline. He took a lot of pitches and made contact almost every time he swung. His power is largely limited to very isolated pulled shots to right. He tore up lefthanders in 1997, though he was often platooned with Charlie Hayes.

Baserunning & Defense

Never an above-average runner, Boggs is even more hampered these days because of persistent leg problems. His range similarly has been weakened in the field, where he had some problems moving to his left in 1997. He takes few chances in terms of stolen bases or extra bases. He remains surehanded on balls he does reach and has a very accurate arm.

1998 Outlook

New York cut Boggs loose after the season, leaving him exactly 200 hits short of the 3,000-hit plateau. With his durability questionable and his lack of run production a handicap at the hot corner, he could have difficulty getting the necessary opportunities to reach the milestone. His best opportunity may come from his hometown team, the expansion Tampa Bay Devil Rays.

Position: 3B/DH
Bats: L **Throws:** R
Ht: 6' 2"   **Wt:** 197

Opening Day Age: 39
Born: 6/15/58 in Omaha, NE
ML Seasons: 16

Overall Statistics

	G	AB	R	H	D	T	HR	RBI	SB	BB	SO	Avg	OBP	Slg
1997	103	353	55	103	23	1	4	28	0	48	38	.292	.373	.397
Career	2227	8453	1422	2800	541	56	109	933	20	1328	668	.331	.420	.447

Where He Hits the Ball

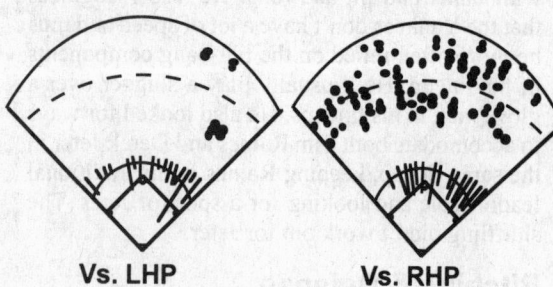

Vs. LHP   **Vs. RHP**

1997 Situational Stats

	AB	H	HR	RBI	Avg		AB	H	HR	RBI	Avg
Home	157	45	0	5	.287	LHP	72	26	1	4	.361
Road	196	58	4	23	.296	RHP	281	77	3	24	.274
First Half	204	49	2	16	.240	Sc Pos	84	20	1	25	.238
Scnd Half	149	54	2	12	.362	Clutch	57	11	0	4	.193

1997 Rankings (American League)

⇒ 2nd in lowest percentage of swings that missed (7.4%) and highest percentage of swings put into play (55.3%)

⇒ 3rd in highest percentage of pitches taken (64.9%) and lowest percentage of extra bases taken as a runner (27.7%)

⇒ 5th in least GDPs per GDP situation (4.0%)

⇒ 10th in lowest batting average in the clutch

⇒ Led the Yankees in least GDPs per GDP situation (4.0%), highest percentage of pitches taken (64.9%), lowest percentage of swings that missed (7.4%) and highest percentage of swings put into play (55.3%)

David Cone

Position: SP
Bats: L **Throws:** R
Ht: 6' 1" **Wt:** 190

Opening Day Age: 35
Born: 1/2/63 in Kansas City, MO
ML Seasons: 12

1997 Season

Until his season was disrupted in mid-August by shoulder problems, David Cone was on his way to another dominating year, cruising along at a 17-win, 250-strikeout pace. He returned to make two abbreviated starts in late September, but bombed in his only postseason start. His shoulder ended up needing only minor repairs, and his solid four months of pitching proved that he had made a full recovery from career-threatening aneurysm surgery the year before.

Pitching

Until his tender shoulder became a problem, Cone was nasty as ever. He continues to throw in the low 90s and can make his fastball hit spots with varying movement and from varying release points. His splitter is one of baseball's best. He mixes in a curve that he throws at two speeds. He can throw it hard with a quick, short break or take a little off and snap off one with a bigger break. He throws fewer sliders than he once did but has gained growing confidence in a cut fastball that can hit 90 MPH. Hitters have a difficult time doing anything with him. They batted just .218 against him in 1997, including a .213 mark by lefthanders.

Defense

Cone has never been adept at holding runners and remains vulnerable to stolen bases. He gave up 22 steals in 30 attempts in 1997, and also helped runners with 14 wild pitches. He's an excellent athlete, but his aggressive delivery often forces him to fall out of fielding position. He also is sometimes prone to mental lapses in the field because he's so focused on his pitching.

1998 Outlook

Early reports on Cone's physical condition have been very positive. Assuming he's fully recovered, he should again be one of the game's premier pitchers and someone the Yankees can count on for 15-20 wins. If healthy, he teams with Andy Pettitte to give New York a pair of aces.

Overall Statistics

	W	L	Pct.	ERA	G	GS	Sv	IP	H	BB	SO	HR	Ratio
1997	12	6	.667	2.82	29	29	0	195.0	155	86	222	17	1.24
Career	148	86	.632	3.13	328	299	1	2189.0	1794	836	2034	171	1.20

How Often He Throws Strikes

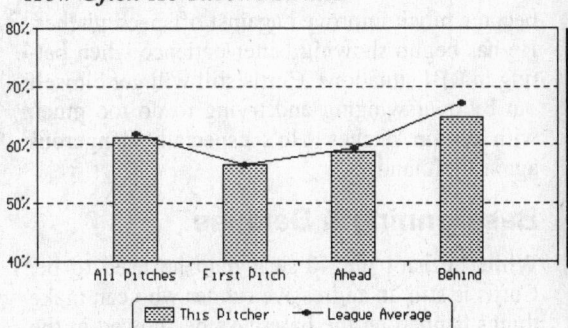

1997 Situational Stats

	W	L	ERA	Sv	IP			AB	H	HR	RBI	Avg
Home	5	2	3.20	0	90.0	LHB		371	79	11	31	.213
Road	7	4	2.49	0	105.0	RHB		339	76	6	29	.224
First Half	8	4	2.55	0	134.1	Sc Pos		163	36	4	44	.221
Scnd Half	4	2	3.41	0	60.2	Clutch		73	21	1	6	.288

1997 Rankings (American League)

⇒ 1st in wild pitches (14) and ERA on the road
⇒ 2nd in least GDPs induced per 9 innings (0.4), most strikeouts per 9 innings (10.2) and lowest batting average allowed vs. lefthanded batters
⇒ 3rd in ERA, strikeouts and lowest batting average allowed (.218)
⇒ Led the Yankees in ERA, walks allowed, strikeouts, wild pitches (14), stolen bases allowed (22), runners caught stealing (8), lowest batting average allowed (.218), lowest slugging percentage allowed (.332), lowest on-base percentage allowed (.305), most strikeouts per 9 innings (10.2), ERA on the road, lowest batting average allowed vs. lefthanded batters and lowest batting average allowed vs. righthanded batters

Chad Curtis

1997 Season

Acquired from Cleveland in early June, Chad Curtis quickly became very valuable to the Yankees. First he was a part-time left fielder, and later he played in center during Bernie Williams' extended down time. He hit so well that he remained a semi-regular even after Williams and Tim Raines returned to the lineup later in the year.

Hitting

Curtis always has had a big swing for a small man, and some believe that his home-run cut has kept him from reaching his potential as a hitter. He'll often chase high fastballs, but he's very dangerous on balls down in the strike zone. He also has become much improved against offspeed pitches. He has begun showing better patience when batting in RBI situations. Curtis still will get himself out by overswinging and trying to do too much with certain pitches. He's especially dangerous against lefthanders.

Baserunning & Defense

While he isn't the 40-steal man he used to be, Curtis is still an aggressive runner who can make things happen on the bases. As he showed in the Division Series against Cleveland, he'll go to any length to break up a double play. As an outfielder, Curtis is sometimes spectacular and sometimes suspect. He still gets to more balls than most outfielders, especially in left where his range is exceptional. He's good at charging grounders and coming up throwing, which makes his strong arm all the more effective.

1998 Outlook

The Yankees liked Curtis' down-and-dirty approach to the game, and his offense was an unexpected plus. New York was quick to pick up his contract option. He should get plenty of work in left field and serve as Williams' caddy in center.

Position: LF/CF
Bats: R **Throws:** R
Ht: 5'10" **Wt:** 175

Opening Day Age: 29
Born: 11/6/68 in Marion, IN
ML Seasons: 6

Overall Statistics

	G	AB	R	H	D	T	HR	RBI	SB	BB	SO	Avg	OBP	Slg
1997	115	349	59	99	22	1	15	55	12	43	59	.284	.362	.481
Career	811	2916	460	779	140	14	75	323	173	341	469	.267	.346	.402

Where He Hits the Ball

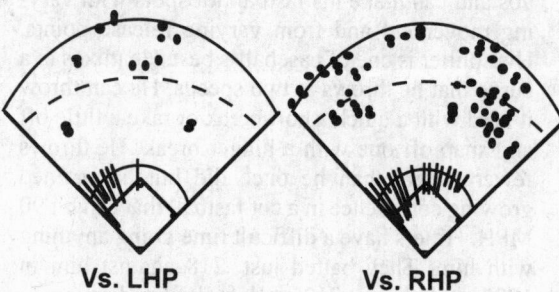

Vs. LHP   Vs. RHP

1997 Situational Stats

	AB	H	HR	RBI	Avg		AB	H	HR	RBI	Avg
Home	149	42	4	19	.282	LHP	105	33	4	18	.314
Road	200	57	11	36	.285	RHP	244	66	11	37	.270
First Half	100	24	5	14	.240	Sc Pos	85	25	3	40	.294
Scnd Half	249	75	10	41	.301	Clutch	45	13	3	6	.289

1997 Rankings (American League)

⇒ 2nd in lowest batting average on an 0-2 count (.032)

Cecil Fielder

1997 Season

Already struggling to escape the worst power drought of his career, Cecil Fielder tore ligaments in his thumb on July 15. The injury required surgery and sidelined him for two months. He returned in September to add three more homers, including the 300th of his career.

Hitting

Fielder seemed to become too enamored with the praise he received during the 1996 postseason for his ability to line opposite-field singles in RBI situations. Because he tried to go the other way so much, his hands slowed down and he was jammed by fastballs he used to drive. Pitchers seemed to catch on to his new approach, and the bigger the situation the more they exploited it to Fielder's disadvantage. Still prone to fishing for breaking balls, he also had difficulty regaining the lift needed for his trademark moonshot homers. Fielder's patience and plate coverage are nice improvements, but he's paid to hit longballs and didn't do that nearly often enough in 1997. He also made poor contact for someone using a singles approach. Usually murder on lefthanders, he batted a feeble .211 with one homer in 90 at-bats against them last year.

Baserunning & Defense

It was odd that Fielder was injured on a slide at the plate, because there have been few more sedentary baserunners in recent years. He's in poor shape, making his dismal speed even worse. He started only eight games at first base in 1997. Though he still possesses soft hands, he's virtually immobile and basically is a designated hitter.

1998 Outlook

A free agent, Fielder killed his market value with his poor season. He could have difficulty finding a team willing to gamble on his girth and declining numbers. Odds seemed to favor him heading back to Japan for a second tour of duty.

Position: DH
Bats: R **Throws:** R
Ht: 6' 3" **Wt:** 250

Opening Day Age: 34
Born: 9/21/63 in Los Angeles, CA
ML Seasons: 12
Nickname: Big Daddy

Overall Statistics

	G	AB	R	H	D	T	HR	RBI	SB	BB	SO	Avg	OBP	Slg
1997	98	361	40	94	15	0	13	61	0	51	87	.260	.358	.410
Career	1353	4741	695	1216	183	6	302	940	2	640	1205	.256	.347	.489

Where He Hits the Ball

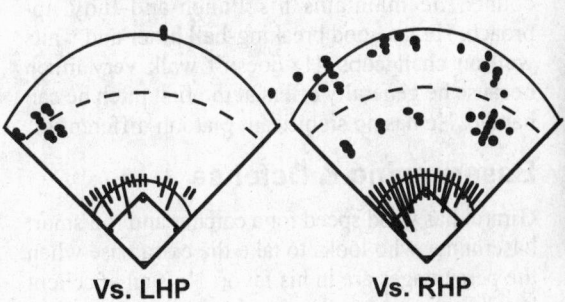

Vs. LHP   **Vs. RHP**

1997 Situational Stats

	AB	H	HR	RBI	Avg		AB	H	HR	RBI	Avg
Home	191	53	6	28	.277	LHP	90	19	1	7	.211
Road	170	41	7	33	.241	RHP	271	75	12	54	.277
First Half	301	78	10	50	.259	Sc Pos	110	28	4	49	.255
Scnd Half	60	16	3	11	.267	Clutch	50	12	1	5	.240

1997 Rankings (American League)

⇒ 5th in lowest percentage of swings put into play (34.4%)
⇒ 8th in highest percentage of swings that missed (27.9%)

Joe Girardi

1997 Season

For the second straight year, Joe Girardi was an important part of the Yankees' nucleus. He was a tough hitter in the clutch and reliably handled a very volatile pitching staff. One low point was that he missed nearly three weeks in September with a broken finger, an injury that bothered him in the postseason.

Hitting

Girardi doesn't have the bat speed to hit for power or battle hard stuff. He's often overmatched by good fastballs. He has made himself into a decent hitter by concentrating on making contact and hitting the ball where it's pitched. Even on hitters' counts, he maintains his Punch-and-Judy approach. He's a good breaking-ball hitter and waits well on changeups. He doesn't walk very much because he generally offers at the first pitch he can handle. He has no significant platoon differential.

Baserunning & Defense

Girardi has good speed for a catcher and is a smart baserunner who looks to take the extra base when the percentages are in his favor. He's an excellent handler of pitchers. The Yankees had a 3.44 ERA with Girardi behind the plate in 1997, compared to 4.68 with backup Jorge Posada. Girardi also has solid skills in blocking balls and framing pitches. A jammed right shoulder suffered in May affected his throwing for the rest of the 1997 season. At his best, Girardi has no cannon but does have a quick release and is accurate. He threw out 34 percent of basestealers last year, slightly above the major league average.

1998 Outlook

Though his playing time may suffer as young catcher Jorge Posada continues to develop, Girardi is one of manager Joe Torre's favorite players. He always will have a key role with this club as long as he remains healthy. The Yankees consider him an extra coach on the field and view whatever he adds offensively as a bonus.

Position: C
Bats: R **Throws:** R
Ht: 5'11" **Wt:** 195

Opening Day Age: 33
Born: 10/14/64 in Peoria, IL
ML Seasons: 9
Pronunciation: jeh-RAR-dee

Overall Statistics

	G	AB	R	H	D	T	HR	RBI	SB	BB	SO	Avg	OBP	Slg
1997	112	398	38	105	23	1	1	50	2	26	53	.264	.311	.334
Career	844	2815	311	765	124	18	21	285	37	183	393	.272	.319	.351

Where He Hits the Ball

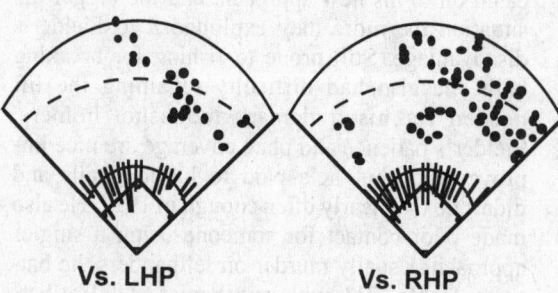

Vs. LHP   Vs. RHP

1997 Situational Stats

	AB	H	HR	RBI	Avg		AB	H	HR	RBI	Avg
Home	198	56	1	24	.283	LHP	103	26	0	11	.252
Road	200	49	0	26	.245	RHP	295	79	1	39	.268
First Half	219	59	1	29	.269	Sc Pos	122	41	0	47	.336
Scnd Half	179	46	0	21	.257	Clutch	71	19	1	9	.268

1997 Rankings (American League)

⇒ 4th in fielding percentage at catcher (.994)
⇒ 9th in errors at catcher (5)

Charlie Hayes

1997 Season

After catching the last out of the 1996 World Series, Charlie Hayes woke up to cold, hard reality in 1997. He had his share of big hits, but spent most of the year fighting Wade Boggs for the third-base job. Hayes found himself in the lineup half the time and in the doghouse just as often.

Hitting

Hayes has solid power. When he's patient and works counts in his favor, he can be a dangerous hitter who can drive the ball to left or right-center. That patience rarely manifests itself, though. He has difficulty maintaining concentration and will fall into stretches where he'll chase high fastballs and breaking balls out of the strike zone. He's dangerous enough against lefthanders to be a decent platoon player, but recently hasn't hit righties well enough to hold onto a regular job.

Baserunning & Defense

When he's interested, Hayes shows above-average baserunning skills and occasionally can steal a base. When he does go, however, his percentage of success is mediocre. He also fell into disfavor with manager Joe Torre in 1997 when he didn't run out several balls. Hayes can be spectacular in the field with his solid range, soft hands and excellent arm. He also can be erratic and mess up routine plays, especially in crucial situations. He also will become too casual with his throws, which accounts for the majority of his errors.

1998 Outlook

After the season, the Yankees traded Hayes to San Francisco for minor league outfielder Chris Singleton. With the Giants, Hayes will compete with Bill Mueller and Mark Lewis for the third-base job. San Francisco will be Hayes' fifth team in five years. If he doesn't improve his hustle and his performance against righthanders, his career could be coming to an end soon.

Position: 3B
Bats: R **Throws:** R
Ht: 6' 0" **Wt:** 224

Opening Day Age: 32
Born: 5/29/65 in Hattiesburg, MS
ML Seasons: 10

Overall Statistics

	G	AB	R	H	D	T	HR	RBI	SB	BB	SO	Avg	OBP	Slg
1997	100	353	39	91	16	0	11	53	3	40	66	.258	.332	.397
Career	1189	4249	458	1128	215	15	117	580	41	289	716	.265	.313	.406

Where He Hits the Ball

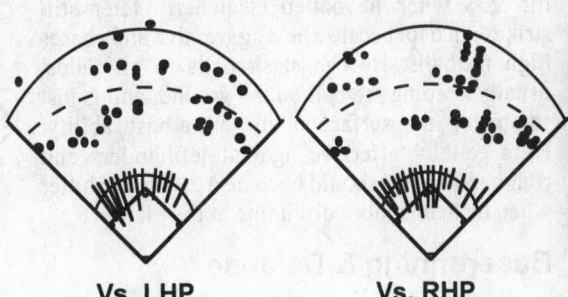

Vs. LHP   **Vs. RHP**

1997 Situational Stats

	AB	H	HR	RBI	Avg		AB	H	HR	RBI	Avg
Home	182	49	5	26	.269	LHP	135	42	8	29	.311
Road	171	42	6	27	.246	RHP	218	49	3	24	.225
First Half	141	39	6	21	.277	Sc Pos	107	22	2	38	.206
Scnd Half	212	52	5	32	.245	Clutch	55	17	5	16	.309

1997 Rankings (American League)

⇒ 7th in lowest batting average on a 3-1 count (.100)
⇒ 8th in errors at third base (13)
⇒ 10th in lowest batting average with runners in scoring position

Derek Jeter

1997 Season

Though his numbers suffered because he was moved around in the batting order, Derek Jeter put together a very solid second season as the Yankees' shortstop. He became only the third player ever to score 100 runs in his first two seasons and was again among the most durable middle infielders in baseball.

Hitting

Manager Joe Torre keeps resisting the idea that Jeter belongs in the leadoff spot, perhaps because of his extra-base potential. But Jeter is clearly more comfortable leading off, and batted .321 with a .394 on-base percentage in that role in 1997. He hit .233 when he batted elsewhere. Jeter still strikes out a lot because he's aggressive and chases high fastballs. He can slash balls to all fields, usually keeping the ball on the ground, and is just scratching the surface of his extra-base ability. He's equally effective against lefthanders and righthanders. He should become a 20-homer hitter when he learns more discipline at the plate.

Baserunning & Defense

Jeter has excellent natural speed and is improving steadily as a basestealer. In 1997, he led the Yankees in swipes and became more efficient as the season wore on. He has outstanding range at shortstop, soft hands and a great feel for situations. He turns the double play well with his strong arm. His throwing does get erratic at times.

1998 Outlook

Jeter's makeup hasn't changed despite his early success. He plays like a veteran in many ways. He's driven to improve and is just beginning to mature physically. With Tim Raines expected to depart New York, Jeter could become a full-time leadoff man in 1998. At a position loaded with remarkable young talent, he holds his own with anyone. He and Seattle's Alex Rodriguez should compete for All-Star berths for the next decade or so.

Position: SS
Bats: R **Throws:** R
Ht: 6' 3" **Wt:** 185

Opening Day Age: 23
Born: 6/26/74 in Pequannock, NJ
ML Seasons: 3
Pronunciation: JEE-ter

Overall Statistics

	G	AB	R	H	D	T	HR	RBI	SB	BB	SO	Avg	OBP	Slg
1997	159	654	116	190	31	7	10	70	23	74	125	.291	.370	.405
Career	331	1284	225	385	60	14	20	155	37	125	238	.300	.368	.415

Where He Hits the Ball

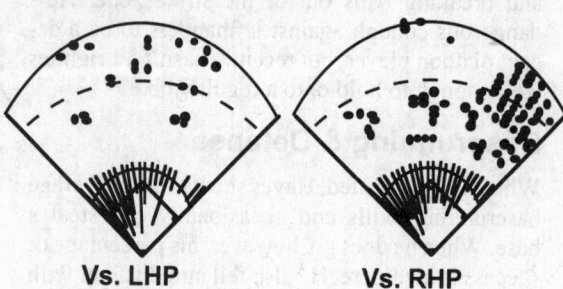

Vs. LHP   Vs. RHP

1997 Situational Stats

	AB	H	HR	RBI	Avg		AB	H	HR	RBI	Avg
Home	313	89	5	39	.284	LHP	169	49	5	21	.290
Road	341	101	5	31	.296	RHP	485	141	5	49	.291
First Half	347	99	4	37	.285	Sc Pos	149	34	2	57	.228
Scnd Half	307	91	6	33	.296	Clutch	99	27	3	14	.273

1997 Rankings (American League)

⇒ 1st in singles, pitches seen (2,923) and plate appearances (748)
⇒ 2nd in highest groundball/flyball ratio (3.0)
⇒ 3rd in at-bats, hits and on-base percentage for a leadoff hitter (.394)
⇒ 4th in runs scored and games played (159)
⇒ 5th in triples and times on base (274)
⇒ Led the Yankees in at-bats, runs scored, hits, singles, triples, sacrifice bunts (8), stolen bases, caught stealing (12), hit by pitch (10), times on base (274), strikeouts, pitches seen (2,923), plate appearances (748), games played (159), highest groundball/flyball ratio (3.0), stolen base percentage (65.7%), most pitches seen per plate appearance (3.91) and bunts in play (14)

Tino Martinez

1997 Season

One of 1997's true superstars was Tino Martinez. He had one of the greatest power seasons in modern Yankees history. He had more RBI than any Yankee since Don Mattingly had 145 in 1985, and his 44 home runs were the most by any Yankee in 36 years. He erased any doubts that he would be able to replace Mattingly, and may be just as good as Donnie Baseball was in his prime.

Hitting

Martinez got into an early home-run groove, hitting 12 homers in his first 30 games, and he stayed locked in for months. He has moved up on the plate slightly and has become exceptionally quick on inside hard stuff. Only a handful of pitchers are willing to try to crowd him any longer. Martinez was especially tough with men on base, with 13 of his homers being three-run shots or grand slams. He can be pitched away with breaking balls, but he generally makes good contact and lays off bad pitches. He always has hit southpaws well for a lefthanded swinger, with little reduction in power.

Baserunning & Defense

With below-average speed, Martinez is no threat to steal. He's a smart baserunner, however, and can take an extra base. He has improved as a first baseman to the point where his defense has become an asset. His range is ordinary, but he has soft hands and a very accurate arm.

1998 Outlook

Already among the better players at one of baseball's deepest positions, Martinez put up numbers that rank with the elite. His challenge will be continuing at the same level. Though he's unlikely to ever match his 1997 homer total, he's a good bet to be a 100-RBI man for several years.

Position: 1B
Bats: L **Throws:** R
Ht: 6' 2" **Wt:** 210

Opening Day Age: 30
Born: 12/7/67 in Tampa, FL
ML Seasons: 8

New York Yankees

Overall Statistics

	G	AB	R	H	D	T	HR	RBI	SB	BB	SO	Avg	OBP	Slg
1997	158	594	96	176	31	2	44	141	3	75	75	.296	.371	.577
Career	856	3085	428	852	165	8	157	570	8	341	469	.276	.347	.488

Where He Hits the Ball

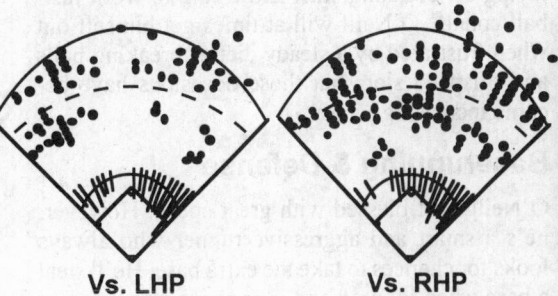

Vs. LHP   **Vs. RHP**

1997 Situational Stats

	AB	H	HR	RBI	Avg		AB	H	HR	RBI	Avg
Home	280	79	18	63	.282	LHP	231	62	12	55	.268
Road	314	97	26	78	.309	RHP	363	114	32	86	.314
First Half	331	100	28	78	.302	Sc Pos	186	59	15	105	.317
Scnd Half	263	76	16	63	.289	Clutch	90	34	8	22	.378

1997 Rankings (American League)

⇒ 1st in sacrifice flies (13)
⇒ 2nd in home runs and RBI
⇒ 3rd in total bases (343) and slugging percentage vs. righthanded pitchers (.636)
⇒ 4th in intentional walks (14), HR frequency (13.5 ABs per HR), batting average in the clutch and fielding percentage at first base (.994)
⇒ Led the Yankees in home runs, total bases (343), RBI, sacrifice flies (13), walks, intentional walks (14), slugging percentage, HR frequency (13.5 ABs per HR), batting average in the clutch, cleanup slugging percentage (.559), slugging percentage vs. righthanded pitchers (.636) and lowest percentage of swings on the first pitch (17.7%)

Paul O'Neill

1997 Season

There are few more quietly productive players in the American League than Paul O'Neill, who kept his game at its usual high level in 1997. He established a career high with 117 RBI, led the majors with a .428 average with men in scoring position and stayed remarkably consistent all year.

Hitting

One of the game's great fastball hitters, O'Neill can turn on inside heat and smash it to right or take hard stuff away and drive it with power to left-center. He also waits well on offspeed stuff. In 1997, he reversed a two-year trend of struggling against lefthanders by being more patient about laying off breaking stuff and trying to work fast-ball counts. O'Neill will at times get himself out when frustrated by a steady diet of breaking balls and offspeed slop, but those occasions have become increasingly rare.

Baserunning & Defense

O'Neill isn't blessed with great speed. However, he's a smart and aggressive runner who always looks for chances to take the extra base. He'll steal a base when ignored and is as tough as anyone in breaking up double plays. O'Neill had five errors in 1997, an unusually high number for him, and all but one came on throws. He remains a quality right fielder with a strong arm. He's one of the most fundamentally sound right fielders in baseball, and almost never misjudges a ball or allows one to get past him.

1998 Outlook

O'Neill has hinted that after his contract expires in 1998, he might consider retirement. Whatever happens, he's in his prime as one of baseball's best hitters and one of the Yankees' true gamers. He leads by example with his intensity and ability to produce consistently in the clutch. He'll likely remain one of New York's most underrated and most irreplaceable players.

Position: RF
Bats: L **Throws:** L
Ht: 6' 4" **Wt:** 215

Opening Day Age: 35
Born: 2/25/63 in Columbus, OH
ML Seasons: 13

Overall Statistics

	G	AB	R	H	D	T	HR	RBI	SB	BB	SO	Avg	OBP	Slg
1997	149	553	89	179	42	0	21	117	10	75	92	.324	.399	.514
Career	1469	5043	720	1448	313	14	199	873	79	670	825	.287	.369	.473

Where He Hits the Ball

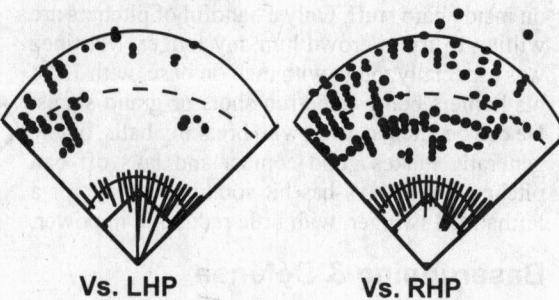

Vs. LHP   **Vs. RHP**

1997 Situational Stats

	AB	H	HR	RBI	Avg			AB	H	HR	RBI	Avg
Home	263	81	10	53	.308		LHP	189	53	4	33	.280
Road	290	98	11	64	.338		RHP	364	126	17	84	.346
First Half	288	90	11	56	.313		Sc Pos	159	68	9	101	.428
Scnd Half	265	89	10	61	.336		Clutch	83	28	2	19	.337

1997 Rankings (American League)

⇒ 1st in batting average with runners in scoring position
⇒ 2nd in batting average vs. righthanded pitchers and fielding percentage in right field (.984)
⇒ 3rd in batting average with two strikes (.273)
⇒ 4th in batting average on the road
⇒ 5th in doubles, batting average on an 0-2 count (.292), on-base percentage vs. righthanded pitchers (.427) and errors in right field (5)
⇒ Led the Yankees in doubles, walks, GDPs (16), batting average with runners in scoring position, batting average vs. righthanded pitchers, batting average on an 0-2 count (.292), on-base percentage vs. righthanded pitchers (.427), batting average at home, batting average with two strikes (.273) and steals of third (2)

Andy Pettitte

1997 Season

Though he didn't match his 21 wins from the year before, Andy Pettitte cut almost a full run off his ERA in 1997 and further established himself as the Yankees' ace. The only negative was a back problem that bothered him late in the year. He didn't win in the final two weeks and didn't pitch well in the postseason.

Pitching

When Pettitte is on, there are few tougher left-handers in the game. He has two fastballs which both are in the 90s, a quick-breaking hard curve, and a slider that can be devastating to righthanders. He gets in trouble when he starts getting breaking balls up in the strike zone, especially to lefthanders. That problem was aggravated by his back troubles, which kept him from keeping his pitches down. Pettitte has excellent control of all his pitches. Because he usually stays ahead of hitters, he usually can get the ball into the closer's hands without going beyond the 120-pitch mark.

Defense

One of the most devastating defensive weapons in baseball is Pettitte's pickoff move, the best in the game. Even baserunners who know it's coming can be tricked. He used the move to pick off 14 men, five more than anyone else in baseball. Pettitte is an excellent athlete with quick defensive reactions and is one of the better fielding pitchers in the American League.

1998 Outlook

Pettitte is a special player, a hugely talented pitcher who is similar to Atlanta's Greg Maddux in his competitive fire and pursuit of perfection. Pettitte is also just entering his prime. Given good health, he stands poised to produce around 20 wins a year for a while. Among active pitchers with 50 or more wins, only Baltimore's Mike Mussina can top Pettitte's .680 winning percentage.

Position: SP
Bats: L **Throws:** L
Ht: 6' 5" **Wt:** 235

Opening Day Age: 25
Born: 6/15/72 in Baton Rouge, LA
ML Seasons: 3
Pronunciation: PET-it

Overall Statistics

	W	L	Pct.	ERA	G	GS	Sv	IP	H	BB	SO	HR	Ratio
1997	18	7	.720	2.88	35	35	0	240.1	233	65	166	7	1.24
Career	51	24	.680	3.58	101	95	0	636.1	645	200	442	45	1.33

How Often He Throws Strikes

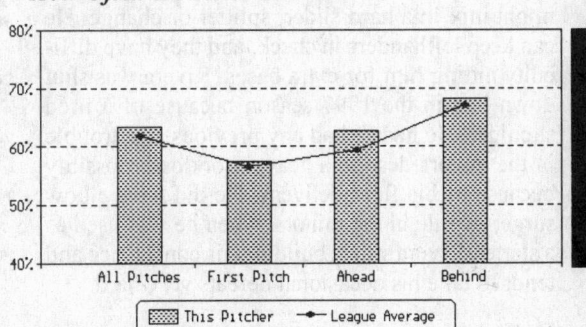

This Pitcher ▬▬ League Average

1997 Situational Stats

	W	L	ERA	Sv	IP		AB	H	HR	RBI	Avg
Home	9	4	2.65	0	118.2	LHB	193	62	1	24	.321
Road	9	3	3.11	0	121.2	RHB	717	171	6	48	.238
First Half	9	5	3.10	0	133.2	Sc Pos	202	56	0	63	.277
Scnd Half	9	2	2.62	0	106.2	Clutch	71	27	0	14	.380

1997 Rankings (American League)

⇒ 1st in games started, GDPs induced (36) and least home runs allowed per 9 innings (.26)
⇒ 2nd in most GDPs induced per 9 innings (1.3)
⇒ 3rd in innings pitched, most run support per 9 innings (6.5) and ERA at home
⇒ Led the Yankees in wins, games started, innings pitched, batters faced (986), pitches thrown (3,629), pickoff throws (211), GDPs induced (36), winning percentage, highest ground-ball/flyball ratio allowed (2.1), lowest stolen base percentage allowed (69.6%), least baserunners allowed per 9 innings (11.3), most run support per 9 innings (6.5), least home runs allowed per 9 innings (.26), most GDPs induced per 9 innings (1.3), most GDPs induced per GDP situation (18.1%) and ERA at home

Mariano Rivera

1997 Season

Yes, he gave up the big Division Series homer to Sandy Alomar that helped send the Yankees on their way out of the postseason. However, Mariano Rivera was otherwise a huge success in his first season as a major league closer. He finished second in the majors with 43 saves, and blew only three opportunities in the second half.

Pitching

Rivera comes hard at every hitter with his rising fastball that routinely reaches the mid-90s. It's one of the best heaters in the game, and few hitters can adjust to it. He'll stray from throwing gas only when his fastball lacks its usual hop. Then he might mix in a hard slider, splitter or change. He can keep lefthanders in check, and they have difficulty hitting him for extra bases. Rivera was shut down late in the 1997 season because of a tired shoulder. He hadn't had any previous arm trouble in the majors despite a heavy workload, possibly because of his fluid delivery. He did have elbow surgery while in the minors, when he was used as a starter. Rivera still is building his confidence and tends to take his occasional defeats very hard.

Defense

The slightly built Rivera is as quick off the mound as any pitcher in the game. He has few equals at fielding bunts. As a closer he usually doesn't have to worry about baserunners. They have had success against him, going 3-for-3 in 1997 and 11-for-14 in his career.

1998 Outlook

Though George Steinbrenner might have grumbled at the playoff failure, it's hard to have anything bad to say about Rivera. He proved more than capable of being New York's closer and he should become even better as he acquires more mental toughness.

Position: RP
Bats: R **Throws:** R
Ht: 6' 2" **Wt:** 168

Opening Day Age: 28
Born: 11/29/69 in Panama City, Panama
ML Seasons: 3

Overall Statistics

	W	L	Pct.	ERA	G	GS	Sv	IP	H	BB	SO	HR	Ratio
1997	6	4	.600	1.88	66	0	43	71.2	65	20	68	5	1.19
Career	19	10	.655	2.96	146	10	48	246.1	209	84	249	17	1.19

How Often He Throws Strikes

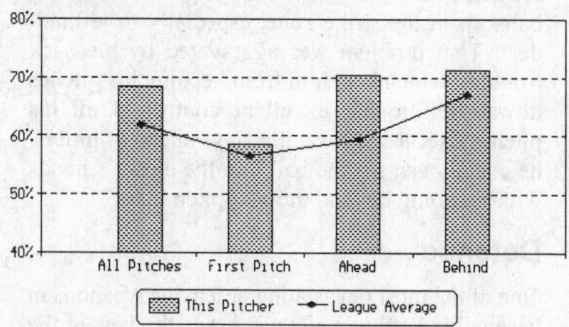

1997 Situational Stats

	W	L	ERA	Sv	IP		AB	H	HR	RBI	Avg
Home	4	3	2.25	23	40.0	LHB	152	37	1	4	.243
Road	2	1	1.42	20	31.2	RHB	122	28	4	15	.230
First Half	2	2	1.96	27	41.1	Sc Pos	73	11	0	13	.151
Scnd Half	4	2	1.78	16	30.1	Clutch	214	52	5	19	.243

1997 Rankings (American League)

⇒ 1st in save opportunities (52)
⇒ 2nd in saves, blown saves (9) and relief ERA (1.88)
⇒ Led the Yankees in saves, games finished (56), save opportunities (52), save percentage (82.7%), blown saves (9), lowest batting average allowed in relief with runners on base (.202), lowest batting average allowed in relief with runners in scoring position (.151), relief ERA (1.88), relief wins (6) and least baserunners allowed per 9 innings in relief (10.7)

Mike Stanley

1997 Season

Mike Stanley's return to New York didn't produce many dividends. After a solid start as a DH and occasional first baseman for the Red Sox, Stanley saw only part-time duty with the Yankees over the final two months. He remained a dangerous hitter, but his value took a dive as physical problems preventing him from catching.

Hitting

Stanley is a good, professional hitter. He handles most fastballs and is willing to take pitches to the opposite field and drive them with power, a big plus for a righthanded hitter playing in Yankee Stadium. He also has excellent power to left and center. He's a disciplined hitter against breaking balls and isn't prone to chasing many pitches outside the strike zone. He does his best hitting when he's able to work the count in his favor and look for a certain pitch. He's always at his best in big situations.

Baserunning & Defense

Shoulder and back problems may have put an end to Stanley's days as a catcher. Even in the best of health, he was never a top-notch backstop. If he does catch now, it likely would be only in an emergency situation. He demonstrated fair ability at first base, where he has decent hands. However, his range is poor and on the few occasions he was forced to throw, he had trouble making the toss to second base. He has below-average speed and is no more than a station-to-station runner.

1998 Outlook

New York may rue parting with pitching prospect Tony Armas Jr. to acquire Stanley, who became a free agent after the season. His future lies as a first baseman or a DH, and thus his marketability could be limited. As a veteran run producer, he should be able to find a job, though his return to the Yankees was uncertain.

Position: DH/C/1B
Bats: R **Throws:** R
Ht: 6' 0" **Wt:** 190

Opening Day Age: 34
Born: 6/25/63 in Ft. Lauderdale, FL
ML Seasons: 12

Overall Statistics

	G	AB	R	H	D	T	HR	RBI	SB	BB	SO	Avg	OBP	Slg
1997	125	347	61	103	25	0	16	65	0	54	72	.297	.393	.507
Career	1096	3016	459	824	161	7	125	505	10	456	641	.273	.370	.456

Where He Hits the Ball

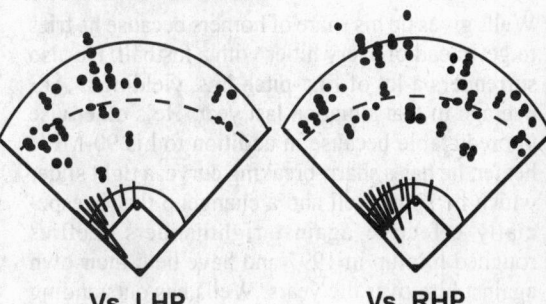

Vs. LHP   **Vs. RHP**

1997 Situational Stats

	AB	H	HR	RBI	Avg		AB	H	HR	RBI	Avg
Home	183	54	6	25	.295	LHP	144	44	6	26	.306
Road	164	49	10	40	.299	RHP	203	59	10	39	.291
First Half	188	60	9	40	.319	Sc Pos	100	35	7	51	.350
Scnd Half	159	43	7	25	.270	Clutch	57	12	1	10	.211

1997 Rankings (American League)

⇒ 4th in lowest percentage of extra bases taken as a runner (27.9%)
⇒ 6th in batting average with runners in scoring position (.350)
⇒ 9th in on-base percentage vs. lefthanded pitchers (.424)
⇒ 10th in lowest batting average on an 0-2 count (.067)

David Wells

1997 Season

The 1997 season was a wild ride for David Wells, who was brought in as a free agent. He had an offseason bar fight in which he broke a finger, brought the infamous Mark Furhman to an Opening Day workout, asked to wear Babe Ruth's retired number 3, and offered to punch out George Steinbrenner. However, Wells survived it all to give the Yankees all they could ask for as a solid No. 3 starter. His 16 wins ranked second on the club and he was able to post a won-lost record identical to that of the man he traded places with, Baltimore's Jimmy Key.

Pitching

Wells gives up his share of homers because he tries to get ahead of every hitter with a fastball. He also surrenders a lot of first-pitch hits, yielding a .413 average in that situation last year. He's otherwise unpredictable because in addition to his 90-MPH heater, he has a sharp-breaking curve, a tight slider which he spots well and a changeup that is especially effective against righthanders. Lefties roughed him up in 1997 and have held their own against him over the years. Wells has outstanding control with all his pitches and maintains his stuff deep into games.

Defense

Wells doesn't look much like a professional athlete and does little to dispel that impression with his fielding. He has no effective move to first, he's slow to the plate and he doesn't field his position consistently. He committed four errors in 1997, more than anyone else on the Yankees' staff.

1998 Outlook

The Yankees hardly are enamored with Wells' off-field activities and conditioning. But he takes the ball, eats innings and wins games, and those are qualities that force management to overlook much of the extraneous distractions. It seems that he'll have to pitch his way out of New York, which he isn't likely to do anytime soon.

Position: SP
Bats: L **Throws:** L
Ht: 6' 4"   **Wt:** 225

Opening Day Age: 34
Born: 5/20/63 in Torrance, CA
ML Seasons: 11

Overall Statistics

	W	L	Pct.	ERA	G	GS	Sv	IP	H	BB	SO	HR	Ratio
1997	16	10	.615	4.21	32	32	0	218.0	239	45	156	24	1.30
Career	106	85	.555	4.02	380	210	13	1631.0	1635	416	1078	189	1.26

How Often He Throws Strikes

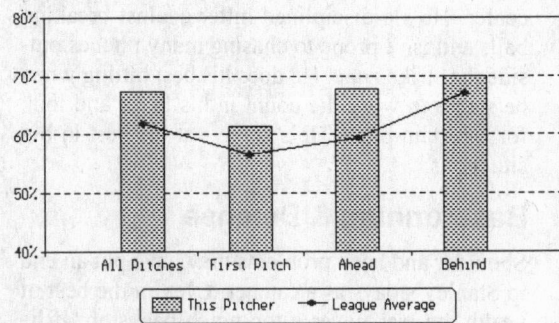

1997 Situational Stats

	W	L	ERA	Sv	IP		AB	H	HR	RBI	Avg
Home	8	5	3.88	0	116.0	LHB	159	52	3	22	.327
Road	8	5	4.59	0	102.0	RHB	702	187	21	78	.266
First Half	9	4	3.82	0	113.0	Sc Pos	209	50	8	74	.239
Scnd Half	7	6	4.63	0	105.0	Clutch	77	22	2	9	.286

1997 Rankings (American League)

⇒ 3rd in complete games (5), shutouts (2) and least pitches thrown per batter (3.52)
⇒ 5th in errors at pitcher (4) and lowest fielding percentage at pitcher (.902)
⇒ 6th in wins and highest strikeout/walk ratio (3.5)
⇒ 7th in hits allowed
⇒ 8th in least GDPs induced per 9 innings (0.5)
⇒ 9th in lowest batting average allowed with runners in scoring position
⇒ 10th in batters faced (922)
⇒ Led the Yankees in losses, complete games (5), shutouts (2), hits allowed, home runs allowed, runners caught stealing (8), highest strikeout/walk ratio (3.5) and least pitches thrown per batter (3.52)

Bernie Williams

Gold Glover

1997 Season

Bernie Williams fought through a persistent hamstring problem to put up another outstanding season as the Yankees' center fielder. After being hampered by injuries for nearly six weeks in June and July, Williams got healthy in the second half and was all but unstoppable down the stretch.

Hitting

Though the switch-hitting Williams has better pure power from the right side, he's a very complete hitter who bats well over .300 from both sides of the plate. As he has matured, he has become a much more selective hitter and increased his walk totals. A good fastball hitter, Williams tends to go to the opposite field more from the left side. He's more easily overpowered by righthanders. Against lefties, he's one of the most dangerous hitters in the game. Used as a leadoff man earlier in his career, he has settled into the No. 3 spot in New York's order.

Baserunning & Defense

Williams has become a more active basestealer. His speed makes him a potential 30-steal player, though he likely never will run enough with the Yankees to reach that level. He also doesn't have quite the success that his speed would indicate he should. He's a superb center fielder and won his first Gold Glove in 1997. He has excellent range and good instincts that allow him to get fine jumps on most balls. He has one of the best center-field arms in the game.

1998 Outlook

Ordinarily, no team would be willing to part with a player of Williams' skill and character. The Yankees, however, are never ordinary. He has become embroiled in a messy contract dispute with George Steinbrenner, so Williams' future in New York isn't etched in stone. Wherever he plays, he'll remain one of the most complete players in the game.

Position: CF
Bats: B **Throws:** R
Ht: 6' 2" **Wt:** 205

Opening Day Age: 29
Born: 9/13/68 in San Juan, PR
ML Seasons: 7

Overall Statistics

	G	AB	R	H	D	T	HR	RBI	SB	BB	SO	Avg	OBP	Slg
1997	129	509	107	167	35	6	21	100	15	73	80	.328	.408	.544
Career	810	3179	537	927	183	33	100	469	82	421	503	.292	.374	.464

Where He Hits the Ball

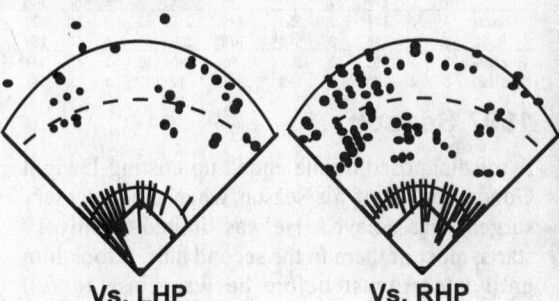

Vs. LHP   **Vs. RHP**

1997 Situational Stats

	AB	H	HR	RBI	Avg		AB	H	HR	RBI	Avg
Home	240	72	13	43	.300	LHP	141	46	9	32	.326
Road	269	95	8	57	.353	RHP	368	121	12	68	.329
First Half	278	85	10	51	.306	Sc Pos	161	54	6	79	.335
Scnd Half	231	82	11	49	.355	Clutch	80	20	2	13	.250

1997 Rankings (American League)

⇒ 2nd in batting average on the road
⇒ 3rd in fielding percentage in center field (.993)
⇒ 4th in batting average and on-base percentage vs. lefthanded pitchers (.443)
⇒ Led the Yankees in batting average, on-base percentage, batting average with the bases loaded (.438), batting average vs. lefthanded pitchers, batting average on a 3-1 count (.600), slugging percentage vs. lefthanded pitchers (.596), on-base percentage vs. lefthanded pitchers (.443), batting average on a 3-2 count (.340), batting average on the road and highest percentage of extra bases taken as a runner (53.3%)

New York Yankees

Dwight Gooden

Position: SP
Bats: R **Throws:** R
Ht: 6' 3" **Wt:** 210

Opening Day Age: 33
Born: 11/16/64 in
Tampa, FL
ML Seasons: 13
Nickname: Doc, Dr. K

Overall Statistics

	W	L	Pct.	ERA	G	GS	Sv	IP	H	BB	SO	HR	Ratio
1997	9	5	.643	4.91	20	19	0	106.1	116	53	66	14	1.59
Career	177	97	.646	3.31	354	351	1	2446.2	2183	792	2067	156	1.22

1997 Situational Stats

	W	L	ERA	Sv	IP		AB	H	HR	RBI	Avg
Home	4	3	3.74	0	55.1	LHB	211	63	8	27	.299
Road	5	2	6.18	0	51.0	RHB	199	53	6	27	.266
First Half	3	1	2.93	0	30.2	Sc Pos	90	30	3	41	.333
Scnd Half	6	4	5.71	0	75.2	Clutch	12	2	1	3	.167

1997 Season

A misdiagnosed hernia ended up costing Dwight Gooden much of his season when the necessary surgery was delayed. He was limited to only 19 starts, most of them in the second half. It took him until late August before he was close to full strength, and he never really put it together for more than a game at a time.

Pitching & Defense

Gooden still can throw in the low 90s and is capable of throwing the great curveball that used to make him so unhittable. However, he has lost much of his aggressiveness and often becomes too tentative when trying to put away hitters. He often nibbles with his slider or changeup, which remain his third- and fourth-best pitches. He always has been easy to run on—though basestealers went just 8-for-13 against him in 1997—but he's an excellent athlete who remains a good fielder.

1998 Outlook

The Yankees didn't tender Gooden a contract after the season, but he was expected to be pursued by a number of clubs. If he stays trouble-free off the field and pays attention to his conditioning, he's capable of paying 13-15-win dividends with the right team.

Hideki Irabu

Position: SP
Bats: R **Throws:** R
Ht: 6' 4" **Wt:** 240

Opening Day Age: 28
Born: 5/5/69 in Hyogo,
Japan
ML Seasons: 1
Pronunciation:
hih-DECK-ee
ee-ROB-oo

Overall Statistics

	W	L	Pct.	ERA	G	GS	Sv	IP	H	BB	SO	HR	Ratio
1997	5	4	.556	7.09	13	9	0	53.1	69	20	56	15	1.67
Career	5	4	.556	7.09	13	9	0	53.1	69	20	56	15	1.67

1997 Situational Stats

	W	L	ERA	Sv	IP		AB	H	HR	RBI	Avg
Home	3	2	6.91	0	27.1	LHB	119	39	9	21	.328
Road	2	2	7.27	0	26.0	RHB	103	30	6	20	.291
First Half	0	0	-	0	0.0	Sc Pos	50	16	4	26	.320
Scnd Half	5	4	7.09	0	53.1	Clutch	12	4	0	1	.333

1997 Season

There were few bigger disappointments in baseball last year than Hideki Irabu. The ballyhooed Japanese pitcher was a bust in his first season in the United States. He cost the Yankees an $8.5 million bonus as part of a $12.8 million contract, as well as top prospects Rafael Medina and Ruben Rivera. After winning his first two starts, Irabu was hammered and seemed to crack under pressure.

Pitching & Defense

Irabu was advertised as having a fastball near 100 MPH, but he rarely topped 91-93 MPH with the Yankees. He has the makings of a devastating splitter, but his mechanics are so unpolished that he has difficulty maintaining his release point. His control was sharp in the minors but not in the majors. His delivery is a balk waiting to happen and he doesn't hold runners well. He's also an awful fielder.

1998 Outlook

The Yankees weren't happy with Irabu's performance, and they were even more disappointed by his attitude. He quickly became disliked in the clubhouse. He does have great physical ability, and if he smooths out his mechanics and grows up, New York's investment in him still could pan out.

Ramiro Mendoza

Position: RP/SP
Bats: R **Throws:** R
Ht: 6' 2" **Wt:** 154

Opening Day Age: 25
Born: 6/15/72 in Los Santos, PN
ML Seasons: 2

Overall Statistics

	W	L	Pct.	ERA	G	GS	Sv	IP	H	BB	SO	HR	Ratio
1997	8	6	.571	4.24	39	15	2	133.2	157	28	82	15	1.38
Career	12	11	.522	4.97	51	26	2	186.2	237	38	116	20	1.47

1997 Situational Stats

	W	L	ERA	Sv	IP		AB	H	HR	RBI	Avg
Home	3	4	3.67	1	76.0	LHB	250	75	7	25	.300
Road	5	2	4.99	1	57.2	RHB	287	82	8	39	.286
First Half	3	4	4.60	0	72.1	Sc Pos	135	37	3	46	.274
Scnd Half	5	2	3.82	2	61.1	Clutch	47	17	0	5	.362

1997 Season

Ramiro Mendoza was a valuable and easily over-looked part of the Yankees' pitching staff in 1997. He went 5-5 and won his last two decisions as a spot starter. He was solid in long and middle relief, compiling a 2.93 ERA in 24 appearances out of the bullpen. His flexibility was appreciated on a staff that was often in a state of flux.

Pitching & Defense

Mendoza has become a more complete pitcher, adding a good slider to a naturally sinking fastball that he throws in the low 90s. His sinker induces .oodles of grounders. He needs to develop a better offspeed pitch before he can be a full-time starter. Basestealers can run on him, but he's a good fielder.

1998 Outlook

Ideally, the Yankees would like to keep Mendoza in the bullpen where he gives them quality innings. However, he has gained confidence as a starter and may be needed in that role. He has the ability to win 12 games at the back of the rotation.

Jeff Nelson

Position: RP
Bats: R **Throws:** R
Ht: 6' 8" **Wt:** 235

Opening Day Age: 31
Born: 11/17/66 in Baltimore, MD
ML Seasons: 6

Overall Statistics

	W	L	Pct.	ERA	G	GS	Sv	IP	H	BB	SO	HR	Ratio
1997	3	7	.300	2.86	77	0	2	78.2	53	37	81	7	1.14
Career	20	24	.455	3.32	377	0	13	415.0	349	198	419	32	1.32

1997 Situational Stats

	W	L	ERA	Sv	IP		AB	H	HR	RBI	Avg
Home	2	2	2.88	0	40.2	LHB	98	23	3	12	.235
Road	1	5	2.84	2	38.0	RHB	179	30	4	22	.168
First Half	2	5	3.02	1	44.2	Sc Pos	95	22	4	31	.232
Scnd Half	1	2	2.65	1	34.0	Clutch	139	34	4	24	.245

1997 Season

In between a brutal first four weeks in which he suffered three defeats and a sluggish finish in which he was plagued by shoulder stiffness, Jeff Nelson was an excellent setup man in the Yankees' bullpen. He worked often and displayed a great ability to bounce back without a day off.

Pitching & Defense

His intimidating sidearm delivery always has been tough on righthanders, but Nelson has had to work hard to improve his effectiveness against lefties. He has started to use a cut fastball against lefties while saving his big-breaking slider for righties, and the results have been good. His sidearm motion gives his slider tremendous lateral movement without a lot of sink, almost like a frisbee. Nelson doesn't hold runners well and his awkward release point makes him struggle to reach grounders.

1998 Outlook

Nelson remains a streaky pitcher, prone to slumps and losses of confidence. But when he's in his groove, he's as good as any setup man in baseball. He'll likely remain a key contributor to the Yankees' relief corps.

Jorge Posada

Position: C
Bats: B **Throws:** R
Ht: 6' 2" **Wt:** 205

Opening Day Age: 26
Born: 8/17/71 in Santurce, PR
ML Seasons: 3
Pronunciation:
HOR-hay poh-SOD-uh

Overall Statistics

	G	AB	R	H	D	T	HR	RBI	SB	BB	SO	Avg	OBP	Slg
1997	60	188	29	47	12	0	6	25	1	30	33	.250	.359	.410
Career	69	202	30	48	12	0	6	25	1	31	39	.238	.345	.386

1997 Situational Stats

	AB	H	HR	RBI	Avg		AB	H	HR	RBI	Avg
Home	78	22	2	9	.282	LHP	42	13	1	5	.310
Road	110	25	4	16	.227	RHP	146	34	5	20	.233
First Half	94	23	1	7	.245	Sc Pos	59	17	3	19	.288
Scnd Half	94	24	5	18	.255	Clutch	28	7	0	2	.250

1997 Season

Jorge Posada is a rare commodity, a switch-hitting catcher with power. He held his own in his rookie season, especially when he was pressed into starting duty after Joe Girardi broke a finger.

Hitting, Baserunning & Defense

Posada appears slightly more comfortable batting righthanded at this point in his career. As a lefty, he has shown promising power. He's a good low fastball hitter from that side, but can be jammed as a righthander. He's unusually patient for a youngster. Posada has decent speed for a catcher and can be used in hit-and-run situations. He has outstanding catching skills to go along with exceptional arm strength and a quick release. He'll be tough to run on as he gains more experience.

1998 Outlook

Yankees brass loves Joe Girardi as its everyday catcher. But Posada could soon make Girardi expendable because of his offensive potential. His catching skills will be equal to Girardi's once Posada gets more time in the majors.

Tim Raines

Position: LF/DH
Bats: B **Throws:** R
Ht: 5' 8" **Wt:** 186

Opening Day Age: 38
Born: 9/16/59 in Sanford, FL
ML Seasons: 19
Nickname: Rock

Overall Statistics

	G	AB	R	H	D	T	HR	RBI	SB	BB	SO	Avg	OBP	Slg
1997	74	271	56	87	20	2	4	38	8	41	34	.321	.403	.454
Career	2186	8238	1475	2439	401	111	159	900	795	1209	872	.296	.386	.430

1997 Situational Stats

	AB	H	HR	RBI	Avg		AB	H	HR	RBI	Avg
Home	149	52	3	22	.349	LHP	59	20	1	4	.339
Road	122	35	1	16	.287	RHP	212	67	3	34	.316
First Half	151	46	1	17	.305	Sc Pos	62	19	0	32	.306
Scnd Half	120	41	3	21	.342	Clutch	35	9	0	5	.257

1997 Season

Tim Raines spent yet another season sidelined by a nagging hamstring injury that disabled him on two different occasions and limited him to 64 starts. However, he managed to return in mid-August to bat .342 the rest of the way.

Hitting, Baserunning & Defense

Age may have robbed Raines of his durability, but when he's able to play he remains a quality hitter from both sides of the plate. Even so, the Yankees have used him primarily against righthanders for two years. Raines remains a great first-pitch fastball hitter and has keen knowledge of the strike zone. He is no more than an occasional basestealer but he had been a high-percentage runner until 1997. Raines is now just an average left fielder with a subpar throwing arm.

1998 Outlook

The Yankees showed little interest in retaining Raines, not offering him a contract and allowing him to become a free agent. Though he probably won't end up as a regular anywhere, he still can hit and should be able to help a team off the bench.

Kenny Rogers
Traded To ATHLETICS

Position: SP/RP
Bats: L **Throws:** L
Ht: 6' 1" **Wt:** 205

Opening Day Age: 33
Born: 11/10/64 in Savannah, GA
ML Seasons: 9

Overall Statistics

	W	L	Pct.	ERA	G	GS	Sv	IP	H	BB	SO	HR	Ratio
1997	6	7	.462	5.65	31	22	0	145.0	161	62	78	18	1.54
Career	88	66	.571	4.20	437	152	28	1267.1	1265	515	850	131	1.40

1997 Situational Stats

	W	L	ERA	Sv	IP		AB	H	HR	RBI	Avg
Home	3	4	5.57	0	72.2	LHB	104	25	3	12	.240
Road	3	3	5.72	0	72.1	RHB	472	136	15	74	.288
First Half	4	4	5.90	0	87.0	Sc Pos	127	45	6	66	.354
Scnd Half	2	3	5.28	0	58.0	Clutch	24	5	0	0	.208

1997 Season

The second season of his four-year Yankees contract was a disaster for Kenny Rogers. He won only three games after May, was yanked from the rotation for nearly two months and was a virtual non-person in New York's bullpen for much of the summer.

Pitching & Defense

When Rogers is aggressive with his fastball and cutter and moves them around in the strike zone, he can set up his outstanding changeup and above-average curve. However, he was tentative much of 1997 and was prone to blowing up at the first sign of trouble. His strength is his ability to throw pitches that look like strikes, so he must get ahead in the count to make hitters expand the strike zone. In the last two years, he simply hasn't done that. Rogers has one of the better pickoff moves in the American League and is also a very solid fielder.

1998 Outlook

After being a bust with the Yankees, Rogers was shipped to Oakland for Scott Brosius during the offseason. Escaping the pressures of New York may transform him back into a solid winner. A lack of confidence, rather than a lack of stuff, has been his biggest problem.

Rey Sanchez

Position: 2B/SS
Bats: R **Throws:** R
Ht: 5' 9" **Wt:** 175

Opening Day Age: 30
Born: 10/5/67 in Rio Piedras, PR
ML Seasons: 7
Pronunciation: RAY SAN-chezz

Overall Statistics

	G	AB	R	H	D	T	HR	RBI	SB	BB	SO	Avg	OBP	Slg
1997	135	343	35	94	21	0	2	27	4	16	47	.274	.307	.353
Career	632	1973	206	524	90	8	7	139	22	101	208	.266	.306	.330

1997 Situational Stats

	AB	H	HR	RBI	Avg		AB	H	HR	RBI	Avg
Home	137	39	1	8	.285	LHP	65	20	1	10	.308
Road	206	55	1	19	.267	RHP	278	74	1	17	.266
First Half	153	41	1	11	.268	Sc Pos	87	24	1	26	.276
Scnd Half	190	53	1	16	.279	Clutch	50	13	0	3	.260

1997 Season

Acquired from the Cubs in August to replace the injured Luis Sojo, Rey Sanchez did a solid job down the stretch as the Yankees' everyday second baseman. He performed his usual magic with the glove and proved surprisingly adept with the bat.

Hitting, Baserunning & Defense

Sanchez has little power and rarely tries to do more than slap a pitch on the ground to try and find a hole. He almost always will swing early in the count. He usually manages to put a pitch into play, but he rarely walks or drives the ball for extra bases. Sanchez has average speed and occasionally will look to steal a base. His defense sets him apart. He's a rare utility infielder who can play either second base or shortstop with exceptional skill. He has a great arm, good range and can turn the double play at either position as well as anyone.

1998 Outlook

Unless the Yankees are forced to look for offense from second base, they can afford to live with Sanchez handling the bulk of the chores. With him at second, they would have the best up-the-middle defense in the American League. Whether they go that route remains to be seen, because Sanchez was a free agent and New York re-signed Sojo.

Luis Sojo

Position: 2B
Bats: R **Throws:** R
Ht: 5'11" **Wt:** 175

Opening Day Age: 32
Born: 1/3/66 in
Barquisimeto, VZ
ML Seasons: 8
Pronunciation: SO-ho

Overall Statistics

	G	AB	R	H	D	T	HR	RBI	SB	BB	SO	Avg	OBP	Slg
1997	77	215	27	66	6	1	2	25	3	16	14	.307	.355	.372
Career	608	1913	226	506	74	10	27	185	23	95	132	.265	.302	.356

1997 Situational Stats

	AB	H	HR	RBI	Avg		AB	H	HR	RBI	Avg
Home	106	34	2	17	.321	LHP	66	15	1	5	.227
Road	109	32	0	8	.294	RHP	149	51	1	20	.342
First Half	118	36	1	16	.305	Sc Pos	62	20	0	21	.323
Scnd Half	97	30	1	9	.309	Clutch	34	4	0	2	.118

1997 Season

Luis Sojo played his way into being the Yankees' everyday second baseman and was on his way to his best season. It all came to an end on August 14, when a Ricky Bones pitch broke his forearm and put him out for the year. All in all, Sojo rebounded from a disastrous 1996 to post a career-high .307 batting average.

Hitting, Baserunning & Defense

Though largely a spray hitter, Sojo occasionally can drive a mistake fastball for power. He usually makes contact and is an aggressive hitter early in the count. Sojo played a solid second base for the Yankees when they needed stability at the position. He's also versatile enough to be plugged in at short, third or left field without hurting his club defensively. He has only average speed and isn't a basestealer.

1998 Outlook

Good teams need players like Sojo, who can play a number of positions, stay on the bench for extended periods and still be ready to produce when needed. The Yankees moved quickly to re-sign him in the offseason after he had become a free agent. He could start at second base for New York or be a valuable utilityman.

Mike Stanton

Position: RP
Bats: L **Throws:** L
Ht: 6' 1" **Wt:** 215

Opening Day Age: 30
Born: 6/2/67 in
Houston, TX
ML Seasons: 9

Overall Statistics

	W	L	Pct.	ERA	G	GS	Sv	IP	H	BB	SO	HR	Ratio
1997	6	1	.857	2.57	64	0	3	66.2	50	34	70	3	1.26
Career	29	26	.527	3.69	471	0	59	456.0	422	183	363	39	1.33

1997 Situational Stats

	W	L	ERA	Sv	IP		AB	H	HR	RBI	Avg
Home	3	0	1.91	0	28.1	LHB	90	14	0	5	.156
Road	3	1	3.05	3	38.1	RHB	154	36	3	16	.234
First Half	5	0	3.03	0	29.2	Sc Pos	70	16	1	19	.229
Scnd Half	1	1	2.19	3	37.0	Clutch	156	35	1	14	.224

1997 Season

Signed before the season to bolster the Yankees' bullpen, Mike Stanton had a breakthrough year that solidified his position as a premier lefthanded reliever. He had separate stretches of nine and 11 games in which he was unscored upon, held lefthanders to a .156 average and allowed only 25 percent of his inherited runners to score.

Pitching & Defense

Stanton's funky delivery makes it difficult for hitters to pick up his pitches. As a result, his high-80s fastball appears much faster. In 1997, he threw fewer sliders and more cut fastballs. He has a rubber arm that thrives on heavy use, and he doesn't need a day off between outings. He has an average pickoff move but he holds runners well. He's usually in poor fielding position, so he makes few plays in the field.

1998 Outlook

He may not have been as imposing a setup man as was Mariano Rivera in 1996, but Stanton was still one of the best in the American League. He was consistent and sometimes overpowering, and did a great job of getting the lead to Rivera. The Yankees will ask him to do the same this year.

Jose Alberro (Pos: RHP, Age: 28)

	W	L	Pct.	ERA	G	GS	Sv	IP	H	BB	SO	HR	Ratio
1997	0	3	.000	7.94	10	4	0	28.1	37	17	11	4	1.91
Career	0	4	.000	7.41	27	5	0	58.1	77	36	23	7	1.94

Claimed on waivers from the Rangers in August, Alberro did exactly nothing to endear himself to the Yankees. Lefthanders hit .349 against him, and there's no such thing as a righty relief specialist. 1998 Outlook: C

Willie Banks (Pos: RHP, Age: 29)

	W	L	Pct.	ERA	G	GS	Sv	IP	H	BB	SO	HR	Ratio
1997	3	0	1.000	1.93	5	1	0	14.0	9	6	8	0	1.07
Career	29	35	.453	4.94	105	84	0	502.2	541	247	352	54	1.57

The third overall pick in the 1987 draft, Banks never has lived up to his promise and missed all of 1996 with a nerve problem in his shoulder. He did look good in September for the Yankees, though. 1998 Outlook: B

Brian Boehringer (Pos: RHP, Age: 28)

	W	L	Pct.	ERA	G	GS	Sv	IP	H	BB	SO	HR	Ratio
1997	3	2	.600	2.63	34	0	0	48.0	39	32	53	4	1.48
Career	5	9	.357	5.54	56	6	0	112.0	109	75	100	15	1.64

Taken by Tampa Bay in the expansion draft, Boehringer then was sent to the Padres in a trade for John Flaherty. He had a 1.77 ERA after his return from arthroscopic elbow surgery and held lefties to a .152 average. 1998 Outlook: A

Joe Borowski (Pos: RHP, Age: 26)

	W	L	Pct.	ERA	G	GS	Sv	IP	H	BB	SO	HR	Ratio
1997	2	3	.400	4.15	21	0	0	26.0	29	20	8	2	1.88
Career	4	7	.364	4.10	49	0	0	59.1	67	37	26	6	1.75

A midseason relief replacement for the Braves, Borowski was claimed by the Yankees after being waived in mid-September. He took the loss in his only appearance for New York. 1998 Outlook: C

Ivan Cruz (Pos: DH, Age: 29, Bats: L)

	G	AB	R	H	D	T	HR	RBI	SB	BB	SO	Avg	OBP	Slg
1997	11	20	0	5	1	0	0	3	0	2	4	.250	.318	.300
Career	11	20	0	5	1	0	0	3	0	2	4	.250	.318	.300

After hitting 83 homers in the last three years in the minors, driving in 90 or more runs each season, Cruz got his first taste of the majors when Cecil Fielder went on the disabled list. 1998 Outlook: C

Mike Figga (Pos: C, Age: 27, Bats: R)

	G	AB	R	H	D	T	HR	RBI	SB	BB	SO	Avg	OBP	Slg
1997	2	4	0	0	0	0	0	0	0	0	3	.000	.000	.000
Career	2	4	0	0	0	0	0	0	0	0	3	.000	.000	.000

Fourth on the Yankees' depth chart at catcher, Figga was recalled after the rosters expanded in September. In his first shot at the big leagues, he fanned three times in four at-bats. 1998 Outlook: C

Andy Fox (Pos: 3B, Age: 27, Bats: L)

	G	AB	R	H	D	T	HR	RBI	SB	BB	SO	Avg	OBP	Slg
1997	22	31	13	7	1	0	0	1	2	7	9	.226	.368	.258
Career	135	220	39	44	5	0	3	14	13	27	37	.200	.290	.264

After playing 113 games for the Yankees in 1996, Fox got just 31 big league at-bats a year later. He can't hit, but he can play just about every position. 1998 Outlook: C

Pete Incaviglia (Pos: DH/RF, Age: 33, Bats: R)

	G	AB	R	H	D	T	HR	RBI	SB	BB	SO	Avg	OBP	Slg
1997	53	154	19	38	4	0	5	12	0	11	46	.247	.308	.370
Career	1264	4203	546	1040	193	21	206	653	33	358	1267	.247	.311	.450

Incaviglia hit 18 homers in 1996, but wore out his welcome in Baltimore and was released in late July. After signing him, it took the Yankees two weeks to discover that his bat speed has decayed. 1998 Outlook: C

Pat Kelly (Pos: 2B/DH, Age: 30, Bats: R)

	G	AB	R	H	D	T	HR	RBI	SB	BB	SO	Avg	OBP	Slg
1997	67	120	25	29	6	1	2	10	8	14	37	.242	.324	.358
Career	591	1719	218	431	97	11	26	183	56	122	354	.251	.309	.365

It's not a good sign when Rey Sanchez and Luis Sojo make you expendable. That's what happened to Kelly, who has been hampered by injuries for three years. He signed a minor league contract with Toronto. 1998 Outlook: B.

Graeme Lloyd (Pos: LHP, Age: 30)

	W	L	Pct.	ERA	G	GS	Sv	IP	H	BB	SO	HR	Ratio
1997	1	1	.500	3.31	46	0	1	49.0	55	20	26	6	1.53
Career	8	19	.296	3.91	242	0	8	248.1	257	78	131	23	1.35

What damaged goods? Lloyd settled in nicely as a lefty setup man for the Yankees. Righties hit .300 off of him, but he posted a 2.89 ERA after the All-Star break. 1998 Outlook: A

Jim Mecir (Pos: RHP, Age: 27)

	W	L	Pct.	ERA	G	GS	Sv	IP	H	BB	SO	HR	Ratio
1997	0	4	.000	5.88	25	0	0	33.2	36	10	25	5	1.37
Career	1	5	.167	5.15	53	0	0	78.2	83	35	66	11	1.50

Mecir seesawed with Hideki Irabu. When Irabu joined the Yankees July 10, Mecir went to Triple-A. When Irabu was demoted July 28, Mecir went back up. When Irabu returned Aug. 13. . . you get the picture. 1998 Outlook: C

Scott Pose (Pos: LF/RF, Age: 31, Bats: L)

	G	AB	R	H	D	T	HR	RBI	SB	BB	SO	Avg	OBP	Slg
1997	54	87	19	19	2	1	0	5	3	9	11	.218	.292	.264
Career	69	128	19	27	4	1	0	8	3	11	15	.211	.273	.258

Pose went back and forth between Triple-A and the majors four times. Waived in October, he'll be best remembered for getting the first hit in Marlins history. 1998 Outlook: C

New York Yankees

Darryl Strawberry (Pos: LF, Age: 36, Bats: L)

	G	AB	R	H	D	T	HR	RBI	SB	BB	SO	Avg	OBP	Slg
1997	11	29	1	3	1	0	0	2	0	3	9	.103	.188	.138
Career	1458	5074	844	1312	240	36	308	937	211	753	1246	.259	.355	.502

Strawberry hit 11 homers in 1996, but missed most of last season with knee problems. He's a free agent whom someone will sign because lefty power is coveted. He may be strictly a DH at this point. 1998 Outlook: B

Mark Whiten (Pos: LF/RF, Age: 31, Bats: B)

	G	AB	R	H	D	T	HR	RBI	SB	BB	SO	Avg	OBP	Slg
1997	69	215	34	57	11	0	5	24	4	30	47	.265	.360	.386
Career	838	2846	430	734	113	20	98	389	76	343	646	.258	.339	.415

Now looking for his ninth major league team, Whiten fell from 22 homers in 1996 to five last season. He was arrested in July on sexual-assault charges that later were dropped. He was cut in August. 1998 Outlook: B

New York Yankees Minor League Prospects

Organization Overview:

The Yankees can develop talent, but they prefer to go out and buy it. The system has produced Derek Jeter, Andy Pettitte, Mariano Rivera and Bernie Williams in the 1990s. Outfielder Ricky Ledee, third baseman Mike Lowell and catcher Jorge Posada all could become regulars in 1998. But because owner George Steinbrenner is so impetuous, it's never certain whether homegrown prospects will be traded for veterans or even given a chance. Steinbrenner decided he had to have Hideki Irabu, so he gave the Padres crown jewels Rafael Mendina and Ruben Rivera, plus cash. Righthander Tony Armas was untouchable—until Steinbrenner coveted Mike Stanley. Ledee and fast-rising lefthander Eric Milton were rumored trade bait in several deals as soon as the regular season ended. Steinbrenner often isn't interested in a player if he doesn't have a high price tag, no matter how talented he is.

Brian Buchanan

Position: OF   **Opening Day Age:** 24
Bats: R **Throws:** R   **Born:** 7/21/73 in Miami,
Ht: 6' 4" **Wt:** 220   FL

Recent Statistics

	G	AB	R	H	D	T	HR	RBI	SB	BB	SO	AVG
96 A Tampa	131	526	65	137	22	4	10	58	23	37	108	.260
97 AAA Columbus	18	61	8	17	1	0	4	7	2	4	11	.279
97 AA Norwich	116	470	75	145	25	2	10	69	11	32	85	.309
97 MLE	134	512	67	143	22	1	11	61	8	25	100	.279

A first-round pick out of the University of Virginia in 1994, Buchanan severely dislocated his left ankle the next season and nearly had to have his foot amputated. He has improved steadily since returning, showing above-average speed and occasional tape-measure power. He's learning to lift balls, which should result in increased homer totals. Strikeouts will be a tradeoff for his power, but he could learn to walk more. He'll spend 1998 in Triple-A and then be ready for the majors.

Rudy Gomez

Position: 2B   **Opening Day Age:** 23
Bats: R **Throws:** R   **Born:** 9/14/74 in
Ht: 5' 11" **Wt:** 180   Hialeah, FL

Recent Statistics

	G	AB	R	H	D	T	HR	RBI	SB	BB	SO	AVG
96 R Yankees	16	58	12	16	6	0	0	10	0	9	7	.276
96 A Tampa	40	130	15	38	9	1	1	24	4	26	12	.292
97 AA Norwich	102	393	65	118	18	7	5	52	11	61	64	.300
97 MLE	102	379	53	104	16	4	4	42	7	41	67	.274

Gomez isn't flashy, but he's the type of steady second baseman the Yankees haven't had since Steve Sax. A 10th-round pick out of the University of Miami in 1996, he handled Double-A in his first full pro season. He hits for average, mixes in some doubles, draws some walks and can steal a base. His biggest need as a hitter is to make better contact. He doesn't have spectacular range at second base, but he gets to his share of balls and makes the plays when he does. Ticketed for Triple-A in 1998, Gomez could challenge for a big league job the following year.

Mike Jerzembeck

Position: P   **Opening Day Age:** 25
Bats: R **Throws:** R   **Born:** 5/18/72 in
Ht: 6' 1" **Wt:** 185   Queens, NY

Recent Statistics

	W	L	ERA	G	GS	Sv	IP	H	R	BB	SO	HR
96 AAA Columbus	0	0	5.40	1	0	0	1.2	1	1	1	0	0
96 AA Norwich	3	6	4.52	14	13	0	69.2	74	38	26	65	9
96 A Tampa	4	2	2.95	12	12	0	73.1	67	26	13	60	4
97 AA Norwich	2	1	1.71	8	8	0	42.0	21	10	16	42	1
97 AAA Columbus	7	5	3.59	20	20	0	130.1	125	55	37	118	14

Two years removed from elbow surgery, Jerzembeck established himself in Triple-A in 1997. A 1993 fifth-round pick out of the University of North Carolina, he throws a 92-94 MPH fastball, a curveball and a changeup. He has good command and needs it to be successful, because his fastball is fairly straight and his curve lacks a tight break. Righthanders hit 135 points higher than lefties did against him in Triple-A, a reverse platoon differential that doesn't seem in line with his stuff. He's not mentioned as a candidate for New York's rotation, so he'll either settle into middle relief or wait on call in Columbus.

Ricky Ledee

Position: OF   **Opening Day Age:** 24
Bats: L **Throws:** L   **Born:** 11/22/73 in
Ht: 6' 2" **Wt:** 160   Ponce, PR

Recent Statistics

	G	AB	R	H	D	T	HR	RBI	SB	BB	SO	AVG
96 AA Norwich	39	137	27	50	11	1	8	37	2	16	25	.365
96 AAA Columbus	96	358	79	101	22	6	21	64	6	44	95	.282
97 R Yankees	7	21	3	7	1	0	0	2	0	2	4	.333
97 AAA Columbus	43	170	38	52	12	1	10	39	4	21	49	.306

Ledee's emergence helped make Ruben Rivera expendable. A 16th-round pick in 1990, Ledee was brought along slowly. He spent four years in short-season leagues, and two more in the Class-A South Atlantic League. He broke out with 29 homers in 1996 and would have put up similar numbers in 1997 if a groin injury hadn't cost him most of the season. He's a slugger first and foremost, but should hit for a decent average despite piling up lots of strikeouts. When he was healthy, his speed and outfield play were much improved last year. If free agent Tim Raines leaves New York, as was expected, Ledee could replace him in left field.

Mike Lowell

Position: 3B **Opening Day Age:** 24
Bats: R **Throws:** R **Born:** 2/24/74 in San
Ht: 6' 4" **Wt:** 195 Juan, PR

Recent Statistics

	G	AB	R	H	D	T	HR	RBI	SB	BB	SO	AVG
96 A Greensboro	113	433	58	122	33	0	8	64	10	46	43	.282
96 A Tampa	24	78	8	22	5	0	0	11	1	3	13	.282
97 AA Norwich	78	285	60	98	17	0	15	47	2	48	30	.344
97 AAA Columbus	57	210	36	58	13	1	15	45	2	23	34	.276
97 MLE	135	476	78	137	26	0	24	75	2	51	65	.288

Lowell is a self-made player who has improved dramatically since signing as a 20th-round pick out of Florida International in 1995. He has moved four levels in the past two seasons, while increasing his home-run output from eight to 30. Knowing he had to add strength, he had spent the previous offseason lifting weights and added 15 pounds. He walks as much as he strikes out, and managers voted him the best hitting prospect in the Double-A Eastern League. A college second baseman, he tracks balls well at third but has questionable range and agility. As a result, he planned to spend this offseason improving his flexibility. Scott Brosius is all that stands between Lowell and a starting job in New York.

Katsuhiro Maeda

Position: P **Opening Day Age:** 26
Bats: R **Throws:** R **Born:** 6/23/71 in Japan
Ht: 6' 2" **Wt:** 215

Recent Statistics

	W	L	ERA	G	GS	Sv	IP	H	R	BB	SO	HR
96 R Yankees	1	1	3.00	2	2	0	9.0	4	3	2	7	1
96 A Tampa	0	0	4.22	2	2	0	10.2	11	5	6	8	0
96 AA Norwich	3	2	4.05	9	9	0	53.1	49	25	21	30	4
97 AA Norwich	8	10	4.56	25	21	0	124.1	117	75	62	76	14

Steinbrenner's fascination with hard-throwing Japanese righthanders didn't begin with Irabu in 1997. The year before, he paid $350,000 to the Seibu Lions and $1.5 million to Maeda. To date, he has distinguished himself more for his Rodmanesque habit of changing his hair color than for his pitching. He throws 93-96 MPH, but you couldn't tell it by his mediocre strikeout totals in Double-A. He lacks a breaking ball as well as confidence. He's already 26, so it's questionable that he'll get much better. Don't bet against Steinbrenner rushing Maeda in an attempt to justify his investment.

Donzell McDonald

Position: OF **Opening Day Age:** 23
Bats: B **Throws:** R **Born:** 2/20/75 in Long
Ht: 6' 0" **Wt:** 165 Beach, CA

Recent Statistics

	G	AB	R	H	D	T	HR	RBI	SB	BB	SO	AVG
96 A Oneonta	74	282	57	78	8	10	2	30	54	43	62	.277
97 A Tampa	77	297	69	88	23	8	3	23	39	48	75	.296

The brother of Darnell McDonald, an Orioles first-round pick in 1997, Donzell is a prospect in his own right. A broken finger limited his exposure last season, but managers voted him the best and fastest baserunner in the Class-A Florida State League. Scouts repeatedly compared him to Kenny Lofton, and not the banged-up version that played for the Braves. A 22nd-round pick out of Yavapai (Ariz.) Junior College in 1995, McDonald can do more than run. He's a switch-hitter who draws walks and has extra-base power, and could be an effective leadoff man if he cuts down on his strikeouts. His speed also allows him to cover the gaps from center field. He's at least two years away.

Eric Milton

Position: P **Opening Day Age:** 22
Bats: L **Throws:** L **Born:** 8/4/75 in State
Ht: 6' 3" **Wt:** 200 College, PA

Recent Statistics

	W	L	ERA	G	GS	Sv	IP	H	R	BB	SO	HR
97 A Tampa	8	3	3.09	14	14	0	93.1	78	35	14	95	8
97 AA Norwich	6	3	3.13	14	14	0	77.2	59	29	36	67	2

Milton signed late after being drafted in the first round out of the University of Maryland in 1996, so he didn't make his pro debut until last season. The wait was worth it, as he went 14-6, 3.11 with 162 strikeouts in 171 innings and finished the year in Double-A. Managers named him the best pitching prospect in the Class-A Florida State League. He has uncommon velocity (low 90s) and command for a lefthander, and also throws a nice changeup and a developing curveball. He needs only to improve his breaking ball to pitch in the majors, and will spend 1998 in Triple-A working on it.

Others to Watch

Homer Bush, 25, came from the Padres as part of the Irabu trade and joined a growing list of Yankees second-base candidates. He can run a little bit and hit a few doubles, but he also strikes out a lot and has an almost pathological fear of walks. Gomez is a better player. . . Righthander **Luis de los Santos** reached Double-A at age 19, throwing 94 MPH all the way. He also showed impeccable control, walking 28 and striking out 116 in 175 1/3 innings in 1997. . . Shortstop **Cristian Guzman** is a switch-hitter who projects to do everything but hit for power. He has 6.4 speed in the 60-yard dash and covers a lot of ground, but he's still learning to hit. He struck out 106 times and walked just 18 while batting .273 in Class-A ball last year at age 19. . . Venezuelan outfielder **Jackson Melian**, 17, signed for $1.6 million in 1996. He made his pro debut in 1997, showing glimpses of 30-30 potential and a strong arm. . . Righthander **Danny Rios**, 25, throws in the low to mid-90s with a hard slider. He lacks the confidence to be a closer, but he could be a good setup man. . . Outfielder **Shane Spencer**, 26, has hit 62 homers at the upper levels of the system in the last two years. He also walks a lot, but the Yankees haven't shown an inclination to give him a shot.

Art Howe

1997 Season

It wasn't hard to see it coming. With the Athletics' recent free-agent losses, Art Howe had to know his team would be in for a rough time. As much as the team struggled, the savvy and patient Howe endured and developed a few potential stars by the time the year came to a close.

Offense

The A's main strength was their power. Even after the trade of Mark McGwire, they were capable of driving the ball long distances. However, Oakland was also a young team which struck out an American League-leading 1,181 times and had a few things to learn about hitting. Howe preferred to advance runners with the bunt rather than the stolen base. The A's ranked first in the AL in sacrifice attempts and second-to-last in steal attempts. He used pinch hitters more than any manager in the league, and they delivered with a .345 average.

Pitching & Defense

Howe oversaw a lot of change. The Opening Day rotation was completely overhauled and five players spent their first year at a new position. The conversion of rookie third baseman Scott Spiezio to second base was a gutsy move, and it worked out surprisingly well. Howe was very active when the A's were in the field, employing the intentional walk as much as any AL manager and ranking second in defensive substitutions. The worst pitching staff in the league required a lot of attention. Howe had the quickest hook in the majors and matched San Francisco's Dusty Baker for the lead in relievers used.

1998 Outlook

The A's endured a lot of lumps last year, but now Howe has a bunch of up-and-coming youngsters who are competing for jobs. He has the makings of an excellent young squad, with only a handful of veterans and a very low base payroll. New GM Billy Beane can actually try to snare a couple of free-agent starters.

Born: 12/15/46 in Pittsburgh, PA

Playing Experience: 1974-1985, Pit, Hou, StL

Managerial Experience: 7 seasons

Manager Statistics

Year Team, Lg	W	L	Pct	GB	Finish
1997 Oakland, AL	65	97	.401	25.0	4th West
7 Seasons	535	599	.472	—	—

1997 Starting Pitchers by Days Rest

	≤3	4	5	6+
Athletics Starts	13	80	39	17
Athletics ERA	4.80	6.34	5.50	6.59
AL Avg Starts	5	89	34	24
AL ERA	4.38	4.60	4.61	5.37

1997 Situational Stats

	Art Howe	AL Average
Hit & Run Success %	42.4	36.5
Stolen Base Success %	66.4	67.3
Platoon Pct.	60.5	59.5
Defensive Subs	38	22
High-Pitch Outings	8	15
Quick/Slow Hooks	29/19	19/15
Sacrifice Attempts	66	53

1997 Rankings (American League)

⇒ 1st in sacrifice bunt attempts (66), intentional walks (40), pinch hitters used (198), quick hooks (29), relief appearances (481), mid-inning pitching changes (264) and first batter platoon percentage (69.6%)

⇒ 2nd in steals of home plate (1), defensive substitutions (38), starting lineups used (133), starts on three days rest (13) and one-batter pitcher appearances (53)

⇒ 3rd in least caught steals of second base (31), least caught steals of home plate (1), hit-and-run percentage (42.4%), slow hooks (19) and saves with over 1 inning pitched (11)

Oakland Athletics

Mark Bellhorn

1997 Season

It was a familiar story for Oakland. The regulars had trouble playing consistent ball, trades ensued and the club's prospects were then brought up to show what they could accomplish. Such was the story with Mark Bellhorn, who shredded Pacific Coast League pitching for a .328 average and 11 homers before a June call-up. He played mostly at third while incumbent Scott Brosius was injured or deployed elsewhere. Bellhorn found major league pitching tougher than in the minors, but also showed flashes of potential.

Hitting

Bellhorn has power and can hit the gaps as well as work the count, but he was inconsistent in 1997. He hits well against righthanders, but isn't as focused against southpaws and becomes passive when he has two strikes. He must correct those flaws to become the quality hitter he had been in the minors.

Baserunning & Defense

A fine baserunner with excellent speed, Bellhorn can take the extra base and is very good at reading pitchers, getting a good jump and stealing bases. He was caught only once in eight tries. He did commit nine errors in limited action, but in Bellhorn's defense he was playing his third position in three years. He should become more comfortable with time. His ability to play shortstop and second base is a plus.

1998 Outlook

A fine athlete, Bellhorn is one of the shining stars in Oakland's farm system. He's only 23 and climbed the minor league ladder quickly. With the trade of Brosius, Bellhorn is the leading candidate to play third base in 1998. With a full season in the majors, watch his hitting and defense improve and stabilize.

Position: 3B/2B
Bats: B **Throws:** R
Ht: 6' 0" **Wt:** 190

Opening Day Age: 23
Born: 8/23/74 in Boston, MA
ML Seasons: 1

Overall Statistics

	G	AB	R	H	D	T	HR	RBI	SB	BB	SO	Avg	OBP	Slg
1997	68	224	33	51	9	1	6	19	7	32	70	.228	.324	.357
Career	68	224	33	51	9	1	6	19	7	32	70	.228	.324	.357

Where He Hits the Ball

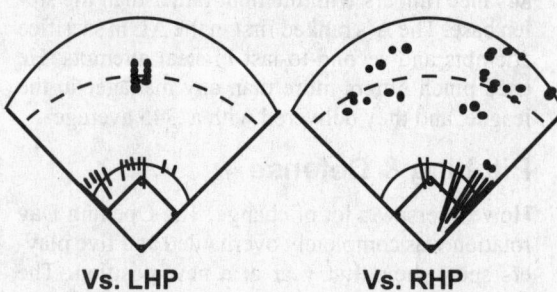

Vs. LHP   **Vs. RHP**

1997 Situational Stats

	AB	H	HR	RBI	Avg		AB	H	HR	RBI	Avg
Home	114	28	3	12	.246	LHP	63	14	2	4	.222
Road	110	23	3	7	.209	RHP	161	37	4	15	.230
First Half	56	18	2	6	.321	Sc Pos	56	12	0	12	.214
Scnd Half	168	33	4	13	.196	Clutch	42	9	0	2	.214

1997 Rankings (American League)
⇒ Did not rank near the top or bottom in any category

Scott Brosius

1997 Season

Ouch. Scott Brosius will want to forget 1997. His average dipped 101 points, enough to make most hitters want to run and hide. Though he was sidelined with a knee problem towards the end of the season, he gutted it out like the pro he is for as long as he could.

Hitting

Brosius developed a hitch in his swing during the spring, and by the time he shed himself of the habit, he had lost a great deal of confidence. All the patience at the plate he had so carefully cultivated went by the wayside, as his walk rate plunged. When he's on his game, Brosius is a good gap-to-gap hitter with decent power. A righthanded hitter, he has developed a puzzling inability to hit lefties.

Baserunning & Defense

Brosius is a fine baserunner with very good speed, capable of stealing 10-15 bases if he gets on base enough. He plays an aggressive third base, often staying near the bag and challenging hitters. Brosius also played shortstop on 30 occasions, and manned the outfield another 23 times. He has a great arm at third, short or right field.

1998 Outlook

It might be hard to imagine a repeat of 1996, but another 1997 is just as unlikely. Brosius' true numbers will probably lie somewhere in between. Oakland figured to use him at a multitude of positions and give him 400 at-bats before trading him to the Yankees in November for Kenny Rogers. He could be New York's everyday third baseman. The Yankees hope that his off year was simply the result of his knee troubles.

Position: 3B/SS/RF
Bats: R **Throws:** R
Ht: 6' 1" **Wt:** 185

Opening Day Age: 31
Born: 8/15/66 in Hillsboro, OR
ML Seasons: 7
Pronunciation: BRO-shus

Overall Statistics

	G	AB	R	H	D	T	HR	RBI	SB	BB	SO	Avg	OBP	Slg
1997	129	479	59	97	20	1	11	41	9	34	102	.203	.259	.317
Career	606	1988	280	494	95	5	76	249	34	178	372	.248	.315	.416

Where He Hits the Ball

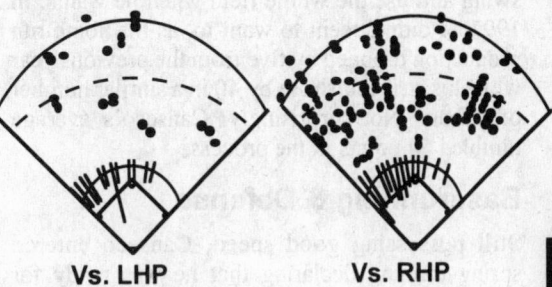

Vs. LHP   **Vs. RHP**

1997 Situational Stats

	AB	H	HR	RBI	Avg		AB	H	HR	RBI	Avg
Home	219	54	7	17	.247	LHP	125	20	2	8	.160
Road	260	43	4	24	.165	RHP	354	77	9	33	.218
First Half	320	67	5	24	.209	Sc Pos	124	15	1	28	.121
Scnd Half	159	30	6	17	.189	Clutch	73	20	3	8	.274

1997 Rankings (American League)

⇒ 1st in lowest batting average, lowest slugging percentage, lowest on-base percentage, lowest batting average with runners in scoring position, lowest batting average vs. lefthanded pitchers, lowest on-base percentage vs. lefthanded pitchers (.215) and lowest batting average on the road

⇒ 2nd in lowest batting average vs. righthanded pitchers, lowest slugging percentage vs. lefthanded pitchers (.232) and highest fielding percentage at third base (.977)

⇒ Led the Athletics in highest groundball/flyball ratio (0.9) and most pitches seen per plate appearance (3.94)

Oakland Athletics

Jose Canseco

1997 Season

The prospect of reuniting Jose Canseco with fellow Bash Brother Mark McGwire helped Oakland begin the season with promise, but nagging injuries to Canseco and the subsequent trade of McGwire left the promise unfilled. Despite adequate numbers, Canseco didn't register enough at-bats to force the automatic renewal of his contract, and his play seemed more often lackadaisical than not.

Hitting

Canseco's body may give him grief, but he's still one of the more dangerous power hitters in the game. A great fastball hitter, he can shorten his swing and use the whole field when he wants. In 1997 he didn't seem to want to, as his home run production dropped by five from the previous year while his strikeouts rose by 40 in a similar number of at-bats. Not surprisingly, Canseco's average tumbled 54 points in the process.

Baserunning & Defense

Still possessing good speed, Canseco entered spring training declaring that he was ready for another 40-40 season. He even challenged speedy teammate Allen Battle to a footrace, an event that never took place. Then Canseco went out and stole a grand total of eight bases. In the field the results were no more encouraging, as he regularly misplayed balls in both right and left field, contributing to the Athletics' dismal season. He throws OK, but not as well as he did before his infamous pitching stint with the Rangers.

1998 Outlook

It's fairly certain that Canseco, who became a free agent, won't return to Oakland in 1998. He has all of the skills and worked judiciously on his defense during the spring of 1997, only to lapse back into bad habits. Canseco is also younger than McGwire, and certainly possesses an equal amount of talent. He'll be a designated hitter somewhere, and if focused and healthy he still can deliver a 30-homer, 100-RBI season.

Position: DH/LF/RF
Bats: R **Throws:** R
Ht: 6' 4" **Wt:** 240

Opening Day Age: 33
Born: 7/2/64 in Havana, Cuba
ML Seasons: 13
Pronunciation: can-SAY-co

Overall Statistics

	G	AB	R	H	D	T	HR	RBI	SB	BB	SO	Avg	OBP	Slg
1997	108	388	56	91	19	0	23	74	8	51	122	.235	.325	.461
Career	1449	5459	920	1470	270	13	351	1107	164	674	1471	.269	.353	.516

Where He Hits the Ball

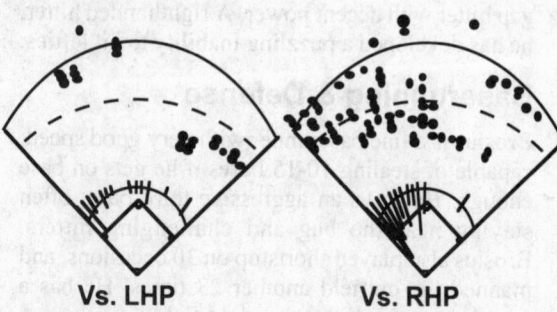

Vs. LHP   **Vs. RHP**

1997 Situational Stats

	AB	H	HR	RBI	Avg		AB	H	HR	RBI	Avg
Home	187	47	10	40	.251	LHP	79	19	2	11	.241
Road	201	44	13	34	.219	RHP	309	72	21	63	.233
First Half	316	76	18	57	.241	Sc Pos	116	28	8	55	.241
Scnd Half	72	15	5	17	.208	Clutch	69	15	5	14	.217

1997 Rankings (American League)

⇒ 5th in errors in right field (5)
⇒ 8th in lowest percentage of swings put into play (35.5%)
⇒ Led the Athletics in strikeouts and GDPs (15)

Jason Giambi

1997 Season

Heads turned when beefed-up Jason Giambi strolled into camp last February. Having spent the offseason pumping iron, emulating his friend and mentor Mark McGwire, Giambi added bulk and lost a little bat speed. He had a slow start, as he switched positions and also suffered nagging injuries during the first half of the year. By the time Geronimo Berroa and McGwire were traded, Giambi had claimed a spot in the order and returned to form, finishing strong with numbers similar to those of his 1996 season.

Hitting

Giambi is a line-drive hitter with gap-to-gap power. He's very consistent, handling all pitches and pitchers very well, and he made great strides in learning to hit lefthanded pitching last year. He knows how to use the entire field, play mental games with enemy hurlers and continually make adjustments at the plate. He draws walks and makes good contact. When he's in a groove, he's impossible to get out.

Baserunning & Defense

As fine a hitter as Giambi is, his defense is at best suspect and his baserunning is just plain terrible. To be sure, Giambi knows his limits, and though he can hit he just isn't either fast or quick. His arm is nothing special. He's fairly innocuous at first base. In left field, the ball pretty much plays him. He also has spent time at third base with little success. Don't look for him to steal any bases, either.

1998 Outlook

Giambi suddenly finds himself a seasoned veteran on a team in the midst of a serious rebuilding process. He already has two seasons under his belt, and in 1997 he played well through the dog days, something that didn't occur during his rookie season. He'll be the first baseman in a young and talented Oakland infield for a few years to come. Down the road, he'll be a designated hitter.

Position: LF/1B/DH
Bats: L **Throws:** R
Ht: 6' 2" **Wt:** 200

Opening Day Age: 27
Born: 1/8/71 in West Covina, CA
ML Seasons: 3
Pronunciation: gee-AHM-bee

Overall Statistics

	G	AB	R	H	D	T	HR	RBI	SB	BB	SO	Avg	OBP	Slg
1997	142	519	66	152	41	2	20	81	0	55	89	.293	.362	.495
Career	336	1231	177	353	88	3	46	185	2	134	215	.287	.359	.475

Where He Hits the Ball

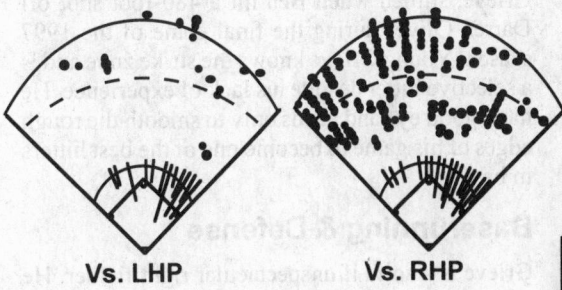

Vs. LHP   **Vs. RHP**

1997 Situational Stats

	AB	H	HR	RBI	Avg		AB	H	HR	RBI	Avg
Home	261	82	14	41	.314	LHP	126	38	6	19	.302
Road	258	70	6	40	.271	RHP	393	114	14	62	.290
First Half	262	79	9	44	.302	Sc Pos	127	35	8	59	.276
Scnd Half	257	73	11	37	.284	Clutch	65	22	6	17	.338

1997 Rankings (American League)

⇒ 7th in lowest percentage of swings on the first pitch (17.0%)
⇒ 8th in doubles and lowest batting average with the bases loaded (.100)
⇒ 10th in lowest groundball/flyball ratio (0.8)
⇒ Led the Athletics in batting average, runs scored, hits, singles, doubles, total bases (257), RBI, sacrifice flies (8), hit by pitch (6), times on base (213), pitches seen (2,289), slugging percentage, on-base percentage, HR frequency (26.0 ABs per HR), batting average with runners in scoring position, batting average in the clutch, batting average vs. lefthanded pitchers, batting average vs. righthanded pitchers, slugging percentage vs. lefthanded pitchers (.492) and slugging percentage vs. righthanded pitchers (.496)

Ben Grieve

1997 Season

Athletics GM Billy Beane and manager Art Howe must take comfort in knowing that youngsters like Ben Grieve and Miguel Tejada will grace their starting lineup for years. Grieve, who has annihilated pitching throughout the minors, appeared in September for Oakland and proceeded to hit three doubles during his debut. He handled big league pitching easily and secured a 1998 job with his exciting and explosive bat.

Hitting

Grieve is a true power hitter, with a quick bat and the ability to drive the ball to the deepest part of the park. Even his father, former Texas GM Tom Grieve, smiled when Ben hit a 480-foot shot off Darren Oliver during the final game of the 1997 season. Young Grieve knows the strike zone and is a selective hitter despite his lack of experience. He has a good eye and needs only to smooth the rough edges of his game to become one of the best hitters in baseball.

Baserunning & Defense

Grieve is a solid if unspectacular right fielder. He reads the ball well off the bat but isn't particularly fast. He does have a strong arm. Grieve's speed isn't overwhelming, so he's not much of a threat to steal anything but the hearts of the hometown fans.

1998 Outlook

Grieve should be in the mix as the everyday right fielder at the start of the season. Like Tejada, he might struggle a bit during his first full campaign. Grieve, however, is more refined than Tejada and enters the year as one of the favorites for American League Rookie of the Year. The only guarantee is that he'll develop and be a joy to watch in the process.

Position: RF
Bats: L **Throws:** R
Ht: 6' 4" **Wt:** 200

Opening Day Age: 21
Born: 5/4/76 in Arlington, Texas
ML Seasons: 1
Pronunciation: GREEVE

Overall Statistics

	G	AB	R	H	D	T	HR	RBI	SB	BB	SO	Avg	OBP	Slg
1997	24	93	12	29	6	0	3	24	0	13	25	.312	.402	.473
Career	24	93	12	29	6	0	3	24	0	13	25	.312	.402	.473

Where He Hits the Ball

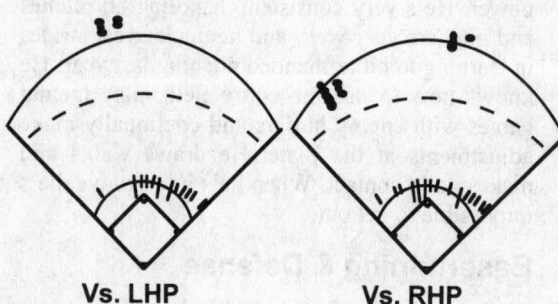

Vs. LHP   **Vs. RHP**

1997 Situational Stats

	AB	H	HR	RBI	Avg		AB	H	HR	RBI	Avg
Home	50	12	3	15	.240	LHP	38	12	1	11	.316
Road	43	17	0	9	.395	RHP	55	17	2	13	.309
First Half	0	0	0	0	-	Sc Pos	31	11	1	18	.355
Scnd Half	93	29	3	24	.312	Clutch	14	4	2	4	.286

1997 Rankings (American League)

⇒ Did not rank near the top or bottom in any category

Steve Karsay

Position: SP
Bats: R **Throws:** R
Ht: 6' 3" **Wt:** 205

Opening Day Age: 26
Born: 3/24/72 in Flushing, NY
ML Seasons: 3
Pronunciation: CAR-say

1997 Season

Despite his 3-12 record, Steve Karsay must look upon 1997 as a triumph. The Athletics didn't want to push Karsay because he had undergone Tommy John surgery in 1995. Though he did spend time on the disabled list at the end of the season with a sore arm, he led the team in starts and finished second in innings, which were encouraging signs.

Pitching

Karsay's ability comes and goes with the health of his arm. His fastball is clocked at 93-94 MPH, and he also has a changeup and curveball that make him a tough pitcher to hit when he's throwing well. For most of 1997, he didn't have solid command of all his pitches to make that happen. When all of Karsay's pitches are falling in place, he's a strike-out pitcher. When not, he gets into trouble. Though he did get hammered regularly—hitters tagged him for a .304 average last year—he made big strides toward returning to the form that once made him a sought-after prospect.

Defense

Karsay doesn't hold runners well at all and has no pickoff move to first. Of the 18 stolen-base attempts off him in 1997, 17 were successful. He has an average glove.

1998 Outlook

Few rotations contain bigger question marks than Oakland's, but Karsay is currently one of their starting five as things now stand. He not only must improve his consistency, but also must show he has completely recovered from the 1995 surgery. Most importantly, he must pitch more aggressively, reducing the number of hits he surrenders in order to stay in the rotation. He certainly has the talent to do it. After throwing less than 200 professional innings over the last four years, he's still catching up on experience.

Overall Statistics

	W	L	Pct.	ERA	G	GS	Sv	IP	H	BB	SO	HR	Ratio
1997	3	12	.200	5.77	24	24	0	132.2	166	47	92	20	1.61
Career	7	16	.304	4.94	36	36	0	209.2	241	71	140	25	1.49

How Often He Throws Strikes

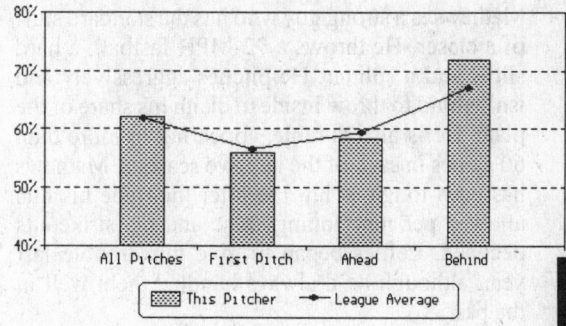

1997 Situational Stats

	W	L	ERA	Sv	IP		AB	H	HR	RBI	Avg
Home	1	5	6.52	0	67.2	LHB	287	85	16	48	.296
Road	2	7	4.98	0	65.0	RHB	259	81	4	31	.313
First Half	2	8	5.49	0	105.0	Sc Pos	137	38	5	56	.277
Scnd Half	1	4	6.83	0	27.2	Clutch	12	5	1	3	.417

1997 Rankings (American League)

⇒ 1st in lowest winning percentage
⇒ 5th in errors at pitcher (4)
⇒ 9th in hit batsmen (9)
⇒ 10th in losses
⇒ Led the Athletics in losses, games started, hit batsmen (9), strikeouts, wild pitches (7), pitches thrown (2,287) and stolen bases allowed (17)

T.J. Mathews

1997 Season

It was an eventful year for T.J. Mathews. He was suspended on Opening Day for headhunting during spring training, then was traded at midseason by St. Louis as the key player in a deal for one of the best-known sluggers in the game, Mark McGwire. Mathews pitched well for the Cardinals prior to his trade, though he did blow three save opportunities without converting one. In Oakland he began in a setup role and eventually took over the closer's job from Billy Taylor. Mathews did convert three saves, but continued to be shaky as a finisher.

Pitching

Mathews is a strong guy who has the standard stuff of a closer. He throws a 92-MPH fastball, a hard slider and a splitter. He pitches aggressively and isn't afraid to throw inside to claim his share of the plate. He is also durable, appearing in more than 60 games in each of the last two seasons. Mathews has been tough to hit, but after the trade his hits allowed per nine innings rose and his strikeouts declined. Lefties began to give him trouble last year, although he'd always handled them well in the past.

Defense

Mathews does more than just pitch aggressively. As a fielder he attacks anything in range, though in his zeal he does throw the ball away on occasion. He's good about covering first base. Mathews has a reputation for being good at holding runners, but basestealers went 13-for-13 against him in 1997.

1998 Outlook

Mathews is in and Taylor is out. Plain and simple, Mathews will be given the ball and asked to close games for the Athletics in 1998. He did have some adjustments after switching leagues, but he should be able to emerge as a solid closer, as Oakland expected when it made the McGwire trade.

Position: RP
Bats: R **Throws:** R
Ht: 6' 2" **Wt:** 200

Opening Day Age: 28
Born: 1/19/70 in Belleville, IL
ML Seasons: 3

Overall Statistics

	W	L	Pct.	ERA	G	GS	Sv	IP	H	BB	SO	HR	Ratio
1997	10	6	.625	3.01	64	0	3	74.2	75	30	70	9	1.41
Career	13	13	.500	2.78	154	0	11	188.0	158	73	178	18	1.23

How Often He Throws Strikes

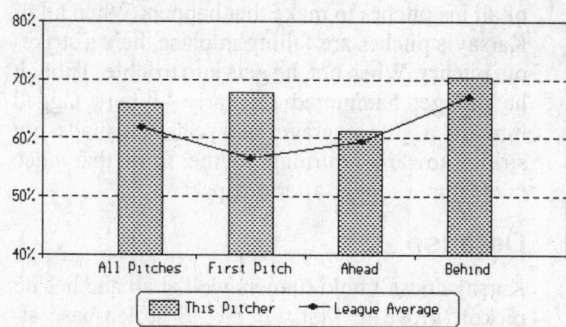

1997 Situational Stats

	W	L	ERA	Sv	IP		AB	H	HR	RBI	Avg
Home	9	3	2.56	2	45.2	LHB	124	40	5	21	.323
Road	1	3	3.72	1	29.0	RHB	164	35	4	12	.213
First Half	3	3	1.73	0	36.1	Sc Pos	93	19	1	21	.204
Scnd Half	7	3	4.23	3	38.1	Clutch	150	43	3	20	.287

1997 Rankings (American League)

⇒ 8th in relief wins (6)

Jason McDonald

1997 Season

Adding another new face to the Athletics' mix, Jason McDonald arrived in May and found himself planted in center field after being a second baseman in college and in the minors. He had trouble adjusting to major league pitching and went down to the minors for a month. When he came back, he was more relaxed and showed more discipline at the plate. McDonald's numbers and playing time rose accordingly.

Hitting

McDonald is an excellent contact hitter who sprays the ball around and uses his speed to help get on base. He's also very selective and knows how to work the count, so if a pitcher will give him nothing to hit he's just as happy to take a walk. Even so, he still has some adjustments to make in order to cut down his strikeout rate. He possesses moderate power and would be hard-pressed to reach double digits in homers.

Baserunning & Defense

McDonald is fast and able to get a good jump on the ball. He made five errors in 166 chances, but should improve as he adjusts to his new position. He has a surprisingly good arm for a former second baseman. McDonald is a good baserunner and can steal a base, but has yet to master reading big league pitchers. He was caught stealing 39 percent of the time in 1997.

1998 Outlook

McDonald is the leading candidate to be both Oakland's starting center fielder and leadoff hitter this year. He has the speed, drive and ability to be successful. However, he will need to improve his strikeout/walk ratio, judge fly balls more accurately and read pitchers better when on base. Look for this to happen and for his performance to improve. At his age, he's not about to develop into a star, but he may establish himself as a useful player.

Position: CF/LF
Bats: B **Throws:** R
Ht: 5' 8" **Wt:** 185

Opening Day Age: 26
Born: 3/20/72 in Modesto, CA
ML Seasons: 1

Overall Statistics

	G	AB	R	H	D	T	HR	RBI	SB	BB	SO	Avg	OBP	Slg
1997	78	236	47	62	11	4	4	14	13	36	49	.263	.361	.394
Career	78	236	47	62	11	4	4	14	13	36	49	.263	.361	.394

Where He Hits the Ball

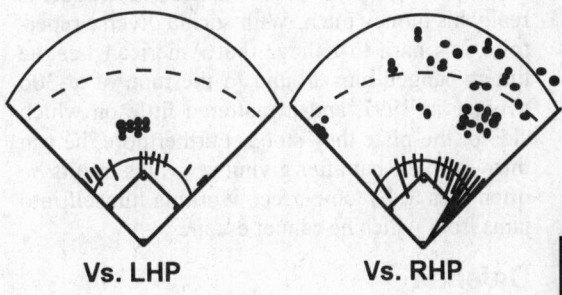

Vs. LHP   **Vs. RHP**

1997 Situational Stats

	AB	H	HR	RBI	Avg		AB	H	HR	RBI	Avg
Home	126	33	1	5	.262	LHP	52	13	0	3	.250
Road	110	29	3	9	.264	RHP	184	49	4	11	.266
First Half	85	19	2	4	.224	Sc Pos	42	10	1	10	.238
Scnd Half	151	43	2	10	.285	Clutch	35	12	1	6	.343

1997 Rankings (American League)

⇒ 5th in errors in center field (4)
⇒ 7th in lowest stolen base percentage (61.9%)
⇒ 10th in bunts in play (18)
⇒ Led the Athletics in triples, stolen bases, caught stealing (8), stolen base percentage (61.9%), bunts in play (18) and steals of third (3)

Ariel Prieto

1997 Season

Probably no one was more disappointed with Ariel Prieto's 1997 campaign than Prieto himself. In 1996, he finished the season strongly despite coming to camp overweight, struggling, and spending time on the disabled list. As a result, expectations last season were high. But there was no carryover, and Prieto's arm gave out again after 22 largely forgettable starts.

Pitching

The prospect of a healthy Prieto is tantalizing, as he offers a full complement of pitches. His fastball arrives around 93 MPH, and he throws both the two- and four-seam varieties. He also mixes in curves, changeups, and sinkers, and a hard slider is really his money pitch. With such a diverse repertoire, it's hard to believe that American League hitters banged him around to the tune of a .306 average in 1997, and it mattered little on which side of the plate they stood. Furthermore, he can throw strikes, but after giving up walks or hits he often tries to be too perfect, working himself into jams from which he cannot escape.

Defense

Despite his size, Prieto gets off the mound quickly and provides good defense, covering both the mound and first base very well. He has a good pickoff move and holds baserunners well.

1998 Outlook

Oakland would dearly love for Prieto to realize his potential and become the pitcher they thought they had snagged with the fifth overall pick in the 1995 draft. He does have talent and will hold down a spot in the rotation going into 1998. Whether he remains, however, will depend on Prieto himself. The A's would like to see him remain healthy and effective over a full season. If he isn't able to do that for them this time around, his next chance may have to come somewhere else.

Position: SP
Bats: R **Throws:** R
Ht: 6' 3" **Wt:** 225

Opening Day Age: 28
Born: 10/22/69 in Havana, Cuba
ML Seasons: 3
Pronunciation: AIR-ee-el pree-AY-toe

Overall Statistics

	W	L	Pct.	ERA	G	GS	Sv	IP	H	BB	SO	HR	Ratio
1997	6	8	.429	5.04	22	22	0	125.0	155	70	90	16	1.80
Career	14	21	.400	4.67	57	52	0	308.2	342	156	202	29	1.61

How Often He Throws Strikes

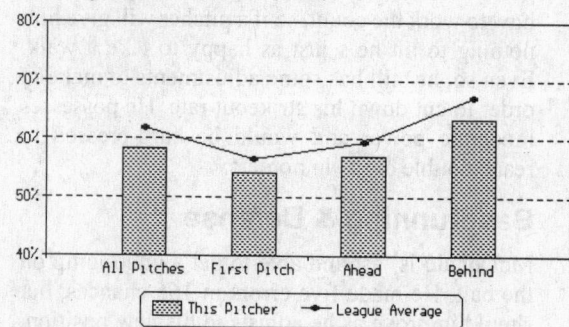

1997 Situational Stats

	W	L	ERA	Sv	IP		AB	H	HR	RBI	Avg
Home	5	2	3.61	0	57.1	LHB	259	80	8	34	.309
Road	1	6	6.25	0	67.2	RHB	247	75	8	38	.304
First Half	6	5	4.73	0	110.1	Sc Pos	142	39	2	52	.275
Scnd Half	0	3	7.36	0	14.2	Clutch	15	6	1	4	.400

1997 Rankings (American League)

⇒ 2nd in errors at pitcher (5) and lowest fielding percentage at pitcher (.848)
⇒ Led the Athletics in walks allowed, wild pitches (7), balks (1), runners caught stealing (5) and lowest batting average allowed with runners in scoring position

Brad Rigby

1997 Season

Like most of the pitchers who ultimately would comprise the Oakland rotation, Brad Rigby wasn't in the majors when the 1997 season began. After 15 solid starts at Triple-A, he was promoted to Oakland and made 14 starts. Poor run support was as much a contributor to his 1-7 record as anything else. He was very consistent and the A's best starter in the second half.

Pitching

Rigby is a large presence on the mound at 6-foot-6, though he could really stand to fill out a little more and hopefully gain a little more velocity. As it is, he has a fastball in the low 90s to go with a changeup, curveball and an above-average slider. Despite Rigby's size and stuff, he's not overpowering. He uses a good mix of pitches, but like many hurlers he gets hit when he tries to be too precise. That tendency shows in the 14 homers he allowed in 77⅔ innings. He needs to improve against lefthanders, who hit him at a .342 clip in the majors and a .323 clip in the minors last year.

Defense

Rigby is very good at holding baserunners, as only two even tried to steal against him. His move to first is similarly effective. He's adequate at fielding his position. He has a decent glove, but his size and delivery don't make it easy for him to cover first on grounders hit to the right side of the infield.

1998 Outlook

Oakland's starting five this year will look nothing like the rotation at the beginning of 1997, and Rigby will be one of the new faces involved. His performance, record aside, really was very good and left the A's impressed with his poise. He'll need to pitch more aggressively, especially to lefties, but is entrenched as a starter. The A's see him as a member of their rotation, hopefully for years to come.

Position: SP
Bats: R **Throws:** R
Ht: 6' 6" **Wt:** 195

Opening Day Age: 24
Born: 5/14/73 in Milwaukee, WI
ML Seasons: 1

Overall Statistics

	W	L	Pct.	ERA	G	GS	Sv	IP	H	BB	SO	HR	Ratio
1997	1	7	.125	4.87	14	14	0	77.2	92	22	34	14	1.47
Career	1	7	.125	4.87	14	14	0	77.2	92	22	34	14	1.47

How Often He Throws Strikes

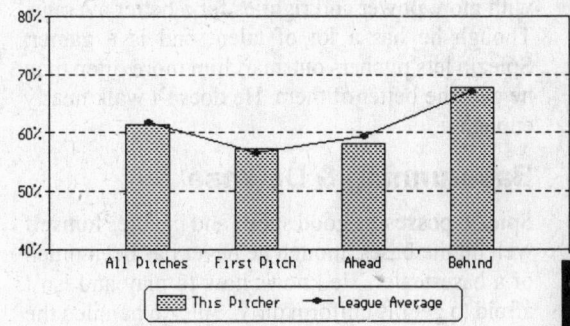

1997 Situational Stats

	W	L	ERA	Sv	IP		AB	H	HR	RBI	Avg
Home	1	4	4.13	0	52.1	LHB	155	53	7	19	.342
Road	0	3	6.39	0	25.1	RHB	150	39	7	20	.260
First Half	0	2	5.25	0	12.0	Sc Pos	71	17	1	23	.239
Scnd Half	1	5	4.80	0	65.2	Clutch	12	3	1	1	.250

1997 Rankings (American League)

⇒ Did not rank near the top or bottom in any category

Scott Spiezio

1997 Season

One of Oakland's big surprises of spring training was the release of second baseman Brent Gates. The A's further surprised observers by giving rookie third baseman Scott Spiezio the everyday job at second base. Spiezio handled the adjustment well, playing excellent defense and hitting with good power for a middle infielder, though his numbers dipped during the second half.

Hitting

Spiezio is a good gap hitter with decent power. He has the ability to turn on anything inside and he can drive outside pitches, but he's had problems maintaining a consistent stroke. He hits lefthanders with more power and righties for a better average. Though he has a lot of talent and is a gamer, Spiezio lets pitchers outsmart him more often than he gets the better of them. He doesn't walk nearly enough.

Baserunning & Defense

Spiezio possesses good speed and handles himself well on the bases, though he never has been much of a basestealer. He knows how to play and isn't afraid to get his uniform dirty. Spiezio handled the tough move from third to second wonderfully, leading American League second basemen with a .990 fielding percentage. He quickly developed the ability to turn the double play.

1998 Outlook

Spiezio enters the season as a regular. He'll probably be at second base, but could return to third base if the Athletics have him switch places with Mark Bellhorn, a shortstop in college. That seems unlikely after his solid glovework at the keystone. Spiezio needs to learn to make adjustments rather than stick with what has worked in the past. He's already got decent power for a middle infielder and he's got the potential to develop even more.

Position: 2B
Bats: B **Throws:** R
Ht: 6' 2" **Wt:** 195

Opening Day Age: 25
Born: 9/21/72 in Joliet, IL
ML Seasons: 2
Pronunciation: SPEE-zee-oh

Overall Statistics

	G	AB	R	H	D	T	HR	RBI	SB	BB	SO	Avg	OBP	Slg
1997	147	538	58	131	28	4	14	65	9	44	75	.243	.300	.388
Career	156	567	64	140	30	4	16	73	9	48	79	.247	.305	.399

Where He Hits the Ball

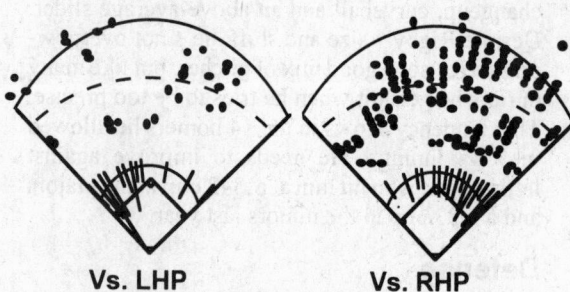

Vs. LHP   Vs. RHP

1997 Situational Stats

	AB	H	HR	RBI	Avg		AB	H	HR	RBI	Avg
Home	280	68	6	39	.243	LHP	149	35	7	24	.235
Road	258	63	8	26	.244	RHP	389	96	7	41	.247
First Half	270	64	8	34	.237	Sc Pos	125	29	3	47	.232
Scnd Half	268	67	6	31	.250	Clutch	86	20	2	7	.233

1997 Rankings (American League)

⇒ 1st in fielding percentage at second base (.990)
⇒ 7th in lowest batting average, lowest on-base percentage and lowest on-base percentage vs. righthanded pitchers (.295)
⇒ 8th in lowest batting average at home and highest percentage of swings put into play (52.1%)
⇒ 9th in lowest groundball/flyball ratio (0.8)
⇒ 10th in lowest batting average vs. lefthanded pitchers and lowest batting average vs. righthanded pitchers
⇒ Led the Athletics in at-bats, triples, plate appearances (590), games played (147), lowest percentage of swings that missed (12.2%) and highest percentage of swings put into play (52.1%)

Matt Stairs

1997 Season

After slamming 10 homers in 137 at-bats in 1996, Matt Stairs finally received an opportunity at more than a couple of hundred gratuitous at-bats. He displayed the power that his previous performances had hinted at. His presence in the lineup somewhat alleviated Mark McGwire's departure, as he was able to help replace McGwire's power in the middle of the order. He also played well defensively in right field in the process.

Hitting

Stairs is an aggressive hitter who swings from the heels, to the extreme that he literally corkscrews as part of his follow-through. Because of that and his exceptional ability to pull the ball, he's able to drive fastballs long distances, especially if they're low. When he's not on his game he hits the ball to left-center, but when in a groove he hits well to all fields. Stairs' pitch selection is inconsistent, but he can draw a walk.

Baserunning & Defense

Possessing a squat, Kirby Puckett-kind of body, Stairs isn't particularly fast but does get the job done in right field. He doesn't make a lot of mistakes and his arm is very strong, as witnessed by the nine assists he racked up last season. Just don't ask him to steal a base. He has four in 252 major league games.

1998 Outlook

Oakland has a lot of choices to make, but following his coming-out party, Stairs probably has earned a spot for himself somewhere in the Oakland lineup. A valuable lefthanded bat, he can be a designated hitter and play the outfield, and could provide valuable veteran leadership to a young Athletics team. The A's will likely bat him cleanup and give him 500 at-bats for the first time in his major league career.

Position: RF/LF/DH
Bats: L **Throws:** R
Ht: 5' 9" **Wt:** 200

Opening Day Age: 30
Born: 2/27/68 in Saint John, New Brunswick, Canada
ML Seasons: 5

Overall Statistics

	G	AB	R	H	D	T	HR	RBI	SB	BB	SO	Avg	OBP	Slg
1997	133	352	62	105	19	0	27	73	3	50	60	.298	.386	.582
Career	252	615	94	174	34	2	38	120	4	80	105	.283	.366	.530

Where He Hits the Ball

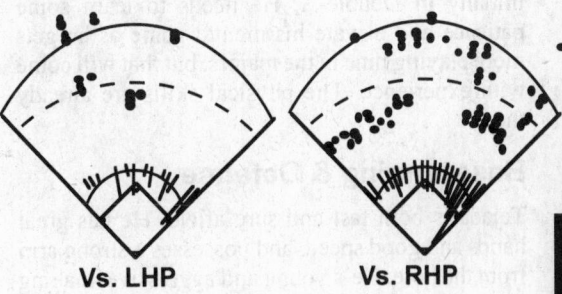

Vs. LHP   **Vs. RHP**

1997 Situational Stats

	AB	H	HR	RBI	Avg		AB	H	HR	RBI	Avg
Home	197	60	20	46	.305	LHP	85	22	8	20	.259
Road	155	45	7	27	.290	RHP	267	83	19	53	.311
First Half	135	48	12	35	.356	Sc Pos	99	27	7	44	.273
Scnd Half	217	57	15	38	.263	Clutch	72	20	6	16	.278

1997 Rankings (American League)

⇒ 5th in lowest cleanup slugging percentage (.427)
⇒ Led the Athletics in least GDPs per GDP situation (6.7%) and highest percentage of pitches taken (60.0%)

Miguel Tejada

1997 Season

Miguel Tejada's appearance in an Athletics uniform was probably as much of a surprise to him as it was to Oakland management. The best shortstop prospect in the game wasn't even slated for a September call-up before injuries forced the team's hand. His short stint in the bigs reflects little on his skills. At Double-A Huntsville, Tejada hit .275-22-97 with 15 stolen bases.

Hitting

If Oakland has a tools player in the system, Tejada is the man. He's capable of hitting for both power and average, and has a quick and explosive bat. He proved to be vulnerable to righthanders during his first month in the majors, but he likewise struggled initially in Double-A. He needs to learn some patience and elevate his mental game as he gets more playing time in the majors, but that will come with experience. The physical skills are already there.

Baserunning & Defense

Tejada is both fast and sure afield. He has great hands and good speed, and possesses a strong arm from the hole. He's young and aggressive, making him prone to the occasional error. Tejada has had modest steal totals in the minors, belying his speed. He'll become more of a threat when he learns to read pitchers.

1998 Outlook

Tejada will be Oakland's shortstop on Opening Day. The Athletics are trying to be cautious and not rush him too fast, but for a team that is really rebuilding they have little to lose by throwing him into the fray. He'll struggle as most talented youngsters do, but watch for him eventually to develop into a star. For 1998, he's capable of hitting for a little bit of power, although it may take another year or two for him to get his average up.

Position: SS
Bats: R **Throws:** R
Ht: 5'10" **Wt:** 170

Opening Day Age: 21
Born: 5/25/76 in Bani, DR
ML Seasons: 1
Pronunciation:
mee-GELL
teh-HA-duh

Overall Statistics

	G	AB	R	H	D	T	HR	RBI	SB	BB	SO	Avg	OBP	Slg
1997	26	99	10	20	3	2	2	10	2	2	22	.202	.240	.333
Career	26	99	10	20	3	2	2	10	2	2	22	.202	.240	.333

Where He Hits the Ball

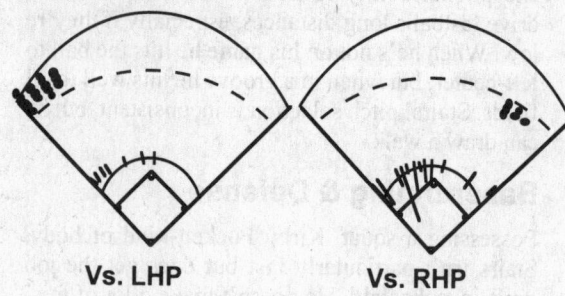

Vs. LHP   **Vs. RHP**

1997 Situational Stats

	AB	H	HR	RBI	Avg		AB	H	HR	RBI	Avg
Home	50	6	1	4	.120	LHP	28	7	1	2	.250
Road	49	14	1	6	.286	RHP	71	13	1	8	.183
First Half	0	0	0	0	-	Sc Pos	22	7	1	9	.318
Scnd Half	99	20	2	10	.202	Clutch	15	3	1	2	.200

1997 Rankings (American League)

⇒ Did not rank near the top or bottom in any category

George Williams

1997 Season

When Terry Steinbach left the A's to sign a free-agent contract with the Twins last winter, George Williams became Oakland's starting catcher by default. Despite a tough 1996 season, his hitting numbers always had been encouraging. Once he got his chance, however, Williams really proved to be no more than a platoon catcher. Plagued by minor injuries, he did hit lefthanders very well (.324) and showed an ability to get on base.

Hitting

Williams is a spray hitter. He has a great deal of patience and knows how to work pitchers, a skill that makes itself evident in his fine on-base percentage. He handles all pitches well and is especially adept at taking offspeed stuff to the opposite field. Williams doesn't have much power, at least at the major league level, and his slugging percentage continues to languish near his on-base percentage.

Baserunning & Defense

Defensively, Williams is less than stellar. He possesses a poor arm and is an easy mark for basestealers. They were successful against him 73 percent of the time in 1997, one of the worst rates against an American League catcher. Worse, he also committed six errors in 498 innings. Williams can get on base, but once there he's not much of a threat to go anywhere unless advanced by a homer. Even at that, it might take him a while to round the bases.

1998 Outlook

Williams has been steady and isn't a bad ball-player, but he certainly isn't a starting catcher. In fact, his overall skills don't seem to point to being a platoon backstop either. He's really more suited to the role of backup. With Brent Mayne aboard, and prospects Ramon Hernandez and A.J. Hinch nearly ready, even that role may be in jeopardy. As a switch-hitting catcher with the ability to reach base, he can be a useful bench player.

Position: C
Bats: B **Throws:** R
Ht: 5'10" **Wt:** 190

Opening Day Age: 28
Born: 4/22/69 in Lacrosse, WI
ML Seasons: 3

Overall Statistics

	G	AB	R	H	D	T	HR	RBI	SB	BB	SO	Avg	OBP	Slg
1997	76	201	30	58	9	1	3	22	0	35	46	.289	.397	.388
Career	161	412	60	101	19	2	9	46	0	74	99	.245	.366	.367

Where He Hits the Ball

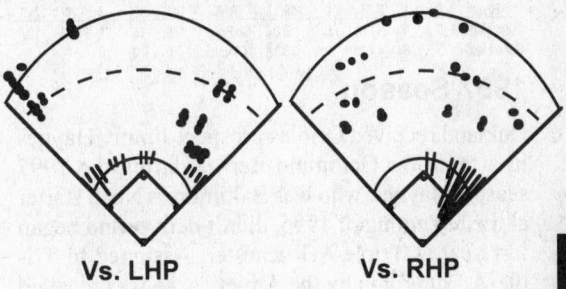

Vs. LHP   **Vs. RHP**

1997 Situational Stats

	AB	H	HR	RBI	Avg		AB	H	HR	RBI	Avg
Home	99	34	2	12	.343	LHP	68	22	2	5	.324
Road	102	24	1	10	.235	RHP	133	36	1	17	.271
First Half	160	41	1	15	.256	Sc Pos	53	14	0	19	.264
Scnd Half	41	17	2	7	.415	Clutch	38	11	0	8	.289

1997 Rankings (American League)
⇒ 7th in errors at catcher (6)

Jimmy Haynes

Position: SP
Bats: R **Throws:** R
Ht: 6' 3" **Wt:** 180

Opening Day Age: 25
Born: 9/5/72 in
LaGrange, GA
ML Seasons: 3

Overall Statistics

	W	L	Pct.	ERA	G	GS	Sv	IP	H	BB	SO	HR	Ratio
1997	3	6	.333	4.42	13	13	0	73.1	74	40	65	7	1.55
Career	8	13	.381	5.99	43	27	1	186.1	207	110	152	23	1.70

1997 Situational Stats

	W	L	ERA	Sv	IP		AB	H	HR	RBI	Avg
Home	1	5	4.91	0	44.0	LHB	141	35	4	13	.248
Road	2	1	3.68	0	29.1	RHB	141	39	3	20	.277
First Half	0	0	-	0	0.0	Sc Pos	76	15	1	25	.197
Scnd Half	3	6	4.42	0	73.1	Clutch	0	0	0	0	-

1997 Season

Oakland received Orioles prospect Jimmy Haynes in a trade for Geronimo Berroa during the 1997 season. Haynes, who was Baltimore's No. 5 starter at the beginning of 1996, didn't deliver and began last year at Triple-A Rochester. Assigned to Triple-A Edmonton by the Athletics, he was recalled in July. Once in the rotation, he delivered steady if unspectacular numbers, establishing himself as a starter.

Pitching & Defense

Haynes brings his fastball at 93 MPH, adding in a slider, changeup and an excellent curveball. The curve is his bread-and-butter pitch. He has fine control and can move the ball around the strike zone. Haynes is an excellent defensive player and has a fine move to first. He keeps runners in check very well.

1998 Outlook

So much was thought of Haynes when the Orioles promoted him in 1996 that his demotion was difficult to accept. Things are different in Oakland, and Haynes merely needs to work some innings to regain his confidence and composure. He still has a live arm and is penciled in as a starter for 1998.

Dave Magadan

Position: 3B/1B/DH
Bats: L **Throws:** R
Ht: 6' 3" **Wt:** 210

Opening Day Age: 35
Born: 9/30/62 in
Tampa, FL
ML Seasons: 12

Overall Statistics

	G	AB	R	H	D	T	HR	RBI	SB	BB	SO	Avg	OBP	Slg
1997	128	271	38	82	10	1	4	30	1	50	40	.303	.414	.391
Career	1245	3542	459	1026	184	12	36	419	10	616	455	.290	.393	.379

1997 Situational Stats

	AB	H	HR	RBI	Avg		AB	H	HR	RBI	Avg
Home	129	39	2	15	.302	LHP	41	9	0	7	.220
Road	142	43	2	15	.303	RHP	230	73	4	23	.317
First Half	114	31	3	9	.272	Sc Pos	62	16	0	23	.258
Scnd Half	157	51	1	21	.325	Clutch	64	19	0	7	.297

1997 Season

Dave Magadan is a smart player who certainly gets the most out of his skills. His experience and hitting knowledge added veteran leadership to a team which lost most of its stars and veterans during the course of the season. Magadan filled in aptly at both corner positions when injuries and trades left Oakland shorthanded, and got on base regularly.

Hitting, Baserunning & Defense

Magadan is a line-drive hitter who can spray the ball to all fields. He has an excellent eye and is disciplined, so a fine on-base percentage usually accompanies his near-.300 batting average. He doesn't have much power and isn't so much of a run producer as he is a valuable bat off the bench and a role player. He's very good in that role. Magadan can make the plays in the field, but his defense is hardly stellar and his speed is limited.

1998 Outlook

Though he briefly became a free agent, Magadan quickly decided to return to Oakland for an encore in 1998. Most of his 12-year career has been spent platooning, subbing, and pinch hitting, and his role next season probably won't be much different.

Damon Mashore

Position: CF/LF
Bats: R **Throws:** R
Ht: 5'11" **Wt:** 195

Opening Day Age: 28
Born: 10/31/69 in Ponce, PR
ML Seasons: 2
Pronunciation: MAY-shore

Overall Statistics

	G	AB	R	H	D	T	HR	RBI	SB	BB	SO	Avg	OBP	Slg
1997	92	279	55	69	10	2	3	18	5	50	82	.247	.370	.330
Career	142	384	75	97	17	3	6	30	9	66	113	.253	.369	.359

1997 Situational Stats

	AB	H	HR	RBI	Avg		AB	H	HR	RBI	Avg
Home	110	25	1	5	.227	LHP	74	22	2	7	.297
Road	169	44	2	13	.260	RHP	205	47	1	11	.229
First Half	251	61	2	16	.243	Sc Pos	51	13	0	14	.255
Scnd Half	28	8	1	2	.286	Clutch	35	11	0	1	.314

1997 Season

Damon Mashore, long ago heralded as Oakland's center fielder of the future, arrived in 1997 at the expense of Ernie Young. Mashore grabbed the starting job and proceeded to tear up the American League for a month. He walked regularly, hit for average and did everything a leadoff hitter should. But the league got wise, Mashore's body gave out and Jason McDonald eventually replaced him.

Hitting, Baserunning & Defense

Mashore is a good opposite-field hitter. Though he can coax a walk from opposing pitchers, he's still inconsistent and can't make adjustments, as witnessed by his falloff after becoming a starter. Mashore is a fast runner and can steal a base, but he often misreads pitchers and gets caught. He's an excellent defender with a terrific arm.

1998 Outlook

For a while it looked like Mashore had really made it, as he played an aggressive center field and hit with authority. His success was short-lived, however, and he played very little over the second half. After the 1997 season, the Athletics optioned him back to Triple-A Edmonton, leaving him unprotected with a questionable future in the majors. He could be a serviceable fourth outfielder.

Brent Mayne

Position: C
Bats: L **Throws:** R
Ht: 6' 1" **Wt:** 190

Opening Day Age: 29
Born: 4/19/68 in Loma Linda, CA
ML Seasons: 8

Overall Statistics

	G	AB	R	H	D	T	HR	RBI	SB	BB	SO	Avg	OBP	Slg
1997	85	256	29	74	12	0	6	22	1	18	33	.289	.343	.406
Career	554	1468	142	375	68	3	15	147	7	124	225	.255	.315	.337

1997 Situational Stats

	AB	H	HR	RBI	Avg		AB	H	HR	RBI	Avg
Home	130	41	4	15	.315	LHP	43	12	0	2	.279
Road	126	33	2	7	.262	RHP	213	62	6	20	.291
First Half	87	17	2	7	.195	Sc Pos	56	12	0	12	.214
Scnd Half	169	57	4	15	.337	Clutch	38	12	0	2	.316

1997 Season

A last-minute addition to the roster, Brent Mayne contributed to the Athletics by catching and providing a lefthanded bat, garnering substantial playing time after injuries felled starting backstop George Williams. After a hot streak in May, Mayne looked like he would grab the spot full-time, but his bat cooled and platooning returned.

Hitting, Baserunning & Defense

Mayne is a spray hitter who effectively lines the ball toward both gaps. He has good patience and knows the art of pitching, so he's adept at getting a good pitch to hit. He doesn't have a lot of power, but Mayne has learned to squeeze a couple of homers out of his 250-plus at-bats each season. He also has learned to hit lefthanders. He doesn't possess much speed, and though he's a good defensive backstop, he doesn't discourage basestealers with his arm.

1998 Outlook

After performing well as a platoon player, Mayne is probably good enough to merit a starting job on many big league clubs. He signed with San Francisco as a free agent and will serve as a backup to Brian Johnson.

Oakland Athletics

Mike Oquist

Position: SP
Bats: R **Throws:** R
Ht: 6' 2" **Wt:** 170

Opening Day Age: 29
Born: 5/30/68 in Lajunta, CO
ML Seasons: 5

Overall Statistics

	W	L	Pct.	ERA	G	GS	Sv	IP	H	BB	SO	HR	Ratio
1997	4	6	.400	5.02	19	17	0	107.2	111	43	72	15	1.43
Career	9	10	.474	4.96	74	26	0	239.1	255	122	150	28	1.58

1997 Situational Stats

	W	L	ERA	Sv	IP		AB	H	HR	RBI	Avg
Home	2	3	4.96	0	49.0	LHB	219	57	8	29	.260
Road	2	3	5.06	0	58.2	RHB	199	54	7	25	.271
First Half	2	2	4.03	0	58.0	Sc Pos	77	24	5	38	.312
Scnd Half	2	4	6.16	0	49.2	Clutch	15	5	0	1	.333

1997 Season

After languishing in the Oriole system for seven years, Mike Oquist signed with the Athletics in 1996 and worked his way into their rotation a year later. A fine athlete, he may have been expendable in Baltimore, but in Oakland, starters are hard to come by. He was a valuable asset and contributed 17 starts.

Pitching & Defense

A classic nibbler, Oquist moves the ball around to ensure success. Since his fastball only reaches 88 MPH, he must use his changeup, curveball and good slider to tie up batters. Oquist doesn't walk a lot of hitters, but he's vulnerable to homers because he's always around the plate. He possesses an excellent move to first and is likewise a fine defender.

1998 Outlook

Based upon his dependable if unspectacular performance in 1997, Oquist will enter spring training with a spot in the A's rotation. There are some questions about his durability after he spent time on the disabled list with a sore shoulder last year, but he was consistent. Oakland likes that and will give him a chance to develop.

Aaron Small

Position: RP
Bats: R **Throws:** R
Ht: 6' 5" **Wt:** 208

Opening Day Age: 26
Born: 11/23/71 in Oxnard, CA
ML Seasons: 4

Overall Statistics

	W	L	Pct.	ERA	G	GS	Sv	IP	H	BB	SO	HR	Ratio
1997	9	5	.643	4.28	71	0	4	96.2	109	40	57	6	1.54
Career	11	8	.579	5.05	91	3	4	133.2	158	70	79	11	1.71

1997 Situational Stats

	W	L	ERA	Sv	IP		AB	H	HR	RBI	Avg
Home	5	1	4.36	2	53.2	LHB	168	55	2	27	.327
Road	4	4	4.19	2	43.0	RHB	203	54	4	23	.266
First Half	6	4	5.13	3	52.2	Sc Pos	115	33	1	41	.287
Scnd Half	3	1	3.27	1	44.0	Clutch	142	37	2	18	.261

1997 Season

Hard as it is to believe, Aaron Small led the Athletics in wins without starting a game. The trend for his season was set in early April after he was promoted. He arrived at the park in the fifth inning, pitched a perfect ninth in a tie game against Boston and walked away with a win. The rest of the year continued in much the same manner, and he proved to be the most dependable Oakland hurler.

Pitching & Defense

Small throws a good fastball which he fires at 92 MPH, and complements it with a sinker, slider, and changeup. He can be overpowering, but lefthanders don't seem to know that and hit him at a .327 clip in 1997. Small's defense is average, but he holds runners fairly well.

1998 Outlook

Small did everything a team could ask of a middle reliever, converting nine seemingly hopeless games into wins while saving another four. He should maintain his setup role and could improve some of his numbers.

Billy Taylor

Position: RP
Bats: R **Throws:** R
Ht: 6' 8" **Wt:** 200

Opening Day Age: 36
Born: 10/16/61 in
Monticello, FL
ML Seasons: 3

Overall Statistics

	W	L	Pct.	ERA	G	GS	Sv	IP	H	BB	SO	HR	Ratio
1997	3	4	.429	3.82	72	0	23	73.0	70	36	66	3	1.45
Career	10	10	.500	3.91	168	0	41	179.2	160	79	181	12	1.33

1997 Situational Stats

	W	L	ERA	Sv	IP		AB	H	HR	RBI	Avg
Home	1	0	4.50	12	40.0	LHB	130	42	2	22	.323
Road	2	4	3.00	11	33.0	RHB	146	28	1	17	.192
First Half	2	4	5.40	16	36.2	Sc Pos	104	28	1	36	.269
Scnd Half	1	0	2.23	7	36.1	Clutch	189	42	2	28	.222

1997 Season

No one in an Oakland uniform mirrored the frustration of the Athletics in 1997 more than Billy Taylor. After enduring an awful spring, he managed to post 23 saves but also blew seven. Despite that and the fact that he was the only A's pitcher to work more than 10 innings with an ERA less than 4.00, he still lost his job as the team's closer to T.J. Mathews.

Pitching & Defense

Taylor is a sinker-slider pitcher who regularly changes his delivery to confuse hitters, especially righties, who batted only .192 against him. He constantly varies his arm angle, reaches 90 MPH with his fastball and mixes in a changeup to keep hitters honest. His defense is adequate and he's fair at holding baserunners.

1998 Outlook

Anyone who witnessed Taylor's inability to put away the Red Sox in an August 20 game knew his closer days were finished. With two out and none on, he went to two strikes on three straight hitters but couldn't get the job done. He never has been a true closer, and setting up Mathews should suit his nature and skills well.

Ernie Young

Position: CF/RF
Bats: R **Throws:** R
Ht: 6' 1" **Wt:** 190

Opening Day Age: 28
Born: 7/8/69 in
Chicago, IL
ML Seasons: 4

Overall Statistics

	G	AB	R	H	D	T	HR	RBI	SB	BB	SO	Avg	OBP	Slg
1997	71	175	22	39	7	0	5	15	1	19	57	.223	.303	.349
Career	249	717	105	163	30	4	26	87	8	80	195	.227	.310	.389

1997 Situational Stats

	AB	H	HR	RBI	Avg		AB	H	HR	RBI	Avg
Home	94	21	3	9	.223	LHP	61	11	0	4	.180
Road	81	18	2	6	.222	RHP	114	28	5	11	.246
First Half	46	6	1	1	.130	Sc Pos	43	6	1	8	.140
Scnd Half	129	33	4	14	.256	Clutch	28	4	0	1	.143

1997 Season

Ernie Young, who traditionally has excelled during second tours of the same level, couldn't get untracked in 1997. He was sent down to the minors after 46 at-bats, and by the time he returned it was late July. Both his confidence and his chances at reclaiming a starting job were gone.

Hitting, Baserunning & Defense

Young hits to right-center field with good power. He's strong and works hard, but is prone to impatience at the plate and can be pitched to. Young is fast and is a good baserunner, but isn't much of a basestealer. He's probably better suited to playing left field than center or right, though he did patrol center for 60 games in 1997. While his defense is average, he has a good arm, as witnessed by the five assists he had as a part-time player.

1998 Outlook

A change of scenery might spell a rebirth for Young. There are few givens on the Oakland roster, so it isn't inconceivable that he could grab a spot on the club, perhaps as a fourth outfielder. If he gets a chance elsewhere, Young has proven he can be a solid contributor given a full season of at-bats.

Other Oakland Athletics

Mark Acre (Pos: RHP, Age: 29)

	W	L	Pct.	ERA	G	GS	Sv	IP	H	BB	SO	HR	Ratio
1997	2	0	1.000	5.74	15	0	0	15.2	21	8	12	1	1.85
Career	9	6	.600	5.17	114	0	2	127.0	135	68	98	16	1.60

The giant-sized righthander struggled early in the '97 season, then was sent to Triple-A Edmonton, where he pitched reasonably well. He was sold to Japan's Yakult Swallows in the winter. 1998 Outlook: D

Willie Adams (Pos: RHP, Age: 25)

	W	L	Pct.	ERA	G	GS	Sv	IP	H	BB	SO	HR	Ratio
1997	3	5	.375	8.18	13	12	0	58.1	73	32	37	9	1.80
Career	6	9	.400	5.81	25	24	0	134.2	149	55	105	20	1.51

After an impressive debut with the A's in 1996, Adams struggled mightily last year and spent a lot of the season in Triple-A Edmonton. Only 25, he'll get another chance this year. 1998 Outlook: B

Rafael Bournigal (Pos: SS, Age: 31, Bats: R)

	G	AB	R	H	D	T	HR	RBI	SB	BB	SO	Avg	OBP	Slg
1997	79	222	29	62	9	0	1	20	2	16	19	.279	.339	.333
Career	225	628	65	161	28	3	1	52	6	42	47	.256	.311	.315

Bournigal seems to define the genre of the good-field, no-hit utility infielder. Though clearly not an everyday player, he filled in well as a parade of starters strolled in and out of the Oakland lineup. 1998 Outlook: B

Tilson Brito (Pos: 2B/3B/SS, Age: 25, Bats: R)

	G	AB	R	H	D	T	HR	RBI	SB	BB	SO	Avg	OBP	Slg
1997	66	172	17	41	5	1	2	14	1	10	38	.238	.285	.314
Career	92	252	27	60	12	1	3	21	2	20	56	.238	.305	.329

Brito began last season with the Blue Jays, then went to the A's on waivers in August. Despite being hampered by a back injury, he hit .283 with good power for his new club. 1998 Outlook: B

Buddy Groom (Pos: LHP, Age: 32)

	W	L	Pct.	ERA	G	GS	Sv	IP	H	BB	SO	HR	Ratio
1997	2	2	.500	5.15	78	0	3	64.2	75	24	45	9	1.53
Career	9	15	.375	5.31	258	15	8	305.0	368	138	194	37	1.66

Groom wasn't nearly as successful last year as he'd been in 1996, but he handled his main job—getting out lefties—well enough to keep him in the majors. 1998 Outlook: A

Gary Haught (Pos: RHP, Age: 27)

	W	L	Pct.	ERA	G	GS	Sv	IP	H	BB	SO	HR	Ratio
1997	0	0	-	7.15	6	0	0	11.1	12	6	11	3	1.59
Career	0	0	-	7.15	6	0	0	11.1	12	6	11	3	1.59

A veteran minor league reliever, Haught didn't impress the A's much in a brief trial last year and they designated him for assignment. Still only 27, he might get a shot with someone this year. 1998 Outlook: C

Dane Johnson (Pos: RHP, Age: 35)

	W	L	Pct.	ERA	G	GS	Sv	IP	H	BB	SO	HR	Ratio
1997	4	1	.800	4.53	38	0	2	45.2	49	31	43	4	1.75
Career	6	2	.750	4.70	63	0	2	67.0	70	47	57	6	1.75

The A's have a fondness for minor league veterans, and they gave the well-traveled Johnson a long look last year. He wasn't overly impressive, and they sold him to the Toronto system in October. 1998 Outlook: C

Tim Kubinski (Pos: LHP, Age: 26)

	W	L	Pct.	ERA	G	GS	Sv	IP	H	BB	SO	HR	Ratio
1997	0	0	-	5.68	11	0	0	12.2	12	6	10	2	1.42
Career	0	0	-	5.68	11	0	0	12.2	12	6	10	2	1.42

Another one of the many minor league veterans to get a shot with the A's last year, Kubinski had some problems but did a nice job of handling lefty swingers. He might stick around this year. 1998 Outlook: B

Patrick Lennon (Pos: LF/RF/DH, Age: 29, Bats: R)

	G	AB	R	H	D	T	HR	RBI	SB	BB	SO	Avg	OBP	Slg
1997	56	116	14	34	6	1	1	14	0	15	35	.293	.374	.388
Career	80	156	21	42	10	1	1	16	0	25	46	.269	.370	.365

A talented hitter who's been set back by injuries and personal problems, Lennon got his first real chance at 29 last year. He hit well enough to possibly fashion a career as a bench player. 1998 Outlook: B

Brian Lesher (Pos: LF, Age: 27, Bats: R)

	G	AB	R	H	D	T	HR	RBI	SB	BB	SO	Avg	OBP	Slg
1997	46	131	17	30	4	1	4	16	4	9	30	.229	.275	.366
Career	72	213	28	49	7	1	9	32	4	14	47	.230	.277	.399

Lesher got a late-season shot with the A's last year and filled in at several positions. He hit for a low average and didn't display much patience, but he did hit with power. 1998 Outlook: B

Andrew Lorraine (Pos: LHP, Age: 25)

	W	L	Pct.	ERA	G	GS	Sv	IP	H	BB	SO	HR	Ratio
1997	3	1	.750	6.37	12	6	0	29.2	45	15	18	2	2.02
Career	3	3	.500	7.35	21	9	0	56.1	78	28	33	9	1.88

Lorraine was once considered a hot prospect, but he was traded a couple of times before surfacing with the A's last year. He was hit hard and Oakland sent him back to the minors. 1998 Outlook: C

Mike Mohler (Pos: LHP, Age: 29)

	W	L	Pct.	ERA	G	GS	Sv	IP	H	BB	SO	HR	Ratio
1997	1	10	.091	5.13	62	10	1	101.2	116	54	66	11	1.67
Career	9	21	.300	4.65	205	20	9	273.0	270	159	191	31	1.57

After a solid 1996 season, Mohler had an ugly '97, going 1-10 and getting lit up by the lefties he's paid to retire. Since he's lefthanded and still breathing, he'll undoubtedly get another chance. 1998 Outlook: B

Izzy Molina (**Pos**: C, **Age**: 26, **Bats**: R)

	G	AB	R	H	D	T	HR	RBI	SB	BB	SO	Avg	OBP	Slg
1997	48	111	6	22	3	1	3	7	0	3	17	.198	.219	.324
Career	62	136	6	27	5	1	3	8	0	4	20	.199	.221	.316

Molina got his first extended major league look last year and struggled mightily at bat. His defense wasn't very good, either. A backup job is all he can realistically hope for. 1998 Outlook: C

Steve Montgomery (**Pos**: RHP, **Age**: 27)

	W	L	Pct.	ERA	G	GS	Sv	IP	H	BB	SO	HR	Ratio
1997	0	1	.000	9.95	4	0	0	6.1	10	8	1	2	2.84
Career	1	1	.500	9.45	12	0	0	20.0	28	21	9	7	2.45

Montgomery had trials with the A's each of the last two seasons, and posted ERAs of 9.22 and 9.95. They dealt him to Cleveland's Buffalo farm club in July, but he didn't impress. 1998 Outlook: D

Carlos Reyes (**Pos**: RHP, **Age**: 28)

	W	L	Pct.	ERA	G	GS	Sv	IP	H	BB	SO	HR	Ratio
1997	3	4	.429	5.82	37	6	0	77.1	101	25	43	13	1.63
Career	14	23	.378	4.93	150	26	1	346.2	377	158	226	52	1.54

Like most A's pitchers, Reyes had a depressing 1997 season. A knee injury which sidelined him for a month didn't help any. He was sent to the minors after the season, but expansion might mean another chance. 1998 Outlook: C

Scott Sheldon (**Pos**: SS, **Age**: 29, **Bats**: R)

	G	AB	R	H	D	T	HR	RBI	SB	BB	SO	Avg	OBP	Slg
1997	13	24	2	6	0	0	1	2	0	1	6	.250	.308	.375
Career	13	24	2	6	0	0	1	2	0	1	6	.250	.308	.375

Sheldon got a brief shot with the A's early last year, but spent most of the year at Triple-A Edmonton, where he swung a powerful bat. He signed a minor league deal with the shortstop-needy Rangers after the season. 1998 Outlook: C

Dave Telgheder (**Pos**: RHP, **Age**: 31)

	W	L	Pct.	ERA	G	GS	Sv	IP	H	BB	SO	HR	Ratio
1997	4	6	.400	6.06	20	19	0	101.0	134	35	55	15	1.67
Career	15	18	.455	5.34	73	44	0	291.2	353	97	153	43	1.54

What does it say about your club's confidence in you when they put you on the *60-day DL* with a blister on your middle finger? AL hitters wept when they heard there'd be no more "Telghede" parties in '97. 1998 Outlook: C

Don Wengert (**Pos**: RHP, **Age**: 28)

	W	L	Pct.	ERA	G	GS	Sv	IP	H	BB	SO	HR	Ratio
1997	5	11	.313	6.04	49	12	2	134.0	177	41	68	21	1.63
Career	13	23	.361	5.57	104	37	2	325.0	407	113	159	53	1.60

Wengert's been with the A's for three years now, and he's pitched a little worse each season. He did have one of Oakland's record-low two complete games last year. Then he got traded to San Diego. 1998 Outlook: C

Steve Wojciechowski (**Pos**: LHP, **Age**: 27)

	W	L	Pct.	ERA	G	GS	Sv	IP	H	BB	SO	HR	Ratio
1997	0	2	.000	7.84	2	2	0	10.1	17	1	5	2	1.74
Career	7	10	.412	5.65	32	24	0	138.2	165	57	48	19	1.60

Wojciechowski began last year at Triple-A Edmonton and was recalled by the A's in July. He made two starts and then went down for the year with an irritated left ulnar nerve. 1998 Outlook: C

Oakland Athletics

Oakland Athletics Minor League Prospects

Organization Overview:

Oakland's deterioration from perennial American League West champs to perennial also-rans is the result of their system being unable to produce pitching. The Athletics have spent 11 of their 14 first-round picks in the 1990s on pitchers, and haven't found an ace in the bunch. Injuries and stalled development ruined their premium arms, and the biggest failure of them all, Todd Van Poppel, leads the group with a mere 18 wins for Oakland. While searching for pitching, the Athletics have done a good job of finding catchers and infielders. They're also among the leaders in grabbing talent in the Dominican Republic. Future all-stars Ben Grieve and Miguel Tejada should become full-time big leaguers in 1998, but Oakland won't win until it finds some pitching.

Eric Chavez

Position: 3B
Bats: L **Throws:** R
Ht: 6' 1" **Wt:** 190

Opening Day Age: 20
Born: 12/7/77 in San Diego, CA

Recent Statistics

	G	AB	R	H	D	T	HR	RBI	SB	BB	SO	AVG
97 A Visalia	134	520	67	141	30	3	18	100	13	37	91	.271

Grieve is on the verge of establishing himself in Oakland, and the system's next star hitting prospect is Chavez. A 1996 first-round pick, he held out that summer while negotiating a $1.14 million bonus and didn't make his pro debut until last year. He was challenged by the high Class-A California League, where he was one of the youngest players at 19, but held his own by hitting .271-18-100. He should develop more power with experience, and likewise should improve his batting eye and average. He doesn't run well and is making the conversion from shortstop to third base. He'll get at least two more years in the minors before being summoned to Oakland.

Ryan Christenson

Position: OF
Bats: R **Throws:** R
Ht: 5' 11" **Wt:** 175

Opening Day Age: 24
Born: 3/28/74 in Redlands, CA

Recent Statistics

	G	AB	R	H	D	T	HR	RBI	SB	BB	SO	AVG
96 A Sou. Oregon	36	136	31	39	11	0	5	21	8	19	21	.287
96 A W Michigan	33	122	21	38	2	2	2	18	2	13	22	.311
97 A Visalia	83	308	69	90	18	8	13	54	20	70	72	.292
97 AA Huntsville	29	120	39	44	9	3	2	18	5	24	23	.367
97 AAA Edmonton	16	49	12	14	2	2	2	5	2	11	11	.286

Christenson wasn't ready to start 1996 in a full-season league, but he ended 1997 expected to contend for Oakland's center-field job in spring training. A 10th-round pick out of Pepperdine in 1995, he batted .310-17-77 with 27 steals while moving from Class-A to Triple-A. He also drew 105 walks, a figure that should warm the heart of any farm director. He's an all-around athlete with good range defensviely, and he endears himself to the Athletics by going all-out all of the time. His primary competition in the spring will be Jason McDonald, who's faster but has less power.

Chris Enochs

Position: P
Bats: R **Throws:** R
Ht: 6' 3" **Wt:** 225

Opening Day Age: 22
Born: 10/11/75 in Weirton, WV

Recent Statistics

	W	L	ERA	G	GS	Sv	IP	H	R	BB	SO	HR
97 A Sou. Oregon	0	0	3.48	3	3	0	10.1	12	4	2	10	0
97 A Modesto	3	0	2.78	10	9	0	45.1	51	20	12	45	0

A West Virginia University product and the 11th overall pick in the 1997 draft, Enochs solidified his status when he outdueled Seton Hall's Jason Grilli, the No. 4 overall pick, in a college game. Enochs quickly signed for $1.204 million, then had no problem pitching in high Class-A. He throws strikes with a 91-93 MPH fastball and a good changeup. He tends to hang his curveball, so the Athletics may have him switch to a slider. Oakland needs starting pitchers and could keep promoting Enochs quickly. He could arrive in the big leagues as soon as mid-1999.

Ramon Hernandez

Position: C
Bats: R **Throws:** R
Ht: 6' 0" **Wt:** 170

Opening Day Age: 21
Born: 5/20/76 in Caracas, Venez

Recent Statistics

	G	AB	R	H	D	T	HR	RBI	SB	BB	SO	AVG
96 A W Michigan	123	447	62	114	26	2	12	68	2	69	62	.255
97 A Visalia	86	332	57	120	21	2	15	85	2	35	47	.361
97 AA Huntsville	44	161	27	31	3	0	4	24	0	18	23	.193

Oakland needs a catcher, and it will be interesting to watch Hernandez battle A.J. Hinch for the starting job. The long-term advantage lies with Hernandez, who's two years younger and has more power in his bat and in his arm. Shoulder tendinitis hampered him in spring training and his elbow bothered him during the year, but it didn't affect his hitting. Even with a weak performance in Double-A, he finished the year at .306-19-109. He also finished in a flurry, going on a homer binge to win Southern League playoff MVP honors. He's still offensive-minded and needs to work on the intracacies of catching, such as running a staff. Only 21, he could get another two full seasons in the minors.

A.J. Hinch

Position: C   **Opening Day Age:** 23
Bats: R **Throws:** R   **Born:** 5/15/74 in
Ht: 6' 1" **Wt:** 195   Waverly, IA

Recent Statistics

	G	AB	R	H	D	T	HR	RBI	SB	BB	SO	AVG
97 A Modesto	95	333	70	103	25	3	20	73	8	42	68	.309
97 AAA Edmonton	39	125	23	47	7	0	4	24	2	20	13	.376

Hinch waited a year to make his pro debut because he spent 1996 as the catcher on the U.S. Olympic team. A third-round pick that year, he played in the Arizona Fall League and didn't impress the Athletics with his strength. That changed in 1997, when he went from Class-A to Triple-A and batted a combined .328-24-97. His best asset may be his intelligence, as he makes adjustments at the plate and expertly handles a pitching staff. He runs well, especially well for a catcher, but his arm has been below average since he dislocated his shoulder two years ago while at Stanford. He doesn't really have 24-homer power, but could be an effective player at half that output. He'll start 1998 in Triple-A and could surface in Oakland late in the year.

Eric Ludwick

Position: P   **Opening Day Age:** 26
Bats: R **Throws:** R   **Born:** 12/14/71 in
Ht: 6' 5" **Wt:** 210   Whiteman AFB, MO

Recent Statistics

	W	L	ERA	G	GS	Sv	IP	H	R	BB	SO	HR
97 AAA Louisville	6	8	2.93	24	11	4	80.0	67	31	26	85	7
97 AAA Edmonton	1	1	3.32	6	3	0	19.0	22	7	4	20	1
97 NL St. Louis	0	1	9.45	5	0	0	6.2	12	7	6	7	1
97 AL Oakland	1	4	8.25	6	5	0	24.0	32	24	16	14	7
97 StL-Oak	1	5	8.51	11	5	0	30.2	44	31	22	21	8

In the past two seasons, Ludwick has proven that he can pitch in Triple-A but hasn't been able to make the jump to the majors. A second-round pick of the Mets in 1993 out of Nevada-Las Vegas, he went to St. Louis in a trade for Bernard Gilkey and joined Oakland at midseason 1997 in a deal for Mark McGwire. He has a power mindset with a 93-94 MPH fastball and a sharp curveball. He also throws a slider and changeup, but neither is effective. A starter for most of his pro career, he may be better suited to be a reliever. Oakland will leave him in the rotation for now and will give him a long look in spring training.

Jamey Price

Position: P   **Opening Day Age:** 26
Bats: L **Throws:** R   **Born:** 2/11/72 in Pine
Ht: 6' 7" **Wt:** 205   Bluff, AR

Recent Statistics

	W	L	ERA	G	GS	Sv	IP	H	R	BB	SO	HR
96 A W Michigan	6	1	1.71	20	16	0	89.1	80	22	19	88	1
97 AA Huntsville	9	3	5.30	20	20	0	110.1	153	71	38	80	16
97 AAA Edmonton	2	0	1.64	2	1	0	11.0	9	3	1	10	0

A sixth-round pick out of the University of Mississippi, Price was put on the fast track because he was nearly 24

when he signed. The biggest question is his health, because he has a history of arm surgeries and still has screws inserted in his elbow. He was shut down for part of the last two seasons, but reached Triple-A at the end of 1997. He throws a low-90s fastball with good sink, a decent curveball and a changeup. He was hit hard last year, but his strikeout and walk totals were fine. He needs to throw less hittable strikes, and will work on doing so in Triple-A in 1998.

Jay Witasick

Position: P   **Opening Day Age:** 25
Bats: R **Throws:** R   **Born:** 8/28/72 in
Ht: 6' 4" **Wt:** 205   Baltimore, MD

Recent Statistics

	W	L	ERA	G	GS	Sv	IP	H	R	BB	SO	HR
97 A Modesto	0	1	4.15	9	2	1	17.1	16	9	5	29	1
97 AAA Edmonton	3	2	4.28	13	1	0	27.1	25	13	15	17	3
97 AL Oakland	0	0	5.73	8	0	0	11.0	14	7	6	8	2

Like Ludwick, Witasick is another former Cardinals prospect who hasn't been able to translate a quality fastball into big league success. A 1993 second-round pick out of Maryland-Baltimore County, he joined the Athletics in the Todd Stottlemyre trade three years later. Witasick throws 94 MPH with good life, but gets pounded when he leaves his fastball up in the strike zone. He has a chance to be Oakland's closer in 1997, but his elbow bothered him in spring training and forced him to change from a slider to a curveball. With T.J. Mathews on the verge of establishing himself with the A's, Witasick may have to settle for being a setup man.

Others to Watch

Righthander **Tom Bennett** has good stuff, though it's hard to tell from his 6-9, 5.71 record in the hitter-friendly, high Class-A California League. He's 21 and throws a fastball in the low to mid-90s and a power curve. . . Playing mainly at Double-A Huntsville, third baseman **Mike Coolbaugh** (.308-30-132), first baseman **D.T. Cromer** (.323-15-121) and outfielder **Mike Neill** (.333-14-83) all put up huge numbers. None is really a prospect, though, because Coolbaugh is the youngest at 25. Cromer probably has the best chance because he's the best hitter of the group, but he'll also be 27 by Opening Day. . . Right fielder **Mario Encarnacion** is another product of Oakland's Dominican efforts. The A's say he's the best tools guy in the system, even better than Tejada, and Encarnacion hit .297-18-78 with 14 steals in the Cal League at age 19. . . Shortstop **Josue Espada**, 22, offers plenty of defense, speed and walks. He has almost no power, however, and won't be able to dethrone Tejada when he reaches the majors.

Lou Piniella

1997 Season

Lou Piniella's Mariners were favored to capture the American League West as long as Randy Johnson was healthy. The Big Unit won 20 games and the Mariners captured their second division title in three years, but it wasn't easy. The Mariners were terrific when Johnson, Jamie Moyer or Jeff Fassero started, but Piniella never was able to fix a disastrous bullpen that nearly overshadowed the game's best offense.

Offense

Seattle set a major league record with 264 home runs and led the AL in runs scored last season. At heart, however, Piniella is a National League manager. He loves to pinch hit and get his bench involved. But he also knows a good thing when he has it, and lets the Mariners slug away. One of his more interesting moves was putting Roberto Kelly in the No. 2 slot, even though it meant putting Kelly and his low on-base percentage in front of Ken Griffey Jr. The move seemed like an attempt to get some speed at the top of the order at all costs.

Pitching & Defense

Seattle's fourth and fifth starters won a total of 13 games, and the bullpen led the AL in blown saves. Piniella's inability to develop young pitchers has been a major cause of Seattle's pitching woes the past two years. While he has little patience with young pitchers, he gives repeated opportunities to veterans such as Bobby Ayala, Norm Charlton and Dennis Martinez. This earns Piniella the respect of the older players, but his decision to keep using Charlton in key situations proved costly.

1998 Outlook

The Mariners have more frontline talent than any team in baseball. A club with Griffey, Johnson, Jay Buhner, Jeff Fassero, Edgar Martinez and Alex Rodriguez should have no problem winning 90 games. Piniella must sort through the bullpen and come up with a solution. If he does, it should mean another AL West title this year.

Born: 8/28/43 in Tampa, FL

Playing Experience: 1964-1984, Bal, Cle, KC, NYA

Managerial Experience: 10 seasons

Nickname: Sweet Lou

Pronunciation: pih-NEL-la

Manager Statistics

Year	Team, Lg	W	L	Pct	GB	Finish
1997	Seattle, AL	90	72	.556	—	1st West
10 Seasons		864	781	.525	—	—

1997 Starting Pitchers by Days Rest

	≤3	4	5	6+
Mariners Starts	5	88	35	24
Mariners ERA	3.95	4.08	4.39	5.22
AL Avg Starts	5	89	34	24
AL ERA	4.38	4.60	4.61	5.37

1997 Situational Stats

	Lou Piniella	AL Average
Hit & Run Success %	29.7	36.5
Stolen Base Success %	69.0	67.3
Platoon Pct.	56.7	59.5
Defensive Subs	27	22
High-Pitch Outings	25	15
Quick/Slow Hooks	14/17	19/15
Sacrifice Attempts	61	53

1997 Rankings (American League)

⇒ 1st in double steals (8) and starts with over 140 pitches (4)

⇒ 2nd in least caught steals of second base (29) and starts with over 120 pitches (25)

⇒ 3rd in steals of third base (17), least caught steals of home plate (1), starts on three days rest (5) and saves with over 1 inning pitched (11)

Jay Buhner (Strong Arm)

1997 Season

While Jay Buhner failed to match his prodigious RBI totals of the past two years, he still put together another fine campaign. He reached 100 RBI for the third straight season and became just the 10th player in major league history to reach 40 homers in three consecutive years. However, his batting average was his lowest since 1992 and his slugging percentage the lowest since 1993.

Hitting

When the media began hammering on Buhner for his low batting average and high strikeout rate, he pointed out that his on-base percentage was good and that he was driving in runs. Buhner has learned to live with his strikeouts. He says he'll often take a pitch early in the game knowing he might see that same pitch later in more crucial situations. Because of his open stance, pitchers constantly work Buhner outside. The result is a lot of whiffs on breaking pitches, but also a ton of walks because of his patience.

Baserunning & Defense

Buhner hasn't swiped a base since 1993, which tells you something about his speed. Defensively, he won his Gold Glove in 1996 based largely on his powerful and accurate right arm, which remains perhaps the best in the American League. He has excellent instincts but his lack of speed means his range is below average. Buhner has mastered the difficult right-field wall and corner at the Kingdome, and holds many potential doubles to singles.

1998 Outlook

Buhner should remain one of the AL's best right fielders. Even if he bats .243 again, he's an outstanding hitter with his combination of power and walks. The Mariners say he may see a little action at first base to reduce the wear and tear on his 33-year-old legs.

Position: RF
Bats: R **Throws:** R
Ht: 6' 3" **Wt:** 210

Opening Day Age: 33
Born: 8/13/64 in Louisville, KY
ML Seasons: 11
Pronunciation: BYEW-ner
Nickname: Bone

Overall Statistics

	G	AB	R	H	D	T	HR	RBI	SB	BB	SO	Avg	OBP	Slg
1997	157	540	104	131	18	2	40	109	0	119	175	.243	.383	.506
Career	1182	4094	674	1053	193	18	253	795	6	618	1128	.257	.357	.499

Where He Hits the Ball

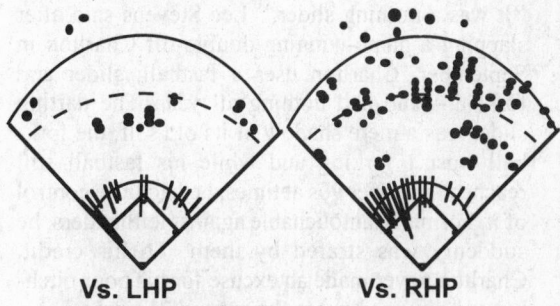

Vs. LHP　　　**Vs. RHP**

1997 Situational Stats

	AB	H	HR	RBI	Avg		AB	H	HR	RBI	Avg
Home	243	57	13	45	.235	LHP	126	40	11	27	.317
Road	297	74	27	64	.249	RHP	414	91	29	82	.220
First Half	301	72	22	64	.239	Sc Pos	161	37	9	70	.230
Scnd Half	239	59	18	45	.247	Clutch	79	17	4	18	.215

1997 Rankings (American League)

⇒ 1st in strikeouts and fielding percentage in right field (.997)
⇒ 2nd in walks, GDPs (23), on-base percentage vs. lefthanded pitchers (.449) and highest percentage of swings that missed (34.0%)
⇒ 3rd in most pitches seen per plate appearance (4.20)
⇒ 4th in home runs, lowest batting average vs. righthanded pitchers and slugging percentage vs. lefthanded pitchers (.627)
⇒ 5th in HR frequency (13.5 ABs per HR)
⇒ Led the Mariners in walks, strikeouts, GDPs (23), games played (157), most pitches seen per plate appearance (4.20) and on-base percentage vs. lefthanded pitchers (.449)

Norm Charlton

1997 Season

On Opening Day, Norm Charlton recorded a save. In his second outing, he surrendered four runs and picked up the loss. It was pretty much all downhill from there, as Charlton became the poster boy for Seattle's bullpen woes. He lost his job as closer with five straight blown saves in late May and early June, though he remained a primary setup man. The low point of his season came on July 30, when Charlton blew a game in Boston. The next day, popular rookie Jose Cruz Jr. was traded. "If I had done my job, he would still be here," Charlton said.

Pitching

"It was a nothing slider," Lee Stevens said after slapping a game-winning double off Charlton in September. Charlton uses a fastball, slider and forkball—and had nothing all year. The darting slider was a mere shadow of its old self, the forkball wasn't forking and while his fastball still reached the lower 90s at times, he had little control of it. Formerly untouchable against lefthanders, he suddenly was strafed by them. To his credit, Charlton never made an excuse for his poor pitching and chugged out to the mound 71 times.

Defense

Charlton improved his ability to hold runners. After allowing 16 steals and catching one runner in his previous three seasons, he permitted only five steals in 10 attempts in 1997. He's in poor fielding position upon finishing his delivery, which leaves him falling toward third base. As a result, he made three errors in 1997.

1998 Outlook

Charlton was given up for dead once before when the Phillies released him in 1995, so he probably shouldn't be placed in the coffin just yet. Manager Lou Piniella has been extremely loyal to Charlton and likely will invite him back, though the Mariners exercised their option to buy out Charlton's $2.9 million contract.

Position: RP
Bats: B **Throws:** L
Ht: 6' 3" **Wt:** 205

Opening Day Age: 35
Born: 1/6/63 in Fort Polk, LA
ML Seasons: 9
Nickname: The Sheriff

Overall Statistics

	W	L	Pct.	ERA	G	GS	Sv	IP	H	BB	SO	HR	Ratio
1997	3	8	.273	7.27	71	0	14	69.1	89	47	55	7	1.96
Career	43	48	.473	3.50	468	37	95	750.0	654	323	667	56	1.30

How Often He Throws Strikes

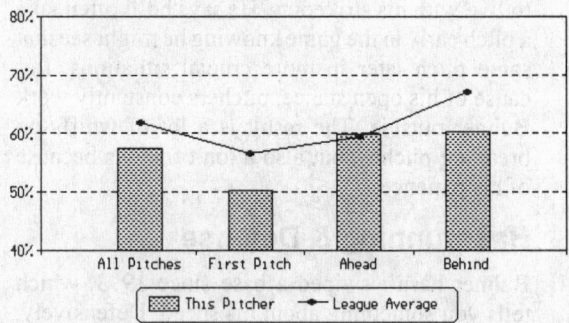

1997 Situational Stats

	W	L	ERA	Sv	IP		AB	H	HR	RBI	Avg
Home	2	6	8.17	7	36.1	LHB	93	29	1	21	.312
Road	1	2	6.27	7	33.0	RHB	192	60	6	39	.313
First Half	2	6	7.43	12	40.0	Sc Pos	102	32	5	58	.314
Scnd Half	1	2	7.06	2	29.1	Clutch	164	49	4	41	.299

1997 Rankings (American League)

⇒ 1st in lowest save percentage (56.0%), blown saves (11), highest relief ERA (7.27) and most baserunners allowed per 9 innings in relief (18.2)

⇒ 2nd in relief losses (8)

⇒ 3rd in highest batting average allowed in relief (.312)

⇒ 5th in highest batting average allowed in relief with runners on base (.338)

⇒ 7th in worst first batter efficiency (.344)

⇒ 10th in errors at pitcher (3)

⇒ Led the Mariners in games pitched, saves, games finished (38), save opportunities (25), save percentage (56.0%), blown saves (11) and relief losses (8)

Joey Cora

1997 Season

On April 21, Joey Cora was hitting a miserable .173. The 10 pounds of muscle he added in the offseason didn't seem to be helping. Then the little second baseman caught fire and after his second four-hit game in four days, he was hitting .379 on May 27. He then became the unlikeliest of All-Stars. "You can't believe you're here. That's why I was taking pictures. To show I was here for real," Cora said.

Hitting

Cora tailed off in the second half and finished near his career norms in batting average and on-base percentage. But his added strength paid off in a .441 slugging percentage, the fourth straight season he has increased that mark. A switch-hitter, he entered 1997 with no career homers batting righthanded, then went deep five times and slugged .617 off southpaws. Cora is a dead fastball hitter. He has learned to work the count a bit deeper, which has resulted in a few more walks and strikeouts. He remains one of the best bunters in the American League.

Baserunning & Defense

Defensively, Cora is subpar. His range is declining, his arm is weak and he's slow turning the double play. While he has a penchant for making the spectacular play, Cora's inability to turn the pivot was costly on several occasions. He still has average speed, but no longer is a threat to steal.

1998 Outlook

With Cora becoming a free agent, the Mariners had a tough decision on whether to re-sign the fan favorite. He's still an effective hitter, but his defensive problems could make him replaceable and his big season made him expensive. His dropoff in the second half may also be cause for concern. Working in Cora's favor was the fact that Seattle had no strong candidate to replace him. Ultimately, the Mariners decided to bring him back.

Position: 2B
Bats: B **Throws:** R
Ht: 5' 8" **Wt:** 162

Opening Day Age: 32
Born: 5/14/65 in Caguas, PR
ML Seasons: 10

Overall Statistics

	G	AB	R	H	D	T	HR	RBI	SB	BB	SO	Avg	OBP	Slg
1997	149	574	105	172	40	4	11	54	6	53	49	.300	.359	.441
Career	964	3132	513	869	144	35	24	262	102	307	276	.277	.346	.369

Where He Hits the Ball

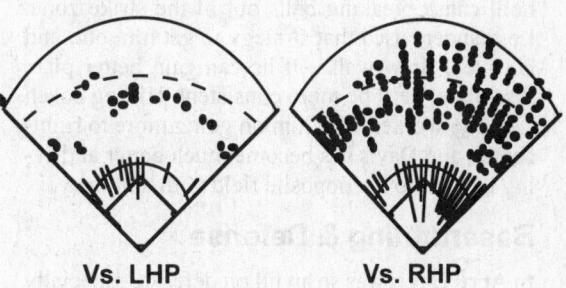

Vs. LHP   **Vs. RHP**

1997 Situational Stats

	AB	H	HR	RBI	Avg		AB	H	HR	RBI	Avg
Home	277	83	4	25	.300	LHP	107	39	5	26	.364
Road	297	89	7	29	.300	RHP	467	133	6	28	.285
First Half	306	101	8	33	.330	Sc Pos	103	32	2	43	.311
Scnd Half	268	71	3	21	.265	Clutch	73	17	0	7	.233

1997 Rankings (American League)

⇒ 1st in lowest fielding percentage at second base (.973) and lowest percentage of swings that missed (6.8%)
⇒ 2nd in errors at second base (17)
⇒ 3rd in highest percentage of swings put into play (54.2%)
⇒ Led the Mariners in singles, doubles, triples, sacrifice bunts (8), on-base percentage for a leadoff hitter (.350), bunts in play (19), lowest percentage of swings that missed (6.8%), highest percentage of swings put into play (54.2%) and highest percentage of extra bases taken as a runner (65.6%)

Russ Davis

1997 Season

After breaking his left fibula early in the 1996 season, Russ Davis was just happy to be back on a baseball field last year. His season was one of ups and downs. He was hitting .323 in early May, but was benched for two games because of his poor defense. He was still hitting better than .300 as late as July 25, but slumped in August. On August 25 he severely sprained his right ankle sliding into home and missed the rest of the season.

Hitting

Davis owns terrific bat speed that ranks with the best on the Mariners. This makes him an excellent fastball hitter, but pitchers eventually realized that he'll chase breaking balls out of the strike zone. Lefthanders used that strategy to get him out, and he rarely drew walks. If he can gain better plate discipline, he'll be more consistent. Hitting coach Lee Elia worked with him on going more to right-center, and Davis has become much better at driving the ball to the opposite field with authority.

Baserunning & Defense

In April Davis was so awful on defense, especially on fielding grounders, that manager Lou Piniella wondered if Davis had developed a mental block. After a brief benching he was solid the rest of the year, though he needs to improve on his .938 fielding percentage. Davis doesn't possess a particularly quick first step but does have a strong arm. He's station-to-station on the bases, but stole six bases in eight tries.

1998 Outlook

The Mariners hope that Davis will keep improving and perhaps even stay healthy for an entire season. However, he's 28 and probably won't get much better unless he improves his strike-zone judgment. Still, there's nothing wrong with his total package.

Position: 3B
Bats: R **Throws:** R
Ht: 6' 0" **Wt:** 195

Opening Day Age: 28
Born: 9/13/69 in Birmingham, AL
ML Seasons: 4

Overall Statistics

	G	AB	R	H	D	T	HR	RBI	SB	BB	SO	Avg	OBP	Slg
1997	119	420	57	114	29	1	20	63	6	27	100	.271	.317	.488
Career	214	699	95	182	43	3	27	94	8	54	180	.260	.317	.446

Where He Hits the Ball

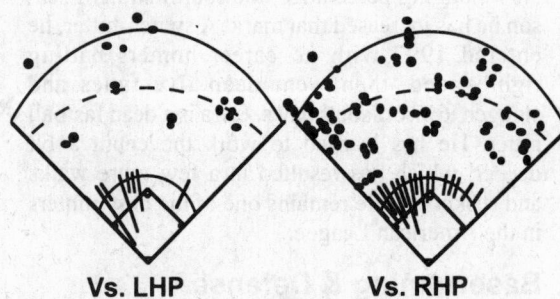

Vs. LHP   **Vs. RHP**

1997 Situational Stats

	AB	H	HR	RBI	Avg		AB	H	HR	RBI	Avg
Home	213	60	11	34	.282	LHP	117	29	5	19	.248
Road	207	54	9	29	.261	RHP	303	85	15	44	.281
First Half	272	84	12	38	.309	Sc Pos	108	31	0	38	.287
Scnd Half	148	30	8	25	.203	Clutch	74	19	5	15	.257

1997 Rankings (American League)

⇒ 2nd in lowest fielding percentage at third base (.938)
⇒ 3rd in batting average on a 3-1 count (.714) and lowest batting average on an 0-2 count (.033)
⇒ 4th in errors at third base (18)
⇒ 8th in batting average with the bases loaded (.571)
⇒ Led the Mariners in batting average on a 3-1 count (.714)

Jeff Fassero

Position: SP
Bats: L **Throws:** L
Ht: 6' 1"   **Wt:** 195

Opening Day Age: 35
Born: 1/5/63 in Springfield, IL
ML Seasons: 7
Pronunciation: fuh-SAIR-oh

1997 Season

Jeff Fassero gave the Mariners exactly what they expected after acquiring him from the Expos in an offseason trade: stability in the rotation, quality innings and wins. Fassero didn't miss a start, pitched more innings than all but two lefthanders in baseball and won a career-high 16 games. He easily could have won 20, but the troubled bullpen blew six leads for him.

Pitching

Fassero has four quality pitches. He throws a low-90s fastball that he likes to spot on the outside corner, another fastball that has more sink to it, a forkball that he uses as an offspeed pitch and a slider. He typically likes to get ahead with the fastball and then go to the forkball or slider, which he runs in on righthanders. Fassero tended to nibble at times last year, leading to an increase in walks. Lefthanders hit him slightly better than righthanders, reversing his career-wide trend, though they still didn't generate much power. Though he lasted 136 pitches in his playoff start against Baltimore, Fassero usually starts getting hit harder after 90 pitches. Opponents hit .205 off him from pitches 76-90, but .286 from pitches 91-105.

Defense

Fassero is an excellent fielder. He has perfect pitching mechanics that leave him ready to react quickly with the glove. He also pays attention to baserunners, who went just 15-for-26 attempting to steal. He threw less often to first than he did in the National League.

1998 Outlook

At 35, Fassero should remain one of the top lefthanders around. He has pitched more than 230 innings two years in a row, so there should be no questions about his durability. He's consistent, throws hard and knows how to pitch. With a bit more luck, this could be the year he wins 20.

Overall Statistics

	W	L	Pct.	ERA	G	GS	Sv	IP	H	BB	SO	HR	Ratio
1997	16	9	.640	3.61	35	35	0	234.1	226	84	189	21	1.32
Career	74	57	.565	3.29	297	135	10	1084.1	1008	358	939	78	1.26

How Often He Throws Strikes

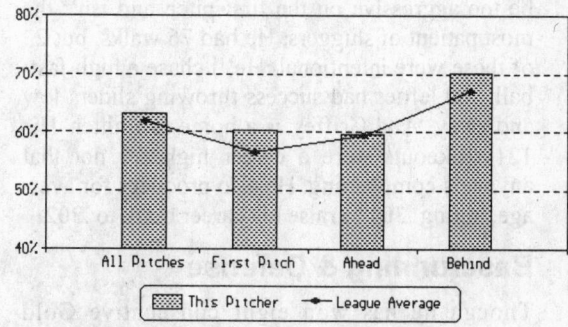

1997 Situational Stats

	W	L	ERA	Sv	IP		AB	H	HR	RBI	Avg
Home	6	5	3.85	0	107.2	LHB	175	46	2	13	.263
Road	10	4	3.41	0	126.2	RHB	731	180	19	81	.246
First Half	8	5	3.99	0	124.0	Sc Pos	220	52	4	69	.236
Scnd Half	8	4	3.18	0	110.1	Clutch	78	16	1	8	.205

1997 Rankings (American League)

⇒ 1st in games started
⇒ 3rd in batters faced (1,010)
⇒ 4th in pitches thrown (3,711)
⇒ 5th in walks allowed, wild pitches (13), balks (2) and runners caught stealing (11)
⇒ Led the Mariners in losses, games started, innings pitched, hits allowed, batters faced (1,010), walks allowed, wild pitches (13), balks (2), pitches thrown (3,711), pickoff throws (132), stolen bases allowed (15), GDPs induced (17), highest groundball/flyball ratio allowed (1.5), least pitches thrown per batter (3.67), least home runs allowed per 9 innings (.81) and most GDPs induced per 9 innings (0.7)

Ken Griffey Jr.

1997 Season

"I'm not a home-run hitter," Ken Griffey Jr. likes to say. Well, he sure isn't a singles hitter. Griffey finally got his MVP Award after leading the American League with 125 runs, 56 home runs, 147 RBI, 393 total bases and a .646 slugging percentage. He erupted with 13 home runs in April, and only a 25-game stretch in June and July when he hit only one homer while battling a sore hamstring prevented him from reaching 61.

Hitting

Junior can crush any pitch. With his bat speed and plate coverage he can pull even outside pitches for home runs. He's not perfect, however. He tends to be too aggressive on the first pitch and isn't the most patient of sluggers. He had 76 walks, but 23 of those were intentional. He'll chase a high fastball, and lefties had success throwing sliders low and away. And Griffey *is* a home-run hitter. His 121 strikeouts were a career high. . . not that anyone's complaining. He also produces for average, hitting .304 to raise his career mark to .302.

Baserunning & Defense

Though he has won eight consecutive Gold Gloves, Griffey's fielding stats didn't match his reputation for a long time. The past two seasons, however, he hasn't played as deep and his fielding numbers have improved. It would be interesting to know if this was a change in philosophy or just a desire to avoid running into outfield walls. His throwing arm is above average and he has excellent speed when he elects to use it to steal bases. He has been successful 72 percent of the time during his career.

1998 Outlook

This will be Junior's 10th year in the big leagues—and he's still just 28. Sit back and enjoy him because once again he'll be one of baseball's best players and a threat to break Roger Maris' home-run record. If he keeps it going, he may one day challenge Hank Aaron's career mark as well.

Position: CF
Bats: L **Throws:** L
Ht: 6' 3" **Wt:** 205

Opening Day Age: 28
Born: 11/21/69 in Donora, PA
ML Seasons: 9
Nickname: Junior, The Kid

Overall Statistics

	G	AB	R	H	D	T	HR	RBI	SB	BB	SO	Avg	OBP	Slg
1997	157	608	125	185	34	3	56	147	15	76	121	.304	.382	.646
Career	1214	4593	820	1389	261	24	294	872	123	580	755	.302	.381	.562

Where He Hits the Ball

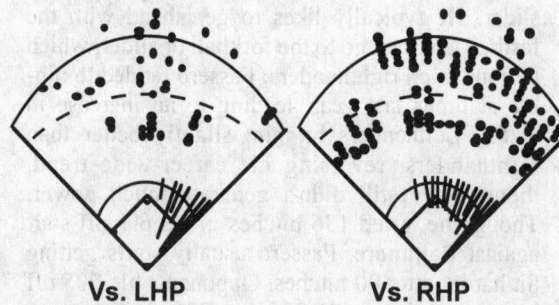

Vs. LHP   Vs. RHP

1997 Situational Stats

	AB	H	HR	RBI	Avg		AB	H	HR	RBI	Avg
Home	289	93	27	72	.322	LHP	196	53	14	39	.270
Road	319	92	29	75	.288	RHP	412	132	42	108	.320
First Half	323	99	30	84	.307	Sc Pos	146	49	12	85	.336
Scnd Half	285	86	26	63	.302	Clutch	80	22	7	16	.275

1997 Rankings (American League)

⇒ 1st in home runs, runs scored, total bases (393), RBI, intentional walks (23), slugging percentage, HR frequency (10.9 ABs per HR), batting average with the bases loaded (.857), slugging percentage vs. righthanded pitchers (.699) and errors in center field (6)

⇒ 2nd in sacrifice flies (12)

⇒ Led the Mariners in home runs, at-bats, runs scored, hits, total bases (393), RBI, sacrifice flies (12), intentional walks (23), plate appearances (704), games played (157), slugging percentage, HR frequency (10.9 ABs per HR), least GDPs per GDP situation (7.3%), batting average with the bases loaded (.857), slugging percentage vs. righthanded pitchers (.699) and batting average at home

Randy Johnson (Unhittable

1997 Season

After undergoing surgery in September 1996 for a herniated disk in his back, Randy Johnson was a huge question mark entering 1997. The Big Unit proved to be as dominating as ever. He recorded two 19-strikeout games and fanned 14 or more four other times. In one five-start stretch he gave up 13 hits and two runs. He won 20 games for the first time and had a career-best 2.28 ERA, finishing second to Toronto's Roger Clemens in the AL Cy Young Award balloting. After bruising his left middle finger in August he missed a few starts and wasn't quite as strong upon his return, losing twice to Baltimore in the playoffs.

Pitching

Johnson is as intimidating a presence as ever has stalked a pitching mound. Six-foot-10 with long hair and a scary glare, he throws as hard as any starter in baseball and isn't afraid to throw inside. He's emotional and will pump his fist after a big strikeout. Everybody knows about Johnson's 96-MPH heater, but it's his slider that makes him unhittable at times. He actually has two breaking balls: a big, sweeping pitch that starts way outside to righthanders before breaking across the corner, and a hard, biting pitch that looks like a strike before turning sharply down and in. Johnson surrendered four homers to lefties in 1997 after giving up just one the three previous years. Yet he still overmatches lefties so much that hitters such as Rafael Palmeiro and Larry Walker took a seat when Johnson was on the mound.

Defense

Johnson played some college basketball at USC. His agility shows as he's surprisingly quick off the mound. He did commit four errors, however. As if Johnson needs to get any tougher, he's now difficult to run on. Of the 29 basestealers who ran against him in 1997, 16 were caught.

1998 Outlook

Johnson is a remarkable 75-20 since 1993 and has gone 43-6 over the past three years. He struck out 291 batters in 213 innings and opponents hit .194 off him in '97. It doesn't get much better than that.

Position: SP
Bats: R **Throws:** L
Ht: 6'10" **Wt:** 230

Opening Day Age: 34
Born: 9/10/63 in Walnut Creek, CA
ML Seasons: 10
Nickname: Big Unit

Overall Statistics

	W	L	Pct.	ERA	G	GS	Sv	IP	H	BB	SO	HR	Ratio
1997	20	4	.833	2.28	30	29	0	213.0	147	77	291	20	1.05
Career	124	68	.646	3.37	262	253	2	1734.0	1320	857	2000	146	1.26

How Often He Throws Strikes

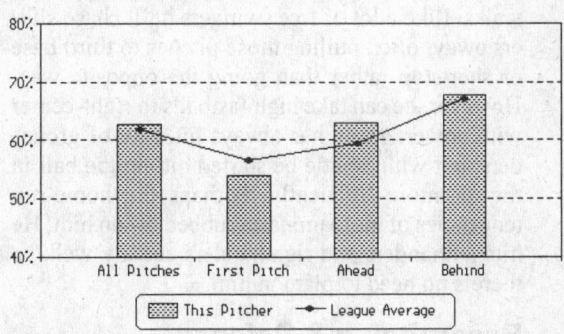

1997 Situational Stats

	W	L	ERA	Sv	IP		AB	H	HR	RBI	Avg
Home	9	1	1.89	0	114.0	LHB	77	20	4	7	.260
Road	11	3	2.73	0	99.0	RHB	681	127	16	49	.186
First Half	12	2	2.20	0	131.0	Sc Pos	143	22	4	34	.154
Scnd Half	8	2	2.41	0	82.0	Clutch	83	18	1	5	.217

1997 Rankings (American League)

⇒ 1st in winning percentage, lowest batting average allowed (.194), most pitches thrown per batter (4.12), most strikeouts per 9 innings (12.3), lowest batting average allowed vs. righthanded batters and lowest batting average allowed with runners in scoring position

⇒ 2nd in ERA, wins, strikeouts, runners caught stealing (16), lowest slugging percentage allowed (.318), lowest on-base percentage allowed (.277), least baserunners allowed per 9 innings (9.9) and ERA at home

⇒ 3rd in complete games (5), shutouts (2), ERA on the road and lowest fielding percentage at pitcher (.871)

⇒ Led the Mariners in ERA, wins, complete games (5), shutouts (2), hit batsmen (10) and strikeouts

Roberto Kelly

1997 Season

The well-traveled Roberto Kelly began the year as Minnesota's semiregular right fielder before being traded to Seattle on Aug. 20 for two minor league pitchers. He filled Seattle's left-field hole and showed surprising pop with the Mariners, slugging seven home runs in just 121 at-bats. His slugging percentage was his highest since 1993 and his 12 home runs were his most since 1991.

Hitting

The Mariners moved Kelly into the No. 2 slot in the batting order in September, but he's ill-suited to that role because of his low on-base percentage. He was overly aggressive as usual, drawing just 22 walks. Like a lot of free swingers he'll chase sliders away, often pulling those pitches to third base or shortstop rather than going the opposite way. However, he can take high fastballs to right-center with power. Kelly has always hit a lot of grounders, but with Seattle he started hitting the ball in the air more frequently. Perhaps the home-run tendencies of his teammates rubbed off on him. He hits lefthanders and righthanders equally well, so there's no need to platoon him.

Baserunning & Defense

One reason manager Lou Piniella moved him up in the order was Kelly's decent speed, but he stole just two bases with the Mariners. Kelly is an adequate outfielder but at times is a little lazy charging grounders. His arm is accurate though not strong.

1998 Outlook

A free agent, Kelly may be joining his eighth team in seven years. With Jose Cruz Jr. traded to Toronto, Seattle still could use Kelly. If he'll sign cheaply enough, the Mariners would like to have him back. If not, they'll have to sign a free agent or take a look at farmhands Raul Ibanez and Shane Monahan.

Position: RF/LF/DH
Bats: R **Throws:** R
Ht: 6' 2" **Wt:** 202

Opening Day Age: 33
Born: 10/1/64 in Panama City, Panama
ML Seasons: 11
Nickname: Gray

Overall Statistics

	G	AB	R	H	D	T	HR	RBI	SB	BB	SO	Avg	OBP	Slg
1997	105	368	58	107	26	2	12	59	9	22	67	.291	.333	.470
Career	1165	4225	594	1217	216	25	99	501	229	287	753	.288	.336	.422

Where He Hits the Ball

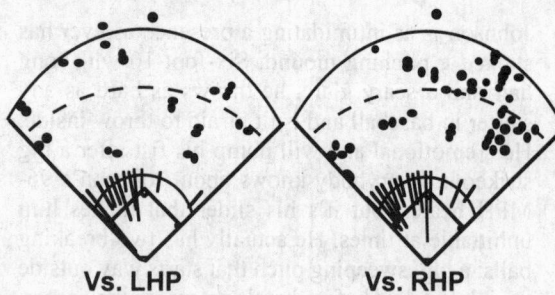

Vs. LHP   Vs. RHP

1997 Situational Stats

	AB	H	HR	RBI	Avg		AB	H	HR	RBI	Avg
Home	188	50	8	30	.266	LHP	124	37	5	24	.298
Road	180	57	4	29	.317	RHP	244	70	7	35	.287
First Half	171	50	1	20	.292	Sc Pos	89	28	3	43	.315
Scnd Half	197	57	11	39	.289	Clutch	55	13	1	8	.236

1997 Rankings (American League)

⇒ Did not rank near the top or bottom in any category

Edgar Martinez

1997 Season

Two-time batting champion Edgar Martinez was once again one of the top hitters in the American League, finishing second to Chicago's Frank Thomas in batting average and on-base percentage, second to Cleveland's Jim Thome in walks, and among league leaders in several other categories. As Seattle's cleanup hitter, he smacked 28 homers, knocked in 108 runs and scored 104.

Hitting

Martinez is a marvel with the bat. If it's an inside pitch, he'll pull it for a home run. Down in the strike zone? Single to center. Slider away? Double to the opposite field. Fastball on the outside corner? In the gap. He's impossible to pitch to because he won't swing at a bad offering. His main weakness is the high fastball, but few pitchers have heat good enough to blow past him. Martinez might have lost a touch of bat speed, however, as his doubles declined. He went up the middle more often, hitting into a career-high 21 double plays, rather than spraying the ball down the lines. He hit much better against righties in 1997, but historically he has been a little better against southpaws.

Baserunning & Defense

Martinez doesn't really run with a piano on his back and he does actually own a fielder's glove. While he's slow, he's a smart runner who doesn't hesitate going from second to home. He played seven games at first base and committed one error. Seattle keeps him out of the field whenever possible to preserve his health.

1998 Outlook

Martinez loves to DH so much that he actually threatened to retire if the Mariners had moved to the National League. With Seattle staying in the AL West, he'll return to his familiar slot in the lineup. He isn't quite the dominating threat he was two years ago, but he remains one of the most productive hitters in the game.

Position: DH
Bats: R **Throws:** R
Ht: 5'11" **Wt:** 200

Opening Day Age: 35
Born: 1/2/63 in New York, NY
ML Seasons: 11

Overall Statistics

	G	AB	R	H	D	T	HR	RBI	SB	BB	SO	Avg	OBP	Slg
1997	155	542	104	179	35	1	28	108	2	119	86	.330	.456	.554
Career	1091	3818	708	1210	291	12	145	592	32	674	551	.317	.423	.513

Where He Hits the Ball

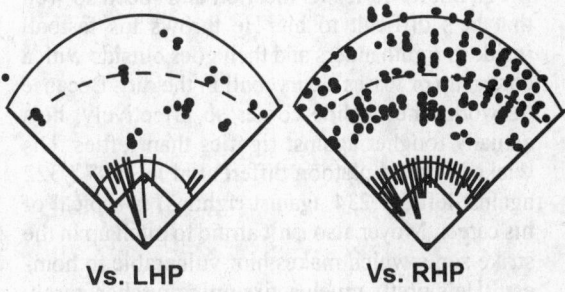

Vs. LHP   **Vs. RHP**

1997 Situational Stats

	AB	H	HR	RBI	Avg		AB	H	HR	RBI	Avg
Home	268	86	12	50	.321	LHP	131	37	4	15	.282
Road	274	93	16	58	.339	RHP	411	142	24	93	.345
First Half	310	106	16	66	.342	Sc Pos	150	46	6	74	.307
Scnd Half	232	73	12	42	.315	Clutch	67	22	1	9	.328

1997 Rankings (American League)

⇒ 1st in times on base (309), on-base percentage vs. righthanded pitchers (.469), highest percentage of pitches taken (66.5%) and lowest percentage of swings on the first pitch (11.9%)

⇒ 2nd in batting average, walks and on-base percentage

⇒ 3rd in batting average vs. righthanded pitchers and batting average on the road

⇒ Led the Mariners in batting average, walks, hit by pitch (11), times on base (309), pitches seen (2,799), on-base percentage, batting average vs. righthanded pitchers, batting average on an 0-2 count (.250), cleanup slugging percentage (.557), on-base percentage vs. righthanded pitchers (.469), batting average on the road and highest percentage of pitches taken (66.5%)

Jamie Moyer

1997 Season

In spring training of 1992, the Cubs asked Jamie Moyer to be their Class-A pitching coach. Moyer thought he still could pitch and declined the offer. While he spent that year out of the big leagues, Moyer is like fine wine—he keeps getting better with age. After beginning 1997 on the disabled list with a strained muscle in his elbow, he posted the best year of his career, going 17-5. In his playoff start against Baltimore, he suffered a strained flexor muscle in his forearm.

Pitching

Hitting is timing, and Moyer's game plan is to disrupt that timing. His fastball doesn't break 85 MPH, but he varies its location and speed so well that he's difficult to hit. He throws his fastball inside to righthanders and then goes outside with a changeup or tosses a curveball in the dirt. Because he works the outside corner so effectively, he's actually tougher against righties than lefties. His wicked reverse platoon differential in 1997 (.322 against lefties, .234 against righties) is typical of his career. Moyer also isn't afraid to pitch up in the strike zone, which makes him vulnerable to homers. He's pretty much a six-inning pitcher, rarely venturing into the seventh and often getting hit when he does.

Defense

Moyer has a fairly slow delivery out of the stretch, and runners stole 14 bases in 20 attempts in 1997. He's reliable with the glove, though when he completes his delivery his feet are spread so far apart that it costs him mobility.

1998 Outlook

The injury Moyer suffered in the playoffs is minor and he'll be ready for spring training. He has gone 30-8 the past two seasons, but it's unreasonable to expect him to continue posting winning percentages around .800. His strikeouts rose dramatically during the second half of 1997, so he shows no signs of slowing down. Moyer should be good for 15 wins.

Position: SP
Bats: L **Throws:** L
Ht: 6' 0" **Wt:** 170

Opening Day Age: 35
Born: 11/18/62 in Sellersville, PA
ML Seasons: 11

Overall Statistics

	W	L	Pct.	ERA	G	GS	Sv	IP	H	BB	SO	HR	Ratio
1997	17	5	.773	3.86	30	30	0	188.2	187	43	113	21	1.22
Career	89	84	.514	4.36	280	228	0	1466.0	1559	477	869	175	1.39

How Often He Throws Strikes

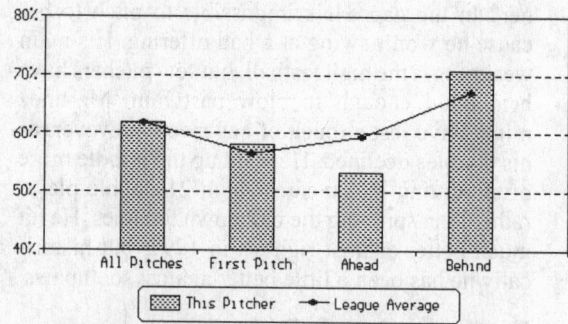

1997 Situational Stats

	W	L	ERA	Sv	IP		AB	H	HR	RBI	Avg
Home	12	2	3.63	0	101.2	LHB	183	59	6	20	.322
Road	5	3	4.14	0	87.0	RHB	547	128	15	50	.234
First Half	8	2	4.34	0	85.0	Sc Pos	154	39	4	48	.253
Scnd Half	9	3	3.47	0	103.2	Clutch	28	9	1	4	.321

1997 Rankings (American League)

⇒ 1st in most run support per 9 innings (7.7) and in fielding percentage at pitcher (1.000)
⇒ 2nd in winning percentage
⇒ 5th in wins
⇒ 7th in lowest on-base percentage allowed (.303)
⇒ 9th in highest strikeout/walk ratio (2.6), lowest slugging percentage allowed (.382), least baserunners allowed per 9 innings (11.3) and least GDPs induced per 9 innings (0.6)
⇒ 10th in lowest batting average allowed vs. righthanded batters
⇒ Led the Mariners in most run support per 9 innings (7.7)

Alex Rodriguez
Future MVP

1997 Season

The expectations were enormous after Alex Rodriguez turned in a .358-36-123 season in 1996, perhaps the best year ever by a shortstop. He might not have duplicated those lofty numbers, but he had an impressive 1997 nonetheless. Though he dropped to .300-23-84, he remains the best offensive shortstop in baseball.

Hitting

Unlike a lot of today's hitters, Rodriguez stands well off the plate. His tremendous bat speed and quick hands allow him to wait on pitches and drill them to the opposite field with power. This approach worked in 1996 when he saw a lot of fastballs, but pitchers fed him a steady diet of breaking balls off the plate in 1997 and he often chased them. Rodriguez isn't a wild swinger, but he needs to make pitchers throw the ball over the plate. He hits lefties and righties equally well, and has displayed much more power at the Kingdome than on the road.

Baserunning & Defense

Rodriguez has a very strong arm and soft hands, but they didn't translate into a sterling defensive performance in 1997. He tends to sling the ball wildly at times, which is why he led American League shortstops with 24 errors. His range was average at best despite his speed. The fastest Mariner, Rodriguez stole 29 bases in 35 attempts and always runs out ground balls.

1998 Outlook

Rodriguez landed on the disabled list in June after suffering a bruised chest wall when he collided with Toronto's Roger Clemens on a play at home plate. That bothered him some the rest of the season. He's certainly capable of better numbers than he produced in 1997, when any other shortstop would have been happy to have Rodriguez' performance.

Position: SS
Bats: R **Throws:** R
Ht: 6' 3" **Wt:** 195

Opening Day Age: 22
Born: 7/27/75 in New York, NY
ML Seasons: 4
Nickname: A-Rod

Overall Statistics

	G	AB	R	H	D	T	HR	RBI	SB	BB	SO	Avg	OBP	Slg
1997	141	587	100	176	40	3	23	84	29	41	99	.300	.350	.496
Career	352	1384	260	435	100	6	64	228	51	109	265	.314	.366	.534

Where He Hits the Ball

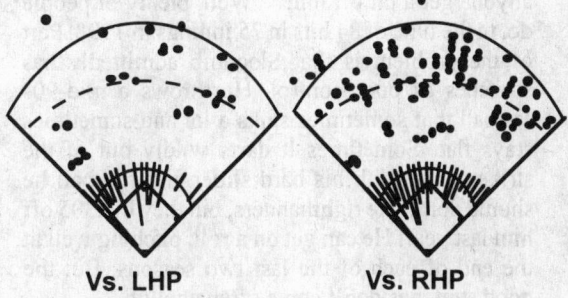

Vs. LHP   **Vs. RHP**

1997 Situational Stats

	AB	H	HR	RBI	Avg		AB	H	HR	RBI	Avg
Home	289	90	16	51	.311	LHP	157	47	8	25	.299
Road	298	86	7	33	.289	RHP	430	129	15	59	.300
First Half	311	97	12	42	.312	Sc Pos	143	43	6	59	.301
Scnd Half	276	79	11	42	.286	Clutch	72	24	3	8	.333

1997 Rankings (American League)

⇒ 1st in errors at shortstop (24) and lowest fielding percentage at shortstop (.962)
⇒ 3rd in steals of third (11)
⇒ 4th in stolen base percentage (82.9%)
⇒ 7th in stolen bases
⇒ 9th in doubles
⇒ Led the Mariners in doubles, stolen bases, highest groundball/flyball ratio (1.4), stolen base percentage (82.9%), batting average in the clutch and steals of third (11)

Seattle Mariners

Heathcliff Slocumb

1997 Season

In 1997, Heathcliff Slocumb had the opportunity to pitch for two teams and fared badly for each of them. He struggled with Boston, going 0-5, 5.79. After getting traded for to Seattle for minor leaguers Derek Lowe and Jason Varitek, he went 0-4, 4.13. He finished with nine losses, six blown saves, a 5.16 overall ERA and 49 walks in 75 innings. The positives were 27 saves in 76 appearances, and a good September. He also converted 10 of 11 save opportunities for the Mariners.

Pitching

When John Marzano first caught Slocumb, his comment was, "His ball moves so much, how does anyone get a hit off him?" Well, plenty of people do, to the tune of 84 hits in 75 innings in 1998. Part of the problem is that Slocumb admittedly has stretches of poor control. He throws a mid-90s fastball that sometimes sinks a lot and sometimes stays flat. Sometimes it darts wildly out of the strike zone. With his hard slider and forkball he should dominate righthanders, but they hit .305 off him last year. He can get on a roll, pitching well at the end of each of the last two seasons. But the good stretches don't come often enough.

Defense

Slocumb always has had problems holding runners. He threw more often to first base in 1997 but that didn't help much. Basestealers still went 11-for-12 against him. He's adequate with the glove, though his delivery causes him to fall off the mound.

1998 Outlook

Slocumb is one of the truly nice guys in baseball but he illustrates exactly why saves are overrated. He simply allows way too many batters to reach base. He's eligible for arbitration and likely will win a multimillion-dollar contract because he has 90 saves in the last three seasons. After getting a firsthand look at him, the Mariners may prefer to pay the money to someone else.

Position: RP
Bats: R **Throws:** R
Ht: 6' 3" **Wt:** 220

Opening Day Age: 31
Born: 6/7/66 in Jamaica, NY
ML Seasons: 7

Overall Statistics

	W	L	Pct.	ERA	G	GS	Sv	IP	H	BB	SO	HR	Ratio
1997	0	9	.000	5.16	76	0	27	75.0	84	49	64	6	1.77
Career	21	26	.447	3.79	376	0	92	432.2	431	238	356	19	1.55

How Often He Throws Strikes

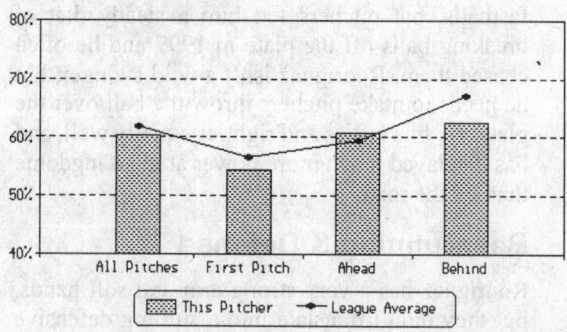

1997 Situational Stats

	W	L	ERA	Sv	IP			AB	H	HR	RBI	Avg
Home	0	4	5.26	12	39.1	LHB	143	38	2	20	.266
Road	0	5	5.05	15	35.2	RHB	151	46	4	29	.305
First Half	0	4	6.57	11	37.0	Sc Pos	111	25	1	41	.225
Scnd Half	0	5	3.79	16	38.0	Clutch	170	44	3	29	.259

1997 Rankings (American League)

⇒ 1st in relief losses (9)
⇒ 2nd in games finished (61) and most baserunners allowed per 9 innings in relief (16.4)
⇒ 3rd in highest relief ERA (5.16)
⇒ 5th in games pitched (76) and lowest save percentage (81.8%)
⇒ 6th in saves (27) and save opportunities (33)
⇒ 9th in blown saves (6) and worst first batter efficiency (.338)
⇒ 10th in wild pitches (10)
⇒ Led the Mariners in lowest batting average allowed in relief with runners on base (.185) and lowest batting average allowed in relief with runners in scoring position (.154)

Paul Sorrento

Position: 1B
Bats: L **Throws:** R
Ht: 6' 2" **Wt:** 220

Opening Day Age: 32
Born: 11/17/65 in Somerville, MA
ML Seasons: 9

1997 Season

Paul Sorrento struggled to find recognition in Seattle's star-studded lineup, but he had another fine season and set career highs with 31 home runs and a .514 slugging percentage. Sorrento once again platooned at first base and rarely played against lefthanders. Usually hitting sixth, he had 80 RBI and thrived in the Kingdome for the second straight year. He was extremely consistent, hitting at least five homers in the last five months of the season.

Hitting

Sorrento sprays the ball around, though most of his home runs go to right field. His plan of attack is simple: swing hard in case he makes contact. He often looks for fastballs and thus can look foolish at times against offspeed pitches. Never effective against lefties, Sorrento did hit four homers in 39 at-bats against them in 1997. But his career average against southpaws still is just .212. His numbers in clutch situations nose-dived, but timely hitting hadn't been a weakness of his in the past.

Baserunning & Defense

A former youth hockey goalie, Sorrento has good hands and is adept at scooping errant throws. He's required to perform the latter skill quite often because of the Mariners' erratic infield arms. He lumbers around the basepaths and hasn't swiped a base since 1995. He does know his limitations and won't make mistakes.

1998 Outlook

Sorrento was a free agent this winter. His power stroke is suited for the friendly right-field porch at the Kingdome, which he has taken full advantage of the past two years. He's a perfect complement to Ken Griffey Jr., Alex Rodriguez and Co., and his numbers most likely would suffer elsewhere.

Overall Statistics

	G	AB	R	H	D	T	HR	RBI	SB	BB	SO	Avg	OBP	Slg
1997	146	457	68	123	19	0	31	80	0	51	112	.269	.345	.514
Career	857	2683	374	709	135	4	138	466	5	323	610	.264	.344	.472

Where He Hits the Ball

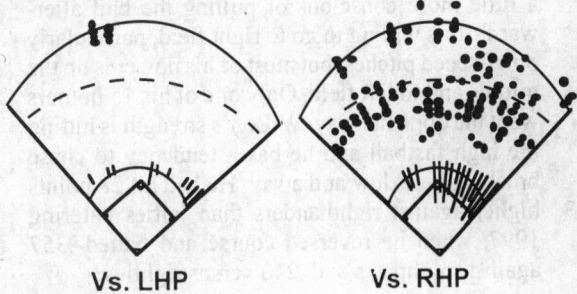

Vs. LHP   **Vs. RHP**

1997 Situational Stats

	AB	H	HR	RBI	Avg		AB	H	HR	RBI	Avg
Home	221	66	18	38	.299	LHP	39	8	4	6	.205
Road	236	57	13	42	.242	RHP	418	115	27	74	.275
First Half	253	71	17	42	.281	Sc Pos	121	24	4	43	.198
Scnd Half	204	52	14	38	.255	Clutch	74	11	1	7	.149

1997 Rankings (American League)

⇒ 1st in lowest batting average in the clutch
⇒ 2nd in fielding percentage at first base (.996)
⇒ 5th in lowest batting average with runners in scoring position
⇒ 6th in HR frequency (14.7 ABs per HR)
⇒ 7th in lowest batting average on an 0-2 count (.048)
⇒ 8th in lowest batting average on the road

Seattle
Mariners

Dan Wilson (Overlooked)

1997 Season

Dan Wilson followed up his All-Star campaign of 1996 with another solid year. He set career bests in several categories and once again proved to be extremely durable. Only Pudge Rodriguez, Mike Piazza and Jason Kendall started more games behind the plate. Unlike previous years Wilson didn't wear down in September, though he went 0-for-13 in the playoffs. With his all-around skills, he's one of the top two or three catchers in the American League.

Hitting

Wilson started off like gangbusters, hitting .349 in April, though with no home runs. He seemed to be a little more conscious of pulling the ball afterward. He's willing to go to right field, particularly on offspeed pitches, but most of his power is up the middle and to left field. Only one of his 15 homers went the opposite way. Wilson's strength is hitting the high fastball and he has a tendency to chase breaking balls low and away. He had hit 28 points higher against righthanders than lefties entering 1997, when he reversed course and batted .357 against southpaws and .240 versus righties.

Baserunning & Defense

Even if Wilson was a below-average hitter, his defense would still make him a valuable asset. His quick release and accurate arm allowed him to throw out 43 percent of basestealers in 1997, the third-best mark in the league. Mariners pitchers love throwing to him, and he allowed just one passed ball despite handling a staff that throws lots of sinkers and sliders. Wilson has good speed for a catcher and his seven steals tied for most among AL backstops. Several of those came on delayed swipes of second.

1998 Outlook

The Mariners talk about finding more rest for Wilson, but don't expect him to get any. He should once again be expected to catch at least 130 games and hit in the .270 range with 15 home runs. With prospects Chris Widger and Jason Varitek traded away in the past year, the catching job definitely continues to be Wilson's.

Position: C
Bats: R **Throws:** R
Ht: 6' 3" **Wt:** 190

Opening Day Age: 29
Born: 3/25/69 in Barrington, IL
ML Seasons: 6

Overall Statistics

	G	AB	R	H	D	T	HR	RBI	SB	BB	SO	Avg	OBP	Slg
1997	146	508	66	137	31	1	15	74	7	39	72	.270	.326	.423
Career	542	1781	189	475	95	6	45	246	11	126	304	.267	.317	.403

Where He Hits the Ball

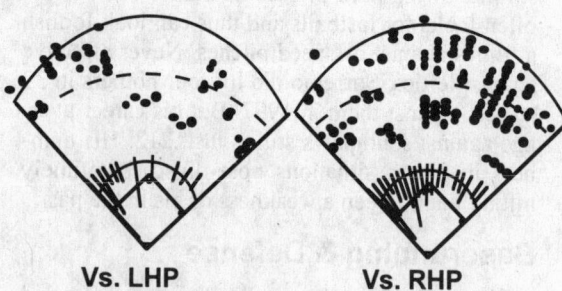

Vs. LHP   Vs. RHP

1997 Situational Stats

	AB	H	HR	RBI	Avg		AB	H	HR	RBI	Avg
Home	253	67	9	45	.265	LHP	129	46	9	28	.357
Road	255	70	6	29	.275	RHP	379	91	6	46	.240
First Half	286	78	6	38	.273	Sc Pos	121	42	5	63	.347
Scnd Half	222	59	9	36	.266	Clutch	81	26	4	13	.321

1997 Rankings (American League)

⇒ 1st in slugging percentage vs. lefthanded pitchers (.651)
⇒ 3rd in fielding percentage at catcher (.995)
⇒ 5th in batting average vs. lefthanded pitchers and lowest slugging percentage vs. righthanded pitchers (.346)
⇒ Led the Mariners in sacrifice bunts (8), batting average with runners in scoring position, batting average vs. lefthanded pitchers, slugging percentage vs. lefthanded pitchers (.651) and batting average with two strikes (.263)

Rich Amaral

Position: LF/1B/2B
Bats: R **Throws:** R
Ht: 6' 0" **Wt:** 175

Opening Day Age: 35
Born: 4/1/62 in Visalia, CA
ML Seasons: 7
Pronunciation: AM-r-all

Overall Statistics

	G	AB	R	H	D	T	HR	RBI	SB	BB	SO	Avg	OBP	Slg
1997	89	190	34	54	5	0	1	21	12	10	34	.284	.327	.326
Career	533	1457	249	405	67	8	10	138	86	141	225	.278	.345	.356

1997 Situational Stats

	AB	H	HR	RBI	Avg		AB	H	HR	RBI	Avg
Home	85	23	0	7	.271	LHP	129	36	1	15	.279
Road	105	31	1	14	.295	RHP	61	18	0	6	.295
First Half	111	28	0	12	.252	Sc Pos	54	11	0	20	.204
Scnd Half	79	26	1	9	.329	Clutch	32	12	0	8	.375

1997 Season

Rich Amaral was a key utilityman for the Mariners for a fifth consecutive season. A contact hitter with speed, he usually played left field, and also filled in at second and first. He's consistent and versatile, ideally suited to helping a team off the bench.

Hitting, Baserunning & Defense

Amaral gets most of his at-bats against lefthanders and hits a lot of hard grounders, making use of his speed. A smart and aggressive baserunner, he can steal a base and is capable of scoring from first in situations where most players stop at third. He has no power, but the Mariners have plenty elsewhere. He covers a lot of ground in the outfield, but he has a weak arm and rarely throws out baserunners. He's below average at second base, where he has difficulty going back on pop flies.

1998 Outlook

At 36, Amaral is at an age where many players experience a sharp dropoff in skills. He's a player who fits in well, so as long as he still can run he'll keep his job. Look for him to see plenty of action as a utility player once again this season.

Bobby Ayala

Position: RP
Bats: R **Throws:** R
Ht: 6' 3" **Wt:** 210

Opening Day Age: 28
Born: 7/8/69 in Ventura, CA
ML Seasons: 6
Pronunciation: eye-YA-luh

Overall Statistics

	W	L	Pct.	ERA	G	GS	Sv	IP	H	BB	SO	HR	Ratio
1997	10	5	.667	3.82	71	0	8	96.2	91	41	92	14	1.37
Career	35	27	.565	4.58	278	14	51	418.2	410	180	394	52	1.41

1997 Situational Stats

	W	L	ERA	Sv	IP		AB	H	HR	RBI	Avg
Home	6	3	5.29	2	47.2	LHB	165	47	7	25	.285
Road	4	2	2.39	6	49.0	RHB	185	44	7	27	.238
First Half	5	2	4.14	6	50.0	Sc Pos	100	23	3	36	.230
Scnd Half	5	3	3.47	2	46.2	Clutch	178	51	5	31	.287

1997 Season

Bobby Ayala was the Mariners' best reliever in 1997, but that isn't saying too much. After an awful start, he pitched his way back into the closer's role in June but bombed in July. Overall he blew four of 12 save chances, which was in line with his career success rate. He pitched very well in middle relief after the Mariners restocked their bullpen at the trade deadline.

Pitching & Defense

Ayala loves his fastball, but the harder he throws it, the less movement he gets. He's successful when he takes a little off the fastball and lets it sink. It often drops out of the strike zone, though, and hitters have learned to sit on his straighter version of the fastball. He rarely throws his slider for strikes. He really struggled to pitch in the Kingdome in 1997, but he was very effective on the road. Ayala's big leg kick makes it hard to hold runners, though he does cover bunts well.

1998 Outlook

Lou Piniella is one of the most loyal managers in baseball. He brought Ayala over from Cincinnati in 1994 and has stuck with him. Ayala isn't a fan favorite, which may be the cause of his Kingdome problems, but look for him to be a decent setup man again.

Seattle Mariners

Mike Blowers

Position: 1B
Bats: R **Throws:** R
Ht: 6' 2" **Wt:** 210

Opening Day Age: 32
Born: 4/24/65 in Wurzburg, Germany
ML Seasons: 9
Pronunciation: BLAU-ers

Overall Statistics

	G	AB	R	H	D	T	HR	RBI	SB	BB	SO	Avg	OBP	Slg
1997	68	150	22	44	5	0	5	20	0	21	33	.293	.376	.427
Career	613	1845	232	483	91	6	65	287	6	205	482	.262	.335	.423

1997 Situational Stats

	AB	H	HR	RBI	Avg		AB	H	HR	RBI	Avg
Home	75	21	5	13	.280	LHP	109	35	5	17	.321
Road	75	23	0	7	.307	RHP	41	9	0	3	.220
First Half	80	19	3	12	.238	Sc Pos	36	10	2	16	.278
Scnd Half	70	25	2	8	.357	Clutch	13	4	1	2	.308

1997 Season

Mike Blowers hit 23 homers and drove in 96 runs for Seattle in 1995, then was traded to Los Angeles in a cost-cutting move. After blowing out his knee with the Dodgers, he re-signed with his hometown Mariners. Used primarily as the righthanded half of a platoon with Paul Sorrento at first base, Blowers also filled in at third base.

Hitting, Baserunning & Defense

Blowers stands off the plate and looks to drive the ball to right-center. Four of his five homers in 1997 went to the opposite field. This approach is particularly effective against lefthanders, against whom Blowers has historically had lots of success. He'll strike out, but he has a good eye and will draw some walks. Blowers never was fast to begin with, so the knee injury didn't have a huge effect on his speed. He's adequate at first or third base, and has a strong throwing arm.

1998 Outlook

Blowers showed he was recovered from his knee injury and may be ready for more playing time in 1998. While his best role may be in a platoon situation at first or third base, he's as good as several regular third basemen out there. He's a free agent, as is Sorrento, so Blowers could become an everyday player again.

Ken Cloude

Position: SP
Bats: R **Throws:** R
Ht: 6' 1" **Wt:** 180

Opening Day Age: 23
Born: 1/9/75 in Baltimore, Maryland
ML Seasons: 1
Pronunciation: CLOUD

Overall Statistics

	W	L	Pct.	ERA	G	GS	Sv	IP	H	BB	SO	HR	Ratio
1997	4	2	.667	5.12	10	9	0	51.0	41	26	46	8	1.31
Career	4	2	.667	5.12	10	9	0	51.0	41	26	46	8	1.31

1997 Situational Stats

	W	L	ERA	Sv	IP		AB	H	HR	RBI	Avg
Home	1	2	5.32	0	23.2	LHB	100	21	3	12	.210
Road	3	0	4.94	0	27.1	RHB	88	20	5	13	.227
First Half	0	0	-	0	0.0	Sc Pos	38	10	2	17	.263
Scnd Half	4	2	5.12	0	51.0	Clutch	6	5	1	1	.833

1997 Season

Recalled from Double-A in early August, Ken Cloude burst onto the scene by taking a no-hitter into the seventh inning of his major league debut. He spent the rest of the year in the Seattle rotation, posting a winning record and pitching better than his 5.12 ERA would indicate.

Pitching & Defense

Extremely poised at age 23, Cloude throws two fastballs, a sharp slider and an occasional change. He has a high fastball that clocks in at 89-92 MPH, and a sinking fastball that's a bit slower. Mixing in a good breaking ball, he kept hitters off balance and limited them to a .218 batting average in his first taste of the majors. Home runs were his biggest problem, so if he can keep the ball in the park he could have a great deal of success. He tended to nibble at times, but wasn't afraid to challenge hitters either. He allowed just two steals in nine starts and is an adequate fielder.

1998 Outlook

Unless he has a terrible spring, Cloude will be Seattle's No. 4 starter. Manager Lou Piniella doesn't have a good track record developing young pitchers, but Cloude appears to have the stuff and makeup to be the exception to the rule.

Brent Gates

Position: 3B/2B
Bats: B **Throws:** R
Ht: 6' 1" **Wt:** 180

Opening Day Age: 28
Born: 3/14/70 in Grand Rapids, MI
ML Seasons: 5

Overall Statistics

	G	AB	R	H	D	T	HR	RBI	SB	BB	SO	Avg	OBP	Slg
1997	65	151	18	36	8	0	3	20	0	14	21	.238	.298	.351
Career	468	1690	197	455	91	9	19	199	14	155	247	.269	.328	.367

1997 Situational Stats

	AB	H	HR	RBI	Avg		AB	H	HR	RBI	Avg
Home	74	18	1	8	.243	LHP	27	4	0	5	.148
Road	77	18	2	12	.234	RHP	124	32	3	15	.258
First Half	84	21	2	11	.250	Sc Pos	40	10	1	17	.250
Scnd Half	67	15	1	9	.224	Clutch	25	6	1	2	.240

1997 Season

Brent Gates found new life in 1997. Unfortunately for him, it was life as a utility infielder. After getting released in spring training by the Athletics, he signed with Seattle and wound up getting the majority of his action at third base.

Hitting, Baserunning & Defense

The promising switch-hitter who hit .290 as a rookie out of Class-A in 1993 is no longer so promising. Gates doesn't generate the bat speed to be a productive big league hitter. He also has struggled against lefthanders and doesn't have extra-base power. His defense at second base is average at best, while at third he displayed the arm of a second baseman. He didn't steal a base.

1998 Outlook

Gates is only 28, so it may be a bit premature to say he's washed up. Still, his days as a starting second baseman appear to be over, even with Joey Cora possibly leaving as a free agent. Gates' newfound ability to play two positions and his ability to bat lefthanded, always a bonus for an infielder, should keep him in the majors for a while longer.

Omar Olivares

Position: SP
Bats: R **Throws:** R
Ht: 6' 1" **Wt:** 190

Opening Day Age: 30
Born: 7/6/67 in Mayaguez, PR
ML Seasons: 8
Pronunciation: oh-lih-VARE-es

Overall Statistics

	W	L	Pct.	ERA	G	GS	Sv	IP	H	BB	SO	HR	Ratio
1997	6	10	.375	4.97	32	31	0	177.1	191	81	103	18	1.53
Career	43	49	.467	4.46	214	143	3	985.0	1015	411	530	94	1.45

1997 Situational Stats

	W	L	ERA	Sv	IP		AB	H	HR	RBI	Avg
Home	4	3	4.20	0	90.0	LHB	370	113	14	60	.305
Road	2	7	5.77	0	87.1	RHB	321	78	4	38	.243
First Half	5	5	4.56	0	106.2	Sc Pos	155	48	8	79	.310
Scnd Half	1	5	5.60	0	70.2	Clutch	32	9	0	1	.281

1997 Season

When the Mariners decided to reconstruct their pitching staff in July, they dealt Scott Sanders and minor leaguer Dean Crow to Detroit for Omar Olivares and Felipe Lira. The two ex-Tigers joined the pennant race and performed miserably, going a combined 1-8. Olivares won just once in 12 starts despite the backing of Seattle's powerful offense.

Pitching & Defense

Olivares isn't overpowering and relies on a sinker. When that pitch is working he can be quite effective, as evidenced by his two shutouts with Detroit. He gets in trouble when he has to go to his slider and fastball. He still can be tough on righthanders but is a soft touch for lefties. He's an excellent athlete, very quick off the mound and one of the best-hitting pitchers in baseball. He has an exceptional pickoff move and eliminates the running game.

1998 Outlook

A free agent, Olivares likely will be searching for employment outside the Pacific Northwest. He pitched poorly the final four months and may be best suited for work out of the bullpen. He never has matched the promise of his first full major league season, when he went 11-7, 3.71 for the Cardinals in 1991.

Paul Spoljaric

Position: RP
Bats: R **Throws:** L
Ht: 6' 3" **Wt:** 205

Opening Day Age: 27
Born: 9/24/70 in
Kelowna, BC
ML Seasons: 3
Pronunciation:
spaul-JARE-ick

Overall Statistics

	W	L	Pct.	ERA	G	GS	Sv	IP	H	BB	SO	HR	Ratio
1997	0	3	.000	3.69	57	0	3	70.2	61	36	70	4	1.37
Career	2	6	.250	4.22	87	1	4	111.0	96	64	110	13	1.44

1997 Situational Stats

	W	L	ERA	Sv	IP		AB	H	HR	RBI	Avg
Home	0	0	4.62	0	37.0	LHB	126	30	3	20	.238
Road	0	3	2.67	3	33.2	RHB	133	31	1	12	.233
First Half	0	3	3.35	2	40.1	Sc Pos	74	15	0	24	.203
Scnd Half	0	0	4.15	1	30.1	Clutch	71	16	3	13	.225

1997 Season

Paul Spoljaric pitched in middle relief with the Blue Jays and then the Mariners after getting traded with Mike Timlin for Jose Cruz Jr. on July 31. After an effective first half, Spoljaric wasn't quite as solid the final two months, making the trade that much more disappointing for Seattle.

Pitching & Defense

The Mariners were excited about Spoljaric's arm and it's easy to see why. He's a lefthander with a 93-MPH fastball, a big curve and a sharp slider. He's effective against righthanders because he'll pound them inside with the fastball and then go to the slider. Lefties don't hit him particularly well either, and he keeps the ball in the ballpark. If Spoljaric can cut down on his walks, he has a chance to be very good. He holds runners well and didn't make an error in 17 chances in 1997.

1998 Outlook

Spoljaric will be an important part of the Seattle pitching staff. There has been talk about turning him into a starter, but the Mariners need bullpen help and likely will keep him in middle relief. He might be worth a chance as the closer if the club can't find one.

Mike Timlin

Position: RP
Bats: R **Throws:** R
Ht: 6' 4" **Wt:** 210

Opening Day Age: 32
Born: 3/10/66 in
Midland, TX
ML Seasons: 7

Overall Statistics

	W	L	Pct.	ERA	G	GS	Sv	IP	H	BB	SO	HR	Ratio
1997	6	4	.600	3.22	64	0	10	72.2	69	20	45	8	1.22
Career	26	24	.520	3.63	331	3	53	419.0	397	172	340	31	1.36

1997 Situational Stats

	W	L	ERA	Sv	IP		AB	H	HR	RBI	Avg
Home	4	1	3.00	4	39.0	LHB	118	31	3	15	.263
Road	2	3	3.48	6	33.2	RHB	151	38	5	17	.252
First Half	2	0	2.41	9	37.1	Sc Pos	66	17	2	24	.258
Scnd Half	4	4	4.08	1	35.1	Clutch	163	48	4	22	.294

1997 Season

When the Mariners panicked and traded outfielder Jose Cruz Jr. to Toronto for relievers Mike Timlin and Paul Spoljaric, they expected to hand Timlin the closer's job he had lost with the Blue Jays. He responded with four blown saves in five chances, which cost him those duties with Seattle and made the Cruz deal all the more regrettable.

Pitching & Defense

Timlin relies on a fastball that tops out at 93 MPH and a hard slider. With the Mariners he didn't have good bite on the slider and struck out just nine batters in 25⅔ innings. He can get into trouble if the slider isn't working because he isn't able to spot his fastball and tends to groove it when he falls behind. He's a decent fielder, and unlike many relievers he doesn't allow many stolen bases.

1998 Outlook

Timlin is probably Seattle's best hope for a closer among the current crop of relievers, though Heathcliff Slocumb, another midseason trade acquisition, filled the role down the stretch. Timlin didn't earn manager Lou Piniella's confidence with two months of mediocre work, and his $2 million salary is a lot to pay for a middle reliever.

Other Seattle Mariners

Rafael Carmona (Pos: RHP, Age: 25)

	W	L	Pct.	ERA	G	GS	Sv	IP	H	BB	SO	HR	Ratio
1997	0	0	-	3.18	4	0	0	5.2	3	2	6	1	0.88
Career	10	7	.588	4.70	72	4	2	143.2	153	91	96	21	1.70

Carmona spent almost all of '97 in the minors after going 8-3 out of the Mariners' bullpen the year before. His work in Triple-A didn't bode well for a comeback. 1998 Outlook: C

Tim Davis (Pos: LHP, Age: 27)

	W	L	Pct.	ERA	G	GS	Sv	IP	H	BB	SO	HR	Ratio
1997	0	0	-	6.75	2	0	0	6.2	6	4	10	1	1.50
Career	6	5	.545	4.62	89	6	2	122.2	136	64	91	11	1.63

Davis missed most of '97 with a torn elbow ligament. If and when he returns, he will still be lefthanded, presumably. 1998 Outlook: C

Rob Ducey (Pos: LF/CF/RF, Age: 32, Bats: L)

	G	AB	R	H	D	T	HR	RBI	SB	BB	SO	Avg	OBP	Slg
1997	76	143	25	41	15	2	5	10	3	6	31	.287	.311	.524
Career	328	636	95	159	42	8	9	52	15	58	154	.250	.310	.384

Ducey returned to the majors for the first time since 1994 and played well as Seattle's fourth outfielder. A notorious batting-practice hitter, he finally produced when it mattered. 1998 Outlook: B

Alvaro Espinoza (Pos: SS/2B, Age: 36, Bats: R)

	G	AB	R	H	D	T	HR	RBI	SB	BB	SO	Avg	OBP	Slg
1997	33	72	3	13	1	0	0	7	1	2	12	.181	.213	.194
Career	942	2478	252	630	105	9	22	201	13	76	324	.254	.279	.331

After hitting .181 off the bench, Espinoza was released by the Mariners in July. Domingo Ramos and Ted Martinez are hopeful that he'll join their support group eventually. 1998 Outlook: D

Mark Holzemer (Pos: LHP, Age: 28)

	W	L	Pct.	ERA	G	GS	Sv	IP	H	BB	SO	HR	Ratio
1997	0	0	-	6.00	14	0	1	9.0	9	8	7	1	1.89
Career	1	4	.200	7.99	56	4	1	65.1	89	36	42	10	1.91

The 28-year-old lefthander appeared in 14 games for the Mariners last year. In 65.1 major league innings, he has a 7.99 ERA. 1998 Outlook: D

Edwin Hurtado (Pos: RHP, Age: 28)

	W	L	Pct.	ERA	G	GS	Sv	IP	H	BB	SO	HR	Ratio
1997	1	2	.333	9.00	13	1	0	19.0	25	15	10	5	2.11
Career	8	9	.471	6.67	43	15	2	144.1	167	85	79	26	1.75

Hurtado bombed at the major league level for the third straight year, although he did pitch well at Triple-A. Elbow surgery held him back in '96; he may get another shot. 1998 Outlook: C

Felipe Lira (Pos: RHP, Age: 25)

	W	L	Pct.	ERA	G	GS	Sv	IP	H	BB	SO	HR	Ratio
1997	5	11	.313	6.34	28	18	0	110.2	132	55	73	18	1.69
Career	20	38	.345	5.20	97	72	1	451.2	487	177	275	65	1.47

Lira ran hot-and-cold all year; after being traded to Seattle in late July, it was mostly cold. A couple of trips to the minors didn't seem to help. He turns 26 this year, and could rebound. 1998 Outlook: B

Mike Maddux (Pos: RHP, Age: 36)

	W	L	Pct.	ERA	G	GS	Sv	IP	H	BB	SO	HR	Ratio
1997	1	0	1.000	10.13	6	0	0	10.2	20	8	7	1	2.63
Career	33	30	.524	4.02	347	48	19	719.0	729	235	469	52	1.34

Greg's big brother signed a minor league contract with the M's and pitched in six games for them before being released in July. He pitched a few games for the Padres' Triple-A team and may surface again. 1998 Outlook: D

Josias Manzanillo (Pos: RHP, Age: 30)

	W	L	Pct.	ERA	G	GS	Sv	IP	H	BB	SO	HR	Ratio
1997	0	1	.000	5.40	16	0	0	18.1	19	17	18	3	1.96
Career	5	6	.455	4.67	93	1	3	129.0	122	67	113	13	1.47

Men all across America cringed in unison when Manzanillo took a line drive to the groin and suffered a lacerated testicle. He went to the minors but couldn't get anyone out. 1998 Outlook: D

Dennis Martinez (Pos: RHP, Age: 42)

	W	L	Pct.	ERA	G	GS	Sv	IP	H	BB	SO	HR	Ratio
1997	1	5	.167	7.71	9	9	0	49.0	65	29	17	8	1.92
Career	241	187	.563	3.68	639	557	6	3908.2	3788	1146	2087	364	1.26

Martinez won one more game for the Mariners, but couldn't get the extra two that he needed to tie Juan Marichal for the all-time record for victories by a Latin American pitcher, and retired. 1998 Outlook: D

John Marzano (Pos: C, Age: 35, Bats: R)

	G	AB	R	H	D	T	HR	RBI	SB	BB	SO	Avg	OBP	Slg
1997	39	87	7	25	3	0	1	10	0	7	15	.287	.340	.356
Career	251	661	66	160	38	1	7	60	0	30	114	.242	.282	.334

Marzano batted .287 as Dan Wilson's backup last year and declared free agency over the winter. A fierce bidding war is not expected to erupt. 1998 Outlook: C

Greg McCarthy (Pos: LHP, Age: 29)

	W	L	Pct.	ERA	G	GS	Sv	IP	H	BB	SO	HR	Ratio
1997	1	1	.500	5.46	37	0	0	29.2	26	16	34	4	1.42
Career	1	1	.500	4.58	47	0	0	39.1	34	20	41	4	1.37

Piniella took out his frustration on McCarthy by shipping him to the minors in July, despite the fact that McCarthy was one of his better relievers at the time. He's a decent lefty. 1998 Outlook: B

Dan Rohrmeier (Pos: 1B, Age: 33, Bats: R)

	G	AB	R	H	D	T	HR	RBI	SB	BB	SO	Avg	OBP	Slg
1997	7	9	4	3	0	0	0	2	0	2	4	.333	.455	.333
Career	7	9	4	3	0	0	0	2	0	2	4	.333	.455	.333

A hard-hitting outfielder who missed his chances, the 32-year-old minor league lifer got a merciful September call-up last year and went 3-for-9. You can bet the grandkids will hear about it. 1998 Outlook: C

Tim Scott (Pos: RHP, Age: 31)

	W	L	Pct.	ERA	G	GS	Sv	IP	H	BB	SO	HR	Ratio
1997	1	1	.500	8.14	17	0	0	21.0	30	7	16	2	1.76
Career	24	13	.649	4.13	276	0	5	314.0	308	133	253	24	1.40

Last year, Scott was released by the Padres and waived by the Rockies, and wasn't able to throw a single pitch for the Mariners due to a sore elbow. If he's recovered, he should hook on somewhere. 1998 Outlook: C

Andy Sheets (Pos: 3B, Age: 26, Bats: R)

	G	AB	R	H	D	T	HR	RBI	SB	BB	SO	Avg	OBP	Slg
1997	32	89	18	22	3	0	4	9	2	7	34	.247	.299	.416
Career	79	199	36	43	11	0	4	18	4	17	75	.216	.279	.332

Moved from shortstop to third base in the minors (for obvious reasons), Sheets sacrificed contact for power. Tampa Bay made him a first-round expansion draft pick, then sent him to San Diego in a trade for John Flaherty. 1998 Outlook: B

Lee Tinsley (Pos: LF, Age: 29, Bats: B)

	G	AB	R	H	D	T	HR	RBI	SB	BB	SO	Avg	OBP	Slg
1997	49	122	12	24	6	2	0	6	2	11	34	.197	.263	.279
Career	361	870	131	210	34	4	13	79	41	88	231	.241	.313	.334

The Mariners' refusal to promote Jose Cruz Jr. in April and their willingness to trade Cruz in July enabled Tinsley to play 34 games in left. He probably won't be so lucky this time. 1998 Outlook: C

Bob Wells (Pos: RHP, Age: 31)

	W	L	Pct.	ERA	G	GS	Sv	IP	H	BB	SO	HR	Ratio
1997	2	0	1.000	5.75	46	1	2	67.1	88	18	51	11	1.57
Career	20	10	.667	5.43	119	21	2	283.2	325	107	189	47	1.52

Wells pitched effectively in July, prompting Lou Piniella to name him the "closer" in one of his weaker moments. Wells didn't do a thing the rest of the year, before or afterward. 1998 Outlook: B

Rick Wilkins (Pos: C, Age: 30, Bats: L)

	G	AB	R	H	D	T	HR	RBI	SB	BB	SO	Avg	OBP	Slg
1997	71	202	20	40	6	0	7	27	0	18	67	.198	.259	.332
Career	677	2021	266	498	93	6	79	261	9	268	543	.246	.335	.416

After hitting so well for the Giants in '96, Wilkins slumped mightily in '97 and was released in August. The Mariners picked him up but he was ill and didn't play much. He should be the backup this year. 1998 Outlook: B

Seattle Mariners Minor League Prospects

Organization Overview:

Seattle's farm system has been productive—for other teams. In the past three years, the Mariners have traded such players as Darren Bragg, Marc Newfield, Desi Relaford, Ron Villone and Chris Widger. The intent has been to help the major league club make a run at the World Series, but some of the deals have been regrettable. Salomon Torres was brought on board from San Francisco for All-Star lefthander Shawn Estes and shortstop prospect Wilson Delgado. In 1997, Seattle stunningly shipped Jose Cruz Jr. to Toronto for setup men Paul Spoljaric and Mike Timlin. Second-tier prospects Dean Crow, Derek Lowe and Jason Varitek also were shipped away last season. The Mariners are fortunate that they have a star-studded big league nucleus that can survive these mistakes.

Ryan Anderson

Position: P
Bats: L **Throws:** L
Ht: 6' 10" **Wt:** 210

Opening Day Age: 18
Born: 7/12/79 in Southfield, MI

Recent Statistics

	W	L	ERA	G	GS	Sv	IP	H	R	BB	SO	HR
97							Did Not Play					

Anderson was projected as a possible No. 1 overall pick in the 1997 draft, but questions about his signability and maturity made him slide. Seattle jumped on him with the 19th pick, eventually signing him for $2.175 million. Because he's a 6-foot-10 lefthander with an overpowering fastball, Anderson repeatedly is compared to Mariners ace Randy Johnson and is known as "Little Unit," a play on Johnson's nickname. Anderson has thrown as hard as 96 MPH, delivers fastballs from three different arm slots and has a hard-biting curve. High school pitchers are a risky lot, especially those with flaky makeups, but Anderson should be entertaining to watch.

Giomar Guevara

Position: SS-2B
Bats: R **Throws:** R
Ht: 5' 9" **Wt:** 158

Opening Day Age: 25
Born: 10/23/72 in Guatire, Miranda, Venez

Recent Statistics

	G	AB	R	H	D	T	HR	RBI	SB	BB	SO	AVG
97 AAA Tacoma	54	176	29	43	5	1	2	13	3	5	39	.244
97 AA Memphis	65	228	30	60	10	4	4	28	5	20	42	.263
97 AL Seattle	5	4	0	0	0	0	0	0	1	0	2	.000
97 MLE	119	398	54	97	15	3	4	38	6	20	88	.244

Guevara knows firsthand that he won't be able to unseat Alex Rodriguez as Seattle's shortstop. He formed a double-play combination with Rodriguez in Class-A ball in 1993. Signed out of Venezuela, Guevara is the same player four years later that he was then. He's a good defensive shortstop with excellent hands and instincts. He shows little aptitude for offense, however, not doing anything particularly well. His only chance as a starter in Seattle would be at second base, but he's more likely to be a utilityman. At best, he's a rich man's Rafael Belliard.

Raul Ibanez

Position: OF
Bats: L **Throws:** R
Ht: 6' 2" **Wt:** 210

Opening Day Age: 25
Born: 6/2/72 in Manhattan, NY

Recent Statistics

	G	AB	R	H	D	T	HR	RBI	SB	BB	SO	AVG
97 AAA Tacoma	111	438	84	133	30	5	15	84	7	32	75	.304
97 AL Seattle	11	26	3	4	0	1	1	4	0	0	6	.154
97 MLE	111	432	77	127	30	3	14	77	5	30	81	.294

Seattle has had trouble finding a left fielder to complement Ken Griffey Jr. and Jay Buhner. Bragg and Cruz could have filled that role, but both were traded away. Ibanez may be the next player to get the chance. A converted catcher, his offense was so far ahead of his defense that it necessitated a move from behind the plate. He's a natural hitter who has put up good numbers in two years in the second-worst hitters' park in the Triple-A Pacific Coast League, though his plate discipline slackened in 1997. He runs decently, but isn't much of a defensive presence. A hot spring could earn him a major league job.

Gil Meche

Position: P
Bats: R **Throws:** R
Ht: 6' 3" **Wt:** 190

Opening Day Age: 19
Born: 9/8/78 in Lafayette, LA

Recent Statistics

	W	L	ERA	G	GS	Sv	IP	H	R	BB	SO	HR
96 R Mariners	0	1	6.00	2	0	0	3.0	4	2	1	4	0
97 A Everett	3	4	3.98	12	12	0	74.2	75	40	24	62	7
97 A Wisconsin	0	2	3.00	2	2	0	12.0	12	5	4	14	1

After the Mariners made him a first-round pick in 1996, Meche concerned them with his lack of velocity in his first pro season. He had thrown 90-92 MPH as a high school junior, but a viral infection and then shoulder tendinitis cost him about 6 MPH. He returned to form in 1997, throwing a consistent 93-96 at low Class-A Everett. He also demonstrated command of a curveball and changeup. Not many 18-year-olds will post a 76-28 strikeout/walk ratio in 87 innings, especially in a league where the hitters generally are three years older. He's still young enough that he needs to be handled with care, but Seattle may have something special in Meche.

Shane Monahan

Position: OF **Opening Day Age:** 23
Bats: L **Throws:** R **Born:** 8/12/74 in
Ht: 6' 1" **Wt:** 200 Syosset, NY

Recent Statistics

	G	AB	R	H	D	T	HR	RBI	SB	BB	SO	AVG
96 A Lancaster	132	585	107	164	31	12	14	97	19	30	124	.280
97 AA Memphis	107	401	52	121	24	6	12	76	14	30	100	.302
97 AAA Tacoma	21	85	15	25	4	0	2	12	5	5	21	.294
97 MLE	128	480	63	140	28	4	13	84	15	29	133	.292

Monahan is another candidate to fill the left-field void. Like Cruz he has good bloodlines, though Monahan's ties are to hockey. His father Hartland played eight seasons in the NHL, and his grandfather (Boom Boom Geoffrion) and great-grandfather (Howie Morenz) are both members of the Hockey Hall of Fame. Monahan was a 1995 second-round pick out of Clemson, and his best attributes are his bat and his burning desire. He rubs opponents and sometimes teammates the wrong way, but his approach works for him. He may be too aggressive at the plate, though. His physical gifts aren't overwhelming, but he gets his share of extra-base hits and steals while playing solid defense. Monahan has little Triple-A experience, so it's unlikely he would make the Opening Day roster.

Marcus Sturdivant

Position: OF **Opening Day Age:** 24
Bats: L **Throws:** L **Born:** 10/29/73 in
Ht: 5' 10" **Wt:** 150 Albemarle, NC

Recent Statistics

	G	AB	R	H	D	T	HR	RBI	SB	BB	SO	AVG
96 A Lancaster	68	292	54	83	19	6	0	31	23	32	35	.284
96 AA Port City	63	243	34	69	11	4	2	23	13	26	33	.284
97 AA Memphis	112	432	71	117	18	5	2	35	21	63	61	.271
97 MLE	112	428	68	113	18	3	2	33	16	52	67	.264

Like Guevara, Sturdivant has no chance of displacing Seattle's incumbent at his position, in his case Griffey. A 28th-round pick in 1992, Sturdivant is an athletic center fielder who lacks the power to play on the corners. He plays the speed game well, drawing walks to get on base and create havoc. Given another year in the minors, he probably could help Seattle as a defensive replacement and pinch runner. Another team might be able to use him as a leadoff man.

Mac Suzuki

Position: P **Opening Day Age:** 22
Bats: R **Throws:** R **Born:** 5/31/75 in Kobe,
Ht: 6' 4" **Wt:** 195 Japan

Recent Statistics

	W	L	ERA	G	GS	Sv	IP	H	R	BB	SO	HR
96 AA Port City	3	6	4.72	16	16	0	74.1	69	41	32	66	10
96 AAA Tacoma	0	3	7.25	13	2	0	22.1	31	19	12	14	3
97 AAA Tacoma	4	9	5.94	32	10	0	83.1	79	60	64	63	13

Suzuki slipped through the Japanese baseball system and was pitching for a U.S. independent team when he became the subject of a bidding war in 1993. The Mari-

ners won out with a signing bonus of $750,000, but have received little return. Elbow and shoulder tendinitis ruined his first two years in the Seattle system. He still has the plus fastball that so many teams coveted, but never has come up with another effective pitch. If he had developed into the closer the Mariners had thought he would, they wouldn't have had to trade Cruz. He pitched poorly at Triple-A in 1997 and isn't ready to contribute as a setup man yet.

Greg Wooten

Position: P **Opening Day Age:** 24
Bats: R **Throws:** R **Born:** 3/30/74 in
Ht: 6' 7" **Wt:** 210 Eugene, OR

Recent Statistics

	W	L	ERA	G	GS	Sv	IP	H	R	BB	SO	HR
96 A Wisconsin	7	1	2.47	13	13	0	83.2	58	27	29	68	3
96 A Lancaster	8	4	3.80	14	14	0	97.0	101	47	25	71	7
97 AA Memphis	11	10	4.47	26	26	0	155.0	166	91	59	98	14

Wooten arrived at Portland State as a shortstop, but left as a pitcher and a third-round pick in 1995. He didn't make his pro debut until the following season, when he led the system with 15 victories for two Class-A clubs. His encore wasn't as successful, as he wasn't able to overpower Double-A hitters. His fastball has average velocity but is effective because it has good movement and is hard to pick up. He also throws a slider, splitter and changeup, all of which need work. He may get another taste of Double-A in 1998.

Others to Watch

Jason Bond struck out 123 in 110 innings at high Class-A Lancaster at age 22. He's a power pitcher for a lefthander and projects as a big league swingman. . . **Chris Dean** is a good hitter for a second baseman, plus he can steal an occasional base and play respectable defense. The downside is that he's 24 and has yet to establish himself in Double-A . . . Unlike Meche, 1996 second-round pick **Jeff Farnsworth** didn't bounce back from shoulder problems. The 22-year-old righthander throws in the mid-90s with a good curveball when healthy, but was limited to 21 innings last season. . . Righthander **Ryan Franklin** almost threw consecutive no-hitters in the Southern League in 1997, but he has average stuff and it was his third tour of Double-A. Relying on command, the 25 year old pitched decently in Triple-A. . . Lefthander **Damaso Marte** is one of the few legitimate pitching prospects in the system. His best pitch is a changeup, and his fastball has good life. At 23, however, he was a bit old for the high Class-A California League. . . Righthander **Denny Stark** was the toughest starter to hit in the minors, holding Class-A Midwest League opponents to a .172 average. He has quick arm action and can throw 94 MPH. He went 7-4, 2.17 with 122 strikeouts in 108 innings. At 22, he was a little old for his league as well.

Larry Rothschild

1997 Season

Larry Rothschild spent 1997 as the Marlins' third-year pitching coach. He oversaw a pitching staff that had its share of success and failure on the way to a World Series championship. Rothschild helped inexperienced youngsters Felix Heredia, Livan Hernandez and Tony Saunders make major contributions. On the other hand, Kevin Brown and Al Leiter weren't as sharp as they had been in '96, Robb Nen's control came and went, and Alex Fernandez suffered a shoulder injury during the playoffs. Shortly before the expansion draft, Tampa Bay hired Rothschild to be its manager.

Offense

Rothschild has no prior managerial experience. He served as a bullpen and pitching coach for the Reds and a minor league pitching instructor for the Braves before joining Florida, so running the offense may be his biggest challenge. The Devil Rays' expansion-draft selections of Miguel Cairo and Quinton McCracken and trades for John Flaherty and Kevin Stocker suggest the club will be built around speed and defense. Fred McGriff is the only proven power hitter, so Rothschild must find other run producers, possibly Brooks Kieschnick, Herbert Perry and Bubba Trammell.

Pitching & Defense

If Rothschild does as well with Tampa Bay's young pitchers as he did with Florida's in 1997, he'll have given the Devil Rays their money's worth. Still, his record of developing young pitchers isn't entirely impressive. Heredia, Hernandez, Saunders and Jay Powell have been his most notable successes, but he was unable to get much out of Rick Helling, Kurt Miller or Marc Valdes. Most of the Marlins staff's improvement under his tenure was the result of free-agent acquisitions.

1998 Outlook

Rothschild's most important task will be to oversee the development of his young pitchers. He should be familiar with Tampa's top pick, Saunders. With little power in his lineup, Rothschild must manage the running game and implement other little-ball strategies.

Born: 3/12/54 in Chicago, IL

Playing Experience: 1981-1982, Det

Managerial Experience: No major league managing experience

Manager Statistics

Year Team, Lg	W	L	Pct	GB	Finish
—	—	—	—	—	—
—	—	—	—	—	—

1997 Starting Pitchers by Days Rest

	≤3	4	5	6+
Devil Rays Starts	—	—	—	—
Devil Rays ERA	—	—	—	—
AL Avg Starts	5	89	34	24
AL ERA	4.38	4.60	4.61	5.37

1997 Situational Stats

	Larry Rothschild	AL Average
Hit & Run Success %	—	36.5
Stolen Base Success %	—	67.3
Platoon Pct.	—	59.5
Defensive Subs	—	22
High-Pitch Outings	—	15
Quick/Slow Hooks	—	19/15
Sacrifice Attempts	—	53

1997 Rankings (American League)

⇒ Did not manage in the majors last year

Wilson Alvarez

1997 Season

Wilson Alvarez was something of a disappointment to the Giants after arriving from the White Sox in a huge July 31 trade. Winning only four of 11 starts after the trade, he complained of shoulder stiffness. His ERA jumped from 2.57 in the first half to 4.65 after the All-Star break. His best pitching came in midseason with Chicago, when he posted a five-game winning streak and didn't allow an earned run in 26⅓ innings.

Pitching

Alvarez can be one of the toughest lefthanders around when he has his best 92-MPH fastball and runs it on the inside and outside corners of the plate. The good fastball sets up his quick-breaking curve and improved changeup. But Alvarez too often will nibble on the corners instead of trusting his fastball. As a result, he wastes too many pitches and usually struggles to last seven innings. Most longball damage against Alvarez is done by righthanders, though lefties hit him for a higher average.

Defense & Hitting

Alvarez' delivery often leaves him in poor fielding position and he's not athletic enough to compensate. He's slow to the plate, but has an above-average pickoff move that helps him compensate. Basestealers went just 11-for-20 against him in 1997. He didn't distinguish himself in his first chance as a big league hitter, going 3-for-26.

1998 Outlook

Alvarez has yet to have the breakthrough season many have predicted for him, but the Devil Rays signed him for $35 million over five years. His late-season shoulder troubles and poor conditioning habits have made him a questionable commodity with many clubs, but he's potentially a big winner waiting to happen.

Position: SP
Bats: L **Throws:** L
Ht: 6' 1" **Wt:** 235

Opening Day Age: 28
Born: 3/24/70 in Maracaibo, VZ
ML Seasons: 8

Overall Statistics

	W	L	Pct.	ERA	G	GS	Sv	IP	H	BB	SO	HR	Ratio
1997	13	11	.542	3.48	33	33	0	212.0	180	91	179	18	1.28
Career	71	54	.568	3.83	197	171	1	1130.1	1035	561	839	113	1.41

How Often He Throws Strikes

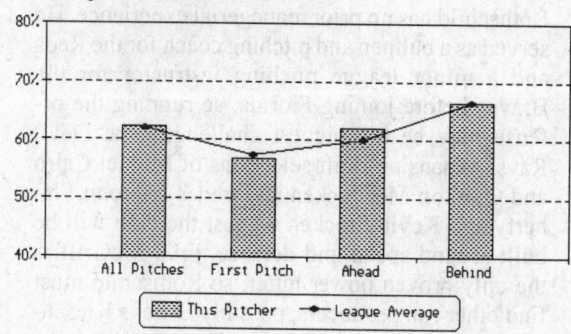

1997 Situational Stats

	W	L	ERA	Sv	IP		AB	H	HR	RBI	Avg
Home	5	6	3.73	0	108.2	LHB	156	39	5	22	.250
Road	8	5	3.22	0	103.1	RHB	629	141	13	64	.224
First Half	7	6	2.57	0	119.0	Sc Pos	157	42	7	69	.268
Scnd Half	6	5	4.65	0	93.0	Clutch	42	9	2	7	.214

1997 Rankings (National League)

⇒ Did not rank near the top or bottom in any category

Rolando Arrojo

Position: SP
Bats: R **Throws:** R
Ht: 6' 4" **Wt:** 210

Opening Day Age: 29
Born: 7/18/68 in Santa Clara, Cuba
ML Seasons: 0
Pronunciation: uh-ROW-hoe

1997 Season

Cuba had lost several pitchers to defections in previous years, so Rolando Arrojo was expected to be the ace of its 1996 Olympic team. But two weeks after stifling Team USA for seven shutout innings in late June, he defected as well. He was granted residency in Costa Rica and declared a free agent by Major League Baseball in mid-April 1997, and soon signed for a $7 million bonus with the Devil Rays. He started slowly but finished strong at high Class-A St. Petersburg, going 5-6, 3.43 with 73 strikeouts in 89⅓ innings.

Pitching

Arrojo threw a consistent 90-91 MPH on the night he dominated Team USA, but improved to 95-96 in the Arizona Fall League after the 1997 season. He'll change speeds off his fastball, sacrificing velocity to add sink. He also has a hard slider that makes him effective against both lefthanders and righthanders. He's working to improve his changeup. He throws quality strikes and avoids walking batters while not giving them much to hit.

Defense

A veteran of years of international play, Arrojo knows how to do the little things. He fields his position, has a good pickoff move and holds runners well. He had no trouble adjusting to U.S. umpires, getting called for just one balk.

1998 Outlook

Because he has big-game experience, Arrojo had figured to get the ball on Opening Day and serve as Tampa Bay's No. 1 starter. The signing of Wilson Alvarez bumped Arrojo down a spot in the rotation, but the Devil Rays' investment in the Cuban looks like it could be worthwhile. The Florida State League wasn't much of a test for a pitcher of Arrojo's age, however, and his age is the subject of debate. Tampa Bay lists him as 29, but Cuban rosters and baseball cards show him to be four years older.

Overall Statistics

	W	L	Pct.	ERA	G	GS	Sv	IP	H	BB	SO	HR	Ratio
1997	—	—	—	—	—	—	—	—	—	—	—	—	—
Career	—	—	—	—	—	—	—	—	—	—	—	—	—

1997 Rankings (American League)
⇒ Did not play in the majors last year

John Flaherty

1997 Season

In his first full season in San Diego, John Flaherty continued the solid play he exhibited after coming from Detroit in a midseason trade in 1996. After getting off to a slow start, he closed with a rush, hitting .320 in the second half to finish with respectable numbers.

Hitting

Never considered much of a hitter, Flaherty has worked hard to make himself productive. He's willing to take pitches to all fields and doesn't try to pull unless he gets a pitch in his inside wheelhouse. Flaherty doesn't walk very much. He can get overpowered upstairs but he has become able to fight some of those pitches off. He's a good breaking-ball hitter with some opposite-field power. He hits his share of home runs when he's able to get a pitch to pull. Flaherty is one of baseball's streakiest hitters, capable of becoming red-hot or ice-cold for months at a time.

Baserunning & Defense

For a catcher, Flaherty has decent speed. He'll take an extra base and occasionally tries to steal one, though he only makes it half the time. He's an outstanding defensive catcher. The entire San Diego staff had confidence in his ability to call games and frame pitches. He also excels at blocking balls in the dirt. His one defensive weakness is throwing. His arm is strong, but he tends to hurry his throws with an erratic delivery that often makes the ball sail for errors.

1998 Outlook

When the Padres gave up Brad Ausmus in the deal for Flaherty, it was clear they wanted Flaherty to fill their void at catcher. Later, they reaffirmed their commitment to him by dealing away Brian Johnson. Then they traded him to Tampa Bay on the night of the expansion draft for Brian Boehringer and Andy Sheets. There's no challenger in sight with the Devil Rays, so Flaherty should hold their starting job for the foreseeable future.

Position: C
Bats: R **Throws:** R
Ht: 6' 1" **Wt:** 200

Opening Day Age: 30
Born: 10/21/67 in New York, NY
ML Seasons: 6
Nickname: Flash

Overall Statistics

	G	AB	R	H	D	T	HR	RBI	SB	BB	SO	Avg	OBP	Slg
1997	129	439	38	120	21	1	9	46	4	33	62	.273	.323	.387
Career	442	1340	125	346	72	2	33	158	7	74	194	.258	.298	.389

Where He Hits the Ball

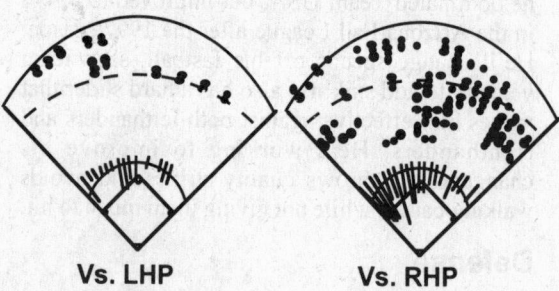

Vs. LHP   **Vs. RHP**

1997 Situational Stats

	AB	H	HR	RBI	Avg		AB	H	HR	RBI	Avg
Home	214	52	4	15	.243	LHP	68	18	1	5	.265
Road	225	68	5	31	.302	RHP	371	102	8	41	.275
First Half	264	64	5	30	.242	Sc Pos	117	31	1	37	.265
Scnd Half	175	56	4	16	.320	Clutch	65	17	0	5	.262

1997 Rankings (National League)

⇒ 3rd in errors at catcher (11) and lowest fielding percentage at catcher (.987)

Roberto Hernandez

1997 Season

A key member of the blockbuster July 31 trade with the White Sox, Roberto Hernandez had only so-so results with San Francisco. After going 27-for-31 in save attempts with Chicago, Hernandez converted only four of eight save opportunities with the Giants, and was often used as a setup man for Rod Beck. Hernandez won five games, including four in September during San Francisco's stretch drive, but then surrendered the game-winning hit in the first two games of the National League Division Series.

Pitching

Hernandez' fastball was clocked as hard as 100 MPH in 1997. He consistently throws in the mid-90s, and when he's spotting his hard splitter he can be as unhittable as any reliever in baseball. He's especially tough on lefthanders, whom he'll bust inside with his riding heat. Hernandez gets in trouble when he tries to overthrow and his fastball straightens. He also shows his inconsistent slider too often, which allows hitters the chance to hurt him with only his third-best pitch. He tends to pitch better in the second half, which was true again last year.

Defense & Hitting

Like so many other closers, Hernandez doesn't worry about basestealers. His big, slow delivery makes him vulnerable to runners who elect to steal in late-inning situations. Hernandez is surprisingly agile for someone his size and fields his position well. He's no factor as a hitter, though he did go 1-for-2 last year in his first major league at-bats.

1998 Outlook

Hernandez has had 30 saves or more in four of his last five seasons. That performance earned him a huge free-agent contract from the Devil Rays, who announced his signing immediately after the expansion draft. His velocity has shown no sign of deteriorating, so he should remain a premier reliever for Tampa Bay.

Position: RP
Bats: R **Throws:** R
Ht: 6' 4" **Wt:** 235

Opening Day Age: 33
Born: 11/11/64 in Santurce, PR
ML Seasons: 7

Overall Statistics

	W	L	Pct.	ERA	G	GS	Sv	IP	H	BB	SO	HR	Ratio
1997	10	3	.769	2.45	74	0	31	80.2	67	38	82	7	1.30
Career	34	26	.567	2.84	373	3	165	437.1	368	170	446	34	1.23

How Often He Throws Strikes

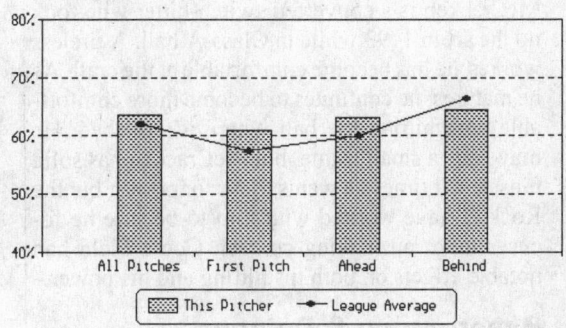

1997 Situational Stats

	W	L	ERA	Sv	IP		AB	H	HR	RBI	Avg
Home	4	0	2.06	17	39.1	LHB	160	31	2	13	.194
Road	6	3	2.83	14	41.1	RHB	138	36	5	20	.261
First Half	5	1	3.05	20	38.1	Sc Pos	100	18	2	26	.180
Scnd Half	5	2	1.91	11	42.1	Clutch	218	48	5	28	.220

1997 Rankings (National League)

⇒ 8th in lowest batting average allowed in relief with runners on base (.197)
⇒ Led the Giants in lowest batting average allowed in relief with runners on base (.197)

Quinton McCracken

1997 Season

Quinton McCracken saw more starts than he might have imagined in his second season with the Rockies. He began the year brilliantly, making contact from both sides of the plate, then becoming a threat to steal whenever he reached base. At midseason, he experienced his first prolonged slump in the major leagues. The question then became whether he could rebound from a slide that saw his average dip from .358 to .258. McCracken did recover, proving to himself that he belongs in the majors by finishing with a .292 average and 28 steals.

Hitting

McCracken is a converted switch-hitter who took up the art in 1993 while in Class-A ball. A tireless worker, he has become comfortable at the craft. As he matures, he continues to become more comfortable with hitting the ball where it's pitched. He may have a small frame, but McCracken has solid muscle. At times he wants to hit for power, but the Rockies have worked with him to be sure he focuses more on making contact. Coors Field had notable effects on both his hitting and his power.

Baserunning & Defense

McCracken has excellent speed and he's a smart baserunner. He knows how to read a pitcher's move and use it to his advantage. He came up as a second baseman before the Rockies converted him to center field. He has become comfortable at the position, though he still is challenged by balls hit directly over his head. McCracken has an accurate arm, but it's not a gun. He has fine leaping ability and the athleticism one would expect from a former defensive back at Duke.

1998 Outlook

McCracken was selected by the Devil Rays with their second pick in the expansion draft and projects as Tampa Bay's everyday center fielder. He proved his value by showing he can play every day and work out of a slump. For a young player he has adjusted well to the times when he has had to come off the bench.

Position: CF
Bats: B **Throws:** R
Ht: 5' 7" **Wt:** 173

Opening Day Age: 28
Born: 3/16/70 in Wilmington, NC
ML Seasons: 3
Nickname: Q

Overall Statistics

	G	AB	R	H	D	T	HR	RBI	SB	BB	SO	Avg	OBP	Slg
1997	147	325	69	95	11	1	3	36	28	42	62	.292	.374	.360
Career	274	609	119	177	24	7	6	76	45	74	125	.291	.368	.383

Where He Hits the Ball

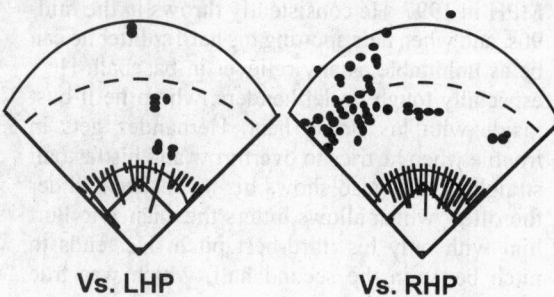

Vs. LHP   Vs. RHP

1997 Situational Stats

	AB	H	HR	RBI	Avg		AB	H	HR	RBI	Avg
Home	157	51	1	21	.325	LHP	86	20	1	6	.233
Road	168	44	2	15	.262	RHP	239	75	2	30	.314
First Half	186	48	3	21	.258	Sc Pos	85	27	0	32	.318
Scnd Half	139	47	0	15	.338	Clutch	54	12	0	3	.222

1997 Rankings (National League)

⇒ 5th in errors in center field (4) and fielding percentage in center field (.980)
⇒ Led the Rockies in batting average on a 3-2 count (.326)

Fred McGriff

1997 Season

It was a frustrating season for Atlanta slugger Fred McGriff. He struggled through a long midseason power drought and finished with only 22 home runs, his lowest total in a decade. His slump led to whispers that he was washed up and brought out criticiscm of his backed-off hitting stance. Though he also racked up 97 RBI, his numbers really weren't all that impressive for a first baseman hitting out of the cleanup slot.

Hitting

McGriff stands well off the plate so that he can fully extend his arms at the point of contact. He likes the ball low and has good power to all fields. He handles southpaws well, except for those with big-breaking curveballs. In an effort to break out of his power outage in 1997, he worked on stepping more toward the plate and driving the ball up the middle. He's one of the most durable players in the majors and always remains in the lineup despite his increasingly frequent aches and pains.

Baserunning & Defense

McGriff makes the routine plays without a problem, but he doesn't have much range to either side. His arm is weak and sometimes erratic. He stole five bases without being caught in 1997, but that's deceptive. In truth, he's a very slow runner who runs as conservatively as anyone in the American League.

1998 Outlook

On the night of the expansion draft, McGriff was traded to his hometown Tampa Bay Devil Rays for a player to be named. Has McGriff begun to yield to Father Time, or was his subpar year a product of the Braves' new ballpark? Turner Field was much less homer-friendly than Fulton County Stadium had been. Regardless, there's no reason to think that McGriff suddenly will recapture the powerful stroke he possessed three years ago. To his credit, he's still a useful run producer and should remain so for a few more seasons.

Position: 1B
Bats: L **Throws:** L
Ht: 6' 3" **Wt:** 215

Opening Day Age: 34
Born: 10/31/63 in Tampa, FL
ML Seasons: 12
Nickname: Crime Dog

Overall Statistics

	G	AB	R	H	D	T	HR	RBI	SB	BB	SO	Avg	OBP	Slg
1997	152	564	77	156	25	1	22	97	5	68	112	.277	.356	.441
Career	1602	5693	946	1622	291	19	339	1007	60	880	1247	.285	.381	.521

Where He Hits the Ball

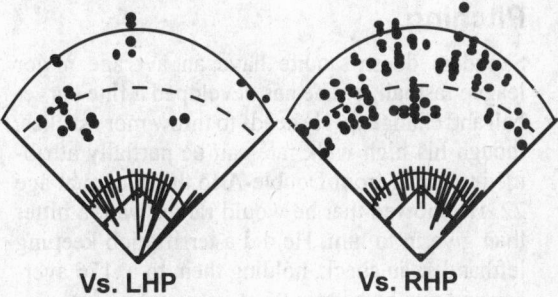

Vs. LHP   **Vs. RHP**

1997 Situational Stats

	AB	H	HR	RBI	Avg		AB	H	HR	RBI	Avg
Home	294	78	8	52	.265	LHP	183	49	6	28	.268
Road	270	78	14	45	.289	RHP	381	107	16	69	.281
First Half	313	88	10	50	.281	Sc Pos	174	45	2	67	.259
Scnd Half	251	68	12	47	.271	Clutch	81	18	5	12	.222

1997 Rankings (National League)

⇒ 1st in GDPs (22), lowest fielding percentage at first base (.990) and lowest percentage of extra bases taken as a runner (23.8%)
⇒ 2nd in errors at first base (13)
⇒ 5th in lowest cleanup slugging percentage (.444)
⇒ Led the Braves in GDPs (22) and cleanup slugging percentage (.444)

Tony Saunders

1997 Season

The Marlins had an open competition in spring training to find a fifth starter, and Tony Saunders made the jump from Double-A to win the job. He had a respectable rookie season that included seven weeks on the disabled list with a strained ligament in his right knee. He was most effective against the Braves, going 3-0, 1.65 against them in four regular-season starts and holding them to two runs in 5⅓ innings in the National League Championship Series. He was bombed in his lone World Series start. Florida originally had planned to protect Saunders, then decided to keep Al Leiter for his trade value. Tampa Bay jumped on Saunders with the No. 1 overall pick in the expansion draft.

Pitching

Saunders doesn't quite have an average major league fastball, but he has developed a fine curveball and changeup. He needs to throw more strikes, though his high walk rate can be partially attributed to going from Double-A to the majors at age 22. He showed that he would rather walk a hitter than give in to him. He did a terrific job keeping lefthanders in check, holding them to a .176 average and two homers in 85 at-bats.

Defense

Saunders was an erratic fielder as a rookie, committing two errors in 15 chances. He did a better job of keeping basestealers in check, allowing only seven swipes in 16 tries. He also picked off two runners. Though he'll rarely hit as an American Leaguer, Saunders did smack a homer in 1997.

1998 Outlook

Saunders tore elbow ligaments in 1994, and the injury forced him to learn how to pitch. He patterns himself after Atlanta's Tom Glavine, knowing he has to hit spots and change speeds. Devil Rays manager and former Marlins pitching coach Larry Rothschild knows Saunders well and obviously has a great deal of confidence in him to endorse him as the top expansion pick. Saunders will be the No. 3 starter for Tampa Bay in 1998, behind Wilson Alvarez and Rolando Arrojo.

Position: SP
Bats: L **Throws:** L
Ht: 6' 2" **Wt:** 205

Opening Day Age: 23
Born: 4/29/74 in Baltimore, MD
ML Seasons: 1

Overall Statistics

	W	L	Pct.	ERA	G	GS	Sv	IP	H	BB	SO	HR	Ratio
1997	4	6	.400	4.61	22	21	0	111.1	99	64	102	12	1.46
Career	4	6	.400	4.61	22	21	0	111.1	99	64	102	12	1.46

How Often He Throws Strikes

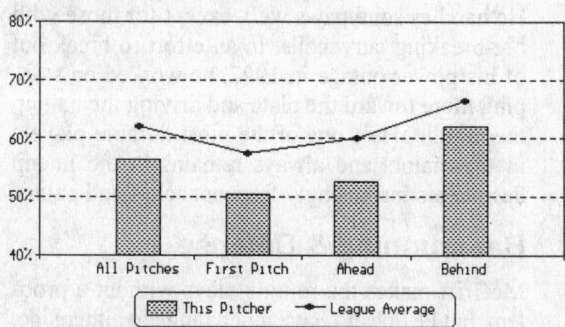

1997 Situational Stats

	W	L	ERA	Sv	IP		AB	H	HR	RBI	Avg
Home	3	4	4.26	0	61.1	LHB	85	15	2	7	.176
Road	1	2	5.04	0	50.0	RHB	320	84	10	49	.263
First Half	2	1	4.38	0	39.0	Sc Pos	102	24	3	40	.235
Scnd Half	2	5	4.73	0	72.1	Clutch	22	9	0	5	.409

1997 Rankings (National League)
⇒ Led the Marlins in balks (1)

Dennis Springer

1997 Season

After 11 seasons in the minors, knuckleballer Dennis Springer finally made a successful jump to the major leagues in 1997. He was a valuable asset to the Angels, working deep into his games and coming back on short rest when injuries hit their rotation. He pitched fairly well in the second half and was a big reason Anaheim was able to remain in contention as long as it did. The Devil Rays selected him in the first round of the expansion draft to eat innings and steady their young staff.

Pitching

Springer throws his knuckler about 75 percent of the time. He can surprise hitters with a curveball here and there, and he'll throw some low-80s fastballs when he's having trouble getting the knuckleball over. Former flutterballers Phil Niekro and Charlie Hough have taught Springer an appreciation for changing speeds with the knuckler, and Springer has been known to throw it at any speed from the mid-70s down to the high 40s. When his pitch is working, he gets tougher as the game goes on. When it won't behave, though, he's prone to giving up homers. He has been effective on three or even two days' rest.

Defense

Springer is an awkward but aggressive fielder, taking gambles when he snares a comebacker with men on base. He controls the running game well for a knuckleballer, and he can catch a runner leaning the wrong way.

1998 Outlook

Like the Marlins did before them, the Devil Rays drafted a knuckleballer to give them a lot of innings in their inaugural year. In a spacious ballpark with a strong defense behind him, Tampa Bay hopes Springer can be reasonably effective and take the ball every five days all season. On a staff that's sure to be unsettled, his durability will be an asset.

Position: SP
Bats: R **Throws:** R
Ht: 5'10" **Wt:** 185

Opening Day Age: 33
Born: 2/12/65 in Fresno, CA
ML Seasons: 3

Overall Statistics

	W	L	Pct.	ERA	G	GS	Sv	IP	H	BB	SO	HR	Ratio
1997	9	9	.500	5.18	32	28	0	194.2	199	73	75	32	1.40
Career	14	18	.438	5.26	56	47	0	311.2	311	125	154	59	1.40

How Often He Throws Strikes

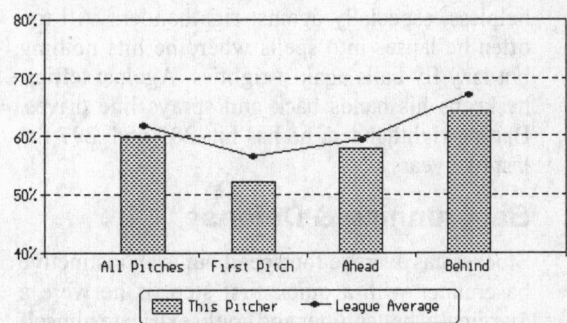

1997 Situational Stats

	W	L	ERA	Sv	IP		AB	H	HR	RBI	Avg
Home	4	4	5.23	0	93.0	LHB	371	100	16	60	.270
Road	5	5	5.13	0	101.2	RHB	375	99	16	52	.264
First Half	4	3	5.82	0	86.2	Sc Pos	179	47	7	79	.263
Scnd Half	5	6	4.67	0	108.0	Clutch	59	16	3	7	.271

1997 Rankings (American League)

⇒ 1st in lowest strikeout/walk ratio (1.0) and least strikeouts per 9 innings (3.5)

⇒ 2nd in lowest groundball/flyball ratio allowed (0.7)

⇒ 3rd in home runs allowed and most home runs allowed per 9 innings (1.48)

⇒ 5th in runners caught stealing (11), highest slugging percentage allowed (.473), least pitches thrown per batter (3.55) and highest ERA on the road

⇒ Led the Angels in complete games (3), shutouts (1), walks allowed, hit batsmen (10), stolen bases allowed (19), runners caught stealing (11), least pitches thrown per batter (3.55) and lowest batting average allowed vs. lefthanded batters

Tampa Bay
Devil Rays

Kevin Stocker

1997 Season

After a brutal 1995 season in which his offense and defense suffered from his poor conditioning efforts, Kevin Stocker has rebounded to become a workmanlike major league shortstop in most respects. He was the Phillies' everyday No. 8 hitter, and was effective at taking walks and turning the lineup over. He made only 11 errors at shortstop and overcame below-average range with expert anticipation and positioning.

Hitting

The key to Stocker's offensive performance is patience. When he fishes for breaking balls out of the strike zone, the switch-hitter can be rendered helpless, especially against righthanders. All too often he lapses into spells where he hits nothing but lazy fly balls against righties. Against lefties, he keeps his hands back and sprays line drives. Batting righthanded, he has hit .283 and .297 the last two years.

Baserunning & Defense

Stocker has average footspeed but is an instinctive baserunner with a quick first step. If he were a marginally better hitter and could extricate himself from the No. 8 hole, he could be a 20-steal guy. He's a technically sound defender who overcomes a lack of raw tools with an excellent grasp of the fundamentals. He turns the double play well, and has soft hands and an accurate arm.

1998 Outlook

Desi Relaford, a flashier, less consistent defender with a strong arm and raw speed, was breathing down Stocker's neck in Philadelphia. As a result, the Phillies traded Stocker to Tampa Bay for outfielder Bob Abreu, a first-round pick in the expansion draft. Stocker should remain a .260 hitter with no power.

Position: SS
Bats: B **Throws:** R
Ht: 6' 1" **Wt:** 175

Opening Day Age: 28
Born: 2/13/70 in Spokane, WA
ML Seasons: 5

Overall Statistics

	G	AB	R	H	D	T	HR	RBI	SB	BB	SO	Avg	OBP	Slg
1997	149	504	51	134	23	5	4	40	11	51	91	.266	.335	.355
Career	545	1840	223	482	82	19	14	172	30	211	339	.262	.347	.350

Where He Hits the Ball

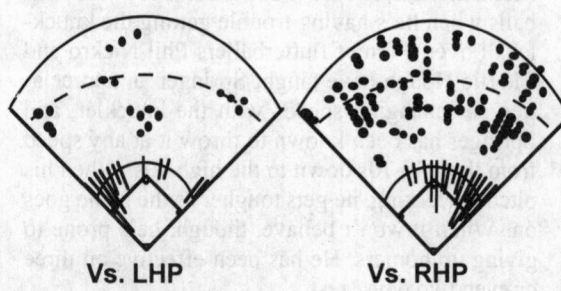

Vs. LHP   **Vs. RHP**

1997 Situational Stats

	AB	H	HR	RBI	Avg		AB	H	HR	RBI	Avg
Home	233	71	2	21	.305	LHP	111	33	1	11	.297
Road	271	63	2	19	.232	RHP	393	101	3	29	.257
First Half	280	70	1	18	.250	Sc Pos	118	29	2	37	.246
Scnd Half	224	64	3	22	.286	Clutch	75	21	0	6	.280

1997 Rankings (National League)

⇒ 1st in lowest batting average on a 3-1 count (.000)
⇒ 2nd in lowest slugging percentage vs. righthanded pitchers (.341)
⇒ 3rd in fielding percentage at shortstop (.981)
⇒ 5th in lowest HR frequency (126.0 ABs per HR) and lowest batting average on the road
⇒ 6th in lowest slugging percentage
⇒ Led the Phillies in intentional walks (7), GDPs (13), batting average at home and bunts in play (19)

Bubba Trammell (Pivotal Season)

1997 Season

After enjoying a monster season in the minors in 1996, Bubba Trammell spent the first month of 1997 with the Tigers as a semi-regular outfielder and designated hitter. He was sent back down in early May, despite the fact that he had played fairly well. Back in Triple-A, he swung for the fences more than ever and boosted his power at the expense of his batting average. That earned him a cursory look in September, but he didn't hit. The Devil Rays grabbed him in the first round of the expansion draft.

Hitting

Trammell may be the best pure hitter taken in the expansion draft. His other tools may be unimpressive, but he's a major league hitter. He's capable of hitting for a decent average with big-time power, and he's ready to hit in the middle of a big league batting order. He'll strike out a lot, but no more so than other power hitters, and he can produce against all types of pitching. Some feel his troubles in Detroit stemmed from trying to pull the ball too much in an effort to impress the brass.

Baserunning & Defense

Trammell's speed is better than one would expect, and he can surprise the defense with a steal every now and then. Even so, he's far from fast and his outfield play is a major weakness. He has a decent arm, but his inability to read fly balls makes him a liability in left or right field. He's best suited to the DH role.

1998 Outlook

Trammell may be one of Tampa Bay's most productive hitters and one of the most surprising players of the year. When Jeff Conine was selected by the Marlins in the 1992 expansion draft, he was quite similar to Trammell. Both were proven hitters in their mid-20s who hadn't gotten much of a chance in the majors due to defensive limitations. Trammell should get a lot of at-bats as Tampa Bay's DH.

Position: RF/LF/DH
Bats: R **Throws:** R
Ht: 6' 2" **Wt:** 220

Opening Day Age: 26
Born: 11/6/71 in Knoxville, TN
ML Seasons: 1
Pronunciation: TRAM-mull

Overall Statistics

	G	AB	R	H	D	T	HR	RBI	SB	BB	SO	Avg	OBP	Slg
1997	44	123	14	28	5	0	4	13	3	15	35	.228	.307	.366
Career	44	123	14	28	5	0	4	13	3	15	35	.228	.307	.366

Where He Hits the Ball

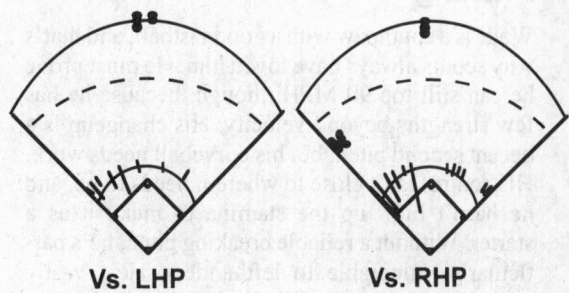

Vs. LHP   **Vs. RHP**

1997 Situational Stats

	AB	H	HR	RBI	Avg		AB	H	HR	RBI	Avg
Home	64	12	2	5	.188	LHP	46	12	3	7	.261
Road	59	16	2	8	.271	RHP	77	16	1	6	.208
First Half	67	16	4	9	.239	Sc Pos	26	5	2	11	.192
Scnd Half	56	12	0	4	.214	Clutch	15	3	0	1	.200

1997 Rankings (American League)

⇒ Did not rank near the top or bottom in any category

Tampa Bay Devil Rays

Terrell Wade

1997 Season

Terrell Wade began 1997 as Atlanta's fifth starter, a position many would envy. He hardly pitched at all during April's light schedule and couldn't find the plate when he joined the rotation for good in May. One month later, he went on the disabled list with a partially torn flexor muscle in his left elbow. During rehab, his shoulder began to bother him as well. He ultimately had season-ending surgery to repair a small tear in his rotator cuff. The Braves left him unprotected in the expansion draft and didn't bother to pull him back after each of the first two rounds, so the Devil Rays decided to take a chance on him in the third.

Pitching

Wade is a southpaw with a good fastball, and that's why scouts always have loved him. He must prove he can still top 90 MPH, though, because he has few strengths beyond velocity. His changeup is a decent second pitch, but his curveball needs work. His control isn't close to where it needs to be, and he hasn't built up the stamina to make it as a starter. Without a reliable breaking pitch, he's particularly vulnerable to lefthanders. He's vastly more hittable from a full windup than he is from the stretch, perhaps because he's been tipping his pitches. He has the raw tools to succeed, though, if he can refine his control and master the breaking ball.

Defense

As a fielder, Wade has decent mobility for a man his size. He should be more surehanded than he's been so far. Baserunners run wild on him, although he is able to pick someone off once in a while.

1998 Outlook

If Wade's arm is sound, Tampa Bay will do its best to smooth off his rough edges and make him into a finished pitcher. He may end up in the bullpen or the rotation, depending upon how he progresses. At age 25 there's no need to rush him, and he still has plenty of time to make good on his potential.

Position: SP
Bats: L **Throws:** L
Ht: 6' 3" **Wt:** 205

Opening Day Age: 25
Born: 1/25/73 in Rembert, SC
ML Seasons: 3

Overall Statistics

	W	L	Pct.	ERA	G	GS	Sv	IP	H	BB	SO	HR	Ratio
1997	2	3	.400	5.36	12	9	0	42.0	60	16	35	6	1.81
Career	7	4	.636	3.89	59	17	1	115.2	120	67	117	16	1.62

How Often He Throws Strikes

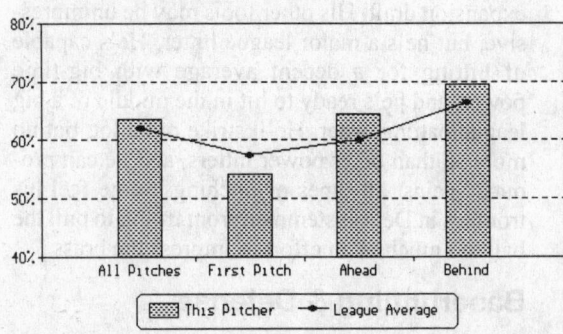

1997 Situational Stats

	W	L	ERA	Sv	IP		AB	H	HR	RBI	Avg
Home	2	2	3.82	0	30.2	LHB	45	22	0	3	.489
Road	0	1	9.53	0	11.1	RHB	127	38	6	21	.299
First Half	2	3	5.36	0	42.0	Sc Pos	36	8	1	14	.222
Scnd Half	0	0	-	0	0.0	Clutch	4	2	0	1	.500

1997 Rankings (National League)

⇒ Did not rank near the top or bottom in any category

Rich Butler

Position: LF
Bats: L **Throws:** R
Ht: 6' 1" **Wt:** 180

Opening Day Age: 24
Born: 5/1/73 in Toronto, Canada
ML Seasons: 1

Overall Statistics

	G	AB	R	H	D	T	HR	RBI	SB	BB	SO	Avg	OBP	Slg
1997	7	14	3	4	1	0	0	2	0	2	3	.286	.375	.357
Career	7	14	3	4	1	0	0	2	0	2	3	.286	.375	.357

1997 Situational Stats

	AB	H	HR	RBI	Avg		AB	H	HR	RBI	Avg
Home	11	4	0	2	.364	LHP	0	0	0	0	-
Road	3	0	0	0	.000	RHP	14	4	0	2	.286
First Half	0	0	0	0	-	Sc Pos	6	3	0	2	.500
Scnd Half	14	4	0	2	.286	Clutch	4	1	0	1	.250

1997 Season

Two years ago, Rich Butler had been all but left for dead. He had flunked two trials at Triple-A before missing almost all of 1996 with a torn rotator cuff. But he re-emerged in 1997 and displayed new-found power, notching 63 extra-base hits in Triple-A while batting an even .300. The Devil Rays surprised many baseball observers when they took him with the 10th overall pick in the expansion draft.

Hitting, Baserunning & Defense

Butler is a slashing line-drive hitter who has improved his plate patience but remains prone to strikeouts. He hasn't proven he can hit lefthanders yet, but he may be a useful bench player because he has the speed to cover all three outfield positions. His arm is strong but not terribly accurate. He's quick enough to steal an occasional base.

1998 Outlook

Butler hadn't hit for power before last season, so there's considerable doubt that he can produce enough to hold down a starting job in the outfield. Still, he projects as a useful fourth outfielder with a little speed, a little pop and a little defense.

Miguel Cairo

Position: 2B
Bats: R **Throws:** R
Ht: 6' 0" **Wt:** 160

Opening Day Age: 23
Born: 5/4/74 in Anaco, Venezuela
ML Seasons: 2
Pronunciation: KY-roh

Overall Statistics

	G	AB	R	H	D	T	HR	RBI	SB	BB	SO	Avg	OBP	Slg
1997	16	29	7	7	1	0	0	1	0	2	3	.241	.313	.276
Career	25	56	12	13	3	0	0	2	0	4	12	.232	.306	.286

1997 Situational Stats

	AB	H	HR	RBI	Avg		AB	H	HR	RBI	Avg
Home	7	5	0	0	.714	LHP	13	2	0	0	.154
Road	22	2	0	1	.091	RHP	16	5	0	1	.313
First Half	2	0	0	0	.000	Sc Pos	9	0	0	1	.000
Scnd Half	27	7	0	1	.259	Clutch	7	0	0	0	.000

1997 Season

Playing for his third organization in as many years, Miguel Cairo batted .279-5-46 with 40 steals at Triple-A Iowa. The Cubs called him up in June and September, and he looked like the frontrunner to succeed Ryne Sandberg at second base. Tampa Bay ended that thought by taking Cairo with the eighth overall pick in the expansion draft.

Hitting, Baserunning & Defense

Cairo has established himself as a contact hitter with some speed. His inability to draw a walk—he had just 24 in 135 Triple-A games in 1997—is the only thing preventing him from being an ideal leadoff candidate. He won't drive many balls out of the park, but he will leg out his share of doubles. He has stolen 167 bases in the minors in the last five seasons, but his success rate is merely average. He's solid defensively and turns the double play well. He could fill in at shortstop if needed.

1998 Outlook

The Cubs were left with no obvious second-base candidate, and Cairo is the only one for the Devil Rays. His only conceivable competition could come from Aaron Ledesma, who has a slightly better bat but is significantly weaker defensively.

Mike Difelice

Position: C
Bats: R **Throws:** R
Ht: 6' 2" **Wt:** 205

Opening Day Age: 28
Born: 5/28/69 in
Philadelphia, PA
ML Seasons: 2
Pronunciation:
dee-fah-LEECE

Overall Statistics

	G	AB	R	H	D	T	HR	RBI	SB	BB	SO	Avg	OBP	Slg
1997	93	260	16	62	10	1	4	30	1	19	61	.238	.297	.331
Career	97	267	16	64	11	1	4	32	1	19	62	.240	.297	.333

1997 Situational Stats

	AB	H	HR	RBI	Avg		AB	H	HR	RBI	Avg
Home	103	22	1	7	.214	LHP	64	15	2	10	.234
Road	157	40	3	23	.255	RHP	196	47	2	20	.240
First Half	122	26	3	13	.213	Sc Pos	59	19	0	22	.322
Scnd Half	138	36	1	17	.261	Clutch	33	5	0	3	.152

1997 Season

One of the Cardinals' more pleasant surprises of the 1997 season, Mike Difelice had spent most of the first six years of his pro career as a backup catcher in the minors. Offensively, he delivered more than anyone expected, which wasn't much. He was solid enough defensively to gain a platoon role.

Hitting, Baserunning & Defense

Difelice never had as many as 250 at-bats in any minor league season, so his 260 in 1997 were a professional high. He didn't make much contact but hit considerably better in the second half. His best work came in the clutch, with 19 of his 30 RBI coming with two out. Difelice is slow but his hitting and running weren't what kept him climbing through the minors. He handles pitchers well and is fundamentally sound behind the plate, throwing out 33 percent of basestealers. He had difficulty blocking pitches in the dirt in the second half, and finished with 12 passed balls.

1998 Outlook

Difelice was a surprise first-round pick in the expansion draft. Tampa Bay traded for John Flaherty later, bumping Difelice to No. 2 on the depth chart. He'll never hit well enough to play regularly, but his defense should make him a capable backup.

Vaughn Eshelman

Position: RP/SP
Bats: L **Throws:** L
Ht: 6' 3" **Wt:** 210

Opening Day Age: 28
Born: 5/22/69 in
Philadelphia, PA
ML Seasons: 3

Overall Statistics

	W	L	Pct.	ERA	G	GS	Sv	IP	H	BB	SO	HR	Ratio
1997	3	3	.500	6.33	21	6	0	42.2	58	17	18	3	1.76
Career	15	9	.625	6.07	83	30	0	212.0	256	111	118	19	1.73

1997 Situational Stats

	W	L	ERA	Sv	IP		AB	H	HR	RBI	Avg
Home	2	2	4.87	0	20.1	LHB	40	9	1	4	.225
Road	1	1	7.66	0	22.1	RHB	136	49	2	25	.360
First Half	2	3	6.26	0	41.2	Sc Pos	55	20	1	26	.364
Scnd Half	1	0	9.00	0	1.0	Clutch	16	8	0	6	.500

1997 Season

Vaughn Eshelman opened 1997 as the last man in Boston's bullpen and was sent to Triple-A in early May with a 9.82 ERA. Back in the minors, he worked as a starter with mixed results before being recalled in June to serve as the Red Sox' fifth starter. He flunked that trial too, and was sent back down in July. The Athletics claimed him on waivers in October before Tampa Bay took him with the last pick of the expansion draft.

Pitching & Defense

Eshelman works the outside corner with a mid-80s fastball and a decent slider and curve. Walks are a necessary evil because anything left over the heart of the plate is liable to be hit hard. He's reasonably effective against lefthanders but lacks a pitch to get righties out. He gets most of his outs when batters beat his breaking pitches into the ground. He grabs his share of comebackers, but wild throws to the bases have always been a problem. Basestealers seemed to figure out his stretch delivery in 1997.

1998 Outlook

Eshelman has never had long-term success in any role at the major league level. His best shot may be to become a one-out specialist. Because he's lefthanded, it's hard to say if he'll run out of trials, but he's going to have to start contributing soon.

Jason Johnson

Position: RP
Bats: R **Throws:** R
Ht: 6' 6" **Wt:** 216

Opening Day Age: 24
Born: 10/27/73 in
Santa Barbara, CA
ML Seasons: 1

Overall Statistics

	W	L	Pct.	ERA	G	GS	Sv	IP	H	BB	SO	HR	Ratio
1997	0	0	-	6.00	3	0	0	6.0	10	1	3	2	1.83
Career	0	0	-	6.00	3	0	0	6.0	10	1	3	2	1.83

1997 Situational Stats

	W	L	ERA	Sv	IP		AB	H	HR	RBI	Avg
Home	0	0	4.50	0	4.0	LHB	7	3	0	1	.429
Road	0	0	9.00	0	2.0	RHB	18	7	2	5	.389
First Half	0	0	-	0	0.0	Sc Pos	5	2	1	5	.400
Scnd Half	0	0	6.00	0	6.0	Clutch	0	0	0	0	-

1997 Season

Jason Johnson's 1997 couldn't have been more surprising. Signed by the Pirates as a nondrafted free agent out of high school, he brought a 15-38 pro record into the season and started the year with his third stint at high Class-A Lynchburg. By August he was in Pittsburgh, surrendering a homer to Mike Piazza on his first big league pitch. Three months later, he was a first-round expansion pick of Tampa Bay.

Pitching & Defense

Johnson's career took off after Pirates prospect Kris Benson showed him a curveball in spring training. With hitters unable to sit on his fastball, Johnson became more of a strikeout pitcher. He throws strikes, but he gives up more hits than his stuff would indicate he should because he's always around the plate. He's huge, which hampers his fielding but not his ability to hold runners. Basestealers were successful 69 percent of the time against him in the minors the last two years, but went 0-for-2 in the majors.

1998 Outlook

Johnson didn't pitch well in the majors and didn't light up Double-A. He could use a full season in Triple-A, but it's unlikely he'll get it. Tampa will need pitching and he's one of their best arms.

Mike Kelly (Pivotal Season)

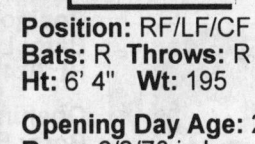
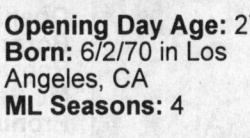

Position: RF/LF/CF
Bats: R **Throws:** R
Ht: 6' 4" **Wt:** 195

Opening Day Age: 27
Born: 6/2/70 in Los
Angeles, CA
ML Seasons: 4

Overall Statistics

	G	AB	R	H	D	T	HR	RBI	SB	BB	SO	Avg	OBP	Slg
1997	73	140	27	41	13	2	6	19	6	10	30	.293	.338	.543
Career	219	403	72	97	33	4	12	52	17	32	107	.241	.303	.432

1997 Situational Stats

	AB	H	HR	RBI	Avg		AB	H	HR	RBI	Avg
Home	90	30	3	13	.333	LHP	64	19	3	11	.297
Road	50	11	3	6	.220	RHP	76	22	3	8	.289
First Half	63	16	2	10	.254	Sc Pos	43	8	1	12	.186
Scnd Half	77	25	4	9	.325	Clutch	31	8	2	7	.258

1997 Season

Long a tease with his athletic ability, Mike Kelly showed flashes of his tools while seeing action in all three outfield positions. He hit a career-high .293, including .325 after the All-Star break. He lost playing time in September with a knee problem.

Hitting, Baserunning & Defense

The second player taken in the 1991 draft, Kelly appears to finally have learned better plate discipline. He used to strike out far too much, but he's making better contact by cutting down his swing and not trying to pull every pitch. He can kill fastballs but is still unproven against good breaking pitches. Kelly is a good athlete who can play anywhere in the outfield, and he's a threat to steal. He has stolen 10 of 11 bases in the last two years.

1998 Outlook

Scouts continue to be intrigued by Kelly's physical tools. So too were the Devil Rays, who made him the first major leaguer they acquired when they traded for him before the expansion draft. The cost was a player to be named, who turned out to be expansion draft choice Dmitri Young.

Brooks Kieschnick

Position: LF
Bats: L **Throws:** R
Ht: 6' 4" **Wt:** 225

Opening Day Age: 25
Born: 6/6/72 in
Robstown, TX
ML Seasons: 2
Pronunciation:
KEESH-nik

Overall Statistics

	G	AB	R	H	D	T	HR	RBI	SB	BB	SO	Avg	OBP	Slg
1997	39	90	9	18	2	0	4	12	1	12	21	.200	.294	.356
Career	64	119	15	28	4	0	5	18	1	15	29	.235	.321	.395

1997 Situational Stats

	AB	H	HR	RBI	Avg		AB	H	HR	RBI	Avg
Home	40	11	3	9	.275	LHP	7	2	0	1	.286
Road	50	7	1	3	.140	RHP	83	16	4	11	.193
First Half	70	14	3	10	.200	Sc Pos	21	7	3	11	.333
Scnd Half	20	4	1	2	.200	Clutch	7	0	0	0	.000

1997 Season

Brooks Kieschnick was one of the best baseball players in the storied history of the University of Texas, but he was unable to win a regular job with the Cubs. He was called up April 11 and hit .295 with three homers through the end of the month. He fell into a 1-for-26 tailspin, was sent back to Triple-A and resurfaced in September. Tampa Bay took him in the third round of the expansion draft.

Hitting, Baserunning & Defense

Kieschnick was chosen 10th overall in the 1993 draft because of his lefthanded power. He has homered 62 times in Triple-A since '95, but just five times in the majors. He strikes out as much as a typical slugger, though he doesn't walk enough to project as more than a .250 hitter. Kieschnick was used as a platoon player by the Cubs and batted just .193 against Triple-A lefthanders in 1997. His homers are the extent of his contributions; he runs poorly and plays even worse defense. He shows a good arm in left field, but he was born to be a designated hitter.

1998 Outlook

Kieschnick is best suited to play for an AL team. First-round expansion draft pick Bubba Trammell has similar tools and probably will get first crack at DH. He could start 1998 as a big league reserve.

Albie Lopez

Position: RP/SP
Bats: R **Throws:** R
Ht: 6' 2" **Wt:** 185

Opening Day Age: 26
Born: 8/18/71 in Mesa, AZ
ML Seasons: 5

Overall Statistics

	W	L	Pct.	ERA	G	GS	Sv	IP	H	BB	SO	HR	Ratio
1997	3	7	.300	6.93	37	6	0	76.2	101	40	63	11	1.84
Career	12	14	.462	5.99	69	31	0	228.1	267	107	173	39	1.64

1997 Situational Stats

	W	L	ERA	Sv	IP		AB	H	HR	RBI	Avg
Home	1	2	6.06	0	35.2	LHB	152	50	7	34	.329
Road	2	5	7.68	0	41.0	RHB	162	51	4	27	.315
First Half	3	4	6.57	0	50.2	Sc Pos	90	32	3	47	.356
Scnd Half	0	3	7.62	0	26.0	Clutch	56	19	6	16	.339

1997 Season

For the fifth straight season, Albie Lopez tried and failed to make the jump from the minors to the majors with Cleveland. Though he has gone 30-15 in Triple-A during that span, his major league record is just 12-14, 5.99. Last year was the first time he was able to stay with Cleveland pretty much from start to finish, though he bombed out of the rotation in June and was hit hard in relief. The Devil Rays selected him in the second round of the expansion draft.

Pitching & Defense

Lopez always has had good stuff, with a 90-MPH fastball, a nice curveball and a changeup. His struggles with Cleveland may have resulted from a lack of confidence combined with the big expectations his minor league exploits created. He has had trouble staying ahead in the count. He has been hit especially hard when he falls behind, and he hasn't been able to deliver strikeouts when he has gotten ahead. He's an erratic fielder, but can be fairly tough to run against.

1998 Outlook

Will Tampa Bay manager Larry Rothschild be able to unlock Lopez' potential? The raw talent is there, but even the Indians gave up on him after five years of patience.

Bryan Rekar

Position: SP
Bats: R **Throws:** R
Ht: 6' 3" **Wt:** 210

Opening Day Age: 25
Born: 6/3/72 in
Oaklawn, Illinois
ML Seasons: 3
Pronunciation:
ree-CAR

Overall Statistics

	W	L	Pct.	ERA	G	GS	Sv	IP	H	BB	SO	HR	Ratio
1997	1	0	1.000	5.79	2	2	0	9.1	11	6	4	3	1.82
Career	7	10	.412	6.54	31	27	0	152.2	193	56	89	25	1.63

1997 Situational Stats

	W	L	ERA	Sv	IP		AB	H	HR	RBI	Avg
Home	0	0	6.75	0	4.0	LHB	21	7	2	3	.333
Road	1	0	5.06	0	5.1	RHB	18	4	1	3	.222
First Half	1	0	5.79	0	9.1	Sc Pos	12	2	2	5	.167
Scnd Half	0	0	-	0	0.0	Clutch	0	0	0	0	-

1997 Season

After shooting through the Colorado system in 1995 and pitching his way back to the minors in 1996, Bryan Rekar spent most of '97 at Triple-A. He pitched decently there, although a tough home park hurt him. The Devil Rays selected him in the second round of the expansion draft, gambling that his failure in Colorado was due more to Coors Field (lifetime 10.16 ERA) than a lack of talent. Tampa Bay hopes that his road performance (lifetime 3.26 ERA) is more indicative of his potential.

Pitching & Defense

Rekar has good stuff and he throws strikes. His moving, high-80s fastball, curveball and changeup give him the weapons to set up hitters and keep them off balance. He needs to maintain the willingness to keep the ball in the strike zone. The move to a pitcher-friendly ballpark may help him gain the confidence to do that. He's an aggressive fielder and one of the toughest pitchers to run on.

1998 Outlook

Still only 26, Rekar may turn out to be one of the most pleasant surprises on the Devil Rays' pitching staff. He'll be managed by a former pitching coach, and it appears he'll have a strong defense behind him.

Bobby Smith

Position: 3B/SS
Bats: R **Throws:** R
Ht: 6' 3" **Wt:** 190

Opening Day Age: 24
Born: 4/10/74 in
Oakland, CA
ML Seasons: 0

Overall Statistics

	G	AB	R	H	D	T	HR	RBI	SB	BB	SO	Avg	OBP	Slg
1997	—	—	—	—	—	—	—	—	—	—	—	—	—	—
Career	—	—	—	—	—	—	—	—	—	—	—	—	—	—

1997 Situational Stats

	AB	H	HR	RBI	Avg		AB	H	HR	RBI	Avg
Home	—	—	—	—	—	LHP	—	—	—	—	—
Road	—	—	—	—	—	RHP	—	—	—	—	—
First Half	—	—	—	—	—	Sc Pos	—	—	—	—	—
Scnd Half	—	—	—	—	—	Clutch	—	—	—	—	—

1997 Season

Bobby Smith's left hand began to bother him during spring training with the Braves. He was diagnosed with a broken hamate bone, which killed his momentum after a terrific Arizona Fall League season in 1996. The injury limited both his playing time and his power at Triple-A Richmond. He hit .246-12-47 in 100 games. Still awaiting his big league debut, he was taken in the first round of the expansion draft by the Devil Rays.

Hitting, Baserunning & Defense

The Braves saw Smith as a power hitter, but he hasn't hit more than 27 doubles or 14 homers in a minor league season. He strikes out often and seldom walks, which keeps his batting average down. He's a good athlete with some speed, but he's a so-so basestealer. He played shortstop in '97, but that was more of a concession that he wouldn't supplant Chipper Jones at third base. Smith is better at the hot corner, showing the arm, hands and range to play there. He also could play in left or right field if needed.

1998 Outlook

Smith hasn't proven he's ready to play in the big leagues, especially every day. Tampa Bay didn't take another third baseman in the expansion draft, so the job is his entering spring training.

Ramon Tatis

Position: RP
Bats: L **Throws:** L
Ht: 6' 3" **Wt:** 195

Opening Day Age: 24
Born: 5/2/73 in
Guayubin, DR
ML Seasons: 1
Pronunciation:
tah-TEEZ

Overall Statistics

	W	L	Pct.	ERA	G	GS	Sv	IP	H	BB	SO	HR	Ratio
1997	1	1	.500	5.34	56	0	0	55.2	66	29	33	13	1.71
Career	1	1	.500	5.34	56	0	0	55.2	66	29	33	13	1.71

1997 Situational Stats

	W	L	ERA	Sv	IP		AB	H	HR	RBI	Avg
Home	1	1	9.00	0	25.0	LHB	80	23	2	9	.288
Road	0	0	2.35	0	30.2	RHB	134	43	11	30	.321
First Half	0	0	4.05	0	33.1	Sc Pos	71	21	4	28	.296
Scnd Half	1	1	7.25	0	22.1	Clutch	33	9	1	7	.273

1997 Season

The Cubs acquired lefthanded reliever Ramon Tatis in the major league Rule 5 draft at the 1996 Winter Meetings. After never having pitched above Class-A, he stuck with Chicago all season. He was hit progressively harder as the year wore on, and pitched in very few important situations in the second half.

Pitching & Defense

Tatis has an average sinking fastball, an unimpressive breaking ball and poor command. He wasn't especially effective against lefthanders, and righties ate him up. When he's on, he gets grounders by keeping the ball away from the heart of the plate. He has an average move to first, but his stretch delivery is tough to read. He can field his position, but hasn't had to hit enough to learn how.

1998 Outlook

The rules of the Rule 5 draft required the Cubs to carry Tatis for the whole season or risk losing him, so he stayed with the team all year. Their efforts went for naught when he went in the second round of the expansion draft to the Devil Rays, who will use him as a setup man.

Esteban Yan

Position: SP
Bats: R **Throws:** R
Ht: 6' 4" **Wt:** 230

Opening Day Age: 23
Born: 6/22/74 in
Campina Del Seibo, DR
ML Seasons: 2
Pronunciation: YAWN

Overall Statistics

	W	L	Pct.	ERA	G	GS	Sv	IP	H	BB	SO	HR	Ratio
1997	0	1	.000	15.83	3	2	0	9.2	20	7	4	3	2.79
Career	0	1	.000	10.89	7	2	0	19.0	33	10	11	6	2.26

1997 Situational Stats

	W	L	ERA	Sv	IP		AB	H	HR	RBI	Avg
Home	0	0	15.19	0	5.1	LHB	22	8	2	7	.364
Road	0	1	16.62	0	4.1	RHB	26	12	1	9	.462
First Half	0	0	-	0	0.0	Sc Pos	17	7	1	13	.412
Scnd Half	0	1	15.83	0	9.2	Clutch	0	0	0	0	-

1997 Season

Esteban Yan never had a winning record until 1997, when he ranked among the Triple-A International League leaders in strikeouts per inning and strikeout/walk ratio. He was recalled in August when Baltimore needed an emergency starter, but was hammered in all three of his big league appearances. Orioles owner Peter Angelos insisted that costly first baseman Rafael Palmeiro be protected in the expansion draft over Yan, who went in the first round to Tampa Bay. Baltimore had planned to trade him to Florida for Al Leiter.

Pitching & Defense

Yan throws an above-average fastball, a hard slider and a changeup for strikes. The Orioles also liked his poise, even though he was rattled in the majors and tried to be too fine with his pitches. He does a decent job of fielding and holding runners. Basestealers have been successful 72 percent of the time against him in the last two seasons.

1998 Outlook

Why Yan lasted until the 18th pick of the expansion draft is a mystery. He was one of the Devil Rays' better selections and figures to be their No. 4 starter behind Wilson Alvarez, Rolando Arrojo and Tony Saunders in 1998.

Tampa Bay Devil Rays Minor League Prospects

Organization Overview:

The Devil Rays started off the expansion draft in fine fashion, taking Marlins lefthander Tony Saunders, then went downhill from there in the consensus of most baseball people. Orioles righthander Esteban Yan was the only other first-rounder truly worth getting excited about, and the second and third rounds didn't provide much. Tampa Bay was more productive trading the picks for veteran talent. The Rays got a good jump in 1996 by getting can't-miss pitching prospect Matt White, albeit for a record bonus of $10.2 million. They've also done a good job of finding talent in Mexico and have done better in the amateur draft than their expansion counterparts in Arizona.

Dan Carlson

Position: P   **Opening Day Age:** 28
Bats: R **Throws:** R   **Born:** 1/26/70 in
Ht: 6' 1" **Wt:** 185   Portland, OR

Recent Statistics

	W	L	ERA	G	GS	Sv	IP	H	R	BB	SO	HR
96 AAA Phoenix	13	6	3.44	33	15	1	146.2	135	61	46	123	18
96 NL San Francisco	1	0	2.70	5	0	0	10.0	13	6	2	4	2
97 A Bakersfield	0	0	0.00	2	2	0	6.0	3	0	1	7	0
97 AAA Phoenix	13	3	3.88	29	14	3	109.0	102	53	36	108	12
97 NL San Francisco	0	0	7.63	6	0	0	15.1	20	14	8	14	5

Carlson is the kind of guy who lived for expansion. He had led Triple-A Phoenix in victories for the last four seasons, but never caught on with the Giants and was going nowhere at 28. Then Tampa Bay rescued him with the final first-round selection in the expansion draft. He was a 33rd-round draft-and-follow who signed out of Mount Hood (Ore.) Community College in 1990. His best pitch is his slider. His fastball and changeup are decent. He has very good command, works quick and does the little things well. He projects more as a swingman, but could wind up as a starter if Tampa Bay needs him in that role.

Steve Cox

Position: 1B   **Opening Day Age:** 23
Bats: L **Throws:** L   **Born:** 10/31/74 in
Ht: 6' 4" **Wt:** 225   Delano, CA

Recent Statistics

	G	AB	R	H	D	T	HR	RBI	SB	BB	SO	AVG
96 AA Huntsville	104	381	59	107	21	1	12	61	2	51	65	.281
97 AAA Edmonton	131	467	84	128	34	1	15	93	1	88	90	.274
97 MLE	131	451	68	112	30	0	11	76	0	70	93	.248

Cox looked like Oakland's possible successor to Mark McGwire when he hit 30 homers at high Class-A Modesto in 1995, but now he looks more like just a steady first baseman. A fifth-round pick in 1992, he makes contact, uses the whole field and draws walks. He has just 27 homers in the last two seasons, so he needs to get stronger. He's average defensively and as a runner. A second-round pick in the expansion draft, Cox will spend 1998 in Triple-A. He's the heir apparent to Fred McGriff and could serve as the Crime Dog's backup at some point this year.

Rick Gorecki

Position: P   **Opening Day Age:** 24
Bats: R **Throws:** R   **Born:** 8/27/73 in
Ht: 6' 3" **Wt:** 167   Evergreen, IL

Recent Statistics

	W	L	ERA	G	GS	Sv	IP	H	R	BB	SO	HR
96			Did Not Play-Injured									
97 A San Berndno	2	3	3.88	14	14	0	51.0	38	22	32	58	4
97 AA San Antonio	4	2	1.39	7	7	0	45.1	26	8	15	33	3
97 NL Los Angeles	1	0	15.00	4	1	0	6.0	9	10	6	6	3

Gorecki's commitment to Northwestern led him to slide until the 19th round of the 1991 draft, but then-Dodgers manager Tom Lasorda schmoozed him and convinced him to sign with Los Angeles. A power curveball enabled Gorecki to reach Triple-A at age 20, but it's also believed to have caused him severe shoulder problems that required surgery in 1995. He missed all of the 1996 season and has made just 31 appearances in the past three years. His fastball and changeup are ordinary, so he needs his curve to survive. He was fairly unhittable in the minors in 1997, giving him hope for the future. Tampa Bay took him in the second round of the expansion draft and could use him as a starter or middle reliever this year.

John LeRoy

Position: P   **Opening Day Age:** 23
Bats: R **Throws:** R   **Born:** 4/19/75 in
Ht: 6' 3" **Wt:** 175   Bellevue, WA

Recent Statistics

	W	L	ERA	G	GS	Sv	IP	H	R	BB	SO	HR
96 A Durham	7	4	3.50	19	19	0	110.2	91	47	52	94	6
96 AA Greenville	1	1	2.98	8	8	0	45.1	43	18	18	38	5
97 AA Greenville	5	5	5.03	29	14	1	98.1	105	59	43	84	20
97 NL Atlanta	1	0	0.00	1	0	0	2.0	1	0	3	3	0

LeRoy seemed to be on his way after leading Braves minor leaguers with a 3.35 ERA in 1996, but had an off year in 1997 and wound up with Tampa Bay as a second-round expansion draft pick. He had been projected to be on Atlanta's 15-man protected list, so his availability was a surprise. At this point, he has a dominant fastball and little else. A 15th-round pick in 1993, he had pitched well in Double-A two years ago, but hitters caught up to him in 1997. He did make one appearance in Atlanta, earning a victory, but needs to improve his command. He gives up too many walks and his strikes are too hittable. LeRoy needs a year in the minors before he can be reasonably expected to contribute to the Devil Rays.

Jose Paniagua

Position: P
Bats: R **Throws:** R
Ht: 6' 2" **Wt:** 185

Opening Day Age: 24
Born: 8/20/73 in San
Jose de Ocoa, DR

Recent Statistics

	W	L	ERA	G	GS	Sv	IP	H	R	BB	SO	HR
96 A Harrisburg	3	0	0.00	3	3	0	18.0	12	1	2	16	0
96 AAA Ottawa	9	5	3.18	15	14	0	85.0	72	39	23	61	7
96 NL Montreal	2	4	3.53	13	11	0	51.0	55	24	23	27	7
97 A West Palm Beach	1	0	0.00	2	2	0	10.0	5	0	2	11	0
97 AAA Ottawa	8	10	4.64	22	22	0	137.2	164	79	44	87	13
97 NL Montreal	1	2	12.00	9	3	0	18.0	29	24	16	8	2

Like most of Montreal's upper-level pitching prospects, Paniagua had a mediocre minor league season in 1997. He also fared poorly after a September callup, though the Devil Rays took him in the second round of the expansion draft. Signed out of the Dominican Republic, he throws a sinking fastball in the low 90s, but his other pitches are inconsistent. His slider can be a good pitch but his command of it is spotty, and his changeup is merely decent. Like his pitches, his performance also was up and down. He had been passed by other pitchers in the Montreal system, but will get a shot to contribute in Tampa Bay in 1998.

Bobby Seay

Position: P
Bats: L **Throws:** L
Ht: 6' 2" **Wt:** 190

Opening Day Age: 19
Born: 6/20/78 in
Sarasota, FL

Recent Statistics

	W	L	ERA	G	GS	Sv	IP	H	R	BB	SO	HR
97 A Chston-SC	3	4	4.55	13	13	0	61.1	56	35	37	64	2

Seay was the first lefthander chosen in the 1996 draft, going 12th overall to the White Sox. When negotiations broke down, he filed a grievance and won free agency. Recipient of a $3 million bonus, his 1997 season was cut short by a stress fracture in his right foot. He returned in instructional league to throw 88-92 MPH with an outstanding curveball. He needs to develop his changeup, but more important questions exist about his work ethic and conditioning. He's two to three years away from Tampa Bay.

Matt White

Position: P
Bats: R **Throws:** R
Ht: 6' 5" **Wt:** 215

Opening Day Age: 19
Born: 8/13/78 in
Waynesboro, PA

Recent Statistics

	W	L	ERA	G	GS	Sv	IP	H	R	BB	SO	HR
97 A Hudson Vall	4	6	4.07	15	15	0	84.0	78	44	29	82	3

White was drafted seventh overall by the Giants in 1996, but followed Seay's path to free agency and signed his record deal with Tampa Bay. His pro debut was delayed by a stress fracture in his lower back, and he lost his first five decisions in the low Class-A New York-Penn League. Then he went 4-1, shaved nearly five runs off his ERA and was voted the league's top prospect by the

managers. His stuff is spectacular, as he has a 95-99 MPH fastball, a power curveball and an above-average changeup. His maturity, poise and command are all well beyond his years. White probably will start 1998 in high Class-A, but he could reach Tampa Bay in 1999.

Randy Winn

Position: OF
Bats: B **Throws:** R
Ht: 6' 2" **Wt:** 175

Opening Day Age: 23
Born: 6/9/74 in Los
Angeles, CA

Recent Statistics

	G	AB	R	H	D	T	HR	RBI	SB	BB	SO	AVG
96 A Kane County	130	514	90	139	16	3	0	35	30	47	115	.270
97 A Brevard Cty	36	143	26	45	8	2	0	15	16	16	28	.315
97 AA Portland	96	384	66	112	15	6	8	36	35	42	92	.292
97 MLE	96	363	45	91	11	5	4	24	22	25	98	.251

Winn originally was a basketball player at Santa Clara, where he switched to baseball and was selected in the third round of the 1995 draft by the Marlins. He was drafted for his speed, and that's why Tampa Bay took him in the third round of the expansion draft as well. Managers named Winn the fastest runner in the Eastern League in 1997. He strikes out too much for a leadoff man but has been a better hitter than expected, drawing walks and providing a little pop. He just needs to make better contact and improve on his basestealing success rate of 65 percent. He has center-field range, but moved to left once he joined Double-A Portland because of the presence of Mark Kotsay. Winn needs time in Triple-A, but he eventually could prove to be a better option than Quinton McCracken in center field.

Others to Watch

Third baseman **Hernando Arrendondo**, 19, was the organization's 1996 minor league player of the year. Signed out of Mexico, he's a line-drive hitter with defensive potential. He could get a look at second base. . . **Cedrick Bowers**, 19, is a raw lefthander. He has a knee-buckling curveball and an average fastball that he locates well. He struck out 164 in 157 innings at Class-A Charleston. . . Signed on the same scouting trip as Arrendondo, righthander **Pablo Ortega** threw the first pitch in organization history. He throws an above-average fastball and slider at age 21. . . Outfielder **Kerry Robinson**, 24, hit .328 with 104 steals in 2½ seasons in the St. Louis system. The speedster was a second-round pick in the expansion draft. . . Outfielder **Alex Sanchez**, 21, led the minors with 92 stolen bases in 1997. He's a Cuban who floated to freedom in the United States on a raft. He'll need to draw more walks and improve his hitting, but managers voted him the fastest runner, best defensive outfielder, best outfield arm and most exciting player in the Class-A South Atlantic League. . . Second baseman/third baseman **Jared Sandberg** is a nephew of Ryne Sandberg. Jared was named MVP in the Rookie-level Appalachian League at age 19, and he can hit for both average and power.

Johnny Oates

1997 Season

While manager Johnny Oates' team enjoyed tremendous success at the box office, his string of five consecutive winning seasons in Baltimore and Texas died despite an all-time high Ranger payroll. Worse yet, Oates' team consistently beat itself with poor fielding, the one failure that most frustrates him. The addition of closer John Wetteland was supposed to reduce late-game tension, yet the Rangers managed to lose 29 one-run games.

Offense

Oates was frustrated by a lack of team speed in 1997. Damon Buford didn't fill the hole left by Darryl Hamilton, and second baseman Mark McLemore, an Oates favorite, battled injuries all year. GM Doug Melvin traded third baseman Dean Palmer for speedster Tom Goodwin on July 25, but the Rangers still lacked a leadoff man and a table-setter with McLemore's skills. The Rangers ranked fifth in the American League in home runs, but seventh in scoring runs.

Pitching & Defense

His fielders don't have to star on ESPN highlight films, but Oates demands they make the routine plays. The Rangers' fielding wasn't the same last year without the steady play of Kevin Elster at shortstop. Benji Gil's inconsistency was unsettling to those around him and sent Melvin searching for a frontline shortstop to build around. Oates doesn't like to push his starting pitchers past 120 pitches. He manages the late innings following traditional pitcher-hitter matchups, generally putting relievers in positions in which they can succeed.

1998 Outlook

Oates got what he wanted when management went beyond its budget to re-sign All-Star catcher Pudge Rodriguez. Now he'll have to live with a top-heavy lineup, as Will Clark, Juan Gonzalez and Rodriguez account for about $20 million in salary. The Rangers don't have any great pitching prospects on the horizon, which could leave them trying to outslug opponents. That's the same formula that failed for seven seasons with Bobby Valentine in charge of the Rangers.

Born: 1/21/46 in Sylva, NC

Playing Experience: 1970-1981, Bal, Atl, Phi, LA, NYA

Managerial Experience: 6 seasons
Nickname: Quaker

Manager Statistics

Year Team, Lg	W	L	Pct	GB	Finish
1997 Texas, AL	77	85	.475	13.0	3rd West
6 Seasons	532	497	.517	—	—

1997 Starting Pitchers by Days Rest

	≤3	4	5	6+
Rangers Starts	2	96	31	23
Rangers ERA	6.39	4.97	4.95	6.25
AL Avg Starts	5	89	34	24
AL ERA	4.38	4.60	4.61	5.37

1997 Situational Stats

	Johnny Oates	AL Average
Hit & Run Success %	32.6	36.5
Stolen Base Success %	66.1	67.3
Platoon Pct.	60.0	59.5
Defensive Subs	12	22
High-Pitch Outings	12	15
Quick/Slow Hooks	17/13	19/15
Sacrifice Attempts	38	53

1997 Rankings (American League)

⇒ 2nd in steals of home plate (1) and squeeze plays (3)

⇒ 3rd in least caught steals of home plate (1), intentional walks (32) and mid-inning pitching changes (207)

Damon Buford

1997 Season

Opportunity proved to be a mixed blessing for Damon Buford. A former prospect of the Orioles when current Texas GM Doug Melvin and manager Johnny Oates were in Baltimore, Buford was given a chance to play every day after Darryl Hamilton departed via free agency. He failed badly, prompting Melvin to trade for center fielder Tom Goodwin at the end of July. Buford ended the season as a part-time player, his role for most of his big league career.

Hitting

Buford not only was expected to replace Hamilton in center field, but also as the leadoff hitter. His inability to get on base proved a major problem for a Texas lineup that struggled to score runs. He couldn't work pitchers for walks. While he seldom swung at the first pitch, he too often fell behind in the count. Buford, who occasionally shows some pop, had trouble hitting righthanders.

Baserunning & Defense

A good baserunner, Buford could steal 30 or more bases if he got on base more often. He gets good jumps against righthanders but sometimes is tentative against lefties. He's always a threat to score from first base. Buford has good range and an average arm.

1998 Season

The Rangers viewed Buford as a fifth outfielder and were considering non-tendering him before including him in the Jim Leyritz-Aaron Sele trade with Boston. With a .232 batting average in 337 games, it appears Buford's value is as a defensive outfielder and pinch runner. The clock is ticking on the career of Don Buford's son.

Position: CF
Bats: R **Throws:** R
Ht: 5'10" **Wt:** 170

Opening Day Age: 27
Born: 6/12/70 in Baltimore, MD
ML Seasons: 5
Pronunciation: BYOO-ford

Overall Statistics

	G	AB	R	H	D	T	HR	RBI	SB	BB	SO	Avg	OBP	Slg
1997	122	366	49	82	18	0	8	39	18	30	83	.224	.287	.339
Career	337	760	129	176	37	0	20	82	38	79	172	.232	.309	.359

Where He Hits the Ball

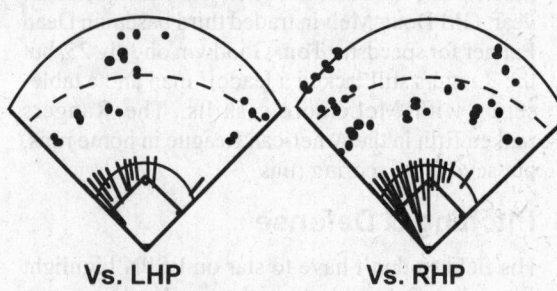

Vs. LHP   Vs. RHP

1997 Situational Stats

	AB	H	HR	RBI	Avg		AB	H	HR	RBI	Avg
Home	178	44	4	23	.247	LHP	139	35	4	14	.252
Road	188	38	4	16	.202	RHP	227	47	4	25	.207
First Half	263	56	5	31	.213	Sc Pos	90	21	1	29	.233
Scnd Half	103	26	3	8	.252	Clutch	46	14	3	5	.304

1997 Rankings (American League)

⇒ Did not rank near the top or bottom in any category

John Burkett

Position: SP
Bats: R **Throws:** R
Ht: 6' 3" **Wt:** 215

Opening Day Age: 33
Born: 11/28/64 in New Brighton, PA
ML Seasons: 9
Pronunciation: BURK-it

1997 Season

John Burkett made 30 starts in his first full season in Texas, but he didn't have the kind of impact the Rangers envisioned when they put together a contract extension to keep him in Arlington through 1999. He was forced out of the rotation for a few turns in August because of a weak shoulder. The Rangers feared he might need surgery, but he returned after making some changes in his conditioning program. When Burkett was healthy, he was hit hard. Before being sidelined, he was on pace to become the first pitcher since Phil Niekro in 1979 to allow 300 hits in a season.

Pitching

Few American League pitchers throw more strikes than Burkett. That should be an asset, but hitters too often jump on him before he can get ahead in the count. He had only 10 more walks than home runs allowed last year, and batters hit .388 when they put his first pitch into play. Opposing managers don't stack their lineups with lefties against Burkett because his running fastball is more effective against them than righthanders. He also uses a good slider against lefties and saves the curveball for righties. He lives at the knees and on the corners.

Defense

Burkett is an average fielder who gives up too many hits up the middle because he falls off to the left side of the mound. He has an average pickoff move, but sometimes gets lazy with Pudge Rodriguez behind the plate. Opponents were successful on nine of their 17 stolen-base attempts.

1998 Outlook

The Rangers hope that Burkett's health problems will cause him to pay more attention to his conditioning. Now 33, he could fade in a hurry if he doesn't pay attention to his off-the-field program. The Rangers need 225 innings and 15 wins from him, a tall order for an aging finesse pitcher.

Overall Statistics

	W	L	Pct.	ERA	G	GS	Sv	IP	H	BB	SO	HR	Ratio
1997	9	12	.429	4.56	30	30	0	189.1	240	30	139	20	1.43
Career	101	80	.558	4.03	257	251	1	1597.2	1702	390	1011	145	1.31

How Often He Throws Strikes

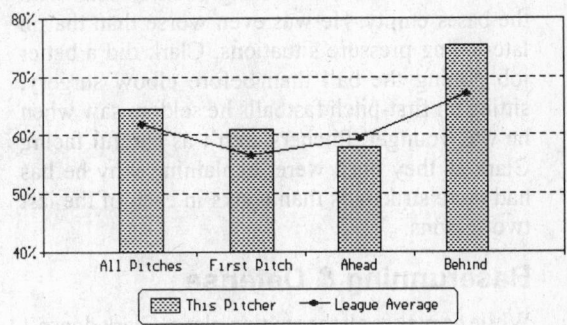

1997 Situational Stats

	W	L	ERA	Sv	IP		AB	H	HR	RBI	Avg
Home	3	5	5.59	0	83.2	LHB	396	118	10	48	.298
Road	6	7	3.75	0	105.2	RHB	387	122	10	44	.315
First Half	6	7	4.62	0	117.0	Sc Pos	171	51	7	71	.298
Scnd Half	3	5	4.48	0	72.1	Clutch	42	15	0	3	.357

1997 Rankings (American League)

⇒ 1st in highest strikeout/walk ratio (4.6)
⇒ 2nd in highest batting average allowed (.307) and highest batting average allowed vs. righthanded batters
⇒ 5th in highest ERA at home
⇒ Led the Rangers in losses, strikeouts, highest strikeout/walk ratio (4.6), lowest slugging percentage allowed (.439), lowest on-base percentage allowed (.333), highest groundball/flyball ratio allowed (1.3), lowest stolen base percentage allowed (52.9%), least baserunners allowed per 9 innings (13.0), most run support per 9 innings (6.1), least home runs allowed per 9 innings (.95), most strikeouts per 9 innings (6.6), ERA on the road and lowest batting average allowed vs. lefthanded batters

Will Clark

1997 Season

Elbow surgery was supposed to put some pop back in Will Clark's bat. But 1997 was another disappointing, injury-plagued season for the fragile first baseman. During the last two seasons he has failed to deliver as many home runs and RBI as his predecessor, Rafael Palmeiro, gave Baltimore in 1996. Clark opened 1997 on the disabled list with a wrist injury and missed the last five weeks with a torn fascia muscle in his right heel. He's been on the DL five times in the last two years.

Hitting

Clark batted a soft .326 in 1997, hitting 92 points worse with runners in scoring position than with the bases empty. He was even worse than that in late-inning pressure situations. Clark did a better job pulling the ball than before elbow surgery, sitting on first-pitch fastballs he seldom saw when he was younger. Pitchers aren't as careful facing Clark as they once were, explaining why he has had more strikeouts than walks in each of the last two seasons.

Baserunning & Defense

While he makes all the routine plays, Clark doesn't cover as much ground as he once did. He and catcher Pudge Rodriguez have an amazing chemistry, allowing Rodriguez to use his arm as a weapon to throw behind runners. Clark does a good job starting 3-6-3 double plays, but seldom responds with good throws when runners force the action in other situations. He's a smart runner despite below-average speed.

1998 Outlook

Expect Clark's tunnel-vision stare to be in prime-time form this year. It's the final season on his five-year contract with Texas, and he needs a big year to convince the Rangers to give him a new deal. Otherwise he'll begin the nomadic phase of his career in 1999.

Position: 1B
Bats: L **Throws:** L
Ht: 6' 1" **Wt:** 200

Opening Day Age: 34
Born: 3/13/64 in New Orleans, LA
ML Seasons: 12
Nickname: The Thrill

Overall Statistics

	G	AB	R	H	D	T	HR	RBI	SB	BB	SO	Avg	OBP	Slg
1997	110	393	56	128	29	1	12	51	0	49	62	.326	.400	.496
Career	1620	5941	970	1795	354	44	230	1004	59	758	982	.302	.381	.493

Where He Hits the Ball

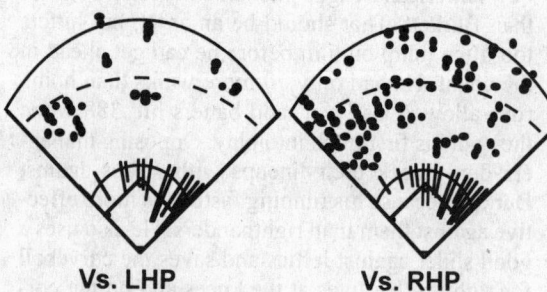

Vs. LHP   Vs. RHP

1997 Situational Stats

	AB	H	HR	RBI	Avg		AB	H	HR	RBI	Avg
Home	202	71	6	26	.351	LHP	129	39	3	16	.302
Road	191	57	6	25	.298	RHP	264	89	9	35	.337
First Half	266	88	8	30	.331	Sc Pos	100	24	4	38	.240
Scnd Half	127	40	4	21	.315	Clutch	63	14	2	8	.222

1997 Rankings (American League)

⇒ 1st in batting average on an 0-2 count (.391)
⇒ 3rd in lowest batting average with the bases loaded (.000) and fielding percentage at first base (.996)
⇒ 7th in intentional walks (11) and batting average on a 3-2 count (.375)
⇒ 10th in least GDPs per GDP situation (5.1%)
⇒ Led the Rangers in intentional walks (11), batting average on an 0-2 count (.391) and batting average on a 3-2 count (.375)

Benji Gil

1997 Season

The Rangers fell in love with the arm strength and range of their former first-round pick, but Benji Gil has yet to return that affection with a solid season. After losing the starting job to Kevin Elster in 1996, he was given his job back last season. He struggled from the start of spring training and failed to hold onto the job. He was bad just about every way a shortstop can be bad: at the plate, in the field and with mental errors on the bases. Gil appeared to crumble mentally after the All-Star break, making it easy for manager Johnny Oates to bench him.

Hitting

Gil is a 150-strikeout season waiting to happen if he ever plays a full season. While blessed with good bat speed, he never has made the adjustments necessary to be a good big league hitter. He strikes out more than half the time when the count goes to two strikes. He swings at too many bad breaking pitches and can be blown away by good fastballs, typified by his nine strikeouts in nine career at-bats against Randy Johnson. He was something of a clutch hitter with Texas in 1995, but has lost that edge.

Baserunning & Defense

Gil has the tools to be an outstanding shortstop. His powerful arm is his best asset and he has the range to make plays going either way. But Gil never has developed the consistency of a frontline shortstop. He boots too many routine grounders, especially in the late innings. His good speed disappeared during the 1997 season, perhaps because of a series of leg injuries.

1998 Outlook

Gil seems likely to be trade bait. He could develop elsewhere, but needs to improve offensively to retain any value. He could become a valuable utilityman, if not a regular, by cutting down on his strikeouts and improving his on-base percentage.

Position: SS
Bats: R **Throws:** R
Ht: 6' 2" **Wt:** 182

Opening Day Age: 25
Born: 10/6/72 in Tijuana, MX
ML Seasons: 4
Pronunciation: GILL

Overall Statistics

	G	AB	R	H	D	T	HR	RBI	SB	BB	SO	Avg	OBP	Slg
1997	110	317	35	71	13	2	5	31	1	17	96	.224	.263	.325
Career	267	794	74	171	33	5	14	80	4	49	266	.215	.261	.322

Where He Hits the Ball

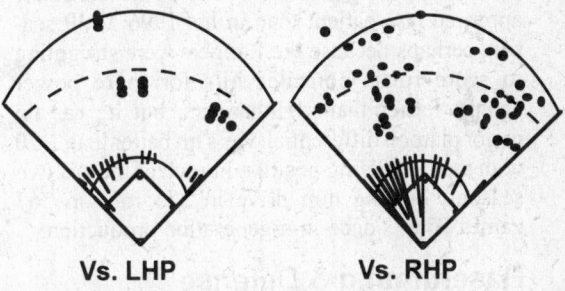

Vs. LHP   Vs. RHP

1997 Situational Stats

	AB	H	HR	RBI	Avg		AB	H	HR	RBI	Avg
Home	165	37	3	15	.224	LHP	74	18	1	5	.243
Road	152	34	2	16	.224	RHP	243	53	4	26	.218
First Half	188	44	3	17	.234	Sc Pos	85	18	2	26	.212
Scnd Half	129	27	2	14	.209	Clutch	27	5	0	1	.185

1997 Rankings (American League)

⇒ 2nd in batting average on a 3-1 count (.750) and lowest fielding percentage at shortstop (.963)
⇒ 5th in errors at shortstop (19)
⇒ 10th in lowest batting average with two strikes (.134)
⇒ Led the Rangers in sacrifice bunts (6) and batting average on a 3-1 count (.750)

Juan Gonzalez — Pure Power

1997 Season

Even after tearing ligaments in his left thumb playing winter ball and opening the season on the disabled list, Juan Gonzalez was one of baseball's most productive hitters. Despite missing all of April, he still managed his fourth 40-plus homer season and his second straight with at least 131 RBI. Gonzalez also hit nine first-pitch homers. He returned as the team's designated hitter, but moved to right field regularly in June.

Hitting

Few guys hit the ball harder than Gonzalez. He can be pitched to, as he'll chase breaking balls in the dirt rather than take a walk, but he's murder on just about everything thrown in the strike zone. He appeared less patient than in his 1996 MVP season, perhaps because the Rangers were struggling to score runs. Gonzalez hits for more power against lefties than righthanders, but he has no major platoon differential. He's hit better than .320 with men in scoring position in each of the last two seasons, helping him drive in 275 runs in 267 games. That's once-in-a-generation production.

Baserunning & Defense

Gonzalez is a one-dimensional player who doesn't attract attention in the field or on the bases. He lacks the range to be an outstanding right fielder, but has a strong enough arm to cut down runners trying to stretch singles into doubles. The risk of injury keeps Texas from trying to run with Gonzalez, who has good speed for a big man.

1998 Outlook

As always, Gonzalez is a legitimate MVP candidate provided he stays healthy. He has played more than 142 games only once since 1991. He appeared strong in the second half of 1997, encouraging the Rangers to believe that 1998 could bring big things. This is the last guaranteed season on his contract, but the Rangers face no pressure to renegotiate because they hold options for the next two years.

Position: DH/RF
Bats: R **Throws:** R
Ht: 6' 3" **Wt:** 220

Opening Day Age: 28
Born: 10/16/69 in Vega Baja, PR
ML Seasons: 9
Nickname: Igor

Overall Statistics

	G	AB	R	H	D	T	HR	RBI	SB	BB	SO	Avg	OBP	Slg
1997	133	533	87	158	24	3	42	131	0	33	107	.296	.335	.589
Career	950	3663	567	1045	196	16	256	790	16	247	716	.285	.334	.557

Where He Hits the Ball

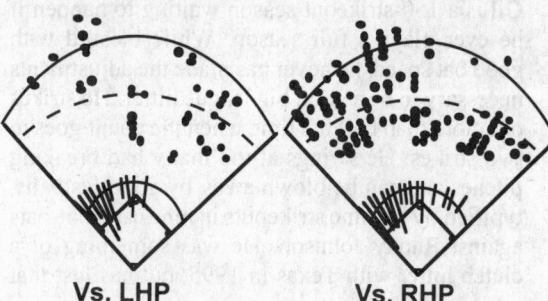

Vs. LHP   Vs. RHP

1997 Situational Stats

	AB	H	HR	RBI	Avg		AB	H	HR	RBI	Avg
Home	246	71	18	57	.289	LHP	148	44	15	40	.297
Road	287	87	24	74	.303	RHP	385	114	27	91	.296
First Half	244	69	20	65	.283	Sc Pos	165	53	10	84	.321
Scnd Half	289	89	22	66	.308	Clutch	80	28	6	22	.350

1997 Rankings (American League)

⇒ 2nd in cleanup slugging percentage (.592) and slugging percentage vs. lefthanded pitchers (.649)

⇒ 3rd in home runs, RBI and HR frequency (12.7 ABs per HR)

⇒ 4th in slugging percentage

⇒ 6th in total bases (314)

⇒ 7th in sacrifice flies (10), lowest groundball/fly-ball ratio (0.7), slugging percentage vs. righthanded pitchers (.566) and errors in right field (4)

⇒ 10th in batting average in the clutch

⇒ Led the Rangers in home runs, RBI, sacrifice flies (10), strikeouts, slugging percentage, HR frequency (12.7 ABs per HR) and batting average with runners in scoring position

Tom Goodwin

Position: CF
Bats: L   **Throws:** R
Ht: 6' 1"   **Wt:** 175

Opening Day Age: 29
Born: 7/27/68 in
Fresno, CA
ML Seasons: 7

1997 Season

After returning from offseason shoulder surgery, Tom Goodwin was having a slightly subpar season for the Royals when he was traded to Texas for free-agent-to-be Dean Palmer on July 25. He was given a trial as the Rangers' leadoff hitter, but Goodwin didn't get on base often enough to earn the job for 1998. He's something of an enigma to managers. He shows flashes of brilliance, yet too often suffers long slumps. He batted only .143 in April and .191 in July. He had another good year in center field and on the bases.

Hitting

A slashing hitter, Goodwin isn't going to scare many people, though former White Sox manager Terry Bevington did give him his first career intentional walk. He also showed more gap power, setting a career high in doubles in 1997. Goodwin's open stance has left him vulnerable to inside fastballs, but he did a decent job fighting them off. He's an excellent bunter who can draw the third baseman in and then slap the ball past him.

Baserunning & Defense

Goodwin might have the best pure speed in the American League. He has stolen at least 50 bases in each of the last three seasons. He didn't gamble quite as often on the bases in 1997. He's a graceful center fielder who should prove valuable in the vast expanses at The Ballpark. His arm strength may be the worst in the majors and often tempts opponents to stretch singles into doubles, but he cuts down his share with accurate throws.

1998 Outlook

After being crowded out of the picture in Kansas City, Goodwin will be the regular center fielder in Texas. The trade of Damon Buford to Boston only increases Goodwin's chances of being in the everyday lineup. The main concern is whether he can get on base often enough to be the leadoff man. If not, he'll hit eighth or ninth.

Overall Statistics

	G	AB	R	H	D	T	HR	RBI	SB	BB	SO	Avg	OBP	Slg
1997	150	574	90	149	26	6	2	39	50	44	88	.260	.314	.336
Career	531	1677	266	458	58	14	7	106	175	128	254	.273	.328	.337

Where He Hits the Ball

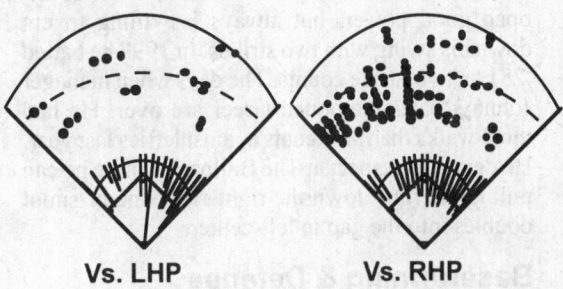

Vs. LHP   **Vs. RHP**

1997 Situational Stats

	AB	H	HR	RBI	Avg		AB	H	HR	RBI	Avg
Home	253	71	0	16	.281	LHP	160	44	0	9	.275
Road	321	78	2	23	.243	RHP	414	105	2	30	.254
First Half	308	87	1	16	.282	Sc Pos	119	31	0	35	.261
Scnd Half	266	62	1	23	.233	Clutch	97	27	0	6	.278

1997 Rankings (American League)

⇒ 1st in lowest HR frequency (287.0 ABs per HR) and bunts in play (41)

⇒ 2nd in caught stealing (16) and lowest on-base percentage for a leadoff hitter (.302)

⇒ 3rd in stolen bases (50) and lowest slugging percentage vs. righthanded pitchers (.338)

⇒ 4th in sacrifice bunts (11), lowest slugging percentage (.336), highest groundball/flyball ratio (2.1) and fielding percentage in center field (.992)

⇒ 5th in steals of third (6)

⇒ Led the Rangers in stolen base percentage (72.7%) and steals of third (3)

Rusty Greer

1997 Season

Day in and day out, Rusty Greer was as valuable as any Ranger not named Ivan Rodriguez. He was as steady as anyone around, batting at least .283 in every month. He's a throwback player with a big heart who seems to always get the most out of his ability. There's not a team in the major leagues that wouldn't make room for Greer, whose game has improved to All-Star caliber.

Hitting

Greer is a complete hitter who adjusts to the situation. He gets good bat speed out of a compact swing and he studies pitchers. While he'll attack the first pitch against some pitchers, he has the ability to work deep into the count. He has developed good power, but always is willing to cut down his swing with two strikes. In 1997 he batted .281 on two-strike counts. The days when manager Johnny Oates platooned Greer are over. He had more walks than strikeouts against lefties last year. He demands respect at The Ballpark, where he can pull home runs down the right-field line or shoot doubles into the gap in left-center.

Baserunning & Defense

Greer is an aggressive fielder with a flair for making diving catches coming in and wall-slamming catches going back. He had an inexplicably poor year in the field in 1997, committing 12 errors. Greer's range allows him to get in position to make mistakes, but a dent in his confidence may have been behind his uncharacteristic troubles. Accurate throws compensate for an average arm. Despite good speed, Greer doesn't run much.

1998 Outlook

Texas is becoming Rusty Greer's team. The Rangers see him as the glue holding together a lineup built around righthanded hitters Juan Gonzalez and Ivan Rodriguez. Greer has averaged 94 RBI the last two years, and his solid production should continue. In an ideal world, every player would have his attitude.

Position: LF/CF
Bats: L **Throws:** L
Ht: 6' 0" **Wt:** 190

Opening Day Age: 29
Born: 1/21/69 in Fort Rucker, AL
ML Seasons: 4

Overall Statistics

	G	AB	R	H	D	T	HR	RBI	SB	BB	SO	Avg	OBP	Slg
1997	157	601	112	193	42	3	26	87	9	83	87	.321	.405	.531
Career	507	1837	302	573	120	12	67	294	21	246	285	.312	.392	.500

Where He Hits the Ball

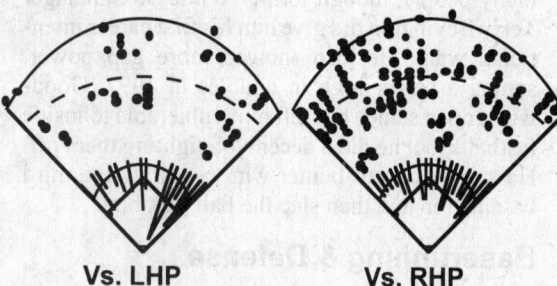

Vs. LHP   Vs. RHP

1997 Situational Stats

	AB	H	HR	RBI	Avg		AB	H	HR	RBI	Avg
Home	300	111	18	54	.370	LHP	178	55	7	19	.309
Road	301	82	8	33	.272	RHP	423	138	19	68	.326
First Half	316	104	13	45	.329	Sc Pos	170	44	7	62	.259
Scnd Half	285	89	13	42	.312	Clutch	91	31	5	14	.341

1997 Rankings (American League)

⇒ 1st in batting average at home, batting average with two strikes (.281), errors in left field (11) and lowest fielding percentage in left field (.963)
⇒ 2nd in hits
⇒ 3rd in times on base (279)
⇒ 5th in runs scored, doubles and total bases (319)
⇒ Led the Rangers in batting average, at-bats, runs scored, hits, doubles, total bases (319), walks, times on base (279), pitches seen (2,739), plate appearances (690), games played (157), on-base percentage, most pitches seen per plate appearance (3.97), batting average vs. righthanded pitchers, on-base percentage vs. lefthanded pitchers (.406), on-base percentage vs. righthanded pitchers (.405), batting average at home and batting average with two strikes (.281)

Mark McLemore

1997 Season

When he's healthy, Mark McLemore can be counted on to be a key player. A string of injuries left him unable to make his usual contributions in 1997, a major reason the Rangers couldn't defend their American League West title. He opened the season playing with a torn ligament in his right hand, which wasn't diagnosed until mid-May. By then, McLemore had set the tone for his year, batting .174 in his first 31 games. His season ended prematurely, as he had surgery on both knees after being shut down on August 18.

Hitting

The switch-hitting McLemore needs his speed to be a threat. He didn't have it in 1997, and it showed. Both McLemore's batting average and on-base percentage dropped severely as he tried to fight through injuries. He's a patient hitter who seldom helps out pitchers. He's generally a little bit tougher from the left side, but demands respect either way when he's healthy. He seemed to be pressing, swinging at more bad pitches than normal. He's a good bunter, but wasn't able to use that weapon last season.

Baserunning & Defense

Late Rangers broadcaster Mark Holtz tagged McLemore as "the Doctor of Defense" for his ability to run far to his left to grab grounders that appeared headed into right field. McLemore is equally good going to his right. He doesn't throw nearly as well as he did early in his career, when he often played the outfield. He can get as good a jump as any baserunner around, but is rapidly losing speed as he gets older.

1998 Outlook

With two years left on his contract, McLemore will return as the regular second baseman. The Rangers hope he'll be rejuvenated after surgery on both knees. It's a major concern, as speed is his game. He and his employers will be anxious about his ability to return to full strength this spring.

Position: 2B
Bats: B **Throws:** R
Ht: 5'11" **Wt:** 207

Opening Day Age: 33
Born: 10/4/64 in San Diego, CA
ML Seasons: 12

Overall Statistics

	G	AB	R	H	D	T	HR	RBI	SB	BB	SO	Avg	OBP	Slg
1997	89	349	47	91	17	2	1	25	7	40	54	.261	.338	.330
Career	1019	3379	492	873	135	25	23	315	152	413	511	.258	.338	.334

Where He Hits the Ball

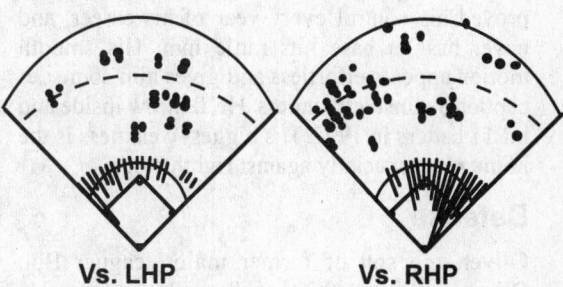

Vs. LHP   **Vs. RHP**

1997 Situational Stats

	AB	H	HR	RBI	Avg		AB	H	HR	RBI	Avg
Home	188	44	0	16	.234	LHP	90	24	0	3	.267
Road	161	47	1	9	.292	RHP	259	67	1	22	.259
First Half	212	53	0	14	.250	Sc Pos	70	15	0	23	.214
Scnd Half	137	38	1	11	.277	Clutch	60	17	0	5	.283

1997 Rankings (American League)

⇒ 6th in highest percentage of swings put into play (52.6%)
⇒ 7th in highest percentage of pitches taken (61.6%)
⇒ 10th in on-base percentage for a leadoff hitter (.355) and errors at second base (8)
⇒ Led the Rangers in sacrifice bunts (6), on-base percentage for a leadoff hitter (.355), highest percentage of pitches taken (61.6%) and highest percentage of swings put into play (52.6%)

Darren Oliver

1997 Season

No longer does Darren Oliver come with the label "Handle With Care." Since rotator-cuff surgery in August 1995, he has turned in two strong seasons and developed into the Rangers' most reliable starter. He established career highs for starts and innings in 1997, and didn't miss a turn in the rotation. There was nothing spectacular about Oliver's effort, but he finished with a winning record for the fourth consecutive season.

Pitching

Oliver is an intelligent pitcher who wins without an overpowering fastball. He uses a fastball in the upper 80s to set up a changeup that's his out pitch. His breaking pitch is a curveball. Oliver has improved his control every year of his career, and never has let base hits rattle him. His smooth motion appears effortless and gives him some deception against lefthanders. He'll throw inside and hit 11 batters in 1997. His biggest weakness is the home run, especially against righthanders.

Defense

Oliver, the son of former major leaguer Bob Oliver, is a good athlete with quick reactions. He sometimes is too aggressive while fielding balls, which leads to errors. He has a terrific pickoff move but allowed opponents to succeed in more than half of their stolen-base attempts in 1997.

1998 Outlook

After surgery for three different injuries during the 1990s, Oliver has been viewed as an injury risk by manager Johnny Oates. But he appears to have turned a corner, allowing Oates to keep him in games longer and breath easier when he develops normal stiffness between starts. Oliver doesn't have the stuff to be a No. 1 or 2 starter, but he does have the best winning percentage in franchise history. The Rangers are counting on 15 victories from him, and there's no reason to believe they won't get them.

Position: SP
Bats: R **Throws:** L
Ht: 6' 2" **Wt:** 200

Opening Day Age: 27
Born: 10/6/70 in Kansas City, MO
ML Seasons: 5

Overall Statistics

	W	L	Pct.	ERA	G	GS	Sv	IP	H	BB	SO	HR	Ratio
1997	13	12	.520	4.20	32	32	0	201.1	213	82	104	29	1.47
Career	35	20	.636	4.28	124	69	2	477.1	492	226	309	57	1.50

How Often He Throws Strikes

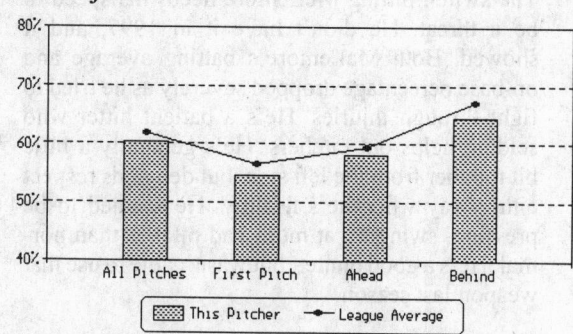

1997 Situational Stats

	W	L	ERA	Sv	IP		AB	H	HR	RBI	Avg
Home	7	6	4.34	0	110.0	LHB	118	29	4	15	.246
Road	6	6	4.04	0	91.1	RHB	669	184	25	83	.275
First Half	5	9	4.07	0	101.2	Sc Pos	185	48	8	67	.259
Scnd Half	8	3	4.33	0	99.2	Clutch	28	9	0	5	.321

1997 Rankings (American League)

⇒ 4th in lowest strikeout/walk ratio (1.3) and least strikeouts per 9 innings (4.6)
⇒ 5th in hit batsmen (11)
⇒ 7th in walks allowed and most baserunners allowed per 9 innings (13.7)
⇒ 8th in highest on-base percentage allowed (.346) and least pitches thrown per batter (3.60)
⇒ 9th in shutouts (1), runners caught stealing (10) and GDPs induced (20)
⇒ 10th in losses, pickoff throws (161) and most home runs allowed per 9 innings (1.30)
⇒ Led the Rangers in ERA, wins, losses, games started, complete games (3), shutouts (1), walks allowed, hit batsmen (11), pickoff throws (161), stolen bases allowed (14), runners caught stealing (10) and GDPs induced (20)

Ivan Rodriguez | Gold Glover

Position: C
Bats: R **Throws:** R
Ht: 5' 9" **Wt:** 205

Opening Day Age: 26
Born: 11/30/71 in Vega Baja, PR
ML Seasons: 7
Nickname: Pudge

1997 Season

Ivan Rodriguez gave the Rangers another vintage performance, and he was rewarded with a $42 million contract in a dramatic signing announced on July 31, the day of the trading deadline. GM Doug Melvin had made it known that Rodriguez would be traded if Texas couldn't sign him to a long-term deal. Rangers fans were overjoyed to keep the AL's best defensive catcher, who hit over .300 for the third straight season. He set a career high in home runs while playing 150 games for a second year in a row.

Overall Statistics

	G	AB	R	H	D	T	HR	RBI	SB	BB	SO	Avg	OBP	Slg
1997	150	597	98	187	34	4	20	77	7	38	89	.313	.360	.484
Career	880	3264	445	948	192	15	88	417	26	181	419	.290	.330	.439

Hitting

Rodriguez is a free swinger who would benefit from a little more discipline. But it's hard to complain when he keeps his swing compact and generally makes contact, hitting the ball to all fields. His strikeouts were up last year, perhaps because of a growing obsession with hitting home runs. While he sacrificed average to reach 20 in 1997, he's always a hitter to be respected. Rodriguez is vulnerable to fastballs inside and breaking pitches away. He likes high fastballs better than low ones.

Where He Hits the Ball

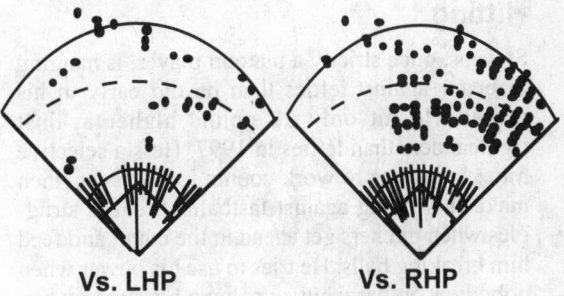

Vs. LHP   Vs. RHP

Baserunning & Defense

Rodriguez is the complete package and has won Gold Gloves in each of his six full seasons in the majors. His ability to cut down basestealers is a big asset that allows Ranger hurlers to concentrate on hitters. He also hinders opponents thinking of going from first to third on singles with snap pickoff throws. He's only average at blocking balls in the dirt, sometimes swiping at balls when he should be shifting his body, but he has become good at blocking runners off the plate. There are catchers who call better games, but few pitchers would prefer anyone to Rodriguez.

1997 Situational Stats

	AB	H	HR	RBI	Avg		AB	H	HR	RBI	Avg
Home	311	108	12	47	.347	LHP	162	52	5	25	.321
Road	286	79	8	30	.276	RHP	435	135	15	52	.310
First Half	341	116	11	40	.340	Sc Pos	128	41	2	54	.320
Scnd Half	256	71	9	37	.277	Clutch	94	34	1	24	.362

1997 Rankings (American League)

⇒ 1st in highest percentage of runners caught stealing as a catcher (51.9%)
⇒ 3rd in batting average at home
⇒ 4th in lowest percentage of pitches taken (43.8%)
⇒ 5th in hits, singles, least pitches seen per plate appearance (3.39) and errors at catcher (7)
⇒ Led the Rangers in singles, hit by pitch (8), GDPs (18), highest groundball/flyball ratio (1.8), batting average in the clutch, batting average with the bases loaded (.556), batting average vs. lefthanded pitchers and highest percentage of extra bases taken as a runner (55.2%)

1998 Outlook

Now that Rodriguez is signed to a five-year contract, the Rangers will have to devote attention to preserving him. He wants to play every day, and manager Johnny Oates has pretty much let him do that. Oates is expected to shift some of the catching chores to young Kevin Brown in 1998, using Rodriguez more often as a DH. That should limit his usual late-season decline at the plate.

Lee Stevens

1997 Season

Nothing was given to Lee Stevens, but the former Angels prospect took advantage of the chances that came his way. After a 32-homer season at Triple-A Oklahoma City in 1996, Stevens produced in spring training to win a crowded battle for a spot on the bench. Then he did an admirable job filling in for Will Clark, Juan Gonzalez and Mickey Tettleton. "Every time I take the field, it's against a team that turned me down," Stevens says. "It's easy to get motivated." He finished the season third on the team in homers and fourth in RBI. He drove in 23 more runs than Clark despite having only 33 more at-bats. Few major league reserves did a better job.

Hitting

Stevens, once strictly a platoon player, is hanging in better against lefties than he did early in his career. He hit only 20 points higher against righthanders than lefties in 1997. He's a selective hitter who tries to work counts in his favor, then makes his living against fastballs. Stevens struggles when pitchers get ahead in the count and feed him breaking balls. He tries to use his power when nobody is on base, but cuts down his swing when men are in scoring position, becoming a tough out.

Baserunning & Defense

Stevens is versatile, playing equally well in the outfield corners and at first base. He doesn't have much range or a great arm, but makes the plays on balls hit toward him. He committed only three errors in 62 games at first base in 1997. He's a base-clogger when he gets on.

1998 Outlook

With bad knees forcing Tettleton into retirement, Stevens should figure in the Rangers' DH mix. He also is a valuable backup for Clark, who has played in only 79 percent of Texas' games the last four years. Stevens will see fewer fastballs than he did in 1997, challenging him to make some adjustments.

Position: 1B/RF/DH
Bats: L **Throws:** L
Ht: 6' 4" **Wt:** 219

Opening Day Age: 30
Born: 7/10/67 in Kansas City, MO
ML Seasons: 5

Overall Statistics

	G	AB	R	H	D	T	HR	RBI	SB	BB	SO	Avg	OBP	Slg
1997	137	426	58	128	24	2	21	74	1	23	83	.300	.336	.514
Career	355	1122	125	285	62	5	38	164	4	86	256	.254	.306	.420

Where He Hits the Ball

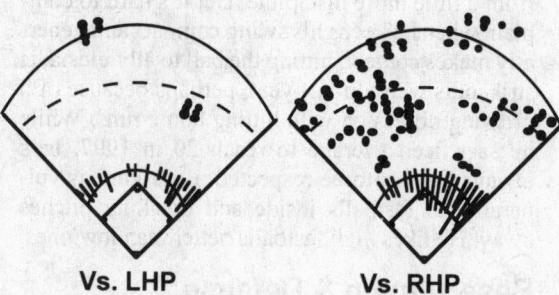

Vs. LHP   Vs. RHP

1997 Situational Stats

	AB	H	HR	RBI	Avg		AB	H	HR	RBI	Avg
Home	218	70	12	40	.321	LHP	67	19	4	12	.284
Road	208	58	9	34	.279	RHP	359	109	17	62	.304
First Half	193	57	10	38	.295	Sc Pos	110	35	6	53	.318
Scnd Half	233	71	11	36	.305	Clutch	57	18	3	12	.316

1997 Rankings (American League)

⇒ 3rd in lowest percentage of pitches taken (43.0%)
⇒ 9th in GDPs (18)
⇒ 10th in most GDPs per GDP situation (17.6%)
⇒ Led the Rangers in GDPs (18)

Fernando Tatis

1997 Season

Rangers GM Doug Melvin thinks enough of Fernando Tatis that he traded Dean Palmer rather than consider a contract extension. Tatis received valuable experience in August and September that should help him as he enters his first full season in the big leagues. He opened the season at Double-A Tulsa, where he showed promising power while hitting for average and taking his walks. He did a decent job after being promoted to Texas, running his home run total to 32 between Tulsa and Arlington. The Rangers were impressed.

Hitting

A switch-hitter when the Rangers signed him, Tatis now bats only righthanded. He hits righthanders about as well as lefties, with good power against righties. Tatis is fairly selective for a young player, but he appeared to press late in close games and sometimes gave away at-bats by chasing pitches. He got most of his hits early in the count, struggling with two strikes.

Baserunning & Defense

Tatis breaks the mold of Rangers third basemen. Buddy Bell, Steve Buechele and Palmer all were lumbering big men who had trouble scoring from first on doubles. Tatis is an athlete who runs well. He stole a combined 20 bases in 1997 and will run against pitchers who neglect him. As a fielder, he's fortunate that he follows the error-prone Palmer instead of Bell and Buechele, who were about as good as it comes. Tatis has a strong arm and quick hands, but could make 15-20 errors over a full season.

1998 Outlook

If Tatis gets off to a good start, he could play 150-plus games. He should benefit from a full year working with hitting instructor Rudy Jaramillo, who has contributed to the development of three MVP performers: Jeff Bagwell, Ken Caminiti and Juan Gonzalez. If Tatis is willing to work, he'll become a more complete hitter.

Position: 3B
Bats: R **Throws:** R
Ht: 6' 1" **Wt:** 175

Opening Day Age: 23
Born: 1/1/75 in San Pedro de Macoris, DR
ML Seasons: 1
Pronunciation: tah-TEEZ

Overall Statistics

	G	AB	R	H	D	T	HR	RBI	SB	BB	SO	Avg	OBP	Slg
1997	60	223	29	57	9	0	8	29	3	14	42	.256	.297	.404
Career	60	223	29	57	9	0	8	29	3	14	42	.256	.297	.404

Where He Hits the Ball

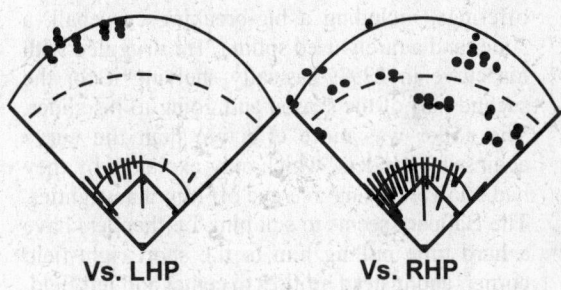

Vs. LHP   Vs. RHP

1997 Situational Stats

	AB	H	HR	RBI	Avg		AB	H	HR	RBI	Avg
Home	95	23	6	12	.242	LHP	61	14	1	5	.230
Road	128	34	2	17	.266	RHP	162	43	7	24	.265
First Half	0	0	0	0	-	Sc Pos	66	17	1	22	.258
Scnd Half	223	57	8	29	.256	Clutch	31	4	1	3	.129

1997 Rankings (American League)

⇒ Did not rank near the top or bottom in any category

John Wetteland

1997 Season

After losing to the Yankees in the 1996 playoffs, the Rangers signed the World Series MVP to fill the hole at the end of their bullpen. While John Wetteland struggled with his curveball throughout the season, he did the job he was hired to do. His lower save total was largely due to the lack of offense that left Texas with a losing record. He finished the season strong, putting to rest any thoughts that the Rangers should have spent their free-agent money elsewhere.

Pitching

Wetteland goes right at hitters with a fastball that's usually in the mid-90s. His fastball is such a good pitch because hitters must be wary of his other offerings, including a big-breaking curveball, a slider and a rarely used splitter. He struggled with his curve in 1997, basically shelving it for the second half of the season and going to his slider. The slider was more effective than the curve against lefthanders, which may explain why they had a lower batting average off him than righties. The Ballpark seems to suit him. Lefthanders have a hard time pulling him to the short right-field corner, and instead hit flies to center and left field, which are spacious.

Defense

With Wetteland pitching and Ivan Rodriguez catching, runners almost never attempt to steal. He gave up only one stolen base last year after allowing eight in 1996 with the Yankees. He doesn't get a lot of grounders back to the mound, but moves well when he does. He's always in the right place, backing up bases and covering first.

1998 Outlook

Wetteland is as reliable as closers come, ranking second in the major leagues with 210 saves since 1992. Pencil him in for another 30-40 as he settles into Arlington. He and setup man Danny Patterson should develop into a late-inning combination to be feared.

Position: RP
Bats: R **Throws:** R
Ht: 6' 2" **Wt:** 215

Opening Day Age: 31
Born: 8/21/66 in San Mateo, CA
ML Seasons: 9
Pronunciation: WET-land

Overall Statistics

	W	L	Pct.	ERA	G	GS	Sv	IP	H	BB	SO	HR	Ratio
1997	7	2	.778	1.94	61	0	31	65.0	43	21	63	5	0.98
Career	35	35	.500	2.81	431	17	211	577.0	435	195	619	48	1.09

How Often He Throws Strikes

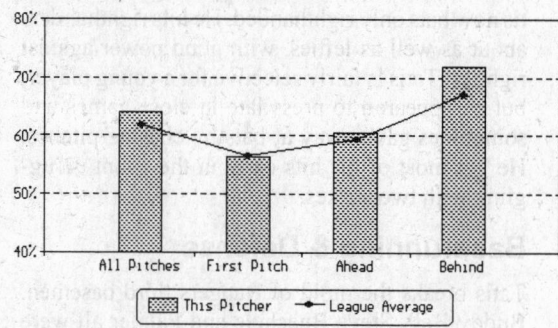

1997 Situational Stats

	W	L	ERA	Sv	IP		AB	H	HR	RBI	Avg
Home	5	0	1.05	15	34.1	LHB	126	21	1	10	.167
Road	2	2	2.93	16	30.2	RHB	110	22	4	12	.200
First Half	4	1	2.57	18	35.0	Sc Pos	46	12	1	16	.261
Scnd Half	3	1	1.20	13	30.0	Clutch	162	35	5	21	.216

1997 Rankings (American League)

⇒ 1st in lowest batting average allowed in relief (.182)
⇒ 2nd in least baserunners allowed per 9 innings in relief (8.9)
⇒ 3rd in games finished (58), first batter efficiency (.107) and relief ERA (1.94)
⇒ 4th in saves and save opportunities (37)
⇒ 5th in relief wins (7)
⇒ Led the Rangers in games pitched, saves, games finished (58), save opportunities (37), save percentage (83.8%), first batter efficiency (.107), lowest batting average allowed in relief with runners on base (.213), relief ERA (1.94), lowest batting average allowed in relief (.182) and least baserunners allowed per 9 innings in relief (8.9)

Bobby Witt

1997 Season

One of the biggest teases in the major leagues over the last decade, Bobby Witt did it again. He began the season as Texas' fifth starter. Unburdened by big expectations, Witt got off to the best start of his career, going 7-0 through May 20. He was the bright spot in a disappointing rotation, which often seemed in chaos because of injuries to Ken Hill and Roger Pavlik and the ineffectiveness of John Burkett. Once the Rangers expected him to make a greater contribution, Witt faded badly in the second half.

Pitching

The older he gets, the more the 33-year-old Witt is becoming a finesse pitcher. He gets beat with hits, not walks, these days. He served up the second-most home runs in the American League in 1997, getting hit hard by lefthanders. Witt's fastball can hit the low 90s but never has had much movement. While his slider always has been a strikeout pitch, he's more inclined to throw sinkers and let hitters put the ball in play.

Defense

Witt never will be confused with Jim Kaat. He's an easy target for basestealers. He has a big leg kick and lots of motion in his delivery, making it tough for even Pudge Rodriguez to cut down runners. He never has been a good fielder and his reactions aren't getting better. He did start two double plays last year, showing he's capable if not reliable.

1998 Outlook

For the third time in four years, Witt filed for free agency. He gambled by turning down a two-year offer from the Rangers at midseason, believing he would find a three-year deal in the winter. Texas still hopes to re-sign him, but it's unlikely the Rangers will add another year on their offer because GM Doug Melvin puts a lot of stock in how players finish the season. A seller's market for starting pitchers might get Witt a three-year deal elsewhere. He's a good bet for 30 starts and 200 innings.

Position: SP
Bats: R **Throws:** R
Ht: 6' 2" **Wt:** 205

Opening Day Age: 33
Born: 5/11/64 in Arlington, VA
ML Seasons: 12

Overall Statistics

	W	L	Pct.	ERA	G	GS	Sv	IP	H	BB	SO	HR	Ratio
1997	12	12	.500	4.82	34	32	0	209.0	245	74	121	33	1.53
Career	124	131	.486	4.63	346	338	0	2109.1	2066	1195	1737	198	1.55

How Often He Throws Strikes

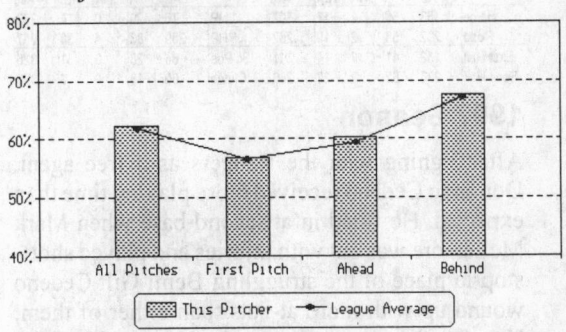

1997 Situational Stats

	W	L	ERA	Sv	IP		AB	H	HR	RBI	Avg
Home	5	7	5.05	0	117.2	LHB	410	137	20	64	.334
Road	7	5	4.53	0	91.1	RHB	423	108	13	49	.255
First Half	10	4	3.62	0	119.1	Sc Pos	192	47	8	78	.245
Scnd Half	2	8	6.42	0	89.2	Clutch	66	18	2	6	.273

1997 Rankings (American League)

⇒ 2nd in home runs allowed and highest slugging percentage allowed (.481)
⇒ 3rd in highest batting average allowed vs. lefthanded batters
⇒ 4th in hits allowed
⇒ 5th in highest batting average allowed (.294)
⇒ Led the Rangers in losses, games started, complete games (3), innings pitched, hits allowed, batters faced (919), home runs allowed, pitches thrown (3,284), stolen bases allowed (14), least pitches thrown per batter (3.57), lowest batting average allowed vs. righthanded batters and lowest batting average allowed with runners in scoring position

Domingo Cedeno

Position: 2B/SS
Bats: B **Throws:** R
Ht: 6' 0" **Wt:** 170

Opening Day Age: 29
Born: 11/4/68 in La Romana, DR
ML Seasons: 5
Pronunciation: suh-DAYN-yoh

Overall Statistics

	G	AB	R	H	D	T	HR	RBI	SB	BB	SO	Avg	OBP	Slg
1997	113	365	49	103	19	6	4	36	3	27	77	.282	.334	.400
Career	315	970	132	250	39	12	10	87	11	63	217	.258	.304	.354

1997 Situational Stats

	AB	H	HR	RBI	Avg		AB	H	HR	RBI	Avg
Home	163	50	2	17	.307	LHP	76	20	0	6	.263
Road	202	53	2	19	.262	RHP	289	83	4	30	.287
First Half	132	41	2	14	.311	Sc Pos	86	28	0	31	.326
Scnd Half	233	62	2	22	.266	Clutch	60	18	0	7	.300

1997 Season

After signing with the Rangers as a free agent, Domingo Cedeno received more playing time than expected. He filled in at second base when Mark McLemore was out with injuries and played shortstop in place of the struggling Benji Gil. Cedeno wound up with more at-bats than either of them. He got off to a good start, but his performance tailed off as he played more in the second half.

Hitting, Baserunning & Defense

A free swinger, the switch-hitting Cedeno could benefit from being more selective at the plate. He strikes out too often for a guy with minimal power. A better hitter from the left side, Cedeno did a good job last season with men in scoring position. He's a versatile fielder who can play second, short and third base, but his 17 errors in 1997 were a concern. He has above-average speed but never has been a basestealer.

1998 Outlook

Cedeno figures to be a reserve infielder. He has raised his batting average in each of the last four seasons, which suggests he could have a long career as a bench player. In Texas, however, he could be crowded out by the development of shortstop prospect Hanley Frias.

Eric Gunderson

Position: RP
Bats: R **Throws:** L
Ht: 6' 0" **Wt:** 190

Opening Day Age: 32
Born: 3/29/66 in Portland, OR
ML Seasons: 7

Overall Statistics

	W	L	Pct.	ERA	G	GS	Sv	IP	H	BB	SO	HR	Ratio
1997	2	1	.667	3.26	60	0	1	49.2	45	15	31	5	1.21
Career	8	7	.533	4.59	169	4	2	145.0	151	61	88	15	1.46

1997 Situational Stats

	W	L	ERA	Sv	IP		AB	H	HR	RBI	Avg
Home	1	1	2.93	0	27.2	LHB	92	23	3	18	.250
Road	1	0	3.68	1	22.0	RHB	95	22	2	10	.232
First Half	1	0	1.78	1	30.1	Sc Pos	53	12	2	23	.226
Scnd Half	1	1	5.59	0	19.1	Clutch	56	14	2	8	.250

1997 Season

Eric Gunderson has resurrected a fading career to become the Rangers' southpaw setup man. Gunderson earned manager Johnny Oates' confidence by throwing strikes and wiggling his way out of others' messes. He baffled AL hitters early in the season, holding them to a .152 average before the All-Star break. It soared to .354 in the second half after advance scouts updated their book on him. A strained ribcage muscle contributed to ugly numbers in August and September.

Pitching & Defense

Gunderson is the classic fastball-sinker lefty who induces grounders. He does a good job of finishing off hitters once he gets ahead in the count, but is vulnerable to hitters who sit on first-pitch fastballs. He does a good job changing speeds against righthanders, who were less effective against him than lefties in 1997. Gunderson has a good pickoff move and is quick to the plate. No one attempted a steal against him last year.

1998 Outlook

Gunderson figures to return as a setup man. The jury's out on what the Rangers can expect. He never has succeeded in one place for long. But then again, Oates and pitching coach Dick Bosman have had success in the past with veteran lefties.

Rick Helling

Position: RP/SP
Bats: R **Throws:** R
Ht: 6' 3" **Wt:** 215

Opening Day Age: 27
Born: 12/15/70 in
Devils Lake, ND
ML Seasons: 4

Overall Statistics

	W	L	Pct.	ERA	G	GS	Sv	IP	H	BB	SO	HR	Ratio
1997	5	9	.357	4.47	41	16	0	131.0	108	69	99	17	1.35
Career	11	16	.407	4.85	64	34	0	243.1	224	111	171	42	1.38

1997 Situational Stats

	W	L	ERA	Sv	IP		AB	H	HR	RBI	Avg
Home	2	4	3.84	0	58.2	LHB	224	49	9	30	.219
Road	3	5	4.98	0	72.1	RHB	239	59	8	33	.247
First Half	2	5	4.74	0	62.2	Sc Pos	105	24	1	41	.229
Scnd Half	3	4	4.21	0	68.1	Clutch	48	13	3	11	.271

1997 Season

After beginning the season in Florida's bullpen, Rick Helling joined the rotation after Al Leiter's injury. Nearly two years after the Marlins acquired him from Texas for John Burkett, the former Rangers first-round pick was reacquired for Ed Vosberg late in the season. He went into the Texas rotation, lasting at least six innings in seven of eight starts.

Pitching & Defense

Helling throws hard but has struggled with his control and his offspeed pitches. His improvement in 1997 was credited in part to a circle changeup and a cut fastball he could rely on more often. Though he's a flyball pitcher, Helling also kept the ball down consistently. His numbers were better as a reliever but he was hard to hit in both roles, allowing opponents to bat just .233 in 1997. Helling moves well coming off the mound, but is sometimes too aggressive trying to cut down the lead runner. Only eight of 21 basestealers succeeded against him last season.

1998 Outlook

Helling showed enough as a Ranger to be a front-runner for a job in the Texas rotation. His versatility is a major asset for any team. He can relieve while waiting to fill a need in the rotation.

Xavier Hernandez

Position: RP
Bats: L **Throws:** R
Ht: 6' 2" **Wt:** 195

Opening Day Age: 32
Born: 8/16/65 in Port
Arthur, TX
ML Seasons: 9

Overall Statistics

	W	L	Pct.	ERA	G	GS	Sv	IP	H	BB	SO	HR	Ratio
1997	0	4	.000	4.56	44	0	0	49.1	51	22	36	7	1.48
Career	34	29	.540	3.93	417	7	34	613.0	578	236	521	62	1.33

1997 Situational Stats

	W	L	ERA	Sv	IP		AB	H	HR	RBI	Avg
Home	0	2	4.26	0	25.1	LHB	73	18	3	11	.247
Road	0	2	4.88	0	24.0	RHB	122	33	4	20	.270
First Half	0	2	3.77	0	43.0	Sc Pos	63	18	2	24	.286
Scnd Half	0	2	9.95	0	6.1	Clutch	94	28	2	16	.298

1997 Season

Signed to a two-year contract by the Rangers, Xavier Hernandez overcame a horrible spring training to put together a decent first half in his return to the American League. Shoulder problems during the second half led to rotator-cuff surgery on August 20. He was winless in 44 chances, pitching mostly in games in which the Rangers trailed. That wasn't what GM Doug Melvin had in mind when he signed Hernandez.

Pitching & Defense

Hernandez long has made his living with a 90-MPH fastball and a splitter. When he's on, he gets lots of grounders. He struggled a little last year with the smaller strike zone of some AL umpires and walked too many men. Hernandez was notorious in the National League for failing to hold runners close. He's a reliable fielder and is excellent at starting double plays on comebackers.

1998 Outlook

The Rangers hope that Hernandez will heal by spring training, but there are no guarantees. The development of Danny Patterson had made Hernandez a secondary part of the bullpen even before his injury, so he comes to camp with his career on the line.

Jim Leyritz

Traded To RED SOX

Position: C/1B/DH
Bats: R **Throws:** R
Ht: 6' 0" **Wt:** 195

Opening Day Age: 34
Born: 12/27/63 in Lakewood, OH
ML Seasons: 8
Pronunciation: LAY-ritz

Overall Statistics

	G	AB	R	H	D	T	HR	RBI	SB	BB	SO	Avg	OBP	Slg
1997	121	379	58	105	11	0	11	64	2	60	78	.277	.379	.393
Career	643	1940	261	521	81	1	68	307	7	253	427	.269	.364	.416

1997 Situational Stats

	AB	H	HR	RBI	Avg		AB	H	HR	RBI	Avg
Home	180	50	3	23	.278	LHP	118	35	5	23	.297
Road	199	55	8	41	.276	RHP	261	70	6	41	.268
First Half	242	68	10	42	.281	Sc Pos	112	34	3	54	.304
Scnd Half	137	37	1	22	.270	Clutch	66	23	0	10	.348

1997 Season

The luggage tags are starting to pile up on Jim Leyritz' suitcase. He was traded to Anaheim after helping New York win the 1996 World Series, then moved to Texas in a July trade for Ken Hill. Leyritz produced for both the Angels and Rangers, delivering clutch hits while starting 65 games at catcher and 17 at first base. His season ended prematurely with torn cartilage in his left knee.

Hitting, Baserunning & Defense

Leyritz generates surprising power from a compact swing. In 1997, his average climbed with men in scoring position, and he was even better in those situations with two outs. He does most of his damage by working counts in his favor, punishing pitchers who make mistakes with breaking balls. Leyritz is a good athlete, but isn't considered strong defensively behind the plate. He can play first, third and the outfield. He rarely steals bases.

1998 Outlook

Texas acquired Leyritz when catcher Ivan Rodriguez was on the trading block. Rodriguez signed a five-year extension, so it was no surprise that Leyritz was traded to Boston with Damon Buford for pitchers Aaron Sele and Mark Brandenburg and catcher Bill Haselman. Leyritz' main competition in Boston will be Scott Hatteberg.

Warren Newson

Position: RF/LF
Bats: L **Throws:** L
Ht: 5' 7" **Wt:** 202

Opening Day Age: 33
Born: 7/3/64 in Newnan, GA
ML Seasons: 7
Nickname: The Deacon

Overall Statistics

	G	AB	R	H	D	T	HR	RBI	SB	BB	SO	Avg	OBP	Slg
1997	81	169	23	36	10	1	10	23	3	31	53	.213	.333	.462
Career	479	971	155	244	39	4	34	118	14	195	287	.251	.376	.405

1997 Situational Stats

	AB	H	HR	RBI	Avg		AB	H	HR	RBI	Avg
Home	93	17	2	8	.183	LHP	13	1	0	0	.077
Road	76	19	8	15	.250	RHP	156	35	10	23	.224
First Half	115	28	4	14	.243	Sc Pos	32	5	1	10	.156
Scnd Half	54	8	6	9	.148	Clutch	27	6	2	4	.222

1997 Season

For a second season, Warren Newson's bat and quiet leadership were valuable to the Rangers' bench. He homered once every 17 at-bats and was an extra-base machine when penciled into the lineup. His season, however, ended with a dive for a sinking liner in late August. He ruptured the biceps tendon in his right arm and had surgery to reattach it, the same surgery that Dean Palmer had in 1995. Newson finished the year on the DL.

Hitting, Baserunning & Defense

Once one of the most respected fastball hitters in the AL, Newson struggled to catch up to good heat in 1997, especially when he came off the bench. He went only 3-for-24 as a pinch hitter and batted .074 when he fell behind in the count. He swings for the fences more often than he did earlier in his career, punishing mistakes but striking out too often. He has limited range and not much of an arm in the outfield, and his fireplug body doesn't make him a basestealing threat.

1998 Outlook

Palmer made a complete recovery after an identical injury. The bad news is Newson must go back on the free-agent market while coming off the injury. He'll have to earn a job in spring training, if he's healthy enough to compete for one.

Danny Patterson

Position: RP
Bats: R **Throws:** R
Ht: 6' 0" **Wt:** 185

Opening Day Age: 27
Born: 2/17/71 in San Gabriel, CA
ML Seasons: 2

Overall Statistics

	W	L	Pct.	ERA	G	GS	Sv	IP	H	BB	SO	HR	Ratio
1997	10	6	.625	3.42	54	0	1	71.0	70	23	69	3	1.31
Career	10	6	.625	3.05	61	0	1	79.2	80	26	74	3	1.33

1997 Situational Stats

	W	L	ERA	Sv	IP		AB	H	HR	RBI	Avg
Home	5	5	4.58	1	37.1	LHB	110	26	0	12	.236
Road	5	1	2.14	0	33.2	RHB	156	44	3	26	.282
First Half	5	3	2.78	1	35.2	Sc Pos	86	22	0	35	.256
Scnd Half	5	3	4.08	0	35.1	Clutch	159	45	3	29	.283

1997 Season

The Rangers were rewarded for their patience in Danny Patterson, who appears to be in the major leagues to stay after seven seasons in the minors. He was a big contributor in his first full season in Texas, finishing third on the staff in both victories and appearances. The Rangers fretted about his right shoulder after finding a partial tear in his labrum in May, but he was tough enough to get outs even when not at top speed.

Pitching & Defense

Patterson's trademark pitch is a "Vulcan" splitter, which he holds between his middle and ring fingers. He also induces grounders with a hard sinker and a good slider. Surprisingly, he was more effective against lefthanders, and he didn't allow a home run in almost 40 innings at The Ballpark in Arlington. Patterson is fairly quick to the plate with runners on base, making him no easy target to steal on. He's an average fielder.

1998 Outlook

Patterson had his shoulder cleaned out in a minor procedure after the season. He's being counted on as the top setup man to John Wetteland. The Rangers will watch his shoulder closely in spring training, but hope a conditioning program will avoid a repeat of his troubles.

Billy Ripken

Position: SS/2B/3B
Bats: R **Throws:** R
Ht: 6' 1" **Wt:** 190

Opening Day Age: 33
Born: 12/16/64 in Havre de Grace, MD
ML Seasons: 11

Overall Statistics

	G	AB	R	H	D	T	HR	RBI	SB	BB	SO	Avg	OBP	Slg
1997	71	203	18	56	9	1	3	24	0	9	32	.276	.300	.374
Career	885	2655	279	654	118	6	20	224	22	169	322	.246	.294	.318

1997 Situational Stats

	AB	H	HR	RBI	Avg		AB	H	HR	RBI	Avg
Home	96	33	1	13	.344	LHP	87	26	0	9	.299
Road	107	23	2	11	.215	RHP	116	30	3	15	.259
First Half	121	37	2	20	.306	Sc Pos	48	13	0	20	.271
Scnd Half	82	19	1	4	.232	Clutch	24	8	0	4	.333

1997 Season

Back problems prevented Billy Ripken from having his best wire-to-wire season since the early 1990s, when he was Baltimore's regular second baseman. He was a key bench player and might have won the shortstop job from Benji Gil if not for two stints on the DL with a herniated disc in his back. Ripken enjoyed a good season at the plate and was as dependable as ever in the field.

Hitting, Baserunning & Defense

Ripken feasted on first-pitch fastballs in 1997, hitting .429 when he put the first pitch in play. That plan of attack wasn't as effective in the second half, as pitchers began starting him off with breaking pitches. Ripken's aggressiveness doesn't lend itself to many walks. His fielding skills that have kept him around all these years. He combines good range with a high fielding percentage, and he's efective at turning double plays. He has below-average speed and a penchant for groin pulls.

1998 Outlook

While eligible for free agency, Ripken could return to Texas. Unselfish and hard-nosed, he's manager Johnny Oates' kind of player. It may be too late to lose his tag as an injury-prone utilityman, but Ripken might surprise people if he got a chance to be a No. 1 shortstop somewhere.

Julio Santana

Position: RP/SP
Bats: R **Throws:** R
Ht: 6' 0" **Wt:** 185

Opening Day Age: 25
Born: 1/20/73 in San Pedro de Macoris, PR
ML Seasons: 1

Overall Statistics

	W	L	Pct.	ERA	G	GS	Sv	IP	H	BB	SO	HR	Ratio
1997	4	6	.400	6.75	30	14	0	104.0	141	49	64	16	1.83
Career	4	6	.400	6.75	30	14	0	104.0	141	49	64	16	1.83

1997 Situational Stats

	W	L	ERA	Sv	IP		AB	H	HR	RBI	Avg
Home	3	2	6.30	0	50.0	LHB	216	70	5	24	.324
Road	1	4	7.17	0	54.0	RHB	221	71	11	48	.321
First Half	3	4	6.51	0	74.2	Sc Pos	129	39	7	61	.302
Scnd Half	1	2	7.36	0	29.1	Clutch	22	7	1	3	.318

1997 Season

The Rangers kept Julio Santana on their roster all season because he was out of options. He failed to take advantage of the exposure, especially when injuries gave him an extended look in the starting rotation. He compiled a 7.36 ERA in 14 starts, lasting five innings or more in only seven of them. He allowed opponents to hit .323 overall and .363 in the second half of the season. A sprained right knee put him on the disabled list briefly in July.

Pitching & Defense

Control problems were the bane of Santana's existence. He regularly worked behind in the count and responded by grooving fastballs. Hitters started to sit on his first pitch, knowing they would get fastballs, and hit .431 when they put the first pitch in play. His offspeed pitches are nothing special. Santana is a converted shortstop who fields comebackers well. He needs to do a better job holding runners.

1998 Outlook

The Rangers want Santana to get his act together in winter ball. If he doesn't pitch well in spring training, don't expect Texas to hand him a roster spot again. Instead they would try to slide him through waivers at the end of spring training, when most clubs have roster problems of their own.

Mike Simms

Position: DH/RF
Bats: R **Throws:** R
Ht: 6' 4" **Wt:** 200

Opening Day Age: 31
Born: 1/12/67 in Orange, CA
ML Seasons: 7

Overall Statistics

	G	AB	R	H	D	T	HR	RBI	SB	BB	SO	Avg	OBP	Slg
1997	59	111	13	28	8	0	5	22	0	8	27	.252	.298	.459
Career	240	472	56	107	22	1	20	75	4	45	127	.227	.298	.405

1997 Situational Stats

	AB	H	HR	RBI	Avg		AB	H	HR	RBI	Avg
Home	59	14	3	10	.237	LHP	81	19	3	13	.235
Road	52	14	2	12	.269	RHP	30	9	2	9	.300
First Half	75	18	4	13	.240	Sc Pos	32	11	1	16	.344
Scnd Half	36	10	1	9	.278	Clutch	18	7	2	9	.389

1997 Season

Mike Simms spent almost all of the season with Texas, but appeared in only 59 games despite getting some additional starts after Mickey Tettleton's knees forced him to retire. Simms started mostly against lefthanders, often in a DH platoon after Tettleton's departure, but hit righties better than he ever had. He did a good job in clutch situations.

Hitting, Baserunning & Defense

Simms feasted on first-pitch fastballs in 1997, batting .462 when he put the first pitch in play. He has good power but doesn't make enough contact to use it. He had two homers and batted .300 as a pinch-hitter in 1997. Simms is a liability anywhere in the field. He's slow and has an average arm.

1998 Outlook

The Rangers dropped Simms to clear some roster space but were hopeful of re-signing him to a minor league contract after he declared free agency. They expect him to be fully recovered from September surgery to repair torn knee cartilage. The trade of Jim Leyritz made it more likely Simms would return.

Other Texas Rangers

Scott Bailes (Pos: LHP, Age: 35)

	W	L	Pct.	ERA	G	GS	Sv	IP	H	BB	SO	HR	Ratio
1997	1	0	1.000	2.86	24	0	0	22.0	18	10	14	2	1.27
Career	38	44	.463	4.86	297	59	13	639.1	697	245	321	84	1.47

Rescued from the "Old Lefties Retirement Home," Bailes returned to the majors last year for the first time since 1992, and pitched pretty well. Ed Vande Berg, there's hope for you. 1998 Outlook: B

Terry Clark (Pos: RHP, Age: 37)

	W	L	Pct.	ERA	G	GS	Sv	IP	H	BB	SO	HR	Ratio
1997	1	7	.125	6.00	13	9	0	57.0	70	23	24	6	1.63
Career	10	23	.303	5.54	91	27	1	232.1	299	89	109	21	1.67

The well-traveled Clark has pitched for six different teams over the last three seasons—two each year. The Rangers got their turn last August, and they've seen enough. Have arm, will travel. 1998 Outlook: C

Mike Devereaux (Pos: RF, Age: 34, Bats: R)

	G	AB	R	H	D	T	HR	RBI	SB	BB	SO	Avg	OBP	Slg
1997	29	72	8	15	3	0	0	7	1	7	10	.208	.275	.250
Career	1077	3727	491	945	169	33	105	479	85	293	633	.254	.307	.401

Signed by the Rangers as a spare outfielder last year, Devereaux didn't hit. When he refused an assignment to the minors, they released him. A comeback is unlikely, but possible. 1998 Outlook: C

Alex Diaz (Pos: RF, Age: 29, Bats: B)

	G	AB	R	H	D	T	HR	RBI	SB	BB	SO	Avg	OBP	Slg
1997	28	90	8	20	4	0	2	12	1	5	13	.222	.268	.333
Career	302	704	94	176	27	7	7	63	38	30	79	.250	.283	.338

The quintessential fifth or sixth outfielder, Diaz joined the Rangers last year and served up his usual combination of speed, good defense and bad hitting. He'll hope to land the same role in '98. 1998 Outlook: C

Bryan Eversgerd (Pos: LHP, Age: 29)

	W	L	Pct.	ERA	G	GS	Sv	IP	H	BB	SO	HR	Ratio
1997	0	2	.000	20.25	3	0	0	1.1	5	3	2	0	6.00
Career	2	5	.286	4.90	68	1	0	90.0	102	32	57	10	1.49

The ex-Cardinal and Expo lefthander spent most of last year with the Rangers' Oklahoma City farm team before joining Texas late in the year. He was hit hard and they dropped him after the season. 1998 Outlook: C

Wilson Heredia (Pos: RHP, Age: 26)

	W	L	Pct.	ERA	G	GS	Sv	IP	H	BB	SO	HR	Ratio
1997	1	0	1.000	3.20	10	0	0	19.2	14	16	8	2	1.53
Career	1	1	.500	3.41	16	0	0	31.2	23	31	14	4	1.71

Heredia, who missed all of 1996 after undergoing ulnar nerve surgery on his right elbow, spent most of '97 at Oklahoma City before joining the Rangers in August. Could be part of the Ranger bullpen this year. 1998 Outlook: B

Henry Mercedes (Pos: C, Age: 28, Bats: R)

	G	AB	R	H	D	T	HR	RBI	SB	BB	SO	Avg	OBP	Slg
1997	23	47	4	10	4	0	0	6	0	6	25	.213	.302	.298
Career	79	146	18	36	8	1	0	17	1	16	55	.247	.325	.315

Being one of Ivan Rodriguez' backups will guarantee you lots of bench time, and Mercedes mostly watched the '97 season from a comfortable seat. He'll be looking for another backup job this year. 1998 Outlook: C

Angel Miranda (Pos: LHP, Age: 28)

	W	L	Pct.	ERA	G	GS	Sv	IP	H	BB	SO	HR	Ratio
1997	0	0	-	3.86	10	0	0	14.0	17	9	8	1	1.86
Career	17	21	.447	4.46	116	47	2	363.1	355	206	243	41	1.54

After getting released by the Brewers last June, Miranda pitched briefly in the Indian system, then was passed on to the Rangers' Oklahoma City farm team. Still only 28, he could come back. 1998 Outlook: C

Roger Pavlik (Pos: RHP, Age: 30)

	W	L	Pct.	ERA	G	GS	Sv	IP	H	BB	SO	HR	Ratio
1997	3	5	.375	4.37	11	11	0	57.2	59	31	35	7	1.56
Career	46	38	.548	4.59	126	125	0	729.0	727	346	518	83	1.47

Pavlik's herky-jerky motion has always left him vulnerable to injury, and he missed most of 1997 with elbow problems. He's good for 10-15 wins when he's healthy, but he'll have to prove it first. 1998 Outlook: C

Marc Sagmoen (Pos: RF, Age: 26, Bats: L)

	G	AB	R	H	D	T	HR	RBI	SB	BB	SO	Avg	OBP	Slg
1997	21	43	2	6	2	0	1	4	0	2	13	.140	.174	.256
Career	21	43	2	6	2	0	1	4	0	2	13	.140	.174	.256

A veteran minor league outfielder, Sagmoen got some fringe duty with the Rangers last year but looked overmatched against major league pitching. He'll probably be back in the minors this year. 1998 Outlook: D

Dave Silvestri (Pos: 3B, Age: 30, Bats: R)

	G	AB	R	H	D	T	HR	RBI	SB	BB	SO	Avg	OBP	Slg
1997	2	4	0	0	0	0	0	0	0	0	1	.000	.000	.000
Career	170	311	42	66	11	3	6	35	4	56	93	.212	.331	.325

Silvestri has a decent amount of power for a middle infielder, but has never had the glove skills to land a major league job. Expansion might help him earn a backup role with someone this year. 1998 Outlook: C

Tanyon Sturtze (Pos: RHP, Age: 27)

	W	L	Pct.	ERA	G	GS	Sv	IP	H	BB	SO	HR	Ratio
1997	1	1	.500	8.27	9	5	0	32.2	45	18	18	6	1.93
Career	2	1	.667	8.47	17	5	0	45.2	63	24	25	10	1.91

The former Athletic and Cub farmhand pitched briefly and ineffectively for Rangers last year. He'll need major improvement if he hopes to land a major league job this year. 1998 Outlook: C

Mickey Tettleton (Pos: DH, Age: 37, Bats: B)

	G	AB	R	H	D	T	HR	RBI	SB	BB	SO	Avg	OBP	Slg
1997	17	44	5	4	1	0	3	4	0	3	12	.091	.167	.318
Career	1485	4698	711	1132	210	16	245	732	23	949	1307	.241	.369	.449

Crippled by knee problems, Tettleton retired in July, putting an end to a useful and distinctive 14-year career. Every Tettleton AB seemed to end either with a walk, a strikeout or a home run. 1998 Outlook: D

Matt Whiteside (Pos: RHP, Age: 30)

	W	L	Pct.	ERA	G	GS	Sv	IP	H	BB	SO	HR	Ratio
1997	4	1	.800	5.08	42	1	0	72.2	85	26	44	4	1.53
Career	14	10	.583	4.61	223	1	9	320.0	348	118	194	31	1.46

Whiteside has been a fringe reliever for the Rangers since 1992, often spending part of the season at Triple-A Oklahoma City. He hasn't pitched well since 1995; how long can this continue? 1998 Outlook: C

Texas Rangers Minor League Prospects

Organization Overview:

Since taking over after the 1994 season, GM Doug Melvin has overhauled Texas' player-development system—and for good reason. A series of poor drafts left the Rangers without many prospects. Most of the rare homegrown players on the big league roster were signed as foreign free agents, such as Juan Gonzalez, Ivan Rodriguez and Fernando Tatis. Rusty Greer is the only key contributor drafted in the 1990s. Tatis made Dean Palmer expendable in 1997, but the system won't produce much else in the next couple of years. The Rangers lost a potential double-play combination when Arizona took Edwin Diaz and Hanley Frias in the expansion draft.

Kevin L. Brown

Position: C **Opening Day Age:** 24
Bats: R **Throws:** R **Born:** 4/21/73 in
Ht: 6' 2" **Wt:** 200 Valparaiso, IN

Recent Statistics

	G	AB	R	H	D	T	HR	RBI	SB	BB	SO	AVG
97 AAA Okla City	116	403	56	97	18	2	19	50	2	38	111	.241
97 AL Texas	4	5	1	2	0	0	1	1	0	0	0	.400
97 MLE	116	397	52	91	16	1	16	46	1	35	115	.229

The Rangers are set behind the plate with Ivan Rodriguez, but Brown still might surface in Texas in 1998. He has the defensive skills to back up Rodriguez and the bat to contribute offense at first base or designated hitter. A 1994 second-round pick out of the University of Southern Indiana, he has good power. His long swing leads to too many strikeouts and he also doesn't walk, preventing him from hitting for average. He's above-average defensively and has a strong arm, so the Rangers won't experience a dropoff if they rest Rodriguez.

Jonathan Johnson

Position: P **Opening Day Age:** 23
Bats: R **Throws:** R **Born:** 7/16/74 in Ocala,
Ht: 6' 0" **Wt:** 180 FL

Recent Statistics

	W	L	ERA	G	GS	Sv	IP	H	R	BB	SO	HR
96 AAA Okla City	1	0	0.00	1	1	0	9.0	2	0	1	6	0
96 AA Tulsa	13	10	3.56	26	25	0	174.1	176	86	41	97	15
97 AAA Okla City	1	8	7.29	13	12	1	58.0	83	54	29	33	6
97 AA Tulsa	5	4	3.52	10	10	0	71.2	70	35	15	47	3

Johnson had been on the fast track since signing as a first-round pick out of Florida State in 1995, but he derailed last year. After moving smoothly up to Double-A, he was annihilated in Triple-A and didn't recover until a demotion. Johnson's curveball is by far his best pitch, as his fastball is slightly below average and his changeup is developing. There was some concern that he was as good as he was going to get when he was drafted, and that may be true. He must prove he can survive in Triple-A before getting a shot in Texas.

Cesar King

Position: C **Opening Day Age:** 20
Bats: R **Throws:** R **Born:** 2/28/78 in La
Ht: 6' 0" **Wt:** 175 Romana, DR

Recent Statistics

	G	AB	R	H	D	T	HR	RBI	SB	BB	SO	AVG
96 A Chston-SC	84	276	35	69	10	1	7	28	8	21	58	.250
97 A Charlotte	91	307	51	91	14	4	6	37	8	35	58	.296
97 AA Tulsa	14	45	6	16	1	0	1	8	0	5	3	.356

King reached Double-A at age 19, which would be cause for excitement if the Rangers weren't set behind the plate already with Ivan Rodriguez. Signed out of the Dominican Republic, King is an above-average catcher with very good receiving and throwing skills. He threw out 50 percent of basestealers in 1997. He also has held his own offensively despite playing against older players, showing doubles power and a good eye at the plate. He needs to make better contact. Overall, he's a better defensive player than Brown. He's not as good offensively, but he's also five years younger. King will start 1998 in Double-A and has the tools to be a regular catcher in the majors.

Brandon Knight

Position: P **Opening Day Age:** 22
Bats: L **Throws:** R **Born:** 10/1/75 in
Ht: 6' 0" **Wt:** 170 Oxnard, CA

Recent Statistics

	W	L	ERA	G	GS	Sv	IP	H	R	BB	SO	HR
96 A Hudson Vall	2	2	4.42	9	9	0	53.0	59	29	21	52	1
96 A Charlotte	4	10	5.12	19	17	0	102.0	118	65	45	74	9
97 A Charlotte	7	4	2.23	14	12	0	92.2	82	33	22	91	9
97 AA Tulsa	6	4	4.50	14	14	0	90.0	83	52	35	84	12

Knight was more of a hitter at Ventura (Calif.) Junior College, but he has focused on pitching since signing as a 14th-round pick in 1995. He throws four pitches, using an above-average fastball along with a curveball, slider and changeup. He had more strikeouts than hits allowed in 1997, even after a promotion to Double-A at age 21. Still relatively inexperienced as a pitcher, Knight mainly needs experience and improved command. He would seem to be at least a year away, but he did make a lot of progress last season. A sore shoulder late in the year kept him out of the Arizona Fall League, but it wasn't considered serious.

Dan Kolb

Position: P   **Opening Day Age:** 23
Bats: R **Throws:** R   **Born:** 3/29/75 in
Ht: 6' 4" **Wt:** 190   Sterling, IL

Recent Statistics

	W	L	ERA	G	GS	Sv	IP	H	R	BB	SO	HR
96 A Chston-SC	8	6	2.57	20	20	0	126.0	80	50	60	127	5
96 A Charlotte	2	2	4.26	6	6	0	38.0	38	18	14	28	1
96 AA Tulsa	1	0	0.77	2	2	0	11.2	5	1	8	7	0
97 AA Tulsa	0	2	4.76	2	2	0	11.1	7	7	11	6	1
97 A Charlotte	4	10	4.87	24	23	0	133.0	146	91	62	83	10

Few minor leaguers throw harder than Kolb, who can consistently throw in the mid-90s and has been clocked at 100 MPH. His signing was the result of a nice piece of scouting by the Rangers, who kept track of him after he dropped out of Sauk Valley (Ill.) Community College and drafted him in the sixth round in 1995. His 1997 performance was puzzling, however, as his fastball dropped to 89-90 MPH at times and left him without an out pitch. His curveball is OK, but he needs a better changeup and command. His fastball alone might make him a successful closer, but Texas plans on keeping him a starter for now.

Ruben Mateo

Position: OF   **Opening Day Age:** 20
Bats: R **Throws:** R   **Born:** 2/10/78 in San
Ht: 6' 0" **Wt:** 170   Cristobal, DR

Recent Statistics

	G	AB	R	H	D	T	HR	RBI	SB	BB	SO	AVG
96 A Chston-SC	134	496	65	129	30	8	8	58	30	26	78	.260
97 A Charlotte	99	385	63	121	23	8	12	67	20	22	55	.314

Mateo is the best position player in the system. He has five-tool potential and the Rangers liken him to the Cubs' Sammy Sosa, who like Mateo was signed as a Dominican teenager by Texas. His power steadily is increasing as he fills out, and he hit .314 in a high Class-A pitchers' league at age 19. His speed allows him to steal bases and track down balls in the outfield, and his arm is a tremendous weapon. His biggest drawback at this point is an unwillingness to take a walk, which could be exploited by more advanced pitchers. Mateo will head to Double-A in 1998 and could be in Texas by the end of the following season.

Eric Moody

Position: P   **Opening Day Age:** 27
Bats: R **Throws:** R   **Born:** 1/6/71 in
Ht: 6' 6" **Wt:** 185   Greenville, SC

Recent Statistics

	W	L	ERA	G	GS	Sv	IP	H	R	BB	SO	HR
97 AAA Okla City	5	6	3.46	35	10	1	112.0	114	49	21	72	13
97 AL Texas	0	1	4.26	10	1	0	19.0	26	10	2	12	4

Moody isn't going to be a focal point of a major league pitching staff, but he has the serviceable type of arm that any team can use. A 24th-round pick in 1993 out of tiny Erskine (S.C.) College, he has moved deliberately through the system. His hits/innings and strikeout/walk

ratio always have been solid if unspectacular. He's 6-foot-6 and delivers pitches from a deceptive arm angle, with his best offering a live fastball. He could pitch at the end of a rotation, but the Rangers broke him into the majors in relief.

Matt Perisho

Position: P   **Opening Day Age:** 22
Bats: L **Throws:** L   **Born:** 6/8/75 in
Ht: 6' 0" **Wt:** 190   Burlington, IA

Recent Statistics

	W	L	ERA	G	GS	Sv	IP	H	R	BB	SO	HR
97 AA Midland	5	2	2.96	10	10	0	73.0	60	26	26	62	5
97 AAA Vancouver	4	4	5.33	9	9	0	52.1	68	42	29	47	3
97 AL Anaheim	0	2	6.00	11	8	0	45.0	59	34	28	35	6

Perisho's career has taken a roller-coaster ride since he was drafted in the third round in 1993 by the Angels. After two decent seasons he needed elbow surgery, then was strafed in 1995. He recovered and dominated the last two years in Double-A Midland, one of the best hitters' parks in the minors. Promotions to Anaheim and Triple-A Vancouver haven't gone nearly as well, because he struggled and lost both his confidence and command. Then the Angels traded him after the season for infielder Mike Bell, who had lost his prospect status with the Rangers. Perisho has four average pitches, but needs to keep his fastball down and tighten his curve. Right now he looks no better than a No. 4 or 5 starter.

Others to Watch

Jorge Carrion was a star two-way player for national champion North Texas Community College in 1996, when he signed with the Rangers as a draft-and-follow for $700,000. His contract dictated that he be allowed to play shortstop, but the Rangers convinced him to take his live arm to the mound last season. He struck out more than a batter per inning at Rookie-level Pulaski at age 20. . . The Rangers discovered that righthander **R.A. Dickey** was missing an elbow ligament after making him a first-round pick in 1996. The 23-year-old Dickey, a former U.S. Olympian, hurt his elbow after eight appearances last year and missed most of the season. . . Lefthander **Corey Lee**, 23, is the best of the four pitchers Texas took in the first two rounds of the 1996 draft. He has an average fastball, command of four pitches and the courage to pitch inside. . . Second baseman **Warren Morris** won the 1996 College World Series with a dramatic ninth-inning homer for Louisiana State, then got a taste of Triple-A at age 23 in his first pro season in 1997. He's a steady player with good hitting skills. . . Righthander **Ted Silva** also performed some CWS heroics, winning the 1995 finale for Cal State Fullerton. Though he's under 6 feet and has average stuff at best, he has gone 35-18 and reached Double-A in three pro seasons. The 23 year old's best pitch is a curve. . . Minor league folk hero **Bubba Smith** hit 27 homers in Triple-A last year. A first baseman still looking for his first major league shot, he's running out of time at 28.

Tim Johnson

1997 Season

Tim Johnson spent 1997 managing the Triple-A Iowa Cubs and leading them to a runner-up finish in the American Association playoffs. He was named the seventh manager in Blue Jays history on November 24, replacing the fired Cito Gaston and interim skipper Mel Queen. Johnson was selected as a result of his superior communication skills, motivational ability and his roots as a former Toronto infielder.

Offense

Johnson says he'll be a proponent of aggressive baserunning and the hit-and-run. He's a believer in using all 25 players on his roster and platooning will be a part of his basic philosophy. His years spent as an Expos advance scout and later as Felipe Alou's bench coach taught him the importance of keeping each player involved. He wants each member of his young Blue Jays team to understand his role right from the outset.

Pitching & Defense

Johnson likes to win games with pitching and defense. He'll begin his managerial tenure with an outstanding rotation led by Roger Clemens and Pat Hentgen, who eat innings and have won the last two American League Cy Young Awards. Johnson relies heavily on scouting reports and will look for platoon matchups with his relievers. He's a stickler for team defense. Glove men will play over sluggers.

1998 Outlook

The Blue Jays have a distinct mix of youngsters and hardened veterans. Johnson's background coming out of East Los Angeles and with the Marine Corps has made him a strong leader. He speaks Spanish fluently, which bodes well for dealing with the many Latin players on the roster. Toronto has nowhere to go but up, so he could have a successful debut.

Born: 7/22/49 in Grand Forks, ND

Playing Experience: 1973-1979, Mil, Tor

Managerial Experience: No major league experience

Manager Statistics

Year	Team, Lg	W	L	Pct	GB	Finish
–	–	–	–	–	–	–
–	–	–	–	–	–	–

1997 Starting Pitchers by Days Rest

	≤3	4	5	6+
Blue Jays Starts	–	–	–	–
Blue Jays ERA	–	–	–	–
AL Avg Starts	5	89	34	24
AL ERA	4.38	4.60	4.61	5.37

1997 Situational Stats

	Tim Johnson	AL Average
Hit & Run Success %	–	36.5
Stolen Base Success %	–	67.3
Platoon Pct.	–	59.5
Defensive Subs	–	22
High-Pitch Outings	–	15
Quick/Slow Hooks	–	19/15
Sacrifice Attempts	–	53

1997 Rankings (American League)

⇒ Did not manage in the majors last year

Joe Carter

1997 Season

Despite crossing the 100-RBI plateau for the 10th time in his 15-year career, Joe Carter did not have a successful season in 1997. His batting average went too far south and his lack of productivity during key moments of the season served to highlight his age and diminished bat speed. He also was portrayed by the Toronto media as a selfish player, not wanting to DH to make room for Carlos Delgado at first base.

Hitting

Carter's .234 batting average, .284 on-base percentage and .399 slugging percentage while batting third or fourth for Toronto exemplified why the Blue Jays were so weak offensively. He hasn't changed much over the years. He's strictly a fly-ball hitter with an obvious weakness for anything pitched outside. With his slower bat, which has diminished his power, he has become virtually helpless when behind in the count.

Baserunning & Defense

Carter roamed between right and left field, as well as first base and DH. He made few errors in the field, but often displayed a lackadaisical manner when challenged with a tough play. His range has become limited and his arm is simply average. His basestealing experience allowed him to take advantage of pitchers with ultra-slow deliveries. He went 8-for-10 in steals in 1997.

1998 Outlook

Carter's contract was extended for one year during the 1996 season. No such luxury was afforded him in 1997, because even if he agreed to a decrease in salary, the Jays still would have to pay him $5.2 million because they couldn't cut his salary more than 20 percent. Therefore, he'll likely be taking his services elsewhere via free agency. He still has another year or two left, but no longer can be counted on to carry a key position in the middle of anyone's batting order.

Position: DH/1B/LF
Bats: R **Throws:** R
Ht: 6' 3"   **Wt:** 215

Opening Day Age: 38
Born: 3/7/60 in Oklahoma City, OK
ML Seasons: 15

Overall Statistics

	G	AB	R	H	D	T	HR	RBI	SB	BB	SO	Avg	OBP	Slg
1997	157	612	76	143	30	4	21	102	8	40	105	.234	.284	.399
Career	2063	8034	1119	2083	410	52	378	1382	227	503	1326	.259	.306	.464

Where He Hits the Ball

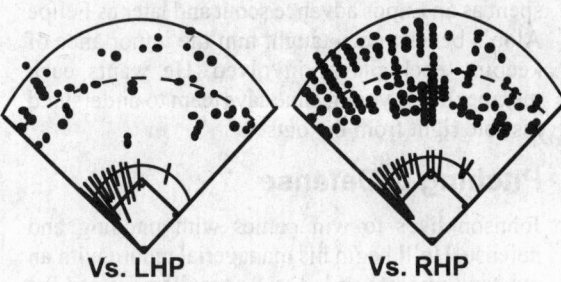

Vs. LHP   **Vs. RHP**

1997 Situational Stats

	AB	H	HR	RBI	Avg		AB	H	HR	RBI	Avg
Home	299	65	11	59	.217	LHP	180	52	6	33	.289
Road	313	78	10	43	.249	RHP	432	91	15	69	.211
First Half	315	74	10	51	.235	Sc Pos	170	45	8	85	.265
Scnd Half	297	69	11	51	.232	Clutch	98	20	1	18	.204

1997 Rankings (American League)

⇒ 1st in lowest groundball/flyball ratio (0.6), lowest batting average vs. righthanded pitchers and lowest percentage of pitches taken (41.8%)
⇒ 2nd in lowest cleanup slugging percentage (.413) and lowest on-base percentage vs. righthanded pitchers (.266)
⇒ 3rd in lowest batting average, highest batting average with the bases loaded (.600) and lowest batting average at home
⇒ Led the Blue Jays in at-bats, hits, RBI, sacrifice flies (9), GDPs (12), plate appearances (668), games played (157), batting average with the bases loaded (.600), batting average vs. lefthanded pitchers and on-base percentage vs. lefthanded pitchers (.328)

Roger Clemens

1997 Season

From a personal standpoint, Roger Clemens will chalk up the 1997 season as perhaps the most satisfying of his illustrious career. After feeling unappreciated by Boston GM Dan Duquette, the free-agent pitcher departed the Red Sox and signed a lucrative three-year contract in Toronto last winter. Despite his team's struggles, Clemens went 21-7, 2.05 for a last-place team to win his fourth Cy Young Award. He showed the baseball world why he is still "The Rocket."

Pitching

Clemens is a premier power pitcher with a full repertoire of offerings, including two fastballs. The running two-seamer is his bread-and-butter pitch. He also throws a hard splitter which he uses anywhere in the count, a nifty slider, and a changeup. His fastball was clocked as high as 97 MPH in 1997, and the splitter usually hits the high 80s. He mixes raw power, generated by the pushoff of his back leg, with an almost flawless command of his pitches. A ferocious competitor, he's special in pressure situations.

Defense

Clemens fields his position well, backs up his fielders and gets to first base as quickly as possible. Because he comes to the plate with predominantly hard stuff, his catcher usually has a good chance to throw out basestealers. His move to first is a typical spin with a lot of zip on this throw.

1998 Outlook

Clemens' debut in Toronto was indeed spectacular, but it wasn't enough to make his new ballclub a contender, nor did it significantly boost attendance. The Blue Jays, however, did get their money's worth. He now has pitched back-to-back seasons with 240-plus innings and 250-plus strikeouts, and shows no signs of tiring. With his absolute dedication to physical fitness, he's possibly in the best shape of his career. There's no reason to expect anything less in 1998.

Position: SP
Bats: R **Throws:** R
Ht: 6' 4" **Wt:** 230

Opening Day Age: 35
Born: 8/4/62 in Dayton, OH
ML Seasons: 14
Nickname: Rocket

Toronto Blue Jays

Overall Statistics

	W	L	Pct.	ERA	G	GS	Sv	IP	H	BB	SO	HR	Ratio
1997	21	7	.750	2.05	34	34	0	264.0	204	68	292	9	1.03
Career	213	118	.644	2.97	417	416	0	3040.0	2563	924	2882	203	1.15

How Often He Throws Strikes

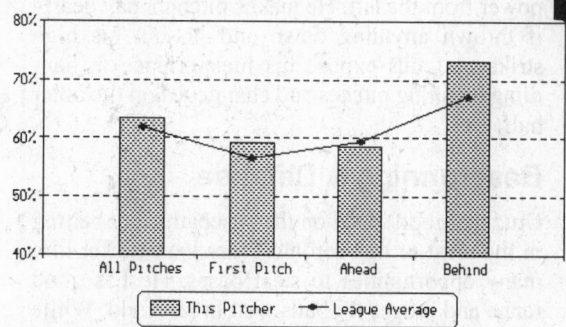

1997 Situational Stats

	W	L	ERA	Sv	IP		AB	H	HR	RBI	Avg
Home	10	4	1.52	0	147.2	LHB	498	102	3	32	.205
Road	11	3	2.71	0	116.1	RHB	459	102	6	27	.222
First Half	13	3	1.69	0	138.1	Sc Pos	194	35	2	48	.180
Scnd Half	8	4	2.44	0	125.2	Clutch	108	21	3	9	.194

1997 Rankings (American League)

⇒ 1st in ERA, wins, complete games (9), shutouts (3), innings pitched, strikeouts, pitches thrown (4,106), lowest slugging percentage allowed (.290), lowest on-base percentage allowed (.273), least baserunners allowed per 9 innings (9.7), ERA at home and lowest batting average allowed vs. lefthanded batters

⇒ 2nd in batters faced (1,044), highest strikeout/walk ratio (4.3), lowest batting average allowed (.213), least home runs allowed per 9 innings (.31) and ERA on the road

⇒ 3rd in winning percentage, most strikeouts per 9 innings (10.0) and lowest batting average allowed with runners in scoring position

⇒ Led the Blue Jays in ERA, wins, complete games (9), shutouts (3) and innings pitched

Jose Cruz Jr.

Position: LF
Bats: B **Throws:** R
Ht: 6' 0" **Wt:** 190

Opening Day Age: 23
Born: 4/19/74 in
Arroyr, PR
ML Seasons: 1

1997 Season

In one of the more surprising trades of 1997, the bullpen-starved Mariners gave up Jose Cruz Jr. for relievers Mike Timlin and Paul Spoljaric just prior to the July 31 trading deadline. Had it not been for Boston's Nomar Garciaparra, Cruz would have been a strong candidate for American League Rookie of the Year with 26 home runs in 104 games.

Hitting

Though not particularly big, Cruz packs a wallop. His quick hands make his bat explode through the strike zone. He's a switch-hitter who makes better contact from the right side, but displays more power from the left. He makes pitchers pay dearly if thrown anything down and in, but his high strikeout totals expose his inexperience in handling breaking pitches and changeups on the outer half.

Baserunning & Defense

Cruz has good speed on the basepaths, but batting in the meat of the Toronto order won't offer him many opportunities to steal bases. He has good range and judges fly balls well in left field. While his arm strength is good, his accuracy is questionable.

1998 Outlook

While Cruz has received rave reviews for his five-tool talent, he'll need time before he hits for average. He has a hitch in his swing which can be exploited by the better pitchers. The trade put him in the spotlight as a key component in the Blue Jays' road back to contention. The Blue Jays will put him in left field, and with Shannon Stewart in center and Shawn Green in right, they hope to develop an outfield unit that could rival their George Bell-Lloyd Moseby-Jesse Barfield threesome of a decade before. He could hit 30 or more homers in 1998.

Overall Statistics

	G	AB	R	H	D	T	HR	RBI	SB	BB	SO	Avg	OBP	Slg
1997	104	395	59	98	19	1	26	68	7	41	117	.248	.315	.499
Career	104	395	59	98	19	1	26	68	7	41	117	.248	.315	.499

Where He Hits the Ball

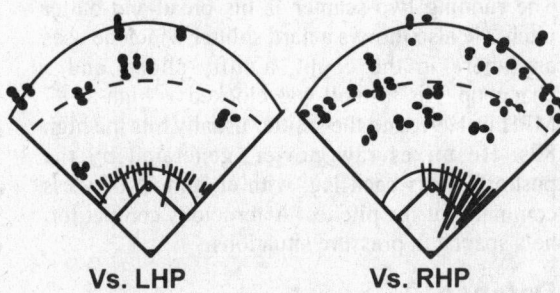

Vs. LHP   **Vs. RHP**

1997 Situational Stats

	AB	H	HR	RBI	Avg		AB	H	HR	RBI	Avg
Home	175	46	11	34	.263	LHP	97	25	5	18	.258
Road	220	52	15	34	.236	RHP	298	73	21	50	.245
First Half	113	29	9	21	.257	Sc Pos	111	21	8	39	.189
Scnd Half	282	69	17	47	.245	Clutch	65	12	3	5	.185

1997 Rankings (American League)

⇒ 3rd in lowest batting average with runners in scoring position (.189) and lowest batting average with the bases loaded (.000)
⇒ 4th in errors in left field (5), lowest fielding percentage in left field (.973), highest percentage of swings that missed (31.0%) and lowest percentage of swings put into play (34.0%)
⇒ 6th in lowest batting average in the clutch (.185)

Carlos Delgado

1997 Season

Since stepping out of a platoon role in 1996, Carlos Delgado has become Toronto's most dangerous hitter. He didn't face the American League's top lefthanders early in the season, but the club's lack of offense led former manager Cito Gaston to use him on an everyday basis. Delgado's batting average dropped sharply during June and July, but he gained confidence as the year wore on and established career highs in home runs, doubles and slugging percentage.

Hitting

Delgado is a typical lefthanded power hitter in that he loves low, inside fastballs. He has terrific bat speed to go with tremendous upper-body strength, enabling him to hit tape-measure shots. He's still an easy strikeout victim and will swing at most anything when behind in the count. More pitchers have been trying to limit his power by coming inside with hard stuff. He has learned to go the opposite way when lefthanders try to throw fastballs on the outer half, but breaking stuff still vexes him.

Baserunning & Defense

While he runs fairly well once he gets going, Delgado isn't a basestealing threat. He doesn't have a quick first step, which limits his range at first, and he's prone to occasional mental lapses in the field. He shared first base with Joe Carter in 1997, and can't help but improve once he plays in the field every day.

1998 Outlook

Delgado will be the first baseman in Toronto this season. Look for him to move from fifth in the order to the cleanup spot unless the Jays acquire a slugger in the offseason. Look for his production against lefties to improve as he enters his third full year of full-time play. Already an accomplished power hitter at 25, he has an extremely bright future.

Position: 1B/DH
Bats: L **Throws:** R
Ht: 6' 3" **Wt:** 206

Opening Day Age: 25
Born: 6/25/72 in Aguadilla, PR
ML Seasons: 5
Pronunciation: del-GAH-doh

Toronto Blue Jays

Overall Statistics

	G	AB	R	H	D	T	HR	RBI	SB	BB	SO	Avg	OBP	Slg
1997	153	519	79	136	42	3	30	91	0	64	133	.262	.350	.528
Career	373	1229	171	311	75	5	67	218	1	154	344	.253	.342	.486

Where He Hits the Ball

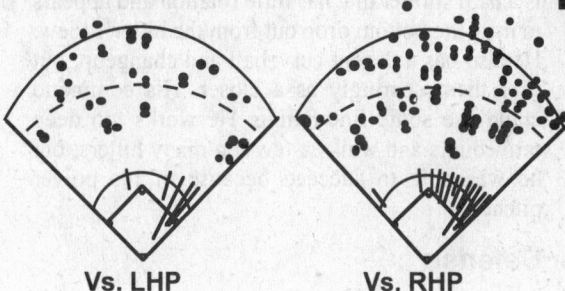

Vs. LHP   Vs. RHP

1997 Situational Stats

	AB	H	HR	RBI	Avg		AB	H	HR	RBI	Avg
Home	258	70	17	52	.271	LHP	134	34	2	16	.254
Road	261	66	13	39	.253	RHP	385	102	28	75	.265
First Half	248	66	16	43	.266	Sc Pos	128	34	10	64	.266
Scnd Half	271	70	14	48	.258	Clutch	89	21	4	14	.236

1997 Rankings (American League)

⇒ 1st in lowest percentage of extra bases taken as a runner (27.1%)
⇒ 2nd in errors at first base (12) and lowest fielding percentage at first base (.988)
⇒ 5th in doubles
⇒ Led the Blue Jays in batting average, home runs, runs scored, doubles, total bases (274), walks, intentional walks (9), times on base (208), strikeouts, pitches seen (2,367), slugging percentage, on-base percentage, HR frequency (17.3 ABs per HR), highest groundball/flyball ratio (0.7), most pitches seen per plate appearance (3.98), batting average vs. righthanded pitchers, cleanup slugging percentage (.500) and slugging percentage vs. righthanded pitchers (.561)

Kelvim Escobar

1997 Season

Seldom have the Blue Jays promoted a pitcher from Double-A Knoxville to Skydome. Kelvim Escobar got his chance because of a shaky closer situation and made the most of his opportunity. He was recalled in late June and pitched well enough to allow the Jays to trade Mike Timlin for outfielder Jose Cruz Jr. A starter in the minors, Escobar converted his first 10 save opportunities and allowed only one run in his first 11 appearances after his call-up.

Pitching

Escobar throws a menacing 96-MPH fastball that busts in on the fists of righthanders. His out pitch is a hard splitter that has little rotation and appears to have the bottom drop out from the hitter's view. He also has a decent curveball and changeup, but uses them sparingly as a closer. His command could use some fine-tuning. He works too deep into counts and walks a few too many hitters, but he was able to succeed because of his power pitches.

Defense

Escobar's concentration is solely on the hitter, which makes him vulnerable to basestealers. Because he throws so hard most of the time and often pitches with a lead, runners still must think twice before taking off. He had limited opportunities to field the ball in 1997, but showed no weakness with his glove or in covering first base in a hurry.

1998 Outlook

After converting 14 of his 17 save opportunities, Escobar showed he's ready to be a big league closer. But the signing of free agent Randy Myers left Escobar's role in doubt. He could be a terrific setup man or become a starter once again. He had arthroscopic elbow surgery last March and showed no ill effects, but the Jays must be careful not to overwork him.

Position: RP
Bats: R **Throws:** R
Ht: 6' 1" **Wt:** 205

Opening Day Age: 21
Born: 4/11/76 in La Guaria, Venezuela
ML Seasons: 1

Overall Statistics

	W	L	Pct.	ERA	G	GS	Sv	IP	H	BB	SO	HR	Ratio
1997	3	2	.600	2.90	27	0	14	31.0	28	19	36	1	1.52
Career	3	2	.600	2.90	27	0	14	31.0	28	19	36	1	1.52

How Often He Throws Strikes

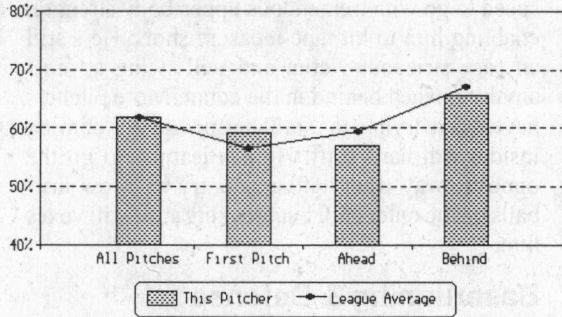

1997 Situational Stats

	W	L	ERA	Sv	IP		AB	H	HR	RBI	Avg
Home	1	0	1.23	8	14.2	LHB	55	12	0	3	.218
Road	2	2	4.41	6	16.1	RHB	63	16	1	8	.254
First Half	2	0	1.08	0	8.1	Sc Pos	34	10	0	9	.294
Scnd Half	1	2	3.57	14	22.2	Clutch	73	20	0	6	.274

1997 Rankings (American League)

⇒ Led the Blue Jays in saves and save opportunities (17)

Carlos Garcia

1997 Season

Perhaps the biggest failure of GM Gord Ash's megatrade with Pittsburgh was second baseman Carlos Garcia. Touted as the man to replace Roberto Alomar, who had left for Baltimore prior to the 1996 season, Garcia reached a season-high .224 average in mid-July after being buried in the .190s for the first two months. He never was able to sustain any consistency at the plate and became despondent over his struggles.

Hitting

Garcia seemed to give up on his swing after the first month of the season. He always had been an impatient contact hitter who managed to avoid striking out too often. However, his swing became so choppy in 1997 that it seemed all he ever did was hit the ball on the ground. As pressure mounted to bring his average up, he walked even less and lost all confidence in letting his swing carry through the zone in normal fashion.

Baserunning & Defense

A nagging calf injury kept Garcia from stealing bases, and his .253 on-base percentage also limited his opportunities. He could be a 20-steal man if he manages to stay healthy and improves his ability to get on base. He was a pleasant surprise in the field, making only eight errors and turning 50 double plays in 96 games. He's not spectacular by any means, but he certainly is dependable.

1998 Outlook

Garcia's dismal season makes second base an ongoing concern for the Blue Jays. While Garcia has another year left on his contract, Mariano Duncan is a free agent. Toronto may have to hold open auditions for the position, as it has for much of the past two seasons, and signed free agents Craig Grebeck and Pat Kelly to minor league contracts. Garcia's confidence needs a major overhaul, and it's not clear that will happen in Toronto. There have always been concerns that he was older than he claimed, and last season did nothing to allay those fears.

Position: 2B
Bats: R **Throws:** R
Ht: 6' 1" **Wt:** 205

Opening Day Age: 30
Born: 10/15/67 in Tachira, VZ
ML Seasons: 8

Toronto Blue Jays

Overall Statistics

	G	AB	R	H	D	T	HR	RBI	SB	BB	SO	Avg	OBP	Slg
1997	103	350	29	77	18	2	3	23	11	15	60	.220	.253	.309
Career	585	2132	269	573	101	17	33	197	71	111	326	.269	.309	.379

Where He Hits the Ball

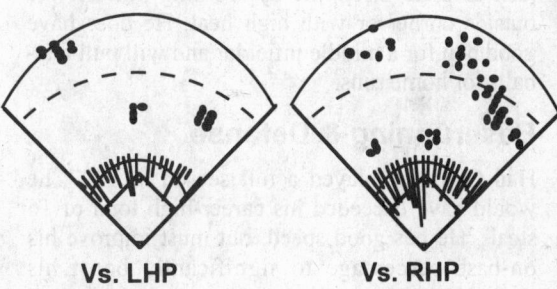

Vs. LHP   **Vs. RHP**

1997 Situational Stats

	AB	H	HR	RBI	Avg		AB	H	HR	RBI	Avg
Home	171	39	0	6	.228	LHP	102	18	1	6	.176
Road	179	38	3	17	.212	RHP	248	59	2	17	.238
First Half	247	53	1	12	.215	Sc Pos	76	11	0	18	.145
Scnd Half	103	24	2	11	.233	Clutch	62	15	1	8	.242

1997 Rankings (American League)

⇒ 8th in sacrifice bunts (10)
⇒ 10th in errors at second base (8)
⇒ Led the Blue Jays in batting average on an 0-2 count (.231)

Alex Gonzalez

1997 Season

After enjoying a productive April, Alex Gonzalez began a steady decline at the plate because of bad habits. He had a hot August after being shifted to the bottom of the order, then fractured his right index finger, taking him out of the lineup until mid-September. He had a sensational year in the field, significantly reducing his errors.

Hitting

Gonzalez isn't selective and chases an inordinate number of pitches outside the strike zone. Because he stands off the plate, he likes the ball inside about knee-high, and consequently has trouble picking up hard sliders on the outer half. Pitchers test his lack of plate discipline by working him off the outside corner or with high heat. He does have good pop for a middle infielder and will pull fastballs for home runs.

Baserunning & Defense

Had Gonzalez played a full season in 1997, he would have exceeded his career-high total of 16 steals. He has good speed, but must improve his on-base percentage to significantly boost his thefts. His range and strong arm are major league caliber, but up until last season he was somewhat error-prone. He made just eight errors in 1997 to post the best fielding percentage at shortstop in the majors.

1998 Outlook

Gonzalez fits in well with Toronto's plan to get younger. His defensive prowess at a demanding position should assure him a lengthy career. Scouts believe he's capable of much more with the bat. His bat has been stuck in neutral for three years, but may be able to make strides under new manager Tim Johnson. Left alone at the bottom of the order, he'll continue his schooling in taking more pitches and getting on base more often.

Position: SS
Bats: R **Throws:** R
Ht: 6' 0" **Wt:** 182

Opening Day Age: 24
Born: 4/8/73 in Miami, FL
ML Seasons: 4

Overall Statistics

	G	AB	R	H	D	T	HR	RBI	SB	BB	SO	Avg	OBP	Slg
1997	126	426	46	102	23	2	12	35	15	34	94	.239	.302	.387
Career	399	1373	168	323	75	12	36	142	38	127	352	.235	.304	.386

Where He Hits the Ball

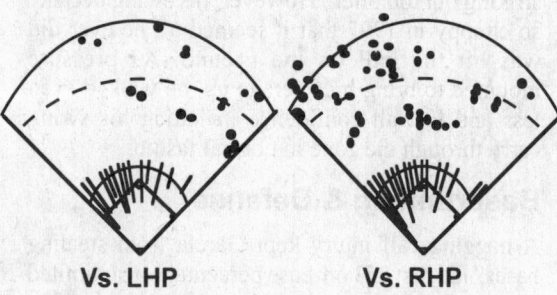

Vs. LHP   **Vs. RHP**

1997 Situational Stats

	AB	H	HR	RBI	Avg		AB	H	HR	RBI	Avg
Home	231	54	4	15	.234	LHP	123	32	3	7	.260
Road	195	48	8	20	.246	RHP	303	70	9	28	.231
First Half	282	68	7	24	.241	Sc Pos	108	21	1	22	.194
Scnd Half	144	34	5	11	.236	Clutch	74	17	4	6	.230

1997 Rankings (American League)

⇒ 1st in batting average on a 3-1 count (1.000) and fielding percentage at shortstop (.986)
⇒ 4th in sacrifice bunts (11) and lowest batting average with runners in scoring position
⇒ 5th in lowest batting average at home
⇒ 9th in lowest batting average with the bases loaded (.100)
⇒ Led the Blue Jays in sacrifice bunts (11) and batting average on a 3-1 count (1.000)

Shawn Green

1997 Season

Shawn Green has been battling the tale of two seasons since he first became a major league regular in 1995. He continually gets off to a slow start, then catches fire by the end of the season. Last year was no exception, except that he proved he is a better ballplayer when given the chance to be in the lineup every day. His .295 batting average after the All-Star break is testimony to that.

Hitting

Green is a spray hitter who likes to wait on the ball and drive it into the gap in left-center. He generates most of his home-run power in that direction as well. He uses his tall, lanky frame to reach out and control the outer portion of the plate, but can be fooled into swinging at inside offspeed pitches in the dirt. He showed up former manager Cito Gaston, who benched him against lefthanders until midseason, by hitting .287 against southpaws, albeit with no home runs.

Baserunning & Defense

Not considered overly quick, Green has enough speed to steal bases and cover decent ground in the outfield. He's an intelligent baserunner who knows when to take advantage. He struggled with errant reads on fly balls early in his career, but now is quite reliable. He also has the best arm among the Blue Jays' corps of young outfielders.

1998 Outlook

Green should be the everyday right fielder in Toronto this season, and will make up one-third of what is sure to be the American League's youngest outfield. Given a full season, he should hit .290 with 20-25 homers. With Gaston gone, Green may finally get the opportunity to do more than just platoon. He likely will move up in the order from the seventh spot, which will translate into better RBI production.

Position: RF/LF/DH
Bats: L **Throws:** L
Ht: 6' 4" **Wt:** 190

Opening Day Age: 25
Born: 11/10/72 in Des Plaines, IL
ML Seasons: 5

Toronto Blue Jays

Overall Statistics

	G	AB	R	H	D	T	HR	RBI	SB	BB	SO	Avg	OBP	Slg
1997	135	429	57	123	22	4	16	53	14	36	99	.287	.340	.469
Career	405	1269	162	353	86	11	42	153	21	90	251	.278	.330	.463

Where He Hits the Ball

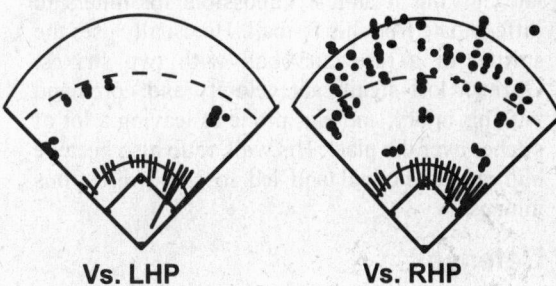

Vs. LHP   **Vs. RHP**

1997 Situational Stats

	AB	H	HR	RBI	Avg		AB	H	HR	RBI	Avg
Home	210	58	10	33	.276	LHP	101	29	0	7	.287
Road	219	65	6	20	.297	RHP	328	94	16	46	.287
First Half	161	44	7	18	.273	Sc Pos	81	23	2	32	.284
Scnd Half	268	79	9	35	.295	Clutch	87	24	7	21	.276

1997 Rankings (American League)

⇒ 1st in lowest batting average with the bases loaded (.000)
⇒ 6th in least GDPs per GDP situation (4.5%)
⇒ Led the Blue Jays in least GDPs per GDP situation (4.5%), batting average with runners in scoring position and batting average with two strikes (.217)

Juan Guzman

1997 Season

Reduced to making just 13 starts, Juan Guzman made two trips to the disabled list in 1997. He had a fractured thumb from which he was able to recover, and then a torn labrum in his shoulder that eventually shelved him for the rest of the year. He was never on target from the very start of the season because of shoulder soreness that inhibited his delivery to the plate.

Pitching

Guzman relies primarily on a fastball, slider and splitter sequence to gain control over the hitters he faces. When healthy, he'll routinely hit 94 MPH on his two-seam fastball. His slider bites hard and late, making it almost impossible for hitters to differentiate from his fastball. He usually uses the splitter or a rare curveball with two strikes. Guzman lost significant velocity and command with his injury, and was prone to leaving a lot of pitches over the plate. His walk ratio also became higher than normal and led to some disastrous innings.

Defense

Lacking an adequate move to first base, Guzman is easy prey for basestealers, who went 12-for-13 against him in 1997. He doesn't maneuver very well coming off the mound, causing him to make errant throws.

1998 Outlook

Guzman underwent shoulder surgery in September and will spend most of the winter in rehab. The prognosis is that he should be ready to go by spring training. Because the surgery was late in the year, it may take him some time to return to 1996 form. The Jays have a lot riding on him because he's one of the best No. 3 starters in baseball. His absence in 1997 hurt deeply. He showed flashes of his old form on several occasions last year, so he's certainly capable of an effective season if healthy.

Position: SP
Bats: R **Throws:** R
Ht: 5'11" **Wt:** 195

Opening Day Age: 31
Born: 10/28/66 in Santo Domingo, DR
ML Seasons: 7
Pronunciation: GOOZ-man

Overall Statistics

	W	L	Pct.	ERA	G	GS	Sv	IP	H	BB	SO	HR	Ratio
1997	3	6	.333	4.95	13	13	0	60.0	48	31	52	14	1.32
Career	70	50	.583	4.03	173	173	0	1070.2	966	481	917	96	1.35

How Often He Throws Strikes

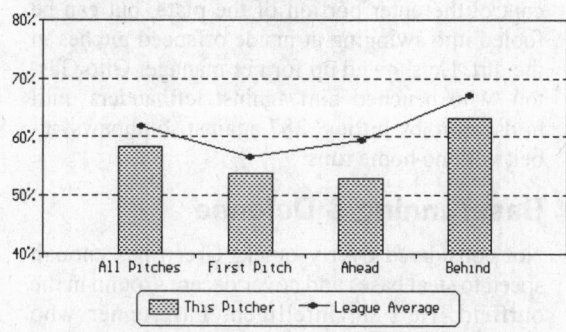

1997 Situational Stats

	W	L	ERA	Sv	IP		AB	H	HR	RBI	Avg
Home	1	3	3.77	0	31.0	LHB	116	25	4	13	.216
Road	2	3	6.21	0	29.0	RHB	109	23	10	24	.211
First Half	3	5	4.13	0	52.1	Sc Pos	51	13	4	24	.255
Scnd Half	0	1	10.57	0	7.2	Clutch	12	2	0	0	.167

1997 Rankings (American League)

⇒ 10th in errors at pitcher (3)
⇒ Led the Blue Jays in stolen bases allowed (12)

Pat Hentgen

1997 Season

While Pat Hentgen didn't produce another Cy Young Award season in 1997, he remained the American League's most durable starter with nine complete games and 264 innings. He led the AL in both categories for the second straight year and continued his string of 156 straight starts without missing his spot in the rotation. On the downside, he did surrender a career-high 31 homers in 1997.

Pitching

Hentgen is known for his superb cut fastball, which bores in on lefthanded hitters at 92 MPH. It nullifies the advantage lefty batters usually have against righty pitchers, which is why Hentgen's numbers in these matchups are better than most. He also throws a rising four-seam fastball at 94 MPH, and uses a big curve and changeup mostly against righties. He does have a tendency to pitch high in the strike zone, which makes him susceptible to homers. He has good control, but his command lacked the precision it had in 1996.

Defense

A good athlete, Hentgen is an adept fielder who's very mobile coming off the mound to charge bunts and slow rollers. He's composed and gets to first base in a hurry. Basestealers are thrown out more often than not against Hentgen because of his velocity and slide-step delivery.

1998 Outlook

Hentgen set a high standard for himself by winning the 1996 AL Cy Young Award and held the mantle as the team's No. 1 starter even though Roger Clemens came aboard. He wasn't far off from his glory year in most areas, and he and Clemens should be the AL's top starter tandem once again. With a better team behind him, Hentgen may return to the 20-win range.

Position: SP
Bats: R **Throws:** R
Ht: 6' 2" **Wt:** 200

Opening Day Age: 29
Born: 11/13/68 in Detroit, MI
ML Seasons: 7

Toronto Blue Jays

Overall Statistics

	W	L	Pct.	ERA	G	GS	Sv	IP	H	BB	SO	HR	Ratio
1997	15	10	.600	3.68	35	35	0	264.0	253	71	160	31	1.23
Career	82	53	.607	3.88	189	159	0	1179.0	1154	423	783	131	1.34

How Often He Throws Strikes

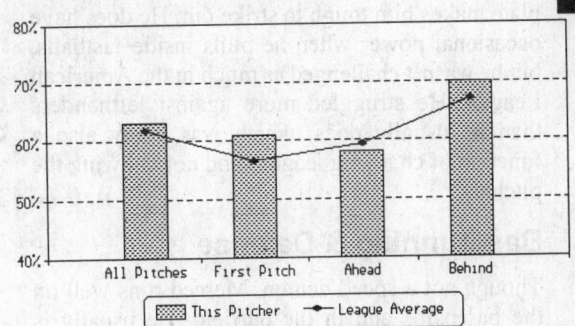

1997 Situational Stats

	W	L	ERA	Sv	IP		AB	H	HR	RBI	Avg
Home	8	5	3.33	0	135.0	LHB	511	123	14	58	.241
Road	7	5	4.05	0	129.0	RHB	484	130	17	49	.269
First Half	8	6	3.27	0	151.1	Sc Pos	188	55	10	79	.293
Scnd Half	7	4	4.23	0	112.2	Clutch	130	43	8	20	.331

1997 Rankings (American League)

⇒ 1st in games started, complete games (9), shutouts (3), innings pitched and batters faced (1,085)
⇒ 2nd in hits allowed and pitches thrown (3,914)
⇒ 3rd in runners caught stealing (15)
⇒ 4th in lowest stolen base percentage allowed (44.4%)
⇒ 5th in home runs allowed, balks (2) and lowest batting average allowed vs. lefthanded batters
⇒ Led the Blue Jays in games started, complete games (9), shutouts (3), innings pitched, hits allowed, batters faced (1,085), home runs allowed, walks allowed, balks (2), pickoff throws (157), stolen bases allowed (12), runners caught stealing (15) and lowest stolen base percentage allowed (44.4%)

Orlando Merced

1997 Season

After batting .283 in seven seasons in Pittsburgh, Orlando Merced was sent to Toronto in a nine-player trade. He was expected to supply the Blue Jays with some much-needed offense as the every-day right fielder, but was slow to come around and was effective only in June. He eventually fell victim to a torn labrum in his right shoulder, which led to season-ending arthroscopic surgery in mid-August.

Hitting

Merced is a line-drive hitter who likes using the opposite field. He keeps his head down throughout his level swing, and his good concentration at the plate makes him tough to strike out. He does have occasional power when he pulls inside fastballs, but he wasn't challenged as much in the American League. He struggled more against lefthanders than he usually does, which was likely also a function of changing leagues and not knowing the pitchers.

Baserunning & Defense

Though not a speed demon, Merced runs well on the basepaths and in the outfield. He usually is successful in his limited stolen-base attempts, and he can be counted on to score from second base on most hits. While he sometimes shows awkwardness with his glove, his aggressive and accurate arm notches him quite a few assists.

1998 Outlook

Merced is now a free agent. With the Blue Jays changing direction in favor of a more youthful outfield, his days in Toronto are probably over. He's likely to sign with a National League team, and is young enough to return to his previous form. It shouldn't be hard for him to find a team that could use a proven run-producer who bats from the left side.

Position: RF
Bats: L **Throws:** R
Ht: 5'11" **Wt:** 183

Opening Day Age: 31
Born: 11/2/66 in San Juan, PR
ML Seasons: 8
Pronunciation: mer-SED

Overall Statistics

	G	AB	R	H	D	T	HR	RBI	SB	BB	SO	Avg	OBP	Slg
1997	98	368	45	98	23	2	9	40	7	47	62	.266	.352	.413
Career	874	2981	441	837	169	21	74	434	42	386	485	.281	.363	.426

Where He Hits the Ball

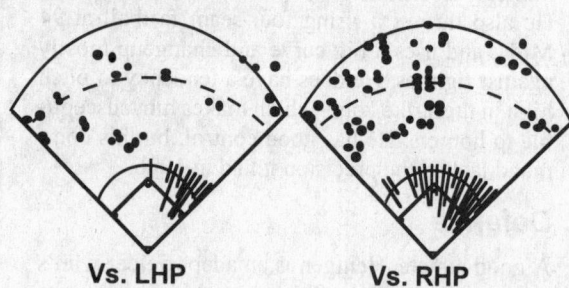

Vs. LHP   **Vs. RHP**

1997 Situational Stats

	AB	H	HR	RBI	Avg		AB	H	HR	RBI	Avg
Home	192	59	3	22	.307	LHP	121	27	4	18	.223
Road	176	39	6	18	.222	RHP	247	71	5	22	.287
First Half	309	87	8	36	.282	Sc Pos	88	18	0	25	.205
Scnd Half	59	11	1	4	.186	Clutch	57	12	0	4	.211

1997 Rankings (American League)

⇒ 6th in lowest batting average with runners in scoring position
⇒ 7th in lowest batting average vs. lefthanded pitchers
⇒ Led the Blue Jays in highest percentage of pitches taken (59.4%)

Benito Santiago

1997 Season

Signed by Toronto as a free agent after hitting a career-high 30 home runs with the Phillies in 1996, Benito Santiago was overwhelmed by the expectations of his new employers. He found changing leagues and getting a read on new pitchers extremely difficult, and hit just .197 with three homers prior to the All-Star break. He improved in the second half, but by then he had been labeled an underachiever.

Hitting

Santiago is a notorious first-pitch swinger who employs a wide-open stance deep and away in the batter's box. His strategy is to keep his front shoulder closed while he brings his front leg toward the plate as he swings. Without good strike-zone judgment, however, his approach usually doesn't breed success. He does have straightaway power when he catches a belt-high fastball, but he invites a lot of outside sliders with his mechanics and location in the box. He also has trouble reaching them.

Baserunning & Defense

Despite a few benchings because of his hitting, Santiago caught the majority of games. He still can throw out runners from his knees on occasion, but his quickness in getting up to make throws has waned over the years. He still threw out nearly 40 percent of basestealers and made only two errors in 1997. He also works well with pitchers and calls a good game. He used to be fast on the basepaths but rarely will attempt to steal any longer.

1998 Outlook

The good news for Santiago is that he has another year remaining on his contract. Also, his .297 average and 10 homers after the All-Star break have the Blue Jays hoping he'll be the player they thought they were getting when they signed him. He'll have to battle free-agent signee Darrin Fletcher for playing time.

Position: C
Bats: R **Throws:** R
Ht: 6' 1" **Wt:** 185

Opening Day Age: 33
Born: 3/9/65 in Ponce, PR
ML Seasons: 12
Pronunciation: sahn-tee-AH-go

Toronto Blue Jays

Overall Statistics

	G	AB	R	H	D	T	HR	RBI	SB	BB	SO	Avg	OBP	Slg
1997	97	341	31	83	10	0	13	42	1	17	80	.243	.279	.387
Career	1343	4766	538	1244	208	25	163	637	78	291	893	.261	.304	.418

Where He Hits the Ball

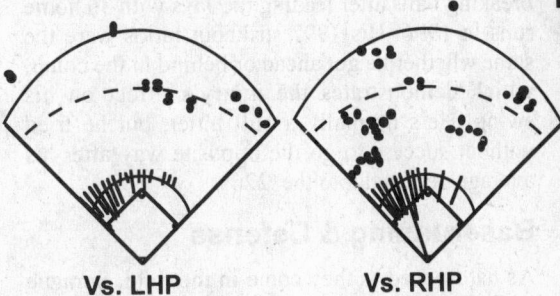

Vs. LHP   **Vs. RHP**

1997 Situational Stats

	AB	H	HR	RBI	Avg		AB	H	HR	RBI	Avg
Home	184	48	7	27	.261	LHP	93	28	6	16	.301
Road	157	35	6	15	.223	RHP	248	55	7	26	.222
First Half	183	36	3	17	.197	Sc Pos	88	18	5	32	.205
Scnd Half	158	47	10	25	.297	Clutch	52	9	4	7	.173

1997 Rankings (American League)

⇒ 1st in fielding percentage at catcher (.997)
⇒ 2nd in lowest batting average in the clutch
⇒ 7th in lowest batting average with runners in scoring position
⇒ 8th in lowest batting average on a 3-2 count (.097)

Ed Sprague

1997 Season

After swinging a hot bat in April, Ed Sprague struggled for the rest of the year. Very few people realized he was playing with an extremely sore shoulder until it finally took him out of the lineup for good in early September. The injury required a visit to the surgeon to repair a torn labrum. After posting career-bests in home runs and RBI in 1996, his production in both departments was cut in half last year.

Hitting

Sprague had difficulty adjusting to more frequent pitch variations than he received in the past. He's a dead-red fastball hitter, but got a steady diet of breaking balls after leading the Jays with 36 home runs in 1996. His 1997 strikeout ratios were the same whether he got ahead or behind in the count, which demonstrates the injury's effect on his swing. He's normally a pull hitter, but he tried without success to go the opposite way after his average declined into the .220s.

Baserunning & Defense

As hard-nosed as they come in the field, Sprague is fearless in positioning himself in front of anything that moves. He'll dive for screeching liners and knock down a majority of would-be doubles down the line. In fact, his penchant for diving led to his shoulder injury. He has a better-than-average glove hand and an accurate arm, but isn't very quick on his feet. Sprague isn't a threat to steal, but he runs hard on every play.

1998 Outlook

Because Sprague decided to play the majority of the season with pain in his shoulder, his statistics are skewed. He's a much more productive player than his numbers would indicate. After successful surgery and a full winter's rest, he should be back to his 1996 form. That means 30 homers and 100 RBI are within reach, and the Blue Jays' anemic attack sorely needs those numbers.

Position: 3B
Bats: R **Throws:** R
Ht: 6' 2" **Wt:** 210

Opening Day Age: 30
Born: 7/25/67 in Castro Valley, CA
ML Seasons: 7
Pronunciation: SPRAYG

Overall Statistics

	G	AB	R	H	D	T	HR	RBI	SB	BB	SO	Avg	OBP	Slg
1997	138	504	63	115	29	4	14	48	0	51	102	.228	.306	.385
Career	783	2774	339	682	150	10	96	367	2	246	574	.246	.317	.411

Where He Hits the Ball

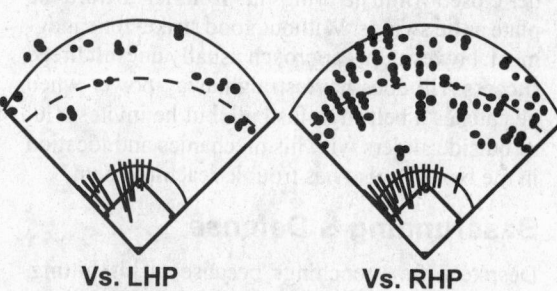

Vs. LHP   **Vs. RHP**

1997 Situational Stats

	AB	H	HR	RBI	Avg		AB	H	HR	RBI	Avg
Home	254	55	5	19	.217	LHP	148	37	7	19	.250
Road	250	60	9	29	.240	RHP	356	78	7	29	.219
First Half	306	72	10	33	.235	Sc Pos	115	20	2	32	.174
Scnd Half	198	43	4	15	.217	Clutch	78	17	1	4	.218

1997 Rankings (American League)

⇒ 2nd in lowest batting average, lowest batting average with runners in scoring position and lowest batting average at home

⇒ 3rd in lowest batting average vs. righthanded pitchers and lowest fielding percentage at third base (.945)

⇒ 4th in lowest slugging percentage vs. righthanded pitchers (.343) and errors at third base (18)

⇒ 6th in lowest groundball/flyball ratio (0.7) and lowest batting average on the road

⇒ 8th in lowest on-base percentage and lowest on-base percentage vs. righthanded pitchers (.297)

⇒ Led the Blue Jays in slugging percentage vs. lefthanded pitchers (.486)

Shannon Stewart

1997 Season

Long considered as Toronto's heir apparent in center field, Shannon Stewart was promoted from Triple-A Syracuse for good in mid-August after Otis Nixon was traded to the Dodgers. Stewart made an immediate impression in the leadoff spot, hitting .295 with a .392 on-base percentage in his first month of regular action. His arrival marked the changing of the guard in the Blue Jay outfield.

Hitting

In the minors, Stewart was an excellent contact hitter with solid strikeout/walk ratios. He continued to show a good eye at the plate for a young player during his short tenure in Toronto. Stewart murders lefthanders and uses his terrific speed to great advantage on grounders. He has extremely quick wrist action in his swing and drives the ball into both gaps. He's adept at keeping his hands in and turning on inside stuff. He lacks home-run power, but he will get extra-base hits.

Baserunning & Defense

With his outstanding speed, Stewart should have no problem stealing 25-30 bases per season. He amassed a club-high seven triples, tying him for fifth in the American League, in just 44 games. He has excellent range in the outfield, but his throwing arm has been questioned so much that it delayed his major league arrival.

1998 Outlook

Stewart is part of a troika of young Toronto outfielders ready for regular duty. With Stewart stationed between Jose Cruz Jr. and Shawn Green, the Blue Jays and their fans will have a lot to look forward to. While Stewart does not possess the power and defensive ability of former Blue Jay Devon White, he'll be a significant upgrade compared to Nixon. With his bat and legs, he should be able to hit for a good average with lots of doubles and triples.

Position: CF
Bats: R **Throws:** R
Ht: 6' 1" **Wt:** 190

Opening Day Age: 24
Born: 2/25/74 in Cincinnati, OH
ML Seasons: 3

Toronto Blue Jays

Overall Statistics

	G	AB	R	H	D	T	HR	RBI	SB	BB	SO	Avg	OBP	Slg
1997	44	168	25	48	13	7	0	22	10	19	24	.286	.368	.446
Career	63	223	29	59	14	7	0	25	13	25	33	.265	.349	.390

Where He Hits the Ball

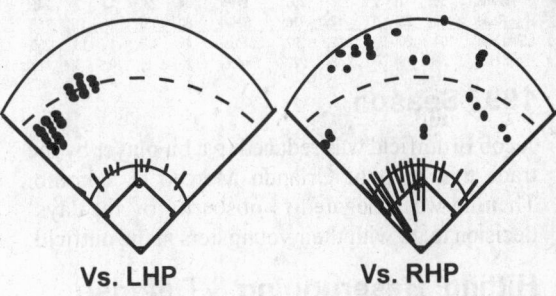

Vs. LHP   **Vs. RHP**

1997 Situational Stats

	AB	H	HR	RBI	Avg		AB	H	HR	RBI	Avg
Home	78	21	0	10	.269	LHP	35	12	0	3	.343
Road	90	27	0	12	.300	RHP	133	36	0	19	.271
First Half	1	0	0	0	.000	Sc Pos	40	14	0	20	.350
Scnd Half	167	48	0	22	.287	Clutch	28	9	0	5	.321

1997 Rankings (American League)

⇒ 4th in batting average on a 3-2 count (.400)
⇒ 5th in triples
⇒ 6th in on-base percentage for a leadoff hitter (.370)
⇒ Led the Blue Jays in triples, on-base percentage for a leadoff hitter (.370) and batting average on a 3-2 count (.400)

Jacob Brumfield

Position: CF/LF
Bats: R **Throws:** R
Ht: 6' 0" **Wt:** 185

Opening Day Age: 32
Born: 5/27/65 in Bogalusa, LA
ML Seasons: 6

Overall Statistics

	G	AB	R	H	D	T	HR	RBI	SB	BB	SO	Avg	OBP	Slg
1997	58	174	22	36	5	1	2	20	4	14	31	.207	.268	.282
Career	488	1388	231	359	83	10	30	142	73	118	246	.259	.320	.398

1997 Situational Stats

	AB	H	HR	RBI	Avg		AB	H	HR	RBI	Avg
Home	55	11	1	8	.200	LHP	94	23	1	9	.245
Road	119	25	1	12	.210	RHP	80	13	1	11	.163
First Half	104	20	1	12	.192	Sc Pos	48	12	1	18	.250
Scnd Half	70	16	1	8	.229	Clutch	29	5	0	3	.172

1997 Season

Jacob Brumfield was reduced to a bit player by the trade that brought Orlando Merced to Toronto. Then he was relegated to obscurity by the Jays' decision to go with their youngsters in the outfield.

Hitting, Baserunning & Defense

Brumfield showed some pop while getting regular duty in 1996. As a seldom-used bench player in 1997, he was too eager to prove himself and fared poorly. He has a lot of difficulty with righthanders pitching him away. He has good speed and is used often in pinch-running situations. Except for an average arm, he has good defensive tools and covers a lot of ground with a reliable glove.

1998 Outlook

Brumfield's future in Toronto has gotten bleaker since the arrival of Jose Cruz Jr. and Shannon Stewart. At best he would be retained as a fifth outfielder, but he's likely to be cast aside as Toronto begins to cut costs. He's getting up in age, but another team may be willing to give him a shot on the strength of his past performance.

Chris Carpenter

Position: SP
Bats: R **Throws:** R
Ht: 6' 6" **Wt:** 215

Opening Day Age: 22
Born: 4/27/75 in Exeter, NH
ML Seasons: 1

Overall Statistics

	W	L	Pct.	ERA	G	GS	Sv	IP	H	BB	SO	HR	Ratio
1997	3	7	.300	5.09	14	13	0	81.1	108	37	55	7	1.78
Career	3	7	.300	5.09	14	13	0	81.1	108	37	55	7	1.78

1997 Situational Stats

	W	L	ERA	Sv	IP		AB	H	HR	RBI	Avg
Home	2	4	4.22	0	42.2	LHB	172	54	4	25	.314
Road	1	3	6.05	0	38.2	RHB	160	54	3	18	.338
First Half	0	2	12.71	0	11.1	Sc Pos	88	27	2	32	.307
Scnd Half	3	5	3.86	0	70.0	Clutch	27	7	0	3	.259

1997 Season

Chris Carpenter has been Toronto's top pitching prospect since the day he was drafted in the first round in 1993. His statistics don't tell the story of the progress he made in 1997. Despite a losing record and high ERA, Carpenter went 2-1, 1.87 in his final five starts.

Pitching & Defense

After getting pummeled in his first eight starts, Carpenter started showing signs of a successful major league pitcher. He began changing speeds with both his two-seam and four-seam fastballs, instead of just airing them out at 94 MPH. He works his cutter in on lefthanders, while his two-seamer rides away from them. A sharp-breaking curveball and a well-hidden changeup are his primary weapons against righties. Despite a high leg kick, he's a decent fielder and surrendered only four steals in 11 attempts in 1997.

1998 Outlook

Carpenter is loaded with potential. He's sure to be in the rotation at the outset as either the fourth or fifth starter, depending on whether the Jays retain Erik Hanson.

Tim Crabtree

Position: RP
Bats: R **Throws:** R
Ht: 6' 4" **Wt:** 195

Opening Day Age: 28
Born: 10/13/69 in
Jackson, MI
ML Seasons: 3

Overall Statistics

	W	L	Pct.	ERA	G	GS	Sv	IP	H	BB	SO	HR	Ratio
1997	3	3	.500	7.08	37	0	2	40.2	65	17	26	7	2.02
Career	8	8	.500	3.99	121	0	3	140.0	154	52	104	12	1.47

1997 Situational Stats

	W	L	ERA	Sv	IP		AB	H	HR	RBI	Avg
Home	2	1	9.00	1	15.0	LHB	78	27	4	19	.346
Road	1	2	5.96	1	25.2	RHB	96	38	3	13	.396
First Half	2	2	8.46	2	22.1	Sc Pos	53	19	1	23	.358
Scnd Half	1	1	5.40	0	18.1	Clutch	65	22	1	5	.338

1997 Season

Another date with the arthroscopic surgeon prevented Tim Crabtree from making a meaningful contribution in 1997. He has been bothered by floating bone chips in his pitching elbow for the last two years, and he spent two months on the disabled list last season.

Pitching & Defense

When healthy, Crabtree has two effective pitches. He has a sinking fastball in the low 90s and a hard slider that make him a tough groundball pitcher. He wasn't able to deliver these pitches with any authority in 1997 because of his elbow problems. He has no special moves to keep runners close, but he's a very good fielder with good mobility.

1998 Outlook

Though ineffective before coming off the disabled list in early August, Crabtree is counted on to come back as part of the righthanded portion of Toronto's setup crew. He should be healthy after a full winter of rest. After pitching so effectively in '96, the Blue Jays believe he can return to form once his arm is fully recovered.

Mariano Duncan

Position: 2B
Bats: R **Throws:** R
Ht: 6' 0" **Wt:** 185

Opening Day Age: 35
Born: 3/13/63 in San
Pedro de Macoris, DR
ML Seasons: 12

Overall Statistics

	G	AB	R	H	D	T	HR	RBI	SB	BB	SO	Avg	OBP	Slg
1997	89	339	36	80	14	0	1	25	6	12	78	.236	.268	.286
Career	1279	4677	619	1247	233	37	87	491	174	201	913	.267	.300	.388

1997 Situational Stats

	AB	H	HR	RBI	Avg		AB	H	HR	RBI	Avg
Home	143	32	1	9	.224	LHP	102	23	0	12	.225
Road	196	48	0	16	.245	RHP	237	57	1	13	.241
First Half	158	39	1	11	.247	Sc Pos	99	28	0	24	.283
Scnd Half	181	41	0	14	.227	Clutch	54	10	0	3	.185

1997 Season

After falling out of favor with the Yankees, Mariano Duncan was traded to Toronto in July and immediately took over at second base in place of the struggling Carlos Garcia. Despite Duncan's elation at getting out of New York, he didn't fare much better with the Blue Jays, hitting just .228.

Hitting, Baserunning & Defense

A frequent strikeout victim, Duncan is an impatient free swinger who seldom takes a walk and has trouble picking up the breaking ball. When he does make contact, he usually will drive the ball into the gap in right-center. Duncan's basestealing days are long over. He now has below-average range in the field, but is relatively surehanded and pivots well on the double play.

1998 Outlook

Duncan is a free agent not likely to be re-signed by the Blue Jays unless they give up on Garcia. It's to his benefit, though, that there's little depth in the farm system at second base. His versatility and pop at the plate should earn him a utility role somewhere.

Erik Hanson

Position: SP
Bats: R **Throws:** R
Ht: 6' 6" **Wt:** 215

Opening Day Age: 32
Born: 5/18/65 in Kinnelon, NJ
ML Seasons: 10

Overall Statistics

	W	L	Pct.	ERA	G	GS	Sv	IP	H	BB	SO	HR	Ratio
1997	0	0	-	7.80	3	2	0	15.0	15	6	18	3	1.40
Career	89	81	.524	4.08	234	230	0	1506.1	1531	475	1154	129	1.33

1997 Situational Stats

	W	L	ERA	Sv	IP		AB	H	HR	RBI	Avg
Home	0	0	7.20	0	5.0	LHB	29	7	1	7	.241
Road	0	0	8.10	0	10.0	RHB	30	8	2	5	.267
First Half	0	0	7.50	0	12.0	Sc Pos	13	6	2	11	.462
Scnd Half	0	0	9.00	0	3.0	Clutch	4	1	1	1	.250

1997 Season

The medical reports just kept getting worse for Erik Hanson last season. What first was thought to be a mild case of shoulder tendinitis during spring training later was discovered to be a torn labrum. Rotator-cuff surgery eventually sidelined him for the majority of the season.

Pitching & Defense

Hanson's forte is a big breaking curveball with a huge downward bend. He also throws a sharp slider and an 89-MPH fastball. He must find the plate with his curve early in the game to be effective. Otherwise, hitters gain confidence and jump on his fastball. He holds runners well with a good move to first and a slide-step delivery to the plate. He's a good athlete who's agile on the mound.

1998 Outlook

The Blue Jays, concerned whether Hanson will be the pitcher he was for Boston two years ago, may try to move him. It's never easy to trade a pitcher coming off surgery, so spring training will determine his market value as well as his future. Keep one thing in mind, though: his best years have all followed seasons in which he didn't pitch many innings. He may surprise.

Charlie O'Brien

Position: C
Bats: R **Throws:** R
Ht: 6' 2" **Wt:** 205

Opening Day Age: 36
Born: 5/1/61 in Tulsa, OK
ML Seasons: 12

Overall Statistics

	G	AB	R	H	D	T	HR	RBI	SB	BB	SO	Avg	OBP	Slg
1997	69	225	22	49	15	1	4	27	0	22	45	.218	.311	.347
Career	702	1976	199	438	109	4	50	237	1	196	302	.222	.308	.357

1997 Situational Stats

	AB	H	HR	RBI	Avg		AB	H	HR	RBI	Avg
Home	97	23	2	9	.237	LHP	75	20	2	10	.267
Road	128	26	2	18	.203	RHP	150	29	2	17	.193
First Half	111	27	3	21	.243	Sc Pos	51	12	2	22	.235
Scnd Half	114	22	1	6	.193	Clutch	46	9	3	11	.196

1997 Season

After undergoing offseason knee surgery, Charlie O'Brien found himself displaced as Toronto's No. 1 backstop after the free-agent signing of Benito Santiago. O'Brien was relegated to serving as Roger Clemens' primary catcher and filling in occasionally when a slumping Santiago became too much of a liability.

Hitting, Baserunning & Defense

O'Brien always has been known as a weak hitter. He has a little bit of power and will draw some walks, but that's not enough to make up for his .222 career average. He's not an adept baserunner either. What makes him useful is that he's a good defensive catcher who calls a good game.

1998 Outlook

The signing of Darrin Fletcher meant that O'Brien, a free agent, won't return to the Blue Jays. However, he has earned a good reputation by catching a Cy Young Award winner in each of the last four seasons, with Clemens his most recent. As a result, he should pick up a backup job somewhere.

Robert Person

Position: SP
Bats: R **Throws:** R
Ht: 6' 0" **Wt:** 185

Opening Day Age: 28
Born: 10/6/69 in St. Louis, MO
ML Seasons: 3

Overall Statistics

	W	L	Pct.	ERA	G	GS	Sv	IP	H	BB	SO	HR	Ratio
1997	5	10	.333	5.61	23	22	0	128.1	125	60	99	19	1.44
Career	10	15	.400	4.93	53	36	0	230.0	216	97	185	36	1.36

1997 Situational Stats

	W	L	ERA	Sv	IP		AB	H	HR	RBI	Avg
Home	2	5	4.54	0	69.1	LHB	251	61	11	35	.243
Road	3	5	6.86	0	59.0	RHB	240	64	8	38	.267
First Half	3	5	4.80	0	65.2	Sc Pos	107	33	4	52	.308
Scnd Half	2	5	6.46	0	62.2	Clutch	45	18	0	6	.400

1997 Season

Acquired from the Mets for John Olerud, Robert Person wound up in the rotation after Juan Guzman and Erik Hanson went down with injuries. Person's lack of control led to an inconsistent 1997 performance.

Pitching & Defense

Person reminds many scouts of Tom Gordon because of his small stature and over-the-top delivery. He doesn't have Gordon's curveball, but his fastball does pop the mitt at 91 MPH and he also throws a tight slider. Command has been his nemesis, and he throws too many hittable fastballs when behind in the count. He's an average fielder with good quickness off the mound, and he has a conventional move to first base that keeps runners honest.

1998 Outlook

With Toronto's rotation expected to be in good health, Person likely will be used in a long-relief role. He'll need to improve his control to keep a regular job in the majors. If he's able to do that, he has good enough stuff to be a quality pitcher.

Dan Plesac

Position: RP
Bats: L **Throws:** L
Ht: 6' 5" **Wt:** 215

Opening Day Age: 36
Born: 2/4/62 in Gary, IN
ML Seasons: 12
Pronunciation: PLEE-sack

Overall Statistics

	W	L	Pct.	ERA	G	GS	Sv	IP	H	BB	SO	HR	Ratio
1997	2	4	.333	3.58	73	0	1	50.1	47	19	61	8	1.31
Career	45	54	.455	3.54	680	14	149	822.2	762	290	742	77	1.28

1997 Situational Stats

	W	L	ERA	Sv	IP		AB	H	HR	RBI	Avg
Home	2	3	5.14	0	21.0	LHB	95	19	4	15	.200
Road	0	1	2.45	0	29.1	RHB	98	28	4	13	.286
First Half	0	3	4.44	1	24.1	Sc Pos	56	13	2	19	.232
Scnd Half	2	1	2.77	0	26.0	Clutch	128	37	6	22	.289

1997 Season

Brought to Toronto as part of the nine-player swap with the Pirates in the 1996-97 offseason, Dan Plesac set a new club record for lefthanders with 73 appearances. Used primarily as a setup man, Plesac posted a 2.77 ERA after the All-Star break.

Pitching & Defense

Plesac is tough on lefthanded hitters, relying on a hard-biting slider as his out pitch. He also throws a two-seam fastball in the low 90s, and an occasional curve and changeup for effect. While he has a decent stepoff move to first, his long delivery makes him a basestealing target. He makes few mistakes with his glove, but isn't quick to first base.

1998 Outlook

Plesac performed well in his first season with the Blue Jays, and Paul Spoljaric's departure to Seattle made him the only viable southpaw in the bullpen. Despite his age, Plesac should continue to succeed in a specialty role that requires few pitches. The Blue Jays can use his veteran's presence in their young bullpen.

Paul Quantrill (Surprise)

Position: RP
Bats: L **Throws:** R
Ht: 6' 1" **Wt:** 185

Opening Day Age: 29
Born: 11/3/68 in London, Ontario, Canada
ML Seasons: 6
Pronunciation: KWON-trill

Overall Statistics

	W	L	Pct.	ERA	G	GS	Sv	IP	H	BB	SO	HR	Ratio
1997	6	7	.462	1.94	77	0	5	88.0	103	17	56	5	1.36
Career	33	51	.393	4.12	259	64	8	642.0	757	186	363	73	1.47

1997 Situational Stats

	W	L	ERA	Sv	IP		AB	H	HR	RBI	Avg
Home	5	2	1.80	2	45.0	LHB	130	41	3	12	.315
Road	1	5	2.09	3	43.0	RHB	217	62	2	18	.286
First Half	4	2	1.64	4	44.0	Sc Pos	108	19	3	28	.176
Scnd Half	2	5	2.25	1	44.0	Clutch	191	62	4	17	.325

1997 Season

1997 was a breakthrough year for Paul Quantrill, who made 77 appearances, the most ever by a Canadian-born pitcher, and posted a career-best 1.94 ERA. He became one of the best setup men in the American League, showing a consistent ability to get men out with runners in scoring position.

Pitching & Defense

Quantrill relies on three pitches. He has a two-seam fastball with good sink, a 92-MPH offering that generates groundouts. He also throws a good slider and changeup to righthanders. He has a tendency to let up against hitters with the bases empty, but he bears down with men on base, allowing just a .201 average in 1997. He is somewhat erratic in the field, and has an average pickoff move.

1998 Outlook

Quantrill's emergence enabled the Blue Jays to trade away Mike Timlin and Paul Spoljaric to get Jose Cruz Jr. Look for Quantrill again to be Toronto's primary righthanded setup man. It will be a major upset if he comes close to posting a sub-2.00 ERA again, but he should remain a useful pitcher.

Woody Williams

Position: SP
Bats: R **Throws:** R
Ht: 6' 0" **Wt:** 190

Opening Day Age: 31
Born: 8/19/66 in Houston, TX
ML Seasons: 5

Overall Statistics

	W	L	Pct.	ERA	G	GS	Sv	IP	H	BB	SO	HR	Ratio
1997	9	14	.391	4.35	31	31	0	194.2	201	66	124	31	1.37
Career	18	25	.419	4.21	134	44	0	403.2	393	170	288	52	1.39

1997 Situational Stats

	W	L	ERA	Sv	IP		AB	H	HR	RBI	Avg
Home	5	8	4.14	0	111.0	LHB	395	107	15	42	.271
Road	4	6	4.63	0	83.2	RHB	353	94	16	47	.266
First Half	3	8	4.59	0	100.0	Sc Pos	166	42	3	55	.253
Scnd Half	6	6	4.09	0	94.2	Clutch	46	14	2	7	.304

1997 Season

Toronto's No. 3 starter after injuries to Juan Guzman and Erik Hanson, Woody Williams had the distinction of receiving the worst run support of any American League starter. The Jays averaged just 3.19 runs during his appearances.

Pitching & Defense

Williams abandoned the use of a splitter he developed in 1996, staying with a standard package with a fastball, slider, curve and changeup. He barely breaks 90 MPH with the fastball, but he does generate good movement. He's prone to mistakes, leading to high home-run totals. He's successful at holding runners, allowing just eight stolen bases in 17 attempts in 1997, and he fields his position well.

1998 Outlook

Williams pitched much better than his 9-14 record would indicate. But if Guzman and Hanson return, Williams will be fighting it out with Chris Carpenter for the final spot in the rotation. He could easily post a better record with better run support.

Other Toronto Blue Jays

Luis Andujar (Pos: RHP, Age: 25)

	W	L	Pct.	ERA	G	GS	Sv	IP	H	BB	SO	HR	Ratio
1997	0	6	.000	6.48	17	8	0	50.0	76	21	28	9	1.94
Career	3	10	.231	5.81	30	20	0	117.2	148	51	48	21	1.69

Andujar rose through the minors as a control pitcher, but has been hit hard in Triple-A and the majors. He had September surgery to remove bone chips in his elbow. 1998 Outlook: C

Huck Flener (Pos: LHP, Age: 29)

	W	L	Pct.	ERA	G	GS	Sv	IP	H	BB	SO	HR	Ratio
1997	0	1	.000	9.87	8	1	0	17.1	40	6	9	3	2.65
Career	3	3	.500	5.51	29	12	0	94.2	115	43	55	12	1.67

It's not a good sign when you're flying to spring training and you chip a collarbone when a briefcase falls out of an overhead compartment. Flener was designated for assignment in July. 1998 Outlook: C

Sandy Martinez (Pos: C, Age: 25, Bats: L)

	G	AB	R	H	D	T	HR	RBI	SB	BB	SO	Avg	OBP	Slg
1997	3	2	1	0	0	0	0	0	0	1	1	.000	.333	.000
Career	141	422	30	98	21	3	5	43	0	24	104	.232	.280	.332

Martinez once was Toronto's catcher of the future, but he can't match Benito Santiago's offense or Charlie O'Brien's defense. His future is probably as a backup, and may be elsewhere. 1998 Outlook: C

Julio Mosquera (Pos: C, Age: 26, Bats: R)

	G	AB	R	H	D	T	HR	RBI	SB	BB	SO	Avg	OBP	Slg
1997	3	8	0	2	1	0	0	0	0	0	2	.250	.250	.375
Career	11	30	2	7	3	0	0	2	0	0	5	.233	.258	.333

Always considered a strong defensive catcher, Mosquera has been getting better with the bat. He doesn't draw a lot of walks, but he hits for a decent average and has doubles power. 1998 Outlook: B

Robert Perez (Pos: LF, Age: 28, Bats: R)

	G	AB	R	H	D	T	HR	RBI	SB	BB	SO	Avg	OBP	Slg
1997	37	78	4	15	4	1	2	6	0	0	16	.192	.192	.346
Career	144	336	36	91	16	1	5	30	3	8	39	.271	.289	.369

Former Florida State and International League batting champ Perez has yet to win a regular job in the majors. After hitting .327 as a semi-regular in 1996, he rotted on the bench in 1997. We guess he won't miss former manager Cito Gaston. 1998 Outlook: C

Tomas Perez (Pos: SS, Age: 24, Bats: B)

	G	AB	R	H	D	T	HR	RBI	SB	BB	SO	Avg	OBP	Slg
1997	40	123	9	24	3	2	0	9	1	11	28	.195	.267	.252
Career	172	516	45	122	19	7	2	36	2	43	75	.236	.297	.312

Perez still could claim the second-base job, as his upside is greater than that of Mariano Duncan or Carlos Garcia. His forte is defense, but he may not hit enough to be a regular for long. 1998 Outlook: B

Bill Risley (Pos: RHP, Age: 30)

	W	L	Pct.	ERA	G	GS	Sv	IP	H	BB	SO	HR	Ratio
1997	0	1	.000	8.31	3	0	0	4.1	3	2	2	2	1.15
Career	12	9	.571	3.56	113	1	1	166.2	128	67	161	24	1.17

1997 marked the fifth time in six years that Risley visited the disabled list. A torn rotator cuff kept him out until late September. When healthy, he's an above-average setup man. 1998 Outlook: B

Ken Robinson (Pos: RHP, Age: 28)

	W	L	Pct.	ERA	G	GS	Sv	IP	H	BB	SO	HR	Ratio
1997	0	0	-	2.70	3	0	0	3.1	1	1	4	1	0.60
Career	2	2	.500	3.91	29	0	0	48.1	35	26	40	8	1.26

Robinson is 28, but his 1997 Triple-A performance can't be overlooked. He led International League relievers in fewest hits per nine innings and ranked second in strikeouts per nine innings. 1998 Outlook: C

Juan Samuel (Pos: DH, Age: 37, Bats: R)

	G	AB	R	H	D	T	HR	RBI	SB	BB	SO	Avg	OBP	Slg
1997	45	95	13	27	5	4	3	15	5	10	28	.284	.364	.516
Career	1677	6031	859	1569	285	102	160	701	383	433	1429	.260	.315	.421

Samuel didn't play much in 1997, but when he did he hit about as well as he ever did. The Jays are going for youth, but Samuel should be able to hook on somewhere. 1998 Outlook: B

Ruben Sierra (Pos: LF/RF, Age: 32, Bats: B)

	G	AB	R	H	D	T	HR	RBI	SB	BB	SO	Avg	OBP	Slg
1997	39	138	10	32	5	3	3	12	0	9	34	.232	.277	.377
Career	1635	6335	880	1707	337	55	235	1036	130	488	951	.269	.318	.451

For a month, the Jays wasted a roster spot on Sierra. Toronto was Sierra's fifth stop in three years, and there may not be a sixth interested in his fading skills and huge ego. 1998 Outlook: C

Toronto Blue Jays Minor League Prospects

Organization Overview:

The Blue Jays produce major league talent as well as any organization. In the past three years alone, they have introduced Chris Carpenter, Carlos Delgado, Kelvim Escobar, Alex Gonzalez, Shawn Green and Shannon Stewart to featured roles in Toronto. That's more than some clubs produce in a decade. Though the Jays can go out and buy a Roger Clemens when they want, next year's club will consist almost entirely of homegrown products or players acquired for prospects. The system is teeming with position-player prospects, especially at the infield corners, and there's a smattering of intriguing arms as well.

Tom Evans

Position: 3B   **Opening Day Age:** 23
Bats: R **Throws:** R   **Born:** 7/9/74 in
Ht: 6' 1" **Wt:** 180   Kirkland, WA

Recent Statistics

	G	AB	R	H	D	T	HR	RBI	SB	BB	SO	AVG
97 A Dunedin	15	42	8	11	2	0	2	4	0	11	10	.262
97 AAA Syracuse	107	376	60	99	17	1	15	65	1	53	104	.263
97 AL Toronto	12	38	7	11	2	0	1	2	0	2	10	.289
97 MLE	107	361	46	84	15	0	11	49	0	40	109	.233

Other than his shoulders, there's little to dislike about Evans. He had rotator-cuff surgery on his right shoulder in 1996 and tore the labrum in his left diving for a ball in 1997. The 1992 fourth-round pick has one of the best eyes in the minors, leading all players with 115 walks two years ago. He has a quick bat that produces line drives, and shows good range and a strong arm at third base. If Ed Sprague, who also battled shoulder problems during a subpar 1997, doesn't rebound, Evans could take his job.

Roy Halladay

Position: P   **Opening Day Age:** 20
Bats: R **Throws:** R   **Born:** 5/14/77 in
Ht: 6' 6" **Wt:** 200   Denver, CO

Recent Statistics

	W	L	ERA	G	GS	Sv	IP	H	R	BB	SO	HR
96 A Dunedin	15	7	2.73	27	27	0	164.2	158	75	46	109	7
97 AA Knoxville	2	3	5.40	7	7	0	36.2	46	26	11	30	4
97 AAA Syracuse	7	10	4.58	22	22	0	125.2	132	74	53	64	13

Halladay has advanced rapidly since being a first-round pick in 1995, reaching Triple-A shortly after he turned 20. He has more than enough stuff to be a frontline starter. His fastball ranges from 92-98 MPH and consistently reaches 95. With that kind of heat, it's almost unfair that he also has a dancing knuckle-curve. He also throws a cut fastball and a changeup, and is toying with a slider. He may have been pushed a bit fast, however,

because his strikeout and hit numbers in Triple-A don't come close to doing justice to his talent. They weren't overwhelming in Class-A ball in 1996 either, which is odd.

Ryan Jones

Position: 1B   **Opening Day Age:** 23
Bats: R **Throws:** R   **Born:** 11/5/74 in
Ht: 6' 3" **Wt:** 220   Torrance, CA

Recent Statistics

	G	AB	R	H	D	T	HR	RBI	SB	BB	SO	AVG
96 AA Knoxville	134	506	70	137	26	3	20	97	2	60	88	.271
97 AAA Syracuse	41	123	8	17	5	1	3	16	0	15	28	.138
97 AA Knoxville	86	328	41	84	19	3	12	51	0	27	63	.256
97 MLE	127	434	35	84	20	2	10	48	0	27	96	.194

Because he's a big, power-hitting first baseman with red hair, Jones has been compared to Mark McGwire since signing as a second-round pick in 1993. Lately the resemblance hasn't gone beyond their faces, however. Jones stalled in 1997, hitting .224 with 15 homers between Double-A and Triple-A as Kevin Witt passed him on the organization's depth chart at first base. Jones does make pretty good contact for a power hitter, and he has worked hard to turn himself into a decent defensive player. He needs to rebound in 1998 to avoid getting lost in the shuffle with the Blue Jays.

Anthony Sanders

Position: OF   **Opening Day Age:** 24
Bats: R **Throws:** R   **Born:** 3/2/74 in Tucson,
Ht: 6' 2" **Wt:** 180   AZ

Recent Statistics

	G	AB	R	H	D	T	HR	RBI	SB	BB	SO	AVG
96 A Dunedin	102	417	75	108	25	0	17	50	16	34	93	.259
96 AA Knoxville	38	133	16	36	8	0	1	18	1	7	33	.271
97 A Dunedin	1	5	0	1	1	0	0	1	0	1	1	.200
97 AA Knoxville	111	429	68	114	20	4	26	69	20	44	121	.266
97 MLE	111	410	48	95	17	3	18	49	13	26	129	.232

Sanders' 1997 accomplishments are all the more impressive considering that they came in the face of tragedy. While he was in spring training, his wife Denise was killed in a skiing accident March 8, leaving behind Sanders and their 3-year-old son Anthony Jr. Sanders missed little time and posted career highs in nearly every offensive category, showing five-tool potential. A seventh-round pick in 1992, he's the best defensive outfielder in the system, a legitimate center fielder with an above-average right-field arm. Toronto envisions him as a player along the lines of a Jim Edmonds or Steve Finley, though the big league outfield is quite crowded with Jose Cruz Jr., Shannon Stewart and Shawn Green.

Andy Thompson

Position: 3B **Opening Day Age:** 22
Bats: R **Throws:** R **Born:** 10/8/75 in
Ht: 6' 3" **Wt:** 210 Oconomowoc, WI

Recent Statistics

	G	AB	R	H	D	T	HR	RBI	SB	BB	SO	AVG
96 A Dunedin	129	425	64	120	26	5	11	50	16	60	108	.282
97 AA Knoxville	124	448	75	128	25	3	15	71	0	63	76	.286
97 MLE	124	426	54	106	21	2	10	51	0	38	81	.249

Though they don't gamble as much these days, the Blue Jays used to hoard talent by pursuing supposedly unsignable players such as Thompson. He lasted until the 23rd round in 1994 because he was ticketed to play quarterback at the University of Minnesota, but Toronto signed him right before he became a Golden Gopher. He's a patient hitter who adjusts well and makes good contact, and he's beginning to tap his considerable power potential. He also has plenty of arm strength at third base. Sprague and Evans are ahead of him in the system, but Thompson will have the bat to play anywhere if he develops as Toronto expects.

Vernon Wells

Position: OF **Opening Day Age:** 19
Bats: R **Throws:** R **Born:** 12/8/78 in
Ht: 6' 1" **Wt:** 195 Shreveport, LA

Recent Statistics

	G	AB	R	H	D	T	HR	RBI	SB	BB	SO	AVG
97 A St. Cathrns	66	264	52	81	20	1	10	31	8	30	44	.307

Toronto took some criticism when they drafted Wells fifth overall in 1997. He was projected to go in the bottom half of the first round and quickly signed for $1.6 million, fueling charges that he was overdrafted because of his signability. The Blue Jays looked pretty smart after Wells' debut in the low Class-A New York-Penn League, where many of the players were three years older than him. He was named the second-best prospect in the league by *Baseball America*, showing all five tools. His bat is his best skill, and his power, speed and arm all project well above average. He already draws walks and makes contact. The Blue Jays love Stewart in center field, but Wells could become an even better player.

Kevin Witt

Position: 1B **Opening Day Age:** 22
Bats: L **Throws:** R **Born:** 1/5/76 in High
Ht: 6' 4" **Wt:** 185 Point, NC

Recent Statistics

	G	AB	R	H	D	T	HR	RBI	SB	BB	SO	AVG
96 A Dunedin	124	446	63	121	18	6	13	70	9	39	96	.271
97 AA Knoxville	127	501	76	145	27	4	30	91	1	44	109	.289
97 MLE	127	475	54	119	23	3	21	65	0	26	116	.251

Witt is another first-round pick (1994) who opened the Blue Jays' eyes in 1997. He crushed 30 homers at Double-A Knoxville, and continues to get bigger and stronger. His strikeout rate is acceptable for a power

hitter, though a few more walks would be preferred. A shortstop who had been converted to third base and showed good hands there, he played more first base at Knoxville because of the presence of Thompson. He tired at the end of the season and needs another year of development, but could surface in Toronto in 1999 and push Delgado to DH.

Joe Young

Position: P **Opening Day Age:** 22
Bats: R **Throws:** R **Born:** 4/28/75 in Ft.
Ht: 6' 4" **Wt:** 205 McMurray, Alberta,
 Canada

Recent Statistics

	W	L	ERA	G	GS	Sv	IP	H	R	BB	SO	HR
96 A Hagerstown	9	9	3.84	21	21	0	122.0	101	64	63	157	7
96 A Dunedin	1	3	5.88	6	6	0	33.2	30	24	17	36	3
97 AA Knoxville	5	4	4.42	19	11	0	59.0	52	38	40	62	4

An accomplished hockey player from Alberta, Young left the ice to sign with Toronto in 1993 as a third-round pick. He's a power pitcher with a solid fastball and hard curveball, and he seemed to turn a corner in 1996 when he finished second in the minors in strikeouts. He continued to pile up whiffs in Double-A until getting shut down with shoulder stiffness that didn't require surgery. He also throws a changeup, and needs to improve his mechanics and command, particularly of his breaking ball. At 22, he has plenty of time.

Others to Watch

Second baseman **Brent Abernathy** has a smooth bat, a good glove and great instincts. He batted .309 with 22 steals at Class-A Hagerstown at age 19. . . Righthander **Carlos Almanzar** could make the Blue Jays as a setup man in 1998. He has posted the second-best strikeout/walk ratio in the Triple-A International League at age 23 last year, using a top-notch changeup and an average fastball. He's very durable and probably would be the only licensed barber in the majors. . . **Felipe Crespo** is part of the cast of thousands Toronto has paraded through second base since Roberto Alomar signed with the Orioles. Crespo, 25, has good pop for a middle infielder, but does little else and is a defensive liability. He's seen as a utilityman now. . . Righthander **Billy Koch's** outlook changed in a hurry. He went from being the fourth overall draft pick and pitching for the U.S. Olympic team in 1996 to tearing an elbow ligament in 1997. Whether the 23 year old can regain his 100-MPH fastball remains to be seen, but surgery went well and he began to throw again in instructional league. . . Opponents batted just .178 off 21-year-old righthander **Yan LaChapelle** in 1997, the second-best mark in the minors. He has a plus fastball and a power curve, and as a marketing bonus he's Canadian. . . First baseman **Luis Lopez** won the batting title (.358) and was named MVP of the Class A South Atlantic League. He's 24 and doesn't have much home-run power for his position, but the Jays like his bat and glove.

National League Players

Buck Showalter

1997 Season

Buck Showalter was hired as Arizona's first manager on November 15, 1995. He has been working ever since to build the organization from the bottom up. There's little doubt that the Diamondbacks franchise will show the order and stability that characterized his four-year run with the Yankees.

Offense

Showalter finds roles in which his players can succeed. Under his guidance, players who lacked the talent to assume full-time roles, such as Jim Leyritz, were turned into productive role players. Showalter's ability to exploit players' strengths without exposing their weaknesses was also evident when he instituted a left-field platoon of Dion James and Gerald Williams. Showalter's favorite offensive strategy is to send the right hitter to the plate at the right time. He likes to keep his bench stocked with pinch hitters, but has little use for stealing, bunting or the hit-and-run.

Pitching & Defense

Despite his success in New York, Showalter's handling of the pitching staff left much to be desired. He had three aces during his four years there—Melido Perez, Jimmy Key and Jack McDowell—and each came down with a major arm injury soon after serving as the anchor of the rotation. Few managers in baseball are more willing to let their starters run up high pitch counts. He also rides his closer and setup men fairly hard. He's not afraid to commit himself to a young pitcher, which will prove useful in Arizona.

1998 Outlook

Showalter's success in New York was the result of both his ability to construct a potent lineup and his ability to maintain a steady hand through periods of high roster turnover. The Diamondbacks' expansion draft yielded some talented hitters like Brent Brede, David Dellucci and Harvey Pulliam who may be ideally suited for Showalter's platoon system. Young pitchers Brian Anderson and Jeff Suppan likely will benefit from Showalter's patience—at least in the short term. There's every reason for optimism in Arizona.

Born: 5/23/56 in DeFuniak Springs, FL

Playing Experience: No major league experience

Managerial Experience: 4 seasons

Manager Statistics

Year Team, Lg	W	L	Pct	GB	Finish
— —	—	—	—	—	—
4 Seasons	313	268	.539	—	—

1997 Starting Pitchers by Days Rest

	≤3	4	5	6+
Diamondbacks Starts	—	—	—	—
Diamondbacks ERA	—	—	—	—
NL Avg Starts	3	90	38	22
NL ERA	4.23	4.05	4.27	4.52

1997 Situational Stats

	Manager	NL Average
Hit & Run Success %	—	36.4
Stolen Base Success %	—	68.4
Platoon Pct.	—	56.3
Defensive Subs	—	26
High-Pitch Outings	—	12
Quick/Slow Hooks	—	18/10
Sacrifice Attempts	—	96
	"	

1997 Rankings (National League)

⇒ Did not manage in the majors last year

Brian Anderson

1997 Season

The Diamondbacks used their first pick (second overall) in the expansion draft to select Brian Anderson. Anderson was considered one of the three best young pitchers available in the draft, and it looks like he'll finally get the chance he's been looking for. Despite pitching very well at Triple-A and decently with the Indians in each of the last two seasons, he never was able to break into their rotation for good. He pitched very well in the 1997 postseason after initially being left off Cleveland's roster, and his performance greatly influenced Arizona's selection.

Pitching

Anderson's best fastball won't crack 90 MPH, but he has excellent control and his curveball and changeup have improved greatly during the past two years. He has a tendency to leave pitches up in the strike zone, and when hitters guess right they can hit him hard. Anderson comes right at hitters and works ahead in the count, but must learn to make the hitters hit his pitch once he gets ahead. His style is similar to Denny Neagle's. Each pitcher works up and down in the zone with fastballs and offspeed stuff.

Defense & Hitting

Anderson was a little shaky in the field when he first came up, but he has settled down and become a solid fielder. He keeps an eye on baserunners and it's very tough to get a good jump against him. He hasn't had a single at-bat as a professional, so he'll need a refresher course on hitting.

1998 Outlook

This is it. After going 18-6 at Triple-A in the last two years, Anderson finally will get the chance to prove his mettle against major league hitters. He has proven he's ready and finally has found a club ready to commit to him. He's expected to be the No. 2 starter on Arizona's starting staff behind Willie Blair this year.

Position: SP
Bats: B **Throws:** L
Ht: 6' 1" **Wt:** 190

Opening Day Age: 25
Born: 4/26/72 in Geneva, OH
ML Seasons: 5

Overall Statistics

	W	L	Pct.	ERA	G	GS	Sv	IP	H	BB	SO	HR	Ratio
1997	4	2	.667	4.69	8	8	0	48.0	55	11	22	7	1.38
Career	20	16	.556	5.25	58	53	0	312.0	354	84	139	54	1.40

How Often He Throws Strikes

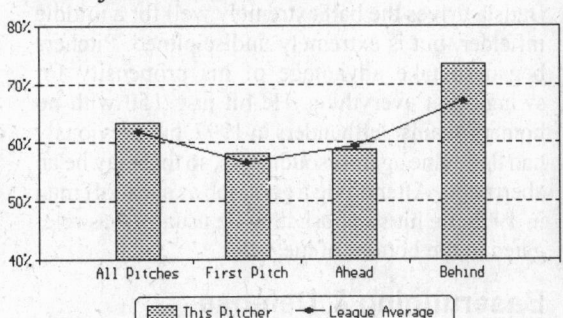

1997 Situational Stats

	W	L	ERA	Sv	IP		AB	H	HR	RBI	Avg
Home	3	2	4.32	0	33.1	LHB	35	11	1	5	.314
Road	1	0	5.52	0	14.2	RHB	148	44	6	23	.297
First Half	3	1	4.18	0	32.1	Sc Pos	38	14	2	20	.368
Scnd Half	1	1	5.74	0	15.2	Clutch	10	3	1	2	.300

1997 Rankings (American League)

⇒ Did not rank near the top or bottom in any category

Tony Batista

1997 Season

After dazzling the Athletics in the second half of 1996, Tony Batista was given Mike Bordick's vacated spot at shortstop. But Batista got complacent, entering spring training overconfident and in poor shape. He hit poorly and injured his lower back, leading to time on the disabled list and a demotion to Triple-A. Batista played sparingly in the final two months after returning to Oakland, often sitting behind Rafael Bournigal. With depth in the infield, the A's didn't protect Batista and watched the Diamondbacks take him in the first round of the expansion draft.

Hitting

Batista drives the ball extremely well for a middle infielder, but is extremely undisciplined. Pitchers began to take advantage of his propensity for swinging at everything. He hit just .150 with no homers against lefthanders in 1997, but previously had done fine against southpaws, so that may be an aberration. After doing a good job as a leadoff man in 1996, he hit so poorly that he usually was relegated to the bottom of the order.

Baserunning & Defense

Batista has above-average speed but isn't a basestealing threat because he doesn't know how to use it. He has above-average range at both second base and shortstop, and is very surehanded. His back problems held him back defensively in 1997, but he still did a creditable job.

1998 Outlook

Batista won't have to worry about playing shortstop after the Diamondbacks signed free agent Jay Bell. Batista has the raw tools to be a very good second baseman. But he must keep himself in shape, develop more plate discipline and hone his basestealing skills. If he doesn't, fellow expansion draftees Edwin Diaz and Danny Klassen aren't too far away from being ready to take Batista's job. He's only 24, but this is a huge season for him.

Position: SS
Bats: R **Throws:** R
Ht: 6' 0" **Wt:** 165

Opening Day Age: 24
Born: 12/9/73 in Puerto Plata, DR
ML Seasons: 2
Pronunciation: bah-TEESE-tah

Overall Statistics

	G	AB	R	H	D	T	HR	RBI	SB	BB	SO	Avg	OBP	Slg
1997	68	188	22	38	10	1	4	18	2	14	31	.202	.265	.330
Career	142	426	60	109	20	3	10	43	9	33	80	.256	.313	.387

Where He Hits the Ball

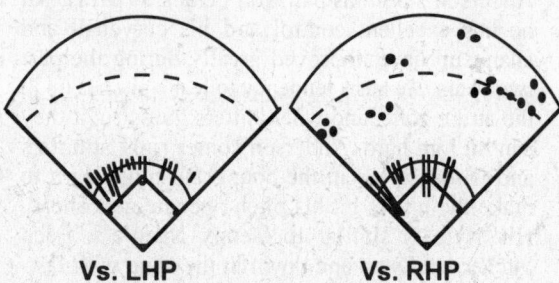

Vs. LHP   Vs. RHP

1997 Situational Stats

	AB	H	HR	RBI	Avg		AB	H	HR	RBI	Avg
Home	107	22	0	5	.206	LHP	60	9	0	2	.150
Road	81	16	4	13	.198	RHP	128	29	4	16	.227
First Half	101	18	4	11	.178	Sc Pos	43	11	2	16	.256
Scnd Half	87	20	0	7	.230	Clutch	22	5	0	0	.227

1997 Rankings (American League)

⇒ Did not rank near the top or bottom in any category

Jay Bell

1997 Season

Jay Bell gave the Royals exactly what they wanted when they acquired him from the Pirates before the 1997 season. He became a defensive anchor at shortstop and an unexpected offensive leader with his best hitting performance ever. He established career highs in several categories, including home runs, RBI and slugging percentage, while also setting many club records for hitting by a shortstop.

Hitting

Bell proved his previous best hitting season (1996 with Pittsburgh) was no fluke by raising the bar even further in 1997. For the first four months of the year, he was the Royals' most consistent offensive threat, hitting for power, smashing line drives to all fields and driving in key runs. Only a late slump diminished his final totals. When he's slumping, Bell will chase bad pitches down and away. He can hit any breaking pitch, though his bat speed appears to be waning.

Baserunning & Defense

Bell's smooth defense and consistent all-around play was a large part of the Royals' team-record .985 fielding percentage. He showed versatility by shifting to third base as the Royals evaluated short-stop prospect Felix Martinez in September, and didn't miss a beat at the hot corner. Bell has average range at shortstop, but has lost a step to his right. He's an adequate baserunner who keeps his head in the game and rarely runs into unnecessary outs.

1998 Outlook

Bell became a hot commodity on the free-agent market after his outstanding 1997 campaign. The Diamondbacks signed him to a five-year deal worth $34 million before the expansion draft. He can't be expected to hit so well every year, but he's clearly among the better major league shortstops in most regards.

Position: SS
Bats: R **Throws:** R
Ht: 6' 0" **Wt:** 182

Opening Day Age: 32
Born: 12/11/65 in Eglin AFB, FL
ML Seasons: 12

Overall Statistics

	G	AB	R	H	D	T	HR	RBI	SB	BB	SO	Avg	OBP	Slg
1997	153	573	89	167	28	3	21	92	10	71	101	.291	.368	.461
Career	1375	5102	752	1369	277	49	104	553	74	528	968	.268	.339	.403

Where He Hits the Ball

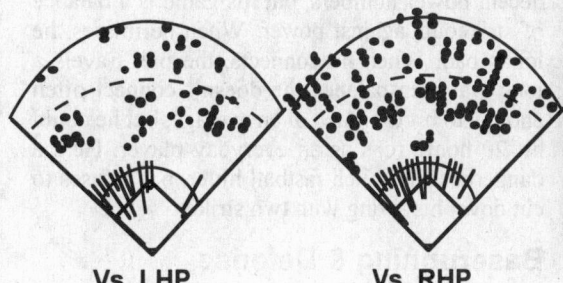

Vs. LHP   **Vs. RHP**

1997 Situational Stats

	AB	H	HR	RBI	Avg		AB	H	HR	RBI	Avg
Home	275	79	10	45	.287	LHP	173	45	4	19	.260
Road	298	88	11	47	.295	RHP	400	122	17	73	.305
First Half	298	83	13	56	.279	Sc Pos	161	49	5	72	.304
Scnd Half	275	84	8	36	.305	Clutch	100	26	2	11	.260

1997 Rankings (American League)

⇒ 3rd in fielding percentage at shortstop (.985)
⇒ 6th in most pitches seen per plate appearance (4.09)
⇒ 10th in pitches seen (2,702)
⇒ Led the Royals in batting average, at-bats, runs scored, hits, singles, total bases (264), times on base (242), strikeouts, pitches seen (2,702), plate appearances (660), most pitches seen per plate appearance (4.09), batting average vs. righthanded pitchers, slugging percentage vs. righthanded pitchers (.500), on-base percentage vs. righthanded pitchers (.384) and lowest percentage of swings on the first pitch (19.5%)

Yamil Benitez

1997 Season

After stagnating at Triple-A in the Montreal organization for two years, Yamil Benitez joined the Royals in an offseason deal. He spent the first half bashing balls over the fence at Triple-A, and was promoted in the second half. He got off to a hot start and showed frequent bursts of power, but tailed off toward the end of the season as his strikeouts piled up. Arizona made him a first-round pick in the expansion draft.

Hitting

Benitez swings from the heels without much concern for whether the pitch is a strike. A quick bat helps him make contact often enough to generate decent power numbers, but his game is a balance of strikeouts against power. When he misses, he looks bad. When he connects, the ball travels a long way. On balance, he doesn't connect often enough to hit for much of an average, but he could hit 20 home runs as an everyday player. He's a dangerous first-pitch fastball hitter, but refuses to cut down his swing with two strikes.

Baserunning & Defense

Benitez has good speed and will steal an occasional base. He's fast enough to cover right field, but has poor instincts and sometimes looks awkward. He has a strong, erratic arm. His throwing, like most of his other skills, remains raw and unrefined.

1998 Outlook

If the Diamondbacks need power, they may look to Benitez. He may end up as a semi-regular or a platoon player in either left or right field. At age 25, it's a bit late to hope that he'll ever be able to truly harness his skills. If Benitez can't get it going, David Dellucci might supplant him.

Position: LF/RF
Bats: R **Throws:** R
Ht: 6' 2" **Wt:** 195

Opening Day Age: 25
Born: 5/10/72 in San Juan, Puerto Rico
ML Seasons: 3
Pronunciation: YAH-mill buh-NEE-tezz

Overall Statistics

	G	AB	R	H	D	T	HR	RBI	SB	BB	SO	Avg	OBP	Slg
1997	53	191	22	51	7	1	8	21	2	10	49	.267	.307	.440
Career	78	242	30	68	9	2	10	30	2	11	60	.281	.315	.459

Where He Hits the Ball

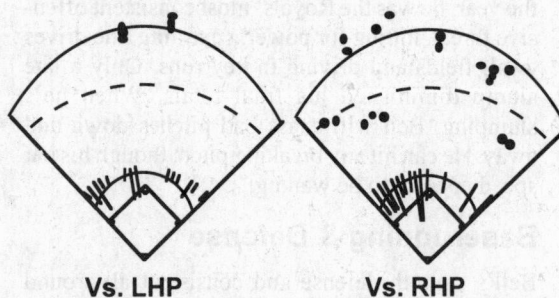

Vs. LHP   **Vs. RHP**

1997 Situational Stats

	AB	H	HR	RBI	Avg		AB	H	HR	RBI	Avg
Home	102	32	5	12	.314	LHP	58	14	3	8	.241
Road	89	19	3	9	.213	RHP	133	37	5	13	.278
First Half	0	0	0	0	-	Sc Pos	40	8	2	13	.200
Scnd Half	191	51	8	21	.267	Clutch	28	9	1	2	.321

1997 Rankings (American League)

⇒ 5th in errors in left field (3)
⇒ 6th in lowest batting average with two strikes (.122)

Jorge Fabregas

1997 Season

Some trades work out better than anyone thinks. The White Sox' mid-May deal with the Angels for Jorge Fabregas and lefty Chuck McElroy paid dividends that Chicago GM Ron Schueler couldn't have imagined. Fabregas had fallen into disfavor in Anaheim, in part because of a difference with hitting coach Rod Carew. He was glad to get a chance elsewhere and took advantage. After hitting only .079 with the Angels, he found his stroke with the Sox, batting .280 the rest of the year. Though he was Chicago's only capable everyday catcher, Fabregas was left unprotected in the expansion draft. Arizona took him in the first round.

Hitting

The lefthanded-hitting Fabregas never has developed into the power hitter he had been with an aluminum bat at the University of Miami. But while the Angels fretted over the change, the Sox were happy with his line-drive hitting. He surprised scouts by pulling the ball to right field more after he joined the Sox, suggesting that his power might eventually return. After averaging one extra-base hit every 32 at-bats in 1996, he improved that ratio to one every 19 at-bats. That's not All-Star material, but it's a major improvement. He loves to hit first-pitch fastballs, but can adjust to make contact with breaking pitches.

Baserunning & Defense

Fabregas is an intelligent guy who wasn't afraid to take charge in his first season with the Sox. He was especially effective with the many young pitchers the Sox paraded to the mound in August and September. He moves somewhat slowly behind the plate, but threw well enough to stem the tide of basestealers who preyed on the Sox when Ron Karkovice was doing most of the catching. He's not afraid to block the plate. Fabregas generally advances one base at a time.

1998 Outlook

For the first time in his career, Fabregas will start 120-130 games if he is healthy. He showed after the trade that he is capable of hitting .275 with 10 home runs and 75 RBI.

Position: C
Bats: L **Throws:** R
Ht: 6' 3" **Wt:** 214

Opening Day Age: 28
Born: 3/13/70 in Miami, FL
ML Seasons: 4
Pronunciation: GEORGE FA-ber-gas

Arizona Diamondbacks

Overall Statistics

	G	AB	R	H	D	T	HR	RBI	SB	BB	SO	Avg	OBP	Slg
1997	121	360	33	93	11	1	7	51	1	14	46	.258	.285	.353
Career	327	968	87	258	30	1	10	115	3	55	119	.267	.304	.331

Where He Hits the Ball

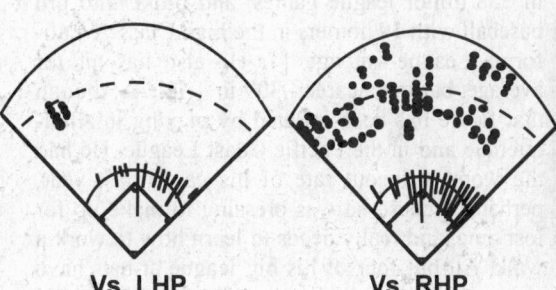

Vs. LHP   **Vs. RHP**

1997 Situational Stats

	AB	H	HR	RBI	Avg		AB	H	HR	RBI	Avg
Home	160	38	1	19	.238	LHP	49	13	1	8	.265
Road	200	55	6	32	.275	RHP	311	80	6	43	.257
First Half	160	37	3	26	.231	Sc Pos	102	27	3	45	.265
Scnd Half	200	56	4	25	.280	Clutch	53	13	3	9	.245

1997 Rankings (American League)

⇒ 2nd in most GDPs per GDP situation (21.1%) and batting average on a 3-2 count (.478)
⇒ 4th in errors at catcher (8) and lowest fielding percentage at catcher (.988)
⇒ Led the White Sox in batting average on a 3-1 count (.625) and batting average on a 3-2 count (.526)

Karim Garcia

1997 Season

Karim Garcia was supposed to take over left field in Los Angeles as early as two years ago. He drew a suspension and a trip to Double-A when he walked out after not getting promoted in 1996, and 1997 marked the third straight year that he began at Triple-A Albuquerque. He was promoted in June, but a shoulder injury cost him the last two months of the season and required reconstructive surgery. It was a mild surprise that the Dodgers didn't protect him in the expansion draft. He lasted nine picks until Arizona chose him.

Hitting

Garcia's best tool is his power. He has 98 homers in 558 minor league games, and broke into pro baseball with 19 homers in the high Class-A California League—at age 17. He also has hit for average, batting a career .309 in Triple-A, though that figure has been inflated by playing in Albuquerque and in the Pacific Coast League. He had the worst strikeout rate of his career last year, perhaps because he was pressing to make up for lost time, and really needs to learn how to work a walk. All but four of his big league at-bats have come against righthanders. He has done OK against lefties in Triple-A, albeit with significantly reduced power.

Baserunning & Defense

Garcia has above-average speed and though he's not an accomplished basestealer by any means, pitchers at least have to pay attention when he's on first base. His biggest asset as a right fielder was his arm strength, which is now questionable after his surgery.

1998 Outlook

Garcia could turn out to be one of the best picks in the expansion draft. He was considered a can't-miss prospect with the Dodgers, who opted to protect several pitchers and may rue keeping Todd Hollandsworth over Garcia. He's just 22—though his age has been questioned since he signed out of Mexico—which buys him plenty of time to heal his shoulder. He should start on an outfield corner for Arizona and bat in the heart of the lineup.

Position: LF
Bats: L **Throws:** L
Ht: 6' 0" **Wt:** 172

Opening Day Age: 22
Born: 10/29/75 in Ciudad Obregon, MX
ML Seasons: 3

Overall Statistics

	G	AB	R	H	D	T	HR	RBI	SB	BB	SO	Avg	OBP	Slg
1997	15	39	5	5	0	0	1	8	0	6	14	.128	.239	.205
Career	29	60	6	9	0	0	1	8	0	6	19	.150	.224	.200

Where He Hits the Ball

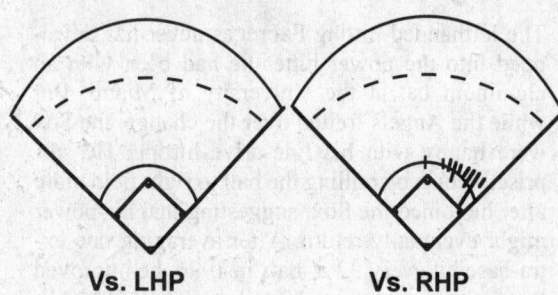

Vs. LHP   **Vs. RHP**

1997 Situational Stats

	AB	H	HR	RBI	Avg		AB	H	HR	RBI	Avg
Home	23	1	0	1	.043	LHP	3	0	0	0	.000
Road	16	4	1	7	.250	RHP	36	5	1	8	.139
First Half	39	5	1	8	.128	Sc Pos	12	3	1	8	.250
Scnd Half	0	0	0	0	-	Clutch	7	0	0	0	.000

1997 Rankings (National League)

⇒ Did not rank near the top or bottom in any category

Travis Lee

1997 Season

The Diamondbacks showed that they were willing to spend money when they signed Travis Lee in the fall of 1996 for $10 million, the second-highest bonus ever paid an amateur. He had been chosen second overall in that year's draft by the Twins, but a contract snafu made him a free agent. He starred at first base for the U.S. Olympic team and won the Golden Spikes Award, college baseball's Heisman Trophy. All that led to huge expectations, and Lee delivered. His first pro season was a rousing success, as he batted .331-32-109 and held his own during a half-season of Triple-A.

Hitting

Lee has a smooth lefthanded swing that reminds some scouts of Cubs first baseman Mark Grace, a fellow San Diego State product. But Lee has much more power potential than Grace ever did. He generates doubles and homers with a short, quick stroke, which is why he had no trouble adjusting to wood bats. He makes very good contact for a slugger, and walks nearly as much as he strikes out. Managers voted him the best prospect, best hitter, best power hitter and most exciting player in the high Class-A California League, where he spent the first half of 1997. Lee struggled against the better lefthanders' breaking balls in Triple-A, batting .184, though he did homer six times in 76 at-bats. He should improve against lefties with experience and doesn't project as a platoon player.

Baserunning & Defense

Cal League managers voted Lee the best defensive first baseman in their circuit as well. Again, he's as smooth as Grace. Lee is agile and has a good arm. He played some center field in his final college season, and could play regularly at an outfield corner in the majors. He runs very well and should lead major league first basemen annually in steals.

1998 Outlook

There's no hole in Lee's game. The National League West features four of the game's top first-base prospects and Lee looks like the best of the bunch. He should be Arizona's Opening Day first baseman and bat either third or fourth in the lineup.

Position: 1B
Bats: L **Throws:** L
Ht: 6' 3" **Wt:** 205

Opening Day Age: 23
Born: 5/26/75 in San Diego, CA
ML Seasons: 0

Overall Statistics

	G	AB	R	H	D	T	HR	RBI	SB	BB	SO	Avg	OBP	Slg
1997	—	—	—	—	—	—	—	—	—	—	—	—	—	—
Career	—	—	—	—	—	—	—	—	—	—	—	—	—	—

1997 Rankings (National League)
⇒ Did not play in the majors last year

Jeff Suppan

1997 Season

The 1997 season was a learning process for Jeff Suppan. In the past, he'd been rushed to the majors and hurt his arm when he was stuck in the bullpen, so he spent last year rebuilding confidence in his stuff. He showed good command of both sides of the plate, and seemed on the verge of becoming a solid major league starter. Boston inexplicably left him unprotected in the expansion draft, so Arizona grabbed him with the third overall pick.

Pitching

Suppan works his 88-90 MPH fastball in and out, and has a good dead-fish changeup that's particularly effective against lefthanders. He throws a slider and a curveball, but they haven't been as sharp since his arm injury in 1996. As a result, he has lost confidence in his breaking pitches. He needs to get them back in order to combat righthanders. Suppan was at his best in the minors when he was unafraid to let the batter make contact, but has nibbled more in the majors. Though he's a fairly efficient worker, he has yet to prove that he has the stamina to pitch into the late innings consistently.

Defense & Hitting

Suppan is an average fielder, but his slow move to the plate is a major concern. Unless he learns to quicken his move to the plate, basestealers will continue to rob him blind. He went 0-for-2 with one strikeout in 1997.

1998 Outlook

Suppan was considered one of the three best talents available in the expansion draft. The Diamondbacks are counting on him, Willie Blair and Brian Anderson to stabilize their rotation.

Position: SP
Bats: R **Throws:** R
Ht: 6' 2" **Wt:** 210

Opening Day Age: 23
Born: 1/2/75 in Oklahoma City, OK
ML Seasons: 3
Pronunciation: soo-PAWN

Overall Statistics

	W	L	Pct.	ERA	G	GS	Sv	IP	H	BB	SO	HR	Ratio
1997	7	3	.700	5.69	23	22	0	112.1	140	36	67	12	1.57
Career	9	6	.600	5.99	39	29	0	157.2	198	54	99	19	1.60

How Often He Throws Strikes

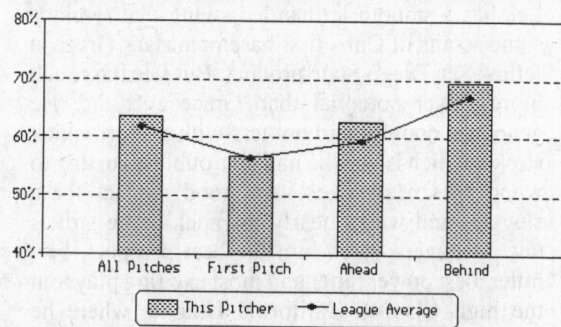

1997 Situational Stats

	W	L	ERA	Sv	IP		AB	H	HR	RBI	Avg
Home	4	2	4.87	0	57.1	LHB	231	64	8	39	.277
Road	3	1	6.55	0	55.0	RHB	228	76	4	23	.333
First Half	2	0	5.65	0	43.0	Sc Pos	119	36	5	51	.303
Scnd Half	5	3	5.71	0	69.1	Clutch	25	6	0	0	.240

1997 Rankings (American League)

⇒ 1st in stolen bases allowed (25)
⇒ 10th in errors at pitcher (3)
⇒ Led the Red Sox in stolen bases allowed (25) and GDPs induced (15)

Devon White

1997 Season

Devon White's offense dropped off rather substantially in 1997 as he contended with a couple of annoying leg injuries. When healthy, he continued to patrol center field with the same grace and ease he has displayed throughout his career. Florida fans no doubt will remember his grand slam that clinched the Division Series against San Francisco. His power numbers were down, however, and his batting average dropped 29 points.

Hitting

White still has more power than the typical center fielder or leadoff man. In general, inside fastballs give him trouble. When he bats from the left side, he can be susceptible to sliders. From the right side, he often chases all types of breaking pitches out of the strike zone. He really struggled against lefthanders in 1997, batting .188 with nearly as many strikeouts as hits. That performance was extremely disappointing, considering he tagged southpaws for a .345 average the year before. He was on pace for a career high in walks before injuries intervened.

Baserunning & Defense

Age has taken a toll on White's speed. He no longer blazes around the bases nor is he a prime basestealing threat, though his wheels are still above average. He remains one of the best center fielders in baseball, with fine leaping ability that allows him to take away potential home runs. He picks up the ball off the bat well, allowing him to get strong jumps. Though his arm isn't what it was, he still throws well with consistent accuracy.

1998 Outlook

This year will show whether White will rebound or if he's headed on a downhill slide. He'll answer that question in Arizona, after being traded for a minor league pitcher on the night of the expansion draft. He's coming off a disappointing postseason that featured little besides the grand slam. His defensive ability is so strong that he can be a valuable everyday player with an average offensive performance, but he should be taken out of the leadoff spot.

Position: CF
Bats: B **Throws:** R
Ht: 6' 2" **Wt:** 190

Opening Day Age: 35
Born: 12/29/62 in Kingston, Jamaica
ML Seasons: 13
Nickname: Devo

Arizona Diamondbacks

Overall Statistics

	G	AB	R	H	D	T	HR	RBI	SB	BB	SO	Avg	OBP	Slg
1997	74	265	37	65	13	1	6	34	13	32	65	.245	.338	.370
Career	1488	5759	903	1500	296	65	154	633	284	423	1211	.260	.315	.415

Where He Hits the Ball

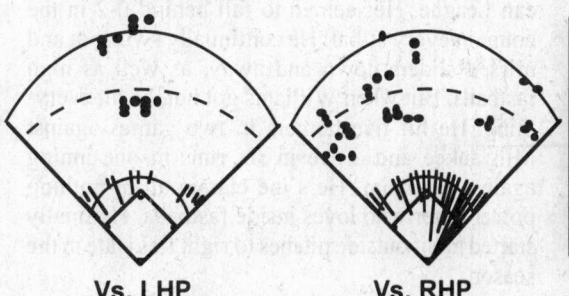

Vs. LHP **Vs. RHP**

1997 Situational Stats

	AB	H	HR	RBI	Avg		AB	H	HR	RBI	Avg
Home	152	38	4	21	.250	LHP	48	9	1	8	.188
Road	113	27	2	13	.239	RHP	217	56	5	26	.258
First Half	70	19	0	5	.271	Sc Pos	52	16	2	30	.308
Scnd Half	195	46	6	29	.236	Clutch	47	10	0	4	.213

1997 Rankings (National League)

⇒ 5th in lowest batting average with two strikes (.118)
⇒ 8th in lowest on-base percentage for a leadoff hitter (.313)
⇒ Led the Marlins in on-base percentage for a leadoff hitter (.313)

1997 Season

Seldom has a talented player looked as bad while having a good year than Matt Williams did in 1997. Acquired in an offseason blockbuster trade with the Giants, he hit .220 from May to July before hitting .309 with 42 RBI in the final two months. He opened the season hitting cleanup for the Tribe, but was dropped to sixth in mid-June. He hit .292 the rest of the season. His roller-coaster campaign included a 1-for-32 slump and a career-high 24-game hitting streak. He then led the club with 13 runs scored in the postseason.

Hitting

Williams struggled in his first year in the American League. He seemed to fall behind 0-2 in the count in every at-bat. He continually swung at and missed sliders down and away, as well as high fastballs. But when Williams got hot, he hit everything. He hit five homers in two games against Milwaukee and drove in six runs in one inning against Anaheim. He's the classic all-or-nothing power hitter who loves inside fastballs. He finally started to hit outside pitches to right field late in the season.

Baserunning & Defense

Williams didn't let his offensive struggles affect his defense. After winning three Gold Gloves in the National League, he won another in his AL debut. He has great range to his left and right, and a strong, sure arm. He routinely made the great play and always made the routine play. Williams set a career high with 12 stolen bases and was one of the most effective baserunners on the team. Not bad for a guy who broke his foot in 1995. He always hustled to first and hit second base hard to break up double plays.

1998 Outlook

Williams went through a divorce in 1997 and wanted to be near his children in Arizona. Cleveland obliged him, trading him to the Diamondbacks for Travis Fryman, Tom Martin and cash. Arizona then signed Williams to a five-year, $45 million contract extension.

Position: 3B
Bats: R **Throws:** R
Ht: 6' 2" **Wt:** 216

Opening Day Age: 32
Born: 11/28/65 in Bishop, CA
ML Seasons: 11

Overall Statistics

	G	AB	R	H	D	T	HR	RBI	SB	BB	SO	Avg	OBP	Slg
1997	151	596	86	157	32	3	32	105	12	34	108	.263	.307	.488
Career	1271	4735	680	1249	211	28	279	837	41	306	980	.264	.312	.497

Where He Hits the Ball

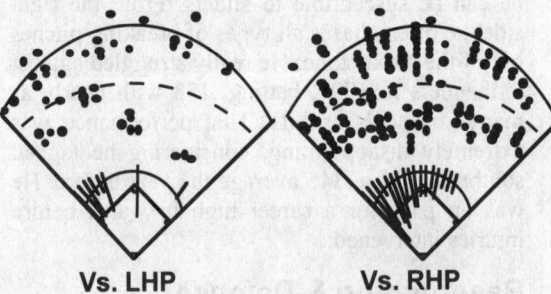

Vs. LHP   Vs. RHP

1997 Situational Stats

	AB	H	HR	RBI	Avg		AB	H	HR	RBI	Avg
Home	272	72	7	38	.265	LHP	139	39	13	31	.281
Road	324	85	25	67	.262	RHP	457	118	19	74	.258
First Half	309	75	20	54	.243	Sc Pos	177	50	7	72	.282
Scnd Half	287	82	12	51	.286	Clutch	79	24	5	20	.304

1997 Rankings (American League)

⇒ 2nd in lowest percentage of pitches taken (43.0%)

⇒ 3rd in slugging percentage vs. lefthanded pitchers (.647), fielding percentage at third base (.970) and highest percentage of swings on the first pitch (43.1%)

⇒ 6th in least pitches seen per plate appearance (3.42)

⇒ 7th in lowest cleanup slugging percentage (.459)

⇒ 9th in lowest on-base percentage and errors at third base (12)

⇒ 10th in lowest on-base percentage vs. righthanded pitchers (.300)

⇒ Led the Indians in at-bats, RBI and slugging percentage vs. lefthanded pitchers (.647)

Joel Adamson

Position: RP/SP
Bats: L **Throws:** L
Ht: 6' 4" **Wt:** 185

Opening Day Age: 26
Born: 7/2/71 in
Lakewood, CA
ML Seasons: 2

Overall Statistics

	W	L	Pct.	ERA	G	GS	Sv	IP	H	BB	SO	HR	Ratio
1997	5	3	.625	3.54	30	6	0	76.1	78	19	56	13	1.27
Career	5	3	.625	4.02	39	6	0	87.1	96	26	63	14	1.40

1997 Situational Stats

	W	L	ERA	Sv	IP		AB	H	HR	RBI	Avg
Home	3	1	4.36	0	33.0	LHB	104	24	5	11	.231
Road	2	2	2.91	0	43.1	RHB	190	54	8	28	.284
First Half	2	1	5.47	0	24.2	Sc Pos	66	16	2	25	.242
Scnd Half	3	2	2.61	0	51.2	Clutch	30	5	1	2	.167

1997 Season

Rookie lefthander Joel Adamson emerged as a solid middle reliever and spot starter in the second half for Milwaukee. Though he proved to be useful, his relatively advanced age and less-than-overpowering stuff caused him to be left unprotected in the expansion draft. Arizona claimed him in the middle of the first round.

Pitching, Defense & Hitting

Adamson's fastball doesn't crack 90 MPH, but he gets by because he mixes it with his a curveball and a changeup. He's fairly effective against lefties, but not enough to be a one-out specialist. He has excellent control but is rather hittable up in the strike zone. He usually worked as a starter in the minors and may be used more extensively in that role in the majors at some point. He's a decent fielder, and he controls the running game well. He hasn't swung the bat well in the minors.

1998 Outlook

Adamson enjoyed a respectable season in 1997, but it remains to be seen whether he can handle a more demanding role. The Diamondbacks may use him as a setup man or try him as a starter. He's a good bet to hold his own, though he almost certainly won't be a star.

Brent Brede

Position: RF/1B
Bats: L **Throws:** L
Ht: 6' 4" **Wt:** 190

Opening Day Age: 26
Born: 9/13/71 in
Belleville, IL
ML Seasons: 2
Pronunciation:
BREE-dee

Overall Statistics

	G	AB	R	H	D	T	HR	RBI	SB	BB	SO	Avg	OBP	Slg
1997	61	190	25	52	11	1	3	21	7	21	38	.274	.347	.389
Career	71	210	27	58	11	2	3	23	7	22	43	.276	.346	.390

1997 Situational Stats

	AB	H	HR	RBI	Avg		AB	H	HR	RBI	Avg
Home	70	22	2	8	.314	LHP	14	4	0	2	.286
Road	120	30	1	13	.250	RHP	176	48	3	19	.273
First Half	86	24	0	7	.279	Sc Pos	52	10	0	16	.192
Scnd Half	104	28	3	14	.269	Clutch	25	12	0	4	.480

1997 Season

Injuries to Marty Cordova and Scott Stahoviak, along with the erratic performance of Rich Becker and Matt Lawton, opened the door for unheralded Brent Brede in 1997. He took advantage of the unexpected playing time and impressed Twins manager Tom Kelly with his line-drive swing, his work ethic and his patience at the plate.

Hitting, Baserunning & Defense

Brede's swing doesn't produce much power, though he can drive the ball if he gets his arms extended. He's usually patient, and held up well in limited exposure to southpaws. He has produced .300 averages in the minors and could do so in the majors. Brede looks more like a basketball player than a baseball man. He has long legs, runs well for a big guy and, like most Twins farm system products, he's a heady baserunner. He's a good defensive player in the outfield and at first base.

1998 Outlook

A first-round expansion draft pick, Brede might get a chance to start for Arizona. More likely, he'll serve as a backup.

<table>
<tr><td>

Hector Carrasco

</td><td>

Chris Clemons

</td></tr>
</table>

Position: RP
Bats: R **Throws:** R
Ht: 6' 2" **Wt:** 180

Opening Day Age: 28
Born: 10/22/69 in San Pedro de Macoris, DR
ML Seasons: 4
Pronunciation: kuh-RASS-koh

Position: RP
Bats: R **Throws:** R
Ht: 6' 4" **Wt:** 225

Opening Day Age: 25
Born: 10/31/72 in Baytown, TX
ML Seasons: 1

Overall Statistics

	W	L	Pct.	ERA	G	GS	Sv	IP	H	BB	SO	HR	Ratio
1997	2	8	.200	4.40	66	0	0	86.0	80	41	76	7	1.41
Career	13	24	.351	3.76	231	0	11	304.0	266	162	240	17	1.41

1997 Situational Stats

	W	L	ERA	Sv	IP		AB	H	HR	RBI	Avg
Home	2	3	3.75	0	48.0	LHB	136	36	4	29	.265
Road	0	5	5.21	0	38.0	RHB	196	44	3	17	.224
First Half	1	2	3.53	0	51.0	Sc Pos	98	24	4	39	.245
Scnd Half	1	6	5.66	0	35.0	Clutch	106	31	3	17	.292

Overall Statistics

	W	L	Pct.	ERA	G	GS	Sv	IP	H	BB	SO	HR	Ratio
1997	0	2	.000	8.53	5	2	0	12.2	19	11	8	4	2.37
Career	0	2	.000	8.53	5	2	0	12.2	19	11	8	4	2.37

1997 Situational Stats

	W	L	ERA	Sv	IP		AB	H	HR	RBI	Avg
Home	0	0	7.20	0	5.0	LHB	31	11	2	6	.355
Road	0	2	9.39	0	7.2	RHB	24	8	2	7	.333
First Half	0	0		0	0.0	Sc Pos	14	5	0	7	.357
Scnd Half	0	2	8.53	0	12.2	Clutch	0	0	0	0	

1997 Season

Hector Carrasco's continuing search for home plate put him in conflict with Reds management once too often, and he was dealt to Kansas City at midseason. The Royals tried him in a setup role, but also were disappointed with his inconsistency.

Pitching, Defense & Hitting

Carrasco hits the mid-90s with his fastball, but struggles to control it. He also throws a hard slider and uses a splitter as a change of pace, but has no command of those pitches either. He's a poor fielder who's often out of position because of his exaggerated delivery, and he's slow to react on grounders through the middle. Basestealers have an edge on Carrasco. He lacks a decent pickoff move and is reluctant to throw to first base. He's 1-for-18 as a big league hitter.

1998 Outlook

Carrasco had found new life in the Royals' overhauled bullpen, but they lost him to Arizona in the second round of the expansion draft. He could be the Diamondbacks' first closer, but will need to throw more strikes to succeed.

1997 Season

Chris Clemons made his major league debut in July, roughly three years after the White Sox had made him a supplemental first-round pick out of Texas A&M. He hadn't pitched that well at Triple-A Nashville, and got bombed in the final three of his five appearances with Chicago. The Diamondbacks selected him in the second round of the expansion draft after the White Sox inexplicably decided not to pull him back.

Pitching, Defense & Hitting

Clemons throws 92-94 MPH with a good slider, and his changeup has potential. He has struggled with command in the minors, and it was a big problem in his first major league stint. His 70/65 strikeout/walk ratio in Triple-A isn't indicative of the quality of his stuff. The White Sox had him throw more changeups, letting hitters get themselves out rather than trying for strikeouts. Clemons is a big man and it takes time to get into fielding position and deliver the ball to the plate. He's not a spectacular fielder and is susceptible to stolen bases. He hasn't batted as a pro.

1998 Outlook

Clemons was more effective as a reliever in college. But Arizona needs starters, so he'll probably begin his Diamondbacks career in the rotation.

Omar Daal

Position: RP/SP
Bats: L **Throws:** L
Ht: 6' 3" **Wt:** 185

Opening Day Age: 26
Born: 3/1/72 in
Maracaibo, VZ
ML Seasons: 5
Pronunciation: DOLL

Overall Statistics

	W	L	Pct.	ERA	G	GS	Sv	IP	H	BB	SO	HR	Ratio
1997	2	3	.400	7.06	42	3	1	57.1	82	21	44	7	1.80
Career	12	11	.522	5.27	205	9	1	213.2	233	99	165	24	1.55

1997 Situational Stats

	W	L	ERA	Sv	IP		AB	H	HR	RBI	Avg
Home	0	2	7.94	0	28.1	LHB	76	28	2	23	.368
Road	2	1	6.21	1	29.0	RHB	163	54	5	20	.331
First Half	1	1	9.21	1	28.1	Sc Pos	78	22	2	35	.282
Scnd Half	1	2	4.97	0	29.0	Clutch	49	21	1	11	.429

1997 Season

After a promising 1996 season when he broke into Montreal's rotation late in the year, lefthander Omar Daal suffered through a nightmarish 1997. He failed to hang on to his starting spot and pitched dreadfully out of the bullpen before being claimed on waivers by the Blue Jays in July. He went back to the minors and pitched magnificently in five starts, and had three strong starts for the Toronto in September. Arizona took him with its second second-round pick in the expansion draft.

Pitching, Defense & Hitting

Though he has pitched out of the bullpen for most of his major league career, Daal's mid-80s sinker and big-breaking curve may be better suited for starting. He's not particularly effective against lefthanders, so the lefty-specialist role he filled in Los Angeles is far from ideal. He has flourished as a starter in the Venezuelan Winter League. He has a quick glove, though he makes his share of misplays. He's fairly tough to run on. As a hitter, he's 1-for-16 with no sacrifices in the majors.

1998 Outlook

Lefties are always in demand, but no major league team has been able to find the right role for Daal. Expansion may give him the best opportunity to find his niche.

David Dellucci

Position: RF/LF
Bats: L **Throws:** L
Ht: 5' 10" **Wt:** 180

Opening Day Age: 24
Born: 10/31/73 in
Baton Rouge, LA
ML Seasons: 1
Pronunciation:
duh-LOO-chee

Overall Statistics

	G	AB	R	H	D	T	HR	RBI	SB	BB	SO	Avg	OBP	Slg
1997	17	27	3	6	1	0	1	3	0	4	7	.222	.344	.370
Career	17	27	3	6	1	0	1	3	0	4	7	.222	.344	.370

1997 Situational Stats

	AB	H	HR	RBI	Avg		AB	H	HR	RBI	Avg
Home	16	3	0	1	.188	LHP	2	0	0	0	.000
Road	11	3	1	2	.273	RHP	25	6	1	3	.240
First Half	23	4	1	2	.174	Sc Pos	8	2	0	2	.250
Scnd Half	4	2	0	1	.500	Clutch	5	1	0	0	.200

1997 Season

David Dellucci was drafted by the Orioles in the 10th round in 1995 out of the University of Mississippi, where he edged Todd Helton for the Southeastern Conference batting crown as a senior. Scouts were concerned about Dellucci's power, and he did nothing to allay those worries when he homered just nine times in his first two pro seasons. Last season saw a breakthrough by Dellucci, who hit 20 homers in 385 Double-A at-bats. He was poised during his major league debut, which featured a homer in his first start.

Hitting, Baserunning & Defense

Dellucci improved all-around in 1997. He added power while topping .300 for his third straight season as a pro. While his homer total increased, he continued to stroke doubles, draw walks and make good contact. His speed also improved, and he stole 11 bases in 15 attempts. He even held his own in center field, though he's more likely to play on one of the corners. His arm is average.

1998 Outlook

Dellucci was Baltimore's most advanced hitting prospect until Arizona took him in the second round of the expansion draft. Yamil Benitez might get first crack at right field for the Diamondbacks, but Dellucci should have a more productive career.

Todd Erdos

Position: RP
Bats: R **Throws:** R
Ht: 6' 1" **Wt:** 190

Opening Day Age: 24
Born: 11/21/73 in Washington, PA
ML Seasons: 1

Overall Statistics

	W	L	Pct.	ERA	G	GS	Sv	IP	H	BB	SO	HR	Ratio
1997	2	0	1.000	5.27	11	0	0	13.2	17	4	13	1	1.54
Career	2	0	1.000	5.27	11	0	0	13.2	17	4	13	1	1.54

1997 Situational Stats

	W	L	ERA	Sv	IP		AB	H	HR	RBI	Avg
Home	1	0	4.91	0	7.1	LHB	28	10	1	8	.357
Road	1	0	5.68	0	6.1	RHB	30	7	0	5	.233
First Half	1	0	7.11	0	6.1	Sc Pos	18	6	0	11	.333
Scnd Half	1	0	3.68	0	7.1	Clutch	7	2	0	3	.286

1997 Season

Todd Erdos recovered from a life-threatening virus to become one of baseball's better closer prospects. He missed the entire 1994 season when a virus attacked his pituitary gland, and wasn't at full strength until two years later. The Padres gave him his first taste of the big leagues in 1997, promoting him in June and again when rosters expanded in September. He pitched much better the second time around. Arizona drafted him in the second round of the expansion draft.

Pitching, Defense & Hitting

Erdos throws 90-92 MPH with a much-improved slider. He also has a very good changeup that ensures that hitters won't sit on his hard stuff. He locates his fastball well. Lefthanders hit .357 against him in the majors, but just .209 off him in Double-A. He's an average fielder who holds runners well. Basestealers have gone just 5-for-8 against him in the last two years. Erdos struck out in his only pro at-bat, which came with San Diego.

1998 Outlook

Sometimes compared to St. Louis' Jeff Brantley, Erdos had his moments in September. Hector Carrasco is the frontrunner to be the Diamondbacks' first closer, but it wouldn't be an upset if Erdos were to win the job.

Marty Janzen

Position: RP
Bats: R **Throws:** R
Ht: 6' 3" **Wt:** 200

Opening Day Age: 24
Born: 5/31/73 in Homestead, FL
ML Seasons: 2

Overall Statistics

	W	L	Pct.	ERA	G	GS	Sv	IP	H	BB	SO	HR	Ratio
1997	2	1	.667	3.60	12	0	0	25.0	23	13	17	4	1.44
Career	6	7	.462	6.39	27	11	0	98.2	118	51	64	20	1.71

1997 Situational Stats

	W	L	ERA	Sv	IP		AB	H	HR	RBI	Avg
Home	1	0	4.63	0	11.2	LHB	46	10	1	1	.217
Road	1	1	2.70	0	13.1	RHB	46	13	3	10	.283
First Half	0	0	2.25	0	4.0	Sc Pos	19	5	0	5	.263
Scnd Half	2	1	3.86	0	21.0	Clutch	6	2	0	1	.333

1997 Season

Regarded as a hot prospect only two years ago, Marty Janzen has fallen a long way. He was optioned to Triple-A at the start of 1997 and flunked out of the Syracuse rotation, but was called up twice when trades and injuries depleted Toronto's staff. He pitched well out of the bullpen over the last two months, and Arizona selected him with its final pick in the expansion draft.

Pitching, Defense & Hitting

When he was the key player in the 1995 David Cone trade, Janzen had great stuff. His fastball reached the low 90s, his curve was voted the best in the Florida State League and he had excellent command. Now his fastball tops out in the high 80s, and he gets by with a decent curveball, a slider and a changeup. It's a mystery how he could have lost his stuff so quickly. He's a solid fielder and a good athlete, and he cuts off the stolen base fairly well. Coming from the American League, he never has had a professional at-bat.

1998 Outlook

Manager Buck Showalter managed the Yankees when Janzen was in the New York system, so he may be able to spot what's gone wrong. Janzen may begin in the bullpen, but he might challenge for a rotation spot if he ever gets it back together.

Chris Jones

Position: RF/LF/CF
Bats: R **Throws:** R
Ht: 6' 2" **Wt:** 210

Opening Day Age: 32
Born: 12/16/65 in Utica, NY
ML Seasons: 7

Overall Statistics

	G	AB	R	H	D	T	HR	RBI	SB	BB	SO	Avg	OBP	Slg
1997	92	152	24	37	9	0	7	25	7	16	45	.243	.322	.441
Career	473	884	135	231	38	10	28	117	24	62	246	.261	.311	.422

1997 Situational Stats

	AB	H	HR	RBI	Avg		AB	H	HR	RBI	Avg
Home	78	18	4	13	.231	LHP	57	13	2	9	.228
Road	74	19	3	12	.257	RHP	95	24	5	16	.253
First Half	89	21	5	17	.236	Sc Pos	44	11	2	18	.250
Scnd Half	63	16	2	8	.254	Clutch	25	4	0	1	.160

1997 Season

Over the last three years, Chris Jones has established himself as one of the National League's most dangerous pinch hitters. He took his act to San Diego in 1997 and established himself as the Padres' top righthanded bat off the bench.

Hitting, Baserunning & Defense

Jones is an aggressive hitter who always guesses fastball. If he gets one early in the count, he can do some damage. He also can get himself quickly into a hole and will strike out a lot when he's behind in the count. Jones never has been a good breaking-ball hitter. He has above-average speed and good aggressiveness as a basestealer. He rarely has had regular outfield duty, but he has decent range and an average arm. He can play both corners.

1998 Outlook

Jones never will be an everyday player, but he has value as a reserve because of his ability to come off the bench and hit. He refused an assignment to the minors after the season, choosing instead to become a free agent. Proven pinch hitters with power and speed are becoming a rare commodity these days, so he was in demand before signing a two-year contract worth $1.4 million with Arizona.

Cory Lidle

Position: RP
Bats: R **Throws:** R
Ht: 5'11" **Wt:** 180

Opening Day Age: 26
Born: 3/22/72 in Hollywood, CA
ML Seasons: 1
Pronunciation: LIE-dell

Overall Statistics

	W	L	Pct.	ERA	G	GS	Sv	IP	H	BB	SO	HR	Ratio
1997	7	2	.778	3.53	54	2	2	81.2	86	20	54	7	1.30
Career	7	2	.778	3.53	54	2	2	81.2	86	20	54	7	1.30

1997 Situational Stats

	W	L	ERA	Sv	IP		AB	H	HR	RBI	Avg
Home	2	1	4.15	1	39.0	LHB	137	44	5	20	.321
Road	5	1	2.95	1	42.2	RHB	177	42	2	22	.237
First Half	3	1	4.06	1	37.2	Sc Pos	91	29	1	32	.319
Scnd Half	4	1	3.07	1	44.0	Clutch	88	21	2	8	.239

1997 Season

Cory Lidle's travels continue. After playing in the Minnesota system, an independent league and the Milwaukee organization, Lidle was traded to the Mets in 1996 and made a solid major league debut in 1997. After being called up in May, he became one of New York manager Bobby Valentine's favorite middle relievers and setup men. Lidle was left unprotected in the expansion draft, however, and Arizona made him a first-round pick.

Pitching, Defense & Hitting

Lidle's fastball only reaches the mid-80s, but he gets grounders with a good curveball and a decent changeup. His main weakness is that he lacks an out pitch against lefthanders. He's very tough on righties. He was an effective starter in the minors and may be able to go back to the rotation at some point. He's a fine fielder who fancies himself a fifth infielder, and he's a real challenge to run on. He went 0-for-5 with four strikeouts at the plate.

1998 Outlook

Lidle figures to be a prominent member of the Diamondbacks' staff, either as a starter or a reliever. The trick will be to find the job he can fill best.

Damian Miller

Position: C
Bats: R **Throws:** R
Ht: 6' 3" **Wt:** 202

Opening Day Age: 28
Born: 10/13/69 in West
Salem, WI
ML Seasons: 1

Overall Statistics

	G	AB	R	H	D	T	HR	RBI	SB	BB	SO	Avg	OBP	Slg
1997	25	66	5	18	1	0	2	13	0	2	12	.273	.282	.379
Career	25	66	5	18	1	0	2	13	0	2	12	.273	.282	.379

1997 Situational Stats

	AB	H	HR	RBI	Avg		AB	H	HR	RBI	Avg
Home	31	8	1	7	.258	LHP	22	4	0	1	.182
Road	35	10	1	6	.286	RHP	44	14	2	12	.318
First Half	0	0	0	0	-	Sc Pos	18	5	1	11	.278
Scnd Half	66	18	2	13	.273	Clutch	4	0	0	0	.000

1997 Season

Rookie catcher Damian Miller began 1997 at Triple-A Salt Lake. Originally drafted in the 20th round in 1990, he made slow progress up the ladder. He hit well at times and showed good defense, but never established himself as a prospect. When Greg Myers was traded to Atlanta, Miller got his shot with the Twins and played well as Terry Steinbach's caddie. Arizona took him in the second round of the expansion draft.

Hitting, Baserunning & Defense

Miller isn't an outstanding offensive player, but he makes contact and can drive a pitch for power if the hurler makes a mistake. He was impatient in the majors, but his walk rate should improve as he gets more comfortable. Like most catchers, he's a station-to-station runner, though he doesn't run himself into outs. Defensively, he owns a strong arm, moves well behind the plate, calls a good game and has the respect of both the pitchers and the coaching staff.

1998 Outlook

Miller isn't a terrific player, but many teams do worse for a backup catcher. He's bright, works hard and could hang around for years as a reserve.

Bob Wolcott

Position: SP
Bats: R **Throws:** R
Ht: 6' 0" **Wt:** 190

Opening Day Age: 24
Born: 9/8/73 in
Huntington Beach, CA
ML Seasons: 3

Overall Statistics

	W	L	Pct.	ERA	G	GS	Sv	IP	H	BB	SO	HR	Ratio
1997	5	6	.455	6.03	19	18	0	100.0	129	29	58	22	1.58
Career	15	18	.455	5.66	56	52	0	286.0	351	97	155	54	1.57

1997 Situational Stats

	W	L	ERA	Sv	IP		AB	H	HR	RBI	Avg
Home	3	2	5.08	0	56.2	LHB	199	64	14	39	.322
Road	2	4	7.27	0	43.1	RHB	212	65	8	27	.307
First Half	4	4	5.53	0	70.0	Sc Pos	104	31	7	45	.298
Scnd Half	1	2	7.20	0	30.0	Clutch	2	1	0	0	.500

1997 Season

Bob Wolcott began the year in Seattle's rotation, but didn't pitch well and was demoted in May. Called back up in June, he spent the remainder of the season bouncing up and down between Seattle and Triple-A Tacoma. He was very inconsistent and concluded his year by getting hammered in August and then not pitching in September. The Diamondbacks selected him in the second round of the expansion draft.

Pitching, Defense & Hitting

Wolcott throws an 87-MPH fastball, a changeup and a curveball that he tends to hang. He has problems with homers, allowing 22 in 100 innings. He doesn't walk many, but hitters know he'll be around the plate and have success when they jump on his first pitch. His stuff isn't awful, but Seattle manager Lou Piniella shows no affection for softtossers. Wolcott is an excellent fielder and allowed three steals in 1997, the first three he's surrendered in the majors. He's 0-for-1 as a major league hitter.

1998 Outlook

Wolcott is just 24. He has been hit hard during stints in the big leagues, but he's smart, has good control and never has been hurt. He'll be given another chance, especially in light of his heroics in the 1995 American League Championship Series.

Arizona Diamondbacks Minor League Prospects

Organization Overview:

The consensus among baseball people was that Arizona had a more successful expansion draft than Tampa Bay. The Diamondbacks' first six picks were solid, and they also made some solid second-round choices such as righthanders Chris Clemons (White Sox) and Todd Erdos (Padres) and outfielder David Dellucci (Orioles). Arizona caught the attention of other teams in 1996, when it spent more than $19 million to sign amateur free agents Travis Lee ($10 million), John Patterson ($6.075 million), Vladimir Nunez ($1.75 million) and Larry Rodriguez ($1.25 million). The Diamondbacks did decently in their first amateur draft in 1996, but their effort last year was rated the worst in the game by *Baseball America*.

Nick Bierbrodt

Position: P
Bats: L **Throws:** L
Ht: 6' 5" **Wt:** 180

Opening Day Age: 19
Born: 5/16/78 in
Tarzana, CA

Recent Statistics

	W	L	ERA	G	GS	Sv	IP	H	R	BB	SO	HR
96 R Diamondback	1	1	1.66	8	8	0	38.0	25	9	13	46	1
96 R Lethbridge	2	0	0.50	3	3	0	18.0	12	4	5	23	0
97 A South Bend	2	4	4.04	15	15	0	75.2	77	43	37	64	4

The first amateur draft pick in Diamondback history, Bierbrodt reaped a lucrative windfall. He signed for $525,000 and got another $521,000 because of a provision in his contract that called for his bonus to be increased by the rise in first-round bonuses from 1995 to 1996. Arizona helped drive the price up by signing Lee and Patterson. Bierbrodt throws 90 MPH, hard for a teenaged lefty. He also has a curveball and changeup that are inconsistent. A ribcage pull in spring training delayed the start of his season, and he had modest success in Class A. He's at least two years away from contributing in Arizona.

Jason Boyd

Position: P
Bats: R **Throws:** R
Ht: 6' 2" **Wt:** 165

Opening Day Age: 25
Born: 2/23/73 in St.
Clair, IL

Recent Statistics

	W	L	ERA	G	GS	Sv	IP	H	R	BB	SO	HR
96 A Clearwater	11	8	3.90	26	26	0	161.2	160	75	49	120	12
97 AA Reading	10	6	4.82	48	7	0	115.2	113	65	64	98	16

A first-round pick in the expansion draft, Boyd took to a move to the bullpen in Double-A last season. A 1994 eighth-round selection by the Phillies out of John A. Logan (Ill.) Community College, he had drawn interest from Nebraska and Penn State as a quarterback. He throws a 92-93 MPH fastball, but needs to throw it more often and for more strikes. He's more comfortable with his slider, and his lack of an offspeed pitch is what prompted his shift from the rotation. He could use a year in Triple-A, but Arizona might press him into major league duty as a setup man.

Edwin Diaz

Position: 2B
Bats: R **Throws:** R
Ht: 5' 11" **Wt:** 170

Opening Day Age: 23
Born: 1/15/75 in
Bayamon, PR

Recent Statistics

	G	AB	R	H	D	T	HR	RBI	SB	BB	SO	AVG
96 AA Tulsa	121	499	70	132	33	6	16	65	8	25	122	.265
97 AAA Okla City	20	73	6	8	3	1	4	1	1	2	27	.110
97 AA Tulsa	105	440	65	121	31	1	15	46	6	33	102	.275
97 MLE	125	498	58	114	29	0	11	41	4	24	136	.229

Diaz quietly had established himself as one of the top second-base prospects in the minors, then regressed in 1997. He batted .110 with a 27-2 strikeout/walk ratio in Triple-A, forcing him to return to Double-A for a second season. When the Rangers didn't protect him from the expansion draft, Arizona snapped him up in the first round. A 1993 second-round pick, he has very good power for a second baseman and uses the whole field. He's average as a runner and as a defender. His plate discipline is a major concern after he fanned 251 times and walked just 60 the past two seasons. Tony Batista will play second base for the Diamondbacks in their inaugural season, but Diaz could supplant him in 1999.

Ben Ford

Position: P
Bats: R **Throws:** R
Ht: 6' 7" **Wt:** 200

Opening Day Age: 22
Born: 8/15/75 in Cedar
Rapids, IA

Recent Statistics

	W	L	ERA	G	GS	Sv	IP	H	R	BB	SO	HR
96 A Greensboro	2	6	4.26	43	0	2	82.1	75	48	33	84	3
97 A Tampa	4	0	1.93	32	0	18	37.1	27	8	14	37	1
97 AA Norwich	4	3	4.22	28	0	1	42.2	35	28	19	38	1

Ford has closer potential, but most baseball people were shocked when Arizona took him in the first round of the expansion draft. They figured the Yankee selected would be five-tool outfielder Donzell McDonald. A 20th-round pick in 1994 out of Indian Hills (Fla.) Community College, Ford throws 92-94 MPH with a nasty breaking ball. He reached Double-A at age 21 in 1997, and has struck out nearly a batter per inning while being consistently tough to hit. He needs at least another year in the minors, but he has the best chance of all the Diamondbacks' expansion draft picks to one day be an effective closer.

Hanley Frias

Position: SS
Bats: B **Throws:** R
Ht: 6' 0" **Wt:** 160

Opening Day Age: 24
Born: 12/5/73 in Villa Altagracia, DR

Recent Statistics

	G	AB	R	H	D	T	HR	RBI	SB	BB	SO	AVG
96 AA Tulsa	134	505	73	145	24	12	2	41	9	30	73	.287
97 AAA Okla City	132	484	64	128	17	4	5	46	35	56	72	.264
97 AL Texas	14	26	4	5	1	0	0	1	0	1	4	.192
97 MLE	132	477	59	121	15	4	4	42	27	52	74	.254

Benji Gil has been a major disappointment at shortstop, so the Rangers may have turned to Frias in 1998. That possibility was eliminated, though, when the Diamondbacks took him in the second round of the expansion draft. Signed out of the Dominican Republic, he has the arm and the range to play a solid shortstop. His power is negligible, but his hitting and on-base skills are decent. He enhances his offensive game with the speed to steal 20 bases in the majors. Arizona is stockpiling talent at shortstop, signing free agent Jay Bell and drafting the offensive-minded Danny Klassen. If Frias doesn't continue to develop as a hitter, he may become a utilityman.

Danny Klassen

Position: SS
Bats: R **Throws:** R
Ht: 6' 0" **Wt:** 175

Opening Day Age: 22
Born: 9/22/75 in Leamington, Ontario, Canada

Recent Statistics

	G	AB	R	H	D	T	HR	RBI	SB	BB	SO	AVG
96 A Stockton	118	432	58	116	22	4	2	46	14	34	77	.269
97 AA El Paso	135	519	112	172	30	6	14	81	16	48	104	.331
97 MLE	135	490	78	143	25	4	9	56	11	28	110	.292

Klassen completed his comeback from major knee surgery in 1995 by batting .331 at Double-A El Paso in 1997, but also made 50 errors. A 1993 second-round pick, he has the hands to play shortstop but must tone down an erratic arm. He can hit some doubles and homers and steal an occasional base, but could improve his knowledge of the strike zone. Arizona took him in the second round of the expansion draft, but also signed Bell and won't have to rush Klassen. He'll spend the entire season in Triple-A trying to improve his glovework. He probably ranks behind Frias on Arizona's current depth chart, but he has a much higher offensive ceiling.

John Patterson

Position: P
Bats: R **Throws:** R
Ht: 6' 6" **Wt:** 200

Opening Day Age: 20
Born: 1/30/78 in Orange, TX

Recent Statistics

	W	L	ERA	G	GS	Sv	IP	H	R	BB	SO	HR
97 A South Bend	1	9	3.23	18	18	0	78.0	63	32	34	95	3

Patterson was the fifth overall pick by Montreal in the 1996 draft, but became a free agent after a contract snafu and signed with Arizona. He didn't pitch professionally in 1996 and started last year in extended spring training, then blew Class A hitters away with a mid-90s fastball and above-average breaking stuff. His 1-9 record was mostly a reflection of his being kept on a strict pitch limit that made it nearly impossible to pick up victories. Like most young pitchers, he needs to improve his changeup, command and stamina. He has better stuff than Bierbrodt and could be on a faster track to the Diamondbacks.

Neil Weber

Position: P
Bats: L **Throws:** L
Ht: 6' 5" **Wt:** 205

Opening Day Age: 25
Born: 12/6/72 in Newport Beach, CA

Recent Statistics

	W	L	ERA	G	GS	Sv	IP	H	R	BB	SO	HR
96 AA Harrisburg	7	4	3.03	18	18	0	107.0	90	37	44	74	8
97 AAA Ottawa	2	5	7.94	9	9	0	39.2	46	46	40	27	7
97 AA Harrisburg	7	6	3.83	18	18	0	112.2	93	56	51	121	17

Weber has a fastball that most lefthanders would kill for, but his record hasn't been on par with his 94-95 MPH heat. He's 37-38 since he was taken by the Expos in the eighth round of the 1993 draft out of Cuesta (Calif.) Community College, and he has spent most of the last three years at Double-A Harrisburg. That's not exactly a sign of progress. Arizona has faith in his fastball, however, and took him in the first round of the expansion draft. Weber also throws a big league curveball as well as a changeup, but he doesn't throw enough strikes or blow as many people away as he should. He walked a batter an inning and his strikeout rate plummeted in Triple-A, an indication he's not nearly ready.

Others to Watch

Outfielders **Stanton Cameron** and **Mike Stoner** smacked 33 homers each in high Class-A, but neither is a true prospect. Cameron is a 28-year-old journeyman with his sixth organization. Stoner, 24, led the minors with 203 hits and 142 RBI. . . Righthander **Vladimir Nunez**, 23, is a much-ballyhooed Cuban defector. He has a mid-90s fastball, but has been hit hard in Class-A for two straight years. . . **Mark Osborne** could supplant Jorge Fabregas' as Arizona's catcher in a couple of years. He got a taste of Double-A at age 19, and hit .253-9-56 last year. . . Righthander **Brad Penny**, 19, went 10-5, 2.73 with 116 strikeouts in 118 2/3 Class-A innings. He's not as touted as Bierbrodt, Nunez or Patterson, but throws in the low 90s. . . Righthander **Larry Rodriguez**, 23, defected from Cuba with Nunez. His stuff isn't as good, but he can top 90 MPH and has a promising slider.

Bobby Cox

1997 Season

A six-game loss to the eventual World Series champion Marlins in the National League Championship Series left many people feeling that the Braves' 1997 season was a disappointment. That perception is the ultimate testament to the consistent excellence of Bobby Cox' club, which won more regular-season games than any team in the majors last year and has been to a record six straight postseasons. The bottom line is that Cox took a team that had been shaken up by some big offseason moves and reshaped it into perhaps the strongest team in baseball.

Offense

Cox uses a set lineup, but isn't afraid to use a hitter in a platoon role if he feels that's all the hitter deserves. He prefers to advance runners via the sacrifice or stolen base rather than the hit-and-run. He values speed on the basepaths, and often will pinch-run in situations where one run is important. He won't tolerate a distinctly below-average offensive player at a corner position.

Pitching & Defense

Cox is sensitive to the needs of his hurlers and has worked with pitching coach Leo Mazzone to keep the Braves' staff as healthy as any in baseball. Many managers have emulated his practice of holding his starters to a strict pitch count. He insists on putting good defensive players up the middle, and likes to match up his catchers with the pitchers they handle the best. He'll ride the hot hand with his bullpen, but shows more patience with established pitchers.

1998 Outlook

If losing the NLCS amounts to a disappointing season, it's obvious what Cox needs to do to be deemed a success. It may be much more difficult for him to bring the Braves back to the World Series in 1998 because they were expected to lose a few key free agents. His ability to make changes on the fly while keeping the team clicking on all cylinders will continue to be tested.

Born: 5/21/41 in Tulsa, OK

Playing Experience: 1968-1969, NYA

Managerial Experience: 16 seasons

Manager Statistics

Year	Team, Lg	W	L	Pct	GB	Finish
1997	Atlanta, NL	101	61	.623	—	1st East
16 Seasons		1312	1089	.546	—	—

1997 Starting Pitchers by Days Rest

	≤3	4	5	6+
Braves Starts	10	96	29	19
Braves ERA	3.14	2.77	3.17	4.31
NL Avg Starts	3	90	38	22
NL ERA	4.23	4.05	4.27	4.52

1997 Situational Stats

	Bobby Cox	NL Average
Hit & Run Success %	31.3	36.4
Stolen Base Success %	65.1	68.4
Platoon Pct.	64.4	56.3
Defensive Subs	29	26
High-Pitch Outings	23	12
Quick/Slow Hooks	13/7	18/10
Sacrifice Attempts	112	96

1997 Rankings (National League)

⇒ 1st in starts with over 120 pitches (23), starts on three days rest (10) and 2+ pitching changes in low scoring games (32)

⇒ 2nd in sacrifice bunt attempts (112) and intentional walks (46)

Atlanta Braves

357

Jeff Blauser

1997 Season

Surprise! Just when Jeff Blauser had been all but written off, he came up with the best year of his career, both at the plate and in the field. Three straight subpar seasons had many convinced that he was on the downslide, but it turned out that all he needed was a return to health.

Hitting

Blauser is a patient hitter who usually takes a strike before he starts hitting. By crowding the plate and striding into the ball, he can reach any pitch. However, quite a few pitches end up reaching various parts of his anatomy as well. He sprays the ball and uses the whole field very well. When healthy he's an ideal No. 2 hitter, but he also filled in capably for leadoff man Kenny Lofton in 1997.

Baserunning & Defense

Free from the knee and hand ailments that plagued him in 1996, Blauser was much improved in the field last year. He won't dazzle you with his range or his arm, but he knows how to position himself and never tries to make plays beyond his capabilites. On the bags, he has decent speed but doesn't go for the extra base or a steal unless he's sure he can make it.

1998 Outlook

Blauser is a free agent who appears to have played his final game for the Braves, who signed Rockies veteran Walt Weiss to a three-year deal to play shortstop. When Blauser's body allows him to play his game, he's a very complete player with few outstanding strengths but hardly any weaknesses. The only real concern is that his wiry frame will remain vulnerable to nagging injuries. Even when healthy, he tends to wear down over the course of a season, and as he edges closer to his mid-30s, his reliability is more of a concern than ever.

Position: SS
Bats: R **Throws:** R
Ht: 6' 1" **Wt:** 180

Opening Day Age: 32
Born: 11/8/65 in Los Gatos, CA
ML Seasons: 11
Pronunciation: BLAU-zer

Overall Statistics

	G	AB	R	H	D	T	HR	RBI	SB	BB	SO	Avg	OBP	Slg
1997	151	519	90	160	31	4	17	70	5	70	101	.308	.405	.482
Career	1184	3961	601	1060	201	28	109	461	61	483	792	.268	.355	.415

Where He Hits the Ball

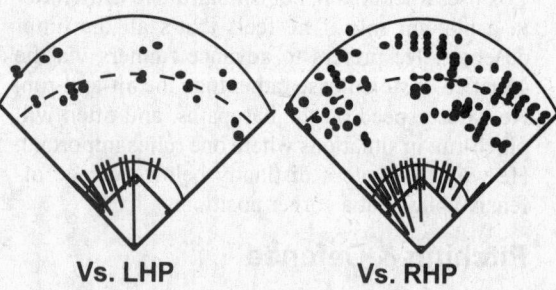

Vs. LHP   **Vs. RHP**

1997 Situational Stats

	AB	H	HR	RBI	Avg		AB	H	HR	RBI	Avg
Home	255	83	9	32	.325	LHP	125	39	7	20	.312
Road	264	77	8	38	.292	RHP	394	121	10	50	.307
First Half	283	98	12	42	.346	Sc Pos	113	32	5	52	.283
Scnd Half	236	62	5	28	.263	Clutch	89	34	3	18	.382

1997 Rankings (National League)

⇒ 2nd in batting average in the clutch
⇒ 4th in hit by pitch (20) and errors at shortstop (16)
⇒ 5th in sacrifice flies (9) and on-base percentage for a leadoff hitter (.391)
⇒ 6th in lowest fielding percentage at shortstop (.973)
⇒ 8th in slugging percentage vs. lefthanded pitchers (.568)
⇒ 9th in on-base percentage vs. lefthanded pitchers (.417)
⇒ 10th in batting average vs. lefthanded pitchers, batting average on an 0-2 count (.269) and batting average at home
⇒ Led the Braves in sacrifice flies (9), hit by pitch (20) and batting average in the clutch

Tom Glavine

1997 Season

Tom Glavine didn't do anything new in 1997. He just kept on pitching masterfully, maintaining his status as one of the top southpaws in baseball. With better support from his offense and bullpen, he easily might have won close to 20 games. As it was, his 14-7 record was hardly a disappointment.

Position: SP
Bats: L **Throws:** L
Ht: 6' 1" **Wt:** 185

Opening Day Age: 32
Born: 3/25/66 in Concord, MA
ML Seasons: 11
Pronunciation: GLA-vin

Pitching

Glavine can be one of the most frustrating pitchers a hitter will face. His game plan is obvious, but knowing what's coming doesn't seem to help batters. His entire philosophy consists of throwing his 90-MPH fastball and changeup just off the outside corner, continually expanding the strike zone to lure hitters into chasing bad pitches. He'll occasionally move a hitter back off the plate, but he'll never give in, even when he falls behind. Keeping the ball down is a big part of his game, and he gets plenty of double plays.

Defense & Hitting

Glavine varies his stretch delivery and is one of the toughest pitchers in baseball for baserunners to read. Very few try to run on him and even fewer are successful. He's as quick as a goalie on defense, and always helps himself with the glove. A three-time recipient of the Silver Slugger award, he batted .222 with seven walks and 17 sacrifice hits in 1997.

1998 Outlook

It's not hard to predict continued success for a player like Glavine, who's consistent, effective and durable. The only possible cause for concern is the fact that he averaged 111 pitches per start in 1997, by far the highest mark of his career. In all probability he'll handle it just fine, but there's a chance that he might show signs of fatigue. On the other hand, the move to more pitcher-friendly Turner Field helped him last year and should continue to shave points off his ERA.

Overall Statistics

	W	L	Pct.	ERA	G	GS	Sv	IP	H	BB	SO	HR	Ratio
1997	14	7	.667	2.96	33	33	0	240.0	197	79	152	20	1.15
Career	153	99	.607	3.40	331	331	0	2196.1	2068	743	1364	147	1.28

How Often He Throws Strikes

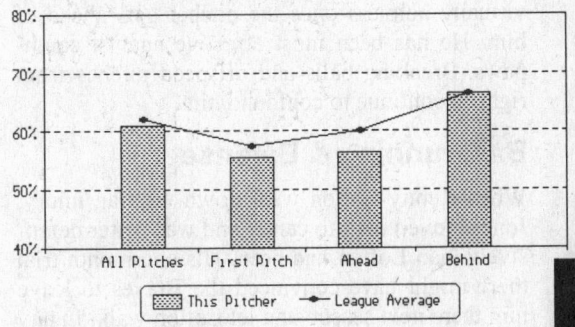

1997 Situational Stats

	W	L	ERA	Sv	IP		AB	H	HR	RBI	Avg
Home	5	2	2.13	0	97.1	LHB	177	42	4	10	.237
Road	9	5	3.53	0	142.2	RHB	693	155	16	64	.224
First Half	9	4	2.62	0	134.0	Sc Pos	164	30	5	54	.183
Scnd Half	5	3	3.40	0	106.0	Clutch	98	22	1	4	.224

1997 Rankings (National League)

⇒ 1st in GDPs induced (33)
⇒ 2nd in sacrifice bunts (17), most GDPs induced per 9 innings (1.2) and lowest batting average allowed with runners in scoring position
⇒ 3rd in ERA at home
⇒ 4th in pitches thrown (3,672) and most GDPs induced per GDP situation (20.2%)
⇒ 5th in shutouts (2), innings pitched, batters faced (970) and walks allowed
⇒ Led the Braves in sacrifice bunts (17), walks allowed, GDPs induced (33), lowest batting average allowed (.226), lowest stolen base percentage allowed (50.0%), most GDPs induced per 9 innings (1.2), most GDPs induced per GDP situation (20.2%), ERA at home and lowest batting average allowed vs. righthanded batters

Andruw Jones

1997 Season

The reviews of Andruw Jones' first full season in the majors were decidedly mixed. On one hand, he played in 153 games, displayed exciting power and defensive skills, and produced as well as a 20 year old could be expected to. On the other hand, however, he wasn't the overnight superstar that some had anticipated. He didn't always hustle, and a late-season slump all but eliminated him from Rookie of the Year considerations.

Hitting

Though he has terrific power for someone so young, Jones is understandably raw at the plate. He does his best hitting early in the count, and he's virtually helpless once the pitcher gets ahead of him. He has been most effective against southpaws. Breaking balls and offspeed pitches from righties continue to confound him.

Baserunning & Defense

When Kenny Lofton went down with an injury, Jones moved over to center and was better defensively than Lofton had been. His one-month trial there might have convinced the Braves to leave him there next season and let Lofton walk. In any of the three outfield positions, Jones has great speed and one of the best throwing arms in the league. He'll show good instincts but also botch some routine plays, and his mishandling of a line drive may have turned the National League Championship Series in the Marlins' favor. Jones has a lot to learn about basestealing, but he was reasonably successful on raw skill alone in 1997.

1998 Outlook

Jones is unquestionably one of the brightest young prospects in the game and will remain a fixture in the Braves' outfield for years to come. Even with his obvious weaknesses, he remains a quality player. It's scary to think of how good he might become with a little more experience and maturity. He is expected to take over as the Braves' full-time center fielder.

Position: RF/CF
Bats: R **Throws:** R
Ht: 6' 1" **Wt:** 185

Opening Day Age: 20
Born: 4/23/77 in Willemstad, Curacao
ML Seasons: 2

Overall Statistics

	G	AB	R	H	D	T	HR	RBI	SB	BB	SO	Avg	OBP	Slg
1997	153	399	60	92	18	1	18	70	20	56	107	.231	.329	.416
Career	184	505	71	115	25	2	23	83	23	63	136	.228	.317	.422

Where He Hits the Ball

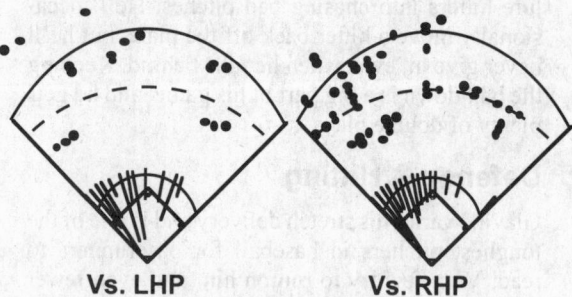

Vs. LHP   **Vs. RHP**

1997 Situational Stats

	AB	H	HR	RBI	Avg		AB	H	HR	RBI	Avg
Home	187	38	5	30	.203	LHP	139	39	7	28	.281
Road	212	54	13	40	.255	RHP	260	53	11	42	.204
First Half	195	53	7	31	.272	Sc Pos	124	29	4	48	.234
Scnd Half	204	39	11	39	.191	Clutch	73	15	3	9	.205

1997 Rankings (National League)

⇒ 3rd in lowest batting average on a 3-2 count (.056) and lowest batting average with two strikes (.112)

⇒ 6th in errors in right field (5) and highest percentage of swings that missed (30.1%)

⇒ 8th in lowest percentage of swings put into play (36.3%)

⇒ 10th in lowest stolen base percentage (64.5%)

Chipper Jones

1997 Season

When your name is Chipper Jones, it's tough to keep up with expectations. All Jones did was put up better numbers than just about every third baseman in the National League while batting third for the winningest team in baseball. But a late slump dropped his average below .300 and he finished with nine fewer homers than he'd hit in 1996. What would have been a superb season for just about any other hitter hardly drew any raves at all for Jones.

Hitting

Jones is a switch-hitter who can handle high pitches from either side of the plate. He has good power to the opposite field, a good eye and an ability to fight off tough two-strike pitches. He has less bat speed from the right side of the plate and doesn't hit with quite the same level of authority as he does lefthanded. The move from hitter-friendly Atlanta-Fulton County Stadium to the more pitcher-friendly Turner Field took a chunk out of his power numbers.

Baserunning & Defense

Jones has good speed and wisely picks his spots to steal. He is one of the best percentage basestealers in the game. He runs the bases aggressively and alertly. A natural shortstop, Jones has both the strong arm and the quick reflexes needed to handle third base, and he plays the position well. His soft hands and natural athletic ability will make him one of the best defensive players in the league if he's able to cut down on his careless errors.

1998 Outlook

If Jones ever refines his righthanded swing to the point where it's on par with his approach from the opposite side of the plate, he'll be a tremendous offensive force. As it is, he's a classic No. 3 hitter who excels in nearly every aspect of the game. He should be a strong MVP candidate for the next few years.

Position: 3B
Bats: B **Throws:** R
Ht: 6' 3" **Wt:** 200

Opening Day Age: 25
Born: 4/24/72 in DeLand, FL
ML Seasons: 4

Overall Statistics

	G	AB	R	H	D	T	HR	RBI	SB	BB	SO	Avg	OBP	Slg
1997	157	597	100	176	41	3	21	111	20	76	88	.295	.371	.479
Career	462	1722	303	502	96	11	74	307	42	237	276	.292	.374	.489

Where He Hits the Ball

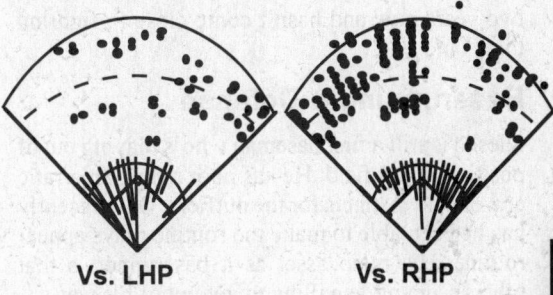

Vs. LHP   Vs. RHP

1997 Situational Stats

	AB	H	HR	RBI	Avg		AB	H	HR	RBI	Avg
Home	304	96	7	56	.316	LHP	196	49	1	21	.250
Road	293	80	14	55	.273	RHP	401	127	20	90	.317
First Half	319	98	14	69	.307	Sc Pos	172	54	6	90	.314
Scnd Half	278	78	7	42	.281	Clutch	90	23	0	15	.256

1997 Rankings (National League)

⇒ 3rd in GDPs (20)
⇒ 5th in fielding percentage at third base (.955)
⇒ 6th in doubles
⇒ 9th in runs scored, games played (157), stolen base percentage (80.0%), batting average vs. righthanded pitchers, lowest slugging percentage vs. lefthanded pitchers (.342) and errors at third base (15)
⇒ 10th in times on base (252), plate appearances (679) and slugging percentage vs. righthanded pitchers (.546)
⇒ Led the Braves in at-bats, runs scored, hits, doubles, total bases (286), RBI, walks, times on base (252), pitches seen (2,437), plate appearances (679), games played (157) and stolen base percentage (80.0%)

Ryan Klesko

1997 Season

A year ago Ryan Klesko seemed on the brink of stardom, but his 1997 campaign marked a definite step backward. Though he remained a useful power threat, his numbers declined across the board and he failed to make any progress in improving any of his weaknesses.

Hitting

Klesko in a sense is the biggest, strongest kid on the playground. He knows he can crush any righthander's fastball to all parts of the park. He doesn't show nearly as much confidence against lefties, and for good reason. They own him. He pulls off their breaking balls and lunges out in front of their offspeed stuff. He has faced them for two years now and hasn't come close to figuring them out.

Baserunning & Defense

Klesko is still a first baseman who's playing out of position in left field. He has poor range, an erratic arm and no instincts for the outfield. Only recently has he been able to make the routine plays appear routine. His main asset as a baserunner is that others seem quite willing to get out of his way.

1998 Outlook

It's time for Klesko to prove that he's something more than a platoon player. His chances of succeeding don't seem nearly as good as they did a year or two ago. Even so, he remains a potential 40-home-run threat, and there aren't too many players who can say that. His hitting might have improved with a return to first base, which opened temporarily with the trade of Fred McGriff to Tampa Bay. Then the Braves signed free agent Andres Galarraga, erasing that possibility.

Position: LF/1B
Bats: L **Throws:** L
Ht: 6' 3" **Wt:** 220

Opening Day Age: 26
Born: 6/12/71 in Westminster, CA
ML Seasons: 6

Overall Statistics

	G	AB	R	H	D	T	HR	RBI	SB	BB	SO	Avg	OBP	Slg
1997	143	467	67	122	23	6	24	84	4	48	130	.261	.334	.490
Career	530	1600	250	447	83	15	100	300	16	192	388	.279	.358	.538

Where He Hits the Ball

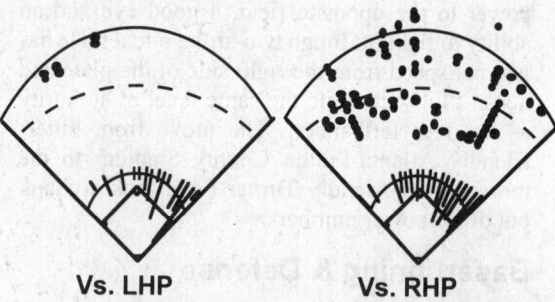

Vs. LHP   Vs. RHP

1997 Situational Stats

	AB	H	HR	RBI	Avg		AB	H	HR	RBI	Avg
Home	230	62	10	44	.270	LHP	106	21	3	14	.198
Road	237	60	14	40	.253	RHP	361	101	21	70	.280
First Half	262	68	14	48	.260	Sc Pos	119	34	7	55	.286
Scnd Half	205	54	10	36	.263	Clutch	58	6	1	3	.103

1997 Rankings (National League)

⇒ 1st in lowest batting average in the clutch and errors in left field (6)
⇒ 2nd in lowest fielding percentage in left field (.969)
⇒ 6th in highest percentage of swings on the first pitch (42.0%)
⇒ 7th in strikeouts
⇒ 8th in lowest batting average on a 3-2 count (.079)
⇒ 10th in lowest percentage of swings put into play (37.0%)
⇒ Led the Braves in home runs, strikeouts, slugging percentage, HR frequency (19.5 ABs per HR) and batting average with the bases loaded (.385)

Mark Lemke

1997 Season

In 1997 Mark Lemke gave the Braves what they've come to expect from him: sporadic offense but slick, flawless defense. That was, until he got injured. Torn ankle ligaments put him on the shelf in August, and he never made a recovery. He missed the entire postseason. Earlier in the year, he was sidelined by a vision problem.

Hitting

Lemke is a weak hitter who uses a dead-level swing to slap high pitches to the opposite field. He's got a bit more power from the right side than from the left, but not enough on either side to worry enemy pitchers. He doesn't draw many walks, but rarely strikes out and knows how to bunt. He has batted second in the order from time to time, but he's best suited to hit near the bottom of the lineup. He really hasn't been an effective offensive player in the last three seasons.

Baserunning & Defense

Lemke's calling card is his textbook defensive play. Naturally low to the ground, he seemingly covers the entire right side of the infield. He glides to the ball off the crack of the bat, gathering it up with his soft hands and whipping it to first with a snap throw. His double-play pivot wastes no time or movement, and ranks with the best in baseball. His straight-line speed is much less impressive, and he's not an aggressive basestealer or baserunner.

1998 Outlook

Lemke's contract was up at the end of the year, and the Braves may opt to save some money by going with a younger second baseman, such as Tony Graffanino. Provided that his leg is sound, Lemke should be able to help a team looking for someone to solidify its infield defense.

Position: 2B
Bats: B **Throws:** R
Ht: 5' 9" **Wt:** 167

Opening Day Age: 32
Born: 8/13/65 in Utica, NY
ML Seasons: 10
Pronunciation: LEM-kee

Overall Statistics

	G	AB	R	H	D	T	HR	RBI	SB	BB	SO	Avg	OBP	Slg
1997	109	351	33	86	17	1	2	26	2	33	51	.245	.306	.316
Career	1038	3139	339	778	121	15	32	263	11	342	326	.248	.319	.327

Where He Hits the Ball

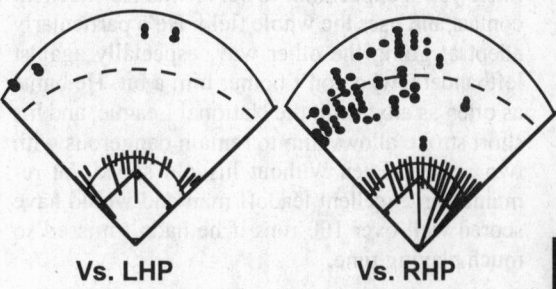

Vs. LHP   **Vs. RHP**

1997 Situational Stats

	AB	H	HR	RBI	Avg		AB	H	HR	RBI	Avg
Home	178	46	2	11	.258	LHP	69	18	1	6	.261
Road	173	40	0	15	.231	RHP	282	68	1	20	.241
First Half	245	55	2	19	.224	Sc Pos	79	20	0	23	.253
Scnd Half	106	31	0	7	.292	Clutch	58	14	0	3	.241

1997 Rankings (National League)

⇒ 6th in fielding percentage at second base (.980)
⇒ 8th in errors at second base (10)

Kenny Lofton

1997 Season

Depending on whom you listen to, Kenny Lofton's 1997 season was either a moderate success or an unmitigated disaster. The expectations were high, no doubt, after he came to Atlanta in a spring deal that sent former Braves leadoff man Marquis Grissom to Cleveland. It was inevitable that both players would be judged in comparison to each other, and both seemed to suffer for it. Hampered all year by groin problems, Lofton hit well and continued to score runs, but his basestealing fell apart completely.

Hitting

As a leadoff man, Lofton is precisely the type of hitter you'd expect him to be. He makes excellent contact and uses the whole field. He's particularly adept at going the other way, especially against lefthanders, who don't bother him a bit. He bunts as often as anyone in the National League, and his short stroke allows him to remain dangerous with two strikes. Even without his old speed, he remained an excellent leadoff man and would have scored well over 100 runs if he hadn't missed so much playing time.

Baserunning & Defense

After Lofton led the American League in steals in each of his first five seasons in the majors, his groin problems were such a hindrance that he stole only 27 bases, half of his previous career low. He also was thrown out stealing 20 times, the most in the majors, and was picked off on three occasions. He remained an aggressive baserunner, though his injuries prevented him from dominating the basepaths like he used to. His range in center field suffered as well, though he remained better than average. Lofton's arm is fairly good and his accuracy improved in 1997.

1998 Outlook

Lofton became a free agent at the end of the season, and it seemed unlikely that would get the $10 million-per-year contract that he once expected. But a number of teams were interested in his services, including the Cleveland Indians. Wherever he ends up, he's a great bet to reclaim his title as one of the top leadoff men in the game.

Position: CF
Bats: L **Throws:** L
Ht: 6' 0" **Wt:** 180

Opening Day Age: 30
Born: 5/31/67 in East Chicago, IN
ML Seasons: 7

Overall Statistics

	G	AB	R	H	D	T	HR	RBI	SB	BB	SO	Avg	OBP	Slg
1997	122	493	90	164	20	6	5	48	27	64	83	.333	.409	.428
Career	822	3314	641	1047	153	48	44	309	354	371	426	.316	.384	.431

Where He Hits the Ball

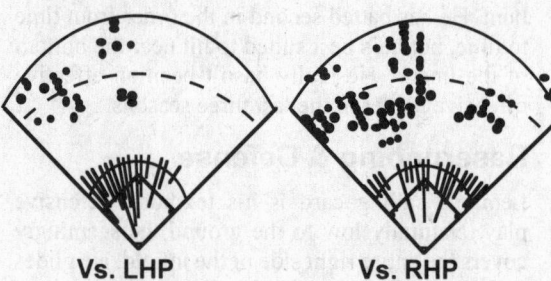

Vs. LHP   **Vs. RHP**

1997 Situational Stats

	AB	H	HR	RBI	Avg		AB	H	HR	RBI	Avg
Home	258	83	3	23	.322	LHP	152	51	2	22	.336
Road	235	81	2	25	.345	RHP	341	113	3	26	.331
First Half	288	99	3	33	.344	Sc Pos	111	39	1	40	.351
Scnd Half	205	65	2	15	.317	Clutch	74	25	0	7	.338

1997 Rankings (National League)

⇒ 1st in caught stealing (20)
⇒ 2nd in highest groundball/flyball ratio (2.2) and lowest stolen base percentage (57.4%)
⇒ 3rd in errors in center field (5)
⇒ 4th in batting average, singles, on-base percentage for a leadoff hitter (.409), batting average on the road and fielding percentage in center field (.983)
⇒ 5th in batting average vs. righthanded pitchers and batting average with two strikes (.267)
⇒ Led the Braves in batting average, singles, stolen bases, caught stealing (20), on-base percentage, highest groundball/flyball ratio (2.2), most pitches seen per plate appearance (3.96), batting average with runners in scoring position and batting average vs. lefthanded pitchers

Javy Lopez

1997 Season

The Braves got another productive season out of their powerful catcher, Javy Lopez. He got off to a terrific start, but wore down a bit in the second half as he suffered a hairline fracture in his thumb and battled other assorted injuries. Still, he showed improvement in his power and plate discipline.

Hitting

Lopez kills low fastballs, and he's slowly learning to lay off the breaking pitches in the dirt that he's always had the impulse to chase. He comes out hacking and is one of the most dangerous first-pitch hitters in the game. He has begun to pull the ball in recent years, but still hits the ball hard to all fields and has excellent power to right-center. His power continued to grow last year as he learned to get better loft on the ball. He hits lefthanders and righthanders equally well, though he has more power against southpaws.

Baserunning & Defense

Lopez' defense gets a bad rap, possibly because he's perceived as an offensive player first and foremost. Still he's adept behind the plate, and does a good job of blocking pitches for a pitching staff that probably throws more balls in the dirt than any other team in the majors. His throwing has improved, and he's not afraid to pick off a napping baserunner. A decent athlete for a catcher, he simply can't steal a base, going 2-for-12 in his major league career.

1998 Outlook

If Lopez didn't have to pay the physical toll that's required of a catcher, he likely would be recognized as one of the game's better all-around hitters. His future development will depend on his ability to stay away from the more serious types of bumps and bruises. If he's able to keep his game at its present level, he's undoubtedly one of the best at his position.

Position: C
Bats: R **Throws:** R
Ht: 6' 3" **Wt:** 200

Opening Day Age: 27
Born: 11/5/70 in Ponce, PR
ML Seasons: 6
Pronunciation: HAH-vee LOE-pezz

Overall Statistics

	G	AB	R	H	D	T	HR	RBI	SB	BB	SO	Avg	OBP	Slg
1997	123	414	52	122	28	1	23	68	1	40	82	.295	.361	.534
Career	458	1545	176	445	70	7	74	227	2	99	287	.288	.335	.486

Where He Hits the Ball

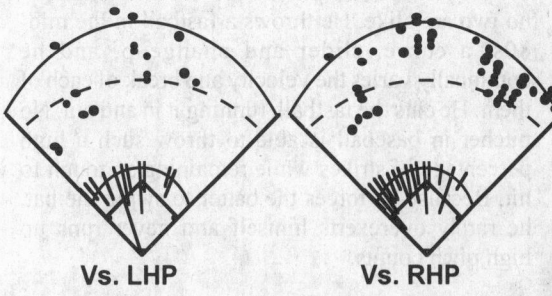

Vs. LHP   Vs. RHP

1997 Situational Stats

	AB	H	HR	RBI	Avg		AB	H	HR	RBI	Avg
Home	183	56	11	34	.306	LHP	97	32	4	14	.330
Road	231	66	12	34	.286	RHP	317	90	19	54	.284
First Half	238	74	14	42	.311	Sc Pos	107	29	5	44	.271
Scnd Half	176	48	9	26	.273	Clutch	73	21	4	8	.288

1997 Rankings (National League)

⇒ 3rd in fielding percentage at catcher (.993)
⇒ 8th in lowest percentage of pitches taken (46.4%)
⇒ 10th in intentional walks (10)
⇒ Led the Braves in intentional walks (10)

Atlanta Braves

Greg Maddux

1997 Season

As it turned out, Greg Maddux' "decline" in 1996 was nothing a little run support couldn't cure. Atlanta scored more runs for him than they had in any season since he joined the Braves, and his won-lost record soared right back up to his normal levels, erasing any doubt that he still ranked among the best in the game. He finished second in the National League Cy Young Award voting to Pedro Martinez.

Pitching

It doesn't seem possible, but Maddux' incomparable control is still improving. He issued a career-low 14 unintentional walks in 1997, three less than the year before. His pitches are like snowflakes—no two are alike. He throws a fastball in the mid-80s, a curve, slider and changeup, and he continually varies the velocity and break of each of them. He cuts the fastball, running it in and out. No pitcher in baseball is able to throw such a high percentage of strikes while remaining so tough to hit. Because he forces the batter to swing the bat, he rarely overexerts himself and never runs up high pitch counts.

Defense & Hitting

Hamstring woes have affected Maddux' mobility off the mound, but he remains one of the top-fielding pitchers in the game. He won his eighth consecutive Gold Glove in 1997. His one weakness on the field is his lack of an an effective pickoff move and an inability to cut off the running game. Normally a good hitter and bunter, he had an off year with the bat despite drawing five walks.

1998 Outlook

Maddux is probably one of the least likely pitchers to break down, because his incredible efficiency helps keep his workloads relatively light. He's constantly looking for new ways to exploit hitters' weaknesses, so what he loses to age he may gain in knowledge. Someday he'll fall back to the ranks of the mortals, but it isn't likely to happen anytime soon.

Position: SP
Bats: R **Throws:** R
Ht: 6' 0" **Wt:** 175

Opening Day Age: 31
Born: 4/14/66 in San Angelo, TX
ML Seasons: 12

Overall Statistics

	W	L	Pct.	ERA	G	GS	Sv	IP	H	BB	SO	HR	Ratio
1997	19	4	.826	2.20	33	33	0	232.2	200	20	177	9	0.95
Career	184	108	.630	2.81	369	365	0	2598.1	2302	609	1820	128	1.12

How Often He Throws Strikes

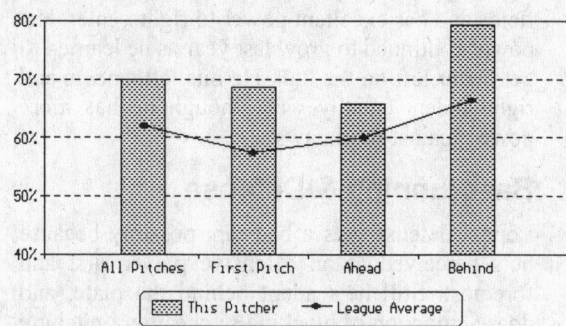

1997 Situational Stats

	W	L	ERA	Sv	IP		AB	H	HR	RBI	Avg
Home	8	3	2.18	0	132.0	LHB	394	84	6	31	.213
Road	11	1	2.24	0	100.2	RHB	455	116	3	25	.255
First Half	11	3	2.36	0	125.2	Sc Pos	159	33	4	47	.208
Scnd Half	8	1	2.02	0	107.0	Clutch	97	18	1	6	.186

1997 Rankings (National League)

⇒ 1st in winning percentage, highest strike-out/walk ratio (8.9), least pitches thrown per batter (3.18) and least home runs allowed per 9 innings (.35)

⇒ 2nd in ERA, wins, lowest slugging percentage allowed (.311), lowest on-base percentage allowed (.256), least baserunners allowed per 9 innings (8.7) and ERA on the road

⇒ 3rd in lowest batting average allowed vs. lefthanded batters

⇒ Led the Braves in ERA, hit batsmen (6), pickoff throws (128), stolen bases allowed (20), winning percentage, highest strikeout/walk ratio (8.9), lowest slugging percentage allowed (.311), lowest on-base percentage allowed (.256) and highest groundball/flyball ratio allowed (2.3)

Denny Neagle

1997 Season

When Denny Neagle was the ace of the Pirates' staff, people predicted that he'd win a lot more games if he ever got to pitch for a good team. In late 1996, the Braves decided to test that theory and acquired him for the stretch run. He pitched poorly in six late-season starts for them, but in 1997 he finally put it all together and led the National League with 20 victories.

Pitching

Neagle delivers a high-80s fastball and a devastating circle change from the same deceptive, three-quarters delivery. The fastball seems much faster and stays up in the zone, while the changeup drops below the hitters' knees. Like Greg Maddux, he'll often use his changeup to set up another, while adding or subtracting a little velocity. Neagle stays mainly on the outside corner, but comes inside much more often than Tom Glavine. He's at his best through his first 90 pitches, but tends to falter if he goes much further.

Defense & Hitting

Neagle is a good bunter, and gets his share of hits and walks as well. He's a decent fielder, but doesn't have to handle many balls himself because he allows so few grounders. Runners can be hung out to dry by Neagle's pickoff move, but he still can be run on at times.

1998 Outlook

What now? Neagle won't go 20-5 every year, but he's a great bet to get 30-35 starts and throw 200 innings. If he's able to do that, he's a virtual lock to remain one of the most successful lefties in the business. The Braves scored a lot of runs for him last year, so he should win fewer games even if he remains just as effective. Neagle had surgery on his non-throwing shoulder after the season, an injury that isn't expected to bother him in 1998.

Position: SP
Bats: L **Throws:** L
Ht: 6' 2" **Wt:** 216

Opening Day Age: 29
Born: 9/13/68 in Gambrills, MD
ML Seasons: 7
Pronunciation: NAY-gull

Overall Statistics

	W	L	Pct.	ERA	G	GS	Sv	IP	H	BB	SO	HR	Ratio
1997	20	5	.800	2.97	34	34	0	233.1	204	49	172	18	1.08
Career	65	44	.596	3.83	234	138	3	989.0	977	278	757	104	1.27

How Often He Throws Strikes

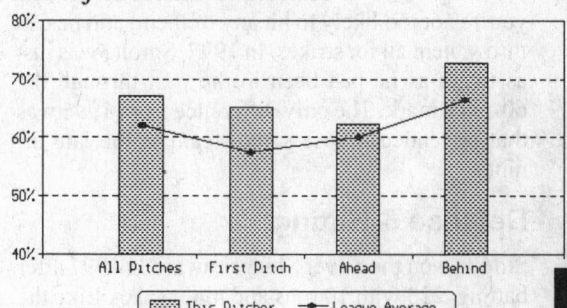

1997 Situational Stats

	W	L	ERA	Sv	IP		AB	H	HR	RBI	Avg
Home	10	1	3.06	0	120.2	LHB	172	41	5	14	.238
Road	10	4	2.88	0	112.2	RHB	702	163	13	66	.232
First Half	12	2	3.20	0	129.1	Sc Pos	172	42	3	54	.244
Scnd Half	8	3	2.68	0	104.0	Clutch	64	18	0	7	.281

1997 Rankings (National League)

⇒ 1st in wins and lowest groundball/flyball ratio allowed (0.9)
⇒ 2nd in shutouts (4), winning percentage and least GDPs induced per 9 innings (0.3)
⇒ 3rd in games started
⇒ 5th in lowest on-base percentage allowed (.277) and least baserunners allowed per 9 innings (10.0)
⇒ Led the Braves in wins, shutouts (4), hit batsmen (6) and most run support per 9 innings (5.7)

Atlanta Braves

John Smoltz  (Workhorse

1997 Season

Until John Smoltz' breakout 1996 season, he'd been viewed as a disappointment for much of his career. So he didn't fret over being viewed that way in 1997, when he was unable to duplicate his fantastic record from the year before. In his heart, he knew that he hadn't declined much at all and that he remains quite capable of posting award-winning numbers in the future.

Pitching

You can't sit on any of Smoltz' pitches, because each one is very deadly. Do you want to hit a moving 95-MPH fastball, a sharp slider, a big-breaking curve or a diving splitter? The truth is you're not too likely to hit any of them, and he can throw them all for strikes. In 1997, Smoltz was just as tough as he had been in the past through the 60-pitch mark. The only difference from 1996 was that he tended to lose some steam in the late innings.

Defense & Hitting

Smoltz won the Silver Slugger award in 1997 after batting .228 with 10 runs and nine walks. Like the rest of the Braves' starters, he's also a fine fielder who's quick off the mound and rarely errs. Baserunners used to drive him to distraction, but he has clamped down on the running game in recent years, developing a more effective pickoff move and a quicker stretch delivery.

1998 Outlook

Simply put, Smoltz is no better than he was in 1996, and no worse than he was last season. That leaves him somewhere in the range of 15-24 wins, making him a good bet to win 20 games again. His ERA dropped off by only eight-hundredths of a run last year, and the real reason his won-lost record declined was a downturn in run support. A little more middle-relief help would be the best thing for him.

Position: SP
Bats: R Throws: R
Ht: 6' 3" Wt: 185

Opening Day Age: 30
Born: 5/15/67 in Warren, MI
ML Seasons: 10

Overall Statistics

	W	L	Pct.	ERA	G	GS	Sv	IP	H	BB	SO	HR	Ratio
1997	15	12	.556	3.02	35	35	0	256.0	234	63	241	21	1.16
Career	129	102	.558	3.40	301	301	0	2060.1	1779	690	1769	171	1.20

How Often He Throws Strikes

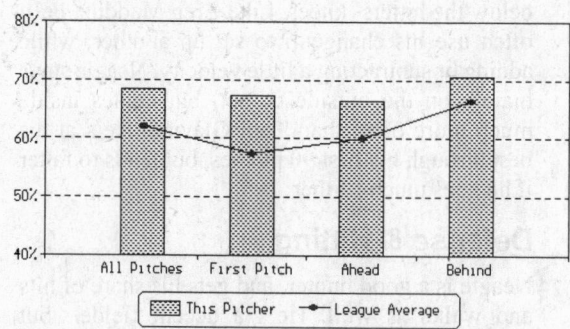

1997 Situational Stats

	W	L	ERA	Sv	IP		AB	H	HR	RBI	Avg
Home	6	7	3.32	0	138.1	LHB	526	130	10	47	.247
Road	9	5	2.68	0	117.2	RHB	440	104	11	41	.236
First Half	8	7	2.92	0	135.2	Sc Pos	213	48	5	68	.225
Scnd Half	7	5	3.14	0	120.1	Clutch	144	45	6	22	.313

1997 Rankings (National League)

⇒ 1st in games started, innings pitched and hits allowed
⇒ 2nd in batters faced (1,043)
⇒ 3rd in complete games (7), strikeouts, wild pitches (10) and pitches thrown (3,698)
⇒ 4th in highest strikeout/walk ratio (3.8) and ERA on the road
⇒ 5th in shutouts (2) and most strikeouts per 9 innings (8.5)
⇒ Led the Braves in losses, games started, complete games (7), innings pitched, hits allowed, batters faced (1,043), home runs allowed, strikeouts, wild pitches (10), balks (1), pitches thrown (3,698), runners caught stealing (11) and most strikeouts per 9 innings (8.5)

Michael Tucker

1997 Season

When the Braves needed a lefthanded hitter to bat second for them, they decided to acquire Michael Tucker from Kansas City. He ended up fitting the bill perfectly. His hot start silenced those who criticized the decision to trade Jermaine Dye for him, and he combined very well with Kenny Lofton to set the table for the heart of the Braves' order. He cooled off after batting .418 in April, batting just .247 in the second half and being platooned for most of the final two months.

Hitting

Tucker has a very quick stroke and is adept at getting on top of high pitches. He hits to all fields against righthanders but can become a little bit too pull-conscious against southpaws. In his limited trials against lefties he has shown an ability to make contact, albeit with much less authority. The Royals' efforts to overhaul his batting style never paid off, and he remains an aggressive hitter.

Baserunning & Defense

Tucker used to run the bases practically until someone tagged him out, but now he runs until he's gone as far as he can go. He hasn't picked up on the finer points of basestealing, but he has the speed to steal 20 or more if he concentrates on that aspect of his game. As a former second baseman, he's still learning in the outfield, but he has come far enough to handle the corners capably. His throwing arm isn't a strength.

1998 Outlook

Unlike the Royals, the Braves have a firm idea of the type of player they want Michael Tucker to become. He had been set back in the past by indecisive handling, so though he'll be 27 this season he may have a few more years of growth left. The Braves will look to Tucker to be their full-time right fielder and No. 2 hitter this year.

Position: RF/LF
Bats: L **Throws:** R
Ht: 6' 2" **Wt:** 185

Opening Day Age: 26
Born: 6/25/71 in South Boston, VA
ML Seasons: 3

Overall Statistics

	G	AB	R	H	D	T	HR	RBI	SB	BB	SO	Avg	OBP	Slg
1997	138	499	80	141	25	7	14	56	12	44	116	.283	.347	.445
Career	308	1015	158	275	53	11	30	126	24	102	236	.271	.344	.433

Where He Hits the Ball

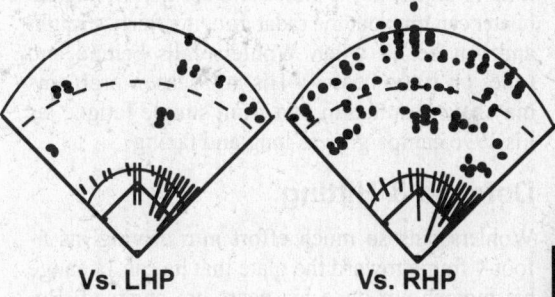

Vs. LHP   **Vs. RHP**

1997 Situational Stats

	AB	H	HR	RBI	Avg		AB	H	HR	RBI	Avg
Home	239	67	5	22	.280	LHP	113	32	0	12	.283
Road	260	74	9	34	.285	RHP	386	109	14	44	.282
First Half	313	95	8	42	.304	Sc Pos	128	33	3	37	.258
Scnd Half	186	46	6	14	.247	Clutch	75	15	1	7	.200

1997 Rankings (National League)

⇒ 2nd in lowest batting average with the bases loaded (.000)
⇒ 3rd in lowest fielding percentage in right field (.979)
⇒ 6th in lowest batting average on an 0-2 count (.050) and highest percentage of extra bases taken as a runner (63.6%)
⇒ 7th in lowest slugging percentage vs. lefthanded pitchers (.327) and highest percentage of swings on the first pitch (41.5%)
⇒ 9th in errors in right field (4)
⇒ 10th in triples and lowest batting average in the clutch
⇒ Led the Braves in triples, least GDPs per GDP situation (5.8%) and highest percentage of extra bases taken as a runner (63.6%)

Mark Wohlers

Position: RP
Bats: R **Throws:** R
Ht: 6' 4" **Wt:** 207

Opening Day Age: 28
Born: 1/23/70 in
Holyoke, MA
ML Seasons: 7
Pronunciation:
WOE-lers

1997 Season

Mark Wohlers has battled his control his entire career, and just when it seemed that he'd finally defeated his arch-enemy, his wildness suddenly began to return. After pitching very well in 1996, he struggled to find the plate last year, particularly in April and September. While Wohlers' numbers remained impressive, Braves manager Bobby Cox seemed to lose confidence in him late in the season.

Pitching

Blessed with one of the most blinding fastballs in the majors, Wohlers can be dominant at times. When his control is on, batters have virtually no time to adjust to his slider and splitter. While his heater can max out the radar gun, it's fairly straight and can be hit when Wohlers falls behind and relies on it too heavily. His late-season problems may have resulted in part from simple fatigue, as his 1996 campaign was long and taxing.

Defense & Hitting

Wohlers puts so much effort into driving his 6-foot-4 frame toward the plate that he can't change his momentum once his gears are engaged. Because a slide step or pickoff move is physically impossible, basestealers rob him blind. All 13 of them were successful against him last year, and during his career only four of 49 have been thrown out. At the plate he has fanned in each of his last eight at-bats, and in the field, he has muffed four of his last 20 chances.

1998 Outlook

With an otherwise thin bullpen, Wohlers is one of the keys to Atlanta's success. That may worry the Braves after witnessing his problems down the stretch in 1997. But they've helped him find his command in the past and probably will get him back on track. Most of his problems stemmed from falling behind in the count, so a mechanical adjustment may be all he needs.

Overall Statistics

	W	L	Pct.	ERA	G	GS	Sv	IP	H	BB	SO	HR	Ratio
1997	5	7	.417	3.50	71	0	33	69.1	57	38	92	4	1.37
Career	31	21	.596	3.33	359	0	104	365.1	312	165	415	18	1.31

How Often He Throws Strikes

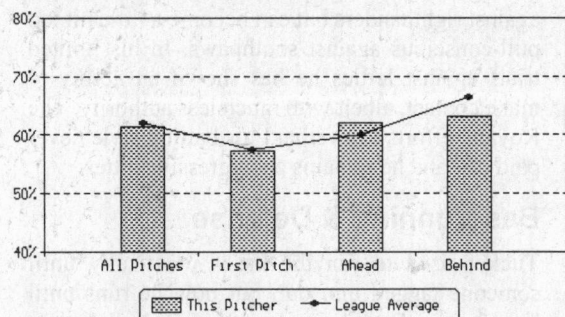

1997 Situational Stats

	W	L	ERA	Sv	IP		AB	H	HR	RBI	Avg
Home	4	4	4.76	15	34.0	LHB	142	32	2	15	.225
Road	1	3	2.29	18	35.1	RHB	112	25	2	12	.223
First Half	2	3	2.17	20	37.1	Sc Pos	74	15	1	21	.203
Scnd Half	3	4	5.06	13	32.0	Clutch	200	47	3	24	.235

1997 Rankings (National League)

⇒ 4th in blown saves (7) and most strikeouts per 9 innings in relief (11.9)
⇒ 7th in games finished (55), lowest save percentage (82.5%) and relief losses (7)
⇒ 9th in saves, save opportunities (40) and lowest batting average allowed in relief (.224)
⇒ Led the Braves in games pitched, saves, games finished (55), save opportunities (40), save percentage (82.5%), blown saves (7), relief ERA (3.50), relief losses (7), relief innings (69.1), lowest batting average allowed in relief (.224) and most strikeouts per 9 innings in relief (11.9)

Mike Cather (Surprise)

Position: RP
Bats: R **Throws:** R
Ht: 6' 2" **Wt:** 195

Opening Day Age: 27
Born: 12/17/70 in San Diego, CA
ML Seasons: 1

Overall Statistics

	W	L	Pct.	ERA	G	GS	Sv	IP	H	BB	SO	HR	Ratio
1997	2	4	.333	2.39	35	0	0	37.2	23	19	29	1	1.12
Career	2	4	.333	2.39	35	0	0	37.2	23	19	29	1	1.12

1997 Situational Stats

	W	L	ERA	Sv	IP		AB	H	HR	RBI	Avg
Home	1	1	2.63	0	24.0	LHB	44	9	1	3	.205
Road	1	3	1.98	0	13.2	RHB	88	14	0	9	.159
First Half	0	0	-	0	0.0	Sc Pos	35	7	0	9	.200
Scnd Half	2	4	2.39	0	37.2	Clutch	71	14	1	10	.197

1997 Season

The emergence of Mike Cather was one of the more remarkable stories of the 1997 season. Signed out of the independent Northern League in 1996, he was called up at the All-Star break last year to help the Braves' faltering bullpen. For the rest of the year he was tremendously effective, holding opponents to a .174 batting average while allowing only one home run in 35 appearances.

Pitching, Defense & Hitting

Hitters proved unable to solve Cather's low-side-arm delivery, pounding grounders into the dirt time after time. His excellent control helped him stay ahead in the count. He relies on a heavy sinker and a slider, and neutralizes lefties with a good changeup. He pays close attention to runners, and no one even tried to steal on him in 1997. He's a decent fielder but a completely unproven hitter.

1998 Outlook

The Braves love what they saw of Cather last year and they want to see more. He'll open 1998 as their primary righthanded setup man.

Brad Clontz

Position: RP
Bats: R **Throws:** R
Ht: 6' 1" **Wt:** 180

Opening Day Age: 26
Born: 4/25/71 in Stuart, VA
ML Seasons: 3

Overall Statistics

	W	L	Pct.	ERA	G	GS	Sv	IP	H	BB	SO	HR	Ratio
1997	5	1	.833	3.75	51	0	1	48.0	52	18	42	3	1.46
Career	19	5	.792	4.51	191	0	6	197.2	201	73	146	19	1.39

1997 Situational Stats

	W	L	ERA	Sv	IP		AB	H	HR	RBI	Avg
Home	2	0	4.01	0	24.2	LHB	74	21	2	17	.284
Road	3	1	3.47	1	23.1	RHB	108	31	1	17	.287
First Half	4	1	4.01	0	33.2	Sc Pos	61	20	1	29	.328
Scnd Half	1	0	3.14	1	14.1	Clutch	47	8	0	7	.170

1997 Season

Brad Clontz slumped heavily in the second half of 1996, but he didn't hit rock-bottom until the Braves demoted him to Triple-A in July 1997. He could have sulked, but instead he allowed just one run in 22 innings to earn a promotion seven weeks later. After rejoining the Braves, he pitched well in middle relief for the remainder of the season.

Pitching, Defense & Hitting

Clontz' biggest asset is his funky sidearm delivery. He gives righties fits with his darting fastball and frisbee slider. Lefties always had given him grief until 1997, when he made an adjustment that allowed him to hang in against them. He's got a rubber arm and is at his best when he pitches to a few hitters at a time, exiting before they become accustomed to his unusual motion. He made an effort to pay more attention to baserunners last year, and it paid off. Though he committed a couple of errors in the field, he's usually adequate with the glove. He has batted five times as a professional and still is looking for his first hit.

1998 Outlook

Clontz was much more effective in the latter half of 1997 and it seems he isn't the same pitcher that looked so helpless in '96. He should remain a valuable middle reliever and setup man this year.

Greg Colbrunn

Position: 1B
Bats: R **Throws:** R
Ht: 6' 0" **Wt:** 200

Opening Day Age: 28
Born: 7/26/69 in Fontana, CA
ML Seasons: 6

Overall Statistics

	G	AB	R	H	D	T	HR	RBI	SB	BB	SO	Avg	OBP	Slg
1997	98	271	27	76	17	0	7	35	1	10	49	.280	.309	.421
Career	546	1786	201	499	92	3	58	265	24	78	288	.279	.316	.432

1997 Situational Stats

	AB	H	HR	RBI	Avg		AB	H	HR	RBI	Avg
Home	130	36	3	17	.277	LHP	124	36	4	19	.290
Road	141	40	4	18	.284	RHP	147	40	3	16	.272
First Half	175	50	4	21	.286	Sc Pos	67	17	2	27	.254
Scnd Half	96	26	3	14	.271	Clutch	40	12	1	4	.300

1997 Season

It's funny how things worked out for Greg Colbrunn. After serving as the Marlins' regular first baseman for two years, he was cut loose and caught on with the Twins at the start of 1997. He was forced to accept a platoon role with the lowly Twins until a mid-August trade sent him to the playoff-bound Braves. In Atlanta, his role was reduced even further, but he flourished as a pinch hitter, delivering many big hits on the way to the first postseason of his career.

Hitting, Baserunning & Defense

Colbrunn's philosophy of hitting is simple. When he gets a strike, he hits it. He doesn't pass very often on a decent pitch, and when he swings he usually makes contact. He hits the ball hard to all fields but doesn't have great power overall. He runs like the former catcher that he is, and his defensive play around first base is strictly average.

1998 Outlook

Colbrunn became a free agent in hopes of landing a more expansive assignment. His skills don't necessarily merit one, so it remained to be seen what he'll be offered. He still could be a valuable bench player if he so chooses.

Alan Embree

Position: RP
Bats: L **Throws:** L
Ht: 6' 2" **Wt:** 190

Opening Day Age: 28
Born: 1/23/70 in Vancouver, WA
ML Seasons: 4
Pronunciation: EMM-bree

Overall Statistics

	W	L	Pct.	ERA	G	GS	Sv	IP	H	BB	SO	HR	Ratio
1997	3	1	.750	2.54	66	0	0	46.0	36	20	45	1	1.22
Career	7	6	.538	4.74	117	4	1	119.2	108	65	113	16	1.45

1997 Situational Stats

	W	L	ERA	Sv	IP		AB	H	HR	RBI	Avg
Home	3	0	2.96	0	27.1	LHB	73	18	1	7	.247
Road	0	1	1.93	0	18.2	RHB	90	18	0	4	.200
First Half	1	1	2.70	0	23.1	Sc Pos	50	7	0	9	.140
Scnd Half	2	0	2.38	0	22.2	Clutch	66	15	1	6	.227

1997 Season

Lefthander Alan Embree turned out to be much more than a mere throw-in in the Kenny Lofton trade with Cleveland. He filled Atlanta's need for a lefthanded specialist and performed well in the role. In fact, he was effective against both lefties and righties, and allowed only five extra-base hits in 66 appearances.

Pitching, Defense & Hitting

Embree is a rare bird, a southpaw with a 95-MPH fastball. Working a few batters at a time, he doesn't need much else and doesn't use his slider very often. His control has been inconsistent throughout his career. As a fielder he handles what he reaches, which isn't much. Basestealers have been successful against him. Can he hit? No one knows. He still hasn't had a single professional at-bat.

1998 Outlook

Embree was so successful as the Braves' one-out lefty that it's hard to see him moving out of the role. If anything, his role may be expanded because he has the skills to be an effective setup man. The only concern would be his stamina. He hasn't been used heavily since undergoing major elbow surgery four years ago.

Tony Graffanino

Position: 2B
Bats: R **Throws:** R
Ht: 6' 1" **Wt:** 175

Opening Day Age: 25
Born: 6/6/72 in
Amityville, NY
ML Seasons: 2
Pronunciation:
graf-a-NEEN-oh

Overall Statistics

	G	AB	R	H	D	T	HR	RBI	SB	BB	SO	Avg	OBP	Slg
1997	104	186	33	48	9	1	8	20	6	26	46	.258	.344	.446
Career	126	232	40	56	10	2	8	22	6	30	59	.241	.326	.405

1997 Situational Stats

	AB	H	HR	RBI	Avg		AB	H	HR	RBI	Avg
Home	99	25	5	11	.253	LHP	59	15	3	7	.254
Road	87	23	3	9	.264	RHP	127	33	5	13	.260
First Half	63	18	2	7	.286	Sc Pos	35	6	0	10	.171
Scnd Half	123	30	6	13	.244	Clutch	36	4	0	0	.111

1997 Season

In the most critical year of his career, things finally began to break right for Tony Graffanino. After overcoming a serious back injury in 1994, he won a spot on the Braves last year as Mark Lemke's backup and showed surprising pop at the plate. When Lemke went down for the year in August, Graffanino took over the bulk of the Braves' second-base chores and performed admirably.

Hitting, Baserunning & Defense

Graffanino is a fastball hitter who prefers the ball down and in. He's capable of putting up decent power numbers for a middle infielder. He has lost a step on the bases since returning from the back injury, and he doesn't steal effectively any more. In the field, he's a smooth defender with a strong arm and good double-play pivot. He's no Lemke, but his glove work won't draw unflattering comparisons, either.

1998 Outlook

If the Braves choose to let Lemke walk as a free agent, Graffanino is first in line for the second-base job. There's no reason to think he won't be able to hold the position and produce both at the plate and in the field.

Keith Lockhart

Position: 2B/3B
Bats: L **Throws:** R
Ht: 5'10" **Wt:** 170

Opening Day Age: 33
Born: 11/10/64 in
Whittier, CA
ML Seasons: 4

Overall Statistics

	G	AB	R	H	D	T	HR	RBI	SB	BB	SO	Avg	OBP	Slg
1997	96	147	25	41	5	3	6	32	0	14	17	.279	.337	.476
Career	355	897	119	256	57	9	21	126	20	62	88	.285	.331	.439

1997 Situational Stats

	AB	H	HR	RBI	Avg		AB	H	HR	RBI	Avg
Home	55	17	3	14	.309	LHP	9	6	1	5	.667
Road	92	24	3	18	.261	RHP	138	35	5	27	.254
First Half	83	19	3	20	.229	Sc Pos	38	11	2	25	.289
Scnd Half	64	22	3	12	.344	Clutch	34	9	1	6	.265

1997 Season

For Keith Lockhart, the March deal that sent him from the Royals to the Braves was both a step down and a step up. It was a demotion from semi-regular play in Kansas City to a more limited role in Atlanta, but it was also a transfer from an also-ran to one of the strongest teams in baseball. Lockhart accepted his new role with the grace of a veteran and flourished in his new surroundings.

Hitting, Baserunning & Defense

Lockhart goes after the first good pitch he sees and usually makes good contact. He can take outside pitches the other way or turn on an inside pitch. He hasn't faced lefties very often and played almost exclusively against righties in 1997. He has served very well in a pinch-hitting capacity. As a second baseman Lockhart has good range and a fair arm, but he's only mediocre at third. His speed is above average, and he also can swipe a base on guile.

1998 Outlook

As a lefthanded hitter who can pinch hit and fill in at two infield positions, Lockhart is a valuable utilityman. The Braves made sure to get him when they traded Jermaine Dye to Kansas City, and they'd love to keep him around for quite a while longer.

Atlanta Braves

Greg Myers

Position: C
Bats: L **Throws:** R
Ht: 6' 2" **Wt:** 215

Opening Day Age: 31
Born: 4/14/66 in Riverside, CA
ML Seasons: 10

Overall Statistics

	G	AB	R	H	D	T	HR	RBI	SB	BB	SO	Avg	OBP	Slg
1997	71	174	24	45	11	1	5	29	0	17	32	.259	.321	.420
Career	654	1882	196	479	99	7	43	234	3	130	308	.255	.300	.383

1997 Situational Stats

	AB	H	HR	RBI	Avg		AB	H	HR	RBI	Avg
Home	86	27	3	18	.314	LHP	15	8	1	4	.533
Road	88	18	2	11	.205	RHP	159	37	4	25	.233
First Half	120	33	3	21	.275	Sc Pos	58	13	1	23	.224
Scnd Half	54	12	2	8	.222	Clutch	29	6	0	4	.207

1997 Season

Greg Myers saw his playing time decrease dramatically in 1997. A platoon catcher the year before with the Twins, he became a reserve when Minnesota signed Terry Steinbach. In September he was traded to Atlanta, where he ranked third on the depth chart behind Javy Lopez and Eddie Perez. Myers received only nine at-bats with the Braves.

Hitting, Baserunning & Defense

Myers has turned in the three highest slugging percentages of his career in the last three seasons, primarily because he had developed a knack for pulling mediocre fastballs out of the park. He's fairly impatient and will chase pitches, resulting in lackluster batting averages, low walk totals and plenty of strikeouts. He's sundial-slow on the bases and hasn't stolen a base since 1993. His instincts aren't good either. He does an acceptable job behind the plate in both throwing out runners and blocking pitches.

1998 Outlook

Myers became a free agent after the season and signed a two-year deal to start for San Diego. He's more suited to be a backup.

Eddie Perez

Position: C
Bats: R **Throws:** R
Ht: 6' 1" **Wt:** 175

Opening Day Age: 29
Born: 5/4/68 in Cuidad Ojeda, VZ
ML Seasons: 3

Overall Statistics

	G	AB	R	H	D	T	HR	RBI	SB	BB	SO	Avg	OBP	Slg
1997	73	191	20	41	5	0	6	18	0	10	35	.215	.259	.335
Career	148	360	40	85	15	1	11	39	0	18	56	.236	.275	.375

1997 Situational Stats

	AB	H	HR	RBI	Avg		AB	H	HR	RBI	Avg
Home	100	26	4	11	.260	LHP	53	9	2	6	.170
Road	91	15	2	7	.165	RHP	138	32	4	12	.232
First Half	96	24	3	8	.250	Sc Pos	47	6	1	13	.128
Scnd Half	95	17	3	10	.179	Clutch	26	5	2	2	.192

1997 Season

The Braves were phenomenally successful when Eddie Perez was behind the plate in 1997. Of course, if Perez was wearing the mask the chances were good that Greg Maddux was toeing the rubber. For the second straight year, Perez served as Maddux' personal receiver as well as Javy Lopez' backup.

Hitting, Baserunning & Defense

Perez has a job solely because of his glove. With only two passed balls in 123 career games, he gives Maddux the confidence to throw his breaking ball and offspeed pitches at any time. Perez isn't the world's best-throwing catcher, but he does reasonably well with Maddux, who doesn't hold runners close or give him much help in throwing out basestealers. Perez runs like he's wearing his catching gear under his uniform, and he has never stolen a base in the majors. He's an impatient hitter who swings with authority.

1998 Outlook

Until Maddux starts getting shelled, Perez' job seems reasonably secure. Manager Bobby Cox likes to keep Lopez' load reasonably light, so Perez should continue to get his share of innings behind the plate.

Danny Bautista (**Pos**: LF, **Age**: 25, **Bats**: R)

	G	AB	R	H	D	T	HR	RBI	SB	BB	SO	Avg	OBP	Slg
1997	64	103	14	25	3	2	3	9	2	5	24	.243	.282	.398
Career	243	618	73	141	21	3	17	69	11	32	140	.228	.268	.354

A frightful beaning in 1996 threatened Bautista's career, but he battled back last season to snag a spot on the Braves' bench, a position he held all year. He has tools but doesn't hit enough to survive a prolonged slump. 1998 Outlook: B

Rafael Belliard (**Pos**: SS, **Age**: 36, **Bats**: R)

	G	AB	R	H	D	T	HR	RBI	SB	BB	SO	Avg	OBP	Slg
1997	72	71	9	15	3	0	1	3	0	1	17	.211	.219	.296
Career	1148	2281	216	503	55	14	2	141	43	136	383	.221	.271	.260

Just as Sammy Byrd was once "Babe Ruth's Legs," Belliard has now become "Jeff Blauser's Glove." He re-signed with the Braves, taking a minor league deal in the offseason. 1998 Outlook: C

Mike Bielecki (**Pos**: RHP, **Age**: 38)

	W	L	Pct.	ERA	G	GS	Sv	IP	H	BB	SO	HR	Ratio
1997	3	7	.300	4.08	50	0	2	57.1	56	21	60	9	1.34
Career	70	73	.490	4.18	347	178	5	1231.0	1236	496	783	116	1.41

Bielecki was Atlanta's most effective middle reliever during the first half, but his performance slipped when his shoulder began hurting. After being diagnosed with a rotator-cuff tear, he retired, but he had second thoughts and was considering a comeback. 1998 Outlook: C

Paul Byrd (**Pos**: RHP, **Age**: 27)

	W	L	Pct.	ERA	G	GS	Sv	IP	H	BB	SO	HR	Ratio
1997	4	4	.500	5.26	31	4	0	53.0	47	28	37	6	1.42
Career	7	6	.538	4.29	86	4	0	121.2	113	56	94	14	1.39

Byrd started out OK in middle relief, then slumped and got sent down. He was recalled a few weeks later, but didn't pitch any better upon his return. He was more effective than his ERA would indicate. 1998 Outlook: C

Chad Fox (**Pos**: RHP, **Age**: 27)

	W	L	Pct.	ERA	G	GS	Sv	IP	H	BB	SO	HR	Ratio
1997	0	1	.000	3.29	30	0	0	27.1	24	16	28	4	1.46
Career	0	1	.000	3.29	30	0	0	27.1	24	16	28	4	1.46

Coverted starter Fox was called up at the All-Star break and proved surprisingly effective over the second half. He should remain in a setup role until he pitches his way out of it. 1998 Outlook: A

Ed Giovanola (**Pos**: 3B, **Age**: 29, **Bats**: L)

	G	AB	R	H	D	T	HR	RBI	SB	BB	SO	Avg	OBP	Slg
1997	14	8	0	2	0	0	0	0	0	2	1	.250	.400	.250
Career	70	104	12	22	2	0	0	7	1	13	19	.212	.303	.231

Giovanola lost out to Mike Mordecai and spent most of the season in the minors. He was claimed on waivers by San Diego after the season. 1998 Outlook: C

Tommy Gregg (**Pos**: LF, **Age**: 34, **Bats**: L)

	G	AB	R	H	D	T	HR	RBI	SB	BB	SO	Avg	OBP	Slg
1997	13	19	1	5	2	0	0	0	1	1	2	.263	.300	.368
Career	446	880	86	214	41	2	20	88	14	71	158	.243	.301	.363

Gregg has made a career out of decimating Triple-A pitching between infrequent stints on major league benches. Eventually, someone will need a pinch hitter, and he'll return for a month or two. 1998 Outlook: C

Kerry Ligtenberg (**Pos**: RHP, **Age**: 26)

	W	L	Pct.	ERA	G	GS	Sv	IP	H	BB	SO	HR	Ratio
1997	1	0	1.000	3.00	15	0	1	15.0	12	4	19	4	1.07
Career	1	0	1.000	3.00	15	0	1	15.0	12	4	19	4	1.07

Signed out of the independent Northern League three years ago, Ligtenberg worked his way up from Double-A to the majors in one year, showing excellent control at every stop. 1998 Outlook: B

Mike Mordecai (**Pos**: 3B, **Age**: 30, **Bats**: R)

	G	AB	R	H	D	T	HR	RBI	SB	BB	SO	Avg	OBP	Slg
1997	61	81	8	14	2	1	0	3	0	6	16	.173	.227	.222
Career	200	268	31	62	13	1	6	25	1	25	56	.231	.294	.354

Mordecai had a poor year as a pinch hitter and backup infielder, but probably won't lose his job until the Braves can come up with someone better. He's better than he showed last year. 1998 Outlook: B

Tim Spehr (**Pos**: C, **Age**: 31, **Bats**: R)

	G	AB	R	H	D	T	HR	RBI	SB	BB	SO	Avg	OBP	Slg
1997	25	49	5	9	1	0	2	6	1	2	16	.184	.231	.327
Career	271	325	42	65	21	1	9	41	7	30	87	.200	.273	.354

Over the last four years, Spehr has appeared in 184 games while accumulating only 164 at-bats. Few teams can afford to carry a third catcher any more, so Spehr may be near the end. 1998 Outlook: C

Atlanta Braves

Atlanta Braves Minor League Prospects

Organization Overview:

After a run of producing talent such as Andruw and Chipper Jones, Ryan Klesko and Javy Lopez, the Braves don't have many reinforcements at the upper levels of their system. They also don't need many, because the major league team is so strong. Most of Atlanta's next wave of top prospects spent 1997 in Class-A ball. That group includes several pitchers who should be ready by the time Greg Maddux and Co. finally start to give out, if that ever happens. Besides working players into their own lineup, the Braves also have done a nice job of trading prospects for established players.

Chris Brock

Position: P
Bats: R **Throws:** R
Ht: 6' 0" **Wt:** 175

Opening Day Age: 28
Born: 2/5/70 in
Orlando, FL

Recent Statistics

	W	L	ERA	G	GS	Sv	IP	H	R	BB	SO	HR
97 AAA Richmond	10	6	3.34	20	19	0	118.2	97	50	51	83	9
97 NL Atlanta	0	0	5.58	7	6	0	30.2	34	23	19	16	2

Primarily an outfielder at Florida State, Brock was drafted in the 12th round in 1992 for his arm strength and immediately converted into a pitcher. He has spent much of the last three seasons in Triple-A, but did receive a six-start trial at the end of Atlanta's rotation in 1997. His best pitch is his curveball, and he can occasionally hit 92-93 MPH but more often pitches around 90. He was a longshot to make the majors, so his career already can be considered a success. He doesn't have the stuff to hold off Kevin Millwood for a starting job, but Brock could factor into the bullpen, Atlanta's biggest weakness.

Bruce Chen

Position: P
Bats: L **Throws:** L
Ht: 6' 2" **Wt:** 180

Opening Day Age: 20
Born: 6/19/77 in
Panama City, Panama

Recent Statistics

	W	L	ERA	G	GS	Sv	IP	H	R	BB	SO	HR
96 A Eugene	4	1	2.27	11	8	0	35.2	23	13	14	55	1
97 A Macon	12	7	3.51	28	28	0	146.1	120	67	44	182	19

The Braves are at the forefront of global scouting, and Chen is a result of their efforts in Panama. With Millwood poised to join the big league rotation, Chen will become the system's top pitching prospect. He made his full-season debut at 19 and held up very well, striking out 182 in 146 innings. His fastball and command are much better than you would expect from a young lefthander and his curveball and changeup also have the

potential to be above-average pitches. He's not a big guy, so he'll need to add strength as he climbs the ladder. Atlanta has no reason to rush him, but if he keeps progressing a level at a time he would reach the majors at 23.

Wes Helms

Position: 3B
Bats: R **Throws:** R
Ht: 6' 4" **Wt:** 210

Opening Day Age: 21
Born: 5/12/76 in
Gastonia, NC

Recent Statistics

	G	AB	R	H	D	T	HR	RBI	SB	BB	SO	AVG
96 A Durham	67	258	40	83	19	2	13	54	1	12	51	.322
96 AA Greenville	64	231	24	59	13	2	4	22	2	13	48	.255
97 AAA Richmond	32	110	11	21	4	0	3	15	1	10	34	.191
97 AA Greenville	86	314	50	93	14	1	11	44	3	13	69	.296
97 MLE	118	402	41	92	14	0	9	40	1	25	88	.229

Atlanta has one of the best young third basemen in the majors in Chipper Jones, and has another good one coming up. Helms, the son of former major leaguer Tommy Helms, already has mastered Double-A at age 22. His 1997 season was delayed by a broken finger, but he showed power and hit to all fields when he returned. The Braves think he'll develop more power once he pulls more pitches. A 10th-round pick in 1994, he started to improve his plate discipline last year. He's a very good defensive third baseman, good enough that he could push Jones to another position. Helms struggled mightily in Triple-A, so he'll spend 1998 at that level.

Damon Hollins

Position: OF
Bats: R **Throws:** L
Ht: 5' 11" **Wt:** 180

Opening Day Age: 23
Born: 6/12/74 in
Fairfield, CA

Recent Statistics

	G	AB	R	H	D	T	HR	RBI	SB	BB	SO	AVG
96 AAA Richmond	42	146	16	29	9	0	0	8	2	16	37	.199
97 AAA Richmond	134	498	73	132	31	3	20	63	7	45	84	.265
97 MLE	134	479	56	113	27	2	15	48	5	34	88	.236

Hollins has been a consistent 20-homer hitter in the minors, save for 1996, when he missed most of the year with a broken left wrist. He returned to form last season, and even made better contact than he had in the past. A 1992 fourth-round pick, he's a career .261 hitter who walks sporadically, so he probably won't hit for a high average in the majors. He runs a tick above-average and has played center in the minors, though he's better suited for right field at the next level. Hollins could get a chance to platoon with Michael Tucker as Andruw Jones assumes an everyday role.

George Lombard

Position: OF
Bats: L **Throws:** R
Ht: 6' 0" **Wt:** 208

Opening Day Age: 22
Born: 9/14/75 in
Atlanta, GA

Recent Statistics

	G	AB	R	H	D	T	HR	RBI	SB	BB	SO	AVG
96 A Macon	116	444	76	109	16	8	15	51	24	36	122	.245
97 A Durham	131	462	65	122	25	7	14	72	35	66	145	.264

Lombard was touted as a future Heisman Trophy candidate when he was recruited by the University of Georgia as a running back, but the Braves scotched those plans by signing him as a 1994 second-round pick. He looked horrible for most of his first two seasons before beginning to turn his career around in the second half of 1996. No longer just a raw talent, he has learned to hit, hit for power and draw a walk. Speed is his most exciting tool, making him a force on the basepaths and in center field. He doesn't throw well, but his arm is playable in center. He's at least two full seasons from helping the Braves.

Kevin Millwood

Position: P
Bats: R **Throws:** R
Ht: 6' 4" **Wt:** 205

Opening Day Age: 23
Born: 12/24/74 in
Bessemer City, NC

Recent Statistics

	W	L	ERA	G	GS	Sv	IP	H	R	BB	SO	HR
97 AA Greenville	3	5	4.11	11	11	0	61.1	59	37	24	61	8
97 AAA Richmond	7	0	1.93	9	9	0	60.2	38	13	16	46	2
97 NL Atlanta	5	3	4.03	12	8	0	51.1	55	26	21	42	1

As if the Braves needed any more pitching, Millwood has developed into the fifth starter they had hoped Jason Schmidt or Terrell Wade would be. After a so-so year in high Class-A in 1996, he jumped from Double-A to the majors last season, tearing up Triple-A along the way. An 11th-round pick in 1993, he throws a consistent 92-93 MPH fastball. His curveball and changeup were much improved, and they and his slider all could become above-average pitches. He limited Triple-A hitters to a .178 average (.120 by righthanders), tops among International League starters, and more than held his own in the majors.

Damian Moss

Position: P
Bats: R **Throws:** L
Ht: 6' 0" **Wt:** 187

Opening Day Age: 21
Born: 11/24/76 in
Darlinghurst, NSW,
Australia

Recent Statistics

	W	L	ERA	G	GS	Sv	IP	H	R	BB	SO	HR
96 A Durham	9	1	2.25	14	14	0	84.0	52	25	40	89	9
96 AA Greenville	2	5	4.97	11	10	0	58.0	57	41	35	48	5
97 AA Greenville	6	8	5.35	21	19	0	112.2	111	73	58	116	13

Two years younger than Millwood, Moss nevertheless had outpitched him on the same teams from 1994-96. Then Moss took a step backward in 1997, trying to pitch through a painful bone chip in the back of his elbow before going on the disabled list in July. His velocity and

command were off, a problem for someone whose fastball is just average to begin with. Signed out of Australia, Moss relies on his curveball and changeup to make his fastball look quicker than it is. He's still just 21, so the temporary setback shouldn't derail his career. He still could reach the majors at a younger age than Millwood did, though his future isn't quite as bright.

Randall Simon

Position: 1B
Bats: L **Throws:** L
Ht: 6' 0" **Wt:** 180

Opening Day Age: 22
Born: 5/26/75 in
Willemstad, Curacao,
Netherlands

Recent Statistics

	G	AB	R	H	D	T	HR	RBI	SB	BB	SO	AVG
97 AAA Richmond	133	519	62	160	45	1	14	102	1	17	76	.308
97 NL Atlanta	13	14	2	6	1	0	0	1	0	1	2	.429
97 MLE	133	496	48	137	39	0	10	79	0	13	79	.276

Willemstad, Curacao, not only produced Andruw Jones but also the Braves' possible successor to McGriff at first base. Simon has a short stroke and a live bat that produce plenty of doubles and occasional homers. He hits lefthanders and righthanders equally well. He makes good contact, but his walk ratios are atrocious and have declined for the past two seasons. He's decent defensively and runs well enough to play left field. The signing of Andres Galarraga precludes Simon from playing every day for Atlanta.

Others to Watch

Righthander **Rob Bell**, 21, tied for the lead on a prospect-studded Class-A Macon staff with 14 wins. He's 6-foot-5 and throws an above-average fastball and knee-buckling curve. . . First baseman **Steve Hacker** and outfielder **Adam Johnson** were low-round college draft picks who have hit well in the minors. Hacker, 23, batted .324-33-119 at Macon. He only offers offense and was about two years too old for his league. Johnson, 22, doesn't have any overwhelming physical gifts but is a more well-rounded player. He hit .281-26-92 with 18 steals at high Class-A Durham. . . Righthander **Jason Marquis**, a 1996 supplemental first-round pick, also won 14 games for Macon and did so at age 18. Managers voted his fastball the best in the South Atlantic League, and his curveball also is above-average at times. . . Signing righthander **Kevin McGlinchy** as a draft-and-follow in 1996 was a coup, but he was mediocre when he was pushed to Durham at age 19. He throws 91-93 MPH, and his curveball and changeup both have potential. . . Yet another Macon pitcher, 19-year-old lefty **Odaliz Perez**, was named the SAL's top reliever after posting a 1.65 ERA and 100 strikeouts in 87 innings. He bounced back from a sore arm in 1996 to throw 94-95 MPH with a solid curve. . . Righthander **Luis Rivera**, another Macon reliever, recovered from blister problems in 1996 to throw 95 MPH at age 19. He also has an above-average changeup, making it difficult for hitters to adjust.

Jim Riggleman

1997 Season

How well respected are Jim Riggleman's managerial abilities? Consider that he began the season with a team that was expected to be much improved, but the club opened the year with 13 straight losses and sank to last place. Through it all, firing Riggleman was never seriously discussed. Few managers could survive such a fiasco, but Riggleman did his best to weather the storm, taking more than his share of the blame while refusing to condemn his players.

Offense

Riggleman is one of the few Cubs managers in recent memory who favors speed over power. Speed at the top of the lineup is especially important to him. He prefers aggressive hitters who put the ball in play and move runners with their outs. He likes to hit and run, and keeps the bench stocked so he can pinch hit often.

Pitching & Defense

Defense is the other fundamental that Riggleman stresses. If a player can't excel in the field, he's not likely to have a regular job no matter how well he hits. The Cubs' early defensive struggles must have been particularly galling for him, and it's no coincidence that some of the club's late-season moves put better glove men in the lineup. He absolutely refuses to allow his starters to run up high pitch counts, and he gives several relievers plenty of work during the last three innings of most games.

1998 Outlook

Riggleman has one thing going for him. No one will expect the Cubs to win in 1998. He'll be growing young players for the future, a role he's well suited for. His patience and professionalism should enable several more youngsters to join 1997's crop. By the end of the year, the end of the tunnel may be in sight.

Born: 11/09/52 in Fort Dix, NJ

Playing Experience: No major league experience

Managerial Experience: 6 seasons

Manager Statistics

Year	Team, Lg	W	L	Pct	GB	Finish
1997	Chicago, NL	68	94	.420	16.0	5th Central
6 Seasons		329	430	.433	—	—

1997 Starting Pitchers by Days Rest

	≤3	4	5	6+
Cubs Starts	3	94	39	16
Cubs ERA	5.94	4.22	4.47	4.97
NL Avg Starts	3	90	38	22
NL ERA	4.23	4.05	4.27	4.52

1997 Situational Stats

	Jim Riggleman	NL Average
Hit & Run Success %	40.6	36.4
Stolen Base Success %	65.9	68.4
Platoon Pct.	47.1	56.3
Defensive Subs	44	26
High-Pitch Outings	2	12
Quick/Slow Hooks	13/5	18/10
Sacrifice Attempts	103	96

1997 Rankings (National League)

⇒ 1st in defensive substitutions (44), mid-inning pitching changes (213) and one-batter pitcher appearances (45)
⇒ 2nd in squeeze plays (12)
⇒ 3rd in sacrifice bunt attempts (103), hit-and-run attempts (143), hit-and-run percentage (40.6%), intentional walks (37) and relief appearances (441)

Terry Adams

1997 Season

Terry Adams began the season as a setup man and pitched 22⅓ innings before allowing his first earned run of the year. After that, he suffered a long downhill slide, even as the meltdown and eventual trade of Mel Rojas gave Adams a greater share of the closer's duties in the second half. Despite converting 18 of 22 save opportunities, he failed to convince the Cubs' brass that he's ready to be a dependable closer just yet.

Pitching

Adams has the classic closer's repertoire, a mid-90s fastball and a hard slider. With his hard stuff and ability to keep the ball down, he induces a good mix of grounders and strikeouts. He encounters occasional bouts of wildness, but his struggles in 1997 came when his fastball tended to lose its life and left him much more hittable. The Cubs can only hope it was a temporary case of fatigue after heavy work over the last two seasons.

Defense & Hitting

Though not spectacularly mobile, Adams hasn't committed an error in 161 big league games. He doesn't have a good enough pickoff move or a quick enough delivery to slow down basestealers, though he did show some improvement in 1997. Fortunately for Cubs fans, his hitting is a non-factor.

1998 Outlook

While the Cubs still regard Adams as their closer of the future, they'd prefer to return him to middle relief for the start of 1998. That would enable him to mature and develop free of pressure. Ideally, his eventual return to the closer's spot would depend more upon his own success than others' failures. Hopefully, last year's decline in effectiveness was just a temporary result of overwork from the year before.

Position: RP
Bats: R **Throws:** R
Ht: 6' 3" **Wt:** 205

Opening Day Age: 25
Born: 3/6/73 in Mobile, AL
ML Seasons: 3

Overall Statistics

	W	L	Pct.	ERA	G	GS	Sv	IP	H	BB	SO	HR	Ratio
1997	2	9	.182	4.62	74	0	18	74.0	91	40	64	3	1.77
Career	6	16	.273	3.92	161	0	23	193.0	197	99	157	9	1.53

How Often He Throws Strikes

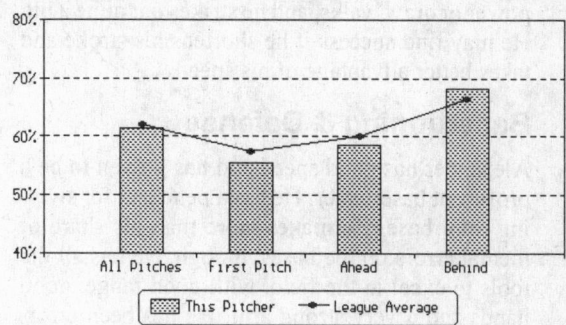

1997 Situational Stats

	W	L	ERA	Sv	IP		AB	H	HR	RBI	Avg
Home	2	5	5.66	6	35.0	LHB	138	41	1	15	.297
Road	0	4	3.69	12	39.0	RHB	159	50	2	24	.314
First Half	1	4	3.60	8	40.0	Sc Pos	97	26	2	35	.268
Scnd Half	1	5	5.82	10	34.0	Clutch	184	59	1	26	.321

1997 Rankings (National League)

⇒ 2nd in relief losses (9) and most baserunners allowed per 9 innings in relief (16.1)
⇒ 3rd in highest batting average allowed in relief (.306)
⇒ 5th in lowest save percentage (81.8%) and lowest percentage of inherited runners scored (16.3%)
⇒ 9th in games pitched
⇒ Led the Cubs in saves, games finished (39), wild pitches (6), save opportunities (22), save percentage (81.8%), lowest percentage of inherited runners scored (16.3%) and relief losses (9)

Manny Alexander

1997 Season

Long-time shortstop prospect Manny Alexander was traded from the Orioles to the Mets before the season began, but the move didn't bring him much more playing time. Instead of being stuck behind Cal Ripken, he was stuck behind Rey Ordonez. Then came a real opportunity, a late-season trade to the Cubs. For the first time in his major league career, he got to play shortstop on a regular basis.

Hitting

Though he never has hit for average in his pro career, Alexander batted .293 with the Cubs, raising hopes that he can hit at an acceptable level. He'll need to because he doesn't hit for much power or draw walks, and he strikes out quite a bit. He may find success if he shortens his stroke and takes better advantage of his speed.

Baserunning & Defense

Alexander has good speed and has proven to be a proficient basestealer. He has a penchant for swiping third base. He makes more than his share of mental errors on the bases, though. He has all the tools to excel in the field, with good range, good hands and a very strong arm. He has been error-prone, but the Cubs hope that will change as his technique improves with experience.

1998 Outlook

Though his position is far from secure, Alexander enters 1998 as the front-runner for the Cubs' shortstop job. Chicago would like him to settle in and become part of their rebuilding effort. With all the rough spots in his game, it may take a lot of patience to allow him the chance to develop into a quality regular. He's never become a part of a major league lineup without sparking controversy. In Baltimore, Cal Ripken was moved to third so that Alexander could play (although the experiment was scrapped a week later). Last year, incumbent shortstop Shawon Dunston belittled Alexander before the Cubs shipped Dunston to Pittsburgh. Hopefully, Alexander will get to play in a less stressful environment this year.

Position: SS/2B
Bats: R **Throws:** R
Ht: 5'10" **Wt:** 160

Opening Day Age: 27
Born: 3/20/71 in San Pedro de Macoris, DR
ML Seasons: 5

Overall Statistics

	G	AB	R	H	D	T	HR	RBI	SB	BB	SO	Avg	OBP	Slg
1997	87	248	37	66	12	4	3	22	13	17	54	.266	.320	.383
Career	242	563	80	131	21	5	6	49	27	40	114	.233	.289	.320

Where He Hits the Ball

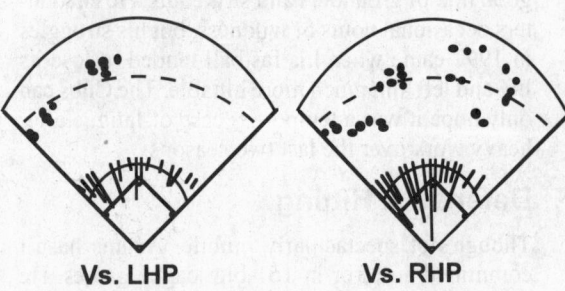

Vs. LHP **Vs. RHP**

1997 Situational Stats

	AB	H	HR	RBI	Avg		AB	H	HR	RBI	Avg
Home	108	26	0	4	.241	LHP	83	20	0	10	.241
Road	140	40	3	18	.286	RHP	165	46	3	12	.279
First Half	119	28	1	9	.235	Sc Pos	57	14	0	17	.246
Scnd Half	129	38	2	13	.295	Clutch	31	9	1	6	.290

1997 Rankings (National League)

⇒ 8th in steals of third (6)

Mark Clark

1997 Season

For the third time in his career, Mark Clark found his groove after a trade brought him a change of scenery. He spent most of the year with the Mets, futilely trying to recapture his 1996 form. But after a late-season deal sent him to the Cubs, he reeled off six wins in nine starts with his new club to finish with even better numbers than he had the year before.

Pitching

Clark doesn't have the stuff to blow hitters away, but with his sinking high-80s fastball, slider and fine command, he gets enough grounders to be successful. He also mixes in a splitter and changeup, but can be hit hard when he falls behind or gets the ball up. The depth of his arsenal and movement of his pitches makes him one of the toughest pitchers to hit on the first pitch of an at-bat.

Defense & Hitting

Clark has been producing grounders for years, and he knows how to handle whatever he can reach. Though he constantly throws to first base, he's no better than average at deterring basestealers. As a hitter, he's pure American League material. He went 2-for-66 last year and his lifetime batting average fell only 15 points as a result. One of his two hits was a stunning homer against the Red Sox.

1998 Outlook

Now comes the tough part. In the past, Clark has had no problem making a favorable first impression with his new teams, but he never has been able to maintain it over the long haul. The Cubs are expecting him to be one of their top three starters, and he should be able to fill that role. He's not cut out to be the ace of the staff, though, despite his hot streak late in 1997. Moving from Shea Stadium to Wrigley Field doesn't figure to improve his stats, either.

Position: SP
Bats: R **Throws:** R
Ht: 6' 5" **Wt:** 225

Opening Day Age: 29
Born: 5/12/68 in Bath, IL
ML Seasons: 7

Overall Statistics

	W	L	Pct.	ERA	G	GS	Sv	IP	H	BB	SO	HR	Ratio
1997	14	8	.636	3.82	32	31	0	205.0	213	59	123	24	1.33
Career	59	45	.567	4.07	159	141	0	914.1	959	261	507	104	1.33

How Often He Throws Strikes

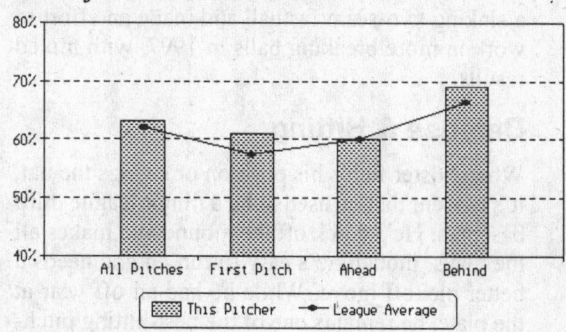

1997 Situational Stats

	W	L	ERA	Sv	IP		AB	H	HR	RBI	Avg
Home	6	4	3.61	0	104.2	LHB	359	107	16	45	.298
Road	8	4	4.04	0	100.1	RHB	431	106	8	40	.246
First Half	7	5	3.94	0	109.2	Sc Pos	175	45	6	58	.257
Scnd Half	7	3	3.68	0	95.1	Clutch	54	16	3	7	.296

1997 Rankings (National League)

⇒ 6th in highest slugging percentage allowed (.443) and least strikeouts per 9 innings (5.4)
⇒ 8th in hits allowed (213) and most GDPs induced per 9 innings (0.9)
⇒ 10th in home runs allowed (24), GDPs induced (21) and highest batting average allowed (.270)
⇒ Led the Cubs in complete games (2)

Chicago Cubs

Kevin Foster

1997 Season

As he has done for his entire career, Kevin Foster ran hot and cold in 1997. He took a 7-3 record into June before slumping in July, then suffered a strained shoulder in August, an injury that all but ended his season. On balance, his campaign left him back in the same frustrating holding pattern that he has been stuck in for three years.

Pitching

Foster's best pitch is a hard four-seam fastball. He doesn't have great command of or confidence in his changeup and breaking ball. As a result he relies heavily on the high heater, giving up a ton of fly balls and far too many homers. He tried to add a sinking two-seam fastball and made an effort to work in more breaking balls in 1997, with mixed results.

Defense & Hitting

When Foster fields his position or swings the bat, it's evident that he used to be a minor league third baseman. He's quick off the mound and makes all the plays, though he's easy to run on and needs a better pickoff move. While he had an off year at the plate, he remains one of the best-hitting pitchers in baseball and even served as a pinch hitter on a few occasions.

1998 Outlook

Foster doesn't have the command to succeed by changing speeds and locations, so his success will depend on whether he's able to add a second pitch that he can throw for strikes. The Cubs believe he can and continue to regard him as a potentially valuable member of the rotation. It's about time for him to start making some progress, though. He's gone as far as he can go with what he's got.

Position: SP
Bats: R **Throws:** R
Ht: 6' 1" **Wt:** 170

Opening Day Age: 29
Born: 1/13/69 in Evanston, IL
ML Seasons: 5

Overall Statistics

	W	L	Pct.	ERA	G	GS	Sv	IP	H	BB	SO	HR	Ratio
1997	10	7	.588	4.61	26	25	0	146.1	141	66	118	27	1.41
Career	32	29	.525	4.71	88	83	0	488.2	471	208	398	85	1.39

How Often He Throws Strikes

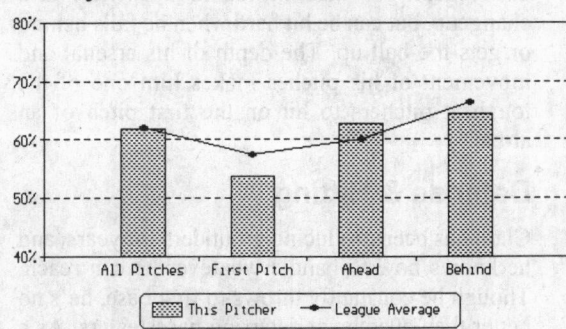

This Pitcher ⬛ — League Average

1997 Situational Stats

	W	L	ERA	Sv	IP		AB	H	HR	RBI	Avg
Home	6	2	3.75	0	81.2	LHB	261	73	13	36	.280
Road	4	5	5.71	0	64.2	RHB	292	68	14	34	.233
First Half	10	5	4.10	0	98.2	Sc Pos	119	25	4	39	.210
Scnd Half	0	2	5.66	0	47.2	Clutch	32	13	1	6	.406

1997 Rankings (National League)

⇒ 3rd in home runs allowed
⇒ 8th in stolen bases allowed (21)
⇒ 10th in sacrifice bunts (11)
⇒ Led the Cubs in sacrifice bunts (11), winning percentage, ERA at home and lowest batting average allowed vs. righthanded batters

Doug Glanville

1997 Season

Chicago's most pleasant surprise in 1997 was out-fielder Doug Glanville, without question. He worked his way out of a platoon role to win the left-field job and became a mainstay at the top of the batting order. With his exciting speed and defensive skills, the Cubs are convinced he's their center fielder of the future.

Hitting

Glanville is an aggressive hitter who makes good contact and protects the plate well with two strikes. He doesn't hit for much power or draw many walks, so he must keep his average up to remain productive. He has the speed to bat leadoff, but until he learns to get on base more he'll remain a below-average tablesetter.

Baserunning & Defense

Glanville doesn't steal bases as often or as effectively as his speed would allow, but he runs intelligently and takes the extra base when it's available. As a natural center fielder with a right fielder's arm, he was one of the most overqualified left fielders in the National League in 1997. The Cubs will move him to center field as soon as the position opens up.

1998 Outlook

With his strong 1997 season, Glanville earned a spot as regular in the Cubs' outfield, possibly for years to come. He's miscast as a left fielder, but should be a good center fielder as soon as he's given the chance. He shouldn't be regarded as a future star, however, because he's 27 and his minor league stats suggest that he's not a true .300 hitter. In left field, he's actually somewhat of an offensive liability, especially since the Cubs have several more promising hitters who can play the position.

Position: LF/CF
Bats: R **Throws:** R
Ht: 6' 2" **Wt:** 170

Opening Day Age: 27
Born: 8/25/70 in Hackensack, NJ
ML Seasons: 2

Overall Statistics

	G	AB	R	H	D	T	HR	RBI	SB	BB	SO	Avg	OBP	Slg
1997	146	474	79	142	22	5	4	35	19	24	46	.300	.333	.392
Career	195	557	89	162	27	6	5	45	21	27	57	.291	.323	.388

Where He Hits the Ball

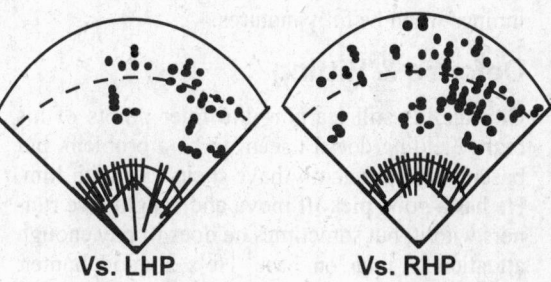

Vs. LHP   Vs. RHP

1997 Situational Stats

	AB	H	HR	RBI	Avg		AB	H	HR	RBI	Avg
Home	254	83	2	25	.327	LHP	156	43	3	11	.276
Road	220	59	2	10	.268	RHP	318	99	1	24	.311
First Half	203	62	2	15	.305	Sc Pos	89	24	0	31	.270
Scnd Half	271	80	2	20	.295	Clutch	76	24	0	10	.316

1997 Rankings (National League)

⇒ 2nd in batting average on an 0-2 count (.359)
⇒ 4th in batting average with two strikes (.277)
⇒ 5th in fielding percentage in left field (.985)
⇒ 6th in lowest HR frequency (118.5 ABs per HR)
⇒ 7th in batting average at home
⇒ 8th in errors in left field (3)
⇒ 9th in highest groundball/flyball ratio (1.8) and lowest stolen base percentage (63.3%)
⇒ Led the Cubs in triples, highest groundball/flyball ratio (1.8), batting average in the clutch, batting average on a 3-1 count (.500), batting average on an 0-2 count (.359), on-base percentage for a leadoff hitter (.344), batting average with two strikes (.277), highest percentage of extra bases taken as a runner (57.4%) and lowest percentage of swings on the first pitch (23.6%)

Jeremi Gonzalez

1997 Season

One of the best things to happen to the Cubs in 1997 was the emergence of young righthander Jeremi Gonzalez. He joined the rotation early in the year and became their most effective starter over the first half of the season. He fell off a bit in the second half, but finished with very respectable numbers for a rookie on a last-place team.

Pitching

Gonzalez has good stuff, a moving fastball in the 90s, a hard slider and a curveball. He throws hard enough to blow his high fastball past hitters on occasion, but gets in trouble when he runs into bouts of wildness. He has good stamina, and the Cubs believe he'll be able to give them a lot of innings when he fully matures.

Defense & Hitting

Gonzalez is still learning the finer points of his craft. Fielding doesn't seem to be a problem, but baserunners frequently have their way with him. He has a good pickoff move and caught five runners with it, but sometimes he doesn't pay enough attention to men on base. He's a good bunter, though he'll never learn to hit.

1998 Outlook

Gonzalez needs to make the adjustments that will enable him to continue to develop and succeed at the major league level, something few Cubs pitchers have been able to do in recent years. He's certainly capable of doing so. If he's able to refine his command, he has the makings of a staff leader. His second-half slide was worrisome, though, especially in light of the numerous Cubs pitchers who've looked good in their first trip around the league recently. Gonzalez' assignment will be to avoid the pitfalls that arrested the development of hurlers like Kevin Foster, Amaury Telemaco and Jim Bullinger.

Position: SP
Bats: R **Throws:** R
Ht: 6' 2"   **Wt:** 200

Opening Day Age: 23
Born: 1/8/75 in Maracaibo, Venezuela
ML Seasons: 1

Overall Statistics

	W	L	Pct.	ERA	G	GS	Sv	IP	H	BB	SO	HR	Ratio
1997	11	9	.550	4.25	23	23	0	144.0	126	69	93	16	1.35
Career	11	9	.550	4.25	23	23	0	144.0	126	69	93	16	1.35

How Often He Throws Strikes

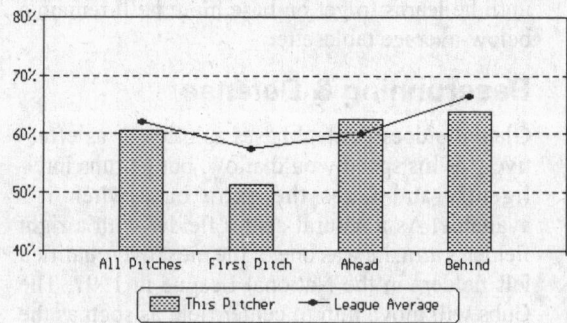

1997 Situational Stats

	W	L	ERA	Sv	IP		AB	H	HR	RBI	Avg
Home	6	3	3.04	0	68.0	LHB	276	64	10	30	.232
Road	5	6	5.33	0	76.0	RHB	257	62	6	29	.241
First Half	5	2	3.12	0	52.0	Sc Pos	114	30	5	43	.263
Scnd Half	6	7	4.89	0	92.0	Clutch	28	9	2	8	.321

1997 Rankings (National League)

⇒ 6th in lowest batting average allowed vs. lefthanded batters
⇒ Led the Cubs in wins, shutouts (1), walks allowed and lowest batting average allowed vs. lefthanded batters

Mark Grace

1997 Season

If you're looking for things you can count on, start with death, taxes and Mark Grace. Once again, Grace batted well over .300 and gave a season-long clinic on fielding at first base. If it wasn't his best season, it was close enough. The only negative was a hamstring pull that cost him a couple of weeks in April.

Hitting

Grace is an equal-opportunity hitter. He hits anybody and everybody. Taking the ball where it's pitched, he sends liners to all fields and waits out a walk if he doesn't see a strike. He doesn't pull the ball or loft it enough to put up flashy power numbers, but he hits the ball hard as consistently as anyone in baseball.

Baserunning & Defense

How slow is Grace? The fact that he's a first baseman is the only thing that prevents him from being the last one off the field at the end of the inning. He's the best slow baserunner in baseball, however, knowing exactly when to take the extra base while rarely getting thrown out trying. At first base, Grace plays with the softest glove around. He digs throws out of the dirt with the best of them, and has both the knowledge and the ability to make all the plays.

1998 Outlook

Despite Grace's continuing productivity, for the first time in a long while the Cubs may be seriously considering trading him. With their lack of power at the corners and the recent signs that a full-fledged rebuilding project is underway, he may be shopped around for younger talent. Cubs fans may cringe at the thought, since Grace is one of the team's two legitimate stars, and is more consistent and less frustrating than the other one, Sammy Sosa. Wherever he lands, everyone will know exactly what to expect from him.

Position: 1B
Bats: L **Throws:** L
Ht: 6' 2" **Wt:** 190

Opening Day Age: 33
Born: 6/28/64 in Winston-Salem, NC
ML Seasons: 10

Overall Statistics

	G	AB	R	H	D	T	HR	RBI	SB	BB	SO	Avg	OBP	Slg
1997	151	555	87	177	32	5	13	78	2	88	45	.319	.409	.465
Career	1448	5458	783	1691	332	34	104	742	59	675	433	.310	.384	.440

Where He Hits the Ball

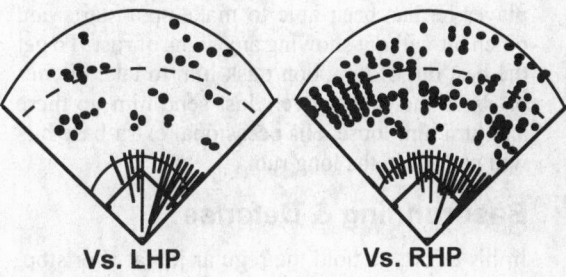

Vs. LHP   Vs. RHP

1997 Situational Stats

	AB	H	HR	RBI	Avg		AB	H	HR	RBI	Avg
Home	276	98	6	43	.355	LHP	143	48	3	19	.336
Road	279	79	7	35	.283	RHP	412	129	10	59	.313
First Half	278	90	9	42	.324	Sc Pos	148	47	0	53	.318
Scnd Half	277	87	4	36	.314	Clutch	73	22	1	9	.301

1997 Rankings (National League)

⇒ 2nd in fielding percentage at first base (.995)
⇒ 4th in batting average at home and lowest percentage of swings that missed (8.8%)
⇒ Led the Cubs in batting average, hits, singles, doubles, triples, sacrifice flies (8), walks, times on base (267), GDPs (18), on-base percentage, batting average vs. lefthanded pitchers, batting average vs. righthanded pitchers, slugging percentage vs. righthanded pitchers (.464), on-base percentage vs. lefthanded pitchers (.412), on-base percentage vs. righthanded pitchers (.408), batting average at home, batting average on the road, highest percentage of pitches taken (59.6%), lowest percentage of swings that missed (8.8%) and highest percentage of swings put into play (52.6%)

Jose Hernandez

1997 Season

In 1996 Jose Hernandez tried and failed to hold the shortstop's job, but out of that failure came success in 1997. Without a regular position, he became sort of a regular non-regular, filling in all over the infield, serving as a defensive replacement and pinch hitting. He fielded capably wherever he was asked to play and showed some sock at the plate as well. He had been the Cubs' regular shortstop for parts of 1996, so manager Jim Riggleman got him into the lineup as often as possible to keep his frustration from building.

Hitting

Hernandez is a pure hacker with decent power. He was prone to slumps as a regular, but as a role player he has been able to make spot starts and pinch hit without showing any signs of rust. To get the best out of him, don't ask him to take pitches or move the runner over. Just send him up there and turn him loose. His occasional extra-base hits will pay off in the long run.

Baserunning & Defense

In his efforts to hold the regular job at shortstop, Hernandez was as slump-prone in the field as he was at the plate. But without so much riding on his glove work in 1997, his fielding was quite acceptable at second base, shortstop and third base. His feet are a bit slow, but his arm is a plus. The only place he's distinctly below-average is on the bases.

1998 Outlook

Hernandez' value lies in the fact that in essence, he covers two bench roles, that of backup infielder and pinch-hitter. It's hard to find a player that can both hit and field enough to perform adequately in both endeavors. His skills may not merit a regular position, but they're good enough to make him a unique and valuable member of the Cubs' bench. Chicago has openings at both middle-infield positions, so he could get quite a bit of playing time.

Position: 3B/2B/SS
Bats: R **Throws:** R
Ht: 6' 1" **Wt:** 180

Opening Day Age: 28
Born: 7/14/69 in Vega Alta, PR
ML Seasons: 6

Overall Statistics

	G	AB	R	H	D	T	HR	RBI	SB	BB	SO	Avg	OBP	Slg
1997	121	183	33	50	8	5	7	26	2	14	42	.273	.323	.486
Career	449	993	148	240	37	14	31	120	9	62	270	.242	.286	.401

Where He Hits the Ball

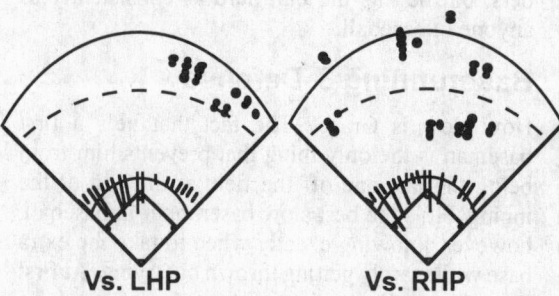

Vs. LHP   **Vs. RHP**

1997 Situational Stats

	AB	H	HR	RBI	Avg		AB	H	HR	RBI	Avg
Home	84	23	4	14	.274	LHP	84	21	3	11	.250
Road	99	27	3	12	.273	RHP	99	29	4	15	.293
First Half	96	27	3	10	.281	Sc Pos	46	10	2	15	.217
Scnd Half	87	23	4	16	.264	Clutch	46	13	1	4	.283

1997 Rankings (National League)

⇒ Led the Cubs in triples

Lance Johnson

1997 Season

For the first time in his career, Lance Johnson was unable to stay healthy enough to play every day. Shin splints hobbled him and put him out of action for a spell in the first half, and a nagging ribcage injury bothered him over much of the second half, even after a late-season trade sent him from the Mets to the Cubs. In between the aches and pains he hit as well as ever, though his basestealing was understandably curtailed.

Hitting

Johnson is an excellent contact hitter who uses the whole field and protects the plate well with two strikes. He hits lefthanders fairly well, though he generates most of his modest extra-base power against righties. As a leadoff man, his career-long weakness has been his inability to wait out walks. He showed improvement in this regard in 1997, though this may not hold up over the long run.

Baserunning & Defense

When he's right, Johnson is a terrific basestealer, piling up dozens of steals while rarely getting caught. His quickness translates into excellent range in center field, though he drops more than his share of fly balls. His arm won't scare anybody, but overall his defense is a real asset.

1998 Outlook

With a glaring need for a power hitter and Doug Glanville ready to take over in center field, the Cubs may look to trade Johnson. His hefty contract is one thing that will make him difficult to move. Wherever he plays, his health is all that can prevent him from returning to his past form. As he enters his mid-30s, he'll remain a useful leadoff man as long as his body allows him to stay in the lineup. He's been tremendously durable in the past, so a return to health seems likely.

Position: CF
Bats: L **Throws:** L
Ht: 5'11" **Wt:** 160

Opening Day Age: 34
Born: 7/6/63 in Cincinnati, OH
ML Seasons: 11

Overall Statistics

	G	AB	R	H	D	T	HR	RBI	SB	BB	SO	Avg	OBP	Slg
1997	111	410	60	126	16	8	5	39	20	42	31	.307	.370	.422
Career	1250	4710	664	1384	155	107	31	442	302	289	335	.294	.334	.392

Where He Hits the Ball

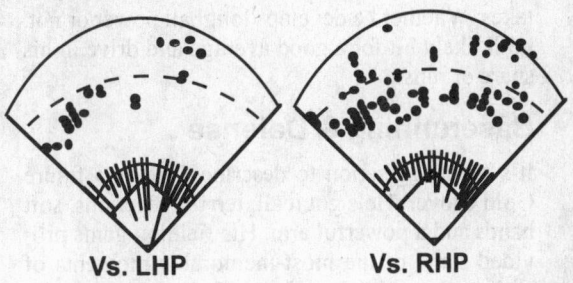

Vs. LHP   **Vs. RHP**

1997 Situational Stats

	AB	H	HR	RBI	Avg		AB	H	HR	RBI	Avg
Home	179	62	4	24	.346	LHP	131	39	1	14	.298
Road	231	64	1	15	.277	RHP	279	87	4	25	.312
First Half	172	51	1	17	.297	Sc Pos	89	30	0	32	.337
Scnd Half	238	75	4	22	.315	Clutch	71	21	0	9	.296

1997 Rankings (National League)

⇒ 2nd in errors in center field (7), lowest fielding percentage in center field (.971) and highest percentage of swings put into play (58.3%)

⇒ 3rd in lowest percentage of swings that missed (8.6%)

⇒ 6th in triples (8) and lowest stolen base percentage (62.5%)

⇒ 8th in on-base percentage for a leadoff hitter (.369) and batting average with two strikes (.254)

⇒ 9th in caught stealing (12) and batting average with runners in scoring position (.337)

Kevin Orie

1997 Season

Third baseman Kevin Orie finally made his long-anticipated arrival at Wrigley Field, and the results were encouraging. Orie overcame a shoulder injury early in the year to post solid numbers while playing top-notch defense. Though he's not the power threat you'd like to have at third, his overall game was so solid that the Cubs expect him to hold down the position for quite a while.

Hitting

Orie generates doubles power with a quick, controlled cut. He makes good contact and shows good strike-zone judgment, and the home runs may come in time. For now he's a line-drive hitter who smacks the ball to all fields and pulls mistakes. Whether he develops longball power or not, he'll likely hit for a good average and drive in his share of runs.

Baserunning & Defense

It's no exaggeration to describe Orie as a future Gold Glover. He's got it all: terrific reactions, soft hands and a powerful arm. His fielding gems provided some of the most memorable moments of Chicago's season, and the Cubs haven't seen leather like his at the hot corner since Ron Santo. A return to his college position—shortstop—has been mentioned, but Orie now sees himself as a third baseman. His speed is below average, but he's far from a liability on the bases.

1998 Outlook

The only thing that might hold Orie back is his health. He has had serious problems with his wrists and shoulder in recent years, and the wrist problems may continue to bother him. He's never played more than 130 games in a season in his professional career, so his durability remains a question mark until he proves otherwise. Apart from that, there's no reason to think he won't become the best third baseman the Cubs have fielded in years.

Position: 3B
Bats: R **Throws:** R
Ht: 6' 4" **Wt:** 210

Opening Day Age: 25
Born: 9/1/72 in West Chester, PA
ML Seasons: 1

Overall Statistics

	G	AB	R	H	D	T	HR	RBI	SB	BB	SO	Avg	OBP	Slg
1997	114	364	40	100	23	5	8	44	2	39	57	.275	.350	.431
Career	114	364	40	100	23	5	8	44	2	39	57	.275	.350	.431

Where He Hits the Ball

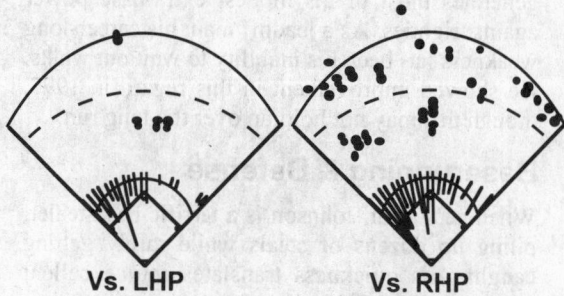

Vs. LHP   Vs. RHP

1997 Situational Stats

	AB	H	HR	RBI	Avg		AB	H	HR	RBI	Avg
Home	204	58	6	27	.284	LHP	87	18	2	10	.207
Road	160	42	2	17	.263	RHP	277	82	6	34	.296
First Half	147	40	3	19	.272	Sc Pos	89	27	1	36	.303
Scnd Half	217	60	5	25	.276	Clutch	68	19	1	9	.279

1997 Rankings (National League)

⇒ 2nd in fielding percentage at third base (.971)
⇒ 5th in most GDPs per GDP situation (20.0%)
⇒ Led the Cubs in triples

Scott Servais

1997 Season

After hitting so well in late 1995 and early 1996, Scott Servais went into a decline that continued through the 1997 season. By the end of the year, he was frequently finding himself benched in favor of Tyler Houston whenever a righthander faced the Cubs. Although he continued to play strong defense and work well with the pitchers, Chicago seemed to be losing patience with his offensive struggles.

Hitting

Servais can give a high fastball a ride every once in a while, but pitchers have learned to keep the ball down on him. If he isn't able to knock a few balls out of the park, he has little to offer because he doesn't make consistent contact or walk enough to get on base very often. He hits lefties surprisingly well. Stamina may be a problem, as his power seems to wane as the season progresses.

Baserunning & Defense

Servais' pitch-calling and excellent rapport with his battery mates are his greatest strengths. These skills are much appreciated by a young Cubs pitching staff. His throwing arm is accurate, if not exceptionally strong, and on balance his throwing is average. On the bases, he has no speed whatsoever and plays strictly station-to-station.

1998 Outlook

Servais' second-half struggles may have resulted in part from a troublesome right knee that was arthroscoped after the season. Or perhaps he simply isn't strong enough to hold up as a starter over a full season. In any case, he begins 1998 as the regular catcher, but his position is far from secure. He may be better suited to a backup role in the long run. Servais might perform well in a platoon role, but Tyler Houston may not be talented enough to hold up the other end of the arrangement.

Position: C
Bats: R **Throws:** R
Ht: 6' 2" **Wt:** 205

Opening Day Age: 30
Born: 6/4/67 in LaCrosse, WI
ML Seasons: 7
Pronunciation: SURR-viss

Overall Statistics

	G	AB	R	H	D	T	HR	RBI	SB	BB	SO	Avg	OBP	Slg
1997	122	385	36	100	21	0	6	45	0	24	56	.260	.311	.361
Career	587	1845	179	455	101	1	50	249	2	133	305	.247	.307	.384

Where He Hits the Ball

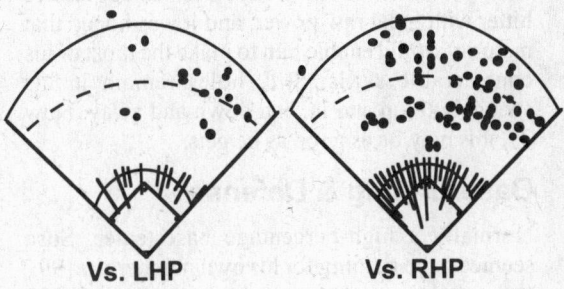

Vs. LHP   **Vs. RHP**

1997 Situational Stats

	AB	H	HR	RBI	Avg		AB	H	HR	RBI	Avg
Home	191	50	4	23	.262	LHP	92	26	3	16	.283
Road	194	50	2	22	.258	RHP	293	74	3	29	.253
First Half	222	60	5	29	.270	Sc Pos	90	23	2	37	.256
Scnd Half	163	40	1	16	.245	Clutch	71	16	1	7	.225

1997 Rankings (National League)

⇒ 3rd in lowest batting average on an 0-2 count (.042)
⇒ 6th in lowest fielding percentage at catcher (.990)
⇒ 7th in errors at catcher (8)
⇒ Led the Cubs in hit by pitch (6)

Chicago Cubs

Sammy Sosa

1997 Season

After hitting 40 homers despite missing the last month of the 1996 season with a broken hand, Sammy Sosa stayed healthy and played in every one of the Cubs' 162 games in 1997. His batting average and power production fell, however, and his frequent strikeouts remained a continuing problem. Chicago signed him to a huge contract extension during the season, but by the end of the year many were wondering if he was worth the money.

Hitting

Sosa showed progress the year before, but seemed to regress in 1997 when he set a team record with 174 strikeouts. He has always been an aggressive hitter with great raw power, and it was hoped that maturity would enable him to make the most of his considerable skills. Still, holes remain in his swing, both up and in, and down and away. Now 29, this may be as good as he gets.

Baserunning & Defense

Normally a high-percentage basestealer, Sosa seemed to be running for his own numbers in 1997 and was thrown out quite a bit in the second half. He has the speed to steal, but chooses to run at odd times and sometimes betrays his intentions. Sosa has one of the best outfield arms in the game, now that his cannon arm has gained accuracy. He has good range, but still commits too many frustrating misplays.

1998 Outlook

For all his faults, Sosa plays hard. Indeed, many of his problems may stem from playing too hard. If he's ever able to stop thinking about his contract, trying to throw out every baserunner, steal every base and hit every ball to the moon, he may become the superstar the Cubs envision. But, on the other hand, he's almost 30 years old, and people have been waiting for him to grow up for a long time. He plays on emotion, so he may push himself to greater heights if the Cubs have a less miserable season this year.

Position: RF
Bats: R **Throws:** R
Ht: 6' 0" **Wt:** 190

Opening Day Age: 29
Born: 11/12/68 in San Pedro de Macoris, DR
ML Seasons: 9

Overall Statistics

	G	AB	R	H	D	T	HR	RBI	SB	BB	SO	Avg	OBP	Slg
1997	162	642	90	161	31	4	36	119	22	45	174	.251	.300	.480
Career	1088	4021	593	1035	162	33	207	642	199	277	1027	.257	.308	.469

Where He Hits the Ball

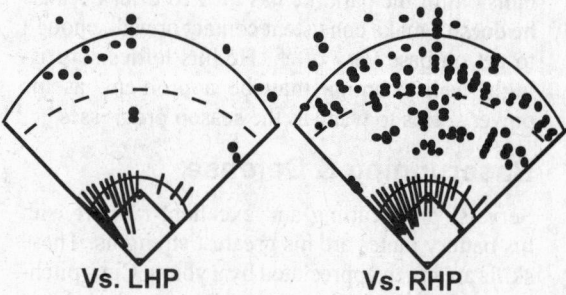

Vs. LHP   Vs. RHP

1997 Situational Stats

	AB	H	HR	RBI	Avg		AB	H	HR	RBI	Avg
Home	312	84	25	85	.269	LHP	141	38	12	34	.270
Road	330	77	11	34	.233	RHP	501	123	24	85	.246
First Half	349	89	17	62	.255	Sc Pos	183	45	9	78	.246
Scnd Half	293	72	19	57	.246	Clutch	96	23	7	20	.240

1997 Rankings (National League)

⇒ 1st in strikeouts, games played (162) and lowest on-base percentage vs. righthanded pitchers (.288)

⇒ 2nd in at-bats, lowest fielding percentage in right field (.977) and highest percentage of swings that missed (31.7%)

⇒ 3rd in lowest on-base percentage

⇒ Led the Cubs in home runs, at-bats, runs scored, total bases (308), RBI, caught stealing (12), intentional walks (9), strikeouts, pitches seen (2,650), plate appearances (694), games played (162), slugging percentage, HR frequency (17.8 ABs per HR), most pitches seen per plate appearance (3.82), cleanup slugging percentage (.498) and slugging percentage vs. lefthanded pitchers (.574)

Kevin Tapani

1997 Season

The season couldn't have gotten off to a worse start for Kevin Tapani. After signing with the Cubs as a free agent to replace Jaime Navarro in the rotation, he underwent surgery on his pitching hand in April and didn't see major league action until July. Amid criticism that his signing had been a waste of money, Tapani became the Cubs' hottest pitcher down the stretch. He finished the year with seven straight victories, including the best game of his career, a one-hit shutout of the Reds on September 16.

Pitching

Tapani used to rely heavily on his split-fingered fastball, but the surgery left him unable to throw the pitch. He compensated admirably, coming up with an impressive straight changeup. By making greater use of his mid-80s fastball and mixing in an occasional slider, he pitched as effectively as ever. His control remains sharp, and he was able to keep the ball in the park better in 1997 than in recent years.

Defense & Hitting

Tapani's delivery puts him in a good position to field and he's quick off the mound, handling many chances with few errors. By tinkering with his stretch delivery, he has become adept at deterring basestealers, even without a good pickoff move. At the plate, he tries not to look too bad and sometimes succeeds.

1998 Outlook

Unless 1997 was a complete fluke, Tapani may prosper at Wrigley Field. He pitched amazingly well there, even with a reduced arsenal. He could be able to justify the Cubs' investment and turn out to be one of the leaders of the staff if he's able to start throwing his splitter again. The half-year's rest probably did his arm some good, and his stabilizing presence will benefit the Cubs' young staff.

Position: SP
Bats: R **Throws:** R
Ht: 6' 0" **Wt:** 189

Opening Day Age: 34
Born: 2/18/64 in Des Moines, IA
ML Seasons: 9
Pronunciation: TAP-uh-nee
Nickname: Tap

Overall Statistics

	W	L	Pct.	ERA	G	GS	Sv	IP	H	BB	SO	HR	Ratio
1997	9	3	.750	3.39	13	13	0	85.0	77	23	55	7	1.18
Career	101	78	.564	4.13	244	238	0	1546.0	1618	372	974	159	1.29

How Often He Throws Strikes

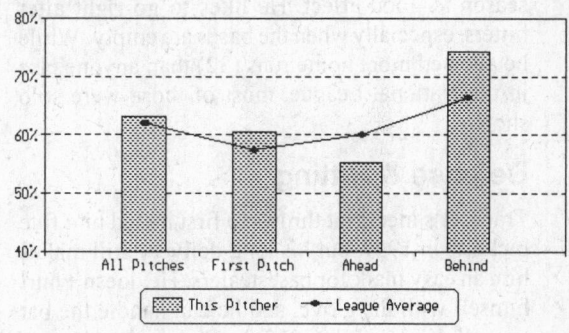

1997 Situational Stats

	W	L	ERA	Sv	IP		AB	H	HR	RBI	Avg
Home	6	0	1.65	0	49.0	LHB	174	40	4	21	.230
Road	3	3	5.75	0	36.0	RHB	144	37	3	9	.257
First Half	0	0	-	0	0.0	Sc Pos	66	17	3	21	.258
Scnd Half	9	3	3.39	0	85.0	Clutch	23	6	1	2	.261

1997 Rankings (National League)
⇒ 8th in balks (2)
⇒ Led the Cubs in shutouts (1) and balks (2)

Steve Trachsel

1997 Season

Steve Trachsel got off to a hot start and made the All-Star team in 1996, but 1997 was just the opposite. He suffered through a terrible April, but pitched decently for the remainder of the season, albeit through consistently tough luck. His performance was better than his stats reflect, and to his credit he never let the frustration of his ill fortune get to him.

Pitching

Trachsel features an average fastball with good movement that he cuts and runs in and out. His splitter is a decent No. 2 pitch, and he worked in more breaking balls over the second half of the season to good effect. He likes to go right after hitters, especially when the bases are empty. While he allowed more home runs (32) than anyone else in the National League, most of those were solo shots.

Defense & Hitting

Trachsel's incessant throws to first netted him five pickoffs in 1997, but his long delivery still makes him an easy mark for basestealers. He doesn't hurt himself with the glove, and he can handle the bat as well. He won't hit .300, but he can lay down a bunt or work a walk better than most pitchers.

1998 Outlook

If anyone on the Cubs is a better pitcher than he showed in 1997, it's Steve Trachsel. A simple change in luck is all that's needed to turn him back into a winning pitcher. He's no big star, but he's durable and throws strikes. The Cubs should be able to count on him to be one of their best starters for the next few years. If he can be a little less preoccupied with avoiding walks and a little more careful when pitching to power hitters, he may return to his All-Star form of 1996.

Position: SP
Bats: R **Throws:** R
Ht: 6' 4" **Wt:** 205

Opening Day Age: 27
Born: 10/31/70 in Oxnard, CA
ML Seasons: 5
Pronunciation: TRACK-sil

Overall Statistics

	W	L	Pct.	ERA	G	GS	Sv	IP	H	BB	SO	HR	Ratio
1997	8	12	.400	4.51	34	34	0	201.1	225	69	160	32	1.46
Career	37	43	.463	3.98	120	119	0	732.2	729	264	531	110	1.36

How Often He Throws Strikes

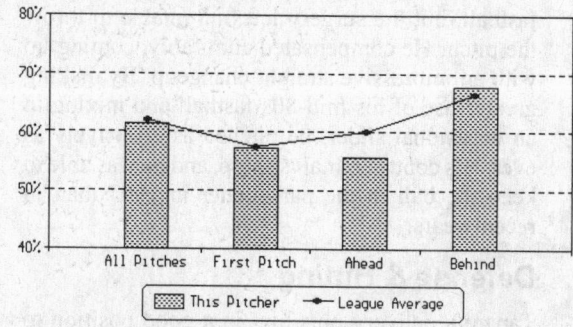

1997 Situational Stats

	W	L	ERA	Sv	IP		AB	H	HR	RBI	Avg
Home	7	4	4.15	0	121.1	LHB	377	98	12	42	.260
Road	1	8	5.06	0	80.0	RHB	408	127	20	59	.311
First Half	4	6	4.76	0	109.2	Sc Pos	171	51	9	74	.298
Scnd Half	4	6	4.22	0	91.2	Clutch	53	18	3	7	.340

1997 Rankings (National League)

⇒ 1st in home runs allowed and most home runs allowed per 9 innings (1.43)

⇒ 2nd in hits allowed and highest batting average allowed vs. righthanded batters

⇒ 3rd in games started and highest slugging percentage allowed (.476)

⇒ Led the Cubs in sacrifice bunts (11), ERA, losses, games started, innings pitched, hits allowed, batters faced (878), home runs allowed, walks allowed, strikeouts, pitches thrown (3,327), pickoff throws (162), stolen bases allowed (27), runners caught stealing (12), GDPs induced (20), highest strikeout/walk ratio (2.3), lowest batting average allowed (.287), lowest slugging percentage allowed (.476) and lowest on-base percentage allowed (.344)

Kent Bottenfield

Position: RP
Bats: R **Throws:** R
Ht: 6' 3" **Wt:** 237

Opening Day Age: 29
Born: 11/14/68 in Portland, OR
ML Seasons: 5

Overall Statistics

	W	L	Pct.	ERA	G	GS	Sv	IP	H	BB	SO	HR	Ratio
1997	2	3	.400	3.86	64	0	2	84.0	82	35	74	13	1.39
Career	14	21	.400	4.20	175	30	5	364.0	379	146	199	43	1.44

1997 Situational Stats

	W	L	ERA	Sv	IP		AB	H	HR	RBI	Avg
Home	1	1	4.93	1	38.1	LHB	124	31	1	9	.250
Road	1	2	2.96	1	45.2	RHB	192	51	12	43	.266
First Half	1	1	2.44	2	55.1	Sc Pos	105	27	1	36	.257
Scnd Half	1	2	6.59	0	28.2	Clutch	47	15	5	16	.319

1997 Season

After being rescued off the scrap heap in 1996, Kent Bottenfield continued to solidify his modest niche in the Cub bullpen. Though he tailed off late in the year, he pitched decently in middle relief and showed good durability.

Pitching, Defense & Hitting

Bottenfield owes his career to his 90 MPH fastball. His slider is a decent enough second pitch, and he has good enough control of both offerings to get by. He has no move to first, however, and basestealers find him an easy mark. As a fielder, he's immobile but surehanded. He has hit well in the past, but went hitless in four trips in 1997.

1998 Outlook

When Bottenfield is no longer qualified to pitch in the majors, the radar gun will let him know immediately. Until then, there's no reason to believe he'll suddenly lose it or become anything more than a decent middle reliever. The Cubs will keep him around but probably won't expand his role.

Brant Brown

Position: LF/1B
Bats: L **Throws:** L
Ht: 6' 3" **Wt:** 205

Opening Day Age: 26
Born: 6/22/71 in Porterville, CA
ML Seasons: 2

Overall Statistics

	G	AB	R	H	D	T	HR	RBI	SB	BB	SO	Avg	OBP	Slg
1997	46	137	15	32	7	1	5	15	2	7	28	.234	.286	.409
Career	75	206	26	53	8	1	10	24	5	9	45	.257	.300	.451

1997 Situational Stats

	AB	H	HR	RBI	Avg		AB	H	HR	RBI	Avg
Home	58	14	3	5	.241	LHP	17	2	0	1	.118
Road	79	18	2	10	.228	RHP	120	30	5	14	.250
First Half	119	26	4	13	.218	Sc Pos	24	6	1	10	.250
Scnd Half	18	6	1	2	.333	Clutch	17	3	0	3	.176

1997 Season

It was a season of missed opportunities for Brant Brown. He hit well in his first major league trial back in 1996, but in 1997 he was unable to hold a job as Doug Glanville's platoon partner in left field. The Cubs sent him down in April and again in June, and he didn't return until the rosters expanded in September.

Hitting, Baserunning & Defense

Brown is capable of hitting for a fairly good average with decent power and very few walks. He's a natural first baseman, but the Cubs asked him to try left field, where he was barely adequate. He's got the arm for the position, but not the range or instincts. He runs the bases with all the speed of a lame catcher.

1998 Outlook

As long as the Cubs have Mark Grace, Brown has little hope of playing regularly. If he can polish his outfield skills, he may be able to help Chicago in a bench role. His bat is potent enough for him to pinch hit and possibly platoon.

Chicago Cubs

Dave Clark

Position: LF
Bats: L **Throws:** R
Ht: 6' 2" **Wt:** 209

Opening Day Age: 35
Born: 9/3/62 in Tupelo, MS
ML Seasons: 12

Overall Statistics

	G	AB	R	H	D	T	HR	RBI	SB	BB	SO	Avg	OBP	Slg
1997	102	143	19	43	8	0	5	32	1	19	34	.301	.386	.462
Career	812	1833	236	491	74	8	62	280	18	208	406	.268	.341	.418

1997 Situational Stats

	AB	H	HR	RBI	Avg		AB	H	HR	RBI	Avg
Home	64	20	1	16	.313	LHP	14	6	0	1	.429
Road	79	23	4	16	.291	RHP	129	37	5	31	.287
First Half	73	22	2	14	.301	Sc Pos	48	15	1	24	.313
Scnd Half	70	21	3	18	.300	Clutch	40	11	2	9	.275

1997 Season

After the Cubs signed Dave Clark over the winter, he gave them exactly what they'd expected—one of the best lefthanded pinch hitters in the business. He came off the bench to bat .308 while amassing a team-record 22 RBI in the pinch.

Hitting, Baserunning & Defense

Clark combines power and patience at the plate, and righthanders haven't found a hole in his stroke yet. He doesn't have enough speed to be useful on the bases or in the outfield, and his strong arm isn't accurate enough to help. Only 25 of his 102 games came at a defensive position.

1998 Outlook

While Clark's advanced age, poor defense and inability to hit lefthanders limit him to duty as a role player, he's one of the best. The Cubs wanted to keep him around as their ace in the hole as long as there are still some game-breaking hits left in his bat. But Houston won his services with a two-year, $1.4 million contract. Count on him to remain one of the most dangerous pinch hitters around.

Dave Hansen

Position: 3B
Bats: L **Throws:** R
Ht: 6' 0" **Wt:** 195

Opening Day Age: 29
Born: 11/24/68 in Long Beach, CA
ML Seasons: 8

Overall Statistics

	G	AB	R	H	D	T	HR	RBI	SB	BB	SO	Avg	OBP	Slg
1997	90	151	19	47	8	2	3	21	1	31	32	.311	.429	.450
Career	584	989	94	264	40	2	15	104	2	132	164	.267	.353	.357

1997 Situational Stats

	AB	H	HR	RBI	Avg		AB	H	HR	RBI	Avg
Home	52	16	1	4	.308	LHP	7	2	0	0	.286
Road	99	31	2	17	.313	RHP	144	45	3	21	.313
First Half	98	27	1	14	.276	Sc Pos	29	9	1	17	.310
Scnd Half	53	20	2	7	.377	Clutch	31	11	1	3	.355

1997 Season

Dave Hansen was signed to replace Dave Magadan as the Cubs' lefthanded-hitting backup third baseman and pinch hitter, and he mirrored Magadan in almost every detail. Playing part-time at third base and coming off the bench to hit, Hansen performed creditably.

Hitting, Baserunning & Defense

Hansen hits for a decent average by using the whole ballpark. He's very patient at the plate but has little power. He has the glove and arm to hold his own at third base, but shows little speed on the basepaths. He also can handle the duties at first base if necessary.

1998 Outlook

Hansen is a useful but eminently replaceable spare part. If Kevin Orie is able to stay healthy, Hansen may become expendable. The fact that he bats lefthanded and plays a little third base should enable him to hook on somewhere whenever the Cubs are done with him.

Tyler Houston

Position: C/3B
Bats: L **Throws:** R
Ht: 6' 2" **Wt:** 210

Opening Day Age: 27
Born: 1/17/71 in Las Vegas, NV
ML Seasons: 2

Overall Statistics

	G	AB	R	H	D	T	HR	RBI	SB	BB	SO	Avg	OBP	Slg
1997	72	196	15	51	10	0	2	28	1	9	35	.260	.290	.342
Career	151	338	36	96	19	1	5	55	4	18	62	.284	.318	.391

1997 Situational Stats

	AB	H	HR	RBI	Avg		AB	H	HR	RBI	Avg
Home	96	24	0	15	.250	LHP	13	2	0	2	.154
Road	100	27	2	13	.270	RHP	183	49	2	26	.268
First Half	90	20	1	16	.222	Sc Pos	47	17	0	25	.362
Scnd Half	106	31	1	12	.292	Clutch	36	7	1	5	.194

1997 Season

Though he didn't keep up his hot hitting from 1996, Tyler Houston remained a useful backup catcher and infielder and gave the Cubs an extra lefthanded bat off the bench. He caught more in the second half, mainly because Scott Servais wore down and stopped hitting.

Hitting, Baserunning & Defense

Houston was never a potent hitter in the minors, and his 1997 stats reflect his true level of ability. He's impatient at the plate, but hits for a decent average with a touch of power. He hasn't been allowed to see many lefthanders, and the platooning should continue. He's a decent backstop with a below-average throwing arm, though he can handle himself capably at first or third base.

1998 Outlook

Houston is your average backup catcher. His best assets are his lefthanded bat and his versatility. The Cubs put his limited skills to good use, and he likely will continue to produce in the limited role he has been given.

Bob Patterson

Position: RP
Bats: R **Throws:** L
Ht: 6' 2" **Wt:** 195

Opening Day Age: 38
Born: 5/16/59 in Jacksonville, FL
ML Seasons: 12

Overall Statistics

	W	L	Pct.	ERA	G	GS	Sv	IP	H	BB	SO	HR	Ratio
1997	1	6	.143	3.34	76	0	0	59.1	47	10	58	9	0.96
Career	38	39	.494	3.96	526	21	27	597.0	583	168	466	68	1.26

1997 Situational Stats

	W	L	ERA	Sv	IP		AB	H	HR	RBI	Avg
Home	1	3	3.34	0	35.0	LHB	96	16	2	16	.167
Road	0	3	3.33	0	24.1	RHB	116	31	7	16	.267
First Half	1	4	3.89	0	34.2	Sc Pos	77	13	2	21	.169
Scnd Half	0	2	2.55	0	24.2	Clutch	121	29	4	17	.240

1997 Season

Ageless lefthander Bob Patterson's job description and performance didn't change a bit. He pitched every other day, facing three or four hitters in the seventh or eighth inning before turning over the game to the closer.

Pitching, Defense & Hitting

Patterson's fastball, slider and changeup are unremarkable, but he stands out for his sharp control and unwavering resilience. He's tough on lefthanders, but righties can hurt him when he gets the ball up in the zone. He committed the very first error of his 12-year career in 1997, but he doesn't get to many balls in the first place. He's got a decent move to first, and shouldn't be allowed to hit.

1998 Outlook

Patterson's arm has less mileage on it than most pitchers his age, and he has shown no signs of slowing down. If he's limited to his present role, he should remain a valuable member of the Cubs' bullpen until he decides to spend more time with the grandkids.

Chicago Cubs

Dave Stevens

Position: RP/SP
Bats: R **Throws:** R
Ht: 6' 3" **Wt:** 205

Opening Day Age: 28
Born: 3/4/70 in
Fullerton, CA
ML Seasons: 4

Overall Statistics

	W	L	Pct.	ERA	G	GS	Sv	IP	H	BB	SO	HR	Ratio
1997	1	5	.167	9.19	16	6	0	32.1	54	26	29	8	2.47
Career	14	14	.500	6.00	145	6	21	201.0	241	106	129	40	1.73

1997 Situational Stats

	W	L	ERA	Sv	IP		AB	H	HR	RBI	Avg
Home	0	3	11.25	0	16.0	LHB	73	26	4	12	.356
Road	1	2	7.16	0	16.1	RHB	73	28	4	19	.384
First Half	1	2	10.32	0	11.1	Sc Pos	49	18	2	25	.367
Scnd Half	0	3	8.57	0	21.0	Clutch	4	3	0	1	.750

1997 Season

The nightmare that began in 1996 worsened in 1997 for Dave Stevens. After losing his grip on the closer's job in Minnesota in 1996, he bombed so badly last year that the Twins demoted him to the minors and ultimately released him in July. The Cubs picked him up on waivers, but he continued to struggle. He earned the dubious distinction of posting a 9.00-plus ERA for two separate teams in the same season.

Pitching, Defense & Hitting

Stevens' 90-plus fastball is the sole reason the Twins saw closer material in him. His inability to add an effective second pitch has been his undoing. His slider and splitter have been inconsistent, and hitters know he won't trust anything but his fastball in a big situation. He's a good athlete and a good fielder, but baserunners have begun to figure out his move to first. As a hitter, he's been weak in the few at-bats he has had.

1998 Outlook

Stevens began his professional career in the Cubs system, and memories of his past promise might have spurred Chicago to give him a second chance. That potential still exists, but to realize it he must harness a second pitch that's eluded him for most of his career.

Amaury Telemaco

Position: SP/RP
Bats: R **Throws:** R
Ht: 6' 3" **Wt:** 210

Opening Day Age: 24
Born: 1/19/74 in
Higuey, DR
ML Seasons: 2
Pronunciation:
ah-MARR-ee
tel-ah-MAH-ko

Overall Statistics

	W	L	Pct.	ERA	G	GS	Sv	IP	H	BB	SO	HR	Ratio
1997	0	3	.000	6.16	10	5	0	38.0	47	11	29	4	1.53
Career	5	10	.333	5.65	35	22	0	135.1	155	42	93	24	1.46

1997 Situational Stats

	W	L	ERA	Sv	IP		AB	H	HR	RBI	Avg
Home	0	2	6.65	0	21.2	LHB	76	23	1	9	.303
Road	0	1	5.51	0	16.1	RHB	79	24	3	17	.304
First Half	0	3	4.68	0	25.0	Sc Pos	47	16	2	22	.340
Scnd Half	0	0	9.00	0	13.0	Clutch	11	3	1	3	.273

1997 Season

Amaury Telemaco was out to prove that he'd recovered from the strained shoulder that struck him in late 1996, but was hit so hard in spring training that the Cubs sent him to Triple-A in mid-March. He was promoted twice during the season, but failed to win a game in 10 appearances, and his work in the minors was unimpressive.

Pitching, Defense & Hitting

When he's right, Telemaco features a 90-MPH fastball and a sharp slider, but he rarely had both pitches working at the same time in 1997. His changeup is nothing more than a third pitch at this point. He doesn't swing the bat or control the running game effectively, though he's a capable enough fielder.

1998 Outlook

Telemaco had a serious setback in 1997, but he's still only 24 and there's plenty of time for him to work his way back. With the Cubs' recent transition to youth, they may have more patience and allow him to work his way back on his own schedule.

Other Chicago Cubs

Miguel Batista (Pos: RHP, Age: 27)

	W	L	Pct.	ERA	G	GS	Sv	IP	H	BB	SO	HR	Ratio
1997	0	5	.000	5.70	11	6	0	36.1	36	24	27	4	1.65
Career	0	5	.000	5.80	21	6	0	49.2	49	34	34	5	1.67

Called up by the Cubs in August, Batista was hit fairly hard in his brief trial, but not as hard as his ERA would suggest. He's the kind of player only a despeRatioe club would take a look at. 1998 Outlook: C

Mike Hubbard (Pos: C, Age: 27, Bats: R)

	G	AB	R	H	D	T	HR	RBI	SB	BB	SO	Avg	OBP	Slg
1997	29	64	4	13	0	0	1	2	0	2	21	.203	.227	.250
Career	65	125	7	21	0	0	2	7	0	4	38	.168	.192	.216

For the third straight year, Hubbard hit fairly well at Triple-A but stunk up the joint in a brief Wrigley audition. The Cubs don't need him as a backup catcher, which leaves him stuck in Iowa again. 1998 Outlook: C

Ramon Morel (Pos: RHP, Age: 23)

	W	L	Pct.	ERA	G	GS	Sv	IP	H	BB	SO	HR	Ratio
1997	0	0	-	4.76	8	0	0	11.1	14	7	7	3	1.85
Career	2	2	.500	4.98	42	0	0	59.2	77	28	32	7	1.76

The Cubs claimed Morel on waivers in September. He's only 23 this year, and had a good year in A-ball four years ago. On the other hand, he didn't pitch very well at Triple-A last year. 1998 Outlook: C

Rodney Myers (Pos: RHP, Age: 28)

	W	L	Pct.	ERA	G	GS	Sv	IP	H	BB	SO	HR	Ratio
1997	0	0	-	6.00	5	1	0	9.0	12	7	6	1	2.11
Career	2	1	.667	4.83	50	1	0	76.1	73	45	56	7	1.55

Myers spent all of '96 with the Cubs as a Rule 5 draftee. Last year, they sent him down so he could be converted back into a starter. The experiment was a moderate success, and he may resurface soon. 1998 Outlook: B

Ryne Sandberg (Pos: 2B, Age: 38)

	G	AB	R	H	D	T	HR	RBI	SB	BB	SO	Avg	OBP	Slg
1997	135	447	54	118	26	0	12	64	7	28	94	.264	.308	.403
Career	2164	8385	1318	2386	403	76	282	1061	344	761	1260	.285	.344	.452

While his season was far from stellar, Sandberg showed flashed of his old form after announcing his retirement plans at midseason. The Cubs have no clear-cut replacement for him. 1998 Outlook: D

Dave Swartzbaugh (Pos: RHP, Age: 30)

	W	L	Pct.	ERA	G	GS	Sv	IP	H	BB	SO	HR	Ratio
1997	0	1	.000	9.00	2	2	0	8.0	12	7	4	1	2.38
Career	0	3	.000	5.72	15	7	0	39.1	43	24	22	4	1.70

Swartzbaugh started two games for the Cubs in April before they realized they'd forgotten to cut him. He had one of his better years at Triple-A, so the Cubs may re-sign him to a minor league contract. 1998 Outlook: C

Chicago Cubs Minor League Prospects

Organization Overview:

The Cubs haven't been to a World Series since World War II, and they're in the midst of their umpteenth rebuilding phase. This time they're trying to win with home-grown players, and the system is making decent progress. In the past two seasons, Doug Glanville and Kevin Orie have won starting jobs while Terry Adams and Jeremi Gonzalez have grabbed important pitching roles. On the downside, Chicago has a number of once-touted players stalling in Triple-A. The strength of the organization is young pitching that for the most part is a few years away. The Cubs need middle infielders and have few options.

Pat Cline

Position: C

Opening Day Age: 23

Bats: R **Throws:** R

Born: 10/9/74 in

Ht: 6' 3" **Wt:** 220

Manatee, FL

Recent Statistics

	G	AB	R	H	D	T	HR	RBI	SB	BB	SO	AVG
96 A Daytona	124	434	75	121	30	2	17	76	10	54	79	.279
97 AAA Iowa	27	95	6	21	2	0	3	10	0	10	24	.221
97 AA Orlando	78	271	39	69	19	0	7	37	2	27	78	.255
97 MLE	105	351	33	75	16	0	7	35	1	24	108	.214

There's a dearth of catching prospects in the minor leagues, but Cline is one of the best. A sixth-round pick in 1993, he has reached double figures in homers each year since he had surgery to correct a left wrist problem in 1994. The Cubs will trade strikeouts for homers, but Cline still whiffs too much and struggled in Double-A. He has an above-average arm to go with his above-average power, but he's more of an offensive player now because he's still learning the intricacies of catching. He had minor hand surgery after the 1997 season. With Scott Servais fading at the major league level, Cline could grab a starting job in 1999.

Courtney Duncan

Position: P

Opening Day Age: 23

Bats: L **Throws:** R

Born: 10/9/74 in Mobile,

Ht: 5' 11" **Wt:** 175

AL

Recent Statistics

	W	L	ERA	G	GS	Sv	IP	H	R	BB	SO	HR
96 A Williamsprt	11	1	2.19	15	15	0	90.1	58	28	34	91	6
97 A Daytona	8	4	1.63	19	19	0	121.2	90	35	35	120	3
97 AA Orlando	2	2	3.40	8	8	0	45.0	37	28	29	45	2

Duncan is a classic example of a sleeper. Taken in the 20th round out of Grambling State in 1996, he has gone 21-7 in 1½ pro seasons and shot up to Double-A. He threw 87-89 MPH in college with a mediocre slider, but as a pro he now hits 92 MPH with better movement and

has an improved breaking ball. He also throws a cut fastball and a changeup. The Cubs expect him to have a solid Triple-A season in 1998 and project him in their major league rotation the following year.

Jason Hardtke

Position: 2B

Opening Day Age: 26

Bats: B **Throws:** R

Born: 9/15/71 in

Ht: 5' 10" **Wt:** 175

Milwaukee, WI

Recent Statistics

	G	AB	R	H	D	T	HR	RBI	SB	BB	SO	AVG
97 AAA Norfolk	97	388	46	107	23	3	11	45	3	40	54	.276
97 AA Binghamton	6	26	3	10	2	0	1	4	0	2	2	.385
97 NL New York	30	56	9	15	2	0	2	8	1	4	6	.268
97 MLE	103	400	42	103	20	2	9	42	2	35	58	.258

Ryne Sandberg's retirement left the Cubs without a clear-cut second baseman, and the loss of Miguel Cairo in the expansion draft cost Chicago one of its top candidates. Hardtke, claimed on waivers from the Mets after the season, may get a chance at the position. A 1990 third-round pick by Cleveland, he's now with his fourth organization. His tools are fairly ordinary across the board, which is why he has just 113 big league at-bats. He projects as a .260 hitter with a little power for a middle infielder. He doesn't have much speed, but he has sure hands and good defensive instincts. Hardtke's main competition in Chicago looks like Jose Hernandez.

Robin Jennings

Position: OF

Opening Day Age: 25

Bats: L **Throws:** L

Born: 4/11/72 in

Ht: 6' 2" **Wt:** 200

Singapore

Recent Statistics

	G	AB	R	H	D	T	HR	RBI	SB	BB	SO	AVG
97 AAA Iowa	126	464	67	128	25	5	20	71	5	56	73	.276
97 NL Chicago	9	18	1	3	1	0	0	2	0	0	2	.167
97 MLE	126	451	55	115	22	3	16	59	4	46	76	.255

Jennings became the first major league player to have been born in Singapore, but just one of several corner-outfield prospects who hasn't been able to make the jump from Triple-A to Wrigley Field. A 33rd-round draft-and-follow out of Manatee (Fla.) Community College in 1991, he broke through as a prospect four years later with a strong Double-A performance and Arizona Fall League batting title. He has continued to hit for decent power, draw walks and make good contact in two years at Triple-A Iowa, but those tools haven't shone through in limited big league trials. He doesn't have all the pop you'd want in a corner outfielder, but he's steady and is the best all-around player in a group of left-field prospects that also includes Brant Brown and Pedro Valdes.

Terrell Lowery

Position: OF   **Opening Day Age:** 27
Bats: R **Throws:** R   **Born:** 10/25/70 in
Ht: 6' 3" **Wt:** 175   Oakland, CA

Recent Statistics

	G	AB	R	H	D	T	HR	RBI	SB	BB	SO	AVG
97 AAA Iowa	110	386	69	116	28	3	17	71	9	65	97	.301
97 NL Chicago	9	14	2	4	0	0	0	0	1	3	3	.286
97 MLE	110	373	57	103	24	2	15	59	6	54	101	.276

A star point guard in Loyola Marymount's fast-paced offense, Lowery opted to pursue a baseball career. He signed with the Rangers as a 1991 second-round pick and eventually became considered as the organization's top prospect. His pure speed was the reason, but he hasn't been as quick since injuring his right Achilles tendon in 1995. He still has good range in center field, but isn't the stolen-base threat he was before the injury. The Cubs picked him up as a minor league Rule 5 draft pick in 1996, and he hit for average and power in Triple-A. He draws enough walks to bat leadoff.

Marc Pisciotta

Position: P   **Opening Day Age:** 27
Bats: R **Throws:** R   **Born:** 8/7/70 in Edison,
Ht: 6' 5" **Wt:** 240   NJ

Recent Statistics

	W	L	ERA	G	GS	Sv	IP	H	R	BB	SO	HR
97 AAA Iowa	6	2	2.36	42	0	22	45.2	29	12	23	48	2
97 NL Chicago	3	1	3.18	24	0	0	28.1	20	10	16	21	1

Before he turned his career around in 1997, Pisciotta's biggest baseball accomplishment was winning the championship game of the 1983 Little League World Series. Drafted by the Pirates in the 19th round out of Georgia Tech in 1991, he was claimed on waivers by the Cubs in November 1996. Triple-A Iowa pitching coach Marty DeMerritt showed him how to use his legs to geneRatioe more power, and Pisciotta's fastball went from the low 90s to 95-97 MPH. He also throws a splitter and slider, and his hard stuff suits him for the closer's role. He should make the Cubs in 1998 as at least a setup man, and could save some games if no one else can handle the responsibility.

Steve Rain

Position: P   **Opening Day Age:** 22
Bats: R **Throws:** R   **Born:** 6/2/75 in Los
Ht: 6' 6" **Wt:** 225   Angeles, CA

Recent Statistics

	W	L	ERA	G	GS	Sv	IP	H	R	BB	SO	HR
96 AA Orlando	1	0	2.56	35	0	10	38.2	32	15	12	48	4
96 AAA Iowa	2	1	3.12	26	0	10	26.0	17	9	8	23	3
97 AAA Iowa	7	1	5.89	40	0	1	44.1	51	30	34	50	8
97 AA Orlando	1	2	3.07	14	0	4	14.2	16	7	8	11	2

While Pisciotta made a quantum leap forward, Rain regressed terribly. After saving a total of 43 games in the previous two seasons, he picked up just five saves in 1997. He's not overpowering, but his fastball and slider have good life and he can throw both pitches for strikes.

He also throws a splitter as a third pitch. The Cubs haven't given up on him, but they no longer believe he can be a big league closer. He needs to reduce his high leg kick to keep runners in check.

Kerry Wood

Position: P   **Opening Day Age:** 20
Bats: R **Throws:** R   **Born:** 6/16/77 in Irving,
Ht: 6' 5" **Wt:** 190   TX

Recent Statistics

	W	L	ERA	G	GS	Sv	IP	H	R	BB	SO	HR
96 A Daytona	10	2	2.91	22	22	0	114.1	72	51	70	136	6
97 AA Orlando	6	7	4.50	19	19	0	94.0	58	49	79	106	2
97 AAA Iowa	4	2	4.68	10	10	0	57.2	35	35	52	80	2

There may not be a better pitching prospect in the minors than Wood, the fourth overall selection in the 1995 draft. Two years later he already had reached Triple-A and would have pitched in Chicago if that wouldn't have exposed him to the expansion draft. Managers in the American Association ranked him as the league's best prospect, while skippers in the Double-A Southern League tabbed him as the loop's top pitching prospect and best fastball. He works at 95-96 MPH and can hit 99, plus he has a Bert Blylevenesque curve when it's on. His curve and changeup need more consistency and he definitely needs more command. The Cubs think he'll throw more strikes once he gets used to his velocity, which keeps increasing. He has a chance to make Chicago's Opening Day rotation at age 20, and the club is banking on him as a No. 1 starter for years to come.

Others to Watch

Second baseman **Dennis Abreu** could fill Ryne Sandberg's shoes in a couple of years. The younger brother of Phillies outfielder Bob Abreu and fellow Cubs farm-hand Nelson Abreu, he showed speed and projectable gap power while batting .321 at Class-A Rockford at age 19. . . Two high school righthanders drafted in the first round did well in the Rookie-level Arizona League. **Jon Garland** (1997) already shows some polish and is a three-pitch pitcher at 18. **Todd Noel** (1996) was named the league's top prospect. He has better stuff, including a 92-93 MPH fastball, but less command. Noel, 19, also had a tender elbow toward the end of the season. . . 24-year-old outfielder **Marty Gazarek** may start to push Jennings and Kieschnick. He's faster and can play right field, plus he's a career .299 hitter with doubles power. . . Because they hit it big with Wood, the Cubs haven't been afraid to draft high school pitchers. Righthander **Chris Gissell** went 6-11, 4.45 at Rockford in his first full pro season at age 19. His two best pitches are an above-average fastball with good movement, and a slider. . . **Justin Speier**, 24, was a catcher at Nicholls State but has thrived as a righthander since the Cubs took him in the 55th round in 1995. He throws a 93-94 MPH fastball and a slider, and is working on a splitter to combat lefties. He's the son of former All-Star shortstop Chris Speier.

Jack McKeon

1997 Season

There was little surprise when the emotional managerial reign of Ray Knight was terminated on July 25. The shock came when his replacement was announced. Jack McKeon, who was a personnel advisor to GM Jim Bowden, was given the job in what was expected to be an interim move. Instead, the 56-year-old McKeon's crusty style and cigar smoke seemed to grow on the Reds. Cincinnati went 33-30 under him, the best record over that period in the mediocre National League Central. He settled down what was an uptight clubhouse under Knight. The Reds played looser ball and the atmosphere improved so much that McKeon had his contract extended for 1998.

Offense

With plenty of speed up and down his roster, McKeon didn't hesitate to press the action with stolen bases and hit-and-runs. He also didn't hesitate to juggle lineups, constantly using different combinations in an effort to not only find out about some unfamiliar players, but also to take advantage of matchups. Under McKeon, there were very few set positions.

Pitching & Defense

With a pitching staff that finished last in the NL in complete games, McKeon used his bullpen frequently. He had his relievers set in their roles and they pitched well under his guidance. As part of his experimenting, McKeon was willing to sacrifice defense at times to look at players in different positions.

1998 Outlook

No one is under any illusions about the Reds, especially with budgetary concerns that could turn over much of the roster. McKeon's job is to put together a foundation for the next few years. If Cincinnati gets some breaks, it could be a surprise team in their wide-open division. Expect the lineup and position shuffling to decrease considerably now that he has a better idea of what his players can do.

Born: 11/23/40 in South Amboy, NJ

Playing Experience: No major league experience

Managerial Experience: 9 seasons
Nickname: Trader Jack

Manager Statistics

Year	Team, Lg	W	L	Pct	GB	Finish
1997	Cincinnati, NL	33	30	.524	8.0	3rd Central
9 Seasons		512	504	.504	—	—

1997 Starting Pitchers by Days Rest

	≤3	4	5	6+
Reds Starts	0	29	22	8
Reds ERA	—	3.97	4.40	4.69
NL Avg Starts	3	90	38	22
NL ERA	4.23	4.05	4.27	4.52

1997 Situational Stats

	Jack McKeon*	NL Average
Hit & Run Success %	37.0	36.4
Stolen Base Success %	72.2	68.4
Platoon Pct.	45.9	56.3
Defensive Subs	7	26
High-Pitch Outings	5	12
Quick/Slow Hooks	13/2	18/10
Sacrifice Attempts	41	96

* McKeon managed the Reds for 63 games

1997 Rankings (National League)

⇒ Did not rank near the top in any category

Bret Boone

1997 Season

Bret Boone's free fall at the plate continued in 1997. After watching his batting average drop in each of the previous two seasons, he hoped to turn things around in 1997. Instead, things got so bad that he was banished to Triple-A Indianapolis when his average fell to .205 61 games into the season. His exile lasted only four days, however, and after the All-Star break he hit a more respectable .258. Defense was another story entirely, as he made a record-low two errors in 136 games.

Hitting

Though built slightly and not possessing outstanding power, Boone insists on taking a big swing and going for the fences. The result is a lot of harmless flyouts and even more strikeouts. He's a good fastball hitter. On those occasions when he's thinking about going up the middle and to right-center, he waits well on breaking stuff. However, he usually falls back into the habit of trying to jerk everything and hits the skids offensively. He really struggled against lefthanders in 1997, with a .210 average and no homers.

Baserunning & Defense

Boone won't scare anybody with his speed, but he'll look to steal occasionally and is aggressive about trying to take the extra base. Other infielders may be flashier, but no one is more dependable. His range is very good, his hands are the best in baseball and he turns the double play well with his strong, accurate arm.

1998 Outlook

The only reason why Boone isn't one of the game's best all-around second basemen is his stubborn insistence on keeping his big swing. Cincinnati has toyed with trading him, but with his father Bob now a manager-in-waiting as a club executive, Boone is likely staying put. He can be an All-Star with some adjustments on offense.

Position: 2B
Bats: R **Throws:** R
Ht: 5'10" **Wt:** 180

Opening Day Age: 28
Born: 4/6/69 in El Cajon, CA
ML Seasons: 6

Overall Statistics

	G	AB	R	H	D	T	HR	RBI	SB	BB	SO	Avg	OBP	Slg
1997	139	443	40	99	25	1	7	46	5	45	101	.223	.298	.332
Career	636	2257	264	572	121	10	62	304	19	162	445	.253	.307	.398

Where He Hits the Ball

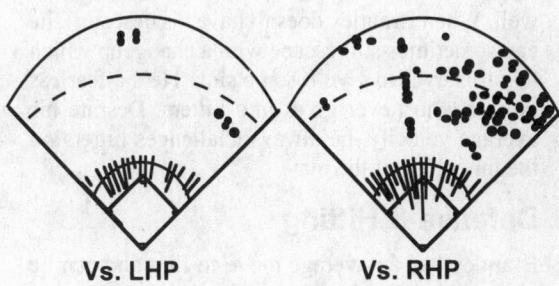

Vs. LHP   **Vs. RHP**

1997 Situational Stats

	AB	H	HR	RBI	Avg		AB	H	HR	RBI	Avg
Home	223	55	4	26	.247	LHP	100	21	0	10	.210
Road	220	44	3	20	.200	RHP	343	78	7	36	.227
First Half	226	43	2	24	.190	Sc Pos	114	20	3	40	.175
Scnd Half	217	56	5	22	.258	Clutch	75	12	1	6	.160

1997 Rankings (National League)

⇒ 1st in lowest batting average vs. righthanded pitchers and fielding percentage at second base (.997)

⇒ 2nd in lowest on-base percentage vs. righthanded pitchers (.288)

⇒ 3rd in lowest batting average with runners in scoring position and lowest batting average in the clutch

⇒ 4th in lowest slugging percentage vs. righthanded pitchers (.344)

⇒ Led the Reds in doubles, sacrifice flies (5), GDPs (12), batting average with the bases loaded (.444) and lowest percentage of swings on the first pitch (18.9%)

Jeff Brantley

Traded To CARDINALS

1997 Season

After re-signing with Cincinnati at below market price near the end of his fantastic 1996 season, Jeff Brantley was never healthy last year. He missed spring training with shoulder troubles. After briefly coming back to pitch in 13 games, he blew his shoulder out May 20 and required major surgery. He managed only one save, 43 fewer than he notched the year before.

Pitching

To be at his best, Brantley needs the arm strength to throw his sharp-breaking splitter and hard slider to righthanders. His shoulder injury kept him from doing that. He has also developed an excellent cut fastball which has made him tough on lefties as well. When Brantley doesn't have his best stuff, he can sometimes still escape with a changeup which he turns over to give it some sink. He's a fearless pitcher who never gives into hitters. Despite his average velocity, he always challenges hitters on the inner part of the plate.

Defense & Hitting

Brantley has an average move to first and can be susceptible to stolen bases. That's especially true if he's used in setup situations instead of save opportunities, when teams are less likely to run. He's quick coming home and is always in good fielding position after delivering a pitch. Brantley rarely hits, which is good because he doesn't handle the bat well.

1998 Outlook

The big question is the status of Brantley's shoulder, and the answer won't be known until spring training. The Reds decided not to wait and traded him to the Cardinals for Dmitri Young in mid-November. If he's able to pitch and Dennis Eckersley signs elsewhere, Brantley could jump back to the 30-save plateau. He was one of the Reds' team leaders, and could become one for the Cardinals if he's not damaged goods.

Position: RP
Bats: R **Throws:** R
Ht: 5'10" **Wt:** 190

Opening Day Age: 34
Born: 9/5/63 in Florence, AL
ML Seasons: 10

Overall Statistics

	W	L	Pct.	ERA	G	GS	Sv	IP	H	BB	SO	HR	Ratio
1997	1	1	.500	3.86	13	0	1	11.2	9	7	16	2	1.37
Career	40	31	.563	3.06	484	18	130	723.2	619	302	601	76	1.27

How Often He Throws Strikes

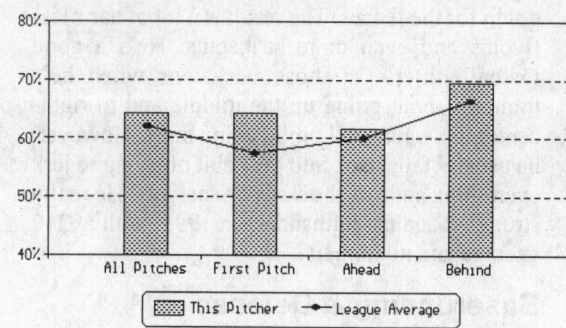

1997 Situational Stats

	W	L	ERA	Sv	IP		AB	H	HR	RBI	Avg
Home	0	0	1.80	0	5.0	LHB	18	1	0	1	.056
Road	1	1	5.40	1	6.2	RHB	26	8	2	5	.308
First Half	1	1	3.86	1	11.2	Sc Pos	8	2	0	4	.250
Scnd Half	0	0	-	0	0.0	Clutch	21	6	1	5	.286

1997 Rankings (National League)

⇒ Did not rank near the top or bottom in any category

Willie Greene

1997 Season

Can't-miss prospect Willie Greene has finally begun meeting the Reds' high expectations. He led the club in home runs and RBI last year, and hit a very respectable .262 over the first half of the season. His batting average dropped after the All-Star break, but his power and production remained steady. He also added to his value by showing himself capable of playing a number of different positions.

Hitting

A free swinger with exceptional strength and bat speed, Greene can crush low fastballs. He tries to pull too many pitches, which is why his batting average isn't better. Greene also is very weak versus lefthanders, batting .172 against southpaws in 1997. Only four of his 49 career homers have come against lefties, and he could become a platoon player if he doesn't improve soon. He piles up strikeouts by chasing breaking balls or high fastballs. However, he has greatly improved his knowledge of the strike zone and has learned to take walks. He also has bettered his ability to cut down his swing and aim for the opposite field.

Baserunning & Defense

Greene is not a burner and is no threat on the bases. He has worked hard on his third-base play, and though his hands are ordinary he showed improvement in his overall skills in the infield. He also improved his throwing mechanics. Greene has no future in the outfield, where he plays occasionally. He appeared to have a clue about how to play first base, where he was able to handle routine plays in a short trial.

1998 Outlook

Cincinnati needs to settle on a place for Greene to play, but there's no question that it needs his bat in the lineup. He's just entering his prime and it would be no surprise if he posted bigger power numbers while topping 100 RBI.

Position: 3B/RF
Bats: L **Throws:** R
Ht: 5'11" **Wt:** 192

Opening Day Age: 26
Born: 9/23/71 in Milledgeville, GA
ML Seasons: 6

Overall Statistics

	G	AB	R	H	D	T	HR	RBI	SB	BB	SO	Avg	OBP	Slg
1997	151	495	62	125	22	1	26	91	6	78	111	.253	.354	.459
Career	334	981	133	238	35	9	49	175	6	135	262	.243	.333	.446

Where He Hits the Ball

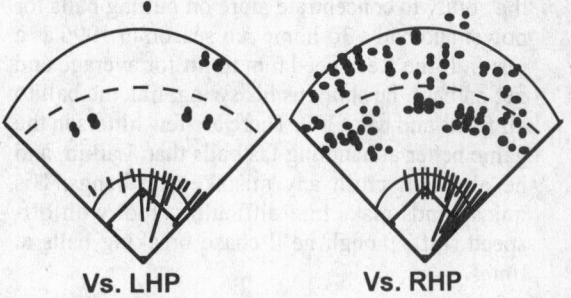

Vs. LHP   Vs. RHP

1997 Situational Stats

	AB	H	HR	RBI	Avg		AB	H	HR	RBI	Avg
Home	243	62	13	44	.255	LHP	99	17	2	9	.172
Road	252	63	13	47	.250	RHP	396	108	24	82	.273
First Half	237	62	13	45	.262	Sc Pos	158	40	7	71	.253
Scnd Half	258	63	13	46	.244	Clutch	68	13	1	4	.191

1997 Rankings (National League)

⇒ 2nd in lowest batting average on an 0-2 count (.033) and lowest fielding percentage at third base (.934)

⇒ Led the Reds in home runs, at-bats, runs scored, total bases (227), RBI, walks, times on base (204), strikeouts, pitches seen (2,199), plate appearances (578), games played (151), slugging percentage, on-base percentage, HR frequency (19.0 ABs per HR), most pitches seen per plate appearance (3.80), batting average with runners in scoring position, batting average vs. righthanded pitchers, slugging percentage vs. righthanded pitchers (.508) and on-base percentage vs. righthanded pitchers (.366)

Barry Larkin

1997 Season

Barry Larkin was never healthy in what was one of the most frustrating seasons of his great career. Problems with his heel and Achilles tendon developed during spring training, and he also missed six weeks with a badly pulled calf muscle and neck spasms. Larkin tried playing through the problems but finally succumbed to heel surgery on September 3. A year after hitting 33 homers and two years removed from an MVP Award, he was limited to just 73 games and hit just four homers.

Hitting

Larkin is the rare kind of hitter who can adjust according to what his team needs. He has shown the ability to concentrate more on pulling balls for power and had a 30-home run season in 1996 as a result. If the Reds need him to hit for average and get on base, he shortens his swing, hits the ball to all fields and bats .300. There are few hitters in the game better at handling fastballs than Larkin, and he also will crush any mistake that hangs. His quick hands make him difficult to fool with off-speed stuff, though he'll chase breaking balls at times.

Baserunning & Defense

Even while hobbling much of last season, Larkin was caught only three times in 17 steal attempts. He's a smart, aggressive runner who's fearless about taking the extra base, especially in late-inning situations. Larkin has few equals at shortstop, where he has great range and a highly accurate arm. Only injuries kept him from contending for his fourth consecutive Gold Glove.

1998 Outlook

Larkin expects to be 100 percent physically when spring training opens. He has voiced uneasiness with the Reds' cost-cutting and suggestions that he might be moved to third base or center field to make room for Pokey Reese at short. It would be very risky for Cincinnati to trade its franchise player when he still has years of quality play ahead of him.

Position: SS
Bats: R **Throws:** R
Ht: 6' 0" **Wt:** 195

Opening Day Age: 33
Born: 4/28/64 in Cincinnati, OH
ML Seasons: 12

Overall Statistics

	G	AB	R	H	D	T	HR	RBI	SB	BB	SO	Avg	OBP	Slg
1997	73	224	34	71	17	3	4	20	14	47	24	.317	.440	.473
Career	1401	5170	862	1547	271	51	139	646	289	592	507	.299	.373	.452

Where He Hits the Ball

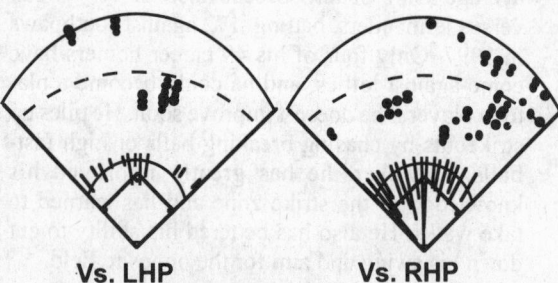

Vs. LHP   Vs. RHP

1997 Situational Stats

	AB	H	HR	RBI	Avg		AB	H	HR	RBI	Avg
Home	110	43	0	12	.391	LHP	47	21	2	11	.447
Road	114	28	4	8	.246	RHP	177	50	2	9	.282
First Half	186	59	4	18	.317	Sc Pos	64	14	1	16	.219
Scnd Half	38	12	0	2	.316	Clutch	33	9	0	1	.273

1997 Rankings (National League)

⇒ 7th in batting average with two strikes (.266)
⇒ Led the Reds in intentional walks (6) and batting average with two strikes (.266)

Hal Morris

1997 Season

A year after turning in one of his best all-around seasons, Hal Morris was bothered by shoulder troubles for most of 1997. He spent most of August and the first part of September on the disabled list, and ended up starting only 89 games at first base. The injury wore on him at the plate, as he hit .276 after entering the season as a career .309 hitter.

Hitting

Morris' biggest negative as a hitter always has been his lack of power. Coming off a career-high 16 homers in 1996, he hit bottom last season. He managed only one home run all season, and that came in April. He also disappeared with runners in scoring position. Morris fell back into the bad habit of swaying too much in his stance, which allowed pitchers to jam him and rob him of the bat speed needed for extra bases. He always has been a good breaking-ball hitter, willing to take balls to the opposite field. He also has a good knowledge of the strike zone.

Baserunning & Defense

Morris has average speed but can surprise with a stolen base if neglected too much. He also is aggressive about trying to take the extra base. Morris is a workmanlike first baseman. His range is ordinary and he can mishandle routine grounders on occasion. He committed seven errors in his limited playing time in 1997. He has an accurate arm and makes the double-play throw to second fairly well.

1998 Outlook

As one of their first cost-cutting moves, the Reds didn't pick up their option on Morris at the end of the season and sent him into free agency. He's not past his prime, but at his best he's no more than an 80-RBI player. That puts him in the lower echelon of first basemen.

Position: 1B
Bats: L **Throws:** L
Ht: 6' 4" **Wt:** 210

Opening Day Age: 32
Born: 4/9/65 in Fort Rucker, AL
ML Seasons: 10

Overall Statistics

	G	AB	R	H	D	T	HR	RBI	SB	BB	SO	Avg	OBP	Slg
1997	96	333	42	92	20	1	1	33	3	23	43	.276	.328	.351
Career	940	3255	451	994	201	18	72	443	44	283	449	.305	.361	.445

Where He Hits the Ball

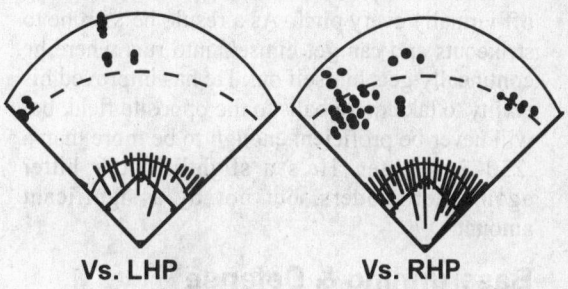

Vs. LHP   Vs. RHP

1997 Situational Stats

	AB	H	HR	RBI	Avg		AB	H	HR	RBI	Avg
Home	167	50	1	19	.299	LHP	72	18	0	12	.250
Road	166	42	0	14	.253	RHP	261	74	1	21	.284
First Half	276	74	1	25	.268	Sc Pos	76	15	0	26	.197
Scnd Half	57	18	0	8	.316	Clutch	57	14	0	3	.246

1997 Rankings (National League)

⇒ 7th in errors at first base (7)
⇒ 10th in most GDPs per GDP situation (17.2%)

Joe Oliver

1997 Season

Joe Oliver opened the 1997 season on the disabled list with a thumb injury, but came back in late April after a rehabilitation stint at Triple-A Indianapolis to have a big first half. He was batting .299 with a .471 slugging percentage at the All-Star break. Then he slumped, batting .224 after the break. He still managed to tie his career high in home runs with 14.

Hitting

Oliver always has been a good high-fastball hitter who can turn on heaters and drive them for power. He never has been able to adjust consistently to breaking balls out of the strike zone, however, because his approach to hitting involves pulling off virtually every pitch. As a result, he's prone to strikeouts and can get himself into ruts where he continually gets himself out. He has improved his ability to take more balls to the opposite field, but will never be proficient enough to be more than a .250-.260 hitter. He's a slightly better hitter against lefthanders, but not by a significant amount.

Baserunning & Defense

Few big league runners are slower than Oliver, who will steal a base or two each year on what are usually bungled hit-and-run plays. However, he's a smart baserunner who usually doesn't make mistakes or get too aggressive. He's a solid receiver who handles pitchers well and is competent in blocking balls in the dirt. He has a very quick release on his throws. If his pitchers give him a chance, Oliver will nab his share of basestealers. He threw out 32 percent of them in 1997.

1998 Outlook

A free agent, Oliver is the kind of veteran receiver with power who can help any number of teams. He accepts his role, works well with pitchers and can supply double-figure home runs from the bottom of the batting order.

Position: C
Bats: R **Throws:** R
Ht: 6' 3" **Wt:** 220

Opening Day Age: 32
Born: 7/24/65 in Memphis, TN
ML Seasons: 9

Overall Statistics

	G	AB	R	H	D	T	HR	RBI	SB	BB	SO	Avg	OBP	Slg
1997	111	349	28	90	13	0	14	43	1	25	58	.258	.313	.415
Career	866	2745	253	685	140	2	84	393	8	205	503	.250	.302	.394

Where He Hits the Ball

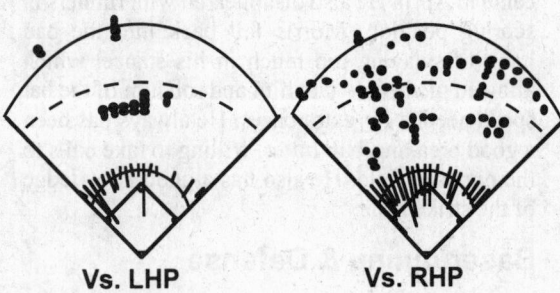

Vs. LHP   Vs. RHP

1997 Situational Stats

	AB	H	HR	RBI	Avg		AB	H	HR	RBI	Avg
Home	169	41	7	23	.243	LHP	86	24	2	8	.279
Road	180	49	7	20	.272	RHP	263	66	12	35	.251
First Half	157	47	7	24	.299	Sc Pos	85	22	3	30	.259
Scnd Half	192	43	7	19	.224	Clutch	65	17	4	9	.262

1997 Rankings (National League)

⇒ 6th in fielding percentage at catcher (.990)
⇒ 9th in errors at catcher (7)
⇒ Led the Reds in sacrifice flies (5)

Eduardo Perez

Position: 1B/LF
Bats: R **Throws:** R
Ht: 6' 4" **Wt:** 215

Opening Day Age: 28
Born: 9/11/69 in
Cincinnati, OH
ML Seasons: 5
Pronunciation:
ed-WAR-doe

1997 Season

For the first time in his five-year big league career, Eduardo Perez got a chance to play regularly, and he made something of his opportunity. He saw time at first base, third base, left field, right field and DH, and set career highs in homers and RBI. His campaign included a big August in which he led the Reds with 24 RBI while becoming the everyday first baseman. Perez struggled down the stretch, however, and ended the season with a 5-for-52 skid.

Hitting

Perez has added strength in the last two years and is now a legitimate power threat. He split his 16 home runs in 1997 equally between lefties and righties. He's a good fastball hitter and has improved his plate discipline to the point where he's able to lay off many of the breaking balls which used to trouble him. He'll chase high fastballs, but he has become a dangerous mistake hitter.

Baserunning & Defense

Though his speed is average, Perez can't be overlooked on the bases. He went 5-for-6 on steals last year and is a smart runner capable of taking an extra base. Chronic problems with his right shoulder have taken Perez away from his original position of third base, where he started only eight times in 1997. He saw most of his action at first base, where he displayed good hands and decent range. He has proven to be barely adequate in spot duty roving the outfield.

1998 Outlook

Perez is no longer just the son of former Reds star Tony Perez. He has made himself into a solid player in his own right. There's still some question about the legitimacy of Perez' newfound power, but Reds brass think Perez can give them 20 homers. The trade for Dmitri Young could cost Perez some playing time at first base.

Overall Statistics

	G	AB	R	H	D	T	HR	RBI	SB	BB	SO	Avg	OBP	Slg
1997	106	297	44	75	18	0	16	52	5	29	76	.253	.321	.475
Career	243	713	87	167	35	3	29	110	13	67	162	.234	.303	.414

Where He Hits the Ball

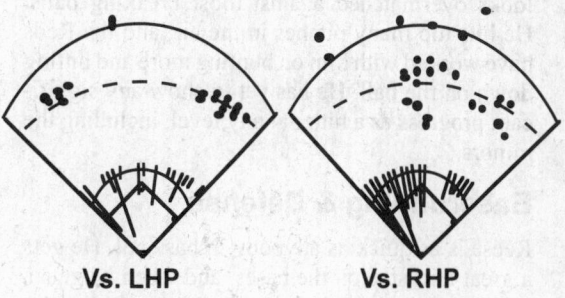

Vs. LHP   **Vs. RHP**

1997 Situational Stats

	AB	H	HR	RBI	Avg		AB	H	HR	RBI	Avg
Home	153	36	7	26	.235	LHP	102	28	8	24	.275
Road	144	39	9	26	.271	RHP	195	47	8	28	.241
First Half	112	29	4	16	.259	Sc Pos	92	23	5	39	.250
Scnd Half	185	46	12	36	.249	Clutch	43	16	3	7	.372

1997 Rankings (National League)

⇒ 7th in cleanup slugging percentage (.512)
⇒ Led the Reds in cleanup slugging percentage (.512)

Pokey Reese

Position: SS
Bats: R **Throws:** R
Ht: 5'11" **Wt:** 180

Opening Day Age: 24
Born: 6/10/73 in Columbia, SC
ML Seasons: 1

1997 Season

Pokey Reese got his first extensive major league playing time in 1997, holding down the everyday shortstop duties for most of the second half during Barry Larkin's absence. Reese led all National League rookies with 25 stolen bases and legged out 15 doubles, but otherwise he struggled offensively. He defense was flashy but erratic.

Hitting

Reese has yet to prove he can hit even average major league stuff. He's slightly built and has little strength or bat speed. He has the bat knocked out of his hands by hard stuff and he strikes out far too often for someone with so little power. Reese also looks overmatched against most breaking balls. He hits too many pitches in the air, and the Reds have worked with him on bunting more and hitting down on the ball. He has yet to show any significant progress as a hitter at any level, including the minors.

Baserunning & Defense

Reese is as quick as anybody in baseball. He gets a great first step on the bases, and when he gets a good jump he's almost impossible to throw out. He can play defensively with any shortstop in baseball. Reese has exceptional range, a great throwing arm and remarkable agility, all of which make him capable of spectacular plays. He can be erratic at times, to which his 15 errors and .966 fielding percentage would attest. His miscues are largely the result of inexperience, which causes him to hurry plays. He also can play second or third.

1998 Outlook

Cincinnati has been waiting for Reese to blossom, but he remains a weak hitter. He's not going to dislodge a healthy Larkin from shortstop. Reese doesn't hit enough to play third and Bret Boone appears to be staying put at second. That means Reese may return to the minors to work on his batting.

Overall Statistics

	G	AB	R	H	D	T	HR	RBI	SB	BB	SO	Avg	OBP	Slg
1997	128	397	48	87	15	0	4	26	25	31	82	.219	.284	.287
Career	128	397	48	87	15	0	4	26	25	31	82	.219	.284	.287

Where He Hits the Ball

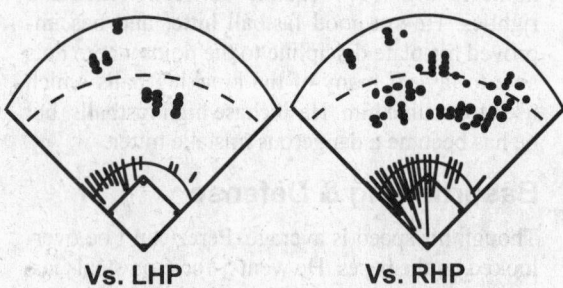

Vs. LHP   **Vs. RHP**

1997 Situational Stats

	AB	H	HR	RBI	Avg		AB	H	HR	RBI	Avg
Home	178	48	3	19	.270	LHP	87	15	1	6	.172
Road	219	39	1	7	.178	RHP	310	72	3	20	.232
First Half	139	33	2	12	.237	Sc Pos	94	16	1	20	.170
Scnd Half	258	54	2	14	.209	Clutch	64	15	1	4	.234

1997 Rankings (National League)

⇒ 1st in lowest on-base percentage for a leadoff hitter (.280)
⇒ 2nd in lowest batting average with runners in scoring position and lowest fielding percentage at shortstop (.966)
⇒ 3rd in least GDPs per GDP situation (2.0%)
⇒ 7th in errors at shortstop (15)
⇒ 8th in steals of third (6)
⇒ 9th in lowest batting average with two strikes (.134)
⇒ 10th in lowest batting average on a 3-1 count (.154)
⇒ Led the Reds in least GDPs per GDP situation (2.0%) and highest percentage of pitches taken (59.4%)

Deion Sanders

1997 Season

His "Prime Time" act may be wearing thin, but there should never be any question about what kind of an athlete Deion Sanders is. After being away from baseball for a year, Sanders returned and stole 56 bases, the second-highest total in the National League. He hit over .300 for much of the first half before slumping badly. He missed the last several weeks with back troubles before rejoining the NFL's Dallas Cowboys.

Hitting

Despite his lack of baseball experience, Sanders has made himself into a better-than-average hitter. He can be overpowered with hard stuff, but he usually puts the ball into play. He has learned to slap balls to the opposite field and try to make things happen with his speed. Sanders falls into slumps when he starts lifting pitches. He simply doesn't have the power to drive many balls for extra bases. He also can be fooled with average breaking balls, and he doesn't draw enough walks to be a top-notch leadoff hitter.

Baserunning & Defense

No player has more pure speed than Sanders. There are few more exciting sights on a baseball field than watching him turn the bases for a triple, something he did seven times in 1997. At times he'll be guilty of taking too many chances on the bases, and he often fails to get good jumps. That said, he was successful on a career-high 81 percent of his steal attempts last season. He's a solid out-fielder in either center or left, and he can outrun most balls. Sanders' arm is below average and runners try to exploit him.

1998 Outlook

The song remains the same for Sanders. It's uncertain whether he'll return to baseball, as he's an All-Pro cornerback first and foremost. Still, he is a remarkable athlete whose speed always will be in demand. If he does play baseball, it almost certainly will be with Cincinnati.

Position: CF/LF
Bats: L **Throws:** L
Ht: 6' 1" **Wt:** 195

Opening Day Age: 30
Born: 8/9/67 in Ft. Myers, FL
ML Seasons: 8
Nickname: Neon Deion, Prime Time

Overall Statistics

	G	AB	R	H	D	T	HR	RBI	SB	BB	SO	Avg	OBP	Slg
1997	115	465	53	127	13	7	5	23	56	34	67	.273	.329	.363
Career	609	2048	302	545	70	43	38	164	183	155	342	.266	.322	.398

Where He Hits the Ball

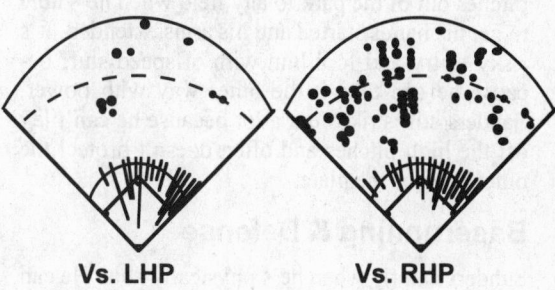

Vs. LHP   **Vs. RHP**

1997 Situational Stats

	AB	H	HR	RBI	Avg		AB	H	HR	RBI	Avg
Home	236	65	0	10	.275	LHP	126	38	1	8	.302
Road	229	62	5	13	.271	RHP	339	89	4	15	.263
First Half	336	100	4	19	.298	Sc Pos	88	18	0	18	.205
Scnd Half	129	27	1	4	.209	Clutch	68	16	0	3	.235

1997 Rankings (National League)

⇒ 1st in steals of third (21)
⇒ 2nd in stolen bases
⇒ 4th in bunts in play (31)
⇒ 5th in lowest batting average with runners in scoring position
⇒ Led the Reds in batting average, hits, singles, triples, stolen bases, caught stealing (13), hit by pitch (6), highest groundball/flyball ratio (1.4), stolen base percentage (81.2%), batting average vs. lefthanded pitchers, on-base percentage for a leadoff hitter (.327), slugging percentage vs. lefthanded pitchers (.357), on-base percentage vs. lefthanded pitchers (.348), batting average at home, batting average on the road, bunts in play (31) and lowest percentage of swings that missed (16.4%)

Cincinnati Reds

Reggie Sanders

1997 Season

Cincinnati spent another season frustrated by Reggie Sanders' inability to remain healthy. He missed three weeks in late April and early May with a back problem, then was sidelined two months with ankle and knee injuries. He came back at the end of July and hit 10 homers in August, but his 19 longballs for the season fell short of the 25-30 the team was expecting.

Hitting

Sanders has trouble getting on top of high fastballs. The book on him remains to pound him up and in with hard stuff. Unlike many righthanders, he's a better low-ball hitter, and he can drive pitches out of the park to any field when he's able to get his hands started and his arms extended. It's risky to try and fool him with offspeed stuff because he can take it the other way with power. Sanders still strikes out a lot because he can't lay off the high pitches and often doesn't protect the outer edge of the plate.

Baserunning & Defense

Sanders can fly when he's physically able. He can steal bases in bunches, though he doesn't always get good jumps. Injuries limited him to just 13 thefts in 1997, but 25-30 aren't out of the question if he gets enough at-bats. He's a premier right fielder with excellent range, the speed to run down balls in the gap and an outstanding throwing arm with a quick, accurate release.

1998 Outlook

No one symbolizes Cincinnati's recent problems more than Sanders. Like so many other Reds, he has been stalled by physical problems and a lack of development. He has the skills to be a star. With the money the Reds have invested in him, they're hoping he re-emerges this season.

Position: RF
Bats: R **Throws:** R
Ht: 6' 1" **Wt:** 185

Opening Day Age: 30
Born: 12/1/67 in Florence, SC
ML Seasons: 7

Overall Statistics

	G	AB	R	H	D	T	HR	RBI	SB	BB	SO	Avg	OBP	Slg
1997	86	312	52	79	19	2	19	56	13	42	93	.253	.347	.510
Career	670	2404	416	652	134	27	111	372	138	295	640	.271	.354	.488

Where He Hits the Ball

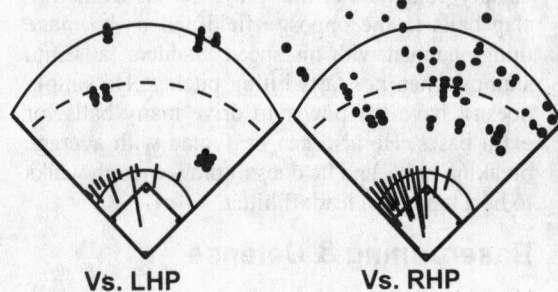

Vs. LHP   **Vs. RHP**

1997 Situational Stats

	AB	H	HR	RBI	Avg		AB	H	HR	RBI	Avg
Home	152	40	11	30	.263	LHP	68	21	4	10	.309
Road	160	39	8	26	.244	RHP	244	58	15	46	.238
First Half	109	25	6	20	.229	Sc Pos	80	22	6	39	.275
Scnd Half	203	54	13	36	.266	Clutch	43	13	5	11	.302

1997 Rankings (National League)

⇒ 6th in lowest batting average with two strikes (.120) and errors in right field (5)
⇒ Led the Reds in batting average in the clutch

Pete Schourek

1997 Season

For a second straight season, Pete Schourek never got going because of arm problems. A triceps injury in mid-May and then the continuation of persistent elbow troubles limited his availability. He made only 17 starts amid two trips to the disabled list and didn't win a game after June 5. After a brilliant 18-7 season in 1995, Schourek has gone 9-13 the last two years.

Pitching

Schourek has outstanding stuff when he's physically able to throw at his best. He can reach the low 90s with both his sinking fastball and a cutter. When he can throw his curve for strikes, he becomes especially tough to hit. He also has a straight change in which he has gained enough confidence to throw in any count. His command wasn't good in 1997, largely because of his physical problems, and he gave up a huge number of home runs. He needs to pitch ahead in the count because he can't overpower hitters unless he's completely healthy.

Defense & Hitting

Like most tall pitchers, Schourek is slow to the plate. He's easy to run on because he lacks a quality pickoff move. Opposing thieves were a perfect 10-for-10 on his watch last season, and are 18-for-20 the past two years. Since compacting his delivery he has become a better fielder, but he doesn't handle an exceptional number of balls up the middle. Schourek can help himself at bat, smacking his second career homer among his four hits in 1997.

1998 Outlook

It has been two years since Schourek was a big winner. With money becoming a growing issue with Cincinnati, the Reds elected not to pick up his contract option. He's a risk for any interested club, but if he's over his elbow troubles he could be a steal. If healthy, Schourek could be a 15-game winner.

Position: SP
Bats: L **Throws:** L
Ht: 6' 5" **Wt:** 205

Opening Day Age: 28
Born: 5/10/69 in Austin, TX
ML Seasons: 7
Pronunciation: SHUR-ek

Overall Statistics

	W	L	Pct.	ERA	G	GS	Sv	IP	H	BB	SO	HR	Ratio
1997	5	8	.385	5.42	18	17	0	84.2	78	38	59	18	1.37
Career	50	46	.521	4.44	179	115	2	774.1	792	268	541	82	1.37

How Often He Throws Strikes

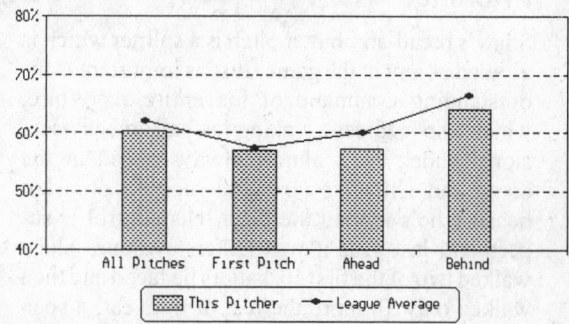

1997 Situational Stats

	W	L	ERA	Sv	IP		AB	H	HR	RBI	Avg
Home	3	4	5.93	0	44.0	LHB	65	18	3	10	.277
Road	2	4	4.87	0	40.2	RHB	259	60	15	40	.232
First Half	5	5	5.14	0	61.1	Sc Pos	68	20	2	27	.294
Scnd Half	0	3	6.17	0	23.1	Clutch	2	0	0	0	.000

1997 Rankings (National League)

⇒ Did not rank near the top or bottom in any category

Jeff Shaw

1997 Season

There were few bigger surprises in baseball last year than Jeff Shaw. He entered 1997 with nine career saves in seven seasons, and once again was slated to be the Reds' top setup man. But when closer Jeff Brantley went down with a shoulder injury, Shaw took over the stopper role and turned in a remarkable performance. His 42 saves and 49 opportunities led the National League. Fourteen of those saves came in September, putting him just one short of the all-time record for a single month. Shaw had saves in 15 straight appearances from late August through late September, and his ERA for September was a sparkling 1.20.

Pitching

Shaw's bread-and-butter pitch is a splitter which is as good as any in the game. Just as important is his outstanding command of his entire repertoire, which also includes a sinking fastball and an occasional slider. He's almost always ahead in the count and will give up home runs on occasion because he's around the plate. His control is superb and last year it was Eckersleyesque. Shaw walked two of the first six batters he faced and then walked only 10 more the rest of the year, a span that covered 360 batters.

Defense & Hitting

Shaw doesn't hold runners well, which isn't a problem when he's a closer. He gets himself into good fielding position and makes all the plays expected of him. His hitting is of no consequence now that he's out of middle relief. He has struck out in 18 of 36 career at-bats.

1998 Outlook

It's not unusual to see great closers emerge late in their careers, and Shaw was nothing short of great last season. Expecting him to save 42 games again is perhaps a reach, but he has the makeup and stuff to be counted upon for at least 30. His emergence opened the door for Jeff Brantley's trade to the Cardinals in mid-November.

Position: RP
Bats: R **Throws:** R
Ht: 6' 2" **Wt:** 200

Opening Day Age: 31
Born: 7/7/66 in Washington Courthouse, OH
ML Seasons: 8

Overall Statistics

	W	L	Pct.	ERA	G	GS	Sv	IP	H	BB	SO	HR	Ratio
1997	4	2	.667	2.38	78	0	42	94.2	79	12	74	7	0.96
Career	23	33	.411	3.77	359	19	51	563.0	558	166	350	60	1.29

How Often He Throws Strikes

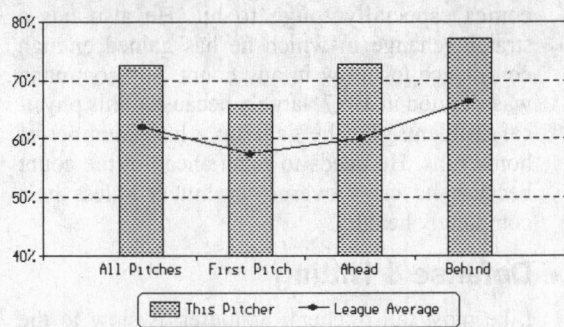

This Pitcher — League Average

1997 Situational Stats

	W	L	ERA	Sv	IP		AB	H	HR	RBI	Avg
Home	2	1	1.90	24	52.0	LHB	178	43	2	18	.242
Road	2	1	2.95	18	42.2	RHB	170	36	5	11	.212
First Half	2	0	1.44	18	56.1	Sc Pos	83	19	0	22	.229
Scnd Half	2	2	3.76	24	38.1	Clutch	239	49	4	18	.205

1997 Rankings (National League)

⇒ 1st in saves, save opportunities (49) and save percentage (85.7%)
⇒ 2nd in least baserunners allowed per 9 innings in relief (8.7)
⇒ 3rd in games pitched and games finished (62)
⇒ 4th in blown saves (7), relief ERA (2.38) and relief innings (94.2)
⇒ Led the Reds in saves, games finished (62), save opportunities (49), save percentage (85.7%), blown saves (7), most GDPs induced per GDP situation (18.0%), relief ERA (2.38) and least baserunners allowed per 9 innings in relief (8.7)

Eddie Taubensee

1997 Season

Eddie Taubensee got a chance to show some versatility in 1997. While continuing to share time at catcher, Taubensee also saw action at first base, left field and right field. All the shuffling didn't seem to hurt him at the plate, as he finished with 10 homers and 34 RBI, totals close to his 1996 figures. He hit .292 after the All-Star break.

Hitting

The power that Taubensee displays usually comes on low fastballs on the inner half of the plate. He also can drive fastballs to the opposite field for extra bases. He can't handle pitches up in the strike zone and never has been able to adjust consistently to offspeed stuff, which is how most clubs approach pitching to him. He rarely gets to hit against lefthanders and is strictly a platoon player. He had just five hits in 31 at-bats against southpaws last season.

Baserunning & Defense

With below-average speed, Taubensee is no threat to steal. He's aggressive on the bases and goes hard into second base to break up double plays. Taubensee's ability to call a game at catcher is suspect. His catching skills are average and his throwing mechanics are poor. His release is slow and he often will sail throws into center field. In 1997, he threw out a mere 13 percent of basestealers. He's no more than a stopgap in the outfield, where his range is poor. He handles the routine plays at first base.

1998 Outlook

Taubensee never will be a full-time player, but he does fill a role as lefthanded option behind the plate. He can produce double-figure home runs, but once he's exposed to regular playing time he usually struggles. His future remains as a utility player with some value.

Position: C
Bats: L **Throws:** R
Ht: 6' 4" **Wt:** 205

Opening Day Age: 29
Born: 10/31/68 in Beeville, TX
ML Seasons: 7
Pronunciation: TAW-ben-see

Overall Statistics

	G	AB	R	H	D	T	HR	RBI	SB	BB	SO	Avg	OBP	Slg
1997	108	254	26	68	18	0	10	34	0	22	66	.268	.323	.457
Career	586	1637	187	432	88	6	53	225	10	142	351	.264	.321	.422

Where He Hits the Ball

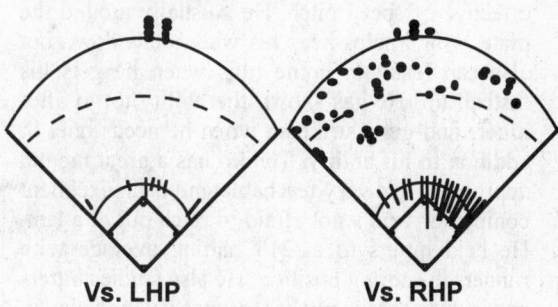

Vs. LHP   Vs. RHP

1997 Situational Stats

	AB	H	HR	RBI	Avg		AB	H	HR	RBI	Avg
Home	127	36	7	21	.283	LHP	31	5	1	2	.161
Road	127	32	3	13	.252	RHP	223	63	9	32	.283
First Half	158	40	6	18	.253	Sc Pos	60	15	1	22	.250
Scnd Half	96	28	4	16	.292	Clutch	42	10	2	7	.238

1997 Rankings (National League)

⇒ 7th in least GDPs per GDP situation (3.8%)
⇒ Led the Reds in sacrifice flies (5)

Brett Tomko

Position: SP
Bats: R **Throws:** R
Ht: 6' 4" **Wt:** 215

Opening Day Age: 24
Born: 4/7/73 in
Cleveland, OH
ML Seasons: 1

1997 Season

Brett Tomko was one of the best rookie pitchers in the baseball. After spending most of April and May with Triple-A Indianapolis, he joined the Reds in early June and never looked back. He went 4-0 in five June starts, and after slipping in July he went 4-2 in August. He finished with the best ERA of any Reds starter, and his 11 victories tied for the club lead.

Pitching

Tomko throws a hard sinker in the low 90s and mixes in a cut fastball that also tops 90 MPH. He's especially tough on lefthanders because of the movement of his cutter. He's still developing an effective offspeed pitch. He's usually around the plate, which helps keep his walk totals down but also can result in home runs when he gets his fastball up. He has shown the ability to go after hitters and get a strikeout when he needs one. In addition to his ability, Tomko has a great mental approach. He's very teachable and is an excellent competitor who's not afraid to pitch out of a jam. He held hitters to a .213 batting average with runners in scoring position. He also studies hitters and is a very heady pitcher for such a young player.

Defense & Hitting

Tomko isn't particularly agile and has a slow delivery, making him vulnerable to the running game. He has worked on improving his pickoff move. He had trouble batting, but managed to make sporadic contact and had three sacrifices.

1998 Outlook

With all the bad news that befell Cincinnati last season, Tomko's emergence was a positive development. With good support and a full season in the rotation, he has the stuff and makeup to be a 15-game winner in 1998 and for years to come.

Overall Statistics

	W	L	Pct.	ERA	G	GS	Sv	IP	H	BB	SO	HR	Ratio
1997	11	7	.611	3.43	22	19	0	126.0	106	47	95	14	1.21
Career	11	7	.611	3.43	22	19	0	126.0	106	47	95	14	1.21

How Often He Throws Strikes

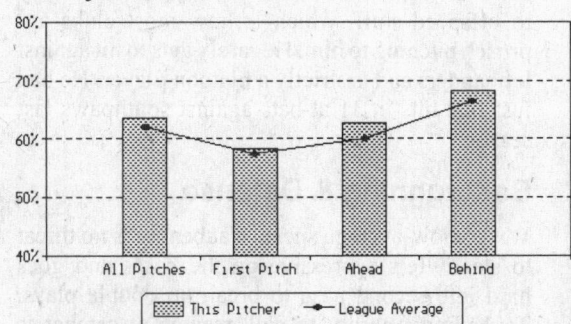

1997 Situational Stats

	W	L	ERA	Sv	IP		AB	H	HR	RBI	Avg
Home	7	4	3.68	0	73.1	LHB	221	42	9	23	.190
Road	4	3	3.08	0	52.2	RHB	232	64	5	24	.276
First Half	5	1	2.51	0	43.0	Sc Pos	89	19	1	30	.213
Scnd Half	6	6	3.90	0	83.0	Clutch	31	10	1	6	.323

1997 Rankings (National League)

⇒ 2nd in lowest batting average allowed vs. lefthanded batters
⇒ Led the Reds in wins, runners caught stealing (7), winning percentage and lowest batting average allowed vs. lefthanded batters

Stan Belinda

Position: RP
Bats: R **Throws:** R
Ht: 6' 3" **Wt:** 215

Opening Day Age: 31
Born: 8/6/66 in Huntingdon, PA
ML Seasons: 9

Overall Statistics

	W	L	Pct.	ERA	G	GS	Sv	IP	H	BB	SO	HR	Ratio
1997	1	5	.167	3.71	84	0	1	99.1	84	33	114	11	1.18
Career	33	25	.569	3.85	460	0	75	534.2	447	217	474	53	1.24

1997 Situational Stats

	W	L	ERA	Sv	IP		AB	H	HR	RBI	Avg
Home	0	4	4.50	0	54.0	LHB	160	42	6	21	.263
Road	1	1	2.78	1	45.1	RHB	207	42	5	27	.203
First Half	0	2	3.42	0	55.1	Sc Pos	112	20	4	39	.179
Scnd Half	1	3	4.09	1	44.0	Clutch	177	38	3	22	.215

1997 Season

Stan Belinda was one of the real finds of 1997. The journeyman reliever was signed by the Reds to a minor league contract in the offseason and ended up finishing second in the National League with 84 appearances. He also led all major league relief pitchers with 114 strikeouts. Belinda wore down in the second half when his ERA rose by nearly a run, but he led the league with 28 holds.

Pitching, Defense & Hitting

A tall sidearmer with a moving fastball in the low 90s, Belinda is very tough on righthanders. He also has a good slider and will cut his fastball against lefties. Belinda usually throws strikes and his strikeout/walk ratio was outstanding in 1997. He makes every fielding play he can reach, and hasn't made a single error in a major league career that now covers 460 games. He's not good at preventing steals, yielding 18 in 22 attempts last year, nearly one per five innings. Belinda can handle the bat in his rare chances to hit.

1998 Outlook

As long as he's kept in middle relief, Belinda can be an imposing performer. The Reds don't intend to change his role and he should be a major part of their bullpen again. If he stays healthy, he should prove his 1997 numbers were no fluke.

Dave Burba

Position: SP
Bats: R **Throws:** R
Ht: 6' 4" **Wt:** 240

Opening Day Age: 31
Born: 7/7/66 in Dayton, OH
ML Seasons: 8

Overall Statistics

	W	L	Pct.	ERA	G	GS	Sv	IP	H	BB	SO	HR	Ratio
1997	11	10	.524	4.73	30	27	0	160.0	157	73	131	22	1.44
Career	49	45	.521	4.26	278	87	1	746.1	702	350	614	78	1.41

1997 Situational Stats

	W	L	ERA	Sv	IP		AB	H	HR	RBI	Avg
Home	7	8	4.67	0	96.1	LHB	294	87	10	34	.296
Road	4	2	4.81	0	63.2	RHB	321	70	12	45	.218
First Half	5	8	5.47	0	105.1	Sc Pos	142	42	7	59	.296
Scnd Half	6	2	3.29	0	54.2	Clutch	24	3	0	2	.125

1997 Season

Until back troubles sidelined him for most of August, Dave Burba was the Reds' most consistent starter. He had two of Cincinnati's major league-low five complete games, and he tied for the club lead in wins. He finished second on the staff in innings and strikeouts.

Pitching, Defense & Hitting

Burba's stuff is above-average. He throws a low-90s fastball that runs all over the place, a quick-breaking slider and an improved changeup. He simply allows his command to waver too often to become a big winner. His walk totals and pitch counts are usually high. Because he falls behind in so many counts, he's prone to allowing home runs when hitters know he has to throw a strike. He is an average fielder with no real move to first and is slow to the plate with his delivery. He led Reds pitchers with nine hits in 1997.

1998 Outlook

The makeup of the Reds' staff is uncertain. With all his inconsistencies, Burba should be expected to eat some innings and win at least 10-12 games. He can't be expected to fill the role of a frontline starter.

Kent Mercker

Position: SP
Bats: L **Throws:** L
Ht: 6' 2" **Wt:** 195

Opening Day Age: 30
Born: 2/1/68 in Dublin, OH
ML Seasons: 9

Overall Statistics

	W	L	Pct.	ERA	G	GS	Sv	IP	H	BB	SO	HR	Ratio
1997	8	11	.421	3.92	28	25	0	144.2	135	62	75	16	1.36
Career	43	42	.506	3.91	285	91	19	730.0	658	342	530	78	1.37

1997 Situational Stats

	W	L	ERA	Sv	IP		AB	H	HR	RBI	Avg
Home	4	5	3.58	0	70.1	LHB	134	36	3	14	.269
Road	4	6	4.24	0	74.1	RHB	405	99	13	39	.244
First Half	6	6	3.19	0	96.0	Sc Pos	118	22	1	34	.186
Scnd Half	2	5	5.36	0	48.2	Clutch	9	1	0	0	.111

1997 Season

Another of GM Jim Bowden's scrap-heap acquisitions, Kent Mercker revived a fading career. After losing five straight decisions in April and May, Mercker settled down and pitched well. He strung together a four-game winning streak in June, and 18 of his 25 starts were quality outings. His 3.92 ERA was a far cry from the 6.98 mark he posted with Baltimore and Cleveland in 1996.

Pitching, Defense & Hitting

With improved arm strength and a more compact delivery, Mercker got his velocity back up into the 90-MPH range. He can cut or sink his fastball, which he throws 75 percent of the time. Mercker will mix in a slider, curve and occasional changeup, but his control and ability to put away hitters can be erratic. Like most pitchers coming out of the Atlanta organization, he fields his position well. He doesn't hold runners well. Mercker gets his share of hits and last season notched his first career triple.

1998 Outlook

Cincinnati was likely to try and retain Mercker, a free agent who demonstrated last year that he's finally capable of winning 12-14 games if he gets run support. He seems to have put a disastrous foray into the American League behind him.

Mike Morgan

Position: SP
Bats: R **Throws:** R
Ht: 6' 2" **Wt:** 220

Opening Day Age: 38
Born: 10/8/59 in Tulare, CA
ML Seasons: 17

Overall Statistics

	W	L	Pct.	ERA	G	GS	Sv	IP	H	BB	SO	HR	Ratio
1997	9	12	.429	4.78	31	30	0	162.0	165	49	103	13	1.32
Career	117	167	.412	4.07	420	359	3	2338.0	2412	785	1189	205	1.37

1997 Situational Stats

	W	L	ERA	Sv	IP		AB	H	HR	RBI	Avg
Home	5	5	4.76	0	75.2	LHB	291	79	7	40	.271
Road	4	7	4.80	0	86.1	RHB	329	86	6	42	.261
First Half	3	5	5.63	0	72.0	Sc Pos	152	46	6	64	.303
Scnd Half	6	7	4.10	0	90.0	Clutch	14	4	0	1	.286

1997 Season

On a pitching staff riddled by injuries, Mike Morgan went to the post for Cincinnati. He led the Reds in starts and innings, all despite a public battle with former manager Ray Knight. Still, Morgan finished with his fourth sub-.500 record in the past five seasons, and for the fourth consecutive campaign he allowed more hits than innings.

Pitching, Defense & Hitting

Morgan's stuff has started showing the wear and tear of a 17-year major league career. His fastball still hits the 90s, but he has increasing difficulty keeping the ball down in the strike zone. That's a necessity with both his sinker and slider. Morgan has good control and that helps him keep his pitch counts down. He's an average fielder who never has done a good job of holding runners. An awful hitter, he actually boasted a triple among his four hits last year.

1998 Outlook

A free agent, Morgan likely can help a club as a fourth or fifth starter. His ability to eat innings and his experience are his main selling points. But at 38 and with his declining ability, he could have difficulty landing a job.

Jon Nunnally

Position: CF/LF/RF
Bats: L **Throws:** R
Ht: 5'10" **Wt:** 190

Opening Day Age: 26
Born: 11/9/71 in
Pelham, NC
ML Seasons: 3

Overall Statistics

	G	AB	R	H	D	T	HR	RBI	SB	BB	SO	Avg	OBP	Slg
1997	78	230	46	71	12	4	14	39	7	31	58	.309	.394	.578
Career	232	623	113	164	32	11	33	98	13	95	169	.263	.363	.509

1997 Situational Stats

	AB	H	HR	RBI	Avg		AB	H	HR	RBI	Avg
Home	94	26	7	18	.277	LHP	31	8	1	8	.258
Road	136	45	7	21	.331	RHP	199	63	13	31	.317
First Half	22	6	0	2	.273	Sc Pos	50	18	1	24	.360
Scnd Half	208	65	14	37	.313	Clutch	34	7	1	7	.206

1997 Season

Jon Nunnally and Chris Stynes were acquired in mid-July from Kansas City in a fortuitous trade for a pair of middle relievers. Nunnally blossomed when he came to the National League, batting .318 with the Reds and playing center field for the injured Deion Sanders. He finished the year with a sparkling .602 slugging percentage in 201 at-bats for Cincinnati.

Hitting, Baserunning & Defense

Nunnally made great strides towards becoming a more complete hitter in 1997. Though much more dangerous against righthanders, he now is showing signs of being able to at least hold his own against lefties. He still strikes out a lot, but he's a dangerous fastball hitter who's starting to adjust to offspeed stuff. He has above-average speed and easily could reach double-digit steal totals. Nunnally played solidly in center field, where his range is adequate. His arm is strong enough to play anywhere in the outfield.

1998 Outlook

Scouts love Nunnally's tools and he may be on the verge of being a solid everyday player. Some Reds officials believe he can hit 25 home runs this year, and he'll likely get the chance to prove them right.

Mike Remlinger

Position: RP/SP
Bats: L **Throws:** L
Ht: 6' 0" **Wt:** 195

Opening Day Age: 32
Born: 3/23/66 in
Middletown, NY
ML Seasons: 5

Overall Statistics

	W	L	Pct.	ERA	G	GS	Sv	IP	H	BB	SO	HR	Ratio
1997	8	8	.500	4.14	69	12	2	124.0	100	60	145	11	1.29
Career	11	16	.407	4.51	113	31	2	247.2	224	139	223	30	1.47

1997 Situational Stats

	W	L	ERA	Sv	IP		AB	H	HR	RBI	Avg
Home	3	3	3.95	1	68.1	LHB	112	27	5	16	.241
Road	5	5	4.37	1	55.2	RHB	336	73	6	34	.217
First Half	3	4	3.00	2	42.0	Sc Pos	112	27	2	36	.241
Scnd Half	5	4	4.72	0	82.0	Clutch	91	14	2	4	.154

1997 Season

One of the Reds' pleasant surprises in 1997 was Mike Remlinger. After a career-high 57 appearances in relief, Remlinger joined the rotation in August. He went 5-4 with two complete games as a starter, and led Cincinnati in strikeouts.

Pitching, Defense & Hitting

Remlinger throws hard, with a 90-plus fastball that has great movement along with a hard slider. He recently developed a changeup to add to the mix. He has always labored with his control, however, and led the National League with 12 wild pitches in 1997. That said, he is beginning to get ahead in the count more consistently. He had six pickoffs last year with his good move to first, and he fields his position well. He's no threat with the bat, with just three hits in 52 career at-bats.

1998 Outlook

There are many examples of lefthanders who struggle for years before finally putting it together later in their career. Remlinger, whose excellent stuff reminds some of Jeff Fassero, could be just such a case. Like Fassero, Remlinger may have been reborn in his early 30s and could be a consistent winner for the next few seasons.

Cincinnati Reds

Chris Stynes

Position: LF
Bats: R **Throws:** R
Ht: 5' 9" **Wt:** 175

Opening Day Age: 25
Born: 1/19/73 in
Queens, NY
ML Seasons: 3

Overall Statistics

	G	AB	R	H	D	T	HR	RBI	SB	BB	SO	Avg	OBP	Slg
1997	49	198	31	69	7	1	6	28	11	11	13	.348	.394	.485
Career	107	325	46	102	14	1	6	36	16	17	21	.314	.355	.418

1997 Situational Stats

	AB	H	HR	RBI	Avg		AB	H	HR	RBI	Avg
Home	75	26	2	9	.347	LHP	41	8	1	6	.195
Road	123	43	4	19	.350	RHP	157	61	5	22	.389
First Half	0	0	0	0	-	Sc Pos	49	19	2	22	.388
Scnd Half	198	69	6	28	.348	Clutch	28	8	1	7	.286

1997 Season

A virtual unknown when he was acquired from Kansas City in mid-July, Chris Stynes surprised the baseball world and certainly the Reds with a remarkable last two months. He failed to hit safely in consecutive games only once while batting .348 and earning everyday playing time.

Hitting, Baserunning & Defense

Stynes shows no hint of having exceptional power, but he demonstrated flashes of extra-base pop that surprised the Reds. He can hit fastballs and has a short stroke that allows him to wait on offspeed pitches and take them the other way. Stynes has above-average speed and is a high-percentage basestealer who was caught just twice in 13 attempts in 1997. He's a very versatile defensive player who can play adequately at left field or second base.

1998 Outlook

Toronto and Kansas City, two of baseball's worst offensive teams, were willing to trade away Stynes, so there has to be some question about the legitimacy of his play with Cincinnati. He quickly became a favorite of both management and fans, and likely will get the chance to play regularly in 1998.

Scott Sullivan

Position: RP
Bats: R **Throws:** R
Ht: 6' 4" **Wt:** 210

Opening Day Age: 27
Born: 3/13/71 in
Tuscaloosa, AL
ML Seasons: 3

Overall Statistics

	W	L	Pct.	ERA	G	GS	Sv	IP	H	BB	SO	HR	Ratio
1997	5	3	.625	3.24	59	0	1	97.1	79	30	96	12	1.12
Career	5	3	.625	3.22	69	0	1	109.0	90	37	101	12	1.17

1997 Situational Stats

	W	L	ERA	Sv	IP		AB	H	HR	RBI	Avg
Home	3	0	3.51	1	51.1	LHB	152	37	7	20	.243
Road	2	3	2.93	0	46.0	RHB	207	42	5	25	.203
First Half	1	2	2.89	1	43.2	Sc Pos	98	24	2	31	.245
Scnd Half	4	1	3.52	0	53.2	Clutch	102	21	2	11	.206

1997 Season

Recalled in mid-May, Scott Sullivan was a solid middle reliever in his first full season with the Reds. After an initial struggle following his promotion, Sullivan settled in. Though he tired somewhat down the stretch, he did go 4-0 in September.

Pitching, Defense & Hitting

Sullivan's sidearm motion makes him very tough on righthanders. His velocity is in the low 90s, so he's not easy prey for lefties. On occasion his fastball will flatten, which can result in a high number of homers. He doesn't possess a good pickoff move, and basestealers went 10-for-10 against him in 1997. Sullivan gets himself into good fielding position despite his unique delivery. He's hitless in nine major league at-bats.

1998 Outlook

Sullivan has strikeout stuff and should be a busy member of Cincinnati's middle-relief corps. A closer in the minors, he doesn't yet have the command necessary to save games in the big leagues. He'll eat innings as a setup man instead.

Other Cincinnati Reds

Giovanni Carrara (Pos: RHP, Age: 30)

	W	L	Pct.	ERA	G	GS	Sv	IP	H	BB	SO	HR	Ratio
1997	0	1	.000	7.84	2	2	0	10.1	14	6	5	4	1.94
Career	3	6	.333	7.61	33	14	0	97.0	132	56	55	25	1.94

Carrara is 30 years old, he can't strike major league hitters out, and he has struggled as both a starter and a reliever in the bigs. In stints with Toronto and Cincinnati, his ERA is a combined 7.61. 1998 Outlook: D

Joey Eischen (Pos: LHP, Age: 27)

	W	L	Pct.	ERA	G	GS	Sv	IP	H	BB	SO	HR	Ratio
1997	0	0	-	6.75	1	0	0	1.1	2	1	2	0	2.25
Career	1	2	.333	4.37	71	0	0	90.2	100	46	69	8	1.61

Elbow and shoulder problems earned Eischen two trips to the DL and helped limit him to a grand total of one appearance for the Reds last season. He pitched very well in his 26 outings in Triple-A. 1998 Outlook: B

Brook Fordyce (Pos: C, Age: 27, Bats: R)

	G	AB	R	H	D	T	HR	RBI	SB	BB	SO	Avg	OBP	Slg
1997	47	96	7	20	5	0	1	8	2	8	15	.208	.267	.292
Career	55	105	8	23	7	0	1	9	2	12	16	.219	.297	.314

Fordyce got a shot with the parent club when Joe Oliver went down with an injury before the start of the season, but a .208 batting average and a trip of his own to the DL did little to solidfy his future. 1998 Outlook: C

Curtis Goodwin (Pos: CF/LF, Age: 25, Bats: Left)

	G	AB	R	H	D	T	HR	RBI	SB	BB	SO	Avg	OBP	Slg
1997	85	265	27	67	11	0	1	12	22	24	53	.253	.316	.306
Career	221	690	87	174	25	3	2	41	59	58	140	.252	.311	.306

Goodwin simply wasn't playing well enough to have a shouting match with manager Jack McKeon and GM Jim Bowden. But he did, and the result was his banishment to the minors. 1998 Outlook: B

Lenny Harris (Pos: LF/1B/2B/3B/RF, Age: 33, Bats: L)

	G	AB	R	H	D	T	HR	RBI	SB	BB	SO	Avg	OBP	Slg
1997	120	238	32	65	13	1	3	28	4	18	18	.273	.327	.374
Career	1067	2582	321	704	101	14	20	232	102	188	221	.273	.323	.346

Harris turned in a typical Lenny Harris-type of season, playing five different positions in the field and seeing plenty of action as a pinch hitter. He's the consummate bench player. 1998 Outlook: A

Mark Johnson (Pos: 1B, Age: 30, Bats: L)

	G	AB	R	H	D	T	HR	RBI	SB	BB	SO	Avg	OBP	Slg
1997	78	219	30	47	10	0	4	29	1	43	78	.215	.345	.315
Career	284	783	117	187	40	1	30	104	12	124	208	.239	.346	.407

An all-or-nothing hitter, Johnson gave the Pirates nothing last year before the Reds picked him up on waivers. The 30-year-old former Dartmouth QB is running out of time and chances in the majors. 1998 Outlook: C

Richie Lewis (Pos: RHP, Age: 32)

	W	L	Pct.	ERA	G	GS	Sv	IP	H	BB	SO	HR	Ratio
1997	2	0	1.000	8.88	18	0	0	24.1	28	18	16	10	1.89
Career	14	15	.483	4.71	215	3	2	288.2	279	186	240	43	1.61

After turning in a surprisingly effective '96 campaign for Detroit, Lewis failed to recapture the magic for either the Athletics or Reds last season. His appearances fell from 72 in '96 to 18 last year. 1998 Outlook: C

Pedro A. Martinez (Pos: LHP, Age: 29)

	W	L	Pct.	ERA	G	GS	Sv	IP	H	BB	SO	HR	Ratio
1997	1	1	.500	9.45	8	0	0	6.2	8	7	4	1	2.25
Career	7	4	.636	3.97	122	1	3	142.2	125	93	114	14	1.53

Oh what a difference a middle name can make. *This* Pedro Martinez was completely inneffective in his short August/September stint with the parent club. Control problems are his downfall. 1998 Outlook: D

Eric Owens (Pos: LF, Age: 27, Bats: R)

	G	AB	R	H	D	T	HR	RBI	SB	BB	SO	Avg	OBP	Slg
1997	27	57	8	15	0	0	0	3	3	4	11	.263	.311	.263
Career	117	264	34	157	19	9	2	36	18	56	49	.220	.293	.242

The '95 American Association MVP has been recalled from, and sent down to, the minors seven times over the last two seasons. He posted a decent batting average last year, but his lack of power limits his options. 1998 Outlook: C

Terry Pendleton (Pos: 3B, Age: 37, Bats: B)

	G	AB	R	H	D	T	HR	RBI	SB	BB	SO	Avg	OBP	Slg
1997	50	113	11	28	9	0	2	12	14	248	.248	.320	.354	
Career	1814	6795	834	1836	346	39	137	917	126	471	930	.270	.316	.393

Pendleton began his 14th season on the DL, and essentially ended it there as well. He underwent surgery on his right knee in March, then his left knee acted up in July and the Reds released him. 1998 Outlook: C

Felix Rodriguez (Pos: RHP, Age: 25)

	W	L	Pct.	ERA	G	GS	Sv	IP	H	BB	SO	HR	Ratio
1997	0	0	-	4.30	26	1	0	46.0	48	28	34	2	1.65
Career	1	1	.500	3.97	37	1	0	56.2	59	33	39	4	1.62

A catcher-turned-pitcher, Rodriguez earned a shot with the Reds after posting a 1.01 ERA in 23 appearances for Indianapolis. He was traded to Arizona before the expansion draft. 1998 Outlook: B

Jeff Tabaka (Pos: LHP, Age: 34)

	W	L	Pct.	ERA	G	GS	Sv	IP	H	BB	SO	HR	Ratio
1997	0	0	-	4.50	3	0	0	2.0	1	1	1	1	1.00
Career	4	3	.571	4.88	94	0	2	94.0	88	59	76	9	1.56

Not even his lefthandedness has been able to save Tabaka from a career spent toiling in the minors. He made all of three appearances for the Reds in '97, and that may be more than he sees this season. 1998 Outlook: D

Ozzie Timmons (Pos: LF, Age: 27, Bats: R)

	G	AB	R	H	D	T	HR	RBI	SB	BB	SO	Avg	OBP	Slg
1997	6	9	1	3	1	0	0	0	0	0	1	.333	.333	.444
Career	148	320	49	76	15	1	15	44	4	28	63	.238	.300	.431

Timmons was traded from the Cubs and started the season on the Reds' roster. He lasted for 13 days before being sent down to Triple-A Indianapolis when Pokey Reese was promoted. 1998 Outlook: B

Gabe White (Pos: LHP, Age: 26)

	W	L	Pct.	ERA	G	GS	Sv	IP	H	BB	SO	HR	Ratio
1997	2	2	.500	4.39	12	6	1	41.0	39	8	25	6	1.15
Career	4	5	.444	5.58	38	12	2	90.1	89	28	67	17	1.30

Is he a starter? Is he a reliever? Does he have the stuff to be either at the big league level? The jury's still out on this once-hot prospect in the Montreal system, but judgment day is quickly approaching. 1998 Outlook: B

Cincinnati Reds Minor League Prospects

Organization Overview:

Marge Schott no longer is in charge, but the Reds are still feeling the effects of her cutbacks on scouting and player development. Cincinnati has few scouts and won't spend the market rate on bonuses, a combination that leads to a fallow farm system. Unless you count feeble-hitting Pokey Reese, rookie Brett Tomko was the only homegrown player with impact potential on the major league team last year. The Reds have few pitching prospects, especially at the upper levels. The trade of John Smiley and Jeff Branson to Cleveland netted Cincinnati four of its best prospects, without whom the Reds would be in even worse shape.

Aaron Boone

Position: 3B	Opening Day Age: 25
Bats: R Throws: R	Born: 3/9/73 in La
Ht: 6' 2" Wt: 190	Mesa, CA

Recent Statistics

	G	AB	R	H	D	T	HR	RBI	SB	BB	SO	AVG
97 AAA Indianapols	131	476	79	138	30	4	22	75	12	40	81	.290
97 NL Cincinnati	16	49	5	12	1	0	0	5	1	2	5	.245
97 MLE	131	463	68	125	28	3	18	64	9	35	82	.270

A third-generation major leaguer and the brother of Reds second baseman Bret Boone, Aaron is the best position player in the system. He needed to add power, so he hit the weights diligently and bashed a career-high 22 homers in 1997. He also continued to hit for average and to stroke doubles, though he still is impatient at the plate. His combination of soft hands, accurate arm and good instincts led managers to name him the best defensive third baseman in the Triple-A American Association. He's ready to battle for a starting job in the majors, though incumbent Willie Greene is coming off a 26-homer season.

Jim Crowell

Position: P	Opening Day Age: 23
Bats: L Throws: L	Born: 5/14/74 in
Ht: 6' 4" Wt: 220	Minneapolis, MN

Recent Statistics

	W	L	ERA	G	GS	Sv	IP	H	R	BB	SO	HR
97 A Kinston	9	4	2.37	17	17	0	114.0	96	41	26	94	4
97 AA Akron	1	0	4.50	3	3	0	18.0	13	12	11	7	2
97 AA Chattanooga	2	1	2.84	3	3	0	19.0	19	6	5	14	2
97 AAA Indianapols	1	1	2.75	3	3	0	19.2	19	7	8	6	1
97 NL Cincinnati	0	1	9.95	2	1	0	6.1	12	7	5	3	2

Crowell entered 1997 without any experience above Class-A and finished with two games in Cincinnati. Signed as a nondrafted free agent out of the University of Indianapolis by the Indians, he dominated at high Class-A Kinston and eventually shot to the majors after the Smiley trade. He throws a 92-MPH fastball and a hard slider, *and* he throws strikes and hits his spots.

Righthanders strafed him for a .500 average during his brief big league trial, but if his confidence wasn't shot he'll have a chance to make a wide-open rotation in spring training.

Damian Jackson

Position: SS	Opening Day Age: 24
Bats: R Throws: R	Born: 8/16/73 in Los
Ht: 5' 10" Wt: 160	Angeles, CA

Recent Statistics

	G	AB	R	H	D	T	HR	RBI	SB	BB	SO	AVG
97 AAA Buffalo	73	266	51	78	12	0	4	13	20	37	45	.293
97 AAA Indianapols	19	71	12	19	6	1	0	7	4	10	17	.268
97 AL Cleveland	8	9	2	1	0	0	0	0	1	0	1	.111
97 NL Cincinnati	12	27	6	6	2	1	1	2	1	4	7	.222
97 MLE	92	331	57	91	16	0	3	18	19	42	64	.275

The key component to the John Smiley trade, Jackson originally signed with Cleveland as a 44th-round draft-and-follow out of Laney (Calif.) Junior College in 1992. He left quite an impression in the American Association last year, as managers voted him the best and fastest baserunner, the top defensive shortstop and the most exciting player. The Reds see him as a leadoff man because of his speed and ability to make contact, but he would need to draw a few more walks to really fill that role. He's a much better hitter than Reese, and thus is Barry Larkin's heir apparent at shortstop. Jackson spent some time at second base in the Arizona Fall League and could step in there if Bret Boone can't break out of his two-year slump.

Brandon Larson

Position: SS	Opening Day Age: 21
Bats: R Throws: R	Born: 5/24/76 in San
Ht: 5' 11" Wt: 190	Angelo, TX

Recent Statistics

	G	AB	R	H	D	T	HR	RBI	SB	BB	SO	AVG
97 AA Chattanooga	11	41	4	11	5	1	0	6	0	1	10	.268

Like Crowell, Larson was relatively unknown at the outset of 1997. After hitting 15 homers in two years at Blinn (Texas) Junior College, he transferred to Louisiana State and set the college baseball world on fire. Larson broke the NCAA record for homers by a shortstop (40) and was named Most Outstanding Player as the Tigers won their second straight College World Series. After drafting him in the first round, the Reds thought enough of him to send him to Double-A, where a sprained ankle ended his pro debut after 11 games. He has legitimate power and can put the bat on the ball. An average runner, he has the arm for shortstop but his range may be more suited for third base. The Reds could have quite a logjam at the hot corner with Boone, Greene and Larson.

Justin Towle

Position: C
Bats: R **Throws:** R
Ht: 6' 3" **Wt:** 210

Opening Day Age: 24
Born: 2/21/74 in
Seattle, WA

Recent Statistics

	G	AB	R	H	D	T	HR	RBI	SB	BB	SO	AVG
96 A Winston-Sal	116	351	60	90	19	1	16	47	17	93	96	.256
97 AA Chattanooga	119	418	62	129	37	5	11	70	5	55	77	.309
97 MLE	119	396	44	107	32	3	7	50	3	34	79	.270

Though Towle has posted fine offensive numbers for the past two seasons, the Reds view him first and foremost as a defensive standout. He's a good receiver with a strong arm, and he nailed 44 percent of the basestealers who ran on him in Double-A. His 11 homers and 37 doubles are all the more impressive when Chattanooga's home park, where extra-base hits go to die, is considered. A 12th-round pick in 1992, he has made steady progress through the system. After a year in Triple-A, he could be Cincinnati's best catching option.

Pat Watkins

Position: OF
Bats: R **Throws:** R
Ht: 6' 2" **Wt:** 185

Opening Day Age: 25
Born: 9/2/72 in Raleigh,
NC

Recent Statistics

	G	AB	R	H	D	T	HR	RBI	SB	BB	SO	AVG
97 AA Chattanooga	46	177	35	62	15	1	7	30	9	15	16	.350
97 AAA Indianapolis	84	325	46	91	14	7	9	35	13	24	55	.280
97 NL Cincinnati	17	29	2	6	2	0	0	1	0	5	.207
97 MLE	130	482	64	133	26	5	11	51	16	30	72	.276

Watkins finally mastered Double-A pitching in his third year at Chattanooga, earning him his first tastes of Triple-A and the majors. A 1993 supplemental first-round pick out of East Carolina, he teased the Reds with 27 homers at hitter-friendly Winston-Salem in his first full pro season. He's a good hitter with some power and average speed, and he may be the best defensive center fielder that Cincinnati has in Triple-A and the majors. Reggie Sanders is the only sure thing in the Reds' outfield, so Watkins should get an opportunity in 1998.

Jason Williams

Position: 2B
Bats: R **Throws:** R
Ht: 5' 8" **Wt:** 180

Opening Day Age: 24
Born: 12/18/73 in Baton
Rouge, LA

Recent Statistics

	G	AB	R	H	D	T	HR	RBI	SB	BB	SO	AVG
97 A Burlington	68	256	49	83	17	1	7	41	9	21	40	.324
97 AA Chattanooga	69	271	38	84	21	1	5	28	5	18	35	.310
97 MLE	69	256	27	69	18	0	3	20	3	11	36	.270

Williams was Larson's predecessor at shortstop for Louisiana State. A 16th-round pick in 1996, he took off that summer to start at short for the U.S. Olympic team. He had no trouble adjusting to professional pitching, batting .317 and reaching Double-A last year. He has good pop for a middle infielder and makes contact, though he could use a little more discipline at the plate. He'll steal an occasional base more on guile than speed.

He's a steady shortstop who doesn't have the flash of a Larkin or Reese or Jackson, and he moved to second base after his promotion. He might have enough bat for third base, but the Reds are loaded at the hot corner. Williams should start the year in Triple-A unless Boone and Jackson don't make the big league roster and need to play every day in the minors.

Scott Winchester

Position: P
Bats: R **Throws:** R
Ht: 6' 2" **Wt:** 210

Opening Day Age: 24
Born: 4/20/73 in
Midland, MI

Recent Statistics

	W	L	ERA	G	GS	Sv	IP	H	R	BB	SO	HR
97 A Kinston	2	1	1.47	34	0	29	36.2	21	6	11	45	2
97 AA Akron	0	0	3.86	6	0	1	7.0	8	3	2	8	1
97 AA Chattanooga	1	0	1.69	9	0	3	10.2	9	4	3	3	0
97 AAA Indianapolis	0	0	0.00	4	0	0	5.2	2	0	2	2	0
97 NL Cincinnati	0	0	6.00	5	0	0	6.0	9	5	2	3	1

Winchester is yet another player received in the Smiley trade. He followed the same path as Crowell, seeing some major league action after starting 1997 in Kinston. He posted 33 saves and a 1.65 ERA between four stops. The Reds say they have clocked Winchester in the mid-90s, though scouts from other teams say his fastball has average velocity. In any case, he combines his fastball with a slider for two power pitches. He has a closer's mentality, and eventually could succeed Jeff Shaw in that role. The best thing for Winchester probably would be to spend 1998 in Triple-A, but the pitching-strapped Reds may call on him. He was taken in the second round of the expansion draft by Arizona, then returned to the Reds in a prearranged deal.

Others to Watch

Righthander **Buddy Carlyle** went 14-5, 2.77 at Class-A Charleston at age 19. He's the best long-term pitching prospect in the system, throwing a live fastball and a hard curve. . . Righthander **Danny Graves**, the fourth player acquired in the Smiley trade, was counted on to use his sinker in a setup role for the Reds. But the 24 year old had rotator-cuff surgery after the season and might miss all of 1998. . . First baseman **Darron Ingram**, 21, was named the best power hitter in the Class-A Midwest League. He went deep 29 times, but has no other positives and struck out 195 times. . . Outfielder **Chad Mottola** was touted as the next Dale Murphy when he was taken in the first round of the 1992 draft. He has a strong arm, but the comparisons pretty much end there. Mottola did hit .317 in Triple-A last year at 25, but he had just 12 homers. . . Former Cubs first-round pick **Jayson Peterson** turned his career around by going 14-6 at Class-A Burlington. The 21-year-old righthander has good stuff but lacks control of his pitches and himself. . . Third baseman **Pete Rose Jr.** finally reached the majors at 27, but don't let his .301-25-99 minor league totals fool you. He's not a prospect, just a good story.

Don Baylor

1997 Season

The Rockies could have gone into the tank after a miserable July, which appeared to end all chances of a postseason run after a promising start. To Don Baylor's credit, the team rallied and won 21 of its final 30 games. While no one wants to make the mistaken impression that the strong finish means the Rockies don't have to shake up the club, it was a good indicator Baylor could motivate his players.

Offense

Baylor manages aggressively and loves to use speed, steal bases and use the hit-and-run. In fact, he used the hit-and-run more than any manager in the game in 1997. He's not a station-to-station strategist in the least, even though his team plays in arguably the best hitters' park of all time. He doesn't sit back and wait for the meat of the order to unload. He always wants to make something happen.

Pitching & Defense

All five members of the Rockies' rotation were hurting at one time or another early in the season, and three went down in one week in early May. Baylor never got Kevin Ritz and Mark Thompson back after they had arthroscopic surgeries, and Bill Swift was released in mid-August to make space on the roster for Pedro Astacio. Baylor has had enough experience handling pitchers that he knows to create matchups he wants. Because he came up with Baltimore and manager Earl Weaver, Baylor values good defense and fundamentals. He knows the little things can mean the difference between winning and losing.

1998 Outlook

Baylor is signed through 1998 and may receive a contract extension soon. He never has entered a season while in the final year of a contract. The Rockies will face some dynamic change, with top prospects Todd Helton and Neifi Perez joining the lineup, and fresh blood added to the pitching staff. The Rockies still believe Baylor is the right man to preside over that change.

Born: 6/28/49 in Austin, TX

Playing Experience: 1970-1988, Bal, Oak, Ana, NYA, Bos, Min

Managerial Experience: 5 seasons
Nickname: Groove

Manager Statistics

Year	Team, Lg	W	L	Pct	GB	Finish
1997	Colorado, NL	83	79	.512	7.0	3rd West
5 Seasons		363	384	.486	—	—

1997 Starting Pitchers by Days Rest

	≤3	4	5	6+
Rockies Starts	2	89	36	24
Rockies ERA	9.28	5.47	5.71	5.66
NL Avg Starts	3	90	38	22
NL ERA	4.23	4.05	4.27	4.52

1997 Situational Stats

	Don Baylor	NL Average
Hit & Run Success %	49.0	36.4
Stolen Base Success %	67.8	68.4
Platoon Pct.	51.7	56.3
Defensive Subs	36	26
High-Pitch Outings	2	12
Quick/Slow Hooks	15/23	18/10
Sacrifice Attempts	93	96

1997 Rankings (National League)

⇒ 1st in steals of home plate (2), double steals (10), hit-and-run attempts (147), hit-and-run percentage (49.0%), pitchouts (113), pitchouts with a runner moving (25) and slow hooks (23)

⇒ 3rd in steals of third base (23) and defensive substitutions (36)

Pedro Astacio

1997 Season

After the Rockies acquired Pedro Astacio for second baseman Eric Young on August 18, Colorado went 6-1 in the games he started. He did allow more hits than innings pitched with Colorado, but he impressed the club with his performance on the road. He had a fairly consistent season except for some rough times in June and August.

Pitching

Astacio's main pitches are a sinking fastball, an above-average curveball and a decent changeup. He's developing a screwball to give hitters a different look and keep them off balance. He's improving in situations when he gets behind in the count, though that's still an area that haunts him. Opponents hit .313 if his first offering to a given batter in 1997 was a ball, and .407 if they were ahead in the count. He has become a little less volatile and emotional on the mound, and he posted the highest strikeout total of his six-year career.

Defense & Hitting

Astacio will change his motion slightly on different pitches. His general delivery, though, doesn't leave him in a good position to field the ball. He hasn't had much luck holding runners during the past couple of seasons. He has a hard time putting the bat on the ball in non-bunting situations. When a sacrifice is required, he can put one down.

1998 Outlook

Astacio may be the best pitcher who's ever worn a Colorado uniform, at least in terms of his performance with the Rockies. Of course, that will change once Darryl Kile takes the mound in 1998. The organization is encouraging Astacio to develop a screwball as an alternative to his changeup. If he can make the pitch work, he'll be that much tougher. He was much more successful at Dodger Stadium than on the road while with Los Angeles, so it will be interesting to see how he does going from one of the best pitchers' parks to the one of the worst.

Position: SP
Bats: R **Throws:** R
Ht: 6' 2" **Wt:** 195

Opening Day Age: 28
Born: 11/28/69 in Hato Mayor, DR
ML Seasons: 6
Pronunciation: uh-STAH-see-oh

Overall Statistics

	W	L	Pct.	ERA	G	GS	Sv	IP	H	BB	SO	HR	Ratio
1997	12	10	.545	4.14	33	31	0	202.1	200	61	166	24	1.29
Career	53	48	.525	3.71	181	139	0	935.1	897	292	649	87	1.27

How Often He Throws Strikes

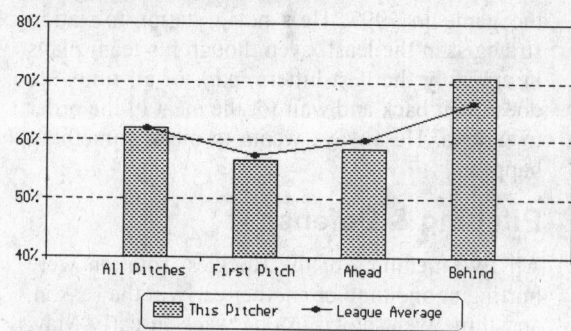

1997 Situational Stats

	W	L	ERA	Sv	IP		AB	H	HR	RBI	Avg
Home	5	5	4.63	0	83.2	LHB	337	91	11	44	.270
Road	7	5	3.79	0	118.2	RHB	439	109	13	47	.248
First Half	5	7	4.07	0	112.2	Sc Pos	180	40	3	59	.222
Scnd Half	7	3	4.22	0	89.2	Clutch	59	10	1	4	.169

1997 Rankings (National League)

⇒ 1st in lowest batting average on an 0-2 count (.000)
⇒ 2nd in balks (3)
⇒ 6th in highest groundball/flyball ratio allowed (2.2)
⇒ 8th in highest ERA at home (4.63)
⇒ 10th in sacrifice bunts (11), home runs allowed (24) and most home runs allowed per 9 innings (1.07)

Roger Bailey

Position: SP
Bats: R **Throws:** R
Ht: 6' 1" **Wt:** 180

Opening Day Age: 27
Born: 10/3/70 in Chattahoochee, FL
ML Seasons: 3

1997 Season

Roger Bailey was an anchor during the first half for a rotation decimated by injury. His success couldn't have been foreseen. The Rockies were waiting for him to realize the potential he had shown at Florida State and through the minors, where he always seemed to make adjustments after adversity. It boiled down to confidence, particularly with his breaking ball. Once he was able to throw it for strikes, Bailey became the aggressive righthander Colorado had sought.

Pitching

Bailey is a sinker/slider pitcher who can succeed when his fastball stays low and produces groundouts. He doesn't have an exceptionally hard fastball, but it can be sneaky quick. He also throws a changeup. Bailey tends to be at his best earlier in games. He struggled in the middle innings in 1997. He needs to cut down on his walks, which nearly outnumber his strikeouts in his career. He did a decent job of keeping lefthanders in check before they figured him out in 1997.

Defense & Hitting

Bailey is athletic and smart. He can be relied upon to keep himself in good shape, knowing that's part of fielding his position. He has good reflexes on balls hit through the box and didn't make an error in 65 chances in 1997. He's still learning to be more conscious of holding runners, who were successful on 16 of 21 steal attempts last season. He does have a good move to first. At the plate, Bailey is no slouch, either. He always has enjoyed hitting and his career average is .206.

1998 Outlook

Bailey won just one game in the second half of 1997, but the Rockies believe he can become a consistent starter. He loves the game, and is willing to work on mechanics and make the mental adjustments needed to succeed. He won't beat himself.

Overall Statistics

	W	L	Pct.	ERA	G	GS	Sv	IP	H	BB	SO	HR	Ratio
1997	9	10	.474	4.29	29	29	0	191.0	210	70	84	27	1.47
Career	18	19	.486	4.90	92	46	1	356.0	392	161	162	43	1.55

How Often He Throws Strikes

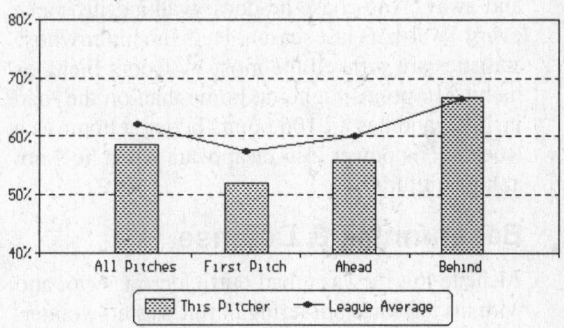

1997 Situational Stats

	W	L	ERA	Sv	IP		AB	H	HR	RBI	Avg
Home	5	3	4.90	0	93.2	LHB	356	112	11	42	.315
Road	4	7	3.70	0	97.1	RHB	385	98	16	49	.255
First Half	8	6	3.50	0	110.2	Sc Pos	184	39	3	59	.212
Scnd Half	1	4	5.38	0	80.1	Clutch	38	12	1	5	.316

1997 Rankings (National League)

⇒ 1st in lowest strikeout/walk ratio (1.2), least strikeouts per 9 innings (4.0) and fielding percentage at pitcher (1.000)

⇒ 2nd in hit batsmen (13)

⇒ 3rd in home runs allowed, GDPs induced (26), highest on-base percentage allowed (.354), least pitches thrown per batter (3.38), most run support per 9 innings (5.9), most home runs allowed per 9 innings (1.27) and most GDPs induced per 9 innings (1.2)

⇒ Led the Rockies in ERA, wins, games started, complete games (5), shutouts (2), innings pitched, hits allowed, batters faced (835), home runs allowed, hit batsmen (13), pitches thrown (2,819), GDPs induced (26), winning percentage and lowest batting average allowed (.283)

Dante Bichette

1997 Season

Coming off October 1996 knee surgery, Dante Bichette quickly learned that the 1997 season would be a struggle. It took quite a while for his old confidence and focus to fall into place. Once they did, he drove in 118 runs and was among National League leaders in a number of categories.

Hitting

The thing that keeps Bichette going is driving in runs. When there are men on base, he can use his compact swing to full advantage. He hit .328 with runners on base in 1997, compared to .289 with the sacks empty. He struggles offensively when he gets caught up in chasing offspeed offerings low and away. And chase he does, walking just once every 19 at-bats last season. He's the hitter whose statistics are inflated the most by Coors Field, as he hit 116 points higher at home than on the road in 1997, and has hit 106 points better at home as a Rockie. His power also disappears when he's not at high altitude.

Baserunning & Defense

Bichette felt he was a bad outfielder in 1996, and with his left knee bothering him it was no wonder. From Opening Day in 1997, he made progress in left field in terms of both his mobility and throwing strength, thanks in part to offseason surgery. He's still better suited to being a designated hitter and produced just four assists in nearly 1,100 innings in the outfield in 1997. The surgery did nothing to improve his speed, as his steal totals declined from a career-high 31 in 1996 to six.

1998 Outlook

It's no wonder Bichette is looking forward to 1998. He doesn't have to spend the offseason in daily six-hour rehabilitation sessions. There was some thought that Colorado might move first-base prospect Todd Helton to left field and then try to trade Bichette, but that possibility ended when Andres Galarraga signed with the Braves.

Position: LF/RF
Bats: R **Throws:** R
Ht: 6' 3" **Wt:** 235

Opening Day Age: 34
Born: 11/18/63 in West Palm Beach, FL
ML Seasons: 10
Pronunciation: DAHN-tay bih-SHET

Overall Statistics

	G	AB	R	H	D	T	HR	RBI	SB	BB	SO	Avg	OBP	Slg
1997	151	561	81	173	31	2	26	118	6	30	90	.308	.343	.510
Career	1130	4160	608	1229	253	20	183	747	125	204	751	.295	.329	.498

Where He Hits the Ball

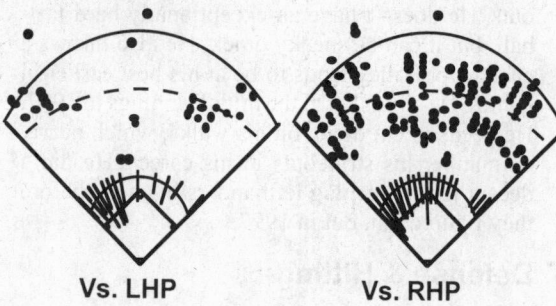

Vs. LHP   Vs. RHP

1997 Situational Stats

	AB	H	HR	RBI	Avg		AB	H	HR	RBI	Avg
Home	301	109	20	87	.362	LHP	133	35	8	28	.263
Road	260	64	6	31	.246	RHP	428	138	18	90	.322
First Half	317	95	12	64	.300	Sc Pos	174	56	6	87	.322
Scnd Half	244	78	14	54	.320	Clutch	66	18	3	15	.273

1997 Rankings (National League)

⇒ 1st in fielding percentage in left field (.991)
⇒ 3rd in batting average at home
⇒ 4th in batting average with the bases loaded (.563)
⇒ 6th in lowest percentage of extra bases taken as a runner (34.9%)
⇒ 7th in batting average vs. righthanded pitchers
⇒ 8th in RBI and lowest on-base percentage vs. lefthanded pitchers (.303)
⇒ 9th in lowest batting average on the road and batting average with two strikes (.252)
⇒ 10th in lowest groundball/flyball ratio (1.0)
⇒ Led the Rockies in sacrifice flies (7), batting average with the bases loaded (.563) and batting average with two strikes (.252)

Ellis Burks

1997 Season

Ellis Burks had to combat nagging injuries early in 1997, but he was able to ease his way back into the lineup because Quinton McCracken became a reliable outfielder in Burks' absence. In the first year of a new two-year contract, Burks proved he may be getting better with age. In 1996, he joined Hank Aaron as the only players to have 200 hits, 40 homers and 30 steals in the same season. His encore would have been nearly as productive had he not missed so much time. Burks finished quite strong, hitting .264 through August before erupting for a .385-7-19 September.

Hitting

Burks remains a deadly fastball hitter. For the first time since coming to Colorado, he hit better against righthanders than lefties. Challenge him inside and he can turn on a ball, but he also likes to use the alleys and basically hits to all fields. In 119 games he homered 32 times, which is especially impressive given that Burks isn't prone to bushels of strikeouts. His power is constant, as he homered the day he came off the disabled list after missing a month with a strained groin. He was much more effective at home in 1997—no surprise—batting 90 points higher at Coors Field than on the road.

Baserunning & Defense

Burks still remains a force on the basepaths, though his steal total plummeted to seven last season and his instincts never have been as considerable as his speed. A growing issue for Burks is the wear and tear of playing center field. He still has decent range at the position, but the presence of McCracken allowed him to see more time in left. His arm isn't much of a factor.

1998 Outlook

There's no reason Burks shouldn't continue to hit. He chose to re-sign with the Rockies in 1996 because he feels he's found a niche in Denver. His family is there and it's obvious he would take special pride in seeing Colorado rebound from two disappointing seasons. He's going into the final year of his contract, and he would like to continue putting up big numbers.

Position: CF/LF
Bats: R **Throws:** R
Ht: 6' 2" **Wt:** 198

Opening Day Age: 33
Born: 9/11/64 in Vicksburg, MS
ML Seasons: 11

Overall Statistics

	G	AB	R	H	D	T	HR	RBI	SB	BB	SO	Avg	OBP	Slg
1997	119	424	91	123	19	2	32	82	7	47	75	.290	.363	.571
Career	1288	4757	822	1378	266	50	209	744	148	474	847	.290	.356	.498

Where He Hits the Ball

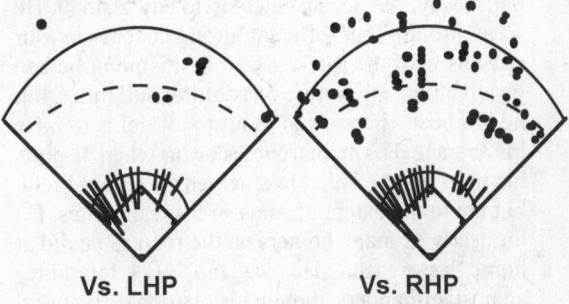

Vs. LHP   **Vs. RHP**

1997 Situational Stats

	AB	H	HR	RBI	Avg		AB	H	HR	RBI	Avg
Home	205	69	17	45	.337	LHP	100	28	5	17	.280
Road	219	54	15	37	.247	RHP	324	95	27	65	.293
First Half	245	62	17	49	.253	Sc Pos	111	36	8	51	.324
Scnd Half	179	61	15	33	.341	Clutch	59	18	4	10	.305

1997 Rankings (National League)

⇒ 8th in home runs

Vinny Castilla

1997 Season

Vinny Castilla is consistent and productive. He topped .300 for the fourth consecutive season, and duplicated his 1996 batting line of .304-40-113. He also was a solid presence defensively at third base. An original Rockie, it's hard to believe he lasted until the second round of the November 1992 expansion draft.

Hitting

Castilla is probably the best high fastball hitter in the National League. Just ask Astros closer Billy Wagner, who challenged him with heat and lost badly, serving up two late-inning homers to Castilla in 1997. He can be susceptible to breaking balls away, but he can catch up to any fastball. He went through four different hitting coaches in four seasons with the Rockies, but at this point he can be left alone. He's more of a natural pull hitter, but he has been encouraged to hit to all fields to raise his average. His main troubles occur when he pulls his head off the ball. He's helped by Coors Field, but not to the extent of some of his teammates. He hit nearly as many homers on the road as he did at home last season. He was the NL's top hitter against lefthanders, though his platoon differential hadn't been that extreme in the past.

Baserunning & Defense

Though Castilla has average range at third, he has a very good, strong arm that's consistently accurate. His defense is no cause for concern. Castilla lacks speed but doesn't cost the Rockies too much on the bases. He's woeful as a basestealer, going 2-for-6 in 1997 and 15-for-35 in his career.

1998 Outlook

Castilla is a better player than anyone realized when the Rockies selected him in the expansion draft. He's settling into his prime as a bona fide offensive star. He once again should produce numbers similar to those of the last two seasons, and his numbers aren't just a Coors Field mirage. He signed a four-year contract extension in the offseason.

Position: 3B
Bats: R **Throws:** R
Ht: 6' 1" **Wt:** 200

Opening Day Age: 30
Born: 7/4/67 in Oaxaca, MX
ML Seasons: 7
Pronunciation: cas-TEE-yah

Overall Statistics

	G	AB	R	H	D	T	HR	RBI	SB	BB	SO	Avg	OBP	Slg
1997	159	612	94	186	25	2	40	113	2	44	108	.304	.356	.547
Career	636	2256	327	674	114	12	124	365	15	130	357	.299	.339	.525

Where He Hits the Ball

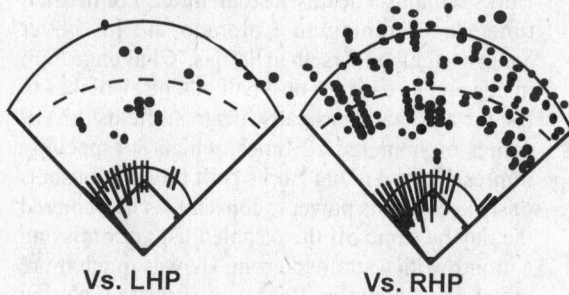

Vs. LHP   Vs. RHP

1997 Situational Stats

	AB	H	HR	RBI	Avg		AB	H	HR	RBI	Avg
Home	316	101	21	62	.320	LHP	129	49	11	31	.380
Road	296	85	19	51	.287	RHP	483	137	29	82	.284
First Half	326	92	22	64	.282	Sc Pos	142	44	6	65	.310
Scnd Half	286	94	18	49	.329	Clutch	91	31	6	15	.341

1997 Rankings (National League)

⇒ 1st in batting average vs. lefthanded pitchers and slugging percentage vs. lefthanded pitchers (.698)
⇒ 3rd in lowest percentage of pitches taken (45.2%) and highest percentage of swings on the first pitch (45.9%)
⇒ Led the Rockies in at-bats, singles, GDPs (18), games played (159), batting average vs. lefthanded pitchers, batting average on a 3-1 count (.556), slugging percentage vs. lefthanded pitchers (.698) and on-base percentage vs. lefthanded pitchers (.434)

Jerry DiPoto

1997 Season

Traded by the Mets for Armando Reynoso, Jerry DiPoto became the Rockies' closer in August. He ascended to the role mostly by default because of Bruce Ruffin's problems, then went 16-for-21 in save opportunities. One of his blown chances was memorable, a grand slam to Bobby Bonilla that allowed the Marlins to come from behind and win in the ninth. The loss effectively ended any prospect of a miracle climb for Colorado past San Francisco and Los Angeles. For the season, hitters batted .288 against him, and he wasn't much more effective against righthanders than lefties.

Pitching

DiPoto is a sinkerball pitcher, but he developed a four-seam fastball that kept hitters from looking down in the zone all the time for his sinking stuff. He also throws a slider and uses a splitter as a changeup. He's extremely durable and seemingly could pitch every day. He's still somewhat un-tested as a closer. DiPoto had struggled as a closer before 1997, converting just 13 of 28 save opportunites. And last season he had the second-worst save percentage in the National League.

Defense & Hitting

Relatively quick to the plate, DiPoto watches runners well. There's nothing special about his defensive ability, though he won't hurt a team with his glove. He rarely bats, finally notching his first major league base hit in 1997.

1998 Outlook

DiPoto is a man who loves to play, loves to have the ball in his hand. He has fought through hard times. He developed thyroid cancer while with the Indians, then saw Jose Mesa develop into a star closer and make him expendable. Though he had some disappointments with the Mets, DiPoto made a lot of his opportunity in Colorado. The question will be whether he can indeed be a true closer as his career continues.

Position: RP
Bats: R **Throws:** R
Ht: 6' 2" **Wt:** 200

Opening Day Age: 29
Born: 5/24/68 in Jersey City, NJ
ML Seasons: 5
Pronunciation: dih-POE-toe

Overall Statistics

	W	L	Pct.	ERA	G	GS	Sv	IP	H	BB	SO	HR	Ratio
1997	5	3	.625	4.70	74	0	16	95.2	108	33	74	6	1.47
Career	20	15	.571	4.12	242	0	29	323.2	359	147	225	14	1.56

How Often He Throws Strikes

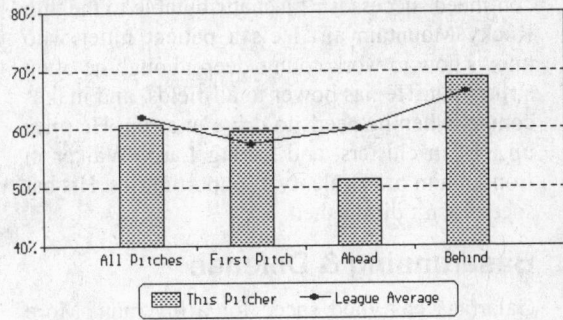

This Pitcher   League Average

1997 Situational Stats

	W	L	ERA	Sv	IP		AB	H	HR	RBI	Avg
Home	5	0	4.08	8	53.0	LHB	190	56	3	35	.295
Road	0	3	5.48	8	42.2	RHB	185	52	3	25	.281
First Half	2	1	4.97	2	50.2	Sc Pos	108	35	4	58	.324
Scnd Half	3	2	4.40	14	45.0	Clutch	145	35	1	14	.241

1997 Rankings (National League)

⇒ 2nd in lowest save percentage (76.2%)
⇒ 3rd in relief innings (95.2)
⇒ 8th in highest batting average allowed in relief (.288)
⇒ 9th in games pitched
⇒ Led the Rockies in games pitched, saves, games finished (33), save opportunities (21), save percentage (76.2%), lowest batting average allowed vs. lefthanded batters, first batter efficiency (.229) and relief innings (95.2)

Andres Galarraga

Position: 1B
Bats: R **Throws:** R
Ht: 6' 3" **Wt:** 235

Opening Day Age: 36
Born: 6/18/61 in Caracas, VZ
ML Seasons: 13
Pronunciation: ON-dres gahl-lah-RAH-guh
Nickname: Big Cat

1997 Season

Andres Galarraga became the first National League player in 14 years to win the RBI title in consecutive seasons. The Big Cat had a complete season at the plate and has been a consistent big league performer ever since he broke in with Montreal in 1985.

Hitting

For anyone at Pro Player Stadium in late May, the memory of Galarraga's mammoth home run off Kevin Brown will endure forever. The drive soared into the upper deck in left field, where no one sits, landing about four rows from the top of the building. The blast showed that Galarraga's continued success isn't just attributable to the thin Rocky Mountain air. He's a patient hitter who knows how to work counts deep, though he often strikes out. He has power to all fields, and makes contact when he needs to drive in a run. He piles up RBI in clusters, and having Larry Walker in front of him offers plenty of opportunities. His bat speed hasn't diminished.

Baserunning & Defense

Galarraga has good speed for a big man. More important, he is a smart baserunner, rarely taking foolish chances. He continues to show good range defensively and knows what he's doing on cutoff plays. He did lead all first basemen with 15 errors last season, so he never had hopes of taking home a Gold Glove. That said, he remains extremely agile, has very soft hands and isn't afraid to throw the ball across the diamond.

1998 Outlook

Galarraga was eligible for free agency, and there's no question the Rockies wanted him back. They offered him a lucrative contract, but he joined the Braves for three years and $24.5 million. It will be interesting to see how he does away from Coors Field.

Overall Statistics

	G	AB	R	H	D	T	HR	RBI	SB	BB	SO	Avg	OBP	Slg
1997	154	600	120	191	31	3	41	140	15	54	141	.318	.389	.585
Career	1621	6074	908	1752	337	29	288	1051	114	404	1469	.288	.342	.496

Where He Hits the Ball

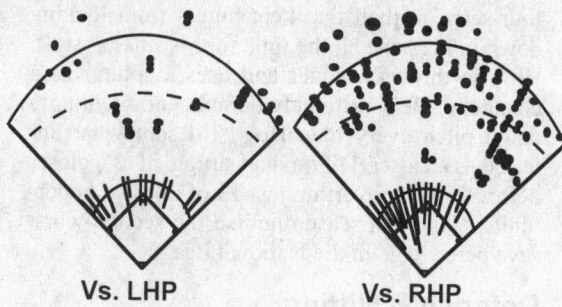

Vs. LHP   **Vs. RHP**

1997 Situational Stats

	AB	H	HR	RBI	Avg		AB	H	HR	RBI	Avg
Home	298	102	21	89	.342	LHP	126	42	10	33	.333
Road	302	89	20	51	.295	RHP	474	149	31	107	.314
First Half	328	106	22	84	.323	Sc Pos	191	55	9	98	.288
Scnd Half	272	85	19	56	.313	Clutch	80	19	4	17	.238

1997 Rankings (National League)

⇒ 1st in RBI and errors at first base (15)
⇒ 2nd in lowest fielding percentage at first base (.991)
⇒ 3rd in home runs, total bases (351) and slugging percentage vs. lefthanded pitchers (.643)
⇒ 4th in runs scored, hits, strikeouts, slugging percentage and cleanup slugging percentage (.555)
⇒ 5th in hit by pitch (17)
⇒ Led the Rockies in RBI, hit by pitch (17), strikeouts, pitches seen (2,504), plate appearances (674), highest groundball/flyball ratio (1.5), most pitches seen per plate appearance (3.72) and cleanup slugging percentage (.555)

Todd Helton

1997 Season

Todd Helton came to the major leagues without missing much of a beat in 1997. He showed with little doubt that he's ready to become an everyday fixture for the Rockies. In just 93 at-bats for the parent club, he hit a solid .280 with five home runs. He also demonstrated that he has the athleticism to play the outfield as well as first base. That kind of versatility should continue to serve the former University of Tennessee quarterback well.

Hitting

Helton has a silky-smooth swing and an extremely businesslike approach. He shows an awareness of situations at the plate way beyond his years. As he came up through Colorado's system, he distinguished himself with his ability to send balls to the alleys and often showed power to the opposite field. Now he's making the adjustment to turn on pitches, which only will enhance his value at Coors Field. He has a lot of self discipline at the plate and can hit with two strikes.

Baserunning & Defense

Not blessed with great speed, Helton is still an alert baserunner. He can move from first to third more on his smarts than on natural talent. At first base, he has good range, a strong arm and the ability to dig balls out of the dirt.

1998 Outlook

Helton will be the everyday first baseman for the Rockies in 1998 with the departure of Andres Galarraga to Atlanta. The combination of his batting stroke and Coors Field should produce a National League batting title at some point in Helton's career.

Position: LF
Bats: L **Throws:** L
Ht: 6' 2" **Wt:** 190

Opening Day Age: 24
Born: 8/20/73 in Knoxville, TN
ML Seasons: 1

Colorado Rockies

Overall Statistics

	G	AB	R	H	D	T	HR	RBI	SB	BB	SO	Avg	OBP	Slg
1997	35	93	13	26	2	1	5	11	0	8	11	.280	.337	.484
Career	35	93	13	26	2	1	5	11	0	8	11	.280	.337	.484

Where He Hits the Ball

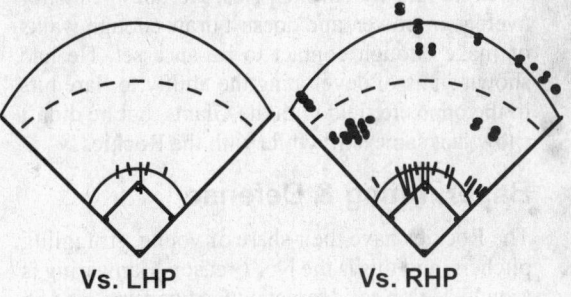

Vs. LHP   **Vs. RHP**

1997 Situational Stats

	AB	H	HR	RBI	Avg		AB	H	HR	RBI	Avg
Home	48	14	3	8	.292	LHP	10	2	0	0	.200
Road	45	12	2	3	.267	RHP	83	24	5	11	.289
First Half	0	0	0	0	-	Sc Pos	28	6	2	8	.214
Scnd Half	93	26	5	11	.280	Clutch	19	7	0	2	.368

1997 Rankings (National League)

⇒ Did not rank near the top or bottom in any category

431

Kirt Manwaring

1997 Season

Kirt Manwaring proved that Coors Field can't make a hitter out of everyone. He hit three points less than he had in 1996 with San Francisco and Houston, and his on-base and slugging percentages declined as well. He platooned with Jeff Reed, and Reed was much more successful with the bat and took the majority of the playing time in the second half.

Hitting

Manwaring never has been a feared hitter and usually is in the lineup for his catching ability. In his defense, he has played through nagging injuries that have hurt his numbers, such as in 1995 when he had five broken ribs. He doesn't hit for average or power, and doesn't draw enough walks or make enough contact to be an asset. He had shown signs of developing the ability to flare hits to the opposite field with the Giants, but he didn't show that same skill while with the Rockies.

Baserunning & Defense

The Rockies have their share of young, struggling pitchers, and this is the No. 1 reason Manwaring is around. He's a solid target with a good arm, and he knows a thing or two about calling a game. He has had some respected mentors, including Terry Kennedy, and he has picked up his share of trade secrets from veteran pitchers such as Mike Krukow and Rick Reuschel. Manwaring is very adept at blocking the plate and blocking balls. He's not much to look at on the basepaths and has just nine steals in 11 years.

1998 Outlook

The Rockies count on Manwaring to shore up an erratic pitching staff—and nothing else. If he doesn't hit better, he could lose more playing time after Jeff Reed re-signed. Manwaring is a much better catcher, but his hitting is too much of a negative. A .226 batting average for someone who plays his home games at Coors Field is laughable.

Position: C
Bats: R **Throws:** R
Ht: 5'11" **Wt:** 203

Opening Day Age: 32
Born: 7/15/65 in Elmira, NY
ML Seasons: 11
Pronunciation: MAN-ware-ing

Overall Statistics

	G	AB	R	H	D	T	HR	RBI	SB	BB	SO	Avg	OBP	Slg
1997	104	337	22	76	6	4	1	27	1	30	78	.226	.291	.276
Career	850	2554	201	620	92	16	17	238	9	193	433	.243	.305	.311

Where He Hits the Ball

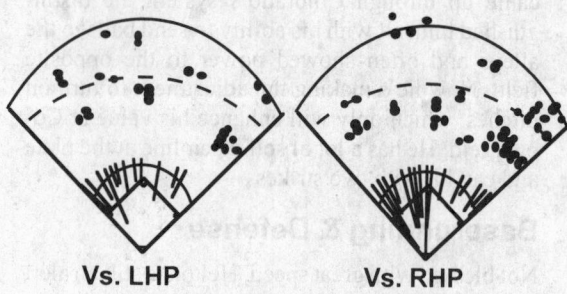

Vs. LHP   Vs. RHP

1997 Situational Stats

	AB	H	HR	RBI	Avg		AB	H	HR	RBI	Avg
Home	175	44	1	14	.251	LHP	117	27	0	7	.231
Road	162	32	0	13	.198	RHP	220	49	1	20	.223
First Half	203	50	1	15	.246	Sc Pos	79	23	0	25	.291
Scnd Half	134	26	0	12	.194	Clutch	38	8	0	0	.211

1997 Rankings (National League)

⇒ 2nd in lowest on-base percentage vs. lefthanded pitchers (.270) and fielding percentage at catcher (.994)

⇒ 3rd in lowest slugging percentage vs. lefthanded pitchers (.256)

⇒ 9th in lowest batting average vs. lefthanded pitchers and lowest batting average on an 0-2 count (.067)

Neifi Perez

1997 Season

Rookie Neifi Perez showed why the Rockies considered him their best position-player prospect. Facing major league pitching didn't faze him and he managed to collect his share of extra-base hits. Defensively he proved he can be Colorado's shortstop of the future. In the short term, he filled in beautifully at second base after the trade of Eric Young to the Dodgers, forming a strong double-play combination with shortstop Walt Weiss.

Hitting

Perez worked closely with Triple-A hitting coach Tony Torchia to become a more disciplined hitter. Early in his pro career, Perez was a free swinger. But Torchia began to teach him that the secret to hitting is waiting for the right pitch, and Perez is making progress. Some scouts think he has tendencies similar to the ones Carlos Baerga had to overcome. He may be on his way, for the new-found success he discovered in Triple-A continued to the majors. He also might be an illusion of Coors Field, hitting .343 with a .509 slugging percentage at home compared to .229 and .368 on the road.

Baserunning & Defense

Perez has a somewhat awkward build, more powerful than the sleek body type often associated with middle infielders from the Dominican Republic. He's not especially fast, though he could reach the double-digit mark in stolen bases and won't cost the Rockies big innings because of his lack of speed. His defense remains his strength. He has a powerful and accurate arm, plus fine range and the ability to handle the hardest of hops. Perez puts himself in a position to field the ball, plants his feet and makes a strong throw.

1998 Outlook

Perez made Weiss expendable and could develop into one of the best all-around players at shortstop in the National League. The Rockies are eager to see how that promise plays out during the course of a full season.

Position: SS/2B
Bats: B **Throws:** R
Ht: 6' 0" **Wt:** 173

Opening Day Age: 23
Born: 2/2/75 in Villa Mella, Dominican Republic
ML Seasons: 2
Pronunciation: NAY-fee per-EZ

Overall Statistics

	G	AB	R	H	D	T	HR	RBI	SB	BB	SO	Avg	OBP	Slg
1997	83	313	46	91	13	10	5	31	4	21	43	.291	.333	.444
Career	100	358	50	98	15	10	5	34	6	21	51	.274	.313	.413

Where He Hits the Ball

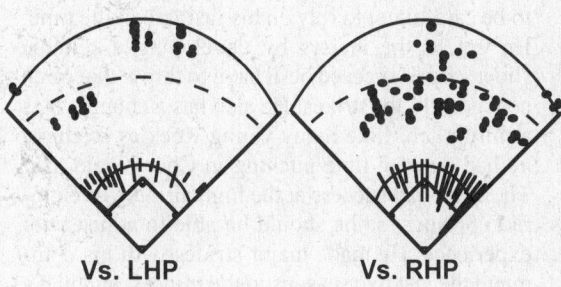

Vs. LHP   **Vs. RHP**

1997 Situational Stats

	AB	H	HR	RBI	Avg		AB	H	HR	RBI	Avg
Home	169	58	3	19	.343	LHP	77	24	2	10	.312
Road	144	33	2	12	.229	RHP	236	67	3	21	.284
First Half	36	9	2	5	.250	Sc Pos	72	19	0	23	.264
Scnd Half	277	82	3	26	.296	Clutch	52	12	0	7	.231

1997 Rankings (National League)

⇒ 2nd in triples
⇒ 10th in least GDPs per GDP situation (5.3%)
⇒ Led the Rockies in triples, least GDPs per GDP situation (5.3%) and bunts in play (16)

John Thomson

1997 Season

John Thomson came up in May from Triple-A Colorado Springs and showed he'll one day be a successful big league pitcher. That's not to say his 1997 performance was anything close to what the Rockies think will be acceptable over the long term. But he did manage to stay in games and earn a respectable 4.71 ERA. Thomson didn't get down when his first four starts all turned into losses. He was especially sharp from late July to early September, when he went 5-2 and threw a complete-game win against the Mets.

Pitching

Thomson has good velocity and was clocked at 92 MPH in the eighth inning of some games. He has to be careful not to rely on his fastball all the time. He got to the majors by developing a reliable slider, and to succeed he'll have to throw that pitch consistently for strikes. He also has a changeup as a third pitch. Like many young Rockies pitchers, he had a rough time pitching in Coors Field. But Thomson had success at the high altitude of Colorado Springs, so he should be able to adjust with experience. He made major strides with his command the last two seasons in the minors, and had a fine strikeout/walk ratio for Colorado.

Defense & Hitting

A conscientious worker, Thomson fields his position well but still is learning to hold runners. He also showed flashes of offensive potential, batting .213 and laying down six sacrifices. In his first career win, he went 4-for-4 with three RBI.

1998 Outlook

If the Rockies are successful in finding a frontline starter to go with Pedro Astacio, Thomson can blend in and be a quiet surprise. He had nothing to be embarrassed about as a rookie. There's a fire inside the man the Rockies call "Red" and those competitive instincts could bode well for him, especially without the pressure of being the No. 1 or 2 man in the rotation.

Position: SP
Bats: R **Throws:** R
Ht: 6' 3" **Wt:** 180

Opening Day Age: 24
Born: 10/1/73 in Vicksburg, VA
ML Seasons: 1
Nickname: Red

Overall Statistics

	W	L	Pct.	ERA	G	GS	Sv	IP	H	BB	SO	HR	Ratio
1997	7	9	.438	4.71	27	27	0	166.1	193	51	106	15	1.47
Career	7	9	.438	4.71	27	27	0	166.1	193	51	106	15	1.47

How Often He Throws Strikes

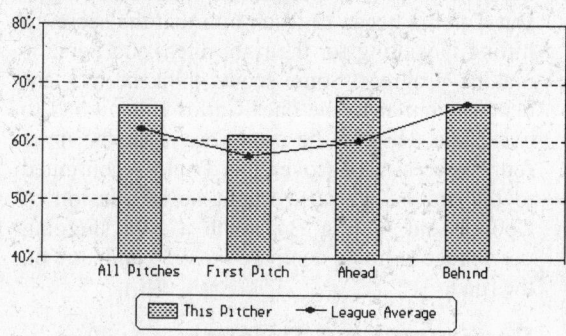

This Pitcher — League Average

1997 Situational Stats

	W	L	ERA	Sv	IP			AB	H	HR	RBI	Avg
Home	4	3	5.90	0	71.2		LHB	354	112	9	49	.316
Road	3	6	3.80	0	94.2		RHB	297	81	6	36	.273
First Half	2	6	6.02	0	61.1		Sc Pos	149	46	3	62	.309
Scnd Half	5	3	3.94	0	105.0		Clutch	35	10	1	5	.286

1997 Rankings (National League)

⇒ 1st in most GDPs induced per 9 innings (1.4)
⇒ 2nd in highest batting average allowed (.296) and highest batting average allowed with runners in scoring position
⇒ Led the Rockies in strikeouts, highest strikeout/walk ratio (2.1), lowest slugging percentage allowed (.433), lowest on-base percentage allowed (.351), lowest stolen base percentage allowed (65.2%), least baserunners allowed per 9 innings (13.5), least home runs allowed per 9 innings (.81), most GDPs induced per 9 innings (1.4) and most strikeouts per 9 innings (5.7)

Larry Walker

1997 Season

Larry Walker always has been a very, very good player, but many baseball observers wondered if he ever would become a truly great player. They stopped wondering in 1997. He had one of the best all-around offensive seasons in the modern era. He was rewarded with the National League Most Valuable Player Award, and also won a Gold Glove for his play in right field.

Hitting

Walker hits with power to all fields, an impressive feat when coupled with his ability to hit for average. He flirted with .400 for half the season and his .366 batting average trailed only San Diego's Tony Gwynn among major leaguers. Perhaps the most amazing thing about Walker's campaign was that Coors Field didn't really help him. He hit .346-29-62 on the road, a stellar full season for most players after hitting just .142 away from Coors Field in 1996. His memorable All-Star at-bat against Randy Johnson aside, he just missed hitting .300 against lefties.

Baserunning & Defense

Walker runs the bases as well as anybody in the game and led the NL in taking extra bases in 1997. His speed allows him to steal bases and turn singles into leg doubles. It also allows him to have fine range in right field. His arm isn't quite the cannon it was early in his career, but it's still a weapon. He's also surehanded, leading NL right fielders with a .992 fielding percentage last season and making just six errors in the past three years.

1998 Outlook

Walker's knees held up in 1997, which made a big difference. He was healthy and learned just how good he can be. In 1998, he'll be eager to show it was no fluke. That's motivation enough for him to continue with the same kind of conditioning program that served him well during last offseason.

Position: RF
Bats: L **Throws:** R
Ht: 6' 3" **Wt:** 225

Opening Day Age: 31
Born: 12/1/66 in Maple Ridge, BC, Canada
ML Seasons: 9

Colorado Rockies

Overall Statistics

	G	AB	R	H	D	T	HR	RBI	SB	BB	SO	Avg	OBP	Slg
1997	153	568	143	208	46	4	49	130	33	78	90	.366	.452	.720
Career	1041	3700	665	1100	242	29	202	673	165	411	694	.297	.374	.542

Where He Hits the Ball

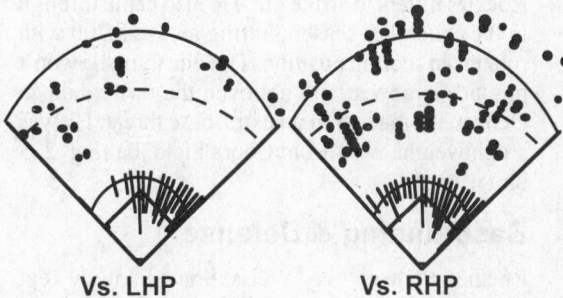

Vs. LHP   **Vs. RHP**

1997 Situational Stats

	AB	H	HR	RBI	Avg		AB	H	HR	RBI	Avg
Home	302	116	20	68	.384	LHP	144	43	6	23	.299
Road	266	92	29	62	.346	RHP	424	165	43	107	.389
First Half	309	123	25	68	.398	Sc Pos	140	51	5	68	.364
Scnd Half	259	85	24	62	.328	Clutch	71	25	7	17	.352

1997 Rankings (National League)

⇒ 1st in home runs, total bases (409), slugging percentage, on-base percentage, HR frequency (11.6 ABs per HR), batting average vs. righthanded pitchers, slugging percentage vs. righthanded pitchers (.788), on-base percentage vs. righthanded pitchers (.470), batting average at home, fielding percentage in right field (.992) and highest percentage of extra bases taken as a runner (70.7%)

⇒ 2nd in batting average, runs scored and hits

⇒ 3rd in doubles, RBI and batting average on the road

⇒ Led the Rockies in batting average, home runs, runs scored, hits, doubles, total bases (409), stolen bases, walks, intentional walks (14), times on base (300) and slugging percentage

Walt Weiss

Signed By
BRAVES

Position: SS
Bats: B **Throws:** R
Ht: 6' 0" **Wt:** 175

Opening Day Age: 34
Born: 11/28/63 in Tuxedo, NY
ML Seasons: 11
Pronunciation: WICE

1997 Season

Walt Weiss continued to be a model of consistency in 1997. He maintained his reputation as one of the surest gloves around, and with the help of Coors Field offered good offense for his position. Decent if not extraordinary range and steady hands are his calling cards.

Hitting

Weiss is flexible when it comes to hitting, capable of filling the leadoff spot when former teammate Eric Young was injured or dropped to the No. 8 hole. Either way, Weiss is a selective hitter whose ability to draw walks makes him valuable. He can hit to all fields and is one of the more difficult Rockies hitters to strike out. He also came through in the clutch last season, hitting an even .300 with runners in scoring position. The one thing he won't produce is power, and not even the rarified air in Denver has made him an extra-base threat. He was a lightweight away from Coors Field, batting .235 on the road.

Baserunning & Defense

Rockies pitchers loved Weiss. Some jokingly kept his baseball card in their locker stall as a token of their appreciation for his rock-steady play at short-stop. Somehow Weiss knows how to be in the right position at the correct time, and while there he fields everything cleanly. He doesn't give away outs. As a runner, he has stopped being a threat for even the occasional stolen base. He has slipped from 15 to 10 to five swipes in the last three seasons.

1998 Outlook

Weiss held the option on the second year of his contract, and decided to shop his services rather than move to second base and make room for Neifi Perez. Weiss signed with the Braves.

Overall Statistics

	G	AB	R	H	D	T	HR	RBI	SB	BB	SO	Avg	OBP	Slg
1997	121	393	52	106	23	5	4	38	5	66	56	.270	.377	.384
Career	1209	3868	492	997	145	23	23	312	81	538	525	.258	.350	.325

Where He Hits the Ball

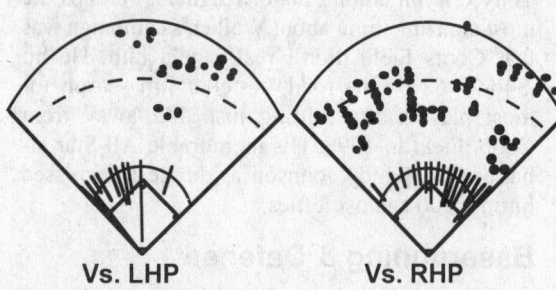

Vs. LHP　　　　**Vs. RHP**

1997 Situational Stats

	AB	H	HR	RBI	Avg		AB	H	HR	RBI	Avg
Home	206	62	2	23	.301	LHP	99	19	1	6	.192
Road	187	44	2	15	.235	RHP	294	87	3	32	.296
First Half	244	62	2	22	.254	Sc Pos	80	24	0	29	.300
Scnd Half	149	44	2	16	.295	Clutch	56	14	0	6	.250

1997 Rankings (National League)

⇒ 2nd in fielding percentage at shortstop (.983)
⇒ 3rd in highest percentage of pitches taken (64.7%)
⇒ 8th in lowest percentage of swings that missed (11.1%) and highest percentage of swings put into play (53.4%)
⇒ Led the Rockies in highest percentage of pitches taken (64.7%)

Jason Bates

Position: 2B/SS
Bats: B **Throws:** R
Ht: 5'11" **Wt:** 185

Opening Day Age: 27
Born: 1/5/71 in Downey, CA
ML Seasons: 3

Overall Statistics

	G	AB	R	H	D	T	HR	RBI	SB	BB	SO	Avg	OBP	Slg
1997	62	121	17	29	10	0	3	11	0	15	27	.240	.338	.397
Career	266	603	78	148	35	5	12	66	5	80	131	.245	.340	.380

1997 Situational Stats

	AB	H	HR	RBI	Avg		AB	H	HR	RBI	Avg
Home	56	17	1	6	.304	LHP	28	5	0	0	.179
Road	65	12	2	5	.185	RHP	93	24	3	11	.258
First Half	80	19	2	8	.238	Sc Pos	25	5	0	7	.200
Scnd Half	41	10	1	3	.244	Clutch	21	4	1	3	.190

1997 Season

Being a utility infielder for the Rockies is a bit like being the Maytag repairman. It can be an idle experience, quite lonely. Jason Bates experienced more of the role that frustrated him in 1996, playing in 62 games and hitting .240 last season. He struck out almost twice as often as he walked.

Hitting, Baserunning & Defense

Bates needs to play often to keep his stroke tuned. If not, he has too many at-bats in which he appears to be overmatched. It's a lot to expect a of 27-year-old overachiever to thrive in a part-time role. Bates does have good speed, but he needs the chance to learn the more subtle aspects of basestealing to be a threat. His best position defensively is second base, where he turns the pivot well.

1998 Outlook

Bates is the first position player the Rockies signed who made it to the big leagues. He can play in the majors if given a chance. He proved that when he played second base every day for the first three months of the 1995 season before a wrist injury to Bates led Colorado to move Eric Young from the outfield to second base. With Young traded and Walt Weiss gone, Bates may get another opportunity to start.

Frank Castillo

Position: SP
Bats: R **Throws:** R
Ht: 6' 1" **Wt:** 200

Opening Day Age: 28
Born: 4/1/69 in El Paso, TX
ML Seasons: 7
Pronunciation: cas-TEE-yoh

Overall Statistics

	W	L	Pct.	ERA	G	GS	Sv	IP	H	BB	SO	HR	Ratio
1997	12	12	.500	5.42	34	33	0	184.1	220	69	126	25	1.57
Career	53	65	.449	4.39	180	175	0	1036.0	1081	307	711	122	1.34

1997 Situational Stats

	W	L	ERA	Sv	IP		AB	H	HR	RBI	Avg
Home	7	6	4.26	0	114.0	LHB	308	81	4	36	.263
Road	5	6	7.29	0	70.1	RHB	426	139	21	68	.326
First Half	6	9	5.28	0	92.0	Sc Pos	170	51	6	74	.300
Scnd Half	6	3	5.56	0	92.1	Clutch	21	6	0	1	.286

1997 Season

Frank Castillo was a welcome addition when the Rockies acquired him from the Cubs in mid-July for a nondescript minor leaguer. In no way was he awed by having to pitch at Coors Field, going 4-2, 4.91 in nine starts in the thin air. Overall, the Rockies went 9-5 in the 14 games he started.

Pitching, Defense & Hitting

Castillo mixes a fastball, curveball and changeup. His stuff is very ordinary, but he has won when he can locate his pitches. He'll be a No. 5 starter at best for most clubs, and he's susceptible to big innings. He's adequate defensively and can shut down the running game. In 1997, just 13 of 28 basestealers were successful against him. His dismal hitting ability often draws jokes, but former Cubs teammate Brian McRae wasn't laughing when he had to give Castillo a BMW he had offered if the pitcher ever homered in batting practice.

1998 Outlook

A free agent, Castillo would give Colorado added depth in the rotation if he re-signs. He's a veteran hand who molds well with a staff of young pitchers, and he can eat plenty of innings.

Darren Holmes

Position: RP/SP
Bats: R **Throws:** R
Ht: 6' 0" **Wt:** 202

Opening Day Age: 31
Born: 4/25/66 in
Asheville, NC
ML Seasons: 8

Overall Statistics

	W	L	Pct.	ERA	G	GS	Sv	IP	H	BB	SO	HR	Ratio
1997	9	2	.818	5.34	42	6	3	89.1	113	36	70	12	1.67
Career	28	22	.560	4.33	358	6	55	464.0	481	185	406	42	1.44

1997 Situational Stats

	W	L	ERA	Sv	IP		AB	H	HR	RBI	Avg
Home	5	1	5.03	2	48.1	LHB	179	61	3	27	.341
Road	4	1	5.71	1	41.0	RHB	181	52	9	29	.287
First Half	3	1	4.08	1	57.1	Sc Pos	106	28	2	41	.264
Scnd Half	6	1	7.59	2	32.0	Clutch	78	29	3	18	.372

1997 Season

During spring training, Darren Holmes was a candidate for the fifth spot in the Colorado rotation. Instead he found himself in the bullpen, where he has spent most of his major league career. Then he went out and allowed 113 hits and 12 homers in 89⅓ innings, troubling numbers for a man whose job is to put out fires. The year proved to be a baffling setback for a pitcher who had fashioned ERAs under 4.00 in two prior seasons for the Rockies.

Pitching, Defense & Hitting

Holmes has an above-average curveball that he mixes with a decent fastball, slider and changeup. When he has command of his curve and can spot it where he wants, he can strike people out in bunches. Too often, however, he was spotting it over the plate. He's one of the poorer defensive pitchers around and doesn't do much to hold runners. Holmes finally got the first hits and the first homer of his eight-year big league career in 1997.

1998 Outlook

Holmes is a free agent and the Rockies likely won't re-sign him. As a former closer, there's no reason he can't do the job as a setup man.

Mark Hutton

Position: RP
Bats: R **Throws:** R
Ht: 6' 6" **Wt:** 240

Opening Day Age: 28
Born: 2/6/70 in
Adelaide, Australia
ML Seasons: 4

Overall Statistics

	W	L	Pct.	ERA	G	GS	Sv	IP	H	BB	SO	HR	Ratio
1997	3	2	.600	4.48	40	1	0	60.1	72	26	39	10	1.62
Career	9	6	.600	4.48	74	16	0	172.2	179	79	108	21	1.49

1997 Situational Stats

	W	L	ERA	Sv	IP		AB	H	HR	RBI	Avg
Home	3	2	6.31	0	35.2	LHB	90	23	2	12	.256
Road	0	0	1.82	0	24.2	RHB	139	49	8	26	.353
First Half	3	1	3.70	0	41.1	Sc Pos	64	18	4	30	.281
Scnd Half	0	1	6.16	0	19.0	Clutch	56	19	5	13	.339

1997 Season

Mark Hutton is getting used to the routine, and it's a troubling one. The Marlins, destined for a World Series title, traded him to Colorado in late July for infielder Craig Counsell. In the summer of 1996, Hutton thought he had survived the trading deadline and would stay with the Yankees, but missed out on a championship there when he was dealt to Florida. All of this movement has done little to help him realize his potential.

Pitching, Defense & Hitting

Hutton is a power pitcher who makes good use of his 6-foot-6 frame. He throws two different fastballs, one that sinks and one that rises. He can throw harder than 90 MPH, but his velocity was below that level with the Rockies. He also throws a slider and an occasional changeup. He has yet to prove himself as a solid, instinctive fielder and is very easy to run on, but the man does like to hit. He owns a career .273 average and a career .409 slugging percentage.

1998 Outlook

Hutton has been a starter, but figures to fit into long relief for the Rockies. Colorado didn't use him much, but he has the kind of hidden talent who could blossom in a place where he gets regular opportunities.

Curt Leskanic

Position: RP
Bats: R **Throws:** R
Ht: 6' 0" **Wt:** 180

Opening Day Age: 29
Born: 4/2/68 in Homestead, PA
ML Seasons: 5
Pronunciation: les-CAN-ik

Overall Statistics

	W	L	Pct.	ERA	G	GS	Sv	IP	H	BB	SO	HR	Ratio
1997	4	0	1.000	5.55	55	0	2	58.1	59	24	53	8	1.42
Career	19	14	.576	5.00	227	11	18	309.1	310	132	283	36	1.43

1997 Situational Stats

	W	L	ERA	Sv	IP		AB	H	HR	RBI	Avg
Home	3	0	5.70	2	30.0	LHB	93	29	4	20	.312
Road	1	0	5.40	0	28.1	RHB	125	30	4	22	.240
First Half	1	0	5.95	1	19.2	Sc Pos	63	21	3	30	.333
Scnd Half	3	0	5.35	1	38.2	Clutch	64	15	3	13	.234

1997 Season

After leading the NL with 76 appearances in 1995, Curt Leskanic had a disappointing encore and then began 1997 on the DL with shoulder problems. He had shoulder and elbow surgery in the offseason. It took a while for things to come around for the five-year veteran, but he finished the season with a flourish, logging 14 straight scoreless outings.

Pitching, Defense & Hitting

Leskanic's improvement in arm strength and general physical condition is important because he needs his fastball to be in the mid-90s. The ball sinks when he reaches that kind of velocity. As a result, he records a high number of groundouts. His slider is known for biting at the last minute. Leskanic fields bunts well and doesn't embarrass himself when he's batting. He has a delivery that can be slow to the plate, but basestealers managed just two steals in five attempts against him in 1997.

1998 Outlook

Leskanic's strong finish showed that he can return to the form that made him an effective setup man and, at one point, Colorado's closer. Middle relievers are probably more important to the Rockies than any other team because of the high scores that prevail at Coors Field.

Jeff Reed

Position: C
Bats: L **Throws:** R
Ht: 6' 2" **Wt:** 190

Opening Day Age: 35
Born: 11/12/62 in Joliet, IL
ML Seasons: 14

Overall Statistics

	G	AB	R	H	D	T	HR	RBI	SB	BB	SO	Avg	OBP	Slg
1997	90	256	43	76	10	0	17	47	2	35	55	.297	.386	.535
Career	928	2357	213	584	101	7	45	231	6	265	383	.248	.324	.354

1997 Situational Stats

	AB	H	HR	RBI	Avg		AB	H	HR	RBI	Avg
Home	132	44	9	31	.333	LHP	29	5	0	0	.172
Road	124	32	8	16	.258	RHP	227	71	17	47	.313
First Half	125	39	7	23	.312	Sc Pos	64	19	5	30	.297
Scnd Half	131	37	10	24	.282	Clutch	39	13	3	8	.333

1997 Season

Jeff Reed is traditionally an offensive catcher, and 1997 saw him turn in another fine performance at the plate. In late August when the Rockies were making a run to get back into the NL West race, he had one stretch where he went 6-for-11 (.545) in three starts. Reed stays in the big leagues not only for his occasional offensive firepower, however, but also because of the way he handles pitchers.

Hitting, Baserunning & Defense

Reed has a compact swing and has developed an ability to drive the ball to the opposite field, though he's traditionally a pull hitter. There's no way to argue with some outstanding numbers: a .297 average, 17 home runs and 47 RBI despite sharing the job with Kirt Manwaring. He makes mistakes on defense that veterans shouldn't make and doesn't block balls exceptionally well. His arm is average. Forget about speed. Reed has just six career steals in 14 major league seasons.

1998 Outlook

Reed declared free agency, then re-signed with the Rockies. He's the kind of veteran who's in demand not only for his professionalism but also for his willingness to do what's asked, whether it's being the No. 1 catcher or serving as the lefthanded half of a platoon.

Colorado Rockies

<table>
<tr><td colspan="2">

Steve Reed

</td><td colspan="2">

Kevin Ritz

</td></tr>
</table>

Position: RP
Bats: R **Throws:** R
Ht: 6' 2" **Wt:** 212

Opening Day Age: 32
Born: 3/11/66 in Los Angeles, CA
ML Seasons: 6

Position: SP
Bats: R **Throws:** R
Ht: 6' 4" **Wt:** 222

Opening Day Age: 32
Born: 6/8/65 in Eatonstown, NJ
ML Seasons: 8

Overall Statistics

	W	L	Pct.	ERA	G	GS	Sv	IP	H	BB	SO	HR	Ratio
1997	4	6	.400	4.04	63	0	6	62.1	49	27	43	10	1.22
Career	26	18	.591	3.62	347	0	15	385.1	348	126	286	53	1.23

1997 Situational Stats

	W	L	ERA	Sv	IP		AB	H	HR	RBI	Avg
Home	1	3	3.45	4	31.1	LHB	100	21	5	10	.210
Road	3	3	4.65	2	31.0	RHB	124	28	5	23	.226
First Half	1	3	5.00	6	36.0	Sc Pos	60	12	0	20	.200
Scnd Half	3	3	2.73	0	26.1	Clutch	112	31	8	26	.277

Overall Statistics

	W	L	Pct.	ERA	G	GS	Sv	IP	H	BB	SO	HR	Ratio
1997	6	8	.429	5.87	18	18	0	107.1	142	46	56	16	1.75
Career	45	54	.455	5.28	149	128	2	744.1	831	375	459	68	1.62

1997 Situational Stats

	W	L	ERA	Sv	IP		AB	H	HR	RBI	Avg
Home	2	4	7.50	0	48.0	LHB	237	85	11	41	.359
Road	4	4	4.55	0	59.1	RHB	193	57	5	23	.295
First Half	6	8	5.87	0	107.1	Sc Pos	117	39	7	52	.333
Scnd Half	0	0		0	0.0	Clutch	2	1	0	1	.500

1997 Season

Steve Reed's control was more of a problem in 1997 than it had been in the past, especially early the season. Reed, whose success depends on his ability to hit spots, had 12 walks in his first 18 2/3 innings. He returned to form and once again was able to give the Rockies lots of innings.

Pitching, Defense & Hitting

Reed is the Colorado franchise's all-time leader in appearances. His durability has made him worthwhile. He's most effective when throwing from a submarine angle, and tends to get hit harder when he uses an overhand delivery. His fastball has more sink than speed, and he keeps hitters off balance with a decent slider and a changeup. He's an average fielder and hasn't hurt the club when it comes to holding runners. As a setup man, his plate appearances are few and far between.

1998 Outlook

Reed may be overpricing himself for a setup man. He has had success, especially when you consider his home park, but made $1.1 million plus $100,000 in incentives in 1997. That's a lot of money for someone in his role, and it may make the Rockies think about his long-term role with the organization.

1997 Season

Arm troubles precluded Kevin Ritz from maintaining his role as the ace of the Colorado rotation. He made 18 appearances before having shoulder surgery to repair a torn right labrum.

Pitching, Defense & Hitting

Ritz' best pitch is a slider, and he can throw a fastball in the high 80s. His challenge is mastering control of his changeup, which he likes to use as a sinker. Wildness and long counts continue to dog him. Ritz hasn't committed an error since 1991, a total of 177 chances, but he doesn't possess a good pickoff move. He gave up more than a steal per game in 1997. Ritz is a good bunter and had been a good hitter by pitchers' standards before going 2-for-35 last season. The shoulder problems may have hindered him.

1998 Outlook

Ritz' recovery from surgery is on course. His healthy return would be a huge bonus for a staff that needs a lot of things to come together for the Rockies to be competitive. If Roger Bailey can prove his success was no fluke and Pedro Astacio continues to pitch well, then the burden on Ritz becomes diminished.

Bruce Ruffin

Position: RP
Bats: B **Throws:** L
Ht: 6' 2" **Wt:** 215

Opening Day Age: 34
Born: 10/4/63 in Lubbock, TX
ML Seasons: 12

Overall Statistics

	W	L	Pct.	ERA	G	GS	Sv	IP	H	BB	SO	HR	Ratio
1997	0	2	.000	5.32	23	0	7	22.0	18	18	31	3	1.64
Career	60	82	.423	4.19	469	152	63	1268.0	1345	565	843	92	1.51

1997 Situational Stats

	W	L	ERA	Sv	IP		AB	H	HR	RBI	Avg
Home	0	0	3.38	2	10.2	LHB	27	8	1	9	.296
Road	0	2	7.15	5	11.1	RHB	55	10	2	7	.182
First Half	0	2	5.32	7	22.0	Sc Pos	22	5	1	13	.227
Scnd Half	0	0		0	0.0	Clutch	33	6	0	8	.182

1997 Season

The Rockies were hard-pressed to explain Bruce Ruffin's lack of control in 1997. He developed a mental block that prevented him from finding the strike zone. It cost him the closer's job, and he went to the minors to work it out. He returned in mid-June, but then an elbow injury landed him on the disabled list. He never returned.

Pitching, Defense & Hitting

In late May Ruffin went to Double-A New Haven, where he had an established relationship with pitching coach Jim Wright. Wright helped him regain the slider that's effective against righthanders, his sinking fastball and his cut fastball. The cutter showed a little more oomph once Ruffin returned to the Colorado 'pen, until arm troubles surfaced. Ruffin is not considered a major defensive liability, but a slow delivery to the plate means opposing runners get too much of a jump. Ruffin is one of the team's weakest-hitting pitchers.

1998 Outlook

Ruffin is eligible for free agency. The Rockies took steps to shore up their bullpen, which helped them make an impressive run down the stretch. That should take some pressure off Ruffin, who will be among several Colorado pitchers coming back from surgery.

Jamey Wright

Position: SP
Bats: R **Throws:** R
Ht: 6' 5" **Wt:** 203

Opening Day Age: 23
Born: 12/24/74 in Oklahoma City, OK
ML Seasons: 2

Overall Statistics

	W	L	Pct.	ERA	G	GS	Sv	IP	H	BB	SO	HR	Ratio
1997	8	12	.400	6.25	26	26	0	149.2	198	71	59	19	1.80
Career	12	16	.429	5.75	42	41	0	241.0	303	112	104	27	1.72

1997 Situational Stats

	W	L	ERA	Sv	IP		AB	H	HR	RBI	Avg
Home	5	7	7.67	0	88.0	LHB	254	100	8	52	.394
Road	3	5	4.23	0	61.2	RHB	351	98	11	47	.279
First Half	4	5	8.17	0	61.2	Sc Pos	167	51	3	75	.305
Scnd Half	4	7	4.91	0	88.0	Clutch	31	11	1	6	.355

1997 Season

In late April, Jamey Wright went up against the Marlins' Kevin Brown and came away with a 7-3 win. He seemed to be on his way in his first full big league season, but he won only once more before the All-Star break, which he entered with an 8.17 ERA. He rebounded in the second half, showing a good deal of composure. He still allowed too many walks and too often pitched up in hitters' power areas for the Rockies' satisfaction, however.

Pitching, Defense & Hitting

Wright throws a two-seam fastball that tops 90 MPH and has good sinking action. When he's on, he has a good breaking ball as well. He has a fluid motion but must work on his location and consistency. He has allowed more walks than strikeouts as a major leaguer and needs a better changeup to help him cope with the difficult pitching environment at home. Wright is athletic enough to field his position well, but falls toward first as he finishes his delivery. He has an excellent pickoff move and is the first to admit he has a horrid swing.

1998 Outlook

The Rockies felt they had no choice but to rush Wright to the big leagues in July 1996. Since then he has grown up mentally, hanging in games where he gives up runs.

Robbie Beckett (**Pos**: LHP, **Age**: 25)

	W	L	Pct.	ERA	G	GS	Sv	IP	H	BB	SO	HR	Ratio
1997	0	0	-	5.40	2	0	0	1.2	1	1	2	0	1.20
Career	0	0	-	11.57	7	0	0	7.0	7	10	8	3	2.43

Beckett has had phenomenal strikeout numbers throughout his minor league career—but his control problems have completely undermined his progress along the way. He could dominate if he finds the strike zone. 1998 Outlook: C

John Burke (**Pos**: RHP, **Age**: 28)

	W	L	Pct.	ERA	G	GS	Sv	IP	H	BB	SO	HR	Ratio
1997	2	5	.286	6.56	17	9	0	59.0	83	26	39	13	1.85
Career	4	6	.400	6.75	28	9	0	74.2	104	33	58	16	1.83

Burke was sent down to the minors for good in July after his appearances turned into home-run derbies; he surrendered 13 longballs in only 59 innings. He fell apart at Triple-A, so his future is iffy. 1998 Outlook: C

Darnell Coles (**Pos**: 3B, **Age**: 35, **Bats**: R)

	G	AB	R	H	D	T	HR	RBI	SB	BB	SO	Avg	OBP	Slg
1997	21	22	1	7	1	0	1	2	0	0	6	.318	.348	.500
Career	957	2891	333	709	142	14	75	368	20	237	445	.245	.307	.382

Coles, who inexplicably has managed to carve out a 14-year career as an error-prone infielder with no power *or* plate discipline, signed to play in Japan last May. Expect a trade embargo any day now. 1998 Outlook: D

Mike DeJean (**Pos**: RHP, **Age**: 27)

	W	L	Pct.	ERA	G	GS	Sv	IP	H	BB	SO	HR	Ratio
1997	5	0	1.000	3.99	55	0	2	67.2	74	24	38	4	1.45
Career	5	0	1.000	3.99	55	0	2	67.2	74	24	38	4	1.45

DeJean pitched decently in 55 games for the Rockies after being called up in May. He rebounded from mid-season elbow problems to post a 2.74 ERA in August/September. 1998 Outlook: A

Rene Gonzales (**Pos**: 3B, **Age**: 36, **Bats**: R)

	G	AB	R	H	D	T	HR	RBI	SB	BB	SO	Avg	OBP	Slg
1997	2	2	0	1	0	0	0	1	0	0	0	.500	.500	.500
Career	705	1539	185	368	59	4	19	136	23	161	230	.239	.315	.320

Gonzales surfaced in Septmember to notch two pinch-hitting appearances with the Rockies. He's only had 135 at-bats in the last four seasons combined. His career looks over at age 36. 1998 Outlook: D

Bobby M. Jones (**Pos**: LHP, **Age**: 25)

	W	L	Pct.	ERA	G	GS	Sv	IP	H	BB	SO	HR	Ratio
1997	1	1	.500	8.38	4	4	0	19.1	30	12	5	2	2.17
Career	1	1	.500	8.38	4	4	0	19.1	30	12	5	2	2.17

The "other" Bobby Jones wasn't nearly as successful as his Met counterpart. Jones spent three weeks in the majors before Rockies manager Don Baylor gave him the hook. His future is questionable. 1998 Outlook: C

Jeff McCurry (**Pos**: RHP, **Age**: 28)

	W	L	Pct.	ERA	G	GS	Sv	IP	H	BB	SO	HR	Ratio
1997	1	4	.200	4.43	33	0	0	40.2	43	20	19	7	1.55
Career	2	8	.200	5.40	90	0	1	105.0	134	52	46	19	1.77

McCurry's strikeout/walk ratio was frightening (19/20), but he didn't pitch too badly in three stints with Colorado last season. Still, there's not much of a reason why he'll see a lot of action in '98. 1998 Outlook: C

Nate Minchey (**Pos**: RHP, **Age**: 28)

	W	L	Pct.	ERA	G	GS	Sv	IP	H	BB	SO	HR	Ratio
1997	0	0	-	13.50	2	0	0	2.0	5	1	1	0	3.00
Career	3	7	.300	6.75	15	12	0	64.0	100	28	38	7	2.00

After a decent season at Triple-A Colorado Springs, Minchey made two appearances near the end of the season and was shelled. He has now surrendered 100 hits in 64 major league innings. Not good. 1998 Outlook: C

Mike Munoz (**Pos**: LHP, **Age**: 32)

	W	L	Pct.	ERA	G	GS	Sv	IP	H	BB	SO	HR	Ratio
1997	3	3	.500	4.53	64	0	2	45.2	52	13	26	4	1.42
Career	14	16	.467	5.24	350	0	7	266.1	292	137	188	26	1.61

Munoz has averaged nearly 60 apperances a year out of the Rockies bullpen over the last four seasons. . . to the delight of Colorado opponents. If he weren't a southpaw, he'd have been finished long ago. 1998 Outlook: B

Harvey Pulliam (**Pos**: LF, **Age**: 30, **Bats**: R)

	G	AB	R	H	D	T	HR	RBI	SB	BB	SO	Avg	OBP	Slg
1997	59	67	15	19	3	0	3	9	0	5	15	.284	.333	.463
Career	123	187	31	49	11	0	8	22	0	13	49	.262	.313	.449

Called up to the majors in May, Pulliam provided the Rockies with outfield help for the remainder of the season. They traded him to Arizona for lefthander Chuck McElroy after the expansion draft. 1998 Outlook: B

Brian Raabe (**Pos**: 2B, **Age**: 30, **Bats**: R)

	G	AB	R	H	D	T	HR	RBI	SB	BB	SO	Avg	OBP	Slg
1997	4	6	0	1	0	0	0	0	0	1	3	.167	.286	.167
Career	17	29	4	6	0	0	0	2	0	2	4	.207	.250	.207

Acquired from Seattle in a late-season trade, Raabe has produced monster numbers in the minors but has just 29 career at-bats in the majors at age 30. 1998 Outlook: C

Mark Thompson (**Pos**: RHP, **Age**: 26)

	W	L	Pct.	ERA	G	GS	Sv	IP	H	BB	SO	HR	Ratio
1997	3	3	.500	7.89	6	6	0	29.2	40	13	9	8	1.79
Career	15	18	.455	5.97	63	41	0	259.1	318	117	143	42	1.68

Thompson's season ended in May after suffering a slight" rotator-cuff tear. His strikeout rates weren't good (4.96 K per 9 IP) *before* the injury, and it's hard to imagine they'll be better in '98. 1998 Outlook: C

John Vander Wal (Pos: RF, Age: 31, Bats: L)

	G	AB	R	H	D	T	HR	RBI	SB	BB	SO	Avg	OBP	Slg
1997	76	92	7	16	2	0	1	11	1	10	33	.174	.255	.228
Career	608	943	113	230	38	11	26	136	15	113	209	.244	.324	.390

Once again Colorado's pinch-hitting specialist, Vander Wal struggled heavily with the bat and was sent down to the minors on July 31. Coming off a poor season at age 31, his future is in doubt. 1998 Outlook: C

Colorado Rockies Minor League Prospects

Organization Overview:

Since their inception, the Rockies have focused on pitching because they figured it always would be easy to attract hitters to Coors Field. Interestingly, they've had more success developing position players. Neifi Perez will start at shortstop in Colorado in 1998, and his double-play partner could be fellow homegrown product Jason Bates. Future batting champion Todd Helton will be in the lineup at first base, and the Rockies also signed and developed Marlins World Series hero Craig Counsell. Three-fifths of their rotation at the end of 1997 were Colorado draftees—Roger Bailey, John Thomson and Jamey Wright—but they haven't had the same kind of impact. Florida gets credit for putting together a deep farm system so quickly, and the Rockies have done nearly as well without nearly as much fanfare.

Mark Brownson

Position: P | **Opening Day Age:** 22
Bats: L **Throws:** R | **Born:** 6/17/75 in West
Ht: 6' 2" **Wt:** 175 | Palm Beach, FL

Recent Statistics

	W	L	ERA	G	GS	Sv	IP	H	R	BB	SO	HR
96 AA New Haven	8	13	3.50	37	19	3	144.0	141	73	43	155	10
97 AA New Haven	10	9	4.19	29	29	0	184.2	172	101	55	170	24

Brownson has delighted the Rockies with his increased velocity since signing as a 30th-round draft-and-follow out of Palm Beach (Fla.) Community College in 1994. He threw 87-88 MPH when he was drafted, and now throws comfortably at 91-93 and can touch 95. He also throws a curveball, slider and changeup, and has exhibited fine command. He split time between starting and relieving until 1997, when Colorado put him in the rotation full-time at Double-A New Haven. He'll head to Triple-A Colorado Springs, and with the way the Rockies use pitchers he could get a call sometime during the season.

Angel Echevarria

Position: OF | **Opening Day Age:** 26
Bats: R **Throws:** R | **Born:** 5/25/71 in
Ht: 6' 4" **Wt:** 215 | Bridgeport, CT

Recent Statistics

	G	AB	R	H	D	T	HR	RBI	SB	BB	SO	AVG
97 AAA Colo Sprngs	77	295	59	95	24	0	13	80	6	28	47	.322
97 NL Colorado	15	20	4	5	2	0	0	0	0	2	5	.250
97 MLE	77	296	46	96	23	0	14	63	4	22	46	.324

Echevarria may be 26, but he has plenty of hits and some power in his bat. He hits line drives and though he doesn't loft a lot of balls, he still could hit 15-20 homers per year. A 17th-round pick out of Rutgers in 1992, he does equal damage to fastballs, breaking balls and changeups. He has seen time in left and right field, and also gotten a look at first base. He probably won't be a starter, but he could serve Colorado as a righthanded pinch hitter who can play three positions.

Derrick Gibson

Position: OF | **Opening Day Age:** 23
Bats: R **Throws:** R | **Born:** 2/5/75 in Winter
Ht: 6' 2" **Wt:** 238 | Haven, FL

Recent Statistics

	G	AB	R	H	D	T	HR	RBI	SB	BB	SO	AVG
96 AA New Haven	122	449	58	115	21	4	15	62	3	31	125	.256
97 AA New Haven	119	461	91	146	24	2	23	75	20	36	100	.317
97 AAA Colo Sprngs	21	78	14	33	7	0	3	12	0	5	9	.423
97 MLE	140	568	108	208	33	2	37	89	16	35	109	.366

A star linebacker who was headed to Auburn, Gibson didn't qualify academically and signed with the Rockies as a 13th-round pick in 1993. He has as much power as anyone in the minors and most anyone in the majors, and uses the John Daly philosophy of "grip it and rip it." It's difficult to say which is more scary, Gibson's tape-measure shots or his strikeout/walk ratio. His 109-41 ratio in 1997 easily was the *best* of his career. Rushed to Double-A in 1996, he settled in there much better last season. His left-field defense, his speed and his arm are all average. If he can close the holes in his swing, Gibson has the power and the major league ballpark (Coors Field) to one day make a run at Roger Maris. That may be a stretch, but Gibson is that strong.

Ben Petrick

Position: C | **Opening Day Age:** 20
Bats: R **Throws:** R | **Born:** 4/7/77 in Salem,
Ht: 6' 0" **Wt:** 195 | OR

Recent Statistics

	G	AB	R	H	D	T	HR	RBI	SB	BB	SO	AVG
96 A Asheville	122	446	74	105	24	2	14	52	19	75	98	.235
97 A Salem	121	412	68	102	23	3	15	56	30	62	100	.248

Look beyond Petrick's .248 batting average and you'll see a very successful season for a 19-year-old catcher in the high Class-A Carolina League. A 1995 second-round pick, he had 41 extra-base hits (including 15 homers), 62 walks and 30 stolen bases. He has very good speed for a catcher, and his agility allows him to excel at blocking pitches. His best tool is his above-average arm. He's at least two years away, but eventually will provide Jeff Reed offense and Kirt Manwaring defense.

Mike Saipe

Position: P **Opening Day Age:** 24
Bats: R **Throws:** R **Born:** 9/10/73 in San
Ht: 6' 1" **Wt:** 190 Diego, CA

Recent Statistics

	W	L	ERA	G	GS	Sv	IP	H	R	BB	SO	HR
96 AA New Haven	10	7	3.07	32	19	3	138.0	114	53	42	126	12
97 AA New Haven	8	5	3.10	19	19	0	136.2	127	57	29	123	18
97 AAA Colo Sprngs	4	3	5.52	10	10	0	60.1	74	42	24	40	10

A 1994 12th-round pick out of the University of San Diego, Saipe has a dominant curveball and durability working for him. His breaking ball was voted the best in the Eastern League by the managers and he led the minors in innings. His fastball is below average at 87 MPH, but he mixes in changeups and succeeds with command. He'll be tested in 1998 with a full year at Triple-A Colorado Springs, which like Coors Field helps hitters and hurts breaking balls. He'll get crushed if his curve isn't effective at high altitude, and that's what happened in 1997.

Steve Shoemaker

Position: P **Opening Day Age:** 25
Bats: L **Throws:** R **Born:** 2/3/73 in
Ht: 6' 1" **Wt:** 195 Phoenixville, PA

Recent Statistics

	W	L	ERA	G	GS	Sv	IP	H	R	BB	SO	HR
96 A Salem	2	7	4.69	25	13	1	86.1	63	49	63	105	6
97 A Salem	3	3	2.77	9	9	0	52.0	31	21	25	76	3
97 AA New Haven	6	4	3.02	14	14	0	95.1	64	36	53	111	6
97 AAA Colo Sprngs	1	1	8.41	5	4	0	20.1	23	19	17	27	5

The Rockies acquired Shoemaker, a 1994 fourth-round pick out of the University of Alabama, from the Yankees in a December 1995 trade for Joe Girardi. Shoemaker had a so-so year at high Class-A Salem in 1996 before blossoming in 1997. He went from Salem to Triple-A, striking out more than a batter per inning at each level. He throws a 93-95 MPH fastball, and took off once he began to refine his curveball and changeup. If his offspeed pitches don't continue to improve, he has the fastball to be a closer. The pounding he took in Colorado Springs showed that he needs a full season there in 1998.

Mike Vavrek

Position: P **Opening Day Age:** 23
Bats: L **Throws:** L **Born:** 4/23/74 in
Ht: 6' 2" **Wt:** 185 Winfield, IL

Recent Statistics

	W	L	ERA	G	GS	Sv	IP	H	R	BB	SO	HR
96 A Salem	10	8	4.87	26	25	0	149.2	167	92	59	103	15
97 A Salem	2	2	2.15	10	9	0	62.2	55	21	18	48	3
97 AA New Haven	12	3	2.57	17	17	0	122.2	94	38	34	101	7

Vavrek is a proven winner, never posting a losing record and going a combined 29-17 since signing as a fifth-round pick out of Lewis (Ill.) University in 1995. He won 12 straight decisions in 1997, though his stuff isn't overpowering. He's your basic cunning lefthander. His fastball is slightly below average, but he cuts it and makes it sink. He throws strikes with his full repertoire, which also includes an above-average changeup and a slider. He challenges hitters, pitching inside even against righthanders. That may just be the mindset needed to succeed in Coors Field, and he's about a year away from finding out.

Edgard Velazquez

Position: OF **Opening Day Age:** 22
Bats: R **Throws:** R **Born:** 12/15/75 in
Ht: 6' 0" **Wt:** 170 Santurce, PR

Recent Statistics

	G	AB	R	H	D	T	HR	RBI	SB	BB	SO	AVG
96 AA New Haven	132	486	72	141	29	4	19	62	6	53	114	.290
97 AAA Colo Sprngs	120	438	70	123	24	10	17	73	6	34	119	.281
97 MLE	120	441	55	126	23	9	18	58	4	27	118	.286

Scouts love to compare Puerto Rican outfield prospects to Roberto Clemente, and that's true even more so in Velazquez' case because he's the nephew of the Hall of Famer. A 1994 10th-round pick, he has a Clemente-like right-field arm and the range to play center field. His offensive potential is nearly as exciting, providing he develops some plate discipline. He has a lightning-quick bat that could do a lot of damage in Coors Field. He has good speed, making him a five-tool player, but is tentative on the bases and isn't a threat to steal. Velazquez could spend another year at Triple-A learning to draw walks.

Others to Watch

Righthander **Heath Bost** reached Triple-A at age 22. He has an above-average fastball and good command, but his other pitches need work. . . Righthander **Shawn Chacon's** fastball has gone from 89-91 MPH to 93-96 since he signed. Just 19, he also has an above-average curveball and a decent change. . . Righthander **Lariel Gonzales**, 21, has the best power arm in the system. He throws 92-97 MPH with a tough splitter. He was a setup man at Salem in 1997 and may be introduced to closing this year. . . Outfielder **Bernard Hutchison**, 23, ranked second in the minors with 81 steals last year. But he also hit .232 in Class-A and offers little but speed. . . Lefthander **Mike Kusiewicz** reached Double-A at age 20. His fastball lacks velocity but has tremendous movement. The Rockies think he'll eventually reach 88-89 MPH, which will make him tough. He already throws four pitches for strikes. . . Righthander **Scott Randall** literally has no-hit stuff, taking part in three such gems in the last two seasons. The 22 year old throws 88-90 MPH with excellent movement and has a good curve.

Jim Leyland

1997 Season

Jim Leyland did it all for Florida. He recognized after the All-Star break that his players were coming to the ballpark flat, looking as if they were about to face a root canal instead of a pennant race. He made them see that contesting for the National League pennant is a privilege. He kept his team believing in itself during the National League Championship Series, even though his top starter (Kevin Brown) had a viral infection and his No. 2 man (Alex Fernandez) tore a rotator cuff. At the time, Leyland was battling walking pneumonia. After 12 years of managing in the majors and three failed trips to the NLCS with the Pirates, Leyland finally reached the World Series and won it all.

Offense

Leyland plays it straight on offense. He was typical of NL managers in most regards. He didn't bunt, steal, hit-and-run or platoon much more or less than the average skipper. He preferred to stand back and not tinker with an offense that had the capacity to explode, even if it finished eighth in the league in scoring. In Pittsburgh and in Florida, he has adapted to the talent around him.

Pitching & Defense

Leyland shows patience and listens to his pitchers. When Livan Hernandez was blowing the Braves away in Game 5 of the NLCS, he left the youngster in to finish the game. When Brown said he had something left in Game 6, Leyland left him in. He made good use of his first true closer, Robb Nen, and spread the work around a deep bullpen to keep the starters and relievers fresh. A strict believer in fundamentals, Leyland loves good defense. That said, he didn't mind putting Bobby Bonilla at third base to boost the lineup.

1998 Outlook

Some thought that Leyland might not return to the Marlins. His contract has an escape clause allowing him to leave if ownership changes, and Wayne Huizenga has put the club up for sale. But Leyland put all the rumors to rest shortly after the Series, announcing that he would be back. Florida's off-season cost-cutting may make him wish he hadn't.

Born: 12/15/44 in Pittsburgh, PA

Playing Experience: No major league experience

Managerial Experience: 12 seasons

Manager Statistics

Year	Team, Lg	W	L	Pct	GB	Finish
1997	Florida, NL	92	70	.568	9.0	2nd East
12 Seasons		943	933	.503	—	—

1997 Starting Pitchers by Days Rest

	≤3	4	5	6+
Marlins Starts	1	90	42	21
Marlins ERA	3.60	3.51	4.58	3.60
NL Avg Starts	3	90	38	22
NL ERA	4.23	4.05	4.27	4.52

1997 Situational Stats

	Jim Leyland	NL Average
Hit & Run Success %	25.3	36.4
Stolen Base Success %	66.5	68.4
Platoon Pct.	55.1	56.3
Defensive Subs	31	26
High-Pitch Outings	18	12
Quick/Slow Hooks	21/12	18/10
Sacrifice Attempts	91	96

1997 Rankings (National League)

⇒ 1st in first batter platoon percentage (64.4%)
⇒ 2nd in least caught steals of third base (4), least caught steals of home plate (1) and quick hooks (21)
⇒ 3rd in starts with over 120 pitches (18)

Moises Alou

1997 Season

Moises Alou took his father's advice in Montreal and left the team his dad managed for better money with a franchise that would spend the money to compete. He then went out and proved himself a worthwhile investment. Alou set a career high with 23 home runs and 115 RBI, enjoying his best year since he hit .339 in 1994. He gave the Marlins 150 solid games and took the offensive load off the struggling Gary Sheffield. After slumping in the first two rounds of the playoffs, Alou exploded in the World Series with three homers and nine RBI.

Hitting

Alou is an experienced hitter who can hit all pitches. He's especially dangerous when high fastballs come his way, because he turns on them and drives them to or over the fence. He's more of a doubles hitter than a home run hitter, 1997 notwithstanding. Pitchers are finding that the best way to handle him is to keep feeding him a steady diet of offspeed pitches. Even so, he's still capable of making adjustments from pitch to pitch and his plate discipline was much improved last season. He'll figure out the pitching pattern, then go on the attack.

Baserunning & Defense

Alou doesn't make a lot of baserunning mistakes. He can occasionally steal a base, but he's not generally considered a big threat. Defensively, Alou is a strength. He reads balls well off the bat and gets good jumps. His arm is rather average, however, and he posted just four assists last season. Normally a left fielder, he subbed in center when Devon White was injured.

1998 Outlook

In the first of many salary-slashing moves, Florida traded Alou to Houston for two minor league pitchers. He'll start in left field for the Astros. There have been concerns that he's losing some of his bat speed, though his 1997 production should quell speculation that his skills are slipping.

Position: LF/CF/RF
Bats: R **Throws:** R
Ht: 6' 3" **Wt:** 195

Opening Day Age: 31
Born: 7/3/66 in Atlanta, GA
ML Seasons: 7
Pronunciation: MOY-sezz ah-LOO

Florida Marlins

Overall Statistics

	G	AB	R	H	D	T	HR	RBI	SB	BB	SO	Avg	OBP	Slg
1997	150	538	88	157	29	5	23	115	9	70	85	.292	.373	.493
Career	760	2687	431	784	167	21	107	488	62	253	389	.292	.354	.489

Where He Hits the Ball

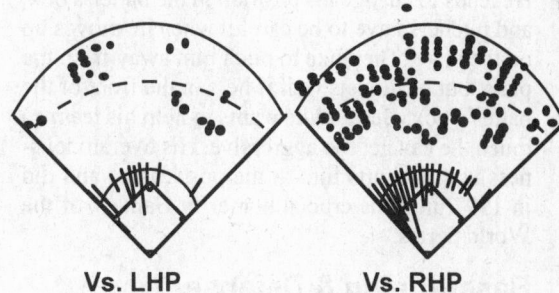

Vs. LHP   **Vs. RHP**

1997 Situational Stats

	AB	H	HR	RBI	Avg		AB	H	HR	RBI	Avg
Home	261	72	12	62	.276	LHP	97	33	5	33	.340
Road	277	85	11	53	.307	RHP	441	124	18	82	.281
First Half	297	87	9	65	.293	Sc Pos	155	51	7	90	.329
Scnd Half	241	70	14	50	.290	Clutch	95	24	2	14	.253

1997 Rankings (National League)

⇒ 8th in batting average with the bases loaded (.444), batting average on the road and errors in left field (3)
⇒ 9th in RBI
⇒ Led the Marlins in home runs, triples, total bases (265), RBI, slugging percentage, batting average with runners in scoring position, batting average with the bases loaded (.444), batting average vs. righthanded pitchers, slugging percentage vs. righthanded pitchers (.463), batting average on the road, highest percentage of swings put into play (45.2%) and highest percentage of extra bases taken as a runner (46.3%)

Bobby Bonilla

1997 Season

Bobby Bonilla signed as a free agent and had an outstanding year, consistently getting big hits and providing a power presence in the Florida lineup. Manager Jim Leyland knew it was a risk putting Bonilla at third base, but Bonilla didn't embarrass himself. Though his home-run production was down, his .468 slugging percentage was a reasonable tradeoff for his 94 strikeouts. Bonilla loves playing for Leyland, especially after a difficult relationship with Davey Johnson in Baltimore.

Hitting

A switch-hitter, Bonilla is much more effective from the right side but also is capable from the left. He tends to change his position in the batter's box, and pitchers have to be careful when he moves up on the plate. They like to pitch him away from the plate, but he adjusts well if he's in the front of the batter's box. Because he wants to help his team so much, he can get too aggressive. His overanxiousness usually hurts him in the postseason, and did in 1997 until his crucial homer in Game 7 of the World Series.

Baserunning & Defense

Bonilla doesn't have great speed because of his size, but he gathers a head of steam when the game is on the line. He certainly doesn't shy away from collisions and has the size to intimidate middle infielders on double plays. His range at third base is limited, and only three players exceeded his 22 errors at the hot corner. Everyone waited for his defense to truly cost Florida, but that never really happened. He made a highlight-film dive and throw from his knees in Game 3 of the World Series.

1998 Outlook

After turmoil in Baltimore, Bonilla found a real fit in Florida and will be back in the same role. His enthusiasm for playing for Leyland serves him well.

Position: 3B
Bats: B **Throws:** R
Ht: 6' 4" **Wt:** 240

Opening Day Age: 35
Born: 2/23/63 in New York, NY
ML Seasons: 12
Pronunciation: buh-NEE-yuh
Nickname: Bobby Bo

Overall Statistics

	G	AB	R	H	D	T	HR	RBI	SB	BB	SO	Avg	OBP	Slg
1997	153	562	77	167	39	3	17	96	6	73	94	.297	.378	.468
Career	1746	6348	993	1810	372	57	262	1061	43	792	1025	.285	.362	.486

Where He Hits the Ball

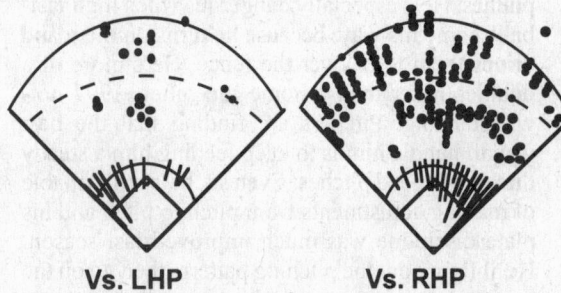

Vs. LHP   **Vs. RHP**

1997 Situational Stats

	AB	H	HR	RBI	Avg		AB	H	HR	RBI	Avg
Home	282	88	8	54	.312	LHP	113	42	6	21	.372
Road	280	79	9	42	.282	RHP	449	125	11	75	.278
First Half	300	93	7	49	.310	Sc Pos	169	48	8	79	.284
Scnd Half	262	74	10	47	.282	Clutch	91	26	3	17	.286

1997 Rankings (National League)

⇒ 3rd in lowest fielding percentage at third base (.937)
⇒ 4th in lowest cleanup slugging percentage (.409) and errors at third base (22)
⇒ 7th in GDPs (18)
⇒ 8th in sacrifice flies (8)
⇒ 9th in doubles
⇒ Led the Marlins in batting average, doubles, sacrifice flies (8), GDPs (18) and batting average at home

Kevin Brown

Position: SP
Bats: R **Throws:** R
Ht: 6' 4" **Wt:** 195

Opening Day Age: 33
Born: 3/14/65 in McIntyre, GA
ML Seasons: 11

1997 Season

Once again, Kevin Brown was the Marlins' ace. He delivered a win whenever the team needed, twice beating Greg Maddux in the National League Championship Series before running out of gas in the World Series. He threw a no-hitter in June against the Giants, and finished the regular season by going a combined 7-0 in August and September. The former chemical-engineering major from Georgia Tech continued to work with scientific precision, striking out 205 and walking just 66.

Pitching

When Brown is on his game, he's essentially unhittable. His hard sinker may be the toughest pitch in baseball. It has extreme movement, not just dropping but also darting for the corners of the plate. His cut fastball, slider and changeup all dance as well. When he gets into trouble, it's usually when he gets tired and his arm angle drops to more of a three-quarters position. If he doesn't come over the top, he loses movement and hangs his slider. He throws strikes and can maintain the quality of his stuff into the late innings.

Defense & Hitting

Brown has no obvious flaws fielding his position. He's athletic and led major league pitchers with 36 putouts and 81 total chances. Though he has a solid pickoff move and is conscious of holding runners, basestealers went 19-for-23 in 1997. That's inexplicable with Charles Johnson behind the plate. He's a career .122 hitter, which isn't terrible considering he came up in the American League.

1998 Outlook

Brown is as good as any pitcher in the game. Poor run support probably cost him the National League Cy Young Award in 1996, and he remained at the top of his game in 1997. He has given the Marlins the chance to win nearly every one of his starts during his two years in Florida, and there's no reason to think that will change.

Florida Marlins

Overall Statistics

	W	L	Pct.	ERA	G	GS	Sv	IP	H	BB	SO	HR	Ratio
1997	16	8	.667	2.69	33	33	0	237.1	214	66	205	10	1.18
Career	121	92	.568	3.42	278	277	0	1921.1	1878	575	1223	113	1.28

How Often He Throws Strikes

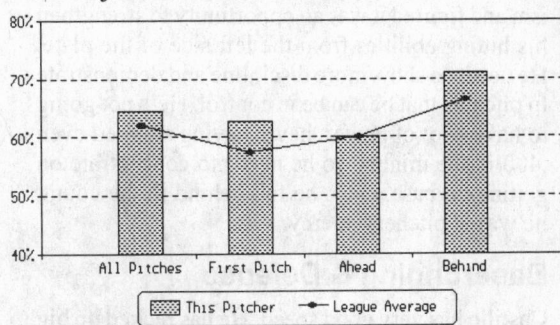

1997 Situational Stats

	W	L	ERA	Sv	IP		AB	H	HR	RBI	Avg
Home	8	4	2.51	0	125.1	LHB	432	106	4	35	.245
Road	8	4	2.89	0	112.0	RHB	458	108	6	36	.236
First Half	8	5	2.67	0	128.0	Sc Pos	201	54	4	62	.269
Scnd Half	8	3	2.72	0	109.1	Clutch	66	9	0	2	.136

1997 Rankings (National League)

⇒ 1st in hit batsmen (14) and highest ground-ball/flyball ratio allowed (3.6)

⇒ 2nd in least home runs allowed per 9 innings (.38)

⇒ 3rd in GDPs induced (26) and highest stolen base percentage allowed (82.6%)

⇒ Led the Marlins in ERA, games started, complete games (6), shutouts (2), innings pitched, hits allowed, batters faced (976), hit batsmen (14), strikeouts, balks (1), pitches thrown (3,551), stolen bases allowed (19), GDPs induced (26), winning percentage, highest strikeout/walk ratio (3.1), lowest slugging percentage allowed (.319), highest groundball/flyball ratio allowed (3.6), least pitches thrown per batter (3.64)and least home runs allowed per 9 innings

Luis Castillo

1997 Season

Luis Castillo was given the chance to be the Marlins' everyday second baseman last year after playing well in the last two months of 1996. It became obvious that at age 21 he needed a little more time in the minors. The Marlins demoted him to Triple-A on July 28 and he stayed there for the remainder of the campaign. Manager Jim Leyland worried that Castillo's confidence could be damaged long-term if he didn't send him down. Castillo proceeded to hit .354 at Charlotte.

Hitting

Castillo is a switch-hitter who's still learning the craft. He handled his demotion with professionalism and figured it was an opportunity to strengthen his hitting abilities from the left side of the plate. He needs to show more discipline and demonstrate to pitchers that he can be in control. He's not going to have a lot of power, never having slugged even .400 in the minors, so he needs to concentrate on getting on base. Once he fell behind in the count, he was at pitchers' mercy.

Baserunning & Defense

Castillo has very good speed. He has racked up big stolen-base totals in the minors, but his success rate has been mediocre. He was caught 10 times in 26 big league tries in 1997, and won't be dangerous until he becomes more efficient. He came up through the minors with shortstop Edgar Renteria, and there are few double-play combinations that are more exciting. Castillo has outstanding range and soft hands, and is very acrobatic turning the double play.

1998 Outlook

The Marlins think Castillo is a potential superstar, but they felt his time at Triple-A was vital. He skipped that level on his way to the major leagues, and it proved costly. With his performance at Charlotte, Castillo put himself back in Florida's second-base mix in 1998.

Position: 2B
Bats: B **Throws:** R
Ht: 5'11" **Wt:** 155

Opening Day Age: 22
Born: 9/12/75 in San Pedro de Macoris, DR
ML Seasons: 2
Pronunciation: cas-TEE-oh

Overall Statistics

	G	AB	R	H	D	T	HR	RBI	SB	BB	SO	Avg	OBP	Slg
1997	75	263	27	63	8	0	0	8	16	27	53	.240	.310	.270
Career	116	427	53	106	10	1	1	16	33	41	99	.248	.314	.283

Where He Hits the Ball

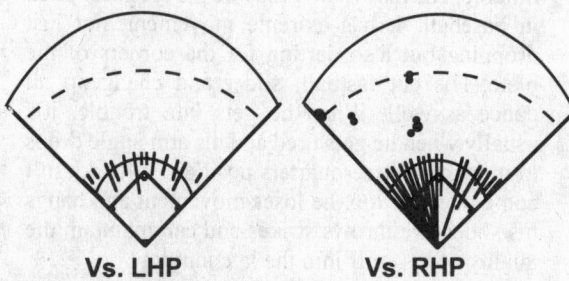

Vs. LHP   Vs. RHP

1997 Situational Stats

	AB	H	HR	RBI	Avg		AB	H	HR	RBI	Avg
Home	138	30	0	3	.217	LHP	45	10	0	1	.222
Road	125	33	0	5	.264	RHP	218	53	0	7	.243
First Half	225	56	0	6	.249	Sc Pos	59	14	0	8	.237
Scnd Half	38	7	0	2	.184	Clutch	40	7	0	2	.175

1997 Rankings (National League)

⇒ 5th in lowest stolen base percentage (61.5%)
⇒ 6th in lowest on-base percentage for a leadoff hitter (.304)
⇒ 9th in errors at second base (9)

Jeff Conine

Position: 1B
Bats: R **Throws:** R
Ht: 6' 1" **Wt:** 220

Opening Day Age: 31
Born: 6/27/66 in
Tacoma, WA
ML Seasons: 7
Pronunciation:
COH-nine

1997 Season

Jeff Conine struggled early in the season, and the Marlins had a difficult decision to make. They wanted more offense from the first-base position, but that meant displacing a man considered the franchise player, "Mr. Marlin." He never complained when Darren Daulton was acquired from the Phillies and ate into his playing time. Instead, Conine picked up his offense late in the season and had some key hits in the postseason. After hitting just .237 before the Daulton trade, Conine hit .254 afterward.

Hitting

Conine has more success against high pitches. Pitchers have been able to retire him by keeping their pitches down in the strike zone. He's also an easy target with two strikes, hitting just .186 in 1997 and .193 over the last five years in those situations. His power declined significantly last season, though he drew a good amount of walks to retain some offensive value. He was dropped to the seventh spot in the order after batting cleanup for most of 1996.

Baserunning & Defense

Conine doesn't have much speed and won't try to steal. He does slide into bases aggressively and he's always aware of the situation. He was more comfortable back at first base than he was in left field, where he played before Moises Alou was signed. Conine's range at first is limited, however. He does have good hands and an averaage arm.

1998 Outlook

A charter member of the Marlins, Conine left the team when he was traded to his original team, the Royals, for a minor league pitcher. He could start at first base or left field for Kansas City.

Overall Statistics

	G	AB	R	H	D	T	HR	RBI	SB	BB	SO	Avg	OBP	Slg
1997	151	405	46	98	13	1	17	61	2	57	89	.242	.337	.405
Career	755	2642	350	765	129	16	98	433	8	287	559	.290	.358	.462

Where He Hits the Ball

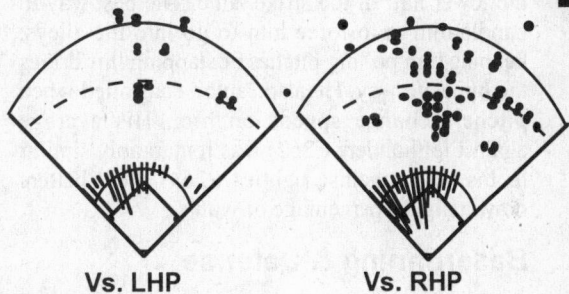

Vs. LHP   Vs. RHP

1997 Situational Stats

	AB	H	HR	RBI	Avg		AB	H	HR	RBI	Avg
Home	190	47	7	26	.247	LHP	105	26	4	15	.248
Road	215	51	10	35	.237	RHP	300	72	13	46	.240
First Half	267	65	8	33	.243	Sc Pos	110	23	3	39	.209
Scnd Half	138	33	9	28	.239	Clutch	85	21	5	14	.247

1997 Rankings (National League)

⇒ 3rd in lowest fielding percentage at first base (.992)
⇒ 6th in errors at first base (8)
⇒ 8th in lowest batting average with runners in scoring position

Darren Daulton

1997 Season

Limited to just five games by knee problems in 1996, Darren Daulton made a strong comeback. Traded from Philadelphia for Billy McMillon, Daulton gave the Marlins more than just added offense when the club wasn't sure if Jeff Conine still could produce. He also brought a presence to the clubhouse and added credibility. His acquisition also offered a further statement that the front office was serious about making a real postseason run.

Hitting

Daulton is dangerous when pitches come near the plate. He'll turn on anything close, especially in the lower half of the strike zone. The best way to handle him is to force him to go into the alleys, keeping him pulling pitches or slapping line drives the opposite way. He also can be controlled when pitchers change speeds on him. His average against lefthanders (.262) was remarkably similar to his mark against righties (.264). Few batters draw a higher percentage of walks.

Baserunning & Defense

Daulton isn't a factor on the bases after years of knee problems, but there were times in 1997 when he traveled far enough running on heart alone. He hit a career-high eight triples and went 6-for-7 stealing bases. He's strictly an offensive player now, with limited range at first base and in the outfield. His knees won't allow him to catch any longer.

1998 Outlook

Daulton hinted at retiring after the Marlins won the World Series, and Florida declined to exercise the 1998 option in his contract. His 1997 statistics indicate that he's far from through as a hitter, but it's uncertain whether he'll decide to play again. He definitely could contribute some offense, and would be a nice fit as a designated hitter for an American League city.

Position: RF/1B
Bats: L **Throws:** R
Ht: 6' 2" **Wt:** 207

Opening Day Age: 36
Born: 1/3/62 in
Arkansas City, KS
ML Seasons: 14
Nickname: Dutch

Overall Statistics

	G	AB	R	H	D	T	HR	RBI	SB	BB	SO	Avg	OBP	Slg
1997	136	395	68	104	21	8	14	63	6	76	74	.263	.378	.463
Career	1161	3630	511	891	197	25	137	588	50	629	726	.245	.357	.427

Where He Hits the Ball

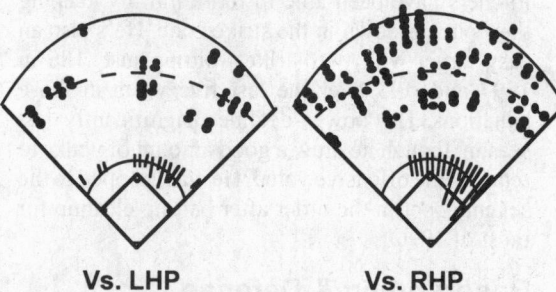

Vs. LHP   Vs. RHP

1997 Situational Stats

	AB	H	HR	RBI	Avg		AB	H	HR	RBI	Avg
Home	182	53	6	28	.291	LHP	84	22	3	10	.262
Road	213	51	8	35	.239	RHP	311	82	11	53	.264
First Half	240	64	11	36	.267	Sc Pos	109	30	3	45	.275
Scnd Half	155	40	3	27	.258	Clutch	55	14	2	10	.255

1997 Rankings (National League)

⇒ 1st in lowest batting average with the bases loaded (.000)
⇒ 5th in sacrifice flies (9)
⇒ 6th in triples (8)
⇒ 8th in least GDPs per GDP situation (3.9%)
⇒ 9th in lowest percentage of extra bases taken as a runner (37.5%)
⇒ 10th in lowest cleanup slugging percentage (.493) and highest percentage of pitches taken (61.1%)

Livan Hernandez

Position: SP
Bats: R **Throws:** R
Ht: 6' 2" **Wt:** 220

Opening Day Age: 23
Born: 2/20/75 in Villa Clara, Cuba
ML Seasons: 2
Pronunciation: LEE-vahn her-NAN-dezz

1997 Season

After defecting from Cuba and getting a $2.5 million bonus, Livan Hernandez disappointed the Marlins by pitching inconsistently in the minors and gaining a lot of weight in 1996. That made his performance last year all the more dramatic. He won his first nine decisions, stabilizing the rotation as Florida made its wild-card run. Then he was named MVP of the National League Championship Series and World Series, striking out 15 to win pivotal Game 5 in the NLCS and adding two victories in the World Series.

Pitching

The zip returned to Hernandez' pitches as he became acclimated to the United States. He learned to deal with the stress of leaving his relatives behind and stopped frequenting fast-food restaurants. His fastball rose to the mid-90s with increased movement, and the bottom started dropping out of his hard slider. At times he looked every bit as dominant as he had with the Cuban national team. His changeup could use some work, but he more than held his own. He even kept lefthanders pretty much in check, though they did hit him better than righties. He pitched better in the majors than he had in the minors, foreshadowing his ability to rise to the occasion.

Defense & Hitting

Hernandez is still young and his defense needs improvement. His pickoff move is adequate and his motion to the plate is somewhat slow. Still, he allowed just four steals in over 96 innings of work. He hits decently for a pitcher, with a career .200 average, and is an adequate bunter.

1998 Outlook

With his fastball and rookie performance, Hernandez has a lot to build on. He has the stuff to pitch in the front of a rotation, though at 23 that may be a lot to ask of him. With Alex Fernandez sidelined and Kevin Brown on the trading block, Hernandez may be asked to become a staff leader sooner than expected.

Overall Statistics

	W	L	Pct.	ERA	G	GS	Sv	IP	H	BB	SO	HR	Ratio
1997	9	3	.750	3.18	17	17	0	96.1	81	38	72	5	1.24
Career	9	3	.750	3.08	18	17	0	99.1	84	40	74	5	1.25

How Often He Throws Strikes

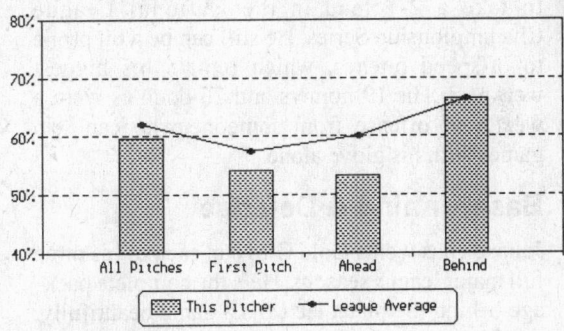

This Pitcher — League Average

1997 Situational Stats

	W	L	ERA	Sv	IP		AB	H	HR	RBI	Avg
Home	5	3	3.45	0	57.1	LHB	157	39	3	11	.248
Road	4	0	2.77	0	39.0	RHB	196	42	2	21	.214
First Half	2	0	4.11	0	15.1	Sc Pos	79	12	1	26	.152
Scnd Half	7	3	3.00	0	81.0	Clutch	10	2	0	0	.200

1997 Rankings (National League)

⇒ Did not rank near the top or bottom in any category

Charles Johnson

1997 Season

As usual, Charles Johnson's arm, knack for handling pitchers and nearly flawless defense were a marvel. He started to get some key hits in July and August, pushing the Marlins toward their first postseason berth. By year's end he had established himself as one of the game's best all-around catchers and not just a defensive star.

Hitting

Substantial progress as a hitter helped make Johnson's season complete. He raised his batting average 32 points, his on-base percentage 55 and his slugging percentage 96. He hit a key three-run homer off of John Smoltz that allowed the Marlins to take a 2-1 lead in the National League Chammpionship Series. He still can be a bit prone to offspeed pitches, which remain his biggest weakness. His 19 homers and 26 doubles were a wealth of offense from someone who can win games with his glove alone.

Baserunning & Defense

Johnson has won a Gold Glove in each of his three full major league seasons. He's the complete package behind the plate. He calls a game beautifully, and it's easy to forget his youth as he leads veteran pitchers. He has a strong arm and an incredibly quick release, which most runners are loathe to test. He threw out 47 percent of basestealers, the second-best figure in the majors. His streak of regular-season games without an error stands at 171, a major league record. Johnson has little speed and needs more experience to learn the finer points of baserunning.

1998 Outlook

What makes Johnson so dynamic is his love for his position and his infectious enthusiasm for defense. How a catcher handles pitchers is one of the most underrated elements in the game. Johnson knows he can be a factor day in and out, even if he goes 0-for-5. The first draft pick in Marlins history turned out to be a wise one.

Position: C
Bats: R **Throws:** R
Ht: 6' 2" **Wt:** 215

Opening Day Age: 26
Born: 7/20/71 in Fort Pierce, Florida
ML Seasons: 4

Overall Statistics

	G	AB	R	H	D	T	HR	RBI	SB	BB	SO	Avg	OBP	Slg
1997	124	416	43	104	26	1	19	63	0	60	109	.250	.347	.454
Career	345	1128	122	272	55	3	44	143	1	147	275	.241	.331	.412

Where He Hits the Ball

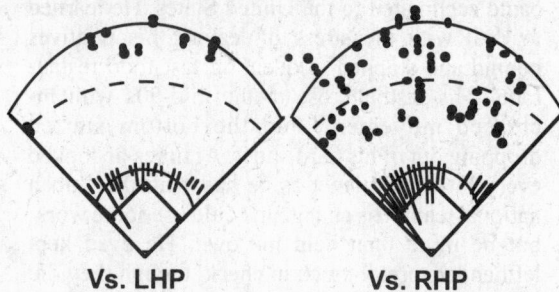

Vs. LHP　　　　**Vs. RHP**

1997 Situational Stats

	AB	H	HR	RBI	Avg		AB	H	HR	RBI	Avg
Home	206	50	7	22	.243	LHP	90	27	5	15	.300
Road	210	54	12	41	.257	RHP	326	77	14	48	.236
First Half	212	48	6	25	.226	Sc Pos	111	25	5	41	.225
Scnd Half	204	56	13	38	.275	Clutch	73	18	3	14	.247

1997 Rankings (National League)

⇒ 1st in lowest batting average with the bases loaded (.000) and fielding percentage at catcher (1.000)
⇒ 6th in lowest batting average vs. righthanded pitchers and lowest percentage of swings put into play (33.6%)
⇒ 7th in lowest batting average on an 0-2 count (.057)
⇒ 10th in lowest batting average with runners in scoring position
⇒ Led the Marlins in strikeouts

Al Leiter

1997 Season

After firing a no-hitter and winning 16 games in 1996, Al Leiter slipped in 1997. He finished 11-9, but his ERA jumped by 1.41. He was ineffective in the postseason until coming up with a strong performance in Game 7 of the World Series. That game, like many of his better outings, came at Pro Player Stadium. He struggled on the road, going 5-7, 6.37. He made two trips to the disabled list, in May with a bruised knee and in August with a pulled groin.

Pitching

Leiter always has had plenty of raw talent. He throws a sinking fastball in the low 90s, a cut fastball, a hard slider and a sharp curve. He still walks too many batters, which would be more disastrous if he wasn't good at limiting homers. He's starting to get more comfortable at working inside. He's relying on his cut fastball more and more, with mixed results. He doesn't have a lot of finesse, so he struggles when he doesn't have his best stuff. He can overmatch hitters, but he generally can't fool them.

Defense & Hitting

Leiter's quick delivery to the plate and the advantage of being a lefthander make him tough to steal on. His talents and Charles Johnson's arm gunned down 16 of 28 basestealers in 1997. Leiter is an agile athlete who likes to field his position. As a hitter, he's just another former American League product trying to learn the craft.

1998 Outlook

Leiter's challenge is to try to recapture his 1996 form. The loss of Alex Fernandez for the entire season makes him the No. 2 starter if Kevin Brown remains. But all those years of power pitching may be taking a toll on Leiter's arm, and he needs his sinking fastball to set up his curve. The 1998 season will determine whether he can rebound or is headed toward a steady decline.

Position: SP
Bats: L **Throws:** L
Ht: 6' 3" **Wt:** 215

Opening Day Age: 32
Born: 10/12/65 in
Toms River, NJ
ML Seasons: 11
Pronunciation: LITE-er

Overall Statistics

	W	L	Pct.	ERA	G	GS	Sv	IP	H	BB	SO	HR	Ratio
1997	11	9	.550	4.34	27	27	0	151.1	133	91	132	13	1.48
Career	60	53	.531	4.01	173	143	2	888.2	776	519	771	67	1.46

How Often He Throws Strikes

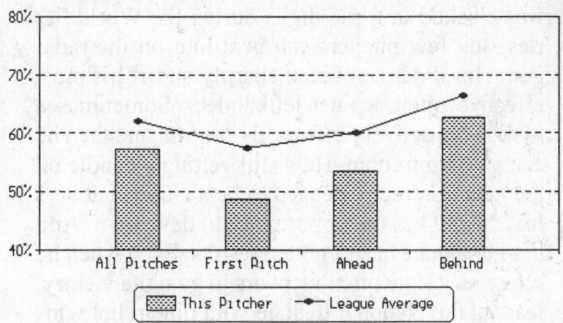

1997 Situational Stats

	W	L	ERA	Sv	IP		AB	H	HR	RBI	Avg
Home	6	2	2.28	0	75.0	LHB	103	21	0	5	.204
Road	5	7	6.37	0	76.1	RHB	449	112	13	67	.249
First Half	7	6	5.02	0	80.2	Sc Pos	139	39	2	55	.281
Scnd Half	4	3	3.57	0	70.2	Clutch	12	0	0	0	.000

1997 Rankings (National League)

⇒ 1st in runners caught stealing (16)
⇒ 3rd in hit batsmen (12)
⇒ 4th in walks allowed (91)
⇒ Led the Marlins in walks allowed and runners caught stealing (16)

Robb Nen

1997 Season

For the second straight year, Robb Nen logged 35 saves in 42 chances. Consistent, right? Well, not exactly. He saw his ERA and walk total nearly double, though he worked fewer innings. He had difficulty at times recovering from adversity, getting rattled on occasion. That said, Nen still was one of the best and most reliable closers in the game. He accounted for all but four of Florida's regular-season saves and survived some wild rides to log four more saves in the postseason.

Pitching

A pure power pitcher, Nen throws a fastball in the upper 90s and a slider in the upper 80s. His heater was clocked in triple digits during the World Series, and few pitchers can beat him on the radar gun. His slider can break sharply and is his most effective pitch against lefthanders. Sometimes a kink in his delivery affects his control, and then he can get into trouble. He's still getting a handle on the mental ferocity needed to be a closer, but he's just 28 and has the opportunity to develop it. And it's not like he hasn't gotten results. Even when he blows saves, he often recovers to gain the victory, leading the National League with nine relief wins in 1997.

Defense & Hitting

Like most closers, Nen does not do an exceptional job of holding runners. Even with the benefit of Charles Johnson's golden arm on his side, he watched basestealers go 9-for-9 against him in 1997. He's an average fielder, limited somewhat by his 6-foot-4 frame. He didn't get an at-bat in 1997 and is 0-for-9 in his career.

1998 Outlook

Florida traded Nen to San Francisco for three minor league pitchers in yet another salary dump. With 70 saves over the last two seasons, he's clearly among baseball's elite closers. The Marlins' postseason exposure made him even more famous. He has the physical tools and arm strength to continue to improve, and is easily capable of repeating his outstanding 1996 campaign.

Position: RP
Bats: R **Throws:** R
Ht: 6' 4" **Wt:** 190

Opening Day Age: 28
Born: 11/28/69 in San Pedro, CA
ML Seasons: 5

Overall Statistics

	W	L	Pct.	ERA	G	GS	Sv	IP	H	BB	SO	HR	Ratio
1997	9	3	.750	3.89	73	0	35	74.0	72	40	81	7	1.51
Career	21	17	.553	3.61	278	4	108	336.2	310	147	340	27	1.36

How Often He Throws Strikes

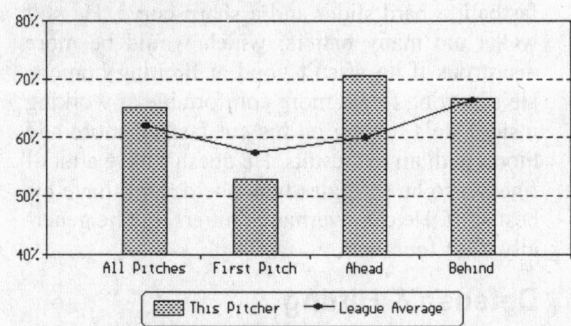

1997 Situational Stats

	W	L	ERA	Sv	IP		AB	H	HR	RBI	Avg
Home	7	1	3.89	16	39.1	LHB	146	32	4	21	.219
Road	2	2	3.89	19	34.2	RHB	142	40	3	23	.282
First Half	5	2	3.92	24	41.1	Sc Pos	111	26	2	37	.234
Scnd Half	4	1	3.86	11	32.2	Clutch	208	51	5	37	.245

1997 Rankings (National League)

⇒ 1st in relief wins (9)
⇒ 2nd in games finished (65)
⇒ 4th in blown saves (7)
⇒ 6th in saves and save opportunities (42)
⇒ 7th in save percentage (83.3%)
⇒ 10th in most strikeouts per 9 innings in relief (9.9)
⇒ Led the Marlins in saves, games finished (65), save opportunities (42), save percentage (83.3%), blown saves (7), relief wins (9) and most strikeouts per 9 innings in relief (9.9)

Edgar Renteria

1997 Season

Edgar Renteria's World Series-winning single is just a first step toward stardom. Like Charles Johnson, he's a highly valued product of the Florida farm system. He's close to Gold Glove level as a shortstop already, and he's developing as a hitter. He showed a knack for performing in the clutch, as his Series winner was one of seven game-winning hits he had in 1997 in the Marlins' final at-bat.

Hitting

As he matures and learns to take a walk, Renteria could become a competent hitter at the top of a lineup. He usually bats in the No. 2 slot, and could succeed Devon White as Florida's leadoff man in the near future. He could develop decent power when he matures physically, and he did stroke 21 doubles at age 22. He's good at taking pitches to the opposite field, but he can be overmatched when fastballs are busted in on his hands. He has been a much better hitter against righthanders early in his career, a reverse platoon differential. If he can improve against lefties, and he should, he could hit close to .300. He's good at getting bunts down, leading the National League in sacrifice bunts.

Baserunning & Defense

Renteria has the speed needed to be a premier basestealer, but needs to refine his technique after getting nailed on 15 of 47 steal attempts. He's still learning to read pitchers and get good jumps. He's magical in the field, especially when he turns the double play. His leaping ability and range are as good as it gets, and he has very soft hands. He looks like a 10-year veteran at shortstop. When he cuts down his errors, he won't have anything resembling a defensive shortcoming.

1998 Outlook

Renteria is yet another reason the Marlins can be optimistic about their future. Sure, they spent huge amounts of money on high-priced veterans, but he's one of the prime examples of why their farm system is considered as good as any in baseball. With Barry Larkin on the decline, Renteria soon could supplant him as the NL's top shortstop.

Position: SS
Bats: R **Throws:** R
Ht: 6' 1" **Wt:** 172

Opening Day Age: 22
Born: 8/7/75 in
Barranquilla, Colombia
ML Seasons: 2
Pronunciation:
ren-ter-REE-uh

Florida Marlins

Overall Statistics

	G	AB	R	H	D	T	HR	RBI	SB	BB	SO	Avg	OBP	Slg
1997	154	617	90	171	21	3	4	52	32	45	108	.277	.327	.340
Career	260	1048	158	304	39	6	9	83	48	78	176	.290	.340	.365

Where He Hits the Ball

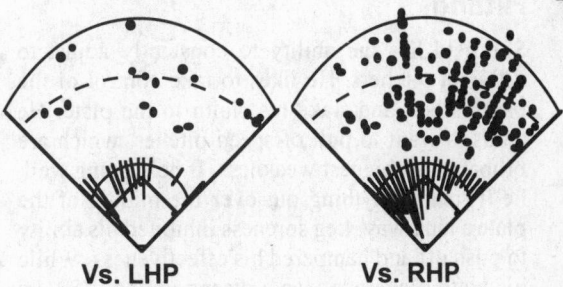

Vs. LHP　　　　**Vs. RHP**

1997 Situational Stats

	AB	H	HR	RBI	Avg		AB	H	HR	RBI	Avg
Home	306	81	3	29	.265	LHP	108	28	0	3	.259
Road	311	90	1	23	.289	RHP	509	143	4	49	.281
First Half	333	88	1	27	.264	Sc Pos	136	40	0	46	.294
Scnd Half	284	83	3	25	.292	Clutch	93	23	1	12	.247

1997 Rankings (National League)

⇒ 1st in sacrifice bunts (19)
⇒ 2nd in singles and caught stealing (15)
⇒ 3rd in lowest slugging percentage, errors at shortstop (17) and bunts in play (32)
⇒ 4th in lowest HR frequency (154.3 ABs per HR) and highest groundball/flyball ratio (2.1)
⇒ 6th in plate appearances (691), lowest slugging percentage vs. righthanded pitchers (.350) and fielding percentage at shortstop (.975)
⇒ 7th in at-bats
⇒ 9th in stolen bases
⇒ Led the Marlins in at-bats, runs scored, hits, singles, sacrifice bunts (19), stolen bases, caught stealing (15), pitches seen (2,485), plate appearances (691), games played (154) and highest groundball/flyball ratio (2.1)

Gary Sheffield

1997 Season

Marlins manager Jim Leyland doesn't like to hear that Gary Sheffield had a terrible 1997 season. Leyland would say Sheffield had a year below his normal standards, but that certainly doesn't mean he didn't make plenty of contributions. His main contribution might have been that his mere presence afforded opportunities for Moises Alou and Bobby Bonilla. Sheffield played through nagging injuries again, and it was obvious that the multi-year deal he signed as the season began placed extra pressure on him to perform. He pressed to justify his salary, and it showed. His production came up a notch in the postseason, offering him a sense that 1997 hardly was a lost season.

Hitting

Sheffield has the ability to constantly adjust to different pitchers. He likes to take control of the batter's box and stake his claim to the plate. He tends to want to pull offspeed pitches, which are probably his biggest weakness. If he's going well, he'll smack anything out over the middle of the plate a long way. Leg soreness inhibited his ability to push off and hampered his effectiveness. While his batting average was a disappointing .250, he did draw 121 walks and finish fifth in the National League with a .424 on-base percentage.

Baserunning & Defense

Sheffield has above-average speed, but he's choosy about when he'll attempt a steal. He does an excellent job of breaking up double plays and he's also aggressive on the bases. Sheffield remains erratic in right field. Balls hit over his head give him some trouble, and he also can overrun some hard-hit singles. His defensive strength is a solid throwing arm, which is most dangerous when he has plenty of time to set up and throw.

1998 Outlook

Sheffield remains one of the game's best hitters. His postseason performance provided a terrific note on which to end a season of struggle. He can spend the winter making sure his hamstring is healthy and return for 1998 on a positive note.

Position: RF
Bats: R **Throws:** R
Ht: 5'11" **Wt:** 190

Opening Day Age: 29
Born: 11/18/68 in Tampa, FL
ML Seasons: 10

Overall Statistics

	G	AB	R	H	D	T	HR	RBI	SB	BB	SO	Avg	OBP	Slg
1997	135	444	86	111	22	1	21	71	11	121	79	.250	.424	.446
Career	1026	3659	603	1048	194	14	180	621	123	561	440	.286	.386	.495

Where He Hits the Ball

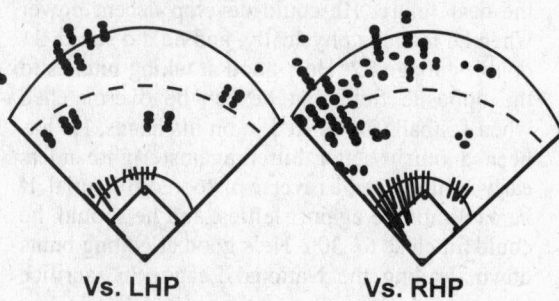

Vs. LHP   Vs. RHP

1997 Situational Stats

	AB	H	HR	RBI	Avg		AB	H	HR	RBI	Avg
Home	214	59	13	33	.276	LHP	67	23	5	13	.343
Road	230	52	8	38	.226	RHP	377	88	16	58	.233
First Half	236	57	9	37	.242	Sc Pos	114	29	5	47	.254
Scnd Half	208	54	12	34	.260	Clutch	68	18	2	10	.265

1997 Rankings (National League)

⇒ 3rd in walks and lowest batting average on the road
⇒ 4th in lowest batting average vs. righthanded pitchers and fielding percentage in right field (.980)
⇒ 5th in on-base percentage and highest percentage of pitches taken (63.5%)
⇒ Led the Marlins in walks, intentional walks (11), hit by pitch (15), times on base (247), on-base percentage, HR frequency (21.1 ABs per HR), most pitches seen per plate appearance (3.92), least GDPs per GDP situation (6.4%), batting average on an 0-2 count (.194), cleanup slugging percentage (.446), on-base percentage vs. righthanded pitchers (.402) and highest percentage of pitches taken (63.5%)

Kurt Abbott

Position: 2B
Bats: R **Throws:** R
Ht: 6' 0" **Wt:** 185

Opening Day Age: 28
Born: 6/2/69 in
Zanesville, OH
ML Seasons: 5

Overall Statistics

	G	AB	R	H	D	T	HR	RBI	SB	BB	SO	Avg	OBP	Slg
1997	94	252	35	69	18	2	6	30	3	14	68	.274	.315	.433
Career	444	1398	184	358	72	19	43	165	15	91	395	.256	.307	.427

1997 Situational Stats

	AB	H	HR	RBI	Avg		AB	H	HR	RBI	Avg
Home	94	26	1	9	.277	LHP	89	28	2	11	.315
Road	158	43	5	21	.272	RHP	163	41	4	19	.252
First Half	151	43	5	21	.285	Sc Pos	66	20	2	23	.303
Scnd Half	101	26	1	9	.257	Clutch	55	19	2	7	.345

1997 Season

When Luis Castillo faltered at second base, the Marlins turned to Kurt Abbott. Eventually he became the righthanded half of a platoon with Craig Counsell, who was acquired from the Rockies in late July. Abbott was steady defensively and offered a bit of offensive punch. His 18 doubles were an outstanding contribution for a part-time player.

Hitting, Baserunning & Defense

Abbott hits for a decent average with good pop for a middle infielder. He strikes out too often, mainly because he has difficulty with breaking balls. He doesn't walk much, but is doing a better job of extending counts and not jumping on first-ball offerings. He has average speed and attempted only four steals in 1997. He can play third base and shortstop, but wasn't needed with Bobby Bonilla and Edgar Renteria as fixtures on the left side of the infield. His range is better suited for second base, and he did a creditable job turning the pivot.

1998 Outlook

Abbott may be expendable. The Marlins could decide to give Castillo his job back or promote Counsell to full-time duty, and prospect Ralph Milliard is knocking on the door. Abbott's power and versatility easily would enable him to find a job elsewhere if he had to.

John Cangelosi

Position: LF/CF
Bats: B **Throws:** L
Ht: 5' 8" **Wt:** 160

Opening Day Age: 35
Born: 3/10/63 in
Brooklyn, NY
ML Seasons: 11

Overall Statistics

	G	AB	R	H	D	T	HR	RBI	SB	BB	SO	Avg	OBP	Slg
1997	103	192	28	47	8	0	1	12	5	19	33	.245	.321	.302
Career	927	1827	309	457	64	15	11	124	152	328	295	.250	.371	.320

1997 Situational Stats

	AB	H	HR	RBI	Avg		AB	H	HR	RBI	Avg
Home	91	25	1	4	.275	LHP	51	12	0	4	.235
Road	101	22	0	8	.218	RHP	141	35	1	8	.248
First Half	103	25	1	8	.243	Sc Pos	44	10	0	11	.227
Scnd Half	89	22	0	4	.247	Clutch	39	6	0	3	.154

1997 Season

John Cangelosi and Marlins manager Jim Leyland were acquainted in Pittsburgh, and Leyland got pretty much what he expected from one of his first options off the bench. Cangelosi offered decent offense, injected a little speed and even added an occasional extra-base burst. For a spot player, he reached base rather consistently.

Hitting, Baserunning & Defense

Cangelosi is just 5-foot-8 and weighs 160 pounds. For someone his size, it's surprising how much he likes to pull pitches. His experience allows him to use his above-average speed and ability to read pitchers to get a good jump on stolen-base attempts. He still has fine range in center field and can go over the wall to bring down a ball. He never has had much arm strength.

1998 Outlook

Cangelosi should be a valuable role player and can look forward to at least a couple of seasons making the most of his part-time duty. Major league clubs can always find a use for a player of his skill and versatility.

Dennis Cook

Position: RP
Bats: L **Throws:** L
Ht: 6' 3" **Wt:** 190

Opening Day Age: 35
Born: 10/4/62 in Lamarque, TX
ML Seasons: 10

Overall Statistics

	W	L	Pct.	ERA	G	GS	Sv	IP	H	BB	SO	HR	Ratio
1997	1	2	.333	3.90	59	0	0	62.1	64	28	63	4	1.48
Career	38	32	.543	3.93	354	71	3	752.0	713	281	488	96	1.32

1997 Situational Stats

	W	L	ERA	Sv	IP			AB	H	HR	RBI	Avg
Home	1	1	2.62	0	34.1	LHB		90	23	1	9	.256
Road	0	1	5.46	0	28.0	RHB		150	41	3	19	.273
First Half	1	2	2.61	0	31.0	Sc Pos		64	17	1	21	.266
Scnd Half	0	0	5.17	0	31.1	Clutch		114	25	1	9	.219

1997 Season

Dennis Cook thrived on being in a pennant race last year. He's an intense competitor who finds pressure satisfying, not stultifying. He gave the Marlins one of several lefthanded options out of the bullpen and even added a couple of huge base hits down the stretch. Most memorable was a pinch-hit single in the bottom of the 12th inning to beat the Braves on August 1.

Pitching, Defense & Hitting

Cook always has been durable, and 1997 was no exception as he appeared in 59 games. His slider remains his best pitch and he also throws a fastball and forkball, but it's the intangibles that make him even more effective. His toughness helps him rise to the occasion. Cook has a decent pickoff move and fields the position well. Put a bat in his hand and he relishes the opportunity. He's one of the best hitting pitchers in baseball, with a career .276 average, and went 5-for-9 last season.

1998 Outlook

Though he's 35, Cook doesn't appear to be in danger of losing the zip on his fastball. He has been an effective lefthander reliever ever since the Indians moved him to the bullpen full-time in 1993. That shouldn't change anytime soon.

Craig Counsell

Position: 2B
Bats: L **Throws:** R
Ht: 6' 0" **Wt:** 170

Opening Day Age: 27
Born: 8/21/70 in South Bend, IN
ML Seasons: 2

Overall Statistics

	G	AB	R	H	D	T	HR	RBI	SB	BB	SO	Avg	OBP	Slg
1997	52	164	20	49	9	2	1	16	1	18	17	.299	.376	.396
Career	55	165	20	49	9	2	1	16	1	19	17	.297	.378	.394

1997 Situational Stats

	AB	H	HR	RBI	Avg			AB	H	HR	RBI	Avg
Home	82	24	1	10	.293	LHP		13	4	0	1	.308
Road	82	25	0	6	.305	RHP		151	45	1	15	.298
First Half	0	0	0	0	-	Sc Pos		43	15	1	16	.349
Scnd Half	164	49	1	16	.299	Clutch		29	5	0	1	.172

1997 Season

Craig Counsell went from afterthought to improbable World Series hero in 1997. His major league career had consisted of one at-bat when the Marlins traded Mark Hutton to the Rockies for him on July 27. Counsell hit .293 in the postseason, driving in the tying run in the bottom of the ninth inning in Game 7 of the World Series and then scoring the game-winner in the 11th.

Hitting, Baserunning & Defense

Counsell is a slap hitter who knows how to work deep into a count and foul off pitches. He made a habit of piling up more walks than strikeouts in the minors and continued that trend with Florida. He has doubles power to the alleys and uses the opposite field. Counsell has decent speed and is aggressive, but is prone to occasional baserunning mistakes. He has good range at second and played his share of shortstop in the minors. He has an average arm and excellent hands, and turns the double play well.

1998 Outlook

Counsell maximizes his limited talent. There's no guarantee of playing time in 1998 with youngsters such as Luis Castillo and Ralph Milliard as options at second base. At worst, he should be able to find a utility job either in Florida or elsewhere.

Jim Eisenreich

Position: LF/1B/RF
Bats: L **Throws:** L
Ht: 5'11" **Wt:** 195

Opening Day Age: 38
Born: 4/18/59 in St. Cloud, MN
ML Seasons: 14
Pronunciation: EYE-zen-rike

Overall Statistics

	G	AB	R	H	D	T	HR	RBI	SB	BB	SO	Avg	OBP	Slg
1997	120	293	36	82	19	1	2	34	0	30	28	.280	.345	.372
Career	1317	3804	471	1119	218	37	51	464	99	308	399	.294	.345	.411

1997 Situational Stats

	AB	H	HR	RBI	Avg		AB	H	HR	RBI	Avg
Home	134	37	2	15	.276	LHP	29	7	0	4	.241
Road	159	45	0	19	.283	RHP	264	75	2	30	.284
First Half	179	50	1	19	.279	Sc Pos	84	22	0	30	.262
Scnd Half	114	32	1	15	.281	Clutch	58	12	0	7	.207

1997 Season

The Marlins signed Jim Eisenreich as a free agent from Philadelphia, knowing that they would get one of the steadier veteran hitters around. With Devon White missing time with an injury and Gary Sheffield struggling, Eisenreich helped lift Florida throughout the summer. His numbers were right in line with what he's produced throughout his career. Especially impressive were his 19 doubles in 293 at-bats.

Hitting, Baserunning & Defense

Eisenreich has been playing pro ball since 1980. He knows how to go with the pitch and send it to all fields. He doesn't have outstanding speed but is a smart baserunner who anticipates situations well. For the first time since 1983, he didn't steal a single base. His arm strength hasn't deteriorated and his outfield range remains adequate.

1998 Outlook

Eisenreich's slugging percentage dropped more than 100 points from 1996 to 1997. But he's perfectly suited for the role in which the Marlins use him, and he remains an important commodity.

Alex Fernandez

Position: SP
Bats: R **Throws:** R
Ht: 6' 1" **Wt:** 215

Opening Day Age: 28
Born: 8/13/69 in Miami Beach, FL
ML Seasons: 8

Overall Statistics

	W	L	Pct.	ERA	G	GS	Sv	IP	H	BB	SO	HR	Ratio
1997	17	12	.586	3.59	32	32	0	220.2	193	69	183	25	1.19
Career	96	75	.561	3.76	231	229	0	1567.0	1499	495	1134	173	1.27

1997 Situational Stats

	W	L	ERA	Sv	IP		AB	H	HR	RBI	Avg
Home	7	6	4.39	0	92.1	LHB	386	112	13	42	.290
Road	10	6	3.02	0	128.1	RHB	426	81	12	42	.190
First Half	9	7	3.63	0	116.2	Sc Pos	174	38	2	53	.218
Scnd Half	8	5	3.55	0	104.0	Clutch	51	12	4	7	.235

1997 Season

Alex Fernandez was a reliable No. 2 starter, winning 17 games and making 32 generally solid starts after joining the Marlins as one of their high-priced free agents last year. But after Atlanta rocked him in Game 2 of the NLCS, he received some devastating news. He had a rotator-cuff tear in his right shoulder, which required surgery and put his 1998 season in jeopardy.

Pitching, Defense & Hitting

When Fernandez doesn't have his best stuff, he finds a way to battle and keep his team in games. He mixes pitches well. His best offerings are an above-average fastball and breaking ball. He likes to tempt hitters to chase fastballs out of the strike zone. He has worked himself into one of the better defensive pitchers in the league, and his deceptive pickoff move helps him. He's decent with the bat, posting six doubles and six walks last year.

1998 Outlook

Fernandez has never been on the DL, but that's where he'll open in 1998. He's expected to miss at least the first half of the season. Though four of the five years on his $36 million contract remain, the Marlins did get a return on their investment as he helped them reach the World Series, even if they won it without him.

Cliff Floyd ⟨Pivotal Season⟩

Position: LF
Bats: L **Throws:** R
Ht: 6' 4" **Wt:** 235

Opening Day Age: 25
Born: 12/5/72 in Chicago, IL
ML Seasons: 5

Overall Statistics

	G	AB	R	H	D	T	HR	RBI	SB	BB	SO	Avg	OBP	Slg
1997	61	137	23	32	9	1	6	19	6	24	33	.234	.354	.445
Career	317	798	104	197	44	9	18	96	26	85	179	.247	.325	.392

1997 Situational Stats

	AB	H	HR	RBI	Avg		AB	H	HR	RBI	Avg
Home	67	16	2	8	.239	LHP	16	4	0	0	.250
Road	70	16	4	11	.229	RHP	121	28	6	19	.231
First Half	86	19	2	5	.221	Sc Pos	34	6	2	11	.176
Scnd Half	51	13	4	14	.255	Clutch	30	7	1	3	.233

1997 Season

Cliff Floyd gave the Marlins a decent power threat off the bench, while showing a little more discipline at the plate than he did with Montreal. His .234 batting average wasn't much to look at, but his .354 on-base percentage and .445 slugging percentage were fine numbers for a part-time player. Considered a potential superstar with the Expos, he's starting to get back on track following a career-threatening wrist injury in 1995.

Hitting, Baserunning & Defense

Floyd offers a mix of tools, with his most exciting being his bat and his power. He's still too aggressive and hurts himself by expanding the strike zone. He has very good speed for a 6-foot-4, 235-pounder, stealing 26 of 32 bases in his major league career. He can play center field, though the Expos used him more as a first baseman. His arm is average.

1998 Outlook

Floyd excelled in a bench role for Florida, but his future holds much more in store for him. He could become the full-time first baseman after the Marlins decided not to bring back Jeff Conine and Darren Daulton. He figured to be a cornerstone player by now, but Floyd is still just 25.

Felix Heredia

Position: RP
Bats: L **Throws:** L
Ht: 6' 0" **Wt:** 165

Opening Day Age: 21
Born: 6/18/76 in Barahona, DR
ML Seasons: 2
Pronunciation: her-EEE-dee-uh

Overall Statistics

	W	L	Pct.	ERA	G	GS	Sv	IP	H	BB	SO	HR	Ratio
1997	5	3	.625	4.29	56	0	0	56.2	53	30	54	3	1.46
Career	6	4	.600	4.30	77	0	0	73.1	74	40	64	4	1.55

1997 Situational Stats

	W	L	ERA	Sv	IP		AB	H	HR	RBI	Avg
Home	2	0	3.06	0	32.1	LHB	69	13	0	6	.188
Road	3	3	5.92	0	24.1	RHB	149	40	3	24	.268
First Half	4	0	1.85	0	34.0	Sc Pos	68	17	0	24	.250
Scnd Half	1	3	7.94	0	22.2	Clutch	80	18	3	10	.225

1997 Season

Felix Heredia was the prototypical situational lefthander, good for setting up the bullpen to finish games or coming in earlier to keep an opponent in check when the Marlins fell behind. His four scoreless appearances in the World Series were crucial in Florida's seven-game victory.

Pitching, Defense & Hitting

Heredia has good raw tools and showed a lot of composure for a young pitcher. His fastball registers in the upper-80s, average for a lefty, and it seems to rise as it approaches the plate. He could throw harder as he matures physically, and uses a slider as his second pitch. He still remains far more effective against lefthanders than righthanders, though the disparity wasn't nearly as significant as it was in 1996. He still allows too many walks for a reliever. His pickoff move is negligible, but he's quick off the mound. He went 1-for-2 with one sacrifice in 1997.

1998 Outlook

Heredia has a long and bright future as a lefty with a lively arm. He has gained a good deal of experience for a 21 year old. If he stays healthy he'll be in demand. A hard-throwing southpaw can find a job in any bullpen.

Jay Powell

Position: RP
Bats: R **Throws:** R
Ht: 6' 4" **Wt:** 225

Opening Day Age: 26
Born: 1/19/72 in
Meridian, MS
ML Seasons: 3

Overall Statistics

	W	L	Pct.	ERA	G	GS	Sv	IP	H	BB	SO	HR	Ratio
1997	7	2	.778	3.28	74	0	2	79.2	71	30	65	3	1.27
Career	11	5	.688	3.73	150	0	4	159.1	149	72	121	8	1.39

1997 Situational Stats

	W	L	ERA	Sv	IP		AB	H	HR	RBI	Avg
Home	5	2	4.67	1	44.1	LHB	92	27	0	7	.293
Road	2	0	1.53	1	35.1	RHB	201	44	3	25	.219
First Half	1	1	2.03	1	44.1	Sc Pos	90	19	1	30	.211
Scnd Half	6	1	4.84	1	35.1	Clutch	160	38	2	19	.238

1997 Season

As righthanded setup man, Jay Powell continued to make progress in adjusting to that role. He initially was projected as closer material when the Orioles made him a first-round draft pick in 1993. He jumped from Double-A to the majors in 1996, then lowered his ERA by more than a run last season.

Pitching, Defense & Hitting

Powell's fastball has excellent movement. He became more effective by improving the bite on his breaking pitches, which helped him hold righthanders to a .219 average. His slow delivery makes him vulnerable to baserunners. He can be a more effective fielder if he learns to land in a position to handle balls as he completes his delivery. He was surprisingly effective as a hitter in 1997, going 2-for-4 after entering the season 0-for-5 in his career.

1998 Outlook

With Nen traded to the Giants, the Marlins could turn to Powell to finish games and feel reasonably confident. Otherwise they'll keep him in the setup role, where he's getting more comfortable.

Gregg Zaun

Position: C
Bats: B **Throws:** R
Ht: 5'10" **Wt:** 170

Opening Day Age: 26
Born: 4/14/71 in
Glendale, CA
ML Seasons: 3

Overall Statistics

	G	AB	R	H	D	T	HR	RBI	SB	BB	SO	Avg	OBP	Slg
1997	58	143	21	43	10	2	2	20	1	26	18	.301	.415	.441
Career	158	386	59	104	24	3	7	49	3	56	52	.269	.366	.402

1997 Situational Stats

	AB	H	HR	RBI	Avg		AB	H	HR	RBI	Avg
Home	61	19	0	11	.311	LHP	14	4	0	2	.286
Road	82	24	2	9	.293	RHP	129	39	2	18	.302
First Half	84	26	2	16	.310	Sc Pos	42	12	0	16	.286
Scnd Half	59	17	0	4	.288	Clutch	38	10	2	7	.263

1997 Season

Gregg Zaun did everything asked of a backup catcher in 1997. He gave Charles Johnson rest on the rare occasion he needed it. Zaun came to work focused every day, whether the job was a rare start or making pitchers comfortable in the bullpen. He was a legitimate offensive presence as a reserve, with a .301 average and 20 RBI in 58 games.

Hitting, Baserunning & Defense

Zaun has a smooth swing with decent power, especially if he's fed a hanging breaking ball. He doesn't have much speed, but doesn't run the Marlins out of opportunities either. He calls a solid game and isn't a pushover when it comes to combating basestealers.

1998 Outlook

Zaun is the kind of player manager Jim Leyland likes, someone who just goes about his job and respects the fact that the 22nd or 23rd man on the roster still can mean a lot. He has been through pennant races with the Orioles and Marlins, and is a valuable commodity as a seasoned catcher who hits well from either side of the plate.

Other Florida Marlins

Antonio Alfonseca (Pos: RHP, Age: 25)

	W	L	Pct.	ERA	G	GS	Sv	IP	H	BB	SO	HR	Ratio
1997	1	3	.250	4.91	17	0	0	25.2	36	10	19	3	1.79
Career	1	3	.250	4.91	17	0	0	25.2	36	10	19	3	1.79

Alfonseca made his major league debut for the Marlins last season, with mixed results. His biggest claim to fame is having six fingers on each hand and six toes on each foot. 1998 Outlook: B

Alex Arias (Pos: 3B/SS, Age: 30, Bats: R)

	G	AB	R	H	D	T	HR	RBI	SB	BB	SO	Avg	OBP	Slg
1997	74	93	13	23	2	0	1	11	0	12	12	.247	.352	.301
Career	455	994	107	266	38	5	9	105	4	98	110	.268	.339	.343

The addition of Bobby Bonilla and the continued development of Edgar Renteria made Arias obsolete last year. 1998 Outlook: C

Kurt Miller (Pos: RHP, Age: 25)

	W	L	Pct.	ERA	G	GS	Sv	IP	H	BB	SO	HR	Ratio
1997	0	1	.000	9.82	7	0	0	7.1	12	7	7	2	2.59
Career	2	7	.222	7.45	37	9	0	73.2	95	47	48	10	1.93

Elbow difficulties cost Miller most of the '97 season. He continued to exhibit serious control problems, then was traded to the Cubs. 1998 Outlook: C

Russ Morman (Pos: RF, Age: 35, Bats: R)

	G	AB	R	H	D	T	HR	RBI	SB	BB	SO	Avg	OBP	Slg
1997	4	7	3	2	1	0	1	2	1	0	2	.286	.286	.857
Career	207	470	51	117	17	4	10	43	3	35	102	.249	.304	.366

Morman has garnered just 13 at-bats in the majors since suffering a knee injury in 1995. He spent just three weeks on the Marlins roster last season, and at age 36, he's probably finished. 1998 Outlook: D

Bob Natal (Pos: C, Age: 32, Bats: R)

	G	AB	R	H	D	T	HR	RBI	SB	BB	SO	Avg	OBP	Slg
1997	4	4	2	2	1	0	1	3	0	2	0	.500	.571	1.500
Career	120	289	13	57	10	3	4	19	2	30	68	.197	.279	.294

After the Marlins acquired Gregg Zaun to handle the backup-catching duties, Natal found himself without a job. He was released after the season. 1998 Outlook: C

Kirt Ojala (Pos: LHP, Age: 29)

	W	L	Pct.	ERA	G	GS	Sv	IP	H	BB	SO	HR	Ratio
1997	1	2	.333	3.14	7	5	0	28.2	28	18	19	4	1.60
Career	1	2	.333	3.14	7	5	0	28.2	28	18	19	4	1.60

Ojala finally reached the majors in August after toiling for eight years in the minor leagues, making five starts for the Marlins in September. He signed with Arizona as a free agent. 1998 Outlook: C

Donn Pall (Pos: RHP, Age: 36)

	W	L	Pct.	ERA	G	GS	Sv	IP	H	BB	SO	HR	Ratio
1997	0	0	-	3.86	2	0	0	2.1	3	1	0	1	1.71
Career	24	22	.522	3.53	305	0	10	472.0	477	132	252	47	1.29

If you blinked at all last season, chances are that you missed Pall's stint in the majors. Pall spent a grand total of five days with Florida before returning to Triple-A Charlotte. The end is near. 1998 Outlook: D

Robby Stanifer (Pos: RHP, Age: 26)

	W	L	Pct.	ERA	G	GS	Sv	IP	H	BB	SO	HR	Ratio
1997	1	2	.333	4.60	36	0	1	45.0	43	16	28	9	1.31
Career	1	2	.333	4.60	36	0	1	45.0	43	16	28	9	1.31

Stanifer was shuttled back-and-forth between Florida and Triple-A Charlotte in '97, with three stops at each location. He's been hit hard, but does possess strong strikeout data. Still fairly young. 1998 Outlook: B

Ed Vosberg (Pos: LHP, Age: 36)

	W	L	Pct.	ERA	G	GS	Sv	IP	H	BB	SO	HR	Ratio
1997	2	3	.400	4.42	59	0	1	53.0	59	21	37	3	1.51
Career	9	13	.409	4.14	194	3	13	184.2	198	78	137	16	1.52

Vosberg was acquired from the Rangers in mid-August to solidify the Marlins' bullpen for the stretch drive and the postseason. He was traded to the Padres after the World Series. 1998 Outlook: A

John Wehner (Pos: RF, Age: 30, Bats: R)

	G	AB	R	H	D	T	HR	RBI	SB	BB	SO	Avg	OBP	Slg
1997	44	36	8	10	2	0	0	2	1	2	5	.278	.333	.333
Career	305	550	70	143	25	4	2	34	11	45	94	.260	.316	.331

Bouncing between the minors and majors throughout his entire career, Wehner occasionally filled in at all three outfield spots for Florida last season. The Marlins cut him in the offseason. 1998 Outlook: C

Florida Marlins Minor League Prospects

Organization Overview:

It would be easy to say Florida bought itself a World Series championship, but that just wouldn't be true. Postseason heroes Livan Hernandez and Edgar Renteria are homegrown Marlins, as are Gold-Glove catcher Charles Johnson and lefty setup man Felix Heredia. Florida wouldn't have won without those players, and plenty more are on the way. The Marlins only began drafting in 1992, but already have a system as good as any in the game. They lost the first player in the expansion draft, and early picks in the next two rounds. GM David Dombrowski and scouting gurus Gary Hughes and Orrin Freeman built up Montreal in the late 1980s and quickly have done the same in Florida. They'll have to keep churning out talent after the Marlins decided to slash salaries.

Manuel Barrios

Position: P　　　　**Opening Day Age:** 23
Bats: R **Throws:** R　　**Born:** 9/21/74 in
Ht: 6' 0" **Wt:** 145　　Cabecera, Panama

Recent Statistics

	W	L	ERA	G	GS	Sv	IP	H	R	BB	SO	HR
97 AAA New Orleans	4	8	3.27	57	0	0	82.2	70	32	34	77	5
97 NL Houston	0	0	12.00	2	0	0	3.0	6	4	3	3	0

Signed out of Panama in 1993, Barrios has put together three straight solid seasons in short relief. He doesn't have the stuff to close in the majors and he's not strong enough to start, but he should be an effective middle reliever for the Marlins, who got him from Houston in the Moises Alou trade. He throws four pitches for strikes and has excellent velocity. Barrios gets the job done against both lefthanders and righthanders, and he showed he can pitch under pressure by leading the system in saves in 1995 and 1996. He should be able to win a role in Florida in spring training.

Todd Dunwoody

Position: OF　　　　**Opening Day Age:** 22
Bats: L **Throws:** L　　**Born:** 4/11/75 in West
Ht: 6' 2" **Wt:** 185　　Lafayette, IN

Recent Statistics

	G	AB	R	H	D	T	HR	RBI	SB	BB	SO	AVG
97 AAA Charlotte	107	401	74	105	16	7	23	62	25	39	129	.262
97 NL Florida	19	50	7	13	2	2	2	7	2	7	21	.260
97 MLE	107	378	49	82	12	5	13	41	16	26	135	.217

For a five-tool prospect, Dunwoody can't seem to generate much attention. A seventh-round pick in 1993, he doesn't have one overwhelming skill but does everything well. He can hit and hit for power, catch and throw in center field, and steal bases. Managers voted him the best hitter and most exiciting player in the Triple-A

International League, and he often is compared to a young Andy Van Slyke. He still chases too many pitches because he sometimes gets too aggressive, but he held his own in a brief big league trial. He'll get a chance to play everyday for the Marlins in left or center.

Joe Fontenot

Position: P　　　　**Opening Day Age:** 21
Bats: R **Throws:** R　　**Born:** 3/20/77 in Scott,
Ht: 6' 2" **Wt:** 185　　LA

Recent Statistics

	W	L	ERA	G	GS	Sv	IP	H	R	BB	SO	HR
96 A San Jose	9	4	4.44	26	23	0	144.0	137	87	74	124	7
97 AA Shreveport	10	11	5.53	26	26	0	151.1	171	105	65	103	12

When the Marlins decided to rid themselves of Robb Nen's salary, they sent him to San Francisco for three prospects. The best of the group was Fontenot, a 1995 first-round pick. He had been moving on a fast track with the Giants, pitching in high Class-A at age 19 and Double-A at 20. His 1997 numbers weren't pretty, but he pitched much better in the second half when his location improved. He has three quality pitches—a mid-90s fastball, a changeup and a curveball—and also throws a cut fastball. He has proven his mental and physical toughness. Fontenot would be best off if he started 1998 in Double-A, but he could reach Florida by September.

Alex Gonzalez

Position: SS　　　　**Opening Day Age:** 21
Bats: R **Throws:** R　　**Born:** 2/15/77 in Cagua,
Ht: 6' 0" **Wt:** 150　　Aragua, Venez

Recent Statistics

	G	AB	R	H	D	T	HR	RBI	SB	BB	SO	AVG
96 R Marlins	10	41	6	16	3	0	0	6	1	2	4	.390
96 A Kane County	4	10	2	2	0	0	0	0	0	2	4	.200
96 AA Portland	11	34	4	8	0	1	0	1	0	2	10	.235
97 AA Portland	133	449	69	114	16	4	19	65	4	27	83	.254
97 MLE	133	428	47	93	12	3	12	45	2	16	88	.217

As good as Renteria is, Gonzalez could be even better. Signed out of Venezuela, he jumped to Double-A despite little full-season experience. He hit 19 homers, showing his developing strength, though some of those longballs should be attributed to the friendly confines of Portland. His offensive skills will be hampered if he can't draw more walks and make better contact, but it's his defense that really excites the Marlins. He could play a solid big league shortstop right now, and may push Renteria to third base when the time comes. Gonzalez needs at least a season in Triple-A to refine his offensive skills. He also has good speed but doesn't use it well as a basestealer.

Oscar Henriquez

Position: P   **Opening Day Age:** 24
Bats: R **Throws:** R   **Born:** 1/28/74 in
Ht: 6' 4" **Wt:** 175   La Guaira, Venez

Recent Statistics

	W	L	ERA	G	GS	Sv	IP	H	R	BB	SO	HR
97 AAA New Orleans	4	5	2.80	60	0	12	74.0	65	28	27	80	4
97 NL Houston	0	1	4.50	4	0	0	4.0	2	2	3	3	0

On the verge of sticking in the big leagues, Henriquez is just happy to be alive. A rare muscle disorder nearly killed him in 1994 and cost the big Venezuelan a season and a half. Since his return he has thrived despite having only one pitch he can trust. That pitch is a fastball that is clocked consistently at 98 MPH and tops out at 100. He has a hard curveball that can surprise hitters, but his control of it is extremely poor. He throws nothing soft and basically dares batters to try to catch up to his heat. Acquired from the Astros in the Moises Alou trade, he could replace Robb Nen as Florida's closer.

Mark Kotsay

Position: OF   **Opening Day Age:** 22
Bats: L **Throws:** L   **Born:** 12/2/75 in
Ht: 6' 0" **Wt:** 180   Woodier, CA

Recent Statistics

	G	AB	R	H	D	T	HR	RBI	SB	BB	SO	AVG
97 AA Portland	114	438	103	134	27	2	20	77	17	75	65	.306
97 NL Florida	14	52	5	10	1	1	0	4	3	4	7	.192
97 MLE	114	411	71	107	21	1	12	53	10	44	69	.260

Kotsay is similar to Dunwoody in that he's a blue-collar center fielder whose skills don't seem to be fully acclaimed. Kotsay led Cal State Fullerton to the 1995 College World Series championship and played on the 1996 U.S. Olympic team, but his lack of physical dominance was questioned along the way. A 1996 first-round pick, he's not the strongest or fastest player around. But few can match his hitting ability and his selective eye, which should add to his developing power. He can steal a base and catch most anything hit to center field. The Marlins showed what they thought of Kotsay when they promoted him in 1997, even though it meant they had to protect him from the expansion draft. He's the leading candidate to replace Devon White in center field.

Ralph Milliard

Position: 2B   **Opening Day Age:** 24
Bats: R **Throws:** R   **Born:** 12/30/73 in
Ht: 5' 10" **Wt:** 160   Willemstad, Curacao, Neth. Ant.

Recent Statistics

	G	AB	R	H	D	T	HR	RBI	SB	BB	SO	AVG
97 AAA Charlotte	33	132	19	35	5	1	4	18	5	9	21	.265
97 AA Portland	19	69	13	19	1	2	0	5	3	7	8	.275
97 NL Florida	8	30	2	6	0	0	0	2	1	3	3	.200

Injuries and Castillo's emergence have taken Milliard out of the limelight the past two seasons, but he's still a viable prospect. Surgery to remove bone chips from his throwing elbow limited him to 60 games in 1997, leaving him unavailable to contribute when Castillo slumped and was demoted. Milliard strikes out a bit much, but he usually compensates with walks. He can hit the occasional homer and steal the occasional base, and he's also a tremendous defensive player. The Curacao native has little left to prove except that he can stay healthy, but might have a tough time supplanting Castillo, Craig Counsell and Kurt Abbott.

John Roskos

Position: C/1B   **Opening Day Age:** 23
Bats: R **Throws:** R   **Born:** 11/19/74 in
Ht: 5' 11" **Wt:** 198   Victorville, CA

Recent Statistics

	G	AB	R	H	D	T	HR	RBI	SB	BB	SO	AVG
96 AA Portland	121	396	53	109	26	3	9	58	3	67	102	.275
97 AA Portland	123	451	66	139	31	4	24	84	4	50	81	.308
97 MLE	123	425	45	113	25	0	16	58	2	29	86	.266

Roskos was a catcher when he signed as a second-round pick in 1993, but Johnson's rapid development sealed that position for the Marlins. In the last two seasons Roskos has spent a lot of time at first base, where a better opportunity awaits in Florida. His best tools are his bat and his power, and his walk and strikeout totals are good for a budding slugger. He can't run much and has had arm problems in the past, but he won't be in the lineup to steal bases or play defense. If the Marlins don't settle on a first baseman, they could turn to Roskos in 1999.

Others to Watch

Lefthander **Brent Billingsley** went 14-7, 3.01 with 175 strikeouts in 171 innings at Class A Kane County. He was 22 and has just an adequate fastball, but he locates it well and has three other effective pitches. . . You can interpret **Josh Booty's** Double-A season any way you want. On one hand, he hit 20 homers at age 22 and managers voted him the Eastern League's best defensive third baseman and best infield arm. On the other, he hit .210 with 27 walks and 166 strikeouts. . . Second baseman **Amaury Garcia**, 22, could have a higher ceiling than Milliard. he has doubles power and stolen-base potential. . . Sluggers **Ryan Jackson** and **Kevin Millar** combined for 58 homers in Portland. Both are 26 but might get a shot. Jackson is a corner outfielder who bounced back from knee surgery. Millar has hit at every level since being signed out of the independent Northern League. He won the Eastern League batting title and hit .342-32-131. . . Dominican righthander **Nelson Lara** has the best arm in the organization. He throws a 97-98 MPH fastball and a low-90s slider, and is still 19. . . The Marlins got lefthander **Jesus Martinez**, 24, from Arizona in exchange for Devon White. Martinez, the younger brother of Pedro and Ramon, has decent velocity but no command. . . **Julio Ramirez**, 20, is yet another five-tool Marlins center fielder. His speed and arm are his best skills.

Larry Dierker

1997 Season

Going from the broadcast booth to the dugout, Larry Dierker piloted the Astros to the National League Central title. Despite that, he's still suspect as a manager in some people's eyes. He was patient with struggling players, and some said he was too patient. His communication skills and willingness to listen to his coaches and players are his biggest assets.

Offense

Dierker wants Houston to win with excellent pitching, speed and defense. His offense can be called aggressive, especially after he gave the team the green light to steal in midsummer. The Astros ended up near the top of the list with 245 stolen-base attempts. He usually doesn't call for the sacrifice bunt in the early innings unless a pitcher is batting. His penchant for staying with the starting pitcher as long as possible cuts down on pinch-hitting opportunities on a team that, at times, had trouble scoring runs.

Pitching & Defense

Dierker thinks starters should pitch as long as he did when he was playing, and he stays with them as long as any manager in the majors. His use of relievers was perplexing, but in fairness the bullpen's performance was inconsistent. He'll go with the hot hand, but otherwise his bullpen roles aren't clearly defined. He seldom double switches or pitches out. Twice in 1997 he forgot to double switch when the situation dictated it, and he still is learning on the job.

1998 Outlook

Dierker is signed through the 1998 season, and owner Drayton McLane already is talking about an extension. The Astros are expected to contend for the division title again, and anything less could land Dierker in hot water.

Born: 9/22/46 in Hollywood, CA

Playing Experience: 1964-1977, Hou, StL

Managerial Experience: 1 season

Pronunciation: DEER-ker

Manager Statistics

Year	Team, Lg	W	L	Pct	GB	Finish
1997	Houston, NL	84	78	.519	—	1st Central
1 Season		84	78	.519	—	—

1997 Starting Pitchers by Days Rest

	≤3	4	5	6+
Astros Starts	5	98	34	16
Astros ERA	2.73	3.55	3.38	5.42
NL Avg Starts	3	90	38	22
NL ERA	4.23	4.05	4.27	4.52

1997 Situational Stats

	Larry Dierker	NL Average
Hit & Run Success %	27.5	36.4
Stolen Base Success %	69.8	68.4
Platoon Pct.	45.4	56.3
Defensive Subs	26	26
High-Pitch Outings	13	12
Quick/Slow Hooks	12/5	18/10
Sacrifice Attempts	96	96

1997 Rankings (National League)

⇒ 1st in stolen base attempts (245), steals of second base (142), steals of third base (29), least caught steals of home plate (0) and double steals (10)

⇒ 2nd in starts on three days rest (5)

⇒ 3rd in starting lineups used (131)

Houston Astros

Bob Abreu

Position: RF
Bats: L **Throws:** R
Ht: 6' 0" **Wt:** 160

Opening Day Age: 24
Born: 3/11/74 in Aragua, Venezuela
ML Seasons: 2
Pronunciation: uh-BRAY-you

1997 Season

After beginning the season as the Astros' starting right fielder, rookie Bob Abreu slumped in May and lost his job. Later in the month he hurt his wrist, and surgery put him out of action until July. After getting seven at-bats in two weeks, he was sent to the minors July 16 and didn't return until September, when he hit .294 in 14 games. The demotion didn't sit with him well.

Hitting

Hitting coach Tom McCraw worked hard with the lefthanded-hitting Abreu so he would be more patient and stop chasing breaking pitches out of the strike zone. The results weren't apparent. He struggled against lefties after hitting them fairly well at Triple-A in 1996. His poor hitting was the single biggest factor in the decision to leave him unprotected during the first round of the expansion draft.

Baserunning & Defense

Abreu once had the best arm in the organization, and still is an above-average thrower despite rotator-cuff surgery in 1993. His outfield play wasn't as impressive in 1997 as it had been in the minors, however. He had just four outfield assists in Houston after recording 18 in 114 games in 1995. He stole just seven bases despite having a green light to go all year. He's a tentative baserunner and the Astros wanted him to work on that area of his game during winter ball.

1998 Outlook

Abreu will get another shot to crack a starting lineup this year, though that opportunity will come in Philadelphia. He was taken sixth overall in the expansion draft by Tampa Bay, then traded for Kevin Stocker. If he stays healthy and plays every day, he has the tools to bat .280 with medium-range power and a fair number of steals. His power development will be critical. He showed great potential four years ago as a 20 year old in Double-A, but since then, his development has stalled. He'll need to add some pop if he hopes to make it as a corner outfielder.

Overall Statistics

	G	AB	R	H	D	T	HR	RBI	SB	BB	SO	Avg	OBP	Slg
1997	59	188	22	47	10	2	3	26	7	21	48	.250	.329	.372
Career	74	210	23	52	11	2	3	27	7	23	51	.248	.325	.362

Where He Hits the Ball

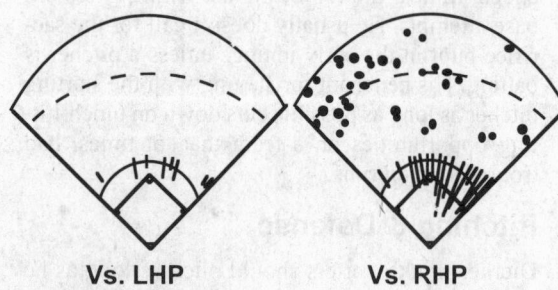

Vs. LHP   **Vs. RHP**

1997 Situational Stats

	AB	H	HR	RBI	Avg		AB	H	HR	RBI	Avg
Home	101	28	3	15	.277	LHP	33	6	0	6	.182
Road	87	19	0	11	.218	RHP	155	41	3	20	.265
First Half	152	36	2	19	.237	Sc Pos	43	15	0	19	.349
Scnd Half	36	11	1	7	.306	Clutch	42	9	1	3	.214

1997 Rankings (National League)

⇒ Did not rank near the top or bottom in any category

Brad Ausmus

1997 Season

Ausmus had the best year of his career, setting peronal highs in several offensive categories. He started the season strong, hitting .344 in April and .284 before the All-Star break, then tailed off somewhat during the the final three months of the season. He helped solidify the catching situation and improve the defense up the middle. His handling of the pitching staff was lauded as Houston's starters ranked among the best in the National League.

Hitting

A line-drive hitter with little power, Ausmus settled into the No. 8 spot and gave the team some production at the bottom of the order. He stands in well against breaking balls but has trouble with good fastballs, particularly if they are high in the strike zone. Lefthanders give him more trouble than righties, a reverse-platoon effect that has lasted throughout his career.

Baserunning & Defense

Ausmus has excellent speed for a catcher and swiped 14 bases in 20 attempts in 1997. He isn't overly aggressive on the bases but is better than most catchers going from first to third. Defensively, he has an average arm but compensates with a quick release that helped him throw out 45 percent of basestealers in 1997, the top figure in the NL. That performance is even more outstanding, considering the number of breaking-ball pitchers on the Houston staff.

1998 Outlook

Ausmus showed he's a solid everyday catcher who's strong defensively, calls a good game and is no slouch with the lumber. He worked very well with the young pitchers, especially Ramon Garcia, Chris Holt and Mike Hampton. The Astros want him to be the everyday catcher again in 1998, and at 28 he should be entering the most productive years of his career.

Position: C
Bats: R **Throws:** R
Ht: 5'11" **Wt:** 190

Opening Day Age: 28
Born: 4/14/69 in New Haven, CT
ML Seasons: 5
Pronunciation: AHHS-muss

Overall Statistics

	G	AB	R	H	D	T	HR	RBI	SB	BB	SO	Avg	OBP	Slg
1997	130	425	45	113	25	1	4	44	14	38	78	.266	.326	.358
Career	508	1615	198	415	77	7	26	149	41	144	297	.257	.320	.362

Where He Hits the Ball

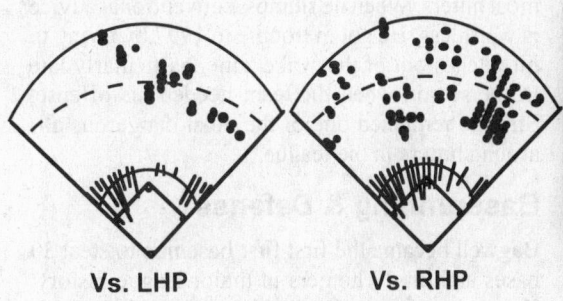

Vs. LHP   **Vs. RHP**

1997 Situational Stats

	AB	H	HR	RBI	Avg		AB	H	HR	RBI	Avg
Home	196	54	1	15	.276	LHP	96	23	1	11	.240
Road	229	59	3	29	.258	RHP	329	90	3	33	.274
First Half	229	65	2	19	.284	Sc Pos	108	28	3	41	.259
Scnd Half	196	48	2	25	.245	Clutch	83	18	2	13	.217

1997 Rankings (National League)

⇒ 1st in highest percentage of runners caught stealing as a catcher (44.7%)
⇒ 9th in errors at catcher (7)

Jeff Bagwell

1997 Season

Though he set several Astro season records and became the franchise's first 30-30 player, Jeff Bagwell didn't have a completely satisfying season in 1997. He started fast but hit only .250 after the All-Star break. On the plus side, he played in all 162 games for the second consecutive year and put up good numbers in the No. 3 spot in the lineup. His 43 homers were a career high and the most ever by an Astro player.

Hitting

Bagwell may have the game's most unorthodox stance. He spreads his feet wide and shortens them up as the pitch approaches, the direct opposite of most hitters. When he slumps, conventional advice is worthless. He got in trouble in 1997 by trying to hit pitches out of the strike zone, particularly late in the season when the team needed his offense. Still, he remained one of the most dangerous all-around hitters in the league.

Baserunning & Defense

Bagwell became the first first baseman to steal 30 bases and hit 30 homers in major league history. He's adept at reading pitchers' moves, and his career-high 31 swipes were largely the product of surprise and good reads rather than speed. He's as aggressive defensively as he is on the basepaths, and cut down his errors from 16 in 1996 to 11 in 1997. He's among the best first basemen in the National League at digging throws out of the dirt.

1998 Outlook

Bagwell is in the prime of his career and should continue to put up All-Star numbers. It's hardly an exaggeration to say that no hitter in baseball means more to his team—Bagwell drove in the highest percentage of his team's runs of any player in the game. The addition of Moises Alou will give the Astros one of the most potent one-two punches in the league.

Position: 1B
Bats: R **Throws:** R
Ht: 6' 0" **Wt:** 195

Opening Day Age: 29
Born: 5/27/68 in Boston, MA
ML Seasons: 7

Overall Statistics

	G	AB	R	H	D	T	HR	RBI	SB	BB	SO	Avg	OBP	Slg
1997	162	566	109	162	40	2	43	135	31	127	122	.286	.425	.592
Career	1008	3657	654	1112	246	20	187	724	109	627	689	.304	.409	.536

Where He Hits the Ball

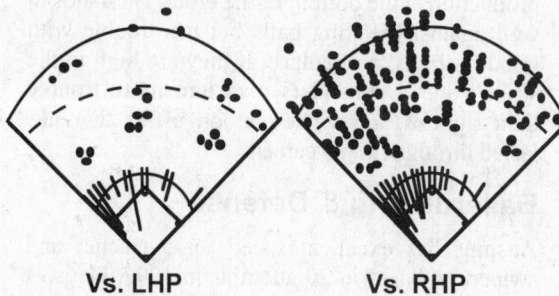

Vs. LHP   **Vs. RHP**

1997 Situational Stats

	AB	H	HR	RBI	Avg		AB	H	HR	RBI	Avg
Home	264	68	22	67	.258	LHP	120	29	5	20	.242
Road	302	94	21	68	.311	RHP	446	133	38	115	.298
First Half	318	100	24	78	.314	Sc Pos	161	50	9	86	.311
Scnd Half	248	62	19	57	.250	Clutch	97	24	5	16	.247

1997 Rankings (National League)

⇒ 1st in pitches seen (2,818) and games played (162)

⇒ 2nd in home runs, RBI, walks, intentional walks (27) and HR frequency (13.2 ABs per HR)

⇒ 3rd in times on base (305), plate appearances (717), slugging percentage, slugging percentage vs. righthanded pitchers (.630) and errors at first base (11)

⇒ Led the Astros in home runs, doubles, total bases (335), RBI, sacrifice flies (8), caught stealing (10), walks, intentional walks (27), strikeouts, pitches seen (2,818), games played (162), slugging percentage, on-base percentage, HR frequency (13.2 ABs per HR), most pitches seen per plate appearance (3.93) and batting average with the bases loaded (.300)

Derek Bell

1997 Season

Derek Bell failed to hold on to the starting center-field job in 1997, didn't produce as a cleanup hitter and was hitting .242 as late as the Fourth of July. He was also unhappy about getting booed by the fans and about moving back to cleanup briefly in September. Depsite all of these problems, he managed to drive in 71 runs despite spending 23 games on the disabled list with a severely bruised left calf. He batted .299 with 10 homers and 45 RBI after the All-Star break.

Hitting

Usually a fast starter, Bell hit .204 in April in what was the most bizarre season of his career. He changed batting stances no fewer than six times, sometimes from at-bat to at-bat. A career .306 hitter against lefties coming into the season, he batted a career-low .235 with one homer in 119 at-bats against southpaws. No one on the Astros hits the ball harder than Bell, but he still strikes out too much and doesn't have the lift to be a 25-30 homer hitter.

Baserunning & Defense

Bell's 15 steals were a career low and he was caught seven times, his worst success rate since breaking into the majors full-time in 1993. He still hasn't learned to read pitchers as well as his teammates and isn't as aggressive on the bases as someone with his speed ought to be. He makes more blunders than he should in right field, but has a very strong arm and isn't reluctant to get his uniform dirty diving for balls.

1998 Outlook

Critics claimed Bell wasn't as hungry after signing a three-year, $13 million contract before the 1997 season. He didn't help matters by insisting he wasn't slumping even when he was hitting .220 early in the year. He seemed to find his niche hitting in the No. 2 spot and may rebound if he's just put there and left alone.

Position: RF/CF
Bats: R **Throws:** R
Ht: 6' 2" **Wt:** 215

Opening Day Age: 29
Born: 12/11/68 in Tampa, FL
ML Seasons: 7

Overall Statistics

	G	AB	R	H	D	T	HR	RBI	SB	BB	SO	Avg	OBP	Slg
1997	129	493	67	136	29	3	15	71	15	40	94	.276	.344	.438
Career	736	2737	369	772	135	12	77	412	131	186	537	.282	.335	.425

Where He Hits the Ball

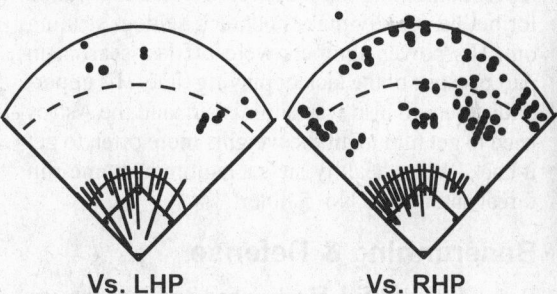

Vs. LHP   Vs. RHP

1997 Situational Stats

	AB	H	HR	RBI	Avg		AB	H	HR	RBI	Avg
Home	241	71	7	40	.295	LHP	119	28	1	9	.235
Road	252	65	8	31	.258	RHP	374	108	14	62	.289
First Half	219	54	5	26	.247	Sc Pos	158	39	3	52	.247
Scnd Half	274	82	10	45	.299	Clutch	92	24	2	9	.261

1997 Rankings (National League)

⇒ 1st in lowest cleanup slugging percentage (.293)
⇒ 3rd in lowest on-base percentage vs. lefthanded pitchers (.270)
⇒ 5th in lowest slugging percentage vs. lefthanded pitchers (.311) and errors in right field (6)
⇒ 10th in lowest batting average vs. lefthanded pitchers
⇒ Led the Astros in highest groundball/flyball ratio (1.6)

Houston Astros

Sean Berry

1997 Season

After third baseman Sean Berry played the entire 1996 season with a torn rotator cuff, but still hit 17 homers and drove in 95 runs in only 431 at-bats, the Astros hoped he would be even better after offseason surgery. But Berry's rehab went slower than anticipated and limited him to 301 at-bats. His .256 average, eight homers and 40 RBI were major league lows in a full season for Berry. He lost his starting job to Bill Spiers and was left unprotected in the expansion draft. He did finish strong, hitting .308 after the All-Star break.

Hitting

Berry has a textbook swing, but his bat speed leaves something to be desired. He doesn't walk a lot but he usually makes contact, seldom striking out. His power numbers were off last season, in part because of the lack of playing time. His upper-body strength also was diminished, and the Astros tried to get him to hit the weights more often to get it back. When healthy, he's a legitimate home-run threat and a solid No. 5 hitter.

Baserunning & Defense

Berry doesn't have much speed and was thrown out five of the six times he attempted to steal in 1997. He obviously has lost a step since stealing 26 bases in 28 attempts during 1993 and 1994. Defensively, he's a liability. His range is minimal, his lack of speed makes him vulnerable to bunts and his erratic throwing arm contributed to his 16 errors in 1997.

1998 Outlook

With Bill Spiers coming off a solid season and prospect Russ Johnson on the horizon, the Astros believe Berry is expendable. With his diminished fielding skills and suspect health, he likely won't be a starter if he returns to Houston. Berry's skills make him more suited to be a designated hitter, a role in which he excelled during interleague games.

Position: 3B
Bats: R **Throws:** R
Ht: 5'11" **Wt:** 200

Opening Day Age: 32
Born: 3/22/66 in Santa Monica, CA
ML Seasons: 8

Overall Statistics

	G	AB	R	H	D	T	HR	RBI	SB	BB	SO	Avg	OBP	Slg
1997	96	301	37	77	24	1	8	43	1	25	53	.256	.318	.422
Career	619	1805	235	497	123	8	65	292	44	154	323	.275	.336	.460

Where He Hits the Ball

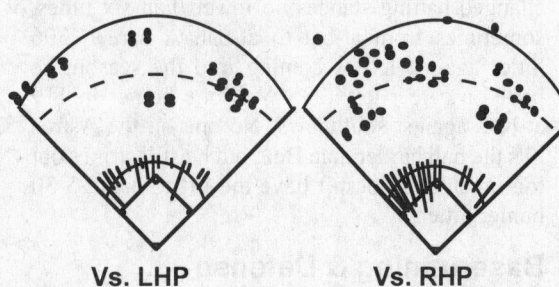

Vs. LHP   Vs. RHP

1997 Situational Stats

	AB	H	HR	RBI	Avg		AB	H	HR	RBI	Avg
Home	156	40	4	25	.256	LHP	75	18	2	12	.240
Road	145	37	4	18	.255	RHP	226	59	6	31	.261
First Half	194	44	5	19	.227	Sc Pos	92	19	1	32	.207
Scnd Half	107	33	3	24	.308	Clutch	44	7	2	6	.159

1997 Rankings (National League)

⇒ 2nd in lowest batting average in the clutch
⇒ 6th in lowest batting average with runners in scoring position
⇒ 7th in errors at third base (16)
⇒ 8th in batting average on an 0-2 count (.280)
⇒ 10th in lowest batting average on a 3-2 count (.100)

Craig Biggio

1997 Season

Craig Biggio was the best all-around player on the National League Central champions. He led the NL in runs for the second time in his career, and his 146 runs were the most by an NL player in 65 years. Biggio set career highs in runs, RBI (81), stolen bases (47) and triples (8). He tied a career high with 22 home runs and helped keep the team near the top of the division when Jeff Bagwell and Derek Bell slumped.

Hitting

Biggio sprays the ball to all fields and crowds the plate as much as any hitter in baseball, which accounted for his club record of getting hit by 34 pitches. He has led the NL in that category three straight seasons. A patient hitter, he has power to the gaps. Though he occasionally can be fooled by sliders inside, he's one of the best leadoff hitters in the game. He does it all, drawing walks, stealing bases and scoring runs—in addition to being a dangerous hitter.

Baserunning & Defense

No Astro reads opposing pitchers better than Biggio. He was successful on 47 of 57 steal attempts in 1997. His speed also showed as he became the first regular in major league history not to ground into a double play in a 162-game season. He's an extremely aggressive baserunner, and will move from first to third on a base hit on even the best arms in the league. He committed a career-high 18 errors last season but still ranked among the best in the NL at his position. He won his fourth straight Gold Glove in 1997.

1998 Outlook

Biggio is in the prime of his career and should continue to shine. The Astros have discussed dropping him to the No. 3 spot in the lineup as a possible way to take advantage of his power. He likes hitting leadoff and might opt to stay put. In any case, he should remain one of the best all-around players in the game.

Position: 2B
Bats: R **Throws:** R
Ht: 5'11" **Wt:** 180

Opening Day Age: 32
Born: 12/14/65 in Smithtown, NY
ML Seasons: 10
Pronunciation: BIDG-jee-oh

Overall Statistics

	G	AB	R	H	D	T	HR	RBI	SB	BB	SO	Avg	OBP	Slg
1997	162	619	146	191	37	8	22	81	47	84	107	.309	.415	.501
Career	1379	5104	874	1470	282	36	116	545	268	634	753	.288	.377	.426

Where He Hits the Ball

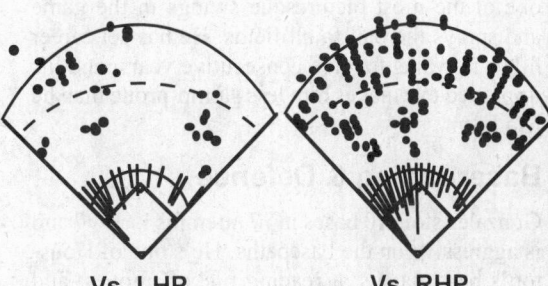

Vs. LHP   **Vs. RHP**

1997 Situational Stats

	AB	H	HR	RBI	Avg		AB	H	HR	RBI	Avg
Home	301	92	7	31	.306	LHP	138	45	6	19	.326
Road	318	99	15	50	.311	RHP	481	146	16	62	.304
First Half	347	106	13	44	.305	Sc Pos	123	44	4	56	.358
Scnd Half	272	85	9	37	.313	Clutch	102	28	5	18	.275

1997 Rankings (National League)

⇒ 1st in runs scored, hit by pitch (34), times on base (309), plate appearances (744), games played (162) and least GDPs per GDP situation (0.0%)

⇒ 2nd in on-base percentage for a leadoff hitter (.418) and highest percentage of extra bases taken as a runner (68.7%)

⇒ 3rd in pitches seen (2,730), on-base percentage vs. lefthanded pitchers (.444), errors at second base (18) and steals of third (14)

⇒ Led the Astros in batting average, at-bats, runs scored, hits, singles, triples, stolen bases, caught stealing (10), hit by pitch (34), times on base (309), plate appearances (744), games played (162), stolen base percentage (82.5%) and least GDPs per GDP situation (0.0%)

Luis Gonzalez

1997 Season

Returning to the Astros after a two-year absence, Luis Gonzalez bounced around the batting order before finally settling in the cleanup spot. Hitting in a role he was unaccustomed to, he had mixed results. His nine homers were the fewest by a full-time No. 4 hitter in baseball. He batted just .232 after the All-Star break, but still contributed by playing outstanding defense and keeping the clubhouse loose.

Hitting

A textbook streak hitter who likes the ball low, Gonzalez is at his best when he isn't expected to provide more than 10-15 homers. He possesses one of the most picturesque swings in the game and sprays the ball to all fields. He has set career highs in walks for five consecutive years, and his improved eye makes him less slump-prone than he had been.

Baserunning & Defense

Gonzalez stole 10 bases in 17 attempts in 1997 and is aggressive on the basepaths. He's one of Houston's best players at reading pickoff moves, and usually gets outstanding jumps. Defensively, he plays a very technically sound left field. He compensates for a subpar throwing arm with accurate throws.

1998 Outlook

A free agent, Gonzalez likely will retain his starter's role because he has proven he can hit lefthanders adequately. He likely will do so elsewhere after Houston traded for Moises Alou. Oddly, in each of the past two years, he's played for teams that have asked him to be a run-producer, when he's really everything *but* one. His defense and his lefty bat are attractive in a righthanded-dominated lineup. Only 30, he still has plenty of baseball left.

Position: LF
Bats: L **Throws:** R
Ht: 6' 2" **Wt:** 185

Opening Day Age: 30
Born: 9/3/67 in Tampa, FL
ML Seasons: 8

Overall Statistics

	G	AB	R	H	D	T	HR	RBI	SB	BB	SO	Avg	OBP	Slg
1997	152	550	78	142	31	2	10	68	10	71	67	.258	.345	.376
Career	968	3317	448	890	202	33	84	479	77	351	477	.268	.342	.425

Where He Hits the Ball

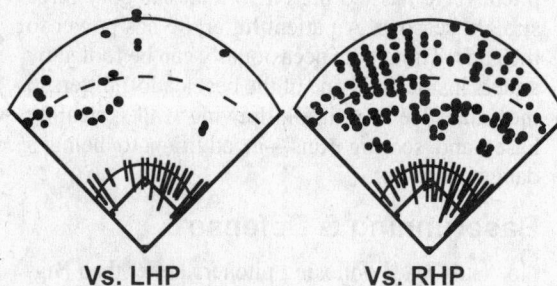

Vs. LHP   **Vs. RHP**

1997 Situational Stats

	AB	H	HR	RBI	Avg		AB	H	HR	RBI	Avg
Home	253	66	4	30	.261	LHP	132	33	3	15	.250
Road	297	76	6	38	.256	RHP	418	109	7	53	.261
First Half	300	84	4	37	.280	Sc Pos	164	40	1	54	.244
Scnd Half	250	58	6	31	.232	Clutch	96	21	1	8	.219

1997 Rankings (National League)

⇒ 3rd in lowest cleanup slugging percentage (.394)
⇒ 4th in errors in left field (5) and lowest fielding percentage in left field (.982)
⇒ 7th in batting average on an 0-2 count (.286)
⇒ 9th in lowest percentage of swings that missed (11.3%)
⇒ 10th in lowest slugging percentage and lowest slugging percentage vs. lefthanded pitchers (.356)
⇒ Led the Astros in cleanup slugging percentage (.394) and lowest percentage of swings that missed (11.3%)

Ricky Gutierrez

1997 Season

Ricky Gutierrez was supposed to back up Pat Listach at shortstop in 1997. After opening the season on the disabled list with a torn ligament in his right thumb, Gutierrez took over as the starter when Listach couldn't cut it. Gutierrez had a good year, batting .261 and showing his versatility by playing shortstop, second or third base as needed. He lost his starter's job to Tim Bogar but came back to start in September after Bogar was felled by an injury.

Hitting

Gutierrez still strikes out too much for a hitter with so little power, and he has a bad habit of chasing balls in the dirt. He's a spray hitter who hits a lot of ground balls. He has trouble with good breaking pitches, but makes contact more often than not.

Baserunning & Defense

Gutierrez has good speed but didn't run much in 1997, stealing successfully in five of his seven attempts. He goes from first to third base well, but isn't an aggressive baserunner. He has an above-average arm and fine range, but his glovework is still the most perplexing thing about his game. It's not bad, but it never has been as dazzling as it was when he was a rookie with the Padres.

1998 Outlook

Gutierrez is a valuable player because he can play several positions adequately and can pinch-hit and pinch-run. He's also a streak hitter who can spark an offense for a week or two on occasion. The Astros will give him another shot to win the starting job, and he'll still have a role if he loses out. On the other hand, they haven't been too eager to let him play in the past. They gave Listach every chance to take the job last year, and settled on Gutierrez only after Bogar got hurt and no other options remained.

Position: SS/3B
Bats: R **Throws:** R
Ht: 6' 1" **Wt:** 175

Opening Day Age: 27
Born: 5/23/70 in Miami, FL
ML Seasons: 5
Pronunciation: goo-tee-AIR-ez

Houston Astros

Overall Statistics

	G	AB	R	H	D	T	HR	RBI	SB	BB	SO	Avg	OBP	Slg
1997	102	303	33	79	14	4	3	34	5	21	50	.261	.315	.363
Career	466	1390	186	360	49	12	10	115	22	136	276	.259	.330	.333

Where He Hits the Ball

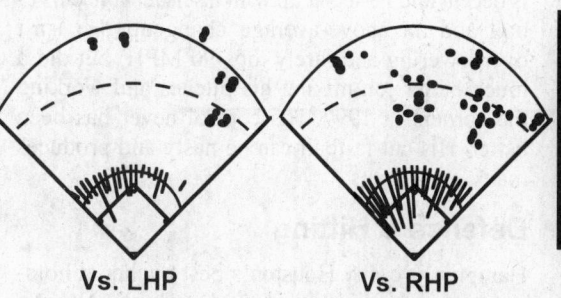

Vs. LHP   **Vs. RHP**

1997 Situational Stats

	AB	H	HR	RBI	Avg		AB	H	HR	RBI	Avg
Home	129	26	0	12	.202	LHP	78	20	1	9	.256
Road	174	53	3	22	.305	RHP	225	59	2	25	.262
First Half	117	30	1	13	.256	Sc Pos	89	21	0	27	.236
Scnd Half	186	49	2	21	.263	Clutch	68	13	0	5	.191

1997 Rankings (National League)

⇒ 1st in most GDPs per GDP situation (22.9%)
⇒ 7th in lowest batting average in the clutch
⇒ Led the Astros in GDPs (17)

475

Mike Hampton

1997 Season

Mike Hampton had a career year as the Astros' No. 2 starter, winning the most games by a National League lefthander not named Shawn Estes or Denny Neagle. Hampton dropped six of his first eight decisions and almost was sent to the bullpen. Manager Larry Dierker, who had tinkered with Hampton's mechanics during spring training, decided to let him go back to his 1996 delivery in early June. He responded by going 11-3 after the All-Star break.

Pitching

Hampton throws four pitches, and his fastball sinks and often is mistaken for a splitter. His slider is decent and he sets it up with a serviceable curveball and an above-average changeup. He isn't overpowering and rarely tops 90 MPH, but did a much better job mixing his pitches and working the corners in 1997. His control never has been better. His cut fastball can be nasty and produces many groundouts.

Defense & Hitting

Hampton is easily Houston's best pitcher at holding runners and is one of the best in the NL. An exceptional athlete, his pickoff move has vastly improved during the last two seasons. As Atlanta manager Bobby Cox put it, "Mike Hampton is impossible to run on any more." For a pitcher, he's no slouch with the bat. He's an above-average bunter and led the staff with a .137 average and eight RBI.

1998 Outlook

Hampton could be the Opening Day starter if Darryl Kile signs elsewhere as a free agent. At age 25, he should be just entering his best years. Hampton was one of the NL's best pitchers after the All-Star break and should pick up where he left off. If he's ever able to develop a pitch that he can throw to lefties, he could take another big step forward.

Position: SP
Bats: R **Throws:** L
Ht: 5'10" **Wt:** 180

Opening Day Age: 25
Born: 9/9/72 in Brooksville, FL
ML Seasons: 5

Overall Statistics

	W	L	Pct.	ERA	G	GS	Sv	IP	H	BB	SO	HR	Ratio
1997	15	10	.600	3.83	34	34	0	223.0	217	77	139	16	1.32
Career	37	32	.536	3.80	142	88	1	592.1	607	208	387	48	1.38

How Often He Throws Strikes

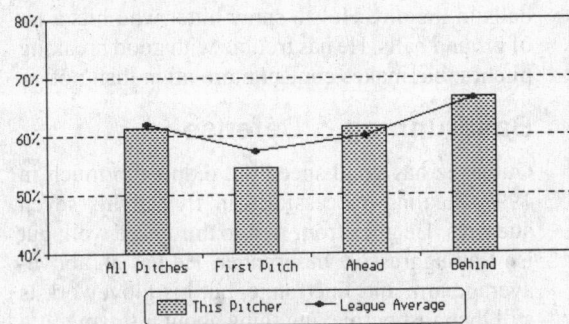

1997 Situational Stats

	W	L	ERA	Sv	IP		AB	H	HR	RBI	Avg
Home	10	2	3.09	0	113.2	LHB	152	47	3	24	.309
Road	5	8	4.61	0	109.1	RHB	692	170	13	64	.246
First Half	4	7	5.19	0	109.1	Sc Pos	187	52	5	70	.278
Scnd Half	11	3	2.53	0	113.2	Clutch	48	13	1	5	.271

1997 Rankings (National League)

⇒ 1st in most run support per 9 innings (6.2)
⇒ 2nd in GDPs induced (27)
⇒ 3rd in games started, complete games (7) and lowest stolen base percentage allowed (36.4%)
⇒ Led the Astros in sacrifice bunts (10), games started, complete games (7), hits allowed, pickoff throws (124), GDPs induced (27), highest groundball/flyball ratio allowed (2.3), lowest stolen base percentage allowed (36.4%), most run support per 9 innings (6.2), least home runs allowed per 9 innings (.65), most GDPs induced per 9 innings (1.1), most GDPs induced per GDP situation (14.6%) and bunts in play (15)

Richard Hidalgo

1997 Season

Richard Hidalgo, the top prospect in the Houston organization, got his first taste of the majors last year and gave management every reason to believe he can step in as a starter in 1998. He quickly played his way into the starting lineup with the Astros, who showed what they thought of him by promoting him early enough to make him eligible for the postseason.

Hitting

The Astros believe Hidalgo has the ability to hit 20 or more homers per season, though he has yet to realize his full power potential. At 22, he still has plenty of time. A line-drive hitter, he has shown more gap power than home-run ability to this point. Hidalgo destroys lefthanders but struggles against even mediocre righties, especially those with good breaking balls. He needs to have more patience at the plate and make more contact. Still, he's a solid offensive prospect who hits to all fields.

Baserunning & Defense

Hidalgo doesn't have above-average speed and is tentative on the basepaths. Defensively, he has good range and gets good jumps on the ball. He can play all three outfield positions, and his arm is strong enough for right field.

1998 Outlook

Hidalgo is a candidate to start in center field. His upside is considerably higher than Chuck Carr's. He was rail-thin when he signed, but he's beginning to fill out, and his power may develop quickly. If he cuts down on his strikeouts and learns to handle curveballs better, he could take some of the pressure off of Jeff Bagwell in the middle of the Houston lineup.

Position: CF
Bats: R **Throws:** R
Ht: 6' 3" **Wt:** 190

Opening Day Age: 22
Born: 7/2/75 in Caracas, Venezuela
ML Seasons: 1

Overall Statistics

	G	AB	R	H	D	T	HR	RBI	SB	BB	SO	Avg	OBP	Slg
1997	19	62	8	19	5	0	2	6	1	4	18	.306	.358	.484
Career	19	62	8	19	5	0	2	6	1	4	18	.306	.358	.484

Where He Hits the Ball

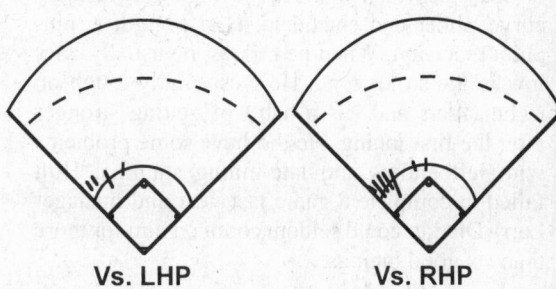

Vs. LHP   **Vs. RHP**

1997 Situational Stats

	AB	H	HR	RBI	Avg		AB	H	HR	RBI	Avg
Home	33	10	0	3	.303	LHP	22	10	1	2	.455
Road	29	9	2	3	.310	RHP	40	9	1	4	.225
First Half	0	0	0	0	-	Sc Pos	13	3	0	3	.231
Scnd Half	62	19	2	6	.306	Clutch	11	2	0	0	.182

1997 Rankings (National League)

⇒ Did not rank near the top or bottom in any category

Chris Holt

1997 Season

Rookie righthander Chris Holt was instrumental in keeping the Astros afloat when two members of the original starting rotation, Sid Fernandez and Shane Reynolds, went on the disabled list early in the season. Holt remained in the rotation when Reynolds returned and was one of the steadiest second-half pitchers in the National League, pitching seven or more innings in nine of his last 14 starts. Poor run support doomed him, as he pitched far better than his 8-12 record. He was only 1-7 in 14 starts after the break despite a 2.61 ERA.

Pitching

Holt isn't overpowering but has excellent control of four pitches. He throws a high-80s fastball, curve, slider and changeup. His strength is pinpoint precision. When he misses, he usually does low in the strike zone. He's especially tough on righthanders and has a habit of getting stronger after the first inning. He did have some problems with lefthanders and late-inning stamina. Holt failed to complete a game last year and manager Larry Dierker could seldom count on him for more than six good innings.

Defense & Hitting

Holt's compact delivery makes him harder than most to run against. He showed improvement in holding runners from previous seasons. He's an above-average fielder, committing only one error in 1997. While his range is adequate at best, he doesn't make many mistakes and reacts quickly. He's a terrible hitter and needs to get better at bunting.

1998 Outlook

Holt showed he can be a starter in the majors and should remain in the rotation for the foreseeable future. He had minor rotator-cuff surgery in the offseason, but is expected to be ready for spring training.

Position: SP
Bats: R **Throws:** R
Ht: 6' 4" **Wt:** 205

Opening Day Age: 26
Born: 9/18/71 in Dallas, TX
ML Seasons: 2

Overall Statistics

	W	L	Pct	ERA	G	GS	Sv	IP	H	BB	SO	HR	Ratio
1997	8	12	.400	3.52	33	32	0	209.2	211	61	95	17	1.30
Career	8	13	.381	3.57	37	32	0	214.1	216	64	95	17	1.31

How Often He Throws Strikes

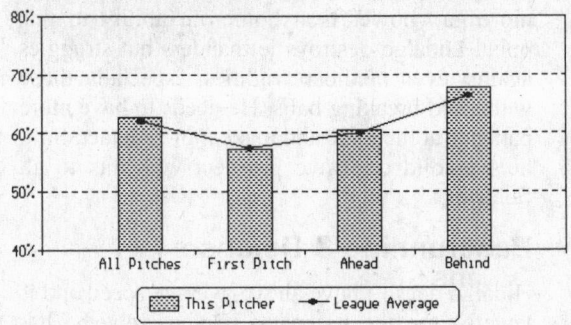

All Pitches · First Pitch · Ahead · Behind

This Pitcher — League Average

1997 Situational Stats

	W	L	ERA	Sv	IP		AB	H	HR	RBI	Avg
Home	3	8	3.52	0	107.1	LHB	391	118	12	55	.302
Road	5	4	3.52	0	102.1	RHB	411	93	5	27	.226
First Half	7	5	4.30	0	113.0	Sc Pos	185	56	2	60	.303
Scnd Half	1	7	2.61	0	96.2	Clutch	57	19	1	5	.333

1997 Rankings (National League)

⇒ 2nd in least strikeouts per 9 innings (4.1)
⇒ 3rd in lowest strikeout/walk ratio (1.6)
⇒ 4th in runners caught stealing (12)
⇒ 5th in lowest winning percentage and lowest batting average on an 0-2 count (.048)
⇒ 6th in losses and highest batting average allowed with runners in scoring position
⇒ 8th in least run support per 9 innings (4.2)
⇒ 9th in hits allowed and highest groundball/flyball ratio allowed (2.1)
⇒ 10th in GDPs induced (21)
⇒ Led the Astros in losses, runners caught stealing (12) and least pitches thrown per batter (3.50)

Darryl Kile

Position: SP
Bats: R **Throws:** R
Ht: 6' 5" **Wt:** 185

Opening Day Age: 29
Born: 12/2/68 in
Garden Grove, CA
ML Seasons: 7

1997 Season

Darryl Kile had a career year in 1997, winning 19 games and setting career bests for starts, complete games, shutouts and innings. As teammate Craig Biggio said last September, "Without D.K. we don't make the playoffs. I'd hate to think where this team would be without him." With Kile signing a three-year, $24 million contract with the Rockies in the offseason, Biggio will find out.

Pitching

Kile's fastball is usually around 95-96 MPH, but it's his curveball that makes him one of the top strikeout pitchers in the game. Better control has contributed to his recent success. His command has improved dramatically since he led the National League in walks in 1994. He was also extremely durable. Kile worked at least seven innings in all but three of his 34 starts, including 29 of the first 30. He attributes his progress to experience and more confidence, the latter as a result of new manager Larry Dierker's hands-off policy.

Defense & Hitting

Kile is a good bunter, and his hitting is improved, although he's still below average. He's quick to the plate, but his curve sometimes is wild and allows runners to take an extra base. His pickoff move is decent. Kile is a solid defensive player and covers bunts well.

1998 Outlook

At 29, Kile figures to be entering the most productive years of his career. He worked harder than ever last year, but arm fatigue is not a major concern, since he remained effective late into games. After improving his control and his performance against lefthanders, he has crossed the only significant barriers between himself and stardom. It couldn't have come at a better time for the free-agent pitcher, who will now try to conquer Coors Field.

Overall Statistics

	W	L	Pct.	ERA	G	GS	Sv	IP	H	BB	SO	HR	Ratio
1997	19	7	.731	2.57	34	34	0	255.2	208	94	205	19	1.18
Career	71	65	.522	3.79	209	182	0	1200.0	1128	562	973	89	1.41

How Often He Throws Strikes

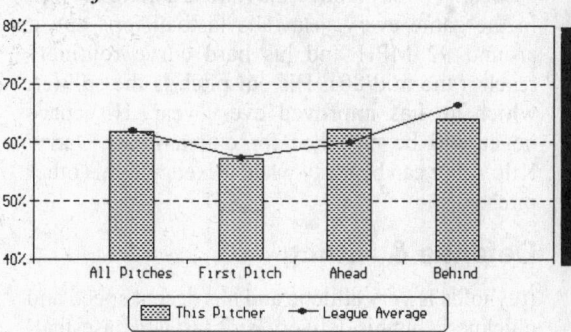

1997 Situational Stats

	W	L	ERA	Sv	IP		AB	H	HR	RBI	Avg
Home	10	3	2.59	0	132.0	LHB	486	113	11	39	.233
Road	9	4	2.55	0	123.2	RHB	438	95	8	37	.217
First Half	10	3	2.17	0	141.1	Sc Pos	210	36	4	56	.171
Scnd Half	9	4	3.07	0	114.1	Clutch	125	29	4	13	.232

1997 Rankings (National League)

⇒ 1st in batters faced (1,056) and lowest batting average allowed with runners in scoring position
⇒ 2nd in wins, shutouts (4), innings pitched, walks allowed, pitches thrown (3,826) and highest stolen base percentage allowed (83.3%)
⇒ 3rd in ERA, games started and ERA on the road
⇒ Led the Astros in sacrifice bunts (10), ERA, wins, games started, shutouts (4), innings pitched, batters faced (1,056), walks allowed, hit batsmen (10), strikeouts, wild pitches (7), pitches thrown (3,826), stolen bases allowed (20), winning percentage, lowest batting average allowed (.225), lowest slugging percentage allowed (.337), lowest on-base percentage allowed (.301), least baserunners allowed per 9 innings (11.0) and ERA at home

Houston Astros

Shane Reynolds

1997 Season

Shane Reynolds hit the skids after a fast start, going 0-4 from May 7 until he was placed on the disabled list June 11. He had arthroscopic surgery to repair a torn meniscus and remove a cyst in his right knee, and returned in mid-July. After that, he recovered slowly and didn't regain his stamina and form until September. He finished the year on a solid note, going 3-1 with a 3.00 ERA in five September starts.

Pitching

Reynolds' forte is his control. He can pinpoint his fastball, splitter and curveball as well as anyone in baseball. His strikeout/walk ratio is among the best in the game every year. His fastball tops out at around 92 MPH and his hard curve routinely reaches the mid-80s. His out pitch is the splitter, which he has improved every year. His curve never will be mistaken for ex-teammate Darryl Kile's, but can be nasty when mixed with his other pitches.

Defense & Hitting

Reynolds is very athletic and has decent speed and quickness, but his delivery isn't fast and basestealers occasionally take advantage of him. He clearly has improved his pickoff move. He fields bunts well and seldom makes errors, mental or otherwise. He's a poor hitter who occasionally hits for power.

1998 Outlook

In hindsight, it appears the Astros rushed Reynolds back too early from his surgery. He believed he was ready, and Houston was in a pennant race and needed Reynolds badly. However, he eventually regained his form and threw as well as any starter on the team in September. Now that he's back to 100 percent, he should revert to his form of 1996, when he won 16 games.

Position: SP
Bats: R **Throws:** R
Ht: 6' 3" **Wt:** 210

Opening Day Age: 30
Born: 3/26/68 in Bastrop, LA
ML Seasons: 6

Overall Statistics

	W	L	Pct.	ERA	G	GS	Sv	IP	H	BB	SO	HR	Ratio
1997	9	10	.474	4.23	30	30	0	181.0	189	47	152	19	1.30
Career	44	39	.530	3.72	141	115	0	769.2	793	161	661	66	1.24

How Often He Throws Strikes

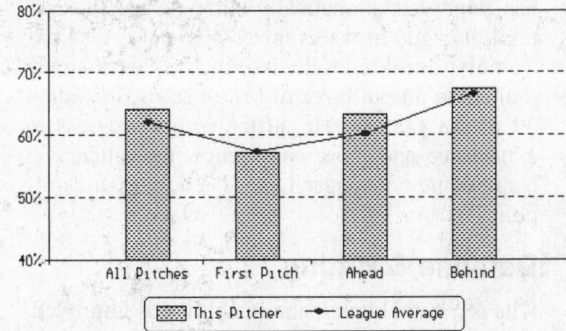

This Pitcher — League Average

1997 Situational Stats

	W	L	ERA	Sv	IP		AB	H	HR	RBI	Avg
Home	6	3	3.40	0	98.0	LHB	370	97	8	48	.262
Road	3	7	5.20	0	83.0	RHB	339	92	11	35	.271
First Half	4	6	3.91	0	94.1	Sc Pos	151	43	1	55	.285
Scnd Half	5	4	4.57	0	86.2	Clutch	53	18	2	8	.340

1997 Rankings (National League)

⇒ 2nd in errors at pitcher (4)
⇒ 4th in highest ERA on the road and lowest fielding percentage at pitcher (.911)
⇒ 7th in highest strikeout/walk ratio (3.2)
⇒ 8th in balks (2) and lowest stolen base percentage allowed (45.5%)
⇒ Led the Astros in balks (2), highest strikeout/walk ratio (3.2) and most strikeouts per 9 innings (7.6)

Billy Wagner

1997 Season

After taking over as Houston's closer early in the 1997 season, Billy Wagner set a major league record with an average of 14.4 strikeouts per nine innings. He also was booed, which gives you an idea of the kind of year the hard-throwing lefthander endured. He was virtually unhittable before the All-Star break, but struggled in the second half and went nearly two months without a save during August and September. Manager Larry Dierker had to employ a closer-by-committee system for a while.

Pitching

Wagner has a 99-MPH fastball and is arguably the hardest-throwing lefthander in the National League. His hard curveball, which usually reaches the high 80s, was very sharp early in the year. He all but abandoned his curve and stayed with his fastball as the season progressed, with disastrous results. Word spread around the National League that Wagner had lost confidence in his breaking ball. When hitters knew they could sit on his powerful fastball, Wagner began to get hit. He insisted his confidence wasn't shaken, yet repeatedly shook off calls for curveballs by Houston catchers. When he did throw the breaking pitch late in the season, it was often out of the strike zone.

Defense & Hitting

Wagner is an average fielder and does pay attention to baserunners, sometimes so much so that he winds up walking hitters. His high leg kick makes him vulnerable to the stolen base. He has decent speed and covers first base and bunts well. As a closer, he rarely hits.

1998 Outlook

Wagner will be Houston's closer when the 1998 season begins. He'll need to improve and trust his curveball if he's to return to the dominating form he displayed in late 1996 and early 1997. When he's on, he's one of the best closers in the game.

Position: RP
Bats: L **Throws:** L
Ht: 5'11" **Wt:** 180

Opening Day Age: 26
Born: 6/25/71 in Tannersville, VA
ML Seasons: 3

Overall Statistics

	W	L	Pct.	ERA	G	GS	Sv	IP	H	BB	SO	HR	Ratio
1997	7	8	.467	2.85	62	0	23	66.1	49	30	106	5	1.19
Career	9	10	.474	2.66	100	0	32	118.1	77	60	173	11	1.16

How Often He Throws Strikes

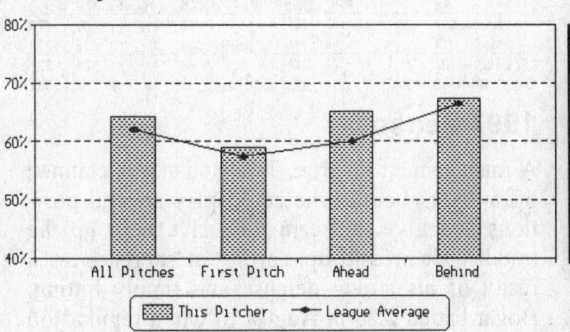

This Pitcher ▦ — League Average

1997 Situational Stats

	W	L	ERA	Sv	IP		AB	H	HR	RBI	Avg
Home	4	4	3.41	10	31.2	LHB	38	9	0	3	.237
Road	3	4	2.34	13	34.2	RHB	202	40	5	28	.198
First Half	5	3	1.83	15	39.1	Sc Pos	71	18	1	25	.254
Scnd Half	2	5	4.33	8	27.0	Clutch	177	40	4	26	.226

1997 Rankings (National League)

⇒ 1st in most strikeouts per 9 innings in relief (14.4)
⇒ 3rd in lowest save percentage (79.3%), relief wins (7), relief losses (8) and lowest batting average allowed in relief (.204)
⇒ 4th in first batter efficiency (.148)
⇒ Led the Astros in games pitched, saves, games finished (49), save opportunities (29), save percentage (79.3%), blown saves (6), first batter efficiency (.148), relief wins (7), relief losses (8), lowest batting average allowed in relief (.204), least baserunners allowed per 9 innings in relief (11.1) and most strikeouts per 9 innings in relief (14.4)

Tim Bogar

Position: SS/3B
Bats: R **Throws:** R
Ht: 6' 2" **Wt:** 198

Opening Day Age: 31
Born: 10/28/66 in
Indianapolis, IN
ML Seasons: 5

Overall Statistics

	G	AB	R	H	D	T	HR	RBI	SB	BB	SO	Avg	OBP	Slg
1997	97	241	30	60	14	4	4	30	4	24	42	.249	.320	.390
Career	394	732	88	179	38	4	10	87	7	59	127	.245	.304	.348

1997 Situational Stats

	AB	H	HR	RBI	Avg		AB	H	HR	RBI	Avg
Home	127	28	3	14	.220	LHP	68	19	1	12	.279
Road	114	32	1	16	.281	RHP	173	41	3	18	.237
First Half	98	21	1	6	.214	Sc Pos	65	18	1	26	.277
Scnd Half	143	39	3	24	.273	Clutch	33	10	0	4	.303

1997 Season

A management favorite, Tim Bogar was claimed off waivers because he could play several positions and give the team defensive help up the middle. He wound up starting at shortstop as a result of his strong defense and timely hitting. Bogar batted .286 in August to win a regular job and was enjoying the best year of his career when he fractured a bone in his forearm September 4. The injury sidelined him for the rest of the season.

Hitting, Baserunning & Defense

Bogar thrives against lefthanders, but he doesn't have any power to speak of and struggles against righties. He's an average baserunner but compensates by being smart. He makes good reads of pitchers' moves and usually runs only in favorable situations. He's solid defensively, with an above-average arm, good range and decent hands. The pitching staff particularly appreciated his defensive contributions.

1998 Outlook

Bogar entered the winter as the frontrunner to start at shortstop. Though Houston is confident he'll return at 100 percent, he's not a lock at shortstop unless he can handle righthanded pitching better than he has in the past.

Chuck Carr

Position: CF
Bats: B **Throws:** R
Ht: 5'10" **Wt:** 165

Opening Day Age: 29
Born: 8/10/68 in San
Bernardino, CA
ML Seasons: 8
Nickname: Chuckie

Overall Statistics

	G	AB	R	H	D	T	HR	RBI	SB	BB	SO	Avg	OBP	Slg
1997	89	238	37	59	14	2	4	17	12	17	48	.248	.305	.374
Career	507	1713	254	435	81	7	13	123	144	149	273	.254	.316	.332

1997 Situational Stats

	AB	H	HR	RBI	Avg		AB	H	HR	RBI	Avg
Home	131	37	3	11	.282	LHP	47	10	0	0	.213
Road	107	22	1	6	.206	RHP	191	49	4	17	.257
First Half	74	14	0	4	.189	Sc Pos	56	12	0	11	.214
Scnd Half	164	45	4	13	.274	Clutch	43	10	1	3	.233

1997 Season

Chuck Carr was signed in June after being waived by Milwaukee. He made an immediate impact and quickly won the starting center-field job, which enabled Derek Bell to move his natural position in right. Carr not only gave the Astros a solid glove in center, but he hit .282 in his final 39 games to help the Astros make the playoffs.

Hitting, Baserunning & Defense

Carr struggles against lefthanders and doesn't have much power, but he has outstanding speed. He sprays the ball to all fields against righthanders, but has a tendency to pull the ball against lefties. Tough to double up, he's an adept bunter and is an above-average basestealer. He covers a lot of ground in center field, but his arm is woefully weak.

1998 Outlook

Carr came to Houston with a reputation as a malcontent, but he was anything but. His hustle and attitude won the respect of his teammates and management while earning him another shot as Houston's starter in center field. He needs to cut down on his strikeouts, and the presence of Richard Hidalgo may relegate him to bench duty.

Tony Eusebio

Position: C
Bats: R **Throws:** R
Ht: 6' 2" **Wt:** 210

Opening Day Age: 30
Born: 4/27/67 in San Jose De Los Llamos, DR
ML Seasons: 5
Pronunciation: you-SAY-bee-oh

Overall Statistics

	G	AB	R	H	D	T	HR	RBI	SB	BB	SO	Avg	OBP	Slg
1997	60	164	12	45	2	0	1	18	0	19	27	.274	.364	.305
Career	296	862	95	245	40	4	13	125	0	82	147	.284	.347	.385

1997 Situational Stats

	AB	H	HR	RBI	Avg		AB	H	HR	RBI	Avg
Home	87	24	0	10	.276	LHP	48	16	1	8	.333
Road	77	21	1	8	.273	RHP	116	29	0	10	.250
First Half	101	28	1	10	.277	Sc Pos	50	15	0	16	.300
Scnd Half	63	17	0	8	.270	Clutch	38	10	0	4	.263

1997 Season

There may be disagreement on whether Tony Eusebio can play every day, but he can hit off the bench. Backing up Brad Ausmus, he was one of Houston's best pinch hitters with a .333 average and five RBI in 12 at-bats.

Hitting, Baserunning & Defense

Eusebio crushes fastballs to the extent that Atlanta's Mark Wohlers hates to face him. Eusebio sprays liners to all parts of the park. He doesn't have much power or any speed, but his on-base percentage usually is among the highest on the Astros. Never a threat to run, he has yet to steal his first major league base. Defense remains Eusebio's weakness and is the reason he hasn't been a starter. He has a strong arm and didn't have a passed ball in 1997, but his game-calling needs work.

1998 Outlook

Former manager Terry Collins once said he'd like to see what kind of numbers Eusebio would put up in a full season. He might get the opportunity this season because of expansion. He's a valuable commodity as a catcher who can hit, but likely will remain a backup if he's still with Houston.

Ramon Garcia Surprise

Position: RP/SP
Bats: R **Throws:** R
Ht: 6' 2" **Wt:** 200

Opening Day Age: 28
Born: 12/9/69 in Guanare, VZ
ML Seasons: 3

Overall Statistics

	W	L	Pct.	ERA	G	GS	Sv	IP	H	BB	SO	HR	Ratio
1997	9	8	.529	3.69	42	20	1	158.2	155	52	120	20	1.30
Career	17	16	.515	4.84	95	37	5	312.2	318	104	200	50	1.35

1997 Situational Stats

	W	L	ERA	Sv	IP		AB	H	HR	RBI	Avg
Home	3	4	3.61	1	77.1	LHB	280	70	10	25	.250
Road	6	4	3.76	0	81.1	RHB	312	85	10	42	.272
First Half	3	7	4.40	1	73.2	Sc Pos	125	31	2	41	.248
Scnd Half	6	1	3.07	0	85.0	Clutch	73	18	1	5	.247

1997 Season

Acquired via the major league Rule 5 draft at the Winter Meetings, Ramon Garcia joined the rotation because of injuries and wound up winning eight times in 20 starts. He was particularly strong after the All-Star break, going 6-1, 3.07 in 14 starts and convincing the Astros to protect him during the expansion draft. He attributed his improvement to gaining the extra innings he believes a five-pitch pitcher needs to be sharp.

Pitching, Defense & Hitting

Garcia throws a four-seam fastball, a splitter, a changeup, a curve and a slider, and usually throws them all for strikes. Garcia's sinking 93-MPH fastball produces a lot of groundouts. He needs to work on his curveball, the least effective of his pitches. He's a so-so fielder but doesn't beat himself. For a former American Leaguer he showed surprising pop at the plate, collecting four hits and five RBI while finishing third on the staff in sacrifice bunts.

1998 Outlook

The Astros are expected to use the durable righthander as a No. 3 or 4 starter. Based on his 1997 finish, he could win 15 games this season. He has proven that he's better suited for starting than relieving.

Houston Astros

Thomas Howard

Position: CF/RF
Bats: L **Throws:** R
Ht: 6' 2" **Wt:** 205

Opening Day Age: 33
Born: 12/11/64 in Middletown, OH
ML Seasons: 8

Overall Statistics

	G	AB	R	H	D	T	HR	RBI	SB	BB	SO	Avg	OBP	Slg
1997	107	255	24	63	16	1	3	22	1	26	48	.247	.323	.353
Career	784	2079	259	556	105	21	30	204	63	138	357	.267	.313	.381

1997 Situational Stats

	AB	H	HR	RBI	Avg		AB	H	HR	RBI	Avg
Home	120	23	0	7	.192	LHP	18	6	0	1	.333
Road	135	40	3	15	.296	RHP	237	57	3	21	.241
First Half	158	39	2	16	.247	Sc Pos	64	10	0	13	.156
Scnd Half	97	24	1	6	.247	Clutch	57	17	0	4	.298

1997 Season

Thomas Howard played all three outfield positions but didn't play any of them effectively enough to earn a full-time starter's job. He led the team in pinch-hit at-bats, but after a strong April he batted .228 the rest of the way.

Hitting, Baserunning & Defense

The lefty-swinging Howard is used pretty much exclusively against righties, though he did well against southpaws last year in limited opportunities. He's a low fastball hitter who usually hits the ball where it's pitched. He has good speed but didn't use it much. Defensively, he has an average arm and good range. His best position is left field.

1998 Outlook

Howard turned 33 in December and is coming off the worst year of his career. He may be hard-pressed to win a job other than as a fourth outfielder. A team may take a flyer on him as a free agent, but he'll have to earn a spot during spring training.

John Hudek

Position: RP
Bats: B **Throws:** R
Ht: 6' 1" **Wt:** 200

Opening Day Age: 31
Born: 8/8/66 in Tampa, FL
ML Seasons: 4
Pronunciation: HOO-dek

Overall Statistics

	W	L	Pct.	ERA	G	GS	Sv	IP	H	BB	SO	HR	Ratio
1997	1	3	.250	5.98	40	0	4	40.2	38	33	36	8	1.75
Career	5	7	.417	4.42	116	0	29	116.0	93	61	118	18	1.33

1997 Situational Stats

	W	L	ERA	Sv	IP		AB	H	HR	RBI	Avg
Home	0	1	3.38	1	21.1	LHB	51	13	2	9	.255
Road	1	2	8.84	3	19.1	RHB	100	25	6	18	.250
First Half	0	0	6.23	4	26.0	Sc Pos	42	11	4	20	.262
Scnd Half	1	3	5.52	0	14.2	Clutch	83	24	6	19	.289

1997 Season

One-time Astros closer John Hudek's 1997 season was marred by control problems and inconsistency. He spent nearly as much time in the minors correcting his troubles as he did in Houston. He never pitched effectively in the major leagues last year.

Pitching, Defense & Hitting

Hudek's best pitch remains a darting fastball in the mid-90s. He needs regular work to be effective, and struggled with his control because he was used infrequently. He's learning to throw a split-fingered fastball, and also throws a slider on occasion. Hudek is excellent with the glove and has gone four years without committing an error. His quick delivery makes him difficult to run on, and he does a good job of holding runners. At the plate, he's 1-for-1 in his career.

1998 Outlook

Hudek is best suited for short stints two or three times a week. Otherwise, his control suffers. He needs to develop the splitter to complement his fastball. He has a closer's mentality and may get a chance to resume that role for another team.

Jose Lima

Position: RP
Bats: R **Throws:** R
Ht: 6' 2" **Wt:** 205

Opening Day Age: 25
Born: 9/30/72 in Santiago, DR
ML Seasons: 4
Pronunciation: LEE-muh

Tom Martin

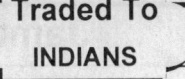

Position: RP
Bats: L **Throws:** L
Ht: 6' 1" **Wt:** 185

Opening Day Age: 27
Born: 5/21/70 in Panama City, FL
ML Seasons: 1

Overall Statistics

	W	L	Pct.	ERA	G	GS	Sv	IP	H	BB	SO	HR	Ratio
1997	1	6	.143	5.28	52	1	2	75.0	79	16	63	9	1.27
Career	9	22	.290	5.92	109	21	5	228.0	262	59	166	34	1.41

1997 Situational Stats

	W	L	ERA	Sv	IP		AB	H	HR	RBI	Avg
Home	0	3	3.89	1	34.2	LHB	122	28	3	17	.230
Road	1	3	6.47	1	40.1	RHB	169	51	6	29	.302
First Half	1	4	4.61	1	52.2	Sc Pos	71	22	2	33	.310
Scnd Half	0	2	6.85	1	22.1	Clutch	66	21	1	9	.318

Overall Statistics

	W	L	Pct.	ERA	G	GS	Sv	IP	H	BB	SO	HR	Ratio
1997	5	3	.625	2.09	55	0	2	56.0	52	23	36	2	1.34
Career	5	3	.625	2.09	55	0	2	56.0	52	23	36	2	1.34

1997 Situational Stats

	W	L	ERA	Sv	IP		AB	H	HR	RBI	Avg
Home	5	2	3.00	1	30.0	LHB	61	16	0	9	.262
Road	0	1	1.04	1	26.0	RHB	144	36	2	21	.250
First Half	2	2	2.00	0	27.0	Sc Pos	66	17	1	28	.258
Scnd Half	3	1	2.17	2	29.0	Clutch	119	33	2	18	.277

1997 Season

Jose Lima's 1997 season was a roller-coaster ride, and there were fewer ups than downs. A versatile pitcher who started, pitched middle relief and even had a few late-inning stints, the Dominican spent most of the season working a mopup role. His stock fell as the year grew shorter and his ERA grew larger.

Pitching, Defense & Hitting

Lima throws an 89-92 MPH fastball, a splitter, a slider and a circle change. His fastball has a sinking action and contributes to most of the groundouts he produces. His best pitch is his changeup, but he relies on it too much. When his fastball doesn't sink, he can get lit up. Lima's defense is fair, but he needs to work on his pickoff move and do a better job holding runners on. He went 0-for-3 in his first taste of major league hitting and is a mediocre bunter.

1998 Outlook

Houston hopes Lima's offseason work on his slider and splitter will help him develop into the starter many envisioned he would become when he was with Detroit. At 25, he'll be on the way out if he doesn't realize his potential soon.

1997 Season

Tom Martin was a pleasant surprise in what for the most part was a disappointing bullpen. A strong spring-training performance landed the hard-throwing lefty on the Opening Day roster, and he responded by not allowing a run in his first 12 appearances. He stumbled in May, when a strained left elbow put him on the disabled list. Except when he tried to pitch through the injury, he was quite impressive.

Pitching, Defense & Hitting

Martin's best pitch is a sharp, rising 90-MPH fastball. He also throws a decent changeup and an occasional slider. Used primarily in a setup role, his performance was better when he worked one-inning stints than when he was asked to go longer. Defensively, he's above-average. His compact delivery helps him get off the mound quickly. He went hitless in three at-bats.

1998 Outlook

With his fastball and good control, Martin may eventually be a closer. The Diamondbacks made him their first pick in the second round of the expansion draft, then sent him to Cleveland in a trade for Matt Williams.

Houston Astros

James Mouton

Position: CF/RF
Bats: R **Throws:** R
Ht: 5' 9" **Wt:** 175

Opening Day Age: 29
Born: 12/29/68 in Denver, Colorado
ML Seasons: 4
Pronunciation: MOO-tawn

Overall Statistics

	G	AB	R	H	D	T	HR	RBI	SB	BB	SO	Avg	OBP	Slg
1997	86	180	24	38	9	1	3	23	9	18	30	.211	.287	.322
Career	411	1088	149	271	53	4	12	100	79	108	213	.249	.321	.338

1997 Situational Stats

	AB	H	HR	RBI	Avg		AB	H	HR	RBI	Avg
Home	78	21	1	13	.269	LHP	99	26	3	15	.263
Road	102	17	2	10	.167	RHP	81	12	0	8	.148
First Half	123	27	2	15	.220	Sc Pos	56	11	0	20	.196
Scnd Half	57	11	1	8	.193	Clutch	36	5	0	2	.139

1997 Season

After three years of waiting for the one-time Pacific Coast League MVP to blossom, the Astros gave up on James Mouton in 1997 and tried to trade him. They couldn't find any takers. He has been giving a starting job in the outfield three times in the past four years and has failed to keep it each time, and 1997 was his poorest season yet. He rarely was used for anything more than a late-inning defensive replacement or pinch runner.

Hitting, Baserunning & Defense

Mouton has a bad habit of chasing pitches low and away, and he's overmatched against run-of-the-mill righthanders. He still has trouble with breaking balls. He strikes out too much, a tragedy considering his speed, and his stolen-base success dropped off considerably in 1997. The one bright spot in Mouton's game is his defense. He covers a lot of ground and cuts off a lot of would-be doubles in the gaps. His arm is average.

1998 Outlook

Mouton's most likely role is as a fifth outfielder for a team that can afford the luxury of a good fielder with speed who can't hit. If he does get another chance in Houston or more likely via the expansion process, it probably will be his last.

Bill Spiers

Position: 3B/SS
Bats: L **Throws:** R
Ht: 6' 2" **Wt:** 190

Opening Day Age: 31
Born: 6/5/66 in Orangeburg, SC
ML Seasons: 9
Pronunciation: SPY-ers

Overall Statistics

	G	AB	R	H	D	T	HR	RBI	SB	BB	SO	Avg	OBP	Slg
1997	132	291	51	93	27	4	4	48	10	61	42	.320	.438	.481
Career	874	2273	314	596	96	23	26	263	69	213	351	.262	.326	.359

1997 Situational Stats

	AB	H	HR	RBI	Avg		AB	H	HR	RBI	Avg
Home	142	44	0	20	.310	LHP	41	13	0	7	.317
Road	149	49	4	28	.329	RHP	250	80	4	41	.320
First Half	150	46	1	18	.307	Sc Pos	78	35	3	46	.449
Scnd Half	141	47	3	30	.333	Clutch	72	25	1	16	.347

1997 Season

Signed as a lefthanded pinch hitter and backup to third baseman Sean Berry, Bill Spiers proved to be a bargain. Not only did he lead the team in hitting, but he helped the club avert disaster when Berry was slow to recover from offseason shoulder surgery.

Hitting, Baserunning & Defense

Spiers lives on fastballs and gets in trouble against breaking pitches, particularly those that are high and inside. He hits equally well against lefties and righties, and is a valuable pinch hitter. Though not a threat to steal, he's an intelligent baserunner. Able to play all four infield positions, he has an average arm and decent range. Few balls get past him.

1998 Outlook

Spiers' 1997 season won him a two-year contract from the Astros. His versatility, good bat and solid defense make him a useful player to have on the roster, whether it's as an everyday player or a utilityman.

Other Houston Astros

Sid Fernandez (Pos: LHP, Age: 35)

	W	L	Pct.	ERA	G	GS	Sv	IP	H	BB	SO	HR	Ratio
1997	1	0	1.000	3.60	1	1	0	5.0	4	2	3	1	1.20
Career	114	96	.543	3.36	307	300	1	1866.2	1421	715	1743	191	1.14

Fernandez made one start for the Astros, felt a twinge in his left arm and never made it back into the rotation. On August 1, he announced his retirement. Adios, El Sid, and thanks for the memories. 1998 Outlook: D

Tommy Greene (Pos: RHP, Age: 30)

	W	L	Pct.	ERA	G	GS	Sv	IP	H	BB	SO	HR	Ratio
1997	0	1	.000	7.00	2	2	0	9.0	10	5	11	2	1.67
Career	38	25	.603	4.14	119	97	0	628.0	591	241	461	62	1.32

After undergoing rotator cuff surgery on his right shoulder for the second time since 1994, Greene's pitching future is bleak at best. His shoulder hasn't lasted a full year since his stellar '93 campaign. 1998 Outlook: D

Randy Knorr (Pos: C, Age: 29, Bats: R)

	G	AB	R	H	D	T	HR	RBI	SB	BB	SO	Avg	OBP	Slg
1997	4	8	1	3	0	0	1	1	0	0	2	.375	.375	.750
Career	176	472	58	108	18	2	17	65	0	37	118	.229	.287	.383

Once pegged as the possible heir-apparent to take over the catching duties from Pat Borders in Toronto, Knorr is no longer more than a serviceable backup. His career average versus righties is just .210. 1998 Outlook: C

Pat Listach (Pos: SS, Age: 30, Bats: B)

	G	AB	R	H	D	T	HR	RBI	SB	BB	SO	Avg	OBP	Slg
1997	52	132	13	24	2	2	0	6	4	11	24	.182	.247	.227
Career	503	1772	250	444	63	13	5	143	116	167	338	.251	.316	.309

The enigmatic former Rookie of the Year was ready for a change of scenery in 1997. It didn't help. Listach began the year as the Astros' everyday shortstop, but hit just .182 and was waived on July 1. 1998 Outlook: C

Mike Magnante (Pos: LHP, Age: 32)

	W	L	Pct.	ERA	G	GS	Sv	IP	H	BB	SO	HR	Ratio
1997	3	1	.750	2.27	40	0	1	47.2	39	11	43	2	1.05
Career	13	19	.406	4.13	231	19	1	373.0	404	136	213	29	1.45

Magnante was called up from the minors on the final day of May and stuck with the parent club for the rest of the season. The lefty specialist went on to post the best numbers of his seven-year career. 1998 Outlook: B

Blas Minor (Pos: RHP, Age: 32)

	W	L	Pct.	ERA	G	GS	Sv	IP	H	BB	SO	HR	Ratio
1997	1	0	1.000	4.50	11	0	1	12.0	13	5	6	1	1.50
Career	13	10	.565	4.40	157	0	5	225.0	231	70	184	29	1.34

Minor's U.S. tour continued in '97, pitching for his fourth organization in as many seasons. He sandwiched 11 outings with Houston in between two stints in the minors, and did little to impress. 1998 Outlook: C

Ray Montgomery (Pos: RF, Age: 28, Bats: R)

	G	AB	R	H	D	T	HR	RBI	SB	BB	SO	Avg	OBP	Slg
1997	29	68	8	16	4	1	0	4	0	5	18	.235	.276	.324
Career	41	82	12	19	5	1	1	8	0	6	23	.232	.275	.354

He saw his first starting duty in the bigs when Derek Bell went down with a bum calf, but two things happened to derail his season: Bell's return and surgery to remove adhesions from Montgomery's rotator cuff. 1998 Outlook: C

Tony Pena (Pos: C, Age: 40, Bats: R)

	G	AB	R	H	D	T	HR	RBI	SB	BB	SO	Avg	OBP	Slg
1997	40	86	6	15	4	0	0	10	0	10	16	.174	.255	.221
Career 1988	6489	667	1687	298	27	107	708	80	455	846	.260	.309	.364

After donning the tools for the better part of 18 seasons in the bigs, it may finally be time for Pena to hang up the pads. His final batting average was below .200 for the second straight year. 1998 Outlook: D

J.R. Phillips (Pos: 1B, Age: 27, Bats: L)

	G	AB	R	H	D	T	HR	RBI	SB	BB	SO	Avg	OBP	Slg
1997	13	15	2	2	0	0	1	4	0	0	7	.133	.125	.333
Career	181	404	43	74	15	1	19	54	2	31	145	.183	.242	.366

Phillips' career is developing a not-so-promising pattern. Over the last four years, he has produced fine numbers in Triple-A but has hit .132, .195, .163 and .133 during his time in the majors. 1998 Outlook: C

Edgar Ramos (Pos: RHP, Age: 23)

	W	L	Pct.	ERA	G	GS	Sv	IP	H	BB	SO	HR	Ratio
1997	0	2	.000	5.14	4	2	0	14.0	15	6	4	3	1.50
Career	0	2	.000	5.14	4	2	0	14.0	15	6	4	3	1.50

The Astros temporarily lost Ramos to the Phillies in the Rule 5 draft, but Philadelphia returned him in early June to make room for Ryan Nye. Ramos was 0-2 in four games in 1997—all with Philly. 1998 Outlook: C

Ken Ramos (Pos: LF, Age: 30, Bats: L)

	G	AB	R	H	D	T	HR	RBI	SB	BB	SO	Avg	OBP	Slg
1997	14	12	0	0	0	0	0	1	0	2	0	.000	.133	.000
Career	14	12	0	0	0	0	0	1	0	2	0	.000	.133	.000

Like Ray Montgomery, Ramos also saw some playing time in the majors during Derek Bell's stint on the DL. Unfortunately for the nine-year minor league vet, he did nothing with it, going hitless in 12 at-bats. 1998 Outlook: D

Luis Rivera (Pos: SS, Age: 34, Bats: R)

	G	AB	R	H	D	T	HR	RBI	SB	BB	SO	Avg	OBP	Slg
1997	7	13	2	3	0	1	0	3	0	1	6	.231	.286	.385
Career	739	2126	235	494	110	12	28	202	19	164	426	.232	.290	.335

Rivera saw his first major league action since 1994 when he appeared in seven games for Houston. After a 3-for-13 showing, he's most likely headed back to the minors once again. 1998 Outlook: D

Russ Springer (Pos: RHP, Age: 29)

	W	L	Pct.	ERA	G	GS	Sv	IP	H	BB	SO	HR	Ratio
1997	3	3	.500	4.23	54	0	3	55.1	48	27	74	4	1.36
Career	10	23	.303	5.34	184	27	6	352.0	380	156	309	52	1.52

For the second straight season, Springer combined a high strikeout total with a high ERA. Go figure. Arizona took him in the third round of the expansion draft and figures to use him in middle relief. 1998 Outlook: A

Donne Wall (Pos: RHP, Age: 30)

	W	L	Pct.	ERA	G	GS	Sv	IP	H	BB	SO	HR	Ratio
1997	2	5	.286	6.26	8	8	0	41.2	53	16	25	8	1.66
Career	14	14	.500	5.00	40	36	0	216.0	256	55	140	30	1.44

A promising '96 campaign saw Wall start the season in the minors and finish in the Houston rotation. He reversed that order last season and was waived. The Reds picked him up and traded him to the Tigers, who then sent him to the Padres. 1998 Outlook: B

Houston Astros Minor League Prospects

Organization Overview:

Though Houston is a small-revenue team, they didn't exactly win the National League Central with home-grown prospects. Ownership won't commit the money to sign amateur talent, and the Astros haven't landed much talent through the draft. The only key players they've introduced in the last two years are pitchers Chris Holt and Billy Wagner. Most of their regulars were either drafted in the 1980s or picked up as spare parts. The Astros do have some talent, and one thing many of the better prospects share in common is Venezuelan ancestry. International scout Andres Reiner has kept the system from wallowing in mediocrity by signing such players as Oscar Henriquez, who was used in the Moises Alou trade, and Richard Hidalgo.

Lance Berkman

Position: OF   **Opening Day Age:** 22
Bats: B **Throws:** L   **Born:** 2/10/76 in Waco,
Ht: 6' 1" **Wt:** 205   TX

Recent Statistics

	G	AB	R	H	D	T	HR	RBI	SB	BB	SO	AVG
97 A Kissimmee	53	184	31	54	10	0	12	35	2	37	38	.293

The Astros didn't have to go far for their 1997 first-round pick, taking Berkman out of local Rice University. He hit .431-41-134 for the Owls, leading NCAA Division I in homers and RBIs while shattering most of Jose Cruz Jr.'s school records. Berkman had no problem hitting for average or power in the high Class A Florida State League, where pitchers usually have the advantage. He also showed a good eye at the plate and did a creditable job in left field after spending most of his college career at first base. It's not inconceivable that Berkman could join Jeff Bagwell and Hidalgo in the heart of Houston's order as early as 1999.

Jose Cabrera

Position: P   **Opening Day Age:** 26
Bats: R **Throws:** R   **Born:** 3/24/72 in La
Ht: 6' 0" **Wt:** 197   Delgada, DR

Recent Statistics

	W	L	ERA	G	GS	Sv	IP	H	R	BB	SO	HR
97 AAA Buffalo	3	0	1.20	5	0	0	15.0	8	2	7	11	2
97 AAA New Orleans	2	2	2.54	31	0	0	46.0	31	13	13	48	2
97 NL Houston	0	0	1.17	12	0	0	15.1	6	2	6	18	1

The Indians never seemed to appreciate Cabrera, assigning him to a co-op team for half of 1996 and trading him to the Astros for Alvin Morman in 1997. Cabrera found a home in Houston, posting a 1.17 ERA and limiting batters to a .125 average in 12 big league appearances. Signed out of the Dominican Republic, he throws a

sinking fastball at 92-93 MPH. His other pitches are below average and won't allow him to be a closer, but his fastball and his command are enough for him to thrive as a setup man. He's a good bet to make the Astros' Opening Day roster.

Scott Elarton

Position: P   **Opening Day Age:** 22
Bats: R **Throws:** R   **Born:** 2/23/76 in Lamar,
Ht: 6' 8" **Wt:** 225   CO

Recent Statistics

	W	L	ERA	G	GS	Sv	IP	H	R	BB	SO	HR
96 A Kissimmee	12	7	2.92	27	27	0	172.1	154	67	54	130	13
97 AA Jackson	7	4	3.24	20	20	0	133.1	103	57	47	141	6
97 AAA New Orleans	4	4	5.33	9	9	0	54.0	51	36	17	50	5

Houston had been pleased with Elarton since making him a 1994 first-round pick, but never could figure out why his velocity dropped 5 MPH after he signed. They don't have to worry any longer, because his fastball was in the low 90s again in 1997. He went from being a good prospect to one of the best in the minors. He learned to pitch without a good fastball, and his changeup and curveball still are better than his heater. He also throws a cut fastball and is praised for his intelligence and athleticism. Though he was hit harder in Triple-A, Elarton could contribute in Houston's rotation by midseason.

Carlos Guillen

Position: SS   **Opening Day Age:** 22
Bats: B **Throws:** R   **Born:** 9/30/75 in
Ht: 6' 0" **Wt:** 150   Maracay, Venez

Recent Statistics

	G	AB	R	H	D	T	HR	RBI	SB	BB	SO	AVG
96 A Quad City	29	112	23	37	7	1	3	17	13	16	25	.330
97 AA Jackson	115	390	47	99	16	1	10	39	6	38	78	.254
97 AAA New Orleans	3	13	3	4	1	0	0	0	0	0	4	.308
97 MLE	118	387	39	87	14	0	6	30	4	23	94	.225

Signed out of Venezuela in 1992, Guillen has been an organization favorite ever since. He's a shortstop with a strong arm and the ability to produce runs and steal bases. Prior to 1997 he just couldn't stay healthy, as shoulder injuries and other ailments restricted him to 77 games in four years. He stayed healthy last season, but his lack of experience showed in Double-A. While he hit .254 and struck out a lot, he did show some power and draw some walks. There's some talk of moving Guillen to third base, but the organization has more pressing needs at shortstop. He probably needs close to two more years in the minors to make up for lost time, though he has the talent to accelerate that timetable.

John Halama

Position: P   **Opening Day Age:** 26
Bats: L **Throws:** L   **Born:** 2/22/72 in
Ht: 6' 5" **Wt:** 195   Brooklyn, NY

Recent Statistics

	W	L	ERA	G	GS	Sv	IP	H	R	BB	SO	HR
96 AA Jackson	9	10	3.21	27	27	0	162.2	151	77	59	110	10
97 AAA New Orleans	13	3	2.58	26	24	0	171.0	150	57	32	126	9

A 23rd round-pick in 1994 out of St. Francis (N.Y.) College, Halama was seen as little more than a situational lefthander until a breakthrough year in 1997. His fastball is merely average and his curveball needs some work, but he can get outs with his changeup. Because his stuff isn't marvelous, he always has done the little things well. He has good life on his pitches, a nice pickoff move and the ability to spot the ball where he wants. The major league rotation may have an open spot this spring, and Halama is first in line.

Russ Johnson

Position: 3B   **Opening Day Age:** 25
Bats: R **Throws:** R   **Born:** 2/22/73 in Baton
Ht: 5' 10" **Wt:** 185   Rouge, LA

Recent Statistics

	G	AB	R	H	D	T	HR	RBI	SB	BB	SO	AVG
97 AAA New Orleans	122	445	72	123	16	6	4	49	7	66	78	.276
97 NL Houston	21	60	7	18	1	0	2	9	1	6	14	.300
97 MLE	122	431	61	109	14	4	3	42	5	54	85	.253

Todd Walker's double-play partner on Louisiana State's 1993 College World Series champions, Johnson was a supplemental first-round pick a year later. He doesn't fit one particular position, as he lacks the range and arm for shortstop and the power for third base. What he is is a hard-nosed player who makes contact and doesn't make mistakes. If he had the footwork to play second base, he could be an All-Star. Don't underestimate his usefulness—he repaired a broken fan belt on the team bus in spring training. He could get the chance to play every day at third for Houston, and also could wind up platooning there with Bill Spiers.

Mitch Meluskey

Position: C   **Opening Day Age:** 24
Bats: B **Throws:** R   **Born:** 9/18/73 in
Ht: 5' 11" **Wt:** 185   Yakima, WA

Recent Statistics

	G	AB	R	H	D	T	HR	RBI	SB	BB	SO	AVG
96 A Kissimmee	74	231	29	77	19	0	1	31	1	29	26	.333
96 AA Jackson	38	134	18	42	11	0	0	21	0	18	24	.313
97 AA Jackson	73	241	49	82	18	0	14	46	1	31	39	.340
97 AAA New Orleans	51	172	22	43	7	0	3	21	0	8	34	.250
97 MLE	124	395	56	107	21	0	11	54	0	39	88	.271

Meluskey batted .340 with 14 homers in half a season of Double-A ball, but the question remains as to whether he can catch in the big leagues. A 12th-round pick by the Indians in 1992, he joined the Astros in a minor league trade in April 1995. He has the physical tools to be a successful backstop, but he doesn't apply himself. Though he gunned down 36 percent of basestealers in 1997, he's still a sloppy receiver. The Astros believe he'll be a hitter, but aren't sure they can keep him behind the plate. He'll spend 1998 catching in Triple-A.

Daryle Ward

Position: 1B   **Opening Day Age:** 22
Bats: L **Throws:** L   **Born:** 6/27/75 in
Ht: 6' 2" **Wt:** 230   Lynwood, CA

Recent Statistics

	G	AB	R	H	D	T	HR	RBI	SB	BB	SO	AVG
96 AAA Toledo	6	23	1	4	0	0	0	1	0	0	3	.174
96 A Lakeland	128	464	65	135	29	4	10	68	1	57	77	.291
97 AA Jackson	114	422	72	139	25	0	19	90	4	46	68	.329
97 AAA New Orleans	14	48	4	18	1	0	2	8	0	7	7	.375
97 MLE	128	445	59	132	22	0	14	76	2	34	83	.297

The son of former All-Star Gary Ward may turn out to be the best player the Astros received in a nine-player, cost-cutting trade in December 1996. A 1994 15th-round pick out of junior-college power Rancho Santiago (Calif.), Ward looks like Mo Vaughn. He hits like him as well, with tremendous bat speed and legitimate power that he's just beginning to tap. Managers named him the best hitting prospect and best power hitter in the Texas League in 1997. Unfortunately for Ward, he also runs like Vaughn, which limits him to first base. If Houston has its way, Bagwell will man that position for another decade. Thus Ward may prove most useful to the Astros as trade bait.

Others to Watch

Another Venezuelan signed by Reiner, lefthander **Alberto Blanco** went 7-4, 2.83 and was one of the toughest pitchers to hit in the Florida State League at age 21. He throws 89-92 MPH with a solid curve, and may be better suited for relief because his elbow can't seem to take a lot of innings. . . Catcher **Ramon Castro** became the first Puerto Rican ever drafted in the first round when the Astros took him in 1994. His offensive game finally started to develop at Class-A Kissimmee, and Houston thinks the 22 year old has Javy Lopez potential with better arm strength. . . Yet another Reiner find in Venezuela, righthander **Freddy Garcia** is 21 and can hold his own with a 92-96 MPH fastball. His other pitches are still rudimentary, but he went 10-8, 2.56 at Kissimmee. . . Righthander **Mark Johnson**, 22, is a workhorse in the Shane Reynolds mold. Johnson throws an 89-92 MPH fastball, a very good slider and a promising changeup. . .Lefthander **Trever Miller**, 24, almost made the Astros in spring training. His best pitch is a curveball. . . A 20th-round find in 1996, righthander **Wade Miller** went 10-2, 1.80 with 76 strikeouts and 14 walks in 100 innings at Kissimmee at age 20. He throws 92-95 MPH with a good slider, plus he's polished.

Bill Russell

1997 Season

In his first full season at the Dodger helm, Bill Russell strove to establish his own managerial style. He shows a taciturn and serious exterior, making it tough for the opponent to discern his next move. On the other hand, his players face the same uncertainty. Down the stretch, Russell relied more and more on established veterans. Ultimately, they didn't get the job done.

Offense

Russell is an aggressive strategist at this early stage of his career. The Dodgers ran more than usual in 1997, but were less successful. He'll hit-and-run with almost anyone, calls for a lot of bunts and absolutely loves the squeeze play. He used a set lineup early in the year before a team-wide slump forced him to try a different mix 18 days in a row in early June. After August trades for Otis Nixon and Eric Young, Russell used the same eight guys almost every day. His substitution strategy is strictly by the book, with little apparent regard for specific matchups.

Pitching & Defense

There has been a fundamental change in the Dodger pitching philosophy in the last few years. The club has become much more aware of pitch counts and now is accused of pulling pitchers too soon. Russell likes distinct roles and stuck with Todd Worrell as his closer though the veteran struggled to get the job done. Russell doesn't make many defensive substitutions, preferring to put the best overall player out there from start to finish.

1998 Outlook

Russell is signed through 1998 and his job should be safe during the ownership transition. However, he faces several challenges. For one, he seems absolutely incapable of inspiring his team. Secondly, he had heated public disputes with pitchers Pedro Astacio (whom the Dodgers wound up trading) and Ismael Valdes. Unless the Dodgers win, his public persona may cost him.

Born: 10/21/48 in Pittsburg, KS

Playing Experience: 1969-1986, LA

Managerial Experience: 2 seasons

Manager Statistics

Year	Team, Lg	W	L	Pct	GB	Finish
1997	Los Angeles, NL	88	74	.543	2.0	2nd West
2 Seasons		137	111	.552	—	—

1997 Starting Pitchers by Days Rest

	≤3	4	5	6+
Dodgers Starts	4	90	43	17
Dodgers ERA	1.98	3.89	3.79	2.91
NL Avg Starts	3	90	38	22
NL ERA	4.23	4.05	4.27	4.52

1997 Situational Stats

	Bill Russell	NL Average
Hit & Run Success %	40.0	36.4
Stolen Base Success %	67.2	68.4
Platoon Pct.	48.6	56.3
Defensive Subs	19	26
High-Pitch Outings	12	12
Quick/Slow Hooks	17/5	18/10
Sacrifice Attempts	132	96

1997 Rankings (National League)

⇒ 1st in sacrifice bunt attempts (132), squeeze plays (13) and 2+ pitching changes in low scoring games (32)

⇒ 2nd in hit-and-run attempts (145)

⇒ 3rd in sacrifice bunt percentage (85.6%), starts on three days rest (4) and one-batter pitcher appearances (35)

Tom Candiotti  Knuckleballer

1997 Season

Tom Candiotti began the year in the bullpen as the odd man out on a loaded staff. After doing a fine job in relief, he returned to the rotation when Ramon Martinez went down and his competent performance allowed the club to trade Pedro Astacio. Candiotti finished with 18 starts, the lowest full-season total of his career, but posted his first winning record as a Dodger and his first this decade. He was consistent all season until September, when he was hammered as Los Angeles' drive for a National League West title came up short.

Pitching

Candiotti tosses his trademark knuckleball about 75 percent of the time. There are actually two versions, one much harder than the other. He mixes in a good curveball, but his fastball gets him in trouble if he doesn't locate it with precision. His success depends on his knuckler, and when it's not dancing he's very vulnerable to the home run. He has a knack for getting tougher with runners on and later in ballgames.

Defense & Hitting

He uses a surprisingly good move to hold runners, though his lack of velocity makes him just average in preventing stolen bases. Though he lacks mobility in the field, he seldom makes mistakes. He's weak with the bat except when it comes to laying down a sacrifice.

1998 Outlook

Candiotti eats up innings and keeps his club in most ballgames. He has been a valuable member of the staff, but his record in six years with the Dodgers is 52-64. In today's market, the 40-year-old free agent should be able to hold a job for as long as he wants the ball. He may even return to Los Angeles. Because he's a knuckleballer, his age isn't really a concern.

Position: RP/SP
Bats: R **Throws:** R
Ht: 6' 2" **Wt:** 221

Opening Day Age: 40
Born: 8/31/57 in Walnut Creek, CA
ML Seasons: 14
Pronunciation: kan-dee-AH-tee

Overall Statistics

	W	L	Pct.	ERA	G	GS	Sv	IP	H	BB	SO	HR	Ratio
1997	10	7	.588	3.60	41	18	0	135.0	128	40	89	21	1.24
Career	136	142	.489	3.54	400	364	0	2452.2	2354	790	1596	206	1.28

How Often He Throws Strikes

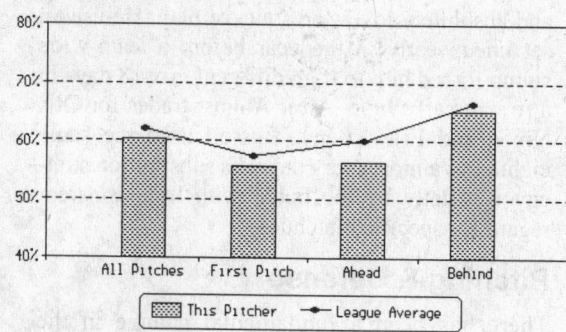

1997 Situational Stats

	W	L	ERA	Sv	IP		AB	H	HR	RBI	Avg
Home	7	3	3.16	0	74.0	LHB	235	62	10	25	.264
Road	3	4	4.13	0	61.0	RHB	282	66	11	27	.234
First Half	5	2	2.80	0	54.2	Sc Pos	125	24	4	32	.192
Scnd Half	5	5	4.15	0	80.1	Clutch	43	9	1	5	.209

1997 Rankings (National League)

⇒ 4th in lowest batting average allowed with runners in scoring position
⇒ 8th in hit batsmen (11)
⇒ Led the Dodgers in hit batsmen (11) and stolen bases allowed (16)

Darren Dreifort

1997 Season

Fully recovered from the elbow surgery that side-lined him for all of 1995, Darren Dreifort finally pitched up to the potential that made him the No. 2 overall pick in the 1993 draft. He filled several roles in the Dodger bullpen, from long relief to setup man to occasional closer. Trevor Hoffman was the only National League reliever with an opponent batting average lower than Dreifort's .202.

Pitching

Dreifort's stuff is just plain nasty. He comes at hitters from a low three-quarters angle, and every-thing he throws is hard. His fastball registers in the mid-90s and has incredible tailing action. His slider breaks in the opposite direction and reaches the high 80s. His pitches have so much movement that it affects his ability to locate them. He basi-cally aims for the middle of the plate and hopes to catch a corner. Both pitches break downward as well, so he gets a lot of grounders. Dreifort has given up just five home runs in his first 115⅔ innings in the majors. He's working on a splitter that will serve as an offspeed pitch.

Defense & Hitting

Dreifort is a thoroughbred athlete and fields his position very well. Though he has a decent move, basestealers have had some success because of his big leg kick and the sharp downward breaking action of his stuff. A talented designated hitter who hit 22 homers in his final year at Wichita State, he still can handle the bat.

1998 Outlook

Dreifort is a real competitor and has the confident demeanor of a closer, and incumbent Todd Wor-rell struggled in 1997. The Dodgers are thinking about moving Dreifort into the rotation, where he would have the leeway to walk a batter or two. He already pitches out of the windup, and having his bat in the lineup would be a bonus. In any case, his role is going to expand in 1998.

Position: RP
Bats: R **Throws:** R
Ht: 6' 2" **Wt:** 205

Opening Day Age: 25
Born: 5/18/72 in Wichita, KS
ML Seasons: 3
Pronunciation: DRY-fort

Overall Statistics

	W	L	Pct.	ERA	G	GS	Sv	IP	H	BB	SO	HR	Ratio
1997	5	2	.714	2.86	48	0	4	63.0	45	34	63	3	1.25
Career	6	11	.353	4.12	94	0	10	115.2	113	61	109	5	1.50

How Often He Throws Strikes

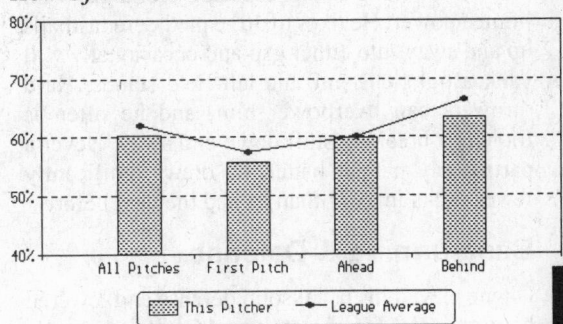

Legend: This Pitcher / League Average

1997 Situational Stats

	W	L	ERA	Sv	IP		AB	H	HR	RBI	Avg
Home	4	0	2.38	2	34.0	LHB	103	19	0	5	.184
Road	1	2	3.41	2	29.0	RHB	120	26	3	19	.217
First Half	3	0	2.35	1	23.0	Sc Pos	64	15	0	18	.234
Scnd Half	2	2	3.15	3	40.0	Clutch	96	24	0	10	.250

1997 Rankings (National League)

⇒ 2nd in first batter efficiency (.128) and lowest batting average allowed in relief (.202)
⇒ 10th in relief ERA (2.86)
⇒ Led the Dodgers in first batter efficiency (.128) and lowest batting average allowed in relief (.202)

Greg Gagne

1997 Season

Greg Gagne's second season with the Dodgers was injury-free and he made his most plate appearances since 1993. The 35 year old wore down, however, and his bat disappeared during the pennant race for the second straight year. While his final offensive numbers look all right, he hit just .161 in September after batting .213 in the final month of 1996. The most alarming aspect of the late-season collapse was his inability to make contact. More than 30 percent of his at-bats in the last two months resulted in a strikeout.

Hitting

Gagne has a long swing, especially for a guy with limited power. He likes to drive mediocre fastballs up and away into either gap and occasionally will yank a tight one into the left-field stands. Hard throwers can overpower him, and he often is fooled by breaking stuff down and away. Never a particularly patient batter, he drew significantly fewer walks in 1997 than he had the year before.

Baserunning & Defense

Gagne played his usual solid defense and lowered his error total from 21 to just 16 last season. He moves well in both directions, making up for diminishing range with a veteran's savvy. His arm is adequate. Though never a burner, Gagne is a heady baserunner. He looks to squeeze out an extra base, yet seldom runs the club out of an inning.

1998 Outlook

Gagne was reportedly talked out of retiring after the 1996 campaign and is leaning in that direction once again. Though he retains most of his skills, the Massachusetts native misses his family. They mean the world to him, as he declined an option to return to Los Angeles for more than $3 million. Gagne wants to play out his career on the East Coast, but his possibilities are limited. After all, guys like Nomar Garciaparra and Derek Jeter aren't going anywhere soon.

Position: SS
Bats: R **Throws:** R
Ht: 5'11" **Wt:** 180

Opening Day Age: 36
Born: 11/12/61 in Fall River, MA
ML Seasons: 15
Pronunciation: GAG-nee

Overall Statistics

	G	AB	R	H	D	T	HR	RBI	SB	BB	SO	Avg	OBP	Slg
1997	144	514	49	129	20	3	9	57	2	31	120	.251	.298	.354
Career	1798	5673	712	1440	296	50	111	604	108	367	1121	.254	.302	.382

Where He Hits the Ball

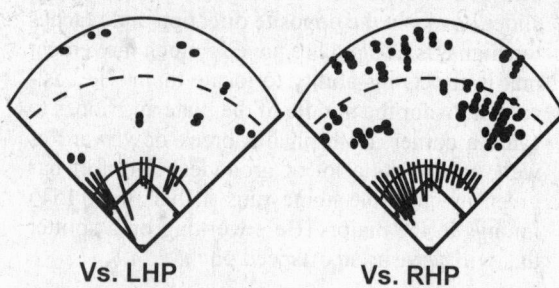

Vs. LHP   Vs. RHP

1997 Situational Stats

	AB	H	HR	RBI	Avg		AB	H	HR	RBI	Avg
Home	260	61	2	20	.235	LHP	133	34	3	14	.256
Road	254	68	7	37	.268	RHP	381	95	6	43	.249
First Half	310	86	5	36	.277	Sc Pos	128	36	1	44	.281
Scnd Half	204	43	4	21	.211	Clutch	91	23	1	9	.253

1997 Rankings (National League)

⇒ 2nd in lowest on-base percentage
⇒ 3rd in lowest slugging percentage vs. righthanded pitchers (.341)
⇒ 4th in lowest on-base percentage vs. righthanded pitchers (.297), lowest batting average at home, errors at shortstop (16) and lowest fielding percentage at shortstop (.971)
⇒ 5th in lowest slugging percentage
⇒ Led the Dodgers in strikeouts, highest ground-ball/flyball ratio (1.6) and batting average with the bases loaded (.467)

Wilton Guerrero

1997 Season

After less than a year of playing second base in Triple-A, Wilton Guerrero opened the 1997 season there for the Dodgers. He strained a shoulder muscle in early May and had to hit almost exclusively from the left side the rest of the way. In June he was caught with a corked bat and suspended by the National League. After the Dodgers traded for Eric Young in August, Guerrero spent a short time at Triple-A Albuquerque, then was relegated mainly to pinch-running duty after his September 2 recall.

Hitting

Guerrero has a bit of pop in his bat, especially for a little guy. Like many switch-hitters, the 23-year old looks like two different hitters from either side of the plate. He steps in the bucket and has a looping swing from the left side, while his righthanded stroke is more compact. Though he walked just eight times in the majors, he's a good hitter and should get better.

Baserunning & Defense

Though listed as the fastest player in the entire organization, Guerrero has a lot to learn on the basepaths. He makes poor decisions and has no clue how to read a pitcher's move. He grew up using a converted milk carton as a glove, making his hands soft and sure. He committed just four errors for the Dodgers and not once muffed a routine play. Not surprisingly, the converted shortstop had a lot of trouble turning the double play from the other side of second base. He moves fluidly, however, and has a strong and accurate arm.

1998 Outlook

Guerrero's image in Los Angeles is eerily similar to a former Dominican Dodger who wore No. 30, Jose Offerman. Guerrero is just 23 and his .291 average was the lowest mark of his pro career, yet talk centers on his inability to turn the double play. Though he's mentioned in a lot of trade rumors, the club may let the talented youngster polish his skills in Triple-A while giving Eric Young the starting role.

Position: 2B
Bats: B **Throws:** R
Ht: 5'11" **Wt:** 155

Opening Day Age: 23
Born: 10/24/74 in Don Gregorio, Dominican Republic
ML Seasons: 2

Overall Statistics

	G	AB	R	H	D	T	HR	RBI	SB	BB	SO	Avg	OBP	Slg
1997	111	357	39	104	10	9	4	32	6	8	52	.291	.305	.403
Career	116	359	40	104	10	9	4	32	6	8	54	.290	.304	.401

Where He Hits the Ball

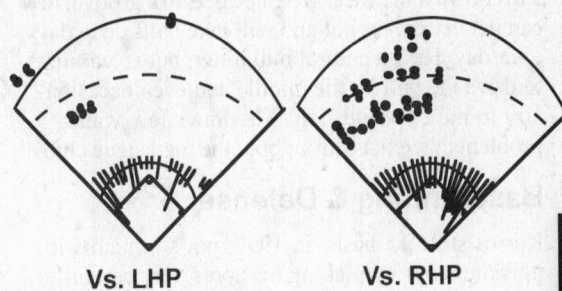

Vs. LHP   Vs. RHP

1997 Situational Stats

	AB	H	HR	RBI	Avg		AB	H	HR	RBI	Avg
Home	176	48	2	13	.273	LHP	91	20	3	8	.220
Road	181	56	2	19	.309	RHP	266	84	1	24	.316
First Half	249	72	2	23	.289	Sc Pos	81	26	0	26	.321
Scnd Half	108	32	2	9	.296	Clutch	60	15	0	4	.250

1997 Rankings (National League)

⇒ 3rd in triples
⇒ 4th in bunts in play (31)
⇒ 5th in sacrifice bunts (13)
⇒ Led the Dodgers in triples

Eric Karros

1997 Season

Eric Karros has turned himself into a very dependable power hitter, reaching 30 home runs and 100 RBI for the third straight campaign in 1997. He overcame his customary slow start and got red-hot in the midsummer months. The burly first baseman plays almost every inning of every game, causing him to wear down at times during the year. In a clutch situation, he's the guy the Dodgers want at the plate.

Hitting

Karros likes the ball up in the strike zone. A real hard thrower can bust him up and in, but the ball had better have some mustard on it. He gets himself in trouble when he starts chasing breaking stuff down and away. When he gets in a groove, he can get extremely hot and will take balls deep day after day. He's a natural pull hitter, but is learning to drive the ball up the middle and even occasionally to the opposite field. He draws few walks, a problem that exists throughout the big league club.

Baserunning & Defense

Karros stole 15 bases in 1997, not so much with quickness but by picking his spots very carefully. An aggressive baserunner, he occasionally will take the club out of an inning. He has made himself into an average first baseman despite his physical limitations. He has very little range and has poor hands, but is smart and does the little things right.

1998 Outlook

The Dodgers signed Karros to a four-year deal before the 1997 season, then shopped him in August. Los Angeles must find room for megaprospect Paul Konerko, whose best position is first base and who offers needed power. Further complicating matters is that Karros' strong work ethic is highly valued on a team that desperately craves leadership. He may be worth more to the Dodgers than he would bring in a trade.

Position: 1B
Bats: R **Throws:** R
Ht: 6' 4" **Wt:** 222

Opening Day Age: 30
Born: 11/4/67 in Hackensack, NJ
ML Seasons: 7
Pronunciation: CARE-ose

Overall Statistics

	G	AB	R	H	D	T	HR	RBI	SB	BB	SO	Avg	OBP	Slg
1997	162	628	86	167	28	0	31	104	15	61	116	.266	.329	.459
Career	891	3371	441	891	165	8	154	535	31	276	596	.264	.319	.455

Where He Hits the Ball

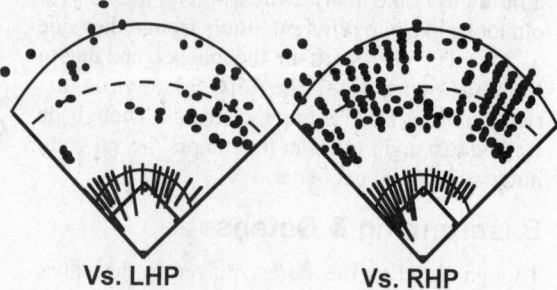

Vs. LHP   Vs. RHP

1997 Situational Stats

	AB	H	HR	RBI	Avg		AB	H	HR	RBI	Avg
Home	296	79	13	48	.267	LHP	153	35	6	26	.229
Road	332	88	18	56	.265	RHP	475	132	25	78	.278
First Half	330	89	20	56	.270	Sc Pos	167	42	7	71	.251
Scnd Half	298	78	11	48	.262	Clutch	98	25	9	18	.255

1997 Rankings (National League)

⇒ 1st in games played (162)
⇒ 3rd in errors at first base (11)
⇒ 4th in at-bats, pitches seen (2,683), plate appearances (700) and lowest fielding percentage at first base (.992)
⇒ 5th in sacrifice flies (9) and lowest groundball/flyball ratio (0.9)
⇒ 7th in lowest batting average vs. lefthanded pitchers
⇒ 9th in home runs and lowest cleanup slugging percentage (.463)
⇒ Led the Dodgers in at-bats, sacrifice flies (9), plate appearances (700), games played (162), stolen base percentage (68.2%), least GDPs per GDP situation (6.6%), cleanup slugging percentage (.463) and steals of third (5)

Ramon Martinez

1997 Season

Ramon Martinez was right in the middle of another fine year when he hit a major speed bump in June. After feeling pain in his shoulder, he was found to have a small tear in the rotator cuff. Instead of season-ending surgery, rest was prescribed. After 10 weeks on the shelf, he returned to pitch surprisingly well. He won four of his last six decisions, though he ran out of gas in his last few starts.

Pitching

Martinez' fastball clocks in at 94 MPH and really tails in on righthanders. When it's really on, he can dominate hitters for a couple of innings on that pitch alone. He has one of the best changeups in the game, and also throws a sloppy slurve. He has command problems, tending to fly open in his delivery and go deep into the count with too many hitters. The constant strain of wriggling out of jams wears him down. He averaged just over six innings per start last season.

Defense & Hitting

Martinez is a bit gangly, but fields his position well. He gets off the mound in good shape and makes accurate throws. His pickoff move is only average, but he keeps a close eye on baserunners. Relying heavily on his fastball certainly helps his catcher. Martinez generally makes contact at the plate, no matter how bad he looks. He's batting solely righthanded again after experimenting with switch-hitting for a few years.

1998 Outlook

Unless his shoulder problem is repaired during the offseason, Martinez would appear to be a ticking time bomb. All those innings he worked for former manager Tom Lasorda early in his career may be catching up to him. His tendency to weaken in the middle innings may be another sign of latent arm troubles. He's signed through 1998 and the Dodgers will continue to rely on his guts and mental toughness.

Position: SP
Bats: R **Throws:** R
Ht: 6' 4" **Wt:** 186

Opening Day Age: 30
Born: 3/22/68 in Santo Domingo, DR
ML Seasons: 10

Overall Statistics

	W	L	Pct	ERA	G	GS	Sv	IP	H	BB	SO	HR	Ratio
1997	10	5	.667	3.64	22	22	0	133.2	123	68	120	14	1.43
Career	116	74	.611	3.48	251	247	0	1630.0	1442	663	1223	140	1.29

How Often He Throws Strikes

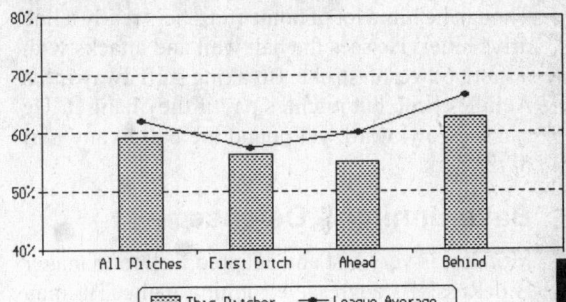

1997 Situational Stats

	W	L	ERA	Sv	IP		AB	H	HR	RBI	Avg
Home	7	3	3.70	0	80.1	LHB	245	66	7	30	.269
Road	3	2	3.54	0	53.1	RHB	262	57	7	22	.218
First Half	6	3	3.42	0	94.2	Sc Pos	142	27	1	37	.190
Scnd Half	4	2	4.15	0	39.0	Clutch	29	3	0	0	.103

1997 Rankings (National League)

⇒ 3rd in lowest batting average allowed with runners in scoring position
⇒ 10th in winning percentage
⇒ Led the Dodgers in winning percentage and lowest batting average allowed with runners in scoring position

Raul Mondesi

1997 Season

Raul Mondesi keeps getting better. He established career highs in several offensive categories in 1997 and played his usual dazzling defense to earn his second Gold Glove. More importantly, he turned it up a notch with the pennant on the line. He also became the first Dodger to have a 30-30 season.

Hitting

Though Mondesi may dawdle on his way to the plate, he wastes no time once he gets in the box. He's a notorious free swinger who helps the pitcher out far too often, and his 44 walks in 1997 may have been his most important career high. Though he hits a lot of home runs, he's really a line drive hitter. He sees the ball well and attacks with a short, powerful stroke. Breaking stuff away is his Achilles heel, but pitchers pay if they hang it. He can look awkward, yet pound the ball to any part of the park.

Baserunning & Defense

Mondesi is very fast and adapted well to manager Bill Russell's aggressive running game. He may not study pitchers' moves, but he can steal a base on sheer speed alone. What he lacks in gracefulness in the field, he makes up for with willpower and determination, not to mention athletic talent. His arm is a gun and he has the quickest release this side of Dan Marino, though he'll sometimes make a reckless throw while trying to show off.

1998 Outlook

Mondesi never leaves anything on the field. If the rest of the club expended the same amount of energy, it might have played deep into October. He's a big crowd favorite and rightfully so. His fine 1997 season might just be the tip of the iceberg, as his potential is vast. He could easily have a year that surpasses what we've seen so far.

Position: RF
Bats: R **Throws:** R
Ht: 5'11" **Wt:** 212

Opening Day Age: 27
Born: 3/12/71 in San Cristobal, DR
ML Seasons: 5
Pronunciation: MAHN-de-see

Overall Statistics

	G	AB	R	H	D	T	HR	RBI	SB	BB	SO	Avg	OBP	Slg
1997	159	616	95	191	42	5	30	87	32	44	105	.310	.360	.541
Career	609	2306	360	690	135	27	100	329	88	129	417	.299	.339	.511

Where He Hits the Ball

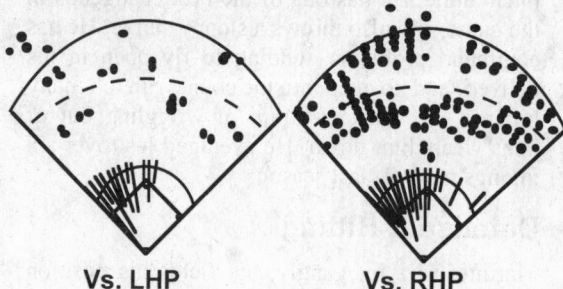

Vs. LHP   Vs. RHP

1997 Situational Stats

	AB	H	HR	RBI	Avg		AB	H	HR	RBI	Avg
Home	304	96	16	40	.316	LHP	148	42	7	23	.284
Road	312	95	14	47	.304	RHP	468	149	23	64	.318
First Half	325	96	17	48	.295	Sc Pos	151	39	4	54	.258
Scnd Half	291	95	13	39	.326	Clutch	110	36	7	17	.327

1997 Rankings (National League)

⇒ 2nd in caught stealing (15) and fielding percentage in right field (.989)
⇒ 4th in hits
⇒ 5th in doubles
⇒ Led the Dodgers in doubles, stolen bases, caught stealing (15), hit by pitch (6), batting average in the clutch and highest percentage of extra bases taken as a runner (63.4%)

Otis Nixon

1997 Season

Otis Nixon was acquired from Toronto in August to jump-start the Dodger offense and patrol center field. In his first week with the Dodgers, he went over the wall to pull two home runs back in a one-run victory. The 39 year old hasn't lost much of his skills. He hit just below his career average and stole 40 bases for the eighth straight year. In fact, his astounding 83 percent success rate was a career high.

Hitting

Batting lefthanded, Nixon has an open stance and then steps further into the bucket. He slaps grounders to the left side and beats out more than his fair share. From the right side, he has a shorter, stronger stroke that produces occasional gap power. He's a rather patient hitter and is able to spoil the pitches that he can't handle. He's always a threat to bunt and if he gets it past the pitcher, it's a base hit.

Baserunning & Defense

Despite his advanced age, Nixon can really fly. He hits warp speed by his second stride and then turns it up a notch. His presence at the plate or on the bases puts pressure on the entire defense. Speed is also his No. 1 weapon in center field. He runs down balls deep into both gaps, and can break the wrong way yet still recover to make a sliding catch. His arm is just average.

1998 Outlook

The Dodgers liked what they saw after renting Nixon for the stretch run. Though not a star, he's a relatively inexpensive solution to two of their voids in center field and the leadoff spot, if they choose to re-sign him as a free agent. If they decide to go in a different direction, he'll find a home elsewhere and no doubt will do a professional job. His legs are his game, as he'll remain useful as long as he retains his speed.

Position: CF
Bats: B **Throws:** R
Ht: 6' 2" **Wt:** 180

Opening Day Age: 39
Born: 1/9/59 in Evergreen, NC
ML Seasons: 15

Overall Statistics

	G	AB	R	H	D	T	HR	RBI	SB	BB	SO	Avg	OBP	Slg
1997	145	576	84	153	18	3	2	44	59	65	78	.266	.337	.318
Career	1515	4516	776	1215	134	20	10	290	557	518	623	.269	.343	.314

Where He Hits the Ball

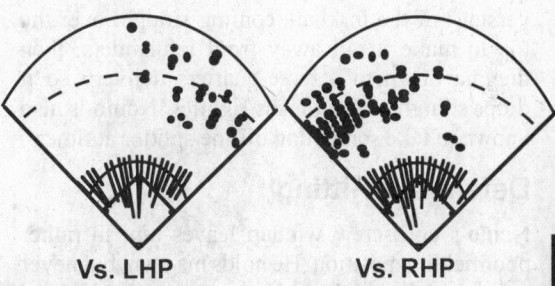

Vs. LHP   **Vs. RHP**

1997 Situational Stats

	AB	H	HR	RBI	Avg		AB	H	HR	RBI	Avg
Home	298	78	0	22	.262	LHP	168	36	1	12	.214
Road	278	75	2	22	.270	RHP	408	117	1	32	.287
First Half	289	77	0	18	.266	Sc Pos	115	31	0	39	.270
Scnd Half	287	76	2	26	.265	Clutch	94	29	0	9	.309

1997 Rankings (National League)

⇒ 5th in lowest batting average on a 3-1 count (.000)
⇒ 8th in bunts in play (24)

Hideo Nomo

1997 Season

Perhaps National League hitters have caught up with Hideo Nomo. He has been progressively less effective in each of his three seasons in the United States and struggled mightily in the second half of 1997. His problems perhaps can be traced to the Scott Rolen liner off his elbow in July. Nomo's subsequent ERA was 5.27, and he underwent elbow surgery after the season.

Pitching

Nomo always has been a two-pitch pitcher. He throws a decent fastball in the low 90s with little movement, and can locate it in all parts of the zone for strikes. He lost velocity late in the year, causing him problems. He actually throws two different versions of the forkball, coming straight over the top to make it tail away from lefthanders, then digging down to a three-quarters delivery so it drops straight down versus righties. Nomo is also known to take something off the splitter at times.

Defense & Hitting

Nomo's corkscrew windup leaves him in rather poor fielding position. He holds his own, but never will win a Gold Glove. He has worked very hard on holding runners, quickening his delivery a great deal from the stretch. Late in the year, he pitched exclusively from the stretch position. Stepping in the bucket when he swings, he seldom connects but has some doubles power when he does. He's a fair bunter at best.

1998 Outlook

Though Nomomania has subsided a bit, he's still very popular in Los Angeles. The 29 year old is signed through 1998 and the club hopes he can return to his previous form. If he could find a happy medium between 1995 and 1997, he still would be one of the game's toughest pitchers. The Dodgers hope that elbow surgery will restore his velocity and effectiveness.

Position: SP
Bats: R **Throws:** R
Ht: 6' 2" **Wt:** 210

Opening Day Age: 29
Born: 8/31/68 in Kobe, Japan
ML Seasons: 3
Pronunciation: hi-DAY-oh NO-mo

Overall Statistics

	W	L	Pct.	ERA	G	GS	Sv	IP	H	BB	SO	HR	Ratio
1997	14	12	.538	4.25	33	33	0	207.1	193	92	233	23	1.37
Career	43	29	.597	3.34	94	94	0	627.0	497	255	703	60	1.20

How Often He Throws Strikes

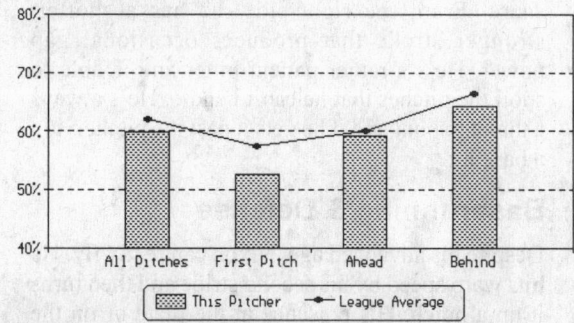

1997 Situational Stats

	W	L	ERA	Sv	IP		AB	H	HR	RBI	Avg
Home	6	7	3.60	0	110.0	LHB	412	104	9	42	.252
Road	8	5	4.99	0	97.1	RHB	383	89	14	49	.232
First Half	8	7	3.81	0	115.2	Sc Pos	191	41	3	60	.215
Scnd Half	6	5	4.81	0	91.2	Clutch	36	10	2	7	.278

1997 Rankings (National League)

⇒ 1st in balks (4) and least GDPs induced per 9 innings (0.2)
⇒ 3rd in walks allowed, wild pitches (10), lowest groundball/flyball ratio allowed (0.9) and most strikeouts per 9 innings (10.1)
⇒ 4th in strikeouts
⇒ 5th in most run support per 9 innings (5.7)
⇒ Led the Dodgers in wins, losses, games started, innings pitched, hits allowed, batters faced (904), walks allowed, strikeouts, wild pitches (10), balks (4), pitches thrown (3,329), runners caught stealing (10), least pitches thrown per batter (3.68), most run support per 9 innings (5.7) and most strikeouts per 9 innings (10.1)

Chan Ho Park

1997 Season

Chan Ho Park began the 1997 season as the fifth man in Los Angeles' rotation. As the year progressed, he became one of the club's most reliable starters. He never had thrown more than 120 innings in a season, and predictably wore down in September.

Pitching

Park had been tentative in the past, but in 1997 he came out and threw strikes. The young Korean cut his walk total despite throwing almost twice as many innings as in 1996. With the best stuff on the Dodger staff, he realized that all he has to do is throw strikes. Opponents batted just .213 against him. Park uses his Tom Seaver-like thighs and classic mechanics to throw his fastball consistently in the mid-90s. His curveball is nice and tight, and when he gets it over he's untouchable. He also throws a slider and an occasional changeup.

Defense & Hitting

Park is very athletic and gets off the mound extremely well. He has developed a good move to first and delivers the ball so quickly to the plate that only six bases were stolen off him in 1997. He takes a wild swing and is dangerous when he connects. He led Los Angeles pitchers with 11 sacrifices and four walks.

1998 Outlook

What a difference a year can make. Every part of Park's game is improving as he learns on the job. Remember, he spent just two seasons in the minors. His talent is awesome and he should just get better. He also has a huge following wherever he pitches, averaging more than 40,000 fans per home start and almost as many on the road. The only imminent problem is Korea's mandatory military stint for its citizens, which still may apply to Park. However, the Dodgers weren't expected to be able to sign him in the first place, and may be able to pull some strings for him.

Position: SP
Bats: R **Throws:** R
Ht: 6' 2" **Wt:** 195

Opening Day Age: 24
Born: 6/30/73 in Kong Ju City, Korea
ML Seasons: 4

Overall Statistics

	W	L	Pct.	ERA	G	GS	Sv	IP	H	BB	SO	HR	Ratio
1997	14	8	.636	3.38	32	29	0	192.0	149	70	166	24	1.14
Career	19	13	.594	3.59	84	40	0	308.2	238	148	298	33	1.25

How Often He Throws Strikes

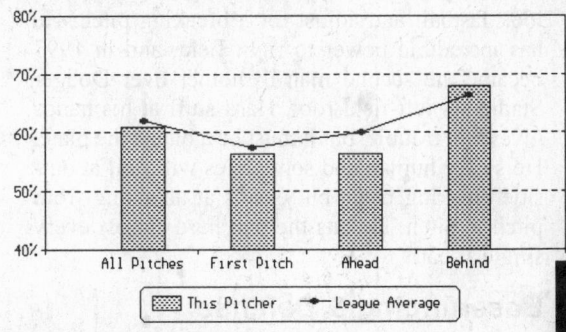

1997 Situational Stats

	W	L	ERA	Sv	IP		AB	H	HR	RBI	Avg
Home	8	3	2.92	0	104.2	LHB	363	86	13	37	.237
Road	6	5	3.92	0	87.1	RHB	337	63	11	34	.187
First Half	5	5	3.29	0	98.1	Sc Pos	109	26	2	40	.239
Scnd Half	9	3	3.46	0	93.2	Clutch	54	11	3	6	.204

1997 Rankings (National League)

⇒ 2nd in lowest batting average allowed (.213) and lowest batting average allowed vs. righthanded batters

⇒ 4th in most pitches thrown per batter (3.94) and least GDPs induced per 9 innings (0.4)

⇒ 5th in lowest groundball/flyball ratio allowed (1.0) and lowest stolen base percentage allowed (37.5%)

⇒ Led the Dodgers in wins, complete games (2), home runs allowed, runners caught stealing (10), lowest batting average allowed (.213), lowest slugging percentage allowed (.354), lowest stolen base percentage allowed (37.5%), lowest batting average allowed vs. lefthanded batters and lowest batting average allowed vs. righthanded batters

Los Angeles Dodgers

Mike Piazza

1997 Season

Mike Piazza's 1997 campaign was probably the greatest offensive year a big league catcher has had in the history of baseball. To put up those numbers in pitcher-friendly Dodger Stadium is all the more astounding. He was at his best in the heat of the pennant race, batting .362 with 18 homers and 54 RBI in the final two months. There's no doubt he's the best hitting catcher in the game, and no backstop ever has matched his first five seasons in the majors.

Hitting

Piazza's combination of strength and quickness are enough to give any pitcher a nightmare. He can look fastball and adjust for a breaking pitch. He has incredible power to right field, and in 1997 became the second man to homer over Dodger Stadium's left-field roof. Hard stuff at his hands gives him trouble, but it must be a bit off the plate. He's only human and sometimes will flail at outside breaking balls, but excels at adjusting from pitch to pitch. He hits the ball hard almost every single at-bat.

Baserunning & Defense

For a catcher, Piazza is slower than quick and faster than lumbering. He stole five bases in 1997, and goes from first to third base pretty well. Bench coach Mike Scioscia has done wonders with his calling and framing of pitches, but Piazza's footwork remains weak and he never blocks the plate. His arm is plenty strong, but he has a slow release and isn't very accurate.

1998 Outlook

After he tired at the tail end of past seasons, Piazza's furious finish temporarily has quieted any talk of moving him out from behind the plate. He has another year left on his contract. If the Dodgers get new ownership, he may be one of the first players to be offered an extension.

Position: C
Bats: R **Throws:** R
Ht: 6' 3" **Wt:** 215

Opening Day Age: 29
Born: 9/4/68 in Norristown, PA
ML Seasons: 6
Pronunciation: pee-AH-za

Overall Statistics

	G	AB	R	H	D	T	HR	RBI	SB	BB	SO	Avg	OBP	Slg
1997	152	556	104	201	32	1	40	124	5	69	77	.362	.431	.638
Career	689	2558	423	854	110	3	168	533	10	272	413	.334	.398	.576

Where He Hits the Ball

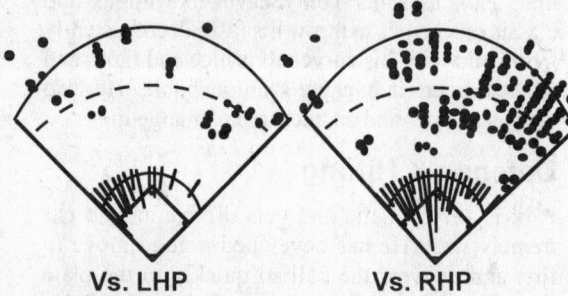

Vs. LHP   Vs. RHP

1997 Situational Stats

	AB	H	HR	RBI	Avg		AB	H	HR	RBI	Avg
Home	279	99	22	61	.355	LHP	124	45	7	27	.363
Road	277	102	18	63	.368	RHP	432	156	33	97	.361
First Half	300	107	16	51	.357	Sc Pos	147	53	11	81	.361
Scnd Half	256	94	24	73	.367	Clutch	84	26	3	19	.310

1997 Rankings (National League)

⇒ 1st in on-base percentage vs. lefthanded pitchers (.450), batting average on the road, errors at catcher (16) and lowest fielding percentage at catcher (.986)

⇒ 2nd in total bases (355), slugging percentage, slugging percentage vs. righthanded pitchers (.644), batting average with two strikes (.311) and lowest percentage of extra bases taken as a runner (25.0%)

⇒ 3rd in batting average, hits, on-base percentage, batting average vs. lefthanded pitchers and batting average vs. righthanded pitchers

⇒ Led the Dodgers in batting average, home runs, runs scored, hits, singles, total bases (355), RBI, intentional walks (11), times on base (273), GDPs (18) and slugging percentage

Ismael Valdes

1997 Season

Ismael Valdes suffered through a frustrating season in 1997. He pitched better than ever before, yet ended up with a sub-.500 record. He had a hamstring pull that sent him to the disabled list for the first time in his career and suffered through a season-long lack of run support. He also had embarrassing confrontations with manager Bill Russell and team leader Eric Karros, who both accused Valdes of lacking the guts to pitch out of tough situations.

Pitching

Valdes has great command of a fastball, curveball, slider and changeup. His 90-MPH, two-seam fastball isn't overpowering but has a nice tail on it. He actually throws two curveballs, a tight little bender and one with a sharper break that he uses as a strikeout pitch. He can locate all his pitches right where he wants, and is a master at moving them and mixing them to keep hitters guessing.

Defense & Hitting

Never spectacular or flashy, Valdes does a competent job of fielding his position. He can get a bit flustered at times and throw a ball away. He makes up for a mediocre pickoff move by keeping a close watch on opposing runners and getting rid of his pitches quickly. He's a weak hitter who is only fair at getting a bunt down.

1998 Outlook

The organization seems to view Valdes as a seven-inning pitcher who falters in clutch situations, but he maintained his effectiveness late in the game when he was left in last year. It has been said that he pitches like a young Greg Maddux. He's a crown jewel and it might be time to start thinking of him that way, though the Dodgers were discussing trading him in the offseason.

Position: SP
Bats: R **Throws:** R
Ht: 6' 3" **Wt:** 207

Opening Day Age: 24
Born: 8/21/73 in Victoria, MX
ML Seasons: 4
Pronunciation: ISH-mail val-DEZZ

Overall Statistics

	W	L	Pct.	ERA	G	GS	Sv	IP	H	BB	SO	HR	Ratio
1997	10	11	.476	2.65	30	30	0	196.2	171	47	140	16	1.11
Career	41	30	.577	3.03	117	91	1	647.2	579	162	491	55	1.14

How Often He Throws Strikes

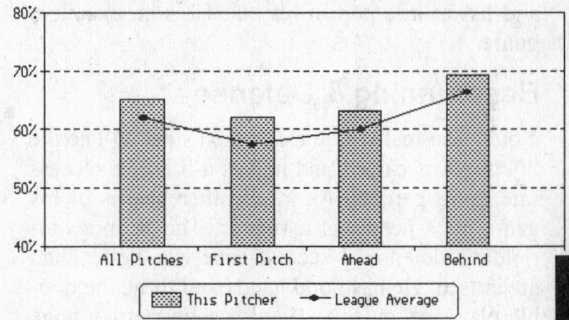

This Pitcher — League Average

1997 Situational Stats

	W	L	ERA	Sv	IP		AB	H	HR	RBI	Avg
Home	5	5	2.07	0	104.1	LHB	367	96	8	36	.262
Road	5	6	3.31	0	92.1	RHB	364	75	8	29	.206
First Half	5	9	2.97	0	112.0	Sc Pos	164	40	1	45	.244
Scnd Half	5	2	2.23	0	84.2	Clutch	76	18	1	1	.237

1997 Rankings (National League)

⇒ 2nd in pickoff throws (213), least run support per 9 innings (3.2) and ERA at home
⇒ 4th in ERA
⇒ Led the Dodgers in ERA, pickoff throws (213), stolen bases allowed (16), GDPs induced (14), highest strikeout/walk ratio (3.0), lowest on-base percentage allowed (.282), highest ground-ball/flyball ratio allowed (1.1), least baserunners allowed per 9 innings (10.1), least home runs allowed per 9 innings (.73), most GDPs induced per 9 innings (0.6), ERA at home and ERA on the road

Eric Young

Great Speed

1997 Season

Nearly five years after losing him in the expansion draft, the Dodgers reacquired Eric Young from the Rockies for Pedro Astacio in an August deal that was intended to ignite the offense. He helped to do just that, bringing an infusion of speed and enthusiasm to a club that desperately needed it.

Hitting

Young is a good fastball hitter who usually makes contact. He can be fooled by breaking balls, but looks to spoil them to prolong an at-bat. Though he walks more than he strikes out, he could learn to become more patient. That said, he gets his share of extra-base hits as he uses the entire field and has a little pop in his bat. He's an excellent bunter.

Baserunning & Defense

Young can really motor. His next steal will be the 200th of his career, and he has a lifetime success rate of 76 percent. As in all other phases of his game, he's heady as a runner. The former outfielder's defense at second base was better than advertised. He has good hands and turns the double play very quickly. He also shows good range to both sides and is a bit better on balls he has to chase than on grounders hit right at him. His arm is short but adequate for second base.

1998 Outlook

Twice in the last five years, the Dodgers have traded a Dominican pitcher named Pedro for a second baseman. They're hoping this deal turns out to be better than the last one, which sent Pedro Martinez to Montreal for Delino DeShields. Young's hitting woes away from Coors Field have been well-chronicled, but if he can match his lifetime road mark of .256 and do all the little things, Los Angeles will be very glad to have him back. His late-season audition probably won Young a spot at or near the top of the 1998 lineup.

Position: 2B
Bats: R **Throws:** R
Ht: 5' 9" **Wt:** 170

Opening Day Age: 30
Born: 5/18/67 in New Brunswick, NJ
ML Seasons: 6
Nickname: E.Y.

Overall Statistics

	G	AB	R	H	D	T	HR	RBI	SB	BB	SO	Avg	OBP	Slg
1997	155	622	106	174	33	8	8	61	45	71	54	.280	.359	.397
Career	699	2406	415	702	107	30	33	254	199	276	181	.292	.372	.402

Where He Hits the Ball

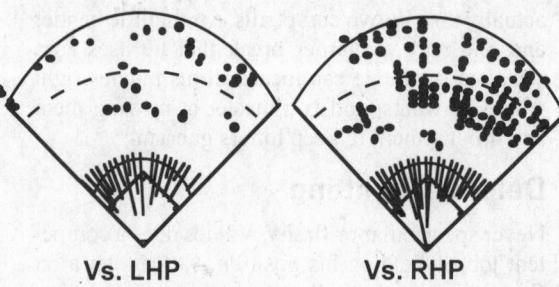

Vs. LHP   Vs. RHP

1997 Situational Stats

	AB	H	HR	RBI	Avg		AB	H	HR	RBI	Avg
Home	277	81	2	32	.292	LHP	157	44	3	15	.280
Road	345	93	6	29	.270	RHP	465	130	5	46	.280
First Half	338	99	4	28	.293	Sc Pos	126	34	0	48	.270
Scnd Half	284	75	4	33	.264	Clutch	76	23	1	10	.303

1997 Rankings (National League)

⇒ 1st in highest percentage of swings put into play (60.3%)
⇒ 2nd in plate appearances (718) and most GDPs per GDP situation (21.2%)
⇒ 3rd in errors at second base (18)
⇒ 4th in caught stealing (14), lowest fielding percentage at second base (.978) and steals of third (10)
⇒ 5th in at-bats (622) and stolen bases (45)

Todd Zeile

1997 Season

After signing a three-year contract to play in his hometown, Todd Zeile stumbled out of the gate. He didn't get going until after the All-Star break, then became one of the club's top performers down the stretch. He hit .345 in the last two months of the season and knocked in 37 runs. It tended to be all or nothing with Zeile. He set a career-high with 31 home runs, but notched just 17 doubles and no triples.

Hitting

Zeile stands straight up at the plate. It almost looks as though he isn't ready and in fact, he seldom takes a hack at the first pitch. He's very selective throughout the at-bat and has a good knowledge of the strike zone. He likes the ball out away from him. After holding his hands too close to his body early in 1997, he made an adjustment and rediscovered his short, powerful stroke. He can hit the ball a long way, mostly to left-center field.

Baserunning & Defense

Like many of his current teammates, Zeile is a station-to-station guy. He's a smart baserunner, but will only take the extra base if he knows he can make it. The former catcher is really a man without a position. At third base, he breaks late on balls hit to either side and especially on anything he must charge. His lack of range and poor hands transform easy plays into tough ones, and tough ones into base hits. His 26 errors at third were exceeded only by Anaheim's Dave Hollins. To his credit, Zeile has a strong and accurate throwing arm.

1998 Outlook

Zeile has been on five teams in three years. His passionless play inspires little affection among Dodgers fans. His presence and sizable contract ultimately may force a trade of Eric Karros. Their skills are very similar and star prospect Paul Konerko is destined to play one of the corner positions soon.

Position: 3B
Bats: R **Throws:** R
Ht: 6' 1" **Wt:** 200

Opening Day Age: 32
Born: 9/9/65 in Van Nuys, CA
ML Seasons: 9
Pronunciation: ZEAL

Overall Statistics

	G	AB	R	H	D	T	HR	RBI	SB	BB	SO	Avg	OBP	Slg
1997	160	575	89	154	17	0	31	90	8	85	112	.268	.365	.459
Career	1159	4185	557	1103	214	13	140	613	42	529	679	.264	.346	.421

Where He Hits the Ball

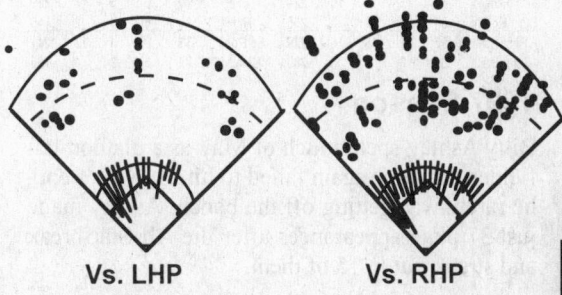

Vs. LHP   **Vs. RHP**

1997 Situational Stats

	AB	H	HR	RBI	Avg		AB	H	HR	RBI	Avg
Home	284	77	17	46	.271	LHP	140	36	5	18	.257
Road	291	77	14	44	.265	RHP	435	118	26	72	.271
First Half	314	72	16	41	.229	Sc Pos	158	36	5	56	.228
Scnd Half	261	82	15	49	.314	Clutch	106	30	7	12	.283

1997 Rankings (National League)

⇒ 1st in errors at third base (26) and lowest fielding percentage at third base (.931)
⇒ 2nd in pitches seen (2,757), highest percentage of pitches taken (65.7%) and lowest percentage of swings on the first pitch (12.9%)
⇒ 3rd in lowest percentage of extra bases taken as a runner (32.7%)
⇒ 4th in most pitches seen per plate appearance (4.10)
⇒ 5th in games played (160)
⇒ Led the Dodgers in walks, hit by pitch (6), GDPs (18), pitches seen (2,757), most pitches seen per plate appearance (4.10), highest percentage of pitches taken (65.7%) and lowest percentage of swings on the first pitch (12.9%)

Billy Ashley

Position: LF
Bats: R **Throws:** R
Ht: 6' 7" **Wt:** 235

Opening Day Age: 27
Born: 7/11/70 in
Taylor, MI
ML Seasons: 6

Overall Statistics

	G	AB	R	H	D	T	HR	RBI	SB	BB	SO	Avg	OBP	Slg
1997	71	131	12	32	7	0	6	19	0	8	46	.244	.293	.435
Career	268	594	53	137	20	1	25	77	0	61	225	.231	.305	.394

1997 Situational Stats

	AB	H	HR	RBI	Avg		AB	H	HR	RBI	Avg
Home	67	15	4	16	.224	LHP	90	26	5	17	.289
Road	64	17	2	3	.266	RHP	41	6	1	2	.146
First Half	96	22	5	16	.229	Sc Pos	38	8	1	12	.211
Scnd Half	35	10	1	3	.286	Clutch	27	5	1	4	.185

1997 Season

Billy Ashley spent much of May as a platoon left fielder, but once again failed to hit. By year's end, he rarely was getting off the bench. Ashley made just 37 plate appearances after the All-Star break and struck out in 15 of them.

Hitting, Baserunning & Defense

It's a lot of fun to watch Ashley hit, at least in batting practice. During games, he doesn't make enough contact. There are many holes in his swing, most notably up and in, and down and away. At some points in 1997, he looked to be making strides toward hitting the ball the other way. Ashley is slow on the basepaths and even slower in the outfield. He's a tentative defender who never looks good and often looks foolish. He does have a strong throwing arm.

1998 Outlook

Ashley has put up big numbers in the thin air of Triple-A Albuquerque, but hasn't shown much in Los Angeles. A fresh start in the American League could do him some good. He's a natural designated hitter.

Roger Cedeno

Position: CF/LF
Bats: B **Throws:** R
Ht: 6' 1" **Wt:** 165

Opening Day Age: 23
Born: 8/16/74 in
Valencia Edo.
Carabobo, VZ
ML Seasons: 3
Pronunciation:
suh-DAYN-yo

Overall Statistics

	G	AB	R	H	D	T	HR	RBI	SB	BB	SO	Avg	OBP	Slg
1997	80	194	31	53	10	2	3	17	9	25	44	.273	.362	.392
Career	206	447	61	115	23	3	5	38	15	52	101	.257	.338	.356

1997 Situational Stats

	AB	H	HR	RBI	Avg		AB	H	HR	RBI	Avg
Home	95	24	3	10	.253	LHP	84	24	2	6	.286
Road	99	29	0	7	.293	RHP	110	29	1	11	.264
First Half	95	22	0	9	.232	Sc Pos	43	14	2	15	.326
Scnd Half	99	31	3	8	.313	Clutch	33	3	0	2	.091

1997 Season

Roger Cedeno looked like a different player in 1997. Gone was the tentativeness of a year before, when he usually looked overmatched and overwhelmed. After playing sporadically early in the season, the young Venezuelan was starting to come on before the Otis Nixon trade put him back on the bench. Then a broken toe ended his season.

Hitting, Baserunning & Defense

The switch-hitting Cedeno has a good eye, especially from the right side. Though he has gap power, he's most effective when he hits down on the ball and uses his speed. Well placed bunts would be a big addition to his offensive arsenal. Though still green on the basepaths, he was safe on nine of 10 steal attempts on raw speed alone. Touted as an outstanding center fielder, he finally is living up to his advance billing. Cedeno gets a good break on most balls, possesses the speed to make up for mistakes and has a decent arm.

1998 Outlook

Who knows what to expect? Lately the Dodgers have been rushing their prospects through the system, only to grow impatient with them after a few months in the big leagues. Cedeno had the fourth-highest on-base percentage on the club and is a better and less expensive player than Nixon.

Tripp Cromer

Position: 2B/SS
Bats: R **Throws:** R
Ht: 6' 2" **Wt:** 170

Opening Day Age: 30
Born: 11/21/67 in Lake City, SC
ML Seasons: 4

Overall Statistics

	G	AB	R	H	D	T	HR	RBI	SB	BB	SO	Avg	OBP	Slg
1997	28	86	8	25	3	0	4	20	0	6	16	.291	.333	.465
Career	145	454	46	105	22	0	9	38	0	21	88	.231	.268	.339

1997 Situational Stats

	AB	H	HR	RBI	Avg		AB	H	HR	RBI	Avg
Home	43	10	2	8	.233	LHP	28	9	3	8	.321
Road	43	15	2	12	.349	RHP	58	16	1	12	.276
First Half	30	11	0	8	.367	Sc Pos	24	14	1	17	.583
Scnd Half	56	14	4	12	.250	Clutch	5	1	0	2	.200

1997 Season

Los Angeles signed free-agent middle infielder Tripp Cromer before the 1997 season, and he came in handy when second baseman Wilton Guerrero got hurt in June. Cromer was called up from Triple-A and played his way into a semi-regular role before spraining his elbow in late July. His glovework was solid as always, and his production at the plate was a pleasant surprise.

Hitting, Baserunning & Defense

Cromer generates more power than expected from a wiry shortstop, but that's mostly because he takes a bigger swing than he ought to. He has little plate discipline and often chases breaking balls in the dirt. He never has hit much at any level and his 1997 performance was probably an aberration. Cromer has below-average speed and isn't much use on the bases. He's a decent defensive second baseman and shortstop with ordinary range. He has good hands and enough arm to play either position.

1998 Outlook

Cromer landed in a good situation last year and made the most of it until he got hurt. The Dodgers still have questions at second base and shortstop, so he may be kept around as a backup infielder.

Mark Guthrie

Position: RP
Bats: R **Throws:** L
Ht: 6' 4" **Wt:** 207

Opening Day Age: 32
Born: 9/22/65 in Buffalo, NY
ML Seasons: 9

Overall Statistics

	W	L	Pct.	ERA	G	GS	Sv	IP	H	BB	SO	HR	Ratio
1997	1	4	.200	5.32	62	0	1	69.1	71	30	42	12	1.46
Career	32	36	.471	4.07	392	43	10	651.2	682	235	505	64	1.41

1997 Situational Stats

	W	L	ERA	Sv	IP		AB	H	HR	RBI	Avg
Home	1	3	3.94	0	29.2	LHB	85	24	3	15	.282
Road	0	1	6.35	1	39.2	RHB	176	47	9	30	.267
First Half	1	2	3.73	0	41.0	Sc Pos	71	19	4	35	.268
Scnd Half	0	2	7.62	1	28.1	Clutch	92	24	6	26	.261

1997 Season

Mark Guthrie began the year as one of the Dodgers' most reliable setup men. By season's end, he had completely fallen apart and was buried deep at the bottom of the bullpen. He was especially vulnerable to homers, giving up 12 in 69⅓ innings.

Pitching, Defense & Hitting

A finesse pitcher, Guthrie doesn't have a great deal of room for error. His fastball is just average, so he relies on a good curveball and splitter to keep batters off balance. Constantly nibbling, he walks his share of hitters. He was often unable to keep his curveball down in 1997, which led to more than a few longballs. He's a decent fielder but has a weak pickoff move for a lefthander. For as few at-bats as he gets, the switch-hitter holds his own at the plate.

1998 Outlook

A hefty contract coupled with a double-digit ERA in September wasn't tempting for the expansion teams. Guthrie will return for the final year of his contract. He has been up and down throughout his career, so it wouldn't be a big surprise to see him pitch effectively once again.

Darren Hall

Position: RP
Bats: R **Throws:** R
Ht: 6' 3" **Wt:** 205

Opening Day Age: 33
Born: 7/14/64 in
Marysville, OH
ML Seasons: 4

Overall Statistics

	W	L	Pct.	ERA	G	GS	Sv	IP	H	BB	SO	HR	Ratio
1997	3	2	.600	2.30	63	0	2	54.2	58	26	39	3	1.54
Career	5	9	.357	3.30	119	0	22	114.2	118	54	90	10	1.50

1997 Situational Stats

	W	L	ERA	Sv	IP			AB	H	HR	RBI	Avg
Home	2	0	0.33	2	27.2	LHB		83	27	1	5	.325
Road	1	2	4.33	0	27.0	RHB		122	31	2	19	.254
First Half	2	2	2.27	2	31.2	Sc Pos		68	19	0	21	.279
Scnd Half	1	0	2.35	0	23.0	Clutch		99	27	1	10	.273

1997 Season

Completely recovered from the elbow surgery that limited him to just 26 appearances in the previous two seasons combined, Darren Hall pitched in a career-high 63 games for the Dodgers in 1997. He averaged under an inning per outing, often coming in to induce a needed ground ball.

Pitching, Defense & Hitting

Hall throws two pitches, a sinker and a slider. Everything is hard and down in the strike zone, so opposing batters tend to pound the ball into the dirt. Lefthanders have given him a lot of trouble since his surgery. His stuff is just average, so he tends to nibble. With an unexceptional move and a good-sized leg kick, he's vulnerable to basestealers. He never has batted as a major leaguer.

1998 Outlook

In the deep Dodger bullpen, Hall is just another middle man. He might be more valuable to a team with less depth, but probably will be invited back to fill the same role. If he leaves, Los Angeles can replace him fairly easily.

Todd Hollandsworth

Position: LF/CF
Bats: L **Throws:** L
Ht: 6' 2" **Wt:** 193

Opening Day Age: 24
Born: 4/20/73 in
Dayton, OH
ML Seasons: 3

Overall Statistics

	G	AB	R	H	D	T	HR	RBI	SB	BB	SO	Avg	OBP	Slg
1997	106	296	39	73	20	2	4	31	5	17	60	.247	.286	.368
Career	296	877	119	236	48	6	21	103	28	68	182	.269	.322	.409

1997 Situational Stats

	AB	H	HR	RBI	Avg			AB	H	HR	RBI	Avg
Home	153	44	1	14	.288	LHP		46	16	1	7	.348
Road	143	29	3	17	.203	RHP		250	57	3	24	.228
First Half	223	51	2	18	.229	Sc Pos		72	19	2	26	.264
Scnd Half	73	22	2	13	.301	Clutch		61	10	0	4	.164

1997 Season

Whether it was the sophomore jinx or simply coming back to earth, Todd Hollandsworth followed up his Rookie-of-the-Year campaign with a disappointing 1997. He began the year as the everyday left fielder, but didn't hit enough to stay in the lineup and earned a demotion to Triple-A Albuquerque. He made it back, then was sidelined most of the last two months with a fractured right elbow.

Hitting, Baserunning & Defense

Hollandsworth has gap power. Like many lefthanders, he likes the ball down and in. He has a long swing that makes it difficult to catch up with high fastballs. He's not very disciplined at the plate and gets himself out too often. Aggressive in all phases of the game, he's a good outfielder and can play all three positions, though his arm isn't strong enough for right field. He's a good baserunner, though not fast enough to steal more than an occasional base.

1998 Outlook

Though he didn't live up to the lofty expectations in LA, Hollandsworth hasn't embarassed himself. The 25 year old deserves a shot at playing daily because he has hit well versus lefthanders in limited opportunities.

Darren Lewis

Position: CF/LF
Bats: R **Throws:** R
Ht: 6' 0" **Wt:** 189

Opening Day Age: 30
Born: 8/28/67 in
Berkeley, CA
ML Seasons: 8

Overall Statistics

	G	AB	R	H	D	T	HR	RBI	SB	BB	SO	Avg	OBP	Slg
1997	107	154	22	41	4	1	1	15	14	17	31	.266	.339	.325
Career	827	2513	380	621	74	26	14	203	186	251	298	.247	.321	.314

1997 Situational Stats

	AB	H	HR	RBI	Avg		AB	H	HR	RBI	Avg
Home	80	21	0	7	.263	LHP	64	17	0	4	.266
Road	74	20	1	8	.270	RHP	90	24	1	11	.267
First Half	56	11	0	4	.196	Sc Pos	33	10	1	14	.303
Scnd Half	98	30	1	11	.306	Clutch	27	6	0	2	.222

1997 Season

Darren Lewis was rescued from purgatory with the White Sox in a late-August trade that thrust him right into the thick of a pennant race. He acquitted himself quite admirably, hitting .299 for the Dodgers while playing his usual fine defense at a new position, left field.

Hitting, Baserunning & Defense

Lewis looks overmatched in many at-bats, but hangs in there and gets his fair share of bloop hits. He uses the whole field, and he just reaches out to make contact when thrown hard stuff on the outer half. He has very little power. Lewis bunts a lot, but needs to work on angling it down the lines. He also can steal a base, but had a rougher time back in the National League. Defensively, the former Gold Glove winner looked right at home in left field. He also is a star in center field. He breaks well on the ball and has a strong and accurate arm.

1998 Outlook

Lewis' stock has dropped considerably over the years. His acquisition by the Dodgers had more to do with their weaknesses than his abilities. A free agent, he'll hook on somewhere as at least a fourth outfielder, if for no other reason than his splendid defense.

Antonio Osuna

Position: RP
Bats: R **Throws:** R
Ht: 5'11" **Wt:** 160

Opening Day Age: 24
Born: 4/12/73 in
Sinaloa, MX
ML Seasons: 3
Pronunciation:
oh-SOO-nuh

Overall Statistics

	W	L	Pct.	ERA	G	GS	Sv	IP	H	BB	SO	HR	Ratio
1997	3	4	.429	2.19	48	0	0	61.2	46	19	68	6	1.05
Career	14	14	.500	3.07	160	0	4	190.1	150	71	199	17	1.16

1997 Situational Stats

	W	L	ERA	Sv	IP		AB	H	HR	RBI	Avg
Home	1	2	2.51	0	28.2	LHB	104	20	2	6	.192
Road	2	2	1.91	0	33.0	RHB	116	26	4	11	.224
First Half	1	3	3.00	0	24.0	Sc Pos	66	6	1	11	.091
Scnd Half	2	1	1.67	0	37.2	Clutch	100	22	1	7	.220

1997 Season

A slow starter, Antonio Osuna spent the whole month of April in Triple-A Albuquerque. Once he returned to his familiar role as the Dodgers' principal righthanded setup man, he got stronger as the year progressed. He posted a 1.67 ERA after the All-Star break.

Pitching, Defense & Hitting

Always pitching from the stretch, the young Mexican gets incredible heat from a compact frame. His fastball travels in the mid-90s, though it lacks movement. He gained more confidence in his curveball in 1997, and he's very tough when he gets his curve and occasional changeup over for strikes. He has a quick move to first and uses it often. Defensively, he's just average. Osuna is 1-for-5 as a big league hitter.

1998 Outlook

Osuna is sought after by many clubs who view him as a closer. However, he's more comfortable in his current, less stressful role. In the era of the six- and seven-inning start, a short reliever like Osuna is very valuable. If Darren Dreifort slides into the starting rotation, Osuna would become indispensable.

Scott Radinsky

Position: RP
Bats: L **Throws:** L
Ht: 6' 3" **Wt:** 204

Opening Day Age: 30
Born: 3/3/68 in
Glendale, CA
ML Seasons: 7
Nickname: Rads

Overall Statistics

	W	L	Pct.	ERA	G	GS	Sv	IP	H	BB	SO	HR	Ratio
1997	5	1	.833	2.89	75	0	3	62.1	54	21	44	4	1.20
Career	34	18	.654	3.34	449	0	36	390.1	367	167	293	24	1.37

1997 Situational Stats

	W	L	ERA	Sv	IP		AB	H	HR	RBI	Avg
Home	2	0	0.65	1	27.2	LHB	87	19	2	16	.218
Road	3	1	4.67	2	34.2	RHB	142	35	2	13	.246
First Half	3	1	3.03	0	35.2	Sc Pos	65	16	1	26	.246
Scnd Half	2	0	2.70	3	26.2	Clutch	106	20	3	12	.189

1997 Season

Scott Radinsky put together another sterling season as the Dodgers' steadiest lefthanded setup man. The calm yet competitive punk rocker had some rocky outings late in the year, but tied for second in the National League with 26 holds. The Los Angeles-area native stands right near the top of the club's bullpen depth chart.

Pitching, Defense & Hitting

Radinsky wastes little motion in delivering the ball, suddenly sending a 93-MPH fastball or hard slider hurtling toward the plate. Everything he throws is hard and his three-quarters release point is very difficult to pick up, especially for lefthanders. He keeps runners honest with a quick move and an offbeat delivery. He's an average fielder at best and fanned in all four of his plate appearances in 1997.

1998 Outlook

Todd Worrell's shoes will be tough to fill and the Dodgers likely will use some money to attract an established closer. It's not out of the realm of possibility for Radinsky and Darren Dreifort to share the role, but it's more likely that Radinsky will retain his job as the lefty setup man.

Dennis Reyes

Position: RP/SP
Bats: R **Throws:** L
Ht: 6' 3" **Wt:** 246

Opening Day Age: 20
Born: 4/19/77 in
Higuera de Zaragoza,
Mexico
ML Seasons: 1
Pronunciation:
RAY-ess

Overall Statistics

	W	L	Pct.	ERA	G	GS	Sv	IP	H	BB	SO	HR	Ratio
1997	2	3	.400	3.83	14	5	0	47.0	51	18	36	4	1.47
Career	2	3	.400	3.83	14	5	0	47.0	51	18	36	4	1.47

1997 Situational Stats

	W	L	ERA	Sv	IP		AB	H	HR	RBI	Avg
Home	1	1	2.84	0	19.0	LHB	43	13	2	6	.302
Road	1	2	4.50	0	28.0	RHB	139	38	2	13	.273
First Half	0	0	-	0	0.0	Sc Pos	41	12	1	14	.293
Scnd Half	2	3	3.83	0	47.0	Clutch	23	8	1	4	.348

1997 Season

Dennis Reyes jumped from Class-A in 1996 to Dodger Stadium a year later. The young Mexican first was called up when Ismael Valdes went on the disabled list, and showed a lot of poise in five starts. Reyes also was very effective in nine relief appearances in September.

Pitching, Defense & Hitting

Reyes is a dead ringer for his idol, Fernando Valenzuela. Though he doesn't have Valenzuela's screwball, there are hints of it when the youngster turns his changeup over. He mostly relies on a cut fastball and curve. None of his pitches are overpowering, so Reyes must move the ball around and throw strikes. Like Valenzuela, he's quite agile for a big man, handling both the glove and bat pretty well. His pickoff move and stretch delivery need work, as big league basestealers went 7-for-7 against him in 1997.

1998 Outlook

Though he doesn't possess the greatest stuff, Reyes has an understanding of his craft well beyond his years. He could use another half-year in the minors, but he wouldn't embarrass himself should he be placed in the Opening Day rotation. He has the potential to be a successful and extremely popular Dodger.

Other Los Angeles Dodgers

Eric Anthony (**Pos**: LF, **Age**: 30, **Bats**: L)

	G	AB	R	H	D	T	HR	RBI	SB	BB	SO	Avg	OBP	Slg
1997	47	74	8	18	3	2	2	5	2	12	18	.243	.349	.419
Career	682	1999	249	462	81	8	78	269	24	217	491	.231	.305	.397

Shuttling back and forth between LA and Triple-A, Anthony provided the Dodgers with pinch-hitting and outfield support. He refused an assignment to the minors at the end of the season. 1998 Outlook: C

Brett Butler (**Pos**: CF/LF, **Age**: 40, **Bats**: L)

	G	AB	R	H	D	T	HR	RBI	SB	BB	SO	Avg	OBP	Slg
1997	105	343	52	97	8	3	0	18	15	42	40	.283	.363	.324
Career	2213	8180	1359	2375	277	131	54	578	558	1129	907	.290	.377	.376

Butler's 17-year major league career finally came to an end in '97 after an assortment of injuries continually sidelined the 40 year old. He's one of the top leadoff men of his generation. 1998 Outlook: D

Juan Castro (**Pos**: SS/2B, **Age**: 25, **Bats**: R)

	G	AB	R	H	D	T	HR	RBI	SB	BB	SO	Avg	OBP	Slg
1997	40	75	3	11	3	1	0	4	0	7	20	.147	.220	.213
Career	121	211	19	38	8	4	0	9	1	18	48	.180	.245	.256

Castro's glove *must* be good, because this utility infielder can't hit a lick; his career batting average is just .180 in 211 big league at-bats. He'll probably compete with Tripp Cromer for a roster spot next season. 1998 Outlook: C

Chip Hale (**Pos**: 3B, **Age**: 33, **Bats**: L)

	G	AB	R	H	D	T	HR	RBI	SB	BB	SO	Avg	OBP	Slg
1997	14	12	0	1	0	0	0	0	0	2	4	.083	.214	.083
Career	333	575	62	159	27	1	7	78	2	58	68	.277	.346	.363

Hale was released in September after getting only a handful of pinch-hit at-bats with the Dodgers. Now 33, he has never garnered more than 186 big league at-bats in a single season. 1998 Outlook: D

Mike Harkey (**Pos**: RHP, **Age**: 31)

	W	L	Pct.	ERA	G	GS	Sv	IP	H	BB	SO	HR	Ratio
1997	1	0	1.000	4.30	10	0	0	14.2	12	5	6	3	1.16
Career	36	36	.500	4.49	131	104	0	656.0	720	225	316	75	1.44

Originally a starter, Harkey operated solely from the bullpen last season for the Dodgers while being bounced to and from the minors. Not many teams out there are clamoring for a mediocre 31-year-old righthander. 1998 Outlook: C

Garey Ingram (**Pos**: LF, **Age**: 27, **Bats**: R)

	G	AB	R	H	D	T	HR	RBI	SB	BB	SO	Avg	OBP	Slg
1997	12	9	2	4	0	0	0	1	1	1	3	.444	.500	.444
Career	82	142	17	37	3	0	3	12	4	17	33	.261	.340	.345

Ingram will be one of dozens competing for the Dodgers' left-field slot next season. He hit well at Double-A San Antonio last year, but at age 27, he'd already be in the majors if he had any potential. 1998 Outlook: C

Wayne Kirby (**Pos**: CF, **Age**: 34, **Bats**: L)

	G	AB	R	H	D	T	HR	RBI	SB	BB	SO	Avg	OBP	Slg
1997	46	65	6	11	2	0	0	4	0	10	12	.169	.280	.200
Career	490	1167	178	296	51	8	14	119	43	97	159	.254	.312	.347

Kirby struggled mightily at the plate during his three stints with LA in 1997. He refused an assignment to the minors at the end of the year; his age (34) and career OBP (.312) won't help his chances. 1998 Outlook: D

Nelson Liriano (**Pos**: 2B, **Age**: 33, **Bats**: B)

	G	AB	R	H	D	T	HR	RBI	SB	BB	SO	Avg	OBP	Slg
1997	76	88	10	20	6	0	1	11	0	6	12	.227	.274	.330
Career	811	2199	296	576	105	27	25	240	59	212	293	.262	.326	.368

Almost exclusively used as a pinch hitter last season, Liriano struggled at the plate and was optioned to the minors at the end of the year. He refused the assignment, and his career looks in jeopardy. 1998 Outlook: C

Eddie Murray (**Pos**: DH, **Age**: 42, **Bats**: B)

	G	AB	R	H	D	T	HR	RBI	SB	BB	SO	Avg	OBP	Slg
1997	55	167	13	37	7	0	3	18	1	15	26	.222	.281	.317
Career	3026	1133	1627	3255	560	35	504	1917	110	1333	1516	.287	.359	.476

Undoubtedly a future Hall-of-Famer, Murray grounded into two critical bases-loaded double plays that helped destroy the Dodgers' playoff hopes. He'll spend 1998 as an Orioles coach. 1998 Outlook: D

Tom Prince (**Pos**: C, **Age**: 33, **Bats**: R)

	G	AB	R	H	D	T	HR	RBI	SB	BB	SO	Avg	OBP	Slg
1997	47	100	17	22	5	0	3	14	0	5	15	.220	.275	.360
Career	285	612	53	122	39	1	9	74	3	53	124	.199	.274	.310

Despite a .199 lifetime batting average, Prince somehow has managed to carve out an 11-year career as a backup catcher. He'll probably be spelling Mike Piazza again in '98. 1998 Outlook: B

Todd Worrell (**Pos**: RHP, **Age**: 38)

	W	L	Pct.	ERA	G	GS	Sv	IP	H	BB	SO	HR	Ratio
1997	2	6	.250	5.28	65	0	35	59.2	60	23	61	12	1.39
Career	50	52	.490	3.09	617	0	256	693.2	608	247	628	65	1.23

Despite recording 35 saves, Worrell had a truly awful season. He fell apart in September, hurting the Dodgers' drive for a division title. He retired in September. 1998 Outlook: D

Los Angeles Dodgers Minor League Prospects

Organization Overview:

The Dodgers are industry leaders in finding worldwide talent and producing Rookies of the Year. Their six main starters in 1997 came from Japan, Mexico, Korea, the Dominican Republic (two) as well as the United States, and they went the extra mile to sign Hideo Nomo and Chan Ho Park. They do spend a lot of money that small-revenue teams can't, but they also avoid embarrassing mistakes such as Hideki Irabu. Second baseman Wilton Guerrero didn't win the National League Rookie of the Year award and may have been overhyped, but the run of five straight from 1992-96 (Eric Karros, Mike Piazza, Raul Mondesi, Hideo Nomo, Todd Hollandsworth) stands as a testament to the club's development skills. Paul Konerko may be the game's best prospect who's on the verge of the majors, and Adrian Beltre may be even better.

Adrian Beltre

Position: 3B **Opening Day Age:** 19
Bats: R **Throws:** R **Born:** 4/7/78 in Santo
Ht: 5' 11" **Wt:** 200 Domingo, DR

Recent Statistics

	G	AB	R	H	D	T	HR	RBI	SB	BB	SO	AVG
96 A Savannah	68	244	48	75	14	3	16	59	4	35	46	.307
96 A San Berndno	63	238	40	62	13	1	10	40	3	19	44	.261
97 A Vero Beach	123	435	95	138	24	2	26	104	25	67	66	.317

There's little that Beltre can't do. He has exciting potential as both a hitter and a slugger and already walks more than he strikes out. At third base, he has above-average arm strength. He even runs well, though he's not a burner and won't be a big baserunning threat. Signed out of the Dominican Republic in 1994, he racked up an impressive list of honors last season as a 19-year-old in the high Class-A Florida State League. He was named MVP, and the managers named him the best batting prospect, the best power prospect, the best defensive third baseman, the best infield arm and the most exciting player in the league. Todd Zeile and Konerko also play third base, but Beltre will move them both out of there when he's ready for the major leagues. He's probably two years away, but his immense talent could allow him to move even quicker.

Kevin Gibbs

Position: OF **Opening Day Age:** 23
Bats: B **Throws:** R **Born:** 4/3/74 in
Ht: 6' 2" **Wt:** 182 Washington, DC

Recent Statistics

	G	AB	R	H	D	T	HR	RBI	SB	BB	SO	AVG
96 A Vero Beach	118	423	69	114	9	11	0	33	60	65	80	.270
97 AA San Antonio	101	358	89	120	21	6	2	34	49	72	48	.335
97 MLE	101	333	66	95	14	2	1	25	33	43	51	.285

A sixth-round pick in 1995 out of Old Dominion, Gibbs has risen quietly through the system. He's a switch-hitter with speed, and he knows the style he needs to play. He makes contact, draws walks and bunts in an effort to get on base, where he can drive a pitcher nuts. He shows fine range in center field and was voted the Double-A Texas League's top defensive outfielder by the managers. He's four months older and two levels behind Roger Cedeno, but Gibbs offers more on-base ability. He could challenge for the starting center-field job in 1999.

Mike Judd

Position: P **Opening Day Age:** 22
Bats: R **Throws:** R **Born:** 6/30/75 in San
Ht: 6' 2" **Wt:** 200 Diego, CA

Recent Statistics

	W	L	ERA	G	GS	Sv	IP	H	R	BB	SO	HR
97 A Vero Beach	6	5	3.53	14	14	0	86.2	67	37	39	104	4
97 AA San Antonio	4	2	2.73	12	12	0	79.0	69	27	33	65	0
97 NL Los Angeles	0	0	0.00	1	0	0	2.2	4	0	0	4	0

The Yankees signed Judd as a ninth-round pick out of Grossmont (Calif.) Junior College in 1995, then peddled him to the Dodgers a year later for reliever Billy Brewer. Brewer made just four appearances for New York, while Judd went from Class-A in 1996 to a September call-up last year. His fastball was rated the best in the high Class-A Florida State League, and he also throws a splitter, slider and changeup. His command could improve, but overall his four-pitch package is tough to hit. He could establish himself in Los Angeles by mid-1999.

Paul Konerko

Position: 3B **Opening Day Age:** 22
Bats: R **Throws:** R **Born:** 3/5/76 in
Ht: 6' 3" **Wt:** 210 Providence, RI

Recent Statistics

	G	AB	R	H	D	T	HR	RBI	SB	BB	SO	AVG
97 AAA Albuquerque	130	483	97	156	31	1	37	127	2	64	61	.323
97 NL Los Angeles	6	7	0	1	0	0	0	0	0	1	2	.143
97 MLE	130	440	60	113	21	0	21	78	1	38	64	.257

Baseball America's 1997 Minor League Player of the Year, Konerko could add to the Dodgers' Rookie-of-the-Year legacy in 1998. That is, if Los Angeles can find a place to play him. The team signed first baseman Eric Karros and third baseman Todd Zeile to long-term contracts after the 1996 season, and Konerko is ready to play on an infield corner now. A 1994 first-round pick as a catcher, he was moved from behind the plate to maximize his considerable offensive talents. The 1997 Pacific Coast League MVP, he's a natural hitter with power to all fields and patience. An acceptable defensive player, he's more likely to wind up at first base, in the short term because Karros may be more tradeable and in the long term because of Beltre.

Jeff Kubenka

Position: P
Bats: R **Throws:** L
Ht: 6' 0" **Wt:** 195

Opening Day Age: 23
Born: 8/24/74 in Weimar, TX

Recent Statistics

	W	L	ERA	G	GS	Sv	IP	H	R	BB	SO	HR
96 A Yakima	5	1	2.51	28	0	14	32.1	20	11	10	61	2
97 A San Berndno	5	1	0.92	34	0	19	39.0	24	4	11	62	1
97 AAA Albuquerque	0	2	8.59	8	0	2	7.1	11	9	2	10	2
97 AA San Antonio	3	0	0.70	19	0	4	25.2	10	2	6	38	1

The Dodgers really scored with a pair of low-round picks in the 1996 draft. Kubenka was a 38th-round selection out of St. Mary's (Texas), and he became the first player from that draft to reach Triple-A. His career numbers couldn't be more impressive: 13-4, 1.90, 65 hits and 29 walks versus 171 strikeouts in 104⅓ innings. He thrives with an unhittable screwball and outstanding command. He also mixes in a below-average fastball and a curveball. He may not have the heat to be a closer, but it wouldn't be wise to bet against him. He probably doesn't need much more time in the minors.

Paul LoDuca

Position: C
Bats: R **Throws:** R
Ht: 5' 10" **Wt:** 193

Opening Day Age: 25
Born: 4/12/72 in Brooklyn, NY

Recent Statistics

	G	AB	R	H	D	T	HR	RBI	SB	BB	SO	AVG
96 A Vero Beach	124	439	54	134	22	0	3	66	8	70	38	.305
97 AA San Antonio	105	385	63	126	28	2	7	69	16	46	27	.327
97 MLE	105	359	46	100	21	1	4	51	11	28	28	.279

It's easy to be overlooked when you're a catcher in Mike Piazza's organization. LoDuca's .327 batting average ranked second to A.J. Hinch's .328 among minor league backstops, and LoDuca led the Double-A Texas League by throwing out 46 percent of basestealers. A 25th-round pick out of Arizona State in 1993, he has hit .305 in his minor league career. He has good gap power, makes excellent contact and draws his share of walks. He handles pitchers and blocks balls well, and has an average arm and a quick release. Managers have voted him the best defensive catcher in the high Class-A Florida State League and the Texas League the last two years. One of the minors' top sleeper prospects, LoDuca will spend 1998 in Triple-A despite having a much higher upside than Dodger backup Tom Prince.

Ted Lilly

Position: P
Bats: L **Throws:** L
Ht: 6' 1" **Wt:** 180

Opening Day Age: 22
Born: 1/4/76 in Lomita, CA

Recent Statistics

	W	L	ERA	G	GS	Sv	IP	H	R	BB	SO	HR
96 A Yakima	4	0	0.84	13	8	0	53.2	25	9	14	75	0
97 A San Berndno	7	8	2.81	23	21	0	134.2	116	52	32	158	9

Lilly was another late-round find in 1996, joining the Dodgers in the 23rd round out of Fresno (Calif.) City College. Bad mechanics were hampering his velocity, which has risen to 92 MPH since he straightened them out. He also throws a good curveball and changeup, and is learning to use his offspeed stuff more often. Hitters have difficulty making solid contact against him, and he won't help them out with walks. He threw a no-hitter and was named Pitcher of the Year in the high Class-A California League in 1997, though he missed the final three weeks with a pinched nerve in his shoulder. Because he's so advanced, he should reach Triple-A by the end of 1998.

Adam Riggs

Position: 2B
Bats: R **Throws:** R
Ht: 6' 0" **Wt:** 190

Opening Day Age: 25
Born: 10/4/72 in Steubenville, OH

Recent Statistics

	G	AB	R	H	D	T	HR	RBI	SB	BB	SO	AVG
97 AAA Albuquerque	57	227	59	69	8	3	13	28	12	29	39	.304
97 NL Los Angeles	9	20	3	4	1	0	0	1	1	4	3	.200
97 MLE	57	208	36	50	5	1	7	17	7	17	40	.240

Riggs is another late-round choice, a 22nd-round pick out of the University of South Carolina at Aiken in 1994. He won the batting title and was named MVP in the Cal League in his first full season, and hasn't stopped hitting since. He's aggressive at the plate and on the basepaths, and shows decent on-base ability and gap power. The Dodgers are pleased with his defensive progress, as he has made himself into an acceptable second baseman. That position is crowded in Los Angeles with Wilton Guerrero and Eric Young, so Riggs may have difficulty getting an opportunity.

Others to Watch

Peter Bergeron, 20, is an organization favorite because of his makeup, and his tools are solid as well. He's an excellent center fielder who can run and throw and get on base. . . Former third baseman **Henry Blanco** has been converted to catcher and was voted the Pacific Coast League's best defensive backstop by the managers. He's 26 and primarily a contact hitter with little power, so he projects as a big league backup. . . **Alex Cora**, the younger brother of Mariners second baseman Joey Cora, is a gifted defender who probably could play shortstop in the majors right now. His hitting was woeful in Double-A at age 21, so he's going to need some time. . . Righthander **Dan Hubbs** continues to get hitters out with his slider, even if his fastball won't catch anyone's attention. He's 27 but could get a shot as a setup man, though maybe not from the loaded Dodgers. . . First baseman **Nick Leach's** bat took him to high Class-A at age 19. He has line-drive power and excellent plate discipline. . . The Dodgers hope that Hawaiian lefthander **Onan Masaoka** develops into the next Sid Fernandez. Masaoka, 20, throws a 92-MPH fastball with movement and has moxie.

Phil Garner

1997 Season

In 1997, Phil Garner did the same thing he's done every year for the past three seasons. He took a young, outmanned, underpaid team and kept it in contention much longer than expected, even as key players went down with injuries. He also continued to work new youngsters into the lineup with success, as Jeromy Burnitz and Mark Loretta made contributions. The Brewers' third-place, 78-83 finish wasn't impressive in and of itself, but it was a fine managing job in light of the talent available to Garner.

Offense

Garner isn't a fanatic about basestealing, but he's big on aggressive baserunning. He especially values speed at the top of the order, and demands that his players be willing and able to lay down a sacrifice when needed. He uses the hit-and-run with good success, and employs the squeeze more often than any manager in the American League.

Pitching & Defense

Garner's experience in his first few years of managing has moved him to put strict pitch limits on his starters. He has the patience to allow a young pitcher to work through his difficulties, and he's very good at matching up a pitcher with his optimal role. Strong defense is very important to him, and he's willing to sacrifice some pop at the plate to keep a glove man in the lineup. He believes in his young players and he's often willing to play them out of position to get them extra at-bats.

1998 Outlook

Garner rightfully is regarded as one of the game's best managers. His style is more typical of the National League than the AL, so switching leagues shouldn't affect him. It's fun to wonder what he might be capable of doing with a normal-sized payroll or a team that could stay healthy all year. Because he remains Milwaukee's manager, we'll probably have to just keep wondering.

Born: 4/30/49 in Jefferson City, TN

Playing Experience: 1973-1988, Oak, Pit, Hou, LA, SF

Managerial Experience: 6 seasons
Nickname: Scrap Iron

Manager Statistics

Year	Team, Lg	W	L	Pct	GB	Finish
1997	Milwaukee, AL	78	83	.484	8.0	3rd Central
6 Seasons		437	469	.482	—	—

1997 Starting Pitchers by Days Rest

	≤3	4	5	6+
Brewers Starts	2	110	12	28
Brewers ERA	2.77	4.68	3.49	4.47
AL Avg Starts	5	89	34	24
AL ERA	4.38	4.60	4.61	5.37

1997 Situational Stats

	Phil Garner	AL Average
Hit & Run Success %	41.8	36.5
Stolen Base Success %	65.2	67.3
Platoon Pct.	59.4	59.5
Defensive Subs	36	22
High-Pitch Outings	6	15
Quick/Slow Hooks	26/12	19/15
Sacrifice Attempts	65	53

1997 Rankings (American League)

⇒ 1st in squeeze plays (7) and 2+ pitching changes in low scoring games (34)

⇒ 2nd in steals of home plate (1), sacrifice bunt attempts (65), pinch hitters used (190) and quick hooks (26)

⇒ 3rd in sacrifice bunt percentage (87.7%), hit-and-run attempts (98), pitchouts (55), pitchouts with a runner moving (12), defensive substitutions (36) and starting lineups used (128)

Jeromy Burnitz

1997 Season

Jeromy Burnitz originally came up as a stud prospect with the Mets during their darkest hour, but lost his job and got traded to Cleveland after the 1994 season. While with the Tribe, he shuttled between the bench and the minors. A trade in late 1996 sent him to Milwaukee. Finally in 1997, at the age of 28, he played regularly all year for the first time in his major league career. He was a smashing success, playing strong defense while leading the club in several offensive categories.

Hitting

Burnitz has a good mix of power and patience. He's very good at working the count in his favor before attacking the ball. Changeups give him the most trouble and he often loses his bat as he tries to check his swing, but he can catch up with anyone's fastball. Burnitz hadn't been allowed to face lefties very often in the past, but he did fairly well against them in 1997 and improved as the year went on. His 72 extra-base hits placed him ahead of such luminaries as Barry Bonds (71), Frank Thomas (70) and Juan Gonzalez (69).

Baserunning & Defense

Burnitz shows good range in right field and boasts a strong, accurate throwing arm. He logged 12 assists in right field in 1997, and added another one while patrolling left. He also has the speed and instincts to cover center field if needed. Most of his errors come when he's a tad too aggressive and lets the ball get past him. He has good speed and can steal a base, but most of his thefts came early in the year before pitchers learned to pay attention to him.

1998 Outlook

Burnitz goes into 1998 with a solid claim on the Brewers' right-field job. He should be able to post numbers comparable to 1997's for the foreseeable future.

Position: RF/CF
Bats: L **Throws:** R
Ht: 6' 0" **Wt:** 190

Opening Day Age: 28
Born: 4/15/69 in Westminster, CA
ML Seasons: 5
Pronunciation: BURR-nitz

Overall Statistics

	G	AB	R	H	D	T	HR	RBI	SB	BB	SO	Avg	OBP	Slg
1997	153	494	85	139	37	8	27	85	20	75	111	.281	.382	.553
Career	387	1107	202	294	66	14	52	178	28	169	269	.266	.367	.491

Where He Hits the Ball

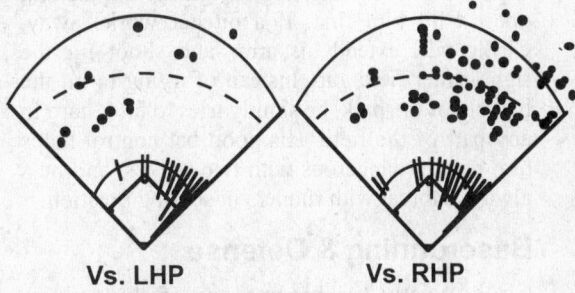

Vs. LHP   Vs. RHP

1997 Situational Stats

	AB	H	HR	RBI	Avg		AB	H	HR	RBI	Avg
Home	245	74	18	56	.302	LHP	121	33	3	20	.273
Road	249	65	9	29	.261	RHP	373	106	24	65	.284
First Half	246	68	12	36	.276	Sc Pos	130	33	4	52	.254
Scnd Half	248	71	15	49	.286	Clutch	79	25	6	13	.316

1997 Rankings (American League)

⇒ 1st in lowest fielding percentage in right field (.968)
⇒ 2nd in errors in right field (7)
⇒ 3rd in triples
⇒ 4th in caught stealing (13)
⇒ 5th in lowest stolen base percentage (60.6%) and slugging percentage vs. righthanded pitchers (.592)
⇒ Led the Brewers in home runs, runs scored, triples, total bases (273), RBI, caught stealing (13), walks, intentional walks (8), strikeouts, slugging percentage, on-base percentage, HR frequency (18.3 ABs per HR), most pitches seen per plate appearance (4.04), batting average in the clutch and slugging percentage vs. righthanded pitchers (.592)

Jeff Cirillo

1997 Season

He wasn't quite as good as the year before, but Jeff Cirillo enjoyed another fine season for Milwaukee at the hot corner. Batting mainly from the second and third spots in the lineup, he contributed his fair share of singles, doubles and walks. He likely would have hit around .300 had it not been for a midsummer slump during his contract negotiations. Cirillo once again proved to be a doubles machine, churning out 46 for the second straight year.

Hitting

Cirillo crowds the plate and dares the pitcher to try to move him back. If a pitcher comes inside, Cirillo will hit the offering to right field if the ball doesn't hit him first. If a pitcher works away, Cirillo will extend his arms and shoot for the right-center field gap. Instead of trying to hit the ball out of the park, he simply tries to hit it hard to any part of the field. His good bat control helps him remain dangerous with two strikes, and he's always a threat with runners in scoring position.

Baserunning & Defense

Cirillo quietly has become one of the premier defensive third basemen in the game. Last year, he fielded more balls cleanly and started more double plays than any other third baseman in the American League. A former pitcher at the University of Southern California, he's got a very strong arm and great reactions. He should get his due in the years to come. A sore knee slowed him once again in 1997, but he has decent speed and runs the bases intelligently. Steals are few and far between, however.

1998 Outlook

The Brewers locked up Cirillo with a long-term deal, ensuring that he'll be a cornerstone to build around for years to come. He has just begun to enter his prime and should have many more good years left. He's always a threat to reach the .300 mark.

Position: 3B
Bats: R **Throws:** R
Ht: 6' 2" **Wt:** 188

Opening Day Age: 28
Born: 9/23/69 in Pasadena, CA
ML Seasons: 4
Pronunciation: suh-RILL-o

Overall Statistics

	G	AB	R	H	D	T	HR	RBI	SB	BB	SO	Avg	OBP	Slg
1997	154	580	74	167	46	2	10	82	4	60	74	.288	.367	.426
Career	476	1600	249	472	120	11	37	216	15	176	201	.295	.372	.453

Where He Hits the Ball

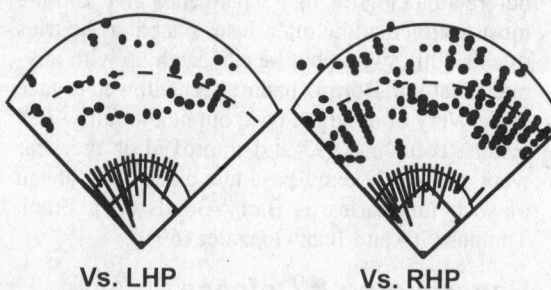

Vs. LHP   Vs. RHP

1997 Situational Stats

	AB	H	HR	RBI	Avg		AB	H	HR	RBI	Avg
Home	300	86	6	42	.287	LHP	165	43	3	13	.261
Road	280	81	4	40	.289	RHP	415	124	7	69	.299
First Half	307	92	6	52	.300	Sc Pos	149	54	4	72	.362
Scnd Half	273	75	4	30	.275	Clutch	101	29	2	18	.287

1997 Rankings (American League)

⇒ 2nd in doubles and batting average with the bases loaded (.625)
⇒ 4th in batting average with runners in scoring position
⇒ 5th in hit by pitch (14) and fielding percentage at third base (.963)
⇒ 6th in errors at third base (17)
⇒ Led the Brewers in batting average, at-bats, hits, singles, doubles, hit by pitch (14), times on base (241), pitches seen (2,457), plate appearances (661), batting average with runners in scoring position, batting average with the bases loaded (.625), on-base percentage vs. lefthanded pitchers (.354), highest percentage of swings put into play (48.8%) and lowest percentage of swings on the first pitch (19.0%)

Cal Eldred

1997 Season

For better or for worse, Cal Eldred returned to the form he showed in 1994 before blowing out his pitching elbow. He's no longer the ravenous innings-eater that he was before the injury, but he's still the solid hurler who takes the mound every five days and gives a solid performance more often than not. Though he did tie for the American League lead with 15 losses, the Brewers apparently are convinced that his rehabbed elbow is sound. They rewarded Eldred with a multi-year deal.

Pitching

Despite the surgery and rehab, Eldred has lost very little off his 90-MPH fastball. He tries to throw the pitch past hitters up in the strike zone, and gives up quite a few homers when he fails—31 last season, to be exact. He releases his overhand curve on the same plane as his fastball, and does his best work when he mixes the two effectively. He'll use a changeup on occasion. Most of his outs come in the air. Phil Garner rarely lets him go much beyond 100 pitches, but Eldred usually manages to get into the seventh inning anyway.

Defense & Hitting

Eldred's high fastballs would seem to enable his catchers to gun down basestealers. But he drives off his back leg, giving runners the extra step they need to beat the throw most of the time. He's a good athlete and a fine fielder who rarely makes an error, physical or mental. In fact, he hasn't been charged with a miscue since 1995. Given his first chance to hit by interleague play, he went 0-for-3 with a sacrifice.

1998 Outlook

The Brewers have chosen to build their staff around Eldred. Despite his less-than-stellar stats, he has the maturity, dedication and approach that defines a staff leader. He was stronger over the second half of 1997, and his performance may continue to improve because he no longer is forced to run up enormous pitch counts.

Position: SP
Bats: R **Throws:** R
Ht: 6' 4" **Wt:** 236

Opening Day Age: 30
Born: 11/24/67 in Cedar Rapids, IA
ML Seasons: 7

Overall Statistics

	W	L	Pct.	ERA	G	GS	Sv	IP	H	BB	SO	HR	Ratio
1997	13	15	.464	4.99	34	34	0	202.0	207	89	122	31	1.47
Career	58	49	.542	4.16	131	131	0	863.2	799	341	540	104	1.32

How Often He Throws Strikes

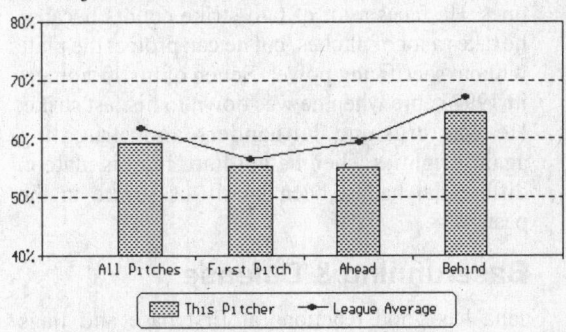

1997 Situational Stats

	W	L	ERA	Sv	IP		AB	H	HR	RBI	Avg
Home	9	5	4.42	0	114.0	LHB	412	101	14	38	.245
Road	4	10	5.73	0	88.0	RHB	365	106	17	59	.290
First Half	8	8	5.50	0	104.2	Sc Pos	179	44	4	59	.246
Scnd Half	5	7	4.44	0	97.1	Clutch	40	11	0	0	.275

1997 Rankings (American League)

⇒ 1st in losses
⇒ 2nd in walks allowed
⇒ 3rd in lowest groundball/flyball ratio allowed (0.8) and highest ERA on the road
⇒ 5th in games started and home runs allowed
⇒ Led the Brewers in wins, losses, games started, shutouts (1), innings pitched, batters faced (885), home runs allowed, walks allowed, hit batsmen (9), strikeouts, pitches thrown (3,436), runners caught stealing (8), lowest batting average allowed (.266), most run support per 9 innings (5.6), lowest batting average allowed vs. lefthanded batters and lowest batting average allowed with runners in scoring position

John Jaha

1997 Season

Only one year after he finally put everything to-gether, John Jaha's left shoulder came apart. He got off to a hot start with six homers in April, then tore the labrum in his left shoulder in late May and missed the rest of the season. The injury was a bitter pill to swallow for both the power-starved Brewers and for Jaha, who's been victimized by ill-timed injuries throughout his pro career.

Hitting

Few hitters have better opposite-field power than Jaha. He goes with the pitch and hits it hard to all parts of the diamond. He's particularly dangerous on high pitches, but can have trouble elevating low ones. He faces a lot of two-strike counts because he takes a lot of pitches, but he can protect the plate without sacrificing power. Seven of his 11 homers in 1997 came when he was down to his last strike. He was crushing lefthanders and struggling against righties when he got hurt, but his platoon differential hadn't been nearly as severe in the past.

Baserunning & Defense

Jaha has good reactions at first base and flags down his share of smashes despite unimpressive foot speed. His fielding percentage has been above .990 for the past three seasons. His arm is reliable. Years of groin and hamstring pulls have relieved him of the urge to steal, and he plays it conservatively on the bases.

1998 Outlook

Jaha's health will be one of the keys to the Brewers' 1998 season. His durability never can be taken for granted because he has a long history of muscle pulls. As long as he's able to stay healthy, he'll likely produce good numbers from the cleanup spot and continue to provide the thunder in Milwaukee's attack.

Position: 1B
Bats: R **Throws:** R
Ht: 6' 1" **Wt:** 222

Opening Day Age: 31
Born: 5/27/66 in Portland, OR
ML Seasons: 6
Pronunciation: JAH-hah

Overall Statistics

	G	AB	R	H	D	T	HR	RBI	SB	BB	SO	Avg	OBP	Slg
1997	46	162	25	40	7	0	11	26	1	25	40	.247	.354	.494
Career	566	1960	332	538	93	4	98	328	32	241	438	.274	.360	.476

Where He Hits the Ball

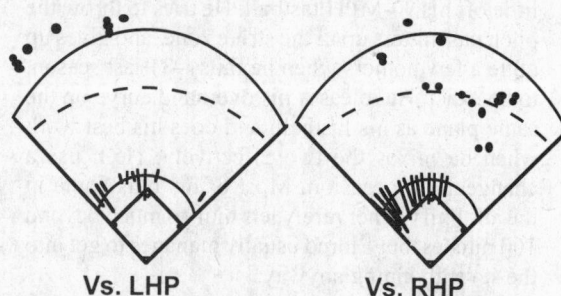

Vs. LHP   Vs. RHP

1997 Situational Stats

	AB	H	HR	RBI	Avg		AB	H	HR	RBI	Avg
Home	76	15	1	7	.197	LHP	42	14	6	11	.333
Road	86	25	10	19	.291	RHP	120	26	5	15	.217
First Half	162	40	11	26	.247	Sc Pos	49	9	2	15	.184
Scnd Half	0	0	0	0	-	Clutch	25	8	3	6	.320

1997 Rankings (American League)

⇒ Did not rank near the top or bottom in any category

Doug Jones

1997 Season

Doug Jones has had enough lives to make Rasputin's cat envious. Last year at age 39, he filled in as the closer for Milwaukee when Mike Fetters was sidelined early in the year. He was so effective that Fetters never got his job back. Jones had one of the best years of his career, saving 36 games in 38 chances, posting his best ERA in five seasons and returning once more to the ranks of the American League's elite closers.

Pitching

If Jones were a stick-shift, he'd have two speeds: first gear and neutral. He throws a change, a change off the change, and a change off the change off the change. With flawless control and an unflappable demeanor, all he does is shoot for the black and try to keep the hitters a fraction of a second out in front of the pitch. When he's on, it can be embarrassing for the hitter. When he isn't, it can be embarrassing for Jones. He was on almost all the time in 1997, striking out 82 batters while walking just nine in 75 appearances. He shut righthanders down to the tune of one home run and a .200 batting average.

Defense & Hitting

To his credit, Jones tries to stay out of the way and leave the fielding to the players behind him who are still young enough to do it. His minimal windup takes two steps off every runner's jump, though, so he shuts down the running game quite effectively. He has batted just five times in 13 seasons, though he does own one hit.

1998 Outlook

Jones became a free agent after the season, and the Brewers wasted no time in re-signing him. We may never know when Jones is washed up, because he always looks washed up to everyone who isn't standing in the batter's box. As soon as he starts taking too little or too much off the ball, he'll start getting hammered again, which should happen sometime between tomorrow and never. In short, his career is as baffling as his stuff.

Position: RP
Bats: R **Throws:** R
Ht: 6' 2" **Wt:** 205

Opening Day Age: 40
Born: 6/24/57 in Covina, CA
ML Seasons: 13

Overall Statistics

	W	L	Pct.	ERA	G	GS	Sv	IP	H	BB	SO	HR	Ratio
1997	6	6	.500	2.02	75	0	36	80.1	62	9	82	4	0.88
Career	56	66	.459	3.10	653	4	278	865.2	864	188	721	53	1.22

How Often He Throws Strikes

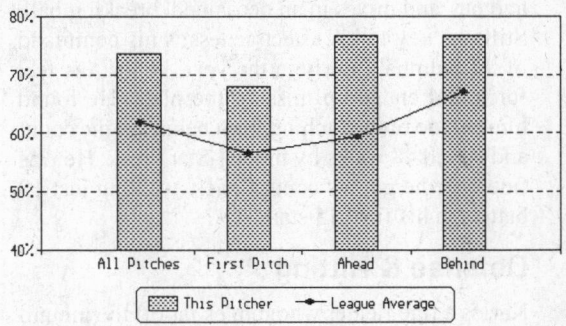

This Pitcher — League Average

1997 Situational Stats

	W	L	ERA	Sv	IP		AB	H	HR	RBI	Avg
Home	6	2	1.55	19	46.1	LHB	149	34	3	12	.228
Road	0	4	2.65	17	34.0	RHB	140	28	1	8	.200
First Half	3	3	2.70	20	43.1	Sc Pos	61	13	1	17	.213
Scnd Half	3	3	1.22	16	37.0	Clutch	183	41	2	14	.224

1997 Rankings (American League)

⇒ 1st in games finished (73) and least baserunners allowed per 9 innings in relief (8.3)
⇒ 2nd in save percentage (94.7%)
⇒ 3rd in saves and save opportunities (38)
⇒ 5th in relief ERA (2.02), relief losses (6), lowest batting average allowed in relief (.215) and most strikeouts per 9 innings in relief (9.2)
⇒ Led the Brewers in games pitched, saves, games finished (73), save opportunities (38), save percentage (94.7%), first batter efficiency (.194), relief ERA (2.02), relief losses (6), lowest batting average allowed in relief (.215), least baserunners allowed per 9 innings in relief (8.3) and most strikeouts per 9 innings in relief (9.2)

Milwaukee Brewers

Scott Karl

1997 Season

For Scott Karl, 1997 was "A Tale of Two Seasons." In the first one, he went 2-10 and nearly lost his spot in Milwaukee's rotation. In the second, he turned it around completely, going 8-3 to finish with numbers very similar to those of the year before. He couldn't match the 13-9 record he produced in 1996, but he lowered his ERA from 4.86 to 4.47.

Pitching

Like Tom Glavine, Karl makes his living throwing changeups to the outside edge of the plate. Karl's change is a deceptive palmball that he mixes with a mid-80s fastball. He cuts and runs the fastball in and out, and mixes in an occasional breaking ball. Still, the key to his effectiveness is his command of the palmball. Early in the year, he lost his feel for it and ended up missing the plate. He found himself too often pitching from behind in the count and issued 48 walks by the All-Star break. He was fine once he got his control back, walking just 19 batters in his final 15 starts.

Defense & Hitting

Karl is a fine fielder who ranges far off the mound and likes to go for the lead runner at second base if possible. He's effective at starting the double play when he has the opportunity. He has one of the best pickoff moves in the American League, but the problem is that he throws the ball away a few times a year. Baserunners don't often try to run on him, and the ones who do often end up paying for it. In his first taste of major league hitting, he went 0-for-4 with three strikeouts in 1997.

1998 Outlook

Karl learned from his struggles in 1997 and may be in line for his best season yet. Much of his future success depends on his ability to maintain the feel of his palmball for an entire season. He doesn't have the stuff to be a world-beater, but he's young, durable and lefthanded. You have to like that combination.

Position: SP
Bats: L **Throws:** L
Ht: 6' 2" **Wt:** 195

Opening Day Age: 26
Born: 8/9/71 in Fontana, CA
ML Seasons: 3

Overall Statistics

	W	L	Pct.	ERA	G	GS	Sv	IP	H	BB	SO	HR	Ratio
1997	10	13	.435	4.47	32	32	0	193.1	212	67	119	23	1.44
Career	29	29	.500	4.55	89	82	0	524.2	573	189	299	62	1.45

How Often He Throws Strikes

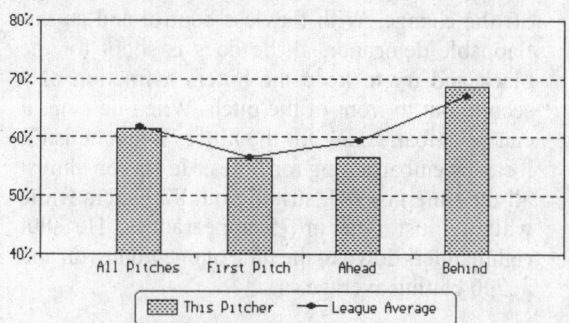

This Pitcher — League Average

1997 Situational Stats

	W	L	ERA	Sv	IP		AB	H	HR	RBI	Avg
Home	5	6	4.32	0	93.2	LHB	119	29	1	6	.244
Road	5	7	4.61	0	99.2	RHB	641	183	22	85	.285
First Half	2	10	5.44	0	97.2	Sc Pos	184	49	3	64	.266
Scnd Half	8	3	3.48	0	95.2	Clutch	36	12	2	6	.333

1997 Rankings (American League)

⇒ 4th in lowest fielding percentage at pitcher (.892)

⇒ 5th in errors at pitcher (4)

⇒ Led the Brewers in ERA, hits allowed, pickoff throws (127), GDPs induced (20), highest strikeout/walk ratio (1.8), lowest slugging percentage allowed (.439), lowest on-base percentage allowed (.340), highest groundball/flyball ratio allowed (1.4), lowest stolen base percentage allowed (53.8%), least pitches thrown per batter (3.83), least baserunners allowed per 9 innings (13.2), least home runs allowed per 9 innings (1.07), most GDPs induced per 9 innings (0.9), most strikeouts per 9 innings (5.5), ERA at home and ERA on the road

Mark Loretta

1997 Season

Going into 1997, it looked like Mark Loretta would be nothing more than a backup for Milwaukee. Then he got two lucky breaks. Shortstop Jose Valentin broke his finger and second baseman Fernando Vina broke his ankle. Loretta subbed for each of them until they returned and pushed his average well over .300 for a time. When the regulars returned, manager Phil Garner did his best to find playing time for Loretta, even using him at first base on occasion.

Hitting

Loretta is a wiry spray hitter with little power but excellent bat control. He has a good eye and takes a lot of pitches, and it can be surprisingly tough to strike him out after the count reaches two strikes. In fact, he ended up hitting .277 with two strikes in 1997. As he matures, he may become a good fit in the No. 2 spot in the batting order. He had a reverse platoon differential last season, having significantly more success against righthanders.

Baserunning & Defense

While he doesn't have spectacular range, Loretta is a surehanded fielder with a good enough arm for third base. He played shortstop throughout the minors, but may be best suited for second base. He turned the double play surprisingly well as a second baseman, considering his lack of experience on that side of the bag. Loretta's speed is unimpressive, and he doesn't try to go much farther on the bases than his legs will allow. When trying to steal, he was caught as many times as he was successful in 1997.

1998 Outlook

Unless another wave of injuries hits the infield, it looks like Loretta will be forced back to the bench for the time being. He should be a more-than-capable backup, though, and has proven that he's quite able to step in and play regularly at several different positions should the opportunity arise.

Position: 2B/1B/3B/SS
Bats: R **Throws:** R
Ht: 6' 0" **Wt:** 175

Opening Day Age: 26
Born: 8/14/71 in Santa Monica, CA
ML Seasons: 3

Overall Statistics

	G	AB	R	H	D	T	HR	RBI	SB	BB	SO	Avg	OBP	Slg
1997	132	418	56	120	17	5	5	47	5	47	60	.287	.354	.388
Career	224	622	89	176	23	5	7	63	8	65	82	.283	.349	.370

Where He Hits the Ball

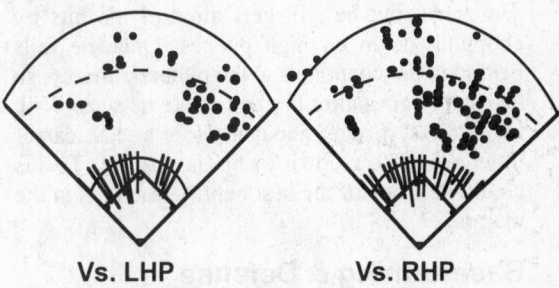

Vs. LHP   **Vs. RHP**

1997 Situational Stats

	AB	H	HR	RBI	Avg		AB	H	HR	RBI	Avg
Home	207	68	2	24	.329	LHP	137	35	1	14	.255
Road	211	52	3	23	.246	RHP	281	85	4	33	.302
First Half	246	73	4	29	.297	Sc Pos	93	27	1	40	.290
Scnd Half	172	47	1	18	.273	Clutch	76	19	1	6	.250

1997 Rankings (American League)

⇒ 2nd in most GDPs per GDP situation (21.1%) and batting average with two strikes (.277)
⇒ 3rd in batting average on a 3-2 count (.421)
⇒ 7th in sacrifice flies (10)
⇒ 10th in lowest slugging percentage vs. lefthanded pitchers (.321)
⇒ Led the Brewers in sacrifice flies (10), GDPs (16), batting average on a 3-2 count (.421), batting average with two strikes (.277), highest percentage of pitches taken (60.3%) and lowest percentage of swings that missed (11.7%)

Milwaukee Brewers

Mike Matheny

1997 Season

The Brewers weren't able to pick up anyone better, so for the second straight year Mike Matheny served as their semi-regular catcher. A new batting stance brought his average up some, but he remained a woefully inadequate hitter. His .294 on-base percentage marked the third time in four major league seasons that it was below .300. His strong throwing and receiving skills helped, but the Brewers often pinch-hit for him in the late innings or benched him when they needed more offense.

Hitting

Matheny is a defensive hitter who has trouble with low pitches. A deeper crouch helped remedy this somewhat, but he still gets most of his hits by chopping down on high pitches. Once he falls behind in the count he's at the pitcher's mercy, so he usually goes after the first strike he sees. With two strikes? Forget about it. He's a .122 career hitter when he's down to his last strike. To his credit, he's one of the best bunting catchers in the majors.

Baserunning & Defense

Matheny's defensive skills are what keep him in the majors. He's a good handler of pitchers and manager Phil Garner likes the way he works with the team's young arms. It helps that Matheny is able to keep breaking balls in front of him as well as gun down a decent number of basestealers. He doesn't have enough speed to steal more than a base or two a year.

1998 Outlook

As a stopgap, Matheny will remain only as long as the gap does. If the Brewers can find a catcher who can both hit and catch, Matheny likely will be relegated to backup duty. Until that happens, he'll continue to play more often than not, if only for his defense.

Position: C
Bats: R **Throws:** R
Ht: 6' 3" **Wt:** 205

Opening Day Age: 27
Born: 9/22/70 in Columbus, OH
ML Seasons: 4
Pronunciation: ma-THEEN-ee

Overall Statistics

	G	AB	R	H	D	T	HR	RBI	SB	BB	SO	Avg	OBP	Slg
1997	123	320	29	78	16	1	4	32	0	17	68	.244	.294	.338
Career	337	852	76	195	43	4	13	101	5	46	189	.229	.277	.335

Where He Hits the Ball

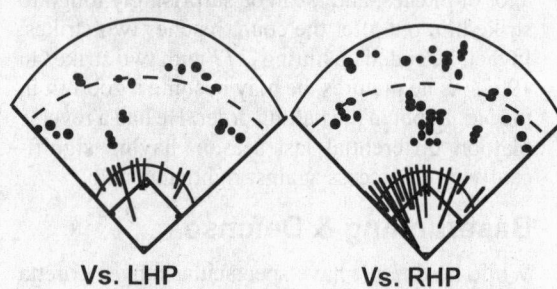

Vs. LHP **Vs. RHP**

1997 Situational Stats

	AB	H	HR	RBI	Avg		AB	H	HR	RBI	Avg
Home	152	36	2	21	.237	LHP	110	29	1	8	.264
Road	168	42	2	11	.250	RHP	210	49	3	24	.233
First Half	180	42	3	17	.233	Sc Pos	79	20	3	30	.253
Scnd Half	140	36	1	15	.257	Clutch	34	9	0	1	.265

1997 Rankings (American League)

⇒ 5th in fielding percentage at catcher (.993)
⇒ 9th in sacrifice bunts (9) and errors at catcher (5)
⇒ Led the Brewers in sacrifice bunts (9) and batting average on an 0-2 count (.269)

Ben McDonald

1997 Season

Once again, injuries and controversy enveloped Ben McDonald. Coming off his solid 1996 season, he began the year as the Brewers' ace and continued to anchor their rotation over the first half of the season, going 6-3 in April and May. Then he tore his rotator cuff and missed the second half, but not before getting a cortisone shot in the shoulder and requesting one more start so that his contract option for 1998 would kick in. The Brewers weren't happy with the way McDonald handled the situation.

Pitching

McDonald is anything but timid. He comes right after hitters with a 90-plus MPH fastball and a hard overhand curve. He's vulnerable to the longball when he leaves pitches up in the zone, but his control has steadily improved. His 1997 walk rate was the lowest of his career. He mixed in breaking balls earlier in the count last year, keeping hitters off balance. He'll also throw an occasional changeup.

Defense & Hitting

McDonald is a fairly mobile fielder for a big man and he can field whatever he reaches. His biggest weakness is his impatience on comebackers, which leads to errors when his throw reaches a base before the fielder does. He has improved in this regard, however. With a high leg kick and long stride, he's a frequent target of basestealers. He yielded 20 steals in 21 starts in 1997. His pickoff move is nothing special, but he nails a runner every now and then, if only because they run on him so much. An all-Louisiana punter in high school and a basketball player at Louisiana State, he should be athletic enough not to embarrass himself at the plate. He struck out in his only major league at-bat, which came last season.

1998 Outlook

McDonald enters the 1998 season with two major question marks. First, how will his surgically repaired shoulder perform? Also, how will his uncomfortable situation with the Brewers be resolved?

Position: SP
Bats: R **Throws:** R
Ht: 6' 7" **Wt:** 214

Opening Day Age: 30
Born: 11/24/67 in Baton Rouge, LA
ML Seasons: 9
Nickname: Big Ben

Overall Statistics

	W	L	Pct.	ERA	G	GS	Sv	IP	H	BB	SO	HR	Ratio
1997	8	7	.533	4.06	21	21	0	133.0	120	36	110	13	1.17
Career	78	70	.527	3.91	211	198	0	1291.1	1186	437	894	138	1.26

How Often He Throws Strikes

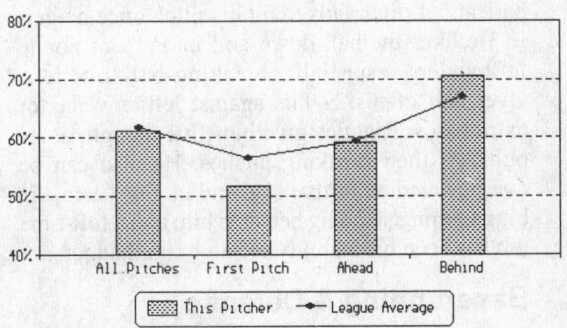

1997 Situational Stats

	W	L	ERA	Sv	IP		AB	H	HR	RBI	Avg
Home	5	2	2.97	0	72.2	LHB	255	66	9	33	.259
Road	3	5	5.37	0	60.1	RHB	251	54	4	25	.215
First Half	7	6	4.24	0	121.0	Sc Pos	104	28	4	41	.269
Scnd Half	1	1	2.25	0	12.0	Clutch	38	9	1	3	.237

1997 Rankings (American League)

⇒ 10th in stolen bases allowed (20)
⇒ Led the Brewers in stolen bases allowed (20)

Matt Mieske

1997 Season

For the fourth straight season, Matt Mieske was given a chance to prove himself in the Brewers' outfield. Once again, he failed to take advantage of the opportunity. In his customary platoon role, Mieske got off to a hot start. He hit .316 in April and followed that up with a .282 May. But as he has done throughout his career, he faded as the season wore on, and finished with his lowest batting average since 1993. He continued to struggle against righthanders, and a hamstring injury all but ended his season in mid-August.

Hitting

At the plate, Mieske is a study in contrasts. He's patient but often fails to hit his pitch once he gets it. He likes the ball down and in and can pound lefthanders, especially breaking-ball pitchers. Over half of his 27 hits against lefties went for extra bases. Righties give him fits, though, as he pulls off their breaking pitches. He also can be overpowered by fastballs up and in. For years, the biggest thing standing between him and a full-time job has been his inability to solve righthanders.

Baserunning & Defense

Recurring hamstring problems have slowed Mieske, who now has only average speed. He rarely attempts to steal any more, which is probably a good thing considering his career success rate currently stands at 30 percent. He's a solid corner outfielder. His arm is fairly good and is his best tool, but his instincts are sometimes questioned. He can appear tentative at times.

1998 Outlook

Mieske's contract was up at the end of 1997, and the Brewers have given him every chance to put it together. He still hasn't been able to prove he's anything more than platoon material, so he'll likely have to try to catch on elsewhere.

Position: RF/LF
Bats: R **Throws:** R
Ht: 6' 0" **Wt:** 192

Opening Day Age: 30
Born: 2/13/68 in Midland, MI
ML Seasons: 5
Pronunciation: MEE-skee

Overall Statistics

	G	AB	R	H	D	T	HR	RBI	SB	BB	SO	Avg	OBP	Slg
1997	84	253	39	63	15	3	5	21	1	19	50	.249	.300	.391
Career	435	1211	175	315	65	8	44	178	7	97	247	.260	.317	.436

Where He Hits the Ball

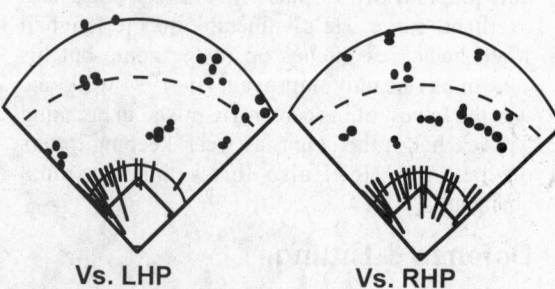

Vs. LHP   Vs. RHP

1997 Situational Stats

	AB	H	HR	RBI	Avg		AB	H	HR	RBI	Avg
Home	116	33	1	10	.284	LHP	106	27	3	11	.255
Road	137	30	4	11	.219	RHP	147	36	2	10	.245
First Half	182	48	2	14	.264	Sc Pos	65	13	0	12	.200
Scnd Half	71	15	3	7	.211	Clutch	42	9	1	2	.214

1997 Rankings (American League)

⇒ 4th in most GDPs per GDP situation (21.1%)

Dave Nilsson

1997 Season

Though his batting average plunged 53 points last year, Dave Nilsson remained one of the better lefty power hitters in the American League. He set career highs with 20 homers and 53 extra-base hits. He continued to be the anchor of the Brewers' lineup, and perhaps more importantly, he stayed healthy all year. That was a satisfying accomplishment for someone who's been felled by any number of odd afflictions during his major league career.

Hitting

Nilsson is a line-drive hitter with power to all fields. He makes excellent contact, and his only real weakness is a tendency to pull off lefthanders' breaking pitches. Consequently, he managed just a .236 batting average against southpaws in 1997. Pitchers who try to work him down and in do so at their own risk. Though he has a big strike zone, he waits for his pitch and takes a walk if he doesn't get it.

Baserunning & Defense

Nilsson is no longer a catcher, but he still runs like one. He always runs hard, though, and many a pivot man has cringed as Nilsson has charged toward second base. Nilsson has been shuffled around since giving up his catchers' mitt in 1994. His best position is first base, but he has been pressed into service in left and right field, where his glaring lack of speed is often exposed. That said, he's one of the best slow outfielders around, cutting off whatever he can get to and flashing a strong, accurate arm.

1998 Outlook

Nilsson wore down last September, and a move to full-time designated hitting would have helped keep the big Australian strong from wire to wire. That's not an option any longer with Milwaukee shifting to the National League. He has the strength to remain above the 20-homer plateau while maintaining a good batting average. He should be able to do both if his health continues to cooperate.

Position: 1B/LF
Bats: L **Throws:** R
Ht: 6' 3" **Wt:** 231

Opening Day Age: 28
Born: 12/14/69 in Brisbane, Queensland, Australia
ML Seasons: 6
Nickname: Thunder
Pronunciation: NILL-son

Overall Statistics

	G	AB	R	H	D	T	HR	RBI	SB	BB	SO	Avg	OBP	Slg
1997	156	554	71	154	33	0	20	81	2	65	88	.278	.352	.446
Career	620	2127	294	600	124	8	72	352	12	234	312	.282	.351	.449

Where He Hits the Ball

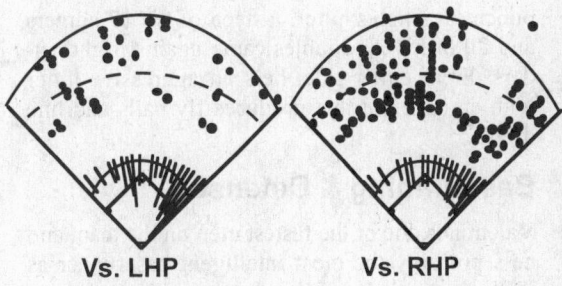

Vs. LHP   **Vs. RHP**

1997 Situational Stats

	AB	H	HR	RBI	Avg		AB	H	HR	RBI	Avg
Home	257	77	5	38	.300	LHP	199	47	4	21	.236
Road	297	77	15	43	.259	RHP	355	107	16	60	.301
First Half	301	84	7	43	.279	Sc Pos	152	36	1	52	.237
Scnd Half	253	70	13	38	.277	Clutch	86	23	2	9	.267

1997 Rankings (American League)

⇒ 6th in lowest on-base percentage vs. lefthanded pitchers (.282)
⇒ 9th in cleanup slugging percentage (.528)
⇒ 10th in errors at first base (6)
⇒ Led the Brewers in intentional walks (8), games played (156), batting average vs. righthanded pitchers and cleanup slugging percentage (.528)

Jose Valentin

1997 Season

After overcoming a broken finger that hampered him early in the season, Jose Valentin put together a solid campaign for the Brewers. Acquired from San Diego in the Gary Sheffield trade in 1992, he continued to hit for power while contributing in many other areas and working on the weaknesses in his game. It was a season of consolidation after a breakthrough year in 1996.

Hitting

The switch-hitting Valentin is two completely different hitters. From the left side, he's one of the most productive power-hitting shortstops in the American League, driving the ball into the gaps and over the fences. From the right side, he has improved by leaps and bounds but remains a punchless singles hitter. Fifteen of his 17 homers and 20 of his 23 doubles came against righthanders. From either side, he's an aggressive hitter with an uppercut that produces fly balls and line drives.

Baserunning & Defense

Valentin is one of the fastest men on the team and he's probably the most intelligent baserunner as well, consistently taking the extra base without going too far. He established a career high with 19 stolen bases in 1997. After some early-season troubles, Valentin settled down to enjoy one of his most solid seasons in the field. He's one of the best glove men in the AL, with good range and a terrific arm. His throws to first are sometimes a bit wild, but his crisp feeds help the Brewers immensely on the double play.

1998 Outlook

In 1997, Valentin made some progress in the two weakest areas of his game: his righthanded hitting and his throwing errors. At age 28, his best years may still be ahead of him. He's one of manager Phil Garner's favorites and should hold down the shortstop position in Milwaukee for years to come.

Position: SS
Bats: B **Throws:** R
Ht: 5'10" **Wt:** 166

Opening Day Age: 28
Born: 10/12/69 in Manati, PR
ML Seasons: 6
Pronunciation: val-en-TEEN

Overall Statistics

	G	AB	R	H	D	T	HR	RBI	SB	BB	SO	Avg	OBP	Slg
1997	136	494	58	125	23	1	17	58	19	39	109	.253	.310	.407
Career	522	1725	268	423	99	13	64	256	65	187	428	.245	.319	.429

Where He Hits the Ball

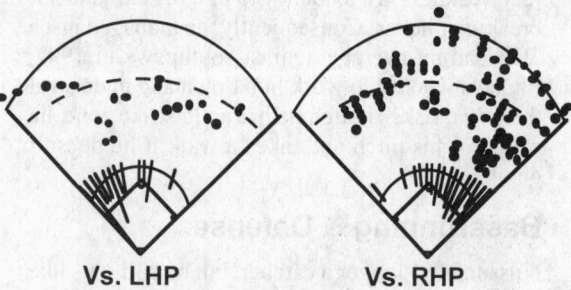

Vs. LHP　　　　**Vs. RHP**

1997 Situational Stats

	AB	H	HR	RBI	Avg		AB	H	HR	RBI	Avg
Home	231	48	4	26	.208	LHP	158	41	2	9	.259
Road	263	77	13	32	.293	RHP	336	84	15	49	.250
First Half	208	56	6	32	.269	Sc Pos	124	32	4	40	.258
Scnd Half	286	69	11	26	.241	Clutch	80	16	1	5	.200

1997 Rankings (American League)

⇒ 1st in lowest batting average at home
⇒ 3rd in lowest groundball/flyball ratio (0.6), errors at shortstop (20) and lowest fielding percentage at shortstop (.967)
⇒ 6th in lowest batting average on a 3-1 count (.077)
⇒ 9th in least GDPs per GDP situation (5.1%) and lowest slugging percentage vs. lefthanded pitchers (.316)
⇒ Led the Brewers in least GDPs per GDP situation (5.1%) and batting average on the road

Fernando Vina

1997 Season

Fernando Vina missed the first half of 1997 after breaking his ankle sliding into second base against the Indians on April 19. He returned after the All-Star game looking as good as new, and picked up where he left off in 1996. The Brewers rewarded him with a multi-year deal at the end of the season.

Hitting

Vina crowds the plate and tries to get on base either by chopping a high pitch through the right side, or by leaning into a pitch. He either hits or gets hit within the first few pitches, so he rarely walks. He can handle the bat, though, and protects the plate effectively with two strikes. He has very little power, lefthanders give him trouble with breaking balls and he gets on base less than most leadoff men. All four of his homers and 11 of his 12 walks last season came against righties. He's not big or strong, and he tends to wear down in the latter part of the year.

Baserunning & Defense

Vina isn't quite as fast as people think a short leadoff man ought to be, so he makes up for it by getting as big a lead as he can at first base. All this does is draw attention to him. He gets picked off quite a bit and doesn't steal bases particularly effectively. He went just 8-for-15 as a basestealer in 1997. Defensively he's the real deal, a wide-ranging glove man and one of the best pivot men in the business.

1998 Outlook

With the freshly signed deal, the Brewers have locked Vina up as part of their infield of the future. Mark Loretta filled in capably during Vina's injury, but make no mistake—Vina enters 1998 as the regular second baseman and leadoff hitter. He's not the ideal leadoff man and he may not last at the top of the batting order, but his glove probably will keep him in the lineup as long as Phil Garner is the manager.

Position: 2B
Bats: L **Throws:** R
Ht: 5' 9" **Wt:** 170

Opening Day Age: 28
Born: 4/16/69 in Sacramento, CA
ML Seasons: 5
Pronunciation: VEEN-yah

Overall Statistics

	G	AB	R	H	D	T	HR	RBI	SB	BB	SO	Avg	OBP	Slg
1997	79	324	37	89	12	2	4	28	8	12	23	.275	.312	.361
Career	435	1335	202	361	46	19	14	111	39	88	100	.270	.334	.365

Where He Hits the Ball

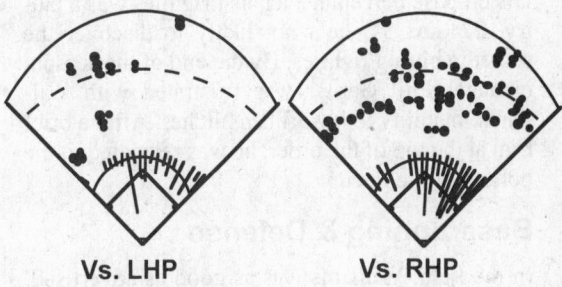

Vs. LHP   **Vs. RHP**

1997 Situational Stats

	AB	H	HR	RBI	Avg		AB	H	HR	RBI	Avg
Home	172	52	1	15	.302	LHP	91	23	0	8	.253
Road	152	37	3	13	.243	RHP	233	66	4	20	.283
First Half	56	18	1	10	.321	Sc Pos	62	19	1	25	.306
Scnd Half	268	71	3	18	.265	Clutch	59	12	0	5	.203

1997 Rankings (American League)

⇒ 3rd in lowest on-base percentage for a leadoff hitter (.311)
⇒ 4th in bunts in play (23)
⇒ Led the Brewers in on-base percentage for a leadoff hitter (.311) and bunts in play (23)

Gerald Williams

1997 Season

The Brewers acquired Gerald Williams from the Yankees in late 1996, and last year they wanted to find out how he'd perform as a full-time center fielder. He had been a platoon player in New York, though he'd shown good speed and defensive skills. The only question was whether he'd be able to hit righthanders. After a full's season's trial that saw him produce a .244 mark against righties, the answer seems to be "no."

Hitting

Williams continued to pound lefties in 1997, hitting for good power. But against righthanders he didn't have nearly as much punch, which made his impatience at the plate all the more unforgivable. His on-base percentage against righties was a paltry .274. At 31, he's not likely to discover the secret to hitting righties. By the end of the season, manager Phil Garner was frustrated with Williams' inability to lay off bad pitches. After a brief trial at the top of the order, he was relegated to the bottom of the lineup.

Baserunning & Defense

In the field, Williams was as good as advertised, displaying ample range and a terrific throwing arm. He registered eight assists in center in 1997, and added three more from left field. He uses his impressive speed both in the field and on the bases, where he runs with abandon.

1998 Outlook

Though Williams is one of the few Brewers' outfielders capable of covering center field, his status as a regular is far from secure. The club seems to have accepted that Williams is no more than a platoon player, and they'll likely explore other alternatives in center. As a result, Williams may be returned to the fourth-outfielder role he filled so well in New York. That may be the spot that suits him best.

Position: CF/LF
Bats: R **Throws:** R
Ht: 6' 2" **Wt:** 190

Opening Day Age: 31
Born: 8/10/66 in New Orleans, LA
ML Seasons: 6

Overall Statistics

	G	AB	R	H	D	T	HR	RBI	SB	BB	SO	Avg	OBP	Slg
1997	155	566	73	143	32	2	10	41	23	19	90	.253	.282	.369
Career	494	1253	186	313	81	11	28	128	42	65	215	.250	.291	.399

Where He Hits the Ball

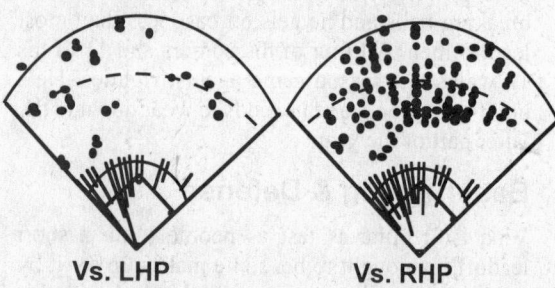

Vs. LHP   Vs. RHP

1997 Situational Stats

	AB	H	HR	RBI	Avg		AB	H	HR	RBI	Avg
Home	267	70	3	19	.262	LHP	157	43	6	15	.274
Road	299	73	7	22	.244	RHP	409	100	4	26	.244
First Half	308	82	7	30	.266	Sc Pos	127	26	1	28	.205
Scnd Half	258	61	3	11	.236	Clutch	100	22	2	10	.220

1997 Rankings (American League)

⇒ 1st in lowest on-base percentage for a leadoff hitter (.283)
⇒ 2nd in lowest slugging percentage vs. righthanded pitchers (.335)
⇒ 3rd in lowest on-base percentage vs. righthanded pitchers (.274)
⇒ 4th in lowest on-base percentage
⇒ Led the Brewers in stolen bases, highest ground-ball/flyball ratio (1.2), stolen base percentage (71.9%), batting average vs. lefthanded pitchers, slugging percentage vs. lefthanded pitchers (.459), steals of third (5) and highest percentage of extra bases taken as a runner (64.6%)

Jeff D'Amico

Position: SP
Bats: R **Throws:** R
Ht: 6' 7" **Wt:** 250

Opening Day Age: 22
Born: 12/27/75 in St. Petersburg, FL
ML Seasons: 2
Pronunciation: duh-MEEK-oh

Overall Statistics

	W	L	Pct.	ERA	G	GS	Sv	IP	H	BB	SO	HR	Ratio
1997	9	7	.563	4.71	23	23	0	135.2	139	43	94	25	1.34
Career	15	13	.536	4.99	40	40	0	221.2	227	74	147	46	1.36

1997 Situational Stats

	W	L	ERA	Sv	IP		AB	H	HR	RBI	Avg
Home	4	2	4.03	0	67.0	LHB	264	71	15	43	.269
Road	5	5	5.37	0	68.2	RHB	262	68	10	32	.260
First Half	6	4	4.39	0	92.1	Sc Pos	103	31	9	53	.301
Scnd Half	3	3	5.40	0	43.1	Clutch	14	1	0	0	.071

1997 Season

Jeff D'Amico's sophomore season was both inconsistent and incomplete, but he gave the club a month-long glimpse of the pitcher he's capable of becoming. After a slow start while learning to control his new two-seam fastball, he put it together and notched six consecutive strong starts in June. Then shoulder problems forced him to be ineffective or out of action the rest of the season.

Pitching, Defense & Hitting

D'Amico throws a high fastball in the 90s with good command, and his sinking two-seamer provides a contrast to his rising four-seamer. He's vulnerable to the home run, though the two-seamer has alleviated the problem somewhat. With a decent slider and changeup, he needs to stay healthy in order to mature into a fine pitcher. He's mobile for a big man and hasn't made an error in 40 big league starts. He's learning the finer points of holding runners. D'Amico went 0-for-4 with three strikeouts and a sacrifice in 1997.

1998 Outlook

If healthy, D'Amico may emerge as one of the best young pitchers in the NL this year. His durability remains a concern due to several injuries during his career. Manager Phil Garner's careful handling should give D'Amico a chance to succeed.

Mike Fetters

Position: RP
Bats: R **Throws:** R
Ht: 6' 4" **Wt:** 224

Opening Day Age: 33
Born: 12/19/64 in Van Nuys, CA
ML Seasons: 9

Overall Statistics

	W	L	Pct.	ERA	G	GS	Sv	IP	H	BB	SO	HR	Ratio
1997	1	5	.167	3.45	51	0	6	70.1	62	33	62	4	1.35
Career	16	25	.390	3.38	335	6	80	450.0	440	201	308	32	1.42

1997 Situational Stats

	W	L	ERA	Sv	IP		AB	H	HR	RBI	Avg
Home	1	1	2.29	4	35.1	LHB	110	34	1	15	.309
Road	0	4	4.63	2	35.0	RHB	144	28	3	13	.194
First Half	1	4	3.96	0	25.0	Sc Pos	76	15	1	24	.197
Scnd Half	0	1	3.18	6	45.1	Clutch	164	44	3	22	.268

1997 Season

Wally Pipp had a headache. Mike Fetters had a torn hamstring. Doug Jones is no Lou Gehrig, but by the time Fetters came off the disabled list in May he had about as much of a chance to get his job back as Pipp had. Jones excelled as the closer, so Fetters simply moved to middle relief and kept on rolling. He ended up posting the kind of numbers one would expect from the nine-year veteran, albeit without the saves.

Pitching, Defense & Hitting

Fetters' splitter has made him a quality short man. He mixes it with his 90-MPH fastball, and hitters never can tell which pitch is coming until it's within 10 feet of the plate. He hasn't developed a good pickoff move, and baserunners continue to take advantage of him. His delivery doesn't give him much of a chance to get to many balls, but he's capable of making all the plays. A career American Leaguer, he's still searching for his first major league at-bat one year into interleague play.

1998 Outlook

At worst, Fetters will give the Brewers a good setup man and an excellent insurance policy for whenever Doug Jones suffers his next meltdown. Fetters gets outs. Whether those outs translate into holds or saves depends only upon how he's used.

Milwaukee Brewers

Bryce Florie

Traded To TIGERS

Position: RP/SP
Bats: R **Throws:** R
Ht: 5'11" **Wt:** 190

Opening Day Age: 27
Born: 5/21/70 in Charleston, SC
ML Seasons: 4
Pronunciation: FLORE-ee

Overall Statistics

	W	L	Pct.	ERA	G	GS	Sv	IP	H	BB	SO	HR	Ratio
1997	4	4	.500	4.32	32	8	0	75.0	74	42	53	4	1.55
Career	8	9	.471	3.90	142	8	1	221.1	196	123	192	16	1.44

1997 Situational Stats

	W	L	ERA	Sv	IP		AB	H	HR	RBI	Avg
Home	0	3	3.86	0	37.1	LHB	133	28	1	18	.211
Road	4	1	4.78	0	37.2	RHB	149	46	3	24	.309
First Half	1	1	5.10	0	30.0	Sc Pos	91	24	2	39	.264
Scnd Half	3	3	3.80	0	45.0	Clutch	33	12	1	6	.364

1997 Season

It looked like a lost season for Bryce Florie until he took over the injured Ben McDonald's spot in the rotation in July. Before then, Florie pitched out of the bullpen, sporadically and ineffectively, struggling with his control. He reeled off a string of seven solid starts before a sore shoulder all but ended his season in late August.

Pitching, Defense & Hitting

Florie's biggest weapon is a sinking fastball that hits the high 80s and runs in on righthanders. The pitch is very difficult to hit in the air, and actually makes him tougher on lefthanders than righties. He complements it with a slider. Both pitches have so much movement that they're hard to hit and hard to control. He was an effective starter in the minors, but has worked mostly out of the bullpen in the majors. He's been somewhat error-prone with the glove. His pickoff move is below average, and basestealers were successful on 15 of 18 occasions in 1997. He came up in the NL with the Padres, but he's 0-for-5 at the plate in his career.

1998 Outlook

Milwaukee swapped Florie to Detroit in a five-player trade that netted the Brewers lefthander Mike Myers. The Tigers may use Florie as a starter.

Julio Franco

Position: 1B/2B
Bats: R **Throws:** R
Ht: 6' 1" **Wt:** 190

Opening Day Age: 36
Born: 8/23/61 in San Pedro de Macoris, DR
ML Seasons: 15

Overall Statistics

	G	AB	R	H	D	T	HR	RBI	SB	BB	SO	Avg	OBP	Slg
1997	120	430	68	116	16	1	7	44	15	69	116	.270	.369	.360
Career	1890	7243	1104	2177	335	47	141	981	260	753	1005	.301	.366	.418

1997 Situational Stats

	AB	H	HR	RBI	Avg		AB	H	HR	RBI	Avg
Home	221	58	5	24	.262	LHP	111	28	0	9	.252
Road	209	58	2	20	.278	RHP	319	88	7	35	.276
First Half	260	75	2	21	.288	Sc Pos	112	32	3	39	.286
Scnd Half	170	41	5	23	.241	Clutch	57	17	0	3	.298

1997 Season

Julio Franco's career remained as wild and unpredictable as ever in 1997. After serving capably as the Indians' designated hitter in 1996, he began last year as their second baseman. His hitting dropped off, he was moved to DH, demoted to the bench and finally released in August. The Brewers immediately picked him up and made him their cleanup hitter, but after a hot start with Milwaukee he faltered badly down the stretch.

Hitting, Baserunning & Defense

Franco covers the plate very well and is particularly adept at taking outside pitches to right field. His swing begins with his hands held high, and his level cut produces a lot of hard-hit grounders and line drives. After experimenting with glasses and posting the lowest full-season batting average and highest strikeout total of his career, his vision is a concern. He's capable at first base, though it takes a toll on his balky hamstrings.

1998 Outlook

Franco's bat is all he has left, so he has to hit to have any value. If he can prove that he can swing the bat like the old Julio Franco, there's probably a team that's willing to gamble on his gimpy legs. He's a free agent and the Brewers don't seem eager to take a second chance on him.

Darrin Jackson

Position: CF/LF
Bats: R **Throws:** R
Ht: 6' 0" **Wt:** 185

Opening Day Age: 34
Born: 8/22/63 in Los Angeles, CA
ML Seasons: 10

Overall Statistics

	G	AB	R	H	D	T	HR	RBI	SB	BB	SO	Avg	OBP	Slg
1997	75	211	26	55	9	1	5	36	4	6	31	.261	.279	.384
Career	773	2276	269	586	92	13	72	281	38	119	423	.257	.295	.404

1997 Situational Stats

	AB	H	HR	RBI	Avg		AB	H	HR	RBI	Avg
Home	122	31	4	24	.254	LHP	97	26	2	16	.268
Road	89	24	1	12	.270	RHP	114	29	3	20	.254
First Half	78	19	3	18	.244	Sc Pos	60	19	3	33	.317
Scnd Half	133	36	2	18	.271	Clutch	35	8	1	4	.229

1997 Season

After two seasons in Japan, Darrin Jackson resumed his nomadic career in the majors. He went to spring training with the Giants and Red Sox before catching on with the Twins. After toiling for them as a part-time outfielder, he was sent to Milwaukee in a minor late-season deal. While their expectations weren't enormous, the Brewers were pleased with his outfield play and timely hitting.

Hitting, Baserunning & Defense

Jackson's defense is the strongest part of his game. He has a strong, accurate arm, and the range to cover any of the three outfield spots. He's a smart, aggressive baserunner, and steals an occasional base while hardly ever getting caught. At the plate, he has decent power and can golf the ball down and in, but his lack of selectivity holds him back, to which his six walks in 211 at-bats in 1997 would attest. He traditionally has been stronger against lefthanders.

1998 Outlook

The Brewers will bring Jackson back as a fourth outfielder. He became a free agent, then was resigned to a minor league contract and invited to spring training.

Jesse Levis

Position: C
Bats: L **Throws:** R
Ht: 5' 9" **Wt:** 180

Opening Day Age: 29
Born: 4/14/68 in Philadelphia, PA
ML Seasons: 6
Pronunciation: LEV-iss

Overall Statistics

	G	AB	R	H	D	T	HR	RBI	SB	BB	SO	Avg	OBP	Slg
1997	99	200	19	57	7	0	1	19	1	24	17	.285	.361	.335
Career	275	558	56	142	21	1	3	50	1	65	47	.254	.333	.312

1997 Situational Stats

	AB	H	HR	RBI	Avg		AB	H	HR	RBI	Avg
Home	80	25	1	7	.313	LHP	18	4	0	1	.222
Road	120	32	0	12	.267	RHP	182	53	1	18	.291
First Half	95	25	1	10	.263	Sc Pos	43	15	0	17	.349
Scnd Half	105	32	0	9	.305	Clutch	63	13	0	4	.206

1997 Season

For the second year in a row, Jesse Levis formed the offensive half of a glove/stick catching platoon with Mike Matheny. Levis caught whenever the club needed some extra offense. The rest of the time, he backed up Matheny and pinch-hit. The role fit his skills perfectly, and he did exactly what he was asked to do.

Hitting, Baserunning & Defense

Levis is no power hitter, but he makes himself productive by pounding balls over and through the infield. He makes good contact and has a good batting eye. He has done well as a pinch hitter and can lay down a sacrifice if asked. Once he reaches base, though, it's evident that his legs are made for squatting rather than running. He's a decent enough handler of pitchers, and while his arm is weak he rarely makes an errant throw.

1998 Outlook

Levis has gone about as far as his skills will take him. As long as the Brewers keep him in his present role, he should be able to help. At the very worst, he'll be a decent backup.

Jose Mercedes

Position: SP/RP
Bats: R **Throws:** R
Ht: 6' 1" **Wt:** 199

Opening Day Age: 27
Born: 3/5/71 in El Seibo, DR
ML Seasons: 4
Pronunciation: mer-SAY-deez

Overall Statistics

	W	L	Pct.	ERA	G	GS	Sv	IP	H	BB	SO	HR	Ratio
1997	7	10	.412	3.79	29	23	0	159.0	146	53	80	24	1.25
Career	9	13	.409	4.21	64	23	0	214.0	200	82	103	35	1.32

1997 Situational Stats

	W	L	ERA	Sv	IP		AB	H	HR	RBI	Avg
Home	4	4	2.74	0	75.2	LHB	313	87	12	35	.278
Road	3	6	4.75	0	83.1	RHB	275	59	12	35	.215
First Half	3	4	4.72	0	74.1	Sc Pos	122	27	4	41	.221
Scnd Half	4	6	2.98	0	84.2	Clutch	37	9	1	3	.243

1997 Season

The biggest surprise on the Brewers' staff last year was righthander Jose Mercedes. Plagued by injuries and ineffectiveness since being selected in the major league Rule 5 draft from the Orioles in 1993, he won the fifth starter's job by default out of spring training. Early results were mixed, but he improved and became one of Milwaukee's best starters in the second half. In nine August and September starts, he had a sparkling 2.69 ERA.

Pitching, Defense & Hitting

With a high-80s fastball and only a fair breaking ball, Mercedes has unimpressive stuff. What enabled him to turn his career around was his control, which used to hamper his game plan. Now he's able to shoot for the corners and hit them often enough to get by. He has good stamina and picks up on hitters' weaknesses, which makes him more effective his second time through the order. Mercedes is an erratic fielder, but basestealers have a tough time taking advantage of him. He struck out in his only two at-bats in interleague play.

1998 Outlook

Mercedes never has been a hot prospect and may not have the potential to do much more than he did in 1997. If his control really has come around, he could remain a useful starter.

Marc Newfield

Position: LF
Bats: R **Throws:** R
Ht: 6' 4" **Wt:** 205

Opening Day Age: 25
Born: 10/19/72 in Sacramento, CA
ML Seasons: 5

Overall Statistics

	G	AB	R	H	D	T	HR	RBI	SB	BB	SO	Avg	OBP	Slg
1997	50	157	14	36	8	0	1	18	0	14	27	.229	.295	.299
Career	262	771	83	194	46	1	19	107	1	50	133	.252	.302	.388

1997 Situational Stats

	AB	H	HR	RBI	Avg		AB	H	HR	RBI	Avg
Home	81	17	0	11	.210	LHP	54	13	0	7	.241
Road	76	19	1	7	.250	RHP	103	23	1	11	.223
First Half	123	29	1	17	.236	Sc Pos	55	11	0	15	.200
Scnd Half	34	7	0	1	.206	Clutch	22	10	0	6	.455

1997 Season

After hitting so well for two months in 1996, young Marc Newfield began 1997 as the Brewers' left fielder. He got off to a good start, but fell into a slump as his right shoulder began to ache. He eventually was diagnosed with a torn rotator cuff, requiring surgery that kept him out of the lineup for the final three months.

Hitting, Baserunning & Defense

When he's healthy, Newfield is an excellent pure hitter with good power to the gaps. He's still learning to wait for his pitch, but he always makes solid contact, sending liners all over the field. His baserunning and defense are things a manager must put up with in order to keep his bat in the lineup. He doesn't have great range or a strong arm, and sometimes misreads fly balls. His speed is average at best.

1998 Outlook

Once again, Newfield will resume his quest to attain a full season as a major league regular. He remains a good offensive prospect and he's young enough to develop into the hitter everyone believes he can be. If his shoulder is right, he once again should enter the season as the Brewers' projected left fielder.

Ron Villone

Position: RP
Bats: L **Throws:** L
Ht: 6' 3" **Wt:** 235

Opening Day Age: 28
Born: 1/16/70 in
Englewood, NJ
ML Seasons: 3
Pronunciation:
va-LONE

Overall Statistics

	W	L	Pct.	ERA	G	GS	Sv	IP	H	BB	SO	HR	Ratio
1997	1	0	1.000	3.42	50	0	0	52.2	54	36	40	4	1.71
Career	4	4	.500	4.09	132	0	3	140.2	129	95	141	21	1.59

1997 Situational Stats

	W	L	ERA	Sv	IP		AB	H	HR	RBI	Avg
Home	0	0	3.52	0	23.0	LHB	71	25	2	13	.352
Road	1	0	3.34	0	29.2	RHB	128	29	2	13	.227
First Half	0	0	5.87	0	23.0	Sc Pos	60	18	2	24	.300
Scnd Half	1	0	1.52	0	29.2	Clutch	46	13	1	7	.283

1997 Season

Ron Villone never has become the star people once predicted he'd become, but he has established himself as a useful middle reliever. He overcame a first-half slump in 1997 to post an excellent second half, compiling a 1.52 ERA in 24 appearances after the All-Star break.

Pitching, Defense & Hitting

Villone throws a live fastball in the 90s, and if he can ever fully harness his heater and develop a good second pitch he might be a good short reliever. His control is spotty, and his changeup and slider aren't particularly impressive. He's no more effective against lefties than righties, so he's not well-suited to be a lefty specialist. His delivery doesn't leave him in a good position to field, but he's a good athlete and reasonably reliable with the glove. The fact that he's a lefty is an asset against the running game, and steal attempts against him are few and far between. He's 0-for-2 with a strikeout in his big league career.

1998 Outlook

Villone has proven to be useful in a limited role, but it's not likely that he'll ever be anything more than a decent middle reliever. The Brewers seem satisfied with him, and will continue to give him as much work as he earns.

Bob Wickman

Position: RP
Bats: R **Throws:** R
Ht: 6' 1" **Wt:** 212

Opening Day Age: 29
Born: 2/6/69 in Green
Bay, WI
ML Seasons: 6

Overall Statistics

	W	L	Pct.	ERA	G	GS	Sv	IP	H	BB	SO	HR	Ratio
1997	7	6	.538	2.73	74	0	1	95.2	89	41	78	8	1.36
Career	41	20	.672	3.91	309	28	12	531.2	533	234	351	42	1.44

1997 Situational Stats

	W	L	ERA	Sv	IP		AB	H	HR	RBI	Avg
Home	5	2	3.69	0	46.1	LHB	146	38	1	19	.260
Road	2	4	1.82	1	49.1	RHB	207	51	7	19	.246
First Half	5	3	3.09	1	46.2	Sc Pos	110	18	2	29	.164
Scnd Half	2	3	2.39	0	49.0	Clutch	240	63	3	24	.263

1997 Season

Acquired in a late-season deal in 1996 from the Yankees, Bob Wickman became one of the most valuable members of the Brewers' bullpen last year. The rubber-armed reliever pitched often and effectively as a setup man. He led the American League with 28 holds. He has a knack for winning, going 41-20 in six seasons.

Pitching, Defense & Hitting

Wickman's stock in trade is a heavy sinker, which results from a childhood accident that cost him the tip of his right index finger. He also throws a slider that's hard to distinguish from the sinker, and the result is a ton of groundouts. His ability to work every day is a major asset. Fatigue costs him velocity but not movement, so it doesn't hurt him much. As a sinkerballer he's used to fielding comebackers, and is quick as a cat when taking one and starting a double play. He owns a below-average pickoff move and is nothing special when it comes to holding runners. His next at-bat in the major leagues will be his first.

1998 Outlook

With manager Phil Garner's heavy reliance on his middle relievers, Wickman should remain a vital member of the bullpen as long as he's effective. He's showing no signs of slowing down.

Mark Davis (**Pos**: LHP, **Age**: 37)

	W	L	Pct.	ERA	G	GS	Sv	IP	H	BB	SO	HR	Ratio
1997	0	0	-	5.51	19	0	0	16.1	21	5	14	4	1.59
Career	51	84	.378	4.17	624	85	96	1145.0	1068	534	1007	129	1.40

After winning the Cy Young Award in '89, Davis got hit hard in '90, '91, '92, '93 and '94. He came back last year, and—surprise!—he got hit hard. His ERA in the '90s is 5.37. 1998 Outlook: D

Eddy Diaz (**Pos**: 2B, **Age**: 26, **Bats**: R)

	G	AB	R	H	D	T	HR	RBI	SB	BB	SO	Avg	OBP	Slg
1997	16	50	4	11	2	1	0	7	0	1	5	.220	.235	.300
Career	16	50	4	11	2	1	0	7	0	1	5	.220	.235	.300

Diaz might hit enough to be a useful backup infielder at some point, but the Brewers didn't need him last year and there's no reason to think they will this year. 1998 Outlook: C

Greg Hansell (**Pos**: RHP, **Age**: 27)

	W	L	Pct.	ERA	G	GS	Sv	IP	H	BB	SO	HR	Ratio
1997	0	0	-	9.64	3	0	0	4.2	5	1	5	1	1.29
Career	3	1	.750	6.22	73	0	3	98.1	117	38	64	20	1.58

The Brewers called Hansell up for a few days in July and August, before slapping themselves and exclaiming, "Oh, *that* Greg Hansell." 1998 Outlook: D

Pete Harnisch (**Pos**: RHP, **Age**: 31)

	W	L	Pct.	ERA	G	GS	Sv	IP	H	BB	SO	HR	Ratio
1997	1	2	.333	7.03	10	8	0	39.2	48	23	22	6	1.79
Career	72	77	.483	3.88	227	224	0	1385.1	1275	532	1003	142	1.30

Harnisch missed most of '97 while suffering from depression, and was unable to get along with Mets manager Bobby Valentine upon his return. Shipped to Milwaukee, he couldn't get the high fastball past anyone any more. 1998 Outlook: B

Jeff Huson (**Pos**: 2B/1B, **Age**: 33, **Bats**: L)

	G	AB	R	H	D	T	HR	RBI	SB	BB	SO	Avg	OBP	Slg
1997	84	143	12	29	3	0	0	11	3	5	15	.203	.238	.224
Career	629	1475	194	344	50	11	7	117	51	157	186	.233	.307	.296

Injuries on the infield forced the Brewers to pick up Huson, and he stuck around for the rest of the year by filling in all over. He signed with the Rockies after the season. 1998 Outlook: C

Jamie McAndrew (**Pos**: RHP, **Age**: 30)

	W	L	Pct.	ERA	G	GS	Sv	IP	H	BB	SO	HR	Ratio
1997	1	1	.500	8.38	5	4	0	19.1	24	23	8	1	2.43
Career	3	4	.429	5.98	15	8	0	55.2	61	35	27	3	1.72

After missing all of '96 with knee problems, McAndrew began the year in the Milwaukee starting rotation but couldn't get the ball over the plate. Sent to the minors, he continued to struggle badly. 1998 Outlook: D

Mike Misuraca (**Pos**: RHP, **Age**: 29)

	W	L	Pct.	ERA	G	GS	Sv	IP	H	BB	SO	HR	Ratio
1997	0	0	-	11.32	5	0	0	10.1	15	7	10	5	2.13
Career	0	0	-	11.32	5	0	0	10.1	15	7	10	5	2.13

The 28-year-old minor league lifer got an unexpected callup in July. He needed only five games to pitch himself off the major league roster. 1998 Outlook: D

Al Reyes (**Pos**: RHP, **Age**: 26)

	W	L	Pct.	ERA	G	GS	Sv	IP	H	BB	SO	HR	Ratio
1997	1	2	.333	5.46	19	0	1	29.2	32	9	28	4	1.38
Career	3	3	.500	4.19	51	0	2	68.2	59	29	59	8	1.28

Last year was Reyes' first full year back after Tommy John surgery. The Brewers called him up in July but he didn't pitch well until September. He could improve and might even be useful this year. 1998 Outlook: B

Kelly Stinnett (**Pos**: C, **Age**: 28, **Bats**: R)

	G	AB	R	H	D	T	HR	RBI	SB	BB	SO	Avg	OBP	Slg
1997	30	36	2	9	4	0	0	3	0	3	9	.250	.308	.361
Career	168	408	46	92	18	3	6	35	4	45	113	.225	.320	.328

For the second straight year, Stinnett had a big offensive year at Triple-A but couldn't catch the Brewers' eye. He did attract the notice of the Diamondbacks, who took him in the third round of the expansion draft. 1998 Outlook: B

Tim Unroe (**Pos**: 1B, **Age**: 27, **Bats**: R)

	G	AB	R	H	D	T	HR	RBI	SB	BB	SO	Avg	OBP	Slg
1997	32	16	3	4	1	0	2	5	2	2	9	.250	.333	.688
Career	48	36	8	8	1	0	2	5	2	6	14	.222	.333	.417

Unroe is a righthanded-hitting first baseman who can't really hit enough to help at first and can't really play third base well enough to help there either. 1998 Outlook: C

Jack Voigt (**Pos**: LF/1B, **Age**: 31, **Bats**: R)

	G	AB	R	H	D	T	HR	RBI	SB	BB	SO	Avg	OBP	Slg
1997	72	151	20	37	9	2	8	22	1	19	36	.245	.331	.490
Career	237	516	77	128	28	3	19	73	2	72	110	.248	.340	.424

Voigt played a little first base and left field for the Brewers in the second half, routinely destroying lefties while waving helplessly at righthanders' offerings. He signed a minor league deal with Oakland in the offseason. 1998 Outlook: C

Milwaukee Brewers Minor League Prospects

Organization Overview:

The Brewers do a pretty good job of developing talent, but get overlooked because they haven't produced any superstars and don't have an abundance of prospects in the system right now. Five of their nine regulars and three members of their starting rotation originally were signed by Milwaukee. The best long-range players are Jeff Cirillo, Jeff D'Amico and Dave Nilsson, solid guys but not the type to earn the system much acclaim. There isn't an impact player on the way and most of the top-level prospects are first-base and left-field types, positions not exactly in short supply, so the small-revenue Brewers may have to splurge on a free agent or two to become a serious contender. They did quietly over-achieve in 1997, thanks mainly to their underrated development program.

Brian Banks

Position: OF   **Opening Day Age:** 27
Bats: B **Throws:** R   **Born:** 9/28/70 in Mesa,
Ht: 6' 3" **Wt:** 200   AZ

Recent Statistics

	G	AB	R	H	D	T	HR	RBI	SB	BB	SO	AVG
97 AAA Tucson	98	378	53	112	26	3	10	63	7	35	83	.296
97 AL Milwaukee	28	68	9	14	1	0	1	8	0	6	17	.206
97 MLE	98	361	39	95	23	2	6	46	5	26	85	.263

Banks is just another face in the Brewers' crowded left-field picture, but his versatility could serve him well. He can play both outfield corners as well as first base and catcher. A 1993 second-round pick out of Brigham Young, he'll also draw a few walks and steal an occasional base. His speed is adequate as are his defensive skills and arm. He won't take the left-field job from Dave Nilsson and he's not as good a prospect as Todd Dunn and Geoff Jenkins, but Banks could carve out a career as a poor man's Jim Leyritz.

Ron Belliard

Position: 2B   **Opening Day Age:** 22
Bats: R **Throws:** R   **Born:** 4/7/75 in New
Ht: 5' 9" **Wt:** 176   York, NY

Recent Statistics

	G	AB	R	H	D	T	HR	RBI	SB	BB	SO	AVG
96 AA El Paso	109	416	73	116	20	8	3	57	26	60	51	.279
97 AAA Tucson	118	443	80	125	35	4	4	55	10	61	69	.282
97 MLE	118	425	58	107	30	3	2	40	7	45	71	.252

Belliard has shot through the system since signing as a 1994 eighth-round pick, beginning a full season in Triple-A at age 21. He's a much better offensive player than his cousin, Braves shortstop Rafael Belliard, but won't turn heads. He makes contact and draws walks, and needs to cut down his swing because he's not going

to hit for power. He'll steal a few bases, but a hamstring injury held him back in 1997. He's very good defensively, with quick hands and a smooth pivot on double plays. Belliard already might be an upgrade on Milwaukee incumbents Mark Loretta and Fernando Vina, but he'll probably spend most of 1998 in Triple-A.

Valerio de los Santos

Position: P   **Opening Day Age:** 22
Bats: L **Throws:** L   **Born:** 10/6/75 in Las
Ht: 6' 4" **Wt:** 185   Matas De Farfan, DR

Recent Statistics

	W	L	ERA	G	GS	Sv	IP	H	R	BB	SO	HR
96 A Beloit	10	8	3.55	33	23	4	164.2	164	83	59	137	11
97 AA El Paso	6	10	5.75	26	16	2	114.1	146	83	38	61	6

De los Santos came out of nowhere in 1996 to emerge as perhaps the best lefthanded pitching prospect in the game. His 1997 was quite forgettable, as he had a lymph node removed from his groin and then developed a staph infection after the surgery. He was roughed up as a starter in Double-A, and wasn't helped by pitching in El Paso, a notorious hitters' park. Signed out of the Dominican Republic, he's now viewed as a short reliever because he doesn't have the offspeed stuff or stamina to pile up a lot of innings in the majors. He has a 93-MPH fastball with command and a tough splitter, enough of an arsenal for a closer. He'll return to El Paso at the start of 1998.

Todd Dunn

Position: OF   **Opening Day Age:** 27
Bats: R **Throws:** R   **Born:** 7/29/70 in Tulsa,
Ht: 6' 5" **Wt:** 220   OK

Recent Statistics

	G	AB	R	H	D	T	HR	RBI	SB	BB	SO	AVG
97 AAA Tucson	93	332	66	101	31	4	18	66	5	39	83	.304
97 AL Milwaukee	44	118	17	27	5	0	3	9	3	2	39	.229
97 MLE	93	316	48	85	27	3	12	48	3	28	86	.269

At 27, Dunn is pushing the envelope to be called a prospect. He got a late start in baseball, originally attending Georgia Tech to play football. He eventually transferred to North Florida, and signed as a supplemental first-round pick in 1993. He won the Texas League batting title in 1996 and hit well in Triple-A last season, mixing tape-measure power with lots of strikeouts. His 39-2 strikeout/walk ratio in Milwaukee indicates his need for better plate discipline. He runs well and has a right-field arm, but reads balls poorly and is more of a left fielder. With Nilsson settling in left and Jeromy Burnitz coming off a fine season in right, there's no starting job available for Dunn.

Geoff Jenkins

Position: OF **Opening Day Age:** 23
Bats: L **Throws:** R **Born:** 7/21/74 in
Ht: 6' 1" **Wt:** 205 Olympia, WA

Recent Statistics

	G	AB	R	H	D	T	HR	RBI	SB	BB	SO	AVG
96 AA El Paso	22	77	17	22	5	4	1	11	1	12	21	.286
96 A Stockton	37	138	27	48	8	4	3	25	3	20	32	.348
97 AAA Tucson	93	347	44	82	24	3	10	56	0	33	87	.236
97 MLE	93	334	32	69	21	2	6	41	0	24	90	.207

Jenkins has perhaps the most vicious swing in the minors, a lefthanded uppercut capable of launching balls great distances. But he has had little opportunity to show his stuff since signing as a 1995 first-round pick out of the University of Southern California, where he ranks second to Mark McGwire in career home runs. Jenkins has had shoulder and knee surgery in the last two years, and he struggled when he got into the Triple-A Tucson lineup in 1997. His bat is his ticket because he's an average runner and left fielder, so he may need to tone down his swing a bit. Four years younger than Dunn, he has a much higher upside and could contend for a starting job in 1998.

Mike Kinkade

Position: 3B **Opening Day Age:** 24
Bats: R **Throws:** R **Born:** 5/6/73 in Livonia,
Ht: 6' 1" **Wt:** 210 MI

Recent Statistics

	G	AB	R	H	D	T	HR	RBI	SB	BB	SO	AVG
96 A Beloit	135	499	105	151	33	4	15	100	23	47	69	.303
97 AA El Paso	125	468	112	180	35	12	12	109	17	52	66	.385
97 MLE	125	438	78	150	29	8	8	76	11	31	69	.342

Kinkade takes offense and defense to the extreme. He led the minors with a .385 batting average and earned Texas League MVP honors. He also led the minors with 60 errors, a total that would have been higher had a sore shoulder not forced him to DH late in the year. El Paso's ballpark contributed to his average, but he really can hit. A 1995 ninth-round pick out of Washington State, he has gap power and a sound concept of the strike zone. He's always going to be stiff in the field, and a transition to first base or left field is in order. He fits the profile of a designated hitter, but lost that option when Milwaukee transferred to the National League. The Brewers have plenty of choices at first and in left, so he may need a change in organizations.

Antone Williamson

Position: 1B **Opening Day Age:** 24
Bats: L **Throws:** R **Born:** 7/18/73 in
Ht: 6' 1" **Wt:** 195 Torrance, CA

Recent Statistics

	G	AB	R	H	D	T	HR	RBI	SB	BB	SO	AVG
97 AAA Tucson	83	304	53	87	20	5	5	41	3	49	41	.286
97 AL Milwaukee	24	54	2	11	3	0	0	6	0	4	8	.204
97 MLE	83	291	39	74	17	3	3	30	2	36	42	.254

Milwaukee GM Sal Bando knows Arizona State third basemen—he was one himself—so he jumped on Williamson, an All-American for the Sun Devils, with the fourth overall pick in the 1994 draft. He hasn't turned out as good as hoped. Bothered by recurring injuries to his shoulder, he hasn't shown any home-run power as a pro. He has a short stroke and can hit some doubles and draw some walks, but needs to get stronger after moving to first base. He has no speed and a soft body, so he won't have a job if he can't hit. At this point, he pales in comparison to Brewers incumbent John Jaha.

Steve Woodard

Position: P **Opening Day Age:** 22
Bats: L **Throws:** R **Born:** 5/15/75 in
Ht: 6' 4" **Wt:** 225 Hartselle, AL

Recent Statistics

	W	L	ERA	G	GS	Sv	IP	H	R	BB	SO	HR
97 AA El Paso	14	3	3.17	19	19	0	136.1	136	56	25	97	8
97 AAA Tucson	1	0	0.00	1	1	0	7.0	3	0	1	6	0
97 AL Milwaukee	3	3	5.15	7	7	0	36.2	39	25	6	32	5

Woodard made a spectacular major league debut on July 28, throwing a one-hitter for eight innings and striking out 12 to beat eventual Cy Young Award winner Roger Clemens and the Blue Jays. He didn't pitch as well before going on the disabled list with a strained ribcage muscle a month later, but the Brewers are high on the 1994 fifth-round pick. His best pitch is an outstanding straight change, and it helped him go 15-3 in the minors. He throws in the upper 80s, and the development of his slurve will determine his future success. Milwaukee probably won't have a rotation opening at the start of 1998, allowing Woodard to gain Triple-A experience.

Others to Watch

First baseman **Kevin Barker**, 22, reached Double-A and drove in 108 runs in his first full season. With another year like that, he'll leapfrog past most of the hitters in the system. . . Center fielder **Chad Green**, 22, has the athleticism that the system sorely needs. He has blazing speed and good range in center field, but he tries to hit too many homers. At high Class-A Stockton he struck out 138 times and walked just 37, not the numbers wanted from a leadoff man. . . Sidearmer **Rick Greene**, acquired in the Bryce Florie trade, may be coming into his own at age 27. A knee injury in the 1992 Olympics sidetracked him, but he limited Triple-A hitters to a .202 average in 1997. . . Right fielder **Scott Krause** got eclipsed by Kinkade at El Paso, but his .361 average ranked second in the minors. He's already 24, but has decent skills across the board. . . Righthander **Sean Maloney** led the minors with 38 saves in 1996, but an emergency appendectomy and shoulder surgery held him to five last season. Now 26, he has a nasty splitter and a 90-91 MPH fastball. . . Righthander **Travis Smith** is a 5-foot-10 righthander who's 25 and has mediocre stuff. That doesn't rate any attention, but his command and 33-10 pro record do.

Felipe Alou

1997 Season

Nobody gets as much out of a limited roster as Felipe Alou. As the Expos' talent base is continually thinned because of financially motivated trades and free-agent losses, he has learned to develop players while maintaining a competitive club. He remains a masterful handler of young pitchers, and the development of Dustin Hermanson and Ugueth Urbina were two of his biggest accomplishments in 1997.

Offense

Alou has always regulated the running game carefully, stressing percentage as opposed to raw totals. He makes do with what he has, which explains why a player like Mark Grudzielanek may lead off while someone like David Segui may hit cleanup. Neither is particularly suited to the role, but Alou believes they represent his best options. The one thing he doesn't tolerate is a player who strikes out a lot.

Pitching & Defense

The sudden development of Hermanson and Urbina were just two more examples of pitchers that Alou has broken in successfully. Expos starters led the majors with 27 complete games in 1997, but that was as much a product of his lack of confidence in his middle relievers as the strong performance of his starters. He's not afraid to bring in his closer as early as the eighth inning, figuring a close game can be decided in the eighth just as easily as in the ninth.

1998 Outlook

This will be another difficult season for Alou, who will be managing a payroll that could be significantly smaller than 1997's scant $17 million. The club may continue to dump veterans in favor of younger players, as the team tries to copy the Pirates with an eye toward becoming the Indians. Alou appeared ready for the challenge at the end of 1997, holding out hope that trades would bring in two or three more young arms.

Born: 5/12/35 in Haina, Dominican Republic

Playing Experience: 1958-1974, SF, Atl, Oak, NYA, Mon, Mil

Managerial Experience: 6 seasons

Pronunciation: fuh-LEE-pay ah-LOO

Manager Statistics

Year	Team, Lg	W	L	Pct	GB	Finish
1997	Montreal, NL	78	84	.481	23.0	4th East
6 Seasons		470	399	.540	—	—

1997 Starting Pitchers by Days Rest

	≤3	4	5	6+
Expos Starts	0	89	50	14
Expos ERA	0.00	3.72	4.40	3.09
NL Avg Starts	3	90	38	22
NL ERA	4.23	4.05	4.27	4.52

1997 Situational Stats

	Felipe Alou	NL Average
Hit & Run Success %	33.3	36.4
Stolen Base Success %	62.0	68.4
Platoon Pct.	58.4	56.3
Defensive Subs	40	26
High-Pitch Outings	15	12
Quick/Slow Hooks	26/13	18/10
Sacrifice Attempts	90	96

1997 Rankings (National League)

⇒ 1st in least caught steals of third base (2), quick hooks (26) and saves with over 1 inning pitched (13)

⇒ 2nd in least caught steals of second base (42), sacrifice bunt percentage (86.7%), defensive substitutions (40) and starting lineups used (138)

⇒ 3rd in least caught steals of home plate (2) and slow hooks (13)

Darrin Fletcher

Position: C
Bats: L **Throws:** R
Ht: 6' 1" **Wt:** 200

Opening Day Age: 31
Born: 10/3/66 in Elmhurst, IL
ML Seasons: 9

1997 Season

When Montreal acquired catcher Chris Widger in the Jeff Fassero trade with Seattle, the incumbent receiver, Darrin Fletcher, found himself in danger of being pushed into the background. Fletcher decided to put the future off for at least one season. He established a career high with 17 homers in just 310 at-bats, posting the highest slugging percentage of any Expos regular.

Hitting

Fletcher is primarily a pull hitter who hits the ball in the air. He hits with an open stance, and he gets good coverage by standing on top of the plate. Like many lefthanded hitters, he likes the ball down. Though he hasn't had many opportunities to face lefties, he has learned to handle their offspeed pitches and can make them pay for mistakes. He makes very good contact, but would be even more dangerous if he wasn't reluctant to draw a walk.

Baserunning & Defense

Fletcher notched his first major league stolen base on July 18, his only swipe in 705 career games. That tells you all you need to know about his speed. He handles pitchers well, but remains a poor thrower because of an inconsistent release and shoddy footwork. He threw out 18 percent of basestealers in 1997, and only Widger posted a worse figure among big league regulars. Like most catchers who came through the Dodgers system, he blocks the plate without fear.

1998 Outlook

Fletcher wanted to stay with the Expos. But the club seemed committed to Widger and couldn't find the money to sign a lefthanded-hitting catcher with a potent bat. As a result, Fletcher signed with Toronto as a free agent. He might be more ideal for a team in the American League, where his throwing deficiencies wouldn't matter as much.

Overall Statistics

	G	AB	R	H	D	T	HR	RBI	SB	BB	SO	Avg	OBP	Slg
1997	96	310	39	86	20	1	17	55	1	17	35	.277	.323	.513
Career	705	2124	205	558	120	6	63	315	1	156	212	.263	.317	.414

Where He Hits the Ball

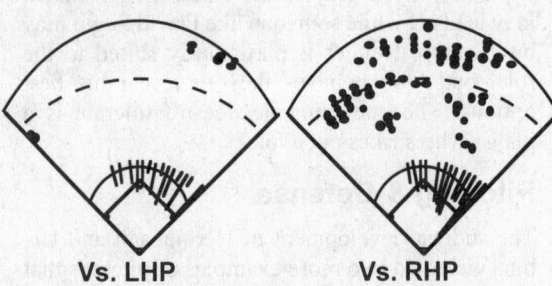

Vs. LHP   **Vs. RHP**

1997 Situational Stats

	AB	H	HR	RBI	Avg		AB	H	HR	RBI	Avg
Home	150	46	10	27	.307	LHP	75	19	4	16	.253
Road	160	40	7	28	.250	RHP	235	67	13	39	.285
First Half	163	47	10	35	.288	Sc Pos	95	29	5	38	.305
Scnd Half	147	39	7	20	.265	Clutch	55	19	3	9	.345

1997 Rankings (National League)

⇒ 2nd in lowest percentage of runners caught stealing as a catcher (14.5%)
⇒ 4th in batting average on a 3-1 count (.778)
⇒ Led the Expos in batting average with runners in scoring position, batting average in the clutch and batting average with the bases loaded (.333)

Mark Grudzielanek

1997 Season

Expectations were high for Mark Grudzielanek after his All-Star season in 1996, but a one-day walkout in spring training set the stage for a tumultuous and in many ways disappointing year. True, he set the major league record for doubles by a shortstop, but by the time the season was over he also had fired his agent, battled through personal problems, committed 32 errors and seen his average drop 33 points from 1996.

Hitting

Grudzielanek's gap power comes from a strong, level swing that generates tremendous bat speed. Both the Expos and Grudzielanek keep quietly expecting to see some of those doubles turn into homers. There's a strong perception that he's miscast at the top of the order, after he drew just 23 walks and posted an on-base percentage of .307 in 1997. He's an aggressive hitter who will work the count in his favor but isn't above chasing a bad pitch.

Baserunning & Defense

Grudzielanek accounted for one-third of Montreal's 75 stolen bases last year, but he's capable of swiping more and he knows it. His range at shortstop has been questioned, but many of his problems are related to poor footwork. He often requires an extra step to set and throw. He can be tentative initiating the double play, but he does possess a strong throwing arm.

1998 Outlook

There are those who believe that Grudzielanek would profit by a move down in the batting order, and manager Felipe Alou has gone on record as saying that he believes Grudzielanek would be better cast as a No. 6 hitter. Nobody should doubt that he has the tools to turn things around, but he must get his head together in the offseason and learn to shut out off-field distractions. In short, he needs to mature.

Position: SS
Bats: R **Throws:** R
Ht: 6' 1" **Wt:** 185

Opening Day Age: 27
Born: 6/30/70 in Milwaukee, WI
ML Seasons: 3
Pronunciation: gruzz-ELL-en-neck

Overall Statistics

	G	AB	R	H	D	T	HR	RBI	SB	BB	SO	Avg	OBP	Slg
1997	156	649	76	177	54	3	4	51	25	23	76	.273	.307	.384
Career	387	1575	202	444	100	9	11	120	66	63	206	.282	.319	.378

Where He Hits the Ball

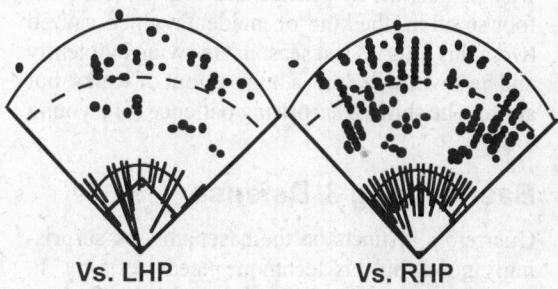

Vs. LHP   **Vs. RHP**

1997 Situational Stats

	AB	H	HR	RBI	Avg		AB	H	HR	RBI	Avg
Home	330	94	1	27	.285	LHP	147	33	1	12	.224
Road	319	83	3	24	.260	RHP	502	144	3	39	.287
First Half	346	100	2	32	.289	Sc Pos	139	33	1	46	.237
Scnd Half	303	77	2	19	.254	Clutch	98	29	2	14	.296

1997 Rankings (National League)

⇒ 1st in at-bats, doubles, lowest on-base percentage vs. lefthanded pitchers (.252), errors at shortstop (32) and lowest fielding percentage at shortstop (.955)

⇒ 3rd in lowest HR frequency (162.3 ABs per HR)

⇒ 4th in least pitches seen per plate appearance (3.29), lowest on-base percentage for a leadoff hitter (.295) and lowest percentage of pitches taken (45.6%)

⇒ Led the Expos in at-bats, hits, singles, doubles, stolen bases, caught stealing (9), pitches seen (2,263), plate appearances (688), games played (156), stolen base percentage (73.5%), lowest percentage of swings that missed (16.7%), highest percentage of swings put into play (47.0%) and steals of third (5)

Montreal Expos

Vladimir Guerrero

1997 Season

The baseball world got a glimpse last year of what a healthy Vladimir Guerrero can do. Unfortunately, it was just a glimpse. One of the most highly touted rookies in the game, he spent 52 games on the disabled list with a broken foot, a pulled right hamstring and a fractured left hand. When he was healthy, though, he looked very much like the five-tool player he was purported to be.

Hitting

Guerrero's long arms give him tremendous plate coverage, allowing him to handle outside pitches and hit with power to all fields. It also explains why he gets hit by pitches and foul balls off his foot so often, the kind of incidents which caused two of his injuries last season. He swings violently and he never will draw a huge amout of walks, but at times he showed surprising patience for a young hitter.

Baserunning & Defense

Guerrero's instincts on the basepaths are surprisingly good, but his technique needs refining. In fact, his tendency to run into bases standing up was one of the major causes of his recurring muscle pulls and strains. He'll steal some bases with good health and more experience. Guerrero's shotgun arm was demonstrated on numerous occasions in his rookie year, but he had some trouble handling balls hit into the corner. Of Guerrero's 12 errors, four were made in a span of four games in May.

1998 Outlook

Guerrero and Rondell White remind some people of Ellis Valentine and Andre Dawson, who starred in the Expos' outfield 20 years ago. It will be interesting to see if both are able to follow Dawson's career path rather than Valentine's. Guerrero hasn't played a lot of baseball since the end of the 1996 season, when a back injury sustained in winter ball began a rash of injuries that extended through last season. He may take extra time off this winter. Rest may help him to carry much of the offensive load in 1998.

Position: RF
Bats: R **Throws:** R
Ht: 6' 2" **Wt:** 195
Opening Day Age: 22
Born: 2/9/76 in Nizao Bani, DR
ML Seasons: 2
Nickname: Miqueas

Overall Statistics

	G	AB	R	H	D	T	HR	RBI	SB	BB	SO	Avg	OBP	Slg
1997	90	325	44	98	22	2	11	40	3	19	39	.302	.350	.483
Career	99	352	46	103	22	2	12	41	3	19	42	.293	.339	.469

Where He Hits the Ball

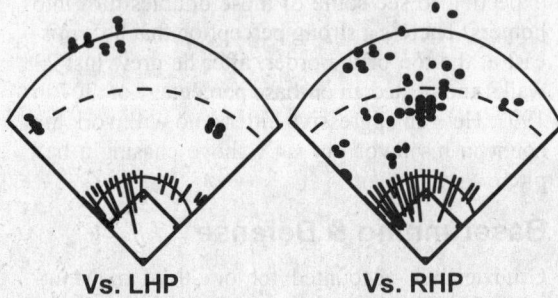

Vs. LHP   Vs. RHP

1997 Situational Stats

	AB	H	HR	RBI	Avg		AB	H	HR	RBI	Avg
Home	166	44	5	21	.265	LHP	93	28	4	12	.301
Road	159	54	6	19	.340	RHP	232	70	7	28	.302
First Half	167	54	6	26	.323	Sc Pos	76	20	2	26	.263
Scnd Half	158	44	5	14	.278	Clutch	57	17	1	5	.298

1997 Rankings (National League)

⇒ 1st in errors in right field (12)
⇒ 10th in batting average on a 3-1 count (.667)
⇒ Led the Expos in batting average with two strikes (.212)

Dustin Hermanson

1997 Season

The Expos knew they had a live arm when they acquired Dustin Hermanson in spring training from the Marlins. Though Hermanson had been a reliever through his first three pro seasons, manager Felipe Alou suggested early that he wanted to take a look at him as a starter. There were early growing pains, but by the time the year was done Hermanson had turned into one of Montreal's most reliable starters.

Pitching

Hermanson has the basic power pitcher's arsenal: a low-90s fastball, a hard slider and a changeup. He's less of a power pitcher against lefthanders, relying more heavily on his change. Indeed, it was the refining of the changeup that was the greatest concern when it was decided he'd start. He gained command of the pitch early and turned it into a fine complement to his hard stuff.

Defense & Hitting

Hermanson is a good athlete who fields his position well, and he became better at controlling the running game as the season progressed. The Expos made a conscious effort not to overload him, preferring he worry instead about getting used to his start. He'll start paying more attention to baserunners in spring training. He goes up to the plate hacking, sometimes making hard contact but usually coming up empty. He can lay down a sacrifice bunt.

1998 Outlook

Hermanson pays a great deal of attention to his physical conditioning, particularly his leg strength, so it stands to reason that he should be able to weather the increased workload on his arm. He still must prove that he can develop the stamina to work late into the ballgame. Last year, almost half of his homers came after he reached the 75-pitch mark. After the trade of Pedro Martinez, Hermanson will go into spring training as no worse than the No. 2 starter. He's bright and willing to learn, and Alou was able to bring him a long way. That should continue in 1998.

Position: SP
Bats: R **Throws:** R
Ht: 6' 2" **Wt:** 195

Opening Day Age: 25
Born: 12/21/72 in Springfield, OH
ML Seasons: 3

Overall Statistics

	W	L	Pct.	ERA	G	GS	Sv	IP	H	BB	SO	HR	Ratio
1997	8	8	.500	3.69	32	28	0	158.1	134	66	136	15	1.26
Career	12	9	.571	4.51	66	28	0	203.2	187	92	166	26	1.37

How Often He Throws Strikes

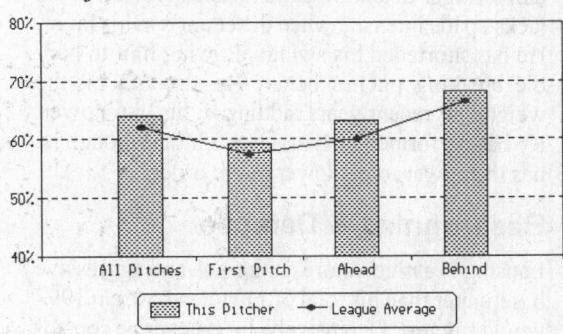

This Pitcher · League Average

1997 Situational Stats

	W	L	ERA	Sv	IP		AB	H	HR	RBI	Avg
Home	3	4	4.12	0	67.2	LHB	276	64	8	33	.232
Road	5	4	3.38	0	90.2	RHB	296	70	7	30	.236
First Half	3	4	3.77	0	76.1	Sc Pos	123	29	3	44	.236
Scnd Half	5	4	3.62	0	82.0	Clutch	13	2	0	0	.154

1997 Rankings (National League)

⇒ 5th in lowest batting average allowed vs. lefthanded batters
⇒ Led the Expos in runners caught stealing (7)

Mike Lansing

1997 Season

When the 1997 season ended, Expos second baseman Mike Lansing was on the trading block. But though it was Lansing's final season in an Expos uniform, it was a great way to bid adieu. He established career highs in doubles, homers and RBI while playing sometimes spectacular defense. He was the heart and soul of the club on and off the field. For the second year in a row he managed to stay clear of the nagging back and leg injuries that dogged him earlier in his career.

Hitting

Lansing has made a transition from being a first-ball swinger to a more patient, selective batter. He jacks up his intensity when the count's in his favor. He has shortened his swing, allowing him to handle breaking pitches better. He also has hit the weights in recent years, adding to his gap power. He has performed well as a No. 2 hitter, though he has the power to bat lower in the order.

Baserunning & Defense

Lansing is a much more dangerous and aggressive baserunner than his total of 11 stolen bases in 1997 would suggest. Defensively, he'll never be considered a textbook defensive second baseman, particularly on the double play, but he has one of the National League's best throwing arms, and that is his equalizer. He's as fearless in the field as he is at the plate, and as he's learned more about playing hitters he's been able to make the best of his range.

1998 Outlook

Lansing has improved his power stats in each of the last four seasons, and people keep waiting for him to come back to earth. It may be a long wait, because he has gotten much stronger and his power gain is real. Better yet for his numbers, he was traded to Colorado for three minor leaguers in the offseason. He was a favorite of manager Felipe Alou, yet the Expos believed they had to unload his salary.

Position: 2B
Bats: R **Throws:** R
Ht: 6' 0" **Wt:** 180

Opening Day Age: 29
Born: 4/3/68 in Rawlins, WY
ML Seasons: 5
Nickname: Laser

Overall Statistics

	G	AB	R	H	D	T	HR	RBI	SB	BB	SO	Avg	OBP	Slg
1997	144	572	86	161	45	2	20	70	11	45	92	.281	.338	.472
Career	677	2565	340	709	165	9	49	265	96	193	335	.276	.333	.405

Where He Hits the Ball

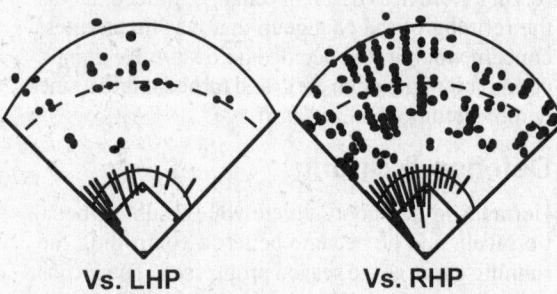

Vs. LHP   Vs. RHP

1997 Situational Stats

	AB	H	HR	RBI	Avg		AB	H	HR	RBI	Avg
Home	259	77	11	32	.297	LHP	117	35	4	16	.299
Road	313	84	9	38	.268	RHP	455	126	16	54	.277
First Half	327	91	12	40	.278	Sc Pos	128	38	3	46	.297
Scnd Half	245	70	8	30	.286	Clutch	93	22	2	13	.237

1997 Rankings (National League)

⇒ 3rd in fielding percentage at second base (.987)
⇒ 4th in doubles and lowest batting average on an 0-2 count (.045)
⇒ 9th in errors at second base (9)
⇒ Led the Expos in runs scored, times on base (211), batting average vs. lefthanded pitchers, batting average at home and lowest percentage of swings on the first pitch (32.9%)

Pedro Martinez

Traded To RED SOX

Position: SP
Bats: R **Throws:** R
Ht: 5'11" **Wt:** 170

Opening Day Age: 26
Born: 10/25/71 in Manoguyabo, DR
ML Seasons: 6

1997 Season

By adding a new pitch to an already fearsome arsenal, Pedro Martinez emerged as the season's most dominant pitcher. He won the National League Cy Young Award and placed at or near the top in every significant pitching statistic in the league. He led the circuit in opponent batting average by a considerable margin. He became only the 13th pitcher since 1900 to record 300 strikeouts, and pitched through a strained thumb ligament in September to keep alive his streak of 117 starts without missing a game because of injury.

Pitching

Martinez already boasted a riding fastball that could reach the mid-90s, a cutter, a hard slider and a curveball. But it was his newly perfected circle changeup that took him to another level. The pitch has screwball action, breaking down and away from lefthanders. He has a rubber arm, and responded well to manager Felipe Alou's decision to let him finish out more games.

Defense & Hitting

Martinez is a nimble athlete who has worked to finish his delivery in better position to field balls. Though he has developed a slide-step move, he remains vulnerable to the running game. He takes a hefty cut at the plate and usually comes up empty, but he knows how to get a bunt down. When he gets on base, he's an extremely aggressive runner.

1998 Outlook

Martinez has taken the final step into the upper echelon of major league starters, and would have won even more games with better support. But the Expos, looking to reduce their already minimal payroll, traded him to Boston in November so they wouldn't have to pay him the huge salary he would command in arbitration. Because of his work ethic, repertoire and competitiveness, there's no reason to think he won't remain one of the best pitchers in baseball.

Overall Statistics

	W	L	Pct.	ERA	G	GS	Sv	IP	H	BB	SO	HR	Ratio
1997	17	8	.680	1.90	31	31	0	241.1	158	67	305	16	0.93
Career	65	39	.625	3.00	185	120	3	912.1	702	306	970	72	1.10

How Often He Throws Strikes

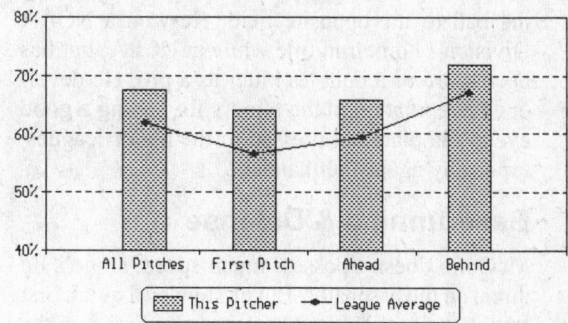

1997 Situational Stats

	W	L	ERA	Sv	IP		AB	H	HR	RBI	Avg
Home	9	5	1.99	0	140.1	LHB	469	86	8	29	.183
Road	8	3	1.78	0	101.0	RHB	391	72	8	33	.184
First Half	10	4	1.74	0	124.0	Sc Pos	161	33	2	43	.205
Scnd Half	7	4	2.07	0	117.1	Clutch	128	26	2	13	.203

1997 Rankings (National League)

⇒ 1st in ERA, complete games (13), lowest batting average allowed (.184), lowest slugging percentage allowed (.277), lowest on-base percentage allowed (.250), least baserunners allowed per 9 innings (8.7), most strikeouts per 9 innings (11.4), ERA at home, ERA on the road, lowest batting average allowed vs. lefthanded batters and lowest batting average allowed vs. righthanded batters

⇒ 2nd in shutouts (4) and strikeouts

⇒ 3rd in highest strikeout/walk ratio (4.6) and least run support per 9 innings (3.5)

⇒ Led the Expos in ERA, wins, complete games (13), innings pitched, batters faced (947), strikeouts, balks (1), pitches thrown (3,631), winning percentage and highest strikeout/walk ratio (4.6)

Montreal Expos

Ryan McGuire

1997 Season

Ryan McGuire came over from the Red Sox before the 1996 season as part of the Wil Cordero trade. After being dropped from the 40-man roster in March 1997, McGuire was called up in June after David Segui hurt his knee. He started hot and became a valuable utility player, starting at first base and in left and center field. He showed himself to be a strong fundamental player capable of contributing offensively.

Hitting

McGuire's textbook swing is smooth, controlled and level. Though physically unimposing, he's a contact hitter with gap power and an ability to take the ball to the opposite field. He won a NCAA Division I home-run title while at UCLA, but has been more of a doubles hitter as a pro. He developed a reputation in the minors for having a good eye at the plate but pressed in the major leagues, especially against lefthanders.

Baserunning & Defense

McGuire doesn't possess much speed, so he's no threat on the basepaths. But he showed a quick first step in the outfield, and he gets a good read on the ball when it leaves the bat. Consequently, he covers a surprising amount of territory. He's a smart player who makes up for his speed and lack of throwing ability by doing things correctly. He showed good instincts around first base and is very smooth at that position.

1998 Outlook

McGuire needs to hit lefties before he'll be able to contribute on an everyday basis. At this point, he doesn't have the power to contribute as a full-time first baseman or left fielder. Still, he bats lefthanded and can hit a little, so Felipe Alou can probably find a role for him. On a Montreal team that could have openings at first base and in left field, he could make things interesting with a good spring training.

Position: 1B/LF/RF
Bats: L **Throws:** L
Ht: 6' 2" **Wt:** 210

Opening Day Age: 26
Born: 11/23/71 in Bellflower, CA
ML Seasons: 1

Overall Statistics

	G	AB	R	H	D	T	HR	RBI	SB	BB	SO	Avg	OBP	Slg
1997	84	199	22	51	15	2	3	17	1	19	34	.256	.320	.397
Career	84	199	22	51	15	2	3	17	1	19	34	.256	.320	.397

Where He Hits the Ball

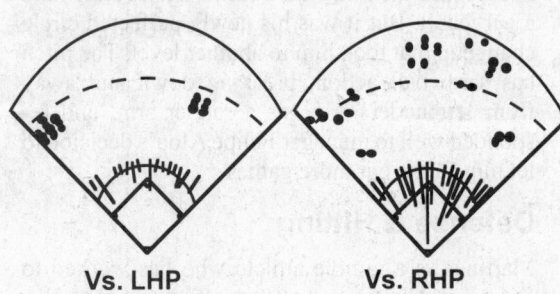

Vs. LHP   Vs. RHP

1997 Situational Stats

	AB	H	HR	RBI	Avg		AB	H	HR	RBI	Avg
Home	88	26	2	8	.295	LHP	65	13	1	2	.200
Road	111	25	1	9	.225	RHP	134	38	2	15	.284
First Half	76	25	3	9	.329	Sc Pos	37	8	0	2	.216
Scnd Half	123	26	0	8	.211	Clutch	40	9	0	2	.225

1997 Rankings (National League)

⇒ Did not rank near the top or bottom in any category

Carlos Perez

1997 Season

After missing all of 1996 following arthroscopic surgery to repair a partial tear of his left rotator cuff and labrum, Carlos Perez' major concern last year was trying to stay healthy. He accomplished that and finished with 207 innings and eight complete games. Perhaps realizing his tenuous situation, he was noticeably less animated in 1997.

Pitching

Perez' mid-to-high-80s fastball is a notch slower than it was before his injury, so he relies more on his offspeed pitches than he used to. He'll throw his changeup for strikes on any count and uses his split-finger fastball to get strikeouts. He's especially tough on lefthanders. His mental approach on the mound is unpredictable and he'll go against the book.

Defense & Hitting

Perez was more controlled on the mound and that carried over to his defensive game. He was able to get himself in better position to make plays on balls hit to either side of the mound. He still makes careless errors, however. He picks off more than his share of runners, though he still needs work on controlling the running game. Perez is a free swinger who attacks the ball at the plate. He even managed to homer last season after adopting an unorthodox stance.

1998 Outlook

Perez will be thrust into an even greater role now that Pedro Martinez has been traded. It will be a true test of Perez' apparently more mature approach. Some baseball people believe he'll be able to add 2-3 MPH to his fastball now that he's an extra year removed from surgery. Felipe Alou handled him carefully last year, keeping him under 120 pitches in every single start. The question is whether he can build on his comeback year and take another step forward.

Position: SP
Bats: L **Throws:** L
Ht: 6' 3" **Wt:** 195

Opening Day Age: 27
Born: 1/14/71 in Nigua, DR
ML Seasons: 2

Overall Statistics

	W	L	Pct.	ERA	G	GS	Sv	IP	H	BB	SO	HR	Ratio
1997	12	13	.480	3.88	33	32	0	206.2	206	48	110	21	1.23
Career	22	21	.512	3.80	61	55	0	348.0	348	76	216	39	1.22

How Often He Throws Strikes

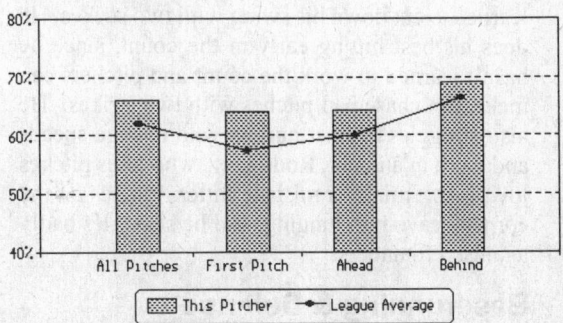

1997 Situational Stats

	W	L	ERA	Sv	IP		AB	H	HR	RBI	Avg
Home	7	5	4.26	0	107.2	LHB	143	29	2	14	.203
Road	5	8	3.45	0	99.0	RHB	650	177	19	87	.272
First Half	8	5	3.52	0	115.0	Sc Pos	175	53	6	78	.303
Scnd Half	4	8	4.32	0	91.2	Clutch	70	18	2	7	.257

1997 Rankings (National League)

⇒ 1st in shutouts (5)
⇒ 2nd in complete games (8) and least pitches thrown per batter (3.35)
⇒ 4th in losses and least strikeouts per 9 innings (4.8)
⇒ 5th in most GDPs induced per 9 innings (1.0) and highest batting average allowed with runners in scoring position
⇒ Led the Expos in losses, games started, shutouts (5), hits allowed, home runs allowed, balks (1), GDPs induced (24), lowest stolen base percentage allowed (73.3%), least pitches thrown per batter (3.35), most run support per 9 innings (4.3), most GDPs induced per 9 innings (1.0) and most GDPs induced per GDP situation (18.5%)

Montreal
Expos

Henry Rodriguez

1997 Season

Henry Rodriguez' production fell off from 1996, but in many ways the seasons were similar: flashes of power, a lack of plate discipline, a high number of strikeouts and substandard defense. He didn't help his cause by missing 19 games with a strained muscle in his right ribcage, and later falling into a severe slump in the second half. Still, it was a decent year overall. Many had expected less after he'd slumped so badly in the second half of '96.

Hitting

At the plate, Rodriguez looks for home runs and first-pitch fastballs. He gets the ball in the air consistently, though he's impatient and still hasn't learned to cut down his swing with two strikes. He does his best hitting early in the count, since he hasn't learned to work the count and pitchers can make him chase bad pitches with two strikes. He also struggles against hurlers who change speeds and work in and out. Rodriguez, who likes pitches low, is essentially a mistake hitter. Pitches on the corners leave him lunging, and he struggles badly against lefthanders.

Baserunning & Defense

Rodriguez is no threat on the bases, especially after fracturing his leg in 1995. He has done little to change his reputation as being defensively challenged, particularly in left field. He gets a poor jump on balls, covers very little territory and makes poor throwing decisions. He often was removed in favor of a late-inning defensive replacement in 1997. First base is his natural position.

1998 Outlook

Despite his shortcomings, Rodriguez remains a fan favorite in Montreal. The club appears set to go in a different direction, and he was left unprotected in the expansion draft. The Expos are willing to go with a cheaper left fielder while attempting to replace Rodriguez' power elsewhere.

Position: LF
Bats: L **Throws:** L
Ht: 6' 1" **Wt:** 205

Opening Day Age: 30
Born: 11/8/67 in Santo Domingo, DR
ML Seasons: 6

Overall Statistics

	G	AB	R	H	D	T	HR	RBI	SB	BB	SO	Avg	OBP	Slg
1997	132	476	55	116	28	3	26	83	3	42	149	.244	.306	.479
Career	555	1774	213	449	105	7	83	287	6	126	464	.253	.303	.461

Where He Hits the Ball

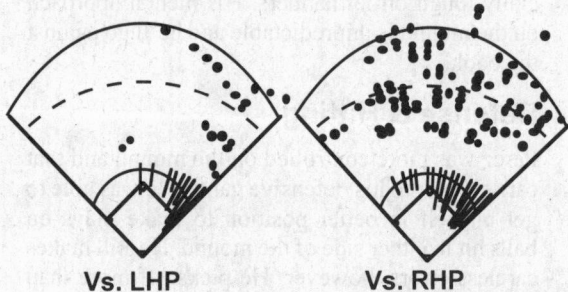

Vs. LHP   **Vs. RHP**

1997 Situational Stats

	AB	H	HR	RBI	Avg		AB	H	HR	RBI	Avg
Home	248	66	14	46	.266	LHP	133	29	5	14	.218
Road	228	50	12	37	.219	RHP	343	87	21	69	.254
First Half	303	82	16	51	.271	Sc Pos	111	33	10	60	.297
Scnd Half	173	34	10	32	.197	Clutch	82	14	3	8	.171

1997 Rankings (National League)

⇒ 1st in batting average on a 3-1 count (1.000), highest percentage of swings that missed (33.2%) and lowest percentage of swings put into play (30.9%)

⇒ 3rd in lowest batting average and strikeouts

⇒ 4th in lowest groundball/flyball ratio (0.8), lowest batting average vs. lefthanded pitchers, fielding percentage in left field (.985) and highest percentage of swings on the first pitch (42.5%)

⇒ 5th in lowest batting average in the clutch

⇒ Led the Expos in RBI, strikeouts, HR frequency (18.3 ABs per HR), most pitches seen per plate appearance (3.79) and batting average on a 3-1 count (1.000)

F.P. Santangelo

1997 Season

It was a productive but painful season for F.P. Santangelo, who once again played a variety of positions (five) and batted in a variety of places in manager Felipe Alou's batting order (six). Santangelo was hobbled by knee troubles most of the season, but he drew 50 walks and was hit by 25 pitches. His on-base percentage of .379 stuck out on a team with an overall .316 mark.

Hitting

Santangelo digs in close on both sides of the plate, forcing pitchers to work him away. He can be too aggressive, but he has some gap power and is capable of driving a fastball over the wall from both sides of the plate. He's much stronger as a lefthanded hitter. An adept bunter, he also will settle for putting the ball in play to advance a runner. His production tailed off dramatically in the second half because he was worn down.

Baserunning & Defense

Santangelo picks his spots to run and is rather aggressive when he healthy. He's an intelligent outfielder with quick reactions. He charges the ball well, enabling him to make strong, accurate throws even though he doesn't have the most powerful arm. He's a gamer in the infield who didn't always appear comfortable at third base. He was willing to sacrifice his body and make up in effort what he lacked in instincts.

1998 Outlook

An unselfish player who has played for Alou in the majors and minors, Santangelo has emerged as a legitimate major leaguer. That's a source of great pride to Alou. With the Expos looking ahead to leaner times, a healthy Santangelo is extremely valuable because of his versatility and ability to switch-hit. The Expos' unsettled roster situation should ensure that Santangelo will continue to get lots of at-bats.

Position: RF/3B/LF/CF
Bats: B **Throws:** R
Ht: 5'10" **Wt:** 168

Opening Day Age: 30
Born: 10/24/67 in El Dorado Hills, CA
ML Seasons: 3
Pronunciation: san-TAN-jel-oh

Overall Statistics

	G	AB	R	H	D	T	HR	RBI	SB	BB	SO	Avg	OBP	Slg
1997	130	350	56	87	19	5	5	31	8	50	73	.249	.379	.374
Career	317	841	121	225	44	11	13	96	14	111	143	.268	.375	.392

Where He Hits the Ball

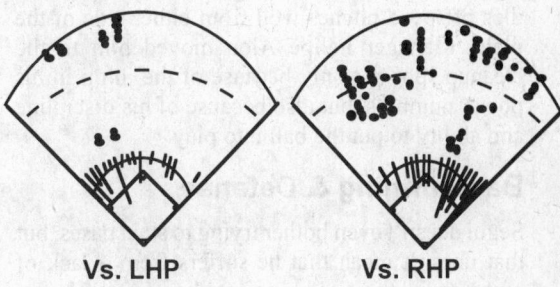

Vs. LHP   **Vs. RHP**

1997 Situational Stats

	AB	H	HR	RBI	Avg		AB	H	HR	RBI	Avg
Home	167	46	5	19	.275	LHP	80	20	2	6	.250
Road	183	41	0	12	.224	RHP	270	67	3	25	.248
First Half	205	63	4	21	.307	Sc Pos	77	12	1	23	.156
Scnd Half	145	24	1	10	.166	Clutch	63	15	0	3	.238

1997 Rankings (National League)

⇒ 1st in lowest batting average with runners in scoring position and on-base percentage for a leadoff hitter (.427)
⇒ 2nd in least GDPs per GDP situation (1.6%)
⇒ 3rd in hit by pitch (25)
⇒ 7th in sacrifice bunts (12)
⇒ Led the Expos in triples, sacrifice bunts (12), hit by pitch (25), least GDPs per GDP situation (1.6%), on-base percentage for a leadoff hitter (.427), bunts in play (18) and highest percentage of pitches taken (56.7%)

David Segui

1997 Season

David Segui was the most consistent Expo hitter in 1997, setting a career high with 21 homers while batting primarily out of the cleanup spot. For the first time in years, he wasn't hounded by nagging hand, wrist and knee ailments. He did have arthroscopic surgery in June to repair a torn meniscus in his left knee, but surprised everyone by returning to the lineup less than three weeks later.

Hitting

Segui always has been able to put a charge into the ball because of his short, powerful stroke. He added a little loft to his swing in 1997 and boosted his homer total as a result. He's a disciplined low-ball hitter who makes good contact and handles offspeed pitches well from either side of the plate. Manager Felipe Alou moved him to the cleanup spot not only because of the jump in his power numbers, but also because of his discipline and ability to put the ball into play.

Baserunning & Defense

Segui doesn't even bother trying to steal bases, but that doesn't mean that he suffers from a lack of mobility in the field. In fact, because of better health he improved his play in the field. He committed only six errors and showed a quick glove hand and deft touch on pickoff throws, as well as a good ability to dig out balls thrown in the dirt. He also has soft hands and an accurate arm.

1998 Outlook

Segui jacked up his value as a free agent with his 1997 performance. His more expensive price tag, along with the development of Brad Fullmer and Ryan McGuire, makes it unlikely that Segui will return to Montreal. That Alou picked him to bat cleanup over Henry Rodriguez and Rondell White shows the respect the manager had in Segui's ability. He may be entering his best years in his early 30s, just as his father Diego did.

Position: 1B
Bats: B **Throws:** L
Ht: 6' 1" **Wt:** 202

Opening Day Age: 31
Born: 7/19/66 in Kansas City, KS
ML Seasons: 8
Pronunciation: suh-GHEE

Overall Statistics

	G	AB	R	H	D	T	HR	RBI	SB	BB	SO	Avg	OBP	Slg
1997	125	459	75	141	22	3	21	68	1	57	66	.307	.380	.505
Career	849	2641	362	738	144	9	69	351	11	291	320	.279	.350	.419

Where He Hits the Ball

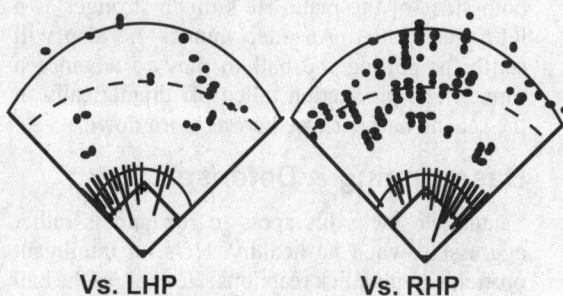

Vs. LHP   **Vs. RHP**

1997 Situational Stats

	AB	H	HR	RBI	Avg		AB	H	HR	RBI	Avg
Home	206	71	10	39	.345	LHP	122	36	5	9	.295
Road	253	70	11	29	.277	RHP	337	105	16	59	.312
First Half	218	70	7	33	.321	Sc Pos	116	30	4	45	.259
Scnd Half	241	71	14	35	.295	Clutch	77	18	2	6	.234

1997 Rankings (National League)

⇒ 5th in batting average on an 0-2 count (.313) and fielding percentage at first base (.995)
⇒ 6th in intentional walks (12)
⇒ 10th in cleanup slugging percentage (.493)
⇒ Led the Expos in batting average, sacrifice flies (6), walks, intentional walks (12), slugging percentage, on-base percentage, batting average vs. righthanded pitchers, batting average on an 0-2 count (.313), cleanup slugging percentage (.493), slugging percentage vs. righthanded pitchers (.519), on-base percentage vs. lefthanded pitchers (.396), on-base percentage vs. righthanded pitchers (.375) and batting average on the road

Ugueth Urbina

1997 Season

Ugueth Urbina did nothing to dissuade those who think he's the next in line to assume the Montreal closer's mantle once held by John Wetteland and Mel Rojas. In his first full season as a closer, Urbina converted 27 of 32 save opportunities and finished with seven saves and two wins in his last 12 appearances. He took the ball whenever it was given to him, no small concern considering that he had surgery while in the winter Venezuelan League to remove loose bodies from his elbow.

Pitching

Urbina has a classic closer's makeup. He comes right at hitters with a high-90s fastball and a nasty slider. He often overmatches righthanders, but he has a great deal of difficulty with lefties because his slider and changeup were ineffective against them. The key to his development is refining his command. His walk rate rose significantly in 1997.

Defense & Hitting

Urbina tends to rush throws at times and has spells where he doesn't pay attention to baserunners, but those are relatively minor problems that can be cured with experience. After toning down his violent delivery, he's now in better position to make a play on balls hit back to him. Urbina can't hit at all, but as a closer he doesn't have to worry about swinging a bat.

1998 Outlook

The Expos made noises about wanting to find another arm in the offseason to take some of the late-inning burden off Urbina. But make no mistake. He'll get the ball in the ninth inning the majority of the time. Urbina's strong second half may be a sign that he's growing more comfortable with his new role. He has the aptitude and the stuff to handle the responsibility. Now that he's smoothed out his mechanics, he may be a star.

Position: RP
Bats: R **Throws:** R
Ht: 6' 2" **Wt:** 185

Opening Day Age: 24
Born: 2/15/74 in Caracas, VZ
ML Seasons: 3
Pronunciation: ooo-GET ur-BEE-nuh

Overall Statistics

	W	L	Pct.	ERA	G	GS	Sv	IP	H	BB	SO	HR	Ratio
1997	5	8	.385	3.78	63	0	27	64.1	52	29	84	9	1.26
Career	17	15	.531	4.02	103	21	27	201.2	180	87	207	33	1.32

How Often He Throws Strikes

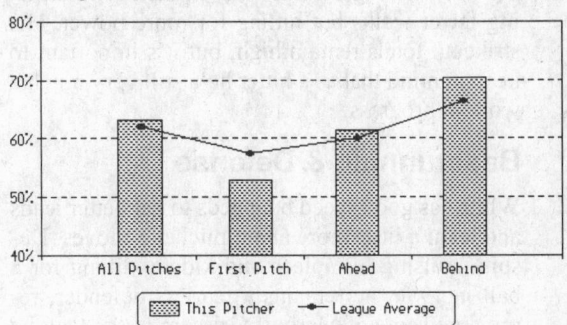

This Pitcher — League Average

1997 Situational Stats

	W	L	ERA	Sv	IP		AB	H	HR	RBI	Avg
Home	5	4	3.38	12	32.0	LHB	103	29	4	17	.282
Road	0	4	4.18	15	32.1	RHB	139	23	5	16	.165
First Half	2	6	4.93	15	34.2	Sc Pos	75	19	4	28	.253
Scnd Half	3	2	2.43	12	29.2	Clutch	183	39	6	27	.213

1997 Rankings (National League)

⇒ 3rd in relief losses (8)
⇒ 4th in save percentage (84.4%)
⇒ 5th in worst first batter efficiency (.339), lowest batting average allowed in relief (.215) and most strikeouts per 9 innings in relief (11.8)
⇒ 9th in lowest batting average allowed in relief with runners on base (.200)
⇒ 10th in games finished (50)
⇒ Led the Expos in saves, games finished (50), save opportunities (32), save percentage (84.4%), blown saves (5), lowest batting average allowed in relief with runners on base (.200), relief losses (8), lowest batting average allowed in relief (.215), least baserunners allowed per 9 innings in relief (11.5) and most strikeouts per 9 innings in relief (11.8)

Montreal Expos

Rondell White

1997 Season

Rondell White took a step forward in 1997, completing the transformation from tablesetter to run producer. His most significant accomplishment was avoiding the injuries that have hampered his career in the past. He put together a healthy season and developed into the kind of power hitter everyone expected him to be.

Hitting

A diligent student of hitting instructor Tommy Harper, White has lightning-quick hands and wrists, and hits with good power to all fields. With his move to the No. 3 spot in the batting order, he became more aggressive early in the count, drawing fewer walks but hitting for more power. His strikeout totals remain high, but it's important to keep in mind that as a hitter he's still very much a work in progress.

Baserunning & Defense

White has good speed but needs to get better leads and learn a little more about pitcher's moves. Despite bruising his spleen and kidney diving for a ball in 1996, he remains a fearless defender, reminding some of Marquis Grissom in the way he tracks down balls hit to deep center. On balls hit over his head, White has learned to turn his back, run to a spot and pick up the ball again. His arm remains the weakest part of his game.

1998 Outlook

White took a major step forward last year and the Expos believe he'll develop into a premier RBI man as he matures. As the only Montreal player to end the 1997 season with a multi-year contract, he's clearly the cornerstone around which the franchise will attempt to rebuild. With Vladimir Guerrero ticketed to hit third, White likely will move to cleanup or fifth in the order. After hitting so well from the No. 3 slot in the order last year, he has convinced the Expos that he can be a top-flight run producer.

Position: CF
Bats: R **Throws:** R
Ht: 6' 1" **Wt:** 205

Opening Day Age: 26
Born: 2/23/72 in Milledgeville, GA
ML Seasons: 5

Overall Statistics

	G	AB	R	H	D	T	HR	RBI	SB	BB	SO	Avg	OBP	Slg
1997	151	592	84	160	29	5	28	82	16	31	111	.270	.316	.478
Career	432	1570	231	444	94	15	51	208	57	110	285	.283	.336	.459

Where He Hits the Ball

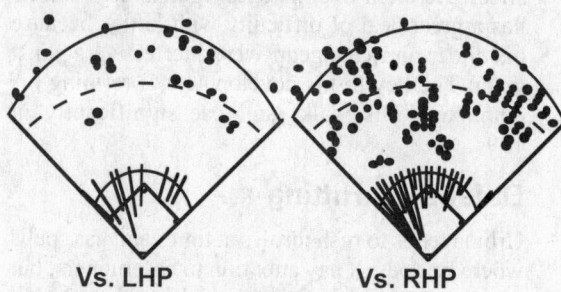

Vs. LHP   **Vs. RHP**

1997 Situational Stats

	AB	H	HR	RBI	Avg		AB	H	HR	RBI	Avg
Home	269	78	9	36	.290	LHP	137	35	10	25	.255
Road	323	82	19	46	.254	RHP	455	125	18	57	.275
First Half	313	83	12	38	.265	Sc Pos	140	29	3	44	.207
Scnd Half	279	77	16	44	.276	Clutch	103	29	7	19	.282

1997 Rankings (National League)

⇒ 1st in fielding percentage in center field (.992)
⇒ 5th in highest groundball/flyball ratio (1.9)
⇒ 7th in GDPs (18) and lowest batting average with runners in scoring position
⇒ 9th in least pitches seen per plate appearance (3.39)
⇒ 10th in lowest on-base percentage vs. lefthanded pitchers (.304)
⇒ Led the Expos in home runs, triples, total bases (283), GDPs (18), highest groundball/flyball ratio (1.9) and slugging percentage vs. lefthanded pitchers (.540)

Chris Widger

1997 Season

After acquiring Chris Widger from Seattle in the Jeff Fassero trade, the Expos decided to let him get used to a new team and new league while not overloading him with too much instruction. His first season in Montreal had mixed results. He was kept busy handling the less experienced members of the pitching staff while showing extra-base potential at the plate.

Hitting

Conventional wisdom held that Widger's defensive game was closer to being ready for the majors than his offensive game. But he showed some extra-base pop and hit well before a late-season slump dragged down his average. He shortened his swing a bit in spring training, but got into trouble during the year when he started to pull off the ball. When he stays on pitches he has enough strength to go to the opposite field. If he's able to do that consistently, his power numbers may improve.

Baserunning & Defense

Widger is no gazelle but moves around the bases well for a catcher and has good awareness when it comes to taking the extra base. There are concerns about his footwork and blocking of pitches, though he was working with many unpolished pitchers in 1997. Widger's defensive stats were unimpressive—no big league catcher had a worst success rate against basestealers than his 13 percent—but he has the tools and arm to be a good defender. He showed he was in need of some refinement in blocking the plate after he often was caught out of position.

1998 Outlook

Widger would have benefited from another year in a quasi-platoon with Darrin Fletcher, but Montreal let Fletcher sign with Toronto. The Expos may try to add a bargain-basement veteran to help with the load, but Widger was acquired at a high price and is expected to take over the starting job.

Position: C
Bats: R **Throws:** R
Ht: 6' 3" **Wt:** 195

Opening Day Age: 26
Born: 5/21/71 in Wilmington, DE
ML Seasons: 3

Overall Statistics

	G	AB	R	H	D	T	HR	RBI	SB	BB	SO	Avg	OBP	Slg
1997	91	278	30	65	20	3	7	37	2	22	59	.234	.290	.403
Career	122	334	33	76	20	3	8	39	2	25	75	.228	.283	.377

Where He Hits the Ball

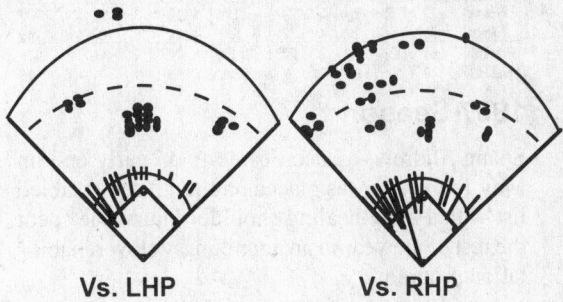

Vs. LHP   **Vs. RHP**

1997 Situational Stats

	AB	H	HR	RBI	Avg		AB	H	HR	RBI	Avg
Home	142	32	4	20	.225	LHP	101	28	4	19	.277
Road	136	33	3	17	.243	RHP	177	37	3	18	.209
First Half	152	41	4	24	.270	Sc Pos	72	24	2	28	.333
Scnd Half	126	24	3	13	.190	Clutch	46	12	1	7	.261

1997 Rankings (National League)

⇒ 1st in lowest percentage of runners caught stealing as a catcher (13.4%)
⇒ 3rd in errors at catcher (11)

Shane Andrews

Position: 3B
Bats: R **Throws:** R
Ht: 6' 1" **Wt:** 215

Opening Day Age: 26
Born: 8/28/71 in
Dallas, TX
ML Seasons: 3
Nickname: Mango

Overall Statistics

	G	AB	R	H	D	T	HR	RBI	SB	BB	SO	Avg	OBP	Slg
1997	18	64	10	13	3	0	4	9	0	3	20	.203	.232	.438
Career	229	659	80	145	28	3	31	104	4	55	207	.220	.281	.413

1997 Situational Stats

	AB	H	HR	RBI	Avg		AB	H	HR	RBI	Avg
Home	29	7	2	5	.241	LHP	10	3	2	4	.300
Road	35	6	2	4	.171	RHP	54	10	2	5	.185
First Half	64	13	4	9	.203	Sc Pos	17	2	0	4	.118
Scnd Half	0	0	0	0		Clutch	8	1	0	0	.125

1997 Season

Shane Andrews' season came to an early end on May 1 when he was placed on the 15-day disabled list with a slow-healing shoulder injury. He spent the rest of the year in an agonizingly slow rehabilitation program.

Hitting, Baserunning & Defense

A notorious free swinger, Andrews has tried to shorten his stroke with decidedly mixed results. He was off to a mediocre start before he was hurt. While he won't make anybody's relay team, he has shown good awareness on the basepaths. He committed six errors in 18 games last year, but if he's healthy he should return to his form of 1996. He made just seven errors from April 27 to the end of that season.

1998 Outlook

Doctors have told Andrews that his injury can take as long as 18 months, so his return date is uncertain. Though he has paid much greater attention to his offseason conditioning in recent years, there's reason to wonder about his response to a prolonged layoff.

Jim Bullinger

Position: SP/RP
Bats: R **Throws:** R
Ht: 6' 2" **Wt:** 190

Opening Day Age: 32
Born: 8/21/65 in New
Orleans, LA
ML Seasons: 6

Overall Statistics

	W	L	Pct.	ERA	G	GS	Sv	IP	H	BB	SO	HR	Ratio
1997	7	12	.368	5.56	36	25	0	155.1	165	74	87	17	1.54
Career	34	40	.459	4.96	184	88	11	636.1	638	304	388	62	1.48

1997 Situational Stats

	W	L	ERA	Sv	IP		AB	H	HR	RBI	Avg
Home	4	4	4.96	0	78.0	LHB	283	75	7	44	.265
Road	3	8	6.17	0	77.1	RHB	314	90	10	45	.287
First Half	5	8	5.77	0	101.1	Sc Pos	169	46	2	64	.272
Scnd Half	2	4	5.17	0	54.0	Clutch	59	12	2	6	.203

1997 Season

Signed as a free agent over the winter, Jim Bullinger went 6-12, 5.68 in 25 starts before he was demoted to the bullpen August 12. He pitched better in relief, but still wasn't terribly effective. He was unable to hold a spot in the rotation and didn't prove useful in relief for the second straight year, which doesn't bode well for his career.

Pitching, Defense & Hitting

In spring training, Bullinger appeared to have corrected a mechanical flaw that had robbed his fastball of its sink. But as his innings increased, his pitches stayed higher in the zone and he often showed his frustration on the mound. He's a fine fielder who never has committed an error, but his slowness to the plate makes him easy pickings for baserunners, who often steal on him. A converted minor league shortstop, Bullinger was once again one of the best-hitting pitchers in the majors.

1998 Outlook

Though Bullinger hasn't set the world on fire as a reliever, his ERA out of the bullpen has been much better than his ERA as a starter the last two seasons. He prefers to start, but there's no saying when he'll be given another chance to do it. He's a free agent, and his future role will depend on the team that signs him.

Mike Johnson

Position: SP/RP
Bats: L **Throws:** R
Ht: 6' 2" **Wt:** 175

Opening Day Age: 22
Born: 10/3/75 in Edmonton, Canada
ML Seasons: 1

Overall Statistics

	W	L	Pct.	ERA	G	GS	Sv	IP	H	BB	SO	HR	Ratio
1997	2	6	.250	6.83	25	16	2	89.2	106	37	57	20	1.59
Career	2	6	.250	6.83	25	16	2	89.2	106	37	57	20	1.59

1997 Situational Stats

	W	L	ERA	Sv	IP		AB	H	HR	RBI	Avg
Home	2	1	4.62	2	48.2	LHB	194	64	10	38	.330
Road	0	5	9.44	0	41.0	RHB	165	42	10	26	.255
First Half	0	1	8.23	2	35.0	Sc Pos	93	27	4	42	.290
Scnd Half	2	5	5.93	0	54.2	Clutch	2	1	1	1	.500

1997 Season

Mike Johnson was selected out of the Blue Jays organization by the Giants as a major league Rule 5 draft choice at the Winter Meetings. San Francisco traded him to the Orioles, who sent him to the Expos at the trade deadline. He made 11 starts and impressed Montreal with his poise, though he was hit.

Pitching, Defense & Hitting

Like fellow Canadian Jason Dickson of the Angels, Johnson throws a curveball, but he's nowhere near as polished. Still, he made the jump to the majors all the way from Class-A, and he held his own considering his inexperience. He showed deceptive arm action with his changeup and will take the next step forward when he develops better command of his fastball. He's a decent fielder because of his poise, but he hasn't had much of a chance to work on his hitting.

1998 Outlook

Johnson has an outside shot at a regular spot in the rotation, but the Expos would prefer to see him open the year at Triple-A Ottawa or Double-A Harrisburg. That way he could mature physically while working on his command.

Joe Orsulak

Position: LF/1B/RF
Bats: L **Throws:** L
Ht: 6' 1" **Wt:** 205

Opening Day Age: 35
Born: 5/31/62 in Glen Ridge, NJ
ML Seasons: 14
Pronunciation: ORR-suh-lack

Overall Statistics

	G	AB	R	H	D	T	HR	RBI	SB	BB	SO	Avg	OBP	Slg
1997	106	150	13	34	12	1	1	7	0	18	17	.227	.310	.340
Career	1494	4293	559	1173	186	37	57	405	93	318	402	.273	.324	.374

1997 Situational Stats

	AB	H	HR	RBI	Avg		AB	H	HR	RBI	Avg
Home	81	16	0	4	.198	LHP	14	0	0	1	.000
Road	69	18	1	3	.261	RHP	136	34	1	6	.250
First Half	103	24	1	7	.233	Sc Pos	32	2	1	7	.063
Scnd Half	47	10	0	0	.213	Clutch	32	8	0	0	.250

1997 Season

Joe Orsulak was picked up at the end of spring training as part of the deal that saw Dustin Hermanson join the Expos in return for Cliff Floyd. The Marlins agreed to pay most of Orsulak's salary, which is the only way a cost-conscious outfit like Montreal could keep a player with his experience all season.

Hitting, Baserunning & Defense

Orsulak's role was limited, but he still showed the things a manager likes out of a veteran. He has a decent eye at the plate and an ability to put the ball in play to all fields. Not much of a threat on the basepaths, Orsulak made 30 starts at three different positions (11 at first base, five in left field and 14 in right) and his moxie was evident at each spot. He still has one of the better outfield arms in the game.

1998 Outlook

A free agent, Orsulak is well respected by his peers and understands what it means to be a role player. Chances are some team will be able to use his lefty bat and experience.

Andy Stankiewicz

Position: 2B/SS
Bats: R **Throws:** R
Ht: 5' 9" **Wt:** 165

Opening Day Age: 33
Born: 8/10/64 in Inglewood, CA
ML Seasons: 6
Pronunciation: STANK-eh-wits

Overall Statistics

	G	AB	R	H	D	T	HR	RBI	SB	BB	SO	Avg	OBP	Slg
1997	76	107	11	24	9	0	1	5	1	4	22	.224	.250	.336
Career	352	699	96	173	40	3	4	51	16	73	108	.247	.325	.330

1997 Situational Stats

	AB	H	HR	RBI	Avg		AB	H	HR	RBI	Avg
Home	53	13	0	3	.245	LHP	35	6	1	3	.171
Road	54	11	1	2	.204	RHP	72	18	0	2	.250
First Half	49	14	0	2	.286	Sc Pos	21	2	0	4	.095
Scnd Half	58	10	1	3	.172	Clutch	26	2	1	2	.077

1997 Season

Andy Stankiewicz served as the Expos' backup middle infielder for the second straight season. Good health by second baseman Mike Lansing and shortstop Mark Grudzielanek limited Stankiewicz' opportunities, as had been the case in 1996 as well.

Hitting, Baserunning & Defense

Stankiewicz doesn't have much pop in his bat and prefers to concentrate on putting the ball in play, but he still struck out 22 times and drew just four walks in 107 at-bats. He was just 5-for-30 as a pinch hitter after going 9-for-29 in 1996, and had trouble catching up with good fastballs. An adept bunter who isn't a threat to steal, he appeared to lose a little range in the field. Still, his overall fundamentals and toughness mean that he won't be a defensive liability.

1998 Outlook

Stankiewicz has committed himself to a strong offseason aerobic program and keeps himself in tremendous physical condition. The prototypical utilityman, he should be able to win a bench job elsewhere if he loses his spot with the Expos.

Doug Strange

Position: 3B
Bats: B **Throws:** R
Ht: 6' 1" **Wt:** 185

Opening Day Age: 33
Born: 4/13/64 in Greenville, SC
ML Seasons: 8

Overall Statistics

	G	AB	R	H	D	T	HR	RBI	SB	BB	SO	Avg	OBP	Slg
1997	118	327	40	84	16	2	12	47	0	36	76	.257	.332	.428
Career	617	1674	185	402	79	7	31	197	13	145	291	.240	.304	.351

1997 Situational Stats

	AB	H	HR	RBI	Avg		AB	H	HR	RBI	Avg
Home	190	51	6	26	.268	LHP	112	28	0	8	.250
Road	137	33	6	21	.241	RHP	215	56	12	39	.260
First Half	162	48	4	23	.296	Sc Pos	82	25	3	33	.305
Scnd Half	165	36	8	24	.218	Clutch	66	16	3	12	.242

1997 Season

Looked upon as a switch-hitting bench player entering the season, Doug Strange found himself the closest thing the Expos had to a regular third baseman after a season-ending injury to Shane Andrews. Strange almost doubled his previous career high in home runs, and by the end of the year manager Felipe Alou was lobbying the team to re-sign him.

Hitting, Baserunning & Defense

Strange always has hit righthanders better than lefties, and in 1997 almost all of his extra-base hits came from the left side. His lefty swing is noticeably shorter than his righty stroke, but Alou had enough confidence to let him bat 112 times from the right side. Slow on the basepaths, Strange showed passable range and a strong throwing arm at third base. He also can play second base and the outfield.

1998 Outlook

The Expos were pleasantly surprised by Strange. He signed a two-year contract with the Pirates and could start for Pittsburgh in 1998.

Anthony Telford

Position: RP
Bats: R **Throws:** R
Ht: 6' 0" **Wt:** 184

Opening Day Age: 32
Born: 3/6/66 in San Jose, CA
ML Seasons: 4

Overall Statistics

	W	L	Pct.	ERA	G	GS	Sv	IP	H	BB	SO	HR	Ratio
1997	4	6	.400	3.24	65	0	1	89.0	77	33	61	11	1.24
Career	7	9	.438	4.07	85	9	1	159.1	158	59	111	21	1.36

1997 Situational Stats

	W	L	ERA	Sv	IP		AB	H	HR	RBI	Avg
Home	2	2	2.90	1	49.2	LHB	138	32	5	15	.232
Road	2	4	3.66	0	39.1	RHB	188	45	6	24	.239
First Half	2	2	2.49	0	47.0	Sc Pos	93	24	0	26	.258
Scnd Half	2	4	4.07	1	42.0	Clutch	130	34	7	18	.262

1997 Season

Anthony Telford had spent the previous three seasons kicking around the minor leagues before staking a claim to a middle-relief job in Montreal with a strong spring training. He finished the year with a team-high 65 appearances and 89 innings in relief, and had become the Expos' primary setup man. He hadn't won a major league game in seven years, then racked up four victories.

Pitching, Defense & Hitting

Telford developed a cut fastball after the 1996 season. It's thrown hard, has a late break and allows him to jam lefthanded hitters. He fields his position decently, but there were times when he appeared tentative throwing the ball to the bases. Opponents stole eight bases in 11 attempts, though that success rate was better against other Montreal pitchers. He's seldom asked to hit and hasn't proven he can get a bunt down.

1998 Outlook

Since he came out of nowhere at 31 and threw a large number of innings in 1997, there's concern about how well Telford's arm will survive the wear and tear. He tired noticeably toward the end of the season, but didn't appear to have lost manager Felipe Alou's confidence.

Marc Valdes

Position: RP/SP
Bats: R **Throws:** R
Ht: 6' 0" **Wt:** 187

Opening Day Age: 26
Born: 12/20/71 in Dayton, OH
ML Seasons: 3

Overall Statistics

	W	L	Pct.	ERA	G	GS	Sv	IP	H	BB	SO	HR	Ratio
1997	4	4	.500	3.13	48	7	2	95.0	84	39	54	2	1.29
Career	5	7	.417	4.18	62	18	2	150.2	164	71	69	8	1.56

1997 Situational Stats

	W	L	ERA	Sv	IP		AB	H	HR	RBI	Avg
Home	2	3	3.76	1	38.1	LHB	136	34	1	13	.250
Road	2	1	2.70	1	56.2	RHB	214	50	1	24	.234
First Half	3	2	3.79	1	38.0	Sc Pos	109	18	0	34	.165
Scnd Half	1	2	2.68	1	57.0	Clutch	43	12	0	-7	.279

1997 Season

The Expos claimed Marc Valdes on waivers from the Marlins over the winter. The one-time first-round pick became an effective and versatile pitcher for Montreal. He eventually found himself in the starting rotation and pitched well in that role during September.

Pitching, Defense & Hitting

Valdes' best pitch is a sinking fastball. When it's on, it makes his slider more effective because hitters tend to be overly aware of the sinker's motion. He needs to improve the arm action on his changeup to round out his repertoire. He fields his position well, but can become careless with men on base. He doesn't handle the bat especially well and hasn't laid down a single sacrifice in his career.

1998 Outlook

The Expos, who face major economic restraints, would like Valdes to begin the season as one of their starters. If he isn't able to do that, he showed enough resiliency in 1997 to assume a responsible role in middle relief.

Montreal Expos

Dave Veres

Position: RP
Bats: R **Throws:** R
Ht: 6' 2" **Wt:** 195

Opening Day Age: 31
Born: 10/19/66 in Montgomery, AL
ML Seasons: 4
Pronunciation: VEER-ez

Overall Statistics

	W	L	Pct.	ERA	G	GS	Sv	IP	H	BB	SO	HR	Ratio
1997	2	3	.400	3.48	53	0	1	62.0	68	27	47	5	1.53
Career	16	10	.615	3.07	225	0	7	284.0	281	96	250	24	1.33

1997 Situational Stats

	W	L	ERA	Sv	IP		AB	H	HR	RBI	Avg
Home	1	1	4.10	0	26.1	LHB	106	31	2	12	.292
Road	1	1	3.03	1	35.2	RHB	139	37	3	18	.266
First Half	2	2	3.14	1	43.0	Sc Pos	74	15	1	25	.203
Scnd Half	0	1	4.26	0	19.0	Clutch	115	29	1	17	.252

1997 Season

With the departure of Mel Rojas to free agency and the burden of the closer's role falling full time on Ugueth Urbina, Dave Veres might have been expected to pick up some additional work as a short reliever. But for the second consecutive season, he was unable to fill the role. He pitched just 19 innings in the second half, when he was bothered by shoulder tightness and knee inflammation.

Pitching, Defense & Hitting

Veres, who throws a split-fingered fastball and slider, saw his strikeout total fall sharply last year. The main problem was a lack of command. When he's on, he can get hitters to chase his splitter in the dirt. In the field, he's not tough to run on and he's sometimes slow to react on balls hit back through the box. He gets little opportunity to bat, but he has done well in his few at-bats.

1998 Outlook

After two seasons of inconsistency from Veres, the Expos may look elsewhere for middle relief in 1998. He had minor arthroscopic sugery after the year to clear out loose bodies from his right knee. He likely will wind up in someone else's bullpen.

Jose Vidro

Position: 3B
Bats: B **Throws:** R
Ht: 6' 0" **Wt:** 185

Opening Day Age: 23
Born: 8/27/74 in Mayaguez, Puerto Rico
ML Seasons: 1
Pronunciation: VEE-dro

Overall Statistics

	G	AB	R	H	D	T	HR	RBI	SB	BB	SO	Avg	OBP	Slg
1997	67	169	19	42	12	1	2	17	1	11	20	.249	.297	.367
Career	67	169	19	42	12	1	2	17	1	11	20	.249	.297	.367

1997 Situational Stats

	AB	H	HR	RBI	Avg		AB	H	HR	RBI	Avg
Home	62	14	0	7	.226	LHP	47	10	0	3	.213
Road	107	28	2	10	.262	RHP	122	32	2	14	.262
First Half	23	3	0	1	.130	Sc Pos	34	9	1	16	.265
Scnd Half	146	39	2	16	.267	Clutch	41	15	2	11	.366

1997 Season

Young switch-hitting infielder Jose Vidro started the year at Triple-A and was promoted briefly in June. He came up for good in July and showed enough to finish the year with 30 starts at third base and a few more at second base and designated hitter.

Hitting, Baserunning & Defense

Vidro has what manager Felipe Alou calls a base-hit swing, especially from the left side of the plate. It's compact and well balanced, thanks to quick hands and wrists that help him generate extra-base power. Vidro was especially strong off the bench, going 9-for-20 as a pinch hitter. He doesn't run much. He has the arm strength to play third base and reacts well to balls down the line.

1998 Outlook

Vidro is a candidate for a utility job. With a strong spring training, he could threaten for a regular turn at third base. He has played second, but may not have enough lateral quickness to do so on a regular basis in the majors.

Other Montreal Expos

Raul Chavez (**Pos**: C, **Age**: 25, **Bats**: R)

	G	AB	R	H	D	T	HR	RBI	SB	BB	SO	Avg	OBP	Slg
1997	13	26	0	7	0	0	0	2	1	0	5	.269	.259	.269
Career	17	31	1	8	0	0	0	2	2	1	6	.258	.273	.258

Defensive specialist Raul Chavez got a brief look with the Expos in September. He's young but hasn't hit enough to deserve a longer look. 1998 Outlook: C

Rheal Cormier (**Pos**: LHP, **Age**: 30)

	W	L	Pct.	ERA	G	GS	Sv	IP	H	BB	SO	HR	Ratio
1997	0	1	.000	33.75	1	1	0	1.1	4	1	0	1	3.75
Career	38	39	.494	4.18	169	108	0	714.2	771	148	425	73	1.29

Cormier got bombed in his first start of the '97 season, and missed the rest of the year after undergoing Tommy John surgery. He is the first Canadian-born player to undergo the procedure. 1998 Outlook: B

Rick DeHart (**Pos**: LHP, **Age**: 28)

	W	L	Pct.	ERA	G	GS	Sv	IP	H	BB	SO	HR	Ratio
1997	2	1	.667	5.52	23	0	0	29.1	33	14	29	7	1.60
Career	2	1	.667	5.52	23	0	0	29.1	33	14	29	7	1.60

The Expos called up throwaway lefty Rick DeHart in the second half last year. His control is decent, but he was hit hard, and at age 28, he's no coming star. 1998 Outlook: C

Steve Falteisek (**Pos**: RHP, **Age**: 26)

	W	L	Pct.	ERA	G	GS	Sv	IP	H	BB	SO	HR	Ratio
1997	0	0	-	3.38	5	0	0	8.0	8	3	2	0	1.38
Career	0	0	-	3.38	5	0	0	8.0	8	3	2	0	1.38

Once a decent prospect, Steve Falteisek's strikeout rate dropped precipitously last year. He may have been worked too hard early in his career. Don't expect much. 1998 Outlook: C

Steve Kline (**Pos**: LHP, **Age**: 25)

	W	L	Pct.	ERA	G	GS	Sv	IP	H	BB	SO	HR	Ratio
1997	4	4	.500	5.98	46	1	0	52.2	73	23	37	10	1.82
Career	4	4	.500	5.98	46	1	0	52.2	73	23	37	10	1.82

The best return the Expos were able to get for Jeff Juden was this guy. He actually pitched well out of the Mont-real bullpen late in the year and could surprise. 1998 Outlook: B

Hensley Meulens (**Pos**: LF, **Age**: 30, **Bats**: R)

	G	AB	R	H	D	T	HR	RBI	SB	BB	SO	Avg	OBP	Slg
1997	16	24	6	7	1	0	2	6	0	4	10	.292	.379	.583
Career	175	481	66	108	17	2	14	52	4	42	159	.225	.295	.356

A man claiming to be Hensley Meulens signed on with the Expos' Triple-A team last year. In order to dispel suspicion, he adopted Meulens' on-field persona, hitting well enough to merit only a brief call-up. 1998 Outlook: C

Sherman Obando (**Pos**: RF, **Age**: 28, **Bats**: R)

	G	AB	R	H	D	T	HR	RBI	SB	BB	SO	Avg	OBP	Slg
1997	41	47	3	6	1	0	2	9	0	6	14	.128	.241	.277
Career	177	355	41	85	13	0	13	49	3	34	100	.239	.310	.386

Obando was left to rot on the Expos' bench for the entire 1997 season. When the season ended, he got up and went home. The Expos offered him a minor league contract, but he became a free agent instead. 1998 Outlook: C

Lee Smith (**Pos**: RHP, **Age**: 40)

	W	L	Pct.	ERA	G	GS	Sv	IP	H	BB	SO	HR	Ratio
1997	0	1	.000	5.82	25	0	5	21.2	28	8	15	2	1.66
Career	71	92	.436	3.03	1022	6	478	1289.1	1133	486	1251	89	1.26

Smith saved five more games to run his all-time-record career total to 478. Then he moseyed off into the sunset. 1998 Outlook: D

Salomon Torres (**Pos**: RHP, **Age**: 26)

	W	L	Pct.	ERA	G	GS	Sv	IP	H	BB	SO	HR	Ratio
1997	0	0	-	9.82	14	0	0	25.2	32	15	11	2	1.83
Career	11	25	.306	5.71	68	43	0	283.2	308	148	159	38	1.61

Torres' wanderings took him to Montreal last year. The Expos traded for him in hopes that Felipe Alou could turn him around, but Torres announced his retirement and it's unclear whether he'll return. 1998 Outlook: C

Montreal Expos Minor League Prospects

Organization Overview:

The only reason the penny-pinching Expos haven't become a complete joke is their farm system. While the organization isn't as strong as it was in the early 1990s, it still produces talent for Montreal—and the rest of baseball. Last September, the starting lineup and key pitchers were all either homegrown Expos or products of trades designed to save money, with the exception of first baseman David Segui. Most of Montreal's next wave of talent needs another half-year to year in the minors, so the Expos really are hurting after trading ace Pedro Martinez and second baseman Mike Lansing. The development staff and manager Felipe Alou always seem to work some magic, though it gets harder every year.

Michael Barrett

Position: C **Opening Day Age:** 21
Bats: R **Throws:** R **Born:** 10/22/76 in
Ht: 6' 3" **Wt:** 185 Atlanta, GA

Recent Statistics

	G	AB	R	H	D	T	HR	RBI	SB	BB	SO	AVG
96 A Delmarva	129	474	57	113	29	4	4	62	5	18	42	.238
97 A Wst Plm Bch	119	423	52	120	30	0	8	61	7	36	49	.284

Barrett never had caught before he was a first-round pick in 1995, but the Expos quickly moved him from shortstop to behind the plate. His arm strength was the reason for the move, and his receiving skills are improving. He was offensively challenged in 1996, when he spent his first full year as a catcher, but he raised his average 46 points last season. He has gap power and could provide 10-15 homers per year once he fills out. He makes good contact, is developing more patience at the plate and runs well for a catcher. Barrett is at least two years away from Montreal.

Hiram Bocachica

Position: SS **Opening Day Age:** 22
Bats: R **Throws:** R **Born:** 3/4/76 in Ponce,
Ht: 5' 11" **Wt:** 165 PR

Recent Statistics

	G	AB	R	H	D	T	HR	RBI	SB	BB	SO	AVG
96 R Expos	9	32	11	8	3	0	0	2	2	5	3	.250
96 A Wst Plm Bch	71	267	50	90	17	5	2	26	21	34	47	.337
97 AA Harrisburg	119	443	82	123	19	3	11	35	29	41	98	.278
97 MLE	119	427	64	107	18	2	7	27	20	28	104	.251

Though he is a shortstop for now, Bocachica could wind up as Lansing's successor at second base. He has had elbow and shoulder problems the last two seasons, though his arm is considered one of his strengths. He has been error-prone throughout his career, and made 27 errors in 57 games at short in 1997. A 1994 first-round pick, his offensive skills are his main ticket, as he has a quick bat, gap power and first-step quickness. He'll make a good leadoff hitter if he makes more contact and draws more walks. Promoting him at the start of 1998 might be rushing things a bit.

Orlando Cabrera

Position: SS **Opening Day Age:** 23
Bats: R **Throws:** R **Born:** 11/2/74 in
Ht: 5' 11" **Wt:** 165 Cartagena, Bolivar,
Columbia

Recent Statistics

	G	AB	R	H	D	T	HR	RBI	SB	BB	SO	AVG
97 A Wst Plm Bch	69	279	56	77	19	2	5	26	32	27	33	.276
97 AA Harrisburg	35	133	34	41	13	2	5	20	7	15	18	.308
97 AAA Ottawa	31	122	17	32	5	2	2	14	8	7	16	.262
97 NL Montreal	16	18	4	4	0	0	0	2	1	1	3	.222
97 MLE	66	245	38	63	16	2	4	25	10	15	35	.257

When Cabrera and Bocachica were both at Double-A Harrisburg, it was Cabrera who played shortstop. He doesn't have Bocachica's arm, but he's a much smoother shortstop. Signed out of Columbia, he jumped from Class A to the majors in 1997. he doesn't have the strength of Bocachica, but he has surprising pop for a 5-foot-9, 150-pounder and runs well. It probably won't be long before Mark Grudzielanek becomes too expensive for Montreal, and Cabrera is the heir apparent. He may be the Expos' starting second baseman after the Lansing trade.

Brad Fullmer

Position: 1B **Opening Day Age:** 23
Bats: L **Throws:** R **Born:** 1/17/75 in Los
Ht: 6' 1" **Wt:** 185 Angeles, CA

Recent Statistics

	G	AB	R	H	D	T	HR	RBI	SB	BB	SO	AVG
97 AA Harrisburg	94	357	60	111	24	2	19	62	6	30	25	.311
97 AAA Ottawa	24	91	13	27	7	0	3	17	1	3	10	.297
97 NL Montreal	19	40	4	12	2	0	3	8	0	2	7	.300
97 MLE	118	431	56	121	28	1	16	61	4	22	36	.281

Fullmer is Montreal's next big prospect, and he heralded his arrival in the big leagues with a homer in his first at-bat. A 1993 second-round pick, he missed his first season with a shoulder injury. He hasn't been much of a defensive player since his return, bouncing from third base to left field to first base, but he has enough bat to play anywhere. He's a polished line-drive hitter who began to develop home-run power in 1997. His ceiling is higher than that of Ryan McGuire, who had his moments with the Expos last season. Fullmer's development makes David Segui expendable, which will save Montreal even more money.

Bob Henley

Position: C
Bats: R **Throws:** R
Ht: 6' 2" **Wt:** 190

Opening Day Age: 25
Born: 1/30/73 in Mobile, AL

Recent Statistics

	G	AB	R	H	D	T	HR	RBI	SB	BB	SO	AVG
96 AA Harrisburg	103	289	33	66	12	1	3	27	1	70	78	.228
97 AA Harrisburg	79	280	41	85	19	0	12	49	5	32	40	.304
97 MLE	79	269	32	74	18	0	8	38	3	22	42	.275

Signed as a draft-and-follow after being a 26th-round pick in the 1991 draft, Henley made consistent progress until a poor offensive season at Double-A Harrisburg in 1996. He rebounded in the Arizona Fall League during the offseason, and had a nice year with the bat in his second shot at Double-A. He's still more of a catch-and-throw guy than an offensive player, but he has gotten stronger. He missed most of the second half after taking a knee in the head during a rundown, which gave him a severe concussion. He needs a full year of Triple-A before he's ready to challenge Chris Widger.

Carl Pavano

Position: P
Bats: R **Throws:** R
Ht: 6' 5" **Wt:** 230

Opening Day Age: 22
Born: 1/8/76 in New Britain, CT

Recent Statistics

	W	L	ERA	G	GS	Sv	IP	H	R	BB	SO	HR
96 AA Trenton	16	5	2.63	27	26	0	185.0	154	66	47	146	16
97 AAA Pawtucket	11	6	3.12	23	23	0	161.2	148	62	34	147	13

When the Expos decided to trade Pedro Martinez, they got Pavano, one of the best pitching prospects in the minors, and a player to be named. A 13th-round pick in 1994, he had middling success in his first two years as a pro. Then he toned his body in the offseason and broke through as the 1996 Eastern League pitcher of the year. In 1997, managers chose him as the International League's top prospect. Pavano overcame a spring-training bout with biceps tendinitis to show a 91-94 MPH fastball that he's not afraid to throw inside, as well as a hard slider and good changeup. He should be a workhorse starter at the front of Montreal's rotation.

Mike Thurman

Position: P
Bats: R **Throws:** R
Ht: 6' 5" **Wt:** 190

Opening Day Age: 24
Born: 7/22/73 in Corvallis, OR

Recent Statistics

	W	L	ERA	G	GS	Sv	IP	H	R	BB	SO	HR
97 AA Harrisburg	9	6	3.81	20	20	0	115.2	102	54	30	85	16
97 AAA Ottawa	1	3	5.49	4	4	0	19.2	17	13	9	15	1
97 NL Montreal	1	0	5.40	5	2	0	11.2	8	9	4	8	3

Thurman was a supplemental first-round pick out of Oregon State in 1994, and has battled nagging injuries ever since. He missed most of his first summer with

shoulder tendinitis, and arthroscopic surgery cost him the first month of 1995. He had some elbow soreness in 1997, which took some of the shine off his performance in Double-A. His stuff is fairly average, but he mixes a fastball, curve and changeup to keep hitters off balance. Because of his elbow and his lackluster Triple-A stint, the Expos probably will bring him along slowly.

Javier Vazquez

Position: P
Bats: R **Throws:** R
Ht: 6' 2" **Wt:** 175

Opening Day Age: 21
Born: 6/25/76 in Ponce, PR

Recent Statistics

	W	L	ERA	G	GS	Sv	IP	H	R	BB	SO	HR
96 A Delmarva	14	3	2.68	27	27	0	164.1	138	64	57	173	12
97 A Wst Plm Bch	6	3	2.16	19	19	0	112.2	98	40	28	100	8
97 AA Harrisburg	4	0	1.07	6	6	0	42.0	15	5	12	47	2

Vazquez has enjoyed plenty of success the last two seasons, leading Expo farmhands in wins and strikeouts in 1996 and topping the entire minors in ERA in 1997. A fifth-round pick in 1994, he has a deep repertoire. He throws a fastball in the low 90s with good movement, but his changeup is a better pitch. For a breaking ball he can turn to either a slider or a curve, and he tightened the latter last season. He has command of all his pitches, as evidenced by his fine hits/innings and strikeouts/walks ratios. He's the best pitching prospect in the system and could advance rapidly.

Others to Watch

25-year-old righthanders **Shayne Bennett** and **Ben Fleetham** combined for 47 saves at the upper levels of the system, but both project as setup men in the major leagues. Bennett's best pitch is a slider, while Fleetham's is a splitter. Both have average fastballs and better moxie. . . Both 20-year-old righthanders acquired from Colorado in the Mike Lansing trade are legitimate prospects. **John Nicholson** has very good command, and his curveball and top-notch changeup are better than his average fastball at this point. **Jake Westbrook** throws a mediocre fastball with good sinking action, and he has an advanced slider and changeup. . . Righthander **Jeremy Powell** already has decent command of three pitches at 21. At 6-foot-6 and 225 pounds, he projects to add a lot of velocity to his fastball. . . **Jon Saffer** is a serviceable left fielder who batted .267 with 15 homers at Triple-A Ottawa. He's 24 and probably more of a platoon player or a reserve, but he does have a useful lefthanded bat. . . Remember first baseman **Fernando Seguignol**, the player acquired from the Yankees in the John Wetteland "trade"? He broke out with 18 homers in the FSL at age 22, nearly as many as he hit in his first two years in the system.

Bobby Valentine

1997 Season

There are few managers more unpopular among opponents than Bobby Valentine. But even the sharpest critics of Valentine's oversized ego would acknowledge that he did an outstanding job in keeping the unheralded Mets in wild-card contention. Valentine won over most of the Mets with his upbeat personality and his ability to put players in situations where they had the best chance of succeeding. However, all was not rosy. Many of his players were aghast at Valentine's inexplicable suggestion that Todd Hundley's lifestyle had a negative effect on his performance. Valentine's harsh handling of Pete Harnisch blew up in an ugly confrontation that led to the pitcher's trade to Milwaukee.

Offense

Valentine is judicious about putting runners into motion, a reflection of his personnel. He doesn't like to give up outs, eschewing the bunt in 1997 more than any National League manager except for St. Louis' Tony La Russa. With the steady improvement of his pitching staff, Valentine showed a tendency to play conservatively for early runs. He was willing to platoon at times when it made sense to ride a particularly hot hand.

Pitching & Defense

Valentine and pitching coach Bob Apodoca got the maximum effort from a rotation of largely underappreciated starters. Valentine had faith in retreads like Rick Reed and Dave Mlicki, and that confidence paid off. For much of the season, the bullpen was a work in progress behind closer John Franco. Valentine shows little hesitation in trying pitchers in different roles, hoping to find the right combination.

1998 Outlook

Valentine is firmly in charge of the Mets. Following the departure of GM Joe McIlvaine, few managers have more influence over their club's personnel decisions than Valentine will have in the coming years. He'll have a chance to build a team to his liking. If he can keep his ego out of the way he's smart enough to help build a winner.

Born: 5/13/50 in Stamford, CT

Playing Experience: 1969-1979, LA, Ana, SD, NYN, Sea

Managerial Experience: 10 seasons

Manager Statistics

Year	Team, Lg	W	L	Pct	GB	Finish
1997	New York, NL	88	74	.543	13.0	3rd East
10 Seasons		681	698	.494	—	—

1997 Starting Pitchers by Days Rest

	≤3	4	5	6+
Mets Starts	2	77	45	27
Mets ERA	3.21	3.65	4.57	3.96
NL Avg Starts	3	90	38	22
NL ERA	4.23	4.05	4.27	4.52

1997 Situational Stats

	Bobby Valentine	NL Average
Hit & Run Success %	45.0	36.4
Stolen Base Success %	56.7	68.4
Platoon Pct.	61.9	56.3
Defensive Subs	23	26
High-Pitch Outings	4	12
Quick/Slow Hooks	16/12	18/10
Sacrifice Attempts	78	96

1997 Rankings (National League)

⇒ 1st in pinch hitters used (313)
⇒ 2nd in hit-and-run percentage (45.0%) and saves with over 1 inning pitched (11)
⇒ 3rd in squeeze plays (11) and starting lineups used (131)

Edgardo Alfonzo

1997 Season

After two mediocre seasons, Edgardo Alfonzo established himself as one of the rising stars in baseball in 1997. After a 2-for-23 start, Alfonso batted .325 over the rest of the season. The only negative was a hamstring injury that cost him a week of playing time. Alfonzo also was one of baseball's best clutch hitters, batting .417 with men in scoring position and .600 with the bases loaded.

Hitting

Alfonzo employs a rare blend of aggressiveness and pitch selection at the plate. He has learned in his brief experience how to take his share of walks. However, he's first and foremost a hacker and can slash balls to all fields for extra bases. His home-run power is still developing, but he already is one of the National League's better fastball hitters and can take good changeups and breaking pitches up the middle. He hit .378 against lefthanders and .292 against righties, and figures to keep getting better.

Baserunning & Defense

The one area of Alfonzo's game which isn't star quality is baserunning. He makes up for his average speed with hustle and smarts. He still had 11 steals and showed an affinity for taking the extra base. After playing well at second in past years, he found a home at the hot corner. Many opposing teams considered him the best-fielding third baseman in the National League. His arm is outstanding, and he's capable of making spectacular plays with his quickness and great hands. He also filled in at shortstop, his position in the minors, when Rey Ordonez was hurt.

1998 Outlook

The sky's the limit for Alfonzo, a model worker with plenty of talent. He should develop into a 20-homer, 90-RBI player this year and has all the tools to become one of the NL's stars into the next century.

Position: 3B/SS
Bats: R **Throws:** R
Ht: 5'11" **Wt:** 187

Opening Day Age: 24
Born: 11/8/73 in St. Teresa, VZ
ML Seasons: 3

Overall Statistics

	G	AB	R	H	D	T	HR	RBI	SB	BB	SO	Avg	OBP	Slg
1997	151	518	84	163	27	2	10	72	11	63	56	.315	.391	.432
Career	375	1221	146	352	55	9	18	153	14	100	149	.288	.342	.392

Where He Hits the Ball

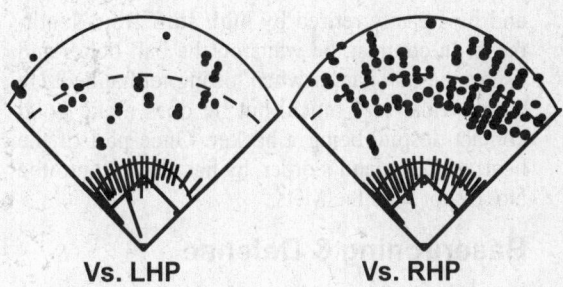

Vs. LHP   **Vs. RHP**

1997 Situational Stats

	AB	H	HR	RBI	Avg		AB	H	HR	RBI	Avg
Home	248	81	4	42	.327	LHP	135	51	4	27	.378
Road	270	82	6	30	.304	RHP	383	112	6	45	.292
First Half	260	85	6	37	.327	Sc Pos	115	48	4	60	.417
Scnd Half	258	78	4	35	.302	Clutch	94	34	2	18	.362

1997 Rankings (National League)

⇒ 2nd in batting average with runners in scoring position, batting average with the bases loaded (.600), batting average vs. lefthanded pitchers and on-base percentage vs. lefthanded pitchers (.448)

⇒ 3rd in fielding percentage at third base (.967)

⇒ Led the Mets in batting average, hits, singles, highest groundball/flyball ratio (1.2), least GDPs per GDP situation (3.7%), batting average with runners in scoring position, batting average in the clutch, batting average with the bases loaded (.600), batting average vs. lefthanded pitchers, on-base percentage vs. lefthanded pitchers (.448), batting average at home, batting average on the road and batting average with two strikes (.267)

Carlos Baerga

1997 Season

After an awful 1996 season, it looked like more of the same for Carlos Baerga when he hit .188 in April. Then, like the rest of the Mets, he turned himself around. He hit .295 from that point on to at least stall the impression that his career was in an irreversible downward spiral. Still, Baerga is not nearly the player he was with the Indians.

Hitting

The switch-hitting Baerga regained much of his lost bat speed through better conditioning. He slimmed down prior to 1997, which helped him get around on the hard stuff. However, Baerga has slipped significantly batting righthanded. He hit just .170 with four RBI against lefties last year, and he's easily retired by high stuff from southpaws. In contrast, he waits on the ball better and drives the ball harder when hitting lefthanded. He won't walk very much, but he does make good contact despite being a hacker. Once part of the heart of Cleveland's order, he has slipped into the No. 6 spot with the Mets.

Baserunning & Defense

Baerga's weight problems and persistent hamstring trouble have combined to eliminate his speed as any kind of weapon. As a result, he has become a very low-percentage basestealer. He never has been a slick second baseman and his defense hasn't gotten better with age. His range is poor. Though he's surehanded, his throwing arm is erratic and he's not smooth at turning double plays.

1998 Outlook

In retrospect, it's amazing how quickly Baerga's skills deteriorated. Though he rebounded in 1997, he never again will be the 200-hit, 100-RBI machine he was in his glory years with Cleveland. He's still capable of producing decent offense for a second baseman if the Mets can continue to live with his defensive mediocrity. If he slips much more, at the plate or in the field, his days as a regular might be numbered.

Position: 2B
Bats: B **Throws:** R
Ht: 5'11" **Wt:** 200

Opening Day Age: 29
Born: 11/4/68 in San Juan, PR
ML Seasons: 8
Pronunciation: by-AIR-ga

Overall Statistics

	G	AB	R	H	D	T	HR	RBI	SB	BB	SO	Avg	OBP	Slg
1997	133	467	53	131	25	1	9	52	2	20	54	.281	.311	.396
Career	1078	4159	603	1231	218	16	114	623	50	219	432	.296	.335	.438

Where He Hits the Ball

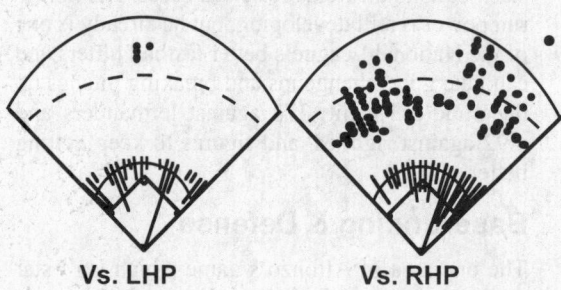

Vs. LHP   **Vs. RHP**

1997 Situational Stats

	AB	H	HR	RBI	Avg		AB	H	HR	RBI	Avg
Home	229	73	4	28	.319	LHP	94	16	1	4	.170
Road	238	58	5	24	.244	RHP	373	115	8	48	.308
First Half	269	78	4	28	.290	Sc Pos	119	34	3	43	.286
Scnd Half	198	53	5	24	.268	Clutch	78	25	1	12	.321

1997 Rankings (National League)

⇒ 3rd in batting average on an 0-2 count (.341) and lowest fielding percentage at second base (.978)
⇒ 6th in errors at second base (14)
⇒ 7th in highest percentage of swings put into play (53.6%)
⇒ 8th in lowest batting average on the road
⇒ Led the Mets in batting average vs. righthanded pitchers and batting average on an 0-2 count (.341)

Carl Everett

1997 Season

Though his season was overshadowed by allegations that he abused his childen, Carl Everett finally established himself as a major league outfielder. Dividing his time between center and right field, Everett posted career highs in several categories. He was inconsistent, batting .212 in the first two months, .314 in the next two and .204 in the final two.

Hitting

A switch-hitter, Everett was much more effective against righthanders and got most of his at-bats against them. He has yet to prove he can hit lefties, though his power is similar from both sides of the plate. He doesn't have consistent discipline from either side and he can be overpowered with hard stuff up in the strike zone. He's a decent breaking-ball hitter from the left side, but needs to cut down his strikeout totals and improve his on-base percentage in order to take more advantage of his speed. Everett has good power to the opposite field from both sides of the plate.

Baserunning & Defense

Everett is just learning the art of basestealing. He went 17-for-26 in 1997, and has the potential to steal 25-30 as he gains more experience and gets on base more often. Everett plays a decent center field but an outstanding right field, where his big-time arm is of more use. He tends to get poor jumps on balls in center, but his speed can make up for many mistakes.

1998 Outlook

There's no question about Everett's physical skills. However, he has had a tendency to sulk when slumping and resist advice. Last year's family difficulties added another cloud over talent that could pay big dividends if he ever matures. He always has been considered a five-tool player, but his sum is less than his parts.

Position: CF/RF
Bats: B **Throws:** R
Ht: 6' 0" **Wt:** 190

Opening Day Age: 26
Born: 6/3/71 in Tampa, FL
ML Seasons: 5

Overall Statistics

	G	AB	R	H	D	T	HR	RBI	SB	BB	SO	Avg	OBP	Slg
1997	142	443	58	110	28	3	14	57	17	32	102	.248	.308	.420
Career	349	994	142	244	50	5	29	133	30	96	246	.245	.319	.393

Where He Hits the Ball

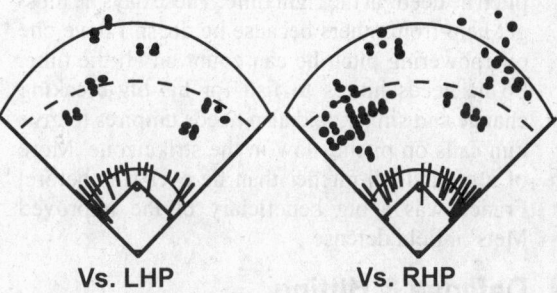

Vs. LHP   **Vs. RHP**

1997 Situational Stats

	AB	H	HR	RBI	Avg		AB	H	HR	RBI	Avg
Home	219	64	11	38	.292	LHP	101	21	2	9	.208
Road	224	46	3	19	.205	RHP	342	89	12	48	.260
First Half	247	69	9	35	.279	Sc Pos	93	26	3	42	.280
Scnd Half	196	41	5	22	.209	Clutch	83	20	4	22	.241

1997 Rankings (National League)

⇒ 3rd in lowest on-base percentage for a leadoff hitter (.294)
⇒ 5th in errors in center field (4)
⇒ 6th in least GDPs per GDP situation (3.7%)
⇒ Led the Mets in stolen bases, stolen base percentage (65.4%) and steals of third (5)

John Franco

Position: RP
Bats: L **Throws:** L
Ht: 5'10" **Wt:** 185

Opening Day Age: 37
Born: 9/17/60 in Brooklyn, NY
ML Seasons: 14

1997 Season

At an age when even the best players start treading water, John Franco got better. Motivated by the Mets' return to competitiveness, he had one of the most consistent seasons of his long career as a closer. After blowing his first save opportunity of the season, he only squandered five more en route to his seventh 30-save year.

Pitching

Franco had trouble with lefthanders in 1997 because he couldn't spot his changeup consistently and was forced to throw too many fastballs. However, that hadn't been a problem in the past and he's uncanny in his ability to usually make the pitch he needs at the right time. These days he must get help from others because he doesn't have one overpowering pitch he can count on all the time. So he needs hitters to fish for his big-breaking change and sinker, and also needs umpires to give him calls on pitches low in the strike zone. More of a groundball pitcher than he ever was before, Franco was a big beneficiary of the improved Mets' infield defense.

Defense & Hitting

Not surprisingly for someone who needs every edge, Franco helps himself in many ways. He's a quick, agile fielder who covers a lot of ground and is especially good at fielding bunts. He also works to negate stolen bases with both a good pickoff move and a quick delivery home. He rarely bats.

1998 Outlook

Franco is more than just an effective closer. He's the Mets' franchise player, a great competitor who never tires of winning and wants nothing more than to keep pitching for his hometown team. He's also the only lefthander ever to reach 300 saves. With New York turning the corner and possibly heading toward contention, he wants to be part of the fun for at least a few more years.

Overall Statistics

	W	L	Pct.	ERA	G	GS	Sv	IP	H	BB	SO	HR	Ratio
1997	5	3	.625	2.55	59	0	36	60.0	49	20	53	3	1.15
Career	77	60	.562	2.57	771	0	359	936.0	855	356	701	51	1.29

How Often He Throws Strikes

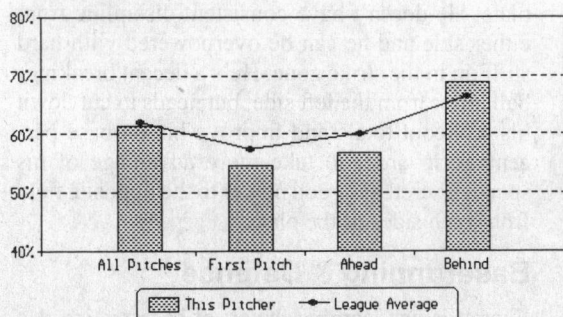

1997 Situational Stats

	W	L	ERA	Sv	IP		AB	H	HR	RBI	Avg
Home	4	0	1.95	17	32.1	LHB	46	14	0	4	.304
Road	1	3	3.25	19	27.2	RHB	171	35	3	15	.205
First Half	1	1	2.86	20	34.2	Sc Pos	63	14	2	17	.222
Scnd Half	4	2	2.13	16	25.1	Clutch	154	35	2	17	.227

1997 Rankings (National League)

⇒ 2nd in save percentage (85.7%)
⇒ 4th in saves and lowest batting average allowed in relief with runners on base (.190)
⇒ 6th in save opportunities (42), worst first batter efficiency (.327) and relief ERA (2.55)
⇒ 7th in least baserunners allowed per 9 innings in relief (10.5)
⇒ 9th in games finished (53)
⇒ 10th in lowest batting average allowed in relief (.226)
⇒ Led the Mets in saves, games finished (53), wild pitches (6), save opportunities (42), save percentage (85.7%), lowest batting average allowed in relief with runners on base (.190), relief ERA (2.55) and lowest batting average allowed in relief (.226)

Bernard Gilkey

1997 Season

Bernard Gilkey went from the best season in his career to his worst. After hitting .317-30-117 in 1996, he couldn't get out of the low .200s until August. His numbers after the All-Star break were more in line with his career performance, and he still managed a decent RBI year. He had his best month in September when the Mets were in the wild-card hunt.

Hitting

Gilkey started pulling off pitches early in the season, perhaps trying to generate more power than he should. It was a bad habit he had difficulty correcting. Always a hitter who could drive the ball to the opposite field, he became unable to reach pitches on the outside corner and also became vulnerable to being busted inside. When he's at his best, Gilkey is capable of generating tremendous power, especially against lefthanders, despite a very short swing. He hit southpaws well even while slumping for so much of the season. He had performed solidly against righthanders before 1997.

Baserunning & Defense

Gilkey has only decent speed and attempts more steals than he should, given his success rate. He's aggressive about taking the extra base and breaking up double plays. He has made himself into a good left fielder with solid range and good hands. His arm strength is good for a left fielder and he's very accurate with a quick release, leading National League outfielders in assists for the second straight year.

1998 Outlook

One of the Mets' solid citizens, Gilkey can be expected to bounce back this season to his previous status as a .280 hitter. He might not approach his 1996 numbers, but 20-plus homers and 90 RBI aren't out of the question.

Position: LF
Bats: R **Throws:** R
Ht: 6' 0" **Wt:** 200

Opening Day Age: 31
Born: 9/24/66 in St. Louis, MO
ML Seasons: 8

New York Mets

Overall Statistics

	G	AB	R	H	D	T	HR	RBI	SB	BB	SO	Avg	OBP	Slg
1997	145	518	85	129	31	1	18	78	7	70	111	.249	.338	.417
Career	891	3222	512	912	201	22	100	445	104	366	527	.283	.358	.452

Where He Hits the Ball

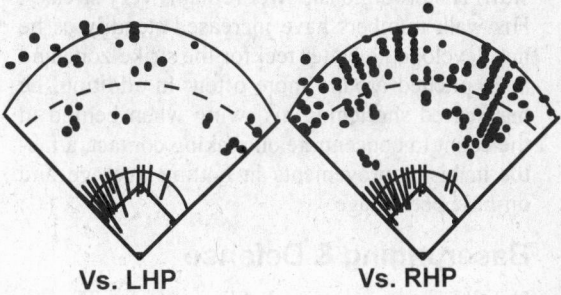

Vs. LHP   **Vs. RHP**

1997 Situational Stats

	AB	H	HR	RBI	Avg		AB	H	HR	RBI	Avg
Home	235	53	7	34	.226	LHP	139	40	9	27	.288
Road	283	76	11	44	.269	RHP	379	89	9	51	.235
First Half	280	59	8	42	.211	Sc Pos	133	36	4	56	.271
Scnd Half	238	70	10	36	.294	Clutch	83	17	3	12	.205

1997 Rankings (National League)

⇒ 1st in sacrifice flies (12)
⇒ 2nd in lowest batting average at home and fielding percentage in left field (.989)
⇒ 5th in lowest batting average and lowest batting average vs. righthanded pitchers
⇒ 7th in lowest groundball/flyball ratio (0.9)
⇒ 8th in errors in left field (3)
⇒ 9th in slugging percentage vs. lefthanded pitchers (.561) and lowest slugging percentage vs. righthanded pitchers (.364)
⇒ Led the Mets in sacrifice flies (12), caught stealing (11) and slugging percentage vs. lefthanded pitchers (.561)

Todd Hundley

1997 Season

Battling through the distraction of his mother's serious illness, a severe elbow injury and needless harrassment by his manager, Todd Hundley gutted out another 30-homer season until his elbow simply wouldn't let him continue in early September. He still had the second-best power numbers of any catcher in the majors, while raising his average 14 points from 1996.

Hitting

The switch-hitting Hundley continues to struggle versus lefthanders but gradually has become a more complete player. He still strikes out a lot and can be neutralized by high fastballs and offspeed stuff. His prodigious power remains very streaky. His walk numbers have increased steadily as he has developed a better feel for the strike zone and been pitched around more often. In addition, he has started shortening his swing when behind in the count to concentrate on making contact, a factor in his improvements in batting average and on-base percentage.

Baserunning & Defense

Hundley isn't a classic plodding catcher. Though his speed is below average, he's aggressive on the bases and doesn't hesitate to take the extra base. Hundley is an excellent defensive catcher in all respects. He's a good handler of pitchers, though he's often second-guessed by manager Bobby Valentine. Hundley blocks balls and frames pitches well. His elbow problems severely limited his throwing last year and are cause for future concern.

1998 Outlook

The best-case scenario for Hundley is that he returns to catching by midseason. However, he had major elbow surgery and might not be able to play for the entire year. If he can, he could be limited to playing first base. The long-term prognosis for Hundley resuming his career is good.

Position: C
Bats: B **Throws:** R
Ht: 5'11" **Wt:** 185

Opening Day Age: 28
Born: 5/27/69 in Martinsville, VA
ML Seasons: 8

Overall Statistics

	G	AB	R	H	D	T	HR	RBI	SB	BB	SO	Avg	OBP	Slg
1997	132	417	78	114	21	2	30	86	2	83	116	.273	.394	.549
Career	776	2425	332	592	114	7	121	385	10	283	569	.244	.326	.447

Where He Hits the Ball

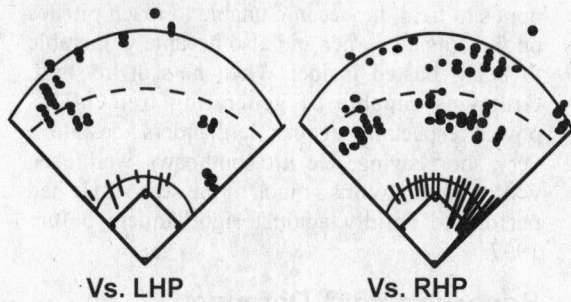

Vs. LHP   Vs. RHP

1997 Situational Stats

	AB	H	HR	RBI	Avg		AB	H	HR	RBI	Avg
Home	196	55	14	39	.281	LHP	96	21	3	14	.219
Road	221	59	16	47	.267	RHP	321	93	27	72	.290
First Half	243	73	19	51	.300	Sc Pos	125	35	9	57	.280
Scnd Half	174	41	11	35	.236	Clutch	75	19	5	15	.253

1997 Rankings (National League)

⇒ 1st in lowest groundball/flyball ratio (0.7) and most pitches seen per plate appearance (4.30)
⇒ 2nd in lowest fielding percentage at catcher (.987)
⇒ 3rd in intentional walks (16) and cleanup slugging percentage (.578)
⇒ Led the Mets in home runs, intentional walks (16), strikeouts, slugging percentage, HR frequency (13.9 ABs per HR), most pitches seen per plate appearance (4.30), cleanup slugging percentage (.578), slugging percentage vs. righthanded pitchers (.601) and on-base percentage vs. righthanded pitchers (.395)

Butch Huskey

1997 Season

Few Mets have come farther than Butch Huskey. Once banished from spring training because of weight problems, he established himself as a legitimate power threat. He saw part-time action for much of the season, but played every day down the stretch. He responded with a .299 average in the last two months. He also excelled as a cleanup hitter, batting .362 in that role.

Hitting

Huskey kills lefthanders and handled righties well in his first extended chance to play every day. Exceptionally strong in the upper body, he waits on pitches and is a very good breaking-ball hitter. He can be busted inside with fastballs but he'll hit mistakes over the plate to all fields with power. Huskey also can reach outside pitches despite his wide-open stance. He has quick hands for a big man and can muscle pitches into the outfield even when he's fooled.

Baserunning & Defense

Huskey's speed is surprising for a big man, and he'll steal a base if he's ignored. He's also aggressive in trying to take extra bases. He'll ground into a lot of double plays, though, because he hits the ball so hard. Huskey is no gazelle at any defensive position but he's at least versatile. He can play both first and third base, though he's especially error-prone at both positions because of an erratic arm. He also can play both outfield corners and saw the most time in right field in 1997. He has made himself into a serviceable outfielder.

1998 Outlook

With his ability to hit for average and power, Huskey has become an important part of the Mets' immediate future. With Todd Hundley sidelined with elbow problems, Huskey will open 1998 as the Mets' biggest homer threat. What position he plays largely will depend on New York's offseason moves. The team will make room for his bat.

Position: RF/1B/3B/LF
Bats: R **Throws:** R
Ht: 6' 3" **Wt:** 244

Opening Day Age: 26
Born: 11/10/71 in Anadarko, OK
ML Seasons: 4

Overall Statistics

	G	AB	R	H	D	T	HR	RBI	SB	BB	SO	Avg	OBP	Slg
1997	142	471	61	135	26	2	24	81	8	25	84	.287	.319	.503
Career	301	1016	114	273	44	4	42	155	10	63	190	.269	.308	.444

Where He Hits the Ball

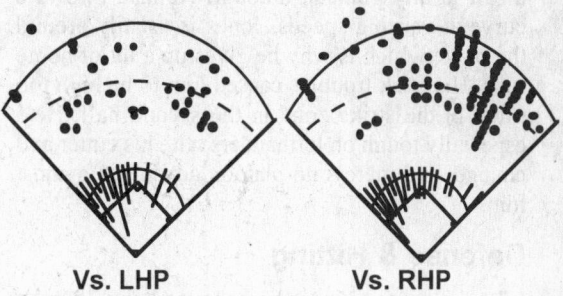

Vs. LHP   Vs. RHP

1997 Situational Stats

	AB	H	HR	RBI	Avg		AB	H	HR	RBI	Avg
Home	235	72	7	36	.306	LHP	139	47	7	26	.338
Road	236	63	17	45	.267	RHP	332	88	17	55	.265
First Half	228	62	10	39	.272	Sc Pos	122	33	1	48	.270
Scnd Half	243	73	14	42	.300	Clutch	88	22	5	13	.250

1997 Rankings (National League)

⇒ 2nd in GDPs (21)
⇒ 4th in most GDPs per GDP situation (20.0%)
⇒ 5th in batting average vs. lefthanded pitchers
⇒ 7th in lowest batting average with two strikes (.126)
⇒ 8th in sacrifice flies (8) and errors in left field (3)
⇒ 10th in least pitches seen per plate appearance (3.41), lowest batting average on an 0-2 count (.068) and slugging percentage vs. lefthanded pitchers (.547)
⇒ Led the Mets in GDPs (21)

Bobby Jones

1997 Season

It was a tale of two seasons for Bobby Jones. He went 12-5, 3.08 in the first half and earned a berth in the All-Star Game. Afterward, he went 3-4, 4.66 and was ineffective for most of July and August. Much of his difficulty stemmed from a back problem. He kept trying to pitch through it, and it cost him a chance to win 20 games.

Pitching

Jones is similar to Greg Maddux in terms of stuff. His fastball rarely exceeds the mid-80s but he has excellent movement on both his sinker and cutter. The consistency with which he can spot the fastball sets up his outstanding changeup, which he'll throw at any point in a count. He also throws a curve at varying speeds. Jones is usually around the plate, which is why he gives up a lot of home runs. His back troubles caused him to be high too often in the strike zone in the second half. He's especially tough on lefthanders with his cutter and change, and there's no platoon advantage against him.

Defense & Hitting

Like most premier pitchers, Jones helps himself out in many ways. He's an excellent fielder who handles many balls up the middle. He also does a solid job of holding runners and has a fair pickoff move. Jones can't be ignored as a hitter either. He had eight hits and four RBI last year. He also can lay down a sacrifice when needed.

1998 Outlook

Jones may never be considered an ace because his stuff is not imposing. However, he's one of the most reliable starters in the National League. Jones has won in double figures for four straight seasons, annually pitches around 200 innings and is a role model for young pitchers with his work ethic.

Position: SP
Bats: R **Throws:** R
Ht: 6' 4" **Wt:** 225

Opening Day Age: 28
Born: 2/10/70 in Fresno, California
ML Seasons: 5

Overall Statistics

	W	L	Pct.	ERA	G	GS	Sv	IP	H	BB	SO	HR	Ratio
1997	15	9	.625	3.63	30	30	0	193.1	177	63	125	24	1.24
Career	51	38	.573	3.86	124	124	0	806.1	823	240	483	86	1.32

How Often He Throws Strikes

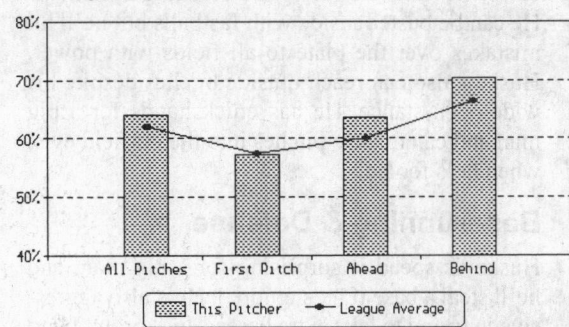

1997 Situational Stats

	W	L	ERA	Sv	IP		AB	H	HR	RBI	Avg
Home	5	4	3.59	0	90.1	LHB	355	84	13	49	.237
Road	10	5	3.67	0	103.0	RHB	375	93	11	34	.248
First Half	12	5	3.08	0	125.2	Sc Pos	142	38	6	59	.268
Scnd Half	3	4	4.66	0	67.2	Clutch	66	13	2	6	.197

1997 Rankings (National League)

⇒ 8th in most home runs allowed per 9 innings (1.12)
⇒ 9th in wins
⇒ 10th in home runs allowed and lowest batting average allowed vs. lefthanded batters
⇒ Led the Mets in wins, complete games (2), shutouts (1), home runs allowed, balks (1), runners caught stealing (6), winning percentage and most run support per 9 innings (4.7)

Brian McRae

1997 Season

Brian McRae never got it going in 1997. He struggled with the Cubs before finally getting dealt to the Mets, where he finished one of his worst seasons. His numbers fell across the board, and his on-base percentage in particular plummeted to a dangerous level—especially for a leadoff hitter. He keeps getting used in that role despite having ordinary on-base percentages.

Hitting

A second-half power surge in 1996 may have sown the seeds for McRae's disappointing 1997 production. He started thinking he was a middle-of-the-order run producer and the result was a bigger swing, less finicky pitch selection and a lack of plate discipline. As a result he hit too many flyballs, swung early and often, and became very easy to pitch to. He often chases pitches out of the strike zone early in the count, so he rarely sees fastballs. A switch-hitter who's better against lefthanders, McRae fell off from both sides of the plate.

Baserunning & Defense

Because he was getting on base less, McRae's stolen-base total and percentage suffered. With his speed and aggressiveness he should be an automatic 30-steal man, but sometimes he uses poor judgment. At times, he had to be urged to run more. McRae has good range in center field and judges balls as well as anyone. His throwing arm is weak, even by center-field standards, but he plays shallow and returns balls to the infield very quickly.

1998 Outlook

The Cubs gave up on McRae just six months after they signed him to a new three-year contract. The Mets weren't impressed by their brief look at him, either. What once was a very promising career seems suddenly at a crossroads. A .242 batting average without a lot of speed and power or the ability to reach base won't keep an outfielder in the lineup on an everyday basis.

Position: CF
Bats: B **Throws:** R
Ht: 6' 0" **Wt:** 196

Opening Day Age: 30
Born: 8/27/67 in Bradenton, FL
ML Seasons: 8

Overall Statistics

	G	AB	R	H	D	T	HR	RBI	SB	BB	SO	Avg	OBP	Slg
1997	153	562	86	136	32	7	11	43	17	65	84	.242	.326	.383
Career	1061	4159	608	1102	211	51	70	405	174	351	648	.265	.327	.391

Where He Hits the Ball

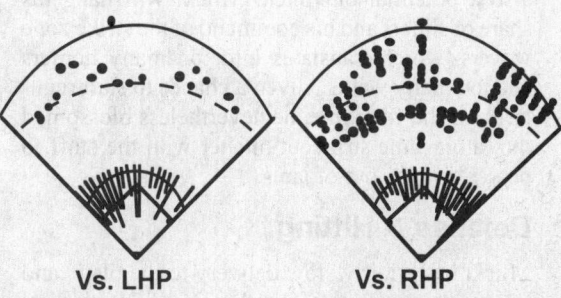

Vs. LHP   Vs. RHP

1997 Situational Stats

	AB	H	HR	RBI	Avg		AB	H	HR	RBI	Avg
Home	297	82	6	23	.276	LHP	144	40	4	9	.278
Road	265	54	5	20	.204	RHP	418	96	7	34	.230
First Half	330	77	4	21	.233	Sc Pos	103	27	1	31	.262
Scnd Half	232	59	7	22	.254	Clutch	80	22	3	7	.275

1997 Rankings (National League)

⇒ 1st in lowest batting average on the road (.204)
⇒ 2nd in lowest batting average (.242) and lowest batting average vs. righthanded pitchers (.230)
⇒ 3rd in fielding percentage in center field (.987)
⇒ 5th in lowest on-base percentage for a leadoff hitter (.304) and errors in center field (4)
⇒ 8th in lowest stolen base percentage (63.0%) and lowest slugging percentage vs. righthanded pitchers (.361)
⇒ 10th in triples (7)

Dave Mlicki

1997 Season

If nothing else, Dave Mlicki's season was made when he shut out the Yankees in the year's most electric interleague game. His 8-12 record was somewhat misleading, because 20 of his 32 outings were quality starts. He was often the victim of poor run support or bad bullpen efforts.

Pitching

Mlicki has the best pure stuff of anybody in the Mets' rotation who managed to finish the 1997 season. He can sink or ride a fastball that can reach the low 90s. He also has a big-breaking curve, a smaller-breaking knuckle-curve, an improving slider and a changeup that by season's end was also a potential out pitch. Mlicki will hang his share of sliders and his command of the strike zone wavers, which translates into too many homers and too many walks. Given a chance to start regularly for the first time, he nevertheless blossomed into a big-time strikeout pitcher with the stuff to power his way out of jams.

Defense & Hitting

Mlicki has a fairly slow delivery to the plate, and basestealers were successful in 26 of 31 attempts against him in 1997. He usually doesn't finish in good fielding position. He strikes out in nearly half his at-bats but can cause damage when he does make contact, managing three doubles last year among his nine hits.

1998 Outlook

Even if New York gets lucky with its bevy of injured young pitchers or acquires an ace, the late-blooming Mlicki will be an important part of the rotation. He may be just coming into his own as a legitimate starter. With his stuff and durability, he could win 13-15 games if he gets any support.

Position: SP
Bats: R **Throws:** R
Ht: 6' 4" **Wt:** 205

Opening Day Age: 29
Born: 6/8/68 in Cleveland, OH
ML Seasons: 5
Pronunciation: mah-LICK-ee

Overall Statistics

	W	L	Pct.	ERA	G	GS	Sv	IP	H	BB	SO	HR	Ratio
1997	8	12	.400	4.00	32	32	0	193.2	194	76	157	21	1.39
Career	23	28	.451	3.98	119	66	1	479.1	483	185	386	58	1.39

How Often He Throws Strikes

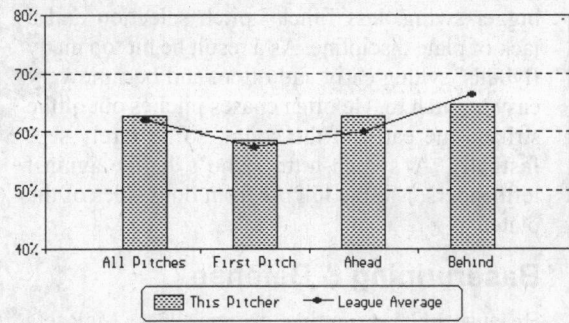

1997 Situational Stats

	W	L	ERA	Sv	IP		AB	H	HR	RBI	Avg
Home	6	5	2.53	0	89.0	LHB	362	89	7	34	.246
Road	2	7	5.25	0	104.2	RHB	386	105	14	45	.272
First Half	4	7	4.65	0	100.2	Sc Pos	174	39	2	54	.224
Scnd Half	4	5	3.29	0	93.0	Clutch	58	17	2	4	.293

1997 Rankings (National League)

⇒ 1st in highest stolen base percentage allowed (83.9%)
⇒ 3rd in highest ERA on the road
⇒ 4th in least run support per 9 innings (3.8)
⇒ 5th in stolen bases allowed (26) and lowest winning percentage
⇒ Led the Mets in losses, games started, shutouts (1), hits allowed, batters faced (838), walks allowed, strikeouts, balks (1), pitches thrown (3,012), stolen bases allowed (26), most strikeouts per 9 innings (7.3), ERA at home and lowest batting average allowed with runners in scoring position

Alex Ochoa

1997 Season

Alex Ochoa has lost his chance to be the Mets' right fielder of the future. He struggled to produce consistently and largely became a part-time player by midseason. He also was hampered by leg problems which took away a significant amount of playing time.

Hitting

Most scouts believe that Ochoa never will be a major power threat and hit more than 10-12 homers a year. That won't lead to everyday play for a corner outfielder. He has some line-drive power, but is undisciplined in his approach and has yet to show any ability to hit offspeed pitches with consistency. Ochoa is more of an opposite-field hitter who only rarely will jerk a fastball to left field. The Mets were disappointed last year that he was unable to make adjustments. He does have a great deal of talent and has the potential to hit 35 doubles in a season.

Baserunning & Defense

Ochoa has excellent speed and could develop into a solid basestealing threat with more experience. His outfield play is outstanding. He has good range, sure hands and sound judgment. Scouts have been talking about his throwing arm since he was first signed by Baltimore. His arm ranks with the best in baseball.

1998 Outlook

The Mets are at a crossroads with Ochoa, who clearly was outplayed by both Butch Huskey and Carl Everett. His lack of power from the right-field slot hurts his value. Giving up on Ochoa's overall ability would be difficult, but he could end up blossoming somewhere else via a trade.

Position: RF
Bats: R **Throws:** R
Ht: 6' 0" **Wt:** 185

Opening Day Age: 26
Born: 3/29/72 in Miami Lakes, FL
ML Seasons: 3
Pronunciation: oh-CHO-uh

Overall Statistics

	G	AB	R	H	D	T	HR	RBI	SB	BB	SO	Avg	OBP	Slg
1997	113	238	31	58	14	1	3	22	3	18	32	.244	.300	.349
Career	206	557	75	152	34	4	7	55	8	37	72	.273	.320	.386

Where He Hits the Ball

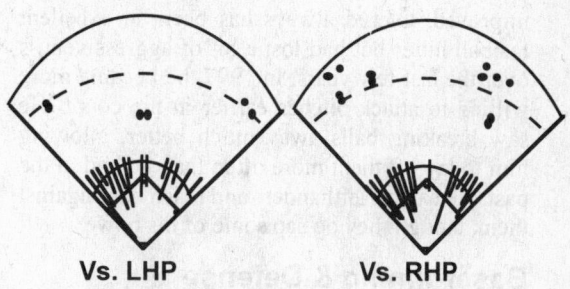

Vs. LHP   **Vs. RHP**

1997 Situational Stats

	AB	H	HR	RBI	Avg		AB	H	HR	RBI	Avg
Home	119	31	1	13	.261	LHP	107	24	1	10	.224
Road	119	27	2	9	.227	RHP	131	34	2	12	.260
First Half	150	33	1	11	.220	Sc Pos	68	13	0	17	.191
Scnd Half	88	25	2	11	.284	Clutch	57	15	1	6	.263

1997 Rankings (National League)

⇒ 5th in batting average on a 3-1 count (.750)
⇒ Led the Mets in batting average on a 3-1 count (.750)

John Olerud

1997 Season

Freed from what had become a negative situation in Toronto, John Olerud revived a slipping career with his best season in four years. Olerud drove in 102 runs, hitting .385 with men in scoring position. Along the way he delivered some of the Mets' most dramatic hits, including a game-winning homer in May that capped a memorable comeback against Colorado. Olerud also achieved a baseball rarity, hitting for the cycle on September 11.

Hitting

Olerud moved up on the plate slightly, which not only made him even quicker on inside pitches but also gave him better plate coverage on outside pitches. As a result, his power numbers were much improved. Olerud always has been an excellent fastball hitter but had lost a bit of aggressiveness over the last few years. In 1997, he became more willing to attack pitches earlier in the count. He saw breaking balls away much better, allowing him to lay off them more often than he had in the past. He can hit lefthanders and reach base against them, though they do sap some of his power.

Baserunning & Defense

Olerud is a smart baserunner, which helps because he's one of the slower players in the National League and no threat to steal. He also grounds into a lot of double plays. He's a solid if unspectacular first baseman with good hands and average range. He'll sometimes have trouble with throws to second but does a good job of digging balls out of the dirt.

1998 Outlook

Olerud fit in well with New York, and though he has a reputation for being reserved, he fell in love with Manhattan. Though the Mets allowed him to become a free agent, they quickly re-signed him for two years and $8 million. He's in his prime and should have years of productive play ahead.

Position: 1B
Bats: L **Throws:** L
Ht: 6' 5" **Wt:** 220
Opening Day Age: 29
Born: 8/5/68 in Seattle, WA
ML Seasons: 9
Pronunciation: OAL-uh-rude

Overall Statistics

	G	AB	R	H	D	T	HR	RBI	SB	BB	SO	Avg	OBP	Slg
1997	154	524	90	154	34	1	22	102	0	85	67	.294	.400	.489
Career	1074	3627	554	1064	247	7	131	573	3	599	497	.293	.396	.474

Where He Hits the Ball

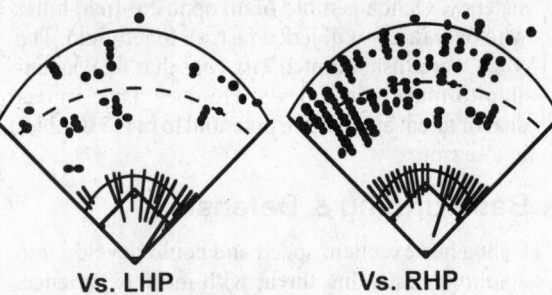

Vs. LHP   Vs. RHP

1997 Situational Stats

	AB	H	HR	RBI	Avg		AB	H	HR	RBI	Avg
Home	247	75	13	57	.304	LHP	145	40	6	38	.276
Road	277	79	9	45	.285	RHP	379	114	16	64	.301
First Half	308	94	13	61	.305	Sc Pos	130	50	7	75	.385
Scnd Half	216	60	9	41	.278	Clutch	94	27	5	21	.287

1997 Rankings (National League)

⇒ 3rd in batting average with runners in scoring position
⇒ 4th in fielding percentage at first base (.995) and highest percentage of pitches taken (64.0%)
⇒ 5th in GDPs (19)
⇒ Led the Mets in at-bats, runs scored, doubles, total bases (256), RBI, walks, hit by pitch (13), times on base (252), pitches seen (2,387), plate appearances (630), games played (154), on-base percentage, highest percentage of pitches taken (64.0%) and highest percentage of swings put into play (53.8%)

Rey Ordonez

1997 Season

Rey Ordonez continued to dazzle in the field, but he also went backward as an offensive player. Amid a pair of long slumps, he wasn't helped by having his season interrupted for six weeks when he broke a bone in his left hand while diving for a ball. He won a Gold Glove despite playing in just 120 games.

Hitting

Ordonez may be the worst hitter among major league regulars. The best that can be said about his skills at the plate is that he makes contact. He's a free swinger who has virtually no power. He can be overmatched by average fastballs and is an automatic out if he hits the ball in the air. He also is guilty of frequently fishing for breaking balls out of the strike zone, and he almost never walks. Since hitting .354 in his first month in the majors, he has batted .228.

Baserunning & Defense

Ordonez has the speed to eventually be a solid basestealer, but his calling card is his glove. He's one of the most exciting defensive talents to come along in years. Ordonez' range may be the best of any shortstop in the game, and his flair is in the same class as that of Cleveland's Omar Vizquel. In addition, Ordonez has an exceptional throwing arm and the ability to make strong and accurate throws from a wide variety of angles. He'll sometimes get himself in trouble by trying to make an impossible play.

1998 Outlook

With two seasons under his belt, it's time for Ordonez to start showing some maturity as a hitter and as a player. He sulked last year when he wasn't immediately put back into the lineup after his return from injury, and he's still erratic enough to worry the Mets. He has the talent to be another Ozzie Smith, or he could wind up being the next Rafael Belliard.

Position: SS
Bats: R **Throws:** R
Ht: 5' 9" **Wt:** 159

Opening Day Age: 25
Born: 11/11/72 in Havana, Cuba
ML Seasons: 2
Pronunciation: RAY or-DOAN-yez

New York Mets

Overall Statistics

	G	AB	R	H	D	T	HR	RBI	SB	BB	SO	Avg	OBP	Slg
1997	120	356	35	77	5	3	1	33	11	18	36	.216	.255	.256
Career	271	858	86	206	17	7	2	63	12	40	89	.240	.275	.283

Where He Hits the Ball

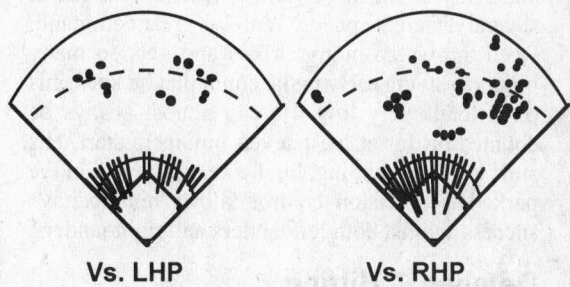

Vs. LHP   **Vs. RHP**

1997 Situational Stats

	AB	H	HR	RBI	Avg		AB	H	HR	RBI	Avg
Home	164	39	1	17	.238	LHP	100	27	0	11	.270
Road	192	38	0	16	.198	RHP	256	50	1	22	.195
First Half	150	38	0	15	.253	Sc Pos	86	24	0	31	.279
Scnd Half	206	39	1	18	.189	Clutch	50	11	0	7	.220

1997 Rankings (National League)

⇒ 1st in fielding percentage at shortstop (.983)
⇒ 4th in sacrifice bunts (14)
⇒ 8th in most GDPs per GDP situation (18.9%)
⇒ Led the Mets in sacrifice bunts (14), batting average on a 3-2 count (.294) and bunts in play (20)

Rick Reed

1997 Season

One of the year's best stories was Rick Reed. A longtime journeyman, Reed was shunned by teammates after serving as a replacement player and was seemingly buried in the minors. But he earned his way back to the majors and was the Mets' most consistent starter in 1997. He led the club in innings and placed among the National League leaders in ERA.

Pitching

Reed's stuff doesn't knock anyone's eyes out, but he has become a master at changing speeds, hitting spots and keeping hitters off balance. His fastball never leaves the 80s, but he has a great changeup and an excellent curve, both of which he throws at several different speeds. With his great command, Reed throws so many strikes and gets so many hitters to swing early in the count that he keeps his pitch totals very low. He can almost always be counted on for at least seven innings a start. His stuff isn't outstanding, but he keeps the ball in the park. His precision control allows him to have success against both lefthanders and righthanders.

Defense & Hitting

The ups and downs of Reed's career have taught him to try and gain every possible edge, which is why he has made himself into a complete pitcher. He's a very poised fielder and does an excellent job of holding runners close. Only nine runners tried to steal against him last year, and just three were successful. Reed also handles the bat well, leading all Mets pitchers in hits, RBI and sacrifices in 1997. He also added a homer.

1998 Outlook

No player in baseball traveled farther last year than Reed, who went from being a fringe Triple-A pitcher to such an important part of the Mets' rotation that he became a no-brain decision to protect in the expansion draft. He's the kind of savvy late bloomer who could be a solid winner for several years.

Position: SP
Bats: R **Throws:** R
Ht: 6' 1" **Wt:** 195

Opening Day Age: 32
Born: 8/16/65 in Huntington, WV
ML Seasons: 9

Overall Statistics

	W	L	Pct.	ERA	G	GS	Sv	IP	H	BB	SO	HR	Ratio
1997	13	9	.591	2.89	33	31	0	208.1	186	31	113	19	1.04
Career	22	24	.478	3.87	94	73	1	474.2	480	89	258	51	1.20

How Often He Throws Strikes

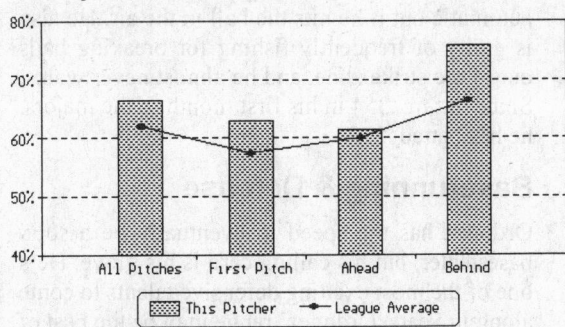

1997 Situational Stats

	W	L	ERA	Sv	IP		AB	H	HR	RBI	Avg
Home	8	5	3.05	0	100.1	LHB	385	89	9	30	.231
Road	5	4	2.75	0	108.0	RHB	393	97	10	38	.247
First Half	6	4	2.93	0	110.2	Sc Pos	156	36	2	43	.231
Scnd Half	7	5	2.86	0	97.2	Clutch	83	18	1	3	.217

1997 Rankings (National League)

⇒ 2nd in lowest stolen base percentage allowed (33.3%)

⇒ 4th in lowest on-base percentage allowed (.272), least pitches thrown per batter (3.39), least baserunners allowed per 9 innings (9.6) and lowest batting average allowed vs. lefthanded batters

⇒ 5th in highest strikeout/walk ratio (3.6), least strikeouts per 9 innings (4.9) and ERA on the road

⇒ Led the Mets in ERA, complete games (2), innings pitched, runners caught stealing (6), GDPs induced (21), highest strikeout/walk ratio (3.6), lowest batting average allowed (.239), lowest slugging percentage allowed (.368) and lowest on-base percentage allowed (.272)

Brian Bohanon

Position: SP/RP
Bats: L **Throws:** L
Ht: 6' 3" **Wt:** 220

Opening Day Age: 29
Born: 8/1/68 in Denton, TX
ML Seasons: 8
Pronunciation: boe-HAN-un

Overall Statistics

	W	L	Pct.	ERA	G	GS	Sv	IP	H	BB	SO	HR	Ratio
1997	6	4	.600	3.82	19	14	0	94.1	95	34	66	9	1.37
Career	18	19	.486	5.35	178	61	2	493.0	564	214	295	55	1.58

1997 Situational Stats

	W	L	ERA	Sv	IP		AB	H	HR	RBI	Avg
Home	2	2	3.38	0	40.0	LHB	75	20	1	8	.267
Road	4	2	4.14	0	54.1	RHB	293	75	8	32	.256
First Half	1	1	6.75	0	13.1	Sc Pos	96	21	2	28	.219
Scnd Half	5	3	3.33	0	81.0	Clutch	35	15	2	5	.429

1997 Season

Through his past association with Mets manager Bobby Valentine in Texas, lefthander Brian Bohanon got another chance in the majors. He didn't waste the opportunity. He was a stopgap option when injuries thinned out New York's rotation. He ended up starting 14 games, during which he averaged six innings per outing and gave New York a chance to win in all but two contests.

Pitching, Defense & Hitting

Bohanon is a lefthander with no margin for error. He doesn't overpower anyone and must hit his spots with his average sinking fastball and changeup. When he gets too much of the plate, he is very hittable. Bohanon is a decent athlete with a fair move to first and can help himself with the bat.

1998 Outlook

Like many other journeyman lefthanders, Bohanon is finding some success later in his career as he learns the art of offspeed pitching. As a spot starter or long reliever, he could be a useful contributor to most staffs.

Matt Franco

Position: 3B/1B
Bats: L **Throws:** R
Ht: 6' 2" **Wt:** 200

Opening Day Age: 28
Born: 8/19/69 in Santa Monica, CA
ML Seasons: 3

Overall Statistics

	G	AB	R	H	D	T	HR	RBI	SB	BB	SO	Avg	OBP	Slg
1997	112	163	21	45	5	0	5	21	1	13	23	.276	.330	.399
Career	142	211	27	56	7	0	6	24	1	14	32	.265	.313	.384

1997 Situational Stats

	AB	H	HR	RBI	Avg		AB	H	HR	RBI	Avg
Home	92	23	3	7	.250	LHP	22	5	0	1	.227
Road	71	22	2	14	.310	RHP	141	40	5	20	.284
First Half	92	29	3	11	.315	Sc Pos	43	13	1	16	.302
Scnd Half	71	16	2	10	.225	Clutch	48	17	1	12	.354

1997 Season

Matt Franco has become one of baseball's best pinch hitters. After going hitless in his first seven opportunities in 1997, he had 19 hits in his next 55, including three homers and 13 RBI. He also filled in occasionally at first and third base.

Hitting, Baserunning & Defense

Franco is used almost exclusively against righthanders and is a good fastball hitter who can drive mistakes a long way. He has trouble with offspeed pitches. Like most good pinch hitters, Franco will swing away early in the count and always looks for fastballs. He's a below-average runner who is aggressive on the bases. He plays a decent first base and has good hands. His play at third is more suspect, because his range is negligible and his arm is erratic.

1998 Outlook

Contenders need good pinch hitters and the Mets have one in Franco, who came through time and again. He accepts his role without complaint, knowing he won't ever be an everyday player.

Jason Isringhausen

Position: SP
Bats: R **Throws:** R
Ht: 6' 3" **Wt:** 196

Opening Day Age: 25
Born: 9/7/72 in Brighton, IL
ML Seasons: 3
Nickname: Izzy
Pronunciation: IS-ring-how-zin

Overall Statistics

	W	L	Pct.	ERA	G	GS	Sv	IP	H	BB	SO	HR	Ratio
1997	2	2	.500	7.58	6	6	0	29.2	40	22	25	3	2.09
Career	17	18	.486	4.43	47	47	0	294.1	318	126	194	22	1.51

1997 Situational Stats

	W	L	ERA	Sv	IP		AB	H	HR	RBI	Avg
Home	2	1	6.08	0	26.2	LHB	69	25	2	13	.362
Road	0	1	21.00	0	3.0	RHB	50	15	1	11	.300
First Half	0	0	-	0	0.0	Sc Pos	35	15	0	18	.429
Scnd Half	2	2	7.58	0	29.2	Clutch	0	0	0	0	-

1997 Season

It was a season in hell for Jason Isringhausen. After breaking his hand when he punched a garbage can, he came down with a form of tuberculosis and also suffered lingering effects from previous elbow troubles. He returned at the end of the year to make six starts, only two of which were decent.

Pitching, Defense & Hitting

Isringhausen still has not developed a good feel for either his changeup or his sinking fastball. He needs both to set up his hard-breaking overhand curve, which is by far his best pitch. He doesn't hold runners well and his fielding skills are poor. He's an outstanding hitter for a pitcher and is capable of hitting a homer.

1998 Outlook

Isringhausen needs to put his lost season behind him in order to regain the luster he had as a promising young pitcher two years ago. He may have to pitch some innings in the minors before the Mets can feel comfortable about his chances of resuming what was a promising career.

Luis Lopez

Position: SS/2B
Bats: B **Throws:** R
Ht: 5'11" **Wt:** 175

Opening Day Age: 27
Born: 9/4/70 in Cidra, PR
ML Seasons: 4

Overall Statistics

	G	AB	R	H	D	T	HR	RBI	SB	BB	SO	Avg	OBP	Slg
1997	78	178	19	48	12	1	1	19	2	12	42	.270	.330	.365
Career	235	595	59	143	32	2	5	51	5	36	124	.240	.291	.326

1997 Situational Stats

	AB	H	HR	RBI	Avg		AB	H	HR	RBI	Avg
Home	96	20	1	7	.208	LHP	51	12	1	4	.235
Road	82	28	0	12	.341	RHP	127	36	0	15	.283
First Half	74	20	0	5	.270	Sc Pos	51	14	0	17	.275
Scnd Half	104	28	1	14	.269	Clutch	42	6	0	3	.143

1997 Season

Luis Lopez proved to be a solid utility infielder in 1997, especially as a fill-in at shortstop when Rey Ordonez was injured. Lopez was recalled from the minors on June 2 and he played well at short, second and occasionally third while hitting a surprising .270.

Hitting, Baserunning & Defense

Though a switch-hitter, Lopez plays almost exclusively against righthanders. He has little home-run power but is capable of producing doubles. He usually makes contact and he's a surprisingly good fastball hitter. He's most comfortable at second base, where he's had more experience. However, he holds his own at short with average range and a solid arm. He has only average speed and doesn't steal bases.

1998 Outlook

Lopez probably won't ever be an everyday player. But his stable defense and occasional offense make him a valuable role player. He so impressed the Mets that he made the more-ballyhooed Manny Alexander expendable last summer.

Greg McMichael

Position: RP
Bats: R **Throws:** R
Ht: 6' 3" **Wt:** 215

Opening Day Age: 31
Born: 12/1/66 in
Knoxville, TN
ML Seasons: 5

Overall Statistics

	W	L	Pct.	ERA	G	GS	Sv	IP	H	BB	SO	HR	Ratio
1997	7	10	.412	2.98	73	0	7	87.2	73	27	81	8	1.14
Career	25	24	.510	2.91	338	0	51	405.1	355	134	369	24	1.21

1997 Situational Stats

	W	L	ERA	Sv	IP		AB	H	HR	RBI	Avg
Home	4	4	1.41	4	44.2	LHB	139	36	3	15	.259
Road	3	6	4.60	3	43.0	RHB	174	37	5	23	.213
First Half	4	6	2.47	4	43.2	Sc Pos	100	18	2	28	.180
Scnd Half	3	4	3.48	3	44.0	Clutch	226	54	6	30	.239

1997 Season

No reliever in baseball had more decisions than Greg McMichael's 17. That was an indication of how often he pitched and how erratic his performance was. His 11 blown saves tied for the major league lead with Seattle's Norm Charlton.

Pitching, Defense & Hitting

McMichael sidearms a constant array of change-ups and sliders, most of them off the low, outside edge of the plate. When he's on, he gets strikeouts in bunches. However, his margin for error is slight and his mistakes are usually costly. McMichael does a professional job of fielding his position, but basestealers went 10-for-11 against him last year. His two hits in 1997 were the first of his career.

1998 Outlook

McMichael still figures to be in the Mets' bullpen mix. His many failures during crunch time likely will push his appearances into earlier innings.

Bill Pulsipher

Position:
Bats: L **Throws:** L
Ht: 6' 3" **Wt:** 208

Opening Day Age: 24
Born: 10/9/73 in Fort
Benning, GA
ML Seasons: 1
Nickname: Pulse
Pronunciation:
PUL-sih-fir

Overall Statistics

	W	L	Pct.	ERA	G	GS	Sv	IP	H	BB	SO	HR	Ratio
1997							Did Not Play						
Career	5	7	.417	3.98	17	17	0	126.2	122	45	81	11	1.32

1997 Situational Stats

	W	L	ERA	Sv	IP		AB	H	HR	RBI	Avg
Home	—	—	—	—	—	LHB	—	—	—	—	—
Road	—	—	—	—	—	RHB	—	—	—	—	—
First Half	—	—	—	—	—	Sc Pos	—	—	—	—	—
Scnd Half	—	—	—	—	—	Clutch	—	—	—	—	—

1997 Season

Long considered one of the top pitching prospects in baseball, Bill Pulsipher had his second straight washout year. Sidelined for half the year by elbow problems, Pulsipher returned to pitch in relief at Triple-A and suffered through horrendous control problems.

Pitching, Defense & Hitting

A hard thrower with a fastball in the low 90s, Pulsipher has constantly struggled to keep his delivery under control and maintain a consistent release point. His control always has been shaky and it completely deteriorated in 1997. Prior to his elbow troubles, he had the makings of an outstanding slider and a decent curve. His violent delivery usually puts him in poor fielding position, and he has yet to develop a good pickoff move. He has also failed to show any hitting ability.

1998 Outlook

Pulsipher was the game's hottest young lefthander in 1995. The Mets would love to see him return to form this spring and once again be on his way to be a dominant pitcher. More realistically, he'll start the season in the minors and possibly be able to help at the major league level late in the season.

Armando Reynoso

Position: SP
Bats: R **Throws:** R
Ht: 6' 0" **Wt:** 204

Opening Day Age: 31
Born: 5/1/66 in San
Luis Potosi, MX
ML Seasons: 7
Pronunciation:
ray-NOH-so

Overall Statistics

	W	L	Pct.	ERA	G	GS	Sv	IP	H	BB	SO	HR	Ratio
1997	6	3	.667	4.53	16	16	0	91.1	95	29	47	7	1.36
Career	39	35	.527	4.69	114	109	1	625.1	703	211	329	79	1.46

1997 Situational Stats

	W	L	ERA	Sv	IP		AB	H	HR	RBI	Avg
Home	3	2	4.75	0	53.0	LHB	150	40	2	13	.267
Road	3	1	4.23	0	38.1	RHB	195	55	5	29	.282
First Half	6	2	3.84	0	82.0	Sc Pos	78	19	1	31	.244
Scnd Half	0	1	10.61	0	9.1	Clutch	21	4	1	3	.190

1997 Season

Shoulder troubles cut short Armando Reynoso's season after 16 starts, the last three of which were affected by his sore arm. Before that Reynoso pitched well, throwing quality starts in 10 of his first 13 outings, including a shutout.

Pitching, Defense & Hitting

The phrase "crafty veteran" must have been coined with Reynoso in mind. He's a thinking man's pitcher who moves his cut fastball, which rarely comes in harder than the low-to-mid 80s, around the strike zone. He also tosses a good forkball and attacks lefthanders with a screwball. In addition, he changes speeds with all his pitches and throws them from an assortment of arm angles. Reynoso also has the best righthanded pick-off move in baseball and is one of the game's best-fielding pitchers. He's also fairly good at getting down sacrifice bunts.

1998 Outlook

Health always has been the question with Reynoso and the Mets won't know if he'll be able to pitch until spring training. If he's physically able, Reynoso is a nice fourth or fifth starter... but that's a big if.

Mel Rojas

Position: RP
Bats: R **Throws:** R
Ht: 5'11" **Wt:** 195

Opening Day Age: 31
Born: 12/10/66 in
Haina, DR
ML Seasons: 8
Pronunciation:
ROH-hahss

Overall Statistics

	W	L	Pct.	ERA	G	GS	Sv	IP	H	BB	SO	HR	Ratio
1997	0	6	.000	4.64	77	0	15	85.1	78	36	93	15	1.34
Career	29	29	.500	3.27	462	0	124	595.0	501	215	511	50	1.20

1997 Situational Stats

	W	L	ERA	Sv	IP		AB	H	HR	RBI	Avg
Home	0	5	4.01	10	51.2	LHB	159	41	8	28	.258
Road	0	1	5.61	5	33.2	RHB	164	37	7	26	.226
First Half	0	2	4.46	9	40.1	Sc Pos	90	26	6	43	.289
Scnd Half	0	4	4.80	6	45.0	Clutch	190	48	9	35	.253

1997 Season

After dominating in the second half of 1996 for the Expos and signing a lucrative free-agent contract with the Cubs, Mel Rojas completely fell apart. He blew six of 19 save opportunities and lost his closer's job with Chicago. Even a trade to the Mets in what amounted to salary dumping by the Cubs couldn't turn him around. He finished the year 0-6 and allowed as many homers as he had saves (15).

Pitching, Defense & Hitting

After allowing a few early-season home runs in Wrigley Field, Rojas never was the same. He lost his aggressiveness with his above-average fastball and started trying to spot it. He also lost confidence in his outstanding forkball, which started hanging more regularly. His stuff remains outstanding when he's relaxed on the mound. Basestealers have a field day against him because of his out-of-control delivery, which also makes him a poor fielder. He occasionally makes contact as a hitter.

1998 Outlook

New York isn't about to give up on Rojas after only a few weeks. There's nothing wrong with his physical ability. The Mets hope that by moving him to a setup role, they can nurse him back to being an elite reliever.

Turk Wendell

Position: RP
Bats: L **Throws:** R
Ht: 6' 2" **Wt:** 195

Opening Day Age: 30
Born: 5/19/67 in Pittsfield, MA
ML Seasons: 5
Pronunciation: WENN-dull

Overall Statistics

	W	L	Pct.	ERA	G	GS	Sv	IP	H	BB	SO	HR	Ratio
1997	3	5	.375	4.36	65	0	5	76.1	68	53	64	7	1.59
Career	11	14	.440	4.45	191	6	23	253.0	243	139	213	29	1.51

1997 Situational Stats

	W	L	ERA	Sv	IP		AB	H	HR	RBI	Avg
Home	3	3	4.50	4	40.0	LHB	114	36	4	20	.316
Road	0	2	4.21	1	36.1	RHB	169	32	3	18	.189
First Half	2	3	4.63	4	44.2	Sc Pos	74	21	3	32	.284
Scnd Half	1	2	3.98	1	31.2	Clutch	97	23	2	19	.237

1997 Season

Like many other members of the Cubs, Turk Wendell started last season uncomfortable and unsuccessful in his role and never got untracked. He joined the Mets as part of the Brian McRae-Lance Johnson trade, but the change of scenery didn't help. His ERA rose 1.52 overall from 1996 and his save total dropped from 18 to five.

Pitching, Defense & Hitting

Wendell's best asset might be his durability. He rarely shows the effects of frequent use. His top pitch is a hard slider that he throws almost exclusively at times. He can have trouble maintaining his release point, causing his slider to flatten. Wendell's fastball and changeup aren't good enough to stand alone. He's an excellent athlete who reaches many balls hit through the middle. He has a good pickoff move and is quick to the plate. Wendell is no threat as a hitter.

1998 Outlook

With his tireless arm, Wendell can be an innings-eater in middle relief. He has neither the consistency nor the overall stuff to be a setup man or closer for an extended period of time.

Paul Wilson

Position: SP
Bats: R **Throws:** R
Ht: 6' 5" **Wt:** 235

Opening Day Age: 25
Born: 3/28/73 in Orlando, FL
ML Seasons: 1

Overall Statistics

	W	L	Pct.	ERA	G	GS	Sv	IP	H	BB	SO	HR	Ratio
1997							Did Not Play						
Career	5	12	.294	5.38	26	26	0	149.0	157	71	109	15	1.53

1997 Situational Stats

	W	L	ERA	Sv	IP		AB	H	HR	RBI	Avg
Home	—	—	—	—	—	LHB	—	—	—	—	—
Road	—	—	—	—	—	RHB	—	—	—	—	—
First Half	—	—	—	—	—	Sc Pos	—	—	—	—	—
Scnd Half	—	—	—	—	—	Clutch	—	—	—	—	—

1997 Season

Shoulder troubles destroyed the 1997 season for Paul Wilson, believed by many baseball people to be the best of the Mets' young pitching prospects. Wilson was able to come back and make some late-season starts in the minors that at least assured New York he had recovered from his arm problems.

Pitching, Defense & Hitting

Wilson has everything it takes to be a big winner in the majors. His fastball has been clocked in the 95-MPH range. He throws a tight, late-breaking slider that will hang occasionally, a hard curveball and a changeup that needs refinement. His pickoff move is still raw, but he's a good athlete who fields his position well. Wilson occasionally can hit a mistake.

1998 Outlook

Wilson has the stuff to be a future ace. Missing an entire year of major league experience was a setback, but if he's healthy he quickly could develop into a 15-game winner.

Other New York Mets

Juan Acevedo (Pos: RHP, Age: 27)

	W	L	Pct.	ERA	G	GS	Sv	IP	H	BB	SO	HR	Ratio
1997	3	1	.750	3.59	25	2	0	47.2	52	22	33	6	1.55
Career	7	7	.500	5.24	42	13	0	113.1	134	42	73	21	1.55

Acevedo spent two brief stints in the majors in support of the Mets bullpen last year. He actually posted better stats with New York last year than with Triple-A Norfolk. 1998 Outlook: B

Steve Bieser (Pos: CF, Age: 30, Bats: L)

	G	AB	R	H	D	T	HR	RBI	SB	BB	SO	Avg	OBP	Slg
1997	47	69	16	17	3	0	0	4	2	7	20	.246	.346	.290
Career	47	69	16	17	3	0	0	4	2	7	20	.246	.346	.290

When you're hitting just .164 in the minors at age 30, that's a sign that your career is in jeopardy. He was designated for reassignment in August. 1998 Outlook: D

Alberto Castillo (Pos: C, Age: 28, Bats: R)

	G	AB	R	H	D	T	HR	RBI	SB	BB	SO	Avg	OBP	Slg
1997	35	59	3	12	1	0	0	7	0	9	16	.203	.304	.220
Career	54	99	6	19	1	0	0	7	1	12	29	.192	.283	.202

Castillo split the catching duties with Todd Pratt after Todd Hundley developed elbow difficulties in September. Nothing short of severe injury problems will force the Mets to call him up in the future. 1998 Outlook: D

Joe Crawford (Pos: LHP, Age: 27)

	W	L	Pct.	ERA	G	GS	Sv	IP	H	BB	SO	HR	Ratio
1997	4	3	.571	3.30	19	2	0	46.1	36	13	25	7	1.06
Career	4	3	.571	3.30	19	2	0	46.1	36	13	25	7	1.06

Crawford pitched well for the Mets both out of the bullpen and as a spot starter. He allowed just 36 hits in 46.1 innings last season— but seven of those hits left the park. He does have good strikeout/walk data. 1998 Outlook: B

Shawn Gilbert (Pos: 2B, Age: 30, Bats: R)

	G	AB	R	H	D	T	HR	RBI	SB	BB	SO	Avg	OBP	Slg
1997	29	22	3	3	0	0	1	1	1	1	8	.136	.174	.273
Career	29	22	3	3	0	0	1	1	1	1	8	.136	.174	.273

New York sure has trouble deciding what it wants, doesn't it? Gilbert was one of a number of Mets who spent the '97 season in continuous limbo between the majors and minors. Not a prospect. 1998 Outlook: D

Ricardo Jordan (Pos: LHP, Age: 27)

	W	L	Pct.	ERA	G	GS	Sv	IP	H	BB	SO	HR	Ratio
1997	1	2	.333	5.33	22	0	0	27.0	31	15	19	1	1.70
Career	4	4	.500	4.30	63	0	1	67.0	67	40	46	4	1.60

Riding a continuous shuttle between Shea Stadium and Triple-A Norfolk, Jordan was hammered in middle relief for the Mets last season. He signed a minor league contract with the Reds in the offseason. 1998 Outlook: C

Takashi Kashiwada (Pos: LHP, Age: 26)

	W	L	Pct.	ERA	G	GS	Sv	IP	H	BB	SO	HR	Ratio
1997	3	1	.750	4.31	35	0	0	31.1	35	18	19	4	1.69
Career	3	1	.750	4.31	35	0	0	31.1	35	18	19	4	1.69

One of four Japanese natives to see action in the majors last season, Kashiwada wasn't particularly effective from the bullpen and struggled with his control. The Mets cut him after the season. 1998 Outlook: C

Barry Manuel (Pos: RHP, Age: 32)

	W	L	Pct.	ERA	G	GS	Sv	IP	H	BB	SO	HR	Ratio
1997	0	1	.000	5.26	19	0	0	25.2	35	13	21	6	1.87
Career	6	2	.750	3.44	83	0	0	133.1	118	46	97	18	1.23

Acquired from Montreal right before the start of the season, Manuel spent two months with the Mets before his lack of success in middle relief earned him a one-way trip to Triple-A Norfolk. 1998 Outlook: C

Carlos Mendoza (Pos: CF, Age: 23, Bats: L)

	G	AB	R	H	D	T	HR	RBI	SB	BB	SO	Avg	OBP	Slg
1997	15	12	6	3	0	0	0	1	0	4	2	.250	.500	.250
Career	15	12	6	3	0	0	0	1	0	4	2	.250	.500	.250

Mendoza saw some action in the Mets' outfield after being called up in September. He has good speed and drew a ton of walks in the minors, and went to Tampa Bay in the expansion draft. 1998 Outlook: B

Kevin Morgan (Pos: 3B, Age: 28, Bats: R)

	G	AB	R	H	D	T	HR	RBI	SB	BB	SO	Avg	OBP	Slg
1997	1	1	0	0	0	0	0	0	0	0	0	.000	.000	.000
Career	1	1	0	0	0	0	0	0	0	0	0	.000	.000	.000

Morgan received his first ever major league at-bat in June during his five-day stay with the Mets. It might have been his last, since he was designated for reassignment in August. 1998 Outlook: D

Yorkis Perez (Pos: LHP, Age: 30)

	W	L	Pct.	ERA	G	GS	Sv	IP	H	BB	SO	HR	Ratio
1997	0	1	.000	8.31	9	0	0	8.2	15	4	7	2	2.19
Career	9	11	.450	4.86	189	0	1	148.0	136	79	145	14	1.45

Perez has always had great strikeout rates, but never found consistent success during his three years in the Marlins' bullpen. He spent most of the '97 season in the minors after developing elbow trouble. 1998 Outlook: C

Todd Pratt (Pos: C, Age: 31, Bats: R)

	G	AB	R	H	D	T	HR	RBI	SB	BB	SO	Avg	OBP	Slg
1997	39	106	12	30	6	0	2	19	0	13	32	.283	.372	.396
Career	141	401	39	96	21	1	11	55	0	40	113	.239	.312	.379

Returning to the majors after a one-year absence, Pratt received steady playing time near the end of '97 and hit well. He's not known for his defense, so his bat will have to stay hot for him to stick around. 1998 Outlook: B

Gary Thurman (Pos: CF, Age: 33, Bats: R)

	G	AB	R	H	D	T	HR	RBI	SB	BB	SO	Avg	OBP	Slg
1997	11	6	0	1	0	0	0	0	0	0	0	.167	.167	.167
Career	424	798	121	194	27	6	2	64	65	61	187	.243	.297	.299

Thurman's professional career appears over after hitting only .212 at Triple-A Ottawa and managing just six at-bats in the majors last season. He has career on-base and slugging averages under .300. 1998 Outlook: D

Andy Tomberlin (Pos: LF, Age: 31, Bats: L)

	G	AB	R	H	D	T	HR	RBI	SB	BB	SO	Avg	OBP	Slg
1997	6	7	0	2	0	0	0	0	0	1	3	.286	.375	.286
Career	160	236	32	56	4	2	9	26	5	23	78	.237	.310	.386

Tomberlin missed nearly the entire season after undergoing surgery to repair a herniated disk in his neck. Even before the injury, he was nothing more than a marginal player. His future looks cloudy. 1998 Outlook: C

Ricky Trlicek (Pos: RHP, Age: 28)

	W	L	Pct.	ERA	G	GS	Sv	IP	H	BB	SO	HR	Ratio
1997	3	4	.429	5.57	27	0	0	32.1	36	23	14	4	1.82
Career	5	8	.385	5.23	87	1	1	125.2	132	65	66	12	1.57

After being acquired in May from the Boston Red Sox, Trlicek's season ended in June after developing tendinitis in his middle finger. He has been very inconsistent throughout his career, but could get a shot. 1998 Outlook: C

New York Mets Minor League Prospects

Organization Overview:

The Mets have remade themselves in the last few years with homegrown prospects such as Edgardo Alfonzo, Todd Hundley, Butch Huskey, Bobby Jones and Rey Ordonez. The team would have been even better off had aces-in-the making Jason Isringhausen, Bill Pulsipher and Paul Wilson not lost most of 1997 to injury. Their successor as the top pitching prospect in the system, Grant Roberts, looked like he might need major elbow surgery. And Jay Payton, their best hitting prospect, missed all year with continuing elbow problems. New York is trying to determine the cause for the rash of injuries, which have curtailed a team that hoped to be a serious contender in the National League East by now.

Fletcher Bates

Position: OF **Opening Day Age:** 24
Bats: B **Throws:** R **Born:** 3/24/74 in
Ht: 6' 1" **Wt:** 193 Wilmington, NC

Recent Statistics

	G	AB	R	H	D	T	HR	RBI	SB	BB	SO	AVG
96 A Columbia	132	491	84	127	21	13	15	72	16	64	162	.259
97 A St. Lucie	70	253	49	76	19	11	11	38	7	33	66	.300
97 AA Binghamton	68	245	44	63	14	2	12	34	9	21	71	.257
97 MLE	68	235	35	53	11	1	9	27	5	17	76	.226

A fifth-round pick in 1993, Bates has put up better numbers in the pros then his former teammate Trot Nixon, Boston's first-round choice that year. Bates wasn't protected on the Mets' 40-man roster after the 1996 season, but slipped through the Rule 5 draft and had a nice year split between high Class-A and Double-A. He's a switch-hitter with power from both sides of the plate and 20-20 potential. He still strikes out a lot on breaking pitches, but he does draw walks. A decent right fielder, he should reach Triple-A at some point in 1998 and could surface in New York the following year.

Arnie Gooch

Position: P **Opening Day Age:** 21
Bats: R **Throws:** R **Born:** 11/12/76 in
Ht: 6' 2" **Wt:** 195 Levittown, PA

Recent Statistics

	W	L	ERA	G	GS	Sv	IP	H	R	BB	SO	HR
96 A St. Lucie	12	12	2.58	26	26	0	167.2	131	74	51	141	7
97 AA Binghamton	10	12	5.09	27	27	0	161.0	179	106	76	98	12

Gooch came to the Mets along with oft-injured righthander Juan Acevedo in the July 1995 Bret Saberhagen trade with the Rockies. A ninth-round pick in 1994, Gooch had a tough time making the jump to Double-A after a banner year in the high Class-A Flor-

ida State League. He put on weight and lost some pop on his fastball, which had average velocity to begin with. When he's on, his fastball has heavy sinking action and his curve breaks sharply. He's still young at 21 and will get another chance in Double-A. His stock has fallen and he now is seen as a No. 4 or 5 starter.

Jay Payton

Position: OF **Opening Day Age:** 24
Bats: R **Throws:** R **Born:** 11/22/72 in
Ht: 5' 10" **Wt:** 190 Zanesville, OH

Recent Statistics

	G	AB	R	H	D	T	HR	RBI	SB	BB	SO	AVG
96 R Mets	3	13	3	5	1	0	1	2	1	0	1	.385
96 AA Binghamton	4	10	0	2	0	0	0	2	0	2	2	.200
96 A St. Lucie	9	26	4	8	2	0	0	1	2	4	5	.308
96 AAA Norfolk	55	153	30	47	6	3	6	26	10	11	25	.307
97				Did Not Play—Injured								

Payton figured to be an everyday big leaguer by now. Instead, he missed all of 1997 and played in just 71 games the year before. He had elbow surgery in 1995 and after the 1996 season, but hurt his elbow again in spring training last year and still felt pain six months later. A 1994 supplemental first-round pick out of Georgia Tech, Payton won batting titles and MVP awards in his first two pro seasons. He's a line-drive hitter with extra-base power and basestealing speed. His arm wasn't much before his elbow problems, and he'll be limited to left field. The Mets don't know what his future holds at this point.

Grant Roberts

Position: P **Opening Day Age:** 20
Bats: R **Throws:** R **Born:** 9/13/77 in El
Ht: 6' 3" **Wt:** 187 Cajon, CA

Recent Statistics

	W	L	ERA	G	GS	Sv	IP	H	R	BB	SO	HR
96 R Kingsport	9	1	2.10	13	13	0	68.2	43	18	37	92	3
97 A Columbia	11	3	2.36	22	22	0	129.2	98	37	44	122	1

Equally dismaying was the news that Roberts needed elbow surgery, which could cost him part of the 1998 season. An 11th-round pick in 1995, he was named the Class-A South Atlantic League's pitcher of the year and top pitching prospect last season. He already threw 94-96 MPH at age 19, and was honing a repertoire that also includes a curveball, slider and changeup. His command was very good for a teenager with his velocity. The Mets say the surgery was minor and will put Roberts in high Class-A when he's ready to pitch. He's two to three years away from the majors.

Jesus Sanchez

Position: P   **Opening Day Age:** 23
Bats: L **Throws:** L   **Born:** 10/11/74 in
Ht: 5' 10" **Wt:** 153   Nazao Bani, DR

Recent Statistics

	W	L	ERA	G	GS	Sv	IP	H	R	BB	SO	HR
96 A St. Lucie	9	3	1.96	16	16	0	92.0	53	22	24	81	6
97 AA Binghamton	13	10	4.30	26	26	0	165.1	146	87	61	176	25

The Mets are in need of inspiration and perhaps Sanchez can provide it. He had reconstructive elbow surgery following the 1995 season, and came back the next year throwing harder than ever. Signed out of the Dominican Republic, he now can get his fastball up to 93 MPH. He likes to establish his heater, and often won't throw his other pitches in the early innings. That can work against him, because his slider and changeup make him more effective. Sanchez continued his comeback in 1997, striking out more than a batter per inning in Double-A. After a year in Triple-A, he could be ready to help the Mets.

Mike Welch

Position: P   **Opening Day Age:** 25
Bats: L **Throws:** R   **Born:** 8/25/72 in
Ht: 6' 2" **Wt:** 207   Haverhill, MA

Recent Statistics

	W	L	ERA	G	GS	Sv	IP	H	R	BB	SO	HR
96 AA Binghamton	4	2	4.59	46	0	27	51.0	55	29	10	53	4
96 AAA Norfolk	0	1	4.15	10	0	2	8.2	8	4	2	6	0
97 AAA Norfolk	2	2	3.66	46	0	20	51.2	53	21	16	35	6

With Derek Wallace sidelined by a shoulder aneurysm, Welch re-emerged as the Mets' top relief prospect in the high minors. Welch didn't pitch until his freshman year at Southern Maine, but developed quickly and was drafted in the third round in 1993. He can hit 93-94 MPH consistently and has command of both two- and four-seam fastballs. He doesn't have good control of his slider and has no offspeed pitch. He's poised and has 64 saves in the last three years, but probably is more cut out for setup duty. He could contribute to the Mets in 1998.

Preston Wilson

Position: OF   **Opening Day Age:** 23
Bats: R **Throws:** R   **Born:** 7/19/74 in
Ht: 6' 2" **Wt:** 193   Bamberg, SC

Recent Statistics

	G	AB	R	H	D	T	HR	RBI	SB	BB	SO	AVG
96 A St. Lucie	23	85	6	15	3	0	1	7	1	8	21	.176
97 A St. Lucie	63	245	32	60	12	1	11	48	3	8	66	.245
97 AA Binghamton	70	259	37	74	12	1	19	47	7	21	71	.286
97 MLE	70	247	29	62	10	0	14	37	4	14	76	.251

A first-round pick in 1992, Wilson finally showed the huge power potential New York always believed he had. The son of Mets icon Mookie Wilson, he went through a series of injuries and played in only 23 games in 1996. Last season, he stayed healthy, hit 30 homers and reached Double-A. He still strikes out too much and rarely walks, but the Mets like his tools and instincts. He's starting to use the whole field as a hitter, he runs well and he has improved defensively. He must stop chasing breaking pitches, and will spend the next couple of years in the minors learning to do so.

Ed Yarnall

Position: P   **Opening Day Age:** 22
Bats: L **Throws:** L   **Born:** 12/4/75 in Lima,
Ht: 6' 4" **Wt:** 220   PA

Recent Statistics

	W	L	ERA	G	GS	Sv	IP	H	R	BB	SO	HR
97 A St. Lucie	5	8	2.48	18	18	0	105.1	93	33	30	114	5
97 AAA Norfolk	0	1	14.40	1	1	0	5.0	11	8	7	2	1
97 AA Binghamton	3	2	3.06	5	5	0	32.1	20	11	11	32	2

Yarnall provided a pleasant surprise to an organization sorely in need of one. A third-round pick out of Louisiana State in 1996, he held out all summer and then looked mediocre in instructional league. When he made his pro debut in 1997, he posted fine numbers and even made a spot start in Triple-A. He doesn't blow hitters away, instead frustrating them with a sinking fastball, a very good changeup and a deceptive delivery. His breaking ball is coming along. Yarnall is progressing faster than the Mets expected, and could be ready by 1999.

Others to Watch

Righthander **Octavio Dotel**, 24, can touch 95 MPH and also has a hard curveball. But after dominating Class-A hitters in 1996, he posted a 5.98 ERA in Double-A. . . Righthander **Brett Herbison** is only 20, but he already has a tremendus changeup and an above-average curveball. If he fills out and picks up velocity, he might be special. . . Lefthander **Kyle Kessel**, 21, went 11-11, 2.72 with 151 strikeouts in 169 innings at Class-A Capital City. Now focused on baseball after two years of playing basketball for Texas A&M, he's a four-pitch pitcher with a good fastball. . . Outfielder **Terrence Long** has five-tool potential but hit a soft .251 at Class-A St. Lucie at age 21. The Mets still believe in him. . . The Mets had a collection of corner infielders who enjoyed strong seasons in 1997: third baseman **Scott McClain** (.280-21-64 in Triple-A), first baseman **Roberto Petagine** (.317-31-100 in Triple-A), third baseman **Matt Raleigh** (.196-37-74 in Double-A) and first baseman **Tate Seefried** (.295-32-92 between Double-A and Triple-A). The 26-year-old Petagine, who was named International League MVP, is the only viable major leaguer. But he may be headed to Japan because he can't find a big league opportunity. . . Righthander **Derek Wallace** was going to be an apprentice to Mets closer John Franco, but a shoulder aneurysm wiped out most of his year. The 26-year-old Wallace was a power pitcher with a 93-95 MPH fastball and a hard slider, but faces a long road back.

Terry Francona

1997 Season

Terry Francona is the prototypical players' manager and had a successful big league debut in 1997. He quickly gained the Phillies' respect with an organized, demanding and professional training camp. He maintained his sense of humor as Philadelphia got off to one of the worst starts in baseball history. He must receive the lions' share of the credit for the team's refusal to die in the second half, as it posted the third-best record (44-33) in the National League after the All-Star break.

Offense

Francona had arguably the most limited arsenal of offensive weapons in baseball, even before Danny Tartabull went down. The Phillies lacked team speed and power, so steals and three-run homers weren't plentiful. Francona knew his team needed to scratch and claw for runs, so the hit-and-run was used throughout the lineup. He liked to use his whole roster, so everyone outside of Scott Rolen could count on being rested once a week.

Pitching & Defense

Francona was in damage-control mode early in the season when his pitchers struggled. He lacked a durable, power reliever for the seventh and eighth innings, and he had only one lefty reliever for most of the season. At least the ninth inning belonged to Ricky Bottalico. Francona is uncomfortable starting players who are poor defensively. Only Ruben Amaro was used often as a defensive replacement in 1997.

1998 Outlook

While he begins the last year of a two-year contract, Francona is expected to be offered a long-term extension. He has the respect of his players and the support of his front office. He's pleased with the Phillies' young pitching and believes that the chief needs for 1998 are a leadoff hitter/center fielder and another run-producing outfielder. The Phils won't be expected to contend but think they can make a run at .500.

Born: 4/22/59 in Aberdeen, SD

Playing Experience: 1981-1990, Mon, ChN, Cin, Cle, Mil

Managerial Experience: 1 season

Manager Statistics

Year	Team, Lg	W	L	Pct	GB	Finish
1997	Philadelphia, NL	68	94	.420	33.0	5th East
1 Season		68	94	.420	—	—

1997 Starting Pitchers by Days Rest

	≤3	4	5	6+
Phillies Starts	1	95	22	29
Phillies ERA	1.13	4.66	4.90	4.49
NL Avg Starts	3	90	38	22
NL ERA	4.23	4.05	4.27	4.52

1997 Situational Stats

	Terry Francona	NL Average
Hit & Run Success %	27.8	36.4
Stolen Base Success %	62.2	68.4
Platoon Pct.	65.5	56.3
Defensive Subs	28	26
High-Pitch Outings	22	12
Quick/Slow Hooks	14/15	18/10
Sacrifice Attempts	91	96

1997 Rankings (National League)

⇒ 1st in steals of home plate (2) and sacrifice bunt percentage (93.4%)

⇒ 2nd in slow hooks (15) and starts with over 120 pitches (22)

⇒ 3rd in least caught steals of home plate (2)

Matt Beech

1997 Season

Shoulder stiffness cost Matt Beech half of spring training, denying him a chance to make the Phillies out of camp. He got his chance after five Triple-A starts and promptly sprained an ankle while running the bases in his first major league start of the year. After pitching in hard luck for much of the season, Beech established himself as a viable big league starter with some excellent late-season performances.

Pitching

Beech has an 88-MPH fastball that moves sharply away from lefthanders. He also throws a hard slider and a slow curve, delivered at an arm angle that's downright unfair to lefties. Beech always has dominated lefties and posted impressive strikeout/walk ratios in the minor leagues, but has been touched for too many homers. When he gets behind in the count he has a tendency to groove fastballs, particularly against righthanders.

Defense & Hitting

Beech is an ordinary defensive pitcher whose follow-through sometimes leaves him out of fielding position. For a southpaw, he handles the running game poorly. His pickoff move is average and his slow delivery gives runners a good jump. He takes a healthy cut at the plate, but hurt himself running the bases on his only extra-base hit of 1997. More importantly, he's an expert bunter.

1998 Outlook

The only lefty starter in the organization who's capable of contributing in the majors, Beech is expected to make the rotation out of spring training. He may be the closest to a sure thing among the team's young hurlers, and must only cut down his homers to become a steady No. 3 starter. His strikeout/walk ratio and potential for above-average control are harbingers of better things to come.

Position: SP
Bats: L **Throws:** L
Ht: 6' 2" **Wt:** 190

Opening Day Age: 26
Born: 1/20/72 in Oakland, CA
ML Seasons: 2

Overall Statistics

	W	L	Pct.	ERA	G	GS	Sv	IP	H	BB	SO	HR	Ratio
1997	4	9	.308	5.07	24	24	0	136.2	147	57	120	25	1.49
Career	5	13	.278	5.51	32	32	0	178.0	196	68	153	33	1.48

How Often He Throws Strikes

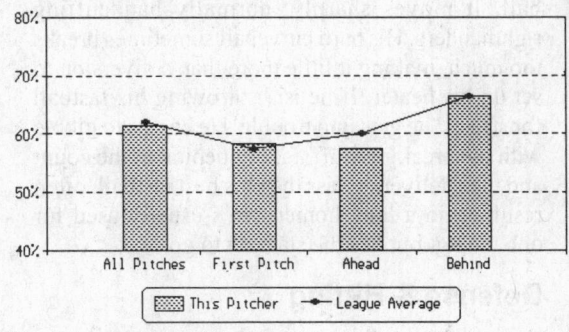

1997 Situational Stats

	W	L	ERA	Sv	IP		AB	H	HR	RBI	Avg
Home	1	3	5.26	0	49.2	LHB	89	20	3	10	.225
Road	3	6	4.97	0	87.0	RHB	438	127	22	62	.290
First Half	0	4	5.72	0	45.2	Sc Pos	124	28	2	39	.226
Scnd Half	4	5	4.75	0	91.0	Clutch	22	7	2	2	.318

1997 Rankings (National League)

⇒ 4th in highest batting average allowed vs. righthanded batters
⇒ 5th in home runs allowed
⇒ 8th in balks (2) and highest ERA on the road
⇒ 10th in sacrifice bunts (11)
⇒ Led the Phillies in home runs allowed and balks (2)

Ricky Bottalico

1997 Season

Though he wasn't the dominant force that he was in his first season as a closer in 1996, Ricky Bottalico still ranked as one of better finishers in the National League despite long stretches of inactivity during the Phillies' atrocious first half. He did endure a dead-arm period around midseason, losing 5 MPH off his fastball. He got his velocity back at about the time the Mariners inexplicably chose the Blue Jays' offer of Paul Spoljaric and Mike Timlin for Jose Cruz Jr. over Philadelphia's offer of Bottalico.

Pitching

Bottalico's best pitch is clearly his 93-MPH fastball. It moves sharply, normally handcuffing righthanders. His hard curveball sometimes breaks too much, making it little more than a diversion to set up his heater. If he isn't throwing his fastball for strikes, he gets into trouble. He begins to nibble with the breaking stuff, falling behind in the count and then delivering less than his best fastball, often resulting in a long homer. He's usually used for one inning, but has the stamina to go two.

Defense & Hitting

Bottalico has a slow, power-pitcher's delivery that affords many steal opportunities. His pickoff move has improved over time, but isn't much of a deterrent. He rarely bats but probably could hold his own. Like a growing number of major league closers, he's a converted catcher.

1998 Outlook

Now that the chance to acquire Cruz has passed, it's unlikely the Phils will deal Bottalico because he's both productive and inexpensive. Expect his command to rebound in 1998. Even more important, the Phils should improve and offer him more save opportunities. Bottalico is in his prime and could have his best season yet in 1998.

Position: RP
Bats: L **Throws:** R
Ht: 6' 1" **Wt:** 208

Opening Day Age: 28
Born: 8/26/69 in New Britain, CT
ML Seasons: 4
Pronunciation: buh-TAL-ih-co

Overall Statistics

	W	L	Pct.	ERA	G	GS	Sv	IP	H	BB	SO	HR	Ratio
1997	2	5	.286	3.65	69	0	34	74.0	68	42	89	7	1.49
Career	11	13	.458	3.02	195	0	69	232.1	168	108	253	20	1.19

How Often He Throws Strikes

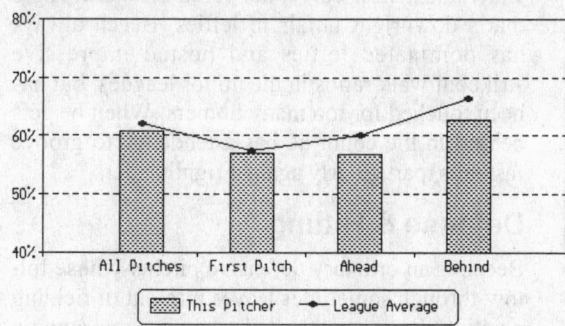

1997 Situational Stats

	W	L	ERA	Sv	IP		AB	H	HR	RBI	Avg
Home	2	3	3.21	17	42.0	LHB	137	35	2	17	.255
Road	0	2	4.22	17	32.0	RHB	140	33	5	21	.236
First Half	1	3	3.82	15	37.2	Sc Pos	75	22	1	28	.293
Scnd Half	1	2	3.47	19	36.1	Clutch	186	46	3	30	.247

1997 Rankings (National League)

⇒ 4th in games finished (61) and blown saves (7)
⇒ 6th in most strikeouts per 9 innings in relief (10.8)
⇒ 8th in saves, save opportunities (41) and save percentage (82.9%)
⇒ Led the Phillies in saves, games finished (61), save opportunities (41), save percentage (82.9%), blown saves (7), relief ERA (3.65), lowest batting average allowed in relief (.245) and most strikeouts per 9 innings in relief (10.8)

Rico Brogna

1997 Season

The Phillies gleefully accepted Rico Brogna in a preseason trade with the Mets for a pair of marginal relievers. Though Brogna remains clearly below average offensively for a first baseman, he was a consistent run producer for Philadelphia against righthanded pitching, and a stud defensively. He toiled in 148 games despite a painful arthritic condition in both knees that could have shut him down at any time.

Hitting

Brogna is a strapping lefthanded hitter who's comfortable hitting the ball where it's pitched. He doesn't turn his hips and pull the ball nearly as often as most lefty power hitters. He's overly aggressive at the plate, especially early in the count. He never has walked more than 39 times in a season. An even worse problem is his utter inability to hit lefthanded pitching. He has sunk below the Mendoza line against southpaws the past two seasons.

Baserunning & Defense

Chronic knee problems compromise Brogna's raw speed. Still, he has exceptional quickness, which serves him well on the bases and in the field. He picked his spots, stealing 12 bases in 1997, and ran the bases intelligently. He was simply brilliant with the glove, showing exceptional range, especially to his left. His uncanny ability to scoop poor throws out of the dirt saved many an error.

1998 Outlook

The Phils consider Brogna to be part of their long-term nucleus. That said, they better recruit some outfielders with good offensive upsides. In a perfect world and on a better team, he would be no better than a platoon player or a defensive replacement. His lack of on-base skills makes him a negative presence in any of the first five spots in a batting order.

Position: 1B
Bats: L **Throws:** L
Ht: 6' 2" **Wt:** 205

Opening Day Age: 27
Born: 4/18/70 in Turner Falls, MA
ML Seasons: 5
Pronunciation: BRONE-yuh

Overall Statistics

	G	AB	R	H	D	T	HR	RBI	SB	BB	SO	Avg	OBP	Slg
1997	148	543	68	137	36	1	20	81	12	33	116	.252	.293	.433
Career	385	1383	177	379	85	6	57	210	13	100	311	.274	.322	.468

Where He Hits the Ball

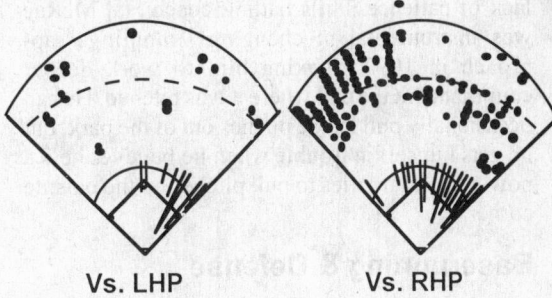

Vs. LHP   Vs. RHP

1997 Situational Stats

	AB	H	HR	RBI	Avg		AB	H	HR	RBI	Avg
Home	252	64	9	38	.254	LHP	116	22	1	11	.190
Road	291	73	11	43	.251	RHP	427	115	19	70	.269
First Half	298	77	9	44	.258	Sc Pos	158	44	7	63	.278
Scnd Half	245	60	11	37	.245	Clutch	77	22	5	13	.286

1997 Rankings (National League)

⇒ 1st in lowest on-base percentage
⇒ 6th in fielding percentage at first base (.994)
⇒ 7th in errors at first base (7)
⇒ 8th in lowest on-base percentage vs. righthanded pitchers (.311)
⇒ 10th in lowest batting average at home
⇒ Led the Phillies in GDPs (13) and slugging percentage vs. righthanded pitchers (.482)

Midre Cummings

1997 Season

Back in 1992, Midre Cummings—not Denny Neagle—was considered the key player obtained by the Pirates from the Twins in the John Smiley trade. A perennial disappointment, Cummings was waived by Pittsburgh before baseball's last-chance station, Philadelphia, intervened in mid-1997. For the first time in his career, Cummings got a chance to play every day as a leadoff man, and he batted .303 as a Phillie. Particularly impressive was his .405 average with two out and runners in scoring position.

Hitting

Cummings always has been undone by his utter lack of patience. Phils batting coach Hal McRae was instrumental in changing Cummings' approach in 1997, coaxing him to work deeper counts and hit the ball where it was pitched. He can occasionally pull inside pitches out of the park, but he gets himself in trouble when he believes he's a power hitter and tries to pull pitches on the outside corner.

Baserunning & Defense

Cummings is a talented baseball player, but not an instinctive one. He has above-average speed, though it doesn't show up in his statistics. Entering the 1997 season, he had attempted exactly one stolen base in his major league career. He's an overly cautious baserunner who seldom takes the extra base. He covers substantial ground in center field, but often takes indirect routes to fly balls. His arm is average at best.

1998 Outlook

Despite playing about as well as he can in his stint with the Phillies, Cummings' production still was insufficient for a starting major league outfielder. Philadelphia desperately needs a leadoff hitter, and Cummings still doesn't reach base enough. The Phils are likely to pursue a free-agent center fielder and leadoff man, but Cummings certainly showed enough to be kept as a fourth outfielder.

Position: CF/LF/RF
Bats: L **Throws:** R
Ht: 6' 0" **Wt:** 203

Opening Day Age: 26
Born: 10/14/71 in St. Croix, Virgin Islands
ML Seasons: 5
Pronunciation: MEE-dray

Overall Statistics

	G	AB	R	H	D	T	HR	RBI	SB	BB	SO	Avg	OBP	Slg
1997	115	314	35	83	22	6	4	31	2	31	56	.264	.330	.411
Career	235	673	75	164	37	8	10	68	3	52	129	.244	.298	.367

Where He Hits the Ball

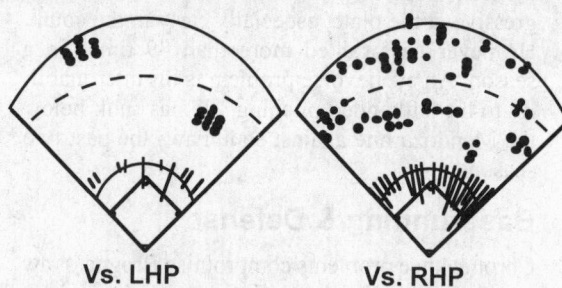

Vs. LHP　　　Vs. RHP

1997 Situational Stats

	AB	H	HR	RBI	Avg		AB	H	HR	RBI	Avg
Home	148	43	3	18	.291	LHP	38	11	0	2	.289
Road	166	40	1	13	.241	RHP	276	72	4	29	.261
First Half	106	20	3	8	.189	Sc Pos	69	22	0	25	.319
Scnd Half	208	63	1	23	.303	Clutch	45	13	1	8	.289

1997 Rankings (National League)

⇒ 7th in on-base percentage for a leadoff hitter (.373)
⇒ Led the Phillies in on-base percentage for a leadoff hitter (.373)

Tyler Green

1997 Season

Tyler Green's future appeared bright when he made the 1995 National League All-Star team, but he then missed a season and a half with shoulder problems that required surgery. He pitched poorly in an early-season stint at Triple-A Scranton/Wilkes-Barre in 1997, but he proved capable of taking a regular turn and pitching deep into ballgames. He was more effective in the majors, throwing four pitches and exhibiting mound savvy he lacked in 1995, when he relied mainly on pure stuff.

Pitching

Known for his lethal knuckle-curve, Green was drafted in the first round out of Wichita State in 1991. He could throw it for strikes on any count, making his 88-MPH fastball seem much faster. When he reached the majors, he couldn't throw his gimmick pitch for strikes and his heater got clobbered. Now the knuckler is a rarely-used relic. Green instead throws many more sliders, slow curves and changeups, and he has regained his velocity on his fastball. However, he's a nibbler with relatively poor command.

Defense & Hitting

Green is a solid athlete and an adequate fielder. His pickoff move isn't particularly impressive, but he has a relatively quick delivery that gives his catcher a fighting chance. He's an excellent hitter. He flirted with the .300 mark all season, and his hits weren't cheap. His bunting ability is underwhelming.

1998 Outlook

Green is clearly a more polished pitcher than he was prior to his 1995 shoulder injury, though his stuff isn't as good. The Phils would love to see him join Schilling and a host of youngsters in their 1998 rotation. Complicating matters is Green's inability to work out of the bullpen because his arm won't allow him to throw on consecutive days.

Position: SP
Bats: R **Throws:** R
Ht: 6' 5" **Wt:** 204

Opening Day Age: 28
Born: 2/18/70 in Springfield, OH
ML Seasons: 3

Overall Statistics

	W	L	Pct.	ERA	G	GS	Sv	IP	H	BB	SO	HR	Ratio
1997	4	4	.500	4.93	14	14	0	76.2	72	45	58	8	1.53
Career	12	13	.480	5.25	43	41	0	224.2	245	116	150	24	1.61

How Often He Throws Strikes

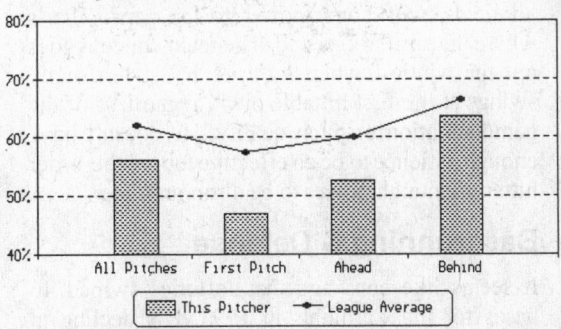

This Pitcher ▨   League Average ●—

1997 Situational Stats

	W	L	ERA	Sv	IP		AB	H	HR	RBI	Avg
Home	1	3	6.42	0	33.2	LHB	133	38	4	16	.286
Road	3	1	3.77	0	43.0	RHB	158	34	4	25	.215
First Half	0	0	-	0	0.0	Sc Pos	77	19	3	33	.247
Scnd Half	4	4	4.93	0	76.2	Clutch	11	5	0	1	.455

1997 Rankings (National League)

⇒ Did not rank near the top or bottom in any category

Gregg Jefferies

1997 Season

For a third straight year, Greg Jefferies was little more than a singles hitter who was difficult to strike out. That's not exactly what the Phillies had in mind when they made him a $5 million-per-year player. Once an authoritative hitter who slammed the ball regularly into the gaps, he seemed content to spray singles to all fields. His once above-average speed was hampered by recurring hamstring pulls.

Hitting

Jefferies was compared to Pete Rose as he exploded through the Mets system over a decade ago. Like Rose, he consistently puts the ball in play to all fields, with some power to the gaps. That's where the similarities end. The team concept goes out the window when Jefferies bats. He usually swings at the first hittable pitch, regardless of the game situation or pitch quality. He doesn't have enough patience to be an effective top-of-the-order hitter or enough power to be a run producer.

Baserunning & Defense

It seems like eons ago that Jefferies swiped 46 bases for the Cardinals in 1993. His decline in stolen-base production is equal parts loss of speed, having his aggressiveness compromised by several injuries, and the general malaise which has defined his Phillies career. Jefferies works hard in left field, often making routine plays difficult by taking circuitous routes. His throwing arm is weak but generally accurate.

1998 Outlook

The Phils asked Jefferies to waive his no-trade clause so that he could be dangled in the expansion draft. He did, but there were no takers. Most likely, manager Terry Francona will pencil him in for left field every day in 1998. He had the best strikeout/walk ratio of any regular player in baseball last year, so it's easy to believe he'll return to the .300 level.

Position: LF
Bats: B **Throws:** R
Ht: 5'10" **Wt:** 184

Opening Day Age: 30
Born: 8/1/67 in Burlingame, CA
ML Seasons: 11
Nickname: Puggsly

Overall Statistics

	G	AB	R	H	D	T	HR	RBI	SB	BB	SO	Avg	OBP	Slg
1997	130	476	68	122	25	3	11	48	12	53	27	.256	.333	.391
Career	1210	4618	649	1346	256	24	109	573	181	414	295	.291	.349	.428

Where He Hits the Ball

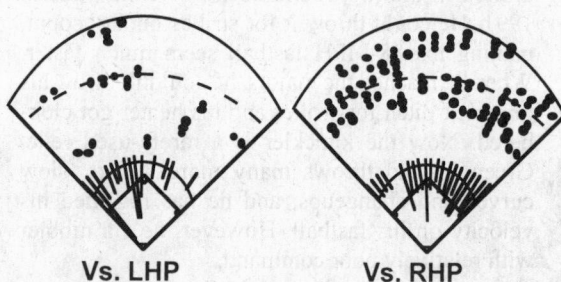

Vs. LHP   **Vs. RHP**

1997 Situational Stats

	AB	H	HR	RBI	Avg		AB	H	HR	RBI	Avg
Home	202	59	2	24	.292	LHP	111	37	5	21	.333
Road	274	63	9	24	.230	RHP	365	85	6	27	.233
First Half	303	76	5	28	.251	Sc Pos	109	26	0	31	.239
Scnd Half	173	46	6	20	.266	Clutch	68	24	2	13	.353

1997 Rankings (National League)

⇒ 2nd in lowest percentage of swings that missed (8.3%)

⇒ 3rd in lowest batting average vs. righthanded pitchers, fielding percentage in left field (.986) and lowest percentage of swings on the first pitch (15.8%)

⇒ Led the Phillies in intentional walks (7), batting average in the clutch, highest percentage of pitches taken (58.7%), lowest percentage of swings that missed (8.3%), highest percentage of swings put into play (57.1%) and lowest percentage of swings on the first pitch (15.8%)

Mark Leiter

1997 Season

Mark Leiter looked like a solid complement to ace Curt Schilling in the early going, but was one of the least effective major league starters over the middle third of the season. He was a true Jekyll-and-Hyde pitcher, likely to either pitch a three-hitter or be in the showers by the third inning in many of his starts. He did take his turn each time around the rotation, averaging six innings per start.

Pitching

Leiter actually has good stuff. His sinking fastball reaches about 87 MPH and has sharp downward movement when his mechanics are sound. He also features a splitter and a slow curve, which make his heater seem much faster. Lack of consistency is his problem. When his mechanics waver, his fastball doesn't sink much and his curve flattens, making him reluctant to change speeds. When that happens, *voila*, you have the Leiter who led the National League in losses (17) and extra-base hits allowed (90) in 1997. Against lefties, the results can be particularly scary. Southpaws have posted slugging percentages better than .500 against him in each of the last two seasons.

Defense & Hitting

Leiter is a below-average fielder whose motion often leaves him out of position. His delivery to the plate is slow, negating a decent pickoff move and making him easy to steal against. He's generally a poor hitter, even by pitchers' standards, but his bunting is acceptable.

1998 Outlook

Though under contract for 1998, Leiter isn't assured of a rotation berth. The Phils will give younger, higher-upside hurlers such as Mike Grace, Matt Beech, Garrett Stephenson and Tyler Green every opportunity to join Schilling in the 1998 rotation. The law of averages dictates that at least one of them will fail, opening a spot for Leiter.

Position: SP
Bats: R **Throws:** R
Ht: 6' 3" **Wt:** 210

Opening Day Age: 34
Born: 4/13/63 in Joliet, IL
ML Seasons: 8
Pronunciation: LITE-er

Overall Statistics

	W	L	Pct.	ERA	G	GS	Sv	IP	H	BB	SO	HR	Ratio
1997	10	17	.370	5.67	31	31	0	182.2	216	64	148	25	1.53
Career	56	67	.455	4.69	244	146	3	1058.1	1104	369	781	141	1.39

How Often He Throws Strikes

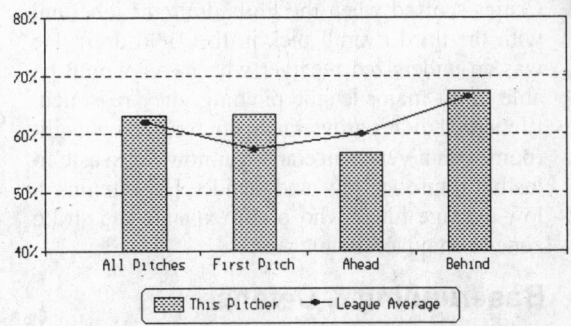

1997 Situational Stats

	W	L	ERA	Sv	IP		AB	H	HR	RBI	Avg
Home	5	7	5.46	0	90.2	LHB	374	118	13	66	.316
Road	5	10	5.87	0	92.0	RHB	366	98	12	55	.268
First Half	4	9	5.89	0	94.2	Sc Pos	198	60	8	96	.303
Scnd Half	6	8	5.42	0	88.0	Clutch	20	4	1	2	.200

1997 Rankings (National League)

⇒ 1st in highest ERA, losses and highest slugging percentage allowed (.491)
⇒ 2nd in wild pitches (11), highest ERA at home and highest ERA on the road
⇒ 3rd in lowest winning percentage, highest batting average allowed (.292) and most baserunners allowed per 9 innings (14.2)
⇒ Led the Phillies in losses, hits allowed, home runs allowed, walks allowed, hit batsmen (9), wild pitches (11), balks (2), pickoff throws (194), stolen bases allowed (19), least pitches thrown per batter (3.59), most run support per 9 innings (5.4) and most GDPs induced per 9 innings (0.6)

Mike Lieberthal

1997 Season

It would be hard to find a major league player who improved more during the 1997 season than Mike Lieberthal. Considered a weak hitter who lacked the clout to command the respect of a pitching staff when the season began, he evolved into a true team leader and a run producer. No less an authority than Curt Schilling raved about Lieberthal's development in the intangible areas that define a catcher's overall worth. Lieberthal allowed only .64 steals per nine innings, a figure bettered by only Brad Ausmus and Charles Johnson in the National League.

Hitting

Critics scoffed when the Phils drafted Lieberthal with the third overall pick in the 1990 draft. He was an undersized receiver who never would be able to hit major league pitching, they reasoned. Lieberthal didn't grow much, but he hit the weight room with a vengeance and can now lay waste to fastballs thrown low and inside. He remains a low-average hitter who often expands the strike zone to an unacceptable size.

Baserunning & Defense

Lieberthal has typical catcher's speed but is an exceedingly smart baserunner. This enables him to take the extra base more often than the bulk of his catching brethren. He's not Charles Johnson, but Lieberthal is among the most technically sound of the mere mortal catchers. His arm strength is only slightly above average, but his exceptionally quick release makes it tough for enemy runners to get a quick jump.

1998 Outlook

Lieberthal probably got a little bit ahead of himself offensively in 1997. His 20 homers could well go down as his career high. However, his offensive contribution is secondary in the Phils' eyes. He's viewed as a steady anchor who can stifle the opposition's running game. Rookie Bobby Estalella will afford him the needed rest as a backup catcher that Mark Parent couldn't in 1997.

Position: C
Bats: R **Throws:** R
Ht: 6' 0" **Wt:** 178

Opening Day Age: 26
Born: 1/18/72 in Glendale, CA
ML Seasons: 4
Pronunciation: LEE-ber-thal

Overall Statistics

	G	AB	R	H	D	T	HR	RBI	SB	BB	SO	Avg	OBP	Slg
1997	134	455	59	112	27	1	20	77	3	44	76	.246	.314	.442
Career	224	747	87	187	40	2	28	109	3	62	116	.250	.310	.422

Where He Hits the Ball

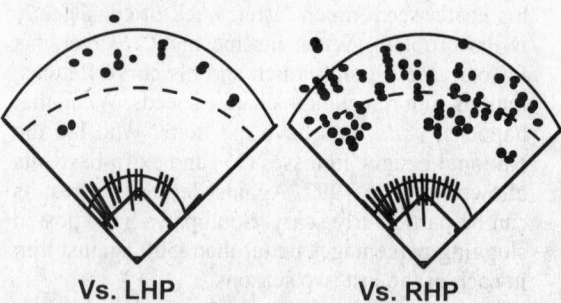

Vs. LHP   Vs. RHP

1997 Situational Stats

	AB	H	HR	RBI	Avg		AB	H	HR	RBI	Avg
Home	219	50	11	35	.228	LHP	106	26	5	25	.245
Road	236	62	9	42	.263	RHP	349	86	15	52	.246
First Half	229	52	12	31	.227	Sc Pos	129	32	9	61	.248
Scnd Half	226	60	8	46	.265	Clutch	74	17	2	9	.230

1997 Rankings (National League)

⇒ 2nd in errors at catcher (12)
⇒ 3rd in batting average on a 3-2 count (.385)
⇒ 4th in lowest batting average and lowest fielding percentage at catcher (.988)
⇒ 8th in lowest batting average on a 3-1 count (.125)
⇒ 9th in lowest on-base percentage vs. righthanded pitchers (.312)
⇒ Led the Phillies in sacrifice flies (7), HR frequency (22.8 ABs per HR), batting average with the bases loaded (.308) and batting average on a 3-2 count (.385)

Billy McMillon

1997 Season

One of the most consistently solid hitters in the minor leagues the past three seasons, Billy McMillon came to the Phillies from Florida for Darren Daulton in mid-1997. McMillon's pure lefthanded stroke has dismantled lefties and righties alike in the minors, but his first extended stay in the majors bore mixed results. He was much less patient than he had been as a minor leaguer, and he saw a steady diet of 0-2 breaking stuff as a result.

Hitting

The short, slim McMillon doesn't look like a hitting machine, but he possesses a quick bat capable of turning around most major league fastballs. His success in Triple-A against lefthanders (.359 in 1996, .286 in 1997) speaks volumes about his swing. He gets into trouble when he gets behind in the count and has to expand his strike zone. He needs to be a .300 hitter to start in the majors, as he lacks the home-run power expected of a corner outfielder.

Baserunning & Defense

McMillon had better hit, because he lacks complementary skills. His raw speed is slightly below average, though his solid baserunning instincts have helped him score plenty of runs in the minors. While he has developed a reputation as a competent outfielder, he looked shaky on the most routine of chances in his 1997 trial. His throwing arm limits him to left field only.

1998 Outlook

McMillon's lackluster 1997 failed to land him the inside track on an everyday role. He likely will have to battle his way onto the major league roster as a part-timer and pinch hitter. He's already 26, so he's not a future legend, but he clearly is a major league-caliber hitter. Expect the Phils to sign at least one free-agent outfielder, and then rely on McMillon and Midre Cummings as backups.

Position: LF
Bats: L **Throws:** L
Ht: 5'11" **Wt:** 172

Opening Day Age: 26
Born: 11/17/71 in Otero, NM
ML Seasons: 2

Overall Statistics

	G	AB	R	H	D	T	HR	RBI	SB	BB	SO	Avg	OBP	Slg
1997	37	90	10	23	5	1	2	14	2	6	24	.256	.293	.400
Career	65	141	14	34	5	1	2	18	2	11	38	.241	.290	.333

Where He Hits the Ball

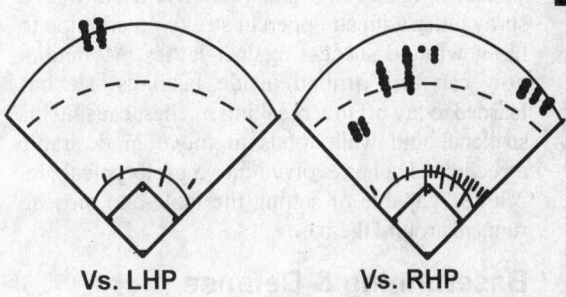

Vs. LHP   **Vs. RHP**

1997 Situational Stats

	AB	H	HR	RBI	Avg		AB	H	HR	RBI	Avg
Home	56	14	2	11	.250	LHP	15	5	1	2	.333
Road	34	9	0	3	.265	RHP	75	18	1	12	.240
First Half	17	2	0	1	.118	Sc Pos	30	7	1	13	.233
Scnd Half	73	21	2	13	.288	Clutch	15	2	0	3	.133

1997 Rankings (National League)

⇒ Did not rank near the top or bottom in any category

Mickey Morandini

1997 Season

Mickey Morandini further established himself as one of the steadiest National League second basemen. He had been overmatched by most lefthanders in the past, but he batted a career-high .304 against them in 1997. He learned to keep his hands back on breaking balls, spraying them the opposite way. Morandini was used in the leadoff spot during the early part of the season and showed the most patience of his career, walking 62 times. His defensive range declined, but he made only six errors.

Hitting

Morandini has whittled away at his offensive shortcomings through the years. He used to be a spray hitter with an uppercut stroke. In addition to his newfound success against lefties, Morandini now can turn around inside fastballs. He has learned to lay off low breaking pitches, causing his strikeout and walk totals to move in desirable directions. He has evolved into a prototypical No. 2 hitter, capable of setting the table and moving runners around the bases.

Baserunning & Defense

Morandini seemingly lost his basestealing form overnight when he collided with Mark Whiten while chasing a pop-up at Coors Field in 1996. He was leading the NL in steals at the time, but he has been both less aggressive and less successful since then. He remains a smart baserunner who aggressively takes the extra base. He makes every play within his somewhat limited range at second base. He made 32 fewer plays in 67 more innings in 1997 than he had in 1996.

1998 Outlook

Though Morandini is an attractive trade property who may be past his prime when the Phils are ready to contend, he's likely to remain their second baseman and No. 2 hitter. Though he may not reach his 1997 marks in batting average and doubles, he should post another solid all-around season.

Position: 2B
Bats: L **Throws:** R
Ht: 5'11" **Wt:** 176

Opening Day Age: 31
Born: 4/22/66 in Leechburg, PA
ML Seasons: 8
Pronunciation: mor-an-DEE-nee

Overall Statistics

	G	AB	R	H	D	T	HR	RBI	SB	BB	SO	Avg	OBP	Slg
1997	150	553	83	163	40	2	1	39	16	62	91	.295	.371	.380
Career	874	3111	403	835	156	41	20	232	98	281	492	.268	.335	.364

Where He Hits the Ball

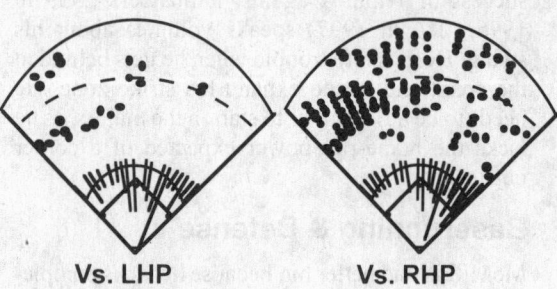

Vs. LHP   Vs. RHP

1997 Situational Stats

	AB	H	HR	RBI	Avg		AB	H	HR	RBI	Avg
Home	267	77	1	22	.288	LHP	125	38	0	17	.304
Road	286	86	0	17	.301	RHP	428	125	1	22	.292
First Half	305	94	1	15	.308	Sc Pos	113	29	1	37	.257
Scnd Half	248	69	0	24	.278	Clutch	62	20	0	12	.323

1997 Rankings (National League)

⇒ 1st in lowest HR frequency (553.0 ABs per HR) and lowest stolen base percentage (55.2%)
⇒ 2nd in fielding percentage at second base (.990)
⇒ 6th in caught stealing (13)
⇒ 7th in doubles and sacrifice bunts (12)
⇒ 8th in on-base percentage vs. lefthanded pitchers (.417)
⇒ 10th in singles
⇒ Led the Phillies in batting average, hits, singles, doubles, sacrifice bunts (12), stolen bases, caught stealing (13), highest groundball/flyball ratio (1.5), batting average vs. lefthanded pitchers, batting average vs. righthanded pitchers, batting average on an 0-2 count (.238), on-base percentage vs. lefthanded pitchers (.417) and batting average on the road

Scott Rolen

1997 Season

The Phillies had high expectations for Scott Rolen entering the 1997 season, and he exceeded them all. He quickly asserted himself as a team leader and as Philadelphia's best offensive and defensive player. Manager Terry Francona initially batted Rolen sixth in the order, but he became the No. 3 hitter for good by May. He showed a consistent line-drive stroke capable of occasional tape-measure power. It was no surprise when he was named National League Rookie of the Year.

Hitting

Rolen has lightning-quick bat speed and uses the entire field. Though he might post a 30-homer season or two before he's done, he's more of a gap hitter who should perennially bat .300. His main weakness is a tendency to strike out chasing high fastballs. He's more than willing to take a walk when the situation dictates, and often was pitched around with runners in scoring position in 1997. He's quite advanced at hitting breaking balls for a youngster.

Baserunning & Defense

These are areas where Rolen separates himself from most young players. He's an instinctive, aggressive baserunner with slightly above-average speed. He demonstrates his understanding of the game with baserunning moves that often appear reckless but are true genius upon reflection. Rolen is a shortstop playing third base. He has incredible reflexes, great range to both sides and a strong arm capable of generating throws from any release point. Still, he must learn to sometimes put the ball in his pocket rather than risk an errant throw.

1998 Outlook

Rolen will continue his march towards superstardom. Hitting .300 with 25 homers and 100 RBI is a reasonable projection for this mature, well-adjusted young man who's not impressed by himself. Others are plenty impressed. Braves shortstop Walt Weiss collects autographed bats from stars, and Rolen is by far the youngest player he has solicited.

Position: 3B
Bats: R **Throws:** R
Ht: 6' 4" **Wt:** 195

Opening Day Age: 22
Born: 4/4/75 in Evansville, IN
ML Seasons: 2
Pronunciation: ROH-len

Philadelphia Phillies

Overall Statistics

	G	AB	R	H	D	T	HR	RBI	SB	BB	SO	Avg	OBP	Slg
1997	156	561	93	159	35	3	21	92	16	76	138	.283	.377	.469
Career	193	691	103	192	42	3	25	110	16	89	165	.278	.367	.456

Where He Hits the Ball

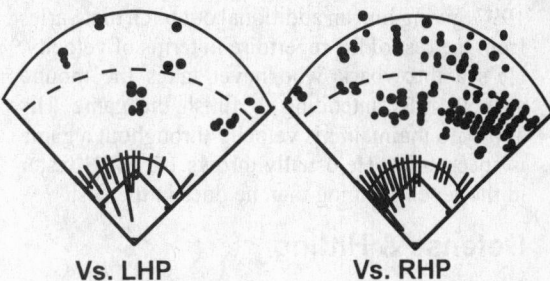

Vs. LHP   **Vs. RHP**

1997 Situational Stats

	AB	H	HR	RBI	Avg		AB	H	HR	RBI	Avg
Home	265	74	11	46	.279	LHP	131	37	3	24	.282
Road	296	85	10	46	.287	RHP	430	122	18	68	.284
First Half	306	87	10	48	.284	Sc Pos	159	51	5	65	.321
Scnd Half	255	72	11	44	.282	Clutch	72	20	2	12	.278

1997 Rankings (National League)

⇒ 2nd in errors at third base (24)
⇒ 3rd in lowest batting average with the bases loaded (.000)
⇒ 5th in strikeouts and highest percentage of extra bases taken as a runner (66.1%)
⇒ Led the Phillies in home runs, at-bats, runs scored, total bases (263), RBI, sacrifice flies (7), stolen bases, walks, hit by pitch (13), times on base (248), strikeouts, pitches seen (2,594), plate appearances (657), games played (156), slugging percentage, on-base percentage, stolen base percentage (72.7%), most pitches seen per plate appearance (3.95), least GDPs per GDP situation (4.0%), batting average with runners in scoring position and slugging percentage vs. lefthanded pitchers (.435)

Curt Schilling

1997 Season

All Curt Schilling did was break the all-time National League record for strikeouts by a righthander with 319. Even when the Phillies were sleepwalking through the first half of the season, his performance was reminiscent of Steve Carlton's tour de force with the 1972 club. Schilling proved to be fully recovered from the rotator-cuff and bone-spur problems that plagued him in 1995 and 1996. He led the majors in pitches thrown by a country mile.

Pitching

Schilling always has been a pure power pitcher, combining a 95-MPH fastball with a nasty slider. He added a splitter in 1996 and perfected it in 1997, giving him an additional out pitch that varies from the rest of his repertoire in terms of velocity. He's a throwback who never takes the mound without fully intending to finish the game. His ability to maintain his velocity throughout a game is spectacular. He usually throws 1-2 MPH faster in the seventh inning than he does in the first.

Defense & Hitting

Schilling is a proud athlete who takes all facets of the game seriously. His reflexes are exceptional, allowing him to spear liners through the middle better than most people not named Maddux. He has an above-average pickoff move and his delivery to the plate is quick for a power pitcher, giving his catcher time to make a play. He's a wild swinger who occasionally can drive the ball, and he is a strong bunter.

1998 Outlook

Though a repeat of his 1997 performance would be an unfair expectation, there's no reason to believe that Schilling's numbers will decline significantly. He has a rare combination of power and control. His record actually could improve as the Phils beef up his supporting cast.

Position: SP
Bats: R **Throws:** R
Ht: 6' 4" **Wt:** 226

Opening Day Age: 31
Born: 11/14/66 in Anchorage, AK
ML Seasons: 10
Pronunciation: SHILL-ing

Overall Statistics

	W	L	Pct.	ERA	G	GS	Sv	IP	H	BB	SO	HR	Ratio
1997	17	11	.607	2.97	35	35	0	254.1	208	58	319	25	1.05
Career	69	63	.523	3.38	267	156	13	1242.2	1088	349	1119	105	1.16

How Often He Throws Strikes

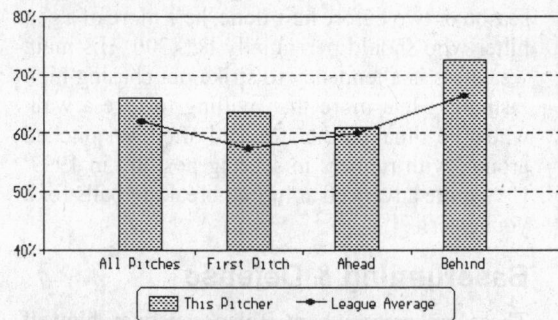

1997 Situational Stats

	W	L	ERA	Sv	IP		AB	H	HR	RBI	Avg
Home	7	6	2.80	0	144.2	LHB	458	107	16	51	.234
Road	10	5	3.20	0	109.2	RHB	472	101	9	41	.214
First Half	9	8	3.59	0	133.0	Sc Pos	187	39	2	59	.209
Scnd Half	8	3	2.30	0	121.1	Clutch	129	30	2	14	.233

1997 Rankings (National League)

⇒ 1st in games started, strikeouts, pitches thrown (4,132) and most pitches thrown per batter (4.10)

⇒ 2nd in highest strikeout/walk ratio (5.5) and most strikeouts per 9 innings (11.3)

⇒ 3rd in complete games (7), innings pitched, batters faced (1,009), lowest on-base percentage allowed (.271) and least baserunners allowed per 9 innings (9.6)

⇒ Led the Phillies in sacrifice bunts (12), ERA, wins, games started, complete games (7), shutouts (2), innings pitched, batters faced (1,009), home runs allowed, strikeouts, pitches thrown (4,132), runners caught stealing (9), GDPs induced (16), winning percentage and highest strikeout/walk ratio (5.5)

Garrett Stephenson

1997 Season

Acquired from the Orioles in 1996 along with Calvin Maduro in exchange for Pete Incaviglia and Todd Zeile, Garrett Stephenson didn't rate a September audition that year. He began 1997 as a swingman for Triple-A Scranton/Wilkes-Barre and was hit hard. Maduro's failure at the major league level made room for Stephenson, who promptly and uncharacteristically struck out 12 Cardinals in an eye-opening first start. He surprised further by maintaining his effectiveness in his second time around the National League.

Pitching

Stephenson has a merely average fastball, but it possesses sharp, sinking movement. Though he shows hitters a slider at times, his key offspeed pitch is his changeup. He'll throw it on any count and in any situation. When he's hitting the corners with his fastball early in the count, the change become a strikeout pitch. Stephenson always has possessed impeccable control, but he could become a batting-practice pitcher in a hurry if he doesn't continuously work on the black.

Defense & Hitting

Stephenson is an ordinary defensive pitcher, showing decent range when fielding bunts. His quick delivery and solid pickoff move enable him to shut down the opponent's running game better than most righthanders. He's an automatic out at the plate, though he has worked hard to make himself an adequate bunter.

1998 Outlook

The Phils will give Stephenson every opportunity to begin 1998 in their starting rotation. When he pitches as he did in 1997, he is a viable third or fourth starter, capable of keeping his club in games for six or seven innings. He has been very inconsistent in the minor leagues, so don't be surprised if the quality of the strikes he throws declines, knocking him out of the rotation.

Position: SP
Bats: R **Throws:** R
Ht: 6' 4" **Wt:** 195

Opening Day Age: 26
Born: 1/2/72 in Takoma Park, MD
ML Seasons: 2

Overall Statistics

	W	L	Pct.	ERA	G	GS	Sv	IP	H	BB	SO	HR	Ratio
1997	8	6	.571	3.15	20	18	0	117.0	104	38	81	11	1.21
Career	8	7	.533	3.65	23	18	0	123.1	117	41	84	12	1.28

How Often He Throws Strikes

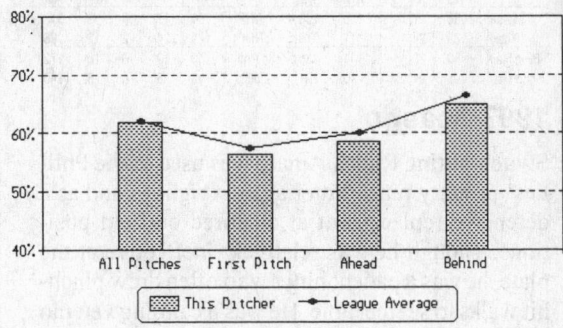

1997 Situational Stats

	W	L	ERA	Sv	IP		AB	H	HR	RBI	Avg
Home	6	3	2.78	0	68.0	LHB	178	43	6	17	.242
Road	2	3	3.67	0	49.0	RHB	248	61	5	25	.246
First Half	2	4	4.02	0	47.0	Sc Pos	84	18	4	33	.214
Scnd Half	6	2	2.57	0	70.0	Clutch	25	6	0	2	.240

1997 Rankings (National League)

⇒ Did not rank near the top or bottom in any category

Ruben Amaro

Position: CF/LF/RF
Bats: B **Throws:** R
Ht: 5'10" **Wt:** 175

Opening Day Age: 33
Born: 2/12/65 in
Philadelphia, PA
ML Seasons: 7

Overall Statistics

	G	AB	R	H	D	T	HR	RBI	SB	BB	SO	Avg	OBP	Slg
1997	117	175	18	41	6	1	2	21	1	21	24	.234	.320	.314
Career	393	820	92	198	38	9	15	90	15	82	113	.241	.321	.365

1997 Situational Stats

	AB	H	HR	RBI	Avg		AB	H	HR	RBI	Avg
Home	86	17	1	10	.198	LHP	54	17	0	9	.315
Road	89	24	1	11	.270	RHP	121	24	2	12	.198
First Half	80	20	2	11	.250	Sc Pos	58	10	0	18	.172
Scnd Half	95	21	0	10	.221	Clutch	43	6	0	3	.140

1997 Season

Switch-hitting Ruben Amaro was used as the Phillies' primary pinch hitter against righties and as a defensive replacement at all three outfield positions. Though he was relatively ineffective at the plate, he was a patient hitter who often drew pinch-hit walks to set the table. He was a calming veteran presence who kept himself ready to play at all times.

Hitting, Baserunning & Defense

Amaro is a limited offensive player whose chief attribute is plate discipline. His once above-average footspeed is in decline, and he never has possessed much extra-base power. He's a smart baserunner who knows when to take the extra base. He's sound defensively with acceptable range at all three outfield positions. His throwing arm is average at best.

1998 Outlook

The Phils are expected to upgrade their outfield prior to the 1998 season. This would likely move a more advanced player into the Amaro role, leaving the veteran looking for work. Even expansion might not save him. There isn't much of a market for outfielders lacking power, speed or exceptional defensive ability.

Wayne Gomes

Position: RP
Bats: R **Throws:** R
Ht: 6' 2" **Wt:** 226

Opening Day Age: 25
Born: 1/15/73 in
Hampton, VA
ML Seasons: 1
Pronunciation:
GOMES

Overall Statistics

	W	L	Pct.	ERA	G	GS	Sv	IP	H	BB	SO	HR	Ratio
1997	5	1	.833	5.27	37	0	0	42.2	45	24	24	4	1.62
Career	5	1	.833	5.27	37	0	0	42.2	45	24	24	4	1.62

1997 Situational Stats

	W	L	ERA	Sv	IP		AB	H	HR	RBI	Avg
Home	3	0	4.32	0	25.0	LHB	64	16	1	12	.250
Road	2	1	6.62	0	17.2	RHB	100	29	3	12	.290
First Half	1	0	3.68	0	14.2	Sc Pos	57	17	2	22	.298
Scnd Half	4	1	6.11	0	28.0	Clutch	52	16	2	7	.308

1997 Season

Former first-round pick Wayne Gomes debuted after a stint as a successful but wild closer at Triple-A Scranton/Wilkes-Barre. Used primarily in middle relief, Gomes was unable to strike out major league hitters despite good stuff, because of a lack of confidence and command.

Pitching, Defense & Hitting

Gomes features a low-90s fastball and a sharp curveball. His inability to throw the curve for strikes in the majors forced him to throw his fastball too often. His mechanics are inconsistent and his fastball tends to be straight. Gomes lacks pinpoint control, so he simply must be a strikeout pitcher to survive. His conditioning has been sub-par, causing him to be an average fielder at best. He has a good pickoff move, which enables him to control the running game despite a slow delivery. As a middle reliever, he rarely will bat.

1998 Outlook

The Phils won't give up on Gomes anytime soon because he possesses a high upside. That said, it's only a remote possibility that Gomes will play an important big league role at the start of the 1998 season. He'll either be the 11th man on the staff or the Triple-A closer.

Rex Hudler

Position: CF/LF
Bats: R **Throws:** R
Ht: 6' 0" **Wt:** 195

Opening Day Age: 37
Born: 9/2/60 in Tempe, AZ
ML Seasons: 12
Nickname: The Wonder Dog

Overall Statistics

	G	AB	R	H	D	T	HR	RBI	SB	BB	SO	Avg	OBP	Slg
1997	50	122	17	27	4	0	5	10	1	6	28	.221	.264	.377
Career	749	1726	259	456	95	10	56	167	107	73	313	.264	.298	.428

1997 Situational Stats

	AB	H	HR	RBI	Avg		AB	H	HR	RBI	Avg
Home	76	22	5	10	.289	LHP	91	23	5	10	.253
Road	46	5	0	0	.109	RHP	31	4	0	0	.129
First Half	55	8	1	1	.145	Sc Pos	24	4	0	3	.167
Scnd Half	67	19	4	9	.284	Clutch	15	6	2	4	.400

1997 Season

Signed as a free agent to provide insurance for untested rookie Wendell Magee and to spell Mickey Morandini at second base against tough lefties, Rex Hudler was a near washout. Torn knee cartilage cost him half of the season, and when healthy he showed a loss of bat and foot speed.

Hitting, Baserunning & Defense

Hudler is a dead fastball hitter who traditionally has destroyed lefthanders. All of his 1997 extra-base hits came against southpaws. Once an offensive catalyst with great speed and a fiery demeanor, Hudler was reduced to an average baserunner last season because of his injury. He may be done at second base because of reduced range, and his weak arm likely limits him to left field.

1998 Outlook

Hudler is signed for 1998. The Phils will try to work him into the lineup on a part-time basis against lefthanders, and will use him as their top righthanded pinch hitter.

Kevin Jordan

Position: 1B/3B
Bats: R **Throws:** R
Ht: 6' 1" **Wt:** 194

Opening Day Age: 28
Born: 10/9/69 in San Francisco, CA
ML Seasons: 3

Overall Statistics

	G	AB	R	H	D	T	HR	RBI	SB	BB	SO	Avg	OBP	Slg
1997	84	177	19	47	8	0	6	30	0	3	26	.266	.273	.412
Career	151	362	40	94	19	0	11	48	2	10	55	.260	.280	.403

1997 Situational Stats

	AB	H	HR	RBI	Avg		AB	H	HR	RBI	Avg
Home	118	29	4	19	.246	LHP	75	18	4	18	.240
Road	59	18	2	11	.305	RHP	102	29	2	12	.284
First Half	63	14	3	9	.222	Sc Pos	66	18	0	22	.273
Scnd Half	114	33	3	21	.289	Clutch	37	12	2	7	.324

1997 Season

Kevin Jordan established himself as a valuable reserve in 1997, becoming the Phillies' best extra-base threat off the bench and a competent defensive replacement at first, second and third base. He also showed a lack of plate discipline, and a substantial loss of speed attributed to a 1996 knee operation.

Hitting, Baserunning & Defense

Jordan will hack at the first—and the second—good pitch he sees. Still, he's a professional hitter who usually makes contact. Interestingly, he consistently performs significantly better against righthanders, making him a versatile pinch-hitting weapon. He never was a speedster, but the jump he once had was robbed by his knee injury. He's surehanded within his limited range, with an adequate arm for a second baseman.

1998 Outlook

The Phils didn't protect Jordan from the expansion draft by most accounts, but that doesn't mean they don't value him. They need his pop off the bench, and he's likely to be the team's primary corner-infield backup in 1998.

Calvin Maduro

Position: SP
Bats: R **Throws:** R
Ht: 6' 0" **Wt:** 175

Opening Day Age: 23
Born: 9/5/74 in Santa Cruz, Aruba
ML Seasons: 2
Pronunciation: mah-DUR-oh

Overall Statistics

	W	L	Pct.	ERA	G	GS	Sv	IP	H	BB	SO	HR	Ratio
1997	3	7	.300	7.23	15	13	0	71.0	83	41	31	12	1.75
Career	3	8	.273	6.57	19	15	0	86.1	96	44	42	13	1.62

1997 Situational Stats

	W	L	ERA	Sv	IP		AB	H	HR	RBI	Avg
Home	3	3	6.80	0	43.2	LHB	112	35	1	14	.313
Road	0	4	7.90	0	27.1	RHB	170	48	11	37	.282
First Half	3	7	7.23	0	71.0	Sc Pos	76	24	3	38	.316
Scnd Half	0	0	-	0	0.0	Clutch	6	1	0	1	.167

1997 Season

Calvin Maduro broke camp as the Phillies' No. 2 starter but he was totally overmatched, lacking power and command. After his return to Triple-A, his mechanics were overhauled to add some velocity and movement to his average fastball.

Pitching, Defense & Hitting

Maduro always has relied on pinpoint precision because his fastball routinely topped out around 85 MPH. He also throws a curveball and changeup, and gets into trouble when he's not throwing them for strikes early in the count. The Phillies took a calculated risk by reinventing Maduro, but they believed he never would experience major league success with his existing repertoire. The early returns were mixed, as he showed better stuff but less command. He's a good athlete who fields his position well. His hitting and bunting are suspect.

1998 Outlook

The Phils would like to see Maduro dominate over a full Triple-A season. They still believe he has a future as a big league starter. He could be the first starter recalled from the minors in 1998.

Wendell Magee

Position: CF
Bats: R **Throws:** R
Ht: 6' 0" **Wt:** 220

Opening Day Age: 25
Born: 8/3/72 in Hattiesburg, MS
ML Seasons: 2
Pronunciation: muh-GHEE

Overall Statistics

	G	AB	R	H	D	T	HR	RBI	SB	BB	SO	Avg	OBP	Slg
1997	38	115	7	23	4	0	1	9	1	9	20	.200	.254	.261
Career	76	257	16	52	11	0	3	23	1	18	53	.202	.253	.280

1997 Situational Stats

	AB	H	HR	RBI	Avg		AB	H	HR	RBI	Avg
Home	56	13	0	5	.232	LHP	20	2	0	3	.100
Road	59	10	1	4	.169	RHP	95	21	1	6	.221
First Half	115	23	1	9	.200	Sc Pos	29	9	0	8	.310
Scnd Half	0	0	0	0	-	Clutch	15	3	1	1	.200

1997 Season

Wendell Magee was given the chance to be an everyday major league center fielder and failed miserably. He showed a total inability to handle major league breaking pitches and appeared to be much slower in center than he was in 1996. His stock dropped so dramatically that he wasn't brought back to the majors in September.

Hitting, Baserunning & Defense

Magee is an exceptional athlete who took up baseball relatively late in life. He easily handled minor league fastballs, but failed to hit breaking pitches. He appears to be a fast runner when he builds up a head of steam in the outfield, but is downright slow to first base and lacks basestealing technique. He's a hustling defender with an average arm.

1998 Outlook

Never again will Magee get such a gift-wrapped opportunity to play in the big leagues. He never will develop into a prolific offensive player, so his only hope for a major league future is as a backup outfielder. He's not in the Phillies' plans.

Ricky Otero

Position: CF
Bats: B **Throws:** R
Ht: 5' 5" **Wt:** 150

Opening Day Age: 25
Born: 4/15/72 in Vega Baja, PR
ML Seasons: 3
Pronunciation: oh-TAIR-oh

Overall Statistics

	G	AB	R	H	D	T	HR	RBI	SB	BB	SO	Avg	OBP	Slg
1997	50	151	20	38	6	2	0	3	0	19	15	.252	.339	.318
Career	189	613	79	157	19	9	2	36	18	56	55	.256	.320	.326

1997 Situational Stats

	AB	H	HR	RBI	Avg		AB	H	HR	RBI	Avg
Home	79	20	0	1	.253	LHP	32	10	0	2	.313
Road	72	18	0	2	.250	RHP	119	28	0	1	.235
First Half	99	23	0	1	.232	Sc Pos	29	3	0	3	.103
Scnd Half	52	15	0	2	.288	Clutch	19	3	0	1	.158

1997 Season

Returned to Triple-A despite being the Phillies' main center fielder in 1996, Ricky Otero suffered compound fractures of two fingers on his left hand in Scranton/Wilkes-Barre's third game. He got a midseason recall, but again was done in by over-aggressiveness at the plate and underaggressiveness on the bases.

Hitting, Baserunning & Defense

Otero is a slap hitter who needs to consistently hit the ball on the ground to succeed. His main problem is his lack of plate discipline. He inexplicably swings at bad pitches when ahead in the count. Despite his speed, his lack of basestealing success has made him unwilling to even try. He has above-average range in center field, but just loves to dive for fly balls, sometimes turning outs into triples. His arm is weak.

1998 Outlook

The Phillies have had it with Otero, as evidenced by the presence of Rob Butler, Midre Cummings and Wendell Magee in center last season. Otero could achieve modest success elsewhere as an extra outfielder.

Mark Parent

Position: C
Bats: R **Throws:** R
Ht: 6' 5" **Wt:** 245

Opening Day Age: 36
Born: 9/16/61 in Ashland, OR
ML Seasons: 12

Overall Statistics

	G	AB	R	H	D	T	HR	RBI	SB	BB	SO	Avg	OBP	Slg
1997	39	113	4	17	3	0	0	8	0	7	39	.150	.198	.177
Career	440	1190	105	254	46	0	52	155	2	88	289	.213	.267	.383

1997 Situational Stats

	AB	H	HR	RBI	Avg		AB	H	HR	RBI	Avg
Home	54	7	0	3	.130	LHP	25	3	0	2	.120
Road	59	10	0	5	.169	RHP	88	14	0	6	.159
First Half	81	12	0	5	.148	Sc Pos	25	6	0	7	.240
Scnd Half	32	5	0	3	.156	Clutch	11	1	0	0	.091

1997 Season

Mark Parent was another free-agent signing who paid the Phils zero dividends in 1997. Always a low-average hitter with home-run power and an average arm, Parent devolved into a low-average hitter with no power and a poor arm. His physical skills simply deteriorated.

Hitting, Baserunning & Defense

Parent is the very definition of the "can't hit his weight" batter. His average has failed to reach his poundage in 10 of his 12 major league seasons. He's an overaggressive hitter who has walked only 88 times in 1,302 career plate appearances. He always salvaged his job with periodic power sprees and reliable handling of pitchers. His movement behind the plate has slowed considerably, and he gave up nearly a steal per game in 1997.

1998 Outlook

The Phils made a two-year commitment to Parent prior to 1997. However, his steep decline and the emergence of both Mike Lieberthal and Bobby Estalella as viable big league catchers likely marks the end of Parent's career.

Mark Portugal

Position: SP
Bats: R **Throws:** R
Ht: 6' 0" **Wt:** 190

Opening Day Age: 35
Born: 10/30/62 in Los
Angeles, CA
ML Seasons: 13

Overall Statistics

	W	L	Pct.	ERA	G	GS	Sv	IP	H	BB	SO	HR	Ratio
1997	0	2	.000	4.61	3	3	0	13.2	17	5	2	0	1.61
Career	92	78	.541	3.83	289	230	5	1509.2	1448	534	951	155	1.31

1997 Situational Stats

	W	L	ERA	Sv	IP		AB	H	HR	RBI	Avg
Home	0	1	4.22	0	10.2	LHB	22	8	0	3	.364
Road	0	1	6.00	0	3.0	RHB	31	9	0	5	.290
First Half	0	2	4.61	0	13.2	Sc Pos	21	7	0	8	.333
Scnd Half	0	0	-	0	0.0	Clutch	0	0	0	0	-

1997 Season

Signed to a two-year contract prior to the 1997 season to eat up innings, Mark Portugal was lost to elbow and knee surgery after just three starts. He was almost ready to pitch by the end of the season.

Pitching, Defense & Hitting

Portugal relies on a variation of speeds and locations to be effective. His fastball is only major league average, but he sets it up well with a combination of curves, sliders and especially change-ups. He throws all of his pitches on the corners with some consistency. He's a six-inning pitcher and hasn't completed more than one game in a season since 1989. Portugal has above-average defensive reactions, but isn't very effective at preventing stolen bases. He handles the bat well, especially in bunting situations.

1998 Outlook

Portugal is under contract for 1998 and is completely recovered from his injuries. His slot in the rotation will be taken by Matt Beech, Garrett Stephenson, Mike Grace or possibly Tyler Green, likely casting Portugal into a setup role.

Jerry Spradlin

Position: RP
Bats: B **Throws:** R
Ht: 6' 7" **Wt:** 240

Opening Day Age: 30
Born: 6/14/67 in
Fullerton, CA
ML Seasons: 4

Overall Statistics

	W	L	Pct.	ERA	G	GS	Sv	IP	H	BB	SO	HR	Ratio
1997	4	8	.333	4.74	76	0	1	81.2	86	27	67	9	1.38
Career	6	9	.400	4.60	120	0	3	139.0	142	38	95	15	1.29

1997 Situational Stats

	W	L	ERA	Sv	IP		AB	H	HR	RBI	Avg
Home	3	2	3.57	0	45.1	LHB	126	34	4	15	.270
Road	1	6	6.19	1	36.1	RHB	188	52	5	31	.277
First Half	1	4	5.02	0	43.0	Sc Pos	94	22	2	33	.234
Scnd Half	3	4	4.42	1	38.2	Clutch	164	45	5	23	.274

1997 Season

Minor league journeyman Jerry Spradlin laid claim to a full-time job in the majors, serving as the Phillies' primary setup man in 1997. Though his ERA was unimpressive, many of those runs scored in a handful of horrendous outings. He was quite durable, ranking among National League leaders in appearances.

Pitching, Defense & Hitting

Spradlin is a behemoth who looks like a power pitcher and he reaches 91-92 MPH, but his fastball comes in straight. He doesn't change speeds effectively, so hitters can zone in easily on the fastball. He also catches too much of the plate with his strikes. He has a slow delivery, but has a decent pickoff move that keeps runners honest. He struck out in his only 1997 at-bat.

1998 Outlook

Among the Phils' deficiencies is an awful setup situation in the bullpen. Spradlin is a major league hurler, but in no way is he capable of pitching the eighth inning of a tie ballgame for a good club. His ability to take the ball nearly every day and pitch multiple innings makes him valuable in a middle-relief role.

Tony Barron (**Pos**: RF, **Age**: 31, **Bats**: R)

	G	AB	R	H	D	T	HR	RBI	SB	BB	SO	Avg	OBP	Slg
1997	57	189	22	54	12	1	4	24	0	12	38	.286	.330	.423
Career	58	190	22	54	12	1	4	24	0	12	39	.284	.329	.421

After posting stellar numbers at Triple-A Scranton, Barron spent the second half of the season in the majors as the Phils' semi-regular right fielder. Does he have a future? Well, uh, he's 31. . . 1998 Outlook: C

Ron Blazier (**Pos**: RHP, **Age**: 26)

	W	L	Pct.	ERA	G	GS	Sv	IP	H	BB	SO	HR	Ratio
1997	1	1	.500	5.03	36	0	0	53.2	62	21	42	8	1.55
Career	4	2	.667	5.38	63	0	0	92.0	111	31	67	14	1.54

A frequent passenger on the continously-running shuttle between Philadelphia and Triple-A Scranton, Blazier has now posted a 5.38 ERA in two seasons out of the bullpen (92 IP). Not too promising. . . 1998 Outlook: C

Billy Brewer (**Pos**: LHP, **Age**: 29)

	W	L	Pct.	ERA	G	GS	Sv	IP	H	BB	SO	HR	Ratio
1997	1	2	.333	4.13	28	0	0	24.0	19	13	17	3	1.33
Career	10	9	.526	4.19	176	0	3	152.2	139	77	109	22	1.41

Brewer pitched decently out of the bullpen after being called up by the Phils in late June, but his season ended in August after suffering an elbow strain. That doesn't sound promising. 1998 Outlook: C

Rob Butler (**Pos**: CF, **Age**: 27, **Bats**: L)

	G	AB	R	H	D	T	HR	RBI	SB	BB	SO	Avg	OBP	Slg
1997	43	89	10	26	9	1	0	13	1	5	8	.292	.326	.416
Career	101	211	31	52	13	2	0	20	3	19	28	.246	.311	.327

Making it back to the majors for the first time in three years, Butler served as the club's fifth outfielder before being sent down in July. He'll be lucky to make it back again. 1998 Outlook: C

Mike Grace (**Pos**: RHP, **Age**: 27)

	W	L	Pct.	ERA	G	GS	Sv	IP	H	BB	SO	HR	Ratio
1997	3	2	.600	3.46	6	6	0	39.0	32	10	26	3	1.08
Career	11	5	.688	3.45	20	20	0	130.1	114	30	82	12	1.10

The oft-injured Phillies starter (is there any other kind?) spent the first half of the season recovering from triceps problems, but pitched well after being called to the majors in August. 1998 Outlook: B

Reggie Harris (**Pos**: RHP, **Age**: 29)

	W	L	Pct.	ERA	G	GS	Sv	IP	H	BB	SO	HR	Ratio
1997	1	3	.250	5.30	50	0	0	54.1	55	43	45	1	1.80
Career	2	3	.400	5.07	72	1	0	103.0	92	72	82	8	1.59

Harris received his first extended stint in the majors since 1990, but don't expect him to stick around for the duration. He walked nearly a batter an inning and posted a 5.30 ERA in middle relief. 1998 Outlook: C

Ryan Karp (**Pos**: LHP, **Age**: 27)

	W	L	Pct.	ERA	G	GS	Sv	IP	H	BB	SO	HR	Ratio
1997	1	1	.500	5.40	15	1	0	15.0	12	9	18	2	1.40
Career	1	1	.500	5.29	16	1	0	17.0	13	12	20	2	1.47

Karp pitched well out of the bullpen after being called up in mid-August, but was hit hard in a series of late-season outings. He has had shoulder problems in the past, but Tampa Bay took him in the second round of the expansion draft. 1998 Outlook: B

Derrick May (**Pos**: RF, **Age**: 29, **Bats**: L)

	G	AB	R	H	D	T	HR	RBI	SB	BB	SO	Avg	OBP	Slg
1997	83	149	8	34	5	1	1	13	4	8	26	.228	.266	.295
Career	686	1971	226	540	95	10	43	283	30	141	224	.274	.322	.398

Strangely enough, May—a player with a career slugging average of .398—racked up a third of his plate appearances from the Phils' cleanup spot. He scored just eight runs in 149 at-bats. 1998 Outlook: C

Michael Mimbs (**Pos**: LHP, **Age**: 29)

	W	L	Pct.	ERA	G	GS	Sv	IP	H	BB	SO	HR	Ratio
1997	0	3	.000	7.53	17	1	0	28.2	31	27	29	6	2.02
Career	12	19	.387	5.03	73	37	1	264.2	274	143	178	29	1.58

Averaging nearly a walk and an earned run per inning, the "Mimbs '97" experiment was officially curtailed in May. Hitters posted an OBP of .424 and slugged .535 against him last season. 1998 Outlook: D

Bobby Munoz (**Pos**: RHP, **Age**: 30)

	W	L	Pct.	ERA	G	GS	Sv	IP	H	BB	SO	HR	Ratio
1997	1	5	.167	8.91	8	7	0	33.1	47	15	20	4	1.86
Career	11	18	.379	4.93	74	30	1	224.1	253	92	126	20	1.54

Munoz' continual struggles prompted the Phils to send the hurler back to the minors in May, but he instead chose to become a free agent and cleared waivers. He didn't make it back to the majors. 1998 Outlook: D

Ryan Nye (**Pos**: RHP, **Age**: 24)

	W	L	Pct.	ERA	G	GS	Sv	IP	H	BB	SO	HR	Ratio
1997	0	2	.000	8.25	4	2	0	12.0	20	9	7	2	2.42
Career	0	2	.000	8.25	4	2	0	12.0	20	9	7	2	2.42

Nye was shelled upon his arrival in Philly, surrendering nine walks and 20 hits in just 12 innings of work. He soon joined the DL with an abdominal strain, so it's possible his problems were injury-related. 1998 Outlook: C

Erik Plantenberg (**Pos**: LHP, **Age**: 29)

	W	L	Pct.	ERA	G	GS	Sv	IP	H	BB	SO	HR	Ratio
1997	0	0	-	4.91	35	0	0	25.2	25	12	12	1	1.44
Career	0	0	-	4.46	61	0	1	42.1	40	31	16	1	1.68

One of the Phils' few lefthanded options out of the bullpen, Plantenberg's less-than-impressive 4.91 ERA got him shipped to the minors in June. He'll be one of hundreds competing for a roster spot next spring. 1998 Outlook: C

Philadelphia Phillies

Mike Robertson (**Pos**: 1B, **Age**: 27, **Bats**: L)

	G	AB	R	H	D	T	HR	RBI	SB	BB	SO	Avg	OBP	Slg
1997	22	38	3	8	2	1	0	4	1	0	6	.211	.268	.316
Career	28	45	3	9	3	1	0	4	1	0	7	.200	.250	.311

Acquired prior to the '97 season from the White Sox, Robertson saw spot duty with the Phils after being called to the majors in late August. As a 27-year-old career minor leaguer, his future is limited at best. 1998 Outlook: D

Scott Ruffcorn (**Pos**: RHP, **Age**: 28)

	W	L	Pct.	ERA	G	GS	Sv	IP	H	BB	SO	HR	Ratio
1997	0	3	.000	7.71	18	4	0	39.2	42	36	33	4	1.97
Career	0	8	.000	8.57	30	9	0	70.1	86	70	46	8	2.22

Ruffcorn was hit progressively harder as the season continued, before going down for the year in August with "numbness in his pitching hand." He's almost out of chances but the Phils need arms. 1998 Outlook: C

Ken Ryan (**Pos**: RHP, **Age**: 29)

	W	L	Pct.	ERA	G	GS	Sv	IP	H	BB	SO	HR	Ratio
1997	1	0	1.000	9.58	22	0	0	20.2	31	13	10	5	2.13
Career	13	14	.481	3.71	208	0	30	247.1	229	133	200	18	1.46

Arguably the Phils' best reliever in '96, Ryan was plagued by a series of elbow problems and was hammered whenever he took the mound. It's questionable whether he'll regain his effectiveness. 1998 Outlook: C

Kevin Sefcik (**Pos**: 2B, **Age**: 27, **Bats**: R)

	G	AB	R	H	D	T	HR	RBI	SB	BB	SO	Avg	OBP	Slg
1997	61	119	11	32	3	0	2	6	1	4	9	.269	.298	.345
Career	110	239	22	65	8	3	2	15	4	13	27	.272	.315	.356

With the ability to play several positions and the ability to hit for a decent average (sans power or walks), Sefcik has been able to carve out a job as the Phils' utilityman over the past couple of seasons. 1998 Outlook: C

Danny Tartabull (**Pos**: RF, **Age**: 35, **Bats**: R)

	G	AB	R	H	D	T	HR	RBI	SB	BB	SO	Avg	OBP	Slg
1997	3	7	2	0	0	0	0	0	0	0	4	.000	.364	.000
Career	1406	5011	756	1366	289	22	262	925	37	768	1362	.273	.368	.496

Signed by Philadelphia to help solve the team's outfield woes, Tartabull was a total waste of his $2.3 million salary last year. A broken foot ended his season after just seven at-bats. 1998 Outlook: C

Darrin Winston (**Pos**: LHP, **Age**: 31)

	W	L	Pct.	ERA	G	GS	Sv	IP	H	BB	SO	HR	Ratio
1997	2	0	1.000	5.25	7	1	0	12.0	8	3	8	4	0.92
Career	2	0	1.000	5.25	7	1	0	12.0	8	3	8	4	0.92

A 31-year-old southpaw, Winston tasted his first big-league action last September when he made seven appearances on the mound. He's a lefty—of which the Phils are in short supply—but he's no prospect. 1998 Outlook: D

Philadelphia Phillies Minor League Prospects

Organization Overview:

For years the Phillies battled the Tigers for the dishonor of having baseball's worst farm system. Not coincidentally, Philadelphia has finished above .500 just twice since its last World Series appearance in 1983 and has posted the National League's worst record for two years running. Scouting director Mike Arbuckle has had some astute drafts since joining the club after the 1992 season, but this kind of decay can't be reversed overnight. NL Rookie of the Year Scott Rolen is a cornerstone the Phillies can build on, but they probably won't contend until the young pitchers deep in their system are ready.

Marlon Anderson

Position: 2B

Bats: L **Throws:** R

Ht: 5' 10" **Wt:** 190

Opening Day Age: 24

Born: 1/3/74 in Montgomery, AL

Recent Statistics

	G	AB	R	H	D	T	HR	RBI	SB	BB	SO	AVG
96 A Clearwater	60	257	37	70	10	3	2	22	26	14	18	.272
96 AA Reading	75	314	38	86	14	3	3	28	17	26	44	.274
97 AA Reading	137	553	88	147	18	6	10	62	27	42	77	.266
97 MLE	137	531	65	125	16	4	7	46	18	26	84	.235

Few prospects are drafted as second basemen, but Anderson is an exception. A 1995 second-round pick out of South Alabama, he's arguably the best position player in the system. He can hit, has good pop for a middle infielder and is a stolen-base threat. If he improves his plate discipline, he would be an ideal No. 1 or 2 hitter. Defensively, he has good range and turns the double play well. After another year of experience, he'll be ready to challenge Mickey Morandini for a big league job.

Ryan Brannan

Position: P

Bats: R **Throws:** R

Ht: 6' 3" **Wt:** 210

Opening Day Age: 22

Born: 4/27/75 in Ann Arbor, MI

Recent Statistics

	W	L	ERA	G	GS	Sv	IP	H	R	BB	SO	HR
97 A Clearwater	0	0	0.33	21	0	10	27.1	20	2	8	25	0
97 AA Reading	4	2	3.10	45	0	20	52.1	52	18	20	39	2

If the Phillies had parted with Ricky Bottalico at the 1997 trading deadline, as had been rumored, Brannan might have made the jump from Double-A to become the team's closer this year. As it stands, the 1996 fourth-round pick out of Long Beach State won't have to do that. He has a very lively fastball that sails and sinks, and

it consistently hits 93 MPH. His slider and changeup could use some refinement, but he won't really need the latter pitch as a short reliever. He has just one season of minor league experience, so he'll probably spend 1998 in Triple-A. If Philadelphia wants to restock with more prospects, it still could trade Bottalico because Brannan is close to ready.

Steve Carver

Position: OF

Bats: L **Throws:** R

Ht: 6' 3" **Wt:** 215

Opening Day Age: 25

Born: 9/27/72 in Houston, TX

Recent Statistics

	G	AB	R	H	D	T	HR	RBI	SB	BB	SO	AVG
96 A Clearwater	117	436	59	121	32	0	17	79	1	52	89	.278
97 AA Reading	79	282	41	74	11	3	15	43	2	36	69	.262
97 MLE	79	271	30	63	10	2	10	32	1	22	75	.232

A 1995 fourth-round pick out of Stanford, Carver was on pace for a 30-homer season in Double-A before he missed half the year after injuring his left shoulder and hand while diving for a fly ball. He's one of the best power hitters in the system, and doesn't have to pull the ball to drive it out of the park. He has below-average speed, but his arm is strong enough for right field. He also has seen some time at first base. Carver was healthy again in instructional league. He's at least another year away from Philadelphia, which needs his type of bat in the lineup.

Bobby Estalella

Position: C

Bats: R **Throws:** R

Ht: 6' 1" **Wt:** 200

Opening Day Age: 23

Born: 8/23/74 in Hialeah, FL

Recent Statistics

	G	AB	R	H	D	T	HR	RBI	SB	BB	SO	AVG
97 AAA Scranton-WB	123	433	63	101	32	0	16	65	3	56	109	.233
97 NL Philadelphia	13	29	9	10	1	0	4	9	0	7	7	.345
97 MLE	123	421	48	89	30	0	12	49	2	42	116	.211

Estalella left a major league calling card when he homered three times in a September game against Montreal, including two shots off Expos ace Pedro Martinez. A 23rd-round draft-and-follow in 1992 out of Miami-Dade Community College South, he's the grandson of former big leaguer Roberto Estalella. Bobby's best tool is his pull power, though he didn't hit for average in Triple-A and always has struck out a lot. He has above-average arm strength and is a leader behind the plate. With Mike Lieberthal coming off a 20-homer season, the Phillies can afford to be patient with Estalella.

Carlton Loewer

Position: P **Opening Day Age:** 24
Bats: B **Throws:** R **Born:** 9/24/73 in
Ht: 6' 6" **Wt:** 220 Lafayette, LA

Recent Statistics

	W	L	ERA	G	GS	Sv	IP	H	R	BB	SO	HR
96 AA Reading	7	10	5.26	27	27	0	171.0	191	115	57	119	24
97 AAA Scranton-WB	5	13	4.60	29	29	0	184.0	198	120	50	152	20

A first-round pick out of Mississippi State in 1994, Loewer has frustrated the Phillies the past two seasons. He has more than enough stuff to win, but lacks the know-how and courage. His fastball can reach 95 MPH, his changeup is solid and he also throws both a curveball and a slider. He throws strikes but gets hit when he can't keep the ball down in the zone. He doesn't do well when confronted by adversity, and the Phillies may have been sending him a message (though they deny it) when they didn't promote him in September. He should see some big league time in 1998.

Desi Relaford

Position: SS **Opening Day Age:** 24
Bats: B **Throws:** R **Born:** 9/16/73 in
Ht: 5' 8" **Wt:** 155 Valdosta, GA

Recent Statistics

	G	AB	R	H	D	T	HR	RBI	SB	BB	SO	AVG
97 AAA Scranton-WB	131	517	82	138	34	4	9	53	29	43	77	.267
97 NL Philadelphia	15	38	3	7	1	2	0	6	3	5	6	.184
97 MLE	131	499	62	120	33	2	6	40	20	32	83	.240

Stuck behind Alex Rodriguez in Seattle, Relaford was liberated by the Phillies in a July 1996 trade for Terry Mulholland. A fourth-round pick in 1991, he was voted the International League's best defensive shortstop and top infield arm last season. He has good speed, but doesn't utilize it enough and plays an offensive game for which he's not suited. He tries to drive the ball instead of focusing on reaching base. With the trade of Kevin Stocker, Relaford will become Philadelphia's starting shortstop in 1998.

Reggie Taylor

Position: OF **Opening Day Age:** 21
Bats: L **Throws:** R **Born:** 1/12/77 in
Ht: 6' 1" **Wt:** 180 Newberry, SC

Recent Statistics

	G	AB	R	H	D	T	HR	RBI	SB	BB	SO	AVG
96 A Piedmont	128	499	68	131	20	6	0	31	36	29	136	.263
97 A Clearwater	134	545	73	133	18	6	12	47	40	30	130	.244

Taylor was considered the best high school athlete available in the 1995 draft, and the Phillies took him with the 14th overall pick. They knew he would be a long-term project, and they were correct. He has yet to put up solid numbers, batting .244 with just 30 walks and 130 strikeouts in 1997. His speed gives him tremendous range in center field, and he'll become a huge basestealing threat

once he hones his instincts. He has extra-base potential, but must correct his habit of pulling off the ball. Like many raw athletes, his ultimate success depends on whether he learns to hit. Philadelphia is willing to wait.

Evan Thomas

Position: P **Opening Day Age:** 23
Bats: R **Throws:** R **Born:** 6/14/74 in Miami
Ht: 5' 10" **Wt:** 175 Fl

Recent Statistics

	W	L	ERA	G	GS	Sv	IP	H	R	BB	SO	HR
96 A Batavia	10	2	2.78	13	13	0	81.0	60	29	23	75	3
97 A Clearwater	5	5	2.44	13	12	0	84.2	68	30	23	89	7
97 AA Reading	3	6	4.12	15	15	0	83.0	98	51	32	83	10

Thomas' curveball is still legendary in college circles. He led NCAA Division I in strikeouts for Florida International in 1996, but lasted until the 10th round of the draft because he's a 5-foot-10 righthander. His hard breaking ball has continued to dominate hitters in the pros, as he has averaged nearly a strikeout per inning and reached Double-A in his first pro season. His fastball is average, his changeup needs improvement and he must keep his pitches down. He's not overwhelming except for his curve, but at worst he looks like a setup man. The Phillies will keep starting him until he fails, which may not happen.

Others to Watch

Righthander **Rob Burger** throws 94 MPH, but doesn't have good command or a consistent breaking ball. Yet he went 11-9, 3.59 at high Class-A Clearwater at age 21 and bears watching. . . If 21-year-old righthander **Dave Coggin** hadn't signed as a supplemental first-round pick in 1995, he would have played quarterback at Clemson. He has the chance to have three above-average pitches, with a 93-94 MPH fastball, good curve and developing changeup. . . Righthander **Adam Eaton**, 20, has the best stuff of any Phillies minor league pitcher. The 1996 first-rounder has a 92 MPH fastball with life and a true power curveball. He went 5-6, 4.16 in his pro debut at Class-A Piedmont. . . Five-foot-eight sparkplug **Jimmy Rollins** is Philadelphia's shortstop of the future. The cousin of Orioles outfielder Tony Tarasco, Rollins is a 19-year-old switch-hitter with speed and good defensive tools. . . Southpaw **Kris Stevens** won 12 games in Class-A last year at age 19. His changeup is his out pitch, and he also has an average fastball and a nice curveball. . . Lefthander **Randy Wolf**, 21, was a second-round steal in the 1997 draft. He went 4-0, 1.58 with 53 strikeouts and eight walks in 40 innings at low Class-A Batavia. He's a three-pitch pitcher with so much polish that he might start his first full season in Double-A. If the Phillies lose out on No. 2 overall pick **J.D. Drew**, a five-tool center fielder who was pursuing free agency, Wolf will make a nice consolation prize.

Gene Lamont

1997 Season

After former manager Jim Leyland was lured by the deep pockets of the Marlins following the 1996 season, the Pirates wanted an experienced manager who had the patience to oversee a massive youth movement. They found the perfect man in their third-base coaching box. Gene Lamont managed the White Sox from 1992-95 and was the AL Manager of the Year in 1993. He was masterful in guiding the Pirates, who had a $9 million payroll and the youngest roster in the majors, to a second-place finish in the National League Central.

Offense

Lamont decided in spring training to stack the top of the batting order with his three fastest players: Tony Womack, Jermaine Allensworth and Al Martin. The move worked perfectly, as the Pirates overcame their lack of power by manufacturing runs all season. The Bucs used the steal and hit-and-run frequently. Once GM Cam Bonifay made some moves at midseason to strengthen a woeful bench, Lamont got the most from his reserves.

Pitching & Defense

Lamont showed a deft touch at handling a starting rotation that didn't have a member over 27 and had only one pitcher (Steve Cooke) who had worked 200 innings in a season. The Pirates maintained the same rotation until late August, when Francisco Cordova went on the DL with elbow inflammation. Lamont never put his starters at risk, lifting Cordova after nine no-hit innings in a July outing against Houston because he had thrown 121 pitches. After some experimenting, Lamont settled on specific roles for his youthful relievers and the bullpen responded by significantly lowering its ERA in the second half.

1998 Outlook

Despite its unexpected run at a division title in 1997, small-market Pittsburgh is committed to its youth movement. Lamont fully understands and endorses that idea, and his reserved manner works very well with young major leaguers. The Pirates only finished 79-83, but it's hard to say that any big-league manager did a better job last season.

Born: 12/25/46 in Rockford, IL

Playing Experience: 1970-1975, Det

Managerial Experience: 5 seasons

Manager Statistics

Year	Team, Lg	W	L	Pct	GB	Finish
1997	Pittsburgh, NL	79	83	.488	5.0	2nd Central
5 Seasons		337	293	.535	—	—

1997 Starting Pitchers by Days Rest

	≤3	4	5	6+
Pirates Starts	0	86	46	23
Pirates ERA	0.00	4.84	3.50	4.15
NL Avg Starts	3	90	38	22
NL ERA	4.23	4.05	4.27	4.52

1997 Situational Stats

	Gene Lamont	NL Average
Hit & Run Success %	33.3	36.4
Stolen Base Success %	76.2	68.4
Platoon Pct.	49.0	56.3
Defensive Subs	14	26
High-Pitch Outings	9	12
Quick/Slow Hooks	16/9	18/10
Sacrifice Attempts	100	96

1997 Rankings (National League)

⇒ 1st in stolen base percentage (76.2%) and intentional walks (48)

⇒ 2nd in steals of third base (27), least caught steals of second base (42) and relief appearances (451)

⇒ 3rd in stolen base attempts (210), steals of second base (133) and mid-inning pitching changes (176)

Jermaine Allensworth

1997 Season

Jermaine Allensworth came to the majors in late July 1996 and played well. After starting off by hitting .286 in April in 1997, he broke a bone in his left hand and was never the same. Allensworth batted just .258 after coming off the disabled list in mid-June and found himself on the bench for nearly all of Pittsburgh's futile chase for the NL Central title over the final two weeks of the season.

Hitting

Allensworth is primarily a singles hitter and wasn't able to hit with any authority after his hand injury. He got into a rut, chasing outside pitches and hitting an endless string of weak grounders and pop-ups. When healthy, he slaps sharp grounders to take advantage of his speed, and slams mistakes into the gaps for extra-base hits. Allensworth doesn't walk enough for a player whose game is built primarily around speed, so he needs to learn better patience at the plate.

Baserunning & Defense

Allensworth has above-average speed and is a threat to steal. However, he became hesitant on the basepaths in 1997 and was shy about running. His defense slipped dramatically after he shined as a rookie. After some early-season territorial disputes with rookie right fielder Jose Guillen, he was tentative about going into the gaps and also had problems fielding grounders. His arm is average at best, and runners can take liberties with him.

1998 Outlook

Allensworth was considered the Pirates' long-term answer in center field at the start of 1997. Then he was the biggest disappointment in an otherwise surprisingly good 1997 season for Pittsburgh. He'll need to work hard this offseason because he will be in a fight to retain his starting job against switch-hitting Adrian Brown, who played well in Allensworth's absence.

Position: CF
Bats: R **Throws:** R
Ht: 6' 0" **Wt:** 190

Opening Day Age: 26
Born: 1/11/72 in Anderson, IN
ML Seasons: 2

Overall Statistics

	G	AB	R	H	D	T	HR	RBI	SB	BB	SO	Avg	OBP	Slg
1997	108	369	55	94	18	2	3	43	14	44	79	.255	.340	.339
Career	169	598	87	154	27	5	7	74	25	67	129	.258	.339	.355

Where He Hits the Ball

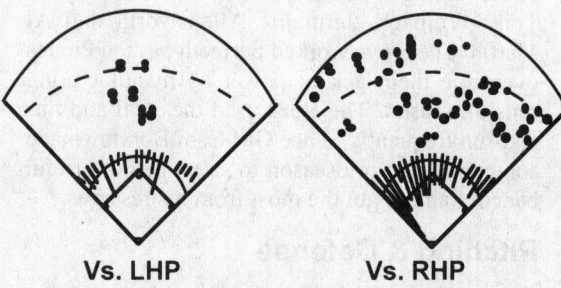

Vs. LHP   Vs. RHP

1997 Situational Stats

	AB	H	HR	RBI	Avg		AB	H	HR	RBI	Avg
Home	186	49	1	18	.263	LHP	97	27	1	6	.278
Road	183	45	2	25	.246	RHP	272	67	2	37	.246
First Half	171	44	2	20	.257	Sc Pos	88	23	0	38	.261
Scnd Half	198	50	1	23	.253	Clutch	52	13	0	6	.250

1997 Rankings (National League)

⇒ 3rd in batting average with the bases loaded (.600) and lowest fielding percentage in center field (.980)
⇒ 5th in errors in center field (4)
⇒ Led the Pirates in sacrifice bunts (9), caught stealing (7) and batting average with the bases loaded (.600)

Steve Cooke

1997 Season

Steve Cooke's career appeared over after he pitched just 72 innings during the 1995-96 seasons combined because of a mystifying nerve problem in his shoulder. Then he showed up for 1997 spring training looking strong after a rigorous off-season rehabilitation program. He earned a spot in the rotation and went 8-9, 3.14 in his first 20 starts. He faded badly down the stretch, going 1-6, 6.84 in his final 12 outings.

Pitching

Cooke is very easy to read. If his pitches are high in the strike zone during the early innings, he's in for a long day. He never was a power pitcher and uses even more finesse since his shoulder problems. He relies on a mid-80s fastball that sinks, a big-breaking curveball, a decent slider and an improving changeup. The curve was his out pitch when he logged 210 innings as a Pirates rookie in 1993, but he doesn't use it as often any longer. He looked like a potential workhorse early in his career, but the shoulder woes and his late-season collapse in 1997 are cause for concern.

Defense & Hitting

Cooke was an all-state performer in three sports as a high school senior in Oregon, and his athletic ability is evident in his defense. He's quick off the mound in fielding bunts and getting to first base. He has a natural advantage in holding runners because he's lefthanded, but his move is nothing special. Cooke's athletic ability doesn't translate to the batter's box, though. He hit .058 in 1997 and usually looks lost at the plate.

1998 Outlook

Cooke looked like a strong candidate for Comeback Player of the Year in the first half of 1997, but his collapse hurt the Pirates' bid for a National League Central crown. He'll be in a fight for a spot in the rotation in spring training. His late-season slide has led to questions whether his shoulder problems have resurfaced.

Position: SP
Bats: R **Throws:** L
Ht: 6' 6" **Wt:** 236

Opening Day Age: 28
Born: 1/14/70 in Kauai, HI
ML Seasons: 5

Overall Statistics

	W	L	Pct.	ERA	G	GS	Sv	IP	H	BB	SO	HR	Ratio
1997	9	15	.375	4.30	32	32	0	167.1	184	77	109	15	1.56
Career	25	36	.410	4.34	103	87	1	543.2	581	191	332	61	1.42

How Often He Throws Strikes

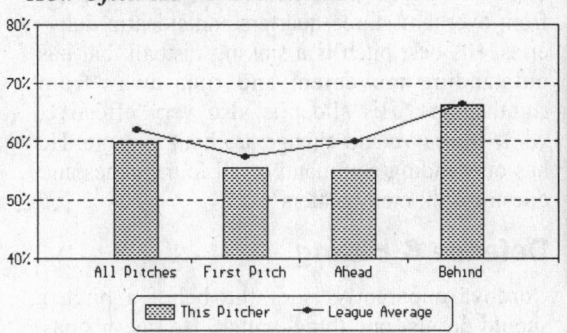

1997 Situational Stats

	W	L	ERA	Sv	IP		AB	H	HR	RBI	Avg
Home	4	9	4.63	0	81.2	LHB	119	34	3	13	.286
Road	5	6	3.99	0	85.2	RHB	527	150	12	65	.285
First Half	7	9	3.10	0	101.2	Sc Pos	178	50	5	63	.281
Scnd Half	2	6	6.17	0	65.2	Clutch	39	11	0	3	.282

1997 Rankings (National League)

⇒ 1st in highest on-base percentage allowed (.366) and most baserunners allowed per 9 innings (14.5)

⇒ 2nd in losses, lowest strikeout/walk ratio (1.4) and highest groundball/flyball ratio allowed (2.9)

⇒ 4th in runners caught stealing (12) and lowest winning percentage

⇒ 5th in highest batting average allowed (.285) and least run support per 9 innings (3.8)

⇒ Led the Pirates in losses, games started, walks allowed, wild pitches (8), runners caught stealing (12) and highest groundball/flyball ratio allowed (2.9)

Francisco Cordova

1997 Season

In his first full season as a starter, Francisco Cordova was one of the National League's top pitchers through the first 2½ months, going 6-5, 2.41 over 15 starts. His season went downhill afterward, with the exception of his nine no-hit innings in a 10-inning no-hitter against Houston on July 12. He went 5-3, 5.21 in his final 14 starts, as he frequently complained of a tired shoulder. He also spent a couple of weeks on the disabled list with an inflamed elbow.

Pitching

No two pitches from Cordova look alike. He throws a fastball, slider, curveball and changeup from overhand, three-quarters and sidearm deliveries. His best pitch is a sinking fastball that has outstanding movement and runs away from righthanders. His slider is also very effective, while his curve and change are both average. He has outstanding command of all four pitches and doesn't walk many batters.

Defense & Hitting

Cordova apparently is of the belief a pitcher should do just one thing—pitch. He doesn't pay much attention to the other aspects of the game. He doesn't hold runners well and can be erratic on his pickoff throws. He's also slow to react to bunts and balls back through the middle. He'll get an occasional hit but usually is bailing out of the box before the pitch is thrown.

1998 Outlook

Cordova has some of the best stuff in the major leagues. When he's on top of his game and rested, he's capable of pitching no-hitters. However, he's on the smallish side and his ability to hold up for the entire season came into question. He can dominate any game but won't be a 225-inning workhorse. His 178⅔ innings were easily a career high, and it was evident that they took a toll on his arm.

Position: SP
Bats: R **Throws:** R
Ht: 5'11" **Wt:** 163

Opening Day Age: 25
Born: 4/26/72 in Veracruz, MX
ML Seasons: 2
Pronunciation: core-DOE-vuh

Overall Statistics

	W	L	Pct.	ERA	G	GS	Sv	IP	H	BB	SO	HR	Ratio
1997	11	8	.579	3.63	29	29	0	178.2	175	49	121	14	1.25
Career	15	15	.500	3.79	88	35	12	277.2	278	69	216	25	1.25

How Often He Throws Strikes

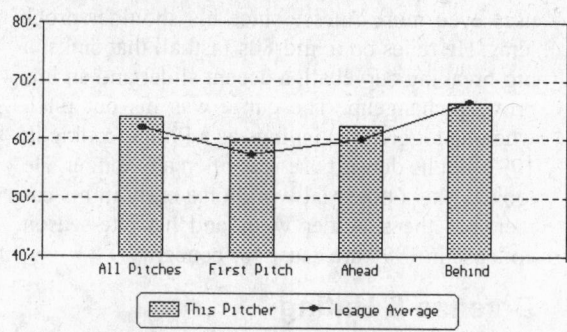

1997 Situational Stats

	W	L	ERA	Sv	IP			AB	H	HR	RBI	Avg
Home	6	6	3.59	0	97.2	LHB	346	103	9	33	.298
Road	5	2	3.67	0	81.0	RHB	330	72	5	36	.218
First Half	6	5	2.82	0	115.0	Sc Pos	141	38	5	51	.270
Scnd Half	5	3	5.09	0	63.2	Clutch	47	10	0	4	.213

1997 Rankings (National League)

⇒ 5th in shutouts (2)
⇒ 6th in errors at pitcher (3)
⇒ 7th in least pitches thrown per batter (3.42)
⇒ 10th in most run support per 9 innings (5.3) and least home runs allowed per 9 innings (.71)
⇒ Led the Pirates in ERA, wins, complete games (2), shutouts (2), GDPs induced (18), winning percentage, lowest batting average allowed (.259), lowest slugging percentage allowed (.386), least pitches thrown per batter (3.42), most run support per 9 innings (5.3), least home runs allowed per 9 innings (.71), most GDPs induced per 9 innings (0.9), ERA at home, ERA on the road and lowest batting average allowed vs. righthanded batters

Shawon Dunston

1997 Season

Just before the Aug. 31 deadline for postseason eligibility, the Pirates acquired Shawon Dunston from the Cubs for a player to be named. Though Pittsburgh's bid to overtake Houston in the National League Central fell short, Dunston did his part by batting .394-5-16 in 18 games with the Bucs.

Hitting

Dunston still showed he had some pop during his September stint with the Pirates, hitting two homers in his first game and consistently driving the ball. Patience never has been a virtue for him, and he has taken that philosophy to the extremes in the latter stages of his career. He swings at everything and didn't draw a walk after joining the Bucs. Dunston can still catch up to good fastballs and will murder hanging breaking pitches. He's an excellent bunter.

Baserunning & Defense

Despite chronic back problems, Dunston still runs well and re-emerged as a stolen-base threat last season. He has above-average speed but primarily swipes bases on his ability to read pitchers' moves. He's aggressive on the bases, always looking to force the issue. Dunston is still a solid defensive player, as well. His range is fine and his throwing arm is far above average, though not quite the cannon it was when he was younger.

1998 Outlook

Dunston showed he had a lot of life left, particularly after joining Pittsburgh for the final month. He became a free agent at the end of the season, and the Pirates are interested in retaining his services if they can fit him into their budget. They would want him back on a one-year basis, then turn shortstop over to prospect Abraham Nunez in 1999. His back always will be a bit of a concern, but he's still capable of playing regularly because he follows a strict exercise regimen. If he's too expensive for Pittsburgh, there's no shortage of teams who gladly would start Dunston at shortstop.

Position: SS
Bats: R **Throws:** R
Ht: 6' 1" **Wt:** 180

Opening Day Age: 35
Born: 3/21/63 in Brooklyn, NY
ML Seasons: 13

Overall Statistics

	G	AB	R	H	D	T	HR	RBI	SB	BB	SO	Avg	OBP	Slg
1997	132	490	71	147	22	5	14	57	32	8	75	.300	.312	.451
Career	1354	4928	604	1333	242	51	117	530	186	184	821	.270	.298	.412

Where He Hits the Ball

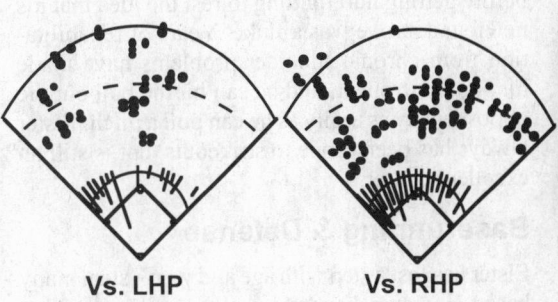

Vs. LHP   **Vs. RHP**

1997 Situational Stats

	AB	H	HR	RBI	Avg		AB	H	HR	RBI	Avg
Home	257	82	10	33	.319	LHP	94	26	3	12	.277
Road	233	65	4	24	.279	RHP	396	121	11	45	.306
First Half	241	71	3	22	.295	Sc Pos	120	33	4	46	.275
Scnd Half	249	76	11	35	.305	Clutch	78	24	0	3	.308

1997 Rankings (National League)

⇒ 2nd in least pitches seen per plate appearance (3.22) and lowest percentage of pitches taken (42.5%)
⇒ 3rd in lowest fielding percentage at shortstop (.969)
⇒ 7th in errors at shortstop (15)
⇒ 8th in stolen base percentage (80.0%)
⇒ 9th in stolen bases (32)
⇒ 10th in lowest on-base percentage (.312) and bunts in play (22)

Pittsburgh Pirates

Kevin Elster

1997 Season

Kevin Elster was signed to a one-year contract as a free agent by the Pirates after having a career year with Texas in 1996, posting 24 home runs and 99 RBI while helping the Rangers to the American League West title. He was everything Pittsburgh wanted before a fractured left wrist ended his season on May 16. At the time, he was leading the club with seven homers and 25 RBI and had committed just one error in 39 games.

Hitting

Elster's power surge in 1996 was a surprise after he hit just 35 homers in his first nine major league seasons. He continued to exhibit his power in 1997 before getting hurt, putting to rest the idea that his newfound stroke was a fluke. Years of rehabilitation from chronic shoulder problems have made him much stronger, and he can hit the ball out the opposite way as easily as he can pull a pitch. Elster always has been prone to strikeouts, but is still an excellent bunter.

Baserunning & Defense

Elster has lost a step with age and won't steal many bases. However, he moves well enough not to clog up the basepaths and is capable of going from first to third on a single. He's still the same steady defender he was when he broke in with the Mets back in 1986, and back then he was considered a glove man only. His range isn't spectacular and his arm is only average, but he positions himself well and is extremely surehanded.

1998 Outlook

Elster was on his way to another solid season when he broke his wrist in May. Both he and Shawon Dunston are free agents, and the Pirates would like to retain one of them as the starting shortstop. Either player would be only a short-term starter, buying time for prospect Abraham Nunez to mature in Triple-A.

Position: SS
Bats: R **Throws:** R
Ht: 6' 2" **Wt:** 200

Opening Day Age: 33
Born: 8/3/64 in San Pedro, CA
ML Seasons: 11

Overall Statistics

	G	AB	R	H	D	T	HR	RBI	SB	BB	SO	Avg	OBP	Slg
1997	39	138	14	31	6	2	7	25	0	21	39	.225	.327	.449
Career	776	2327	270	529	118	11	66	307	14	224	444	.227	.294	.373

Where He Hits the Ball

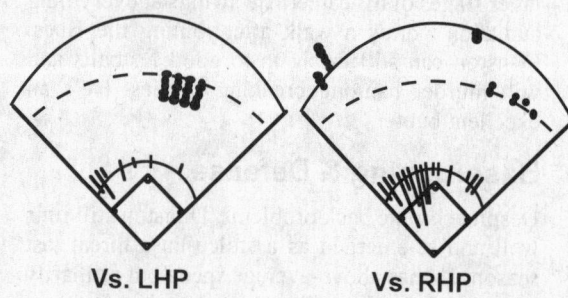

Vs. LHP   **Vs. RHP**

1997 Situational Stats

	AB	H	HR	RBI	Avg		AB	H	HR	RBI	Avg
Home	56	10	3	9	.179	LHP	26	5	0	1	.192
Road	82	21	4	16	.256	RHP	112	26	7	24	.232
First Half	138	31	7	25	.225	Sc Pos	39	9	1	16	.231
Scnd Half	0	0	0	0	-	Clutch	25	8	1	7	.320

1997 Rankings (National League)

⇒ Did not rank near the top or bottom in any category

Jose Guillen

1997 Season

The Pirates stunned many by naming Jose Guillen their Opening Day right fielder even though he was making the jump from Class-A Lynchburg, where he won Carolina League MVP honors in 1996. He wound up leading National League rookies with 39 multi-hit games, and his 70 RBI ranked second behind Philadelphia's Scott Rolen. Guillen looked overmatched early and was hitting just .234 in early June before batting .290 in his final 85 games.

Hitting

Guillen takes the concepts of "see ball hit ball" to the extreme. He swings at nearly every pitch thrown to him and draws walks as infrequently as Greg Maddux issues them. Once Guillen learns to quit getting himself out, he has a chance to be an offensive force. He has quick wrists, good bat speed and the ability to hit with authority to all fields. Like many young hitters, he'll chase breaking and offspeed pitches off the plate, but he's still learning.

Baserunning & Defense

Guillen has good speed but didn't use it in 1997. He hardly ever tried to steal and was usually a station-to-station runner on the bases. He arrived in Pittsburgh with a reputation as one of the best outfield arms in the game. His arm is indeed strong, but extremely scattershot and he tends to make unnecessary throws. Guillen is erratic in chasing fly balls, going all-out one minute, then pulling up early in the next.

1998 Outlook

Guillen skipped over both Double-A and Triple-A on his way to the majors, and his lack of experience showed. He must exhibit more patience at the plate and work on his sometimes-shaky defense. He has a great enthusiasm for the game and should improve in 1998. Eventually he can be counted on for 25 homers and 90 RBI per season.

Position: RF
Bats: R **Throws:** R
Ht: 5'11" **Wt:** 185

Opening Day Age: 21
Born: 5/17/76 in San Cristobal, DR
ML Seasons: 1
Pronunciation: GHEY-un

Overall Statistics

	G	AB	R	H	D	T	HR	RBI	SB	BB	SO	Avg	OBP	Slg
1997	143	498	58	133	20	5	14	70	1	17	88	.267	.300	.412
Career	143	498	58	133	20	5	14	70	1	17	88	.267	.300	.412

Where He Hits the Ball

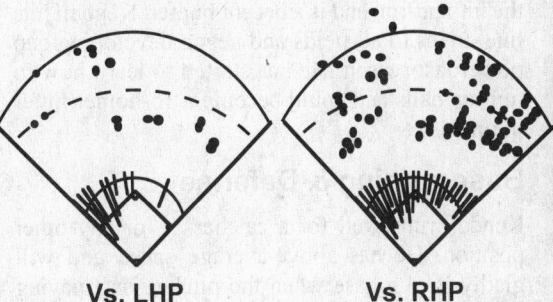

Vs. LHP   **Vs. RHP**

1997 Situational Stats

	AB	H	HR	RBI	Avg		AB	H	HR	RBI	Avg
Home	242	65	5	32	.269	LHP	99	26	3	13	.263
Road	256	68	9	38	.266	RHP	399	107	11	57	.268
First Half	283	74	7	35	.261	Sc Pos	154	37	5	55	.240
Scnd Half	215	59	7	35	.274	Clutch	93	23	1	10	.247

1997 Rankings (National League)

⇒ 1st in least pitches seen per plate appearance (3.13), lowest fielding percentage in right field (.963), lowest percentage of pitches taken (40.4%) and highest percentage of swings on the first pitch (47.8%)

⇒ 2nd in errors in right field (9)

⇒ 4th in lowest on-base percentage

⇒ 5th in lowest on-base percentage vs. righthanded pitchers (.300)

⇒ 7th in highest groundball/flyball ratio (1.8)

⇒ 9th in lowest batting average on a 3-1 count (.125)

⇒ Led the Pirates in GDPs (16), HR frequency (35.6 ABs per HR) and highest groundball/flyball ratio (1.8)

Jason Kendall

1997 Season

Jason Kendall followed up a solid rookie year in 1996, when he hit .300 and played in the All-Star Game, with another fine season. He led the Pirates with 36 doubles and hit .326 in his final 76 games after his average had dropped to .258 in late June. Kendall's 18 stolen bases were the most ever by a Pittsburgh catcher, and he also established a club record by being hit by 31 pitches.

Hitting

Despite his young age, Kendall is one of the toughest hitters in baseball to strike out. He has an extremely good understanding of the strike zone and rarely chases bad pitches. He's excellent on the hit-and-run and is a decent bunter. Kendall hits line drives to all fields and began developing gap power last season. He has started to learn how to turn on balls and could become a 15-homer hitter in time.

Baserunning & Defense

Kendall runs well for a catcher. . . or any other position. He has above-average speed and will gladly steal a base when the pitcher isn't paying attention. He's also an alert baserunner and rarely runs himself into an out. Kendall's throwing improved dramatically in 1997 after he made some mechanical adjustments with his footwork during spring training. He's excellent at blocking balls and handles the pitching staff extremely well.

1998 Outlook

After his rookie season, there were rumors that Kendall would move to second base a la Craig Biggio. It's now clear Kendall isn't going anywhere, either position-wise or team-wise. The Pirates signed him to a four-year contract extension in July and he figures to gradually assume the mantle of team leader. He improved in all phases of the game and should be one of the better all-around catchers in baseball for many years.

Position: C
Bats: R **Throws:** R
Ht: 6' 0" **Wt:** 181

Opening Day Age: 23
Born: 6/26/74 in San Diego, CA
ML Seasons: 2

Overall Statistics

	G	AB	R	H	D	T	HR	RBI	SB	BB	SO	Avg	OBP	Slg
1997	144	486	71	143	36	4	8	49	18	49	53	.294	.391	.434
Career	274	900	125	267	59	9	11	91	23	84	83	.297	.382	.419

Where He Hits the Ball

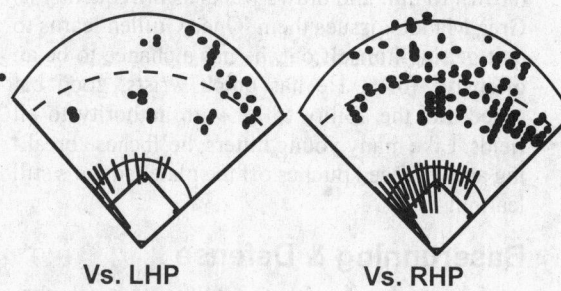

Vs. LHP   **Vs. RHP**

1997 Situational Stats

	AB	H	HR	RBI	Avg		AB	H	HR	RBI	Avg
Home	234	72	5	24	.308	LHP	101	30	3	10	.297
Road	252	71	3	25	.282	RHP	385	113	5	39	.294
First Half	261	70	2	27	.268	Sc Pos	121	31	0	38	.256
Scnd Half	225	73	6	22	.324	Clutch	75	28	0	12	.373

1997 Rankings (National League)

⇒ 1st in lowest percentage of swings on the first pitch (12.4%)
⇒ 2nd in hit by pitch (31)
⇒ 3rd in batting average in the clutch, errors at catcher (11) and highest percentage of runners caught stealing as a catcher (34.9%)
⇒ Led the Pirates in batting average, doubles, walks, hit by pitch (31), slugging percentage, on-base percentage, most pitches seen per plate appearance (3.81), batting average in the clutch, on-base percentage vs. righthanded pitchers (.395), batting average at home, batting average on the road, batting average with two strikes (.242), highest percentage of pitches taken (59.5%) and lowest percentage of swings that missed (12.1%)

Esteban Loaiza

1997 Season

After leading the National League with 31 starts as a rookie in 1995 and then spending a majority of 1996 in the minors, Esteban Loaiza returned to Pittsburgh and led the staff in innings pitched. Loaiza started and finished strongly, going 2-0, 1.83 in five April starts and 1-2, 2.88 in five September outings. He went 8-9, 5.01 in 22 starts in between.

Pitching

Loaiza seemingly has the tools to be a dominant pitcher. He throws a 90-MPH fastball with good sink and a tight slider, and his splitter and curveball also are effective pitches. His biggest problem is still concentration. He'll sail along for three or four innings, and then suddenly lose his focus and get tagged with a five-run inning. This is increasingly frustrating for the Pirates, who even tried banishing Loaiza to the Mexican League in 1996 in an attempt to get him to start realizing his potential. That didn't work, either.

Defense & Hitting

Loiaza is a good athlete, quick on and off the mound, with an idea of how to swing the bat and run the bases. He pays close attention to runners, but has a slow delivery to the plate. He was adequate against basestealers in 1997, as they were successful on 20 of 30 attempts.

1998 Outlook

The Pirates have touted Loaiza as a potential ace since he was in Class-A. It's increasingly doubtful that he'll develop into a frontline pitcher, though he's durable and has a fluid delivery. He still retains value as a starter who can eat up 200 innings a season. If he ever decides to apply himself, he could become a consistent winner as well. He may have the best combination of stuff and stamina on Pittsburgh's staff.

Position: SP
Bats: R **Throws:** R
Ht: 6' 4" **Wt:** 190

Opening Day Age: 26
Born: 12/31/71 in Tijuana, MX
ML Seasons: 3
Pronunciation: low-EYE-zuh

Overall Statistics

	W	L	Pct.	ERA	G	GS	Sv	IP	H	BB	SO	HR	Ratio
1997	11	11	.500	4.13	33	32	0	196.1	214	56	122	17	1.38
Career	21	23	.477	4.65	75	73	0	421.2	484	130	239	49	1.46

How Often He Throws Strikes

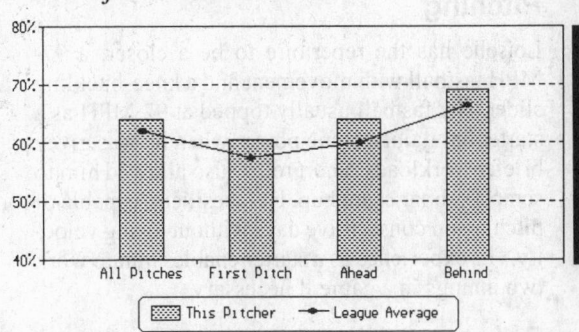

1997 Situational Stats

	W	L	ERA	Sv	IP		AB	H	HR	RBI	Avg
Home	4	6	4.69	0	86.1	LHB	405	117	7	39	.289
Road	7	5	3.68	0	110.0	RHB	361	97	10	53	.269
First Half	6	5	4.04	0	107.0	Sc Pos	189	50	1	66	.265
Scnd Half	5	6	4.23	0	89.1	Clutch	38	15	1	5	.395

1997 Rankings (National League)

⇒ 2nd in balks (3)
⇒ 3rd in hit batsmen (12)
⇒ 5th in highest ERA at home
⇒ 6th in hits allowed
⇒ 7th in highest batting average allowed (.279)
⇒ 8th in pickoff throws (173) and least strikeouts per 9 innings (5.6)
⇒ 9th in stolen bases allowed (20), highest on-base percentage allowed (.335) and most baserunners allowed per 9 innings (12.9)
⇒ Led the Pirates in wins, games started, innings pitched, hits allowed, batters faced (851), hit batsmen (12), balks (3), pickoff throws (173), stolen bases allowed (20) and lowest batting average allowed with runners in scoring position

Rich Loiselle

1997 Season

Few players in the major leagues saw their fortunes change more than Rich Loiselle. Acquired in a 1996 trade with Houston for Danny Darwin, he came to spring training as the favorite for the No. 5 starter's job but lost out to a resurgent Steve Cooke. Loiselle started the season in middle relief, then was thrust into the closer's job in late April when John Ericks was lost for the season with a herniated disc in his neck. Loiselle went on to record the second-highest save total ever by a rookie, behind only Todd Worrell's 36 for St. Louis in 1986. Loiselle also set a Pirates rookie record with 72 appearances.

Pitching

Loiselle has the repertoire to be a closer, a 97-MPH fastball with movement and a knee-buckling slider. His fastball usually topped at 92 MPH as a starter but gained some power when he was given briefer workloads. Short relief also allowed him to scrap a subpar changeup. He's resilient, capable of pitching on consecutive days without losing velocity. His experience as a starter enables him to work two innings in a game if necessary.

Defense & Hitting

Loiselle is a big man who doesn't get off the mound quickly, and his move to first is on the slow side. He also tends to rush pickoff throws, sending some in the dirt. Those drawbacks aren't serious for a closer, and neither is the fact that he's nothing special with a bat in his hands.

1998 Outlook

Loiselle will be the Pirates' closer after his sensational and unexpected 1997 season. Pittsburgh has been searching for a consistent relief ace since Kent Tekulve was in his heyday, and Loiselle might be that guy. He has a great arm and doesn't get rattled in pressure situations, which is why he excels in the role.

Position: RP
Bats: R **Throws:** R
Ht: 6' 5" **Wt:** 225

Opening Day Age: 26
Born: 1/12/72 in Neenah, WI
ML Seasons: 2
Pronunciation: loy-SELL

Overall Statistics

	W	L	Pct.	ERA	G	GS	Sv	IP	H	BB	SO	HR	Ratio
1997	1	5	.167	3.10	72	0	29	72.2	76	24	66	7	1.38
Career	2	5	.286	3.09	77	3	29	93.1	98	32	75	10	1.39

How Often He Throws Strikes

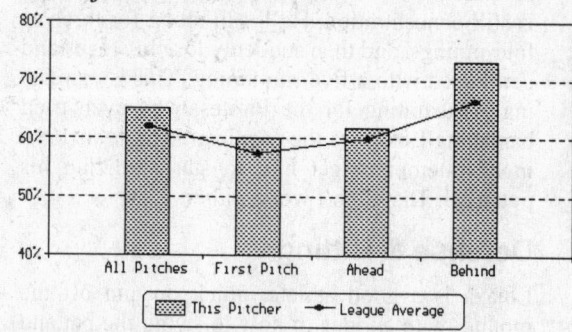

1997 Situational Stats

	W	L	ERA	Sv	IP		AB	H	HR	RBI	Avg
Home	0	2	3.44	14	34.0	LHB	123	38	2	18	.309
Road	1	3	2.79	15	38.2	RHB	160	38	5	21	.238
First Half	1	1	3.13	10	37.1	Sc Pos	74	26	0	29	.351
Scnd Half	0	4	3.06	19	35.1	Clutch	198	53	5	27	.268

1997 Rankings (National League)

⇒ 3rd in save percentage (85.3%)
⇒ 6th in games finished (58) and errors at pitcher (3)
⇒ 10th in saves and save opportunities (34)
⇒ Led the Pirates in games pitched, saves, games finished (58), save opportunities (34), save percentage (85.3%), blown saves (5) and relief ERA (3.10)

Al Martin

1997 Season

Al Martin became the player the Pirates planned to build around after dismantling their club during the final four months of 1996. He signed a two-year contract extension immediately after that season ended and then tacked on another year last July, keeping him in Pittsburgh until 2000. But he didn't have a season befitting a franchise player in 1997. A sprained right hand forced him to the disabled list in late May and never completely healed.

Hitting

Martin is a dead-red fastball hitter all the way. He goes to the plate looking for fastballs he can drive and will pull mediocre heaters over the right-field fence. However, pitchers have grown wise to his approach and his continuing inability to handle breaking and offspeed pitches. He has a hard time slowing his bat down for changeups, and usually can be made to chase even the most mediocre curveballs and sliders. He has improved his concentration against lefthanders to the point where he no longer needs to be platooned.

Baserunning & Defense

Martin has outstanding speed and is capable of 30-steal seasons. He's extremely aggressive on the bases, sliding hard into second to break up double plays and always looking to take an extra base. He's one of the worst left fielders in the National League, however. He has a hard time tracking fly balls and has particular trouble going toward the line. His arm is below average and he doesn't help matters by not charging the ball well.

1998 Outlook

The Pirates thought Martin was ready to emerge as a star after he batted .300 with 40 doubles, 18 homers, 72 RBI and 38 steals in 1996. But he backslid in 1997 and at age 30 it's doubtful he'll suddenly burst into a superstar. He's a productive major leaguer, but the Pirates would consider dealing him as they continue their youth movement.

Position: LF
Bats: L **Throws:** L
Ht: 6' 2" **Wt:** 210

Opening Day Age: 30
Born: 11/24/67 in West Covina, CA
ML Seasons: 6

Overall Statistics

	G	AB	R	H	D	T	HR	RBI	SB	BB	SO	Avg	OBP	Slg
1997	113	423	64	123	24	7	13	59	23	45	83	.291	.359	.473
Career	629	2260	369	652	127	24	71	271	112	219	474	.288	.352	.460

Where He Hits the Ball

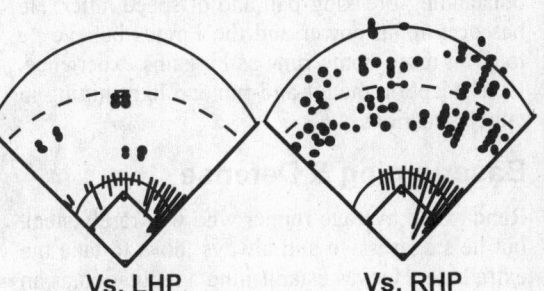

Vs. LHP   Vs. RHP

1997 Situational Stats

	AB	H	HR	RBI	Avg		AB	H	HR	RBI	Avg
Home	202	61	8	32	.302	LHP	92	30	1	16	.326
Road	221	62	5	27	.281	RHP	331	93	12	43	.281
First Half	176	52	7	26	.295	Sc Pos	125	35	5	48	.280
Scnd Half	247	71	6	33	.287	Clutch	61	14	0	5	.230

1997 Rankings (National League)

⇒ 1st in errors in left field (6) and lowest fielding percentage in left field (.957)
⇒ 10th in triples
⇒ Led the Pirates in caught stealing (7) and intentional walks (7)

Joe Randa

Position: 3B/2B
Bats: R **Throws:** R
Ht: 5'11" **Wt:** 190

Opening Day Age: 28
Born: 12/18/69 in
Milwaukee, WI
ML Seasons: 3

1997 Season

Acquired in a six-player trade with Kansas City in December 1996, Joe Randa got off to a slow start while adjusting to the National League. His batting average stood at .190 in late April, then he hit .348 in May and .309 the rest of the way to finish above .300 for the second time in as many full major league seasons. He missed most of July with a broken left little finger, and his power production slipped afterward.

Hitting

Randa is a line-drive hitter who sprays the ball to all fields. While he can be overpowered by above-average fastballs, he stays back well and is an outstanding breaking-ball and offspeed hitter. He has occasional power and the Pirates believe he may hit more home runs as he gains experience. He is adept on the hit-and-run and likes hitting in clutch situations.

Baserunning & Defense

Randa is an average runner who will rarely steal, but he's aggressive and always looks to take the extra base. He was establishing a reputation as an above-average defensive third baseman in the American League, but didn't display those skills in his first NL season. He had serious trouble on artificial turf, which hurt his range and also made it difficult for him to adjust to balls that hit the dirt cutout around the bag. His arm is average but accurate. Randa has also had limited time at second base and is able to turn the double play well.

1998 Outlook

Randa is unheralded but steady. He doesn't provide the power wanted in a corner infielder, but the Pirates believed his home-run stroke still could develop. Pittsburgh allowed Arizona to take him in the third round of the expansion draft, and the Diamondbacks traded him to Detroit in a deal for Travis Fryman. Randa could be a regular for many more years if he adds a little pop. Even if he doesn't, he is still a viable long-term utility candidate. The Pirates likely will replace him with either Freddy Garcia, Aramis Ramirez or free-agent signee Doug Strange.

Overall Statistics

	G	AB	R	H	D	T	HR	RBI	SB	BB	SO	Avg	OBP	Slg
1997	126	443	58	134	27	9	7	60	4	41	64	.302	.366	.451
Career	270	850	100	248	53	10	14	112	17	73	128	.292	.349	.427

Where He Hits the Ball

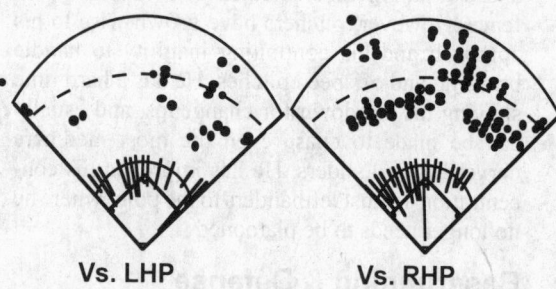

Vs. LHP   Vs. RHP

1997 Situational Stats

	AB	H	HR	RBI	Avg		AB	H	HR	RBI	Avg
Home	227	69	5	37	.304	LHP	99	23	2	10	.232
Road	216	65	2	23	.301	RHP	344	111	5	50	.323
First Half	249	74	5	34	.297	Sc Pos	120	38	1	50	.317
Scnd Half	194	60	2	26	.309	Clutch	75	24	1	10	.320

1997 Rankings (National League)

⇒ 3rd in triples
⇒ 4th in lowest fielding percentage at third base (.938)
⇒ 5th in errors at third base (21)
⇒ 6th in batting average vs. righthanded pitchers
⇒ 9th in highest percentage of swings put into play (53.0%)
⇒ Led the Pirates in triples, batting average with runners in scoring position, batting average vs. righthanded pitchers, slugging percentage vs. righthanded pitchers (.480) and highest percentage of swings put into play (53.0%)

Jason Schmidt

Position: SP
Bats: R **Throws:** R
Ht: 6' 5" **Wt:** 185

Opening Day Age: 25
Born: 1/29/73 in Kelso, WA
ML Seasons: 3

1997 Season

Jason Schmidt had a scare in spring training, as he was forced to return to Pittsburgh for testing after he was discovered to have an irregular heartbeat. He checked out fine, but missing nearly two weeks of exhibition games seemed to hamper him early in the season, as he went 1-3, 5.47 in his first 10 starts. He went 9-6, 4.28 afterward but finished on a sour note with a combined 5.81 ERA in August and September.

Pitching

Schmidt has the makings of a classic power pitcher with a 95-MPH fastball and a hard slider. However, he has a tendency to overthrow those pitches, causing the fastball to run out of the strike zone and the slider to bounce. He still is working on his changeup and sometimes gets into trouble because of it. He can become so intent on proving he can change speeds that he starts throwing too many changeups and gets away from his strengths. His control still needs refinement, but once he gets his pitch counts down he'll pile up his share of complete games.

Defense & Hitting

Though a big man, Schmidt was flawless in the field last season. He gets off the mound rather quickly and is attentive to situations. However, he has a slow delivery to the plate and runners can take liberties on him. Schmidt worked hard on his hitting, but the results were just a .107 average. He'd be better served to just worry about his pitching.

1998 Outlook

Schmidt has the physical ability to become the ace of a young Pirates staff. However, the jury is still out on his mental approach. He's an extremely bright guy with a keen sense of humor. Those qualities, though, also cause him to outthink himself on the mound at times and raise questions about his intensity. He's still young and his future looks very bright.

Overall Statistics

	W	L	Pct.	ERA	G	GS	Sv	IP	H	BB	SO	HR	Ratio
1997	10	9	.526	4.60	32	32	0	187.2	193	76	136	16	1.43
Career	17	17	.500	5.04	60	51	0	309.0	328	147	229	28	1.54

How Often He Throws Strikes

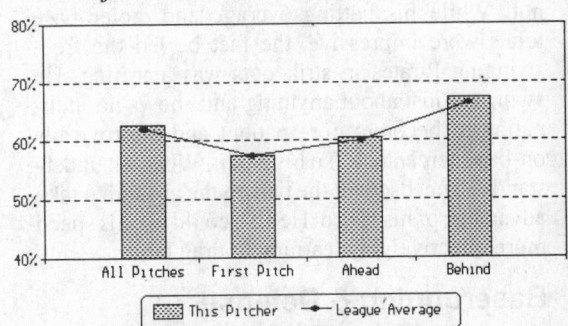

1997 Situational Stats

	W	L	ERA	Sv	IP			AB	H	HR	RBI	Avg
Home	7	6	5.20	0	98.2	LHB		359	98	11	41	.273
Road	3	3	3.94	0	89.0	RHB		368	95	5	52	.258
First Half	4	4	4.25	0	89.0	Sc Pos		171	49	1	65	.287
Scnd Half	6	5	4.93	0	98.2	Clutch		43	8	1	3	.186

1997 Rankings (National League)
⇒ 1st in fielding percentage at pitcher (1.000)
⇒ 3rd in highest ERA at home
⇒ 4th in lowest strikeout/walk ratio (1.8)
⇒ 5th in highest ERA
⇒ 7th in highest on-base percentage allowed (.341) and most baserunners allowed per 9 innings (13.3)
⇒ 8th in walks allowed
⇒ 9th in wild pitches (8)
⇒ 10th in least GDPs induced per 9 innings (0.5)
⇒ Led the Pirates in sacrifice bunts (9), games started, complete games (2), wild pitches (8), pitches thrown (3,080), lowest stolen base percentage allowed (50.0%) and lowest batting average allowed vs. lefthanded batters

Tony Womack

1997 Season

Tony Womack entered spring training in a three-way battle with rookies Lou Collier and Brandon Cromer for the Pirates' second-base job. He wound up playing in the All-Star Game and became the first Pittsburgh player to lead the National League in stolen bases since Omar Moreno in 1979. Womack set a club record by stealing 32 consecutive bases without being caught, and tied another with four steals in a September game at Cincinnati.

Hitting

Womack's speed makes him an ideal leadoff hitter, but his total lack of strike-zone judgment does not. While his batting average and stolen-base totals were impressive, the fact he led the free-swinging Pirates in strikeouts was alarming. He swings at just about anything and shows no inclination to become more patient and improve his on-base percentage. To his credit, Womack understands he needs to hit the ball on the ground to take advantage of his speed. He also could use his speed more effectively by learning to drag bunt.

Baserunning & Defense

Womack has explosive speed and is a first-rate basestealing threat. He reads pitchers' moves extremely well and is rarely picked off. Despite his quickness, he's a poor defensive second baseman. He often is fooled by the direction of balls off the bat, though his speed and reflexes help him recover. He has above-average range but his hands are stiff and he has trouble turning the double play with a substandard arm. He also needs work on tracking down pop flies.

1998 Outlook

Womack was supposed to be a one-year stopgap in 1997 until Collier or prospect Chad Hermansen was ready to take over. Now Womack has cemented his position as the starting second baseman through at least 1998. His speed makes him a weapon, but he won't be a long-term fixture unless he improves his plate discipline and defense.

Position: 2B
Bats: L **Throws:** R
Ht: 5' 9" **Wt:** 155

Opening Day Age: 28
Born: 9/25/69 in Danville, VA
ML Seasons: 4

Overall Statistics

	G	AB	R	H	D	T	HR	RBI	SB	BB	SO	Avg	OBP	Slg
1997	155	641	85	178	26	9	6	50	60	43	109	.278	.326	.374
Career	192	707	105	194	29	10	6	58	64	54	116	.274	.329	.369

Where He Hits the Ball

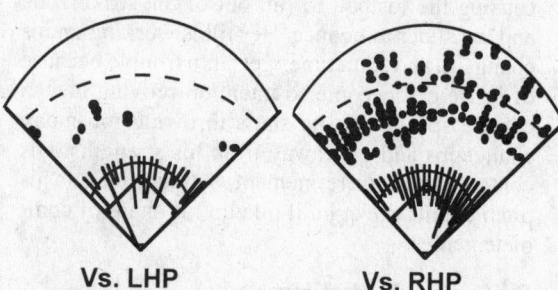

Vs. LHP   Vs. RHP

1997 Situational Stats

	AB	H	HR	RBI	Avg		AB	H	HR	RBI	Avg
Home	314	87	5	26	.277	LHP	129	40	0	14	.310
Road	327	91	1	24	.278	RHP	512	138	6	36	.270
First Half	342	93	3	29	.272	Sc Pos	139	41	1	44	.295
Scnd Half	299	85	3	21	.284	Clutch	94	21	0	11	.223

1997 Rankings (National League)

⇒ 1st in stolen bases, stolen base percentage (89.6%) and errors at second base (20)
⇒ 2nd in lowest fielding percentage at second base (.974) and steals of third (16)
⇒ 3rd in at-bats, singles and triples
⇒ Led the Pirates in at-bats, runs scored, hits, singles, triples, total bases (240), stolen bases, caught stealing (7), times on base (224), strikeouts, pitches seen (2,613), plate appearances (689), games played (155), stolen base percentage (89.6%), batting average vs. lefthanded pitchers, batting average on a 3-1 count (.667), on-base percentage for a leadoff hitter (.326), slugging percentage vs. lefthanded pitchers (.357) and on-base percentage vs. lefthanded pitchers (.360)

Kevin Young

Position: 1B/3B
Bats: R **Throws:** R
Ht: 6' 2" **Wt:** 219

Opening Day Age: 28
Born: 6/16/69 in Alpena, MI
ML Seasons: 6

1997 Season

Kevin Young came full circle in 1997, returning to Pittsburgh after once being considered the cornerstone of the team's previous rebuilding process as a rookie four years earlier. Released by the Pirates in the spring of 1996 and again by Kansas City at the end of that season, Young began 1997 as a reserve but moved into a starting role at first base in late June when Mark Johnson was demoted to the minors. Despite missing five weeks in midsummer with a torn ligament in his right thumb, Young led the Pirates in home runs and RBI.

Hitting

Young blossomed into a power hitter in 1997. During his first trial with the Pirates, he had serious contact problems and was happy just to spray an occasional line drive. The new and improved Young now can pull fastballs left out over the plate, and he can take hanging breaking pitches the other way. He still has a slow swing and is susceptible to good inside fastballs. However, he has learned to wait for good pitches and no longer routinely gets himself out.

Baserunning & Defense

Young runs well for a big man. He's extremely aggressive on the basepaths and is a threat to steal. He's a first-rate defensive first baseman with outstanding range and quickness to go with sure hands. He also shows good range at third, though he tends to be erratic with long throws across the diamond. He also has played some outfield during his career and is adequate on the corners.

1998 Outlook

Young forced his way into the Pirates' plans by having a surprisingly good season. He figures to be the starting first baseman while power prospect Ron Wright develops at Triple-A.

Overall Statistics

	G	AB	R	H	D	T	HR	RBI	SB	BB	SO	Avg	OBP	Slg
1997	97	333	59	100	18	3	18	74	11	16	89	.300	.332	.535
Career	418	1224	147	309	64	8	39	181	18	81	290	.252	.303	.413

Where He Hits the Ball

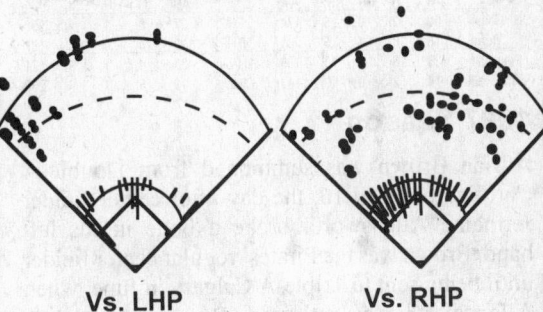

Vs. LHP   **Vs. RHP**

1997 Situational Stats

	AB	H	HR	RBI	Avg		AB	H	HR	RBI	Avg
Home	173	48	11	41	.277	LHP	86	31	5	19	.360
Road	160	52	7	33	.325	RHP	247	69	13	55	.279
First Half	206	63	10	43	.306	Sc Pos	107	32	5	54	.299
Scnd Half	127	37	8	31	.291	Clutch	60	20	4	20	.333

1997 Rankings (National League)

⇒ 1st in lowest batting average on a 3-1 count (.000)
⇒ 6th in cleanup slugging percentage (.517)
⇒ 8th in sacrifice flies (8)
⇒ Led the Pirates in home runs, RBI, sacrifice flies (8), least GDPs per GDP situation (7.0%) and cleanup slugging percentage (.517)

Adrian Brown

Position: CF
Bats: B **Throws:** R
Ht: 6' 0" **Wt:** 175

Opening Day Age: 24
Born: 2/7/74 in McComb, MS
ML Seasons: 1

Overall Statistics

	G	AB	R	H	D	T	HR	RBI	SB	BB	SO	Avg	OBP	Slg
1997	48	147	17	28	6	0	1	10	8	13	18	.190	.273	.252
Career	48	147	17	28	6	0	1	10	8	13	18	.190	.273	.252

1997 Situational Stats

	AB	H	HR	RBI	Avg		AB	H	HR	RBI	Avg
Home	69	12	0	5	.174	LHP	27	8	1	4	.296
Road	78	16	1	5	.205	RHP	120	20	0	6	.167
First Half	133	26	1	10	.195	Sc Pos	33	4	1	9	.121
Scnd Half	14	2	0	0	.143	Clutch	19	5	1	3	.263

1997 Season

Adrian Brown was summoned from Double-A Carolina on May 16, the day after center fielder Jermaine Allensworth broke a bone in his left hand. Brown was the Pirates' regular center fielder until being sent to Triple-A Calgary in June, when Allensworth was activated. Brown returned to Pittsburgh in September but played sparingly.

Hitting, Baserunning & Defense

Brown was originally a righthanded batter. Now a switch-hitter, he's still more comfortable from the right side. Brown is a slap hitter who swings down on the ball to take advantage of his speed. He can handle most fastballs, but is still baffled by sliders and curves. He has above-average speed, though he's still learning the art of reading pitchers and stealing bases. Brown is an outstanding fielder with superior range and an adequate arm.

1998 Outlook

Brown's statistics as a rookie aren't eye-opening, but he caught the Pirates' attention with his steady improvement. Allensworth is coming off a subpar season and Brown will be given a chance to unseat him as a starter. Should Allensworth fend off the challenge, Brown would still be a viable option as a fourth outfielder because of his speed and ability to play the corner spots.

John Ericks

Position: RP
Bats: R **Throws:** R
Ht: 6' 7" **Wt:** 251

Opening Day Age: 30
Born: 9/16/67 in Oak Lawn, IL
ML Seasons: 3

Overall Statistics

	W	L	Pct.	ERA	G	GS	Sv	IP	H	BB	SO	HR	Ratio
1997	1	0	1.000	1.93	10	0	6	9.1	7	4	6	1	1.18
Career	8	14	.364	4.78	57	22	14	162.0	171	73	132	19	1.51

1997 Situational Stats

	W	L	ERA	Sv	IP		AB	H	HR	RBI	Avg
Home	1	0	2.70	2	3.1	LHB	21	4	0	1	.190
Road	0	0	1.50	4	6.0	RHB	14	3	1	1	.214
First Half	1	0	1.93	6	9.1	Sc Pos	10	1	0	1	.100
Scnd Half	0	0			0.0	Clutch	20	4	1	1	.200

1997 Season

John Ericks began 1997 as the Pirates' closer after failing as a starter the previous two seasons. He took to the job well, converting six of seven save opportunities, but didn't pitch after April 28 due to a herniated disc in his neck. He had surgery in May, but never totally regained his velocity during injury-rehabilitation assignments with Rookie-level Bradenton and Triple-A Calgary.

Pitching, Defense & Hitting

When healthy, Ericks has a 95-MPH fastball and hard slider. His success depends on his velocity, which plunged to 87 MPH after his neck surgery. Moved to the bullpen midway through the 1996 season, he has an aggressive mentality that's perfect for the job. He never made it as a starter because of his inability to develop an offspeed pitch. Ericks is below-average defensively and is a poor hitter.

1998 Outlook

Ericks is a mystery heading into 1998. He looked ready to emerge as a closer before succumbing to the neck surgery. While he was out, rookie Rich Loiselle became one of the most reliable short men in the National League. Ericks' future will be tied to his velocity, and there's no guarantee he'll automatically supplant Loiselle if it returns.

Jon Lieber

Position: SP
Bats: L **Throws:** R
Ht: 6' 3" **Wt:** 220

Opening Day Age: 27
Born: 4/2/70 in Council Bluffs, IA
ML Seasons: 4
Pronunciation: LEE-burr

Overall Statistics

	W	L	Pct.	ERA	G	GS	Sv	IP	H	BB	SO	HR	Ratio
1997	11	14	.440	4.49	33	32	0	188.1	193	51	160	23	1.30
Career	30	33	.476	4.45	122	76	1	511.2	568	118	370	61	1.34

1997 Situational Stats

	W	L	ERA	Sv	IP			AB	H	HR	RBI	Avg
Home	6	5	4.25	0	95.1		LHB	378	115	15	48	.304
Road	5	9	4.74	0	93.0		RHB	356	78	8	37	.219
First Half	6	8	4.08	0	106.0		Sc Pos	161	43	5	63	.267
Scnd Half	5	6	5.03	0	82.1		Clutch	38	8	0	1	.211

1997 Season

More by default than merit, Jon Lieber was the Pirates' Opening Day starter. He was the oldest and most experienced member of the youngest rotation in the major leagues. He had an up-and-down season, as evidenced by his monthly ERAs: April (3.28), May (6.28), June (3.28), July (7.13), August (3.49) and September (4.91).

Pitching, Defense & Hitting

Lieber relies on a combination of late-breaking sliders and hard sinkers, and gets into serious trouble when he fails to keep them low in the strike zone. His changeup is below average. He has decent control, but his lack of dedication to conditioning causes him to tire in the late innings and may eventually force him to the bullpen. Lieber isn't a great athlete, but he makes the plays he should make. He needs to work on both his pickoff move and in speeding his delivery to the plate. Lieber is a decent hitter and can bunt when needed.

1998 Outlook

When Lieber broke into the major leagues in 1994, former Pirates manager Jim Leyland called him a young Tom Seaver. Lieber, though, too often looks more like Jon Horrific than Tom Terrific. At best he's a No. 4 starter, and he'll be pushed for his spot in Pittsburgh's rotation this spring.

Kevin Polcovich

Position: SS
Bats: R **Throws:** R
Ht: 5' 9" **Wt:** 168

Opening Day Age: 27
Born: 6/28/70 in Auburn, NY
ML Seasons: 1
Pronunciation: POLE-ka-vich

Overall Statistics

	G	AB	R	H	D	T	HR	RBI	SB	BB	SO	Avg	OBP	Slg
1997	84	245	37	67	16	1	4	21	2	21	45	.273	.350	.396
Career	84	245	37	67	16	1	4	21	2	21	45	.273	.350	.396

1997 Situational Stats

	AB	H	HR	RBI	Avg			AB	H	HR	RBI	Avg
Home	116	30	0	9	.259		LHP	56	16	2	7	.286
Road	129	37	4	12	.287		RHP	189	51	2	14	.270
First Half	100	29	1	7	.290		Sc Pos	62	13	1	17	.210
Scnd Half	145	38	3	14	.262		Clutch	35	7	1	3	.200

1997 Season

The Pirates had a roster full of surprises but none were bigger than Kevin Polcovich, a career minor leaguer. He started the season at Double-A Carolina, moved up to Triple-A Calgary and then was called up to Pittsburgh in May after starting shortstop Kevin Elster suffered a season-ending wrist injury. Polcovich was the Pirates' regular shortstop until a sprained left ankle forced him out of action in September.

Hitting, Baserunning & Defense

Polcovich is a contact hitter who looks to slap the ball on the ground and run. He has occasional pop, and can turn around a high fastball or hanging slider. He has above-average speed and is particularly aggressive going from second to home and first to third on singles. Polcovich is an average defensive player with decent range and arm strength, though he's much better going to his right than left.

1998 Outlook

Polcovich is viewed as a utility player by the Pirates despite his unexpected success during his three-month run as their starting shortstop. The Pirates will try to re-sign free agents Shawon Dunston or Kevin Elster and play one until prospect Abraham Nunez is ready for full-time duty.

Ricardo Rincon

Position: RP
Bats: L **Throws:** L
Ht: 6' 0" **Wt:** 190

Opening Day Age: 27
Born: 4/13/70 in
Veracruz, Mexico
ML Seasons: 1

Overall Statistics

	W	L	Pct.	ERA	G	GS	Sv	IP	H	BB	SO	HR	Ratio
1997	4	8	.333	3.45	62	0	4	60.0	51	24	71	5	1.25
Career	4	8	.333	3.45	62	0	4	60.0	51	24	71	5	1.25

1997 Situational Stats

	W	L	ERA	Sv	IP		AB	H	HR	RBI	Avg
Home	4	3	2.51	2	32.1	LHB	81	19	2	10	.235
Road	0	5	4.55	2	27.2	RHB	141	32	3	12	.227
First Half	2	4	4.06	4	31.0	Sc Pos	56	11	0	14	.196
Scnd Half	2	4	2.79	0	29.0	Clutch	139	34	2	13	.245

1997 Season

After seven seasons in the Mexican League, Ricardo Rincon emerged as the Pirates' top lefthanded reliever in 1997. He had four saves and a 2.16 ERA in his first 21 games before posting no saves and a 4.37 ERA in his final 41 appearances. He spent several weeks on the disabled list during the summer with an inflamed shoulder.

Pitching, Defense & Hitting

Rincon is the epitome of a crafty southpaw. He throws a variety of breaking balls from different angles, making an average fastball look even faster. Rincon's best pitch is a slider that's almost impossible for lefthanders to touch when he's throwing well. Rincon is a good defensive pitcher and has a quick move to first base. He has batted just once in his major league career.

1998 Outlook

Rincon was a revelation for the Pirates in 1997, handling the transition from the Mexican League to the majors well. He has a live arm and the perfect temperament to be a quality lefthanded reliever for many years to come.

Matt Ruebel

Position: RP
Bats: L **Throws:** L
Ht: 6' 2" **Wt:** 180

Opening Day Age: 28
Born: 10/16/69 in
Cincinnati, OH
ML Seasons: 2
Pronunciation:
ROO-bull

Overall Statistics

	W	L	Pct.	ERA	G	GS	Sv	IP	H	BB	SO	HR	Ratio
1997	3	2	.600	6.32	44	0	0	62.2	77	27	50	8	1.66
Career	4	3	.571	5.49	70	7	1	121.1	141	52	72	15	1.59

1997 Situational Stats

	W	L	ERA	Sv	IP		AB	H	HR	RBI	Avg
Home	1	0	6.11	0	35.1	LHB	82	22	2	21	.268
Road	2	2	6.59	0	27.1	RHB	173	55	6	31	.318
First Half	2	2	8.69	0	29.0	Sc Pos	87	28	3	44	.322
Scnd Half	1	0	4.28	0	33.2	Clutch	55	16	2	13	.291

1997 Season

Matt Ruebel spent the entire 1997 season with the Pirates, but was definitely the 12th man on a 12-man pitching staff. He pitched just three times in September, including only once in the last 22 games. The high point of the year for Ruebel, who spent most of May on the disabled with an inflamed shoulder, was a team-high 5⅔-inning relief stint in an August game against Colorado.

Pitching, Defense & Hitting

Ruebel's fastball is below average, and his curveball and slider are inconsistent. His best pitch is a changeup, but it doesn't really help him much in relief. He's durable and can provide four or five innings from the bullpen if necessary. He has trouble rushing throws on bunts and isn't quick on balls hit back through the box, though he does have a decent pickoff move. Ruebel is a decent bunter but isn't much of a threat with a bat in his hands.

1998 Outlook

Ruebel is better suited for the rotation because his strengths lie in changing speeds and hitting his spots. However, his stuff really isn't big-league caliber and he'll have a hard time sticking in the majors, even if he does provide some value by eating up innings in long relief.

Mark Smith

Position: RF/LF
Bats: R **Throws:** R
Ht: 6' 3" **Wt:** 205

Opening Day Age: 27
Born: 5/7/70 in Pasadena, CA
ML Seasons: 4

Overall Statistics

	G	AB	R	H	D	T	HR	RBI	SB	BB	SO	Avg	OBP	Slg
1997	71	193	29	55	13	1	9	35	3	28	36	.285	.374	.503
Career	138	382	49	99	20	1	16	62	6	43	80	.259	.339	.442

1997 Situational Stats

	AB	H	HR	RBI	Avg		AB	H	HR	RBI	Avg
Home	73	21	6	16	.288	LHP	66	14	5	10	.212
Road	120	34	3	19	.283	RHP	127	41	4	25	.323
First Half	53	16	2	11	.302	Sc Pos	57	21	5	30	.368
Scnd Half	140	39	7	24	.279	Clutch	44	13	4	10	.295

1997 Season

Mark Smith was acquired from the Padres in a four-player trade on the last day of spring training and began the season at Triple-A Calgary. He was summoned to Pittsburgh on May 22, and then pulled a hamstring the next day and went on the disabled list for a month. He started 20 games in left field, 15 in right and six at first base.

Hitting, Baserunning & Defense

The knock on Smith, a former Orioles first-round pick, was that he never lived up to his power potential. That changed in 1997, after he added the strength to turn on pitches during an offseason conditioning program. He's a fastball hitter but is learning to hang in better against offspeed stuff. He also has shown a flair for dramatic late-inning hits during his brief tenure in the majors. Smith has heavy legs and doesn't run particularly well. He's an adequate corner outfielder with a decent arm and went to instructional league in an effort to learn first base.

1998 Outlook

Smith still is looking for a chance at regular major league duty after spending parts of the last four years with Baltimore and Pittsburgh. He's capable, but his chances with the Pirates seem limited with Al Martin and Jose Guillen on the outfield corners.

Dale Sveum

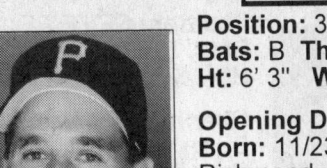

Signed By YANKEES

Position: 3B/1B/SS
Bats: B **Throws:** R
Ht: 6' 3" **Wt:** 185

Opening Day Age: 34
Born: 11/23/63 in Richmond, CA
ML Seasons: 10
Pronunciation: SWAYM

Overall Statistics

	G	AB	R	H	D	T	HR	RBI	SB	BB	SO	Avg	OBP	Slg
1997	126	306	30	80	20	1	12	47	0	27	81	.261	.319	.451
Career	783	2397	292	573	120	12	66	324	10	216	612	.239	.301	.382

1997 Situational Stats

	AB	H	HR	RBI	Avg		AB	H	HR	RBI	Avg
Home	149	31	5	19	.208	LHP	51	10	2	9	.196
Road	157	49	7	28	.312	RHP	255	70	10	38	.275
First Half	138	42	6	22	.304	Sc Pos	93	19	4	33	.204
Scnd Half	168	38	6	25	.226	Clutch	70	20	2	8	.286

1997 Season

Dale Sveum spent his first full season in the major leagues since 1991 and proved to be a key reserve for the Pirates. He made 39 starts at third base, 13 at shortstop, nine at first base and two at second.

Hitting, Baserunning & Defense

The switch-hitting Sveum bats much better from the left side of the plate. He has good power against righthanders and is a threat to pull balls over the fence. From the right side, he just hopes to make contact and is usually content with slapping pitches the other way. Leg injuries and age have slowed him to a crawl, but he's a smart baserunner and doesn't take many risks. Sveum is below average defensively at this stage of his career. His glovework is acceptable on the infield corners, but barely passable up the middle.

1998 Outlook

Sveum seemed destined for stardom until suffering a broken left leg in 1988 with Milwaukee. He resurrected his career in 1997 by becoming a valuable bench player as a switch-hitter capable of playing all four infield positions. He became a free agent and signed with the Yankees for two years and $1.6 million.

<table>
</table>

Turner Ward

Position: CF/LF/RF
Bats: B **Throws:** R
Ht: 6' 2" **Wt:** 182

Opening Day Age: 32
Born: 4/11/65 in
Orlando, FL
ML Seasons: 8

Overall Statistics

	G	AB	R	H	D	T	HR	RBI	SB	BB	SO	Avg	OBP	Slg
1997	71	167	33	59	16	1	7	33	4	18	17	.353	.420	.587
Career	412	1085	163	275	52	8	28	152	25	138	179	.253	.338	.394

1997 Situational Stats

	AB	H	HR	RBI	Avg		AB	H	HR	RBI	Avg
Home	83	35	5	19	.422	LHP	24	9	1	7	.375
Road	84	24	2	14	.286	RHP	143	50	6	26	.350
First Half	14	6	1	2	.429	Sc Pos	47	19	1	24	.404
Scnd Half	153	53	6	31	.346	Clutch	38	15	2	9	.395

1997 Season

Journeyman Turner Ward's career appeared finished when the White Sox released him after failing to sell his contract to a Japanese team. The Pirates signed him to a Triple-A Calgary contract April 22 and promoted him to Pittsburgh on July 2. Used in all three outfield spots and as a pinch hitter, he batted a career-high .353.

Hitting, Baserunning & Defense

The switch-hitting Ward swings the bat effectively from either side of the plate. He has more pop from the left side but also makes solid contact from the right. He's an aggressive hitter who looks for fastballs early in the count, but has enough patience to lay off bad pitches. Ward is an above-average runner and will steal an occasional base. He's average defensively at all three outfield spots, though he's most comfortable in center field. His arm is mediocre and his range is decent, but he makes up for shortcomings through hustle.

1998 Outlook

Having recovered from reconstructive shoulder surgery that limited him to just 43 games with Milwaukee in 1996, Ward was a valuable bench player for the Pirates. Eligible for arbitration, he'll gladly be welcomed back in Pittsburgh if his salary demands aren't outrageous.

Marc Wilkins

Position: RP
Bats: R **Throws:** R
Ht: 5'11" **Wt:** 200

Opening Day Age: 27
Born: 10/21/70 in
Mansfield, OH
ML Seasons: 2

Overall Statistics

	W	L	Pct.	ERA	G	GS	Sv	IP	H	BB	SO	HR	Ratio
1997	9	5	.643	3.69	70	0	2	75.2	65	33	47	7	1.30
Career	13	8	.619	3.76	117	2	3	150.2	140	69	109	13	1.39

1997 Situational Stats

	W	L	ERA	Sv	IP		AB	H	HR	RBI	Avg
Home	5	0	4.05	1	40.0	LHB	113	28	2	11	.248
Road	4	5	3.28	1	35.2	RHB	156	37	5	16	.237
First Half	6	1	4.69	1	40.1	Sc Pos	62	14	2	22	.226
Scnd Half	3	4	2.55	1	35.1	Clutch	109	22	2	10	.202

1997 Season

In his first full major league season, Marc Wilkins emerged as the Pirates' top righthanded setup man. Wilkins became the first Pittsburgh reliever to start a season 5-0 since Dave Giusti in 1973 but also gave up seven home runs in his 48 appearances. However, Wilkins did not allow a homer in his last 22 appearances and was scored upon just three times in his last 20 games.

Pitching, Defense & Hitting

Wilkins induces plenty of groundball outs with a sinking fastball that reaches 93 MPH, a big-breaking curveball, and a slider. When Wilkins has control of his curve, he is particularly tough, as the pitch drops straight down and is equally effective against both righthanded and lefthanded batters. Wilkins has yet to make an error in two major league seasons and is attentive to baserunners. He also is decent with the bat.

1998 Outlook

Wilkins has established himself as a first-rate setup man out of the Pirates' bullpen and is again poised to be the key component in the bridge between the starters and closer Rich Loiselle. Whether Wilkins has the stuff to eventually becomes a closer is open to debate, but he figures to have a long career in the majors regardless.

Other Pittsburgh Pirates

Emil Brown (Pos: LF, Age: 23, Bats: R)

	G	AB	R	H	D	T	HR	RBI	SB	BB	SO	Avg	OBP	Slg
1997	66	95	16	17	2	1	2	6	5	10	32	.179	.304	.284
Career	66	95	16	17	2	1	2	6	5	10	32	.179	.304	.284

Obtained from Oakland in the '96 major league Rule 5 draft, Brown stuck with the Pirates because they didn't want to risk having to give him back. He sorely needs more seasoning, but his speed is enticing. 1998 Outlook: C

Jason Christiansen (Pos: LHP, Age: 28)

	W	L	Pct.	ERA	G	GS	Sv	IP	H	BB	SO	HR	Ratio
1997	3	0	1.000	2.94	39	0	0	33.2	37	17	37	2	1.60
Career	7	6	.538	4.69	135	0	0	134.1	142	70	128	14	1.58

Christiansen came off the DL in mid-June following surgery on his shoulder and was a steady lefty middle man for Pittsburgh. He gave up runs in just six of 39 appearances, registering 37 Ks. 1998 Outlook: A

Elmer Dessens (Pos: RHP, Age: 26)

	W	L	Pct.	ERA	G	GS	Sv	IP	H	BB	SO	HR	Ratio
1997	0	0	-	0.00	3	0	0	3.1	2	0	2	0	0.60
Career	0	2	.000	7.31	18	3	0	28.1	42	4	15	2	1.62

Dessens spent much of '97 with Carolina and Calgary before finishing the season in the Pittsburgh bullpen. He began his career as a starter, but any future he may have probably lies in relief work. 1998 Outlook: C

Jeff Granger (Pos: LHP, Age: 26)

	W	L	Pct.	ERA	G	GS	Sv	IP	H	BB	SO	HR	Ratio
1997	0	0	-	18.00	9	0	0	5.0	10	8	4	3	3.60
Career	0	1	.000	9.09	27	2	0	31.2	47	26	19	8	2.31

The Yo-Yo, up-and-down-from-the-minors career of Jeff Granger continued in '97. The Pirates hoped he would work as a lefty option out of the bullpen, but a 9.00 ERA had him in Calgary by the end of April. 1998 Outlook: C

Keith Osik (Pos: C, Age: 29, Bats: R)

	G	AB	R	H	D	T	HR	RBI	SB	BB	SO	Avg	OBP	Slg
1997	49	105	10	27	9	1	0	7	0	9	21	.257	.322	.362
Career	97	245	28	68	23	2	1	21	1	23	43	.278	.344	.400

Osik once again spent the year as Jason Kendall's backup, but was unable to match his 1996 numbers. His average fell from .293 to .257, which still isn't too bad for a part-time catcher. 1998 Outlook: B

Chris Peters (Pos: LHP, Age: 26)

	W	L	Pct.	ERA	G	GS	Sv	IP	H	BB	SO	HR	Ratio
1997	2	2	.500	4.58	31	1	0	37.1	38	21	17	6	1.58
Career	4	6	.400	5.24	47	11	0	101.1	110	46	45	15	1.54

Talk about a guy who never unpacked his bags! Peters was called up from Triple-A Calgary three different times in '97. In between flights and bus rides, he managed to make 31 appearances for the Pirates. 1998 Outlook: B

Clint Sodowsky (Pos: RHP, Age: 25)

	W	L	Pct.	ERA	G	GS	Sv	IP	H	BB	SO	HR	Ratio
1997	2	2	.500	3.63	45	0	0	52.0	49	34	51	6	1.60
Career	5	7	.417	5.96	58	13	0	99.2	113	72	74	15	1.86

Sodowsky was much more effective in relief last year than he had been as a starter in the past. Arizona took him in the second round of the expansion draft. 1998 Outlook: B

Paul Wagner (Pos: RHP, Age: 30)

	W	L	Pct.	ERA	G	GS	Sv	IP	H	BB	SO	HR	Ratio
1997	1	0	1.000	4.50	16	0	0	18.0	20	13	9	4	1.83
Career	27	40	.403	4.59	144	75	3	538.2	568	221	415	54	1.46

After spending the first half of 1997 on the DL recovering from reconstructive elbow surgery, Wagner worked in the Pirate bullpen in July and August before landing with the Brewers. 1998 Outlook: C

David Wainhouse (Pos: RHP, Age: 30)

	W	L	Pct.	ERA	G	GS	Sv	IP	H	BB	SO	HR	Ratio
1997	0	1	.000	8.04	25	0	0	28.0	34	17	21	2	1.82
Career	1	2	.333	7.78	47	0	0	56.2	65	36	40	6	1.78

Wainhouse started the season as a righthanded option out of Gene Lamont's bullpen, but by the end of May he was in Lamont's doghouse. An 8.04 ERA in 25 outings earned him a trip to the minors in mid-June. 1998 Outlook: D

Eddie Williams (Pos: 1B, Age: 33, Bats: R)

	G	AB	R	H	D	T	HR	RBI	SB	BB	SO	Avg	OBP	Slg
1997	38	96	12	23	5	0	3	12	1	11	25	.240	.327	.385
Career	378	1117	145	284	47	2	39	147	2	99	210	.254	.322	.405

Williams saw time in the majors with both the Dodgers and Pirates. When he wasn't struggling with major league pitching, he was tearing apart the PCL, but at 33 his chances to prove himself are dwindling. 1998 Outlook: C

Pittsburgh Pirates Minor League Prospects

Organization Overview:

When many teams dump salary, they're usually content just to get rid of veterans. Not the Pirates, who have done an excellent job of adding prospects while they trim salary. They turned Denny Neagle into Jason Schmidt and Ron Wright; Carlos Garcia and Orlando Merced into Abraham Nunez, Jose Pett, Jose Silva and Craig Wilson; and Jay Bell and Jeff King into Jeff Wallace. They even turned Danny Darwin into Rich Loiselle. GM Cam Bonifay's trades, some astute first-round picks and good work on the international market have given the Pirates a farm system as good as any in the game—without paying exorbitant signing bonuses. Pittsburgh has mined Mexico as well as any team, finding players such as Francisco Cordova, Esteban Loaiza and Ricardo Rincon.

Kris Benson

Position: P   **Opening Day Age:** 23
Bats: R **Throws:** R   **Born:** 11/7/74 in Duluth,
Ht: 6' 4" **Wt:** 190   MN

Recent Statistics

	W	L	ERA	G	GS	Sv	IP	H	R	BB	SO	HR
97 A Lynchburg	5	2	2.58	10	10	0	59.1	49	20	13	72	1
97 AA Carolina	3	5	4.98	14	14	0	68.2	81	49	32	66	11

Unlike some small-revenue teams have in the past, the Pirates didn't flinch when they had the No. 1 overall draft pick. They used the top 1996 pick to draft Benson out of Clemson, and spent the going rate (a club-record $2 million) to sign him. He was the most advanced college pitching prospect in years, and some scouts thought he could have joined the Pirates immediately if he hadn't taken the summer off to pitch in the Olympics. That didn't happen, but he did reach Double-A in his first season. Benson throws 92-93 MPH with good life on his fastball. His curveball and command are outstanding, and his changeup is a good third pitch. He's a student of the game who understands what he needs to do to succeed, and he learns from his mistakes. His biggest shortcoming may be a lack of stamina that seemed to sap his strength in the second half of 1997, when he also was bothered by hamstring pulls. He'll probably join Pittsburgh as a September call-up.

Lou Collier

Position: SS   **Opening Day Age:** 24
Bats: R **Throws:** R   **Born:** 8/21/73 in
Ht: 5' 10" **Wt:** 170   Chicago, IL

Recent Statistics

	G	AB	R	H	D	T	HR	RBI	SB	BB	SO	AVG
97 AAA Calgary	112	397	65	131	31	5	1	48	12	37	47	.330
97 NL Pittsburgh	18	37	3	5	0	0	0	3	1	1	11	.135
97 MLE	112	375	46	109	27	3	0	34	8	26	49	.291

Collier has been one of the system's top position players since signing as a 31st-round draft-and-follow out of Triton (Ill.) Community College in 1993, but he may be squeezed out of a spot in Pittsburgh. Since being acquired from the Blue Jays, dazzling gloveman Abraham Nunez has staked a claim to shortstop, Collier's natural position. And slugger Chad Hermansen is converting to second base, Collier's other option. Collier hits line drives, and has slightly above-average speed and a strong arm. He could get a shot at short before Nunez is ready, and if he does he better make the most of it.

Chad Hermansen

Position: OF   **Opening Day Age:** 20
Bats: R **Throws:** R   **Born:** 9/10/77 in Salt
Ht: 6' 2" **Wt:** 185   Lake City, UT

Recent Statistics

	G	AB	R	H	D	T	HR	RBI	SB	BB	SO	AVG
96 A Augusta	62	226	41	57	11	3	14	41	11	38	65	.252
96 A Lynchburg	66	251	40	69	11	3	10	46	5	29	56	.275
97 AA Carolina	129	487	87	134	31	4	20	70	18	69	136	.275
97 MLE	129	470	67	117	28	3	15	54	12	45	145	.249

A first-round pick in 1995, Hermansen has proven that he can hit and that he can't play shortstop. He made 53 errors in 1996 and 23 in 36 games at short last season. The Pirates tried to convert him to center field, which didn't take, but he seemed to find a home at second base. He's an exceptional hitter for a middle infielder, and more than held his own in Double-A despite being the youngest player in the Southern League. He has 20-20 potential, though he needs to cut down on his strikeouts. His development has been rapid, and he could supplant Tony Womack as Pittsburgh's second baseman in 1999 at age 21.

Abraham Nunez

Position: SS   **Opening Day Age:** 22
Bats: B **Throws:** R   **Born:** 3/16/76 in Santo
Ht: 5' 11" **Wt:** 160   Domingo, DR

Recent Statistics

	G	AB	R	H	D	T	HR	RBI	SB	BB	SO	AVG
97 A Lynchburg	78	304	45	79	9	4	3	32	29	23	47	.260
97 AA Carolina	47	198	31	65	6	1	1	14	10	20	28	.328
97 NL Pittsburgh	19	40	3	9	2	2	0	6	1	3	10	.225

Nunez was the best player acquired by Pittsburgh in a nine-player trade with Toronto in December 1996. Signed out of the Dominican Republic by the Blue Jays, he's an outstanding shortstop who covers a lot of range and has a good arm. His best offensive tool is his speed, and he batted .328 in Double-A after he learned to stop expanding the strike zone. He has no power to speak of, and his extra-base hits usually are the result of quickness not strength. The Pirates would like to see him spend a full season in Triple-A before making him their regular shortstop in 1999.

Aramis Ramirez

Position: 3B
Bats: R **Throws:** R
Ht: 6' 1" **Wt:** 176

Opening Day Age: 19
Born: 6/25/78 in Santo Domingo, DR

Recent Statistics

	G	AB	R	H	D	T	HR	RBI	SB	BB	SO	AVG
96 A Erie	61	223	37	68	14	4	9	42	0	31	41	.305
96 A Augusta	6	20	3	4	1	0	1	2	0	1	7	.200
97 A Lynchburg	137	482	85	134	24	2	29	114	5	80	103	.278

Another Dominican signee, Ramirez was named the New York-Penn League's top prospect in 1996 and the Carolina League's MVP in 1997 at age 19. He's capable of producing several seasons similar to his .278-29-114 year. Ramirez also is willing to draw a walk when pitchers won't challenge him, though he's not much of a runner. Defensively, he has the hands and arm to be a solid third baseman once he smooths some rough edges out with experience. With Joe Randa lost in the expansion draft, the Pirates will accelerate Ramirez' development and may promote him straight to the majors.

Jose Silva

Position: P
Bats: R **Throws:** R
Ht: 6' 5" **Wt:** 210

Opening Day Age: 24
Born: 12/19/73 in Tijuana, BC, Mexico

Recent Statistics

	W	L	ERA	G	GS	Sv	IP	H	R	BB	SO	HR
97 AAA Calgary	5	1	3.41	17	11	0	66.0	74	27	22	54	3
97 NL Pittsburgh	2	1	5.94	11	4	0	36.1	52	26	16	30	4

Another component of the nine-player trade with Toronto, Silva has had problems staying healthy since he signed as a sixth-round pick in 1991. A severe automobile accident and then shoulder problems cost him most of the 1995 and 1996 seasons, and soreness in his elbow limited him to 66 innings last season. When he's healthy he can throw in the mid-90s, and managers rated his fastball the best in the Triple-A Pacific Coast League. His lost innings have cost him the opportunity to improve his curveball and changeup, which can become average pitches. If they don't come along he may be better suited for the bullpen, but the Pirates won't rule him out as a starter.

Jeff Wallace

Position: P
Bats: L **Throws:** L
Ht: 6' 2" **Wt:** 237

Opening Day Age: 21
Born: 4/12/76 in Wheeling, WV

Recent Statistics

	W	L	ERA	G	GS	Sv	IP	H	R	BB	SO	HR
97 A Lynchburg	5	0	1.65	9	0	1	16.1	9	3	10	13	0
97 AA Carolina	4	8	5.40	38	0	3	43.1	43	37	36	39	3
97 NL Pittsburgh	0	0	0.75	11	0	0	12.0	8	2	8	14	0

Wallace hasn't been acclaimed as a "hot prospect," but he could make the Bell-King trade with Kansas City look awfully good for the Pirates. He throws comfortably at 94-96 MPH and peaks at 98, and Randy Johnson and Billy Wagner are perhaps the only lefthanders who throw harder. A 1995 25th-round pick used primarily as a starter by the Royals, Wallace became a power reliever with the Pirates and made 11 solid major league appearances at age 21. His only other pitch is a hard slider. He strained an elbow ligament toward the end of the season and has pitched only 226 minor league innings (none above Double-A), yet it may be tempting for Pittsburgh to keep him on the Opening Day roster.

Ron Wright

Position: 1B
Bats: R **Throws:** R
Ht: 6' 0" **Wt:** 215

Opening Day Age: 22
Born: 1/21/76 in Delta, UT

Recent Statistics

	G	AB	R	H	D	T	HR	RBI	SB	BB	SO	AVG
96 A Durham	66	240	47	66	15	2	20	62	1	37	71	.275
96 AA Greenville	63	232	39	59	11	1	16	52	1	38	73	.254
96 AA Carolina	4	14	1	2	0	0	0	0	0	2	7	.143
97 AAA Calgary	91	336	50	102	31	0	16	63	0	24	81	.304
97 MLE	91	319	35	85	27	0	11	44	0	17	85	.266

When the Pirates sent Denny Neagle to Atlanta in August 1996, part of the return was one of the top sluggers in the minor leagues. A seventh-round pick in 1994, Wright was headed for a third consecutive 30-homer season in 1997 before his left wrist was broken by a pitch. There's not much more to his game, as he walks little, strikes out a lot and doesn't play first base or run well. But his power, generated from a short, quick stroke, is very attractive all by itself. If Kevin Young asks for too much money in arbitration or gets off to a slow start, Pittsburgh will quickly turn to Wright.

Others to Watch

Lefthander **Jimmy Anderson** has a 91-92 MPH fastball and a hard slider, but Triple-A hitters caught up to him. He's still only 22, and taking another crack at the Pacific Coast League won't hurt him. . . Skinny righthander **Bronson Arroyo** has a projectable fastball, and indeed it picked up 2-3 MPH in 1997 to reach 90. He also has an above-average curveball and changeup, and very good command. After going 12-4, 3.31 for high Class-A Lynchburg at age 20, he could move quickly. . . Third baseman **Freddy Garcia** spent 1996 in the majors as a major league Rule 5 draft pick, and hit 24 homers in the minors in 1997. He's a bit old at 25, however, and won't stand in Ramirez' way. . . First baseman **Garrett Long** turned down a Yale scholarship to sign as a second-round pick in 1995. Shoulder surgery a year later has impeded his power potential, but he did hit .300 with 61 walks in 83 games at Class-A Augusta in 1997 at the age of 20. . . Brazilian righthander **Jose Pett** was much ballyhooed when the Blue Jays signed him at age 16 in 1992, but he has gone just 23-36 in the minors. His fastball and slider are good, hard pitches, but he hasn't put it all together. . . Like Pett, catcher **Craig Wilson** joined the Pirates as part of the Garcia-Merced trade with the Blue Jays. He hit 19 homers at Lynchburg at age 20 and is making progress behind the plate.

Tony La Russa

1997 Season

Tony La Russa guaranteed St. Louis would win the National League Central in the spring, then was as befuddled as anyone by his team's inability to score runs or handle the fundamentals. La Russa juggled his lineup, worked the percentages, played hunches, mixed in numerous youngsters when injuries or potential warranted and kept running out his tried-and-true veterans. His strategies didn't work this time.

Offense

La Russa gradually is becoming accustomed to the NL's brand of baseball. He now uses a running game, something made easier with Delino DeShields in the leadoff spot, and doesn't waste many hit-and-run opportunities. Veteran sluggers might be called upon to lay down a bunt and big galoots like Mark McGwire occasionally will be on the run. La Russa delights in double-switches and likes a power-packed lineup with as many proven winners as he can find.

Pitching & Defense

When it comes to the team's moundsmen, La Russa and pitching coach Dave Duncan are co-managers. Despite Duncan's vast and valuable input, La Russa decides who pitches when and for how long. He likes starters who work deep into games and a bullpen tailored for specific situations. He puts a premium on defense and won't tolerate a player who can't master fundamentals.

1998 Outlook

La Russa believes the 1997 Cardinals were about unfulfilled potential and broken promises. His club let down in its fundamental approach at the plate, on the bases and in the field. Look for him to stress a back-to-basics approach and build an offense based largely on the Brian Jordan-Mark McGwire-Ray Lankford trio. His pitching-first mentality will also drive him to develop a rotation that will create consistent winning opportunities for his club. La Russa still thinks the Cardinals can reach a World Series, and he'll manage the team with that objective in mind.

Born: 10/04/44 in Tampa, FL

Playing Experience: 1963-1973, Oak, Atl, ChN

Managerial Experience: 19 seasons

Manager Statistics

Year	Team, Lg	W	L	Pct	GB	Finish
1997	St. Louis, NL	73	89	.451	11.0	4th Central
19 Seasons		1,481	1,346	.524	—	—

1997 Starting Pitchers by Days Rest

	≤3	4	5	6+
Cardinals Starts	3	98	34	15
Cardinals ERA	5.29	3.73	3.60	5.17
NL Avg Starts	3	90	38	22
NL ERA	4.23	4.05	4.27	4.52

1997 Situational Stats

	Tony La Russa	NL Average
Hit & Run Success %	33.6	36.4
Stolen Base Success %	73.2	68.4
Platoon Pct.	54.1	56.3
Defensive Subs	18	26
High-Pitch Outings	16	12
Quick/Slow Hooks	18/9	18/10
Sacrifice Attempts	77	96

1997 Rankings (National League)

⇒ 1st in steals of home plate (2), double steals (10) and starting lineups used (146)

⇒ 2nd in stolen base attempts (224), stolen base percentage (73.2%), steals of second base (140), pitchouts with a runner moving (22) and pinch hitters used (307)

⇒ 3rd in pitchouts (79) and first batter platoon percentage (62.7%)

Alan Benes

1997 Season

Alan Benes needed only one season to solve his bout with big-league inconsistency. He matured from an enigmatic rookie in 1996 to an often-dominating sophomore hurler. Few pitchers were better through their first 20 starts. Mild alarms went off when he hit a stretch of three starts that ranked noticeably below the standards he'd established for himself. Eventually Benes learned he needed surgery on a slightly torn rotator cuff, and ended the season with his right arm in a sling.

Pitching

Benes mixed a mid-90s fastball, a cut fastball and a splendid curveball to create a baffling blend of possibilities. What pushed him into consideration among the league's elite was his veteran's attitude. Always a precocious pitcher, the former first-round draft pick seemed to benefit immensely from the influence of staff mates such as big brother Andy, Todd Stottlemyre and Dennis Eckersley. He maintained consistent poise even throughout numerous frustrating starts with poor run support, and showed marked improvement working to lefthanders.

Defense & Hitting

Benes is improving defensively, though it's still not something to consider a strength. On the other hand, his knack for keeping runners from stealing bases is a huge asset. Of the 22 who dared try to steal last season, only 10 were successful, thanks in part to a shorter step and the zip on his fastball. Cardinals pitchers are competitive about their offensive numbers and Benes brought up the rear, with only two sacrifice hits and 16 strikeouts.

1998 Outlook

Benes didn't plan to start throwing until January after his September surgery. Once his arm is in shape and his pitches are polished, he should step right back onto the mound to battle the best opposing teams can offer. His next challenge is to find a way to win tough pitching duels.

Position: SP
Bats: R **Throws:** R
Ht: 6' 5"   **Wt:** 215

Opening Day Age: 26
Born: 1/21/72 in Evansville, IN
ML Seasons: 3
Pronunciation: BENN-ess

Overall Statistics

	W	L	Pct.	ERA	G	GS	Sv	IP	H	BB	SO	HR	Ratio
1997	9	9	.500	2.89	23	23	0	161.2	128	68	160	13	1.21
Career	23	21	.523	4.17	60	58	0	368.2	344	159	311	42	1.36

How Often He Throws Strikes

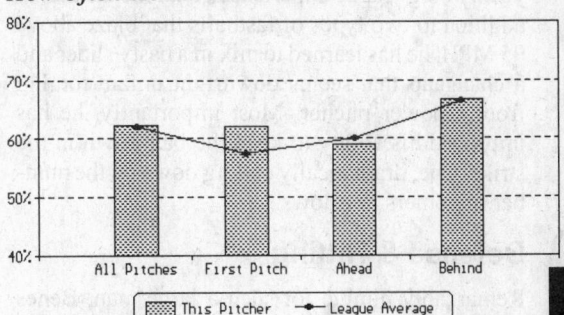

Legend: This Pitcher — League Average

1997 Situational Stats

	W	L	ERA	Sv	IP		AB	H	HR	RBI	Avg
Home	3	6	2.68	0	84.0	LHB	292	68	8	30	.233
Road	6	3	3.13	0	77.2	RHB	293	60	5	27	.205
First Half	7	7	2.55	0	127.0	Sc Pos	116	25	2	40	.216
Scnd Half	2	2	4.15	0	34.2	Clutch	67	13	1	5	.194

1997 Rankings (National League)

⇒ 4th in runners caught stealing (12)
⇒ 5th in lowest batting average allowed vs. righthanded batters
⇒ 6th in wild pitches (9)
⇒ 8th in balks (2)
⇒ 9th in ERA at home and lowest batting average allowed vs. lefthanded batters
⇒ Led the Cardinals in losses, wild pitches (9), runners caught stealing (12), ERA at home and lowest batting average allowed vs. lefthanded batters

Andy Benes

1997 Season

Andy Benes entertained Cy Young Award possibilities at the opening of spring camp. Then a strained ribcage muscle put him on the disabled list for the start of the regular season, and led to a slow start when he returned to the rotation. Once he settled into a groove, Benes found himself frustrated because of poor offensive support. He still managed to finish 10-7 before his season ended prematurely with a broken finger.

Pitching

He's big, he's a workhorse, he throws hard. . . and now Benes has begun applying the wisdom of nine years of big league experience. That means that in addition to two types of fastballs that blaze above 95 MPH, he has learned to mix in a nasty slider and a changeup that seems downright unfair coming from a power pitcher. Most importantly, he has improved his ability to keep the ball down in the strike zone, dramatically cutting down on the number of homers he allows.

Defense & Hitting

Remarkably nimble for such a large man, Benes has quick reflexes in pursuit of line drives and bunts to either side of the mound. He has had to work on holding runners throughout his career and has been inconsistent. He was most surprising at the plate in 1997, posting a .218 average, driving in five runs and having a team-high eight sacrifice bunts.

1998 Outlook

A free agent following the 1997 season, Benes seems to be in his prime. He still might need to prove to some doubters that he can be a consistent big winner and a dominant No. 1 starter able to win close games. To Benes, it's important mainly to work 200 innings and give his team a chance to win most of his outings. He's dependable in that way.

Position: SP
Bats: R **Throws:** R
Ht: 6' 6" **Wt:** 245
Opening Day Age: 30
Born: 8/20/67 in Evansville, IN
ML Seasons: 9
Pronunciation: BENN-ess
Nickname: Big Train, Rain Man

Overall Statistics

	W	L	Pct.	ERA	G	GS	Sv	IP	H	BB	SO	HR	Ratio
1997	10	7	.588	3.10	26	26	0	177.0	149	61	175	9	1.19
Career	104	94	.525	3.64	261	258	1	1705.1	1564	573	1416	160	1.25

How Often He Throws Strikes

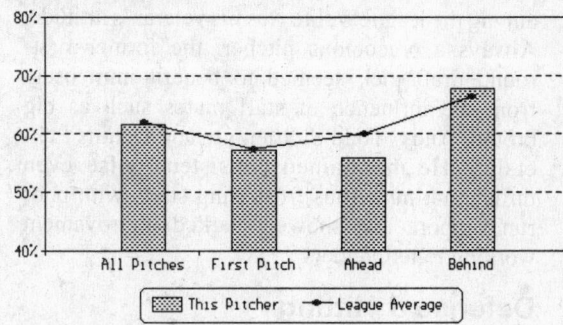

1997 Situational Stats

	W	L	ERA	Sv	IP		AB	H	HR	RBI	Avg
Home	7	2	2.82	0	89.1	LHB	336	82	6	39	.244
Road	3	5	3.39	0	87.2	RHB	312	67	3	21	.215
First Half	6	3	3.16	0	94.0	Sc Pos	151	30	1	46	.199
Scnd Half	4	4	3.04	0	83.0	Clutch	54	16	0	9	.296

1997 Rankings (National League)

⇒ 2nd in most pitches thrown per batter (3.98)
⇒ 3rd in least home runs allowed per 9 innings (.46)
⇒ 4th in most strikeouts per 9 innings (8.9)
⇒ 5th in lowest slugging percentage allowed (.330) and lowest batting average allowed with runners in scoring position
⇒ Led the Cardinals in sacrifice bunts (8), ERA, strikeouts, pickoff throws (105), stolen bases allowed (22), winning percentage, highest strikeout/walk ratio (2.9), lowest batting average allowed (.230), lowest slugging percentage allowed (.330), lowest on-base percentage allowed (.298) and least baserunners allowed per 9 innings (10.9)

Royce Clayton

1997 Season

Royce Clayton was rewarded with his first All-Star selection in 1997. He reached career highs in doubles and home runs as he became a key part of the offense. The Cardinals found a niche for him in the No. 8 spot, where he could drive in runs and make good use of his baserunning abilities. He also started to take on a leadership role as a defensive anchor at shortstop.

Hitting

Clayton has wanted to fit into the batting order as a leadoff or No. 2 hitter, but hasn't succeeded when been given those opportunities in the past. He really doesn't make enough contact and he's better suited as a second leadoff man at the bottom of the order. Blazing fastballs still beat him. He doesn't draw nearly as many walks as he could if he'd start to lay off breaking balls out of the strike zone. A shorter batting stroke has helped his progress.

Baserunning & Defense

Clayton is a good basestealer, as he has a quick jump and the intelligence to pick his spots well. Fast down the line, he had 21 infield hits in 1997. His range, confidence and savvy make him one of the better defensive shortstops in the big leagues. He routinely gets to shots in the hole and then fires strong throws to first. His extremely strong arm occasionally gets him into trouble with wild throws.

1998 Outlook

More contact and improved pitch selection could turn Clayton into a premier shortstop, the kind the Cardinals might want to lock up with a long-term contract. But their farm system also is loaded at his position. Even if he doesn't seize that second spot in the order or bat .300 with improved run production, he still should be a key to a successful infield.

Position: SS
Bats: R **Throws:** R
Ht: 6' 0" **Wt:** 183

Opening Day Age: 28
Born: 1/2/70 in Burbank, CA
ML Seasons: 7

Overall Statistics

	G	AB	R	H	D	T	HR	RBI	SB	BB	SO	Avg	OBP	Slg
1997	154	576	75	153	39	5	9	61	30	33	109	.266	.306	.398
Career	789	2857	318	734	131	27	33	280	129	199	541	.257	.306	.356

Where He Hits the Ball

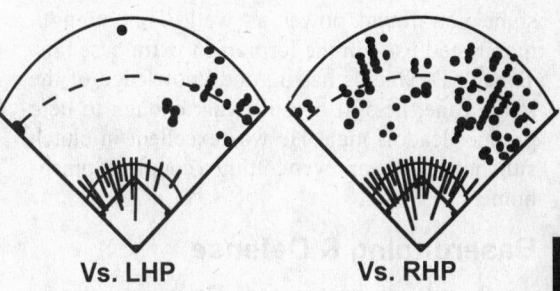

Vs. LHP   Vs. RHP

1997 Situational Stats

	AB	H	HR	RBI	Avg		AB	H	HR	RBI	Avg
Home	262	78	5	32	.298	LHP	139	35	2	10	.252
Road	314	75	4	29	.239	RHP	437	118	7	51	.270
First Half	322	85	6	36	.264	Sc Pos	139	32	0	46	.230
Scnd Half	254	68	3	25	.268	Clutch	114	28	1	11	.246

1997 Rankings (National League)

⇒ 2nd in lowest on-base percentage for a leadoff hitter (.285) and errors at shortstop (19)
⇒ 5th in GDPs (19), lowest on-base percentage vs. lefthanded pitchers (.295) and lowest fielding percentage at shortstop (.973)
⇒ Led the Cardinals in at-bats, doubles, games played (154), highest groundball/flyball ratio (1.8), batting average with the bases loaded (.316), batting average on an 0-2 count (.227) and batting average at home

Delino DeShields

1997 Season

In their quest to fill desperate needs at second base and the leadoff position, the Cardinals signed Delino DeShields prior to last season. Their faith proved well placed. He looked a lot closer to the promising talent who wore a Montreal uniform from 1990-93 than the player who was a bust in Los Angeles from 1994-96. DeShields matched his career high in batting average, set career highs in triples and homers, and was a threat on the bases with 55 steals. He struggled in the field, however.

Hitting

DeShields swung with renewed confidence in 1997. Not only did he put the ball into play more frequently than he ever has, but he also displayed some new-found power as well. This strength manifested itself in the form of 51 extra-base hits. Though DeShields has a good knowledge of the strike zone, he still doesn't walk enough to be a premier leadoff man. He was excellent in clutch situations last year, even hitting a couple of pinch-homers.

Baserunning & Defense

As the season progressed, DeShields clearly gained more and more confidence on the basepaths. He always has been able to run, and his lively legs carried him to a National League-best 14 triples and 14 bunt hits. Defensively, he has good range and can make the tough play. However, he has some trouble with routine grounders, has a weak arm and is average at best at turning double plays.

1998 Outlook

Perhaps being a part of a contender will help DeShields develop the concentration he needs to succeed in the field. If he improves there, the Cardinals gladly will accept a repeat of his 1997 offensive performance. He has shown a determination to play through injuries and a willingness to stir things up on the bases. As a result, he could score more than 100 runs this season.

Position: 2B
Bats: L **Throws:** R
Ht: 6' 1" **Wt:** 175

Opening Day Age: 29
Born: 1/15/69 in Seaford, DE
ML Seasons: 8
Pronunciation: duh-LINE-oh

Overall Statistics

	G	AB	R	H	D	T	HR	RBI	SB	BB	SO	Avg	OBP	Slg
1997	150	572	92	169	26	14	11	58	55	55	72	.295	.357	.448
Career	1058	3971	593	1063	146	53	49	350	356	512	751	.268	.352	.368

Where He Hits the Ball

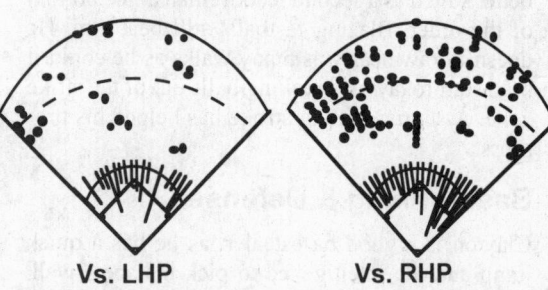

Vs. LHP   **Vs. RHP**

1997 Situational Stats

	AB	H	HR	RBI	Avg		AB	H	HR	RBI	Avg
Home	277	79	6	28	.285	LHP	118	33	1	12	.280
Road	295	90	5	30	.305	RHP	454	136	10	46	.300
First Half	303	88	5	28	.290	Sc Pos	109	35	4	49	.321
Scnd Half	269	81	6	30	.301	Clutch	96	29	3	13	.302

1997 Rankings (National League)

⇒ 1st in triples, lowest fielding percentage at second base (.972) and bunts in play (40)
⇒ 2nd in errors at second base (19)
⇒ 3rd in stolen bases
⇒ 4th in caught stealing (14)
⇒ 5th in highest percentage of swings put into play (55.8%) and steals of third (9)
⇒ Led the Cardinals in batting average, hits, singles, triples, sacrifice flies (6), stolen bases, caught stealing (14), plate appearances (643), stolen base percentage (79.7%), batting average with runners in scoring position, batting average vs. righthanded pitchers, on-base percentage for a leadoff hitter (.353), batting average on the road, bunts in play (40) and highest percentage of pitches taken (60.9%)

Dennis Eckersley

1997 Season

As one of the oldest players in the big leagues in 1997, Dennis Eckersley probably surpassed any reasonable expectations. He still ranked among the National League's leaders in saves, struck out almost a batter an inning and put on another season-long clinic on commanding the strike zone. But it wasn't a completely satisfying season for Eckersley, who yielded an uncharacteristic nine homers.

Pitching

Once the premier control pitcher in baseball, Eckersley now finds himself pitching deeper into counts than ever. His fastball has retained most of its movement if not its old speed, but he has shown an increasing amount of trouble putting his slider where he wants. When that slider is on, he rides it in on righthanders' fists and makes it unhittable for them. Lefties hit just .217 against him in 1997, but that probably was an aberration. They batted .324 against Eckersley in the previous four seasons.

Defense & Hitting

Eckersley is a terrific athlete who fields his position impeccably. He never has shown much of a knack for keeping baserunners close and didn't pick off any runners in 1997. He used to hit decently for a pitcher, but didn't bat at all last season.

1998 Outlook

There's no reason to think that Eckersley, who keeps himself in supreme condition and works as hard as any professional athlete, can't parlay his experience and skills into another season as a closer. That said, he probably shouldn't be the only capable closer in his bullpen, which is why St. Louis traded for Jeff Brantley. A free agent, Eckersley no longer can just rack up saves automatically, but he could prove to be an excellent setup man if he slips into that role.

Position: RP
Bats: R **Throws:** R
Ht: 6' 2" **Wt:** 195

Opening Day Age: 43
Born: 10/3/54 in Oakland, CA
ML Seasons: 23
Nickname: The Eck

Overall Statistics

	W	L	Pct.	ERA	G	GS	Sv	IP	H	BB	SO	HR	Ratio
1997	1	5	.167	3.91	57	0	36	53.0	49	8	45	9	1.08
Career	193	170	.532	3.49	1021	361	389	3246.0	3030	730	2379	341	1.16

How Often He Throws Strikes

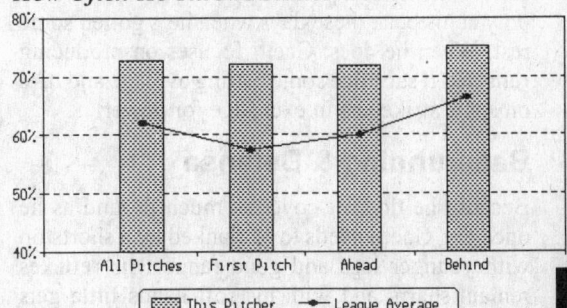

1997 Situational Stats

	W	L	ERA	Sv	IP		AB	H	HR	RBI	Avg
Home	0	5	5.02	20	28.2	LHB	106	23	2	12	.217
Road	1	0	2.59	16	24.1	RHB	100	26	7	13	.260
First Half	0	3	4.28	18	27.1	Sc Pos	55	13	2	16	.236
Scnd Half	1	2	3.51	18	25.2	Clutch	161	39	8	23	.242

1997 Rankings (National League)

⇒ 4th in saves, blown saves (7) and least GDPs induced per GDP situation (0.0%)
⇒ 5th in save opportunities (43)
⇒ 6th in save percentage (83.7%)
⇒ Led the Cardinals in saves, games finished (47), save opportunities (43), save percentage (83.7%) and blown saves (7)

Gary Gaetti

1997 Season

After two remarkable seasons full of power and run production, Gary Gaetti started to fall victim to Father Time in 1997. Showing some decline in his bat speed in the middle of the season, Gaetti experienced some power slumps. He also lost some range at third base, but was still one of the most dependable defenders at the hot corner.

Hitting

Gaetti always has been one of the better mistake hitters in the game, as well as a talented pull hitter when he sees a fat fastball. At his best, he tortured pitchers by swinging a quick bat through the strike zone with a classic power uppercut. However, he's only at his peak these days when he's gotten some rest. When he does, Gaetti focuses on producing runs. He'll sacrifice some batting average and take on some strikeouts in exchange for power.

Baserunning & Defense

Because he doesn't cover as much ground as he once did, Gaetti needs to be flanked by a shortstop with younger legs and good range. His reflexes remain sharp, and with his soft hands little gets past him if he can reach it. His quick release and consistently strong, accurate throws place him a notch above most third basemen, and he's also serviceable at first base. Though lacking speed, he's a smart runner who won't make mistakes on the bases.

1998 Outlook

Gaetti went into the winter as a free agent. He would be a good investment—at least better than most 40-year-old third basemen—as long as he's only asked to play 100-110 games. He'll still provide plenty of power and RBI. He also adds the intangible benefit of a veteran who understands the game and likes to talk about its nuances with teammates young and old.

Position: 3B/1B
Bats: R **Throws:** R
Ht: 6' 0" **Wt:** 200

Opening Day Age: 39
Born: 8/19/58 in Centralia, IL
ML Seasons: 17
Pronunciation: guy-ETT-ee

Overall Statistics

	G	AB	R	H	D	T	HR	RBI	SB	BB	SO	Avg	OBP	Slg
1997	148	502	63	126	24	1	17	69	7	36	88	.251	.305	.404
Career	2261	8227	1048	2101	400	37	332	1224	95	570	1486	.255	.307	.434

Where He Hits the Ball

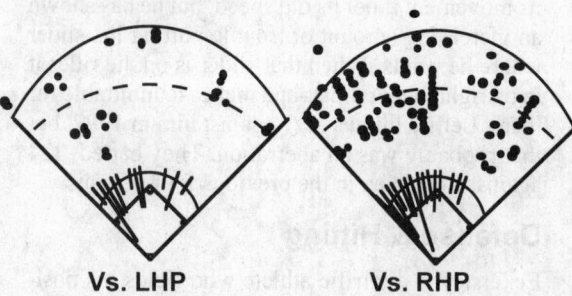

Vs. LHP   **Vs. RHP**

1997 Situational Stats

	AB	H	HR	RBI	Avg		AB	H	HR	RBI	Avg
Home	256	64	7	37	.250	LHP	112	31	5	18	.277
Road	246	62	10	32	.252	RHP	390	95	12	51	.244
First Half	258	66	6	32	.256	Sc Pos	146	36	3	53	.247
Scnd Half	244	60	11	37	.246	Clutch	100	27	4	14	.270

1997 Rankings (National League)

⇒ 1st in fielding percentage at third base (.978)
⇒ 2nd in highest percentage of swings on the first pitch (46.7%)
⇒ 3rd in GDPs (20) and lowest on-base percentage vs. righthanded pitchers (.289)
⇒ 5th in lowest on-base percentage, least pitches seen per plate appearance (3.33) and lowest percentage of pitches taken (46.0%)
⇒ 7th in most GDPs per GDP situation (19.6%)
⇒ 9th in lowest batting average vs. righthanded pitchers and lowest batting average at home
⇒ 10th in lowest batting average
⇒ Led the Cardinals in sacrifice flies (6), hit by pitch (6) and GDPs (20)

Ron Gant

1997 Season

The Cardinals' 1996 investment in a rich five-year contract for Ron Gant took a nasty hit last year. Coming off a 30-homer season, he was expected to step up as the team's top run producer. Instead, he set a club record with 162 strikeouts and had a dismal .388 slugging percentage. A knee injury hindered him some, but he never looked comfortable at the plate.

Hitting

Feed Gant fastballs up in the strike zone and he's still capable of busting a laser-beam, tape-measure shot. But where he once was equally dangerous when pitchers worked him inside, Gant struggled to make contact when they challenged him on his fists last year. He frequently bailed out and continued to flail helplessly at breaking balls down and away. His power virtually disappeared during the second half, and it was all he could do to simply make contact. He hits much better when he's relaxed, though he hasn't fared well against lefties for a couple of years.

Baserunning & Defense

Though some might blame the broken leg he suffered in 1994 for his reduced stolen-base totals, Gant swiped 23 bases as recently as 1995. Managers have sent in late-inning defensive replacements for Gant in recent years. Never considered an outstanding left fielder, he chases balls into the gap with gusto and doesn't hesitate to dive for a catch. His arm is only average.

1998 Outlook

In the middle of a projected lineup with Mark McGwire, Ray Lankford and Brian Jordan, Gant won't feel the pressure of having to be the top run producer. That could help him settle into the form he enjoyed several years ago with the Braves, when he was only a complementary player and responded with a couple of 30-homer, 100-RBI seasons. Getting Gant to cut down on his strikeouts will be new hitting coach Dave Parker's priority. It's basically a matter of returning to his once-productive approach to hitting.

Position: LF
Bats: R **Throws:** R
Ht: 6' 0" **Wt:** 200

Opening Day Age: 33
Born: 3/2/65 in Victoria, TX
ML Seasons: 10

Overall Statistics

	G	AB	R	H	D	T	HR	RBI	SB	BB	SO	Avg	OBP	Slg
1997	139	502	68	115	21	4	17	62	14	58	162	.229	.310	.388
Career	1238	4523	736	1167	212	37	223	712	207	505	968	.258	.333	.469

Where He Hits the Ball

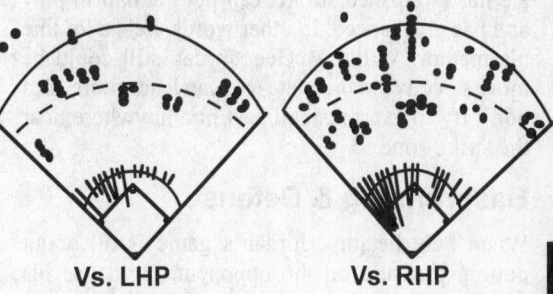

Vs. LHP   **Vs. RHP**

1997 Situational Stats

	AB	H	HR	RBI	Avg		AB	H	HR	RBI	Avg
Home	244	57	11	34	.234	LHP	122	24	5	15	.197
Road	258	58	6	28	.225	RHP	380	91	12	47	.239
First Half	288	66	12	40	.229	Sc Pos	130	35	5	45	.269
Scnd Half	214	49	5	22	.229	Clutch	114	26	4	21	.228

1997 Rankings (National League)

⇒ 1st in lowest batting average and errors in left field (6)
⇒ 2nd in strikeouts and lowest batting average on the road
⇒ 3rd in most pitches seen per plate appearance (4.17), lowest batting average vs. lefthanded pitchers, lowest batting average at home and lowest fielding percentage in left field (.977)
⇒ 4th in least GDPs per GDP situation (2.3%) and lowest on-base percentage vs. lefthanded pitchers (.295)
⇒ 5th in highest percentage of swings that missed (30.1%)
⇒ Led the Cardinals in strikeouts and least GDPs per GDP situation (2.3%)

Brian Jordan

1997 Season

The absence of Brian Jordan left a glaring hole in the Cardinals' 1997 plans. Plagued by injuries throughout his early baseball career, he received a taste of the past from persistent wrist and bulging-disc problems. He tried to play through the pain three different times, but never was able to drive the ball. Jordan's season ended for good in August.

Hitting

Before his wrist sapped him of much of his power, Jordan had turned into that most feared of hitters, a line-drive artist able to drive the ball to any field. While trying to contribute in some way to the 1997 club, he helped out early as a decent contact hitter. He has a polished stroke, can put the ball in play and has great speed. In other words, he's a lot like his mentor, Willie McGee. Jordan still could be more selective at the plate and can learn more. But don't try to get a fastball past him anywhere near the strike zone.

Baserunning & Defense

When he's healthy, Jordan's game is all about putting pressure on the opponent. He'll use his excellent speed to steal a base or force an outfielder into a rushed throw. It doesn't make much sense challenging Jordan on defense. An outstanding and daring athlete, he can run down fly balls, loves making highlight catches at the wall and will lay his body out for diving grabs. His throwing arm is among the best for National League right fielders.

1998 Outlook

Jordan's wrist should be strong again after surgery. He hopes his back will be ready after several months of dedicated, careful rehabilitation. He figures to be stronger and better-conditioned against possible future injuries after a winter of grueling workouts. It might be too much to expect another year such as 1996, when he batted .422 with runners in scoring position. But Jordan might be one of the most dangerous No. 2 hitters in the game, and the team will benefit even more from his enthusiastic leadership.

Position: RF/CF
Bats: R **Throws:** R
Ht: 6' 1" **Wt:** 215

Opening Day Age: 31
Born: 3/29/67 in Baltimore, MD
ML Seasons: 6

Overall Statistics

	G	AB	R	H	D	T	HR	RBI	SB	BB	SO	Avg	OBP	Slg
1997	47	145	17	34	5	0	0	10	6	10	21	.234	.311	.269
Career	493	1742	246	493	88	17	59	276	69	99	307	.283	.330	.455

Where He Hits the Ball

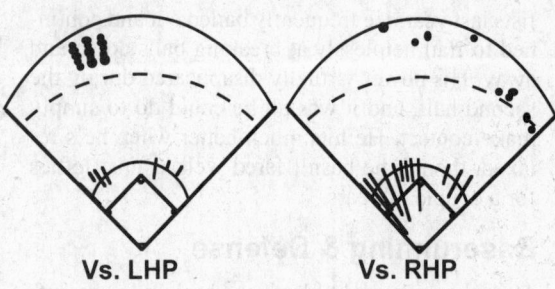

Vs. LHP   Vs. RHP

1997 Situational Stats

	AB	H	HR	RBI	Avg		AB	H	HR	RBI	Avg
Home	72	18	0	8	.250	LHP	35	10	0	3	.286
Road	73	16	0	2	.219	RHP	110	24	0	7	.218
First Half	114	29	0	9	.254	Sc Pos	41	10	0	9	.244
Scnd Half	31	5	0	1	.161	Clutch	29	6	0	2	.207

1997 Rankings (National League)

⇒ Led the Cardinals in hit by pitch (6)

Ray Lankford

1997 Season

Ray Lankford went from being a question mark to an exclamation point for St. Louis in 1997. He started the season on the disabled list while rehabilitating his shoulder after winter surgery to repair a torn rotator cuff. The only ill effect of the injury turned out to be to his throwing arm, as he swung a hot bat from the moment he returned to the lineup. His 31 homers set a club record for center fielders and he fell just short of his first 100-RBI season.

Hitting

Lankford's first All-Star berth arrived because he developed some patience at the plate and learned to handle lefties. After hitting no home runs against lefthanders in 1996, he had 12 last year and actually had a higher batting mark against southpaws than he did against righties. It was a matter of improved concentration, better pitch selection and an ability to stay back on the ball longer. His power comes from superb bat speed and an aggressive approach to fastballs, though that also results in his high strikeout totals. However, Lankford also walked nearly 100 times in 1997 and consistently strokes about 30 doubles a year.

Baserunning & Defense

Lankford isn't a blazer, but he's daring, fast and learning more each year about picking the right situations in which to run. Catchers know better than to stand in the way of this former junior-college running back when he's headed home. Defensively, he can track down fly balls and make leaping, homer-stealing catches as well as any center fielder. His usually powerful arm wasn't at full strength last season after the surgery and opposing baserunners took advantage.

1998 Outlook

There's no reason to consider 1997 a fluke, because Lankford has been touted as an MVP candidate for several years. He'll get more RBI chances than ever batting cleanup behind Brian Jordan and Mark McGwire. While the Cardinals would settle for a repeat season, Lankford is capable of moving into the National League's top echelon of hitters.

Position: CF
Bats: L **Throws:** L
Ht: 5'11" **Wt:** 200

Opening Day Age: 30
Born: 6/5/67 in Los Angeles, CA
ML Seasons: 8

Overall Statistics

	G	AB	R	H	D	T	HR	RBI	SB	BB	SO	Avg	OBP	Slg
1997	133	465	94	137	36	3	31	98	21	95	125	.295	.411	.585
Career	993	3606	610	982	222	43	135	535	199	502	880	.272	.361	.470

Where He Hits the Ball

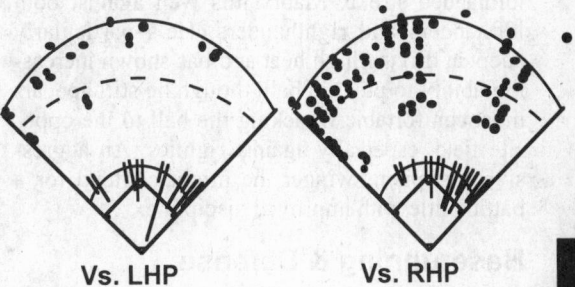

Vs. LHP   **Vs. RHP**

1997 Situational Stats

	AB	H	HR	RBI	Avg		AB	H	HR	RBI	Avg
Home	259	75	10	45	.290	LHP	136	41	12	38	.301
Road	206	62	21	53	.301	RHP	329	96	19	60	.292
First Half	240	80	17	61	.333	Sc Pos	114	31	11	70	.272
Scnd Half	225	57	14	37	.253	Clutch	93	23	3	12	.247

1997 Rankings (National League)

⇒ 1st in errors in center field (9) and lowest fielding percentage in center field (.970)
⇒ 2nd in most pitches seen per plate appearance (4.25), cleanup slugging percentage (.578) and slugging percentage vs. lefthanded pitchers (.662)
⇒ 3rd in on-base percentage vs. righthanded pitchers (.426), highest percentage of swings that missed (30.6%) and lowest percentage of swings put into play (32.5%)
⇒ Led the Cardinals in home runs, runs scored, total bases (272), RBI, walks, intentional walks (10), times on base (232), pitches seen (2,408), slugging percentage, on-base percentage, HR frequency (15.0 ABs per HR) and most pitches seen per plate appearance (4.25)

John Mabry

1997 Season

Touted as a Mark Grace-type hitter capable of challenging for a batting championship while also earning his keep as a solid defensive first baseman, John Mabry encountered several hurdles in his third big league season. He fell into a deep run-producing slump, with only one RBI after the All-Star break. His season was cut short when he suffered a broken jaw in August. To top it off, he soon found himself without a position when Mark McGwire took over at first base and Brian Jordan figured to reclaim right field.

Hitting

A hard-working hitter with a sweet, natural lefthanded stroke, Mabry hits well against both lefthanders and righthanders. He's particularly adept at driving high heat and has shown increasing ability to pull the ball, though he still appears most comfortable whacking the ball to the opposite field, especially against righties. An aggressive first-pitch swinger, he might contend for a batting title with improved discipline.

Baserunning & Defense

Good luck in finding any non-catcher who runs more slowly than Mabry. He hits an inordinate number of hard grounders, leading to numerous double plays. An excellent, strong-armed right fielder, Mabry was also developing into a good first baseman. He was most adept at scooping low throws. Now he's learning yet another position and will try to follow the footsteps of the likes of Joe Torre and Todd Zeile as players the Cardinals converted into third basemen while in the big leagues.

1998 Outlook

Reports on Mabry's work at third base during the 1997 fall instructional league were good. His contribution this season hinges almost directly on how well he makes that move, because that's the one position where he figures to get extensive playing time. Mabry also can get into the lineup as a backup first baseman and in left and right field. He should see enough action to further polish his .300 stroke and produce at least 50 RBI.

Position: RF/1B
Bats: L **Throws:** R
Ht: 6' 4" **Wt:** 205

Opening Day Age: 27
Born: 10/17/70 in Wilmington, DE
ML Seasons: 4
Pronunciation: MAY-bree

Overall Statistics

	G	AB	R	H	D	T	HR	RBI	SB	BB	SO	Avg	OBP	Slg
1997	116	388	40	110	19	0	5	36	0	39	77	.284	.352	.371
Career	402	1342	140	397	73	3	23	154	3	102	210	.296	.347	.406

Where He Hits the Ball

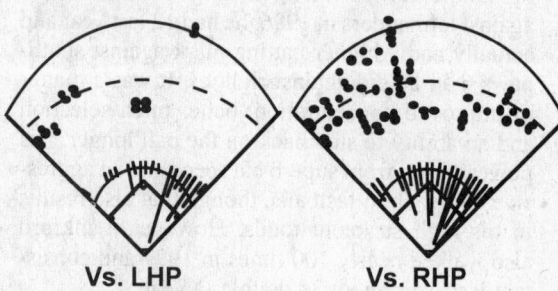

Vs. LHP   Vs. RHP

1997 Situational Stats

	AB	H	HR	RBI	Avg		AB	H	HR	RBI	Avg
Home	192	56	5	20	.292	LHP	94	25	0	10	.266
Road	196	54	0	16	.276	RHP	294	85	5	26	.289
First Half	285	84	5	35	.295	Sc Pos	82	23	2	31	.280
Scnd Half	103	26	0	1	.252	Clutch	67	21	0	6	.313

1997 Rankings (National League)

⇒ 5th in lowest percentage of extra bases taken as a runner (34.1%)
⇒ Led the Cardinals in batting average in the clutch and batting average on a 3-2 count (.346)

Mark McGwire

1997 Season

Upon signing a long-term contract with the Cardinals late in the season, Mark McGwire continually used the word "overwhelming" to describe the way fans had convinced him to continue playing in St. Louis. Well, McGwire was rather overwhelming himself. Switching leagues right before the trading deadline, he quickly adjusted to new surroundings and teammates to prove he's the best power hitter on the planet. His 58 homers—24 of which were hit in his two months with the Cardinals—included a handful of blasts that traveled more than 500 feet.

Hitting

He's not just muscles and homers. McGwire generates most of his power with uncommon bat speed. He's a patient hitter who's very selective at the plate. He can drive the ball in clutch situations and takes equal satisfaction in reaching base with a walk. Like most power hitters, he strikes out fairly often. The tradeoff, however, is worth it.

Baserunning & Defense

No one will withhold money from McGwire's paycheck because he doesn't steal bases, though he actually swiped a couple with St. Louis. He's not fast, but he has enough baseball savvy to avoid running into blatant outs. Perhaps his power overshadows his defensive work at first base. He's remarkably nimble and has a long reach, so not much gets past him. He also has an above-average arm relative to his position.

1998 Outlook

Crazy as it sounds, McGwire could turn in an even more productive set of numbers this season than he did in 1997. Topping 58 home runs sounds like a longshot, but he'll be more comfortable in the NL and won't be facing as many pitchers for the first time in his career. He'll have even more pressure to live up to the team's grandiose expectations. History says McGwire's batting average should be up and his strikeout rate down from his marks with the Cardinals last season.

Position: 1B
Bats: R **Throws:** R
Ht: 6' 5" **Wt:** 250

Opening Day Age: 34
Born: 10/1/63 in Pomona, CA
ML Seasons: 12

Overall Statistics

	G	AB	R	H	D	T	HR	RBI	SB	BB	SO	Avg	OBP	Slg
1997	156	540	86	148	27	0	58	123	3	101	159	.274	.393	.646
Career	1380	4622	811	1201	198	5	387	983	10	890	1104	.260	.382	.556

Where He Hits the Ball

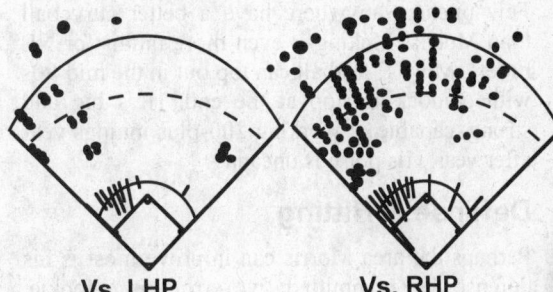

Vs. LHP   **Vs. RHP**

1997 Situational Stats

	AB	H	HR	RBI	Avg		AB	H	HR	RBI	Avg
Home	248	78	30	60	.315	LHP	117	33	12	27	.282
Road	292	70	28	63	.240	RHP	423	115	46	96	.272
First Half	299	86	31	71	.288	Sc Pos	142	33	11	63	.232
Scnd Half	241	62	27	52	.257	Clutch	87	23	8	19	.264

1997 Rankings (National League)

⇒ 5th in batting average on a 3-1 count (.750)
⇒ 10th in lowest batting average with two strikes (.135)
⇒ Led the Cardinals in batting average on a 3-1 count (.750)

Matt Morris

1997 Season

It's not that the Cardinals didn't expect Matt Morris to come in as a rookie and be able to win 12 games or pitch 200 innings or strike out twice as many batters as he walked. It's not that they didn't think he could one day be the best pitcher on their staff. They just didn't expect it to happen so soon and all at once. Morris was supposed to only spend part of April with the big league club before its top five starters were healthy, but he was so impressive that St. Louis couldn't send him back to Triple-A Louisville. He led all National League rookie pitchers in wins, strikeouts and ERA.

Pitching

Few pitchers anywhere have a better curveball than Morris. Making it even more unfair for NL hitters, Morris' fastball can top out in the mid-90s with a mocking hop at the end. He's big and strong, capable of working 200-plus innings year after year. His poise is uncanny.

Defense & Hitting

Perhaps the area Morris can improve most is his defense. He committed five errors as a rookie, most of them coming on wild throws while rushing off the mound in pursuit of a bunt. He also ran into trouble when pitching from the stretch, as he committed three balks. With only 11 of 18 basestealers successful against him, Morris generally did good work at keeping runners close to the bag. He tried telling everyone he wasn't much of a hitter, but then his performance hinted he wasn't that bad: a .205 batting average and six RBI.

1998 Outlook

With the polish that comes from improved consistency and a better offspeed pitch, Morris can become a big winner for a long time. He's probably ahead of where teammate Alan Benes was at a similar stage. Morris has been able to harness his intensity on the mound while remaining calm off it, qualities that should help him make rapid improvement. If it's possible for a second-year pitcher to be considered an ace of a staff, he's got that opportunity.

Position: SP
Bats: R **Throws:** R
Ht: 6' 5" **Wt:** 210

Opening Day Age: 23
Born: 8/9/74 in Middletown, NY
ML Seasons: 1

Overall Statistics

	W	L	Pct.	ERA	G	GS	Sv	IP	H	BB	SO	HR	Ratio
1997	12	9	.571	3.19	33	33	0	217.0	208	69	149	12	1.28
Career	12	9	.571	3.19	33	33	0	217.0	208	69	149	12	1.28

How Often He Throws Strikes

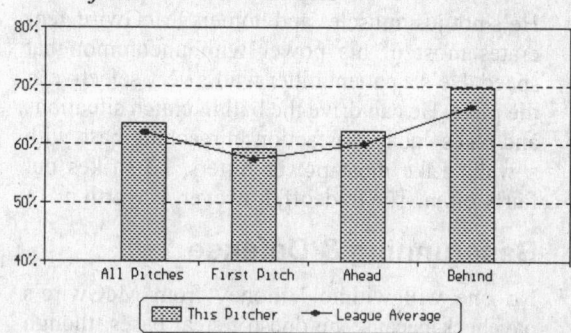

1997 Situational Stats

	W	L	ERA	Sv	IP		AB	H	HR	RBI	Avg
Home	9	5	2.73	0	141.2	LHB	405	105	8	55	.259
Road	3	4	4.06	0	75.1	RHB	401	103	4	26	.257
First Half	6	5	2.82	0	105.1	Sc Pos	189	54	3	26	.286
Scnd Half	6	4	3.55	0	111.2	Clutch	79	23	2	8	.291

1997 Rankings (National League)

⇒ 1st in errors at pitcher (5)
⇒ 2nd in balks (3) and lowest fielding percentage at pitcher (.868)
⇒ 4th in least home runs allowed per 9 innings (.50)
⇒ 5th in GDPs induced (25)
⇒ Led the Cardinals in wins, losses, games started, complete games (3), innings pitched, hits allowed, batters faced (900), walks allowed, balks (3), pitches thrown (3,290), GDPs induced (25), highest groundball/flyball ratio allowed (1.9), lowest stolen base percentage allowed (61.1%), least pitches thrown per batter (3.66), most GDPs induced per 9 innings (1.0) and most GDPs induced per GDP situation (17.2%)

Todd Stottlemyre

1997 Season

Todd Stottlemyre produced another admirable season as one of the most competitive pitchers in the game. After a decent first half, he was one of the better hurlers in the National League for an impressive midsummer stretch marked by excellent control and a load of strikeouts. Only a late-season bout with shoulder fatigue kept him from a shot at a third consecutive 14-victory, 200-inning showing.

Pitching

Hanging near pitching coach Dave Duncan's locker is a poster of Stottlemyre with "Bulldog" written over it. Yes, Stottlemyre has honed a fastball that still reaches 93 MPH. He also has sharpened an untouchable splitter and polished his curveball and changeup under Duncan's tutelage over the last several seasons. But Stottlemyre's success as a low-hit, control/power pitcher is a credit to his ability to harness his once-wild emotions and channel them into his performance. He has a fiery intensity; he loves to pitch deep into a game and detests losing.

Defense & Hitting

A good athlete, Stottlemyre learned long ago that he needed every edge he could possibly get and thus has developed strong defensive work. He comes out of his delivery in good fielding position. He's not particularly adept at holding runners. He takes great pride in his hitting, and batted .236 with eight walks and four RBI last season.

1998 Outlook

Not many teams will be able to match the Cardinals at the No. 4 starting slot. Stottlemyre has spent 10 seasons in the big leagues and is almost a lock to deliver 200 innings and a top-10 finish in strikeouts. His tired arm was the result of a recurring shoulder problem, something that probably will be solved by a new arm-strengthening regimen. He could win 15 games for the first time since 1991.

Position: SP
Bats: L **Throws:** R
Ht: 6' 3" **Wt:** 200

Opening Day Age: 32
Born: 5/20/65 in Yakima, WA
ML Seasons: 10
Pronunciation: STAH-till-my-er

Overall Statistics

	W	L	Pct.	ERA	G	GS	Sv	IP	H	BB	SO	HR	Ratio
1997	12	9	.571	3.88	28	28	0	181.0	155	65	160	16	1.22
Career	109	97	.529	4.29	299	267	1	1753.0	1756	652	1221	187	1.37

How Often He Throws Strikes

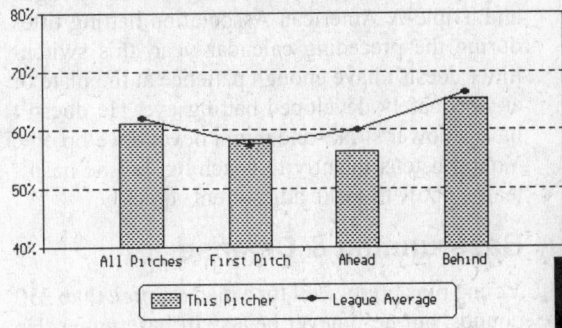

1997 Situational Stats

	W	L	ERA	Sv	IP		AB	H	HR	RBI	Avg
Home	4	5	4.89	0	70.0	LHB	359	96	11	51	.267
Road	8	4	3.24	0	111.0	RHB	312	59	5	30	.189
First Half	7	6	3.95	0	123.0	Sc Pos	135	43	6	64	.319
Scnd Half	5	3	3.72	0	58.0	Clutch	51	17	1	5	.333

1997 Rankings (National League)

⇒ 1st in highest batting average allowed with runners in scoring position
⇒ 3rd in hit batsmen (12) and lowest batting average allowed vs. righthanded batters
⇒ 6th in least GDPs induced per 9 innings (0.4)
⇒ 7th in most strikeouts per 9 innings (8.0)
⇒ 8th in lowest batting average allowed (.231)
⇒ 10th in lowest slugging percentage allowed (.356), lowest groundball/flyball ratio allowed (1.3) and ERA on the road
⇒ Led the Cardinals in wins, losses, home runs allowed, hit batsmen (12), ERA on the road and lowest batting average allowed vs. righthanded batters

St. Louis Cardinals

Dmitri Young

1997 Season

Considered a Rookie-of-the-Year candidate, Dmitri Young frustrated St. Louis and was flustered by the big leagues. He opened the season with a chance to play every day as the team's first baseman, but he never showed much power or a knack for driving in runs. His .256 batting average with runners in scoring position and his frequent lapses in the field sent him to the bench and eventually back to the minors.

Hitting

Young called his rookie season one filled with hard lessons. The Cardinals learned plenty about Young, too. Despite his Mexican Pacific League and Triple-A American Association batting titles during the preceding calendar year, this switch-hitter doesn't have enough patience at the plate or an adequately-developed batting eye. He doesn't have a power stroke and might never develop one. Young listens intently to coaching, but he hasn't learned how to make adjustments quickly.

Baserunning & Defense

Young runs pretty well for a man of more than 230 pounds, but he'll never be a swift baserunner. He stole only six bases, a weak output for a player who hit only five homers. Defensively, he's a first baseman who has played the outfield on occasion—only because the National League doesn't feature a designated hitter. Young might improve enough to keep steady work, but he'll never be a good defensive first baseman.

1998 Outlook

After trading for Mark McGwire, the Cardinals didn't really have a spot for Young. They traded him to Cincinnati, where he could start or platoon with Eduardo Perez, for reliever Jeff Brantley. Young was taken by Tampa Bay in the first round of the expansion draft, but returned to the Reds in a prearranged deal.

Position: 1B
Bats: B **Throws:** R
Ht: 6' 2" **Wt:** 240

Opening Day Age: 24
Born: 10/11/73 in Vicksburg, MS
ML Seasons: 2

Overall Statistics

	G	AB	R	H	D	T	HR	RBI	SB	BB	SO	Avg	OBP	Slg
1997	110	333	38	86	14	3	5	34	6	38	63	.258	.335	.363
Career	126	362	41	93	14	3	5	36	6	42	68	.257	.337	.354

Where He Hits the Ball

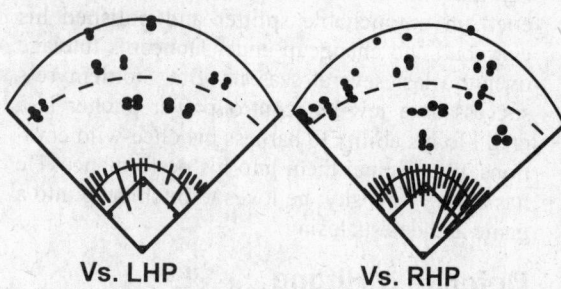

Vs. LHP   Vs. RHP

1997 Situational Stats

	AB	H	HR	RBI	Avg		AB	H	HR	RBI	Avg
Home	175	42	2	15	.240	LHP	83	22	1	9	.265
Road	158	44	3	19	.278	RHP	250	64	4	25	.256
First Half	208	60	3	25	.288	Sc Pos	82	21	0	28	.256
Scnd Half	125	26	2	9	.208	Clutch	64	13	0	5	.203

1997 Rankings (National League)

⇒ 5th in errors at first base (10)

Tony Fossas

Position: RP
Bats: L **Throws:** L
Ht: 6' 0" **Wt:** 198

Opening Day Age: 40
Born: 9/23/57 in
Havana, Cuba
ML Seasons: 10

Overall Statistics

	W	L	Pct.	ERA	G	GS	Sv	IP	H	BB	SO	HR	Ratio
1997	2	7	.222	3.83	71	0	0	51.2	62	26	41	7	1.70
Career	16	21	.432	3.70	521	0	7	392.0	398	163	301	37	1.43

1997 Situational Stats

	W	L	ERA	Sv	IP		AB	H	HR	RBI	Avg
Home	2	4	3.18	0	22.2	LHB	94	25	0	6	.266
Road	0	3	4.34	0	29.0	RHB	114	37	7	19	.325
First Half	1	1	1.88	0	28.2	Sc Pos	69	13	1	16	.188
Scnd Half	1	6	6.26	0	23.0	Clutch	104	32	3	13	.308

1997 Season

Injuries forced the Cardinals into summoning Tony Fossas from the bullpen more often and for longer stints than orginally planned. He led the NL by allowing only six of 60 inherited runners to score, but pitched far too often against righties who batted .325 and belted seven homers off him.

Pitching, Defense & Hitting

Fossas has his best success against some of the NL's top lefthanders, who have trouble reaching his tailing slider and somehow can't track the movement of the relatively lightweight fastball that he likes to throw on their fists. He still can hold his own against lefties, but lacks the ability to work righthanders to make him anything more than a speciality reliever. He fields what he can reach. Runners like to try to run on him, and 10 of 14 stole successfully last season. As a hitter, he got as far as the on-deck circle once in 1997.

1998 Outlook

Nothing is certain for 40-year-old pitchers coming off a 2-7 season. Fossas, a free agent, will get a crack at a big league job with a team willing to pay a veteran's wages for a man who pitches to one or two batters every few days. The Cardinals might look at re-signing him, considering their lack of lefthanders.

John Frascatore

Position: RP
Bats: R **Throws:** R
Ht: 6' 1" **Wt:** 210

Opening Day Age: 28
Born: 2/4/70 in
Queens, NY
ML Seasons: 3
Pronunciation:
fras-ka-TORE-ee

Overall Statistics

	W	L	Pct.	ERA	G	GS	Sv	IP	H	BB	SO	HR	Ratio
1997	5	2	.714	2.48	59	0	0	80.0	74	33	58	5	1.34
Career	6	4	.600	3.41	74	5	0	116.0	120	51	81	10	1.47

1997 Situational Stats

	W	L	ERA	Sv	IP		AB	H	HR	RBI	Avg
Home	3	0	2.82	0	38.1	LHB	116	25	1	11	.216
Road	2	2	2.16	0	41.2	RHB	183	49	4	22	.268
First Half	3	2	2.66	0	40.2	Sc Pos	97	18	0	28	.186
Scnd Half	2	0	2.29	0	39.1	Clutch	98	25	1	11	.255

1997 Season

After several years of promise followed by disappointment, John Frascatore earned a prominent spot in the big league bullpen at just about the time the Cardinals were ready to give up on him. He became particularly important as the top righthanded setup man after T.J. Mathews was traded to Oakland.

Pitching, Defense & Hitting

The Cardinals couldn't seem to decide if they wanted Frascatore to be a starter or a closer, so they alternated him between the rotation and bullpen in the minors. His live arm tempted them to make him into a starter, but his fiery attitude could point him toward the closer's role in the future. He likes the bullpen, where he can emerge with fastballs blazing and breaking balls baffling. Somewhat of a workhorse, he'll be able to work in long- and short-relief situations. Frascatore doesn't have any glaring shortcomings defensively, but he needs to work on holding basestealers. He's hitless in 11 major league at-bats.

1998 Outlook

Frascatore could return to the same role with the Cardinals and improve on his 1997 performance.

Tom Lampkin

Position: C
Bats: L **Throws:** R
Ht: 5'11" **Wt:** 185

Opening Day Age: 34
Born: 3/4/64 in
Cincinnati, OH
ML Seasons: 8

Overall Statistics

	G	AB	R	H	D	T	HR	RBI	SB	BB	SO	Avg	OBP	Slg
1997	108	229	28	56	8	1	7	22	2	28	30	.245	.335	.380
Career	389	786	95	179	29	3	19	92	14	91	105	.228	.314	.345

1997 Situational Stats

	AB	H	HR	RBI	Avg		AB	H	HR	RBI	Avg
Home	119	23	2	9	.193	LHP	36	9	0	4	.250
Road	110	33	5	13	.300	RHP	193	47	7	18	.244
First Half	159	36	5	15	.226	Sc Pos	43	9	0	12	.209
Scnd Half	70	20	2	7	.286	Clutch	56	11	1	4	.196

1997 Season

The Cardinals wanted Tom Lampkin for his lefthanded bat and veteran's presence behind the plate. He satisfied those needs with some power against righthanders and hit .286 during the second half of the season. Thanks to Tom Pagnozzi's injuries, St. Louis used Lampkin in a catching platoon and to provide a key late-inning spark.

Hitting, Baserunning & Defense

Lampkin cuts a muscular presence and has surprising pop in his bat despite being used in spot situations. His keen eye allows him to draw walks and generally put the ball in play. He always seemed in the midst of late-inning rallies in 1997, though he batted just .209 with runners in scoring position. He's a smart baserunner, if not particularly swift. Lampkin is a capable catcher defensively in part because he knows how to call a game. He's average in terms of combating basestealers.

1998 Outlook

Lampkin's defensive skills might not be enough to help him make the Cardinals. His lefthanded bat might not be consistently good enough for their bench, either. However, the combination of all that he offers should be an attractive possibility for any club with a young pitching staff.

Willie McGee

Position: RF/LF/CF
Bats: B **Throws:** R
Ht: 6'1" **Wt:** 185

Opening Day Age: 39
Born: 11/2/58 in San
Francisco, CA
ML Seasons: 16

Overall Statistics

	G	AB	R	H	D	T	HR	RBI	SB	BB	SO	Avg	OBP	Slg
1997	122	300	29	90	19	4	3	38	8	22	59	.300	.347	.420
Career	1949	7109	958	2118	333	93	76	802	338	417	1129	.298	.336	.403

1997 Situational Stats

	AB	H	HR	RBI	Avg		AB	H	HR	RBI	Avg
Home	128	43	2	18	.336	LHP	95	26	1	12	.274
Road	172	47	1	20	.273	RHP	205	64	2	26	.312
First Half	155	47	3	21	.303	Sc Pos	84	26	1	34	.310
Scnd Half	145	43	0	17	.297	Clutch	84	22	2	11	.262

1997 Season

The "Willie McGee Story" continued, as Cardinals fans continued to shower him with affectionate ovations at the very mention of his name. McGee responded with effort, humility and a steady supply of base hits. Though he prefers to play in a reserve role, he played considerably in stretches and still managed to hit .300.

Hitting, Baserunning & Defense

A complete player with power and speed in his younger days, McGee focuses now on putting the ball in play and making the most of his vast experience. Primarily a first-pitch hitter, he's most dangerous in taking any fastball where it's pitched and using the entire field. He's an excellent pinch hitter, particularly in clutch situations. McGee doesn't run as often as in the past but he still runs almost as well. Defensively, he still can track down fly balls in the gap. Though his arm isn't necessarily strong, it's accurate.

1998 Outlook

McGee, who re-signed as a free agent, will be at his best if he can stay a fourth outfielder for the entire season. If the Cards can save the wear and tear on his legs that way, he should not only provide another .300 average for up to 200 at-bats, but also set an exemplary approach for his teammates.

Donovan Osborne

Position: SP
Bats: L **Throws:** L
Ht: 6' 2" **Wt:** 195

Opening Day Age: 28
Born: 6/21/69 in
Roseville, CA
ML Seasons: 5

Overall Statistics

	W	L	Pct.	ERA	G	GS	Sv	IP	H	BB	SO	HR	Ratio
1997	3	7	.300	4.93	14	14	0	80.1	84	23	51	10	1.33
Career	41	38	.519	3.84	123	118	0	727.0	733	199	454	81	1.28

1997 Situational Stats

	W	L	ERA	Sv	IP		AB	H	HR	RBI	Avg
Home	2	1	3.18	0	34.0	LHB	37	12	0	2	.324
Road	1	6	6.22	0	46.1	RHB	270	72	10	41	.267
First Half	1	2	3.60	0	35.0	Sc Pos	79	21	2	31	.266
Scnd Half	2	5	5.96	0	45.1	Clutch	5	0	0	0	.000

1997 Season

The Cardinals were left wondering what might have been had Donovan Osborne stayed healthy. They were teased by a mostly injury-free 1996 season in which Osborne seemed to emerge as one of the National League's top lefties. In 1997, he made only 14 starts and was never able to find any consistency.

Pitching, Defense & Hitting

No one has questioned Osborne's arsenal, which includes a dandy fastball and a nasty slider. He has a competitive nature that he's learned to channel instead of letting it get the best of him. During his successful streaks, which can last for weeks, he's as crafty in the strike zone as any lefty. But there remain questions concerning his health and response to big-game situations. A good athlete, he handles his defensive responsibilities well and is so adept at holding runners that they rarely try to steal against him. A two-way player at UNLV, Osborne swings the bat better than most pitchers.

1998 Outlook

Osborne should have little trouble rebounding from hernia surgery, and his most recent injuries haven't affected his arm. He might not ever be a 200-inning workhorse, but he can win 12-14 games if he gets regular work.

Tom Pagnozzi

Position: C
Bats: R **Throws:** R
Ht: 6' 1" **Wt:** 195

Opening Day Age: 35
Born: 7/30/62 in
Tucson, AZ
ML Seasons: 11
Pronunciation:
pag-NAHZ-ee

Overall Statistics

	G	AB	R	H	D	T	HR	RBI	SB	BB	SO	Avg	OBP	Slg
1997	25	50	4	11	3	0	1	8	0	1	7	.220	.235	.340
Career	876	2736	240	698	144	11	43	310	18	175	413	.255	.300	.363

1997 Situational Stats

	AB	H	HR	RBI	Avg		AB	H	HR	RBI	Avg
Home	28	8	1	4	.286	LHP	14	5	0	2	.357
Road	22	3	0	4	.136	RHP	36	6	1	6	.167
First Half	8	2	0	0	.250	Sc Pos	19	4	0	6	.211
Scnd Half	42	9	1	8	.214	Clutch	7	1	0	2	.143

1997 Season

Tom Pagnozzi found out how difficult catching can be when trying to play with a torn hip flexor. Thanks to his injury, the veteran spent more time swinging a bat on injury rehab at Double-A Arkansas than in St. Louis.

Hitting, Baserunning & Defense

When healthy, Pagnozzi has been able to put his experience to use at the plate. He never has had a quick bat, but he has been an intelligent guess hitter who's learned to stop chasing pitches out of the strike zone. That has made for flashes of power and good work in clutch situations. The problem is that Pagnozzi has been injured in four of the last five seasons. There's no benefit in his running ability. The Cardinals have missed him behind the plate, where he has won Gold Gloves and has a good feel for handling pitchers. He doesn't have a lot of arm strength, but he's very accurate.

1998 Outlook

Pagnozzi can't be counted on to work 100 games anymore. The Cardinals have top prospect Elieser Marrero nearly ready to take over, but they aren't sure they can win a pennant with a rookie catcher. They'd like Pagnozzi to return in top condition and give them a veteran first option who's able to play sound defense and contribute offensively.

St. Louis
Cardinals

Mark Petkovsek

Position: RP
Bats: R **Throws:** R
Ht: 6' 0" **Wt:** 195

Opening Day Age: 32
Born: 11/18/65 in Beaumont, TX
ML Seasons: 5
Pronunciation: pet-KY-zik

Overall Statistics

	W	L	Pct.	ERA	G	GS	Sv	IP	H	BB	SO	HR	Ratio
1997	4	7	.364	5.06	55	2	2	96.0	109	31	51	14	1.46
Career	24	16	.600	4.70	159	30	2	363.2	392	114	187	45	1.39

1997 Situational Stats

	W	L	ERA	Sv	IP		AB	H	HR	RBI	Avg
Home	2	1	3.77	0	45.1	LHB	168	44	3	18	.262
Road	2	6	6.22	2	50.2	RHB	205	65	11	43	.317
First Half	4	4	3.40	1	55.2	Sc Pos	87	33	3	45	.379
Scnd Half	0	3	7.36	1	40.1	Clutch	85	27	4	15	.318

1997 Season

Mark Petkovsek prides himself on dependability but he fell short in 1997. He worked a variety of situations, as is his custom, but didn't do particularly well in any of them. He struggled to keep the ball down and yielded 14 homers in 96 innings.

Pitching, Defense & Hitting

Petkovsek is only effective if his control is precise and his sinker stays down in the strike zone. As well as he managed that in 1996, when he went 11-2 for the Cardinals, he couldn't find any consistent success last season. The rest of his repertoire features a fastball, slider and changeup so indistinguishable that it's difficult for him to succeed without sharpness on his bread-and-butter pitches. He fields his position well enough and has made strides in holding baserunners. Petkovsek can handle a bat but doesn't get many opportunities.

1998 Outlook

Considering his durability and flexibility at serving a pitching staff in several roles, Petkovsek should expect to find a spot in the St. Louis bullpen. His tenure there could be brief, though, if he doesn't quickly show some of the form that made him so valuable two years ago.

Danny Sheaffer

Position: 3B/LF
Bats: R **Throws:** R
Ht: 6' 0" **Wt:** 195

Opening Day Age: 36
Born: 8/2/61 in Jacksonville, FL
ML Seasons: 7
Pronunciation: shay-FIR

Overall Statistics

	G	AB	R	H	D	T	HR	RBI	SB	BB	SO	Avg	OBP	Slg
1997	76	132	10	33	5	0	0	11	1	8	17	.250	.296	.288
Career	389	946	87	219	38	5	13	110	6	60	122	.232	.278	.323

1997 Situational Stats

	AB	H	HR	RBI	Avg		AB	H	HR	RBI	Avg
Home	55	16	0	6	.291	LHP	63	14	0	4	.222
Road	77	17	0	5	.221	RHP	69	19	0	7	.275
First Half	74	21	0	4	.284	Sc Pos	33	11	0	11	.333
Scnd Half	58	12	0	7	.207	Clutch	27	11	0	5	.407

1997 Season

The Cardinals couldn't shake loose of Danny Sheaffer. They were fortunate they couldn't. Twice they sent him to Triple-A Louisville, but both times he returned to the big league club immediately afterward and contributed at a variety of positions. His .250 batting average got a boost from a .333 mark with runners in scoring position.

Hitting, Baserunning & Defense

With more time in the minor leagues than the majors, Sheaffer has a clear understanding of his role. He lacks power, never has run particularly well and has drawn only 18 walks in his last 350 plate appearances. Because he's such an aggressive swinger, Sheaffer isn't valued as a pinch hitter, but he has helped in clutch situations. More importantly, he has provided a safety net defensively. Once a solid catcher, he's more of a utility player now, able to play all three outfield positions, second base and third base. Scheaffer has a strong arm but no other distinguishing assets.

1998 Outlook

Valued by St. Louis as a quiet, hard-working player, Sheaffer will probably make their club this season only if injuries create a need for a versatile reserve. His future may lead him to coaching, though he still could help someone on the bench.

Other St. Louis Cardinals

Jose Bautista (Pos: RHP, Age: 33)

	W	L	Pct.	ERA	G	GS	Sv	IP	H	BB	SO	HR	Ratio
1997	2	2	.500	6.66	32	0	0	52.2	70	14	23	8	1.59
Career	32	42	.432	4.62	312	49	3	685.2	732	171	328	106	1.32

Bautista could offer neither the Tigers nor the Cardinals the same thing he gave the Giants in 1996: quality middle innings. His 6.66 ERA for the season bedeviled both clubs. 1998 Outlook: C

David Bell (Pos: 3B/2B/SS, Age: 25, Bats: R)

	G	AB	R	H	D	T	HR	RBI	SB	BB	SO	Avg	OBP	Slg
1997	66	142	9	30	7	2	1	12	1	10	28	.211	.261	.310
Career	169	433	34	97	20	4	4	40	3	24	75	.224	.268	.316

Hoping to finally prove that he could hit at the major league level, Bell batted just .136 in April before breaking his left hand. He returned in July, but hit just .225 with one homer the rest of the way. 1998 Outlook: C

Rigo Beltran (Pos: LHP, Age: 28)

	W	L	Pct.	ERA	G	GS	Sv	IP	H	BB	SO	HR	Ratio
1997	1	2	.333	3.48	35	4	1	54.1	47	17	50	3	1.18
Career	1	2	.333	3.48	35	4	1	54.1	47	17	50	3	1.18

After six-plus seasons in the minors, lefty middle man Rigo Beltran got the call in late-May and stuck. His effectiveness went a long way towards compensating for the loss of Rick Honeycutt. 1998 Oulook: A

Jeff Berblinger (Pos: 2B, Age: 27, Bats: R)

	G	AB	R	H	D	T	HR	RBI	SB	BB	SO	Avg	OBP	Slg
1997	7	5	1	0	0	0	0	0	0	0	1	.000	.000	.000
Career	7	5	1	0	0	0	0	0	0	0	1	.000	.000	.000

Berblinger got his first shot at Triple-A last season, and displayed the same qualities that he flashed in Single- and Double-A: the ability to hit for average and smack a fair share of extra-base hits. 1998 Outlook: B

Mike Busby (Pos: RHP, Age: 25)

	W	L	Pct.	ERA	G	GS	Sv	IP	H	BB	SO	HR	Ratio
1997	0	2	.000	8.79	3	3	0	14.1	24	4	6	2	1.95
Career	0	3	.000	10.80	4	4	0	18.1	33	8	10	6	2.24

Busby has now made four career starts in the majors and lost three of them while posting a 10.80 ERA. His record at Louisville is 8-15 over the past three years, and he continues to walk a lot of batters. 1998 Outlook: D

Micah Franklin (Pos: RF, Age: 25, Bats: B)

	G	AB	R	H	D	T	HR	RBI	SB	BB	SO	Avg	OBP	Slg
1997	17	34	6	11	0	0	2	2	0	3	10	.324	.378	.500
Career	17	34	6	11	0	0	2	2	0	3	10	.324	.378	.500

The Cardinals finally gave Franklin his first taste of the show, and he took a big bite, hitting .324 in 17 games. He has age on his side, but his high strikeout totals make him a proverbial longshot. 1998 Outlook: B

Mike Gallego (Pos: 2B, Age: 37, Bats: R)

	G	AB	R	H	D	T	HR	RBI	SB	BB	SO	Avg	OBP	Slg
1997	27	43	6	7	2	0	0	1	0	1	6	.163	.178	.209
Career	1111	2931	374	700	111	12	42	282	24	326	465	.239	.320	.328

The light-hitting second baseman who always seemed to find a spot on a Tony La Russa roster couldn't even hit his weight last season. He drove in one run in 43 at-bats and was waived at the end of July. 1998 Outlook: D

Mike Gulan (Pos: 3B, Age: 27, Bats: R)

	G	AB	R	H	D	T	HR	RBI	SB	BB	SO	Avg	OBP	Slg
1997	5	9	2	0	0	0	0	1	0	1	5	.000	.100	.000
Career	5	9	2	0	0	0	0	1	0	1	5	.000	.100	.000

Gulan was one of a seemingly endless parade of players called up to spell Gary Gaetti at third base. His 0-for-9 stint with five strikeouts did nothing to belie his lack of discipline at the plate. 1998 Outlook: D

Rick Honeycutt (Pos: LHP, Age: 43)

	W	L	Pct.	ERA	G	GS	Sv	IP	H	BB	SO	HR	Ratio
1997	0	0	-	13.50	2	0	0	2.0	5	1	2	0	3.00
Career	109	143	.433	3.72	797	268	38	2160.0	2183	657	1038	185	1.31

A string of 19 consecutive seasons with at least 20 appearances finally came to an end when Honeycutt's left shoulder gave out at the beginning of the season. He announced his retirement in late September. 1998 Outlook: D

Scott Livingstone (Pos: 3B, Age: 32, Bats: L)

	G	AB	R	H	D	T	HR	RBI	SB	BB	SO	Avg	OBP	Slg
1997	65	67	4	11	2	0	0	6	1	3	11	.164	.194	.194
Career	597	1423	162	408	70	4	17	165	9	84	174	.287	.323	.377

Livingstone spent parts of the '97 season with San Diego, St. Louis, Rancho Cucamonga, Louisville and on the disabled list. His at-bat totals in the majors have decreased in each of the last five seasons. 1998 Outlook: D

Sean Lowe (Pos: RHP, Age: 27)

	W	L	Pct.	ERA	G	GS	Sv	IP	H	BB	SO	HR	Ratio
1997	0	2	.000	9.35	6	4	0	17.1	27	10	8	2	2.13
Career	0	2	.000	9.35	6	4	0	17.1	27	10	8	2	2.13

Lowe followed up a mediocre performance at Louisville with a forgettable end-of-the-season stint with the Cards. He gave up 18 earned runs and 10 walks in his first 15⅔ innings of work in the majors. 1998 Outlook: C

Tom McGraw (Pos: LHP, Age: 30)

	W	L	Pct.	ERA	G	GS	Sv	IP	H	BB	SO	HR	Ratio
1997	0	0	-	0.00	2	0	0	1.2	2	1	0	0	1.80
Career	0	0	-	0.00	2	0	0	1.2	2	1	0	0	1.80

At the ripe "young" age of 29, McGraw finally saw his first career action in the bigs, making two appearances for the Cardinals before being shipped back down to Triple-A. Hope he enjoyed the show. 1998 Outlook: D

St. Louis Cardinals

Roberto Mejia (**Pos**: 2B, **Age**: 25, **Bats**: R)

	G	AB	R	H	D	T	HR	RBI	SB	BB	SO	Avg	OBP	Slg
1997	7	14	0	1	1	0	0	2	0	0	5	.071	.067	.143
Career	133	411	47	90	24	6	10	40	7	28	118	.219	.270	.380

The well-traveled Mejia lasted for seven games in early April before going on the DL, and he underwent shoulder surgery in May that ended his season. The question now becomes whether it will end his career. 1998 Outlook: D

Lance Painter (**Pos**: LHP, **Age**: 30)

	W	L	Pct.	ERA	G	GS	Sv	IP	H	BB	SO	HR	Ratio
1997	1	1	.500	4.76	14	0	0	17.0	13	8	11	1	1.24
Career	14	11	.560	5.58	106	22	1	225.2	267	78	152	36	1.53

Painter went on the DL in early April with a bum hamstring, came back in late-May, made one appearance, felt the hammy go again, and went right back on the DL. Needless to say, '97 was a lost season. 1998 Outlook: C

Phil Plantier (**Pos**: RF/LF, **Age**: 29, **Bats**: L)

	G	AB	R	H	D	T	HR	RBI	SB	BB	SO	Avg	OBP	Slg
1997	52	121	13	30	8	0	5	5	0	13	30	.248	.331	.438
Career	610	1883	260	457	90	3	91	91	13	237	476	.243	.332	.439

Injuries dogged Phil Plantier again in 1997, as they have since he showed great promise with the Red Sox and Padres in the early 1990s. Acquired from San Diego in the Fernando Valenzuela-Danny Jackson trade in June, he had a strong September and flashed occasional power. 1998 Outlook: C

Steve Scarsone (**Pos**: 2B, **Age**: 31, **Bats**: R)

	G	AB	R	H	D	T	HR	RBI	SB	BB	SO	Avg	OBP	Slg
1997	5	10	0	1	0	0	0	0	1	2	5	.100	.250	.100
Career	304	762	101	184	39	4	20	80	6	61	242	.241	.303	.382

After two mildly productive years with the Giants, Scarsone's bat appears to have run out of gas. He couldn't stick with the Cardinals and signed a minor league deal with the Angels. 1998 Outlook: C

Fernando Valenzuela (**Pos**: LHP, **Age**: 37)

	W	L	Pct.	ERA	G	GS	Sv	IP	H	BB	SO	HR	Ratio
1997	2	12	.143	4.96	18	18	0	89.0	106	46	61	12	1.71
Career	173	153	.531	3.54	453	424	2	2930.0	2718	1151	2074	226	1.32

A resurgent 1996 campaign gave way to a disastrous '97 season. After going 2-8 with the Padres, Valenzuela was dealt to the Cards, where he proceeded to go 0-4 in five starts before being waived. 1998 Outlook: D

St. Louis Cardinals Minor League Prospects

Organization Overview:

The Cardinals have one of the deepest farm systems in the game. In the last two years, they have produced Rigo Beltran, Alan Benes, Mike Difelice, John Frascatore, Matt Morris and Dmitri Young. In 1998, they'll introduce players such as Manny Aybar and Eli Marrero into their regular mix for the long term. They seem to produce a talented pitcher each year, and signing Rick Ankiel as a second-round pick in 1997 added to their stable of arms. The never-ending pipeline should allow them to contend for a while in the mediocre National League Central, even if they have to jettison some costly veterans in the future.

Rick Ankiel

Position: P
Bats: L **Throws:** L
Ht: 6' 1" **Wt:** 210
Opening Day Age: 18
Born: 7/19/79 in Ft. Pierce, FL

Recent Statistics

	W	L	ERA	G	GS	Sv	IP	H	R	BB	SO	HR
97					Did Not Play							

Ankiel may have been the most astute pick in the 1997 draft. Projected as a possible No. 1 overall selection, he lasted until the 72nd pick because he reportedly wanted as much as $6 million to sign. St. Louis bided its time and got him for $2.5 million, a record for a drafted player who didn't become a free agent. In instructional league, he lived up to the scouting reports. Ankiel threw 92 MPH—remember that he's a high school lefthander—and showed an outstanding curveball. He has hit 95 MPH, and if his command is as good as expected he could rocket through the minors.

Manny Aybar

Position: P
Bats: R **Throws:** R
Ht: 6' 1" **Wt:** 165
Opening Day Age: 23
Born: 10/5/74 in Bani, DR

Recent Statistics

	W	L	ERA	G	GS	Sv	IP	H	R	BB	SO	HR
97 AAA Louisville	5	8	3.48	22	22	0	137.0	131	60	45	114	10
97 NL St. Louis	2	4	4.24	12	12	0	68.0	66	33	29	41	8

Signed out of the Dominican as a shortstop, Aybar hit .203 in his first season in the Dominican Summer League and was converted to pitching in 1993. The Cardinals made the move because he had a strong arm, but were surprised at how quickly he showed command. He has good movement on a fastball that consistently reaches the low 90s and at times hits the mid-90s. He has

a slider that can be an above-average pitch, and he knows he needs a changeup. He pitched well for a rookie in the St. Louis rotation in 1997 and will be the first candidate to fill an opening this year.

Scarborough Green

Position: OF
Bats: B **Throws:** R
Ht: 5' 10" **Wt:** 170
Opening Day Age: 23
Born: 6/9/74 in Creve Coeur, MO

Recent Statistics

	G	AB	R	H	D	T	HR	RBI	SB	BB	SO	AVG
97 AA Arkansas	76	251	45	77	14	4	2	29	11	36	48	.307
97 AAA Louisville	52	209	26	53	11	2	3	13	10	22	55	.254
97 NL St. Louis	20	31	5	3	0	0	0	1	0	2	5	.097
97 MLE	128	443	56	113	23	3	3	33	14	41	108	.255

Green has two things going for him: a cool first name and blazing speed. A 10th-round draft-and-follow signed out of St. Louis-Meramec Community College in 1993, he was a .230 career hitter as a pro before batting .283 in the minors last season. He still needs to make more of his running ability by making better contact, drawing more walks and improving his ability to steal bases. A natural righthanded hitter, he became a switch-hitter after signing and now is better from the left side. He's a stellar center fielder with an average arm. Managers voted him the fastest runner and most exciting player in the Double-A Texas League, and he definitely plays with flair. Green will spend 1998 in Triple-A working on perfecting the little man's game.

Curtis King

Position: P
Bats: R **Throws:** R
Ht: 6' 5" **Wt:** 205
Opening Day Age: 27
Born: 10/25/70 in Philadelphia, PA

Recent Statistics

	W	L	ERA	G	GS	Sv	IP	H	R	BB	SO	HR
97 AA Arkansas	2	3	4.46	32	0	16	36.1	38	19	10	29	7
97 AAA Louisville	2	1	2.05	16	0	3	22.0	19	5	6	9	1
97 NL St. Louis	4	2	2.76	30	0	0	29.1	38	14	11	13	0

Scouts can hunt out talent anywhere, and the Cardinals found King at the Philadelphia College of Textiles, which isn't exactly a baseball hotbed. A 1994 fifth-round pick, King started in his first two pro seasons before converting to relief in in 1996. He led the organization with 31 saves that year, and continued to pitch well in 1997. He throws a fastball that has good life if he keeps it low in the strike zone, as well as a splitter and slider. He was hit harder in the majors than his 2.76 ERA would indicate, but should pitch as a setup man in St. Louis again this year.

Braden Looper

Position: P
Bats: R **Throws:** R
Ht: 6' 5" **Wt:** 225

Opening Day Age: 23
Born: 10/28/74 in Weatherford, OK

Recent Statistics

	W	L	ERA	G	GS	Sv	IP	H	R	BB	SO	HR
97 A Pr William	3	6	4.48	12	12	0	64.1	71	38	25	58	6
97 AA Arkansas	1	4	5.91	19	0	5	21.1	24	14	7	20	2

The closer on the 1996 U.S. Olympic team, Looper was the third overall draft pick that year. The Wichita State product didn't debut until 1997, when he began the year as a starter for the sake of innings. He didn't pitch particularly well, then fared worse when he was promoted to Double-A and put in the bullpen. The Cardinals say that Looper just had a tired arm and wasn't able to showcase his excellent stuff. He throws in the mid-90s with good movement low in the strike zone and also has a very good changeup. He's working on a slider as a second power pitch. His arm is fine now and he'll continue working toward being St. Louis' closer of the future in 1998. The Marlins reportedly offered ace Kevin Brown for Aybar and Looper, but the Cardinals turned them down.

Eli Marrero

Position: C
Bats: R **Throws:** R
Ht: 6' 1" **Wt:** 180

Opening Day Age: 24
Born: 11/17/73 in Cuba

Recent Statistics

	G	AB	R	H	D	T	HR	RBI	SB	BB	SO	AVG
97 AAA Louisville	112	395	60	108	21	7	20	68	4	25	53	.273
97 NL St. Louis	17	45	4	11	2	0	2	7	4	2	13	.244
97 MLE	112	381	48	94	19	4	15	54	2	20	55	.247

Marrero may be the best catching prospect in the minors and showed in a brief 1997 major league trial that he may be ready to play in St. Louis this year. A 1993 third-round pick, he was voted the Triple-A American Association's best defensive catcher by the managers. His arm strength is his best tool, and he also has a quick release and good accuracy. He's getting better as a power hitter and makes good contact, but he's too impatient at this point to hit for a high average. He also runs well for a catcher and is durable. If he doesn't begin the year as the Cardinals' starting catcher, he definitely should finish it in that role.

Luis Ordaz

Position: SS
Bats: R **Throws:** R
Ht: 5' 11" **Wt:** 170

Opening Day Age: 22
Born: 8/12/75 in Maracaibo, Venez

Recent Statistics

	G	AB	R	H	D	T	HR	RBI	SB	BB	SO	AVG
97 AA Arkansas	115	390	44	112	20	6	4	58	11	22	39	.287
97 NL St. Louis	12	22	3	6	1	0	0	1	3	1	2	.273
97 MLE	115	376	35	98	18	4	3	46	7	15	41	.261

Ordaz was a throw-in in a three-way Rule 5 draft trade in 1995 between the Cardinals, Reds and Royals. Signed out of Venezuela, he had shown little hitting ability while in the Cincinnati chain. But in two years with St. Louis he has batted .279 in the minors and even hit .273 during a September callup last year. He still needs to get stronger and improve his batting eye. Despite average speed, he's a top-notch shortstop with great hands, a strong arm and good range. He's at least a year away from being able to play regularly in the majors, but he should provide a decent alternative should Royce Clayton become too expensive for the Cardinals.

Brady Raggio

Position: P
Bats: R **Throws:** R
Ht: 6' 4" **Wt:** 210

Opening Day Age: 25
Born: 9/17/72 in Los Angeles, CA

Recent Statistics

	W	L	ERA	G	GS	Sv	IP	H	R	BB	SO	HR
97 AAA Louisville	8	11	4.17	22	22	0	138.0	145	68	32	91	18
97 NL St. Louis	1	2	6.89	15	4	0	31.1	44	24	16	21	1

Raggio is fortunate to be alive after falling off a cliff in 1992. He messed up his knee, elbow and back, but didn't damage his pitching arm and made a remarkable recovery. A 20th-round pick out of Chabot (Calif.) Junior College in 1992, his best pitch is a slider. His fastball has below-average velocity, but it moves and he can locate it well. He throws strikes but can be hittable, as was very much the case when he pitched for St. Louis in 1997. He has a future as a major league swingman.

Others to Watch

Lefthander **Armando Almanza** led the minors with 36 saves and posted a 1.67 ERA in high Class-A at age 24. He needs to be challenged at a tougher level, but throws an above-average fastball with life and a slider. . . Precocious shortstop **Brent Butler** continued to dazzle the Cardinals with his bat, hitting .306-15-71 at Class-A Peoria at age 19. He has tremendous discipline, but a lack of speed may necessitate a move to third base. . . First basemen **Nate Dishington** and **Joe Freitas** slammed 28 and 33 homers, respectively in 1997. Dishington, 22, is a former second-round pick who has a shot, while the 24-year-old Freitas was a bit old for the Class-A Midwest League. . . Righthander **Keith Glauber**, 26, keeps adding velocity and now throws 93 MPH. He also has a sharp-breaking curveball and could make a decent setup man. . . **Placido Polanco**, 22, was named the Texas League's best defensive second baseman by the managers. He formed a slick double-play combination with Luis Ordaz, and is a good fastball hitter who uses the whole field. . . Righthander **Cliff Politte's** age (23) took a little of the shine off his Pitcher of the Year award in the high Class-A Carolina League. But he also pitched well in Double-A, going a combined 15-2, 2.22 with 144 strikeouts in 158 innings. His fastball has improved from 86-87 to 91-92 MPH, and he also has a tough slider.

Bruce Bochy

1997 Season

It was a far-from-satisfying year for Bruce Bochy, the National League co-Manager of the Year in 1996. Injuries were a constant problem for the Padres, who never contended seriously to repeat as National League West champions. Bochy particularly had to struggle to piece together a pitching staff that was among the worst in the league. However, he also deserved credit for not quitting on the season. He was able to learn about several younger players who could pay dividends down the road after they gained the confidence instilled by Bochy's patience.

Offense

Bochy had his offense in motion more often last year in an attempt to manufacture more runs. That was partly because he had more speed in his lineup, and partly because injuries at times crippled the heart of the order. The Padres attempted 200 stolen bases and finished second in the NL in scoring. He didn't hesitate to use his bench and had the league's best pinch-hitting production.

Pitching & Defense

The inability of several Padres pitchers to improve ended up being a huge problem and resulted in the firing of pitching coach Dan Warthen. With an inconsistent staff, Bochy liked to use a quick hook. He was at times unconventional in his use of closer Trevor Hoffman, who made 70 appearances, many of which weren't save opportunities. Hoffman also was asked frequently to pitch more than one inning. Bochy emphasizes defense, but the Padres had the second-worst fielding percentage in the NL.

1998 Outlook

Though entrenched as Padres manager, Bochy needs a better season and there will be great pressure to contend this year. There's not a lot of patience from top management and Bochy's often placid managing style might wear thin if another season starts unraveling.

Born: 4/16/55 in Landes de Bussac, France

Playing Experience: 1978-1987, Hou, NYN, SD

Managerial Experience: 3 seasons

Pronunciation: BOE-chee

Manager Statistics

Year	Team, Lg	W	L	Pct	GB	Finish
1997	San Diego, NL	76	86	.469	14.0	4th West
3 Seasons		237	231	.506	—	—

1997 Starting Pitchers by Days Rest

	≤3	4	5	6+
Padres Starts	4	93	27	28
Padres ERA	11.25	4.62	5.82	5.72
NL Avg Starts	3	90	38	22
NL ERA	4.23	4.05	4.27	4.52

1997 Situational Stats

	Bruce Bochy	NL Average
Hit & Run Success %	31.9	36.4
Stolen Base Success %	70.0	68.4
Platoon Pct.	59.7	56.3
Defensive Subs	9	26
High-Pitch Outings	3	12
Quick/Slow Hooks	20/13	18/10
Sacrifice Attempts	81	96

1997 Rankings (National League)

⇒ 2nd in saves with over 1 inning pitched (11)

⇒ 3rd in pinch hitters used (291), slow hooks (13), quick hooks (20) and starts on three days rest (4)

San Diego Padres

653

Andy Ashby

1997 Season

After notching a quality start in in each of his first eight appearances, Andy Ashby came down with elbow trouble that sidelined him for nearly a month. When he returned, he pitched poorly for two months before salvaging his season with a strong September. When all was said and done, his season was like most of the others he's had in San Diego: decent overall numbers but a disappointing record.

Pitching

Ashby has a presence about him that makes him a stabilizing force in San Diego's rotation. Though he wasn't physically sound for much of 1997, he still managed to pitch 200 innings. When healthy, he has outstanding stuff, led by a 90-MPH cut fastball that makes him especially tough on righthanders. He also throws a sinking fastball, and mixes in a slider and changeup. His frequent elbow problems have caused Ashby to be slightly tentative, particularly with his cutter. He remains a good strikeout pitcher but needs to be more aggressive.

Defense & Hitting

Ashby has improved at holding runners, varying his delivery to keep baserunners guessing, but they seemed to figure him out last year and ran with more success than they had in the past. He also handles many balls through the middle and is athletic on the mound. He makes infrequent contact as a hitter but has become a decent bunter.

1998 Outlook

San Diego gave a three-year contract to Ashby, who has pitched through injuries to become the closest thing the Padres have to an ace. He seemed to be over his elbow troubles by the end of 1997. He could break through this year and finally become the big winner he's always had the potential to be.

Position: SP
Bats: R **Throws:** R
Ht: 6' 5" **Wt:** 190

Opening Day Age: 30
Born: 7/11/67 in Kansas City, MO
ML Seasons: 7

Overall Statistics

	W	L	Pct.	ERA	G	GS	Sv	IP	H	BB	SO	HR	Ratio
1997	9	11	.450	4.13	30	30	0	200.2	207	49	144	17	1.28
Career	41	55	.427	4.18	159	146	1	910.1	930	284	627	97	1.33

How Often He Throws Strikes

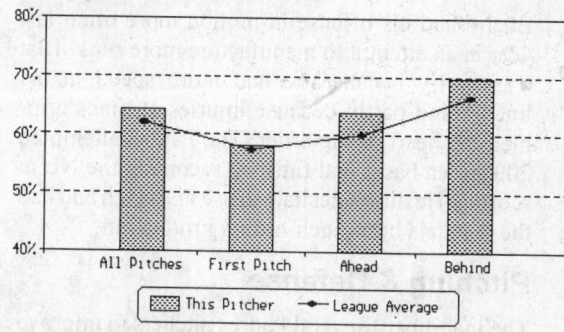

1997 Situational Stats

	W	L	ERA	Sv	IP		AB	H	HR	RBI	Avg
Home	5	4	3.29	0	109.1	LHB	409	117	14	55	.286
Road	4	7	5.12	0	91.1	RHB	369	90	3	39	.244
First Half	4	5	3.54	0	96.2	Sc Pos	192	47	3	72	.245
Scnd Half	5	6	4.67	0	104.0	Clutch	68	19	1	8	.279

1997 Rankings (National League)

⇒ 3rd in stolen bases allowed (30) and highest groundball/flyball ratio allowed (2.4)
⇒ 5th in highest ERA on the road
⇒ Led the Padres in ERA, losses, games started, complete games (2), innings pitched, hits allowed, batters faced (851), strikeouts, stolen bases allowed (30), highest strikeout/walk ratio (2.9), lowest batting average allowed (.266), lowest slugging percentage allowed (.382), lowest on-base percentage allowed (.311), highest groundball/flyball ratio allowed (2.4), least pitches thrown per batter (3.43), least baserunners allowed per 9 innings (11.7), most run support per 9 innings (5.2) and least home runs allowed per 9 innings (.76)

Ken Caminiti

1997 Season

Despite ongoing shoulder troubles and assorted other aches and pains that cost him 25 games, Ken Caminiti played through much of the pain for another big-time season. He batted .350-15-38 in the season's final two months. He probably returned too quickly from offseason shoulder surgery, and his slow start accelerated the Padres' early exit from the National League West race.

Hitting

Caminiti's shoulder troubles robbed him of much of his power from the right side. He hit .306 against southpaws, but 20 of his 26 homers came when he batted lefthanded. He remains capable of some awesome bombs, like the upper-deck blast he hit in Philadelphia last season. Caminiti will strike out more than 100 times a year, but he never gets cheated with his swings. He pulls from both sides of the plate and can be crowded up in the strike zone. In clutch spots, he'll cut down his swing and occasionally go to the opposite field. He also is patient about taking walks.

Baserunning & Defense

There are times when it seems Caminiti can barely drag himself from the on-deck circle to the batter's box. But no matter his physical condition, he always is aggressive on the bases. Caminiti is a high-percentage basestealer and is fearless about breaking up double plays and taking extra bases. He's a great third baseman with an all-world arm and terrific range on plays to either side and on slow rollers. He won his third Gold Glove in 1997.

1998 Outlook

Look out for Caminiti this season. He had solid numbers in 1997 despite never being fully healthy. Now he'll have a full winter of conditioning without having to rehab a major injury. It will be no surprise if he passes the 30-homer and 100-RBI plateaus.

Position: 3B
Bats: B **Throws:** R
Ht: 6' 0" **Wt:** 200

Opening Day Age: 34
Born: 4/21/63 in Hanford, CA
ML Seasons: 11
Pronunciation: kam-un-NET-ee

Overall Statistics

	G	AB	R	H	D	T	HR	RBI	SB	BB	SO	Avg	OBP	Slg
1997	137	486	92	141	28	0	26	90	11	80	118	.290	.389	.508
Career	1374	4999	684	1374	278	15	167	759	73	525	875	.275	.343	.437

Where He Hits the Ball

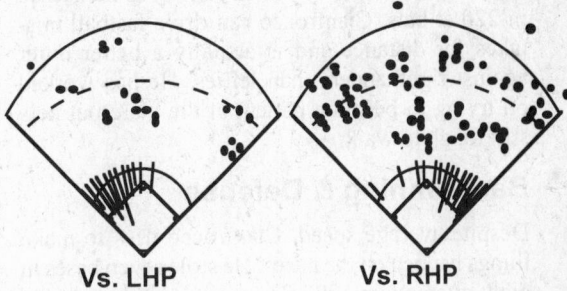

Vs. LHP   **Vs. RHP**

1997 Situational Stats

	AB	H	HR	RBI	Avg		AB	H	HR	RBI	Avg
Home	230	71	15	46	.309	LHP	144	44	6	24	.306
Road	256	70	11	44	.273	RHP	342	97	20	66	.284
First Half	235	58	6	35	.247	Sc Pos	138	42	8	67	.304
Scnd Half	251	83	20	55	.331	Clutch	79	17	0	10	.215

1997 Rankings (National League)

⇒ 2nd in errors at third base (24)
⇒ 5th in cleanup slugging percentage (.519) and lowest fielding percentage at third base (.940)
⇒ 9th in lowest percentage of swings put into play (36.7%)
⇒ 10th in batting average with the bases loaded (.444) and highest percentage of extra bases taken as a runner (61.7%)
⇒ Led the Padres in walks, strikeouts, HR frequency (18.7 ABs per HR), cleanup slugging percentage (.519) and on-base percentage vs. lefthanded pitchers (.404)

San Diego Padres

Archi Cianfrocco

1997 Season

Archi Cianfrocco played quite a bit of first, second and third base for the Padres early in the year. His playing time dwindled as the season progressed, largely because he produced so little. He got just 49 at-bats and hit .224 after the All-Star break.

Hitting

Cianfrocco always has been a early-count fastball hitter and never has made adjustments otherwise. As a result, he rarely sees first-pitch heat and instead gets a steady diet of breaking balls and offspeed stuff. When he falls behind in the count, he'll start chasing pitches out of the strike zone and strikes out quite often as a result. In 1997, the whiffs got completely out of control as he had 80 in 220 at-bats. Cianfrocco can drive fastball mistakes for distance and is actually a better hitter against righthanders than lefties. He has worked on trying to be more patient at the plate but he's still tough to walk.

Baserunning & Defense

Despite average speed, Cianfrocco tries to make things happen on the bases. He stole seven bases in eight attempts in 1997. He doesn't have great defensive skills, but his versatility is an asset. His best position is first base. He also can play third adequately with average range and an erratic arm. He also has appeared at second base and in the outfield.

1998 Outlook

Role players are more valuable than ever with rosters turning over so much. Cianfrocco has been a decent utilityman because of his versatility and occasional power. The Padres quickly re-signed him after he became a free agent. In his five seasons in San Diego, Cianfrocco has played every position except pitcher and center field. He'll remain the Padres' supersub for at least one more year.

Position: 1B/2B/3B
Bats: R **Throws:** R
Ht: 6' 5" **Wt:** 215

Opening Day Age: 31
Born: 10/6/66 in Rome, NY
ML Seasons: 6
Pronunciation: AR-key sin-FROCK-oh

Overall Statistics

	G	AB	R	H	D	T	HR	RBI	SB	BB	SO	Avg	OBP	Slg
1997	89	220	25	54	12	0	4	26	7	25	80	.245	.328	.355
Career	460	1204	132	299	56	7	33	180	15	75	338	.248	.298	.389

Where He Hits the Ball

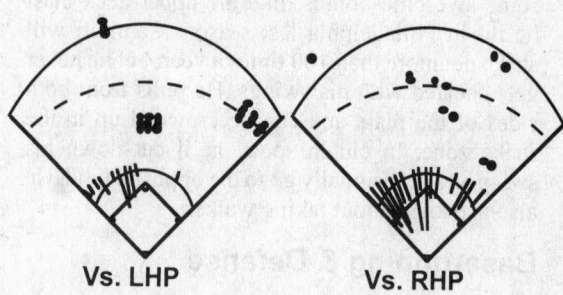

Vs. LHP   **Vs. RHP**

1997 Situational Stats

	AB	H	HR	RBI	Avg		AB	H	HR	RBI	Avg
Home	121	31	3	18	.256	LHP	68	14	3	5	.206
Road	99	23	1	8	.232	RHP	152	40	1	21	.263
First Half	171	43	3	23	.251	Sc Pos	55	15	1	21	.273
Scnd Half	49	11	1	3	.224	Clutch	32	7	0	4	.219

1997 Rankings (National League)

⇒ 1st in lowest batting average with two strikes (.097)

Steve Finley

1997 Season

Despite a big-time power season that included a pair of three-home run games, Steve Finley also had difficulty maintaining consistency. A second-half slump pulled his batting average down to .261, his lowest average in seven years. Nevertheless, he was able to maintain the surprising power stroke that he'd discovered the year before and remained one of the best all-around center fielders in the National League.

Hitting

Finley has added upper-body strength and moved up on the plate, looking to pull pitches whenever possible. He kills low fastballs and he looks to jerk any pitch left over the plate. The other side of Finley's new-found status as a power hitter is his refusal to take pitches to the opposite field. As a result, he has fallen into the bad habit of trying to pull breaking pitches away and ends up grounding them to second. He also can be pitched up in the strike zone and moved off the plate with hard stuff.

Baserunning & Defense

An outstanding baserunner, Finley is one of the better percentage basestealers around. He always uses good judgment on the bases and looks to take the extra base, placing among the NL leaders in triples in most seasons. Finley has outstanding range and an excellent arm in center field. He's capable of making spectacular plays, including home run-saving catches, and is one of the game's best defensive outfielders.

1998 Outlook

Finley has made a conscious decision to sacrifice power for average, but the power potential has always been there. During his days with the Astros, the 'Dome muted his developing power. Now, he's finally learned to tap into it. As he adjusts to this new approach, look for him to bring his average back up to his customary levels while maintaining his run production.

Position: CF
Bats: L **Throws:** L
Ht: 6' 2" **Wt:** 180

Opening Day Age: 33
Born: 3/12/65 in Union City, TN
ML Seasons: 9

Overall Statistics

	G	AB	R	H	D	T	HR	RBI	SB	BB	SO	Avg	OBP	Slg
1997	143	560	101	146	26	5	28	92	15	43	92	.261	.313	.475
Career	1223	4579	713	1276	203	69	105	479	222	361	569	.279	.332	.422

Where He Hits the Ball

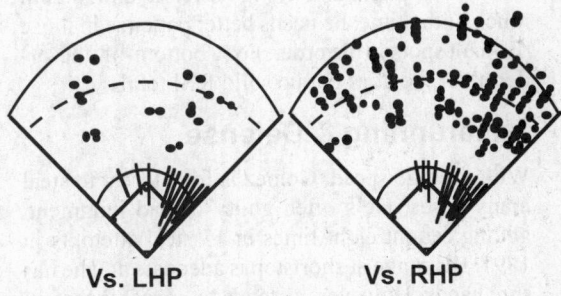

Vs. LHP   **Vs. RHP**

1997 Situational Stats

	AB	H	HR	RBI	Avg		AB	H	HR	RBI	Avg
Home	273	59	5	30	.216	LHP	152	40	5	20	.263
Road	287	87	23	62	.303	RHP	408	106	23	72	.260
First Half	280	78	16	55	.279	Sc Pos	145	40	7	66	.276
Scnd Half	280	68	12	37	.243	Clutch	91	25	2	15	.275

1997 Rankings (National League)

⇒ 1st in lowest batting average at home
⇒ 2nd in fielding percentage in center field (.989)
⇒ 3rd in highest percentage of extra bases taken as a runner (67.7%)
⇒ 5th in errors in center field (4)
⇒ 8th in runs scored and lowest groundball/flyball ratio (0.9)
⇒ Led the Padres in home runs, runs scored, triples and highest percentage of extra bases taken as a runner (67.7%)

Chris Gomez

1997 Season

On the way to career highs in several offensive categories, Chris Gomez also gave hints that an increased workload may have worn him down. He batted .240 and didn't hit homer in the second half. He also continued to struggle mightily against righthanders, hitting .242.

Hitting

Gomez strikes out far too often for someone who hits so few homers. At times he looks overmatched against good hard stuff, and he can be handled with good fastballs on the corners. He's a decent breaking-ball hitter because he doesn't try to pull too much, concentrating more on hitting the ball where it's pitched. Hitting seventh and eighth much of the time, he needs better patience in those difficult spots in the order. For a bottom-of-the-order hitter, he does put up solid RBI totals.

Baserunning & Defense

With average speed, Gomez is little threat to steal many bases. He's often guilty of bad judgment, getting caught eight times in 13 steal attempts in 1997. His range at shortstop is adequate and he has sure hands. However, he tends to hurry his throws or throw from an improper arm angle which often results in errant tosses. Even slick-fielding first baseman Wally Joyner can prevent only so many of those misfires from becoming errors.

1998 Outlook

In recent years, a number of the most outstanding athletes to play baseball in decades have broken into the majors as shortstops. Gomez isn't an eye-popping talent, but he's solid and easily overlooked. The power he flashed during his days in Detroit seems to have been an illusion, but the Padres accept his limitations. He does a workmanlike job, and until someone better comes along he'll be San Diego's starter.

Position: SS
Bats: R **Throws:** R
Ht: 6' 1" **Wt:** 188

Opening Day Age: 26
Born: 6/16/71 in Los Angeles, CA
ML Seasons: 5

Overall Statistics

	G	AB	R	H	D	T	HR	RBI	SB	BB	SO	Avg	OBP	Slg
1997	150	522	62	132	19	2	5	54	5	53	114	.253	.326	.326
Career	540	1833	207	453	86	6	28	213	19	193	375	.247	.324	.346

Where He Hits the Ball

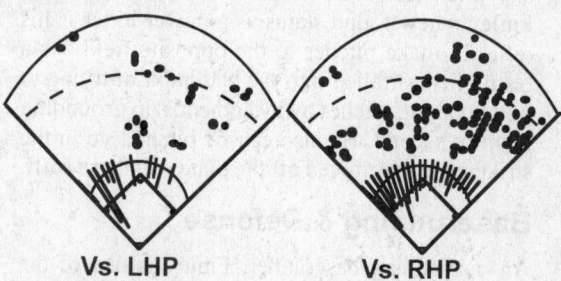

Vs. LHP   Vs. RHP

1997 Situational Stats

	AB	H	HR	RBI	Avg		AB	H	HR	RBI	Avg
Home	266	63	2	26	.237	LHP	109	32	2	15	.294
Road	256	69	3	28	.270	RHP	413	100	3	39	.242
First Half	318	83	5	37	.261	Sc Pos	141	33	1	44	.234
Scnd Half	204	49	0	17	.240	Clutch	78	26	0	8	.333

1997 Rankings (National League)

⇒ 1st in lowest slugging percentage and lowest slugging percentage vs. righthanded pitchers (.308)
⇒ 4th in fielding percentage at shortstop (.978)
⇒ 6th in lowest batting average with the bases loaded (.067), lowest on-base percentage vs. righthanded pitchers (.309) and lowest batting average at home
⇒ 7th in errors at shortstop (15)
⇒ 8th in lowest batting average vs. righthanded pitchers
⇒ 9th in lowest HR frequency (104.4 ABs per HR) and most pitches seen per plate appearance (3.95)
⇒ Led the Padres in GDPs (16) and games played (150)

Tony Gwynn

1997 Season

At a time when you'd expect Tony Gwynn to be slowing down, he instead came up with arguably the best season of his Hall of Fame career. Gwynn not only led the league in hitting for the eighth time, tying Honus Wagner's National League record, but he also set career highs in doubles, homers, RBI and total bases.

Hitting

Gwynn keeps adding to his credentials as the greatest pure hitter of his generation. He has batted at least .300 in 15 straight seasons, with only Ty Cobb and Stan Musial having longer streaks. He needs 220 hits to reach 3,000 for his career. In 1997 he added power to his repertoire, making one of his many adjustments in his stance to allow him to pull the ball with more regularity. As usual, Gwynn hardly ever struck out and was machine-like in slapping balls where they were pitched. He also batted .459 with men in scoring position, the highest mark in the majors by a safe margin.

Baserunning & Defense

His history of leg and weight problems has robbed Gwynn of some of his speed but he still can steal bases in key situations. His physical troubles also have cut down his range in the outfield, but he remains one of the NL's best right fielders because of his excellent judgment and great hands. He doesn't have a cannon for an arm, but he's always accurate with his throws.

1998 Outlook

The baseball world has run out of superlatives to describe Gwynn. Though his body seems to be breaking down a little more each year, his bat can't be slowed. Reaching 3,000 hits is his next milestone, as is a record ninth batting crown. He keeps rolling along like few hitters in baseball history.

Position: RF
Bats: L **Throws:** L
Ht: 5'11" **Wt:** 220

Opening Day Age: 37
Born: 5/9/60 in Los Angeles, CA
ML Seasons: 16

Overall Statistics

	G	AB	R	H	D	T	HR	RBI	SB	BB	SO	Avg	OBP	Slg
1997	149	592	97	220	49	2	17	119	12	43	28	.372	.409	.547
Career	2095	8187	1237	2780	460	84	107	973	308	707	389	.340	.390	.455

Where He Hits the Ball

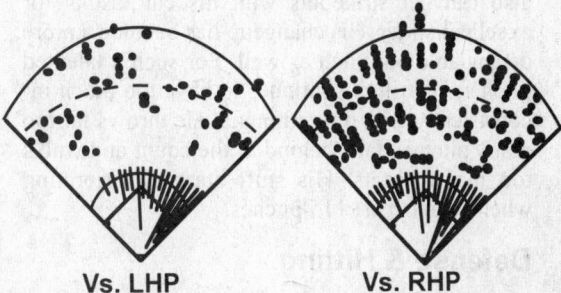

Vs. LHP   **Vs. RHP**

1997 Situational Stats

	AB	H	HR	RBI	Avg		AB	H	HR	RBI	Avg
Home	296	112	8	63	.378	LHP	163	58	6	48	.356
Road	296	108	9	56	.365	RHP	429	162	11	71	.378
First Half	330	130	13	71	.394	Sc Pos	146	67	9	99	.459
Scnd Half	262	90	4	48	.344	Clutch	86	34	4	30	.395

1997 Rankings (National League)

⇒ 1st in batting average, hits, singles, sacrifice flies (12), batting average with runners in scoring position, batting average in the clutch, batting average with the bases loaded (.615), batting average on an 0-2 count (.400), batting average with two strikes (.358) and lowest percentage of swings that missed (8.0%)

⇒ 2nd in doubles, batting average vs. righthanded pitchers, batting average at home and batting average on the road

⇒ 3rd in least pitches seen per plate appearance (3.28), fielding percentage in right field (.983) and highest percentage of swings put into play (58.0%)

San Diego Padres

Joey Hamilton

1997 Season

After missing nearly a month with shoulder troubles, Joey Hamilton came back to be the best starter in what was a motley Padres rotation. He led the staff in wins, including a memorable last-week gem against the Dodgers in Los Angeles. However, Hamilton won only two of his last 10 starts and once again failed to have the big year that's expected of him.

Pitching

There are few better sinking fastballs than Hamilton's when he's at his best. He throws his sinker in the low 90s and it explodes with late, sharp movement that can result in a parade of groundouts. He also can get strikeouts with his cut fastball or excellent slider. His changeup has become a more dependable out pitch as well. For such a talented pitcher, Hamilton continues to have too much inconsistency with his command. He throws far too many pitches, falls behind in the count and walks too many hitters. His stuff starts deteriorating when he gets past 115 pitches.

Defense & Hitting

Hamilton has worked to improve his pickoff move and does a much better job of holding runners than he did when he first joined the Padres. He remains a very uncoordinated fielder against whom some clubs consciously try to bunt for basehits. He has worked hard to improve his hitting and had two home runs among his seven hits in 1997, a stunning achievement for a hitter whose ineptitude was once legendary.

1998 Outlook

Despite winning 27 games in the last two years, Hamilton is viewed by many as an underachiever. He's a prime reason why the Padres changed pitching coaches after the season. He needs to adopt a more mature attitude. With the proper mindset he can be a star, and it's getting to the time for him to step up and realize his full potential.

Position: SP
Bats: R **Throws:** R
Ht: 6' 4" **Wt:** 230

Opening Day Age: 27
Born: 9/9/70 in Statesboro, GA
ML Seasons: 4
Nickname: Big Daddy

Overall Statistics

	W	L	Pct.	ERA	G	GS	Sv	IP	H	BB	SO	HR	Ratio
1997	12	7	.632	4.25	31	29	0	192.2	199	69	124	22	1.39
Career	42	31	.575	3.70	112	108	0	717.1	692	237	492	65	1.30

How Often He Throws Strikes

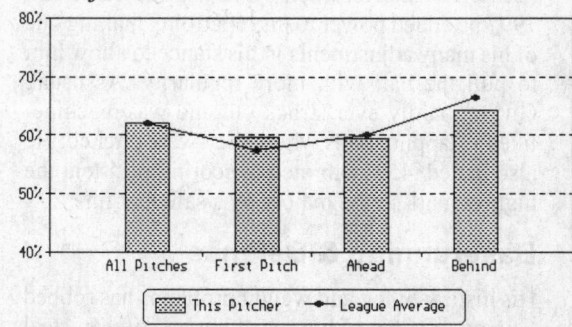

1997 Situational Stats

	W	L	ERA	Sv	IP		AB	H	HR	RBI	Avg
Home	3	6	4.56	0	102.2	LHB	360	110	14	52	.306
Road	9	1	3.90	0	90.0	RHB	374	89	8	38	.238
First Half	6	3	4.21	0	87.2	Sc Pos	175	45	4	67	.257
Scnd Half	6	4	4.29	0	105.0	Clutch	55	15	1	5	.273

1997 Rankings (National League)

⇒ 3rd in hit batsmen (12)
⇒ 4th in runners caught stealing (12)
⇒ 5th in lowest strikeout/walk ratio (1.8)
⇒ 7th in highest batting average allowed vs. lefthanded batters
⇒ 8th in highest on-base percentage allowed (.340) and most baserunners allowed per 9 innings (13.1)
⇒ 9th in highest batting average allowed (.271) and highest ERA at home
⇒ Led the Padres in sacrifice bunts (9), wins, walks allowed, hit batsmen (12), wild pitches (7), pitches thrown (2,973), runners caught stealing (12), GDPs induced (14), winning percentage, lowest stolen base percentage allowed (52.0%) and most GDPs induced per 9 innings (0.7)

Sterling Hitchcock

1997 Season

Sterling Hitchcock had another bout of elbow trouble on the way to a so-so season in which he won 10 games but posted a 5.20 ERA. He seemed on his way to salvaging his season in mid-August, but suffered through a truly awful September. In his final six appearances, he went 0-3, 10.34.

Pitching

A cranky elbow has caused Hitchcock to throw what used to be a decent splitter less frequently. He throws more sinkers and sliders, with his fastball usually staying in the high 80s. He also has a good straight change. Hitchcock has become gun-shy about pitching inside and tends to leave too many pitches over the outer half of the plate, pitches which often get hit for distance. His control is usually solid in terms of walks, but Hitchcock isn't as efficient as he should be, resulting in fairly high pitch counts. He doesn't have great stamina, and his stuff usually starts fading once he gets past 110 pitches.

Defense & Hitting

Though he's lefthanded, Hitchcock is easy to run on. Opponents stole 26 bases in 35 attempts in 1997. He's a good athlete who uses his motion to get into fielding position. In his first year swinging the bat, he was even more awful than anyone could have expected. He did prove to be an adequate bunter.

1998 Outlook

It's rare to see such a talented young lefthander already pitching for his third team. Hitchcock likely will stay put in San Diego. The Padres think better coaching and a healthy elbow can make him into the 15-game winner scouts have predicted Hitchcock would be for years. Still, it's worrisome to see a hurler forced to become a sinker-slider pitcher at such a young age. He hasn't been quite the same since working so hard in '95, and after beginning his career as a strikeout pitcher, he's now gone 35 starts without striking out more than six men in a game.

Position: SP
Bats: L **Throws:** L
Ht: 6' 1" **Wt:** 192

Opening Day Age: 26
Born: 4/29/71 in Fayetteville, NC
ML Seasons: 6

Overall Statistics

	W	L	Pct.	ERA	G	GS	Sv	IP	H	BB	SO	HR	Ratio
1997	10	11	.476	5.20	32	28	0	161.0	172	55	106	24	1.41
Career	39	35	.527	5.07	126	104	2	619.1	675	245	428	82	1.49

How Often He Throws Strikes

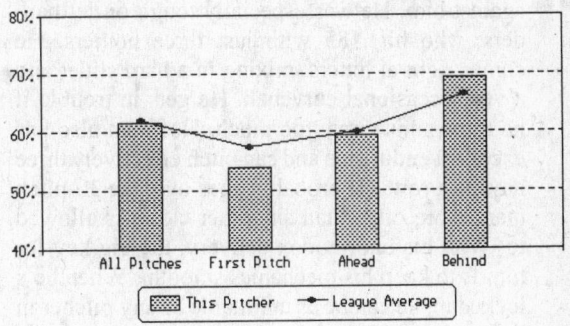

1997 Situational Stats

	W	L	ERA	Sv	IP		AB	H	HR	RBI	Avg
Home	6	4	4.04	0	75.2	LHB	117	37	4	12	.316
Road	4	7	6.22	0	85.1	RHB	506	135	20	76	.267
First Half	5	5	4.64	0	83.1	Sc Pos	152	39	5	62	.257
Scnd Half	5	6	5.79	0	77.2	Clutch	29	7	0	3	.241

1997 Rankings (National League)

⇒ 1st in highest ERA on the road
⇒ 5th in stolen bases allowed (26)
⇒ 8th in balks (2)
⇒ 10th in home runs allowed
⇒ Led the Padres in losses and home runs allowed

San Diego Padres

Trevor Hoffman

1997 Season

There's little doubt that Trevor Hoffman has established himself as one of baseball's best closers. His save numbers were down from 1996, more a reflection of his team's struggles than his own. Hoffman converted 27 of his last 28 save opportunities after blowing five of his first 16. After saving 16 games with a 4.06 ERA before the All-Star break, he had 21 saves and a 1.44 ERA in the second half.

Pitching

Hoffman was somewhat more hittable and gave up nine home runs in 1997 because he lost his release point at times, costing him movement on his mid-90s fastball. Still, opponents batted just .200 against him. He was especially tough on lefthanders, who hit .185 with just three homers. He comes right at hitters, mixing in a hard slider and a very occasional curveball. He gets in trouble if he throws his curve too much. Hoffman also has excellent endurance and can pitch effectively three days in a row. He probably goes over the 30-pitch mark more often than any other closer is allowed to. With his unorthodox delivery, the big key for him is to keep his mechanics smooth. When he's locked in, he can be as unhittable as any pitcher in baseball, as evidenced by his annually overpowering strikeout numbers.

Defense & Hitting

Hoffman's delivery isn't exactly suited for efficient fielding. He's helped by his experience as a former infielder, and has very good hands and instincts for making plays. He doesn't hold runners especially well, usually not a problem for a closer. He rarely gets a chance to bat but handles himself reasonably well as a hitter.

1998 Outlook

Hoffman is in his physical prime and has awesome stuff. No National League reliever has had more saves over the last two seasons. If the Padres rebound into contention, he should get back over 40 saves again.

Position: RP
Bats: R **Throws:** R
Ht: 6' 0" **Wt:** 205

Opening Day Age: 30
Born: 10/13/67 in Bellflower, CA
ML Seasons: 5

Overall Statistics

	W	L	Pct.	ERA	G	GS	Sv	IP	H	BB	SO	HR	Ratio
1997	6	4	.600	2.66	70	0	37	81.1	59	24	111	9	1.02
Career	30	23	.566	3.03	309	0	135	368.2	276	128	421	39	1.10

How Often He Throws Strikes

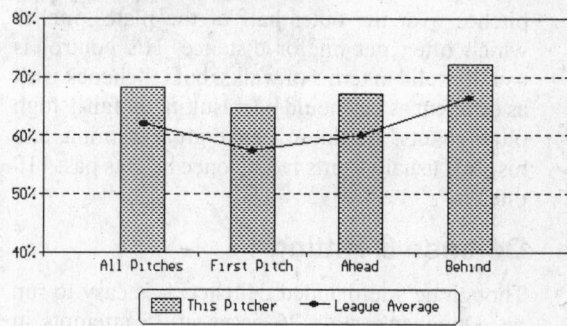

1997 Situational Stats

	W	L	ERA	Sv	IP		AB	H	HR	RBI	Avg
Home	6	0	2.85	16	41.0	LHB	157	29	3	17	.185
Road	0	4	2.45	21	40.1	RHB	138	30	6	19	.217
First Half	3	3	4.06	16	37.2	Sc Pos	77	17	4	27	.221
Scnd Half	3	1	1.44	21	43.2	Clutch	216	40	5	29	.185

1997 Rankings (National League)

⇒ 1st in lowest batting average allowed in relief (.200)
⇒ 2nd in saves and most strikeouts per 9 innings in relief (12.3)
⇒ 3rd in save opportunities (44), first batter efficiency (.147) and least baserunners allowed per 9 innings in relief (9.2)
⇒ 4th in blown saves (7)
⇒ 5th in games finished (59) and save percentage (84.1%)
⇒ Led the Padres in games pitched, saves, games finished (59), wild pitches (7), save opportunities (44), save percentage (84.1%), blown saves (7), lowest batting average allowed in relief with runners on base (.219), relief ERA (2.66), relief wins (6) and relief innings (81.1)

Wally Joyner

1997 Season

Wally Joyner missed two weeks early in the year with an ankle sprain, but he'll otherwise remember the 1997 season fondly. He batted a career-high .327 to finish fifth in the National League batting race. Though he didn't come close to matching the 34 homers he hit in 1987, this may have been his best all-around season in the majors.

Hitting

Joyner is a true professional hitter who doesn't try to do too much with any pitch. He can pull a low fastball with authority, but he's more content to hit breaking balls and high fastballs to the opposite field. Lefthanders sap what power he has and take a bite out of his batting average. Teams like to pitch Joyner high and tight, but if the ball is left over the plate he'll put it into play. He's always been a good hitter in the clutch and 1997 was no exception. He batted .353 with runners in scoring position.

Baserunning & Defense

Joyner has below-average speed and is no threat as a basestealer, but he's a heady baserunner who will take an extra base when the percentages are with him. There are few slicker first basemen. He has great hands and digs throws out of the dirt as well as anyone. He also has good range around the bag and makes the double-play throw to second look routine.

1998 Outlook

The Padres renewed their option on Joyner for 1998 and there's no argument about the decision. First-base prospect Derrek Lee has been slow in his development. It's a given that Joyner will miss two or three weeks each season with minor aches and pains, but the Padres appreciate what he delivers when he's in there. Joyner has become an important part of the Padres as both a stabilizing force in the infield and a solid bat in the lineup.

Position: 1B
Bats: L **Throws:** L
Ht: 6' 2" **Wt:** 200

Opening Day Age: 35
Born: 6/16/62 in Atlanta, GA
ML Seasons: 12

Overall Statistics

	G	AB	R	H	D	T	HR	RBI	SB	BB	SO	Avg	OBP	Slg
1997	135	455	59	149	29	2	13	83	3	51	51	.327	.390	.486
Career	1620	5993	843	1750	348	22	179	937	58	680	678	.292	.363	.447

Where He Hits the Ball

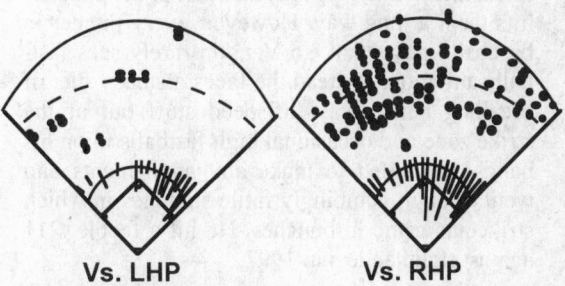

Vs. LHP   **Vs. RHP**

1997 Situational Stats

	AB	H	HR	RBI	Avg		AB	H	HR	RBI	Avg
Home	216	70	6	34	.324	LHP	80	21	3	15	.263
Road	239	79	7	49	.331	RHP	375	128	10	68	.341
First Half	246	83	8	49	.337	Sc Pos	133	47	3	65	.353
Scnd Half	209	66	5	34	.316	Clutch	75	26	0	13	.347

1997 Rankings (National League)

⇒ 1st in fielding percentage at first base (.996)
⇒ 3rd in sacrifice flies (10)
⇒ 4th in batting average vs. righthanded pitchers
⇒ 5th in batting average and batting average on the road
⇒ 6th in batting average on an 0-2 count (.303)
⇒ 7th in batting average with runners in scoring position
⇒ 8th in lowest batting average with the bases loaded (.100)
⇒ 10th in on-base percentage vs. righthanded pitchers (.407)

San Diego Padres

663

Greg Vaughn

1997 Season

There have been few bigger free-agent busts than Greg Vaughn. Signed to a new three-year contract by the Padres, Vaughn struggled to keep his average above .200 for much of the year and ultimately was relegated to part-time duty in left field. A trade to the Yankees fell through when the Yanks insisted that he wasn't physically sound. He was signed to be a run producer, but failed to convince the Padres that they could count on him at all. If there was a bright spot, it was that he had his best overall month in September, batting .262-4-17.

Hitting

Vaughn tries to pull everything. When he gets mistake fastballs over the inner half of the plate, he hits them a long way. However, every pitcher in baseball knows that, so Vaughn rarely sees fastballs any more. Instead, he faces a steady diet of breaking balls away, offspeed stuff out of the strike zone and occasional high fastballs in on his hands. He failed to make any adjustments and went through numbingly futile stretches in which strikeouts came in bunches. He hit a feeble .211 against righthanders in 1997.

Baserunning & Defense

With only average speed, Vaughn is just an occasional basestealing threat. He has decent range but is a subpar left fielder otherwise. A history of shoulder problems has left him with a weak throwing arm and he's prone to misjudge fly balls as well, making it risky to play him regularily in left.

1998 Outlook

Few baseball people could understand why the Padres were so quick to give Vaughn a new long-term contract. In his eight months in the National League, he has batted .213 with 28 homers. Pitchers have been getting him out the same way for so long that the Padres may be reaching their breaking point with him. He needs to make adjustments.

Position: LF
Bats: R **Throws:** R
Ht: 6' 0" **Wt:** 202

Opening Day Age: 32
Born: 7/3/65 in Sacramento, CA
ML Seasons: 9

Overall Statistics

	G	AB	R	H	D	T	HR	RBI	SB	BB	SO	Avg	OBP	Slg
1997	120	361	60	78	10	0	18	57	7	56	110	.216	.322	.393
Career	1066	3746	608	906	171	14	197	645	73	501	902	.242	.332	.453

Where He Hits the Ball

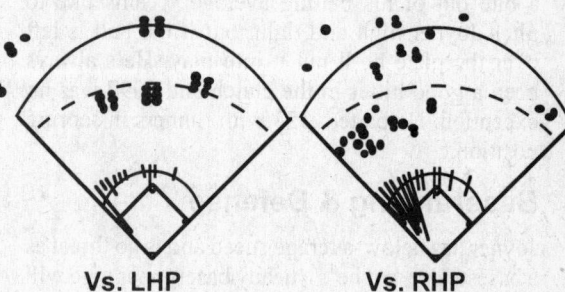

Vs. LHP   **Vs. RHP**

1997 Situational Stats

	AB	H	HR	RBI	Avg		AB	H	HR	RBI	Avg
Home	163	33	11	29	.202	LHP	76	18	8	20	.237
Road	198	45	7	28	.227	RHP	285	60	10	37	.211
First Half	196	44	10	24	.224	Sc Pos	108	23	3	38	.213
Scnd Half	165	34	8	33	.206	Clutch	67	17	3	9	.254

1997 Rankings (National League)

⇒ 2nd in lowest batting average with two strikes (.106) and lowest percentage of swings put into play (32.0%)
⇒ 4th in lowest batting average on a 3-2 count (.058) and highest percentage of swings that missed (30.6%)
⇒ 9th in lowest batting average with runners in scoring position
⇒ Led the Padres in least GDPs per GDP situation (6.3%)

Quilvio Veras

1997 Season

In the middle of June, a light went off in Quilvio Veras' head. After struggling through the first two months of the year and hearing complaints from his own teammates about his inadequacy as a lead-off man, he resuscitated his career with a strong two-month run in midsummer. He hit nearly .300 from June on, posting career highs in hits, doubles and RBI while rediscovering his basestealing aggressiveness.

Hitting

The switch-hitting Veras strikes out too much for a leadoff hitter and continues to struggle against lefthanders. However, he's a good fastball hitter and has a knack for working walks. He can surprise at times with his extra-base pop, and also has become an occasionally dangerous breaking-ball hitter. He can lay down a bunt from time to time, rarely grounds into double plays and can get on via the hit-by-pitch.

Baserunning & Defense

The Marlins gave up on Veras because he became hesitant to run, but as 1997 wore on he regained much of the aggressiveness that once made him the National League stolen-base leader. Healthy hamstrings had a lot to do with that. He gets a quick first step and has good speed. His percentage should improve as he regains his confidence. Veras has good hands and range at second. He makes many of his errors by trying to do too much on certain plays. He's very acrobatic in turning double plays.

1998 Outlook

No one ever has questioned Veras' physical skills. Now over hamstring problems and possessing new maturity and confidence, he could be on the verge of becoming an exciting leadoff man. He has the potential to score 100 runs and steal 50 bases. The key for him is to remain healthy and in a good frame of mind.

Position: 2B
Bats: B **Throws:** R
Ht: 5' 9" **Wt:** 166

Opening Day Age: 26
Born: 4/3/71 in Santo Domingo, DR
ML Seasons: 3
Pronunciation: KILL-vee-oh VARE-ess

Overall Statistics

	G	AB	R	H	D	T	HR	RBI	SB	BB	SO	Avg	OBP	Slg
1997	145	539	74	143	23	1	3	45	33	72	84	.265	.357	.328
Career	342	1232	200	322	51	9	12	91	97	203	194	.261	.372	.347

Where He Hits the Ball

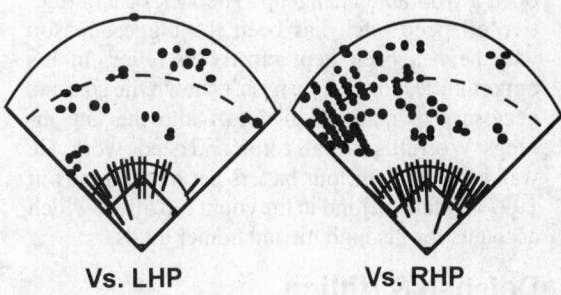

Vs. LHP   Vs. RHP

1997 Situational Stats

	AB	H	HR	RBI	Avg		AB	H	HR	RBI	Avg
Home	261	72	3	18	.276	LHP	124	24	0	5	.194
Road	278	71	0	27	.255	RHP	415	119	3	40	.287
First Half	271	73	3	26	.269	Sc Pos	116	31	0	39	.267
Scnd Half	268	70	0	19	.261	Clutch	89	25	0	13	.281

1997 Rankings (National League)

⇒ 1st in lowest slugging percentage vs. lefthanded pitchers (.234)
⇒ 2nd in lowest slugging percentage, lowest HR frequency (179.7 ABs per HR) and lowest batting average vs. lefthanded pitchers
⇒ 3rd in highest groundball/flyball ratio (2.1)
⇒ 5th in fielding percentage at second base (.984) and steals of third (9)
⇒ Led the Padres in sacrifice bunts (9), stolen bases, caught stealing (12), hit by pitch (7), pitches seen (2,527), highest groundball/flyball ratio (2.1), most pitches seen per plate appearance (4.00), bunts in play (21), steals of third (9) and lowest percentage of swings on the first pitch (21.8%)

San Diego Padres

Tim Worrell

Position: RP/SP
Bats: R **Throws:** R
Ht: 6' 4" **Wt:** 220

Opening Day Age: 30
Born: 7/5/67 in
Pasadena, CA
ML Seasons: 5
Pronunciation:
wor-RELL

1997 Season

Tim Worrell had been bounced between starting and relieving, but the Padres finally seemed to settle on using him as a middle reliever in 1997. He made a career-high 50 relief appearances and was on his way to a solid season when he hit the wall at the end of the year. He pitched well over the second half before closing the season with four disastrous appearances that inflated his ERA.

Pitching

Finally over his serious elbow troubles, Worrell again is throwing consistently in the low to mid-90s. He has a running fastball which he can also sink. He also throws a hard slider and has developed a workable changeup. The lack of an effective offspeed pitch has been the biggest reason why he has been kept mostly in relief. In his opportunities to start, he hasn't shown the stamina necessary to maintain his stuff into the late innings. Worrell's overall command needs work. He walked more than four batters per nine innings in 1997 and falls behind in the count too often, which accounts for his high hit and homer totals.

Defense & Hitting

Worrell is an excellent fielding pitcher who handles many balls through the middle and is very adept at coming off the mound to field bunts. He has a quick move to first and a quick delivery home, though basestealers went 16-for-22 against him in 1997. Worrell occasionally can help himself at the plate, though he's hardly a threat as a hitter.

1998 Outlook

Worrell remains convinced he should be a starter, but the Padres believed otherwise. He hasn't made much of his opportunities in the rotation. It's uncertain what role he'll perform in Detroit after the Tigers traded Dan Miceli and Donne Wall for him in the offseason.

Overall Statistics

	W	L	Pct.	ERA	G	GS	Sv	IP	H	BB	SO	HR	Ratio
1997	4	8	.333	5.16	60	10	3	106.1	116	50	81	14	1.56
Career	16	23	.410	4.30	143	40	4	356.0	354	143	259	36	1.40

How Often He Throws Strikes

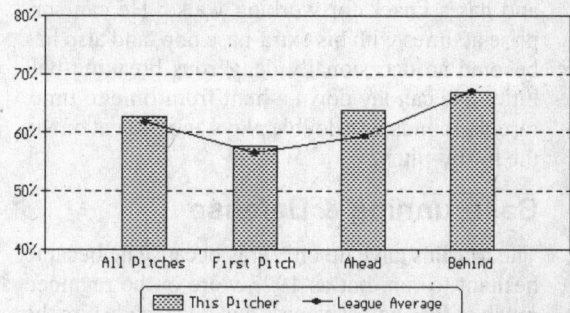

This Pitcher — League Average

1997 Situational Stats

	W	L	ERA	Sv	IP		AB	H	HR	RBI	Avg
Home	4	7	4.76	0	64.1	LHB	195	59	5	28	.303
Road	0	1	5.79	3	42.0	RHB	219	57	9	39	.260
First Half	3	6	5.30	2	74.2	Sc Pos	132	35	2	50	.265
Scnd Half	1	2	4.83	1	31.2	Clutch	123	34	2	19	.276

1997 Rankings (National League)

⇒ 1st in lowest fielding percentage at pitcher (.867)
⇒ 2nd in errors at pitcher (4)
⇒ 8th in worst first batter efficiency (.318) and most baserunners allowed per 9 innings in relief (15.1)
⇒ 9th in highest relief ERA (5.10) and highest batting average allowed in relief (.286)
⇒ 10th in highest batting average allowed vs. lefthanded batters
⇒ Led the Padres in holds (16)

Sean Bergman

Position: RP/SP
Bats: R **Throws:** R
Ht: 6' 4" **Wt:** 230

Opening Day Age: 27
Born: 4/11/70 in Joliet, IL
ML Seasons: 5

Doug Bochtler

Traded To ATHLETICS

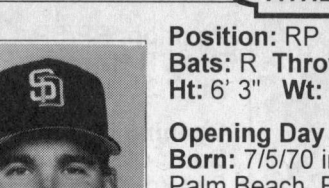

Position: RP
Bats: R **Throws:** R
Ht: 6' 3" **Wt:** 200

Opening Day Age: 27
Born: 7/5/70 in West Palm Beach, FL
ML Seasons: 3
Pronunciation: BOCK-ler

Overall Statistics

	W	L	Pct.	ERA	G	GS	Sv	IP	H	BB	SO	HR	Ratio
1997	2	4	.333	6.09	44	9	0	99.0	126	38	74	11	1.66
Career	18	27	.400	5.22	125	60	0	405.0	483	168	276	52	1.61

1997 Situational Stats

	W	L	ERA	Sv	IP		AB	H	HR	RBI	Avg
Home	1	4	5.40	0	46.2	LHB	165	47	4	30	.285
Road	1	0	6.71	0	52.1	RHB	234	79	7	39	.338
First Half	2	3	5.01	0	64.2	Sc Pos	114	40	3	55	.351
Scnd Half	0	1	8.13	0	34.1	Clutch	19	8	1	7	.421

Overall Statistics

	W	L	Pct.	ERA	G	GS	Sv	IP	H	BB	SO	HR	Ratio
1997	3	6	.333	4.77	54	0	2	60.1	51	50	46	3	1.67
Career	9	14	.391	3.78	151	0	6	171.1	134	108	159	14	1.41

1997 Situational Stats

	W	L	ERA	Sv	IP		AB	H	HR	RBI	Avg
Home	1	3	4.18	1	32.1	LHB	114	28	3	18	.246
Road	2	3	5.46	1	28.0	RHB	109	23	0	16	.211
First Half	1	4	5.50	2	37.2	Sc Pos	80	20	0	29	.250
Scnd Half	2	2	3.57	0	22.2	Clutch	118	23	2	14	.195

1997 Season

It was largely a dreadful season for Sean Bergman, who pitched his way into the Padres' rotation in June but got hammered until he was sent back to the bullpen in mid-July. For the remainder of 1997, he got shelled as he worked in a mop-up role.

Pitching, Defense & Hitting

A sinkerballer with velocity in the high 80s and a hard slider, Bergman needs good command to be effective. He pitches from behind in the count too often. His stuff is good enough to get him his share of strikeouts, but his control isn't consistent enough to allow him to fulfill his potential. Bergman doesn't have a good pickoff move and is slow coming to the plate. He's only a fair fielder, but isn't a bad hitter for a pitcher.

1998 Outlook

Since coming out of Southern Illinois University, the knock on Bergman has been that he has good stuff but doesn't know how to win. Nothing has happened since to change that impression. Bergman is young enough to still blossom but time is beginning to run out on him. The Padres may be tiring of his inconsistency.

1997 Season

Doug Bochtler missed two weeks with a leg injury but otherwise was a solid setup man in the Padres' bullpen. He made 54 appearances and was more effective than his ERA would suggest, with opponents batting only .229 against him.

Pitching, Defense & Hitting

Bochtler has an awful-looking delivery and his poor mechanics have contributed to his frequent shoulder troubles. They also have caused him to constantly struggle with his release point, which is a big reason for his horrendous walk totals in 1997. He can throw in the low-90s and his slider is tough on righthanders. He does an adequate job of holding runners and fields his position well. He hasn't had an at-bat in two years.

1998 Outlook

As long as Bochtler struggles with his control, he never will be more than a middle reliever. No team wants its setup man to average nearly a walk per inning or give up more free passes than strikeouts. Still, he has the stuff to be effective and could take on a greater load if he's able to master his control. San Diego inexplicably traded him in a deal for Oakland's Don Wengert after the season.

San Diego Padres

Wil Cunnane

Position: RP/SP
Bats: R **Throws:** R
Ht: 6' 2" **Wt:** 175

Opening Day Age: 23
Born: 4/24/74 in Suffern, NY
ML Seasons: 1

Overall Statistics

	W	L	Pct.	ERA	G	GS	Sv	IP	H	BB	SO	HR	Ratio
1997	6	3	.667	5.81	54	8	0	91.1	114	49	79	11	1.78
Career	6	3	.667	5.81	54	8	0	91.1	114	49	79	11	1.78

1997 Situational Stats

	W	L	ERA	Sv	IP		AB	H	HR	RBI	Avg
Home	2	1	3.63	0	34.2	LHB	164	47	4	26	.287
Road	4	2	7.15	0	56.2	RHB	210	67	7	40	.319
First Half	4	2	6.29	0	58.2	Sc Pos	100	37	3	54	.370
Scnd Half	2	1	4.96	0	32.2	Clutch	25	7	0	3	.280

1997 Season

A major league Rule 5 draftee out of the Marlins' organization, lefthander Wil Cunnane was a useful pickup for the Padres. He was hit hard as a starter, but didn't embarrass himself in the bullpen. He ran out of gas in September, posting a 10.57 ERA in eight appearances.

Pitching, Defense & Hitting

Cunnane doesn't have an overpowering pitch and has to get by with good command and control. His velocity rarely exceeds the mid-80s, but he can be effective when he's hitting his spots with his sinker or changeup. He's something of a nibbler and walks too many hitters for someone with his limited stuff. He has an average lefthander's move to first and fields his position well. Cunnane proved to be an excellent hitter with five hits and four RBI in 14 at-bats in 1997.

1998 Outlook

San Diego thinks Cunnane could have a future as a lefty middle reliever. They likely will have him spend some time in the minors trying to add needed velocity.

Carlos Hernandez

Position: C
Bats: R **Throws:** R
Ht: 5'11" **Wt:** 215

Opening Day Age: 30
Born: 5/24/67 in San Felix, Bolivar, VZ
ML Seasons: 8

Overall Statistics

	G	AB	R	H	D	T	HR	RBI	SB	BB	SO	Avg	OBP	Slg
1997	50	134	15	42	7	1	3	14	0	3	27	.313	.328	.448
Career	284	612	45	151	21	1	12	54	1	26	107	.247	.283	.343

1997 Situational Stats

	AB	H	HR	RBI	Avg		AB	H	HR	RBI	Avg
Home	65	18	2	7	.277	LHP	37	12	1	1	.324
Road	69	24	1	7	.348	RHP	97	30	2	13	.309
First Half	72	21	1	5	.292	Sc Pos	30	9	0	9	.300
Scnd Half	62	21	2	9	.339	Clutch	22	6	0	0	.273

1997 Season

Despite missing a month with a calf strain, Carlos Hernandez had a solid season as the Padres' backup catcher. He had a career-high .313 batting average—raising his career mark to .247—and logged more at-bats than he had since 1992.

Hitting, Baserunning & Defense

Hernandez won't scare anyone with his power, but he occasionally will get a fastball he can pull out of the park. He never has been a good breaking-ball hitter and rarely walks. He showed improvement in hitting more balls where they were pitched, rather than constantly trying to pull the ball. Hernandez doesn't run well, especially after serious back problems a few years ago. He's a solid receiver with a strong arm and a quick release, and he threw out 35 percent of basestealers in 1997.

1998 Outlook

Hernandez is physically able to play only once or twice a week, which means he won't replace the departed John Flaherty as the starter. He's a solid backup who accepts his role and is especially good at shutting down opposing running games. He became a free agent after the season, but the Padres quickly re-signed him.

Paul Menhart

Position: SP
Bats: R **Throws:** R
Ht: 6' 2" **Wt:** 190

Opening Day Age: 29
Born: 3/25/69 in St.
Louis, MO
ML Seasons: 3

Overall Statistics

	W	L	Pct.	ERA	G	GS	Sv	IP	H	BB	SO	HR	Ratio
1997	2	3	.400	4.70	9	8	0	44.0	42	13	22	6	1.25
Career	5	9	.357	5.47	41	23	0	164.2	169	85	90	24	1.54

1997 Situational Stats

	W	L	ERA	Sv	IP			AB	H	HR	RBI	Avg
Home	2	1	4.55	0	27.2	LHB		72	18	1	8	.250
Road	0	2	4.96	0	16.1	RHB		92	24	5	13	.261
First Half	0	0	-	0	0.0	Sc Pos		40	10	0	13	.250
Scnd Half	2	3	4.70	0	44.0	Clutch		1	1	0	0	1.000

1997 Season

Journeyman Paul Menhart was recalled in August despite an undistinguished minor league record. He made eight late-season starts and pitched decently. He averaged around six innings per start and kept his ERA below 5.00, which by Padres standards in 1997 was pretty good.

Pitching, Defense & Hitting

Menhart was once a highly regarded pitching prospect with Toronto before arm troubles sidetracked his career. His velocity now doesn't rise above the mid-80s, so he gets by with a sinker-slider combination. He needs to hit spots and get ahead of hitters to be successful, and he demonstrated surprisingly good control with the Padres. He's a solid fielder who works hard to hold runners. Getting a chance to bat for the first time, Menhart went 0-for-12 with two sacrifices.

1998 Outlook

As a long-relief option, Menhart may have a chance of landing a job. However, it's a reach to expect him to be part of the rotation in San Diego or anywhere else. He likely will remain on the fringes.

Craig Shipley

Position: SS/2B
Bats: R **Throws:** R
Ht: 6' 1" **Wt:** 190

Opening Day Age: 35
Born: 1/7/63 in
Sydney, Australia
ML Seasons: 10

Overall Statistics

	G	AB	R	H	D	T	HR	RBI	SB	BB	SO	Avg	OBP	Slg
1997	63	139	22	38	9	0	5	19	1	7	20	.273	.306	.446
Career	505	1198	137	326	56	5	18	121	33	42	169	.272	.302	.372

1997 Situational Stats

	AB	H	HR	RBI	Avg		AB	H	HR	RBI	Avg
Home	53	17	3	11	.321	LHP	47	12	3	6	.255
Road	86	21	2	8	.244	RHP	92	26	2	13	.283
First Half	33	11	2	4	.333	Sc Pos	42	12	1	14	.286
Scnd Half	106	27	3	15	.255	Clutch	35	8	1	2	.229

1997 Season

Utilityman Craig Shipley spent more than a third of the season on the disabled list with hamstring and hip injuries. He still managed to hit a career-high five homers and finished the season strong by batting .300 in September.

Hitting, Baserunning & Defense

Shipley has underrated strength, especially to right-center, where he deposits breaking balls and fastballs away and up in the strike zone. He has never been a good offspeed hitter but he has made himself effective with his willingness to take pitches up the middle. Shipley is just an average baserunner. He doesn't have a strong defensive position. His range at short is inadequate, his arm at third is subpar and he doesn't have the skills to be more than a stopgap outfielder.

1998 Outlook

There are worse utility players than Shipley, a decent player with some power. He always gives his all, which endears him to managers. However, he was a free agent and teams can find younger and cheaper alternatives.

San Diego
Padres

Pete Smith

Position: RP/SP
Bats: R **Throws:** R
Ht: 6' 2" **Wt:** 200

Opening Day Age: 32
Born: 2/27/66 in
Weymouth, MA
ML Seasons: 10

Overall Statistics

	W	L	Pct.	ERA	G	GS	Sv	IP	H	BB	SO	HR	Ratio
1997	7	6	.538	4.81	37	15	1	118.0	120	52	68	16	1.46
Career	42	66	.389	4.46	194	151	1	937.1	941	370	575	114	1.40

1997 Situational Stats

	W	L	ERA	Sv	IP		AB	H	HR	RBI	Avg
Home	2	3	5.16	0	61.0	LHB	223	60	6	29	.269
Road	5	3	4.42	1	57.0	RHB	226	60	10	31	.265
First Half	2	1	5.70	1	36.1	Sc Pos	111	35	4	44	.315
Scnd Half	5	5	4.41	0	81.2	Clutch	40	13	0	7	.325

1997 Season

Pete Smith was one of the few pleasant surprises on the Padres' pitching staff in 1997. Recalled as bullpen help in early May, he was forced into the rotation in mid-July and proved to be a solid innings-eater over the second half of the season. His seven wins tied his career high.

Pitching, Defense & Hitting

A former first-round draft pick, Smith has pitched for several organizations and worked through several injuries before catching on with San Diego. Formerly a hard thrower, Smith now relies on a decent splitter, a slider and a changeup. He has decent command, though he does run deep counts and walks his share of hitters. He won't give in to hitters when behind in the count. Smith handles himself well in the field and has an average move to first. He can do some damage with the bat when he makes contact.

1998 Outlook

No one expects Smith, a free agent, to suddenly become a big winner. But with so many pitching questions, the Padres likely will look at him as a possible fifth starter, a role that would seem to best fit his ability.

Mark Sweeney

Position: RF/1B/LF
Bats: L **Throws:** L
Ht: 6' 1" **Wt:** 195

Opening Day Age: 28
Born: 10/26/69 in
Framingham, MA
ML Seasons: 3

Overall Statistics

	G	AB	R	H	D	T	HR	RBI	SB	BB	SO	Avg	OBP	Slg
1997	115	164	16	46	7	0	2	23	2	20	32	.280	.358	.360
Career	250	411	53	112	18	0	7	58	6	63	76	.273	.369	.367

1997 Situational Stats

	AB	H	HR	RBI	Avg		AB	H	HR	RBI	Avg
Home	74	19	2	12	.257	LHP	7	2	0	1	.286
Road	90	27	0	11	.300	RHP	157	44	2	22	.280
First Half	80	19	0	6	.238	Sc Pos	55	18	0	19	.327
Scnd Half	84	27	2	17	.321	Clutch	36	15	1	8	.417

1997 Season

Mark Sweeney came to San Diego in the Fernando Valenzuela-Danny Jackson trade with St. Louis in June. He was a sterling bench player for the Padres, leading the majors with 22 pinch hits, including two home runs and 14 RBI. He's a lifetime .348 pinch hitter and is capable of filling in at first base and the outfield corners.

Hitting, Baserunning & Defense

Sweeney has a short, quick stroke that can occasionally turn around fastballs for extra bases. He's aggressive early in the count. He can be enticed to chase breaking balls, but when he has a pitcher in a fastball count he's very dangerous. He rarely is used against lefthanders, but has a .333 career average against southpaws. Sweeney's speed is unremarkable and he's a mediocre basestealer. His best defensive position is first base, where he has good hands and overall skills. He also can play left or right field, but his arm is just adequate.

1998 Outlook

With his outstanding season off the bench, Sweeney may have found his niche as one of baseball's best reserves. He can fill in at a number of positions, and his pinch-hitting ability is invaluable.

George Arias (**Pos**: 3B, **Age**: 26, **Bats**: R)

	G	AB	R	H	D	T	HR	RBI	SB	BB	SO	Avg	OBP	Slg
1997	14	28	3	7	1	0	0	3	0	0	1	.250	.250	.286
Career	98	280	22	67	9	1	6	31	2	16	51	.239	.280	.343

Once the Angels' heir apparent at third base, Arias was dealt to San Diego in mid-August for catcher Angelo Encarnacion. He has some power, but he won't challenge Ken Caminiti for a starting job. 1998 Outlook: C

Richard Batchelor (**Pos**: RHP, **Age**: 30)

	W	L	Pct.	ERA	G	GS	Sv	IP	H	BB	SO	HR	Ratio
1997	3	1	.750	5.97	23	0	0	28.2	40	14	18	2	1.88
Career	5	1	.833	5.03	43	0	0	53.2	63	18	33	3	1.51

Batchelor led the Triple-A American Association in saves in 1996. Traded to the Padres by the Cardinals in June 1997, he lasted a month in San Diego before he was banished to the minors, never to return. He was waived in the offseason and signed with Cleveland. 1998 Outlook: C

Jim Bruske (**Pos**: RHP, **Age**: 33)

	W	L	Pct.	ERA	G	GS	Sv	IP	H	BB	SO	HR	Ratio
1997	4	1	.800	3.63	28	0	0	44.2	37	25	32	4	1.39
Career	4	1	.800	4.14	48	0	1	67.1	66	32	49	6	1.46

Promoted in late June, Bruske pitched well in middle relief. The only downside was a three-week stint on the disabled list with biceps tendinitis. The Dodgers claimed him on waivers after the season. 1998 Outlook: B

Terry Burrows (**Pos**: LHP, **Age**: 29)

	W	L	Pct.	ERA	G	GS	Sv	IP	H	BB	SO	HR	Ratio
1997	0	2	.000	10.45	13	0	0	10.1	12	8	8	1	1.94
Career	4	4	.500	6.42	50	3	1	68.2	85	38	35	15	1.79

Among San Diego's last cuts in spring training, Burrows spent a month in the majors between May and June. Lefties hit .692 off him, and with a career ERA of 6.42, he's running out of chances. 1998 Outlook: C

Danny Jackson (**Pos**: LHP, **Age**: 36)

	W	L	Pct.	ERA	G	GS	Sv	IP	H	BB	SO	HR	Ratio
1997	2	9	.182	7.58	17	13	0	67.2	98	28	32	11	1.86
Career	112	131	.461	4.01	353	324	1	2072.2	2110	816	1225	133	1.41

Jackson began the season on the disabled list with the Cardinals, then was traded to San Diego in mid-June as part of the Fernando Valenzuela blockbuster. Two months later, he retired. 1998 Outlook: D

Joey Long (**Pos**: LHP, **Age**: 27)

	W	L	Pct.	ERA	G	GS	Sv	IP	H	BB	SO	HR	Ratio
1997	0	0	-	8.18	10	0	0	11.0	17	8	8	1	2.27
Career	0	0	-	8.18	10	0	0	11.0	17	8	8	1	2.27

Long was recalled in late April when fellow reliever Dario Veras went on the disabled list. Long didn't impress the Padres, who demoted him a month later and removed him from the 40-man roster in October. 1998 Outlook: C

Mandy Romero (**Pos**: C, **Age**: 30, **Bats**: B)

	G	AB	R	H	D	T	HR	RBI	SB	BB	SO	Avg	OBP	Slg
1997	21	48	7	10	0	0	2	4	1	2	18	.208	.240	.333
Career	21	48	7	10	0	0	2	4	1	2	18	.208	.240	.333

In his 10th pro season, Romero finally made the majors when backup catcher Carlos Hernandez went on the disabled list. Romero homered in front of his hometown Florida fans, the highlight of his career. 1998 Outlook: C

Terry Shumpert (**Pos**: 2B, **Age**: 31, **Bats**: R)

	G	AB	R	H	D	T	HR	RBI	SB	BB	SO	Avg	OBP	Slg
1997	13	33	4	9	3	0	1	6	0	3	4	.273	.324	.455
Career	345	858	101	191	40	8	17	92	44	59	178	.223	.276	.347

Shumpert got his yearly allotment of 30 or so at-bats, though he didn't return to San Diego after he was demoted May 27. He can run a little and play several positions, so he'll probably surface again. 1998 Outlook: C

Don Slaught (**Pos**: C, **Age**: 39, **Bats**: R)

	G	AB	R	H	D	T	HR	RBI	SB	BB	SO	Avg	OBP	Slg
1997	20	20	2	0	0	0	0	0	0	5	4	.000	.200	.000
Career	1327	4063	415	1151	235	28	77	476	18	311	559	.283	.338	.412

Sluggo made the Padres as a nonroster player, then earned his release by May 20. A very useful backup in 1996, he went 0-for-20 last season. At 39, he's probably done. 1998 Outlook: D

Jorge Velandia (**Pos**: SS, **Age**: 23, **Bats**: R)

	G	AB	R	H	D	T	HR	RBI	SB	BB	SO	Avg	OBP	Slg
1997	14	29	0	3	2	0	0	0	0	1	7	.103	.133	.172
Career	14	29	0	3	2	0	0	0	0	1	7	.103	.133	.172

While the Padres were waiting for Craig Shipley to get healthy, they gave Velandia a two-week trial. He has a slick glove but an incredibly weak bat, and was traded to Oakland. 1998 Outlook: C

Dario Veras (**Pos**: RHP, **Age:** 25)

	W	L	Pct.	ERA	G	GS	Sv	IP	H	BB	SO	HR	Ratio
1997	2	1	.667	5.11	23	0	0	24.2	28	12	21	5	1.62
Career	5	2	.714	3.86	46	0	0	53.2	52	22	44	8	1.38

After showing promise as a middle reliever in 1996, Veras missed much of the 1997 season with shoulder troubles. He ended up making only 23 appearances, though his work in August and September was encouraging. 1998 Outlook: B

San Diego Padres

San Diego Padres Minor League Prospects

Organization Overview:

If the Padres hadn't decided to reverse course since their fire sale of 1993, they might have become baseball's worst team. That's because they haven't produced much talent as of late. The only homegrown players who were major factors in the lineup last year were Tony Gwynn and Joey Hamilton. The system is rebounding thanks to a series of strong drafts, the first few of which earned scouting director Kevin Towers a promotion to GM. San Diego has four of the game's best advanced prospects in righthander Matt Clement, first baseman Derrek Lee, righthander Rafael Medina and outfielder Ruben Rivera. The latter two came in the Hideki Irabu trade with the Yankees, which looks incredibly one-sided in the Padres' favor.

Matt Clement

Position: P
Opening Day Age: 23
Bats: R **Throws:** R
Born: 8/12/74 in Pittsburgh, PA
Ht: 6' 3" **Wt:** 190

Recent Statistics

	W	L	ERA	G	GS	Sv	IP	H	R	BB	SO	HR
96 A Clinton	8	3	2.80	16	16	0	96.1	66	31	52	109	3
96 A Rancho Cuca	4	5	5.59	11	11	0	56.1	61	40	26	75	8
97 A Rancho Cuca	6	3	1.60	14	14	0	101.0	84	30	31	109	3
97 AA Mobile	6	5	2.56	13	13	0	88.0	83	37	32	92	4

Clement is one of the biggest breakthrough prospects of the 1997 season. A third-round pick four years earlier, he struck out 201 in 189 innings and pitched very well after a promotion to Double-A. He throws a sinking fastball at 92 MPH, and it gives righthanders a lot of difficulty because it tails away from them. He also has a hard, late-breaking slider, and could get even better if he develops a changeup to fill his need for an offspeed pitch. His command had been erratic in the past but got better in 1997, allowing him to work both sides of the plate effectively. He's at least a year away from San Diego, but looks like the best Padres-developed pitcher since Hamilton.

Ben Davis

Position: C
Opening Day Age: 21
Bats: B **Throws:** R
Born: 3/10/77 in Chester, PA
Ht: 6' 4" **Wt:** 205

Recent Statistics

	G	AB	R	H	D	T	HR	RBI	SB	BB	SO	AVG
96 A Rancho Cuca	98	353	35	71	10	1	6	41	1	31	89	.201
97 A Rancho Cuca	122	474	67	132	30	1	17	76	3	28	107	.278

High school catchers drafted in the first round usually fail miserably, and Davis seemed headed down that path when he hit .201 in high Class-A in 1996. He was in over his head as a 19-year-old, and also was bothered by elbow tendinitis. The No. 2 overall pick in the 1995 draft, he rebounded last season. He began to make adjustments to breaking pitches and raised his average 77 points at the same level. He nearly tripled his homer output, though he could use better plate discipline. Always considered a defensive standout, he showed dazzling arm strength and sharp receiving skills. He even runs well for a catcher. He'll go to Double-A in 1998 and is on course to reach the majors at age 23.

Marc Kroon

Position: P
Opening Day Age: 24
Bats: B **Throws:** R
Born: 4/2/73 in Bronx, NY
Ht: 6' 2" **Wt:** 175

Recent Statistics

	W	L	ERA	G	GS	Sv	IP	H	R	BB	SO	HR
97 AAA Las Vegas	1	3	4.54	46	0	15	41.2	34	22	22	53	5
97 NL San Diego	0	1	7.15	12	0	0	11.1	14	9	5	12	2

Few minor leaguers throw harder than Kroon, part of an otherwise forgettable Mets-Padres trade involving five minor leaguers in December 1993. A supplemental second-round pick in 1991, he never really blossomed until the Padres moved him to the bullpen full-time in 1996. The role suited him perfectly, because he has a consistent 93-95 MPH fastball that can hit 97-98, as well as a hard slider. His control was inconsistent and he never mastered a changeup, flaws that aren't as glaring in the bullpen. He's working on a splitter to give him some semblance of an offspeed pitch. He won't supplant Hoffman, but Kroon has a power arm and could be an efficient setup man. He'll get the chance in 1998.

Derrek Lee

Position: 1B
Opening Day Age: 22
Bats: R **Throws:** R
Born: 9/6/75 in Sacramento, CA
Ht: 6' 5" **Wt:** 220

Recent Statistics

	G	AB	R	H	D	T	HR	RBI	SB	BB	SO	AVG
97 AAA Las Vegas	125	472	86	153	29	2	13	64	17	60	116	.324
97 NL San Diego	22	54	9	14	3	0	1	4	0	9	24	.259
97 MLE	125	449	65	130	23	1	11	48	11	44	120	.290

Outside of getting a taste of the big leagues when Wally Joyner went on the disabled list, Lee had a disappointing season. Disappointing for a 1993 first-round pick and 1996 Southern League MVP. Despite playing at hitter-friendly Las Vegas in the hitter-friendly Pacific Coast League, he dropped from 34 to 13 homers. He was getting out in front of too many pitches before he corrected the flaw in August, though he did make much better contact than he had previously. He did hit .324 and showed some basestealing ability, and would be a good first baseman if he could cure his penchant for nonchalance. Joyner had his option picked up and will spend another year at first base for San Diego, but Lee should be starting for the Padres in 1999.

Rafael Medina

Position: P   **Opening Day Age:** 23
Bats: R **Throws:** R   **Born:** 2/15/75 in
Ht: 6' 3" **Wt:** 194   Panama City, Panama

Recent Statistics

	W	L	ERA	G	GS	Sv	IP	H	R	BB	SO	HR
96 AA Norwich	5	8	3.06	19	19	0	103.0	78	48	55	112	7
97 A Rancho Cuca	2	0	2.00	3	3	0	18.0	13	4	5	14	1
97 AAA Las Vegas	4	5	7.56	13	13	0	66.2	90	60	39	50	12

Adding Medina alone for Irabu would have worked out well for the Padres, who also got Rivera and cash. Medina was shelled in Triple-A during the season, but he excelled in the Arizona Fall League afterward. He has an easy delivery, a consistent 95-MPH fastball and a hard slurve, and fits right in with San Diego's corps of young power pitchers. Signed out of Panama by the Yankees, his two biggest needs are developing an off-speed pitch and controlling his weight. If he can do both, he could become a frontline starter.

Juan Melo

Position: SS   **Opening Day Age:** 21
Bats: B **Throws:** R   **Born:** 11/5/76 in Bani,
Ht: 6' 3" **Wt:** 185   DR

Recent Statistics

	G	AB	R	H	D	T	HR	RBI	SB	BB	SO	AVG
96 A Rancho Cuca	128	503	75	153	27	6	8	75	6	22	102	.304
97 AAA Las Vegas	12	48	6	13	4	0	1	6	0	1	10	.271
97 AA Mobile	113	456	52	131	22	2	7	67	7	29	90	.287
97 MLE	125	479	42	119	20	1	5	53	4	17	104	.248

The son of the Padres' Dominican scout of the same name, Melo is an all-around shortstop who should be able to take Chris Gomez' job in the next few years. A switch-hitter, Melo should develop decent power from both sides of the plate once he fills out. He'll also be better once he stops chasing pitches out of the strike zone. An average runner with good range, he has a cannon arm that makes him an above-average shortstop. He'll get a full season in Triple-A at age 22, then may be ready to put the heat on Gomez.

Heath Murray

Position: P   **Opening Day Age:** 24
Bats: L **Throws:** L   **Born:** 4/19/73 in Troy,
Ht: 6' 4" **Wt:** 205   OH

Recent Statistics

	W	L	ERA	G	GS	Sv	IP	H	R	BB	SO	HR
97 AAA Las Vegas	6	8	5.45	19	19	0	109.0	142	72	41	99	10
97 NL San Diego	1	2	6.75	17	3	0	33.1	50	25	21	16	3

Will the real Heath Murray please stand up? After a fine Double-A season in 1996, he was shelled in Triple-A and the majors last year. A 1994 third-round pick out of the University of Michigan, he uses four pitches and relies on location to succeed. When he left his fastball high in the strike zone and started missing the corners of the plate, he got pounded. He has below-average velocity, but his cut fastball and curveball are effective and he uses his changeup as an out pitch. He'll get another shot at Triple-A this year and will have to prove he can remain a starter at the game's higher levels. Otherwise he'll become a middle reliever.

Ruben Rivera

Position: DH   **Opening Day Age:** 24
Bats: R **Throws:** R   **Born:** 11/14/73 in
Ht: 6' 3" **Wt:** 190   Chorrera, Panama

Recent Statistics

	G	AB	R	H	D	T	HR	RBI	SB	BB	SO	AVG
97 A Rancho Cuca	6	23	6	4	1	0	1	3	1	3	9	.174
97 AAA Las Vegas	12	48	6	12	5	1	1	6	1	1	20	.250
97 NL San Diego	17	20	2	5	1	0	0	1	2	2	9	.250

Rivera has been considered one of baseball's top prospects since 1994, but the Yankees parted with him to get Irabu. Signed out of Panama, Rivera has been hampered in the past two years by shoulder problems and a questionable attitude that soured when he felt New York demoted him unfairly. His shoulder limited him to 35 games in 1997, but he still showed plenty of tools. His combination of power and speed make him a 30-30 man just waiting to happen, and he was considered a better defensive center fielder than former teammate Bernie Williams. He's not the most selective hitter, but at 24 he has time to work on patience. The brother of Yankees closer Mariano Rivera should be starting for the Padres by midseason at the latest.

Others to Watch

Outfielder **Mike Darr** was a revelation after coming from Detroit in the Jody Reed trade. He batted .344-15-94 with 23 stolen bases in high Class-A ball at age 21, showing plenty of polish and a good right-field arm. . . **Aaron Guiel** was another outfielder acquired in 1997 by the Padres, who got him from Anaheim for catcher Angelo Encarnacion. Guiel hit .333-23-94 in Double-A at age 24 and continued to hit doubles and draw walks as well. . . Righthander **Rodrigo Lopez** might bear watching. He had 123 strikeouts in 121⅔ innings at Class-A Clinton at age 21. . . Righthander **Jason Middlebrook**, 22, is a possible coup. Once touted as the possible No. 1 pick in the 1996 draft, he slid to the ninth round because of elbow problems. San Diego gambled and signed him for $750,000, and his fastball is back up to 94 MPH and his curveball also looks strong. . . Second baseman **David Newhan**, acquired in the trade that sent Doug Bochtler to Oakland, is a fairly polished hitter. He hits for average and draws walks, and he also has good plate discipline.

Dusty Baker

1997 Season

Dusty Baker was an easy choice for National League Manager of the Year. While incorporating a constant parade of new faces, Baker got the Giants out of the gate quickly in April and never looked back. Leaning heavily on his bullpen, Baker took San Francisco to an eight-game lead in the NL West. After getting caught and passed by the Dodgers, Baker kept the Giants emotionally involved and they were able to regain the lead and win the division.

Offense

With his improved starting pitching, Baker often utilized one-run strategies early in a game, bunting with anyone in the lineup except for Barry Bonds and Jeff Kent. He always has liked to put his runners in motion and will use the hit-and-run with virtually any combination of players. Baker doesn't hesitate to employ platoons. By midseason in 1997, he was alternating players at both third base and right field.

Pitching & Defense

If there's one criticism of Baker, it's that he'll ride his bullpen hard. Four of his relievers last year had more than 70 appearances and a fifth had 63. The Giants tied the Athletics for the most relief appearances in the majors in 1997. He uses the pitchout as much as any manager in the National League, and he's also not afraid to issue an intentional walk. He demands versatility out of his bench.

1998 Outlook

Baker has had success relating with veterans and showing patience with youngsters. With the Giants likely to experience another sizeable turnover in their roster, his flexibility and the respect he commands should become even more valuable to the organization. He and GM Brian Sabean aren't always on the same wavelength but work well together. Baker has become firmly established not only as San Francisco's leader but also as one of the NL's most solid managers.

Born: 6/15/49 in Riverside, CA

Playing Experience: 1968-1986, Atl, LA, SF, Oak

Managerial Experience: 5 seasons

Manager Statistics

Year	Team, Lg	W	L	Pct	GB	Finish
1997	San Francisco, NL	90	72	.556	—	1st West
5 Seasons		383	362	.514	—	—

1997 Starting Pitchers by Days Rest

	≤3	4	5	6+
Giants Starts	2	84	38	30
Giants ERA	5.87	4.39	3.67	4.64
NL Avg Starts	3	90	38	22
NL ERA	4.23	4.05	4.27	4.52

1997 Situational Stats

	Dusty Baker	NL Average
Hit & Run Success %	36.4	36.4
Stolen Base Success %	71.2	68.4
Platoon Pct.	70.7	56.3
Defensive Subs	22	26
High-Pitch Outings	17	12
Quick/Slow Hooks	20/3	18/10
Sacrifice Attempts	84	96

1997 Rankings (National League)

⇒ 1st in least caught steals of second base (40) and relief appearances (481)

⇒ 2nd in least caught steals of third base (4), pitchouts (93), mid-inning pitching changes (203), first batter platoon percentage (63.2%) and one-batter pitcher appearances (36)

⇒ 3rd in stolen base percentage (71.2%), hit-and-run attempts (143), pitchouts with a runner moving (21), intentional walks (37), quick hooks (20) and 2+ pitching changes in low scoring games (30)

Rod Beck

1997 Season

After a fast start that included 11 saves in April, Rod Beck struggled so much during the second half that he often was booed at 3Com Park. The bottom line was that he turned in one of his best seasons, one that included a career high in wins and the second-best save total in the National League. His high point came during a September 18 game against Los Angeles, when he escaped a bases-loaded, none-out jam and went on to pitch three scoreless innings for a critical extra-inning win.

Pitching

Beck's velocity has been slipping for several years and so have his strikeout numbers. He continues to remain effective by utilizing his other weapons: a good splitter, a curve which he throws at varying speeds, excellent control and outstanding competitiveness. Beck might get defeated, but he never carries a loss into his next game. His increased reliance on his curve has resulted in more homers allowed. He typically is much tougher on lefthanders. Batters had success when they put Beck's first pitch in play, batting .366 in 1997, but hit just .228 otherwise.

Defense & Hitting

Despite his lumbering appearance, Beck does an adequate job of fielding his position. He has no real move to first and is slow to the plate, so he can be run on. Basestealers were perfect in three attempts against him in 1997. He didn't get an at-bat last season but is a career .235 hitter.

1998 Outlook

Beck and co-closer Roberto Hernandez became free agents after the season, and the Giants decided to go in a different direction by trading prospects to the Marlins for Robb Nen. Beck is something of a risk because of his suspect conditioning and dwindling velocity, though he has been a big part of San Francisco's success.

Position: RP
Bats: R **Throws:** R
Ht: 6' 1" **Wt:** 236

Opening Day Age: 29
Born: 8/3/68 in Burbank, CA
ML Seasons: 7

Overall Statistics

	W	L	Pct.	ERA	G	GS	Sv	IP	H	BB	SO	HR	Ratio
1997	7	4	.636	3.47	73	0	37	70.0	67	8	53	7	1.07
Career	21	28	.429	2.97	416	0	199	463.0	404	93	393	52	1.07

How Often He Throws Strikes

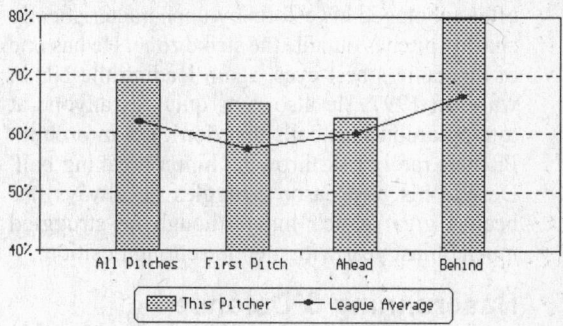

1997 Situational Stats

	W	L	ERA	Sv	IP		AB	H	HR	RBI	Avg
Home	4	1	2.72	21	39.2	LHB	137	32	2	14	.234
Road	3	3	4.45	16	30.1	RHB	132	35	5	19	.265
First Half	4	2	2.43	29	37.0	Sc Pos	56	18	2	27	.321
Scnd Half	3	2	4.64	8	33.0	Clutch	169	43	4	24	.254

1997 Rankings (National League)

⇒ 1st in games finished (66)
⇒ 2nd in saves and save opportunities (45)
⇒ 3rd in blown saves (8) and relief wins (7)
⇒ 5th in least baserunners allowed per 9 innings in relief (9.9)
⇒ 6th in lowest save percentage (82.2%)
⇒ Led the Giants in saves, games finished (66), save opportunities (45), save percentage (82.2%), blown saves (8), relief wins (7), lowest batting average allowed in relief (.249) and least baserunners allowed per 9 innings in relief (9.9)

Barry Bonds

Gold Glover

1997 Season

The general consensus was that 1997 was an off year for Barry Bonds. Most players would be happy to have such a disappointing season. Bonds topped 100 RBI for the seventh time in his career and had his fifth 40-30 year in home runs and steals. He produced when it mattered, hitting seven homers and racking up 11 RBI in the Giants' last 11 games as they clinched the National League West. He also won his seventh Gold Glove.

Hitting

For the first time in a while, teams had success when they attacked Bonds with hard stuff on the inside part of the plate. During his slow start, he often sabotaged his efforts by uncharacteristically chasing pitches outside the strike zone. He has one of the game's best eyes, again leading the NL in walks in 1997. He also is as quick as anyone at turning around fastballs that don't get in on him. Pitchers rarely risk throwing him a breaking ball. Despite his postseason struggles he always has been a great clutch hitter, though he struggled much of last year with men in scoring position.

Baserunning & Defense

If he wanted to concentrate on stealing bases, Bonds could probably swipe 50 a year without a problem. However, he picks his spots, resulting in fewer steals but a high success rate. In 1997, he was caught only eight times in 45 attempts. When he's at the top of his game, Bonds is one of the best left fielders in history. He has exceptional range and an accurate arm.

1998 Outlook

Too much has been made of Bonds' mercurial personality rather than his remarkable ability. He has settled into San Francisco as a franchise player. Barring major injury, he should have several superstar seasons remaining, and he probably already has clinched future induction in the Hall of Fame.

Position: LF
Bats: L **Throws:** L
Ht: 6' 1" **Wt:** 190

Opening Day Age: 33
Born: 7/24/64 in Riverside, CA
ML Seasons: 12

Overall Statistics

	G	AB	R	H	D	T	HR	RBI	SB	BB	SO	Avg	OBP	Slg
1997	159	532	123	155	26	5	40	101	37	145	87	.291	.446	.585
Career	1742	6069	1244	1750	359	56	374	1094	417	1227	958	.288	.408	.551

Where He Hits the Ball

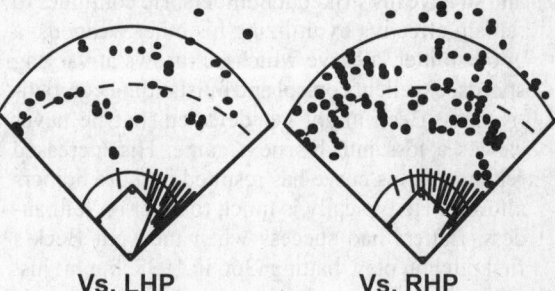

Vs. LHP   Vs. RHP

1997 Situational Stats

	AB	H	HR	RBI	Avg		AB	H	HR	RBI	Avg
Home	264	86	24	61	.326	LHP	166	49	11	26	.295
Road	268	69	16	40	.257	RHP	366	106	29	75	.290
First Half	287	79	20	46	.275	Sc Pos	135	33	7	57	.244
Scnd Half	245	76	20	55	.310	Clutch	81	27	3	11	.333

1997 Rankings (National League)

⇒ 1st in walks, intentional walks (34) and cleanup slugging percentage (.579)
⇒ 2nd in times on base (308), on-base percentage and on-base percentage vs. righthanded pitchers (.455)
⇒ 3rd in runs scored, HR frequency (13.3 ABs per HR) and lowest groundball/flyball ratio (0.8)
⇒ 4th in home runs and errors in left field (5)
⇒ 5th in stolen base percentage (82.2%), slugging percentage vs. lefthanded pitchers (.584) and lowest fielding percentage in left field (.984)
⇒ 6th in stolen bases, games played (159), slugging percentage, slugging percentage vs. righthanded pitchers (.585), on-base percentage vs. lefthanded pitchers (.427) and highest percentage of pitches taken (62.4%)

Shawn Estes

1997 Season

In his first full major league season, Shawn Estes emerged as one of the major leagues' top pitchers. He made the All-Star team and had 19 victories to become San Francisco's winningest lefthander in more than two decades. He went 4-0 in April, June and August. The only blemish on his season was a bout of late-season shoulder stiffness that caused him to miss a September start.

Pitching

Few young lefties have come along recently with nastier stuff than Estes. He throws his fastball in the mid-90s and can make it sink away from righthanders or run away from lefties. He also fires a very hard, sharp-breaking curveball, with which he generates most of his strikeouts. He occasionally will offer a changeup, but it's his least-developed pitch. The one problem Estes has is control. He not only walked a National League-high 100 batters but also ran very deep counts, which inflated his pitch totals and curtailed his ability to hurl complete games. That may have worn him out in the second half, when his ERA rose to 4.01 from 2.51 in the first half. He was very tough on righties.

Defense & Hitting

Estes does an excellent job of holding runners. With his solid pickoff move, he largely negates the running game. He gave up just eight steals in 20 attempts in 1997. A good athlete, Estes usually puts himself into good fielding position. He can handle the bat effectively and slammed a homer for his first hit last season.

1998 Outlook

The sky seems to be the limit for Estes, provided he avoids the injuries that plagued him early in his career. He needs to pay attention to conditioning, which has the Giants somewhat concerned. Barring any setbacks, he'll be San Francisco's ace for years to come.

Position: SP
Bats: R **Throws:** L
Ht: 6' 2" **Wt:** 185

Opening Day Age: 25
Born: 2/18/73 in San Bernardino, CA
ML Seasons: 3
Pronunciation: EST-us

Overall Statistics

	W	L	Pct.	ERA	G	GS	Sv	IP	H	BB	SO	HR	Ratio
1997	19	5	.792	3.18	32	32	0	201.0	162	100	181	12	1.30
Career	22	13	.629	3.50	46	46	0	288.1	241	144	255	17	1.34

How Often He Throws Strikes

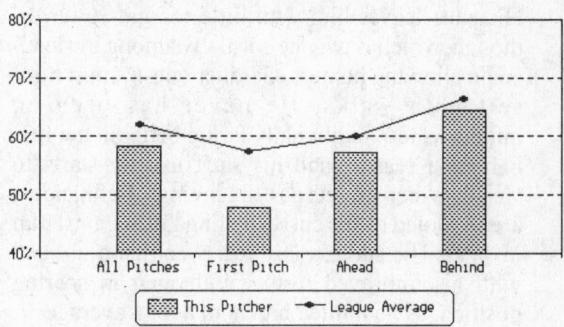

Legend: ▨ This Pitcher — ◆ League Average

1997 Situational Stats

	W	L	ERA	Sv	IP		AB	H	HR	RBI	Avg
Home	11	1	2.33	0	104.1	LHB	161	39	1	20	.242
Road	8	4	4.10	0	96.2	RHB	565	123	11	46	.218
First Half	12	2	2.51	0	111.1	Sc Pos	167	38	3	50	.228
Scnd Half	7	3	4.01	0	89.2	Clutch	49	7	0	2	.143

1997 Rankings (National League)

⇒ 1st in walks allowed
⇒ 2nd in wins and most run support per 9 innings (6.0)
⇒ 3rd in wild pitches (10), winning percentage, lowest batting average allowed (.223), lowest slugging percentage allowed (.311) and most pitches thrown per batter (3.96)
⇒ 4th in runners caught stealing (12)
⇒ 5th in shutouts (2), least home runs allowed per 9 innings (.54) and ERA at home
⇒ 6th in most strikeouts per 9 innings (8.1)
⇒ 7th in lowest strikeout/walk ratio (1.8) and lowest stolen base percentage allowed (40.0%)
⇒ 8th in strikeouts and balks (2)
⇒ 9th in pitches thrown (3,365)

Mark Gardner

Position: SP
Bats: R **Throws:** R
Ht: 6' 1" **Wt:** 205

Opening Day Age: 36
Born: 3/1/62 in Los Angeles, CA
ML Seasons: 9

1997 Season

Over the season's first half, Mark Gardner was as valuable as any Giants pitcher. Through July, he had a 11-4 record that included a six-game winning streak. But Gardner wore down later in the season because of arm fatigue. He also had to struggle with his wife's serious illness, which forced him to the sidelines after September 13. He still managed career highs in starts, wins and innings.

Pitching

Gardner is at his best when he's hitting his spots with his outstanding curveball, setting up a mid-80s fastball that he can throw inside effectively. His stuff leaves him with little margin for error, though, which is why he's usually among the leaders in allowing homers. Gardner doesn't hurt himself with walks. He never has been an innings-eater, traditionally faring better in the first half of a season, and his stuff usually starts to weaken when he gets past six innings. Lefthanders aren't fooled by his curve, batting .305 against him in 1997. His success last year went hand in hand with his improved results with men in scoring position, as he limited hitters to a .234 average.

Defense & Hitting

Gardner throws a lot of breaking balls and is fairly slow to the plate, but he keeps basestealers honest. They were caught in half of their 32 attempts against him in 1997. He's a solid fielder who doesn't get rattled when he needs to make a play. Gardner will get a few occasional hits by accident, but he's little threat at all as a hitter.

1998 Outlook

With their staff overflowing with free agents, the Giants elected to pick up their option on Gardner for 1998. If he's able to stay as a third or fourth starter and if his workload is monitored, he should be able to win 12-15 games.

Overall Statistics

	W	L	Pct.	ERA	G	GS	Sv	IP	H	BB	SO	HR	Ratio
1997	12	9	.571	4.29	30	30	0	180.1	188	57	136	28	1.36
Career	65	64	.504	4.37	230	186	1	1173.0	1159	430	874	148	1.35

How Often He Throws Strikes

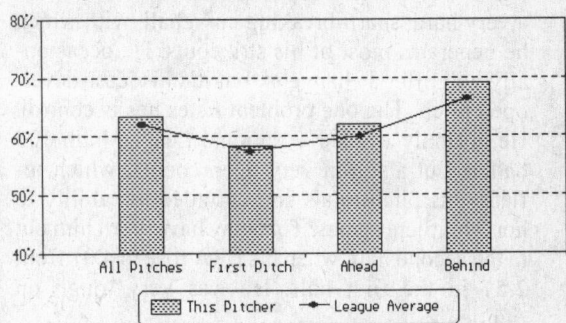

1997 Situational Stats

	W	L	ERA	Sv	IP		AB	H	HR	RBI	Avg
Home	6	4	4.19	0	96.2	LHB	334	102	13	38	.305
Road	6	5	4.41	0	83.2	RHB	356	86	15	44	.242
First Half	9	4	3.73	0	111.0	Sc Pos	141	33	6	51	.234
Scnd Half	3	5	5.19	0	69.1	Clutch	51	16	4	6	.314

1997 Rankings (National League)

⇒ 1st in pickoff throws (220), fielding percentage at pitcher (1.000) and runners caught stealing (16)

⇒ 2nd in home runs allowed, balks (3) and most home runs allowed per 9 innings (1.40)

⇒ 3rd in least GDPs induced per 9 innings (0.4)

⇒ 4th in lowest groundball/flyball ratio allowed (1.0)

⇒ 5th in highest slugging percentage allowed (.449) and most pitches thrown per batter (3.93)

⇒ Led the Giants in losses, home runs allowed, balks (3), pickoff throws (220), runners caught stealing (16), highest strikeout/walk ratio (2.4) and lowest batting average allowed vs. lefthanded batters

Darryl Hamilton

1997 Season

Limited by a thumb injury early in the season, Darryl Hamilton came on to be a key player for the Giants in the second half. He hit .346 in July, including a 14-game hitting streak, and was one of San Francisco's big guns in their final-week drive to the National League West title. He scored 11 runs and drove in eight in the final nine games.

Hitting

Hamilton isn't a prototypical leadoff hitter because he doesn't work many walks. He can be counted on to consistently put the ball into play. If a fastball is left down and in, he can surprise with some power to right field and extra-base pop to the alleys. Hamilton is also a solid hitter in the clutch, hitting .320 with men in scoring position in 1997. He is also a threat to push a bunt up the third-base side if the defense gives it to him.

Baserunning & Defense

Considered a big-time stolen-base threat after a 41-steal season for Milwaukee in 1992, Hamilton has been limited by frequent hamstring injuries. He remains a decent basestealer, though he tends to use bad judgment in deciding when to run. As a center fielder, Hamilton has few peers. He had a 204-game errorless streak snapped last June when he misplayed a ball against Anaheim. Hamilton is aggressive on balls hit in front of him. His arm is below average but he compensates by getting to balls quickly.

1998 Outlook

There are better leadoff hitters in baseball than Hamilton and the Giants had hoped for more consistent offensive production. However, he's a solid defensive player and a career .288 hitter. San Francisco will have to accept that he's more of a complement than a catalyst, because he has another year on his contract.

Position: CF
Bats: L **Throws:** R
Ht: 6' 1" **Wt:** 185

Opening Day Age: 33
Born: 12/3/64 in Baton Rouge, LA
ML Seasons: 9

Overall Statistics

	G	AB	R	H	D	T	HR	RBI	SB	BB	SO	Avg	OBP	Slg
1997	125	460	78	124	23	3	5	43	15	61	61	.270	.354	.365
Career	939	3280	495	945	146	28	34	347	139	321	342	.288	.351	.381

Where He Hits the Ball

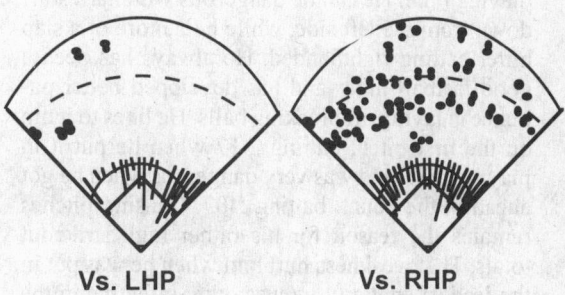

Vs. LHP   **Vs. RHP**

1997 Situational Stats

	AB	H	HR	RBI	Avg		AB	H	HR	RBI	Avg
Home	203	51	1	14	.251	LHP	104	26	1	12	.250
Road	257	73	4	29	.284	RHP	356	98	4	31	.275
First Half	214	59	2	18	.276	Sc Pos	100	32	2	37	.320
Scnd Half	246	65	3	25	.264	Clutch	68	20	1	10	.294

1997 Rankings (National League)

⇒ 3rd in lowest stolen base percentage (60.0%) and errors in center field (5)
⇒ 4th in lowest fielding percentage in center field (.980) and lowest percentage of swings on the first pitch (16.1%)
⇒ 5th in most pitches seen per plate appearance (4.02)
⇒ Led the Giants in caught stealing (10), most pitches seen per plate appearance (4.02), batting average with runners in scoring position, on-base percentage for a leadoff hitter (.350), batting average with two strikes (.238), lowest percentage of swings that missed (9.6%), highest percentage of swings put into play (48.4%) and lowest percentage of swings on the first pitch (16.1%)

S. F. Giants

Stan Javier

1997 Season

After losing his center-field job to free-agent signee Darryl Hamilton, Stan Javier ended up playing himself into regular duty as part of a platoon in right. He went on to have one of the best seasons of his career, setting career highs in a number of categories, including games, hits and walks. He also helped the Giants down the stretch, emerging from a long August slump to hit .310 in September.

Hitting

The switch-hitting Javier is a much more effective hitter from the left side, where most of his power is generated and where he gets the majority of his playing time. He can be dangerous with hard stuff down from the left side, while he's more of a slap hitter batting righthanded. He always has been a good fastball hitter and has developed better patience in laying off breaking balls. He likes to jump on the first pitch, batting .317 when he put it in play in 1997, and was very dangerous when he got ahead in the count, batting .407. Chasing pitches remains the reason for his rather high strikeout totals. That weakness hurt him when he was put in the leadoff spot, but he was quite effective in the No. 6 hole.

Baserunning & Defense

Many players have better speed than Javier, but few are better runners. He's one of baseball's best percentage basestealers, successfully swiping 25 in only 28 attempts in 1997. Javier is as sure-handed as any outfielder and his range is more than adequate. But he's playing out of position when he's in right field, where his mediocre arm is exposed.

1998 Outlook

One of the Giants' many free agents, Javier re-signed for two years. He's one of manager Dusty Baker's favorites, a veteran role player capable of productive offensive streaks. He's also a solid defensive player.

Position: RF/CF
Bats: B **Throws:** R
Ht: 6' 0" **Wt:** 185

Opening Day Age: 34
Born: 1/9/64 in San Francisco de Macoris, DR
ML Seasons: 13
Pronunciation: HAH-vee-air

Overall Statistics

	G	AB	R	H	D	T	HR	RBI	SB	BB	SO	Avg	OBP	Slg
1997	142	440	69	126	16	4	8	50	25	56	70	.286	.368	.395
Career	1302	3610	552	948	161	27	41	347	194	397	602	.263	.337	.356

Where He Hits the Ball

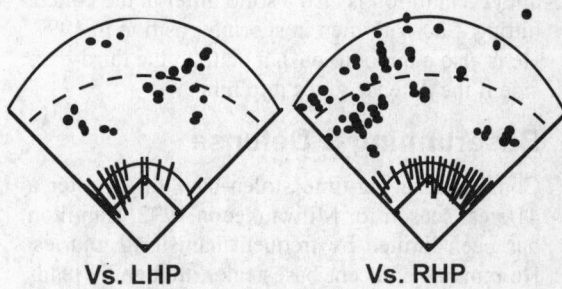

Vs. LHP   **Vs. RHP**

1997 Situational Stats

	AB	H	HR	RBI	Avg		AB	H	HR	RBI	Avg
Home	220	67	6	27	.305	LHP	135	34	2	10	.252
Road	220	59	2	23	.268	RHP	305	92	6	40	.302
First Half	209	65	5	22	.311	Sc Pos	102	28	2	41	.275
Scnd Half	231	61	3	28	.264	Clutch	77	23	1	15	.299

1997 Rankings (National League)

⇒ 2nd in stolen base percentage (89.3%)

⇒ 8th in lowest slugging percentage vs. lefthanded pitchers (.341) and steals of third (6)

⇒ Led the Giants in stolen base percentage (89.3%), least GDPs per GDP situation (6.0%), steals of third (6) and highest percentage of extra bases taken as a runner (61.0%)

Brian Johnson

1997 Season

Every pennant race has its share of heroes, and one of San Francisco's biggest was Brian Johnson. Acquired from Detroit on July 16 for backup catcher Marcus Jensen, Johnson hit two of the season's biggest home runs. He smacked an extra-inning blast to beat the Dodgers on September 18 and put the Giants into first place in the National League West, then rapped a ninth-inning game-winner a week later against Colorado. He became San Francisco's regular catcher and hit .279 after the trade.

Hitting

Johnson has the power to hit 15-plus homers a year. As he has gained more experience, he has learned not to swing for the fences. He has worked over the last two seasons to shorten his swing, and has improved against breaking balls and offspeed pitches. Johnson has always been a solid fastball hitter, and though he doesn't walk very much he usually puts the ball into play. He hit just .226 off lefthanders in 1997, reversing a career-long trend in which he had been tougher on southpaws than righties.

Baserunning & Defense

Johnson has above-average speed for a catcher and finally stole his first major league base last season. He's becoming an outstanding handler of pitchers, and is especially good at blocking balls in the dirt and framing pitches. He also has worked hard to improve his throwing mechanics and his strong, accurate arm was much improved in 1997. He threw out 33 percent of basestealers after joining the Giants.

1998 Outlook

Even if Johnson never does another thing, he'll live on in San Francisco lore for his September heroics. The Giants believe he's ready to become a solid everyday catcher, a role they think he can fill for the next few years. He could also be capable of emerging as an offensive factor at the position as well. Though Oakland's Brent Mayne was signed as a free agent, he was brought in strictly as a backup.

Position: C
Bats: R **Throws:** R
Ht: 6' 2"   **Wt:** 210

Opening Day Age: 30
Born: 1/8/68 in Oakland, CA
ML Seasons: 4

Overall Statistics

	G	AB	R	H	D	T	HR	RBI	SB	BB	SO	Avg	OBP	Slg
1997	101	318	32	83	13	3	13	45	1	19	45	.261	.303	.443
Career	287	861	77	224	39	5	27	125	1	39	141	.260	.293	.411

Where He Hits the Ball

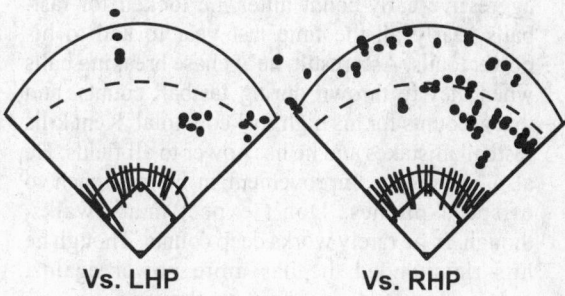

Vs. LHP   Vs. RHP

1997 Situational Stats

	AB	H	HR	RBI	Avg		AB	H	HR	RBI	Avg
Home	158	42	8	23	.266	LHP	93	21	1	10	.226
Road	160	41	5	22	.256	RHP	225	62	12	35	.276
First Half	139	33	2	18	.237	Sc Pos	87	14	1	28	.161
Scnd Half	179	50	11	27	.279	Clutch	60	19	4	9	.317

1997 Rankings (National League)

⇒ Did not rank near the top or bottom in any category

Jeff Kent

1997 Season

The term "career year" was made for Jeff Kent's 1997 season. He shattered every conceivable personal best, driving in 41 more runs than his previous high and hitting nine more homers than he ever had before—setting a franchise record for second basemen in the process. Kent got off to a hot start with 26 RBI in April and never really slowed down, even in September when he still managed 17 RBI despite hitting .216. He was the major reason the widely-criticized Matt Williams trade worked out for the Giants.

Hitting

Kent gears his short stroke to hitting fastballs. An aggressive early-count hitter, he looked for fastballs nearly all the time last year to add to his power totals. As a result, he'll chase breaking balls when they're thrown during fastball counts, and that accounts for his high strikeout total. Kent kills fastball mistakes and he has power to all fields. He also has shown improvement in his approach to offspeed pitches. Don't expect many walks, though, as he rarely works deep counts. Though he hits righthanded, he has more power against righties than he does against southpaws.

Baserunning & Defense

Despite average speed, Kent is a smart baserunner who can steal a base if opposing pitchers are inattentive. He always has had the rap of being a poor second baseman, but Kent played solidly for the Giants and proved he could turn the tough double play. His hands and throwing accuracy, however, can be erratic.

1998 Outlook

No one can expect Kent to repeat his 29-home-run, 121-RBI season. He was very comfortable batting cleanup behind Barry Bonds in the Giants' lineup, and there's no reason to believe he can't produce at least 20 homers and drive in 90-100 runs.

Position: 2B/1B
Bats: R **Throws:** R
Ht: 6' 1" **Wt:** 185

Opening Day Age: 30
Born: 3/7/68 in Bellflower, CA
ML Seasons: 6

Overall Statistics

	G	AB	R	H	D	T	HR	RBI	SB	BB	SO	Avg	OBP	Slg
1997	155	580	90	145	38	2	29	121	11	48	133	.250	.316	.472
Career	757	2705	386	728	156	13	107	439	27	188	548	.269	.324	.455

Where He Hits the Ball

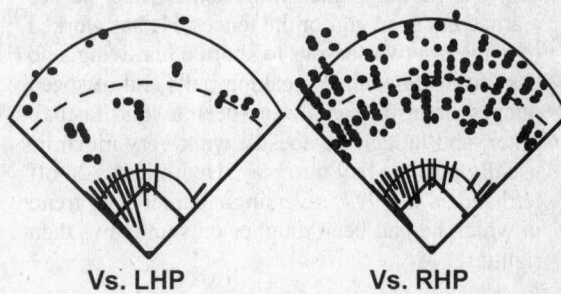

Vs. LHP   **Vs. RHP**

1997 Situational Stats

	AB	H	HR	RBI	Avg		AB	H	HR	RBI	Avg
Home	281	69	13	58	.246	LHP	148	34	6	21	.230
Road	299	76	16	63	.254	RHP	432	111	23	100	.257
First Half	298	75	18	64	.252	Sc Pos	199	54	8	91	.271
Scnd Half	282	70	11	57	.248	Clutch	89	21	4	21	.236

1997 Rankings (National League)

⇒ 2nd in lowest groundball/flyball ratio (0.7)
⇒ 3rd in sacrifice flies (10)
⇒ 5th in RBI, batting average with the bases loaded (.500) and errors at second base (16)
⇒ 6th in lowest batting average, strikeouts and lowest fielding percentage at second base (.979)
⇒ 7th in lowest cleanup slugging percentage (.455) and lowest batting average at home
⇒ 8th in lowest batting average vs. lefthanded pitchers
⇒ 9th in hit by pitch (13)
⇒ 10th in highest percentage of swings that missed (27.0%)
⇒ Led the Giants in at-bats, doubles, RBI, sacrifice flies (10), hit by pitch (13), and strikeouts

Kirk Rueter

1997 Season

Other Giants might have better stuff, but down the stretch Kirk Rueter emerged as San Francisco's best big-game pitcher. The Giants won 20 of his 32 starts and he was at his best during the stretch drive. He went 4-0, 1.97 in five September starts, including an epic 2-1 win over Los Angeles. He has rather ordinary stuff, but he's 39-20 in 94 career starts.

Pitching

Rueter rarely tops the mid-80s with his fastball, but his changeup is so good that he'll throw it at any point in the count. His outstanding change makes his fastball look harder than it is, and he fearlessly throws inside to both lefthanders and righthanders. He's equally effective against both types of hitters. Rueter also throws an effective curveball, mostly against righties. He has a history of being a six-inning pitcher, but worked a career-high 190 innings last year. When he lasted into the seventh, he remained strong.

Defense & Hitting

Rueter does a good job of holding runners with both a solid pickoff move and a slide-step delivery. Only 4-of-11 basestealers succeeded against him in 1997, and they're only 15-of-41 against him in his career. He gets himself into solid fielding position and makes all the required plays for his position. Rueter poses little danger with the bat, though he did manage to drive in five runs last year.

1998 Outlook

It has been five years since Rueter broke into the majors with a 8-0 record for Montreal. He's still just 27 and has matured physically to where he's much more durable. He's a terrific competitor whom the Giants believe can win 15 games this season.

Position: SP
Bats: L **Throws:** L
Ht: 6' 3" **Wt:** 195

Opening Day Age: 27
Born: 12/1/70 in Centralia, IL
ML Seasons: 5
Pronunciation: REE-ter

Overall Statistics

	W	L	Pct.	ERA	G	GS	Sv	IP	H	BB	SO	HR	Ratio
1997	13	6	.684	3.45	32	32	0	190.2	194	51	115	17	1.28
Career	39	20	.661	3.72	95	94	0	518.0	532	128	270	48	1.27

How Often He Throws Strikes

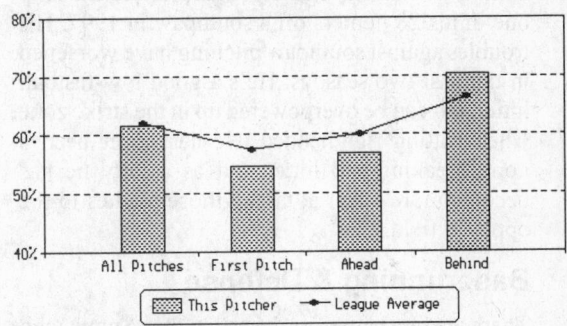

1997 Situational Stats

	W	L	ERA	Sv	IP		AB	H	HR	RBI	Avg
Home	7	4	3.00	0	102.0	LHB	141	39	4	18	.277
Road	6	2	3.96	0	88.2	RHB	593	155	13	49	.261
First Half	5	3	3.80	0	97.0	Sc Pos	149	32	3	48	.215
Scnd Half	8	3	3.07	0	93.2	Clutch	31	6	1	2	.194

1997 Rankings (National League)

⇒ 1st in fielding percentage at pitcher (1.000)
⇒ 3rd in pickoff throws (210)
⇒ 4th in lowest stolen base percentage allowed (36.4%)
⇒ 6th in winning percentage
⇒ 7th in most run support per 9 innings (5.6) and least strikeouts per 9 innings (5.4)
⇒ 8th in most pitches thrown per batter (3.82)
⇒ Led the Giants in games started, hits allowed, GDPs induced (19), lowest on-base percentage allowed (.311), lowest stolen base percentage allowed (36.4%), least pitches thrown per batter (3.82), least baserunners allowed per 9 innings (11.6), most GDPs induced per 9 innings (0.9), ERA on the road and lowest batting average allowed with runners in scoring position

S. F. Giants

J.T. Snow

1997 Season

After beginning his year by getting drilled in the face by a Randy Johnson pitch in spring training, things definitely took a turn for the better for J.T. Snow. He came back from his harrowing experience to have a huge inaugural year in the National League, setting career bests in homers and RBI. He was one of three Giants to surpass 100 RBI. Though Snow's batting average skidded toward the end of the year, he drove in 44 runs in the season's last two months.

Hitting

The switch-hitting Snow is far more dangerous batting lefthanded than righthanded. He hit only one of his 28 homers off a southpaw in 1997. His troubles against southpaw pitching have worsened in the past two seasons. He's a good low-fastball hitter, but can be overpowered up in the strike zone when batting righthanded. He has never been a good breaking-ball hitter, but as a lefty he has become more adept at taking those pitches to the opposite field.

Baserunning & Defense

There are few better first basemen than Snow, who was given much credit for holding together what was at times an erratic Giants infield. He won a Gold Glove after previously earning two with the Angels. He has great hands and an accurate arm, and he consistently digs low throws out of the dirt. Snow has below-average speed, though he'll occasionally attempt to steal a base.

1998 Outlook

Snow has long flirted with developing into a complete hitter, and he had his best season yet in 1997. The Giants have every reason to expect more of the same. Despite his struggles against lefties, Snow should be counted on for 20 homers and 90 RBI. Another season like last year would be viewed as a bonus.

Position: 1B
Bats: B **Throws:** L
Ht: 6' 2" **Wt:** 202

Opening Day Age: 30
Born: 2/26/68 in Long Beach, CA
ML Seasons: 6

Overall Statistics

	G	AB	R	H	D	T	HR	RBI	SB	BB	SO	Avg	OBP	Slg
1997	157	531	81	149	36	1	28	104	6	96	124	.281	.387	.510
Career	652	2306	313	606	101	5	93	362	12	283	452	.263	.344	.432

Where He Hits the Ball

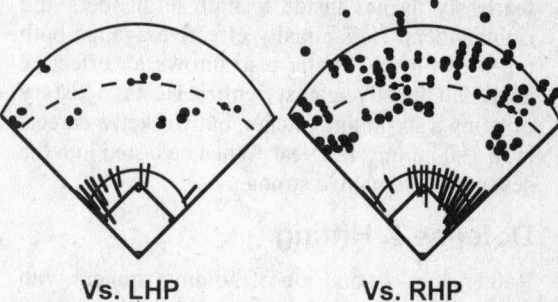

Vs. LHP   Vs. RHP

1997 Situational Stats

	AB	H	HR	RBI	Avg		AB	H	HR	RBI	Avg
Home	257	70	14	50	.272	LHP	133	25	1	16	.188
Road	274	79	14	54	.288	RHP	398	124	27	88	.312
First Half	288	86	13	47	.299	Sc Pos	144	40	7	75	.278
Scnd Half	243	63	15	57	.259	Clutch	82	18	1	9	.220

1997 Rankings (National League)

⇒ 1st in lowest batting average vs. lefthanded pitchers
⇒ 2nd in lowest slugging percentage vs. lefthanded pitchers (.256)
⇒ 3rd in fielding percentage at first base (.995)
⇒ 4th in walks
⇒ 5th in intentional walks (13) and slugging percentage vs. righthanded pitchers (.595)
⇒ Led the Giants in pitches seen (2,550), batting average vs. righthanded pitchers and slugging percentage vs. righthanded pitchers (.595)

Jose Vizcaino

1997 Season

In a very underrated season as the Giants' every-day shortstop, Jose Vizcaino set personal bests in numerous categories. He held up well over the season, playing a career-high 151 games and driving in several big runs for San Francisco down the stretch. He also was a stable force in the infield, making only one error in the Giants' last 40 games.

Hitting

A slap hitter who chases too many pitches for someone with so little power, Vizcaino still manages to contribute offensively. A switch-hitter, he's usually more dangerous batting lefthanded, where his modest pop usually surfaces. He's also a tough out in RBI situations, batting .318 with runners in scoring position last year. He has good bunting ability and is a decent fastball hitter, but chases too many breaking balls to make him an especially consistent top-of-the-order hitter. San Francisco usually used him in the No. 2 slot despite his mediocre on-base percentage. Vizcaino also strikes out far too often for a non-power hitter. He has his most success when he jumps on the first pitch, but is hopeless when he falls behind in the count.

Baserunning & Defense

Vizcaino has above-average speed but isn't aggressive about stealing bases. He's a solid if unspectacular, shortstop with sure hands and an accurate throwing arm. He also has surprising range, helped by experience that has taught him where to play hitters. Vizcaino also can play a solid second base and fill in at third or the outfield.

1998 Outlook

One of the many Giants' free agents, Vizcaino was likely to stay in San Francisco. He's a dependable shortstop who can occasionally produce some offense.

Position: SS
Bats: B **Throws:** R
Ht: 6' 1" **Wt:** 180

Opening Day Age: 30
Born: 3/26/68 in Palenque de San Cristobal, DR
ML Seasons: 9
Pronunciation: vis-kah-EE-no

Overall Statistics

	G	AB	R	H	D	T	HR	RBI	SB	BB	SO	Avg	OBP	Slg
1997	151	568	77	151	19	7	5	50	8	48	87	.266	.323	.350
Career	907	3071	371	839	105	32	17	267	50	220	440	.273	.321	.345

Where He Hits the Ball

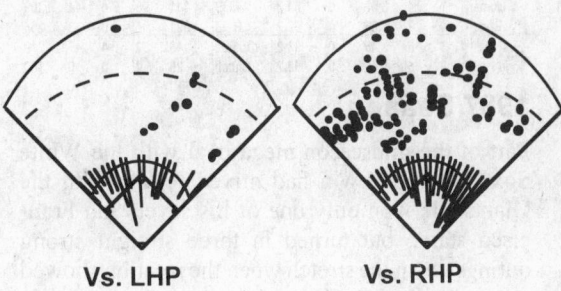

Vs. LHP   **Vs. RHP**

1997 Situational Stats

	AB	H	HR	RBI	Avg		AB	H	HR	RBI	Avg
Home	279	66	1	21	.237	LHP	125	30	0	12	.240
Road	289	85	4	29	.294	RHP	443	121	5	38	.273
First Half	303	79	2	23	.261	Sc Pos	132	42	1	41	.318
Scnd Half	265	72	3	27	.272	Clutch	95	35	1	12	.368

1997 Rankings (National League)

⇒ 1st in highest groundball/flyball ratio (2.3)
⇒ 4th in lowest slugging percentage, lowest slugging percentage vs. lefthanded pitchers (.288) and errors at shortstop (16)
⇒ 5th in sacrifice bunts (13), batting average in the clutch, lowest batting average at home and fielding percentage at shortstop (.976)
⇒ 7th in lowest HR frequency (113.6 ABs per HR)
⇒ 8th in bunts in play (24)
⇒ 10th in singles, triples and lowest slugging percentage vs. righthanded pitchers (.368)
⇒ Led the Giants in singles, triples, sacrifice bunts (13), highest groundball/flyball ratio (2.3), batting average on the road and bunts in play (24)

Danny Darwin

Position: SP/RP
Bats: R **Throws:** R
Ht: 6' 3" **Wt:** 202

Opening Day Age: 42
Born: 10/25/55 in
Bonham, TX
ML Seasons: 20

Overall Statistics

	W	L	Pct.	ERA	G	GS	Sv	IP	H	BB	SO	HR	Ratio
1997	5	11	.313	4.35	31	24	0	157.1	181	45	92	26	1.44
Career	163	172	.487	3.75	683	346	32	2868.0	2775	825	1861	298	1.26

1997 Situational Stats

	W	L	ERA	Sv	IP		AB	H	HR	RBI	Avg
Home	1	4	3.62	0	64.2	LHB	311	96	16	44	.309
Road	4	7	4.86	0	92.2	RHB	321	85	10	33	.265
First Half	3	6	3.46	0	93.2	Sc Pos	146	32	4	46	.219
Scnd Half	2	5	5.65	0	63.2	Clutch	25	4	0	0	.160

1997 Season

Part of the midseason mega-deal with the White Sox, Danny Darwin had mixed results with the Giants. He won only one of his seven San Francisco starts, but turned in three straight strong outings down the stretch when the rotation showed signs of fading. Earlier in the season, Darwin made 17 starts for Chicago, in which he pitched much better than his 4-8 AL record suggests.

Pitching, Defense & Hitting

Though now in his 40s, Darwin has remained a useful pitcher because he has an unorthodox delivery and command of the strike zone. His velocity is only average, but he'll still try to bust hitters off the plate. He can be effective on the inside part of the plate, but a slight mistake can result in a home run. He also throws a good slider and forkball. Darwin does a solid job of holding runners and has always been a good fielder. He has kept himself in good shape despite his age. He's rarely a threat with the bat, though he did have two RBI in his brief stint with the Giants.

1998 Outlook

If he wants to keep pitching and if he stays healthy, Darwin should find work as a spot starter or middle reliever. His savvy and toughness would be a nice fit on any number of pitching staffs.

Osvaldo Fernandez

Position: SP
Bats: R **Throws:** R
Ht: 6' 2" **Wt:** 190

Opening Day Age: 29
Born: 11/4/68 in
Holguin, Cuba
ML Seasons: 2

Overall Statistics

	W	L	Pct.	ERA	G	GS	Sv	IP	H	BB	SO	HR	Ratio
1997	3	4	.429	4.95	11	11	0	56.1	74	15	31	9	1.58
Career	10	17	.370	4.70	41	39	0	228.0	267	72	137	29	1.49

1997 Situational Stats

	W	L	ERA	Sv	IP		AB	H	HR	RBI	Avg
Home	2	3	6.15	0	33.2	LHB	112	29	5	23	.259
Road	1	1	3.18	0	22.2	RHB	124	45	4	12	.363
First Half	3	4	4.95	0	56.1	Sc Pos	65	18	3	28	.277
Scnd Half	0	0	-	0	0.0	Clutch	17	5	0	1	.294

1997 Season

It was largely a washout year for Cuban righthander Osvaldo Fernandez, who blew out his elbow after making 11 starts and was lost for the season. Before going down, Fernandez struggled with both his command and velocity, an indication he was likely hurting all along.

Pitching, Defense & Hitting

Even at his best, Fernandez doesn't have eye-popping stuff. He has excellent pitching savvy and is a good competitor. He throws a fastball that only rarely touches 90 MPH, but he doesn't hesitate to throw inside. He has worked on being more aggressive with all his pitches, including a good overhand curve and a slider. Fernandez has a solid pickoff move, limiting basestealers to three swipes in 10 tries in 1997, and fields his position very well. He's largely helpless at the plate, though he's capable of laying down a sacrifice bunt.

1998 Outlook

The Giants are optimistic that Fernandez will make a total recovery from elbow surgery and be ready to compete for a spot in their rotation this spring. They hope he can win the 10-12 games they thought he was capable of last year. They list his age as 29, but Cuban national team rosters from international play indicate that he's 33.

Doug Henry

Signed By ASTROS

Position: RP
Bats: R **Throws:** R
Ht: 6' 4" **Wt:** 205

Opening Day Age: 34
Born: 12/10/63 in Sacramento, CA
ML Seasons: 7

Overall Statistics

	W	L	Pct.	ERA	G	GS	Sv	IP	H	BB	SO	HR	Ratio
1997	4	5	.444	4.71	75	0	3	70.2	70	41	69	5	1.57
Career	18	31	.367	4.07	363	0	77	400.0	379	188	327	40	1.42

1997 Situational Stats

	W	L	ERA	Sv	IP		AB	H	HR	RBI	Avg
Home	4	2	3.30	1	43.2	LHB	104	25	2	15	.240
Road	0	3	7.00	2	27.0	RHB	164	45	3	21	.274
First Half	2	3	3.43	2	42.0	Sc Pos	72	21	2	31	.292
Scnd Half	2	2	6.59	1	28.2	Clutch	124	37	2	20	.298

1997 Season

No bullpen was busier last year than San Francisco's, and Doug Henry was one of the Giants' workhorses. He made a career-high 75 appearances, but the workload got to him. He had a 1.26 ERA in the first two months and a 7.07 mark afterward, earning a demotion to middle relief.

Pitching, Defense & Hitting

Henry was a hard thrower when he first broke in with the Brewers. Arm injuries have changed his style to a breaking-ball pitcher who likes to change speeds. He gets his share of strikeouts with his splitter or slider. Henry has become something of a nibbler, and he walks too many and is easy to hit when he can't throw his breaking pitches for strikes. He's slightly more effective against lefthanders. He's an average fielder with a so-so move to first. As a hitter he's 1-for-11 in his career.

1998 Outlook

One of the Giants' many free agents, Henry has value as a middle man. However, his rocky second half may have soured San Francisco on trying to re-sign him. He wound up in Houston instead.

Glenallen Hill

Position: RF
Bats: R **Throws:** R
Ht: 6' 2" **Wt:** 220

Opening Day Age: 33
Born: 3/22/65 in Santa Cruz, CA
ML Seasons: 9

Overall Statistics

	G	AB	R	H	D	T	HR	RBI	SB	BB	SO	Avg	OBP	Slg
1997	128	398	47	104	28	4	11	64	7	19	87	.261	.297	.435
Career	821	2706	373	711	144	17	118	415	90	201	609	.263	.315	.459

1997 Situational Stats

	AB	H	HR	RBI	Avg		AB	H	HR	RBI	Avg
Home	193	44	3	24	.228	LHP	111	30	4	17	.270
Road	205	60	8	40	.293	RHP	287	74	7	47	.258
First Half	282	70	8	48	.248	Sc Pos	104	33	0	45	.317
Scnd Half	116	34	3	16	.293	Clutch	62	22	2	22	.355

1997 Season

Glenallen Hill struggled for consistency for much of 1997, managing only 15 RBI from June through July. He ended the season platooning with Stan Javier in right field. Hill seemed to play better in the part-time situation, batting .312 in his last 35 starts. Eight of his 11 homers either tied games or gave the Giants a lead.

Hitting, Baserunning & Defense

Hill can crush inside fastballs low in the strike zone. But he also will chase breaking balls away and doesn't catch up to high, hard stuff. He rarely works deep counts and never has had a good feel for the strike zone. Hill has above-average speed but has become a sporadic basestealer who lacks aggressiveness. He's prone to making mistakes in right field, especially in the tough conditions at 3Com Park. His defensive play at home earned him several boos in 1997. He does have an outstanding throwing arm.

1998 Outlook

Despite detractors throughout the organization, Hill has had a strong backer in manager Dusty Baker. But even Baker couldn't live with Hill's ups and downs in 1997. He was a free agent and may have played his last game for the Giants.

S. F. Giants

Mark Lewis

Position: 3B/2B
Bats: R **Throws:** R
Ht: 6' 1" **Wt:** 185

Opening Day Age: 28
Born: 11/30/69 in
Hamilton, OH
ML Seasons: 7

Overall Statistics

	G	AB	R	H	D	T	HR	RBI	SB	BB	SO	Avg	OBP	Slg
1997	118	341	50	91	14	6	10	42	3	23	62	.267	.318	.431
Career	584	1909	229	516	100	11	31	200	19	128	338	.270	.318	.383

1997 Situational Stats

	AB	H	HR	RBI	Avg		AB	H	HR	RBI	Avg
Home	152	36	4	21	.237	LHP	124	36	1	15	.290
Road	189	55	6	21	.291	RHP	217	55	9	27	.253
First Half	190	54	6	23	.284	Sc Pos	88	24	2	32	.273
Scnd Half	151	37	4	19	.245	Clutch	54	20	2	11	.370

1997 Season

One of the Giants' many new acquisitions in 1997, Mark Lewis split time at third base with Bill Mueller and had a decent season offensively. He closed the season with a flourish, batting .333 in September.

Hitting, Baserunning & Defense

Lewis has produced double-figure homer totals in the last two seasons, but he's not really a power hitter. He tries to pull the ball too often, and that results in too a high strikeout rate for a non-slugger. He's an aggressive hitter who looks for fastballs early in the count, and he can be fooled by offspeed or breaking pitches. Lewis is adequate at most infield positions, possessing decent range and a solid arm. He has had trouble at third base, where his reactions often seemed a step too slow. He's an average baserunner with little basestealing ability.

1998 Outlook

The Giants don't view Lewis as an everyday player. They see him as a utilityman and may not want to go to arbitration with him. If he returns, he'll compete with Mueller and Charlie Hayes for time at third base.

Bill Mueller

Position: 3B
Bats: B **Throws:** R
Ht: 5'11" **Wt:** 175

Opening Day Age: 27
Born: 3/17/71 in
Maryland Heights, MO
ML Seasons: 2
Pronunciation:
MILL-err

Overall Statistics

	G	AB	R	H	D	T	HR	RBI	SB	BB	SO	Avg	OBP	Slg
1997	128	390	51	114	26	3	7	44	4	48	71	.292	.369	.428
Career	183	590	82	180	41	4	7	63	4	72	97	.305	.380	.424

1997 Situational Stats

	AB	H	HR	RBI	Avg		AB	H	HR	RBI	Avg
Home	189	55	5	24	.291	LHP	85	24	2	10	.282
Road	201	59	2	20	.294	RHP	305	90	5	34	.295
First Half	185	50	2	18	.270	Sc Pos	96	25	1	36	.260
Scnd Half	205	64	5	26	.312	Clutch	67	22	1	13	.328

1997 Season

Bill Mueller emerged as the Giants' most dependable player at third base last year. He showed some power for the first time in his career and hit .312 after the All-Star break, including a big August in which he batted .349 with 15 RBI.

Hitting, Baserunning & Defense

The switch-hitting Mueller is equally effective from both sides of the plate. He has gap power to all fields and is a good contact hitter who has always been able to work a walk. He's a difficult hitter to defense because of his ability to hit balls where they're pitched. He's a solid fastball hitter, but also can punch breaking balls to the opposite field. Mueller is a heady baserunner but is little threat to steal. Defensively, he can play either second or third base. At the hot corner, he has decent range and compiled one of the National League's best fielding percentages because of his good hands and accurate arm.

1998 Outlook

The Giants would like more power out of their third baseman, however, Mueller does get on base and will get his share of doubles. He signed a three-year contract in the offseason. But after trading with the Yankees for Charlie Hayes, San Francisco may platoon Hayes and Mueller in 1998.

Terry Mulholland

Position: SP/RP
Bats: R **Throws:** L
Ht: 6' 3" **Wt:** 212

Opening Day Age: 35
Born: 3/9/63 in
Uniontown, PA
ML Seasons: 11

Overall Statistics

	W	L	Pct.	ERA	G	GS	Sv	IP	H	BB	SO	HR	Ratio
1997	6	13	.316	4.24	40	27	0	186.2	190	51	99	24	1.29
Career	87	102	.460	4.29	303	257	0	1707.2	1807	430	891	173	1.31

1997 Situational Stats

	W	L	ERA	Sv	IP		AB	H	HR	RBI	Avg
Home	2	5	3.43	0	94.1	LHB	140	38	2	11	.271
Road	4	8	5.07	0	92.1	RHB	571	152	22	81	.266
First Half	6	9	3.72	0	118.2	Sc Pos	161	44	1	61	.273
Scnd Half	0	4	5.16	0	68.0	Clutch	60	23	5	8	.383

1997 Season

His 6-13 won-lost record leaves a somewhat mis-leading impression on Terry Mulholland's season. Before being acquired on waivers by San Francisco in August, Mulholland had been a solid starter for the Cubs. His record in Chicago was 6-12, but he allowed two runs or fewer in 12 of his 25 starts and was plagued by the worst run support of any National Leaguer. He pitched largely in relief for San Francisco.

Pitching, Defense & Hitting

Mulholland still can be effective when he spots his sneaky fastball and then mixes in a good slider, changeup and forkball. He has good control but his stuff has deteriorated to the point where he must pitch on the corners and change speeds. He's well-known for having one of the best pickoff moves in the game and has permitted just seven stolen bases in the last six years. Chronic knee problems have robbed him of any agility in the field. Mulholland can occasionally help himself with the bat.

1998 Outlook

A free agent, Mulholland remains an excellent competitor who rarely gets himself in trouble with control lapses. He still can be a serviceable fourth or fifth starter on a good club. It's a reach to expect him to help as a reliever.

Pat Rapp

Position: SP
Bats: R **Throws:** R
Ht: 6' 3" **Wt:** 215

Opening Day Age: 30
Born: 7/13/67 in
Jennings, LA
ML Seasons: 6

Overall Statistics

	W	L	Pct.	ERA	G	GS	Sv	IP	H	BB	SO	HR	Ratio
1997	5	8	.385	4.83	27	25	0	141.2	158	72	92	16	1.62
Career	38	47	.447	4.31	128	123	0	708.2	741	353	415	58	1.54

1997 Situational Stats

	W	L	ERA	Sv	IP		AB	H	HR	RBI	Avg
Home	1	3	4.92	0	64.0	LHB	257	76	7	29	.296
Road	4	5	4.75	0	77.2	RHB	291	82	9	44	.282
First Half	4	6	4.38	0	102.2	Sc Pos	147	34	2	54	.231
Scnd Half	1	2	6.00	0	39.0	Clutch	20	9	2	4	.450

1997 Season

The acquisition of Pat Rapp was one of the many pennant-race moves engineered by Giants GM Brian Sabean that didn't make much of an impact. Immediately upon arriving from Florida in July, Rapp pulled a ribcage muscle in his first start and landed on the disabled list. When he returned in August, he was demoted to the minors 10 days later. Recalled in September, he would win only once in six total San Francisco starts.

Pitching, Defense & Hitting

Rapp lives and dies with his curveball, which can be outstanding but too often flattens in the strike zone. He has a high-maintenance delivery which can desert him at any point. His fastball rarely tops the mid-80s. Rapp has an excellent move to first and comes home quickly, making him tough on basestealers. He's a solid fielder and a career .123 hitter.

1998 Outlook

When he's pitching well, Rapp can eat innings and keep his team in most of his starts. Most likely he will return to San Francisco, and he's capable of winning 10-12 games at the back end of the rotation.

Rich Rodriguez

Position: RP
Bats: L **Throws:** L
Ht: 6' 0" **Wt:** 200

Opening Day Age: 35
Born: 3/1/63 in
Downey, CA
ML Seasons: 7

Overall Statistics

	W	L	Pct.	ERA	G	GS	Sv	IP	H	BB	SO	HR	Ratio
1997	4	3	.571	3.17	71	0	1	65.1	65	21	32	7	1.32
Career	19	17	.528	3.20	355	2	5	422.0	395	169	244	37	1.34

1997 Situational Stats

	W	L	ERA	Sv	IP		AB	H	HR	RBI	Avg
Home	3	2	2.73	0	33.0	LHB	103	32	3	14	.311
Road	1	1	3.62	1	32.1	RHB	143	33	4	21	.231
First Half	3	3	1.76	1	41.0	Sc Pos	75	22	1	28	.293
Scnd Half	1	0	5.55	0	24.1	Clutch	103	23	2	10	.223

1997 Season

After appearing in just one major league game in the previous two years, Rich Rodriguez earned a job with the Giants as a nonroster player and produced one of the best seasons of his journeyman career. He appeared in a career-high 71 games and survived the heavy workload. He worked 16 scoreless outings in his last 19 appearances.

Pitching, Defense & Hitting

Rodriguez isn't a specialty lefthanded reliever. He always has held his own against righthanders and was much more effective against them in 1997, limiting them to a .231 average while southpaws hit .311 against him. His out pitch is a screwball with a late, short break, and he also has an average fastball that he often tries to sink. Rodriguez is a competent fielder at his position. He has an average move to first and a quick delivery home, and basestealers went 0-for-4 against him last year. He got the first hit of his career in 1997, improving his lifetime average to .050.

1998 Outlook

Rodriguez is one of those veteran lefty relievers who seemingly has nine lives. He re-established himself as a durable situational pitcher. He re-signed as a free agent with the Giants for a two-year contract.

Julian Tavarez

Position: RP
Bats: L **Throws:** R
Ht: 6' 2" **Wt:** 165

Opening Day Age: 24
Born: 5/22/73 in
Santiago, DR
ML Seasons: 5
Pronunciation:
tuh-VAR-ez

Overall Statistics

	W	L	Pct.	ERA	G	GS	Sv	IP	H	BB	SO	HR	Ratio
1997	6	4	.600	3.87	89	0	0	88.1	91	34	38	6	1.42
Career	22	16	.579	4.31	206	12	0	292.2	327	91	171	30	1.43

1997 Situational Stats

	W	L	ERA	Sv	IP		AB	H	HR	RBI	Avg
Home	3	1	4.95	0	40.0	LHB	125	32	0	18	.256
Road	3	3	2.98	0	48.1	RHB	204	59	6	38	.289
First Half	2	2	3.97	0	45.1	Sc Pos	101	26	2	51	.257
Scnd Half	4	2	3.77	0	43.0	Clutch	147	41	2	18	.279

1997 Season

No pitcher was busier in 1997 than Julian Tavarez, who led the majors and set a Giants record with 89 appearances. Aside from a rough May, he remained consistent throughout the season. His best stretch came from late May through mid-July, during which he had a streak of 24 straight scoreless outings.

Pitching, Defense & Hitting

Tavarez' best pitch is a hard, sinking fastball that usually is clocked in the low 90s. He has struggled in recent years to maintain a consistent slider and splitter, but when he has all his pitches working, his stuff is as good as anyone's. He gets into trouble when he hangs his slider. Righthanders had more success than lefthanders did against him in 1997, reversing a career trend. Tavarez fields his position well and is quick to the plate, but basestealers went 5-for-5 against him last year. He struck out in his only major league plate appearance.

1998 Outlook

Many clubs believe that Tavarez' natural stuff is so good that he can either be a starter or a closer when he matures. The Giants view him more as a reliever, and he'll remain a setup man after the trade for Robb Nen.

Other San Francisco Giants

Rene Arocha (**Pos**: RHP, **Age**: 32)

	W	L	Pct.	ERA	G	GS	Sv	IP	H	BB	SO	HR	Ratio
1997	0	0	-	11.32	6	0	0	10.1	17	5	7	2	2.13
Career	18	17	.514	4.11	124	36	11	331.0	363	75	190	37	1.32

Traded from St. Louis before the season, Arocha spent three weeks in the majors, where he struggled immensely. He was sent to Triple-A Phoenix and didn't return. 1998 Outlook: C

Rich Aurilia (**Pos**: SS, **Age**: 26, **Bats**: R)

	G	AB	R	H	D	T	HR	RBI	SB	BB	SO	Avg	OBP	Slg
1997	46	102	16	28	8	0	5	19	1	8	15	.275	.321	.500
Career	160	439	47	113	18	1	10	49	6	34	69	.257	.309	.371

Aurilia's playing time last year was curtailed after suffering a stress fracture of the back near the end of '96, but he had a good year with the bat in a limited role. He drove in 19 runs in only 102 at-bats. 1998 Outlook: B

Cory Bailey (**Pos**: RHP, **Age**: 27)

	W	L	Pct.	ERA	G	GS	Sv	IP	H	BB	SO	HR	Ratio
1997	0	1	.000	8.38	7	0	0	9.2	15	4	5	1	1.97
Career	5	5	.500	4.28	77	0	0	90.1	96	51	63	4	1.63

Traded from Texas in late July, Bailey saw a smattering of major league action after being called up in September. He pitched effectively in 51 games with St. Louis in '96, but struggled last season. 1998 Outlook: C

Marvin Benard (**Pos**: RF/LF, **Age**: 28, **Bats**: L)

	G	AB	R	H	D	T	HR	RBI	SB	BB	SO	Avg	OBP	Slg
1997	84	114	13	26	4	0	1	13	3	13	29	.228	.315	.289
Career	232	636	107	160	23	4	7	44	29	73	120	.252	.333	.333

Benard went from being a regular in '96 to a fifth outfielder/pinch hitter last season. As a career .252 hitter with very little power, his long-term future is in jeopardy. 1998 Outlook: C

Damon Berryhill (**Pos**: C/1B, **Age**: 34, **Bats**: B)

	G	AB	R	H	D	T	HR	RBI	SB	BB	SO	Avg	OBP	Slg
1997	73	167	17	43	8	0	3	23	0	20	29	.257	.335	.359
Career	683	2030	175	488	106	6	47	257	3	139	409	.240	.288	.368

After missing all of 1996 with an injury, Berryhill returned and put up typical Berryhill numbers. That may not be enough to find him work this year. 1998 Outlook: C

Doug Creek (**Pos**: LHP, **Age**: 29)

	W	L	Pct.	ERA	G	GS	Sv	IP	H	BB	SO	HR	Ratio
1997	1	2	.333	6.75	3	3	0	13.1	12	14	14	1	1.95
Career	1	4	.200	5.93	72	3	0	68.1	59	49	62	12	1.58

Creek was traded to the White Sox in early November and sold to Japan's Hanshin Tigers a month later. He has good strikeout data, but his control problems (6.5 BB per 9 IP for his career) are horrific. 1998 Outlook: D

John Johnstone (**Pos**: RHP, **Age**: 29)

	W	L	Pct.	ERA	G	GS	Sv	IP	H	BB	SO	HR	Ratio
1997	0	0	-	3.24	18	0	0	25.0	22	14	19	1	1.44
Career	2	4	.333	4.82	55	0	0	74.2	85	44	55	9	1.73

Johnstone started the season with the Giants, was eventually designated for reassigment, and found his way back to San Francisco after a brief stop in Oakland. He's never gotten more than 25 innings per year. 1998 Outlook: C

Jim Poole (**Pos**: LHP, **Age**: 31)

	W	L	Pct.	ERA	G	GS	Sv	IP	H	BB	SO	HR	Ratio
1997	3	1	.750	7.11	63	0	0	49.1	73	25	26	6	1.99
Career	18	8	.692	3.87	316	0	3	276.2	258	122	199	28	1.37

Poole made 63 appearances for the Giants last year. What's baffling is. . . why?? He surrendered 13.4 hits per 9 IP and posted an ERA over 7.00. Is it really that easy for a southpaw to keep a job? 1998 Outlook: C

Joe Roa (**Pos**: RHP, **Age**: 26)

	W	L	Pct.	ERA	G	GS	Sv	IP	H	BB	SO	HR	Ratio
1997	2	5	.286	5.21	28	3	0	65.2	86	20	34	8	1.61
Career	2	6	.250	5.40	30	4	0	73.1	99	25	34	9	1.69

Acquired from Cleveland after the '96 season, Roa was hammered in 28 appearances (mostly from the bullpen) before being sent down to the minors for good in August. 1998 Outlook: C

William VanLandingham (**Pos**: RHP, **Age**: 27)

	W	L	Pct.	ERA	G	GS	Sv	IP	H	BB	SO	HR	Ratio
1997	4	7	.364	4.96	18	17	0	89.0	80	59	52	11	1.56
Career	27	26	.509	4.54	84	81	0	477.1	470	220	300	46	1.45

VanLandingham was booted out of the Giants' starting rotation after failing to bounce back from his disappointing 1996 campaign. He spent most of the second half of the season in the minors. 1998 Outlook: C

San Francisco Giants Minor League Prospects

Organization Overview:

The Giants may have the worst collection of minor league talent in baseball. That's in part because they had little before GM Brian Sabean arrived in 1993, and in part because they have traded away what they acquired since. The National League West championship team featured just one homegrown Giant in a prominent role: Bill Mueller. They were the last team to have a player chosen in each of the expansion draft's first two rounds. Sabean sacrificed six players, including quality prospects Lorenzo Barcelo, Mike Caruso and Ken Vining, to get Wilson Alvarez, Danny Darwin and Roberto Hernandez from the White Sox for the stretch drive. When co-closers Hernandez and Rod Beck hit the free-agent market, Sabean traded three of his best remaining arms: Joe Fontenot, Mick Pageler and Mike Villano yielded Robb Nen from the Marlins. The Giants don't have the deep pockets of the Diamondbacks, Dodgers or Rockies, so they could be in for a huge fall when the major league team stops contending.

Darin Blood

Position: P
Bats: B **Throws:** R
Ht: 6' 2" **Wt:** 205

Opening Day Age: 23
Born: 8/31/74 in
Spokane, WA

Recent Statistics

	W	L	ERA	G	GS	Sv	IP	H	R	BB	SO	HR
96 A San Jose	17	6	2.65	27	25	0	170.0	140	59	71	193	4
97 AA Shreveport	8	10	4.33	27	27	0	156.0	152	89	83	90	12

Blood excelled in his first two pro seasons, going a combined 23-9 and being named high Class-A California League Pitcher of the Year in 1996. A 1995 third-round pick out of Gonzaga, he hit the wall a bit in Double-A. He throws four pitches: a sinking fastball, curveball, slider and changeup. His velocity is average at best, but his fastball has life and he can locate it where he wants. His previously solid command slipped in Shreveport, and he had nearly as many walks as strikeouts. Though he won't blow hitters away, he needs to establish his fastball more often. If he can't develop further, he may have to settle for being a middle reliever.

Jason Brester

Position: P
Bats: L **Throws:** L
Ht: 6' 3" **Wt:** 190

Opening Day Age: 21
Born: 12/7/76 in
Lincoln, NE

Recent Statistics

	W	L	ERA	G	GS	Sv	IP	H	R	BB	SO	HR
96 A Burlington	10	9	3.96	27	27	0	157.0	139	78	64	143	14
97 A San Jose	9	9	4.24	26	26	0	142.1	164	80	52	172	4

With the massive exodus of pitchers from the Giants, Brester is now their top mound prospect. A 1995 second-round pick, he more than held his own in the California League at age 20. He has an above-average fastball which he locates well, and his curveball is a strikeout pitch. He fanned 172 hitters in 142⅓ innings in 1997 and has averaged more than a whiff per inning as a pro. He also throws a straight change, and his arm speed is very deceptive. He has good composure, as evidenced by how well he handled a hitters' league with older players. Brester should advance to Double-A in 1998 and be ready for San Francisco by 2000.

Troy Brohawn

Position: P
Bats: L **Throws:** L
Ht: 6' 1" **Wt:** 190

Opening Day Age: 25
Born: 1/14/73 in
Cambridge, MD

Recent Statistics

	W	L	ERA	G	GS	Sv	IP	H	R	BB	SO	HR
96 AA Shreveport	9	10	4.60	28	28	0	156.2	163	99	49	82	30
97 AA Shreveport	13	5	2.56	26	26	0	169.0	148	57	64	98	10

Brohawn was a two-way player at the University of Nebraska, but he has focused on pitching since signing as a 1994 fourth-round pick. He's a lefthanded version of Blood who outsmarts hitters rather than overpowering them. Brohawn's best pitch is his straight change, and he also throws a fastball, cutter and curveball. That repertoire allowed him to lead all Double-A and Triple-A pitchers with a 2.56 ERA in 1997. If there was a downside, it was that it was his second year in Shreveport. How well Brohawn performs in Triple-A in 1998 will go a long way to determining whether he stays a starter or becomes a middle reliever.

Jacob Cruz

Position: OF
Bats: L **Throws:** L
Ht: 6' 0" **Wt:** 175

Opening Day Age: 25
Born: 1/28/73 in
Oxnard, CA

Recent Statistics

	G	AB	R	H	D	T	HR	RBI	SB	BB	SO	AVG
97 AAA Phoenix	127	493	97	178	45	3	12	95	18	64	64	.361
97 NL San Francisco	16	25	3	4	1	0	0	3	0	3	4	.160
97 MLE	127	464	75	149	38	1	9	74	12	50	67	.321

The Triple-A Pacific Coast League batting champion with a .361 average, Cruz is San Francisco's best prospect. A 1994 supplemental first-round pick out of Arizona State, he has gap-to-gap power and could hit 15-20 homers per year if he gets a little stronger. He walks as much as he strikes out, and he can steal an occasional base. He's also a solid right fielder with an above-average arm. With his good tools across the board and two years of Triple-A experience, Cruz is ready to compete for a starting job with the Giants. He could wrest right field from Glenallen Hill and Stan Javier.

Wilson Delgado

Position: SS
Bats: B **Throws:** R
Ht: 5' 11" **Wt:** 165

Opening Day Age: 22
Born: 7/15/75 in Santo Domingo, DR

Recent Statistics

	G	AB	R	H	D	T	HR	RBI	SB	BB	SO	AVG
97 AAA Phoenix	119	416	47	120	22	4	9	59	9	24	70	.288
97 NL San Francisco	8	7	1	1	1	0	0	0	0	0	2	.143
97 MLE	119	396	36	100	18	2	6	46	6	19	74	.253

As if the Shawn Estes-Salomon Torres trade with Seattle wasn't one-sided enough, the Giants also received Delgado in the deal. Signed out of the Dominican Republic, he went from Class-A to the majors in 1996, his first full season with San Francisco. He can handle the bat and has a little pop for a middle infielder. His ability to draw walks will determine whether he becomes a No. 2 or a No. 8 hitter. He's not particularly fast, but he gets to balls at shortstop and has an accurate arm. The presence of Jose Vizcaino will allow the Giants to give Delgado more Triple-A experience in 1998.

Jason Grilli

Position: P
Bats: R **Throws:** R
Ht: 6' 4" **Wt:** 185

Opening Day Age: 21
Born: 11/11/76 in Royal Oak, MI

Recent Statistics

	W	L	ERA	G	GS	Sv	IP	H	R	BB	SO	HR
97					Did Not Play							

The son of former big leaguer Steve Grilli, Jason was drafted fourth overall in 1997. The Seton Hall product signed for a club-record $1.875 million bonus. He has yet to make his pro debut, but he looked very sharp in instructional league. He's a strikeout pitcher who broke Charles Nagy's Big East Conference single-game record with 18 this spring. Grilli throws a 90-91 MPH sinking fastball with ease, and also has a hard sliider. The Giants are pleased with his control and composure as well. He'll need to improve his changeup and his consistency, but that's usually true of amateur pitchers. He likely will start in the California League in 1998 and could reach the majors quickly.

Russ Ortiz

Position: P
Bats: R **Throws:** R
Ht: 6' 1" **Wt:** 200

Opening Day Age: 23
Born: 6/5/74 in Van Nuys, CA

Recent Statistics

	W	L	ERA	G	GS	Sv	IP	H	R	BB	SO	HR
96 A San Jose	0	0	0.25	34	0	23	36.2	16	2	20	63	0
96 AA Shreveport	1	2	4.05	26	0	13	26.2	22	14	21	29	0
97 AA Shreveport	2	3	4.13	12	12	0	56.2	52	28	37	50	3
97 AAA Phoenix	4	3	5.51	14	14	0	85.0	96	57	34	70	11

A setup man on the 1994 College World Series champion Oklahoma Sooners, Ortiz had blossomed since signing as a fourth-round pick the following year. He consistently has shown a 95-96 MPH fastball, making him an ideal closer candidate. He excelled in that role in his first two pro seasons before the Giants made him a starter in 1997. He was hit harder than in the past, but continued to pile up strikeouts. San Francisco officials say they made the switch to get him more innings and to have him work on his curveball and changeup. With that mission accomplished, he probably will return to Triple-A as a reliever in 1998. He could be helping to set up Nen later in the season.

Dante Powell

Position: OF
Bats: R **Throws:** R
Ht: 6' 2" **Wt:** 185

Opening Day Age: 24
Born: 8/25/73 in Long Beach, CA

Recent Statistics

	G	AB	R	H	D	T	HR	RBI	SB	BB	SO	AVG
97 AAA Phoenix	108	452	91	109	24	4	11	42	34	52	105	.241
97 NL San Francisco	27	39	8	12	1	0	1	3	1	4	11	.308
97 MLE	108	434	70	91	20	2	8	32	24	40	111	.210

Powell has always dazzled observers with his tools and confounded them with his inconsistent effort. A 1994 first-round pick out of Cal State Fullerton, he made huge strides in Double-A in 1996 but regressed in Triple-A last year. He has power and plenty of speed, but didn't hit for a good average and struck out too much. He covers plenty of ground in center field and throws well to boot. He also has a reputation for not hustling at all times and for being slow to make adjustments. Powell needs more time in Triple-A before he can challenge Darryl Hamilton for San Francisco's center-field job.

Others to Watch

Third baseman-turned-left fielder **Mike Glendenning** put up huge .258-33-100 numbers in the Cal League at age 20. He has power to all fields and started to improve when he became less pull-conscious. . . **Ramon Martinez**, 25, is a decent all-around shortstop who batted .315 in 1997 while playing mostly in Double-A. He's a good contact hitter and is steady in the field. . . First baseman **Damon Minor** is the twin brother of Orioles prospect Ryan Minor. Damon has similar power, bashing 31 homers in the Cal League at age 23. His bat will have to carry him. . . Catcher **Doug Mirabelli**, 27, began to show offensive potential in 1996. He's also a good receiver who can take charge of a pitching staff. . . Lefthander **Ricky Pickett**, 28, has yet to pitch in the majors despite some sharp minor league numbers: 341 innings, 237 hits, 422 strikeouts. His control comes and goes, but he has a very deceptive fastball and a nice curveball. . . Outfielder **Armando Rios** has produced in consecutive seasons at Double-A, but he's running out of time at 26. He's a doubles hitter with a strong arm.

Expansion Draft Picks

The Arizona Diamondbacks and Tampa Bay Devil Rays stocked their rosters during baseball's sixth expansion draft, held November 18 at the Phoenix Civic Plaza. Arizona won a predraft coin toss and opted to take the second and third selections. Tampa Bay got the first and fourth picks, and the Diamondbacks and Devil Rays alternated choices after that.

Players were eligible to be drafted if they had major league experience, if they had signed at age 19 or older and had at least three years of pro experience, or if they had signed at age 18 or younger and had at least four years of pro experience. Each existing team was allowed to protect 15 players, and had to keep any player who had the right to veto a trade unless the player waived that right.

Each existing team could lose no more than one player in each round. After each of the first two rounds, existing teams could protect another three players. The third round lasted 14 picks, during which neither league could lose more than seven players.

The order of selection:

Tampa Bay Devil Rays

First Round
1. Tony Saunders, lhp, Marlins
4. Quinton McCracken, of, Rockies
6. Bobby Abreu, of, Astros
8. Miguel Cairo, 2b, Cubs
10. Rich Butler, of, Blue Jays
12. Bobby Smith, 3b, Braves
14. Jason Johnson, rhp, Pirates
16. Dmitri Young, 1b, Reds
18. Esteban Yan, rhp, Orioles
20. Mike Difelice, c, Cardinals
22. Bubba Trammell, of, Tigers
24. Andy Sheets, ss, Mariners
26. Dennis Springer, rhp, Angels
28. Dan Carlson, rhp, Giants

Second Round
30. Brian Boehringer, rhp, Yankees
32. Mike Duvall, lhp, Marlins
34. John LeRoy, rhp, Braves
36. Jim Mecir, rhp, Red Sox
38. Bryan Rekar, rhp, Rockies
40. Rick Gorecki, rhp, Dodgers
42. Ramon Tatis, lhp, Cubs
44. Kerry Robinson, of, Cardinals
46. Steve Cox, 1b, Athletics
48. Albie Lopez, rhp, Indians
50. Jose Paniagua, rhp, Expos
52. Carlos Mendoza, of, Mets
54. Ryan Karp, lhp, Phillies
56. Santos Hernandez, rhp, Giants

Arizona Diamondbacks

First Round
2. Brian Anderson, lhp, Indians
3. Jeff Suppan, rhp, Red Sox
5. Gabe Alvarez, 3b, Padres
7. Jorge Fabregas, c, White Sox
9. Karim Garcia, of, Dodgers
11. Edwin Diaz, 2b, Rangers
13. Cory Lidle, rhp, Mets
15. Joel Adamson, lhp, Brewers
17. Ben Ford, rhp, Yankees
19. Yamil Benitez, of, Royals
21. Neil Weber, lhp, Expos
23. Jason Boyd, rhp, Phillies
25. Brent Brede, of, Twins
27. Tony Batista, ss, Athletics

Second Round
29. Tom Martin, lhp, Astros
31. Omar Daal, lhp, Expos
33. Scott Winchester, rhp, Reds
35. Clint Sodowsky, rhp, Pirates
37. Danny Klassen, ss, Brewers
39. Matt Drews, rhp, Tigers
41. Todd Erdos, rhp, Padres
43. Chris Clemons, rhp, White Sox
45. David Dellucci, of, Orioles
47. Damian Miller, c, Twins
49. Hector Carrasco, rhp, Royals
51. Hanley Frias, ss, Rangers
53. Bob Wolcott, rhp, Mariners
55. Mike Bell, 3b, Angels

Tampa Bay Devil Rays

Third Round

58. Randy Winn, of, Marlins
60. Terrell Wade, lhp, Braves
62. Aaron Ledesma, 2b, Orioles
64. Brooks Kieschnick, of, Cubs
66. Luke Wilcox, of, Yankees
68. Herbert Perry, 1b, Indians
70. Vaughn Eshelman, lhp, Athletics

Arizona Diamondbacks

Third Round

57. Joe Randa, 3b, Pirates
59. Jesus Martinez, lhp, Dodgers
61. Russ Springer, rhp, Astros
63. Bryan Corey, rhp Tigers
65. Kelly Stinnett, c, Brewers
67. Chuck McElroy, lhp, White Sox
69. Marty Janzen, rhp, Blue Jays

Previous Expansion Draft No. 1 Picks

1960

Los Angeles Angels—Eli Grba, rhp, Yankees
Washington Senators—Bobby Shantz, lhp, Yankees

1961

Houston Colt .45s—Eddie Bressoud, ss, Giants
New York Mets—Hobie Landrith, c, Giants

1968

San Diego Padres—Ollie Brown, of, Giants
Montreal Expos—Manny Mota, of, Pirates
Kansas City Royals—Roger Nelson, rhp, Orioles
Seattle Pilots—Don Mincher, 1b, Angels

1976

Seattle Mariners—Ruppert Jones, of, Royals
Toronto Blue Jays—Bob Bailor, ss, Orioles

1992

Colorado Rockies—David Nied, rhp, Braves
Florida Marlins—Nigel Wilson, of, Blue Jays

About STATS, Inc.

STATS, Inc. is the nation's leading independent sports information and statistical analysis company, providing detailed sports services for a wide array of commercial clients.

As one of the fastest-growing sports companies—in 1994, we ranked 144th on the "Inc. 500" list of fastest-growing privately held firms—STATS provides the most up-to-the-minute sports information to professional teams, print and broadcast media, software developers and interactive service providers around the country. Some of our major clients are ESPN, the Associated Press, Fox Sports, Electronic Arts, MSNBC, SONY and Topps. Much of the information we provide is available to the public via STATS On-Line. With a computer and a modem, you can follow action in the four major professional sports, as well as NCAA football and basketball. . . as it happens!

STATS Publishing, a division of STATS, Inc., produces 12 annual books, including the *Major League Handbook*, *The Scouting Notebook*, the *Pro Football Handbook*, the *Pro Basketball Handbook* and the *Hockey Handbook* as well as the *STATS Fantasy Insider* magazine. These publications deliver STATS' expertise to fans, scouts, general managers and media around the country.

In addition, STATS offers the most innovative—and fun—fantasy sports games and support products around, from *Bill James Fantasy Baseball* and *Bill James Classic Baseball* to *STATS Fantasy Football* and *STATS Fantasy Hoops*. Check out the latest STATS and Bill James fantasy game, *Stock Market Baseball* and our immensely popular Fantasy Portfolios.

Information technology has grown by leaps and bounds in the last decade, and STATS will continue to be at the forefront as a supplier of the most up-to-date, in-depth sports information available. For those of you on the information superhighway, you can always catch STATS in our area on America Online or at our Internet site.

For more information on our products, or on joining our reporter network, contact us on:

America On-Line — (Keyword: STATS)

Internet — www.stats.com

Toll Free in the USA at 1-800-63-STATS (1-800-637-8287)

Outside the USA at 1-847-676-3383

Or write to:

STATS, Inc.
8131 Monticello Ave.
Skokie, IL 60076-3300

Castro, Juan	511	Cruz, Nelson	109		Foulke, Keith	105
Castro, Nelson	45	Cruz Jr., Jose	316		Fox, Andy	219
Castro, Ramon	490	Cummings, John	152	**E**	Fox, Chad	375
Catalanotto, Frank	153	Cummings, Midre	588		Franco, John	564
Cather, Mike	371	Cunnane, Will	668	Easley, Damion	139	Franco, Julio	530
Cedeno, Domingo	304	Curtis, Chad	202	Eaton, Adam	606	Franco, Matt	575
Cedeno, Roger	506			Echevarria, Angel	444	Francona, Terry	584
Chacon, Shawn	445			Eckersley, Dennis	635	Franklin, Micah	649
Charlton, Norm	248			Edmonds, Jim	28	Franklin, Ryan	268
Chavez, Anthony	44	**D**		Eenhoorn, Robert	43	Frascatore, John	645
Chavez, Eric	244			Eischen, Joey	419	Freitas, Joe	652
Chavez, Raul	557	D'Amico, Jeff	529	Eisenreich, Jim	461	Frias, Hanley	356
Checo, Robinson	89	Daal, Omar	351	Elarton, Scott	489	Frye, Jeff	83
Chen, Bruce	376	Damon, Johnny	158	Eldred, Cal	517	Fryman, Travis	141
Christenson, Ryan	244	Darr, Mike	673	Elster, Kevin	612	Fullmer, Brad	558
Christiansen, Jason	627	Darwin, Danny	686	Embree, Alan	372	Fussell, Chris	67
Cianfrocco, Archi	656	Darwin, Jeff	109	Encarnacion, Angelo	43	
Cirillo, Jeff	516	Daulton, Darren	452	Encarnacion, Juan	140	
Clark, Dave	394	Davis, Ben	672	Encarnacion, Mario	245	
Clark, Mark	381	Davis, Chili	159	Enochs, Chris	244	**G**
Clark, Terry	309	Davis, Eric	61	Erdos, Todd	352	
Clark, Tony	137	Davis, Mark	534	Ericks, John	622	
Clark, Will	292	Davis, Russ	250	Erickson, Scott	52	Gaetti, Gary	636
Clayton, Royce	633	Davis, Tim	265	Erstad, Darin	29	Gagne, Greg	494
Clemens, Roger	315	de la Maza, Roland	176	Escobar, Kelvim	318	Gaillard, Eddie	152
Clement, Matt	672	de los Santos, Luis	222	Eshelman, Vaughn	282	Galarraga, Andres	430
Clemons, Chris	350	de los Santos, Valerio	535	Espada, Josue	245	Gallego, Mike	649
Cline, Pat	398	Dean, Chris	268	Espinoza, Alvaro	265	Gant, Ron	637
Clontz, Brad	371	DeHart, Rick	557	Estalella, Bobby	605	Garces, Rich	87
Cloude, Ken	262	DeJean, Mike	442	Estes, Shawn	677	Garcia, Amaury	466
Clyburn, Danny	67	Delgado, Carlos	317	Eusebio, Tony	483	Garcia, Carlos	319
Coggin, Dave	606	Delgado, Wilson	693	Evans, Tom	334	Garcia, Freddy	629
Colbrunn, Greg	372	Delluci, David	351	Everett, Carl	563	Garcia, Freddy (Hou)	490
Coleman, Michael	89	DeLucia, Rich	43	Eversgerd, Bryan	309	Garcia, Karim	344
Coleman, Vince	152	DeShields, Delino	634	Eyre, Scott	105	Garcia, Ramon	483
Coles, Darnell	442	Dessens, Elmer	627		Garciaparra, Nomar	73
Collier, Lou	628	Devereaux, Mike	309		Gardner, Mark	678
Collins, Terry	24	Diaz, Alex	309		Garland, Jon	399
Colon, Bartolo	126	Diaz, Eddy	534	**F**	Garner, Phil	514
Cone, David	201	Diaz, Edwin	355		Gates, Brent	263
Conine, Jeff	451	Diaz, Einar	131	Fabregas, Jorge	343	Gazarek, Marty	399
Converse, Jim	173	Dickey, R.A.	312	Falkenborg, Brian	68	Giambi, Jason	227
Cook, Dennis	460	Dickson, Jason	26	Falteisek, Steve	557	Giambi, Jeremy	176
Cooke, Steve	609	Dierker, Larry	467	Farnsworth, Jeff	268	Gibbs, Kevin	512
Coolbaugh, Mike	245	Difelice, Mike	282	Fasano, Sal	173	Gibson, Derrick	444
Coomer, Ron	180	DiPoto, Jerry	429	Fassero, Jeff	251	Gil, Benji	293
Cooper, Scott	173	DiSarcina, Gary	27	Fernandez, Alex	461	Gilbert, Shawn	580
Coppinger, Rocky	66	Dishman, Glenn	152	Fernandez, Osvaldo	686	Giles, Brian	115
Cora, Alex	513	Dishington, Nate	652	Fernandez, Sid	487	Gilkey, Bernard	565
Cora, Joey	249	Dotel, Octavio	583	Fernandez, Tony	114	Giovanola, Ed	375
Cordero, Francisco	153	Drabek, Doug	104	Fetters, Mike	529	Girardi, Joe	204
Cordero, Wil	72	Dreifort, Darren	493	Fick, Robert	154	Gissell, Chris	399
Cordova, Francisco	610	Drew, J.D.	606	Fielder, Cecil	203	Glanville, Doug	383
Cordova, Marty	181	Drews, Matt	154	Figga, Mike	219	Glauber, Keith	652
Cormier, Rheal	557	Drumright, Mike	154	Finley, Chuck	30	Glaus, Troy	44
Corsi, Jim	83	Ducey, Rob	265	Finley, Steve	657	Glavine, Tom	359
Counsell, Craig	460	Duncan, Courtney	398	Flaherty, John	272	Glendenning, Mike	693
Cox, Bobby	357	Duncan, Mariano	329	Flener, Huck	333	Gomes, Wayne	598
Cox, Steve	287	Dunn, Todd	535	Fleetham, Ben	559	Gomez, Chris	658
Crabtree, Tim	329	Dunston, Shawon	611	Fletcher, Darrin	538	Gomez, Rudy	221
Crawford, Joe	580	Dunwoody, Todd	465	Florie, Bryce	530	Gonzales, Rene	442
Creek, Doug	691	Duran, Roberto	152	Floyd, Cliff	462	Gonzalez, Alex	320
Crespo, Felipe	335	Durham, Ray	96	Fontenot, Joe	465	Gonzalez, Alex (Fla)	465
Cromer, D.T.	245	Dye, Jermaine	160	Fonville, Chad	109	Gonzalez, Jeremi	384
Cromer, Tripp	507			Ford, Ben	355	Gonzalez, Juan	294
Crow, Dean	153			Fordham, Tom	110	Gonzalez, Lariel	445
Crowell, Jim	421			Fordyce, Brook	419	Gonzalez, Luis	474
Cruz, Deivi	138			Fossas, Tony	645	Gooch, Arnie	582
Cruz, Ivan	219			Foster, Jim	68	Gooden, Dwight	214
Cruz, Jacob	692			Foster, Kevin	382	Goodwin, Curtis	419

Goodwin, Tom	295
Gordon, Tom	74
Gorecki, Rick	287
Grace, Mark	385
Grace, Mike	603
Graffanino, Tony	373
Granger, Jeff	627
Graves, Danny	422
Grebeck, Craig	39
Green, Chad	536
Green, Scarborough	651
Green, Shawn	321
Green, Tyler	589
Greene, Charlie	66
Greene, Rick	536
Greene, Todd	31
Greene, Tommy	487
Greene, Willie	403
Greer, Rusty	296
Gregg, Tommy	375
Greisinger, Seth	154
Grieve, Ben	228
Griffey Jr., Ken	252
Grilli, Jason	693
Grissom, Marquis	116
Groom, Buddy	242
Gross, Kevin	43
Grudzielanek, Mark	539
Grundt, Ken	87
Guardado, Eddie	192
Gubicza, Mark	43
Guerrero, Vladimir	540
Guerrero, Wilton	495
Guevara, Giomar	267
Guiel, Aaron	673
Guillen, Carlos	489
Guillen, Jose	613
Guillen, Ozzie	97
Gulan, Mike	649
Gunderson, Eric	304
Guthrie, Mark	507
Gutierrez, Ricky	475
Guzman, Cristian	222
Guzman, Juan	322
Gwynn, Tony	659

H

Hacker, Steve	377
Halama, John	490
Hale, Chip	511
Hall, Darren	508
Hall, Joe	152
Halladay, Roy	334
Halter, Shane	173
Hamelin, Bob	142
Hamilton, Darryl	679
Hamilton, Joey	660
Hammond, Chris	84
Hammonds, Jeffrey	53
Hampton, Mike	476
Haney, Chris	173
Hansell, Greg	534
Hansen, Dave	394
Hansen, Jed	161
Hanson, Erik	330
Hardtke, Jason	398

Hargrove, Mike	112
Harkey, Mike	511
Harnisch, Pete	534
Harris, Lenny	419
Harris, Pep	43
Harris, Reggie	603
Hasegawa, Shigetoshi	40
Haselman, Bill	84
Hatteberg, Scott	75
Haught, Gary	242
Hawkins, LaTroy	192
Hayes, Charlie	205
Haynes, Jimmy	238
Helling, Rick	305
Helms, Wes	376
Helton, Todd	431
Hemphill, Bret	44
Henderson, Rickey	32
Henley, Bob	559
Henriquez, Oscar	466
Henry, Butch	85
Henry, Doug	687
Hentgen, Pat	323
Herbison, Brett	583
Heredia, Felix	462
Heredia, Wilson	309
Hermansen, Chad	628
Hermanson, Dustin	541
Hernandez, Carlos	668
Hernandez, Fernando	152
Hernandez, Jose	386
Hernandez, Livan	453
Hernandez, Ramon	244
Hernandez, Roberto	273
Hernandez, Xavier	305
Hershiser, Orel	117
Hidalgo, Richard	477
Higginson, Bob	143
Hill, Glenallen	687
Hill, Ken	33
Hinch, A.J.	245
Hitchcock, Sterling	661
Hocking, Denny	193
Hoffman, Trevor	662
Hoiles, Chris	54
Hollandsworth, Todd	508
Hollins, Damon	376
Hollins, Dave	34
Holmes, Darren	438
Holt, Chris	478
Holtz, Mike	43
Holzemer, Mark	265
Honeycutt, Rick	649
Houston, Tyler	395
Howard, David	169
Howard, Thomas	484
Howe, Art	223
Howell, Jack	40
Howry, Bobby	111
Hubbard, Mike	397
Hubbard, Trent	130
Hubbs, Dan	513
Hudek, John	484
Hudler, Rex	599
Hudson, Joe	87
Hundley, Todd	566
Hunter, Brian L.	144
Hunter, Torii	197
Hurst, Jimmy	89
Hurtado, Edwin	265

Huskey, Butch	567
Huson, Jeff	534
Hutchins, Norm	45
Hutchison, Bernard	445
Hutton, Mark	438

I

Ibanez, Raul	267
Incaviglia, Pete	219
Ingram, Darron	422
Ingram, Garey	511
Irabu, Hideki	214
Isringhausen, Jason	576

J

Jackson, Damian	421
Jackson, Danny	671
Jackson, Darrin	531
Jackson, Mike	126
Jackson, Ryan	466
Jacome, Jason	130
Jaha, John	518
James, Mike	41
Janzen, Marty	352
Jarvis, Kevin	152
Javier, Stan	680
Jefferies, Gregg	590
Jefferson, Reggie	76
Jenkins, Geoff	536
Jennings, Robin	398
Jensen, Marcus	147
Jerzembeck, Mike	221
Jeter, Derek	206
Johnson, Adam	377
Johnson, Brian	681
Johnson, Charles	454
Johnson, Dane	242
Johnson, Jason	283
Johnson, Jonathan	311
Johnson, Lance	387
Johnson, Mark	419
Johnson, Mark (Chi/AL)	111
Johnson, Mark (Hou)	490
Johnson, Mike	553
Johnson, Randy	253
Johnson, Russ	490
Johnson, Tim	313
Johnstone, John	691
Jones, Andruw	360
Jones, Bobby	568
Jones, Bobby M.	442
Jones, Chipper	361
Jones, Chris	353
Jones, Doug	519
Jones, Jacque	197
Jones, Ryan	334
Jones, Todd	145
Jordan, Brian	638
Jordan, Kevin	599
Jordan, Ricardo	580
Joyner, Wally	663
Judd, Mike	512

Juden, Jeff	127
Justice, David	118

K

Kamieniecki, Scott	62
Kapler, Gabe	154
Karchner, Matt	98
Karkovice, Ron	106
Karl, Scott	520
Karp, Ryan	603
Karros, Eric	496
Karsay, Steve	229
Kashiwada, Takashi	580
Keagle, Greg	147
Kelly, Mike	283
Kelly, Pat	219
Kelly, Roberto	254
Kelly, Tom	177
Kendall, Jason	614
Kent, Jeff	682
Kessel, Kyle	583
Key, Jimmy	55
Kieschnick, Brooks	284
Kile, Darryl	479
King, Cesar	311
King, Curtis	651
King, Jeff	162
Kingsale, Eugene	67
Kinkade, Mike	536
Kinney, Matt	90
Kirby, Wayne	511
Klassen, Danny	356
Klesko, Ryan	362
Kline, Steve	557
Knight, Brandon	311
Knight, Marcus	45
Knoblauch, Chuck	182
Knorr, Randy	487
Koch, Billy	335
Kolb, Dan	312
Konerko, Paul	512
Kotsay, Mark	466
Krause, Scott	536
Kreuter, Chad	41
Krivda, Rick	66
Kroon, Marc	672
Kubenka, Jeff	513
Kubinski, Tim	242
Kusiewicz, Mike	445

L

La Russa, Tony	630
LaChapelle, Yan	335
Lacy, Kerry	87
Laker, Tim	66
Lamont, Gene	607
Lampkin, Tom	646
Langston, Mark	35
Lankford, Ray	639
Lansing, Mike	542
Lara, Nelson	466
Larkin, Barry	404
Larson, Brandon	421

Latham, Chris	196		
Lawton, Matt	183		
Leach, Nick	513		
LeBron, Juan	176		
Ledee, Ricky	221		
Ledesma, Aaron	66		
Lee, Carlos	110		
Lee, Corey	312		
Lee, Derrek	672		
Lee, Travis	345		
Leiter, Al	455		
Leiter, Mark	591		
Lemke, Mark	363		
Lennon, Patrick	242		
LeRoy, John	287		
Lesher, Brian	242		
Leskanic, Curt	439		
Levine, Al	109		
Levis, Jesse	531		
Lewis, Darren	509		
Lewis, Marc	198		
Lewis, Mark	688		
Lewis, Richie	419		
Leyland, Jim	446		
Leyritz, Jim	306		
Lidle, Cory	353		
Lieber, Jon	623		
Lieberthal, Mike	592		
Liefer, Jeff	111		
Ligtenberg, Kerry	375		
Lilly, Ted	513		
Lima, Jose	485		
Liniak, Cole	89		
Lira, Felipe	265		
Liriano, Nelson	511		
Listach, Pat	487		
Livingstone, Scott	649		
Lloyd, Graeme	219		
Loaiza, Esteban	615		
Lockhart, Keith	373		
LoDuca, Paul	513		
Loewer, Carlton	606		
Lofton, Kenny	364		
Loiselle, Rich	616		
Lombard, George	377		
Long, Garrett	629		
Long, Joey	671		
Long, Ryan	173		
Long, Terrence	583		
Looper, Braden	652		
Lopez, Albie	284		
Lopez, Javy	365		
Lopez, Luis	576		
Lopez, Luis (Tor)	335		
Lopez, Mendy	176		
Lopez, Rodrigo	673		
Loretta, Mark	521		
Lorraine, Andrew	242		
Lowe, Derek	87		
Lowe, Sean	649		
Lowell, Mike	222		
Lowery, Terrell	399		
Ludwick, Eric	245		

M

Mabry, John	640	McKeel, Walt	87
Macfarlane, Mike	169	McKeon, Jack	400
Machado, Robert	109	McLemore, Mark	297
Mack, Shane	85	McMichael, Greg	577
Maddux, Greg	366	McMillon, Billy	593
Maddux, Mike	265	McRae, Brian	569
Maduro, Calvin	600	Meares, Pat	184
Maeda, Katsuhiro	222	Meche, Gil	267
Magadan, Dave	238	Mecir, Jim	219
Magee, Wendell	600	Medina, Rafael	673
Magnante, Mike	487	Mejia, Roberto	650
Mahay, Ron	87	Melian, Jackson	222
Mahomes, Pat	87	Melo, Juan	673
Malave, Jose	87	Meluskey, Mitch	490
Maloney, Sean	536	Mendoza, Carlos	580
Manto, Jeff	130	Mendoza, Ramiro	265
Manuel, Barry	580	Menhart, Paul	669
Manuel, Jerry	91	Merced, Orlando	324
Manwaring, Kirt	432	Mercedes, Henry	309
Manzanillo, Josias	265	Mercedes, Jose	532
Marquis, Jason	377	Mercker, Kent	416
Marrero, Eli	652	Mesa, Jose	119
Marte, Damaso	268	Meulens, Hensley	557
Martin, Al	617	Miceli, Dan	148
Martin, Norberto	106	Middlebrook, Jason	673
Martin, Tom	485	Mieske, Matt	524
Martinez, Dave	99	Millar, Kevin	466
Martinez, Dennis	265	Miller, Damian	354
Martinez, Edgar	255	Miller, David	132
Martinez, Felix	176	Miller, Kurt	464
Martinez, Jesus	466	Miller, Orlando	148
Martinez, Pedro	543	Miller, Ray	46
Martinez, Pedro A.	419	Miller, Travis	197
Martinez, Ramon	497	Miller, Trever	490
Martinez, Ramon (SF)	693	Miller, Wade	490
Martinez, Sandy	333	Milliard, Ralph	466
Martinez, Tino	207	Mills, Alan	63
Martinez, Willie	132	Millwood, Kevin	377
Marzano, John	265	Milton, Eric	222
Masaoka, Onan	513	Mimbs, Michael	603
Mashore, Damon	239	Minchey, Nate	442
Mateo, Ruben	312	Minor, Blas	487
Matheny, Mike	522	Minor, Damon	693
Mathews, T.J.	230	Minor, Ryan	67
Mathews, Terry	62	Mirabelli, Doug	693
Matthews, Mike	132	Miranda, Angel	309
May, Darrell	43	Misuraca, Mike	534
May, Derrick	603	Mitchell, Kevin	130
Mayne, Brent	239	Mlicki, Dave	570
McAndrew, Jamie	534	Moehler, Brian	149
McCarthy, Greg	265	Mohler, Mike	242
McClain, Scott	583	Molina, Izzy	243
McCracken, Quinton	274	Molitor, Paul	185
McCurry, Jeff	442	Monahan, Shane	268
McDill, Allen	173	Mondesi, Raul	498
McDonald, Ben	523	Montgomery, Jeff	163
McDonald, Darnell	68	Montgomery, Ray	487
McDonald, Donzell	222	Montgomery, Steve	243
McDonald, Jason	231	Moody, Eric	312
McDowell, Jack	130	Morandini, Mickey	594
McElroy, Chuck	107	Mordecai, Mike	375
McGee, Willie	646	Morel, Ramon	397
McGlinchy, Kevin	377	Moreno, Julio	68
McGraw, Tom	649	Morgan, Kevin	580
McGriff, Fred	275	Morgan, Mike	416
McGuire, Ryan	544	Morgan, Scott	132
McGwire, Mark	641	Morman, Alvin	130
		Morman, Russ	464
		Morris, Hal	405
		Morris, Matt	642

Morris, Warren	312
Mosquera, Julio	333
Moss, Damian	377
Mottola, Chad	422
Mouton, James	486
Mouton, Lyle	109
Moyer, Jamie	256
Mueller, Bill	688
Mulholland, Terry	689
Munoz, Bobby	603
Munoz, Mike	442
Munro, Peter	90
Murray, Eddie	511
Murray, Heath	673
Muser, Tony	155
Mussina, Mike	56
Myers, Greg	374
Myers, Mike	152
Myers, Randy	57
Myers, Rod	170
Myers, Rodney	397

N

Naehring, Tim	77
Nagy, Charles	120
Natal, Bob	464
Naulty, Dan	193
Navarro, Jaime	100
Neagle, Denny	367
Neill, Mike	245
Nelson, Jeff	215
Nen, Robb	456
Nevin, Phil	149
Newfield, Marc	532
Newhan, David	673
Newson, Warren	306
Nicholson, John	559
Nieves, Melvin	150
Nilsson, Dave	525
Nixon, Otis	499
Nixon, Trot	90
Noel, Todd	399
Nomo, Hideo	500
Norton, Greg	111
Nunez, Abraham	628
Nunez, Vladimir	356
Nunnally, Jon	417
Nye, Ryan	603

O

O'Brien, Charlie	330
O'Leary, Troy	78
O'Neill, Paul	208
Oates, Johnny	289
Obando, Sherman	557
Ochoa, Alex	571
Offerman, Jose	164
Ogea, Chad	127
Ojala, Kirt	464
Olerud, John	572
Olivares, Omar	263
Oliver, Darren	298
Oliver, Joe	406

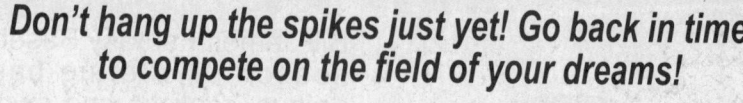
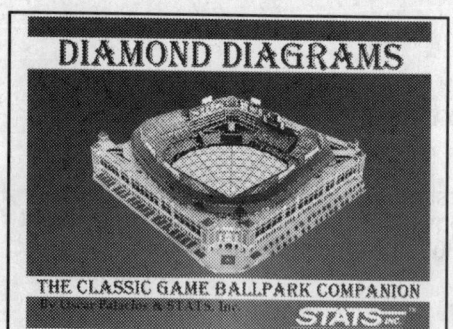

Get Into STATS Fantasy Hoops!

Soar into next season with STATS Fantasy Hoops! SFH lets YOU make the calls. Don't just sit back and watch Grant Hill, Shawn Kemp and Michael Jordan—get in the game and coach your team to the top!

How to Play SFH:
1. Sign up to coach a team
2. You'll receive a full set of rules and a draft form with SFH point values for all eligible players—anyone who played in the NBA last year, plus all NBA draft picks
3. Complete the draft form and return it to STATS
4. You will take part in the draft with nine other owners, and we will send you league rosters
5. You make unlimited weekly transactions including trades, free-agent signings, activations, and benchings
6. Six of the 10 teams in your league advance to postseason play, with two teams ultimately advancing to the Finals

SFH point values are based on actual NBA results, mirroring the real thing. Weekly reports will tell you everything you need to know to lead your team to the SFH Championship!

PLAY STATS Fantasy Football!

STATS Fantasy Football puts YOU in charge! You draft, trade, cut, bench, activate players and even sign free agents each week. SFF pits you head-to-head against 11 other owners.

STATS' scoring system applies realistic values, tested against actual NFL results. Each week, you'll receive a superb in-depth report telling you all about both team and league performances.

How to Play SFF:
1. Sign up today!
2. STATS sends you a draft form listing all eligible NFL players
3. Fill out the draft form and return it to STATS, and you will take part in the draft along with 11 other team owners
4. Go head-to-head against the other owners in your league. You'll make week-by-week roster moves and transactions through STATS' Fantasy Football experts, via phone, fax, or on-line!

STATS Fantasy Football on the Web? Check it out! www.stats.com

Order from STATS INC. Today!

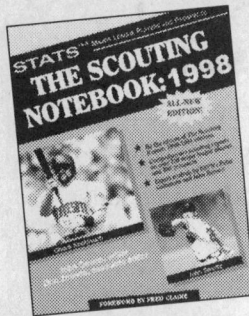

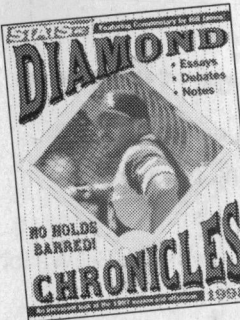
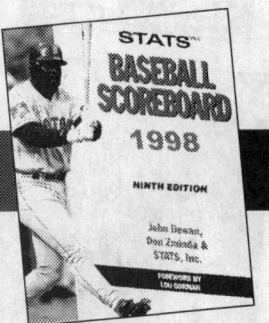

ROUNDING OUT THE STARTING LINEUP...

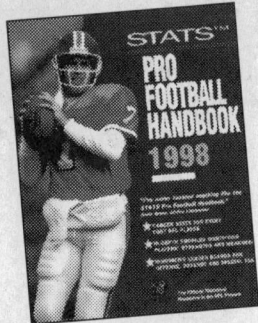

STATS Pro Football Handbook 1998

- A complete season-by-season register for every active NFL player
- Numerous statistical breakdowns for hundreds of NFL players
- Leader boards in a number of innovative and traditional categories
- Exclusive evaluations of offensive linemen
- **Item #FH98, $19.95, Available 2/1/98**

STATS Pro Football Revealed 1998
The 100-Yard War

- Profiles each team, complete with essays, charts and play diagrams
- Detailed statistical breakdowns on players, teams and coaches
- Essays about NFL trends and happenings by leading experts
- Same data as seen on ESPN's *Sunday Night Football* broadcasts
- **Item #PF98, $19.95, Available 7/1/98**

STATS Pro Basketball Handbook 1997-98

- Career stats for every player who logged minutes during 1996-97
- Team game logs with points, rebounds, assists and much more
- Leader boards from points per game to triple doubles
- Essays cover the hottest topics facing the NBA. Foreword by Bill Walton
- **Item #BH98, $19.95, Available Now!**

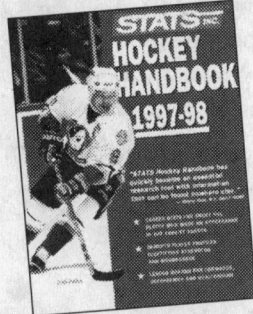

STATS Hockey Handbook 1997-98

- Complete career register for every 1996-97 NHL player and goalie
- Exclusive breakdowns identify player strengths and weaknesses
- Specific coverage for each team, plus league profiles
- Standard and exclusive leader boards
- **Item #HH98, $19.95, Available Now!**

Order from STATS INC. Today!

Use Order Form in This Book, or Call 1-800-63-STATS or 847-676-3383 or visit www.stats.com

STATS, Inc. Order Form

PUBLICATIONS (STATS books include FREE first class shipping; magazines — add $2)

Qty.	Product Name	Item #	Price	Total
	STATS All-Time Major League Handbook	ATHA	$54.95	
	STATS All-Time Baseball Sourcebook	ATSA	$54.95	
	STATS All-Time Major League COMBO (BOTH books!)	ATCA	$99.95	
	STATS Major League Handbook 1998	HB98	$19.95	
	STATS Major League Handbook 1998 (Comb-bound)	HC98	$21.95	
	STATS Projections Update 1998 (MAGAZINE)	PJUP	$9.95	
	The Scouting Notebook: 1998	SN98	$19.95	
	The Scouting Notebook: 1998 (Comb-bound)	SC98	$21.95	
	STATS Minor League Scouting Notebook 1998	MN98	$19.95	
	STATS Minor League Handbook 1998	MH98	$19.95	
	STATS Minor League Handbook 1998 (Comb-bound)	MC98	$21.95	
	STATS Player Profiles 1998	PP98	$19.95	
	STATS Player Profiles 1998 (Comb-bound)	PC98	$21.95	
	STATS 1998 BVSP Match-Ups!	BP98	$19.95	
	STATS Baseball Scoreboard 1998	SB98	$19.95	
	STATS Diamond Chronicles 1998	CH98	$19.95	
	Pro Football Revealed: The 100 Yard War (1998 Edition)	PF98	$19.95	
	STATS Pro Football Handbook 1998	FH98	$19.95	
	STATS Pro Football Handbook 1998 (Comb-bound)	FC98	$21.95	
	STATS Basketball Handbook 1997-98	BH98	$19.95	
	STATS Hockey Handbook 1997-98	HH98	$19.95	
	STATS Diamond Diagrams 1998	DD98	$19.95	
	STATS Fantasy Insider: 1998 Major League Baseball Edition (MAGAZINE)	IB98	$5.95	
	STATS Fantasy Insider: 1998 Pro Football Edition (MAGAZINE)	IF98	$5.95	
	Prior Editions (Please circle appropriate year)			
	STATS Major League Handbook '90 '91 '92 '93 '94 '95 '96 '97		$9.95	
	The Scouting Report/Notebook '94 '95 '96 '97		$9.95	
	STATS Player Profiles '93 '94 '95 '96 '97		$9.95	
	STATS Minor League Handbook '92 '93 '94 '95 '96 '97		$9.95	
	STATS BVSP Match-Ups! '94 '95 '96 '97		$5.95	
	STATS Baseball Scoreboard '92 '93 '94 '95 '96 '97		$9.95	
	STATS Basketball Scoreboard/Handbook '93-'94 '94-'95 '95-'96 '96-'97		$9.95	
	Pro Football Revealed: The 100 Yard War '94 '95 '96 '97		$9.95	
	STATS Pro Football Handbook '95 '96 '97		$9.95	
	STATS Minor League Scouting Notebook '95 '96 '97		$9.95	
	STATS Hockey Handbook '96-'97		$9.95	

FANTASY GAMES

Qty.	Product Name	Item Number	Price	Total
	Bill James Classic Baseball	BJCB	$129.00	
	STATS Fantasy Hoops	SFH	$79.00	
	STATS Fantasy Football	SFF	$69.00	
	Bill James Fantasy Baseball	BJFB	$89.00	

1st Fantasy Team Name (ex. Colt 45's):_____ _____

   What Fantasy Game is this team for?_____

2nd Fantasy Team Name (ex. Colt 45's):_____ _____

   What Fantasy Game is this team for?_____

      NOTE: $1.00/player is charged for all roster moves and transactions.

For Bill James Fantasy Baseball:

Would you like to play in a league drafted by Bill James?   ❑ Yes   ❑ No

MULTIMEDIA PRODUCTS (Prices include shipping & handling charges)

Qty.	Product Name	Item Number	Price	Total
	Bill James Encyclopedia CD-Rom	BJCD	$49.95	

TOTALS	Price	Total
Product Total (excl. Fantasy Games)		
Canada—all orders—add:	$2.50/book	
Magazines—shipping—add:	$2.00/each	
Order 2 or more books—subtract:	$1.00/book	
(**NOT** to be combined with other specials)		
Subtotal		
Fantasy Games Total		
IL residents add 8.5% sales tax		
GRAND TOTAL		

NOTE: *Orders for shipments outside of the USA or Canada are Credit Card only.*
Actual shipping charges will be added to the product cost.